W9-AYA-430

PrincetonReview.com

THE BEST 376 COLLEGES

2012 Edition

By Robert Franek,

Laura Braswell, Seamus Mullarkey, and

The Staff of The Princeton Review

Random House, Inc., New York
2012 Edition

The Princeton Review, Inc.
111 Speen Street, Suite 550
Framingham, MA 01701
E-mail: editorialsupport@review.com

ISBN 978-0-375-42839-5

Senior VP—Publisher: Robert Franek
Editors: Seamus Mullarkey, Laura Braswell
Production: Deborah A. Silvestrini
Production Editor: Michelle Krapf
Data Collection: David Soto

Printed in the United States of America on partially recycled paper.

9 8 7 6 5 4 3 2 1

2012 Edition

ACKNOWLEDGMENTS

Each year we assemble an awe-inspiringly talented group of colleagues who work together to produce our guidebooks; this year is no exception. Everyone involved in this effort—authors, editors, data collectors, production specialists, and designers—gives so much more than is required to make *The Best 376 Colleges* an exceptional student resource guide. This new edition gives prospective college students what they really want: The most honest, accessible, and pertinent information about the colleges they are considering attending.

My sincere thanks go to the many who contributed to this tremendous project. I know our readers will benefit from our collective efforts to collect the opinions of current students at the outstanding schools we profile. A special thank you goes to our authors, Julie Doherty, Eric Owens, Anne DeWitt, Kristen O'Toole, Alexander Fletcher, and Andrea Kornstein, for their dedication in pouring through tens of thousands of surveys to produce the campus culture narratives of each school profiled. Very special thanks go to Seamus Mullarkey and Laura Braswell for their editorial commitment and vision. A warm and special thank you goes to our Student Survey Team, Anya Yurchyshyn, Caroline Seklir, Lincoln Michel, Anne DeWitt, Abe Koogler, and Steven Aglione, who continue to work in partnership with school administrators and students alike. My continued thanks go to our data collection pro, David Soto, for his successful efforts in collecting and accurately representing the statistical data that appear with each college profile. The enormousness of this project and its deadline constraints could not have been realized without the calm presence of our production partners at Penn Foster: Deborah Silvestrini and Michelle Krapf. Jeff Orr and his team's dedication, focus, and most important, careful eyes, continue to delight and remind me of what a pleasure it is to work on this project each year. Special thanks also go to Jeanne Krier, our Random House publicist, for the dedicated work she continues to do on this book and the overall series since its inception. Jeanne continues to be my trusted colleague, media advisor, and friend. I would also like to make special mention of Tom Russell and Nicole Benhabib, our Random House publishing team, for their continuous investment and faith in our ideas. Last, I thank my TPR Partner Team, Scott Kirkpatrick, Michael Bleyhl, Paul Kanarek, Brian Healy, and Lev Kaye for their confidence in me and my content team and for their commitment to providing students the resources they need to find the right fit school for them. Again, to all who contributed so much to this publication, thank you for your efforts; they do not go unnoticed.

Robert Franek
Senior VP—Publisher
Lead Author—*The Best 376 Colleges*

DOONESBURY   By Garry Trudeau

Contents

PART I: INTRODUCTION

Getting into Selective Colleges: A Guide for High School Students

What we've put together in this book is a guide to the nation's 376 most academically outstanding institutions so that you can be informed about the unique opportunities these schools offer and what it's really like to be a student at them. As selective as you'll be about choosing the right college for you, know that many of the colleges we profile will be selective in choosing the students right for them. While some of the schools you'll read about here admit upwards of eighty percent of their applicants, the majority have many more applicants than they have seats to fill and some admit less than ten percent of the students who apply. That means—depending on which colleges you're pinning your hopes on attending—you are likely going to have to put quite a bit of effort into getting in. High grades in challenging courses are just the beginning!

If you're like most of the two million (and growing!) high school students who apply to college each year, you're probably wondering what college admissions officers are really looking for in an applicant. What exactly does it take to get into college? What can I do to make my application stand out? Once I get accepted, how do I know which college is best for me?

In order to get you started on the road to a successful application, we're going to give you a few goals, suggestions and tips for checkpoints along the way. This brief primer will help you know what you should be doing year by year in high school to prepare yourself for admission to your "best" college.

6 STEPS TO GETTING INTO COLLEGE

Sure, high school is supposed to be fun, but putting some effort into your schoolwork and extracurricular experiences can make applying to your choice colleges a lot less stressful. Though it might sound like boring advice, the following steps are extremely important!

1. Work hard for good grades.

2. Enroll in challenging courses.

3. Spend time preparing for the SAT or the ACT and SAT Subject Tests.

4. Polish your writing skills.

5. Establish relationships with teachers and advisors who can write strong letters of recommendation for you.

6. Get involved in some activities, community service, or work experiences that will enable you to show your values, talents, and skills.

NEED MORE HELP?

For more information on how you can make the most of your high school years and turn those experiences into a successful college application, check out our offering of college admissions books at PrincetonReviewBooks.com.

Freshman Year

Getting a good start is the best way to get a strong finish! You don't want to have to play catch-up during your junior and senior years when you're supposed to be focusing on bigger things. During your freshman year, make sure you concentrate on your studies and work hard to earn good grades. Get to know your teachers and ask for their help if you are having trouble in a subject—as well as if you just really enjoy it and want to learn more. They'll most certainly want to help you do your best. If there is an honor roll at your school, make it a goal to get on it. And if your grades are so good that you qualify for membership in the National Honor Society, pat yourself on the back and don't think twice about accepting the invitation to join. Make it a point to meet your guidance counselor so you can begin pinpointing colleges you may be interested in and studying for the courses and admission tests they require. The great thing about freshman year is that you have plenty of time to focus on projects that can make your admissions applications during your senior year look the best they can. Make sure you take hold of that opportunity!

> "During your freshman year, make sure you concentrate on your studies and work hard to earn good grades."

Read a Good Book! (or two)

Strong vocabulary and reading skills are essential to doing well on the SAT and ACT (and most tests you'll take for that matter—even math tests require good reading skills!). By cracking open a few good books, you can do some early prep for both tests. Here are some books we love by interesting authors. Not only will you learn some stuff by reading them, but we think you'll love them too!

- *The Curious Incident of the Dog in the Night-Time: A Novel* by Mark Haddon

- *A Heartbreaking Work of Staggering Genius* by Dave Eggers

- *Life of Pi* by Yann Martel

- *Reading Lolita in Tehran* by Azar Nafisi

- *White Teeth* by Zadie Smith

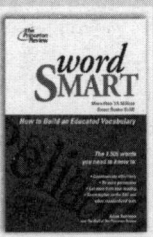

Another Good Book

For extra practice building your vocabulary, check out our *Word Smart* books. Our flagship *Word Smart* book has more than 1,500 words including our "SAT Hit Parade": words most frequently on the SAT.

Sophomore Year

As a sophomore, you'll need to stay focused on your studies. If you didn't earn strong grades during your freshman year, start doing so this year. Scope out the Advanced Placement courses that are offered at your school. You'll want to sign up for as many AP courses as you can reasonably take, starting in your junior year. In sophomore year, you'll also want to choose one or more extracurriculars that interest you. Admissions officers tell us they look favorably on involvement in student government, student newspaper, community service, and sports. What you don't want to do is overload your schedule with activities just to rack up a long list of extracurriculars. Colleges would much rather see you focus on a few worthwhile extracurriculars than divide your time among a bunch of different activities that you're not passionate about. Your sophomore year is when you'll have an opportunity to take the PSAT. Given every October, the PSAT is a shortened version of the SAT. It is used to predict how well you will do on the SAT, and it determines eligibility

> "Colleges would much rather see you focus on a few worthwhile extracurriculars than divide your time among a bunch of different activities that you're not passionate about."

for National Merit Scholarships. While your PSAT scores won't count until you retake the test in your junior year, you should approach this as a test run for the real thing, because the real thing is coming, and it's coming fast. Sophomore year will be over before you know it, and you'll soon have to step it up and be running strong in the critical part of the race to reach the application finish line.

What Should You Do This Summer?

Ahhh, summer. The possibilities seem endless. You can get a job, intern, travel, study, volunteer, or do nothing at all. Here are a few ideas to get you started:

- **Go to college:** No, not for real. However, you can participate in summer programs at colleges and universities at home and abroad. Programs can focus on anything from academics (stretch your brain by taking an intensive science or language course) to sports to admissions guidance. This is also a great opportunity to explore college life firsthand, especially if you get to stay in a dorm.

- **Prep for the PSAT, SAT, or ACT:** So maybe it's not quite as adventurous as trekking around Patagonia for the summer (it's also not as expensive!) or as cool as learning to slam dunk at basketball camp, but hey, there's nothing adventurous or cool about being rejected from your top-choice college because of unimpressive test scores. Plus, you'll be ahead of the game if you can return to school with much of your PSAT, SAT, and ACT preparation behind you.

- **Research scholarships:** College is expensive. While you should never rule out a school based on cost, the more scholarship money you can secure beforehand, the more college options you will have. You'll find loads of info on financial aid and scholarships (including a scholarship search tool) on our site, PrincetonReview.com.

Get Help

Admissions officers will want to see that you've earned high grades in challenging classes. The Princeton Review's Cracking the AP Exam series offers test-prep guides to the most popular AP subject tests to help give you a leg up on passing the exams. High AP scores can boost your chances of admission, plus they are used for placement in college courses and for awarding college credit (ka-ching! ka-ching!) saving on tuition costs! We also offer *Cracking the PSAT/NMSQT,* which has two full-length practice tests and tips on how to score your best on the test. And a great vocabulary will help you with both AP classes and the PSAT, so sign up for the Princeton Review's Vocab Minute on PrincetonReview.com.

Junior Year

Your junior year is going to be exciting and challenging and extremely important in your academic career. You'll start the year off by taking the PSAT in October. High PSAT scores in junior year qualify you for the National Merit Scholarship competition. To become a finalist, you also need great grades and a recommendation from your school. It's critical that your junior-year grades are solid. When colleges look at your transcripts they put a heavy emphasis on junior-year grades. Decisions are made before admissions officers see your second-semester, senior-year grades and possibly before they see your first-semester, senior-year grades! During your junior year, you'll probably take the SAT or ACT test for the first time. Most colleges require scores from one of these tests for admission and/or scholarship award decisions. Also take time during your junior year to research colleges, and, if possible, visit schools high on your "hopes" list. When researching colleges, you'll want to consider a variety of factors besides whether or not you can get in, including location, school size, majors or programs offered that interest you, and cost and availability of financial aid. It helps to visit schools because it's the best way to learn whether a school may be right for you. If you can schedule an interview with an admissions officer during your visit, it may help him or her discover how right you may be for the school.

ACT or SAT?

Not sure which test to take? First make sure that all the schools to which you're applying accept both tests (nearly all colleges now do so, but it's best to check). Then take the test on which you do better. Visit PrincetonReview.com to take a free assessment test that will help you identify whether the ACT or SAT is better for you. We also have a new book on this very subject: *ACT or SAT? Choosing the Right Exam for You.* More and more students are opting to take the ACT in addition to, or instead of, the SAT. No matter which test you end up taking, you should plan to spend 3 to 12 weeks preparing for the tests.

About the SAT: The SAT is comprised of Math, Critical Reading, and Writing sections. Colleges will see your individual section scores and your composite score, but generally they'll be most concerned with your composite score. Currently, a new "Score Choice" policy is in place. It allows students to choose which scores (of a complete SAT test, not of one section of a test) will be sent to colleges. However, some colleges are asking to see all of your test scores, so be sure to check this out on a per-school basis.

About the ACT: The ACT has an English, Reading, Math, and Science section, plus the optional Writing section. (Some schools require the essay, so be sure to ask before you take the test.) You can take the ACT several times and choose which of your scores will be sent to the colleges.

About SAT Subject Tests: Most highly selective colleges also require you to take three SAT Subject Tests in addition to the SAT or ACT. If you have SAT Subject Tests to take, plan now. You can't take the SAT and SAT Subject Tests on the same day.

Senior Year

It's finally here! Senior year! It's now time to get serious about pulling everything together on your applications. Deadlines will vary from school to school, and you will have a lot to keep track of, so make checklists of what's due when. If you're not happy with your previous SAT scores, you should take the October SAT. If you still need to take any SAT Subject Tests, now's the time.

When you ask teachers to write recommendations for you, give them everything they need. Tell them your application deadline and include a stamped, addressed envelope, or directions on how to submit the recommendation online, and be sure to send them a thank-you note after you know the recommendation was turned in.

Your essay, on the other hand, is the one part of your application you have total control over. Don't repeat information from other parts of your application. And by all means, proofread! You'll find tips from admissions officers on what they look for (and what peeves them the most) about college applicants' essays in our book, *College Essays That Made a Difference*.

If you have found the school of your dreams and you're happy with your grades and test scores, consider filing an early decision application. Many selective colleges commit more than half of their admissions spots to early decision applicants. To take this route, you must file your application in early November. By mid-December, you'll find out whether you got in—but there's a catch. If you're accepted early decision to a college, you must withdraw all applications to other colleges. This means that your financial aid offer might be hard to negotiate, so be prepared to take what you get. Regardless of which route you decide to take, have a backup plan. Make sure you apply to at least one safety school—one that you feel confident you can get into and afford. Another option is to apply early decision at one school, but apply to other colleges during the regular decision period in the event that you are rejected from the early decision college.

We know how exciting but stressful that decision can be. If you're having a difficult time choosing between two colleges, try to visit each of them one more time. Can you imagine yourself walking around that campus, building a life in that community, and establishing friendships with those people? Finally, decide and be happy. Don't forget to thank your recommenders and tell them where you'll be going to school. Some of the best times of your life await!

Our Other "Majorly" Helpful Books

The college admissions process is overwhelming, and counselor appointments can be few and far between at some schools. That's why The Princeton Review got more than 200 top college counselors to share their secrets about getting that crucial acceptance letter! *The Portable Guidance Counselor* helps you maximize your college chances with answers to key questions: What should I look for during college visits? How many AP classes should I take? What do college admissions officers really want to see on an application?

Our *K & W Guide to Colleges for Students with Learning Disabilities or Attention Deficit Disorders* profiles more than 300 schools and includes advice from specialists in the field of learning disabilities, and strategies to help students identify and successfully apply to the best programs for their needs.

Our *Gay & Lesbian Guide to College Life* addresses challenges that LGBT students face from finding and applying to colleges to dealing with campus life issues. Appendixes provide lists of LGBT scholarships, support networks, advocacy groups, and academic/career resources.

Our *Guide to College Majors* profiles more than 350 undergraduate majors and covers high school preparation for them, college courses you'll likely take, career options, and salary prospects.

   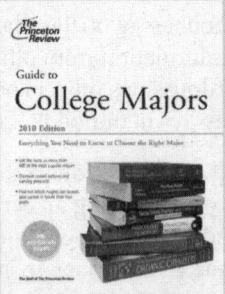

You'll find information about these and our more than 150 guidebooks at PrincetonReviewBooks.com.

Paying for College: Savvy Strategies for Financial Aid

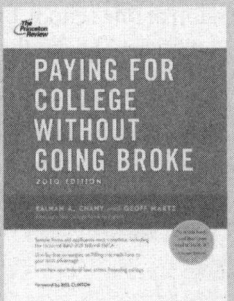

The Princeton Review's *Paying for College Without Going Broke* is the only annually updated guide to financial aid that has detailed, line-by-line strategies for completing the highly complicated FAFSA for the upcoming school year (as well as the CSS/PROFILE form) to one's best advantage. It explains how the financial aid process works and reveals strategies—all legal—for maximizing your eligibility for aid. Authored by Kal Chany, one of the nation's most widely sourced experts on college funding, it also includes annually updated information on education tax breaks, college savings programs, and student and parent loans.

Check out Kal Chany's "26 Tips for Getting Financial Aid . . ." on pages 7-10.

26 TIPS FOR GETTING FINANCIAL AID, SCHOLARSHIPS, AND GRANTS AND FOR PAYING LESS FOR COLLEGE

by Kalman A. Chany, author of *Paying for College Without Going Broke*

(Random House/Princeton Review Books)

Getting financial aid

1. Learn how the aid process works. The more and the sooner you know about the process, the better you can take steps to maximize your aid eligibility.

2. Apply for financial aid no matter what your circumstances. Some merit-based aid can only be awarded if the applicant has submitted financial aid application forms.

3. Don't wait until your child is accepted to apply for financial aid. Do it when applying for admission.

4. Complete all the required aid applications. All students seeking aid must submit the FAFSA (Free Application for Federal Student Aid); other forms may also be required. Check with each college to see what's required and when.

5. Get the best scores you can on the SAT or ACT. They are used not only in decisions for admission but also financial aid. If your scores and other stats exceed the school's admission criteria, you are likely to get a better aid package than a marginal applicant.

6. Apply strategically to colleges. Your chances of getting aid will be better at schools that have generous financial aid budgets. (Check the "Best Value Colleges" list and Financial Aid Ratings for schools in this book and on princetonreview.com.)

7. Don't rule out any school as too expensive. A generous aid award from a pricey private school can make it less costly than a public school with a lower sticker price.

8. Take advantage of education tax benefits. A dollar saved on taxes is worth the same as a dollar in scholarship aid. Look into Coverdells, education tax credits, and loan deductions.

Scholarships and grants

9. Get your best possible score on the PSAT: It is the National Merit Scholarship Qualifying Test and also used in the selection of students for other scholarships and recognition programs.

10. Check your eligibility for grants and scholarships from your state. Some (but not all) states will allow you to use such funds out of state.

11. Look for scholarships locally. Find out if your employer offers scholarships or tuition assistance plans for employees or family members. Also look into scholarships from your church, community groups, and high school.

12. Look for outside scholarships realistically: they account for less than five percent of aid awarded. Research them at princetonreview.com or other free sites. Steer clear of scholarship search firms that charge fees and "promise" scholarships.

Paying for college

13. Start saving early when the student is an infant. Too late? Start now. The more you save, the less you'll have to borrow.

14. Invest wisely. Considering a 529 plan? Compare your own state's plan which may have tax benefits with other states' programs. Get info at savingforcollege.com.

15. If you have to borrow, first pursue federal education loans (Perkins, Stafford, PLUS). Avoid private loans at all costs.

16. Never put tuition on a credit card. The debt is more expensive than ever given recent changes to interest rates and other fees some card issuers are now charging.

17. Try not to take money from a retirement account or 401(k) to pay for college. In addition to likely early distribution penalties and additional income taxes, the higher income will reduce your aid eligibility.

Paying less for college

18. Attend a community college for two years and transfer to a pricier school to complete the degree. Plan ahead: Be sure the college you plan to transfer to will accept the community college credits.

19. Look into "cooperative education" programs. Over 900 colleges allow students to combine college education with a job. It can take longer to complete a degree this way but graduates generally owe less in student loans and have a better chance of getting hired.

20. Take as many AP courses as possible and get high scores on AP exams. Many colleges award course credits for high AP scores. Some students have cut a year off their college tuition this way.

21. Earn college credit via "dual enrollment" programs available at some high schools. These allow students to take college level courses during their senior year.

22. Earn college credits by taking CLEP (College-Level Examination Program) exams. Depending on the college, a qualifying score on any of the thirty-three CLEP exams can earn students three to twelve college credits. (See Princeton Review's *Cracking the CLEP*-5th Edition.)

23. Stick to your college and your major. Changing colleges can result in lost credits. Aid may be limited/not available for transfer students at some schools. Changing majors can mean paying for extra courses to meet requirements.

24 . Finish college in three years if possible. Take the maximum number of credits every semester, attend summer sessions, and earn credits via online courses. Some colleges offer three-year programs for high-achieving students.

25. Let Uncle Sam pay for your degree. ROTC (Reserve Officer Training Corps) programs available from U.S. Armed Forces branches (except the Coast Guard) offer merit-based scholarships up to full tuition via participating colleges in exchange for military service after you graduate.

26. Better yet: Attend a tuition-free college. Check out the nine institutions in this book on the "Tuition-Free Schools Honor Roll" list—p. 51

Want to Search by Tuition?

We say it over and over: Never rule out applying to a college because of its "sticker" price. Many schools are very generous with their financial aid, and it can cost less to attend an expensive private college than an inexpensive public university. Check out our list of "Best Value Colleges" at Princeton-Review.com/best-value-colleges.aspx to see the 100 institutions (50 public, 50 private) we saluted in February 2011 as our recommended "best value" picks in the nation. You'll also find the list in this book on page 52. (Also in that section of the book, check out our list "Great Financial Aid" on p. 39: it names the top twenty schools at which students we surveyed were happiest with their financial aid awards.) In this book, in addition to giving you tons of facts and stats about the schools' financial aid offerings and policies (we even have a Financial Aid Rating) in the school profiles, we also offer an index of colleges in this book sorted by tuition. You'll find it on page 816.

There is also an index by location!

Great Schools for 15 of the Most Popular Undergraduate Majors

Worried about having to declare a major on your college application? Relax. Most colleges won't require you to declare a major until the end of your sophomore year, giving you plenty of time to explore your options. However, problems may arise if you are thinking about majoring in a program that limits its enrollment—meaning that if you don't declare that major early on, you might not get into that program at a later date.

On the flip side, some students declare a major on their application because they believe it will boost their chances of gaining admission. This is a slippery slope to climb, however. If you later decide to change your major and it involves switching from one school within the college to another (from the school of arts and sciences to the school of business, for example), it can be tricky.

Never choose a college solely on the perceived prestige of a particular program. College will expose you to new and exciting learning opportunities. To choose a school based on a major before you even know what else is out there would limit you in many ways. (Choosing a school based on program availability is a different story.) You may also want to investigate opportunities to design your own major.

How Did We Compile These Lists?

Each year we collect data from more than a thousand colleges on the subject of—among many other things—undergraduate academic offerings. We ask colleges not only to report which undergraduate majors they offer, but also which of their majors have the highest enrollment. The list below identifies (in alphabetical order) fifteen of the forty "most popular" majors that the schools responding to our survey reported to us. We also conduct our own research on college majors. We look at institutional data, and we consult with our in-house college admissions experts as well as our National College Counselor Advisory Panel (whom we list in our index, page 806) for their input on schools offering great programs in these majors. We thank them and all of the guidance counselors, college admissions counselors, and education experts across the country whose recommendations we considered in developing these lists. Of the roughly 3,500 schools across the United States, those on these lists represent only a snapshot of the many offering great programs in these majors. Use our lists as a starting point for further research. Some schools on these lists may not appear in the *Best 376 Colleges* (these are marked with an asterisk*), but you can find profiles of them in our *Complete Book of Colleges*, 2012 Edition.

Great Schools for Accounting Majors

- Alfred University
- Auburn University
- Babson College
- Baylor University
- Birmingham-Southern College
- Boston College
- Boston University
- Brigham Young University
- Bucknell University
- Calvin College
- Claremont McKenna College
- Clemson University
- College of Charleston
- Cornell University
- DePaul University
- Drexel University
- Duquesne University
- Elon University
- Emory University
- Fordham University
- Georgetown University
- Indiana University—Bloomington
- Iowa State University
- James Madison University
- Lehigh University
- Michigan State University
- New York University
- Northeastern University
- Pennsylvania State University
- Pepperdine University
- Rider University
- Rochester Institute of Technology
- Seton Hall University
- Suffolk University
- Temple University
- Texas A&M University—College Station
- University of Houston
- University of Illinois at Urbana-Champaign
- University of Michigan—Ann Arbor
- University of Pennsylvania
- University of Southern California
- The University of Texas at Austin

Great Schools for Biology Majors

- Agnes Scott College
- Albion College
- Austin College
- Baylor University
- Brandeis University
- Carleton College
- Christopher Newport University
- Colby College
- Cornell University
- Drexel University
- Duke University
- Guilford College
- Harvard College
- Haverford College
- Howard University
- Illinois Wesleyan University
- Indiana University—Bloomington
- Johns Hopkins University
- Louisiana State University
- Loyola University—Chicago
- Massachusetts Institute of Technology
- Mount Holyoke College
- Ohio University—Athens
- The Ohio State University—Columbus
- Pomona College
- Reed College
- Rice University
- Swarthmore College
- Temple University
- Texas A&M University—College Station
- University of California—Davis
- The University of Chicago
- University of Dallas
- University of Delaware
- University of Denver
- University of Houston
- University of New Mexico
- University of the Pacific
- Wofford College
- Xavier University of Louisiana

Schools marked with an asterisk do not appear in the *Best 376 Colleges.*
You can find those school profiles in *Complete Book of Colleges,* 2012 Edition.

Great Schools for Business/Finance Majors

- Babson College
- Bentley College
- Boston College
- Carnegie Mellon University
- Champlain College
- Christopher Newport University
- City University of New York—
  Baruch College
- Cornell University
- DePaul University
- Emory University
- Florida State University
- Indiana University—Bloomington
- Iowa State University
- Lehigh University
- Massachusetts Institute of
  Technology
- Miami University (OH)
- Michigan State University
- New York University
- Northwestern University
- Ohio University—Athens
- Portland State University
- Rice University
- Roanoke College
- Seattle University
- University of California—Berkeley
- University of California—
  Los Angeles
- University of Chicago
- University of Florida
- University of Houston
- University of Illinois at
  Urbana-Champaign
- University of Michigan
- University of Pennsylvania
- University of Southern California
- The University of Texas at Austin
- University of Virginia
- Washington University in St. Louis

Great Schools for Communications Majors

- Augsburg College*
- Baylor University
- Boise State University*
- Boston University
- Bradley University
- City University of New York—
  Hunter College
- Clemson University
- College of Charleston
- Cornell University
- Denison University
- DePaul University
- Duquesne University
- Eckerd College
- Emerson College
- Fairfield University
- Fordham University
- Gonzaga University
- Gustavus Adolphus College
- Hollins University
- Indiana University—Bloomington
- Iowa State University
- Ithaca College
- James Madison University
- Lake Forest College
- Loyola University—New Orleans
- Michigan State University
- Muhlenberg College
- New York University
- Northwestern University
- Pepperdine University
- Ripon College
- Salisbury University
- Seton Hall University
- St. John's University (NY)
- Stanford University
- Suffolk University
- Syracuse University
- University of California—San Diego
- University of California—
  Santa Barbara
- University of Iowa
- University of Maryland—
  College Park
- University of Southern California
- The University of Texas at Austin
- University of Utah

Schools marked with an asterisk do not appear in the *Best 376 Colleges*.
You can find those school profiles in *Complete Book of Colleges*, 2012 Edition.

Great Schools for Computer Science/Computer Engineering Majors

- Auburn University
- Boston University
- Bradley University
- Brown University
- California Institute of Technology
- Carnegie Mellon University
- Clemson University
- Drexel University
- Florida State University
- George Mason University
- Georgia Institute of Technology
- Gonzaga University
- Hampton University
- Harvey Mudd College
- Iowa State University
- Johns Hopkins University
- Lehigh University
- Massachusetts Institute of Technology
- Michigan State University
- New Jersey Institute of Technology
- Northeastern University
- Northwestern University
- Princeton University
- Rice University
- Roanoke College
- Rochester Institute of Technology
- Rose-Hulman Institute of Technology
- Seattle University
- Stanford University
- State University of New York at Binghamton
- State University of New York—University at Buffalo
- Texas A&M University—College Station
- United States Air Force Academy
- University of Arizona
- University of California—Berkeley
- University of California—Los Angeles
- University of California—Riverside
- University of Illinois at Urbana-Champaign
- University of Massachusetts Amherst
- University of Michigan—Ann Arbor
- University of Washington

Great Schools for Criminology Majors

- American University
- Auburn University
- City University of New York—John Jay College of Criminal Justice*
- North Carolina State University
- The Ohio State University—Columbus
- Ohio University—Athens
- Quinnipiac University
- Sam Houston State University*
- Suffolk University
- University of California—Irvine*
- University of Delaware
- University of Denver
- University of Maryland—College Park
- University of Miami
- University of New Hampshire
- University of South Florida
- University of Utah
- Valparaiso University

Schools marked with an asterisk do not appear in the *Best 376 Colleges*.
You can find those school profiles in *Complete Book of Colleges*, 2012 Edition.

Great Schools for Education Majors

- Adelphi University*
- Alma College*
- Arcadia University*
- Ashland University*
- Auburn University
- Augsburg College*
- Barnard College
- Bethany College (WV)*
- Bryn Athyn College of the New Church*
- Bucknell University
- California State University—Sacramento*
- Carthage College*
- City University of New York—Brooklyn College
- City University of New York—Hunter College
- Colgate University
- College of William & Mary
- Columbia College (MO)
- Columbia University
- Cornell College
- Cornell University
- Duquesne University
- Elon University
- Franklin Pierce College*
- Gonzaga University
- Goucher College
- Hardin-Simmons University*
- Hillsdale College
- Indiana University—Bloomington
- Jewish Theological Seminary—Albert A. List College*
- LaSalle University*
- Loyola Marymount University
- Marquette University
- McGill University
- Miami University (OH)
- Montana State University—Bozeman*
- Nazareth College
- New York Institute of Technology*
- New York University
- Northeastern University
- Northwestern University
- The Ohio State University—Columbus
- San Francisco State University*
- Simmons College
- Skidmore College
- Smith College
- State University of New York—New Paltz*
- Trinity University (Washington, D.C.)*
- Trinity University (San Antonio, TX)
- University of Maine
- The University of Montana—Missoula
- University of St. Thomas (TX)*
- University of Toledo*
- Vanderbilt University
- Villanova College
- Wagner College
- Wellesley College
- Xavier University (OH)

Great Schools for Engineering Majors

- California Institute of Technology
- California Polytechnic State University*
- Carnegie Mellon University
- Columbia University
- Cooper Union
- Cornell University
- Drexel University
- Duke University
- Franklin W. Olin College of Engineering
- Georgia Institute of Technology
- Harvard College
- Harvey Mudd College
- Illinois Institute of Technology
- Johns Hopkins University
- Massachusetts Institute of Technology
- Pennsylvania State University
- Princeton University
- Purdue University—West Lafayette
- Rose-Hulman Institute of Technology
- Stanford University
- Texas A&M University—College Station
- University of California—Berkeley
- University of California—Los Angeles
- The University of Texas at Austin
- University of Wisconsin—Madison
- Worcester Polytechnic Institute

Schools marked with an asterisk do not appear in the *Best 376 Colleges*.
You can find those school profiles in *Complete Book of Colleges*, 2012 Edition.

Great Schools for English Literature and Language Majors

- Amherst College
- Auburn University
- Bard College (NY)
- Barnard College
- Bennington College
- Boston College
- Brown University
- City University of New York—
  Hunter College
- Claremont McKenna College
- Clemson University
- Colby College
- Colgate University
- Columbia University
- Cornell University
- Dartmouth College
- Denison University
- Duke University
- Emory University
- Eugene Lang College
  The New School for Liberal Arts
- Fordham University
- George Mason University
- Gettysburg College
- Harvard College
- Johns Hopkins University
- Kenyon College
- Pitzer College
- Pomona College
- Princeton University
- Rice University
- Stanford University
- Syracuse University
- Tufts University
- University of California—Berkeley
- The University of Chicago
- University of Michigan—Ann Arbor
- University of Notre Dame
- University of Utah
- Vassar College
- Washington University in St. Louis
- Wellesley College
- Yale University

Great Schools for History Majors

- Bowdoin College
- Brown University
- Centre College
- Colgate University
- College of the Holy Cross
- Columbia University
- Drew University
- Furman University
- Georgetown University
- Grinnell College
- Hampden-Sydney College
- Harvard College
- Haverford College
- Hillsdale College
- Kenyon College
- Oberlin College
- Princeton University
- Trinity College (CT)
- Tulane University
- University of Virginia
- Wabash College
- Washington and Lee University*
- Yale University

Schools marked with an asterisk do not appear in the *Best 376 Colleges*.
You can find those school profiles in *Complete Book of Colleges*, 2012 Edition.

Great Schools for Journalism Majors

- American University
- Boston University
- Carleton College
- Columbia University
- Emerson College
- Hampton University
- Howard University
- Indiana University—Bloomington
- Loyola University—New Orleans
- Middle Tennessee State University*
- Northwestern University
- Ohio University—Athens
- Pennsylvania State University
- Samford University
- St. Bonaventure University
- Syracuse University
- Temple University
- University of Florida
- University of Maryland—College Park
- University of Missouri—Columbia
- The University of North Carolina at Chapel Hill
- University of Oregon
- University of Southern California
- The University of Texas at Austin
- University of Wisconsin—Madison

Great Schools for Marketing and Sales Majors

- Babson College
- Baylor University
- Bentley College
- Duquesne University
- Fairfield University
- Hofstra University
- Indiana University—Bloomington
- Iowa State University
- James Madison University
- Miami University (OH)
- Providence College
- Seattle University
- Siena College
- Syracuse University
- Texas A&M University
- University of Central Florida
- University of Michigan—Ann Arbor
- University of Mississippi
- University of Pennsylvania
- University of South Florida
- The University of Texas at Austin

Great Schools for Mechanical Engineering Majors

- Bradley University
- California Institute of Technology
- Clarkson University
- Colorado School of Mines*
- Drexel University
- Franklin W. Olin College of Engineering
- Georgia Institute of Technology
- Harvey Mudd College
- Iowa State University
- Lehigh University
- Massachusetts Institute of Technology
- New Jersey Institute of Technology
- North Carolina State University
- Purdue University—West Lafayette
- Rose-Hulman Institute of Technology
- Stanford University
- State University of New York— University at Buffalo
- Stevens Institute of Technology
- United States Military Academy
- University of California—Berkeley
- University of Illinois at Urbana-Champaign
- University of Michigan—Ann Arbor
- University of Missouri—Rolla*
- Worcester Polytechnic Institute

Schools marked with an asterisk do not appear in the *Best 376 Colleges*.
You can find those school profiles in *Complete Book of Colleges*, 2012 Edition.

Great Schools for Political Science/Government Majors

- American University
- Amherst College
- Bard College (NY)
- Bates College
- Bowdoin College
- Brigham Young University (UT)
- Bryn Mawr College
- Carleton College
- Claremont McKenna College
- College of the Holy Cross
- Columbia University
- Davidson College
- Dickinson College
- Drew University
- Furman University
- George Mason University
- George Washington University
- Georgetown University
- Gettysburg College
- Gonzaga University
- Harvard College
- Kenyon College
- Macalester College
- Princeton University
- Stanford University
- Swarthmore College
- Syracuse University
- University of Arizona
- University of California—Berkeley
- University of California—Los Angeles
- University of Washington
- Vassar College
- Yale University

Great Schools for Psychology Majors

- Albion College
- Bates College
- Carnegie Mellon University
- Christopher Newport University
- Clark University
- Colorado State University
- Columbia University
- Cornell University
- Dartmouth College
- Duke University
- George Mason University
- Gettysburg College
- Harvard College
- James Madison University
- Lewis & Clark College
- Loyola University—Chicago
- New York University
- Pitzer College
- Portland State University
- Princeton University
- Roanoke College
- Smith College
- Stanford University
- University of California—Davis
- University of California—Los Angeles
- University of California—Riverside
- University of California—Santa Barbara
- University of California—Santa Cruz
- University of Houston
- University of Michigan—Ann Arbor
- University of Southern California
- The University of Texas at Austin
- University of Utah
- Washington University in St. Louis
- Yale University

Schools marked with an asterisk do not appear in the *Best 376 Colleges*.
You can find those school profiles in *Complete Book of Colleges*, 2012 Edition.

HOW AND WHY WE PRODUCE THIS BOOK

This Year's Edition

In the nineteen years since the first edition of this book, our Best Colleges guide has grown considerably. We've added more than 100 colleges to the guide and deleted several along the way. How we choose the schools for the book, and how we produce it, however, has not changed significantly over the years (with the exception of how we conduct our student survey—more on this follows).

To determine which schools will be in each edition, we don't use mathematical calculations or formulas. Instead we rely on a wide range of input, both quantitative and qualitative. Every year we collect data from nearly 2,000 colleges that we use for our *Complete Book of Colleges*, this book, and our web-based profiles of schools. We visit dozens of colleges and meet with their admissions officers, deans, presidents and college students. We talk with hundreds of high school counselors, parents, and students. Colleges also submit information to us requesting consideration for inclusion in the book. As a result, we are able to maintain a constantly evolving list of colleges to consider adding to each new edition of the book. Any college we add to the guide, however, must agree to support our efforts to survey its students via our anonymous student survey. (Sometimes a college's administrative protocols will not allow it to participate in our student survey; this has caused some academically outstanding schools to be absent from the guide.) Finally, we work to ensure that our roster of colleges in the book presents a wide representation of institutions by region, character, and type. Here you'll find profiles of public and private schools, Historically Black Colleges and Universities, men's and women's colleges, science- and technology-focused institutions, nontraditional colleges, highly selective schools, and some with virtually open-door admissions policies.

For this year's edition we added six schools to the guide: Champlain College, Christopher Newport University, Portland State University, Roanoke College, University of Houston, and one international school, National University of Ireland, Maynooth.

Our ranking lists in this edition are based on our surveys of 122,000 students attending the 376 colleges in the book. We surveyed about 330 students per campus on average, though that number varies depending on the size of the student population. We've surveyed anywhere from twenty-some students at Deep Springs College (100 percent of the all-male student body) to more than 1,000 collegians at such colleges as Drexel University, Clemson University, and the United States Military Academy.

All of the institutions in this guide are academically terrific in our opinion. The 376 schools featured—our picks of the cream of the crop colleges and universities—comprise only the top fifteen percent of all colleges in the nation. Not every college will appeal to every student but that is the beauty of it. These are all very different schools with many different and wonderful things to offer. We hope you will use this book as a starting point (it will certainly give you a snapshot of what life is like at these schools) but not as the final word on any one school. Check out other resources. Visit as many colleges as you can. Talk to students at those colleges—ask what they love and what bothers them most about their schools. Finally, form your own opinions about the colleges you are considering. At the end of the day, it's what YOU think about the schools that matters most, and that will enable you to answer that all-important question: "Which college is best for me?"

> *"We worked to create a guide that would help people who couldn't always get to the campus nonetheless get in-depth campus feedback to find the schools best for them."*

The History of This Book

When we published the first edition of this book in 1992, there was a void in the world of college guides (hard to believe, but true!). No publication provided college applicants with statistical data from colleges that covered academics, admissions, financial aid, and student demographics along with narrative descriptions of the schools based on comprehensive surveys of students attending them. Of course, academic rankings of colleges had been around for some time. They named the best schools on hierarchical lists, from 1 to 200 and upwards, some in tiers. Their criteria factored in such matters as faculty salaries, alumni giving, and peer reviews (i.e., what college administrators thought of the schools that, in many cases, they competed with for students). But no one was polling students at these terrific colleges about their experiences on campus—both inside and outside the classroom. We created our first Best Colleges guide to address that void. It was born out of one very obvious omission in college guide publishing and two very deep convictions we held then and hold even more strongly today:

- One: The key question for students and parents researching colleges shouldn't be "What college is best, academically?" The thing is, it's not hard to find academically great schools in this country. (There are hundreds of them.) The key question—and one that is truly tough to answer—is "What is the best college for me?"

- Two: We believe the best way for students and parents to know if a school is right—and ultimately best—for them is to visit it. Travel to the campus, get inside a dorm, audit a class, browse the town and—most importantly—talk to students attending the school. In the end it's the school's customers—its students—who are the real experts about the college. Only they can give you the most candid and informed feedback on what life is really like on the campus.

Guided by these convictions, we worked to create a resource that would help people who couldn't always get to the campus nonetheless get in-depth campus feedback to find the schools best for them. We culled an initial list of 250 academically great schools, based on our own college knowledge and input from fifty independent college counselors. We gathered institutional data from those schools and surveyed 30,000 students attending them (about 120 per campus on average). We wrote the school profiles, incorporating school data and extensive quotes from surveyed students, and we compiled for the book more than sixty ranking lists of top twenty schools in various categories based on our surveys of students at the schools.

With support from nearly a million students who've participated in our student surveys over the years, and administrators at nearly 400 colleges, we're pleased to offer what we continue to believe is the most substantive resource you can find to know which of these 376 schools may be best for you.

About Our Student Survey for Our "Best Colleges" Books

Our undergraduate student survey is a mammoth undertaking. In the first few years that we published this book, we formally surveyed students at all of the colleges and universities in the book on an annual basis. By the time we had gone through a few editions, we found that barring some grand upheaval or administrative change on campus, there's little change in student opinion from one year to the next, but that shifts emerge in a third or fourth year (as surveyed students leave or matriculate). With this in mind, we switched to a three-year cycle for formally resurveying each campus. Thus, each year we target about 150 campuses for resurveying. We resurvey colleges more often than that if colleges request it (and we can accommodate the request) or if we believe it is warranted for one reason or another.

In the early years, our surveys were conducted on campuses and on paper, but the launch in the late 1990s of our online survey (http://survey.review.com), has made it possible for students to complete a survey anytime and anywhere. Now all of our student surveys are now completed online.

Online surveys submitted by students outside of a school's normal survey cycle and independent of any solicitation on our part are factored into the subsequent year's rankings and ratings calculations. In that respect, our surveying is a continuous process. All colleges and universities whose students we plan to survey are notified about the survey through our administrative contacts at the schools. We depend upon them for assistance either in notifying the student body about the availability of the online survey via e-mail.

The survey has more than eighty questions divided into four sections: "About Yourself," "Your School's Academics/Administration," "Students," and "Life at Your School." We ask about all sorts of things, from "How many out-of-class hours do you spend studying each day?" to "How do you rate your campus food?" Most questions offer students a five-point grid on which to indicate their answer choices (headers may range from "Excellent" to "Awful"). Eight questions offer students the opportunity to expand on their answers with narrative comment. These essay-type responses are the sources of the student quotations that appear in the school profiles. Once the surveys have been completed and responses stored in our database, every college is given a score (similar to a grade point average) for its students' answers to each question. This score enables us to compare students' responses to a particular question from one college to the next. We use these scores as an underlying data point in our calculation of the ratings in the profile sidebars and the ranking lists in the section of the book titled "School Rankings and Lists."

Once we have the student survey information in hand, we write the college profiles. Student quotations in each profile are chosen because they represent the sentiments expressed by the majority of survey respondents from the college; or, they illustrate one side or another of a mixed bag of student opinion, in which case there will also appear a counterpoint within the text. In order to guard against producing a write-up that's off the mark for any particular college, we send our administrative contact at each school a copy of the profile we intend to publish prior to its publication date, with ample opportunity to respond with corrections, comments, and/or outright objections. In every case in which we receive requests for changes, we take careful measures to review the school's suggestions against the student survey data we collected and make appropriate changes when warranted.

HOW THIS BOOK IS ORGANIZED

Each of the colleges and universities in this book has its own two-page profile. To make it easier to find and compare information about the schools, we've used the same profile format for every school. Look at the sample pages below: Each profile has nine major components. First, at the very top of the profile you will see the school's address, telephone, and fax numbers for the admissions office, the telephone number for the financial aid office, and the school's website and/or e-mail address. Second, there are two sidebars (the narrow columns on the outside of each page, which consist mainly of statistics) divided into the categories of Campus Life, Academics, Selectivity, and Financial Facts. Third, there are four headings in the narrative text: Students Say, Admissions, Financial Aid, and From the Admissions Office. Here's what you'll find in each part:

The Sidebars

The sidebars contain various statistics culled from our surveys of students attending the school and from questionnaires that school administrators complete at our request in the fall of each year. Keep in mind that not every category will appear for every school—in some cases the information is not reported or not applicable. We compile the eight ratings—Quality of Life, Fire Safety, Green Rating, Academic, Profs Interesting, Profs Accessible, Admissions Selectivity, and Financial Aid—listed in the sidebars based on the results from our student surveys and/or institutional data we collect from school administrators.

These ratings are on a scale of 60–99. If a 60* (60 with an asterisk) appears as any rating for any school, it means that the school reported so few of the rating's underlying data points by our deadline that we were unable to calculate an accurate rating for it. (These measures are outlined in the ratings explanation below.) Be advised that because the Admissions Selectivity Rating is a factor in the computation that produces the Academic Rating, a school that has 60* (60 with an asterisk) as its Admissions Selectivity Rating will have an Academic Rating that is lower than it should be. Also bear in mind that each rating places each college on a continuum for purposes of comparing colleges within this edition only. Since our ratings computations may change from year to year, it is invalid to compare the ratings in this edition to those that appear in any prior or future edition.

Finally, these ratings are quite different from the ranking lists that appear in Part 2 of the book, "School Rankings and Lists." The ratings are numerical measures that show how a school "sizes up," if you will, on a fixed scale. Our sixty-two ranking lists report the top twenty (or in some cases bottom twenty) schools of the 376 in the book (not of all schools in the nation) in various categories. They are based on our surveys of students at the schools and/or institutional data. We don't rank the schools in the book 1 to 376 hierarchically. Here is what each heading in the sidebar tells you, in order of their appearance:

Quality of Life Rating

On a scale of 60–99, this rating is a measure of how happy students are with their campus experiences outside the classroom. To compile this rating, we weighed several factors, all based on students' answers to questions on our survey. They included the students' assessments of: their overall happiness; the beauty, safety, and location of the campus; comfort of dorms; quality of food; ease of getting around campus and dealing with administrators; friendliness of fellow students; and the interaction of different student types on campus and within the greater community.

> *"Ratings are quite different from the ranking lists. The ratings are numerical measures that show how a school "sizes up," if you will, on a fixed scale. Our sixty-two ranking lists report the top twenty (or in some cases bottom twenty) schools of the 376 in the book (not of all schools in the nation) in various categories."*

Fire Safety Rating

On a scale of 60–99, this rating measures how well prepared a school is to prevent or respond to campus fires, specifically in residence halls. We asked schools several questions about their efforts to ensure fire safety for campus residents. We developed the questions in consultation with the Center for Campus Fire Safety (www.campusfiresafety.org). Each school's responses to eight questions were considered when calculating its Fire Safety Rating. They cover:

1. The percentage of student housing sleeping rooms protected by an automatic fire sprinkler system with a fire sprinkler head located in the individual sleeping rooms.

2. The percentage of student housing sleeping rooms equipped with a smoke detector connected to a supervised fire alarm system.

3. The number of malicious fire alarms that occur in student housing per year.

4. The number of unwanted fire alarms that occur in student housing per year.

5. The banning of certain hazardous items and activities in residence halls, like candles, smoking, halogen lamps, etc.

6. The percentage of student housing fire alarm systems that, if activated, result in a signal being transmitted to a monitored location, where security investigates before notifying the fire department.

7. The percentage of student housing fire alarm systems that, if activated, result in a signal being transmitted immediately to a continuously monitored location, which can then immediately notify the fire department to initiate a response.

8. How often fire safety rules-compliance inspections are conducted each year.

Schools that did not report answers to a sufficient number of questions receive a Fire Safety Rating of 60* (60 with an asterisk). You can also find Fire Safety Ratings for the *Best 376 Colleges* (and several additional schools) in our *Complete Book of Colleges*, 2012 Edition. On page 51 of this book, you'll find a list of the schools with 99 (the highest score) Fire Safety Ratings.

Green Rating

We asked all the schools we collect data from annually to answer a number of questions that evaluate the comprehensive measure of their performance as an environmentally aware and responsible institution. The questions were developed in consultation with ecoAmerica, a research and partnership-based environmental nonprofit that convened an expert committee to design this comprehensive rating system, and cover: 1) whether students have a campus quality of life that is both healthy and sustainable; 2) how well a school is preparing students not only for employment in the clean energy economy of the twenty-first century, but also for citizenship in a world now defined by environmental challenges; and 3) how environmentally responsible a school's policies are. Each school's responses to ten questions were considered when calculating its Green Rating. They cover:

1. The percentage of food expenditures that go toward local, organic, or otherwise environmentally preferable food.

2. Whether the school offers programs including free bus passes, universal access transit passes, bike sharing/renting, car sharing, carpool parking, vanpooling, or guaranteed rides home to encourage alternatives to single-passenger automobile use for students.

3. Whether the school has a formal committee with participation from students that is devoted to advancing sustainability on campus.

4. Whether new buildings are required to be LEED Silver certified or comparable.

5. The schools overall waste diversion rate.

6. Whether the school has an environmental studies major, minor or concentration.

7. Whether the school has an 'environmental literacy' requirement.

8. Whether a school has produced a publicly available greenhouse gas emissions inventory and adopted a climate action plan consistent with eighty percent greenhouse gas reductions by 2050 targets.

9. What percentage of the school's energy consumption, including heating/cooling and electrical, is derived from renewable resources (this definition included 'green tags' but not nuclear or large scale hydro power).

10. Whether the school employs a dedicated full-time (or full-time equivalent) sustainability officer.

Colleges that did not supply answers to a sufficient number of the green campus questions for us to fairly compare them to other colleges receive a Green Rating of 60*. On page 51 of this book, you'll find a list of the schools with 99 (the highest score) Green Ratings.

Type of school
Whether the school is public or private.

Affiliation
Any religious order with which the school is affiliated.

Environment
Whether the campus is located in an urban, suburban, or rural setting.

Total undergrad enrollment
The total number of degree-seeking undergraduates who attend the school.

"% male/female" through "# countries represented"
Demographic information about the full-time undergraduate student body, including male to female ratio, ethnicity, and the number of countries represented by the student body. Also included are the percentages of the student body who are from out of state, attended a public high school, live on campus, and belong to Greek organizations.

Survey Says . . .
A snapshot of key results of our student survey. This list shows what the students we surveyed felt unusually strongly about, both positively and negatively, at their schools (see the end of this section for a detailed explanation of items on the list).

Academic Rating
On a scale of 60–99, this rating is a measure of how hard students work at the school and how much they get back for their efforts. The rating is based on results from our surveys of students and data we collect from administrators. Factors weighed included how many hours students reported that they study each day outside of class, students' assessments of their professors' teaching abilities and of their accessibility outside the classroom and the quality of students the school attracts as measured by admissions statistics.

4-year graduation rate
The percentage of degree-seeking undergraduate students graduating in four years or less.

6-year graduation rate
The percentage of degree-seeking undergraduate students graduating within six years.

Calendar
The school's schedule of academic terms. A "semester" schedule has two long terms, usually starting in September and January. A "trimester" schedule has three terms, one usually beginning before Christmas and two after. A "quarterly" schedule has four terms, which go by very quickly: the entire term, including exams, usually lasts only nine or ten weeks. A "4-1-4" schedule is like a semester schedule, but with a month-long term in between the fall and spring semesters. (Similarly, a 4-4-1 has a short term following two longer semesters.) It is always best to call the admissions office for details.

Student/faculty ratio
The ratio of full-time undergraduate instructional faculty members to all undergraduates.

Profs interesting rating

On a scale of 60–99, this rating is based on levels of surveyed students' agreement or disagreement with the statement: "Your instructors are good teachers."

Profs accessible rating

On a scale of 60–99, this rating is based on levels of surveyed students' agreement or disagreement with the statement: "Your instructors are accessible outside the classroom."

Most common regular class size; Most common lab size

The most commonly occurring class size for regular courses and for labs/discussion sections.

Most Popular Majors

The majors with the highest enrollments at the school.

Admissions Selectivity Rating

On a scale of 60–99, this rating is a measure of how competitive admission is at the school. This rating is determined by several factors, including the class rank of entering freshmen, test scores, and percentage of applicants accepted.

% of applicants accepted

The percentage of applicants to whom the school offered admission.

% of acceptees attending

The percentage of accepted students who eventually enrolled at the school.

accepting a place on wait list

The number of students who decided to take a place on the wait list when offered this option.

% admitted from wait list

The percentage of applicants who opted to take a place on the wait list and were subsequently offered admission. These figures will vary tremendously from college to college, and should be a consideration when deciding whether to accept a place on a college's wait list.

of early decision applicants

The number of students who applied under the college's early decision or early action plan.

% accepted early decision

The percentage of early decision or early action applicants who were admitted under this plan. By the nature of these plans, the vast majority who are admitted ultimately enroll.

Range SAT Critical Reading, Range SAT Math, Range SAT Writing, Range ACT Composite

The average and the middle fifty percent range of test scores for entering freshmen.

Don't be discouraged from applying to the school of your choice even if your combined SAT scores are 80 or even 120 points below the average, because you may still have a chance of getting in. Remember that many schools value other aspects of your application (e.g., your grades, how good a match you make with the school) more heavily than test scores.

Minimum TOEFL

The minimum test score necessary for entering freshmen who are required to take the TOEFL (Test of English as a Foreign Language). Most schools will require all international students or non-native English speakers to take the TOEFL in order to be considered for admission.

Average HS GPA

The average grade point average of entering freshman. We report this on a scale of 1.0–4.0 (occasionally colleges report averages on a 100 scale, in which case we report those figures). This is one of the key factors in college admissions.

% graduated top 10%, top 25%, top 50% of class

Of those students for whom class rank was reported, the percentage of entering freshmen who ranked in the top tenth, quarter, and half of their high school classes.

Early decision/action deadlines

The deadline for submission of application materials under the early decision or early action plan.

Early decision, early action, priority, and regular admission deadlines

The dates by which all materials must be postmarked (we'd suggest "received in the office") in order to be considered for admission under each particular admissions option/cycle for matriculation in the fall term.

Early decision, early action, priority, and regular admission notification

The dates by which you can expect a decision on your application under each admissions option/cycle.

Nonfall registration

Some schools will allow incoming students to register and begin attending classes at times other than the fall term, which is the traditional beginning of the academic calendar year. Other schools will allow you to register for classes only if you can begin in the fall term. A simple "yes" or "no" in this category indicates the school's policy on nonfall registration.

Applicants also look at

These lists are based on information we receive directly from the colleges. Admissions officers are annually given the opportunity to review and suggest alterations to these lists for their schools, as most schools track as closely as they can other schools to which applicants they accepted applied, and whether the applicants chose their school over the other schools, or vice versa.

Financial Aid Rating

On a scale of 60–99, this rating is a measure of the financial aid the school awards and how satisfied students are with the aid they receive. It is based on school-reported data on financial aid and students' responses to the survey question, "If you receive financial aid, how satisfied are you with your financial aid package?" On page 51 of this book you'll find a list of the schools with 99 (the highest score) Financial Aid Ratings.

Annual in-state tuition

The tuition at the school, or for public colleges, the cost of tuition for a resident of the school's state. Usually much lower than out-of-state tuition for state-supported public schools.

Annual out-of-state tuition

For public colleges, the tuition for a nonresident of the school's state. This entry appears only for public colleges, since tuition at private colleges is generally the same regardless of state of residence.

Required fees

Any additional costs students must pay beyond tuition in order to attend the school. These often include fitness center fees and the like. A few state schools may not officially charge in-state students tuition, but those students are still responsible for hefty fees.

Tuition and fees

In cases when schools do not report separate figures for tuition and required fees, we offer this total of the two.

Comprehensive fee

A few schools report one overall fee that reflects the total cost of tuition, room and board, and required fees. If you'd like to see how this figure breaks down, we recommend contacting the school.

Room and board

Estimated annual room and board costs.

Books and supplies

Estimated annual cost of necessary textbooks and/or supplies.

% frosh receiving need-based aid

The percentage of all degree-seeking freshmen who applied for financial aid, were determined to have financial need, and received any sort of aid, need-based or otherwise.

% UG receiving need-based aid

The percentage of all degree-seeking undergrads who applied for financial aid, were determined to have financial need, and received any sort of aid, need-based or otherwise.

% receiving non-need-based aid

The percentage of all degree-seeking undergrads who received any non-need-based scholarship or grant aid.

% receiving need-based self-help aid

The percentage of all degree-seeking undergrads who received any need-based self-help aid.

% receiving any financial aid

The percentage of all degree-seeking undergrads receiving any financial aid (need-based, merit-based, gift aid).

Avg Indebtedness

The average per-borrower cumulative undergraduate indebtedness of those who borrowed at any time through any loan programs (institutional, state, Federal Perkins, Federal Stafford Subsidized and Unsubsidized, private loans that were certified by your institution, etc.; exclude parent loans).

Nota Bene: The statistical data reported in this book, unless otherwise noted, was collected from the profiled colleges from the fall of 2010 through the spring of 2011. In some cases, we were unable to publish the most recent data because schools did not report the necessary statistics to us in time, despite our repeated outreach efforts. Because the enrollment and financial statistics, as well as application and financial aid deadlines, fluctuate from one year to another, we recommend that you check with the schools to make sure you have the most current information before applying.

Students Say

This section shares the straight-from-the-campus feedback we get from the school's most important customers: The students attending them. It summarizes the opinions of freshman through seniors we've surveyed and it includes direct quotes from scores of them. When appropriate, it also incorporates statistics provided by the schools. The Students Say section is divided into three subsections: Academics, Life, and Student Body. The Academics section describes how hard students work and how satisfied they are with the education they are getting. It also often tells you which programs or academic departments students rated most favorably and how professors interact with students. Student opinion regarding administrative departments also works its way into this section. The Life section describes life outside the classroom and addresses questions ranging from "How comfortable are the dorms?" to "How popular are fraternities and sororities?" In this section, students describe what they do for entertainment both on-campus and off, providing a clear picture of the social environment at their particular school. The Student Body section will give you the lowdown on the types of students the school attracts and how the students view the level of interaction among various groups, including those of different ethnic, socioeconomic, and religious backgrounds.

All quotations in these sections are from students' responses to open-ended questions on our survey. We select quotations based on the accuracy with which they reflect overall student opinion about the school as conveyed in the survey results.

Admissions

This section lets you know which aspects of your application are most important to the admissions officers at the school. It also lists the high school curricular prerequisites for applicants, which standardized tests (if any) are required, and special information about the school's admissions process (e.g., Do minority students and legacies, for example, receive special consideration? Are there any unusual application requirements for applicants to special programs?).

Financial Aid

Here you'll found out what you need to know about the financial aid process at the school, namely what forms you need and what types of merit-based aid and loans are available. Information about need-based aid is contained in the financial aid sidebar. This section includes specific deadline dates for submission of materials as reported by the colleges. We strongly encourage students seeking financial aid to file all forms—federal, state, and institutional—carefully, fully, and on time.

The Inside Word

This section gives you the inside scoop on what it takes to gain admission to the school. It reflects our own insights about each school's admissions process and acceptance trends. (We visit scores of colleges each year and talk with hundreds of admissions officers in order to glean this info.) It also incorporates information from institutional data we collect and our surveys over the years of students at the school.

From the Admissions Office

This section presents the key things the school's admissions office would like you to know about their institution. For schools that did not respond to our invitation to supply text for this space, we excerpted an appropriate passage from the school's catalog, web site, or other admissions literature. For this section, we also invited schools to submit a brief paragraph explaining their admissions policies regarding the SAT (especially the Writing portion of the exam) and the SAT Subject Tests. We are pleased that nearly every school took this opportunity to clarify its policies as we know there has been some student and parent confusion about how these scores are evaluated for admission.

Survey Says

Our Survey Says list, located in the Campus Life sidebar on each school's two-page spread, is based entirely on the results of our student survey. In other words, the items on this list are based on the opinions of the students we surveyed at those schools (not on any quantitative analysis of library size, endowment, etc.). These items reveal popular or unpopular trends on campus for the purpose of providing a snapshot of life on that campus only. The appearance of a Survey Says item in the sidebar does not reflect the popularity of that item relative to its popularity amongst the student bodies at other schools. To ascertain the relative popularity of certain items/trends on campus, see the appropriate ranking (e.g., for the Survey Says item "Library needs improving," see the "This is a Library?" ranking). Some of the terms that appear on the Survey Says list are not entirely self-explanatory; these terms are defined below.

Different types of students interact: We asked students whether students from different class and ethnic backgrounds interacted frequently and easily. When students' collective response is "yes," the heading "Different types of students interact" appears on the list. When the collective student response indicates there are not many interactions between students from different class and ethnic backgrounds, the phrase "Students are cliquish" appears on the list.

No one cheats: We asked students how prevalent cheating is at their school. If students reported cheating to be rare, the term "No one cheats" shows up on the list.

Students are happy: This category reflects student responses to the question "Overall, how happy are you?"

Students are very religious or Students aren't religious: We asked students how religious students are at their school. Their responses are reflected in this category.

Diverse student types on campus: We asked students whether their student body is made up of a variety of ethnic groups. This category reflects their answers to this question. This heading shows up as "Diversity lacking on campus" or "Diverse student types on campus." It does not reflect any institutional data on this subject.

Students get along with local community: This category reflects student responses to a question concerning how well the student body gets along with residents of the college town or community.

Career services are great: This category reflects student opinion on the quality of career/job placement services on campus. This heading shows up as "Career services are great."

ABOUT THOSE COLLEGE RANKING LISTS

Finding a college that has terrific academics is easy. There are hundreds of academically great colleges out there. Their campus cultures, student bodies, and school offerings, however, differ widely. Finding the academically great school that is right for you is the tough part. Hence, we compile not one ranking list but sixty-two unique lists, each one reporting the top twenty (or in some cases bottom twenty) schools from our Best Colleges book in a specific category.

None of the lists are based on what we think of the schools (though members of the media, the public, and school administrators mistakenly credit or blame us for the results, saying "According to The Princeton Review, X school is the best in the nation for…" or "The Princeton Review ranks Y school the 10th most…."). In fact, the only thing we say is that all of the 376 colleges in this book are outstanding (hence, the "Best" designation). It's what students think of their schools—how they rate various aspects of their colleges' offerings and what they report to us about their campus experiences—that results in a school's appearance on our ranking lists.

Here you won't find the colleges in the book ranked hierarchically, 1 to 376. We think such lists—particularly those driven by and perpetuating a "best academics" mania—are not useful for the people they are supposed to serve (college applicants). More and more college administrators—including several at schools ranked high on these lists—agree. In fact, the primary reason we developed this book was to give applicants and parents better and broader information that will help them winnow a list of colleges right for them.

About eighty-five percent of the schools in our book end up on one or more of the lists in each edition. The students are the raters—we are simply the folks who compile the ranking lists based on their opinions. To college officials happy about the lists their schools are on, we say don't thank us, we're just the messengers. To college officials unhappy about the lists their schools are on (and unsurprisingly, it is mainly they who say our student survey has no validity whatsoever), we say don't blame us, we're just the messengers.

All of these ranking lists are based entirely on students' answers to questions on our surveys (e.g., our "Best Campus Food" list and inverse list, "Is it Food?" are each based on the single survey question, "How do you rate your campus food?") or students' answers to a combination of survey questions (e.g., our "Party Schools" list and our inverse list, "Stone-Cold Sober Schools" are each based on students' answers to survey questions concerning the use of alcohol and drugs on their campuses, the popularity of the frat/sorority scene on their campuses, and the number of hours they say they study each day outside of class time).

Each list, even those with somewhat irreverent titles (such as "Dorms Like Dungeons"), covers one of many aspects of a college's character that can be helpful in deciding if it's the right or wrong place for an individual student. The lists report on a wide range of issues that may be important, either singly or, more likely, in combination. Our ranking lists cover: financial aid, campus facilities and amenities, extracurriculars, town-gown relations, the student body's political leanings, social life, race/class relations, gay-friendly (or not so friendly) atmosphere, career services, athletic facilities, and more.

> *"It's what students think of their schools—how they rate various aspects of their colleges' offerings and what they report to us about their campus experiences—that results in a school's appearance on our ranking lists."*

Our newest addition is one ranking list category: "Best Health Services."

The ranking list category that media covers the most (though it appears 57th among the lists in our "School Rankings and Lists" section, and is only referenced briefly in our press materials) is the "Party Schools" list. It's even been the subject of a Doonesbury cartoon (which appears on the frontispiece of this book) as well as a USA TODAY editorial in which the paper commended us for reporting the list, calling it "a public service." Our "Party Schools" list draws a wide range of reaction every year. Some students complain that their college didn't make the list, while others are irate because their college did. One reporter from the *Washington Post* whose alma mater was #1 on the list several years back wrote a column in which he argued that the ranking was grossly undeserved: He had recently visited his campus and pronounced the then current student body lame as "partiers" compared to the revelers of his day.

Many incorrectly assume that an institution that shows up on the "Party Schools" list is not an advisable college to attend. We recommend all 376 schools in this book as outstanding institutions at which to earn one's college degree. But just as the schools on our "LGBT-Unfriendly" list may not be ideal campuses for gay students, the schools on our "Party Schools" list may not be ideal for students seeking a campus at which the use of alcohol and drugs and the frat/sorority scene is, well, less exuberant.

On the other hand, no one should make the mistake of assuming that the colleges and universities that don't show up on our "Party Schools" list are in any way insulated from the influences of alcohol and drugs on their campuses. An oft-quoted Harvard University School of Public Health study published in 2000 found that forty-five percent of undergraduates, in general, binge drink (consume five or more alcoholic beverages in one sitting for men, four drinks or more for women).[1] These facts are alarming, as they should be. College administrators face tremendous challenges in creating and enforcing campus alcohol and drug use/abuse policies. Many struggle with problems resulting from the prevalence of bars and liquor stores near their campuses; at some universities that have appeared on our "Party Schools" list there are more than 100 such establishments within a few miles from the campus. "Dry campus" policies often exacerbate the problem, driving drinking off-campus, making it even more dangerous for students.

Despite the claims of some administrators at colleges that have repeatedly made our "Party School" list that our reporting this list promotes drinking on campuses (a group of such administrators receiving funding through the American Medical Association to address their campus alcohol problems made the news several years back with this claim, after which USA TODAY published the editorial praising our ranking as a "public service"), we neither encourage nor discourage students who wish to drink. None of our lists promote behavior: They report on it, plain and simple. What we promote is information.

What we do say to college students—as we have said in this very section of this book for more than 10 years—is this: If you're going to drink, do it safely, smartly, responsibly, and legally. If you're going off campus to drink, don't drive back drunk—get a designated driver. Don't let a peer situation (fraternity rush, etc.) put you in jeopardy—it's simply not worth it. Don't use alcohol or drugs as a badge of your coolness—there's not much of a fine line between someone who's socially engaging and someone who's totally disengaging because he or she has performed a chemical auto-lobotomy. Last, don't simply take responsibility for yourself; remember to keep an eye on your friends, and never leave them passed out and alone.

---

1 *Harvard University School of Public Health. "College Student Binge Drinking Rates Remain High Despite Efforts by School Administrations." www.hsph.harvard.edu/news/press-releases/2000-releases/press03142000.html.*

Finally, we would like to thank all the college officials, college counselors, advisors, students, and parents, who have made this annual guide possible by supporting us these past nineteen years. Our ranking lists have, collectively, been based on surveys of more than 750,000 students whose input has been vital to our publication of this book. We know that it has helped students find great colleges perfect for them, and it has brought to the colleges in our book many outstanding students who otherwise may not have considered attending their institutions.

WE WANT TO HEAR FROM YOU

To all of our readers, we welcome your feedback on how we can continue to improve this guide. We hope you will share with us your comments, questions, and suggestions. Please contact us at editorialsupport@review.com. We welcome it.

To college applicants, we wish you all the best in your college search. And when you get to your campuses and settle in to your college life, come back to us online; participate in our survey for this book at http://survey.review.com. Let your honest comments about your schools guide prospective students who want your help answering the $64,000 question (goodness knows, the sticker price at some schools may be that high or even higher!): "Which is the best college for me?"

PART 2

School Rankings and Lists

We present our 62 "Top 20" ranking lists in eight categories.

Schools by Type

Under each list heading, we tell you the survey question or assessment that we used to tabulate the list. We tally student responses to several questions on our survey for our lists "Best Classroom Experience," "Best Quality of Life," and the six lists in our Schools by Type rankings (including our "Party Schools" and "Stone-Cold Sober Schools" lists). Be aware that all of our 62 ranking lists are based entirely on our student surveys. They do not reflect our opinions of the schools. They are entirely the result of what students attending these schools tell us about them: It's how students rate their own schools and what they report to us about their campus experiences at them that make our ranking lists so unusual. After all, what better way is there to judge a school than by what its customers—its students—say about it?

Honor Rolls

Best Value Colleges List

ACADEMICS/ADMINISTRATION

Best Classroom Experience

Based on a combination of survey questions concerning teachers, classroom/lab facilities, classes attended, and amount of in-class discussion

1. United States Military Academy
2. Stanford University
3. Franklin W. Olin College of Engineering
4. Reed College
5. University of Richmond
6. Princeton University
7. Mount Holyoke College
8. Bard College (NY)
9. Williams College
10. Pomona College
11. Wellesley College
12. Colby College
13. Swarthmore College
14. Grinnell College
15. Colgate University
16. St. John's College (MD)
17. Champlain College
18. Hamilton College
19. Bates College
20. Sweet Briar College

Students Study the Most

How many out-of-class hours do you spend studying each day?

1. Harvey Mudd College
2. Massachusetts Institute of Technology
3. Franklin W. Olin College of Engineering
4. Harvard College
5. Princeton University
6. Davidson College
7. United States Military Academy
8. Haverford College
9. University of Chicago
10. California Institute of Technology
11. Swarthmore College
12. Cornell University
13. Bryn Mawr College
14. Middlebury College
15. Reed College
16. Bard College (NY)
17. Carnegie Mellon University
18. Mount Holyoke College
19. Rhodes College
20. Grove City College

Students Study the Least
How many out-of-class hours do you spend studying each day?

1. University of North Dakota
2. Salisbury University
3. The University of Alabama—Tuscaloosa
4. University of Central Florida
5. University of South Florida
6. University of Mississippi
7. University of Iowa
8. Louisiana State University
9. Florida State University
10. University of Maryland—College Park
11. Rider University
12. Ohio University—Athens
13. West Virginia University
14. University of Florida
15. University of Georgia
16. The University of Texas at Austin
17. James Madison University
18. Catawba College
19. Loyola Marymount University
20. University of Maine

Professors Get High Marks
Are your instructors good teachers?

1. Wellesley College
2. Harvey Mudd College
3. Reed College
4. Franklin W. Olin College of Engineering
5. Kenyon College
6. Colby College
7. Sarah Lawrence College
8. Millsaps College
9. Rose-Hulman Institute of Technology
10. Hamilton College
11. Carleton College
12. College of William & Mary
13. Middlebury College
14. Sweet Briar College
15. Austin College
16. Wofford College
17. New College of Florida
18. Hillsdale College
19. Whitman College
20. Centre College

Professors Get Low Marks
Are your instructors good teachers?

1. New Jersey Institute of Technology
2. United States Merchant Marine Academy
3. University of Illinois at Urbana-Champaign
4. Indiana University of Pennsylvania
5. University of California—San Diego
6. Rutgers, The State University of New Jersey—New Brunswick
7. University of Oregon
8. University of Connecticut
9. Georgia Institute of Technology
10. Iowa State University
11. California Institute of Technology
12. University of California—Riverside
13. University of Rhode Island
14. Illinois Institute of Technology
15. Case Western Reserve University
16. Purdue University—West Lafayette
17. Stevens Institute of Technology
18. University of Kentucky
19. University of Iowa
20. Washington State University

Most Accessible Professors
Are your instructors accessible outside the classroom?

1. United States Military Academy
2. United States Coast Guard Academy
3. Pomona College
4. United States Naval Academy
5. United States Air Force Academy
6. Reed College
7. Sweet Briar College
8. Skidmore College
9. Southern Methodist University
10. Williams College
11. Sarah Lawrence College
12. Wabash College
13. Claremont McKenna College
14. Amherst College
15. Franklin & Marshall College
16. Webb Institute
17. Colgate University
18. Hampden-Sydney College
19. Ohio University—Athens
20. Muhlenberg College

Least Accessible Professors
Are your instructors accessible outside the classroom?

1. United States Merchant Marine Academy
2. New Jersey Institute of Technology
3. Georgia Institute of Technology
4. University of Toronto
5. St. John's University (NY)
6. Illinois Institute of Technology
7. Rutgers, The State University of New Jersey—New Brunswick
8. Sonoma State University
9. Howard University
10. Stevens Institute of Technology
11. McGill University
12. Temple University
13. The University of North Carolina at Greensboro

14. Case Western Reserve University
15. University of Maine
16. State University of New York—Stony Brook University
17. University of South Florida
18. University of Kentucky
19. The University of South Dakota
20. Tuskegee University

Class Discussions Encouraged
How much of your overall class time is devoted to discussion as opposed to lectures?

1. Sarah Lawrence College
2. Eugene Lang College
3. Champlain College
4. Wagner College
5. University of Redlands
6. Green Mountain College
7. Prescott College
8. Hampshire College
9. Colorado College
10. Reed College
11. Sweet Briar College
12. Thomas Aquinas College
13. Wesleyan College
14. Wells College
15. Oglethorpe University
16. United States Military Academy
17. Seattle University
18. Whitman College
19. Pitzer College
20. St. John's College (MD)

Most Popular Study Abroad Program
How popular is studying abroad at your school?

1. Goucher College
2. Dartmouth College
3. Kalamazoo College
4. Elon University
5. Marist College
6. Colby College
7. Tufts University
8. University of Dallas
9. Bates College
10. Georgetown University
11. Pepperdine University
12. Wofford College
13. University of Denver
14. Austin College
15. Middlebury College
16. Eckerd College
17. Colgate University
18. Indiana University—Bloomington
19. University of Delaware
20. Claremont McKenna College

Best Health Services
Based on students' assessments of student health services/facilities on campus

1. University of California—Los Angeles
2. Whitman College
3. United States Military Academy
4. The University of Texas at Austin
5. Pennsylvania State University—University Park
6. Georgia Institute of Technology
7. University of Pittsburgh—Pittsburgh Campus
8. Susquehanna University
9. University of Georgia
10. University of Florida
11. North Carolina State University
12. Colby College
13. University of California—Santa Barbara
14. University of Minnesota—Twin Cities
15. Villanova University
16. Wofford College
17. Stanford University
18. Rice University
19. California State University Stanislaus
20. Virginia Tech

Best Career Services
Based on students' rating of campus career/job-placement services

1. University of Florida
2. Northeastern University
3. Pennsylvania State University—University Park
4. The University of Texas at Austin
5. Barnard College
6. Claremont McKenna College
7. Rochester Institute of Technology
8. Bentley University
9. Clemson University
10. University of Richmond
11. Missouri University of Science and Technology
12. Spelman College
13. Yale University
14. Cornell University
15. Lafayette College
16. University of Missouri—Columbia
17. Worcester Polytechnic Institute
18. American University
19. Southern Methodist University
20. Franklin W. Olin College of Engineering

Best College Library
Based on students' assessment of library facilities

1. Harvard College
2. Columbia University

3. Brigham Young University (UT)
4. Cornell University
5. Duke University
6. Princeton University
7. Stanford University
8. United States Military Academy
9. Emory University
10. Yale University
11. Hampden-Sydney College
12. Middlebury College
13. University of Chicago
14. University of Virginia
15. Pennsylvania State University—University Park
16. West Virginia University
17. The University of Texas at Austin
18. University of Wisconsin—Madison
19. Colgate University
20. University of Maryland—College Park

This Is a Library?
Based on students' assessment of library facilities

1. Clarkson University
2. Bradley University
3. Tuskegee University
4. College of the Atlantic
5. Seattle University
6. Birmingham-Southern College
7. Montana Tech of the University of Montana
8. Hampshire College
9. Wells College
10. Howard University
11. Spelman College
12. Drexel University
13. United States Merchant Marine Academy
14. Duquesne University
15. Bard College (NY)
16. United States Coast Guard Academy
17. William Jewell College
18. Salisbury University
19. Prescott College
20. Marywood University

Great Financial Aid
Based on students' assessments of how satisfied they are with their financial aid package

1. Swarthmore College
2. Princeton University
3. University of Virginia
4. Yale University
5. New College of Florida
6. Franklin W. Olin College of Engineering
7. Columbia University
8. University of Mississippi
9. Harvard College
10. Thomas Aquinas College

11. Pomona College
12. Cornell College
13. Rice University
14. University of Puget Sound
15. Washington University in St. Louis
16. Claremont McKenna College
17. Wabash College
18. Lake Forest College
19. University of Redlands
20. City University of New York—Hunter College

Financial Aid Not So Great
Based on students' assessments of how satisfied they are with their financial aid package

1. Pennsylvania State University—University Park
2. Quinnipiac University
3. New York University
4. Elon University
5. Duquesne University
6. University of Maryland—College Park
7. Sonoma State University
8. DePaul University
9. Miami University (OH)
10. Grove City College
11. California State University Stanislaus
12. Hofstra University
13. Auburn University
14. Villanova University
15. Spelman College
16. Howard University
17. Washington State University
18. The College of New Jersey
19. University of Kentucky
20. Westminster College (PA)

School Runs Like Butter
Overall, how smoothly is your school run?

1. Washington University in St. Louis
2. Pomona College
3. Elon University
4. The University of North Carolina at Chapel Hill
5. Rice University
6. Claremont McKenna College
7. University of Southern California
8. United States Coast Guard Academy
9. United States Air Force Academy
10. Stanford University
11. Clemson University
12. Middlebury College
13. Princeton University
14. Amherst College
15. Carleton College
16. Wheaton College (IL)

17. Virginia Tech
18. United States Military Academy
19. Pennsylvania State University—University Park
20. United States Naval Academy

Long Lines and Red Tape
Overall, how smoothly is your school run?

1. New York University
2. University of New Orleans
3. Eugene Lang College
4. Wells College
5. Fisk University
6. Hampton University
7. St. John's University (NY)
8. Hampshire College
9. Randolph College
10. United States Merchant Marine Academy
11. State University of New York—Purchase College
12. Manhattanville College
13. City University of New York—Baruch College
14. The Catholic University of America
15. Illinois Institute of Technology
16. University of New Mexico
17. Rutgers, The State University of New Jersey—New Brunswick
18. Hiram College
19. Lake Forest College
20. University of Rhode Island

QUALITY OF LIFE

Happiest Students
Overall, how happy are you?

1. Rice University
2. Clemson University
3. Brown University
4. Stanford University
5. Bowdoin College
6. Loyola Marymount University
7. Pennsylvania State University—University Park
8. Franklin W. Olin College of Engineering
9. Pomona College
10. University of Mississippi
11. University of California—Santa Barbara
12. Claremont McKenna College
13. Macalester College
14. The University of Texas at Austin
15. Ohio Wesleyan University
16. Hamilton College
17. Yale University
18. Colgate University

19. Tufts University
20. University of Pittsburgh—Pittsburgh Campus

Least Happy Students
Overall, how happy are you?

1. New Jersey Institute of Technology
2. Marywood University
3. United States Merchant Marine Academy
4. United States Coast Guard Academy
5. Montana Tech of the University of Montana
6. Clarkson University
7. United States Naval Academy
8. Indiana University of Pennsylvania
9. Illinois Institute of Technology
10. City University of New York—Baruch College
11. New York University
12. Alfred University
13. Fisk University
14. Tuskegee University
15. United States Air Force Academy
16. University of California—Riverside
17. University of Maine
18. The University of South Dakota
19. Whittier College
20. University of New Orleans

Most Beautiful Campus
Based on students' rating of campus beauty

1. Florida Southern College
2. Lewis & Clark College
3. University of California—Santa Cruz
4. Mount Holyoke College
5. Princeton University
6. Sweet Briar College
7. Vassar College
8. Colgate University
9. Sewanee—The University of the South
10. University of San Diego
11. Ohio University—Athens
12. College of the Holy Cross
13. University of Mississippi
14. University of Richmond
15. Rhodes College
16. University of Notre Dame
17. Saint Anselm College
18. Roanoke College
19. Flagler College
20. Pepperdine University

Least Beautiful Campus
Based on students' rating of campus beauty

1. Clarkson University
2. State University of New York—Purchase College

3. Harvey Mudd College
4. University of Dallas
5. Howard University
6. New Jersey Institute of Technology
7. Case Western Reserve University
8. Rochester Institute of Technology
9. City University of New York—Hunter College
10. State University of New York at Albany
11. University of Tennessee
12. University of Alabama at Birmingham
13. Rider University
14. State University of New York—University at Buffalo
15. University of Massachusetts Amherst
16. Eugene Lang College
17. Missouri University of Science and Technology
18. Temple University
19. Purdue University—West Lafayette
20. North Carolina State University

Easiest Campus to Get Around
Based on students' assessments of ease of getting around their campus

1. Wabash College
2. Skidmore College
3. Webb Institute
4. Franklin W. Olin College of Engineering
5. Dartmouth College
6. Susquehanna University
7. Prescott College
8. Davidson College
9. Stevens Institute of Technology
10. The George Washington University
11. St. John's College (MD)
12. Reed College
13. Austin College
14. Connecticut College
15. The College of Idaho
16. Hillsdale College
17. Macalester College
18. Centre College
19. Muhlenberg College
20. University of Puget Sound

Best Campus Food
Based on students' rating of campus food

1. Wheaton College (IL)
2. Bowdoin College
3. Virginia Tech
4. Bryn Mawr College
5. James Madison University
6. University of Georgia
7. Washington University in St. Louis
8. Cornell University
9. Colby College

10. University of Massachusetts Amherst
11. Saint Anselm College
12. University of Scranton
13. Boston University
14. University of Richmond
15. Kansas State University
16. Scripps College
17. University of New Hampshire
18. Goucher College
19. St. Olaf College
20. University of Notre Dame

Is It Food?
Based on students' rating of campus food

1. Hampton University
2. New College of Florida
3. United States Merchant Marine Academy
4. Wells College
5. State University of New York at Albany
6. Wesleyan College
7. Fordham University
8. Catawba College
9. Alfred University
10. Flagler College
11. Amherst College
12. Hampden-Sydney College
13. Missouri University of Science and Technology
14. Hiram College
15. Drew University
16. The Catholic University of America
17. Fisk University
18. Xavier University of Louisiana
19. Bard College (NY)
20. Hollins University

Dorms Like Palaces
Based on students' rating of dorm comfort

1. Bryn Mawr College
2. Loyola University—Maryland
3. Smith College
4. Bennington College
5. Washington University in St. Louis
6. Christopher Newport University
7. Bowdoin College
8. Scripps College
9. Skidmore College
10. Franklin W. Olin College of Engineering
11. Amherst College
12. Rose-Hulman Institute of Technology
13. Sweet Briar College
14. Yale University
15. The George Washington University
16. Pomona College
17. Mount Holyoke College
18. Dartmouth College

19. Sonoma State University
20. Reed College

Dorms Like Dungeons
Based on students' rating of dorm comfort

1. University of New Mexico
2. United States Merchant Marine Academy
3. Hampton University
4. Tuskegee University
5. United States Coast Guard Academy
6. University of Washington
7. Prescott College
8. State University of New York at Albany
9. Fisk University
10. Xavier University of Louisiana
11. College of the Ozarks
12. Clarkson University
13. The Evergreen State College
14. United States Naval Academy
15. Whittier College
16. Alfred University
17. Spelman College
18. Rider University
19. Cornell College
20. University of Rhode Island

Best Quality of Life
Based on The Princeton Review's QUALITY OF LIFE RATING (page 22)

1. Rice University
2. Bowdoin College
3. Macalester College
4. Auburn University
5. Barnard College
6. Claremont McKenna College
7. Dartmouth College
8. Davidson College
9. Emory University
10. Agnes Scott College
11. Brown University
12. Columbia University
13. Franklin W. Olin College of Engineering
14. Kansas State University
15. Smith College
16. University of Mississippi
17. University of Pittsburgh—Pittsburgh Campus
18. Vanderbilt University
19. Virginia Tech
20. Washington University in St. Louis

POLITICS

Most Conservative Students
Based on students' assessment of their personal political views

1. Hillsdale College
2. Thomas Aquinas College
3. Texas A&M University—College Station
4. Grove City College
5. United States Air Force Academy
6. University of Dallas
7. United States Merchant Marine Academy
8. Hampden-Sydney College
9. Brigham Young University (UT)
10. Angelo State University
11. Samford University
12. College of the Ozarks
13. United States Military Academy
14. Southern Methodist University
15. Pepperdine University
16. Wheaton College (IL)
17. Baylor University
18. United States Coast Guard Academy
19. The Catholic University of America
20. Lynchburg College

Most Liberal Students
Based on students' assessment of their personal political views

1. Macalester College
2. Warren Wilson College
3. New College of Florida
4. Eugene Lang College
5. Sarah Lawrence College
6. Hampshire College
7. Bard College (NY)
8. University of Puget Sound
9. Pitzer College
10. Prescott College
11. Oberlin College
12. Bennington College
13. Skidmore College
14. The Evergreen State College
15. McGill University
16. Lewis & Clark College
17. Green Mountain College
18. Scripps College
19. Marlboro College
20. Reed College

Most Politically Active Students
How popular are political/activist groups?

1. The George Washington University
2. Georgetown University
3. New College of Florida
4. College of the Atlantic
5. American University

6. United States Military Academy
7. University of Chicago
8. Harvard College
9. Bates College
10. Hampshire College
11. George Mason University
12. Mills College
13. Warren Wilson College
14. Claremont McKenna College
15. Grinnell College
16. Amherst College
17. University of Southern California
18. University of Dallas
19. United States Air Force Academy
20. University of Colorado—Boulder

Election? What Election?
How popular are political/activist groups?

1. University of Scranton
2. Stonehill College
3. Salisbury University
4. Sacred Heart University
5. Ohio Northern University
6. Fisk University
7. Alfred University
8. College of the Ozarks
9. Rose-Hulman Institute of Technology
10. Worcester Polytechnic Institute
11. Wagner College
12. Coe College
13. University of Rhode Island
14. Lehigh University
15. Moravian College
16. Susquehanna University
17. James Madison University
18. Michigan Technological University
19. Simmons College
20. Purdue University—West Lafayette

DEMOGRAPHICS

Lots of Race/Class Interaction
Do different types of students (black/white, rich/ poor) interact frequently and easily?

1. Loyola University—New Orleans
2. Stanford University
3. University of Miami
4. Franklin W. Olin College of Engineering
5. University of Alabama at Birmingham
6. Rice University
7. St. Mary's College of Maryland
8. City University of New York—Hunter College
9. Pitzer College

10. Temple University
11. City University of New York—Queens College
12. Beloit College
13. University of New Mexico
14. Whitman College
15. DePaul University
16. Suffolk University
17. University of Charleston
18. Babson College
19. Illinois Institute of Technology
20. State University of New York—Stony Brook University

Little Race/Class Interaction
Do different types of students (black/white, rich/ poor) interact frequently and easily?

1. Providence College
2. University of New Hampshire
3. Fairfield University
4. Trinity College (CT)
5. Boston College
6. Miami University
7. Gettysburg College
8. Quinnipiac University
9. University of Denver
10. Lehigh University
11. Rollins College
12. Samford University
13. Wake Forest University
14. Villanova University
15. Texas Christian University
16. Vanderbilt University
17. Bucknell University
18. Chapman University
19. Furman University
20. The Catholic University of America

LGBT-Friendly
Do students, faculty and administrators treat all persons equally, regardless of their sexual orientation and gender identity/expression?

1. New York University
2. Stanford University
3. Emerson College
4. Wellesley College
5. Bennington College
6. University of Wisconsin—Madison
7. Macalester College
8. New College of Florida
9. Prescott College
10. Sarah Lawrence College
11. Bryn Mawr College
12. Grinnell College
13. St. John's College (MD)

14. Franklin W. Olin College of Engineering
15. Smith College
16. Hampshire College
17. Swarthmore College
18. Boston University
19. Mount Holyoke College
20. Bard College at Simon's Rock (MA)

LGBT-Unfriendly

Do students, faculty and administrators treat all persons equally, regardless of their sexual orientation and gender identity/expression?

1. Wheaton College (IL)
2. Grove City College
3. Brigham Young University (UT)
4. Hampden-Sydney College
5. College of the Ozarks
6. University of Notre Dame
7. Thomas Aquinas College
8. Boston College
9. University of Dallas
10. Texas A&M University—College Station
11. Providence College
12. Southern Methodist University
13. Samford University
14. University of Rhode Island
15. The Catholic University of America
16. Calvin College
17. Pepperdine University
18. University of Wyoming
19. University of Kentucky
20. Fairfield University

Most Religious Students

Are students very religious?

1. Brigham Young University (UT)
2. Hillsdale College
3. Thomas Aquinas College
4. Wheaton College (IL)
5. Grove City College
6. University of Dallas
7. College of the Ozarks
8. University of Notre Dame
9. Calvin College
10. Baylor University
11. Pepperdine University
12. Samford University
13. Furman University
14. The Catholic University of America
15. United States Military Academy
16. Saint Louis University
17. Creighton University
18. Gonzaga University
19. University of Scranton
20. City University of New York—Brooklyn College

Least Religious Students

Are students very religious?

1. Bennington College
2. Reed College
3. Bard College (NY)
4. Vassar College
5. Sarah Lawrence College
6. Bard College at Simon's Rock (MA)
7. Emerson College
8. Pomona College
9. Grinnell College
10. Macalester College
11. Hampshire College
12. Eugene Lang College
13. Connecticut College
14. Hamilton College
15. Haverford College
16. Lewis & Clark College
17. College of the Atlantic
18. University of California—Santa Barbara
19. Skidmore College
20. Bowdoin College

TOWN LIFE

Great College Town

Based on students' assessment of the surrounding city or town

1. Columbia University
2. Georgetown University
3. Tulane University
4. The George Washington University
5. Boston University
6. New York University
7. Barnard College
8. Southern Methodist University
9. University of Minnesota—Twin Cities
10. American University
11. DePaul University
12. Stevens Institute of Technology
13. Vanderbilt University
14. City University of New York—Hunter College
15. University of Michigan—Ann Arbor
16. The University of North Carolina at Asheville
17. Eugene Lang College
18. The University of Texas at Austin
19. University of Denver
20. University of Colorado—Boulder

College Town Not So Great

Based on students' assessment of the surrounding city or town

1. Tuskegee University
2. Wabash College

3. United States Coast Guard Academy
4. Hofstra University
5. University of Notre Dame
6. Wheaton College (MA)
7. New Jersey Institute of Technology
8. Bates College
9. Albion College
10. Ohio Northern University
11. Union College (NY)
12. Baylor University
13. Clark University
14. United States Military Academy
15. Lehigh University
16. DePauw University
17. Wittenberg University
18. University of the Pacific
19. Rensselaer Polytechnic Institute
20. Duke University

Town-Gown Relations Are Great
Do students get along well with members of the local community?

1. Clemson University
2. Kansas State University
3. College of the Ozarks
4. Virginia Tech
5. Rice University
6. Saint Michael's College
7. University of Alabama at Birmingham
8. Macalester College
9. Wheaton College (IL)
10. Franklin W. Olin College of Engineering
11. St. Olaf College
12. Agnes Scott College
13. Westminster College (PA)
14. Nazareth College
15. Catawba College
16. The University of North Carolina at Asheville
17. Bellarmine University
18. William Jewell College
19. Millsaps College
20. University of New Orleans

Town-Gown Relations Are Strained
Do students get along well with members of the local community?

1. Duke University
2. Lehigh University
3. Trinity College (CT)
4. Northwestern University
5. Union College (NY)
6. Sarah Lawrence College
7. Fairfield University
8. University of Notre Dame
9. Providence College
10. University of Maryland—College Park

11. DePauw University
12. Franklin & Marshall College
13. The College of Wooster
14. Syracuse University
15. University of New Hampshire
16. Johns Hopkins University
17. Dickinson College
18. Wesleyan University
19. University of Rochester
20. University of Delaware

EXTRACURRICULARS

Best Athletic Facilities
Based on students' rating of campus athletic facilities

1. Georgia Institute of Technology
2. University of Maryland—College Park
3. United States Military Academy
4. Wabash College
5. The Ohio State University—Columbus
6. Ohio University—Athens
7. University of Missouri—Columbia
8. Rice University
9. Pennsylvania State University—University Park
10. Loyola University—Maryland
11. Calvin College
12. West Virginia University
13. University of Illinois at Urbana-Champaign
14. Southern Methodist University
15. University of Georgia
16. University of Florida
17. Boston University
18. St. Lawrence University
19. University of Denver
20. Stanford University

Students Pack the Stadiums
How popular are intercollegiate sports?

1. University of Notre Dame
2. University of Florida
3. Pennsylvania State University—University Park
4. Auburn University
5. University of Connecticut
6. Florida State University
7. University of Mississippi
8. Clemson University
9. The University of North Carolina at Chapel Hill
10. University of Michigan—Ann Arbor
11. Syracuse University
12. University of Illinois at Urbana-Champaign
13. Virginia Tech
14. University of Iowa

15. The University of Texas at Austin
16. West Virginia University
17. University of Southern California
18. The Ohio State University—Columbus
19. University of Maryland—College Park
20. Villanova University

Intercollegiate Sports Unpopular or Nonexistent
How popular are intercollegiate sports?

1. Bennington College
2. New College of Florida
3. College of the Atlantic
4. Champlain College
5. Bard College (NY)
6. Reed College
7. St. John's College (MD)
8. New York University
9. Sarah Lawrence College
10. University of Chicago
11. Harvey Mudd College
12. The Evergreen State College
13. Emerson College
14. Barnard College
15. Suffolk University
16. Clark University
17. Carnegie Mellon University
18. Brandeis University
19. State University of New York—Purchase College
20. Missouri University of Science and Technology

Everyone Plays Intramural Sports
How popular are intramural sports?

1. Pennsylvania State University—University Park
2. University of Notre Dame
3. Clemson University
4. United States Military Academy
5. Grove City College
6. Gonzaga University
7. The University of North Carolina at Chapel Hill
8. University of Connecticut
9. Iowa State University
10. Florida Southern College
11. University of Nebraska—Lincoln
12. Wabash College
13. Mercer University
14. Brigham Young University (UT)
15. Florida State University
16. United States Naval Academy
17. Villanova University
18. Angelo State University
19. University of Florida
20. Creighton University

Nobody Plays Intramural Sports
How popular are intramural sports?

1. Sarah Lawrence College
2. New College of Florida
3. Bard College at Simon's Rock (MA)
4. Eugene Lang College
5. Prescott College
6. Fisk University
7. The Cooper Union for the Advancement of Science and Art
8. Randolph College
9. New York University
10. Emerson College
11. Suffolk University
12. College of the Atlantic
13. Bryn Mawr College
14. Xavier University of Louisiana
15. Spelman College
16. Barnard College
17. The Evergreen State College
18. Manhattanville College
19. Agnes Scott College
20. Portland State University

Best College Radio Station
How popular is the radio station?

1. St. Bonaventure University
2. DePauw University
3. Ithaca College
4. Emerson College
5. Hofstra University
6. Knox College
7. Brown University
8. University of Puget Sound
9. The College of Wooster
10. Fordham University
11. Providence College
12. Stanford University
13. Sacred Heart University
14. Carleton College
15. University of Kansas
16. Wellesley College
17. Flagler College
18. Denison University
19. Chapman University
20. Westminster College (PA)

Best College Newspaper
How popular is the newspaper?

1. The University of North Carolina at Chapel Hill
2. Yale University
3. University of Wisconsin—Madison
4. Brown University
5. Texas A&M University—College Station
6. Pennsylvania State University—University Park

7. Northwestern University
8. University of Maryland—College Park
9. University of Florida
10. The University of Texas at Austin
11. University of Minnesota—Twin Cities
12. Ohio University—Athens
13. Cornell University
14. University of Mississippi
15. University of Connecticut
16. University of Kansas
17. University of South Carolina—Columbia
18. Syracuse University
19. Howard University
20. Tufts University

Best College Theater
How popular are college theater productions?

1. Muhlenberg College
2. Drew University
3. Bennington College
4. Yale University
5. Wagner College
6. Emerson College
7. Northwestern University
8. Carnegie Mellon University
9. Indiana University—Bloomington
10. State University of New York—Purchase College
11. Brown University
12. Knox College
13. Kenyon College
14. City University of New York—Brooklyn College
15. Elon University
16. St. Olaf College
17. New York University
18. Ithaca College
19. Sarah Lawrence College
20. The College of Idaho

SOCIAL SCENE

Lots of Beer
How widely used is beer?

1. Ohio University—Athens
2. University of New Hampshire
3. Claremont McKenna College
4. Pennsylvania State University—University Park
5. West Virginia University
6. University of Florida
7. Providence College
8. Florida State University
9. University of Georgia
10. The University of Texas at Austin

11. Bucknell University
12. Colgate University
13. Syracuse University
14. University of Iowa
15. University of California—Santa Barbara
16. Lehigh University
17. Indiana University—Bloomington
18. University of Wisconsin—Madison
19. DePauw University
20. Miami University (OH)

Got Milk?
How widely used is beer?

1. Brigham Young University (UT)
2. College of the Ozarks
3. Wheaton College (IL)
4. United States Air Force Academy
5. City University of New York—Brooklyn College
6. Wesleyan College
7. Xavier University of Louisiana
8. Spelman College
9. City University of New York—Queens College
10. University of Houston
11. Grove City College
12. City University of New York—Baruch College
13. Thomas Aquinas College
14. Calvin College
15. Pepperdine University
16. Christopher Newport University
17. United States Coast Guard Academy
18. California State University Stanislaus
19. Simmons College
20. Mills College

Lots of Hard Liquor
How widely used is hard liquor?

1. Providence College
2. Ohio University—Athens
3. Trinity College (CT)
4. Tulane University
5. St. Bonaventure University
6. University of Georgia
7. Indiana University—Bloomington
8. University of Iowa
9. University of Wisconsin—Madison
10. University of Mississippi
11. Southern Methodist University
12. The University of Texas at Austin
13. University of California—Santa Barbara
14. University of Illinois at Urbana-Champaign
15. West Virginia University
16. Pennsylvania State University—University Park

17. Louisiana State University
18. University of Florida
19. Syracuse University
20. Quinnipiac University

Scotch and Soda, Hold the Scotch
How widely used is hard liquor?

1. Brigham Young University (UT)
2. Grove City College
3. City University of New York—Baruch College
4. Wheaton College (IL)
5. United States Air Force Academy
6. City University of New York—Brooklyn College
7. Simmons College
8. University of Utah
9. Wesleyan College
10. College of the Ozarks
11. Marywood University
12. Illinois Institute of Technology
13. University of Houston
14. Calvin College
15. City University of New York—Queens College
16. Thomas Aquinas College
17. United States Coast Guard Academy
18. Xavier University of Louisiana
19. United States Military Academy
20. City University of New York—Hunter College

Reefer Madness
How widely used is marijuana?

1. Colorado College
2. University of California—Santa Cruz
3. University of California—Santa Barbara
4. University of Colorado—Boulder
5. Bard College (NY)
6. Lewis & Clark College
7. Warren Wilson College
8. Eckerd College
9. New College of Florida
10. University of Vermont
11. The Evergreen State College
12. New York University
13. Reed College
14. Syracuse University
15. Skidmore College
16. Pitzer College
17. Arizona State University
18. University of Illinois at Urbana-Champaign
19. Sarah Lawrence College
20. Grinnell College

Don't Inhale
How widely used is marijuana?

1. United States Air Force Academy
2. United States Coast Guard Academy
3. Thomas Aquinas College
4. Brigham Young University (UT)
5. College of the Ozarks
6. United States Naval Academy
7. United States Military Academy
8. Wheaton College (IL)
9. United States Merchant Marine Academy
10. The University of Tulsa
11. Ohio Northern University
12. Hillsdale College
13. Creighton University
14. University of Notre Dame
15. Calvin College
16. Samford University
17. Centenary College of Louisiana
18. University of Louisiana at Lafayette
19. City University of New York—Baruch College
20. City University of New York—Queens College

Major Frat and Sorority Scene
How popular are fraternities/sororities?

1. Vanderbilt University
2. Transylvania University
3. University of Mississippi
4. Sewanee—The University of the South
5. Wake Forest University
6. DePauw University
7. Lehigh University
8. Texas Christian University
9. University of Illinois at Urbana-Champaign
10. University of Georgia
11. Ohio University—Athens
12. Pennsylvania State University—University Park
13. University of Iowa
14. Arizona State University
15. Florida State University
16. Birmingham-Southern College
17. Wofford College
18. Bucknell University
19. Albion College
20. University of South Carolina—Columbia

SCHOOLS BY TYPE

Party Schools
Based on a combination of survey questions concerning the use of alcohol and drugs, hours of study each day, and the popularity of the Greek system

1. Ohio University—Athens
2. University of Georgia
3. University of Mississippi
4. University of Iowa
5. University of California—Santa Barbara
6. West Virginia University
7. Pennsylvania State University—University Park
8. Florida State University
9. University of Florida
10. The University of Texas at Austin
11. University of Illinois at Urbana-Champaign
12. Syracuse University
13. Louisiana State University
14. University of Wisconsin—Madison
15. DePauw University
16. Indiana University—Bloomington
17. Arizona State University
18. University of Maryland—College Park
19. University of Vermont
20. University of South Carolina—Columbia

Stone-Cold Sober Schools
Based on a combination of survey questions concerning the use of alcohol and drugs, hours of study each day, and the popularity of the Greek system

1. Brigham Young University (UT)
2. Wheaton College (IL)
3. Wesleyan College
4. United States Coast Guard Academy
5. United States Military Academy
6. United States Naval Academy
7. Calvin College
8. Grove City College
9. Pepperdine University
10. City University of New York—Brooklyn College
11. The Cooper Union for the Advancement of Science and Art
12. United States Merchant Marine Academy
13. United States Air Force Academy
14. Franklin W. Olin College of Engineering
15. City University of New York—Queens College
16. Thomas Aquinas College
17. University of Dallas
18. Agnes Scott College
19. College of the Ozarks
20. Gustavus Adolphus College

Jock Schools
Based on a combination of survey questions concerning intercollegiate and intramural sports, and the popularity of the Greek system

1. University of Florida
2. Clemson University
3. University of Nebraska—Lincoln
4. Virginia Tech
5. Pennsylvania State University—University Park
6. University of Dayton
7. Washington & Jefferson College
8. University of Kansas
9. The University of North Carolina at Chapel Hill
10. Florida State University
11. Auburn University
12. Wabash College
13. University of Kentucky
14. The University of Alabama—Tuscaloosa
15. University of Georgia
16. Washington State University
17. Union College (NY)
18. Iowa State University
19. The Ohio State University—Columbus
20. University of Maryland—College Park

Dodgeball Targets
Based on a combination of survey questions concerning intercollegiate and intramural sports, and the popularity of the Greek system

1. New College of Florida
2. Eugene Lang College
3. Bard College at Simon's Rock (MA)
4. Bennington College
5. St. John's College (NM)
6. Marlboro College
7. Prescott College
8. Reed College
9. New York University
10. The Evergreen State College
11. Vassar College
12. Oberlin College
13. Franklin W. Olin College of Engineering
14. Suffolk University
15. Rollins College
16. Champlain College
17. Randolph College
18. Clark University
19. Hollins University
20. The Cooper Union for the Advancement of Science and Art

Future Rotarians and Daughters of the American Revolution

Based on a combination of survey questions concerning the political persuasion, the use of drugs, the popularity of student government, and the level of acceptance of the gay community on campus

1. Hillsdale College
2. Wheaton College (IL)
3. Thomas Aquinas College
4. Brigham Young University (UT)
5. Grove City College
6. United States Naval Academy
7. United States Air Force Academy
8. United States Coast Guard Academy
9. United States Military Academy
10. College of the Holy Cross
11. Calvin College
12. Baylor University
13. United States Merchant Marine Academy
14. Pepperdine University
15. Ohio Northern University
16. Hampden-Sydney College
17. Westminster College (PA)
18. Furman University
19. Wabash College
20. Mercer University

Birkenstock-Wearing, Tree-Hugging, Clove-Smoking Vegetarians

Based on a combination of survey questions concerning the political persuasion, the use of drugs, the popularity of student government, and the level of acceptance of the gay community on campus

1. New College of Florida
2. Eugene Lang College The New School for Liberal Arts
3. Bard College at Simon's Rock (MA)
4. Beloit College
5. Colorado College
6. Bennington College
7. Reed College
8. Oberlin College
9. Bard College (NY)
10. Warren Wilson College
11. Sarah Lawrence College
12. Skidmore College
13. The Evergreen State College
14. University of Central Florida
15. Lewis & Clark College
16. Grinnell College
17. Pitzer College
18. Green Mountain College
19. Eckerd College
20. University of Vermont

Deep Springs Honor Roll

Since Deep Springs is a two-year college (and the only one in The Best 376 Colleges), we remove it from our rankings tallies in order to avoid comparing "apples and oranges." Instead we present this list of some ranking categories in which Deep Springs ranks high (or low, as it were) among the best colleges in our book.

Town-Gown Relations Are Great
Most Beautiful Campus
Easiest Campus to Get Around
Most Accessible Professors
Best Campus Food
LGBT-Friendly
Most Liberal Students
Stone-Cold Sober Schools
Scotch and Soda, Hold the Scotch
Got Milk?
Don't Inhale
Dodgeball Targets
Intercollegiate Sports Unpopular or Nonexistent
Least Religious Students
This Is a Library?

PRINCETON REVIEW'S "FINANCIAL AID RATING," "FIRE SAFETY RATING," AND "GREEN RATING" HONOR ROLLS

We salute theses schools that received a 99 (the highest score) in the tallies for our "Financial Aid," "Fire Safety," and "Green" Ratings—three of eight ratings on some of the school profiles in this book as well as in our *Complete Book of Colleges*, 2012 edition, and at www.PrincetonReview.com. Our school ratings are numerical scores (Note: They are not ranking lists) that show how a school "sizes up" on a fixed scale. They are comparable to grades and based primarily on institutional data we collect directly from the colleges.

Financial Aid Honor Roll
Schools are listed in alphabetical order. See p. 26 for information on how our "Financial Aid Rating" is determined.

Carleton College
Claremont McKenna College
Columbia University
Franklin W. Olin College of Engineering
Pomona College
Princeton University
Swarthmore College
Thomas Aquinas College
Vassar College
Yale University

Fire Safety Honor Roll
Schools are listed in alphabetical order. See p. 22 for information on how our "Fire Safety Rating" is determined.

Adelphi University*
Bay Path College*
Bentley University
College of Mount St. Joseph*
Dominican University of California*
Duquesne University
Georgia College & State University*
Husson College*
Kennesaw State University*
Milwaukee School of Engineering*
Mountain State University*
The Ohio State University—Newark*
Saint Mary-of-the-Woods College*
Sweet Briar College
University of Maine—Fort Kent*
University of Minnesota, Morris*
Wheeling Jesuit University*

Green Honor Roll
Schools are listed in alphabetical order. See p. 23 for information on how our "Green Rating" is determined.

American University
Arizona State University
College of the Atlantic
Dickinson College
Georgia Institute of Technology
Harvard College
Northeastern University
Oregon State University*
San Francisco State University*
State University of New York at Binghamton
University of California—Santa Cruz
University of Maine
University of Washington
University of Wisconsin—Stevens Point*
Virginia Tech
Warren Wilson College

Tuition-Free Schools Honor Roll
The following schools have been excluded from our ranking lists dealing with financial aid:

Berea College
College of the Ozarks
The Cooper Union for the Advancement
  of Science and Art
United States Air Force Academy
United States Coast Guard Academy
United States Merchant Marine Academy
United States Military Academy
United States Naval Academy
Webb Institute

We commend these schools on their ability to do the seemingly impossible: not charge tuition. While some charge students for room and board and other fees, the overall cost of attendance at these schools is very low, and at some schools: free! (Note: We do not include these schools in our ranking lists dealing with financial aid, since they would have an unfair advantage over schools that charged even a moderate tuition.)

Schools marked with an asterisk do not appear in the *Best 376 Colleges*.

You can find those school profiles in *Complete Book of Colleges*, 2012 Edition.

The Princeton Review and USA TODAY have collaborated to bring you this list of 100 Best Value Colleges. We selected the 100 schools (50 private and 50 public) in February 2011 based on 30 factors covering academics, costs, and financial aid. For information about each school and an exclusive analysis in an interactive database and map, go to www.bestvaluecolleges.usatoday.com

Top 50 Private

Amherst College
Boston College
Bowdoin College
Brandeis University
Brown University
Bryn Mawr College
California Institute of Technology
Carleton College
Claremont McKenna College
College of the Holy Cross
Colorado College
Columbia University
Dartmouth College
Davidson College
DePauw University
Duke University
Emory University
Gettysburg College
Grinnell College
Hamilton College
Harvard College
Harvey Mudd College
Johns Hopkins University
Lafayette College
Macalester College
Massachusetts Institute of Technology
Mount Holyoke College
Pomona College
Princeton University
Rice University
Scripps College
Sewanee—The University of the South
Smith College
Stanford University
Swarthmore College
Trinity College (CT)
University of Chicago
University of Pennsylvania
University of Richmond
Vanderbilt University
Vassar College
Wabash College
Wake Forest University
Washington University in St. Louis
Wellesley College
Wesleyan College
Wesleyan University
Whitman College
Williams College
Yale University

Top 50 Public

Appalachian State University*
California State University—Long Beach*
City University of New York—Hunter College
The College of New Jersey
College of William & Mary
Florida State University
Georgia Institute of Technology
Iowa State University
James Madison University
Michigan State University
New College of Florida
New Mexico Institute of Mining & Technology*
North Carolina State University
The Ohio State University—Columbus
St. Mary's College of Maryland
State University of New York at Binghamton
State University of New York at Geneseo
State University of New York—Stony Brook University
Texas A&M University—College Station
Truman State University
University of California—Berkeley
University of California—Davis
University of California—Irvine*
University of California—Los Angeles
University of California—San Diego
University of California—Santa Barbara
University of Central Florida
University of Colorado—Boulder
University of Connecticut
University of Delaware
University of Florida
University of Georgia
University of Illinois at Urbana-Champaign
University of Maryland—Baltimore County
University of Maryland—College Park
University of Michigan—Ann Arbor
University of Minnesota—Twin Cities
The University of North Carolina at Asheville
The University of North Carolina at Chapel Hill
University of North Carolina—Wilmington*
University of North Florida*
University of Oklahoma
University of Pittsburgh—Pittsburgh Campus
University of South Carolina—Columbia
University of Tennessee
The University of Texas at Austin
University of Virginia
University of Washington
University of Wisconsin—Madison
Virginia Tech

Schools marked with an asterisk do not appear in the *Best 376 Colleges*.

You can find those school profiles in *Complete Book of Colleges*, 2012 Edition.

PART 3

THE BEST
376 COLLEGES

AGNES SCOTT COLLEGE

141 EAST COLLEGE AVENUE, DECATUR, GA 30030-3797 • ADMISSIONS: 404-471-6285 • FAX: 404-471-6414

CAMPUS LIFE

Quality of Life Rating	98
Fire Safety Rating	95
Green Rating	94
Type of school	private
Affiliation	Presbyterian
Environment	metropolis

STUDENTS

Total undergrad enrollment	892
% male/female	0/100
% from out of state	39
% from public high school	77
% live on campus	86
% African American	28
% Asian	3
% Caucasian	43
% Hispanic	6
% international	10
# of countries represented	37

SURVEY SAYS . . .
No one cheats
Lab facilities are great
Students get along with local
community
Students love Atlanta/Decatur, GA
Great off-campus food
Dorms are like palaces
Campus feels safe

ACADEMICS

Academic Rating	90
% students graduating within 4 years	59
% students graduating within 6 years	68
Calendar	semester
Student/faculty ratio	10:1
Profs interesting rating	95
Profs accessible rating	96
Most common reg class size	10–19 students
Most common lab size	10–19 students

MOST POPULAR MAJORS
political science, psychology

STUDENTS SAY ". . ."

Academics

"Great location. Gorgeous campus. Superb academics." That's how a typical Scottie sums up the argument for Agnes Scott College, a small all-women's school located a stone's throw from Atlanta. "The [school's] mission statement sums it up perfectly," one student writes: "Agnes Scott educates women to think deeply, live honorably, and engage the intellectual and social challenges of their times." Nowhere is this more apparent than in Agnes Scott's Honor Code, ("our greatest strength," one student writes), which "is moderated by the student-run Honor Court." The code "has many benefits," including "self-scheduled and unproctored exams," infusing the campus with a sense of mutual trust. It also helps students manage their demanding academic workloads. As one student warns, "Courses are challenging and the...workload is heavy, especially during midterms and exams. Most classes are back-heavy, so if you don't do homework during the semester then finals can become incredibly stressful." A caring and attentive faculty and administration also help. "To say they are committed and available is an understatement," one student tells us. "All the deans and most faculty members know students by name." The consensus among students is that faculty members are all dedicated to their field and to teaching, and they're skilled at both. Finally, the school's "huge endowment" has many here bragging about the school's "amazing financial aid packages," another plus.

Life

Scott is "a quiet campus" where students "are dedicated to their own pursuits, which makes it an environment conducive to being productive and focused, but it's next to Atlanta, so [we're] never at a loss for things to do." Challenging academics mean students "stay on campus and study and get things done during the week. Everyone studies, goes to class, is involved in clubs, and chills out in each others' dorms" from Monday through Thursday. Then, "on the weekends, everyone leaves campus," often to socialize with students from "another college such as Georgia Tech, Emory, Georgia State, or Morehouse." Because of the school's "great location, students are able to easily get off campus and refresh themselves with the city life," although some feel a car "is pretty much a must" to reap full benefits, which include "concerts, clubs, and movies in Atlanta. If you like to shop, you definitely shop in Atlanta. Lenox Square Mall, Atlantic Station, and Perimeter Mall are some of the more popular places to shop." Students also love Atlanta's funky little Five Points neighborhood and even have some favorite hot spots in hometown Decatur, an upscale Atlanta satellite that's home to a variety of coffee shops and eateries.

Student Body

"It's almost impossible to describe a typical student" at Agnes Scott, where "you'll find everyone from preppy, Southern Baptist, Republican, in-state student debutantes to radical, vegan, communist lesbians, and everyone in between." As one student puts it, "We vary from women in pearls and plaid skirts to women in black parachute pants and metal in their noses." "Diversity is definitely one of Agnes Scott's strong points," students here agree. These "ambitious high-achievers" "not only consistently attend classes, but they are also involved in so many things—clubs, student government, taking more than the standard number of classes, work-study, etc.—that they barely have time to get everything done. Nearly everyone on campus is concerned about and dedicated to one issue or another, whether it's gender equality, the environment, or refugee women in Atlanta." They're "an intense and passionate bunch" that "fully [expects] to make advances in whatever it is they want to do."

FINANCIAL AID: 404-471-6395 • E-MAIL: ADMISSION@AGNESSCOTT.EDU • WEBSITE: WWW.AGNESSCOTT.EDU

THE PRINCETON REVIEW SAYS

Admissions

Very important factors considered include: Academic GPA, application essay, class rank, recommendation(s), rigor of secondary school record, character/personal qualities, talent/ability. Students must submit one of the following: a) SAT or ACT with writing component or b) graded writing assignment or have an evaluative interview. *Important factors considered include:* Extracurricular activities, volunteer work, work experience. *Other factors considered include:* Alumni/ae relation, first generation, geographical residence, interview, level of applicant's interest, racial/ethnic status, state residency. TOEFL required of all international applicants. High school diploma is required, and GED is accepted. *Academic units recommended:* 4 English, 3 mathematics, 2 science (2 science labs), 2 foreign language, 2 social studies, 2 history.

Financial Aid

Students should submit: FAFSA. Regular filing deadline is February 15. The Princeton Review suggests that all financial aid forms be submitted as soon as possible after January 1. *Need-based scholarships/grants offered:* Federal Pell, SEOG, state scholarships/grants, private scholarships, school scholarship or grant aid from institutional funds. *Loan aid offered:* Direct Subsidized Stafford, Direct Unsubsidized Stafford, Direct PLUS. Applicants will be notified of awards on a rolling basis beginning March 1. Federal Work-Study Program available. Off-campus job opportunities are excellent.

The Inside Word

Agnes Scott waives the application fee for those who apply online; all it will cost you is your time. Take the time to craft a solid application if you want to be considered seriously, as this is a very competitive school where admissions officers give each candidate a very careful look. A strong application that creates a compelling portrait may well overcome moderate shortcomings in high school grades or test scores, especially if bolstered by an enthusiastic interview during a campus visit.

THE SCHOOL SAYS "..."

From the Admissions Office

"Who will you become? If you are looking for a liberal arts college that will help you explore, strive, and surpass what you think is your potential, then consider Agnes Scott College. Our students and alumnae say it best:

"'I found the academic program to be extremely challenging at Agnes Scott; but it's not overwhelming—it's easy to go to your teachers and ask for help because they know who you are and take a personal interest.'—Evan Joslin, Class of 2008, Atlanta, Georgia.

"'Agnes Scott College didn't teach me what to think. They taught me how to think,' says Jessica Owens, class of 1998, who majored in biology at ASC, received a master's degree in cancer biology from Stanford and an MBA from Harvard.

"Students find their passions and their voices through guaranteed internships, international study experiences, and collaborative learning in places like the science center, facilities that were designed expressly to facilitate faculty-student research. Your next four years are about you. We invite you to come for a visit and imagine the possibilities for you."

SELECTIVITY

Admissions Rating	90
# of applicants	2,117
% of applicants accepted	46
% of acceptees attending	27
# accepting a place on wait list	0

FRESHMAN PROFILE

Range SAT Critical Reading	540–670
Range SAT Math	530–650
Range SAT Writing	550–650
Range ACT Composite	24–29
Average HS GPA	3.60
% graduated top 10% of class	34
% graduated top 25% of class	69
% graduated top 50% of class	92

DEADLINES

Early action	
Deadline	11/15
Notification	12/15
Regular	
Priority	3/1
Nonfall registration?	yes

APPLICANTS ALSO LOOK AT
AND OFTEN PREFER
Emory University, Georgia State University, University of Georgia

AND SOMETIMES PREFER
Georgia Institute of Technology

AND RARELY PREFER
Mercer University—Macon

FINANCIAL FACTS

Financial Aid Rating	87
Annual tuition	$31,980
Room and board	$10,150
Required fees	$215
Books and supplies	$1,000
% frosh rec. need-based scholarship or grant aid	75
% UG rec. need-based scholarship or grant aid	73
% frosh rec. non-need-based scholarship or grant aid	25
% UG rec. non-need-based scholarship or grant aid	27
% frosh rec. need-based self-help aid	63
% UG rec. need-based self-help aid	64
% frosh rec. any financial aid	100
% UG rec. any financial aid	99
% UG borrow to pay for school	69
Average cumulative indebtedness	$26,493

ALBION COLLEGE

611 EAST PORTER, ALBION, MI 49224 • ADMISSIONS: 517-629-0321 • FAX: 517-629-0569

STUDENTS SAY ". . ."

Academics

Albion College, a small liberal arts school with "a great biology department" and "wonderful programs in the sciences and pre-law," has "an amazing ability to provide the 'small school' intimacy with peers and instructors while delivering world-class education that competes with major universities," according to its students. Albion boasts of "professors that would make many bigger schools drool," and "Since it's strictly an undergraduate institution, Albion's services are all geared toward the students." Indeed, "the entire faculty and staff always make time for students and even acknowledge you by name when you walk past them on campus," and "The professors seem to genuinely envision a greater academic career for all students and strongly encourage further schooling after attaining the four-year degree." Students also enjoy a "number of available opportunities, in class and out of class, for internships and studying abroad, even after the students leave here," thanks to a strong alumni network. As one undergrad explains, "Albion is about connections. Even though it is a small school, everyone knows someone who goes to or has graduated from Albion. Even though it is out of the way, we are very connected to the wider world." A solid selection of study abroad and research opportunities also "puts us on the cutting edge of this shrinking world." The Albion curriculum is flexible enough to "emphasize the freedom of choice for every individual. It allows students to express themselves in various ways and allows students to get hands-on experience of specific areas of work" while completing their studies.

Life

"There isn't a lot to do in the city of Albion itself," but students tell us that "there is always something happening on campus" to compensate. Greek life "is a very large part of Albion, and there are always things going on at the frats;" about one-third of all students join Greek organizations. Other options include "concerts, comedians, and other activities put on by Union Board, an event planning committee sponsored with student activity funds." The school works hard to draw big-name entertainment and in recent years has hosted performances by Dane Cook, Pablo Francisco, OAR, and Less Than Jake. While "a lot of people drink and party because they don't know what else to do," students insist that those who choose not to drink have plenty of options. Hometown Albion "is a small one-horse town where there isn't a whole bunch for the residents to do, let alone the student body."

Student Body

"I think one word can describe the Albion student: involved," one student writes, adding, "Nearly every Albion student is involved with multiple organizations that engage in community outreach, philosophical discussions, diversity awareness, hobby enthusiasts, and nearly every other aspect of a social organization you can think of." Most here "seem to come from either wealthy backgrounds or are from the surrounding town and are from low-income families," with the balance tilted firmly toward the former group. "There is not a dominant religion" on campus, "but Albion College was founded as a Christian school," meaning, "Many of the students are Christian." Most "are white, and many "have always lived in Michigan" and "could be described as the attractive, popular, smart kid in school" who "came to Albion to be a big fish in a small pond."

FINANCIAL AID: 517-629-0440 • E-MAIL: ADMISSION@ALBION.EDU • WEBSITE: WWW.ALBION.EDU

THE PRINCETON REVIEW SAYS

Admissions

Very important factors considered include: Academic GPA, application essay, recommendation(s), rigor of secondary school record, standardized test scores, character/personal qualities. *Important factors considered include:* Class rank, extracurricular activities, first generation, talent/ability, volunteer work. *Other factors considered include:* Alumni/ae relation, geographical residence, level of applicant's interest, racial/ethnic status, state residency, work experience. SAT or ACT required; ACT with or without writing component accepted. TOEFL required of all international applicants. High school diploma is required, and GED is accepted. *Academic units required:* 4 English, 3 mathematics, 3 science (2 science labs), 2 foreign language, 3 social studies. *Academic units recommended:* 4 English, 4 mathematics, 4 science (2 science labs), 3 foreign language, 4 social studies.

Financial Aid

Students should submit: FAFSA. The Princeton Review suggests that all financial aid forms be submitted as soon as possible after January 1. *Need-based scholarships/grants offered:* Federal Pell, SEOG, state scholarships/grants, private scholarships, school scholarship or grant aid from institutional funds. *Loan aid offered:* Direct Subsidized Stafford, Direct Unsubsidized Stafford, Direct PLUS, Federal Perkins. Applicants will be notified of awards on a rolling basis beginning March 15. Federal Work-Study Program available. Off-campus job opportunities are fair.

The Inside Word

Albion fills each incoming class with students who had a solid—if not exceptional—high school career. Albion applicants are a self-selecting group, which explains the schools eighty-plus percent acceptance rate. Borderline candidates can improve their chances by presenting an impressive roster of extracurriculars and volunteer work, strong essays, and a strong interview. A campus visit is highly encouraged.

THE SCHOOL SAYS "..."

From the Admissions Office

"Some schools are for jocks and others for geeks and some for average Joes, at Albion, we are for thinkers! No matter how else you describe yourself, if you are a thinker, then Albion could be the perfect college for you. We are thinking about sustainability, mating habits of nurse sharks, and how the time of day affects test performance...we are thinking about grad schools, alternative spring breaks, the ethics of genetic cloning and myriad other topics...so the question is: What are you thinking? Albion is home to six interdisciplinary and experiential institutes for business, public policy and service, environmental studies, premedical and health care studies, teacher education and honors. Albion is among the top eighty-five liberal arts colleges for the number of alumni who are corporate executives. Our graduates are admitted to top-notch medical, dental and law schools at a ninety-five percent clip. In a typical year forty-five percent of our graduates go directly to graduate school, attending institutions such as Harvard, Vanderbilt, Northwestern, and Stanford. A full-service, eighty-stall equestrian center opened in 2004. Our equestrian teams compete in IHSA events. Our Division III sports teams compete in the Michigan Intercollegiate Athletic Association and field twenty-one varsity sports. Recent athletic programs to compete in NCAA post-season tournaments include football, men's and women's basketball, women's soccer, both tennis teams, numerous swimmers, and track and field athletes. Albion has more than 120 student organizations that encompass the full array of service, religious, academic and athletic interests."

SELECTIVITY

Admissions Rating	75
# of applicants	2,305
% of applicants accepted	68
% of acceptees attending	24
# accepting a place on wait list	0

FRESHMAN PROFILE

Range SAT Critical Reading	540–600
Range SAT Math	610–630
Range SAT Writing	510–590
Range ACT Composite	25–28
Minimum paper TOEFL	550
Minimum computer TOEFL	270
Minimum web-based TOEFL	79

DEADLINES

Early action	
Deadline	12/1
Notification	11/1
Regular	
Notification	11/1
Nonfall registration?	yes

APPLICANTS ALSO LOOK AT AND OFTEN PREFER
University of Michigan—Ann Arbor
AND SOMETIMES PREFER
Hope College, Kalamazoo College, Michigan State University

FINANCIAL FACTS

Financial Aid Rating	84
Annual tuition	$30,650
Room and board	$8,842
Required fees	$536
Books and supplies	$900
% frosh rec. need-based scholarship or grant aid	74
% UG rec. need-based scholarship or grant aid	68
% frosh rec. non-need-based scholarship or grant aid	70
% UG rec. non-need-based scholarship or grant aid	63
% frosh rec. need-based self-help aid	58
% UG rec. need-based self-help aid	57
% frosh rec. any financial aid	99
% UG rec. any financial aid	99
% UG borrow to pay for school	50
Average cumulative indebtedness	$34,282

ALFRED UNIVERSITY

ALUMNI HALL, ONE SAXON DRIVE, ALFRED, NY 14802-1205 • ADMISSIONS: 607-871-2115 • FAX: 607-871-2198

CAMPUS LIFE

Quality of Life Rating	72
Fire Safety Rating	65
Green Rating	71
Type of school	private
Environment	rural

STUDENTS

Total undergrad enrollment	1,846
% male/female	49/51
% from out of state	30
% live on campus	77
% African American	5
% Asian	2
% Caucasian	68
% Hispanic	3
% international	2
# of countries represented	18

SURVEY SAYS . . .
Students are friendly
Frats and sororities are unpopular
or nonexistent
College radio is popular

ACADEMICS

Academic Rating	77
% students graduating within 4 years	5
% students graduating within 6 years	69
Calendar	semester
Student/faculty ratio	12:1
Profs interesting rating	81
Profs accessible rating	80
Most common reg class size	10–19 students
Most common lab size	10–19 students

MOST POPULAR MAJORS
business/commerce, ceramics, psychology

STUDENTS SAY ". . ."

Academics

Alfred University is a small school with an impressive range of world-class majors. The school is known for its "excellent art program," particularly its ceramics and glass majors, as well as for its engineering and psychology programs. While some students at Alfred focus only on their majors, students happily report that there are a "variety of academic opportunities" and that it's "easy to take subjects outside your major." This is appreciated by many, including one art student who likes that Alfred offers "other majors versus a traditional art [school] setting. If I had decided to change majors, Alfred has almost every opportunity." Alfred's "outstanding, talented, dedicated" faculty is one of its biggest draws. An English writing student gushes that professors "bring a level of vibrancy and academic encouragement through enthusiasm to the classroom." "The professors are always pushing you to reach your full potential" and are "always willing to put time into student independent projects." Students also rave about the small classes sizes. "It is the closest to one-on-one teaching you can get," a clinical and counseling psychology major notes, and "The classroom size is perfect for a more personalized education."

Life

Alfred's "beautiful," "small" campus and its "somewhat rural location" are big draws for students looking for a quieter academic experience with a strong "sense of community." Of course, its location means the weather isn't exactly tropical. One student notes that it can feel like "it's basically winter here for about eighty percent of the school year, and it snows constantly." Luckily, "There is always something to do on weekends and week days," for distraction, such as "student club productions…and fundraisers and an excellent selection of movies shown on campus." On top of that, "There are so many clubs and options that you can find something to do," and "Every sports team is supported, and superfans are at every event." "The facilities are amazing," particularly the "great" art buildings and the engineering facilities. Alfred's "strong equestrian program" and barn are also a big draw. Students find some of Alfred's dorms to be "pretty outdated," and there's a bit of grumbling about the "hit-or-miss" and "expensive" dining facilities.

Student Body

Alfred has a "warm" atmosphere, and "You can't go down the street without receiving a smile." Students are "friendly, outgoing, and involved," and many do community service work and are active in one of Alfred's many clubs or organizations. The prominent art school means that there's a large presence of creative types on campus, and the equally prominent engineering school ensures a good mix of personalities. One student notes, "A pretty significant gap between the prevalent, spunky art students and the more reclusive engineers," but another adds that this means students are "well-acquainted with people from a variety of studies and backgrounds and with a variety of interests." Most people believe that "everyone finds their own little niche," but they appreciate that it "definitely does not mean they stay there—you are allowed to float between everything." In fact, "More often than not, you'll see engineers rubbing elbows with philosophy majors and artists chilling with math and chemistry majors."

ALFRED UNIVERSITY

FINANCIAL AID: 607-871-2159 • E-MAIL: ADMISSIONS@ALFRED.EDU • WEBSITE: WWW.ALFRED.EDU

THE PRINCETON REVIEW SAYS

Admissions

Very important factors considered include: Academic GPA, class rank, rigor of secondary school record, character/personal qualities, extracurricular activities. *Important factors considered include:* Application essay, recommendation(s), standardized test scores, volunteer work, work experience. *Other factors considered include:* First generation, interview, level of applicant's interest, racial/ethnic status, talent/ability. SAT or ACT required; ACT with or without writing component accepted. TOEFL required of all international applicants. High school diploma is required, and GED is accepted. *Academic units required:* 4 English, 2 mathematics, 2 science (2 science labs), 2 social studies. *Academic units recommended:* 4 mathematics, 3 science (3 science labs), 3 social studies.

Financial Aid

Students should submit: FAFSA, institution's own financial aid form. Regular filing deadline is March 15. The Princeton Review suggests that all financial aid forms be submitted as soon as possible after January 1. *Need-based scholarships/grants offered:* Federal Pell, SEOG, state scholarships/grants, private scholarships, school scholarship or grant aid from institutional funds. *Loan aid offered:* Direct Subsidized Stafford, Direct Unsubsidized Stafford, Direct PLUS, Federal Perkins, university loans from institutional funds. Applicants will be notified of awards on a rolling basis beginning February 15. Federal Work-Study Program available. Off-campus job opportunities are poor.

The Inside Word

Alfred is a fine university with a solid local reputation. The allure for arts students is obvious—Alfred's programs in the arts are especially well-regarded—and as a result, competition is fiercest among applicants for these programs. A killer portfolio, even more than great grades and standardized test scores, is your most likely ticket in. Competition for the engineering school is also tight. Applicants will need to have thrived in a rigorous high school program.

THE SCHOOL SAYS " . . ."

From the Admissions Office

"The admissions process at Alfred University is the foundation for the personal attention each student can expect during their time at AU. Each applicant is evaluated individually and receives genuine, individual care and consideration.

"The best way to discover all Alfred University has to offer is to come to campus. We truly have something for everyone with more than sixty courses of study, twenty-two intercollegiate athletic teams, and 100 clubs and organizations. You can tour campus; meet current students, faculty, coaches, and staff; attend a class; and eat in our dining hall—experience first hand what life at AU is like.

"Alfred University is a place where students are free to pursue their dreams and interests—all of them—no matter how varied or different. Academics, athletics, study abroad, special interests—they're all part of what makes you who you are and who you are going to become."

SELECTIVITY
Admissions Rating	80
# of applicants	2,825
% of applicants accepted	70
% of acceptees attending	27
# accepting a place on wait list	0
# of early decision applicants	34
% accepted early decision	91

FRESHMAN PROFILE
Range SAT Critical Reading	480–590
Range SAT Math	500–610
Range SAT Writing	470–570
Range ACT Composite	21–26
Minimum paper TOEFL	550
Minimum computer TOEFL	213
Minimum web-based TOEFL	80
Average HS GPA	3.19
% graduated top 10% of class	20
% graduated top 25% of class	52
% graduated top 50% of class	86

DEADLINES
Early decision	
Deadline	12/1
Notification	12/15
Regular	
Priority	2/1
Notification	11/15
Nonfall registration?	yes

APPLICANTS ALSO LOOK AT
AND OFTEN PREFER
Clarkson University, Rochester Institute of Technology
AND SOMETIMES PREFER
Ithaca College, State University of New York—University at Buffalo
AND RARELY PREFER
Hartwick College, State University of New York—New Paltz

FINANCIAL FACTS
Financial Aid Rating	83
Annual tuition	$25,974
Room and board	$11,498
Required fees	$910
Books and supplies	$1,050
% frosh rec. need-based scholarship or grant aid	78
% UG rec. need-based scholarship or grant aid	76
% frosh rec. non-need-based scholarship or grant aid	50
% UG rec. non-need-based scholarship or grant aid	43
% frosh rec. need-based self-help aid	72
% UG rec. need-based self-help aid	70
% frosh rec. any financial aid	92
% UG rec. any financial aid	90
% UG borrow to pay for school	80
Average cumulative indebtedness	$30,731

AMERICAN UNIVERSITY

4400 MASSACHUSETTS AVENUE, NORTHWEST, WASHINGTON, D.C. 20016-8001 • ADMISSIONS: 202-885-6000 • FAX: 202-885-1025

STUDENTS SAY ". . ."

Academics

American University exploits its Washington, D.C., location—that facilitates a strong faculty, prestigious guest lecturers, and "a wealth of internship opportunities"—to offer "incredibly strong programs" in political science and international relations. "The poli-sci kids are all going to be president one day, and the international studies ones are all going to save the world," a student insists. The school of communication also excels, and the school works hard to accommodate "interdisciplinary majors and the opportunities associated with studying them," which include "taking advantage of the resources of the city. The school values learning out of the classroom as much as learning in the classroom." As you might expect from a school with a strong international relations program, "AU's study abroad program is one of the best." Although AU "does not have the automatically recognizable prestige of nearby Georgetown," that's not necessarily a drawback; on the contrary, "The administration and professors go out of their way to ensure a great academic experience," in part because the school is trying to "climb in the rankings and gain recognition as one of the nation's top universities." However, some concede, "The university could improve programs in other fields, aside from its specialties in international studies, public affairs, business, and communication."

Life

"The greatest strength of AU is the activity level both politically and in the community," students tell us, noting that during the most recent election the campus "was a proxy holy war...Whether it was signs in windows, talk in the class or in the hallways, t-shirts, or canvassing in Metro-accessible Virginia, students on both sides took November 4 religiously." As one student explains, "Let's put it this way: A politician who comes to campus is likely to draw about ninety percent of the student population [and] an AU basketball game, about nine [percent]." Students get involved in the community through "campus outreach by student-run organizations," which many see as "the school's greatest asset." The typical undergrad is "incredibly engaged and active...Students seek internships in every line of work, becoming actively involved in a field of interest before graduation." When it's time to relax, "Washington, D.C., offers limitless opportunities to explore." Many "enjoy partying and hanging out off-campus and on campus (even though AU is a 'dry campus')," but there are also "a lot of people who don't drink and have a very good time just using what D.C. has to offer: museums, restaurants, parks, cinemas, theaters, and shops." As one student sums it up: "The city is the school's greatest resource. You will never run out of things to do in Washington."

Student Body

AU attracts a crowd that "tends to be very ideologically driven." "Liberals run the show," most here agree, although they add that "Plenty of students don't fit this mold, and I've never seen anyone rejected for what they believe." The campus "is very friendly to those with alternative lifestyles (GLBT, vegetarian, green-living, etc.)," but students with more socially conservative inclinations note that "while AU boasts about the many religious groups on campus, there is still a general antipathy toward piety." The perception that some departments outshine others is reflected in the way students perceive each other; one says, "You have the political studies know-it-alls, the international studies student who thinks he is going to save the world, the artsy film/communication students, and the rest [who] are unhappy students who couldn't get into George Washington or Georgetown."

FINANCIAL AID: 202-885-6100 • E-MAIL: AFA@AMERICAN.EDU • WEBSITE: WWW.AMERICAN.EDU

THE PRINCETON REVIEW SAYS

Admissions

Very important factors considered include: Academic GPA, rigor of secondary school record, standardized test scores, level of applicant's interest. *Important factors considered include:* Application essay, recommendation(s), extracurricular activities, volunteer work. *Other factors considered include:* Alumni/ae relation, character/personal qualities, first generation, geographical residence, racial/ethnic status, talent/ability, work experience. SAT or ACT required; ACT with writing component required. TOEFL required of all international applicants. High school diploma is required, and GED is accepted. *Academic units required:* 4 English, 3 mathematics, 3 science (2 science labs), 2 foreign language, 2 social studies, 3 academic elective. *Academic units recommended:* 4 English, 4 mathematics, 4 science, 3 foreign language, 4 social studies, 4 academic elective.

Financial Aid

Students should submit: FAFSA, CSS/Financial Aid PROFILE. Regular filing deadline is February 15. The Princeton Review suggests that all financial aid forms be submitted as soon as possible after January 1. *Need-based scholarships/grants offered:* Federal Pell, SEOG, state scholarships/grants, private scholarships, school scholarship or grant aid from institutional funds. *Loan aid offered:* Direct Subsidized Stafford, Direct Unsubsidized Stafford, Direct PLUS, Federal Perkins, university loans from institutional funds. Applicants will be notified concurrent with their offer of admission. Federal Work-Study Program available. Off-campus job opportunities are excellent.

The Inside Word

Despite strong competition from other area powerhouses, American sees a strong application pool that allows it to be very selective. Admissions rates have declined significantly in recent years. In addition to asking students to indicate their intended field of study, the university is also interested in clear demonstrations of interest on the part of applicants.

THE SCHOOL SAYS "..."

From the Admissions Office

"American University is located in the residential 'Embassy Row' neighborhood of Washington, D.C. Nestled among embassies and ambassadorial residences, AU's campus offers a safe, suburban environment with easy access to Washington's countless cultural destinations via the Metrorail subway system. A global center of government, Washington, D.C., stands unmatched in academics, professional, and cultural resources. AU's faculty includes scholars, journalists, artists, diplomats, authors, and scientists. Combining a liberal arts core curriculum with in-depth professional programs, academics at AU provide the necessary balance between theoretical study and hands-on experience. Our Career Center will work with you to enhance this experience with access to unique internship opportunities available only in Washington. Combine this with our diverse national and international student body and our world-class study abroad program, and AU can open up a world of possibilities."

SELECTIVITY

Admissions Rating	93
# of applicants	16,924
% of applicants accepted	43
% of acceptees attending	20
# accepting a place on wait list	277
% admitted from wait list	0
# of early decision applicants	565
% accepted early decision	73

FRESHMAN PROFILE

Range SAT Critical Reading	590–710
Range SAT Math	580–680
Range SAT Writing	580–690
Range ACT Composite	27–31
Minimum paper TOEFL	550
Minimum web-based TOEFL	80
Average HS GPA	3.80
% graduated top 10% of class	49
% graduated top 25% of class	82
% graduated top 50% of class	98

DEADLINES

Early decision	
Deadline	11/15
Notification	12/31
Regular	
Deadline	1/15
Nonfall registration?	yes

APPLICANTS ALSO LOOK AT

AND OFTEN PREFER
Boston College, Brown University, College of William and Mary, Georgetown University, The George Washington University, Tufts University

AND SOMETIMES PREFER
Syracuse University, Tulane University

AND RARELY PREFER
Fordham University, Northeastern University, New York University, University of Maryland—College Park

FINANCIAL FACTS

Financial Aid Rating	82
Annual tuition	$37,554
Room and board	$14,066
Books and supplies	$517
% frosh rec. need-based scholarship or grant aid	32
% UG rec. need-based scholarship or grant aid	25
% frosh rec. non-need-based scholarship or grant aid	28
% UG rec. non-need-based scholarship or grant aid	22
% frosh rec. need-based self-help aid	48
% UG rec. need-based self-help aid	44
% UG borrow to pay for school	60
Average cumulative indebtedness	$36,206

AMHERST COLLEGE

CAMPUS BOX 2231, PO BOX 5000, AMHERST, MA 01002 • ADMISSIONS: 413-542-2328 • FAX: 413-542-2040

CAMPUS LIFE

Quality of Life Rating	90
Fire Safety Rating	72
Green Rating	66
Type of school	private
Environment	town

STUDENTS

Total undergrad enrollment	1,795
% male/female	49/51
% from out of state	89
% from public high school	58
% live on campus	99
% African American	11
% Asian	11
% Caucasian	39
% Hispanic	11
% international	9
# of countries represented	28

SURVEY SAYS . . .
No one cheats
School is well-run
Dorms are like palaces
Campus feels safe
Low cost of living
Musical organizations are popular

ACADEMICS

Academic Rating	98
% students graduating within 4 years	89
% students graduating within 6 years	94
Calendar	4-1-4
Student/faculty ratio	8:1
Profs interesting rating	87
Profs accessible rating	93
Most common reg class size	10–19 students

MOST POPULAR MAJORS
economics, history,
English, biology

STUDENTS SAY ". . ."

Academics
With just more than 1,700 students, Amherst College "has a strong sense of community born of its small size" that goes hand-in-hand with an atmosphere that "encourages discussion and cooperation." Many here are quick to praise the "fantastic" professors and "supportive" administration. "Professors come here to teach," says one undergrad, "not just to do research." The "enriching" academics are bolstered by the "dedicated" faculty, but slackers be warned: You must be "willing to sit down and read a text forward and backward and firmly grasp it" as "skimming will do you no good." Besides having "easily accessible" professors, some students also appreciate that "registration is done by paper" as "it forces you to talk to your advisor." Another student notes, "I'm amazed at how easy it is to sit down for a casual lunch with anyone in the administration without there having to be a problem that needs to be discussed." Indeed, most here agree, "The support for students is as good as anyone could expect." However, some mention that despite the "administration, staff, and faculty" being "accessible and receptive to student input on every level," the "realities of running a small school in this economic climate mean a lot of suggestions won't be acted upon any time soon." Nevertheless, Amherst's alumni have a solid track record when it comes to obtaining postgraduate degrees—so much so that some think of the college "as prep school for grad school."

Life
While students at Amherst are "focused first and foremost on academics, nearly every student is active and enjoys life outside of the library." "There's a club or organization for every interest" here, and students assure us that if there isn't one that you're interested in, "the school will find the money for it." Students also praise the "awesome" dorms (some say they're "as spacious, well-maintained, and luxurious as many five-star hotels"), for being "designed to facilitate social interaction." Coincidentally, the dorms tend to serve as the school's social hub, particularly since Greek organizations were banned back in 1985. Amherst makes up for the lack of frat houses with "a number of socials put on by student government and I-Club (International Club) that are held throughout the year at bars downtown." And don't worry if you don't have a car since these events "have free buses that transport students to and from the bars." Some bemoan that the town of Amherst is "incredibly small" and doesn't feature much in the way of fun. Others take solace in "the many eateries in town that feature lots of ethnically diverse foods" and "go to sporting events." And since Amherst is part of the Five Colleges consortium, there's "an extended social life to be had," however "not that many people go out of their way to experience it." For those who like liquor with their extracurricular activities, most "drink on campus instead of off campus" thanks to some "huge apartment parties."

Student Body
Traditionally, the student body at Amherst has been known by the "stereotype of the preppy, upper-middle-class, white student," but many here note that the school is "at least as racially diverse as the country and more economically diverse than people think." That's not to say that the college doesn't have "a sizeable preppy population fresh from East Coast boarding schools," but overall students here report, "Diversity—racial, ethnic, geographic, socioeconomic—is more than a buzzword here." The campus is also "a politically and environmentally conscious" place, as well as a "highly athletic one." The school's small size "means that no group is isolated and everyone interacts and more or less gets along." Others, however, aren't as convinced about the student body's unity. "There is definitely a divide in the student body," says one undergrad. "The typical Amherst student is either an extremely quiet, bookish nerd or a lumbering, backward-baseball-cap-wearing jock." That said, the school is filled with "open-minded, intellectually passionate, and socially conscious critical thinkers." As one student puts it, "Most students—even our most drunken athletes and wild party-goers—are concerned about learning and academics."

FINANCIAL AID: 413-542-2296 • E-MAIL: ADMISSION@AMHERST.EDU • WEBSITE: WWW.AMHERST.EDU

THE PRINCETON REVIEW SAYS

Admissions

Very important factors considered include: Academic GPA, application essay, recommendation(s), rigor of secondary school record, standardized test scores, character/personal qualities, extracurricular activities, first generation, talent/ability. *Important factors considered include:* Class rank, alumni/ae relation, volunteer work. *Other factors considered include:* Geographical residence, state residency, work experience. ACT with writing component recommended. TOEFL required of all international applicants. High school diploma or equivalent isn't required. *Academic units recommended:* 4 English, 4 mathematics, 3 science (1 science lab), 4 foreign language, 2 social studies, 2 history.

Financial Aid

Students should submit: FAFSA, CSS/Financial Aid PROFILE. The Princeton Review suggests that all financial aid forms be submitted as soon as possible after January 1. *Need-based scholarships/grants offered:* Federal Pell, SEOG, state scholarships/grants, private scholarships, school scholarship or grant aid from institutional funds. *Loan aid offered:* Direct Subsidized Stafford, Direct Unsubsidized Stafford, Direct PLUS, Federal Perkins, university loans from institutional funds. Federal Work-Study Program available. Off-campus job opportunities are excellent.

The Inside Word

Membership certainly has its benefits at Amherst College. For the price of entry to this school students also gain entrance to the prestigious Five Colleges consortium, which allows enrolled students to take courses for credit at no additional cost at any of the four participating consortium members (Hampshire College, Mount Holyoke College, Smith College, and the University of Massachusetts—Amherst). And this deal isn't just confined to the classroom: Students can use other schools' libraries, eat meals at the other cafeterias, and participate in extracurricular activities offerred at the other schools. And don't worry about how you'll get there—your bus fare is covered, too.

THE SCHOOL SAYS ". . ."

From the Admissions Office

"Amherst College looks, above all, for men and women of intellectual promise who have demonstrated qualities of mind and character that will enable them to take full advantage of the college's curriculum…Admission decisions aim to select from among the many qualified applicants those possessing the intellectual talent, mental discipline, and imagination that will allow them most fully to benefit from the curriculum and contribute to the life of the college and of society. Whatever the form of academic experience—lecture course, seminar, conference, studio, laboratory, independent study at various levels—intellectual competence and awareness of problems and methods are the goals of the Amherst program, rather than the direct preparation for a profession.

"Applicants must submit scores from the SAT plus two SAT Subject Tests. Students may substitute the ACT with the writing component."

SELECTIVITY

Admissions Rating	99
# of applicants	8,099
% of applicants accepted	15
% of acceptees attending	39
# accepting a place on wait list	471
% admitted from wait list	3
# of early decision applicants	440
% accepted early decision	34

FRESHMAN PROFILE

Range SAT Critical Reading	670–770
Range SAT Math	670–770
Range SAT Writing	680–770
Range ACT Composite	30–34
Minimum paper TOEFL	600
Minimum computer TOEFL	250
Minimum web-based TOEFL	100
% graduated top 10% of class	87
% graduated top 25% of class	97
% graduated top 50% of class	100

DEADLINES

Early decision	
Deadline	11/1
Notification	12/15
Regular	
Priority	1/1
Deadline	4/1
Nonfall registration?	yes

APPLICANTS ALSO LOOK AT AND OFTEN PREFER

Harvard College, Princeton University, Yale University

AND SOMETIMES PREFER

Brown University, Dartmouth College, Stanford University, Williams College

FINANCIAL FACTS

Financial Aid Rating	96
Annual tuition	$40,160
Room and board	$10,660
Required fees	$702
Books and supplies	$1,000
% frosh rec. need-based scholarship or grant aid	39
% UG rec. need-based scholarship or grant aid	55
% frosh rec. need-based self-help aid	50
% UG rec. need-based self-help aid	50
% frosh rec. any financial aid	60
% UG rec. any financial aid	57
% UG borrow to pay for school	42
Average cumulative indebtedness	$12,843

ANGELO STATE UNIVERSITY

2601 WEST AVENUE N, SAN ANGELO, TX 76909 • ADMISSIONS: 325-942-2041 • FAX: 325-942-2078

STUDENTS SAY ". . ."

Academics
Angelo State University, a member of the Texas Tech University System, is "a small school with big opportunities." "Bang for your buck" is reportedly ample. In addition to a "relatively cheap tuition price compared to other public universities in Texas," ASU offers tremendous financial aid and "excellent scholarship opportunities." Academically, this place is a "science haven." "The technology here is great." The on-campus planetarium is one of the biggest and best at any school, anywhere. Students also praise the education, agriculture, and nursing programs. "Classes are generally small." Professors "are on a first-name basis with their students" and "get to know you personally." As far as teaching, some profs are "pretty much awesome" while others are merely "subject matter experts, not teachers." The administration is "relatively well-organized." On the whole, students tell us that they feel "supported and encouraged." "I'm uber-happy to be at Angelo State and can't imagine being anywhere else," gloats an accounting major.

Life
ASU's campus is "very small and easy to navigate." Students note "it can be really hard to find a parking space on campus" and note the need for "more student parking around certain buildings." Some facilities are "not big enough." Students also warn, "Be cautious of the cafeteria food." "Campus life is very active." "ASU does an excellent job of trying to involve its students." "Many people play intramural sports." The University Center is popular for "killing time." Activities on offer include ping pong, a wealth of video games, and "Texas hold 'em tournaments." For nature lovers, there's a state park nearby with biking and hiking trails. By the time the weekend rolls around, some people "go to the bars and clubs." "House parties" are also frequent. On the other hand, Greek life is paltry. One student describes the surrounding city of San Angelo as "a very 'old person' town." Another student says that "people coming from small towns to San Angelo are able to keep entertained outside of school fairly easily," observes a shrewd first-year student. "Conversely, people coming from larger cities find it hard to have fun because, out here, you do need some creativity in finding things to do." For serious leisure, "You have to drive three hours to Austin."

Student Body
While drawing students from throughout Texas, including the major metropolitan areas, the typical student at ASU attended "a very small high school" in "a tiny west Texas town." Most come from "lower- to middle-class" families. Almost three-quarters receive financial aid. Students describe themselves as "friendly, hardworking," and "career oriented." They tend to be "conservative." "There aren't a whole lot of cowboy hats, but it's relatively traditional," explains a junior. "There is nothing too radical around here." There are some "dullards," but "Academics are pretty important" to most students. It's not uncommon for students to "use ASU as a bridge or a stepping stone and transfer to a larger university after one or two years to finish their degrees." Nontraditional students are quite common as well. "There are all different types of people and all different ages," notes a junior. "This makes it easier to fit in."

FINANCIAL AID: 325-942-2246 • E-MAIL: ADMISSIONS@ANGELO.EDU • WEBSITE: WWW.ANGELO.EDU

THE PRINCETON REVIEW SAYS

Admissions

Very important factors considered include: Class rank, rigor of secondary school record, standardized test scores. SAT or ACT required; ACT with or without writing component accepted. TOEFL required of all international applicants. High school diploma is required, and GED is accepted. *Academic units recommended:* 4 English, 4 mathematics, 4 science, 3.5 social studies, 2 foreign language, 1 visual/performing arts.

Financial Aid

Students should submit: FAFSA. Regular filing deadline is April 1. The Princeton Review suggests that all financial aid forms be submitted as soon as possible after January 1. *Need-based scholarships/grants offered:* Federal Pell, SEOG, state scholarships/grants, private scholarships, school scholarship or grant aid from institutional funds, Federal Nursing Scholarships. *Loan aid offered:* Federal Perkins, Federal Nursing Loans, state loans, university loans from institutional funds. Applicants will be notified of awards on a rolling basis beginning April 1. Federal Work-Study Program available. Off-campus job opportunities are excellent.

The Inside Word

The admissions process at Angelo State embodies an inclusive attitude that encourages students who may not have established their full academic potential in high school to invest in attaining a higher degree. Students in the top ten percent of their class are granted automatic admission. Those applicants who don't meet general admission requirements may apply for alternative admission. In this case, leadership activities, community service, talents and awards, extenuating circumstances, and employment history play a large role.

THE SCHOOL SAYS "..."

From the Admissions Office

"Angelo State University remains an affordable institution with a superb record of sending graduates on to success in business, agribusiness, health care, and education as well as in medical, law, and professional school. ASU maintains strong academic programs in traditional fields, such as physics, biology, mathematics, education, business, agriculture, and nursing, while developing innovative offerings like the computer science department's computer gaming design sequence, ranked by The Princeton Review as one of the top fifty in the nation.

"Because of strong academics and a substantial gift aid program, including the Carr Scholarship Program, which annually awards scholarships totaling approximately $4 million, ASU remains one of the top educational values in Texas. About sixty-seven percent of ASU students receive gift aid, financial support which does not have to be repaid to the university. ASU targets students in the top forty-five percent of their class or with 990–1100 SAT and 21–24 ACT scores for gift aid. Additionally, ASU offers its Blue and Gold Guarantee program for students from low income families.

"Because of its low twenty to one student/faculty ratio and individualized instruction, ASU attracts many first-generation students, who benefit from special programs and scholarships. A quarter of the student body is Hispanic, enhancing the university's overall diversity. Comprehensive academic advising and numerous opportunities for international study enhance the college experience on the 268-acre Angelo State campus known for its safety and modern academic, residential and recreational facilities."

SELECTIVITY

Admissions Rating	65
# of applicants	3,128
% of applicants accepted	95
% of acceptees attending	50

FRESHMAN PROFILE

Range SAT Critical Reading	410–530
Range SAT Math	430–540
Range ACT Composite	18–23
Minimum paper TOEFL	550
Minimum computer TOEFL	213
Minimum web-based TOEFL	79
% graduated top 10% of class	12
% graduated top 25% of class	36
% graduated top 50% of class	72

DEADLINES

Regular	
Deadline	8/22
Notification	9/1
Nonfall registration?	yes

FINANCIAL FACTS

Financial Aid Rating	76
Annual in-state tuition	$3,645
Annual out-of-state tuition	$11,085
Room and board	$6,666
Required fees	$2,027
Books and supplies	$1,150
% frosh rec. need-based scholarship or grant aid	57
% UG rec. need-based scholarship or grant aid	35
% frosh rec. non-need-based scholarship or grant aid	54
% UG rec. non-need-based scholarship or grant aid	36
% frosh rec. need-based self-help aid	60
% UG rec. need-based self-help aid	41
% frosh rec. any financial aid	87
% UG rec. any financial aid	81
% UG borrow to pay for school	43
Average cumulative indebtedness	$10,712

ARIZONA STATE UNIVERSITY

PO Box 870112, Tempe, AZ 85287-0112 • Admissions: 480-965-7788 • Fax: 480-965-3610

STUDENTS SAY ". . ."

Academics

Arizona State University's "greatest strength is the great depth of its faculty and wealth of opportunities offered to students." Many students say they chose ASU because it "offers a huge range of classes and majors at a reasonable cost for in-state students." Students also say the university provides "the best of both worlds: a large research university and an honors program tailored for individual needs." The Honors College and The Walter Cronkite School of Journalism and Mass Communication stand out as notable programs that offer "targeted education." Despite this, a Russian major points out, "The school still has a reputation for partying, which is not totally undeserved. The student body is not full of future Einsteins." Many ASU students, however, believe you get from the university what you put into it and say, "A large number of students truly care about the education they are receiving." While "for the most part, ASU is home to engaging professors that are genuinely concerned with the success of their students," "the large auditorium classes are an absolute joke."

Life

At ASU, "There is always something happening on campus," and students say, "ASU is all about diversity and open doors; there are a million distinct opportunities to get involved in whatever you're passionate about." Many rave, "Campus life is amazing. There is always something to do, someone to hang out with, or places to be," adding, "The weather is nice enough to sit outside and study a lot." A kinesiology majors says, "The overall culture is very Southern California," but "The west side of campus has more of a Portland feel, which is more individual and artsy. It all depends on where you decide to get plugged in." Despite praise for ASU's dedication to "pursuing new ways to become more sustainable and encouraging 'going green' throughout campus, classrooms, and offices," many students feel, "ASU should concentrate on renovating old buildings, which are falling apart" and gripe about inconsistent air conditioning during the hottest months. Some students complain that ASU needs to "improve in advising and the overall process of changing a major," and some say, "The red tape can be very frustrating, especially as a new student."

Student Body

With an enrollment of more than 50,000 undergraduates, "It's hard to define typical" when it comes to describing the ASU student body. "Due to the huge student population size and plethora of social events and organizations, any student can find a niche and a group of people with similar interests." Some say, "There is a minority of students who work hard and care about their educations surrounded by a majority only concerned with drinking, partying, and getting a better tan." It's also pointed out that "because the party atmosphere is so huge, those students seem to have the largest voice." However, others say, "Even the party kids care about their grades," and the typical student is "laid-back but invested in their future." One political science major jokes, "I would say the hardest part for students fitting in is dealing with the heat." Most agree, "The 'dry campus' rules are *far* from followed, and even for those who don't break those rules, there are places right across the street for students to drink at their leisure," adding, "Tempe is great—if you're in college," and "Tempe has many fun activities both indoors and outdoors, depending on the weather! From hiking to biking, all kinds of sports, going downtown and being around the museums and history, to having a good time hanging out with friends on Mill Avenue."

ARIZONA STATE UNIVERSITY

FINANCIAL AID: 480-965-3355 • E-MAIL: ADMISSIONS@ASU.EDU • WEBSITE: WWW.ASU.EDU

THE PRINCETON REVIEW SAYS

Admissions

Very important factors considered include: Academic GPA, class rank, standardized test scores. *Important factors considered include:* State residency. TOEFL required of all international applicants. High school diploma is required, and GED is accepted. *Academic units required:* 4 English, 4 mathematics, 3 science (3 science labs), 2 foreign language, 1 social studies, 1 history, 1 fine arts.

Financial Aid

Students should submit: FAFSA. Regular filing priority date is March 1. The Princeton Review suggests that all financial aid forms be submitted as soon as possible after January 1. *Need-based scholarships/grants offered:* Federal Pell, SEOG, state scholarships/grants, private scholarships, school scholarship or grant aid from institutional funds, Federal Nursing Scholarship. *Loan aid offered:* Direct Subsidized Stafford, Direct Unsubsidized Stafford, Direct PLUS, Federal Perkins, Federal Nursing Loans, state loans. Applicants will be notified of awards on a rolling basis. Federal Work-Study Program available. Off-campus job opportunities are good.

The Inside Word

ASU clearly outlines all the requirements for admission on its website. The applications of students who meet all the requirements go under "individual review" and are carefully evaluated by the admissions team. Students interested in Barrett, The Honors College may apply for admission only after submitting an application to ASU.

THE SCHOOL SAYS ". . ."

From the Admissions Office

"ASU is breaking down the walls of the traditional academic experience to increase the impact of education and research in local and global communities. As the New American University, ASU is committed to interdisciplinary connections, academic excellence, and societal impact. We are bold and forward-thinking, and we see challenges as opportunities.

"With 250-plus undergraduate majors, ASU is a learning environment where personal expression is valued as much as research and discovery. ASU champions intellectual and cultural diversity and welcomes students from all fifty states and 120-plus nations. Our distinguished faculty receives prestigious honors including the Nobel Prize and membership in the National Academies. Student achievements include Goldwater, Rhodes, Marshall, and Fulbright scholars.

"ASU has four unique campuses in metropolitan Phoenix. State-of-the-art living and learning facilities are found at ASU's Downtown Phoenix campus. The campus creates strong learning and career connections for 11,500-plus students with media, health care, corporate, and government organizations.

"The Polytechnic campus, located in Mesa, Arizona, is home to 9,000-plus students who are exploring professional and technical programs. Thousands of square feet of new laboratory space make way for project-based learning.

"ASU welcomes 55,000-plus students studying at the historic Tempe campus. The Sun Devils athletic complex, performing arts facilities, and high-tech research space create a dynamic and engaging learning environment.

"At the West campus in northwest Phoenix, ASU offers business, education, and interdisciplinary arts and science programs to 10,000-plus students. The campus's award-winning architecture and lush landscaping are designed to create a close-knit learning community."

SELECTIVITY

Admissions Rating	78
# of applicants	29,771
% of applicants accepted	87
% of acceptees attending	37

FRESHMAN PROFILE

Range SAT Critical Reading	480–600
Range SAT Math	490–620
Range ACT Composite	21–27
Minimum paper TOEFL	500
Minimum computer TOEFL	173
Minimum web-based TOEFL	61
Average HS GPA	3.39
% graduated top 10% of class	28
% graduated top 25% of class	56
% graduated top 50% of class	85

DEADLINES

Scholarship	
Priority	2/1
Regular	
Priority	5/1
Notification	9/15
Nonfall registration?	yes

FINANCIAL FACTS

Financial Aid Rating	76
Annual in-state tuition	$7,793
Annual out-of-state tuition	$20,257
Room and board	$9,706
Required fees	$339
Books and supplies	$1,290
% frosh rec. need-based scholarship or grant aid	54
% UG rec. need-based scholarship or grant aid	44
% frosh rec. non-need-based scholarship or grant aid	17
% UG rec. non-need-based scholarship or grant aid	13
% frosh rec. need-based self-help aid	32
% UG rec. need-based self-help aid	36
% frosh rec. any financial aid	84
% UG rec. any financial aid	76
% UG borrow to pay for school	46
Average cumulative indebtedness	$18,542

AUBURN UNIVERSITY

202 MARY MARTIN HALL, AUBURN, AL 36849-5149 • ADMISSIONS: 334-844-4080 • FAX: 334-844-6179

STUDENTS SAY ". . ."

Academics

Auburn University, students agree, "provides excellence in academics, athletics, and social experiences, all in one of the friendliest towns in the country." In fact, some students would go further, insisting that the Auburn community isn't "a 'nation,' as many schools and fan bases are, and we do not wish to be because we pride ourselves on being something closer: a family." An Auburn education unites "a community of strangers with the same heartbeat for tradition, character, honor, and education, who find commonality as they represent their university," according to its many loyal undergraduates. This sense of community helps make Auburn "a large school with a small feel" that "offers amenities only a large school has to offer" without forsaking the personal touches. Professors, for example, are "willing to bend over backwards to make sure [you] get everything out of the learning experience that [you] want," while administrators actively work with "students and the [school's] multiple student organizations" on campus. Academics are "challenging and rewarding," with Auburn's "great engineering program" receiving especially high marks. The school's many business undergrads appreciate "the real-world aspect that many teachers try to bring into the classroom." With all these assets, it's no wonder Auburn students brag that "Auburn prepares you for life and any educational aspirations after [the] undergraduate [years], such as a graduate program, medical school, or law school."

Life

"People are very friendly on campus" at Auburn, where the "Greek community is very strong," and fortunately, "There is no animosity between Greek and non-Greek students." It's this "family atmosphere," the "tradition and friendliness of the alumni, fans, and students on school days and game days" that students say "is unrivaled…anywhere else." There are "plenty of things to do on campus, whether getting involved with a student organization or going to a sports event." Auburn hosts "several hundred student organizations on campus, so it is really easy to get involved," and people do; this student body "thrives on campus involvement and community service. After all, Auburn isn't just a university, it is a way of life." There's also "lots of tailgating" for college football games, of course—the games are "extremely important" to just about everyone on campus—and other intercollegiate sports "from swimming to gymnastics to baseball to basketball" have their enthusiastic adherents as well. Intramurals are very popular with Auburn's active, fitness-minded student body. Undergrads love hometown Auburn, "a small college town" with "plenty of things for students to do…There are great local restaurants, and the downtown area is really being revived with shops and nightlife." Students "also travel to places like Atlanta or nearby beaches just to get away for a weekend."

Student Body

"The most common quality among Auburn students is friendliness, as it is truly a place where you can get along with almost everyone," students here assure us. Your standard issue Auburn undergrad is a "white, Southern, religious, and politically conservative" student who "loves football," "likes to have fun," and "absolutely loves his or her university. Auburn students do anything they can to get involved in both school and the community." Many here "take time with their appearance for the day," and as a result, the student body comes across as "fairly attractive and healthy; to be honest, more attractive than most other schools I have seen." The stereotype applies most accurately to students in the Greek system, undergrads tell us. Beyond the norm, there are those who "don't wear shoes and act like it is normal, so we treat it like it is normal, but it is still a bit gross!" One student observed that minority students "do fit in well" at Auburn.

FINANCIAL AID: 334-844-4367 • E-MAIL: ADMISSIONS@AUBURN.EDU • WEBSITE: WWW.AUBURN.EDU

THE PRINCETON REVIEW SAYS

Admissions

Very important factors considered include: Academic GPA, application essay, standardized test scores. *Important factors considered include:* Rigor of secondary school record, alumni/ae relation, character/personal qualities, extracurricular activities, first generation, geographical residence, level of applicant's interest, state residency, talent/ability, volunteer work, work experience. *Other factors considered include:* Recommendation(s). SAT or ACT required; ACT with writing component required. TOEFL required of all international applicants. High school diploma is required, and GED is accepted. *Academic units required:* 4 English, 3 mathematics, 2 science (1 science lab), 3 social studies. *Academic units recommended:* (2 science labs), 1 foreign language, 4 social studies.

Financial Aid

Students should submit: FAFSA. The Princeton Review suggests that all financial aid forms be submitted as soon as possible after January 1. *Need-based scholarships/grants offered:* Federal Pell, SEOG, state scholarships/grants, private scholarships, school scholarship or grant aid from institutional funds. *Loan aid offered:* Direct Subsidized Stafford, Direct Unsubsidized Stafford, Direct PLUS, Federal Perkins, Federal Nursing Loans, university loans from institutional funds. Applicants will be notified of awards on a rolling basis beginning October 2. Federal Work-Study Program available. Off-campus job opportunities are good.

The Inside Word

Auburn admissions officers have more than 15,000 applications to sort through each year. Applicants meeting certain baseline GPA, curricular, and standardized test score levels are admitted without consideration of their applications. Applicants who fall far short of these baselines are nearly always rejected, except for those with unique talents and traits that will contribute substantially to campus life. Letters of recommendation, essays, and extracurricular activities are the make-or-break point for borderline candidates. Starting in 2012, applicant's test scores must be submitted directly from the testing agencies.

THE SCHOOL SAYS "..."

From the Admissions Office

"Auburn University is a comprehensive land-grant university serving Alabama and the nation. The university is especially charged with the responsibility of enhancing the economic, social, and cultural development of the state through its instruction, research, and extension programs. In all of these programs, the university is committed to the pursuit of excellence. The university assumes an obligation to provide an environment of learning in which the individual and society are enriched by the discovery, preservation, transmission, and application of knowledge; in which students grow intellectually as they study and do research under the guidance of competent faculty, and in which the faculty develop professionally and contribute fully to the intellectual life of the institution, community, and state. This obligation unites Auburn University's continuing commitment to its land-grant traditions and the institution's role as a dynamic and complex, comprehensive university."

SELECTIVITY
Admissions Rating	88
# of applicants	15,784
% of applicants accepted	79
% of acceptees attending	34

FRESHMAN PROFILE
Range SAT Critical Reading	535–650
Range SAT Math	560–660
Range SAT Writing	530–640
Range ACT Composite	24–30
Minimum paper TOEFL	550
Minimum computer TOEFL	213
Minimum web-based TOEFL	79
Average HS GPA	3.78
% graduated top 10% of class	46
% graduated top 25% of class	69
% graduated top 50% of class	91

DEADLINES
Early action	
Deadline	10/1
Notification	10/15
Regular	
Priority	2/1
Deadline	6/1
Notification	rolling
Nonfall registration?	yes

APPLICANTS ALSO LOOK AT AND SOMETIMES PREFER
Clemson University, Georgia Institute of Technology, University of Alabama—Tuscaloosa, University of Florida, University of Georgia, University of Tennessee—Knoxville

FINANCIAL FACTS
Financial Aid Rating	66
Annual in-state tuition	$7,008
Annual out-of-state tuition	$21,024
Room and board	$9,630
Required fees	$892
Books and supplies	$1,100
% frosh rec. need-based scholarship or grant aid	26
% UG rec. need-based scholarship or grant aid	23
% frosh rec. non-need-based scholarship or grant aid	6
% UG rec. non-need-based scholarship or grant aid	3
% frosh rec. need-based self-help aid	21
% UG rec. need-based self-help aid	27
% frosh rec. any financial aid	62
% UG rec. any financial aid	54
% UG borrow to pay for school	46
Average cumulative indebtedness	$23,491

AUSTIN COLLEGE

900 NORTH GRAND AVE, SUITE 6N SHERMAN, TX 75090-4400 • ADMISSIONS: 903-813-3000 • FAX: 903-813-3198

STUDENTS SAY ". . ."

Academics

Austin College, a "small school with a huge amount of opportunities," "is about active learning and creating unique experiences for each student" through "unsurpassed opportunities for internships, studying abroad, and a personalized learning experience," students tell us. "A strong premed program" attracts many undergraduates to this campus; psychology, political science, international relations, environmental studies, language programs featuring "the Jordan Family Language House, the language tables in the cafeteria, conversation classes, and incredibly easy access to study abroad," and an education program "where one can get a [master's degree in teaching]" also earn students' accolades. Students are especially enthusiastic about AC's "JanTerm," "where for the month of January students take one intensive course," and "Many students take the opportunity to go abroad or do internships or directed studies of their choice." Best of all, students benefit from "matched tuition when abroad," which means that "all scholarships and loans remain in place for your tuition abroad." Academics entail "a well-rounded and difficult curriculum that really gives students…bang for their buck," combined with "tough classes, hard work, and great people." The end result, undergraduates explain, is "a fun yet academically challenging place that is more home than school."

Life

Campus life at Austin College is pretty much what you would expect at a small school in a small town. Undergraduates "generally chill out at their friend's places" or "house hop, have dinner parties, [or attend] writer's circles, Friday Night Happy Hour, painting circles, garden parties, tea parties, [and other] quaint little things." AC also has "a great Greek community, although it's entirely local" (that is, unaffiliated with national Greek organizations) and an effective campus activities board that "has some kind of event planned for almost every night (bingo, movies, etc.). They also get tickets for midnight showings at Cinemark and free bowling at the local alley." Hometown Sherman contributes "a dollar cinema, which isn't too shabby" and "local bars and restaurants [that] run nightly specials," but otherwise it "is not a very active or exciting town, so you have to try a little harder to enjoy yourself." Students note, "We're only an hour away from Dallas and Denton, and an hour-and-a-half to Fort Worth, so a large city isn't too hard to reach." All in all, things are pretty low key at AC. "In general, a lot of people spend a lot of time on school-work and studying, at an on-campus job, at some sort of service organization, or [participating in] an extracurricular," one student sums up.

Student Body

Though small, Austin College is large enough to "host a regular buffet of savant-level geniuses, artistic hippie types, and driven athletes." Undergrads tend to be "very studious" to the point that "everyone here is a bit of a nerd." One student elaborates: "Take every nerd from every high school…and put them all in one place. That's Austin College, and once all the fresh eccentric kids arrive, they reassemble into what a 'normal' school should look like, with jocks, theater groups, musicians, academics, class clowns, homecoming queens, and library workers." They're also "pretty liberal, aware of social issues…and focused on the importance of service to others." Though, in the past, students have noted that there's "not much racial diversity among students due to the size, price, and location of the school." Recent efforts to increase minority representation on campus have been a big success. "Though Presbyterian, Austin College is very religiously diverse, and students of all religions (including the irreligious) are accepted." Most here "are from the Dallas/Fort Worth area."

FINANCIAL AID: 903-813-2900 • E-MAIL: ADMISSION@AUSTINCOLLEGE.EDU • WEBSITE: WWW.AUSTINCOLLEGE.EDU

THE PRINCETON REVIEW SAYS

Admissions

Very important factors considered include: Academic GPA, rigor of secondary school record. *Important factors considered include:* Application essay, class rank, recommendation(s), standardized test scores, character/personal qualities, extracurricular activities, talent/ability. *Other factors considered include:* Alumni/ae relation, first generation, geographical residence, interview, racial/ethnic status, religious affiliation/commitment, state residency, volunteer work, work experience. SAT or ACT required; ACT with writing component required. TOEFL required of all international applicants. High school diploma is required, and GED is accepted. *Academic units required:* 4 English, 3 mathematics, 3 science (2 science labs), 2 foreign language, 2 social studies, 1 visual/performing arts, 1 academic elective. *Academic units recommended:* 4 English, 4 mathematics, 4 science (3 science labs), 3 foreign language, 3 social studies, 2 visual/performing arts.

Financial Aid

Students should submit: FAFSA. The Princeton Review suggests that all financial aid forms be submitted as soon as possible after January 1. *Need-based scholarships/grants offered:* Federal Pell, SEOG, state scholarships/grants, private scholarships, school scholarship or grant aid from institutional funds. *Loan aid offered:* Direct Subsidized Stafford, Direct Unsubsidized Stafford, Direct PLUS, Federal Perkins, state loans, university loans from institutional funds. Applicants will be notified of awards on a rolling basis beginning March 1. Federal Work-Study Program available. Off-campus job opportunities are good.

The Inside Word

The admissions process at Austin College is similar to the process at most competitive, small, private colleges. Rigor of high school curriculum, grades, and standardized test scores are paramount, but admissions officers also dig down into essays, recommendations, and record of extracurricular achievement in search of a more complete portrait of each applicant. A campus visit, including an interview with an admissions officer, is a good way to signal your serious interest in attending AC.

THE SCHOOL SAYS "..."

From the Admissions Office

"Few schools the size of Austin College offer a greater emphasis on all things global, highlighted by a nationally recognized study abroad program. Three-quarters of the class of 2009 studied abroad while attending Austin College, and an average seventy percent of students in the past ten years have studied abroad, exploring more than fifty countries on six continents. In fact, Austin College has been ranked number one in the nation four of the past six years by the Institute of International Education for percentage of study abroad participation among liberal arts colleges.

"Study abroad takes many forms at Austin College, including January Term, internship programs, and service opportunities such as the new Global Outreach summer program that has sent students on self-designed international service projects in Costa Rica, Ethiopia, Ghana, Guatemala, India, Kenya, Lebanon, Nigeria, Pakistan, Peru, Russia, South Africa, Thailand, and Vietnam. In 2010 alone, Austin College students once again furthered their educations on nearly every continent, including North America, South America, Europe, Asia, Africa, and Australia. For January Term, students visited twenty-five countries on five continents—all except Australia and Antarctica. Austin College biology professor George Diggs covered the coldest continent with a January sabbatical trip to Antarctica, where his research involved capturing videos of penguins, leopard seals, and humpback whales, as well as photos of animals and a small tuft of grass he found on the Antarctic Peninsula."

SELECTIVITY

Admissions Rating	87
# of applicants	1,750
% of applicants accepted	80
% of acceptees attending	30
# accepting a place on wait list	18
% admitted from wait list	39

FRESHMAN PROFILE

Range SAT Critical Reading	560–680
Range SAT Math	570–670
Range SAT Writing	540–650
Range ACT Composite	24–28
Minimum paper TOEFL	550
Minimum computer TOEFL	213
Minimum web-based TOEFL	80
Average HS GPA	3.56
% graduated top 10% of class	41
% graduated top 25% of class	70
% graduated top 50% of class	92

DEADLINES

Early action	
Deadline	1/15
Notification	3/1
Priority	1/15
Deadline	5/1
Notification	12/15
Nonfall registration?	yes

APPLICANTS ALSO LOOK AT

AND OFTEN PREFER
Southwestern University

AND SOMETIMES PREFER
Baylor University, Texas A&M University—College Station, Texas Christian University

FINANCIAL FACTS

Financial Aid Rating	96
Annual tuition	$29,075
Room and board	$9,549
Required fees	$160
Books and supplies	$1,200
% frosh rec. need-based scholarship or grant aid	68
% UG rec. need-based scholarship or grant aid	61
% frosh rec. non-need-based scholarship or grant aid	41
% UG rec. non-need-based scholarship or grant aid	3
% frosh rec. need-based self-help aid	49
% UG rec. need-based self-help aid	48
% frosh rec. any financial aid	97
% UG rec. any financial aid	98

BABSON COLLEGE

LUNDER UNDERGRADUATE ADMISSION CENTER, BABSON PARK, MA 02457 • ADMISSION: 781-239-5522 • FAX: 781-239-4135

STUDENTS SAY ". . ."
Academics
Babson is a school well-suited to the age of specialization. Its business is business; if you're looking for a well-regarded undergraduate degree in business, Babson can serve your needs because the school "offers multiple opportunities for students to gear their own educations" to develop "a complete set of management skills." As one student puts it, "When I took a quick look at the curriculum, I was positive whatever I wanted to study in business could be found" at Babson. The school is best known for its emphasis on entrepreneurship; all freshmen must undertake the school's Foundations in Management and Entrepreneurship immersion course, during which undergrads create their own startups. Those who choose to pursue the field further can jockey for space in E-Tower, a "community of twenty-one highly motivated entrepreneurs chosen to live together" and immerse themselves in all things entrepreneurial (similar housing options are available for students in, among others, finance and green business). Internship opportunities are abundant thanks to the school's reputation and proximity to Boston, providing students "a hands-on experience of how things work in the real world." Professors "want nothing more than to see their students learn and do well. Many…refer to themselves as 'pracademics' because they have had such amazing real-world experience from which they can draw on in the classroom. From executives of Fortune 500 companies to entrepreneurs who own multimillion dollar companies, the knowledge of professors at Babson is only rivaled by their desire to see students do well." Career placement services here "are really strong."

Life
Babson is in the "perfect location," "near Boston but not in it." One student explains: "We are not in the busy city life on a daily basis, but we are able to get into Boston very easily, whether it's driving, taking the T, or the Babson Shuttle that drops you off right in the center of Fanueil Hall." (The shuttle runs only on weekends.) Campus life, once considered sub-par, "is definitely a lot better. [Student government] sponsors and hosts many events throughout the months to keep students entertained and involved," including "Knight Parties, where there are monthly dance parties in one of our large auditoriums" and "spring, winter, and fall weekend, where they have entertainment and bands come to the school. This year we even had Jimmy Fallon come for a comedy concert in the fall—the show was packed; it was standing room only." Students report, "A favorite hangout on a Thursday night is the pub, where there is entertainment and food. Babson [provides] supervised drinking for those of legal drinking age." The school's numerous student-run clubs "are very motivated, providing diverse and educating events" such as mixers and symposia.

Student Body
"It is hard to pinpoint a typical student, as Babson is so diverse," but the common thread is that "we all view business as a primary, shared strand that can link our interests and passions in order to help us make a difference in the world." Babson "is an international college. Outside of our library, there is a flag tree where the flags of different students represented on our campus are flown to show our diversity. We have students from about sixty-seven different countries," and students "learn from each others' differences. It is one of the great pieces of knowledge we are able to pick up at Babson." The "dominant domestic students will be the preppy white boy and girl who treat their designer clothes like aprons," while "international students are mostly of Indian and Hispanic descent who do not refrain from displaying their wealth," all supplemented by "a small population of students that are swimming in personal debt to attend Babson or could never place a foot on the campus if it weren't for their financial aid."

BABSON COLLEGE

FINANCIAL AID: 781-239-4219 • E-MAIL: UGRADADMISSION@BABSON.EDU • WEBSITE: WWW.BABSON.EDU

THE PRINCETON REVIEW SAYS

Admissions

Very important factors considered include: Academic GPA, application essay, recommendation(s), rigor of secondary school record, standardized test scores, character/personal qualities. *Important factors considered include:* Class rank, extracurricular activities. *Other factors considered include:* Alumni/ae relation, first generation, geographical residence, interview, level of applicant's interest, racial/ethnic status, state residency, talent/ability, volunteer work, work experience. SAT or ACT required; TOEFL required of all international applicants. High school diploma is required, and GED is accepted. *Academic units recommended:* 4 English, 4 mathematics, 4 science (3 science labs), 4 foreign language, 2 social studies, 2 history.

Financial Aid

Students should submit: FAFSA, CSS/Financial Aid PROFILE. Regular filing deadline is February 15. The Princeton Review suggests that all financial aid forms be submitted as soon as possible after January 1. *Need-based scholarships/grants offered:* Federal Pell, SEOG, state scholarships/grants, private scholarships, school scholarship or grant aid from institutional funds. *Loan aid offered:* Direct Subsidized Stafford, Direct Unsubsidized Stafford, Direct PLUS, Federal Perkins, state loans. Federal Work-Study Program available. Off-campus job opportunities are good.

The Inside Word

Babson's national profile is ascending quickly, resulting in a substantial uptick in the number of applications received each year. Expect admissions standards to rise in accordance. The school considers writing ability a strong indicator of preparedness for college; proceed accordingly.

THE SCHOOL SAYS "..."

From the Admissions Office

"Nationally recognized as a Top 20 Business Program and the number one school in entrepreneurship for fourteen years, Babson College defines entrepreneurship education for the world. Our learning concepts provide students with the ability to adapt to ever-changing business environments, the experience to hit the ground running upon graduation, and the know-how to discover opportunities that will create economic and social value everywhere. We believe, as do our graduates and their employers, in the value of an integrated approach combined with experiential education. As a business school where one-half of the classes are in liberal arts, Babson emphasizes creativity, imagination, and risk-taking as essential to learning the foundation of business.

"Babson's close-knit community provides students with the opportunity to form close relationships with faculty and staff. An average class size of twenty-nine and student/faculty ratio of fourteen to one allow faculty to serve as role models and mentors committed to helping our students grow. With about ninety percent holding a doctoral degree, these accomplished business executives, authors, entrepreneurs, scholars, researchers, and artists bring an intellectual diversity and real-world experience that adds depth to Babson's programs. Most importantly, faculty members teach 100 percent of the courses.

"At Babson, students receive a world-class education that is innovative and creative, yet practical. They study business, learn about leadership, and undertake a transformative life experience preparing them to create an authentic, powerful brand of success. Our students make friends, find mentors, and develop long-lasting relationships that will thrive long after graduation."

SELECTIVITY

Admissions Rating	94
# of applicants	4,061
% of applicants accepted	40
% of acceptees attending	31
# accepting a place on wait list	338
% admitted from wait list	0
# of early decision applicants	180
% accepted early decision	69

FRESHMAN PROFILE

Range SAT Critical Reading	570–660
Range SAT Math	630–720
Range SAT Writing	600–684
Range ACT Composite	26–30
Minimum paper TOEFL	600
Minimum computer TOEFL	250
Minimum web-based TOEFL	100
Average HS GPA	A–/B+
% graduated top 10% of class	53
% graduated top 25% of class	87
% graduated top 50% of class	99

DEADLINES

Early decision	
Deadline	11/1
Notification	12/15
Early action	
Deadline	11/1
Notification	1/1
Regular	
Priority	11/1
Deadline	1/1
Nonfall registration?	yes

FINANCIAL FACTS

Financial Aid Rating	89
Annual tuition	$40,400
Room and board	$13,330
Books and supplies	$1,020
% frosh rec. need-based scholarship or grant aid	52
% UG rec. need-based scholarship or grant aid	50
% frosh rec. non-need-based scholarship or grant aid	8
% UG rec. non-need-based scholarship or grant aid	7
% frosh rec. need-based self-help aid	43
% UG rec. need-based self-help aid	43
% frosh rec. any financial aid	45
% UG rec. any financial aid	48
% UG borrow to pay for school	47
Average cumulative indebtedness	$30,357

BARD COLLEGE

OFFICE OF ADMISSIONS, ANNANDALE-ON-HUDSON, NY 12504 • ADMISSIONS: 845-758-7472 • FAX: 845-758-5208

CAMPUS LIFE

Quality of Life Rating	70
Fire Safety Rating	82
Green Rating	90
Type of school	private
Environment	village

STUDENTS

Total undergrad enrollment	1,928
% male/female	43/57
% from out of state	67
% from public high school	64
% live on campus	74
% African American	3
% Asian	3
% Caucasian	57
% Hispanic	3
% Native American	1
% international	12
# of countries represented	66

SURVEY SAYS . . .

Lots of liberal students
No one cheats
Students aren't religious
Campus feels safe
Frats and sororities are unpopular
or nonexistent
Political activism is popular

ACADEMICS

Academic Rating	96
% students graduating within 4 years	66
% students graduating within 6 years	76
Calendar	semester
Student/faculty ratio	10:1
Profs interesting rating	88
Profs accessible rating	87
Most common reg class size	10–19 students
Most common lab size	15 students

MOST POPULAR MAJORS

languages and literature, social
sciences, visual and performing arts

STUDENTS SAY ". . ."

Academics

Students come to Bard seeking "a liberal arts college with a left-leaning student body of creative thinkers who are all actively interested in political and social activism and learning/academia for its own sake," and "we find it," they tell us. Those yearning for "an atmosphere of curious individuals striving for knowledge," a place where "there are intelligent discussions both inside and outside the classroom" will find a home at this small liberal arts school in the scenic Hudson Valley. All students start their educations here building a solid grounding, starting with a three-week orientation and intensive communication and research workshop, followed by the year-long freshman seminar that is a survey of history's "great ideas." As one student observes, "The curriculum at Bard is set up to give students a broad foundation of knowledge," a foundation they get to test when completing their senior project in their final year. As at many elite small schools, "The administration and professors are amazingly accessible. A simple e-mail can get you an appointment with the dean of students, and the professors encourage students to ask for help or to discuss any ideas they may have." Students aren't coddled, however; writes one, "One reason that the school doesn't run as 'smoothly' [as other schools] is that this place isn't about handing life's jewels to everyone. All the students must put some effort into their work to get the real payoff. It's a bit like real life in that manner." As one student puts it, "Bard, more than any other school, is what you make of it. If you wish to make a big splash, the school will provide you with the proper equipment (large boulders, diving boards, etc.). It is up to you, though, to take advantage of it."

Life

Bard "has a gorgeous campus," and undergrads "take full advantage of that when the weather is warm. Blithewood, our Italian-style gardens, is often full of students picnicking and playing Frisbee, and elsewhere on campus most trees have at least one student reading, or perhaps playing an instrument, in the shade. Other popular pastimes/attractions include the on-campus art museum, the waterfall, and many winding, hilly hiking trails that snake around Blithewood and along the Hudson River." The campus hosts a rich cultural life; the "student-run entertainment space—a converted auto garage known as SMOG—holds many fantastic music shows (both student bands and musical guests), as well as the very popular themed dance parties," and "Art is everywhere. Students frequently have the opportunities to see world-class performances by the American Symphony Orchestra for free or for a mere five dollars." All this activity makes up for the fact that "the campus is a little isolated," as does the fact that "shuttles run to nearby towns rather frequently." Undergrads tell us that "This is not a beer-pong school. Rather than the norm being the stereotypical frat-style college party, many 'parties' are just friends sitting together; drinking boxed wine; listening to jazz or indie rock; and discussing philosophy, art, current events, etc." When they need to get away, "Many kids go to New York City for the weekends."

Student Body

"Bard is a safe haven for all hipsters, serious intellectuals, artists, and dreamers," so it should come as no surprise that "Everyone at Bard was atypical in high school, and consequently it's difficult to classify anyone as either typical or atypical. Students here are brilliant, enthusiastic, passionate, and genuinely different." They tend to be "very passionate about their specific interests and work hard to manifest them in the community," with "an unbelievable sensitivity to the subtleties of, and a passion for, language." "It's 'cool' to be intellectual, artistic, and well-read" here, and "'hipster' fashion is in style." Occasionally some "do try to be a little too philosophical, and some kids can border on pretentious or self-righteous, but most are absolutely amazing people with fascinating backgrounds."

FINANCIAL AID: 845-758-7526 • E-MAIL: ADMISSION@BARD.EDU • WEBSITE: WWW.BARD.EDU

THE PRINCETON REVIEW SAYS

Admissions

Very important factors considered include: Academic GPA, application essay, recommendation(s), rigor of secondary school record, character/personal qualities, extracurricular activities, talent/ability. *Important factors considered include:* Volunteer work, work experience. *Other factors considered include:* Class rank, standardized test scores, alumni/ae relation, first generation, geographical residence, interview, level of applicant's interest, racial/ethnic status, religious affiliation/commitment, state residency. ACT with or without writing component accepted. TOEFL required of all international applicants. High school diploma is required, and GED is accepted. *Academic units recommended:* 4 English, 4 mathematics, 4 science (3 science labs), 4 foreign language, 4 social studies, 4 history.

Financial Aid

Students should submit: FAFSA, CSS/Financial Aid PROFILE. Regular filing deadline is February 15. The Princeton Review suggests that all financial aid forms be submitted as soon as possible after January 1. *Need-based scholarships/grants offered:* Federal Pell, SEOG, state scholarships/grants, private scholarships, school scholarship or grant aid from institutional funds. *Loan aid offered:* Direct Subsidized Stafford, Direct Unsubsidized Stafford, Direct PLUS, Federal Perkins. Federal Work-Study Program available. Off-campus job opportunities are good.

The Inside Word

Bard receives more than enough applications from students with the academic credentials to gain admission, so the school has the luxury of focusing on matchmaking. The goal is to find students who can handle the independence allowed here and who will thrive in an intellectually intensive environment. The school requires two application essays; expect both to be very carefully scrutinized by the admissions office.

THE SCHOOL SAYS "..."

From the Admissions Office

"An alliance with Rockefeller University, the renowned graduate scientific research institution, gives Bardians access to Rockefeller's professors and laboratories and to places in Rockefeller's Summer Research Fellows Program. Almost all our math and science graduates pursue graduate or professional studies; ninety percent of our applicants to medical and health professional schools are accepted.

"The Globalization and International Affairs (BGIA) Program is a residential program in the heart of New York City that offers undergraduates a unique opportunity to undertake specialized study with leading practitioners and scholars in international affairs and to gain internship experience with international-affairs organizations. Topics in the curriculum include human rights, international economics, global environmental issues, international justice, managing international risk, and writing on international affairs, among others. Internships/tutorials are tailored to students' particular fields of study.

"Student dormitory and classroom facilities are in Bard Hall, 410 West Fifty-Eighth Street, a newly renovated eleven-story building near the Lincoln Center District in New York City.

"Bard College does not require SAT scores to be submitted for admissions consideration. Students may choose to submit scores, and, if submitted, we will consider them in the context of the overall application. "

SELECTIVITY
Admissions Rating	97
# of applicants	5,570
% of applicants accepted	35
% of acceptees attending	25
# accepting a place on wait list	213
% admitted from wait list	23

FRESHMAN PROFILE
Range SAT Critical Reading	680–740
Range SAT Math	650–680
Minimum paper TOEFL	600
Minimum computer TOEFL	250
Average HS GPA	3.50
% graduated top 10% of class	64
% graduated top 25% of class	81
% graduated top 50% of class	97

DEADLINES
Early action	
Deadline	11/1
Notification	1/1
Regular	
Deadline	1/15
Nonfall registration?	no

APPLICANTS ALSO LOOK AT AND OFTEN PREFER
Brown University

AND SOMETIMES PREFER
New York University, Oberlin College, Reed College, Vassar College

FINANCIAL FACTS
Financial Aid Rating	91
Annual tuition	$42,476
Room and board	$12,286
Required fees	$830
Books and supplies	$950
% frosh rec. need-based scholarship or grant aid	64
% UG rec. need-based scholarship or grant aid	59
% frosh rec. need-based self-help aid	56
% UG rec. need-based self-help aid	58
% frosh rec. any financial aid	73
% UG rec. any financial aid	68
% UG borrow to pay for school	49
Average cumulative indebtedness	$24,311

BARD COLLEGE AT SIMON'S ROCK

84 ALFORD ROAD, GREAT BARRINGTON, MA 01230 • ADMISSIONS: 413-528-7228 • FAX: 413-541-0081

STUDENTS SAY ". . ."

Academics

Bard College at Simon's Rock is a tiny, "rigorous," and "unique" bastion of the liberal arts and sciences that allows high-school-aged students "the opportunity to start their college careers and broaden their academic horizons a bit earlier than is orthodox." At Simon's Rock, you can enroll after completing tenth or eleventh grade. "I wasn't learning anything in high school," explains an art history major. "Simon's Rock recognizes that and provides you with another option." Students receive an AA degree after two years and a BA degree after four. The college offers an incredible amount of freedom to design your own course of study. There are more than forty majors. The arts programs are "very strong." Students in the engineering program can spend three years at Simon's Rock and then two years at Columbia University. Several outstanding study abroad opportunities send juniors to places such as Turkey, England, and China. Many people "only stay here two years," long enough to earn an associate's degree. After that, they transfer to a more traditional college. However, you can also stick around at SR to get your bachelor's degree. Either way, "The academic expectations are formidable." Course work is "challenging" and "requires a lot of time input out of class." There's quite a bit of reading. Seniors must complete a self-designed thesis. Classes are small—the average size is a mere ten students—and they're filled with "engaging" discussion. "Simon's Rock professors are generally very supportive and understanding." They provide "up-close and personal attention" and "go out of their way to be available out of the classroom."

Life

The "gorgeous" campus here can be "a bit of a bubble" and, at times, "small to the point of claustrophobia," but students promise that there is much to do. There's "a large number of clubs for the size of the school," and "New clubs and interests are always forming." "The athletic center is top-notch." Winters are hard, but "The spring is pure glory." Hikes "in the beautiful woods" are common, weather permitting. Equally common is "just hanging out." Often, students will "simply sit around talking about random stuff, ranging from the weather to Marx." "Drugs and alcohol are a major form of recreation and stress relief." However, the party scene is "relatively low-key." Often, it's "sneaking around under night skies" to darkened party spots. Students also emphasize that it's "possible to have fun and attend parties without being pressured" into consuming anything you would rather avoid. The "very small town" of Great Barrington is a little less than two miles away. "Befriending car-endowed people is a good skill." With or without wheels, though, "There is very little to do off campus." Simon's Rock is "isolated" in the Berkshire Mountains of "rural" western Massachusetts, roughly in "in the middle of nowhere." On the plus side, New York City and Boston are reasonably easy to reach. Older students frequently make treks to those cities on the weekends.

Student Body

For the students here, "Simon's Rock is a blissful release from the institutional hell of high school." Students come here from forty or so states. They're "brilliant and creative" and "excited to learn." "Lots of people come from their high school used to being the smartest person in the room," explains one student, "and then they realize that, wow, there are lots of really smart people here, and now you have someone to talk to about serious stuff." Students describe themselves as "strong individuals who lean toward nonconformity." They're "a little misunderstood." They "tend to be liberal," and they're "very aware and educated in current politics." "Some people are very, very androgynous." "Many are artists." Many are "hippies." Ultimately, Simon's Rock is filled with "kids who think outside the box." "Most people walk to their own beat." "Brightly dyed hair, body piercings, tattoos, girls with buzz cuts, guys in skirts, and crazy clothing ensembles are SR trademarks."

FINANCIAL AID: 413-528-7297 • E-MAIL: ADMIT@SIMONS-ROCK.EDU • WEBSITE: WWW.SIMONS-ROCK.EDU

THE PRINCETON REVIEW SAYS

Admissions

Very important factors considered include: Application essay, recommendation(s), rigor of secondary school record, character/personal qualities, interview, talent/ability. *Important factors considered include:* Academic GPA, class rank, level of applicant's interest. *Other factors considered include:* Standardized test scores (optional), alumni/ae relation, extracurricular activities, first generation, racial/ethnic status, volunteer work, work experience. ACT with or without writing component accepted. TOEFL required of all international applicants. High school diploma or equivalent isn't required. *Academic units recommended:* 2 English, 2 mathematics, 2 science (1 science lab), 2 foreign language, 2 social studies, 2 history.

Financial Aid

Students should submit: FAFSA and CSS/Financial Aid PROFILE or International Student Application for Financial Aid and International Student Certification of Finances. The Princeton Review suggests that all financial aid forms be submitted as soon as possible after January 1. *Need-based scholarships/grants offered:* Federal Pell, SEOG, state scholarships/grants, private scholarships, school scholarship or grant aid from institutional funds. *Loan aid offered:* Direct Subsidized Stafford, Direct Unsubsidized Stafford, Direct PLUS, Federal Perkins, state loans. Applicants will be notified of awards on a rolling basis beginning April 15. Federal Work-Study Program available. Off-campus job opportunities are good.

The Inside Word

Because Simon's Rock boasts healthy application numbers, it's in a position to concentrate on matchmaking. To that end, admissions officers seek students with independent and inquisitive spirits. Applicants who exhibit academic ambition while extending their intellectual curiosity beyond the realm of the classroom are particularly appealing. Successful candidates typically have several honors and advanced placement courses on their transcripts, as well as strong letters of recommendation and well-written personal statements.

THE SCHOOL SAYS " . . ."

From the Admissions Office

"Bard College at Simon's Rock is the only four-year college of the liberal arts and sciences specifically designed to provide bright, highly motivated students with the opportunity to begin college in a residential environment immediately after the tenth or eleventh grade.

"Approximately half of our students transfer after the sophomore year and complete their junior and senior years of college elsewhere. The most common transfer destinations are Bard College, Brown University, Cornell University, New York University, Smith College, Stanford University, University of California—Berkeley, and University of Chicago. For those who choose to complete the BA at Simon's Rock, the graduation rate exceeds ninety percent."

SELECTIVITY

Admissions Rating	91
# of applicants	204
% of applicants accepted	80
% of acceptees attending	55
# accepting a place on wait list	0

FRESHMAN PROFILE

Range SAT Critical Reading	560–690
Range SAT Math	530–680
Range ACT Composite	25–30
Minimum paper TOEFL	600
Minimum computer TOEFL	100
Average HS GPA	3.36
% graduated top 10% of class	60
% graduated top 25% of class	82
% graduated top 50% of class	94

DEADLINES

Regular	
Priority	2/1
Deadline	5/31
Notification	rolling
Nonfall registration?	yes

FINANCIAL FACTS

Financial Aid Rating	83
Annual tuition	$41,160
Required fees	$1,372
Books and supplies	$2,000
% frosh rec. need-based scholarship or grant aid	57
% UG rec. need-based scholarship or grant aid	57
% frosh rec. non-need-based scholarship or grant aid	51
% UG rec. non-need-based scholarship or grant aid	51
% frosh rec. need-based self-help aid	63
% UG rec. need-based self-help aid	61
% frosh rec. any financial aid	87
% UG rec. any financial aid	84
% UG borrow to pay for school	69
Average cumulative indebtedness	$25,000

BARNARD COLLEGE

3009 BROADWAY, NEW YORK, NY 10027 • ADMISSIONS: 212-854-2014 • FAX: 212-854-6220

STUDENTS SAY ". . ."

Academics

Life is lived in the fast lane at Barnard, an all-women's liberal arts college partnered with Columbia University that incorporates "a small school feel with big school resources and incorporates both campus and city life." Nestled in the Morningside Heights neighborhood of Manhattan on a gated (main) campus, the school maintains an "independent spirit" while providing a "nurturing environment," and its partnership with a larger research university gives it the "best of both worlds" and affords its students the opportunities, course options, and resources that many colleges don't have. The academic experience at Barnard is simply "wonderful," according to the students. Teachers here are "experts in their field" and "value their positions as both teachers and mentors," to the extent "they make you want to stay on Barnard's campus for class and not take classes at Columbia." "I've never been in an environment where there is such a reciprocal relationship between students wanting to learn and be challenged and professors wanting to teach and help," says a junior. Though underclassmen typically aren't able to get into as many of the small classes (the process of which "is a nightmare"), one student claims that "some of the best classes I've had have been in large lecture halls." The administration gets thumbs-up nearly across the board for their accessibility and compassion for students. Deans are always available to students wanting to meet, and the alumni network and career services are singled out for their efficacy. "Every time there is an issue on campus that students care about or an event that has happened, we get e-mails and town-hall style meetings devoted to discussing the issues." "Barnard is New York—busy, exciting, full of opportunity," says one student.

Life

Not much goes on around campus, to the chagrin of a few, but as one freshman puts it, "Why stay on campus when you're in New York?" Students take advantage of the resources available to them in New York City, from Broadway shows and Central Park to museums and restaurants; "The possibilities are endless," and can "make it impossible to stick to a budget." Theater and a capella are also very big here, and many students are involved with clubs and organizations at Columbia, sometimes even dominating them. There are some complaints that facilities and dorms are "crumbling," but the recently opened Diana Center building has fast become a hub of student activities, including studying, learning, socializing, dining, and relaxing. "Life at Barnard is probably sixty to seventy-five percent academic and around twenty-five to forty percent free."

Student Body

Even though it's all women here, Barnard is "the anti-women's college," as "very, very few students are here for the single-sex education"—they're here for the academics and New York. There's a definite liberal slant on campus, and these "usually politically savvy," "very cultured," "energetic and motivated" women are "ambitious and opinionated," with career and leadership goals at the top of their agenda. "Barnard students are not lazy" and have no problems booking their days full of study and activities. Most here learn to "fit into the mad rush" very quickly and take advantage of their four short years. Although quite a few students are from the tristate area and the majority are white, "there is still a sense of diversity" thanks to a variety of different backgrounds, both cultural and geographical; there's also a "tiny gay community" that seems easily accepted.

FINANCIAL AID: 212-854-2154 • E-MAIL: ADMISSIONS@BARNARD.EDU • WEBSITE: WWW.BARNARD.EDU

THE PRINCETON REVIEW SAYS

Admissions

Very important factors considered include: Academic GPA, recommendation(s), rigor of secondary school record, character/personal qualities, extracurricular activities. *Important factors considered include:* Application essay, class rank, standardized test scores, talent/ability, volunteer work. *Other factors considered include:* Interview (optional), alumni/ae relation, first generation, geographical residence, level of applicant's interest, racial/ethnic status, work experience. SAT and SAT Subject Tests or ACT with writing component required. TOEFL required of all international applicants. High school diploma or equivalent is required. *Academic units required: Academic units recommended:* 4 English, 3 mathematics, 3 science (2 science labs), 3 foreign language.

Financial Aid

Students should submit: FAFSA, CSS/Financial Aid PROFILE. Regular filing deadline is February 1. The Princeton Review suggests that all financial aid forms be submitted as soon as possible after January 1. *Need-based scholarships/grants offered:* Federal Pell, SEOG, state scholarships/grants, private scholarships, school scholarship or grant aid from institutional funds. *Loan aid offered:* Federal Perkins, Federal Stafford loans. Applicants will be notified of awards in late March. Federal Work-Study Program available. Off-campus job opportunities are excellent.

The Inside Word

As at many top colleges, early decision applications have increased at Barnard—although the admissions standards are virtually the same as for their regular admissions cycle. The college's admissions staff is suprisingly open and accessible for such a highly selective college with as long and impressive a tradition of excellence. The admissions committee's expectations are high, but their attitude reflects a true interest in who potential students are and what's on their minds. Students have a much better experience throughout the admissions process when treated with sincerity and respect—perhaps this is why Barnard continues to attract and enroll some of the best students in the country.

THE SCHOOL SAYS "..."

From the Admissions Office

"Barnard College is a small, distinguished liberal arts college for women that is partnered with Columbia University and located in the heart of New York City. The college enrolls women from all over the United States, Puerto Rico, and the Caribbean. More than thirty countries, including France, England, Hong Kong, and Greece, are also represented in the student body. Students pursue their academic studies in more than forty majors and are able to cross register at Columbia University.

"Applicants for the entering class must submit scores from the SAT Reasoning Test and two SAT Subject Tests of their choice or the ACT with the writing component."

SELECTIVITY

Admissions Rating	96
# of applicants	4,618
% of applicants accepted	28
% of acceptees attending	45
# accepting a place on wait list	555
% admitted from wait list	9
# of early decision applicants	396
% accepted early decision	53

FRESHMAN PROFILE

Range SAT Critical Reading	630–730
Range SAT Math	620–710
Range SAT Writing	650–750
Range ACT Composite	28–32
Minimum paper TOEFL	600
Minimum computer TOEFL	250
% graduated top 10% of class	81
% graduated top 25% of class	95
% graduated top 50% of class	98

DEADLINES

Early decision	
Deadline	11/15
Notification	12/15
Regular	
Deadline	1/1
Nonfall registration?	no

APPLICANTS ALSO LOOK AT AND OFTEN PREFER

Brown University, Columbia University, Harvard College, University of Pennsylvania, Yale University

AND SOMETIMES PREFER

Northwestern University, Princeton University, Stanford University, Tufts University, University of Chicago, Wellesley College, Wesleyan University

AND RARELY PREFER

Boston College, Bryn Mawr College, Fordham University, University of California—Berkeley, Vassar College

FINANCIAL FACTS

Financial Aid Rating	96
Annual tuition	$38,868
Room and board	$12,950
Required fees	$1,678
Books and supplies	$1,146
% frosh rec. need-based scholarship or grant aid	41
% UG rec. need-based scholarship or grant aid	40
% frosh rec. need-based self-help aid	42
% UG rec. need-based self-help aid	42
% frosh rec. any financial aid	55
% UG rec. any financial aid	51
% UG borrow to pay for school	48
Average cumulative indebtedness	$14,142

BATES COLLEGE

23 CAMPUS AVENUE, LINDHOLM HOUSE, LEWISTON, ME 04240 • ADMISSIONS: 207-786-6000 • FAX: 207-786-6025

STUDENTS SAY ". . ."

Academics

"You will not find it hard to gain access to resources" at Bates College, a small school in Maine that "tries to be unique in the homogeneous world of New England's small liberal arts colleges by weaving together academics with real-world experience." First-year seminars, mandatory senior theses, service-learning, and a range of interdisciplinary majors are part of the academic experience. About two-thirds of the students here study abroad at some point before graduation. "Research and internship opportunities" are absurdly abundant. A fairly unusual 4-4-1 calendar includes two traditional semesters and an "incredible" five-week spring term that provides really cool opportunities. Examples include studying marine biology on the Maine coast, Shakespearean drama in England, or economics in China and Taiwan. The "brilliant, accessible, and friendly" faculty does "whatever it takes to actually teach you the material instead of just lecturing and leaving." "The professors at Bates are here because they are passionate about their field and want to be teaching," explains a politics major. "I have never met so many professors who are willing to dedicate endless time outside of class to their students," gushes a psychology major. Course selection can be sparse, but the "regularly available" administration is "responsive to student concerns" as well.

Life

"The library is the place to be during the week because everyone is there." The academic workload is reportedly substantial, but "it is entirely manageable and does not restrict you from participating in athletics, clubs, or just having some down time." Parties are common on the weekends, and students "stand mashed up against everyone else in the keg line." There's a great college radio station—91.5 on your FM dial—and many students get involved. "Bates also has a lot of traditions that students get excited about." In the winter, during Puddle Jump, just for instance, Batesies who feel especially courageous can take the plunge into the frigid water of Lake Andrews. Otherwise, "Dances, comedians, and trivia challenges are shockingly well-attended because there's not a whole lot else to do." The biggest social complaint here centers on the surrounding area. It's the kind of place where "you wouldn't want to be walking alone at three in the morning." Also, relations between Batesies and local residents are reportedly strained. "The interaction between the town and college is relatively minimal," relates a junior. When students feel they just have to get away, they can "hit up the nearby ski slopes." The great outdoors is another option. Bates rents "tents, sleeping bags, kayaks, climbing gear, stoves, vans—really anything you want for outdoor fun." Also, Boston and some smaller cities such as Freeport and Portland are easily accessible.

Student Body

Students tell us, "Bates needs to improve its ethnic diversity." Most of the students here are white. In the last three years, however, the percentage of students who identify as Asian, African, Native, and/or Latino/a American has increased. "Your typical Batesie owns at least two flannel shirts" and "likes to have fun on the weekends." There are "a lot of jocks," and some "take the sports teams here way too seriously." Students here call themselves "down-to-earth" yet "intellectually driven." They enjoy "participating in academics, sports, and clubs." They "love the outdoors." However, this campus is "eclectic," and "Bates students are by no means monolithic in character." "We have everyone from the prep-school spoiled brat to the hippie environmentalist, from people with all different gender and sexual preferences and orientations to the former or current goth," observes a junior. "There are dorks, brains, goof-offs, and class clowns." There are "plenty of kids who apparently haven't found the dorm showers," too. "There are few, if any, cliques on campus." "Crossing boundaries" is quite common. "There are different groups but none of them are exclusive in any way." "Even those who do not fit into any specific social group are widely accepted."

FINANCIAL AID: 207-786-6096 • E-MAIL: ADMISSIONS@BATES.EDU • WEBSITE: WWW.BATES.EDU

THE PRINCETON REVIEW SAYS

Admissions

Very important factors considered include: Academic GPA, application essay, class rank, recommendation(s), rigor of secondary school record, character/personal qualities, extracurricular activities, interview, level of applicant's interest, talent/ability. *Other factors considered include:* Standardized test scores, alumni/ae relation, first generation, geographical residence, racial/ethnic status, state residency, volunteer work, work experience. ACT with or without writing component accepted. TOEFL required of all international applicants. *Academic units required:* 4 English, 3 mathematics, 3 science (2 science labs), 2 foreign language, 3 social studies. *Academic units recommended:* 4 English, 4 mathematics, 4 science (3 science labs), 4 foreign language, 4 social studies.

Financial Aid

Students should submit: FAFSA, CSS/Financial Aid PROFILE, non-custodial profile. Regular filing deadline is February 1. The Princeton Review suggests that all financial aid forms be submitted as soon as possible after January 1. *Need-based scholarships/grants offered:* Federal Pell, SEOG, state scholarships/grants, private scholarships, school scholarship or grant aid from institutional funds. *Loan aid offered:* Direct Subsidized Stafford, Direct Unsubsidized Stafford, Direct PLUS, Federal Perkins, state loans. Applicants will be notified of awards on a rolling basis beginning on or about April 1. Federal Work-Study Program available. Institutional employment available. Off-campus job opportunities are good.

The Inside Word

While holding its applicants to lofty standards, Bates strives to adopt a personal approach to the admissions process. Officers favor qualitative information and focus more on academic rigor, essays, and recommendations than GPA and test scores. The school seeks students who look for challenges and take advantage of opportunities in the classroom and beyond. Interviews are strongly encouraged—candidates who opt out may place themselves at a disadvantage.

THE SCHOOL SAYS "..."

From the Admissions Office

"Bates College is widely recognized as one of the finest liberal arts colleges in the nation. The curriculum and faculty challenge students to develop the essential skills of critical assessment, analysis, expression, aesthetic sensibility, and independent thought. Founded by abolitionists in 1855, Bates graduates have always included men and women from diverse ethnic and religious backgrounds. Bates highly values its study abroad programs, unique calendar (4-4-1), and the many opportunities available for one-on-one collaboration with faculty through seminars, research, service-learning, and the capstone experience of senior thesis. Co-curricular life at Bates is rich; most students participate in club or varsity sports; many participate in performing arts; and almost all students participate in one of more than 110 student-run clubs and organizations. More than two-thirds of alumni enroll in graduate study within ten years.

"The Bates College Admissions Staff reads applications very carefully; the high school record and the quality of writing are of particular importance. Applicants are strongly encouraged to have a personal interview, either on campus or with an alumni representative. Students who choose not to interview may place themselves at a disadvantage in the selection process. Bates offers tours, interviews, and information sessions throughout the summer and fall. Drop-ins are welcome for tours and information sessions. Please call ahead to schedule an interview. At Bates, the submission of standardized testing (the SAT, SAT Subject Tests, and the ACT) is not required for admission. After two decades of optional testing, our research shows no differences in academic performance and graduation rates between submitters and nonsubmitters."

SELECTIVITY

Admissions Rating	94
# of applicants	4,517
% of applicants accepted	32
% of acceptees attending	34
# accepting a place on wait list	265
% admitted from wait list	12
# of early decision applicants	486
% accepted early decision	48

FRESHMAN PROFILE

Range SAT Critical Reading	620–710
Range SAT Math	620–700
Range SAT Writing	638–713
Range ACT Composite	29–32
% graduated top 10% of class	66
% graduated top 25% of class	92
% graduated top 50% of class	100

DEADLINES

Early decision	
Deadline	11/15
Notification	12/20
Regular	
Deadline	1/1
Nonfall registration?	yes

APPLICANTS ALSO LOOK AT

AND OFTEN PREFER
Brown University, Dartmouth College, Williams College

AND SOMETIMES PREFER
Bowdoin College, Middlebury College, Wesleyan University

AND RARELY PREFER
Bucknell University, Connecticut College, Trinity College (CT)

FINANCIAL FACTS

Financial Aid Rating	95
Annual comprehensive tuition	$53,300
% frosh rec. need-based scholarship or grant aid	41
% UG rec. need-based scholarship or grant aid	42
% frosh rec. need-based self-help aid	40
% UG rec. need-based self-help aid	43
% frosh rec. any financial aid	43
% UG rec. any financial aid	45
% UG borrow to pay for school	36
Average cumulative indebtedness	$18,699

BAYLOR UNIVERSITY

ONE BEAR PLACE #97056, WACO, TX 76798-7056 • ADMISSIONS: 254-710-3435 • FAX: 254-710-3436

CAMPUS LIFE

Quality of Life Rating	74
Fire Safety Rating	90
Green Rating	82
Type of school	private
Environment	city

STUDENTS

Total undergrad enrollment	12,376
% male/female	42/58
% from out of state	19
% live on campus	38
# of fraternities	22
# of sororities	20
% African American	7
% Asian	7
% Caucasian	66
% Hispanic	13
% international	2
# of countries represented	86

SURVEY SAYS . . .

Lab facilities are great
Great computer facilities
Athletic facilities are great
School is well-run
Students are friendly
Students are very religious
Students are happy
Intramural sports are popular
Frats and sororities dominate
social scene
Student publications are popular

ACADEMICS

Academic Rating	77
% students graduating within 4 years	50
% students graduating within 6 years	71
Calendar	semester
Student/faculty ratio	14:1
Profs interesting rating	80
Profs accessible rating	81
Most common reg class size	10–19 students
Most common lab size	20–29 students

MOST POPULAR MAJORS
biology, marketing, psychology

STUDENTS SAY ". . ."

Academics

One typical Baylor student describes her school as "a globally active research university [that] boasts a multitude of intelligent student minds. The spiritual foundations of Baylor attract only the most approachable and helpful student body and faculty." Baylor is praised by undergrads as a place in which to "grow as a student and a person simultaneously." Small class sizes and professors' genuine interest creates "a top-notch, all-encompassing educational experience." Professors are "engaging and passionate about their area of expertise…they infuse the importance of academic and moral integrity into all that they teach." The Honors College, premed, and entrepreneurship program continue to be stand-out features as well as engineering and "strong science programs." "Professors are really accessible and the university provides many tutoring resources and help when needed." Faculty and overall academics are consistently praised, though the prevailing Christian themes are sometimes fuel for criticism: "While the professors are knowledgeable, almost no one at Baylor seems capable of considering possibilities outside of the Christian paradigm," notes a senior. However, a sociology major emphatically states, "If a student wants a good academic education at the university level, with teachers who care about their classes, Baylor is the great choice!" Though there are signs of change on the horizon with the addition of Ken Starr (of White House notoriety) as the new president, "The relationship between the students and administration has started taking a turn for the better."

Life

Undergrads are tired of hearing about the "Baylor Bubble" and point out that it's mainly because some students haven't bothered to explore off-campus destinations. Attractions include the Waco Mammoth Site as well as "the amazing Cameron Park…and various cultural festivals in downtown Waco—such as an annual Greek food festival." "There are so many different intramural sports here, and many people love to get competitive." Academic life is rigorous, so students blow off steam via the numerous biking and running trails circling the well-manicured campus (including the famous Bear Trail.) "Everyone has a great time going to sporting events, whether it's cheering on our highly ranked women's basketball team or our always exciting football team." Make no mistake, "Greek life is big," states one senior. "The social scene is largely off-campus and dominated by the Greek system." Though "there is a good mix of students to provide anyone [with] a group to plug into, but the closer you are to the typical student, the better off you are." Acceptance of other lifestyles and faiths is an underlying theme of the small amount of discontent voiced by students, "This is not a welcoming community if you don't conform." Students living a "fringe lifestyle" tend to feel pressure to keep those differences to themselves.

Student Body

"People here…like to have fun just being with people, so students can always be seen in common areas chilling or even doing homework. Playing some sport is the next most popular activity." Though there's a sense that some undergrads are naïve about the world outside of their "bubble." They're criticized for being "pretty homogeneous" and intolerant of those who "cuss" or don't go to church. Yet Baylor is consistently admired for fostering an embracing student body. "Life at Baylor is great," gushes one student. Overall, most undergrads agree that the community and environment are supportive and welcoming—and studious. "Baylor emphasizes having fun while getting your education. It is well-run, has great facilities, and faculty and staff that care about the students." As one sophomore neatly wraps it up, "Once you're here, you're family."

BAYLOR UNIVERSITY

FINANCIAL AID: 254-710-2611 • E-MAIL: ADMISSIONS@BAYLOR.EDU • WEBSITE: WWW.BAYLOR.EDU

THE PRINCETON REVIEW SAYS

Admissions

Very important factors considered include: Class rank, rigor of secondary school record, standardized test scores. *Important factors considered include:* Academic GPA. *Other factors considered include:* Application essay, recommendation(s), alumni/ae relation, character/personal qualities, extracurricular activities, first generation, interview, level of applicant's interest, religious affiliation/commitment, talent/ability, volunteer work. SAT or ACT required; ACT with writing component required. TOEFL required of some international applicants. High school diploma is required, and GED is accepted. *Academic units required:* 4 English, 4 mathematics, 4 science (2 science labs), 2 foreign language, 2 social studies, 1 history.

Financial Aid

Students should submit: FAFSA. The Princeton Review suggests that all financial aid forms be submitted as soon as possible after January 1. *Need-based scholarships/grants offered:* Federal Pell, SEOG, state scholarships/grants, private scholarships, school scholarship or grant aid from institutional funds. *Loan aid offered:* Direct Subsidized Stafford, Direct Unsubsidized Stafford, Direct PLUS, Federal Perkins, Federal Nursing Loans, state loans. Applicants will be notified of awards on a rolling basis beginning March 1. Federal Work-Study Program available. Off-campus job opportunities are fair

The Inside Word

Baylor wants to see applicants who are at the top of their class with strong SAT or ACT scores. Expect to convey your academic commitment and curiosity as well as display your achievements outside of school and within your community. Though not mandatory, you may wish to augment your application by submitting a resume or recommendation letters via your Baylor online account. One advantage to getting your application in early is you'll secure your spot via first-round acceptance and be at the front of the line for your housing application.

THE SCHOOL SAYS ". . ."

From the Admissions Office

"Baylor University is a Christian university in the Baptist tradition and is affiliated with the Baptist General Convention of Texas. As the oldest institution of higher learning in the state, Baylor's founders sought to establish a college dedicated to Christian principles, superior academics, and a shared sense of community. Students come from all fifty states and some ninety foreign countries. Baylor's nationally recognized academic divisions offer 151 undergraduate degree programs, 76 master's degree programs, and 33 doctoral degree programs. Baylor ranks in the top 100 percent of colleges and universities participating in the National Merit Scholarship program. Baylor is one of the select eleven percent of U.S. colleges and universities with a Phi Beta Kappa chapter. The Templeton Foundation repeatedly names Baylor as one of America's top character-building colleges. Baylor's undergraduate programs emphasize the central importance of vocation (calling) and service in students' lives, helping them explore their value and role in society. Baylor is a charter member of the Independent 529 Tuition Plan, a prepaid college tuition plan. Baylor's tuition is one of the lowest of any major private university in the Southwest and one of the least expensive in the nation. Approximately ninety percent of Baylor students receive student financial assistance. The approximately 1,000-acre main campus adjoins the Brazos River near downtown Waco, a Central Texas city of 110,000 people. "

SELECTIVITY

Admissions Rating	83
# of applicants	34,145
% of applicants accepted	48
% of acceptees attending	20
# accepting a place on wait list	164
% admitted from wait list	0

FRESHMAN PROFILE

Range SAT Critical Reading	540–650
Range SAT Math	570–670
Range SAT Writing	530–640
Range ACT Composite	24–29
Minimum paper TOEFL	540
Minimum computer TOEFL	207
Minimum web-based TOEFL	76
% graduated top 10% of class	36
% graduated top 25% of class	71
% graduated top 50% of class	95

DEADLINES

Early action	
Deadline	11/1
Notification	1/15
Nonfall registration?	yes

FINANCIAL FACTS

Financial Aid Rating	75
Annual tuition	$28,720
Room and board	$8,664
Required fees	$2,938
Books and supplies	$1,390
% frosh rec. need-based scholarship or grant aid	62
% UG rec. need-based scholarship or grant aid	55
% frosh rec. non-need-based scholarship or grant aid	6
% UG rec. non-need-based scholarship or grant aid	5
% frosh rec. need-based self-help aid	52
% UG rec. need-based self-help aid	47
% frosh rec. any financial aid	96
% UG rec. any financial aid	88

BELLARMINE UNIVERSITY

2001 NEWBURG ROAD, LOUISVILLE, KY 40205 • ADMISSIONS: 502-272-8131 • TOLL-FREE: 800-274-4723 • FAX: 502-272-8002

CAMPUS LIFE

Quality of Life Rating	88
Fire Safety Rating	88
Green Rating	75
Type of school	private
Affiliation	Roman Catholic
Environment	metropolis

STUDENTS

Total undergrad enrollment	2,612
% male/female	36/64
% from out of state	31
% from public high school	66
% live on campus	44
# of fraternities	1
# of sororities	1
% African American	3
% Asian	2
% Caucasian	82
% Hispanic	3
% international	1
# of countries represented	32

SURVEY SAYS . . .

*Students get along with local
community
Students love Louisville, KY
Great off-campus food
Low cost of living
Very little drug use*

ACADEMICS

Academic Rating	85
% students graduating within 4 years	52
% students graduating within 6 years	65
Calendar	semester
Student/faculty ratio	13:1
Profs interesting rating	92
Profs accessible rating	89
Most common reg class size	21 students
Most common lab size	21 students

MOST POPULAR MAJORS

business, nursing, communication,
biology, psychology

STUDENTS SAY ". . ."

Academics

A "small, private, Catholic university," in the heart of vibrant Louisville, Kentucky, Bellarmine University has a curriculum that casts an eye toward the future and provides a "well-rounded education" that is not only "demanding in academic excellence" but also "prepares students for the real-world, both mentally and socially." Bellarmine's unique combination of "service, academics, and learning" ensures that "each student is fully prepared to excel in their job opportunities, as well as in life." A "premier college" with an academic lens that merges rigorous education and spiritual awareness toward practical ends, students note the curriculum's "real-world" focus on "teaching students to become professional adults." Professors are "friendly and approachable," with "a genuine love of their craft" and an investment in "ensuring an enriching experience for students beyond the classroom." Bellarmine is "a small school with big-school quality and ambitions," and students benefit from "small classes" and "personalized attention" and are often drawn to Bellarmine for its "great reputation" and "generous scholarships." With an academic mission that focuses on "exploration, discovery, and growth in yourself and your understanding of the world," Bellarmine encourages its students to continue their educations outside the university setting. Its "study abroad programs are fantastic." The university also has "a great physical therapy and nursing program," according to students.

Life

A "tight-knit community" with "a beautiful campus," Bellarmine balances big city sophistication with an active, conscientious student body. As one student aptly summarizes, "Bellarmine is all about creating the small school atmosphere on an academically strong campus in the heart of a big city." Students are quick to note the campus's proximity to Louisville's Bardstown Road where there is a plethora of "restaurants, stores, and coffee shops" "within walking distance from campus." On the weekends, students "frequent [Louisville's] opera and theater productions and visit museums." On campus, "life at Bellarmine is very upbeat." The university sponsors "a large variety of sports and extracurricular events." "Students are extremely interested in getting involved," and "intramurals are very popular." For many, due to its small size, Bellarmine embodies "a home away from home." Though students note that Bellarmine has a somewhat "homogeneous population," "the part of the city of Louisville where Bellarmine is located is a very liberal art oriented." Bellarmine champions a commitment to "community; how you are involved in it, how you can change it for the better, and what it can do for you."

Student Body

Like the academic curriculum itself, Bellarmine students are "willing to broaden the mind and be introduced to new experiences." The typical Bellarmine student is "friendly, helpful, and intellectual." With an eye toward advancement and applying education in a real-world setting, students describe themselves as "hardworking" and "dedicated to making good grades, graduating, and starting a career." However, Bellarmine's students acknowledge that it's not all nose in the book at Bellarmine. In the words of one student, "Bellarmine students like to relax *and* achieve." Students are "extremely motivated," "take pride in their work," and still "can enjoy good times outside of school." A typical Bellarmine student might be found "sitting on the grass in the quad, playing Frisbee, in the library, or in their studio working on their next big project." By and large, students describe the population at Bellarmine as "upper-middle-class Caucasian" with "lots of athletes." Due to the school's religious foundation, many students come from "private Catholic schools" in the Louisville vicinity. Though students remark that there are "not a lot of atypical students," those who march to the beat of a different drummer "do find a place to fit in." "Open-minded and personable," "most students who attend Bellarmine are there for a reason—to succeed."

FINANCIAL AID: 502-452-8124 • E-MAIL: ADMISSIONS@BELLARMINE.EDU • WEBSITE: WWW.BELLARMINE.EDU

THE PRINCETON REVIEW SAYS

Admissions

Very important factors considered include: Academic GPA, recommendation(s), rigor of secondary school record, standardized test scores, character/personal qualities, level of applicant's interest. *Important factors considered include:* Class rank, extra-curricular activities. *Other factors considered include:* Application essay, alumni/ae relation, first generation, geographical residence, interview, racial/ethnic status, state residency, talent/ability, volunteer work, work experience. SAT or ACT required; ACT with or without writing component accepted. TOEFL required of all international applicants. High school diploma is required, and GED is accepted. *Academic units required:* 4 English, 3 mathematics, 3 science (2 science labs), 2 foreign language, 2 social studies, 1 history, 5 academic elective. *Academic units recommended:* 4 English, 4 mathematics, 4 science (2 science labs), 2 foreign language, 3 social studies, 2 history, 7 academic elective.

Financial Aid

Students should submit: FAFSA. The Princeton Review suggests that all financial aid forms be submitted as soon as possible after January 1. *Need-based scholarships/grants offered:* Federal Pell, SEOG, state scholarships/grants, private scholarships, school scholarship or grant aid from institutional funds. *Loan aid offered:* Federal Perkins, state loans, university loans from institutional funds. Applicants will be notified of awards on a rolling basis beginning April 1. Federal Work-Study Program available. Off-campus job opportunities are excellent.

The Inside Word

Admissions at Bellarmine University is competitive. However, much like their mission statement, Bellarmine's admissions committee views applicants' profiles from a composite perspective and is looking for a well-rounded candidate whose qualifications reflect more than the sum total of a GPA and test scores. Recommendations and personal statements—which present a stronger picture of the students' educational goals—volunteer experiences, and extracurricular commitments, hold significant weight. Candidates with strong grades and diverse interests are likely to earn acceptance.

THE SCHOOL SAYS " . . ."

From the Admissions Office

"Bellarmine University prepares its students for success with a broad, liberal arts education combined with training for mastery in a specialized area. We engage students in the classroom and expand their horizons through internship and study-abroad opportunities. State-of-the-art facilities like the Norton Health Sciences Center and a Service Learning Clinic offer real-life, hands on experience for nursing and doctor of physical therapy students. Bellarmine delivers this world-class education just five miles from downtown Louisville, the nation's 16th-largest city. The 135-acre campus is set in a safe, historic, and eclectic neighborhood and features a fitness center, indoor and outdoor tennis courts, a sand volleyball court, athletics fields and a beautiful new dining hall. Recent additions to the campus reflect the university's academic emphasis on a liberal arts core curriculum surrounded by competitive graduate and professional schools, while the campus library houses the largest collection of works by and about internationally renowned author and Trappist monk Thomas Merton. With more than fifty clubs and organizations on campus and eighteen NCAA Division II athletic teams, and Division I men's lacrosse, Bellarmine offers a variety of recreational opportunities for all students. Students who live on campus also find a Bellarmine difference in the living arrangements. From traditional college residence halls to apartment-style and suite living arrangements, students have many housing options. The university has completed a major new residence hall complex that surrounds a Tuscan-style piazza. As Bellarmine attracts more residential students, the university has created more spaces for them to hang out, such as the café on the ground floor of the Siena Primo residence hall."

SELECTIVITY

Admissions Rating	86
# of applicants	6,816
% of applicants accepted	51
% of acceptees attending	16

FRESHMAN PROFILE

Range SAT Critical Reading	480–610
Range SAT Math	500–605
Range ACT Composite	22–26
Minimum paper TOEFL	550
Minimum computer TOEFL	213
Minimum web-based TOEFL	80
Average HS GPA	3.52
% graduated top 10% of class	20
% graduated top 25% of class	54
% graduated top 50% of class	83

DEADLINES

Early action	
Deadline	11/1
Notification	11/15
Regular	
Priority	2/1
Deadline	8/15
Notification	10/1
Nonfall registration?	yes

FINANCIAL FACTS

Financial Aid Rating	75
Annual tuition	$26,190
Room and board	$9,070
Required fees	$1,150
Books and supplies	$876
% frosh rec. need-based scholarship or grant aid	83
% UG rec. need-based scholarship or grant aid	75
% frosh rec. non-need-based scholarship or grant aid	44
% UG rec. non-need-based scholarship or grant aid	45
% frosh rec. need-based self-help aid	56
% UG rec. need-based self-help aid	51
% frosh rec. any financial aid	100
% UG rec. any financial aid	96
% UG borrow to pay for school	67
Average cumulative indebtedness	$23,925

BELOIT COLLEGE

700 COLLEGE STREET, BELOIT, WI 53511 • ADMISSIONS: 608-363-2500 • FAX: 608-363-2075

CAMPUS LIFE

Quality of Life Rating	82
Fire Safety Rating	71
Green Rating	68
Type of school	private
Environment	town

STUDENTS

Total undergrad enrollment	1,308
% male/female	43/57
% from out of state	77
% from public high school	79
% live on campus	94
# of fraternities	3
# of sororities	3
% African American	3
% Asian	2
% Caucasian	73
% Hispanic	7
% international	9
# of countries represented	45

SURVEY SAYS . . .
No one cheats
Students are friendly
Different types of students interact
Students aren't religious
Low cost of living
Political activism is popular

ACADEMICS

Academic Rating	89
% students graduating within 4 years	67
% students graduating within 6 years	77
Calendar	semester
Student/faculty ratio	10:1
Profs interesting rating	91
Profs accessible rating	95
Most common reg class size	10–19 students
Most common lab size	10–15 students

MOST POPULAR MAJORS
anthropology, international relations, political science

STUDENTS SAY ". . ."

Academics

"Professors and the general administration are always very open to students" at Beloit College, a school whose community "feels like a big family." Professors, in fact, "often prefer to be thought of as friends and advisors (for example, all of my professors insist on being called by their first names rather than by honorifics)." One student's experiences are typical: "My Chinese professor requires a fifteen-minute private conference with each student weekly to practice conversation. My First Year Initiative leader conferences with us about every draft of every paper and tells us how to improve. My psych teacher gives us essay tests and specific comments on how to improve." These touches make "the academic experience at Beloit is very personal and friendly," placing the emphasis "on cooperating while at the same time developing each unique individual however his/her potential/interest leads." Even though professors have a range of teaching styles, "Classes are very interdisciplinary and often unintentionally work well in conjunction with other courses." Standout disciplines include political science, international relations (bolstered by "a great study abroad program to match a great language arts department"), anthropology, and chemistry; "what sets these departments apart from most schools is that there are research-related classes that provide interesting extracurricular experiences" and give students the opportunity "to explore social, academic, and occupational aspects of life in an experiential, hands-on manner."

Life

Life at Beloit is fairly low-key; it's "generally about going to classes that you appreciate, hanging out with friends, playing some type of sport and doing homework." Low-key doesn't mean boring, though; on the contrary, "Weekends are a lot of fun, partly because you can drink wherever, whenever, and whatever you like" thanks to an "extremely lenient" drinking policy (students hasten to add that "Beloit students are rarely irresponsible or obnoxious and usually look out for each other"). Those uninterested in the party scene will find "some substance-free housing and a lot of fun and crazy stuff to do (ranging from Friday night movies to sledding on cafeteria trays)." Weeknights are generally given over to "all sorts of presentations [and] lectures by guests," that capture the interest of many undergrads or to hanging at "the Java Joint, the campus coffee shop, [where students] play chess, board games, or do a puzzle." When they need a change of scenery, students take the bus or find a friend with a car and road trip to Madison, Milwaukee, or Chicago to go out on the town. When they're not relaxing, "People are very politically active; they encourage voting and the signing of a ridiculous amount of petitions."

Student Body

"Everybody has a niche at Beloit, whether you're interested in Greek life or LARPing on Saturday nights, and everything in between," and students "are really friendly, even (if not especially) with others who have wildly different interests" because "Beloit students are generally very curious about and accepting of the unfamiliar, with the single exception of religion. Christians at Beloit sometimes feel they need to hide their faith or risk being judged as conservative, judgmental, or uptight." Indeed, most here are "very liberal," which can make "discussion hard sometimes because so many people have the same ideas. Those with more conservative ideas either don't talk about their political views or are very bad at it." As far as diversity in its traditional sense is concerned, "There are lots of rich kids, but the school does a good job recruiting (and financing) students from lower socioeconomic classes."

BELOIT COLLEGE

FINANCIAL AID: 608-363-2500 • E-MAIL: ADMISS@BELOIT.EDU • WEBSITE: WWW.BELOIT.EDU

THE PRINCETON REVIEW SAYS

Admissions

Very important factors considered include: Academic GPA, application essay, recommendation(s), rigor of secondary school record. *Important factors considered include:* Class rank, standardized test scores, interview. *Other factors considered include:* Alumni/ae relation, character/personal qualities, extracurricular activities, first generation, level of applicant's interest, talent/ability, volunteer work, work experience. SAT or ACT required; ACT with or without writing component accepted. TOEFL required of all international applicants. High school diploma is required, and GED is accepted. *Academic units recommended:* 4 English, 4 mathematics, 3 science, 2 foreign language, 4 social studies.

Financial Aid

Students should submit: FAFSA, institution's own financial aid form. Regular filing deadline is March 1. The Princeton Review suggests that all financial aid forms be submitted as soon as possible after January 1. *Need-based scholarships/ grants offered:* Federal Pell, SEOG, state scholarships/grants, private scholarships, school scholarship or grant aid from institutional funds. *Loan aid offered:* Direct Subsidized Stafford, Direct Unsubsidized Stafford, Direct PLUS, Federal Perkins, university loans from institutional funds. Applicants will be notified of awards on a rolling basis beginning April 1. Federal Work-Study Program available. Off-campus job opportunities are good.

The Inside Word

Beloit takes a well-rounded approach to the admissions game. Realizing that applicants are more than statistics on a page, the college works diligently to assess the total package. While most weight is given to a candidate's secondary school transcript, which is evaluated not only for grades but also for academic rigor, significant attention is also paid to essays and recommendations. Counselors strive to find students who not only demonstrate success in the classroom but also display strong character and leadership skills.

THE SCHOOL SAYS "..."

From the Admissions Office

"Beloiters spend four years challenged to explore their passions, excel in their studies, and apply the lessons of the classroom to the larger world, in their careers, and in service to others. That focus—putting the liberal arts into practice—has long set this college and its graduates apart. Study abroad, internships, research, service, and work opportunities are typical examples of the ways the Beloit experience extends beyond the classroom. Beloit students are more apt to value learning for its own sake and at the same time, understand the connection between college and the rest of their lives as citizens of the world.

"Beloit College uses the Common Application exclusively. Although students must submit test scores from the ACT or SAT, standardized test scores are less important than the strength of the academic program and performance, the essays, and recommendations. Beloit offers two nonbinding early action plans with deadlines of either November 1 or December 1; notification is six weeks hence. Applicants who wish to be considered for merit scholarships are urged to apply under one of the early action plans. The preferred deadline for regular decision applicants in January 15."

SELECTIVITY

Admissions Rating	90
# of applicants	2,003
% of applicants accepted	72
% of acceptees attending	23
# accepting a place on wait list	23
% admitted from wait list	43

FRESHMAN PROFILE

Range SAT Critical Reading	570–700
Range SAT Math	620–680
Range ACT Composite	24–30
Minimum paper TOEFL	550
Minimum computer TOEFL	213
Minimum web-based TOEFL	80
Average HS GPA	3.42
% graduated top 10% of class	42
% graduated top 25% of class	71
% graduated top 50% of class	94

DEADLINES

Early action I	
Deadline	11/1
Notification	12/15
Early action II	
Deadline	12/1
Notification	1/15
Regular	
Priority	1/15
Notification	2/15
Nonfall registration?	yes

APPLICANTS ALSO LOOK AT AND OFTEN PREFER
Carleton College
AND SOMETIMES PREFER
Grinnell College, Macalester College, Oberlin College

FINANCIAL FACTS

Financial Aid Rating	94
Annual tuition	36,444
Room and board	$7,502
Required fees	$230
Books and supplies	$600
% frosh rec. need-based scholarship or grant aid	70
% UG rec. need-based scholarship or grant aid	66
% frosh rec. non-need-based scholarship or grant aid	28
% UG rec. non-need-based scholarship or grant aid	25
% frosh rec. need-based self-help aid	70
% UG rec. need-based self-help aid	66
% frosh rec. any financial aid	94
% UG rec. any financial aid	90
% UG borrow to pay for school	69
Average cumulative indebtedness	$19,564

THE BEST 376 COLLEGES ■ 87

BENNINGTON COLLEGE

OFFICE OF ADMISSIONS, BENNINGTON, VT 05201 • ADMISSIONS: 800-833-6845 • FAX: 802-440-4320

CAMPUS LIFE

Quality of Life Rating	81
Fire Safety Rating	82
Green Rating	81
Type of school	private
Environment	town

STUDENTS

Total undergrad enrollment	668
% male/female	33/67
% from out of state	95
% from public high school	53
% live on campus	94
% African American	2
% Asian	2
% Caucasian	81
% Hispanic	3
% Native American	1
% international	7
# of countries represented	30

SURVEY SAYS . . .
Lots of liberal students
Class discussions encouraged
Students aren't religious
Dorms are like palaces
Low cost of living
Intercollegiate sports are unpopular
or nonexistent
Frats and sororities are unpopular
or nonexistent
Theater is popular

ACADEMICS

Academic Rating	98
% students graduating within 4 years	55
% students graduating within 6 years	60
Calendar	trimester
Student/faculty ratio	10:1
Profs interesting rating	94
Profs accessible rating	92
Most common reg class size	10–19 students
Most common lab size	10–19 students

MOST POPULAR MAJORS
social sciences, English language and
literature, visual and performing arts

STUDENTS SAY ". . ."

Academics
Bennington caters to students who want maximum control over their academic endeavors; all students here participate in the Plan Process, "which allows students to create their own course of study." Here's how it works: "Either a student devises his own personalized set of requirements, or [the requirements] are recommended by a 'plan committee' of usually three faculty members personally assigned to each student." The idea is to "leave up to the student the chance to connect ideas and classes that would normally be left out of a core curriculum," and unsurprisingly, students here love it—for many it is the primary reason they choose to attend Bennington. The Field Work Term internship program is another compelling factor. This "seven-week internship term in the winter" gives students "the ideal opportunity to connect with professionals in our areas of interest and learn what you are (and what you aren't) interested in pursuing" while also building a resume. The social sciences, humanities, and performing/creative arts are strongest here, but students insist that the hard sciences are also "strong…and more popular than one might think for a small 'alternative' liberal arts school." Bennington professors "range from being very available to ridiculously available," and "most are extremely active and respected in their fields, and all are willing to meet outside of class and help a motivated student find professional connections."

Life
Bennington undergrads are "very focused on work. All students share a passion for what they are doing," to the extent that "The class doesn't end when we leave the classroom. Discussions often continue, and people are always talking about their classes and their work." Because Bennington is a small school "people are generally friendly and very interested in one another and their work," and because the campus "is a little isolated" "there isn't much to do off-campus," so students must be "good at entertaining themselves." Fortunately, "There is always plenty to do on campus. Sometimes there are too many events to choose from: dance concerts, plays, readings, themed parties, art openings, and many more events, on campus and off." Some party intensely "to blow off some steam" because "we all work so exceedingly hard," but most here agree the situation is under control; students can't ignore academics for too long because "with the way our academic system works, you can be kicked out for getting too many C's." When they need to get away, undergrads "are most likely to take day trips to nearby Brattleboro and Williamstown, each of which are very close and offer all sorts of diversions."

Student Body
"Self-motivated, voraciously curious, and open to growth," the typical Bennington student "is very devoted to his work and personally invested in creating something meaningful with [his] time. A stereotype for the general student body could be 'indie kid,' but that doesn't quite fit because the students here have a broader awareness of disciplines and interests outside of their own due to the cross-disciplinary nature of [the] studies." To some, it seems that "Everyone here is a total nerd: art nerd, science nerd, lit nerd, language nerd, math nerd, drama nerd, dance nerd. Nerds of all shapes, types, and aesthetic genres." They are "the type of people who would rather dance in polyester or read a book than go to a basketball game." There are "probably fewer than a handful of Republicans on campus, and there are definitely no Abercrombie & Fitch sweatshirts around."

FINANCIAL AID: 802-440-4325 • E-MAIL: ADMISSIONS@BENNINGTON.EDU • WEBSITE: WWW.BENNINGTON.EDU

THE PRINCETON REVIEW SAYS

Admissions

Very important factors considered include: Academic GPA, application essay, class rank, recommendation(s), rigor of secondary school record, character/personal qualities, extracurricular activities, interview, talent/ability. *Other factors considered include:* Standardized test scores, alumni/ae relation, first generation, geographical residence, level of applicant's interest, racial/ethnic status, volunteer work, work experience. ACT with or without writing component accepted. TOEFL required of all international applicants. High school diploma is required, and GED is accepted. *Academic units recommended:* 4 English, 4 mathematics, 3 science, 2 foreign language, 4 social studies, 4 history.

Financial Aid

Students should submit: FAFSA, institution's own financial aid form, CSS/Financial Aid PROFILE. Regular filing deadline is February 15. The Princeton Review suggests that all financial aid forms be submitted as soon as possible after January 1. *Need-based scholarships/grants offered:* Federal Pell, SEOG, state scholarships/grants, private scholarships, school scholarship or grant aid from institutional funds. *Loan aid offered:* Direct Subsidized Stafford, Direct Unsubsidized Stafford, Direct PLUS, university loans from institutional funds. Applicants will be notified of awards on a rolling basis beginning April 1. Federal Work-Study Program available. Off-campus job opportunities are good.

The Inside Word

Bennington students need to be academically accomplished, driven, and self-directed to handle the academic freedom granted by the curriculum. The admissions office seeks all these qualities in applicants and, because of the school's prestige, typically finds them in all admitted students. A campus visit isn't required but is strongly recommended as an excellent way to demonstrate your interest in the school and to provide admissions officers with the personal contact they prefer in evaluating candidates.

THE SCHOOL SAYS "..."

From the Admissions Office

"At Bennington, your education is unified and fueled by your intellect and imagination, guided by a rigorous and ongoing conversation with your faculty, and shaped by your experience working in the world each year. Bennington is the only college to require that its students spend a term—every year—at work in the world. And its new Center for the Advancement of Public Action provides a unique opportunity for students to explore how the questions that matter to them come together with the questions that matter to the world. Rooted in an abiding faith in the talent, imagination, and responsibility of the individual, Bennington invites students to pursue and shape their own intellectual inquiries and, in doing so, to discover the profound interconnection of things.

"Submission of standardized test scores (the SAT, SAT Subject Tests, or the ACT) is optional."

SELECTIVITY

Admissions Rating	90
# of applicants	1,089
% of applicants accepted	65
% of acceptees attending	24
# accepting a place on wait list	15
% admitted from wait list	67
# of early decision applicants	69
% accepted early decision	59

FRESHMAN PROFILE

Range SAT Critical Reading	610–740
Range SAT Math	530–650
Range SAT Writing	600–710
Range ACT Composite	26–30
Minimum paper TOEFL	577
Minimum computer TOEFL	233
Average HS GPA	3.41
% graduated top 10% of class	33
% graduated top 25% of class	63
% graduated top 50% of class	88

DEADLINES

Early decision	
Deadline	11/15
Notification	12/15
Early action	
Deadline	12/1
Notification	2/1
Regular	
Deadline	1/3
Notification	4/1
Nonfall registration?	yes

APPLICANTS ALSO LOOK AT

AND OFTEN PREFER
Bard College

AND SOMETIMES PREFER
Lewis & Clark College, Sarah Lawrence College, University of Vermont

AND RARELY PREFER
Eugene Lang College The New School for Liberal Arts, Hampshire College, Marlboro College

FINANCIAL FACTS

Financial Aid Rating	79
Annual tuition	$40,280
Room and board	$11,550
Required fees	$1,070
Books and supplies	$800
% frosh rec. need-based scholarship or grant aid	56
% UG rec. need-based scholarship or grant aid	62
% frosh rec. non-need-based scholarship or grant aid	2
% UG rec. non-need-based scholarship or grant aid	4
% frosh rec. need-based self-help aid	53
% UG rec. need-based self-help aid	58
% frosh rec. any financial aid	84
% UG rec. any financial aid	82
% UG borrow to pay for school	74
Average cumulative indebtedness	$26,224

BENTLEY UNIVERSITY

175 FOREST STREET, WALTHAM, MA 02452-4705 • ADMISSIONS: 781-891-2244 • FAX: 781-891-3414

CAMPUS LIFE

Quality of Life Rating	92
Fire Safety Rating	99
Green Rating	89
Type of school	private
Environment	town

STUDENTS

Total undergrad enrollment	4,196
% male/female	59/41
% from out of state	52
% from public high school	72
% live on campus	79
# of fraternities	6
# of sororities	5
% African American	3
% Asian	7
% Caucasian	62
% Hispanic	6
% international	11
# of countries represented	92

SURVEY SAYS . . .

Great computer facilities
Great library
Athletic facilities are great
Career services are great
School is well-run
Dorms are like palaces
Campus feels safe

ACADEMICS

Academic Rating	77
% students graduating within 4 years	79
% students graduating within 6 years	88
Calendar	semester
Student/faculty ratio	14:1
Profs interesting rating	81
Profs accessible rating	85
Most common reg class size	20–29 students

MOST POPULAR MAJORS
accounting, finance, marketing

STUDENTS SAY ". . ."

Academics

"If you're looking to work in business in the Boston area, desire a beautiful campus, state-of-the-art trading room, and technologically advanced university, Bentley University is the place for you," one student assures us. Bentley is known for its business program, and many students cite the program's excellent reputation as their reason for choosing to attend college here, as well as strong career services and professional internship opportunities. Students are pleased with Bentley's abilities to create a "career-bound student while instilling the importance of liberal studies," and to "prepare you and help you earn a job with all the technical and educational background you need." They also "love that most of the professors have worked outside of academia and can bring...real-world experience and examples to the classroom." Professors are "great role models and have had a lot of experience in the business world," and "all professors hold office hours, and they are all responsive to e-mail and phone messages." "Class sizes are capped at thirty-five, which gives students a solid relationship with each professor," and "a lot of classes are discussion-based and force you to think about real-world applications." Some students note that classes can be challenging, but that "many of the departments have tutoring labs available for students at all levels." The administration also receives high marks: It's "truly concerned with students' wants," "engaging and open to new ideas," and "very communicative."

Life

Bentley students study hard and are "very business-like" during week, so they use weekends to blow off a little steam. Many seek fun in the local sports teams (Red Sox, Patriots, and Celtics), local bars on Moody Street, and regular shuttles into Cambridge (Boston is also easily accessible via public transportation). "This university really strikes a great balance of fun and work." While students are happy to have a city like Boston nearby, with its "bars, historical sites, theatres, restaurants, clubs, etc.," there's plenty of activity on campus, too, and "entertainment is limitless." "Students are extremely involved at Bentley." "Most students participate in more than one club, and many hold administrative positions in the club. These clubs lead to not only good friends but also networking opportunities." "Many people participate in very competitive intramural sports." Bentley does have a Greek system, though frat houses are located off campus.

Student Body

A typical student at Bentley "is an intelligent, white New Englander." Moreover, they're "very driven and know what they want to do with their life," and they "know how to have ats appear to be the same: serious business students working all the time," good time and balance that with schoolwork." "On the surface, most studenand they're "involved in a few extracurriculars." However, look beneath the surface and you'll notice a significant international population and "a lot of atypical students" who "fit in with the rest of the students perfectly." Some students say they think the majority of their peers come from wealth, but most feel that Bentley is fairly balanced: "While walking through campus, you may see tons of individuals driving expensive cars or walking to class dressed to the nines, [but] you will also encounter people driving inexpensive cars and walking to class dressed in sweats."

BENTLEY UNIVERSITY

FINANCIAL AID: 781-891-3441 • E-MAIL: UGADMISSION@BENTLEY.EDU • WEBSITE: WWW.BENTLEY.EDU

THE PRINCETON REVIEW SAYS

Admissions
Very important factors considered include: Academic GPA, rigor of secondary school record, standardized test scores. *Important factors considered include:* Application essay, recommendation(s), character/personal qualities, extracurricular activities, level of applicant's interest, talent/ability, volunteer work. *Other factors considered include:* Class rank, alumni/ae relation, first generation, geographical residence, interview, racial/ethnic status, state residency, work experience. SAT or ACT required; ACT with writing component required. TOEFL required of all international applicants. High school diploma is required, and GED is accepted. *Academic units recommended:* 4 English, 4 mathematics, 3 science (3 science labs), 3 foreign language, 3 social studies.

Financial Aid
Students should submit: FAFSA, CSS/Financial Aid PROFILE. Regular filing deadline is February 1. The Princeton Review suggests that all financial aid forms be submitted as soon as possible after January 1. *Need-based scholarships/grants offered:* Federal Pell, SEOG, state scholarships/grants, private scholarships, grant aid from institutional funds. *Loan aid offered:* Direct Subsidized Stafford, Direct Unsubsidized Stafford, Direct PLUS, Federal Perkins, state loans. Applicants will be notified of awards beginning mid-March. Federal Work-Study Program available. Off-campus job opportunities are good. Non-need-based academic scholarships are offered from institutional funds (no financial aid application required).

The Inside Word
If you have a bunch of electives available to you senior year, you may think that choosing business classes is the best way to impress the Bentley admissions office. Not so; the school would prefer you take a broad range of challenging classes—preferably at the AP level—in English, history/social sciences, math, lab sciences, and foreign language. The school enjoys a sizable applicant pool, so you'll need solid grades and test scores to gain admission.

THE SCHOOL SAYS "..."

From the Admissions Office
"Bentley University is a national leader in business education, providing an unparalleled fusion of business and the arts and science. Bentley blends the breadth and technological strength of a university with the values and student focus of a small college.

"Many Bentley students choose both a business major and our nationally acclaimed Liberal Studies major (LSM), gaining a competitive edge in their future careers by building meaningful connections across disciplines. Bentley students also embrace internships, service learning, study abroad, and corporate partnerships. More than eighty percent of Bentley undergraduates complete at least one internship.

"In 2010, Bentley was ranked number six nationally by The Princeton Review for 'Best Career Services.' Also in 2010, ninety-nine percent of Bentley students found employment or enrolled in graduate school within six months of graduation. Their median annual salary was more than $50,000.

"Approximately ninety-eight percent of freshmen live on campus. Students live and learn in a multicultural environment that prepares them to thrive in today's diverse work world. International students representing more than eighty countries are part of the Bentley community. There are more than 100 student organizations, as well as abundant intramurals, recreational sports, and twenty-three varsity teams in NCAA Divisions I and II.

"Bentley's location in Waltham, Massachusetts—just minutes from Boston—puts the city's many resources within easy reach. Bentley's free shuttle makes regular trips to Harvard Square in Cambridge, just a subway ride from the heart of Boston. Boston also offers students many opportunities for internships and jobs after graduation."

SELECTIVITY	
Admissions Rating	86
# of applicants	6,203
% of applicants accepted	46
% of acceptees attending	33
# accepting a place on wait list	815
% admitted from wait list	1
# of early decision applicants	126
% accepted early decision	79

FRESHMAN PROFILE	
Range SAT Critical Reading	530–630
Range SAT Math	590–670
Range SAT Writing	540–630
Range ACT Composite	25–28
Minimum paper TOEFL	550
Minimum computer TOEFL	213
Minimum web-based TOEFL	80
% graduated top 10% of class	34
% graduated top 25% of class	74
% graduated top 50% of class	97

DEADLINES	
Early decision	
Deadline	11/1
Notification	12/17
Early action	
Deadline	11/15
Notification	1/15
Regular	
Deadline	1/15
Nonfall registration?	yes

APPLICANTS ALSO LOOK AT AND SOMETIMES PREFER
Babson College, Boston College, Boston University, Bryant University, Northeastern University, University of Massachusetts Amherst, Villanova University

FINANCIAL FACTS	
Financial Aid Rating	87
Annual tuition	$35,580
Room and board	$12,180
Required fees	$1,478
Books and supplies	$1,100
% frosh rec. need-based scholarship or grant aid	41
% UG rec. need-based scholarship or grant aid	41
% frosh rec. non-need-based scholarship or grant aid	16
% UG rec. non-need-based scholarship or grant aid	15
% frosh rec. need-based self-help aid	45
% UG rec. need-based self-help aid	45
% frosh rec. any financial aid	77
% UG rec. any financial aid	75
% UG borrow to pay for school	64
Average cumulative indebtedness	$32,710

BEREA COLLEGE

CPO 2220, BEREA, KY 40404 • ADMISSIONS: 859-985-3500 • FAX: 859-985-3512

STUDENTS SAY ". . ."

Academics
Berea College in central Kentucky is "about bringing underprivileged high school graduates from the Appalachian region and beyond together for a chance at a higher education, a career, and a better life." Thanks to a labor program that requires all students to work ten to fifteen hours each week and a ton of donated cash, tuition here is "free." "Each student receives a laptop to use while in school" as well. "No tuition does not mean a full ride," though. "Extra costs such as technology fees, insurance, food plans, etc., add up quickly," advises a business major. About two-thirds of the students receive additional financial aid. Berea's administration is efficient, but it "tends to be too parental in nature," and can be overly concerned with image. "Donors hear a story of poor kids who are getting help from a school that sometimes styles itself as a charity," explains a junior. In addition to a decent range of liberal arts and sciences majors, there are several career-oriented programs. The academic atmosphere is "rigorous." Class attendance is mandatory. A few "hardcore" professors "abuse the idea of homework." Others "need refresher courses on how to deal with people." On the whole, though, faculty members are "witty," and they "have a strong passion for what they are teaching." "Everyone who I've had has been completely accessible outside of class," describes a nursing major. "Students are able to get so much more one-on-one time than at larger colleges."

Life
"Buildings, facilities, and technology are not always the newest, nicest, or most expensive" on this "tiny campus." There's no cable television in the dorm rooms, and the "crazy" visitation policy for members of the opposite sex is "borderline nineteenth century." Academics take up a lot of time, and "every student is required to have an on-campus job." Some students make stoneware pottery. Others "feed sheep and goats" on the college farm. However, "janitorial work," computer support, and similarly mundane jobs are more typical. "With work, classes, and studying, there's not much time left for anything else." "There are many clubs" and several religious groups. "Movie marathons" and "dances" are common. "Pick-up games" and intramurals are popular. "Some of us go camping when it's nice out, that kind of thing," says a first-year student. Otherwise, "Life at Berea is generally regarded as boring." "If it weren't for videogames, I'd go nuts," speculates a junior. The surrounding town is "very small." "There is not even a movie theater." "Someone from a big city would be in for a shock." Freshmen can't bring cars at all, and generally, only students who live far away can ever have vehicles. The county is dry, and there are no bars. Berea's alcohol polices are theoretically harsh but more lenient in practice. "If you can hide it, you can drink it." However, alcohol and drug usage is "very low." "We're not a party school," says a junior. "Basically, our weekends consist of walking down to Wal-Mart," explains a sophomore, "and that's if we're really ready for a crazy night."

Student Body
"The typical student at Berea College is broke" but "has big dreams." "Most people are from working-class families." They were "raised in backwoods hollows" around "the Appalachian area." "We are all here because we have no money but are equipped with the hope for a bright future and a desire to learn," declares a senior. Students at Berea are "sleep deprived" and "too busy to really have the time to slack off (though there are some that still manage it)." They're "bright, hardworking," and "studious." "Most of us are nerds," admits a senior. There are "quite a few Bible thumpers." At the same time, Berea is "probably more liberal than conservative," and this is something of "a hippie school." "People are really big about recycling, sustainability, and the environment." Students tell us that Berea has "more diversity than most schools." "There is a very large homeschool population." There are quite a few "young married students." There's also a noticeable contingent of international students and "a large population of African Americans." Most students claim that minorities "blend in well."

FINANCIAL AID: 859-985-3310 • E-MAIL: ADMISSIONS@BEREA.EDU • WEBSITE: WWW.BEREA.EDU

THE PRINCETON REVIEW SAYS

Admissions

Very important factors considered include: Interview. *Important factors considered include:* Academic GPA, application essay, class rank, rigor of secondary school record, standardized test scores, character/personal qualities. *Other factors considered include:* Recommendation(s), extracurricular activities, first generation, geographical residence, level of applicant's interest, racial/ethnic status, state residency, talent/ability, volunteer work, work experience. SAT or ACT required; ACT with or without writing component accepted. TOEFL required of all international applicants. High school diploma is required, and GED is accepted. *Academic units recommended:* 4 English, 3 mathematics, 2 science (2 science labs), 2 foreign language, 1 social studies, 1 history.

Financial Aid

Students should submit: FAFSA. Regular filing deadline is May 1. The Princeton Review suggests that all financial aid forms be submitted as soon as possible after January 1. *Need-based scholarships/grants offered:* Federal Pell, SEOG, state scholarships/grants, private scholarships, school scholarship or grant aid from institutional funds. *Loan aid offered:* Direct Subsidized Stafford, Direct Unsubsidized Stafford, Direct PLUS, Federal Perkins, university loans from institutional funds. Applicants will be notified of awards on a rolling basis beginning April 15.

Inside Word

The full-tuition scholarship that every student receives understandably attracts a lot of applicants. Competition among candidates is intense. To make matters worse, you may be too wealthy to get admitted here. Berea won't admit students whose parents can afford to send them elsewhere. Financially qualified applicants should apply as early as possible.

THE SCHOOL SAYS "..."

From the Admissions Office

"Founded in 1855 by ardent abolitionists, Berea College was the first racially integrated coeducational college in the South. Over the past 150 years, Berea's has evolved into one of the most distinctive colleges in the United States. Serving students primarily from the Appalachian region, Berea College seeks to serve students who possess great academic promise but have access to limited financial resources. Berea provides an inviting and personal educational experience, evidenced in part by a ten to one student/faculty ratio and extensive, faculty-led advising and orientation programs.

"In support of students with limited financial resources, every enrolling student receives a full-tuition scholarship, a laptop computer, as well as a paid on-campus job. Students pay room, board, and fee charges to the extent that they are able as determined by their FAFSA results. Any remaining room, board, and fee charges are covered through scholarships and grant-based aid. Students may use earnings from their jobs to assist with their portion of room, board, and fee charges; books and supplies; and other personal expenses.

"As a result of this combination of academic reputation and generous financial assistance, Berea attracts many more applicants than are able to be accepted, so admission is competitive. The best means of improving the chances for admission is to complete the application process as early as possible, preferably by November 30 of the senior year.

"Applicants must submit scores from the SAT or ACT (with or without the writing components from either test)."

SELECTIVITY

Admissions Rating	93
# of applicants	3,264
% of applicants accepted	17
% of acceptees attending	76

FRESHMAN PROFILE

Range SAT Critical Reading	520–650
Range SAT Math	500–620
Range SAT Writing	480–615
Range ACT Composite	21–26
Minimum paper TOEFL	500
Minimum computer TOEFL	173
Minimum web-based TOEFL	61
Average HS GPA	3.42
% graduated top 10% of class	31
% graduated top 25% of class	71
% graduated top 50% of class	96

DEADLINES

Regular	
Deadline	4/30
Notification	11/1
Nonfall registration?	no

FINANCIAL FACTS

Financial Aid Rating	91
Annual tuition	$24,100
Room and board	$5,768
Required fees	$876
Books and supplies	$700
% frosh rec. need-based scholarship or grant aid	100
% UG rec. need-based scholarship or grant aid	100
% frosh rec. need-based self-help aid	100
% UG rec. need-based self-help aid	100
% frosh rec. any financial aid	100
% UG rec. any financial aid	100
% UG borrow to pay for school	73
Average cumulative indebtedness	$5,836

BIRMINGHAM-SOUTHERN COLLEGE

900 ARKADELPHIA ROAD, BIRMINGHAM, AL 35254 • ADMISSIONS: 205-226-4696 • FAX: 205-226-3074

STUDENTS SAY "..."

Academics

Birmingham-Southern College "is an institution that cares for its students and provides them with a high-quality education and opportunities to succeed." A double-major in art and psychology says, "I chose BSC because I wanted a small liberal arts college where I would know my teachers personally and where I would gain a well-rounded education and experience to help me further my career in life." Most students rave about the "academic reputation and the small class sizes that allow for personalized interaction with the professors." The college is known for its strong premed and theater programs, and students say BSC has a "reputation for sending students to some of the most prestigious and reputable graduate and professional schools in the country." Professors get high marks across the board. Students say, "The professors here make BSC what it is" and add, "They're always willing to help you out and meet with you if you need extra help. They make the academic experience here completely fabulous and well worth the hard work you have to put into your studies." Academic standards are considered rigorous, and students say BSC "demands the best from the professors and the best from the students. The faculty is fantastic, and the campus is beautiful."

Life

BSC "is a gated/closed campus, so living on campus is preferred by most students—and many of the activities happen at night for this reason." Students describe the atmosphere on campus as, "welcoming [and] intelligent, where assumptions are challenged, and individuals [are] supported" and say, "In order to 'fit in' one *must* get involved in something." Many students say the small size of the college "allows for a lot of opportunities for students to get involved and become an active part of campus." Clubs and intramurals are popular, and students say, "It definitely never gets boring here on campus." One student adds, "Even if you can't think of anything to do, the school is always having some kind of event that's usually free and pretty fun." The administration earns some grumbles, with students saying, "There is a disconnect with administration and the student population." Better communication around campus "is something students have been looking for in the past few years." A collaborative education major says, "We've recently had some financial troubles, and it has exposed some gaping holes in the way the administration deals with the student body"; however, some are optimistic that "steps have been taken this year to improve that situation." A common complaint is the cafeteria, where students feel frustrated by high prices and a lack of quality.

Student Body

At BSC, typical students are "goal-oriented and focused," but also "hard workers" who "find time for play." One student says, "Simply put, a BSC student is a laid-back workaholic who knows how to have a good time." Another adds, "The model Birmingham-Southern student is over-committed, because at BSC it's cool to be busy." Students say they're "heavily involved in Greek life and student organizations" and that the small student body allows for more leadership roles in extracurricular activities. Despite the popularity of the Greek system and the fact that "most people at BSC drink," drinking is "not required to have friends or fun," and "Students fit in well at BSC regardless of their personal preferences, usually." Most students are "Southern, both in origin and in nature—warm hellos from strangers are a part of life on campus. Overall, it's a pretty likeable" and "smart bunch." Although, "The typical student comes from an upper-middle-class background," one student says, "There are many (like myself) who are here through extensive scholarships and financial aid." Birmingham gets praise as a vibrant community with a local art scene, and a psychology major says, "There is a great coffeehouse scene in Birmingham, and during exams you can often find students studying at various locally owned coffeehouses."

BIRMINGHAM-SOUTHERN COLLEGE

FINANCIAL AID: 205-226-4688 • E-MAIL: ADMISSION@BSC.EDU • WEBSITE: WWW.BSC.EDU

THE PRINCETON REVIEW SAYS

Admissions

Very important factors considered include: Academic GPA, application essay, recommendation(s), rigor of secondary school record, standardized test scores. *Important factors considered include:* Character/personal qualities. *Other factors considered include:* Extracurricular activities, interview, level of applicant's interest, talent/ability, work experience. SAT or ACT required; ACT with writing component recommended. TOEFL required of all international applicants. High school diploma is required, and GED is accepted. *Academic units required:* 4 English. *Academic units recommended:* 4 mathematics, 4 science (2 science labs), 2 foreign language, 2 social studies, 2 history, 1 academic elective.

Financial Aid

Students should submit: FAFSA. The Princeton Review suggests that all financial aid forms be submitted as soon as possible after January 1. *Need-based scholarships/grants offered:* Federal Pell, SEOG, state scholarships/grants, private scholarships, school scholarship or grant aid from institutional funds, United Negro College Fund. *Loan aid offered:* Direct Subsidized Stafford, Direct Unsubsidized Stafford, Direct PLUS, Federal Perkins. Applicants will be notified of awards on a rolling basis beginning March 1. Federal Work-Study Program available. Off-campus job opportunities are excellent.

The Inside Word

BSC is a small college that caters to prospective students during the application process. Admissions counselors routinely "hit the road" traveling to meet students across the country and working with high schools to organize informational sessions about BSC. They put a strong emphasis on the campus visit and offer to help potential applicants plan every aspect of their visit, from transportation to dining.

THE SCHOOL SAYS "..."

From the Admissions Office

"Respected publishers continue to recognize Birmingham-Southern College as one of the top-ranked liberal arts colleges in the nation. One guide highlights our small classes and the fact that we still assign each student a 'faculty-mentor,' to assure individualized attention to our students. One notable aspect of our academic calendar is our January interim term, a four-week period in which students can participate in special projects in close collaboration with faculty members, either on or off campus. One dimension of Birmingham-Southern's civic focus is the commitment to volunteerism. The Center for Leadership Studies assists students in realizing their leadership potential by combining the academic study of leadership with significant community service.

"Freshman applicants must present acceptable scores on the SAT or the ACT; they must also submit an original essay and a satisfactory recommendation from the high school."

SELECTIVITY

Admissions Rating	85
# of applicants	2,101
% of applicants accepted	69
% of acceptees attending	31

FRESHMAN PROFILE

Range SAT Critical Reading	520–540
Range SAT Math	510–630
Range ACT Composite	23–28
Minimum paper TOEFL	500
Minimum computer TOEFL	173
Minimum web-based TOEFL	61
Average HS GPA	3.40
% graduated top 10% of class	32
% graduated top 25% of class	53
% graduated top 50% of class	82

DEADLINES

Regular	
Priority	1/1
Notification	7/1
Nonfall registration?	yes

APPLICANTS ALSO LOOK AT AND OFTEN PREFER
Rhodes College, Vanderbilt University
AND SOMETIMES PREFER
Auburn University, University of Alabama—Tuscaloosa

FINANCIAL FACTS

Financial Aid Rating	91
Annual tuition	$28,250
Required fees	$946
Books and supplies	$1,100
% frosh rec. need-based scholarship or grant aid	44
% UG rec. need-based scholarship or grant aid	38
% frosh rec. non-need-based scholarship or grant aid	53
% UG rec. non-need-based scholarship or grant aid	48
% frosh rec. need-based self-help aid	41
% UG rec. need-based self-help aid	38
% frosh rec. any financial aid	99
% UG rec. any financial aid	98
% UG borrow to pay for school	79
Average cumulative indebtedness	$27,798

BOSTON COLLEGE

140 COMMONWEALTH AVENUE, DEVLIN HALL 208, CHESTNUT HILL, MA 02467-3809 • ADMISSIONS: 617-552-3100

CAMPUS LIFE
Quality of Life Rating	89
Fire Safety Rating	91
Green Rating	85
Type of school	private
Affiliation	Roman Catholic-Jesuit
Environment	city

STUDENTS
Total undergrad enrollment	9,099
% male/female	48/52
% from out of state	72
% from public high school	51
% live on campus	83
% African American	5
% Asian	10
% Caucasian	65
% Hispanic	9
% international	3
# of countries represented	91

SURVEY SAYS . . .
Students love Chestnut Hill, MA
Campus feels safe
Everyone loves the Eagles
Frats and sororities are unpopular
or nonexistent
Student publications are popular

ACADEMICS
Academic Rating	84
Calendar	semester
Student/faculty ratio	13:1
Profs interesting rating	83
Profs accessible rating	85
Most common	
reg class size	10–19 students

MOST POPULAR MAJORS
communication studies, English
language and literature, finance

STUDENTS SAY ". . ."

Academics

Boston College, a small Jesuit school on the outskirts of Boston, "is all about educating the person as a whole." Its strong core curriculum ensures all students receive a "well-rounded" liberal arts education regardless of their chosen major. Boston College's well-respected education and business school attract a lot of students, and there are many other strong programs, including English and communication. Students think Boston College is a "great experience academically" and gush about their "phenomenal professors." A secondary education major student says, "Boston College's professors are truly exceptional and are devoted to undergraduate learning." They're "engaging, challenging, and understanding, [and] are genuinely interested in the student as a whole person." Boston College's "prestigious" academics come with "high expectations," but if students need help professors are "easily accessible outside of classes." Students "feel prepared for whatever is next" and note that their "well-connected" teachers and strong alumni network help with the job search. One student, who was drawn to Boston College because of its stellar reputation, finds it "even better than expected." Another adds, "I have always revered Boston College's academic and athletic reputation, and coming here, I have not been disappointed."

Life

Boston College's "gorgeous campus" and "perfect'" suburban location has created a very rich campus life and given the school a "strong community feel." There's "a superb sense of school spirit, which truly sets it apart." One students raves, "There is just so much school spirit and love for the university!" Boston College's "incredible sports teams" are well-supported by "superfans at every event." "There is also a large service component," to life at Boston College, which allows students "to serve the community in Boston and communities all around the world." Boston College offers a "plethora of extracurricular activities," and students think "there's a club or group for everyone here." The school has "great facilities" and "state-of-the-art resources." Dorms are generally well-reviewed, though students think the housing lottery could be more "fair." Students often go into Boston for all of its entertainment and cultural activities but are happy to return to their "close-knit college" where they "feel very at home."

Student Body

Boston College has gotten some flak for its "preppy," "white," and "homogenous" student body, and a communication student admits, "The school's nickname as 'J. Crew U.' isn't entirely unwarranted." Boston College could definitely use "greater racial diversity," but one student says that each year "the student body becomes more and more diverse." A student double-majoring in economics and German says, "Once you've settled in you'll find that it's not at all difficult to find a group of friends" no matter who you are. "There is a large religious/spiritual community," because of the school's Jesuit affiliation, but "It is only one group of many." Boston College's Division I ranking means there are plenty of athletes and sports fans. Students warn that Boston College is "not the place to go to class in your pajamas." People, particularly women, are "very well-dressed" and "stylish." Students say their peers are "really ambitious" and "hardworking." "The majority of students seem intelligent and academically driven as well as dedicated to and passionate about one or more extracurricular activities." Though people at Boston College are "academically oriented," they're "also into having a good time, and "have a "work hard, play hard mentality." There's a moderate amount of drinking on campus and off, but students say that no matter what, everyone "definitely [has] school as a top priority."

FAX: 617-552-0798 • FINANCIAL AID: 800-294-0294 • WEBSITE: WWW.BC.EDU

THE PRINCETON REVIEW SAYS

Admissions

Very important factors considered include: Academic GPA, rigor of secondary school record, standardized test scores. *Important factors considered include:* Application essay, class rank, recommendation(s), alumni/ae relation, character/personal qualities, extracurricular activities, religious affiliation/commitment, talent/ability, volunteer work. *Other factors considered include:* First generation, racial/ethnic status, work experience. ACT with writing component required. TOEFL required of all international applicants. High school diploma is required, and GED is accepted. *Academic units recommended:* 4 English, 4 mathematics, 4 science (4 science labs), 4 foreign language, 4 social studies, 4 history.

Financial Aid

Students should submit: FAFSA, CSS/Financial Aid PROFILE. The Princeton Review suggests that all financial aid forms be submitted as soon as possible after January 1. *Need-based scholarships/grants offered:* Federal Pell, SEOG, state scholarships/grants, private scholarships, school scholarship or grant aid from institutional funds. *Loan aid offered:* Federal Perkins, Federal Nursing Loans, state loans. Federal Work-Study Program available. Off-campus job opportunities are good.

The Inside Word

Boston College is one of many selective schools that eschew set admissions formulae. While a challenging high school curriculum and strong test scores are essential for any serious candidate, the college seeks students who are passionate and make connections between academic pursuits and extracurricular activities. The application process should reveal a distinct, mature voice and a student whose interest in education goes beyond the simple desire to earn an A.

THE SCHOOL SAYS " . . . "

From the Admissions Office

"Boston College students achieve at the highest levels with honors including two Rhodes scholarship winners, nine Fulbrights, and one each for Marshall, Goldwater, Madison, and Truman Postgraduate Fellowship Programs. Junior Year Abroad and Scholar of the College Program offer students flexibility within the curriculum. Facilities opened in the past ten years include the Merkert Chemistry Center, Higgins Hall (housing the Biology and Physics departments), three new residence halls, the Yawkey Athletics Center, the Vanderslice Commons Dining Hall, the Hillside Cafe, and a state-of-the-art library. Students enjoy the vibrant location in Chestnut Hill with easy access to the cultural and historical richness of Boston.

"Boston College requires freshman applicants to take the SAT with writing (or the ACT with the writing exam required). Two SAT Subject Tests are required; students are encouraged to take Subject Tests in fields in which they excel."

SELECTIVITY

Admissions Rating	96
# of applicants	29,933
% of applicants accepted	31
% of acceptees attending	25
# accepting a place on wait list	2,686
% admitted from wait list	4

FRESHMAN PROFILE

Range SAT Critical Reading	610–700
Range SAT Math	640–730
Range SAT Writing	630–720
Range ACT Composite	29–32
Minimum paper TOEFL	600
Minimum computer TOEFL	250
Minimum web-based TOEFL	100
% graduated top 10% of class	79
% graduated top 25% of class	95
% graduated top 50% of class	100

DEADLINES

Early action	
Deadline	11/1
Notification	12/25
Regular	
Deadline	1/1
Nonfall registration?	yes

APPLICANTS ALSO LOOK AT
AND OFTEN PREFER
Cornell University, Georgetown University, Northwestern University, University of Notre Dame
AND SOMETIMES PREFER
New York University, Tufts University, University of Michigan—Ann Arbor
AND RARELY PREFER
Boston University, Villanova University

FINANCIAL FACTS

Financial Aid Rating	94
Annual tuition	$39,880
Room and board	$12,082
Required fees	$1,092
Books and supplies	$900
% frosh rec. need-based scholarship or grant aid	39
% UG rec. need-based scholarship or grant aid	37
% frosh rec. non-need-based scholarship or grant aid	1
% UG rec. non-need-based scholarship or grant aid	1
% frosh rec. need-based self-help aid	39
% UG rec. need-based self-help aid	37
% frosh rec. any financial aid	61
% UG rec. any financial aid	66
% UG borrow to pay for school	49
Average cumulative indebtedness	$19,514

BOSTON UNIVERSITY

121 BAY STATE ROAD, BOSTON, MA 02215 • ADMISSIONS: 617-353-2300 • FAX: 617-353-9695

STUDENTS SAY ". . ."

Academics

Boston University shrugs off the dichotomy that generally separates public and private institutions, offering both the diversity and choice that only a large school can, while also offering the friendliness, security, and personal attention you would expect from a pricey, private college. The key to BU's success is the varied yet close-knit academic departments: "Boston University is a huge institution full of opportunities to learn and experience the city, but it's also made up of small academic and extracurricular communities that offer students a home away from home." A junior adds, "BU has so many choices when it comes to majors and classes that I find myself struggling to pick just four classes a semester." In addition to coursework, "Internship and study abroad opportunities are easily accessible," and there are "dual-degree and MA/BA opportunities within our many colleges and schools." Despite their prestigious names and careers, "Professors at BU are here to teach, not to research. Students are their primary concern, and that shows through their work." Outside of class, professors "have office hours, but are more than happy to meet if that doesn't match with my schedule," one student shares. When it comes to the nuts and bolts of administering this stellar educational experience, students should be mindful that BU is "a large university with tons of offices" so it can be "difficult to quickly get an answer to a pressing question." At the same time, "The administration does not stay in their offices; they are readily accessible and easy to converse with." Of particular note, the "Dean of Students…is a great resource on campus and is actively working to participate in events with the students."

Life

Academics come first at BU, but social life is a close second. With an urban campus located "in the heart of Boston," students love heading off campus and "exploring places like Chinatown, Quincy Market, the North End, and Boston Common." If you want to mix and mingle with other undergraduates, there's no better atmosphere: "Whether it is on our campus or across the river at Harvard or across town at Northeastern, there is always some kind of social event to attend." On campus, dorms are comfortable, cafeteria food is good, and "There are 525 clubs and organizations that are constantly meeting." Of particular note, "There is a great community service center, which offers many different programs that cater to your schedule." While many students spend their free time in the city, campus activities at BU include such sundry offerings as "free concerts at our own mini-club, BU Central, or the laser light show at the BU Beach." In addition, "The different culture clubs at BU will occasionally host themed dances…which are fun and a great opportunity to learn about the culture of your fellow peers." Sports enthusiasts on campus are plentiful—especially when it comes to BU's champion ice hockey team—and "Students with the sports pass, which is normally included in tuition…can even pick up hockey tickets for free and just enjoy the game."

Student Body

Set in one of the world's best college towns, you'll meet kids "from all over America and all over the globe" at BU. At the same time, BU draws "a lot of people from the Northeast coast, and especially from the Boston area," who already know and love the city. Size and diversity make the social experience inclusive and accepting: "There are no real stigmas or cliques on campus because everyone is so diverse." No matter how unique your interests, you're sure to find like minds: "There are an amazing amount of clubs that meet every night of the week—including quidditch, astronomy, camping, religious/ethnic clubs, and many, many more." In fact, many students tell us, "We have such a large student body that there really is someone for everyone here." At the same time, academics are priority number one for most students. A current student explains, "BU is so diverse, but one thing that so many people have in common is a drive to succeed. Grades are competitive and students are driven to succeed, not only in school but also in internships."

FINANCIAL AID: 617-353-2965 • E-MAIL: ADMISSIONS@BU.EDU • WEBSITE: WWW.BU.EDU

THE PRINCETON REVIEW SAYS

Admissions

Very important factors considered include: Rigor of secondary school record. *Important factors considered include:* Academic GPA, application essay, class rank, recommendation(s), standardized test scores. *Other factors considered include:* Alumni/ae relation, character/personal qualities, extracurricular activities, first generation, geographical residence, level of applicant's interest, racial/ethnic status, state residency, volunteer work, work experience. SAT and two SAT Subject Tests required; ACT with writing component required. TOEFL required of all international applicants. High school diploma is required, and GED is accepted. *Academic units required:* 4 English, 3 mathematics, 3 science (3 science labs), 2 foreign language, 3 social studies. *Academic units recommended:* 4 English, 4 mathematics, 4 science (4 science labs), 4 foreign language, 4 social studies.

Financial Aid

Students should submit: FAFSA, CSS/Financial Aid PROFILE. Regular filing deadline is February 15. The Princeton Review suggests that all financial aid forms be submitted as soon as possible after January 1. *Need-based scholarships/grants offered:* Federal Pell, SEOG, state scholarships/grants, private scholarships, school scholarship or grant aid from institutional funds. *Loan aid offered:* Direct Subsidized Stafford, Direct Unsubsidized Stafford, Direct PLUS, Federal Perkins, state loans. Applicants will be notified of awards on a rolling basis beginning April 1. Federal Work-Study Program available. Off-campus job opportunities are excellent.

The Inside Word

At BU, your academic performance in high school is the single most important factor in an admissions decision. Competitive applicants are those who pursued the most challenging curriculum available at their school. Admissions requirements vary depending on the school or program to which you apply (though students are welcome to apply "undeclared"), so prospective students should check the school's website.

THE SCHOOL SAYS "..."

From the Admissions Office

"Boston University is a world-recognized, private teaching and research university committed to excellence in undergraduate education. Students study with distinguished faculty that include Fulbright Scholars, Pulitzer Prize winners, MacArthur Fellows, Nobel Prize winners, and a former Poet Laureate. In nine undergraduate schools and colleges, BU offers students more than 250 programs of study, cutting-edge research with faculty mentors, internships in the U.S. and abroad, and one of the nation's most extensive study abroad programs. Housing is guaranteed for four years in a variety of on-campus residences, including high-rise buildings and historic brownstones. BU students are engaged with their campus community through nearly 500 student organizations, club and intramural sports, and twenty-three NCAA Division I sports teams. Students experience the city of Boston as an extension of campus for study, internships, employment, and cultural and recreational activities.

BU requires freshman applicants to take the SAT and two SAT Subject Tests. Students may submit the results of the ACT (with writing) in lieu of the SAT and SAT Subject Tests. Students applying to the Accelerated Medical or Dental Programs are required to submit Subject Tests in chemistry, math (Level 2), and a foreign language (recommended). Candidates for the College of Fine Arts must present a portfolio or participate in an audition.

SELECTIVITY

Admissions Rating	95
# of applicants	38,275
% of applicants accepted	58
% of acceptees attending	20
# accepting a place on wait list	1,151
% admitted from wait list	1
# of early decision applicants	897
% accepted early decision	44

FRESHMAN PROFILE

Range SAT Critical Reading	580–670
Range SAT Math	600–700
Range SAT Writing	590–680
Range ACT Composite	26–30
Minimum paper TOEFL	550
Minimum computer TOEFL	215
Minimum web-based TOEFL	78
Average HS GPA	3.52
% graduated top 10% of class	57
% graduated top 25% of class	88
% graduated top 50% of class	99

DEADLINES

Early decision	
Deadline	11/1
Notification	12/15
Regular	
Deadline	1/1
Nonfall registration?	yes

APPLICANTS ALSO LOOK AT

AND OFTEN PREFER
New York University, The George Washington University, University of Southern California

AND SOMETIMES PREFER
Boston College, Cornell University, Northeastern University, Syracuse University, Tufts University

AND RARELY PREFER
Brown University, University of Massachusetts Amherst

FINANCIAL FACTS

Financial Aid Rating	86
Annual tuition	$39,314
Room and board	$12,260
Required fees	$550
Books and supplies	$940
% frosh rec. need-based scholarship or grant aid	46
% UG rec. need-based scholarship or grant aid	44
% frosh rec. non-need-based scholarship or grant aid	18
% UG rec. non-need-based scholarship or grant aid	11
% frosh rec. need-based self-help aid	44
% UG rec. need-based self-help aid	42
% frosh rec. any financial aid	69
% UG rec. any financial aid	66
% UG borrow to pay for school	54
Average cumulative indebtedness	$31,809

BOWDOIN COLLEGE

5000 COLLEGE STATION, BOWDOIN COLLEGE, BRUNSWICK, ME 04011-8441 • ADMISSIONS: 207-725-3100 • FAX: 207-725-3101

CAMPUS LIFE
Quality of Life Rating	99
Fire Safety Rating	94
Green Rating	96
Type of school	private
Environment	village

STUDENTS
Total undergrad enrollment	1,751
% male/female	50/50
% from out of state	88
% from public high school	58
% live on campus	93
% African American	5
% Asian	7
% Caucasian	65
% Hispanic	12
% international	3
# of countries represented	31

SURVEY SAYS . . .
School is well-run
Great food on campus
Dorms are like palaces
Frats and sororities are unpopular
or nonexistent

ACADEMICS
Academic Rating	99
% students graduating within 4 years	90
% students graduating within 6 years	93
Calendar	semester
Student/faculty ratio	9:1
Profs interesting rating	96
Profs accessible rating	97
Most common reg class size	10–19 students
Most common lab size	10–19 students

MOST POPULAR MAJORS
biology, economics, political science

STUDENTS SAY ". . ."

Academics
Bowdoin students lavish praise on their prestigious small school, celebrating the "range and rigor" of the academic programs, the beautiful Maine setting, and the "vibrant group of faculty and students." They even love the cafeteria food! A classic liberal arts school, the academic curriculum at Bowdoin is "very challenging, discussion-oriented, and [it] demands creativity from the students." Despite the school's small size, you'll find a "varied and interesting course selection" within its more than thirty-five major and minor programs. In addition, students "have the ability to self-design classes and majors" and to participate in "some of the best undergraduate research opportunities liberal arts schools have to offer." According to their adoring students, Bowdoin professors are "extremely intelligent, well-spoken, and effective teachers," who are also "very enthusiastic about their work and welcome students to chat or ask questions one-on-one." At Bowdoin, "Professors put their students first and always make time to meet, whether to talk about a paper, or for coffee, or both." "Academics are highly rigorous," and major programs are typified by "challenging courses with professors who expect a high level of work." Fortunately, the "environment is very laid-back," and students are usually "competitive with themselves but not competitive with others." A current senior adds, "Academically, Bowdoin is very challenging, but I've loved having to put in my best effort to do well. It's good to be challenged!" Throughout the faculty and administration, "student opinions are highly valued and sought out." The school's popular president "invests a significant amount of time in us, the students," and "The first-year deans…make it a point to meet with each first-year student one-on-one, preferably in the first semester."

Life
College life is incredibly comfortable for Bowdoin undergraduates. On this pretty Maine campus, "freshmen dorms are very luxurious," and "facilities are great, including new athletic fields and [a] new fitness center." Cafeteria food gets rave reviews, and the dining services department is "excellent about listening to student opinions and promoting sustainability." A senior admits, "I will probably never eat this well again in my life." While there aren't any fraternities and sororities at Bowdoin, "There are social houses, where many sophomores, juniors, and (some) seniors live. These former Greek houses put on multiple events each week, from themed parties with several kegs, to coffee houses, movies, and discussions with professors." "Work hard, play hard" is a popular mantra on campus, and "There are always multiple parties going on Thursday, Friday, and Saturday nights." Alternately, "Getting outside and exploring Maine is very popular with our outdoorsy student body." In surrounding Brunswick, students enjoy "amazing restaurants and coffee shops on and around Maine Street." In addition, "Portland is thirty minutes away and is a great city with lots of resources." Echoing the sentiments of many happy Bowdoin students, a satisfied sophomore tells us, "I wish I could stay in college forever."

Student Body
You'll meet a lot of "wealthy, athletic, New Englanders" at Bowdoin College. In fact, students joke, "Everyone seems to be from a small town right outside Boston." Those outside the dominant demographic admit that there seems to be "a divide between the typical New England kid and the 'diverse' kids, who come from other states are less well-off, or are racially diverse." However, "Students here work really hard to create a community that is open and accepting," and the majority of students have "no trouble fitting in." On that note, "Bowdoin students truly are nice. We often marvel at how there do not seem to be mean or unfriendly people here." Student athletes are common, and "around seventy percent of the campus is involved in some kind of sport," from intramurals to the outing club. Nonetheless, academics are top priority: "No matter if they are a theater kid or hockey player, everyone can be found in the library during the week." In addition to schoolwork, Bowdoin students are "always passionate about something, be it music, rock-climbing, or volunteer work."

BOWDOIN COLLEGE

FINANCIAL AID: 207-725-3273 • E-MAIL: ADMISSIONS@BOWDOIN.EDU • WEBSITE: WWW.BOWDOIN.EDU

THE PRINCETON REVIEW SAYS

Admissions

Very important factors considered include: Academic GPA, application essay, class rank, recommendation(s), rigor of secondary school record, character/personal qualities, extracurricular activities, talent/ability. *Important factors considered include:* Alumni/ae relation, first generation. *Other factors considered include:* Geographical residence, interview, racial/ethnic status, state residency. Standardized tests are optional. ACT with or without writing component accepted. TOEFL required of all international applicants. *Academic units recommended:* 4 English, 4 mathematics, 4 science (3 science labs), 4 foreign language, 4 social studies.

Financial Aid

Students should submit: FAFSA, CSS/Financial Aid PROFILE. Regular filing deadline is February 15. The Princeton Review suggests that all financial aid forms be submitted as soon as possible after January 1. *Need-based scholarships/grants offered:* Federal Pell, SEOG, state scholarships/grants, private scholarships, school scholarship or grant aid from institutional funds. *Loan aid offered:* Direct Subsidized Stafford, Direct Unsubsidized Stafford, Federal Perkins, state loans. Federal Work-Study Program available. Off-campus job opportunities are good.

The Inside Word

Many students feel instantly at home on the Bowdoin campus. A current freshman reports, "Bowdoin was a great fit for me on paper, and I fell in love with the campus and student body when I visited." A senior agrees, "I had visited over twenty colleges, and they all start to look the same academically, but Bowdoin stood out because of the people." During the admissions process, prospective students can schedule a tour and personal interview with admissions staff or a Bowdoin senior. If it's a fit, the school offers the option to apply early decision.

THE SCHOOL SAYS "..."

From the Admissions Office

"A Bowdoin education is best summed up by 'The Offer of the College':"

> To be at home in all lands and all ages;
> To count Nature a familiar acquaintance,
> And Art an intimate friend;
> To gain a standard for the appreciation of others' work
> And the criticism of your own;
> To carry the keys of the world's library in your pocket,
> And feel its resources behind you in whatever task you undertake;
> To make hosts of friends...
> Who are to be leaders in all walks of life;
> To lose yourself in generous enthusiasms
> And cooperate with others for common ends—
> This is the offer of the college for the best four years of your life."

Adapted from the original 'Offer of the College'
by William DeWitt Hyde
President of Bowdoin College 1885–1917"

SELECTIVITY

Admissions Rating	98
# of applicants	6,018
% of applicants accepted	20
% of acceptees attending	43
# of early decision applicants	740
% accepted early decision	31

FRESHMAN PROFILE

Range SAT Critical Reading	650–750
Range SAT Math	660–750
Range SAT Writing	660–750
Range ACT Composite	30–33
Minimum paper TOEFL	600
Minimum computer TOEFL	250
Minimum web-based TOEFL	100
Average HS GPA	3.80
% graduated top 10% of class	83
% graduated top 25% of class	97
% graduated top 50% of class	100

DEADLINES

Early decision	
Deadline	11/15
Notification	12/31
Regular	
Deadline	1/1
Notification	4/5
Nonfall registration?	no

APPLICANTS ALSO LOOK AT AND OFTEN PREFER
Harvard College, Princeton University, Yale University

AND SOMETIMES PREFER
Brown University, Dartmouth College, Williams College

AND RARELY PREFER
Amherst College, Middlebury College, Wesleyan University

FINANCIAL FACTS

Financial Aid Rating	97
Annual tuition	$41,150
Room and board	$11,315
Required fees	$415
Books and supplies	$820
% frosh rec. need-based scholarship or grant aid	47
% UG rec. need-based scholarship or grant aid	43
% frosh rec. non-need-based scholarship or grant aid	40
% UG rec. non-need-based scholarship or grant aid	40
% frosh rec. need-based self-help aid	35
% UG rec. need-based self-help aid	34
% frosh rec. any financial aid	44
% UG rec. any financial aid	47
% UG borrow to pay for school	43
Average cumulative indebtedness	$18,229

BRADLEY UNIVERSITY

1501 WEST BRADLEY AVENUE, PEORIA, IL 61625 • ADMISSIONS: 309-677-1000 • FAX: 309-677-2797

STUDENTS SAY ". . ."

Academics

"A medium-sized school with the personality of a large "state" Division I school" for many students, Bradley boasts the affordability of an in-state education with "the prestige and community" of a small-school atmosphere due to its "intimate class settings" and "devoted professors." Often noted for its "great nursing program," Bradley and its academic offerings are united by "passion, tradition, and a striving for consistent improvement and excellence." With a focus on providing students with "everything they need to be successful out in the 'real-world,'" Bradley is "great at making students feel welcome" while providing alums with "lessons to build upon for a lifetime." "Bradley is all about teaching the individual student" and "developing one's intellect for what comes next." Students are often drawn to Bradley for its "job placement, good facilities, diverse areas of study, student/teacher relationships, and class sizes." Professors are "very knowledgeable and have a vested interest in every student's learning." Many students champion the school's new president and administration for the scope of their vision as well as their renewed commitment to soliciting student opinion. President Glasser "makes an excellent role model for young women." She is "very in tune" and "makes [students] her number one priority."

Life

Life at Bradley provides "the resources of a large university with the familiarity that comes from a small liberal arts school." With a student body of approximately 5,000, "Bradley has a wide variety of students. If you need study partners we have those; if you want to party on Friday night, we have those students; if you want to stay in and watch a movie, we have plenty of those. You can easily find someone with the same interests." "Bradley is all about community." As one student says, Bradley provides a "'salad bowl' environment because people from all backgrounds generally get along." Due to "the variety of campus clubs, activities, and organizations," "everyone finds a niche." "Almost everyone on campus is associated with some sort of Greek organization or athletic team. Spending time with the group of friends that each person develops is the most common idea of fun." When it comes to facilities, though students remark that "the library needs to be updated with more and better computers," the recreation center is the "beauty of the campus" and "offers hundreds of activities to join." "The new Markin Fitness Center is very popular."

Student Body

When it comes to describing the typical Bradley student, one shoe doesn't fit all. Benefiting from its size and diversity, there's a "huge variety in student types at Bradley," including "some students from big city suburbs [and] some from small farm towns, with the income base varying greatly no matter where they came from." The "typical student is intelligent, but yet very sociable and easy to get along with," and "involved in at least one outside organization." Though variety seems to be the norm, others note, in general, "There are two types [of students]: The suburban type—usually from St. Louis or Chicago. This type is more trendy and into the latest fads and such. Then there is the small-town type. These tend to be very interesting people who are laid-back yet conservative."

BRADLEY UNIVERSITY

FINANCIAL AID: 309-677-3089 • E-MAIL: ADMISSIONS@BRADLEY.EDU • WEBSITE: WWW.BRADLEY.EDU

THE PRINCETON REVIEW SAYS
Admissions

Very important factors considered include: Academic GPA, rigor of secondary school record. *Important factors considered include:* Class rank, standardized test scores. *Other factors considered include:* Application essay, recommendation(s), alumni/ae relation, character/personal qualities, extracurricular activities, first generation, geographical residence, interview, level of applicant's interest, racial/ethnic status, talent/ability, volunteer work. SAT or ACT required; ACT with or without writing component accepted. TOEFL required of all international applicants. High school diploma is required, and GED is accepted. *Academic units required:* 4 English, 3 mathematics, 2 science (2 science labs), 2 social studies. *Academic units recommended:* 5 English, 4 mathematics, 3 science (3 science labs), 2 foreign language, 3 social studies, 2 history.

Financial Aid

Students should submit: FAFSA. The Princeton Review suggests that all financial aid forms be submitted as soon as possible after January 1. *Need-based scholarships/grants offered:* Federal Pell, SEOG, state scholarships/grants, private scholarships, school scholarship or grant aid from institutional funds. *Loan aid offered:* Direct Subsidized Stafford, Direct Unsubsidized Stafford, Direct PLUS, Federal Perkins, Federal Nursing Loans. Federal Work-Study Program available.

The Inside Word

With much regional appeal, the vast majority of students at Bradley originate from Illinois. With an active eye toward broadening the student body's geographic demographics, the school presents an opportunity for out-of-staters seeking to attend an excellent university without having to endure the grueling admissions process of many private universities. Above-average students should find that gaining admission here is a relatively painless experience.

THE SCHOOL SAYS "..."
From the Admissions Office

"Unlike many smaller private colleges, Bradley offers the academic variety of more than 100 undergraduate and thirty graduate programs of study. In addition to the traditional liberal arts and sciences, academic programs include business, communication, education, engineering, fine and performing arts, and health sciences. Unique programs include entrepreneurship, health science with a direct entry to the Doctorate of Physical Therapy, interactive media, and sports communication. "While Bradley offers the academic choices of a larger university, it also provides students the guidance and mentoring of faculty that only a smaller university can provide. Bradley classes average just twenty-three students.

"Beyond a great academic experience, students also choose Bradley for opportunities to be involved in a very active campus life. Bradley hosts more than 230 student organizations, including more than sixty dedicated to student leadership and community service.

"Integration of career development is central to the Bradley experience. One measurable outcome of this career development integration is that ninety-three percent of graduates begin work, graduate school, or other postgraduate experiences of their choice within six months of graduation.

"Located in a residential neighborhood on the west bluff of the Illinois River, the eighty-five-acre campus is just one mile from downtown Peoria. The city is a diverse community of more than 360,000 people. Both Chicago and St. Louis are less than a three-hour drive. The distinctive feel of Bradley comes from a blend of large school opportunities with the quality, personal attention, and challenge of a small, private college."

SELECTIVITY

Admissions Rating	80
# of applicants	6,343
% of applicants accepted	72
% of acceptees attending	25
# accepting a place on wait list	0

FRESHMAN PROFILE

Range SAT Critical Reading	480–630
Range SAT Math	490–640
Range ACT Composite	23–28
Minimum paper TOEFL	550
Minimum computer TOEFL	197
Average HS GPA	3.62
% graduated top 10% of class	29
% graduated top 25% of class	63
% graduated top 50% of class	92

DEADLINES

Regular	
Priority	3/1
Notification	10/1
Nonfall registration?	yes

APPLICANTS ALSO LOOK AT AND OFTEN PREFER
Purdue University—West Lafayette,
University of Illinois at Urbana-Champaign

AND SOMETIMES PREFER
Augustana College (IL), Butler University, DePaul University, Drake University, Illinois Wesleyan University, Loyola University of Chicago, Marquette University, Saint Louis University, University of Illinois at Chicago

AND RARELY PREFER
Illinois State University, Iowa State University, Northern Illinois University, University of Iowa, University of Missouri—Columbia

FINANCIAL FACTS

Financial Aid Rating	78
Annual tuition	$25,150
Room and board	$7,950
Books and supplies	$1,200
% frosh rec. need-based scholarship or grant aid	68
% UG rec. need-based scholarship or grant aid	70
% frosh rec. non-need-based scholarship or grant aid	9
% UG rec. non-need-based scholarship or grant aid	8
% frosh rec. need-based self-help aid	61
% UG rec. need-based self-help aid	56
% frosh rec. any financial aid	96
% UG rec. any financial aid	93
% UG borrow to pay for school	86
Average cumulative indebtedness	$17,859

BRANDEIS UNIVERSITY

415 SOUTH STREET, MS003, WALTHAM, MA 02454 • ADMISSIONS: 781-736-3500 • FAX: 781-736-3536

STUDENTS SAY ". . ."

Academics

"Strong academics and an activist spirit" imbue Brandeis University, where "quirk and politically and socially aware students actually [go] to classes they really have a desire to attend," because they care "about learning both inside and outside the classroom, about other people, and about the world around us." No touchy-feely granola institution, Brandeis is "a top research university" as well as "a strong liberal arts school," and its students are serious about the future: "If you're thinking about business, law, or medical school, you'll fit right in with the pack" here. Brandeis' independent undergrads love that the "curriculum is flexible and allows you to do what you want." One explains: "The core curriculum is only composed of eight categories, which makes it easy for students to jump into classes of their interest, rather than get tied up in general or required courses. Not to mention that those eight requirements are incredibly flexible: I took Intro to 3-D Animation last semester for my science requirement!" Brandeis' impressive academics "encourage [students] to think outside of the box and try new things," an approach that jibes with the "overall intellectual" environment created by students and faculty. Because "Brandeis is primarily an undergraduate institution," students don't feel that they need to compete with grad students for their professors' attention. "The fact that I can have such close contact on a daily basis with such incredibly talented individuals is something that occasionally astounds me," one undergrad writes.

Life

"There is definitely a strong campus life" at Brandeis, where "there is always something going on." Campus activity "is diverse. One Saturday you might go to a party and then the next day you might play a board game with your friends until three in the morning; or a concert one night and an art history lecture the next night." As one student puts it, "There are people who go out and party hard all week, [and] there are people who stay in on weekend nights to do work. The truth is Brandeis is a place where just about anyone can find someone like them." Students place a premium on creativity; fortunately, "there is always something creative to do." Undergrads "ice skate, dance, sing in an a cappella group, perform in a play, play a club or intramural sport, work on campus, have an internship off campus," or simply hang out in the campus coffeehouse located in "a replica of a Scottish castle." The Brandeis Shuttle allows students to "go into Boston on the weekends…the average student makes it to Boston once or twice a month" in order to "see a movie, have a meal, go to a museum or Quincy Market, [and] go to bars or clubs (only if you're over twenty-one…Boston is strict)." Hometown Waltham isn't half bad either; we're told that "the food is great and there's a movie theater, bars, and Lizzy's Ice Cream" nearby.

Student Body

"There is no 'typical student' except that generally people are driven and creative," Brandeis undergrads tell us. Most here "are passionate about something and have many interests, though those interests are varied." Students tend to be "involved in a variety of activities" that include "community service or a peace group of some sort." Most are "probably double-majoring;" are "into dance, singing, or a musical band of some sort;" and have "frequent contact with leaders, administrators, and faculty." They're also likely to be "quirky… the reason they come to Brandeis is because they're drawn to these qualities… What other university would host a silent dance in their Campus Center where everyone's listening to their own iPod?" As one student sums up, "The typical student is studious, liberal, and passionate. Also Jewish. But not *everyone* is Jewish. There are atypical students, but the great thing about Brandeis is that we don't care if you're different. If you're a good person who has something interesting to offer, [someone] will be your friend."

BRANDEIS UNIVERSITY

FINANCIAL AID: 781-736-3700 • E-MAIL: ADMISSIONS@BRANDEIS.EDU • WEBSITE: WWW.BRANDEIS.EDU

THE PRINCETON REVIEW SAYS
Admissions
Very important factors considered include: Academic GPA, class rank, rigor of secondary school record, standardized test scores, character/personal qualities. *Important factors considered include:* Application essay, recommendation(s), extracurricular activities, level of applicant's interest, talent/ability, volunteer work, work experience. *Other factors considered include:* Alumni/ae relation, first generation, geographical residence, interview, racial/ethnic status. SAT or ACT required; ACT with writing component required. TOEFL required of all international applicants. High school diploma is required, and GED is accepted. *Academic units recommended:* 4 English, 4 mathematics, 4 science (2 science labs), 4 foreign language, 4 social studies.

Financial Aid
Students should submit: CSS/Financial Aid PROFILE. Regular filing deadline is February 1. The Princeton Review suggests that all financial aid forms be submitted as soon as possible after January 1. *Need-based scholarships/grants offered:* Federal Pell, SEOG, state scholarships/grants, private scholarships, school scholarship or grant aid from institutional funds. *Loan aid offered:* Direct Subsidized Stafford, Direct Unsubsidized Stafford, Direct PLUS, Federal Perkins, state loans, university loans from institutional funds. Federal Work-Study Program available.

The Inside Word
Brandeis used to be considered the "safety school" for kids who hoped to gain admission to at least one of the Ivies. That was back when Brandeis was accepting three-quarters of its applicants, but those days are long gone. Admissions standards have risen at all top schools, and Brandeis is no exception: If you expect to get in here, you've got your work cut out for you. Your application should give evidence of both the ability and enthusiasm to handle demanding academics. A clear demonstration of writing ability will also help a lot.

THE SCHOOL SAYS "..."
From the Admissions Office
"Education at Brandeis is personal, combining the intimacy of a small liberal arts college and the intellectual power of a large research university. Classes are small and are taught by professors, ninety-eight percent of whom hold the highest degree in their fields. They give students personal attention in state-of-the-art resources, giving them the tools to succeed in a variety of postgraduate endeavors.

"This vibrant, free-thinking, intellectual university was founded in 1948. Brandeis University reflects the values of the first Jewish Supreme Court Justice Louis Brandeis, which are passion for learning, commitment to social justice, respect for creativity and diversity, and concern for the world.

"Brandeis has an ideal location on the commuter rail nine miles west of Boston; state-of-the-art sports facilities; and internships that complement interests in law, medicine, government, finance, business, and the arts.

"Brandeis meets 100 percent of demonstrated need for all admitted students."

SELECTIVITY
Admissions Rating	98
# of applicants	7,753
% of applicants accepted	35
% of acceptees attending	25
# accepting a place on wait list	469
% admitted from wait list	38
# of early decision applicants	411
% accepted early decision	48

FRESHMAN PROFILE
Range SAT Critical Reading	630–730
Range SAT Math	640–730
Range SAT Writing	640–730
Range ACT Composite	28–32
Minimum paper TOEFL	600
Minimum computer TOEFL	250
Minimum web-based TOEFL	100
Average HS GPA	3.77
% graduated top 10% of class	84
% graduated top 25% of class	97
% graduated top 50% of class	100

DEADLINES
Early decision	
Deadline	11/15
Notification	12/15
Regular	
Deadline	1/15
Nonfall registration?	yes

FINANCIAL FACTS
Financial Aid Rating	82
Annual tuition	$38,994
Room and board	$11,214
Required fees	$1,280
Books and supplies	$1,000
% frosh rec. need-based scholarship or grant aid	57
% UG rec. need-based scholarship or grant aid	45
% frosh rec. non-need-based scholarship or grant aid	6
% UG rec. non-need-based scholarship or grant aid	3
% frosh rec. need-based self-help aid	51
% UG rec. need-based self-help aid	41
% frosh rec. any financial aid	55
% UG rec. any financial aid	58
% UG borrow to pay for school	70
Average cumulative indebtedness	$21,351

BRIGHAM YOUNG UNIVERSITY (UT)

A-153 ASB, PROVO, UT 84602-1110 • ADMISSIONS: 801-422-2507 • FAX: 801-422-0005

CAMPUS LIFE

Quality of Life Rating	94
Fire Safety Rating	67
Green Rating	60*
Type of school	private
Affiliation	The Church of Jesus Christ of Latter-day Saints
Environment	city

STUDENTS

Total undergrad enrollment	30,409
% male/female	51/49
% from out of state	67
% live on campus	19
% African American	<1
% Asian	6
% Caucasian	87
% Hispanic	5
% Native American	<1
% international	6
# of countries represented	121

SURVEY SAYS . . .

Students are very religious
Musical organizations are popular
Very little beer drinking
Very little hard liquor
Very little drug use

ACADEMICS

Academic Rating	81
% students graduating within 4 years	31
% students graduating within 6 years	78
Calendar	semester
Student/faculty ratio	21:1
Profs interesting rating	85
Profs accessible rating	77
Most common reg class size	20–29 students

MOST POPULAR MAJORS

business/commerce, elementary education and teaching, exercise physiology

STUDENTS SAY ". . ."

Academics

Brigham Young University is a Mormon school that's "all about putting religion and education together" and learning "about secular subjects through spiritual eyes." The school provides a "high-quality" education in a "challenging" academic atmosphere. Students at Brigham Young strive for academic excellence. As one student explains, "Brigham Young pushes us to realize that our 'best' can be a lot better than we ever dreamed, and I love that!" The school offers a wide range of majors, and its education, business, and mathematics programs get great reviews, as does their language program. Classes are generally a "healthy mix of discussion and lecture," and the education classes in particular have "a lot of group work." The school doesn't focus only on classroom learning, however. "Hands-on experience, internships, and study abroad are highly encouraged," and many students take advantage of these opportunities. There are also "tons of undergraduate research opportunities." Professors are "passionate about what they're teaching," and they "really care about their students' success." Another adds, "Professors really do take a genuine interest in their students," and "The vast majority are also very willing to help out students individually." While students at Brigham Young appreciate the academic attention they receive from professors, they also like that it "is committed to spiritual and academic learning for the benefit and betterment of everyone" and that they're being taught to "pursue lifelong learning and service."

Life

Students at Brigham Young love the "atmosphere of spirituality that unites everyone" and "the kindness of those around you." Brigham Young provides a "safe environment," but students "still get to have real-world experiences." Recreationally, "There are multiple clubs across campus to fit the taste of different people," "tons of…performing events," and "fun student body activities, which are cheap." There are also "exceptional weekly devotions and forums." Brigham Young's athletics are well-supported and are a place where "students love to have fun." Students rave about the library and the "Adlab," but more than anything they appreciate that there are "good people everywhere you go."

Student Body

Brigham Young has an extremely conservative "Honor Code" derived from the Mormon Church that requires, among other things, abstinence from drugs, alcohol, tobacco, and caffeine, as well as "inappropriate" "sexual activity, including sex outside of marriage and homosexuality." The Honor Code is a plus for students seeking a like-minded peer group, such as this art education student who "didn't want to have to worry about walking in on my roommate sleeping with someone or have to hold her head up while she was puking her guts out into the toilet." The Honor Code also demands honesty and respect for others, which means the student body is "friendly, outgoing," and "concerned for others." Students are "smart and very confident in their intelligence," as well as "hardworking" and "goal-oriented." Mormon traditions mean that many students are married, and people appreciate that "the school caters…really well to the average Latter-day Saint student coming in and working with those wanting to get married [or] go on missions." Marriage is definitely on many people's minds. A family studies major notes, "We are constantly encouraged to date." People generally think that "students mesh together well and it is easy to make new friends," though one concedes, "I can see how it could be hard to fit in if you are not used to the Mormon culture or beliefs."

BRIGHAM YOUNG UNIVERSITY (UT)

FINANCIAL AID: 801-422-4104 • E-MAIL: ADMISSIONS@BYU.EDU • WEBSITE: WWW.BYU.EDU

THE PRINCETON REVIEW SAYS

Admissions

Very important factors considered include: Academic GPA, rigor of secondary school record, standardized test scores, character/personal qualities, interview, religious affiliation/commitment. *Important factors considered include:* Application essay, recommendation(s), extracurricular activities, racial/ethnic status, volunteer work. *Other factors considered include:* First generation, geographical residence, level of applicant's interest, state residency, talent/ability, work experience. ACT with writing component recommended. TOEFL required of all international applicants. *Academic units recommended:* 4 English, 4 mathematics, 2 science (2 science labs), 2 foreign language, 2 history.

Financial Aid

Students should submit: FAFSA. Regular filing deadline is February 15. The Princeton Review suggests that all financial aid forms be submitted as soon as possible after January 1. *Need-based scholarships/grants offered:* Federal Pell, private scholarships, school scholarship or grant aid from institutional funds. *Loan aid offered:* Direct Subsidized Stafford, Direct Unsubsidized Stafford, Direct PLUS. Applicants will be notified of awards on a rolling basis beginning April 1.

The Inside Word

An applicant pool of more than 10,000 necessitates a reliance on numbers, especially during the first round of cuts. Much of the matchmaking done at other schools isn't necessary here, as a highly self-selecting applicant pool typically precludes those who would make a poor fit. Still, admissions officers want to see at least respect (if not reverence) for LDS principles, without which survival here would be difficult indeed.

THE SCHOOL SAYS "..."

From the Admissions Office

"The mission of Brigham Young University—founded, supported, and guided by The Church of Jesus Christ of Latter-day Saints—is to assist individuals in their quest for perfection and eternal life. That assistance should provide a period of intensive learning in a stimulating setting where a commitment to excellence is expected and the full realization of human potential is pursued. All instruction, programs, and services at BYU, including a wide variety of extracurricular experiences, should make their own contribution toward the balanced development of the total person. Such a broadly prepared individual will not only be capable of meeting personal challenge and change but will also bring strength to others in the tasks of home and family life, social relationships, civic duty, and service to mankind.

"Freshman applicants are required to take either the ACT (with the optional writing section) or the SAT. The highest composite score will be used in admissions decisions."

SELECTIVITY

Admissions Rating	93
# of applicants	10,913
% of applicants accepted	64
% of acceptees attending	75

FRESHMAN PROFILE

Range SAT Critical Reading	570–680
Range SAT Math	580–690
Range ACT Composite	26–30
Minimum paper TOEFL	500
Minimum computer TOEFL	173
Average HS GPA	3.77
% graduated top 10% of class	52
% graduated top 25% of class	84
% graduated top 50% of class	98

DEADLINES

Regular	
Priority	12/1
Deadline	2/1
Nonfall registration?	yes

APPLICANTS ALSO LOOK AT AND SOMETIMES PREFER
University of Utah

FINANCIAL FACTS

Financial Aid Rating	69
Annual tuition	$4,560
Room and board	$7,120
Books and supplies	$900
% frosh rec. need-based scholarship or grant aid	13
% UG rec. need-based scholarship or grant aid	33
% frosh rec. non-need-based scholarship or grant aid	19
% UG rec. non-need-based scholarship or grant aid	18
% frosh rec. need-based self-help aid	8
% UG rec. need-based self-help aid	15
% frosh rec. any financial aid	53
% UG rec. any financial aid	64
% UG borrow to pay for school	31
Average cumulative indebtedness	$13,354

BROWN UNIVERSITY

PO Box 1876, 45 PROSPECT STREET, PROVIDENCE, RI 02912 • ADMISSIONS: 401-863-2378 • FAX: 401-863-9300

CAMPUS LIFE

Quality of Life Rating	98
Fire Safety Rating	79
Green Rating	92
Type of school	private
Environment	city

STUDENTS

Total undergrad enrollment	6,318
% male/female	48/52
% from out of state	96
% from public high school	56
% live on campus	79
# of fraternities	8
# of sororities	2
% African American	10
% Asian	15
% Caucasian	44
% Hispanic	9
% Native American	1
% international	10
# of countries represented	110

SURVEY SAYS . . .
No one cheats
Students are friendly
Great off-campus food
Students are happy
College radio is popular
Student publications are popular
Political activism is popular

ACADEMICS

Academic Rating	95
% students graduating within 4 years	86
% students graduating within 6 years	96
Calendar	semester
Student/faculty ratio	9:1
Profs interesting rating	88
Profs accessible rating	89
Most common reg class size	10–19 students

MOST POPULAR MAJORS
biology, economics, international relations

STUDENTS SAY ". . ."

Academics

Known for its somewhat unconventional (but still highly regarded) approaches to life and learning, Brown University remains the slightly odd man out of the Ivy League, and the school wouldn't have it any other way. The school's willingness to employ and support different, methods such as the shopping period, the first two weeks of the semester where anyone can drop into any class to "find out if it's something they're interested in enrolling in," or the *Critical Review*, a student publication that produces reviews of courses based on evaluations from students who have completed the course, is designed to treat students "like an adult" through "freedom and choice." This open-minded environment allows them "to practice passion without shame or fear of judgment," the hallmark of a Brown education. Even if students do find themselves exploring the wrong off-the-beaten path, "There are multitudes of built-in support measures to help you succeed despite any odds." Even grades are a non-issue here, "except amongst paranoid premeds."

Professors are mostly hits with a few misses, but there are "amazing professors in every department, and they're not hard to find"; it's just "up to students to find the teaching styles that work for them." "Academics at Brown are what you make of them," and even though students are diligent in their academic pursuits and feel assured they're "getting a wonderful education with the professors," most agree that their education is "really more about the unique student body and learning through active participation in other activities." The administration gets cautiously decent reviews for their accessibility and general running of the school, but it also gets scolded for getting "distracted by the long term." The president, however, is absolutely loved by students for being "an incredible person with a great vision for the school."

Life

Thinking—yes, thinking—and discussing take up a great deal of time at Brown. "People think about life, politics, society at large, global affairs, the state of the economy, developing countries, animals, plants, rocket science, math, poker, each other, sex, sexuality, the human experience, gender studies, what to do with our lives, etc.," says a senior anthropology major. "Most people here don't go home that often," and like any school, "There are people who go out five nights a week and people who go out five nights a semester." "Alcohol and weed are pretty embedded in campus life," and most parties are dorm room events, even though partying "never gets in the way of academics or friendship. If you don't drink/smoke, that's totally cool." There's also plenty of cultural activities, such as indie bands, student performances, jazz, swing dancing, and speakers. Themed housing (art house, tech house, interfaith house) and co-ops are also popular social mediators.

Student Body

It's a pretty unique crowd here, where "athletes, preps, nerds, and everyone in between come together" because they "love learning for the sake of learning, and [they] love Brown equally as much." "The 'mainstream' is full of people who are atypical in sense of fashion, taste in music, and academic interests," says a junior. Unsurprisingly, everyone here's "very smart," as well as "very quirky and often funny," and "a great amount are brilliant and passionate about their interests;" "most have interesting stories to tell." People here are "curious and open about many things," which is perhaps why sexual diversity is a "strong theme" among Brown interactions and events. The overall culture "is pretty laid-back and casual," and "most of the students are friendly and mesh well with everyone."

BROWN UNIVERSITY

FINANCIAL AID: 401-863-2721 • E-MAIL: ADMISSION_UNDERGRADUATE@BROWN.EDU • WEBSITE: WWW.BROWN.EDU

THE PRINCETON REVIEW SAYS

Admissions

Very important factors considered include: Rigor of secondary school record, character/personal qualities, level of applicant's interest, talent/ability. *Important factors considered include:* Academic GPA, application essay, class rank, recommendation(s), standardized test scores, extracurricular activities. *Other factors considered include:* Alumni/ae relation, first generation, geographical residence, interview, racial/ethnic status, state residency, volunteer work, work experience. ACT with writing component required. TOEFL required of all international applicants. *Academic units required:* 4 English, 3 mathematics, 3 science (2 science labs), 3 foreign language, 2 history, 1 academic elective. *Academic units recommended:* 4 English, 4 mathematics, 4 science (3 science labs), 4 foreign language, 2 history, 1 visual/performing arts, 1 academic elective.

Financial Aid

Students should submit: FAFSA, CSS/Financial Aid PROFILE. Regular filing deadline is February 1. The Princeton Review suggests that all financial aid forms be submitted as soon as possible after January 1. *Need-based scholarships/grants offered:* Federal Pell, SEOG, state scholarships/grants, private scholarships, school scholarship or grant aid from institutional funds. *Loan aid offered:* Direct Subsidized Stafford, Direct Unsubsidized Stafford, Direct PLUS, Federal Perkins, university loans from institutional funds. Federal Work-Study Program available. Off-campus job opportunities are excellent.

The Inside Word

The cream of just about every crop applies to Brown. Gaining admission requires more than just a superior academic profile from high school. Some candidates, such as the sons and daughters of Brown graduates (who are admitted at virtually double the usual acceptance rate), have a better chance for admission than most others. Minority students benefit from some courtship, particularly once admitted. Ivies like to share the wealth and distribute offers of admission across a wide range of constituencies. Candidates from states that are overrepresented in the applicant pool, such as New York, have to be particularly distinguished in order to have the best chance at admission. So do those who attend high schools with many seniors applying to Brown, as it is rare for several students from any one school to be offered admission.

THE SCHOOL SAYS "..."

From the Admissions Office

"Founded in 1764, Brown is a private, coeducational, Ivy League university in which the intellectual development of undergraduate students is fostered by a dedicated faculty on a traditional New England campus.

"Applicants will be required to submit results of the SAT Reasoning Test and any two SAT Subject Tests (except for the SAT Subject Test Writing). Students may substitute any SAT tests with the ACT with the writing component."

SELECTIVITY
Admissions Rating	98
# of applicants	30,946
% of applicants accepted	9
% of acceptees attending	53
# accepting a place on wait list	600
% admitted from wait list	5
# of early decision applicants	2,803
% accepted early decision	22

FRESHMAN PROFILE
Range SAT Critical Reading	660–760
Range SAT Math	670–770
Range SAT Writing	670–770
Range ACT Composite	29–33
Minimum paper TOEFL	600
Minimum computer TOEFL	250
Minimum web-based TOEFL	100
% graduated top 10% of class	93
% graduated top 25% of class	99
% graduated top 50% of class	100

DEADLINES
Early decision	
Deadline	11/1
Notification	12/15
Regular	
Deadline	1/1
Nonfall registration?	no

APPLICANTS ALSO LOOK AT AND OFTEN PREFER
Harvard College, Princeton University, Stanford University, Yale University

FINANCIAL FACTS
Financial Aid Rating	93
Annual tuition	$39,928
Room and board	$11,432
% frosh rec. need-based scholarship or grant aid	48
% UG rec. need-based scholarship or grant aid	40
% frosh rec. need-based self-help aid	39
% UG rec. need-based self-help aid	40
% frosh rec. any financial aid	49
% UG rec. any financial aid	46
Average cumulative indebtedness	$20,836

BRYANT UNIVERSITY

1150 DOUGLAS PIKE, SMITHFIELD, RI 02917 • ADMISSIONS: 401-232-6100 • FAX: 401-232-6741

CAMPUS LIFE

Quality of Life Rating	77
Fire Safety Rating	89
Green Rating	76
Type of school	private
Environment	village

STUDENTS

Total undergrad enrollment	3,332
% male/female	59/41
% from out of state	85
% live on campus	82
# of fraternities	6
# of sororities	3
% African American	4
% Asian	3
% Caucasian	80
% Hispanic	4
% international	6
# of countries represented	61

SURVEY SAYS . . .

Great computer facilities
Great library
Athletic facilities are great
Career services are great
School is well-run
Campus feels safe
Lots of beer drinking
Hard liquor is popular

ACADEMICS

Academic Rating	78
% students graduating within 4 years	72
% students graduating within 6 years	76
Calendar	semester
Student/faculty ratio	16:1
Profs interesting rating	79
Profs accessible rating	84
Most common reg class size	30–39 students
Most common lab size	fewer than 10 students

MOST POPULAR MAJORS

accounting, international business, speech, communication

STUDENTS SAY ". . ."

Academics

Bryant University's College of Business is "regarded as one of the best business schools not only in Rhode Island but in the country." The university is "all about real-world application" and "is a technologically advanced school that prepares you in every way for a competitive job market and/or competitive graduate schools." "The career center here is also phenomenal and well-renowned" and the school has a high rate of job placement for graduates. Although business is the focus—"Business. Business. Business," as one student puts it—"students receive a great liberal art education as well." Most students praise the classes at Bryant, whose small "sizes allow for a high level of inter-action between students and professors, as well as students and other students." Students tend to rate the faculty highly, although some students are lukewarm in their assessment. "There are some professors who have engaged me to learn far more than I expected to, however there are some 400-level classes where professors have challenged me less than 200-level classes I have taken." Many students note the ease and importance of networking on campus. "It is extremely easy to network with professors and alumni because everyone is really involved." One student sums Bryant University up as "the right mix of Division I athletics, academics, friendly students, and beautiful campus."

Life

Located "close to Providence," Bryant has a small "picturesque campus" where "there are always people around who want to have fun whether it's drinking their faces off or going to some student programming event. Those two activities are really the main things for fun on campus." Some students agree with this assessment: "Friday and Saturday nights are meant for party-ing, Sunday it's back to work. People study hard, but don't stress too much and can take a step back and relax." The student body tends to be active in athletics and clubs, with most students being "involved in at least one club or activity on campus, and typically students (especially business students) are extremely focused on obtaining full-time employment and internship opportu-nities." When it comes to improvements, students feel the school could use "healthier food options" and "additional dining halls."

Student Body

Bryant's student body comes "generally from the New England/New York/New Jersey area, however it is not out of the ordinary to find others from different states and countries." The school was recently made a Division I athletic school, so "there are many athletes on campus, either varsity or club/intramurals. Everyone stays in shape and is very active." The student body is "financially well-off" with a preppy style, often involving "North Face and Ugg boots," dominating campus. Although some students note the student population "lacks diversity" and the school is "socially still catching up," many students claim "a strong sense of community, and most students know each other, and everyone is really friendly." "I wanted a small school with students that are open-minded and kind," one student explains. "When I visited [campus] everyone met this expectation, and since attending I still feel this is true." Although, another student suggests Bryant is "filled with students who are only concerned about getting ahead in life by securing a high-paying job." "Students fit in by joining groups with similar interests and by being involved," and "there are definitely a lot of cliques." However, one student claims that no matter what you do, "it is hard to not fit in."

BRYANT UNIVERSITY

FINANCIAL AID: 401-232-6020 • E-MAIL: ADMISSION@BRYANT.EDU • WEBSITE: ADMISSION.BRYANT.EDU

THE PRINCETON REVIEW SAYS

Admissions

Very important factors considered include: Academic GPA, rigor of secondary school record. *Important factors considered include:* Application essay, class rank, recommendation(s), standardized test scores. *Other factors considered include:* Alumni/ae relation, character/personal qualities, extracurricular activities, first generation, geographical residence, interview, level of applicant's interest, racial/ethnic status, state residency, talent/ability, volunteer work, work experience. SAT or ACT required; ACT with or without writing component accepted. TOEFL required of all international applicants. High school diploma is required, and GED is accepted. *Academic units required:* 4 English, 4 mathematics, 2 science (2 science labs), 2 foreign language, 2 history. *Academic units recommended:* 4 English, 4 mathematics, 3 science (2 science labs), 2 foreign language, 3 history.

Financial Aid

Students should submit: FAFSA. Regular filing deadline is February 15. The Princeton Review suggests that all financial aid forms be submitted as soon as possible after January 1. *Need-based scholarships/grants offered:* Federal Pell, SEOG, state scholarships/grants, private scholarships, school scholarship or grant, aid from institutional funds. *Loan aid offered:* Direct Subsidized Stafford, Direct Unsubsidized Stafford, Direct PLUS, Federal Perkins. Federal Work-Study Program available. Off-campus job opportunities are fair.

The Inside Word

Bryant University touts its ability to "shatter the thinking" that liberal arts and business are incompatible. Prospective students who want to learn about business without sacrificing a strong education in other fields will want to put Bryant on their list. The university boasts a whopping ninety-six percent job-placement rate, which is no small thing in this economy.

THE SCHOOL SAYS "..."

From the Admissions Office

"Founded in 1863, Bryant University empowers students to realize their personal best in life and their chosen professions. Bryant is the one university that is driving a paradigm shift in undergraduate education by shattering the thinking that liberal arts and business are separate paths. The University's innovative real-world curriculum is made more profound by an unwavering focus on character and ethics.

"The College of Arts and Sciences offers degrees in applied economics, actuarial mathematics, applied mathematics and statistics, applied psychology, biology, Chinese, communication, environmental science, global studies, history, literary and cultural studies, politics and law, sociology, and Spanish. The College of Business offers a degree in business administration with concentrations in accounting, computer information systems, entrepreneurship, finance, financial services, management, and marketing; a degree in information technology; and an international business degree with concentrations in computer information systems, finance, management, and marketing.

"Bryant's academic programs are accredited by the New England Association of Schools and Colleges. The College of Business is accredited by AACSB International—The Association to Advance Collegiate Schools of Business, a distinction earned by only five percent of universities. In addition, Bryant's International Business degree program is a member of CUIBE—The Consortium for Undergraduate International Business Education.

"Bryant has internships and recruiting partnerships with 350 companies; nearly 100 student clubs and organizations; Northeast Conference NCAA Division I, intramural, and club sports; and service learning and leadership development programs. Qualified students can study abroad for a semester, a summer, or an academic year in one of forty-five countries.

"Bryant is on a beautiful 428-acre campus in Smithfield, Rhode Island, and is fifteen minutes away from the state capital, Providence; forty-five minutes from Boston; and three hours from New York City."

SELECTIVITY
Admissions Rating	87
# of applicants	5,050
% of applicants accepted	69
% of acceptees attending	24
# accepting a place on wait list	197
% admitted from wait list	25
# of early decision applicants	231
% accepted early decision	73

FRESHMAN PROFILE
Range SAT Critical Reading	500–590
Range SAT Math	540–630
Range SAT Writing	510–590
Range ACT Composite	22–26
Minimum paper TOEFL	550
Minimum computer TOEFL	213
Minimum web-based TOEFL	80
Average HS GPA	3.34
% graduated top 10% of class	23
% graduated top 25% of class	57
% graduated top 50% of class	92

DEADLINES
Early decision	
Deadline	11/15
Notification	1/7
Early action	
Deadline	12/1
Notification	1/15
Regular	
Deadline	2/1
Nonfall registration?	yes

APPLICANTS ALSO LOOK AT AND OFTEN PREFER
Babson College, Bentley College, Boston University, Northeastern University

AND SOMETIMES PREFER
Fairfield University, Providence College, Stonehill College, University of Connecticut, University of Massachusetts Amherst

AND RARELY PREFER
Quinnipiac University, Roger Williams University, University of New Hampshire, University of Rhode Island

FINANCIAL FACTS
Financial Aid Rating	75
Annual tuition	$34,288
Room and board	$12,829
Required fees	$336
Books and supplies	$1,300
% frosh rec. need-based scholarship or grant aid	54
% UG rec. need-based scholarship or grant aid	57
% frosh rec. non-need-based scholarship or grant aid	30
% UG rec. non-need-based scholarship or grant aid	25
% frosh rec. need-based self-help aid	57
% UG rec. need-based self-help aid	61
% frosh rec. any financial aid	66
% UG rec. any financial aid	68
Average cumulative indebtedness	$39,490

BRYN MAWR COLLEGE

101 NORTH MERION AVENUE, BRYN MAWR, PA 19010-2859 • ADMISSIONS: 610-526-5152 • FAX: 610-526-7471

STUDENTS SAY ". . ."

Academics

Bryn Mawr is all about "empowering women to achieve their dreams." The school has a "reputation for strong academics," and students confirm that work there's "no joke." Bryn Mawr is a small college, which means there's not "a huge variety of classes," but it also means that classes are small. One student reports that most of hers have "around ten people," and another says her largest lecture class had forty students. This leads to "deep discussions [and] meaningful relationships [being] formed with peers and colleagues." Classes are "very interactive," and "great student-teacher relationships [are] established by the way classes are conducted." The faculty is "amazing and no doubt brilliant," and "They go a long way to make sure you don't only feel like students but also like a mini-family." An East Asian studies student says she feels "comfortable talking to faculty members/professors about anything." Students think one of the best parts about Bryn Mawr is the "amazing academic opportunities within the tri-co," the system that lets them take classes at Haverford and University of Pennsylvania. All of these great attributes combine to make Bryn Mawr a fantastic college experience. As one student puts it, Bryn Mawr "compels me to be extraordinary in an environment of equally extraordinary students."

Life

Academics are the focus of life at Bryn Mawr, but that doesn't mean students are "a bunch of nuns who sit around studying all day." "We do a lot of studying," a student explains, "but we also enjoy our time here." Not only are there "tons of school-sponsored activities," but there are opportunities to "go to a big party with tons of dancing and tons of people," at Bryn Mawr or at Haverford. "Meals here are really important," adds a student. "Dinner can be the only time we'll see each other, [which] can easily go on for an hour and a half." Bryn Mawr's "amazing food" probably has something to do with that. Bryn Mawr has an "absolutely beautiful campus," with great facilities, including a new gym with an "Olympic-sized swimming pool…TVs, large windows…and state-of-the-art machines that are built for women." Though Bryn Mawr has a suburban location, "The proximity and ease in traveling to Philadelphia, New York, and Washington, D.C. is beyond fantastic." Students love Bryn Mawr's traditions, two of which are the Self-Government Association and the Honor Code. The Self-Government Association, the oldest student government in America, "allows…students to have an input on many aspects of how the college is run." The Honor Code, which every student must sign, emphasizes respect and integrity. The code creates "a strong community" and a safe one. One student says, "I don't lock my door!" Another adds, "You could lose a ring anywhere on campus and just send an e-mail out to the student body and have it back in the next few hours."

Student Body

"There is no typical student," at Bryn Mawr, "aside from women with a passion for learning and a commitment to excellence." A German student reports, "The variety of people here is enormous," and this "creates the…uniqueness that Bryn Mawr prides itself on." People's thoughts on racial diversity, however, "are kind of conflicting." One student explains, "Coming from a big city…Bryn Mawr did not seem very diverse, but my roommate came from a very small town and thought Bryn Mawr was extremely diverse." What students do agree on is that they're "friendly and welcoming," "creative," and "a little quirky." Though the intense workload means students are "very interested in… academics and work hard to get good grades," they "are also social" and "take time to build up strong friendships with other students." Students at Bryn Mawr really respect each other's individuality and love that their peers "have a purposive direction in regards to what they want to do with their future."

BRYN MAWR COLLEGE

FINANCIAL AID: 610-526-5245 • E-MAIL: ADMISSIONS@BRYNMAWR.EDU • WEBSITE: WWW.BRYNMAWR.EDU

THE PRINCETON REVIEW SAYS

Admissions

Very important factors considered include: Recommendation(s), rigor of secondary school record. *Important factors considered include:* Academic GPA, application essay, character/personal qualities, extracurricular activities. *Other factors considered include:* Class rank, standardized test scores, alumni/ae relation, first generation, geographical residence, interview, racial/ethnic status, talent/ability, volunteer work, work experience. ACT with or without writing component accepted. TOEFL or IELTS is required of students for whom English is a second language, and whose primary language of instruction hasn't been English. High school diploma is required, and GED is accepted. *Academic units recommended:* 4 English, 4 mathematics, 3 science (1 science lab), 3 foreign language, 2 social studies, 2 history, 2 academic elective.

Financial Aid

Students should submit: FAFSA, CSS/Financial Aid PROFILE. Regular filing deadline is March 1. The Princeton Review suggests that all financial aid forms be submitted as soon as possible after January 1. *Need-based scholarships/grants offered:* Federal Pell, SEOG, state scholarships/grants, school scholarship or grant aid from institutional funds. *Loan aid offered:* Direct Subsidized Stafford, Direct Unsubsidized Stafford, Direct PLUS, Federal Perkins. Federal Work-Study Program available. Off-campus job opportunities are available.

The Inside Word

Bryn Mawr's student body is among the academically best in the nation. Outstanding preparation for graduate study draws an applicant pool that's well-prepared and intellectually curious. Interviews are strongly recommended but not required. If you're still unsure of how to stand out in the crowd, the school offers a service where you can e-mail current students your questions, so take advantage of that to make sure that the school is right for you.

THE SCHOOL SAYS "..."

From the Admissions Office

"Bryn Mawr's extraordinary academics, vibrant and diverse community, and focus on global leadership prepare students to challenge convention and take their places in the world. Every year 1,300 women from around the world gather on the college's historic campus to study with leading scholars, conduct advanced research, and expand the boundaries of what is possible. A Bryn Mawr woman is defined by a rare combination of personal characteristics: an intense intellectual commitment; a purposeful vision of her life; and a desire to make a meaningful contribution to the world. Consistently producing outstanding scholars, Bryn Mawr is ranked among the top ten of all colleges and universities in percentage of graduates who go on to earn a PhD, and is considered excellent preparation for the nation's top law, medical and business schools. More than 500 students collaborate with faculty on independent projects every year, and to augment an already strong curriculum, students may choose from more than 5,000 courses offered through nearby Haverford and Swarthmore colleges, as well as the University of Pennsylvania.

"Minutes outside of Philadelphia and only two hours by train from New York City and Washington, D.C., Bryn Mawr is recognized by many as one of the most stunning college campuses in the United States.

"Bryn Mawr has a "Test Flexible" admissions policy, which allows students the option of using AP exam scores at Bryn Mawr. See the website for full details: www.brynmawr.edu/admissions/test_policy.shtml."

SELECTIVITY
Admissions Rating	92
# of applicants	2,271
% of applicants accepted	48
% of acceptees attending	34
# accepting a place on wait list	392
% admitted from wait list	5
# of early decision applicants	147
% accepted early decision	61

FRESHMAN PROFILE
Range SAT Critical Reading	590–720
Range SAT Math	580–700
Range SAT Writing	600–700
Range ACT Composite	26–30
Minimum paper TOEFL	600
Minimum computer TOEFL	250
Minimum web-based TOEFL	90
% graduated top 10% of class	64
% graduated top 25% of class	92
% graduated top 50% of class	100

DEADLINES
Early decision I	
Deadline	11/15
Notification	12/15
Early decision II	
Deadline	1/1
Regular	
Deadline	1/15
Nonfall registration?	no

APPLICANTS ALSO LOOK AT
AND OFTEN PREFER
Brown University, University of Pennsylvania
AND SOMETIMES PREFER
Haverford College, Smith College, Swarthmore College, Wellesley College
AND RARELY PREFER
Mount Holyoke College, Vassar College

FINANCIAL FACTS
Financial Aid Rating	97
Annual comprehensive tuition	$51,780
Books and supplies	$1,000
% frosh rec. need-based scholarship or grant aid	65
% UG rec. need-based scholarship or grant aid	59
% frosh rec. non-need-based scholarship or grant aid	50
% UG rec. non-need-based scholarship or grant aid	50
% frosh rec. need-based self-help aid	63
% UG rec. need-based self-help aid	54
% frosh rec. any financial aid	79
% UG rec. any financial aid	69
% UG borrow to pay for school	59
Average cumulative indebtedness	$23,509

BUCKNELL UNIVERSITY

FREAS HALL, BUCKNELL UNIVERSITY, LEWISBURG, PA 17837 • ADMISSIONS: 570-577-1101 • FAX: 570-577-3538

CAMPUS LIFE

Quality of Life Rating	81
Fire Safety Rating	85
Green Rating	87
Type of school	private
Environment	village

STUDENTS

Total undergrad enrollment	3,487
% male/female	49/51
% from out of state	76
% from public high school	66
% live on campus	88
# of fraternities	12
# of sororities	8
% African American	3
% Asian	3
% Caucasian	81
% Hispanic	4
% international	4
# of countries represented	52

SURVEY SAYS . . .
Athletic facilities are great
Low cost of living
Frats and sororities dominate
social scene

ACADEMICS

Academic Rating	94
% students graduating within 4 years	89
% students graduating within 6 years	91
Calendar	semester
Student/faculty ratio	10:1
Profs interesting rating	90
Profs accessible rating	92
Most common reg class size	10–19 students
Most common lab size	10–19 students

MOST POPULAR MAJORS
biology, business administration and management, economics

STUDENTS SAY "..."

Academics
Bucknell University delivers the quintessential East Coast college experience, with a balanced combination of "great academics, a liberal arts education, beautiful campus, sterling reputation, and a great social scene." At this prestigious small school, instruction is top notch because "teachers are all interested in their subject matter and are always willing to let class discussion take its course." If you need extra help or just some words of advice, "professors are incredibly available. They will always drop whatever they are doing to take as much time as is needed to help a student." In fact, "You get so close to some teachers that you babysit their kids or have meals with them." Bucknell offers a challenging yet non-competitive environment, where "students are always willing to help a classmate who is struggling, which is a rare characteristic on today's elite campuses." Additionally, Bucknell's excellent facilities and ample co-curricular opportunities—including a "fantastic" overseas program—complement the undergraduate experience. A senior adds, "I've had the opportunity to do research, and this is one of the best experiences I've had at Bucknell." The school runs well, and there's "very little red tape" holding up administrative functions—a rarity in the world of higher education. Bucknell staff members are "always willing to help you," and the administration is generally student-oriented.

Life
An idyllic place to work and live, the Bucknell campus is "gorgeous," and when the weather is nice, "People are always playing football on the quad or reading textbooks on benches with their Ray-Bans on." Whether you like cinema, chess, or soccer, "There are over 130 clubs and organizations, so there is something for everyone." In addition, "Fitness in general is very popular here," and "Many students will go to the gym in their free time." While student interests may vary, there is one uniting factor: "Greek life is really big on campus," and the party scene is hopping. A current student elaborates, "Weekends are when the books are tossed on the shelf and every student on campus...hightails it to various fraternity parties." That said, students acknowledge that Greek life isn't for everyone. One student reassures us that while "Greek life is definitely a visible part of the social life at Bucknell," it's "not the only option," and "it's not necessary to go Greek in order to have a social life here." Whether affiliated or not, students may choose to "attend university-sponsored movie showings or go to the theater downtown, watch a movie with friends in our hall lounge, go to the 7th Street Cafe for a smoothie, or go to other university-sponsored events, like concerts." In downtown Lewisburg, students enjoy "all types of little shops and restaurants, as well as one of the only original art deco movie theaters left in the country." If you want to take a break from the "bubble," "Bucknell also provides plenty of opportunities to get off campus with trips to NYC, D.C., local hockey games, skiing areas, and other events."

Student Body
While there are exceptions to any rule, Bucknell students are predominantly "white, upper-middle class, and from the Northeast." Attracting many likeminded recruits, Bucknellians are "rich but never flashy, classic preppy, intellectual, driven, friendly, social, and very active." Bucknell undergraduates also claim to be a particularly attractive set. Says one, "Our school seems to defy nature with the number of beautiful people on campus." On the whole, most Bucknell undergraduates "find a good balance between school and social life, and they are often dedicated to extracurriculars." Greek life is huge, and many undergraduates "party as hard as they study." However, academics are always first priority, and "a student who skips class on a regular basis is very rare." On this small Pennsylvania campus, "There really isn't a lot of diversity," and a student jokes, "It looks like we go to school at a country club." Still, "The school works hard to bring minority students and international students here through various scholarship programs."

FINANCIAL AID: 570-577-1331 • E-MAIL: ADMISSIONS@BUCKNELL.EDU • WEBSITE: WWW.BUCKNELL.EDU

THE PRINCETON REVIEW SAYS

Admissions

Very important factors considered include: Academic GPA, application essay, class rank, rigor of secondary school record, standardized test scores, character/personal qualities, talent/ability. *Important factors considered include:* Recommendation(s), extracurricular activities, level of applicant's interest, volunteer work, work experience. *Other factors considered include:* Alumni/ae relation, first generation, geographical residence, racial/ethnic status, religious affiliation/commitment. SAT or ACT required; ACT with writing component required. TOEFL required of all international applicants. High school diploma is required, and GED is accepted. *Academic units required:* 4 English, 3 mathematics, 2 science, 2 foreign language, 2 social studies, 2 history, 1 academic elective. *Academic units recommended:* 4 English, 4 mathematics, 3 science, 4 foreign language, 2 social studies, 2 history, 1 academic elective.

Financial Aid

Students should submit: FAFSA, CSS/Financial Aid PROFILE. Regular filing deadline is January 15. The Princeton Review suggests that all financial aid forms be submitted as soon as possible after January 1. *Need-based scholarships/grants offered:* Federal Pell, SEOG, state scholarships/grants, private scholarships, school scholarship or grant aid from institutional funds. *Loan aid offered:* Direct Subsidized Stafford, Direct Unsubsidized Stafford, Direct PLUS, Federal Perkins. Federal Work-Study Program available. Off-campus job opportunities are poor.

The Inside Word

Admission to Bucknell is competitive, and admissions officers will cast a keen eye on the quality of your application, including your performance in a hopefully rigorous secondary school curriculum, as well as your SAT or ACT test scores. The university is interested in assessing both your aptitude for college-level study in general and your ability to contribute to the Bucknell experience, in particular. It's wise to learn a bit about Bucknell before applying: Bucknell's supplement to the Common Application asks you to explain why the school is a good fit for you.

THE SCHOOL SAYS ". . ."

From the Admissions Office

"Bucknell combines the personal experience of a small liberal arts college with the breadth and opportunity typically found at larger research universities. With a low student/faculty ratio, students gain exceptional hands-on experience, working closely with faculty in an environment enhanced by first-class academic, residential, and athletic facilities. Together, the College of Arts and Sciences and the College of Engineering offer fifty-six majors and sixty-five minors. Learning opportunities permeate campus life in and out of the classroom and across the disciplines. For example, engineering students participate in music ensembles, theater productions, and poetry readings, while arts and sciences students take engineering courses, conduct scientific research in the field, and produce distinctive creative works. Students also pursue their interests in more than 150 organizations and through athletic competition in the prestigious Division I Patriot League. These activities constitute a comprehensive approach to learning that teaches students how to think critically and develop their leadership skills so that they are prepared to make a difference locally, nationally, and globally."

SELECTIVITY

Admissions Rating	96
# of applicants	7,178
% of applicants accepted	31
% of acceptees attending	41
# accepting a place on wait list	621
% admitted from wait list	13
# of early decision applicants	623
% accepted early decision	63

FRESHMAN PROFILE

Range SAT Critical Reading	590–670
Range SAT Math	630–710
Range SAT Writing	600–690
Range ACT Composite	27–31
Minimum paper TOEFL	550
Minimum computer TOEFL	213
Minimum web-based TOEFL	106
Average HS GPA	3.50
% graduated top 10% of class	65
% graduated top 25% of class	89
% graduated top 50% of class	100

DEADLINES

Early decision	
Deadline	11/15
Notification	12/15
Regular	
Deadline	1/15
Nonfall registration?	no

APPLICANTS ALSO LOOK AT

AND OFTEN PREFER
Boston College, Cornell University, Johns Hopkins University, Tufts University, University of Virginia, Washington University in St. Louis

AND SOMETIMES PREFER
Carnegie Mellon University, Colgate University, University of Richmond, Villanova University, Wake Forest University

AND RARELY PREFER
Lafayette College, Lehigh University, Penn State—University Park, University of Delaware, University of Maryland—College Park

FINANCIAL FACTS

Financial Aid Rating	93
Annual tuition	$43,628
Room and board	$10,374
Required fees	$238
Books and supplies	$900
% frosh rec. need-based scholarship or grant aid	45
% UG rec. need-based scholarship or grant aid	43
% frosh rec. non-need-based scholarship or grant aid	6
% UG rec. non-need-based scholarship or grant aid	6
% frosh rec. need-based self-help aid	45
% UG rec. need-based self-help aid	46
% frosh rec. any financial aid	62
% UG rec. any financial aid	62
% UG borrow to pay for school	61
Average cumulative indebtedness	$18,900

CALIFORNIA INSTITUTE OF TECHNOLOGY

1200 EAST CALIFORNIA BOULEVARD, MAIL CODE 10-90, PASADENA, CA 91125 • ADMISSIONS: 626-395-6341 • FAX: 626-683-3026

CAMPUS LIFE
Quality of Life Rating	76
Fire Safety Rating	65
Green Rating	65
Type of school	private
Environment	metropolis

STUDENTS
Total undergrad enrollment	967
% male/female	60/40
% from out of state	65
% from public high school	70
% live on campus	95
% African American	1
% Asian	39
% Caucasian	37
% Hispanic	6
% international	12
# of countries represented	32

SURVEY SAYS . . .
Class discussions are rare
No one cheats
Lab facilities are great
Students are friendly
Campus feels safe
Frats and sororities are unpopular
or nonexistent

ACADEMICS
Academic Rating	93
% students graduating within 4 years	81
% students graduating within 6 years	90
Calendar	quarter
Student/faculty ratio	3:1
Profs interesting rating	61
Profs accessible rating	66
Most common reg class size	fewer than 10 students
Most common lab size	20–29 students

MOST POPULAR MAJORS
mathematics, mechanical engineering, physics

STUDENTS SAY "..."

Academics
According to students at the California Institute of Technology, their tiny school is "the greatest research university out there." "Caltech's math, science, and engineering programs are indisputably first-rate," gloats a senior. "If you like science and know that you want some sort of career in research, engineering, or academia, this is one of the best places to come in the world." The mandatory core curriculum is heavy on math, physics, and chemistry. It also includes a humanities requirement. Beyond that, students can choose from a host of majors and minors. Whatever path you choose, "The resources are incredible," and "lab facilities are top-notch." There are fabulous opportunities "for students to conduct research at every class level," too. Be prepared for "a crippling workload," though. The academic atmosphere here is "probably the most intense you could hope to find." It's "like trying to drink from a fire hose" ("even if this is an overused cliché"). "There is no grade inflation." "Caltech has the ability to crush your own opinion of how smart you are." "If you were the top student all your life, prepare to experience a big dose of humility because you'll have to work hard just to stay in the middle of the pack." "Introductory classes are often taught by Nobel laureates" and world renowned scientists. "The quality of professors as teachers, rather than brilliant researchers, however, is often hit-or-miss," explains an applied physics major. Professors "tend to be very passionate about their subjects," but "only a select few professors teach well."

Life
Life at Caltech "involves doing a lot of homework." "A sizable population of the school does not come out of their rooms much." Clubs and extracurricular activities run the gamut, though, and it's very easy to get involved "no matter your experience." "Computer games, card games, role-playing games," and the like are popular. Otherwise, social life relies heavily on Caltech's unique housing system. First-year students are required to live on campus, in one of eight houses. "The houses combine the feel and purpose of a dorm with the pride and spirit of a fraternity." "Each house plans social events" and "provides the main social community" for students. When Caltech students throw a party, "It's a major operation." "Most parties here involve two weeks of prior planning and construction," and the end result is "usually pretty epic." Off campus, Caltech's location in sunny Pasadena provides ample opportunities for outdoor activities. There are "beaches, mountains, and desert all within a two-hour drive." The proximity of Los Angeles provides a ready escape as well. "Once in a while we'll all pile in a car and go to Los Angeles for a concert or something," notes a senior, "and that's a lot of fun." "Plotting pranks" is another common pastime here. Techers have a notorious reputation for "amusing" and generally harmless mischief. Students once altered the famous Hollywood Sign to read "Caltech." In another instance, they adjusted the scoreboard at the Rose Bowl to show Caltech leading hated MIT by an impressive score of 38-9.

Student Body
Caltech is home to "lots of whites and Asians," and the student population is overwhelmingly male. "The ratio sucks," laments a lonely senior. "Your typical student here was the math team/science team/quiz bowl type in high school." "This is nerd heaven." "Everyone's a scientist," and "every student is brilliant." Students also describe themselves as "hardworking," "quirky," and "slightly eccentric." You'll find a wide variety, though, "from cool party types, to scary hardcore nerds, to cool party types who build massive railguns in their spare time." Some students are "terribly creative." Some are "socially inept" and "very strange." Ultimately, it's a hard group to pigeonhole. "You will meet someone who you might think is a total jock if you saw him or her on the street, but [he or she] works late at night on homework and aces exams," promises one student. "If you come here with stereotypes in mind, they will be broken."

CALIFORNIA INSTITUTE OF TECHNOLOGY

FINANCIAL AID: 626-395-6280 • E-MAIL: UGADMISSIONS@CALTECH.EDU • WEBSITE: ADMISSIONS.CALTECH.EDU

THE PRINCETON REVIEW SAYS

Admissions

Very important factors considered include: Rigor of secondary school record. *Important factors considered include:* Academic GPA, application essay, class rank, recommendation(s), standardized test scores, character/personal qualities, extracurricular activities. *Other factors considered include:* First generation, racial/ethnic status, talent/ability, volunteer work, work experience. SAT or ACT required; ACT with or without writing component accepted. High school diploma or equivalent isn't required. *Academic units required:* 3 English, 4 mathematics, 2 science (1 science lab), 1 social studies, 1 history. *Academic units recommended:* 4 English, 4 science, 3 foreign language, 3 social studies, 1 history.

Financial Aid

Students should submit: FAFSA, institution's own financial aid form, CSS/Financial Aid PROFILE. The Princeton Review suggests that all financial aid forms be submitted as soon as possible after January 1. *Need-based scholarships/grants offered:* Federal Pell, SEOG, state scholarships/grants, private scholarships. *Loan aid offered:* Direct Subsidized Stafford, Direct Unsubsidized Stafford, Direct PLUS, Federal Perkins, university loans from institutional funds. Federal Work-Study Program available.

The Inside Word

Each Caltech application receives three independent reads before it's presented to the admissions committee. This ensures that all candidates receive a thorough evaluation. The school values the unique drive and energy of its current students and desires applicants who display a similar combination of creativity and intellect. Stellar academic credentials are a must, and prospective students must display an aptitude for math and science.

THE SCHOOL SAYS "..."

From the Admissions Office

"Admission to the freshman class is based on many factors—some quantifiable, some not. What you say in your application is important! Because we don't interview students for admission, your letters of recommendation are weighed heavily. High school academic performance is very important, as is a demonstrated interest in math, science, and/or engineering. We are also interested in your character, maturity, and motivation. We are very proud of the process we use to select each freshman class. It's very individual, it has great integrity, and we believe it serves all the students who apply. If you have any questions about the process or about Caltech in general, write us a letter or give us a call. We'd like to hear from you!

"Freshman applicants must submit scores from either the SAT or ACT. In addition, students must submit the results of two SAT Subject Tests: mathematics IIC and one of the following—biology (ecological or molecular), chemistry, or physics."

SELECTIVITY

Admissions Rating	98
# of applicants	4,859
% of applicants accepted	12
% of acceptees attending	36
# accepting a place on wait list	337
% admitted from wait list	7

FRESHMAN PROFILE

Range SAT Critical Reading	700–780
Range SAT Math	770–800
Range SAT Writing	710–780
Range ACT Composite	34–35
% graduated top 10% of class	96
% graduated top 25% of class	100

DEADLINES

Early action	
Deadline	11/1
Notification	12/15
Regular	
Deadline	1/3
Notification	3/15
Nonfall registration?	no

APPLICANTS ALSO LOOK AT AND OFTEN PREFER
Harvard College, Massachusetts Institute of Technology, Stanford University
AND SOMETIMES PREFER
Princeton University

FINANCIAL FACTS

Financial Aid Rating	97
Annual tuition	$36,387
Room and board	$11,676
Required fees	$1,317
Books and supplies	$1,323
% frosh rec. need-based scholarship or grant aid	53
% UG rec. need-based scholarship or grant aid	53
% UG rec. non-need-based scholarship or grant aid	2
% frosh rec. need-based self-help aid	39
% UG rec. need-based self-help aid	49
% frosh rec. any financial aid	53
% UG rec. any financial aid	55
% UG borrow to pay for school	43
Average cumulative indebtedness	$10,760

CALIFORNIA STATE UNIVERSITY STANISLAUS

ONE UNIVERSITY CIRCLE, TURLOCK, CA 95382 • ADMISSIONS: 209-667-3070 OR 800-300-7420 (CA ONLY) • FAX: 209-667-3394

CAMPUS LIFE

Quality of Life Rating	84
Fire Safety Rating	95
Green Rating	87
Type of school	public
Environment	town

STUDENTS

Total undergrad enrollment	6,963
% male/female	36/64
% from public high school	93
% live on campus	9
# of fraternities	7
# of sororities	9
% African American	3
% Asian	11
% Caucasian	39
% Hispanic	34
% Native American	1
% international	2
# of countries represented	25

SURVEY SAYS . . .

Diverse student types on campus
Low cost of living
Very little drug use

ACADEMICS

Academic Rating	67
% students graduating within 4 years	24
% students graduating within 6 years	50
Calendar	semester
Student/faculty ratio	21:1
Profs interesting rating	81
Profs accessible rating	75
Most common reg class size	20–29 students
Most common lab size	20–29 students

MOST POPULAR MAJORS
business/commerce, liberal arts and sciences

STUDENTS SAY ". . ."

Academics

"Best known for its nursing, criminal justice, and psychology programs" as well as what many students believe is "one of the best teacher credential programs in California," California State University Stanislaus provides to its 7,000 undergraduates "a very practical education" in "a friendly environment." Small in comparison to many state universities, CSU Stanislaus can offer "small class sizes that allow better communication with both professors and fellow classmates," which is a huge plus. A "friendly, accessible faculty" is another; professors are "well-educated, well-written, and have the experience to back up what they teach. When students stop in to ask a question, the professors stop what they are doing and give their full attention to the student." Programs are designed with the goal of accommodating a wide variety of students; the school "has a main campus and two satellite campuses and offers both day and night classes" so that part-time students can access the same educational opportunities as traditional full-timers. As at many state schools, budgetary problems occasionally impose hardships, such as course cancellations that result in "a lack of classes [required] to graduate. Budget cuts have made this tough for a lot of students, and many of my friends will now have to attend the college for an additional year in order to graduate."

Life

CSU Stanislaus students who live on campus tell us, "The dorms and the school provide students with tons of activities and fun events to attend. Stanislaus really makes an effort to get their students involved and become well-rounded individuals" by offering "lots of activities put on by the Student Union and lots more put on by the Residential Life people or by specific floors in the dorms." Intramural sports are very popular. Students add, "There are also lots of clubs and organizations to get involved with on campus." Hometown Turlock is "a small town" with "not a ton of things to do" other than "a decent movie theater," but "it's only a short drive to Modesto where there really are tons of things to do," including "some great restaurants." Commuters have a rougher time integrating into campus life; "It's hard to build friendships with people because more often [than] not they live pretty far away," one explains. Currently, less than ten percent of all students live in on-campus housing.

Student Body

"A CSU Stanislaus poster student would be a white female in her twenties"—two in three students here are women—but "there is a wide range of diversity on this campus," including a substantial Hispanic population. Undergrads "all seem to fit in well with each other." "The are two types of students at CSU Stanislaus: the commuter and the one who's incredibly involved." Commuters tend to focus on getting] their degree and getting] into their career," and can be a "bit disconnected from the social life on campus." However, other students are "involved in almost everything," are "in clubs and are active in student government." The prevailing attitude here is low-key and business-like; "Everyone is down-to-earth, relaxed, and chill" but also "more focused and driven than the average twenty-year-old."

CALIFORNIA STATE UNIVERSITY STANISLAUS

FINANCIAL AID: 209-667-3336 • E-MAIL: OUTREACH_HELP_DESK@CSUSTAN.EDU • WEBSITE: WWW.CSUSTAN.EDU

THE PRINCETON REVIEW SAYS

Admissions

Very important factors considered include: Academic GPA, rigor of secondary school record, standardized test scores. *Important factors considered include:* Class rank. ACT with or without writing component accepted. TOEFL required of all international applicants. High school diploma is required, and GED is accepted. *Academic units required:* 4 English, 3 mathematics, 2 science (2 science labs), 2 foreign language, 1 social studies, 1 history, 1 visual/performing arts, 1 academic elective.

Financial Aid

Students should submit: FAFSA. The Princeton Review suggests that all financial aid forms be submitted as soon as possible after January 1. *Need-based scholarships/grants offered:* Federal Pell, SEOG, state scholarships/grants, private scholarships, school scholarship or grant aid from institutional funds. *Loan aid offered:* Federal Perkins, university loans from institutional funds. Applicants will be notified of awards on a rolling basis beginning March 15. Federal Work-Study Program available. Off-campus job opportunities are good.

The Inside Word

Like most state schools, CSU Stanislaus admissions practices are fairly straightforward. The university adheres to the eligibility index as defined by the California state system, so applicants who meet GPA and standardized test score minimums are automatically granted admission. Out-of-state candidates face more stringent requirements, as do those applying for highly competitive majors and programs, such as the Pre-Licensure Nursing Program.

THE SCHOOL SAYS "..."

From the Admissions Office

"CSU Stanislaus was recognized by the American Association of State Colleges and Universities as one of twelve public universities nationwide that demonstrate exceptional performance in retention and graduation rates. Student success is facilitated by a dense network of on-campus resources including consistent advising, a strong first-year program, frequent and meaningful contact with professors, and supportive staff and administrators.

"CSU Stanislaus has thirteen nationally accredited programs and is widely recognized for its quality academics. A new state-of-the-art science building opened in 2007 along with a new bookstore in 2008 and student recreation complex in 2009. The campus is widely known as the most beautiful and friendly of the CSU campuses, blending modern facilities with the pastoral charm of the countryside. The campus enjoys an ideal location in the heart of California's Central Valley, a short distance from the San Francisco Bay Area, Monterey, the Sierra Nevada mountains, and Yosemite National Park. The proximity allows for hiking, skiing, snowboarding, kayaking, surfing, and other outdoor sports and activities.

"CSU Stanislaus awarded more than $24.5 million in merit- and need-based grants and scholarships for the 2008–2009 school year. Approximately sixty-eight percent of freshmen received need-based aid and the average gift aid for the group was $5,190. Scholarships range from full tuition, board, and books through the President's Scholarship to hundreds of other scholarships ranging from $100 to $5,000 per school year. The CSU Stanislaus experience can be summed up as providing a small private school atmosphere at a public school price."

SELECTIVITY

Admissions Rating	78
# of applicants	4,896
% of applicants accepted	34
% of acceptees attending	63

FRESHMAN PROFILE

Range SAT Critical Reading	400–510
Range SAT Math	410–530
Range SAT Writing	410–520
Range ACT Composite	17–22
Minimum paper TOEFL	550
Minimum computer TOEFL	173
Minimum web-based TOEFL	61
Average HS GPA	3.30

DEADLINES

Regular	
Priority	11/30
Deadline	11/30
Notification	1/1
Nonfall registration?	yes

FINANCIAL FACTS

Financial Aid Rating	65
Annual in-state tuition	$5,407
Room and board	$8,880
Books and supplies	$1,650
% frosh rec. need-based scholarship or grant aid	47
% UG rec. need-based scholarship or grant aid	65
% frosh rec. non-need-based scholarship or grant aid	3
% UG rec. non-need-based scholarship or grant aid	4
% frosh rec. need-based self-help aid	27
% UG rec. need-based self-help aid	64
% frosh rec. any financial aid	60
% UG rec. any financial aid	76
% UG borrow to pay for school	25
Average cumulative indebtedness	$16,500

CALVIN COLLEGE

3201 BURTON STREET SOUTHEAST, GRAND RAPIDS, MI 49546 • ADMISSIONS: 616-526-6106 • FAX: 616-526-6777

CAMPUS LIFE

Quality of Life Rating	85
Fire Safety Rating	73
Green Rating	75
Type of school	private
Affiliation	Christian Reformed
Environment	metropolis

STUDENTS

Total undergrad enrollment	3,839
% male/female	47/53
% from out of state	42
% from public high school	43
% live on campus	58
% African American	3
% Asian	4
% Caucasian	79
% Hispanic	2
% international	10
# of countries represented	54

SURVEY SAYS . . .

*Students get along with local
community
Great off-campus food
Low cost of living
Frats and sororities are unpopular
or nonexistent
Musical organizations are popular
Very little drug use*

ACADEMICS

Academic Rating	84
% students graduating within 4 years	58
% students graduating within 6 years	77
Calendar	4-1-4
Student/faculty ratio	11:1
Profs interesting rating	86
Profs accessible rating	89
Most common reg class size	20–29 students
Most common lab size	10–19 students

MOST POPULAR MAJORS

business, engineering,
nursing, education, biology,
psychology, communication

STUDENTS SAY "..."

Academics

Calvin College is a small liberal arts college with "an excellent reputation as a Christian and academic institute." The college is associated with the Christian Reformed Church and has a definite Christian focus. "Calvin prepares people for successful lives of service and building of the Kingdom of God." Calvin takes academics seriously and works to engage "the entire academic world without compromising its Christian worldview." At the same time, "Academic freedom is somewhat limited by the school's religious affiliation." Calvin works hard to make college "affordable for everyone that comes here" and "has a very beautiful campus with amazing people. "I always feel as if I have support and guidance in any of my choices," one student says. Students are very high on the professors, who "make their subjects fascinating" and "genuinely care about the students." "Not only do they know their stuff, but they will go above and beyond to help you." However, students disagree on the rigor of the academics. "Good professors, but [the class work is] very rigorous. Sometimes the standards are unattainably high," one student complains. Another student counters, saying, "Academics aren't always as rigorous as I might hope, but my professors are engaging and enthusiastic." One student sums Calvin up simply: "Small class sizes, good faculty, and good facilities all contribute to make this a strong school."

Life

Campus life at Calvin is influenced by its faith commitments. "If you want to go out and party like the stereotypical college life, you'll have to get off campus" because "if you do drink alcohol or smoke weed, you get kicked out immediately." There are many events on campus and "tons of fun activities to do with people in your dorm—floor dates with crazy Salvation Army outfits, ice skating, weekend retreats, roller skating, and serenading other dorms on campus." Off campus, the streets are "loaded with malls, movie theaters, bowling alleys, restaurants, and stores, so there is never a dull moment." Students look forward to "receiving a good education toward [their] major as well as spiritual growth." The college makes sure that "there are tons of opportunities and organizations for students to get involved [in] outside of the classroom. It builds community very efficiently and rapidly." In general, the small "student body and campus size promote a social atmosphere wherein each student may feel a strong sense of community, friendship and belonging."

Student Body

Most students at Calvin "have grown up in Christian homes" and "are largely from the same mold: religiously steadfast, politically center-right, and Midwestern in values (if not origin)." Although the school is affiliated with the Christian Reformed, there's a range of evangelical students and a spectrum of political leanings. "Calvin students are really into social justice issues," one student proudly says. "They want to change the world." Many students appreciate the religious atmosphere. "I feel Christ around me every day, all the time," one student says. However, for others, "The Christian atmosphere can be restricting." Some students lovingly joke, "The stereotypical Calvin student is tall, blond, and Dutch and grew up within a thirty-mile radius of Grand Rapids," but at the same time, "There are plenty of internationals and students from other states, too." The school could still do more to bring "in a more diverse student body. Not only racially, but regionally as well. It seems that most of the students are from Michigan or the surrounding states." However, the small student body creates a close community. "We are learning to live, and living to learn: socially, academically, and spiritually together."

FINANCIAL AID: 616-957-6134 • E-MAIL: ADMISSIONS@CALVIN.EDU • WEBSITE: WWW.CALVIN.EDU

THE PRINCETON REVIEW SAYS

Admissions

Very important factors considered include: Academic GPA, rigor of secondary school record, standardized test scores, religious affiliation/commitment. *Important factors considered include:* Application essay, recommendation(s), character/personal qualities, extracurricular activities. *Other factors considered include:* Class rank, level of applicant's interest, volunteer work, work experience. SAT or ACT required; ACT with or without writing component accepted. TOEFL required of all international applicants. High school diploma is required, and GED is accepted. *Academic units required:* 3 English, 3 mathematics, 2 science, 2 social studies, 3 academic elective. *Academic units recommended:* 4 English, 3 mathematics, 2 science (1 science lab), 2 foreign language, 3 social studies, 3 academic elective.

Financial Aid

Students should submit: FAFSA. Regular filing deadline is February 15. The Princeton Review suggests that all financial aid forms be submitted as soon as possible after January 1. *Need-based scholarships/grants offered:* Federal Pell, SEOG, state scholarships/grants, private scholarships, school scholarship or grant aid from institutional funds. *Loan aid offered:* Direct Subsidized Stafford, Direct Unsubsidized Stafford, Direct PLUS, Federal Perkins, university loans from institutional funds. Applicants will be notified of awards on a rolling basis beginning March 15. Federal Work-Study Program available. Off-campus job opportunities are excellent.

The Inside Word

Calvin College's website sports the following slogan: "Distinctively Christian, Academically Excellent, Always Reforming." Christian students who seek academic excellence without sacrificing their religious values should find a nurturing environment and a strong education at Calvin.

THE SCHOOL SAYS ". . ."

From the Admissions Office

"Calvin's respected faculty, innovative core curriculum, and well-qualified student body come together in an environment that links intellectual freedom with a heart for service. Calvin's 400-acre campus is home to nearly 4,000 students and 380 professors who chose Calvin because of its international reputation for academic excellence combined with faith-shaped learning.

"Calvin students come from near and far, with a record-setting 2010–2011 class that included ten percent international students and nearly twelve percent racial or ethnic minorities. Calvin encourages students to explore all things and offers nearly 100 majors, minors, and accredited professional programs to choose among.

"Quality teaching and accessibility to students are considered top priorities by faculty members. More than eighty-two percent of Calvin professors hold the highest degree in their field, the student/faculty ratio is eleven to one, and the average class size is twenty-two. In the past four years, Calvin has produced seven Fulbright Scholars. Calvin professors lead thirteen different semester-long study abroad programs and more than thirty January interim courses that take students into other countries and cultures. The Open Doors report of the Institute for International Education consistently ranks Calvin among the top five baccalaureate colleges for the number of students who complete a short-term study abroad.

"Before they graduate, more than eighty percent of Calvin students report having at least one internship, a great way for students to try their individual gifts in the workplace while gaining professional experience. In a survey of recent graduates, nearly 100 percent of responders report that they had either secured a job or begun graduate school within six months of graduation. Calvin is among the top five percent of four-year private colleges in the number of graduates who go on to earn a PhD."

SELECTIVITY

Admissions Rating	82
# of applicants	2,566
% of applicants accepted	92
% of acceptees attending	39

FRESHMAN PROFILE

Range SAT Critical Reading	510–650
Range SAT Math	540–670
Range ACT Composite	23–29
Minimum paper TOEFL	550
Minimum computer TOEFL	213
Minimum web-based TOEFL	80
Average HS GPA	3.60
% graduated top 10% of class	31
% graduated top 25% of class	58
% graduated top 50% of class	84

DEADLINES

Regular	
Deadline	8/15
Notification	11/1
Nonfall registration?	yes

APPLICANTS ALSO LOOK AT AND OFTEN PREFER
Wheaton College (IL)

AND SOMETIMES PREFER
Grand Valley State University, Hope College, University of Michigan—Ann Arbor

AND RARELY PREFER
Michigan State University, Western Michigan University

FINANCIAL FACTS

Financial Aid Rating	77
Annual tuition	$25,340
Room and board	$8,760
Required fees	$225
Books and supplies	$1,000
% frosh rec. need-based scholarship or grant aid	70
% UG rec. need-based scholarship or grant aid	65
% frosh rec. non-need-based scholarship or grant aid	7
% UG rec. non-need-based scholarship or grant aid	5
% frosh rec. need-based self-help aid	63
% UG rec. need-based self-help aid	61
% frosh rec. any financial aid	95
% UG rec. any financial aid	92
% UG borrow to pay for school	66
Average cumulative indebtedness	$27,700

CARLETON COLLEGE

100 SOUTH COLLEGE STREET, NORTHFIELD, MN 55057 • ADMISSIONS: 507-222-4190 AND 800-995-2275 • FAX: 507-222-4526

STUDENTS SAY ". . ."

Academics

Students interested in "discovering what it is you want to learn and then learning it within a wide context" are drawn to Carleton College, a small and extremely rigorous school that's "strongly liberal arts oriented" but also boasts "serious science departments." One freshman explains the reasoning behind choosing Carleton: "I could truly explore what I wanted to do without feeling as though I would have to have a sub-par education in science, if that was what I chose to major in." The "intensely passionate" undergrads of Carleton enjoy "a sense of community that's hard to find elsewhere." One undergraduate says, "You'll find yourself striking up conversations with complete strangers at the post office, in town, and along sidewalks in the middle of a snowy night. New friends are found everywhere." This is true even among the faculty; "Carleton is not a research college, so while professors do some research, they are much more focused on students." Carleton operates on a trimester calendar, which students endorse. "It's nice to be only taking three classes, though more intensely, rather than spreading yourself over four or five." Students also love the "great study abroad office," which has provided students here with "opportunities to travel to China, Thailand, Spain, and Africa."

Life

"Small and quaint" are two words Carleton students frequently use to describe their school's hometown. "Northfield is not that exciting," cedes a freshman, "but I'm not sure anyone wants to change that." Most students are content simply to find "nice restaurants" and "locals [who] are darn helpful in about any situation" in town. This might be because things are much livelier on campus. "An evening doesn't go by without some kind of event, whether it be musical, artistic, theatrical, or political," a sophomore writes. The notoriously heavy workload means "people study most of the time on weekdays" and occasionally "lose it. This comes more in the form of weird, creative outlets than it does self-destructive behavior, though. There are a lot of naked Winter Olympics, pranks, traditions, and general goofing off." Students are proud of this "little bit of eccentricity [that] makes everything fun." Intramurals "are really hot at Carleton; the people who aren't playing them are much fewer and [farther] between than the people who are." Ultimate Frisbee and broomball are the games of choice. There are also "plenty of parties," and while a portion "of the student body will be drunk on a typical weekend," there's "absolutely no pressure to drink if you don't want to." One freshman tells us that for fun she "makes a smoothie run to the Sayles-Hill Student Center," then later stops by "Dacie Moses House, a place where students gather to bake cookies." Students are even upbeat about the harsh winters here, describing them as "a uniting element [because] it's negative fifty degrees outside."

Student Body

The "creative, warm, compassionate, and helpful" undergrads of Carleton are "quirky," but "Everyone is accepting of these little eccentricities." "Everyone's surprising," writes one student, "and that can be a little exhausting at times," but mostly students embrace the challenges their peers present. They "don't form cliques based on [conventional] criteria" such as "socioeconomic background, race, gender, [or] sexual orientation." An upbeat studio-art major writes, "We have a wonderful mix of people that reaches from nerds to jocks, people who dye their hair to [those] who swear by Abercrombie, people who are Republican to those who are Democrat to those who are Independent to those who don't care; we have vegetarians, and we have people who would live on steak if you let them. We have a truly rich mix of all sorts of people, and we all enjoy each other and end up with the most amazing groups of friends."

FINANCIAL AID: 507-222-4138 • E-MAIL: ADMISSIONS@CARLETON.EDU • WEBSITE: WWW.CARLETON.EDU

THE PRINCETON REVIEW SAYS

Admissions

Very important factors considered include: Academic GPA, class rank, rigor of secondary school record. *Important factors considered include:* Application essay, recommendation(s), standardized test scores, alumni/ae relation, character/personal qualities, extracurricular activities, racial/ethnic status, talent/ability, volunteer work, work experience. *Other factors considered include:* First generation, geographical residence, interview, state residency. SAT or ACT required; ACT with writing component required. TOEFL required of all international applicants. High school diploma is required, and GED is accepted. *Academic units recommended:* 4 English, 3 mathematics, 3 science (1 science lab), 3 foreign language.

Financial Aid

Students should submit: FAFSA, CSS/Financial Aid PROFILE. Regular filing deadline is February 15. The Princeton Review suggests that all financial aid forms be submitted as soon as possible after January 1. *Need-based scholarships/grants offered:* Federal Pell, SEOG, state scholarships/grants, private scholarships, school scholarship or grant aid from institutional funds. *Loan aid offered:* Direct Subsidized Stafford, Direct Unsubsidized Stafford, Direct PLUS, Federal Perkins, state loans, university loans from institutional funds. Federal Work-Study Program not available.

The Inside Word

Carleton admissions are highly competitive. It's possible to get in without stellar high school grades and test scores if you have some exceptional talent or show tremendous promise, but most successful applicants have all of these qualities. High school record is most important here; standardized test scores weigh heavily, as does your personal essay. Interviews aren't required, but they're recommended. Sit for one, even if you can't schedule a campus visit; a local rep should be able to interview you in or near your hometown.

THE SCHOOL SAYS ". . ."

From the Admissions Office

"In an annual college freshmen survey, Carleton students identify themselves as everything from conservatives to liberals, with a majority of them falling in the moderate to liberal range. Although individualistic and energetic Carls take their academics seriously, they don't take themselves seriously. Participation in athletics, theater or music, religious events, or dining hall discussions marks the Carleton experience. The College recently opened two new LEED-certified, environmentally friendly residence halls. With nearly three-fifths of the student body receiving need-based grant aid, there is a broad socioeconomic representation across the student body. Eight percent of all students are international, and twenty-one percent come from traditionally underrepresented groups, and about eight percent are first-generation students. A look at majors in the past decade shows that graduates cover all areas, with about one-third of them in each of the following: math/science, humanities and arts, and social sciences. More than two-thirds of all students will spend time earning class credits off campus; Carleton participates in programs worldwide from Asia to Africa. You can scuba dive off the Great Barrier Reef or walk the Great Wall of China. Within ten years of graduating, about seventy-five percent of alumni pursue graduate or professional degrees. Carleton ranks third among liberal arts colleges in the number of PhDs earned by its alumni."

SELECTIVITY

Admissions Rating	96
# of applicants	4,856
% of applicants accepted	30
% of acceptees attending	34
# accepting a place on wait list	368
% admitted from wait list	14
# of early decision applicants	443
% accepted early decision	47

FRESHMAN PROFILE

Range SAT Critical Reading	650–750
Range SAT Math	650–750
Range SAT Writing	650–740
Range ACT Composite	29–33
Minimum paper TOEFL	600
Minimum computer TOEFL	250
Minimum web-based TOEFL	100
% graduated top 10% of class	76
% graduated top 25% of class	93
% graduated top 50% of class	100

DEADLINES

Early decision	
Deadline	1/15
Notification	12/15, 2/15
Regular	
Deadline	1/15
Nonfall registration?	no

APPLICANTS ALSO LOOK AT AND OFTEN PREFER
Williams College, Yale University

AND SOMETIMES PREFER
Washington University in St. Louis

AND RARELY PREFER
Macalester College

FINANCIAL FACTS

Financial Aid Rating	99
Annual tuition	$42,690
Room and board	$11,238
Required fees	$252
Books and supplies	$1,460
% frosh rec. need-based scholarship or grant aid	52
% UG rec. need-based scholarship or grant aid	55
% frosh rec. non-need-based scholarship or grant aid	5
% UG rec. non-need-based scholarship or grant aid	10
% frosh rec. need-based self-help aid	50
% UG rec. need-based self-help aid	54
% frosh rec. any financial aid	57
% UG rec. any financial aid	62
% UG borrow to pay for school	44
Average cumulative indebtedness	$19,436

CARNEGIE MELLON UNIVERSITY

5000 FORBES AVENUE, PITTSBURGH, PA 15213 • ADMISSIONS: 412-268-2082 • FAX: 412-268-7838

STUDENTS SAY "..."

Academics

CMU is an academic powerhouse that "pushes [students] to a much greater level of understanding." Undergrads are quick to reason that this is due to "outstanding faculty who are extremely passionate about their fields of study." Of course, this passion "transfers to rigorous and interesting courses." Indeed, "one definitely develops an excellent work ethic by attending this institution." A bio and psych double-major concurs stating, "Every student works hard: It is unavoidable." Fortunately, he goes on to say, "I have never had any trouble accessing any of my professors. They are quick to answer e-mails and are more than willing to meet with you outside of class and office hours." The university "offers a huge variety of top-ranked programs, such as the business school, the engineering school, the computer science school, and the music and drama departments." Naturally this "makes it easy to take a variety of classes but still get a quality education." And as one student puts it, "At the end of the day knowledge is oozing from my pores. I love it!" One senior did reveal that signing up for class can be a hassle because "the registration system is pretty much from the '80s." However, he did assure us that the administration is aware of the issues and "working on it." Overall, students are fairly happy with the "accessible" administration. One happy sophomore shares that those on the faculty "listen to students' requests and move to make changes on campus accordingly." And a computer science major sums up by stating, "The administration is helpful when you need it and never too intrusive."

Life

Though undergrads at Carnegie Mellon are "very focused on their education and their [future] careers" many students are still able to strike "a balance." Indeed, one senior assures us that he and his peers "know how to have fun too." Students in need of a study break can find distraction in a myriad of campus events. The residential staff (residential assistants and faculty advisors) often host activities like "movie nights, stressball crafting, and snowball fights." Additionally, undergrads can participate in anything from "intramural sports teams, to building racing vehicles [and] designing computer games." Performances from the many "a capella and drama groups" are also well-attended. Though one junior admits, "We're not big partiers comparatively," plenty of students "do go to frat parties on the weekend." And many undergrads revel in CMU traditions, such as carnival when "classes are cancelled for two days, and week-long parties occur." Impressively, "Public transportation is free for Carnegie Mellon students" making Pittsburgh highly accessible. The city offers a number "of museums to visit," and "the Waterfront, where there's great shopping, a movie theater, and various restaurants are only a bus ride away." Finally, those who are twenty-one can take advantage of "the vast number of bars, lounges, and clubs in the area."

Student Body

Carnegie Mellon seems to attract "focused, intelligent" students who are "ambitious, goal-oriented" and "maybe a little too smart for [their] own good." In short, the university is "a utopia for nerds." And while this might mean you'll encounter a few "socially awkward" peers, one sophomore assures us that it's "a very comfortable, friendly environment." Though a number of undergrads proclaim that there's "no typical student," there are "two common types—the artsy student and the total computer geek." Don't be misled, however; these kids can't easily be pigeonholed. "Some are engineers, some are actors, some are scientists, and some are writers." "Everyone is unique and interesting." Indeed, quick to praise their "quirky" and "well-rounded" fellow students, many undergrads here greatly appreciate the fact that people "are passionate about a variety of subjects." Impressively, "Students are not only ethnically and religiously diverse, but every person here has some unique or interesting characteristic." Moreover, "Everyone is really accepting of students that are different than them." And, as a content chemical engineering major shares, "Everyone finds their place."

FINANCIAL AID: 412-268-2068 • E-MAIL: UNDERGRADUATE-ADMISSIONS@ANDREW.CMU.EDU • WEBSITE: WWW.CMU.EDU

THE PRINCETON REVIEW SAYS

Admissions

Very important factors considered include: Academic GPA, class rank, rigor of secondary school record, standardized test scores. *Important factors considered include:* Application essay, recommendation(s), alumni/ae relation, character/personal qualities, extracurricular activities, first generation, interview, level of applicant's interest, racial/ethnic status, talent/ability, volunteer work, work experience. SAT or ACT required; SAT Subject Tests required. ACT with writing component required. TOEFL required of all international applicants. High school diploma is required, and GED is accepted. *Academic units required:* 4 English, 4 mathematics, 3 science (3 science labs), 2 foreign language, 3 academic elective. *Academic units recommended:* 4 English, 4 mathematics, 3 science (3 science labs), 2 foreign language, 4 academic elective.

Financial Aid

Students should submit: FAFSA, CSS PROFILE. Regular filing deadline is May 1. The Princeton Review suggests that all financial aid forms be submitted as soon as possible after January 1. *Need-based scholarships/grants offered:* Federal Pell, SEOG, state scholarships/grants, private scholarships, school scholarship or grant aid from institutional funds. *Loan aid offered:* Federal Perkins. Federal Work-Study Program available. Off-campus job opportunities are good.

The Inside Word

Don't be misled by Carnegie Mellon's acceptance rate. Although relatively high for a university of this caliber, the applicant pool is fairly self-selecting. If you haven't loaded up on demanding courses in high school, you're not likely to be a serious contender. The admissions office explicitly states that it doesn't use formulas when making decisions. That said, a record of strong academic performance in the area of your intended major is key.

THE SCHOOL SAYS "..."

From the Admissions Office

"If you're looking for an intellectual environment that blends academic and artistic richness with classroom innovation, explore Carnegie Mellon. Consistently ranked as a top twenty-five institution, Carnegie Mellon is world-renowned for its unique approach to education and research. Left-brain and right-brain thinking unite within our collaborative culture, and is the foundation of learning at Carnegie Mellon."

"As a student, you will acquire a depth and breadth of knowledge while sharpening your problem-solving, critical thinking, creative and quantitative skills. You will develop sound critical judgment, resourcefulness and professional ethics through a collaborative and hands-on education. As a graduate, you will be one of the innovative leaders and problem-solvers of tomorrow."

"While a Carnegie Mellon education is marked by a strong focus on fundamental and versatile problem-solving skills in a particular discipline, your talents and interests don't remain confined to one area. The university respects academic diversity and provides opportunities for you to explore more than one field of study. Carnegie Mellon consists of seven colleges (six undergraduate): Carnegie Institute of Technology (engineering), College of Fine Arts, College of Humanities and Social Sciences (combining liberal arts education with professional specializations), Tepper School of Business, Mellon College of Science, the School of Computer Science, and the Heinz College. Here, music, molecular science, acting, analysis, opera and organic chemistry weave in and out of the lives and minds of Carnegie Mellon students on a daily basis."

"The university's 150-acre main campus is located in the Oakland area of Pittsburgh, five miles from downtown."

SELECTIVITY

Admissions Rating	97
# of applicants	15,496
% of applicants accepted	33
% of acceptees attending	29
# accepting a place on wait list	563
% admitted from wait list	12
# of early decision applicants	1,258
% accepted early decision	21

FRESHMAN PROFILE

Range SAT Critical Reading	620–720
Range SAT Math	680–780
Range SAT Writing	630–730
Range ACT Composite	29–33
Minimum paper TOEFL	600
Minimum computer TOEFL	250
Minimum web-based TOEFL	102
Average HS GPA	3.62
% graduated top 10% of class	72
% graduated top 25% of class	93
% graduated top 50% of class	99

DEADLINES

Early decision	
Deadline	11/1
Notification	12/15
Regular	
Deadline	1/1
Nonfall registration?	no

FINANCIAL FACTS

Financial Aid Rating	80
Annual tuition	$41,500
Room and board	$11,110
Required fees	$850
Books and supplies	$2,400
% frosh rec. need-based scholarship or grant aid	56
% UG rec. need-based scholarship or grant aid	47
% frosh rec. non-need-based scholarship or grant aid	21
% UG rec. non-need-based scholarship or grant aid	19
% frosh rec. need-based self-help aid	53
% UG rec. need-based self-help aid	48
% frosh rec. any financial aid	54
% UG rec. any financial aid	49
% UG borrow to pay for school	47
Average cumulative indebtedness	$30,744

CASE WESTERN RESERVE UNIVERSITY

103 TOMLINSON HALL, 10900 EUCLID AVENUE, CLEVELAND, OH 44106-7055 • ADMISSIONS: 216-368-4450 • FAX: 216-368-5111

CAMPUS LIFE

Quality of Life Rating	70
Fire Safety Rating	77
Green Rating	93
Type of school	private
Environment	metropolis

STUDENTS

Total undergrad enrollment	4,125
% male/female	58/42
% from out of state	51
% from public high school	77
% live on campus	78
# of fraternities	16
# of sororities	8
% African American	5
% Asian	16
% Caucasian	55
% Hispanic	3
% international	6
# of countries represented	26

SURVEY SAYS . . .

Lab facilities are great
Great computer facilities
Great library
Great off-campus food
Low cost of living
Student publications are popular
Student government is popular

ACADEMICS

Academic Rating	77
% students graduating within 4 years	65
% students graduating within 6 years	82
Calendar	semester
Student/faculty ratio	9:1
Profs interesting rating	68
Profs accessible rating	72
Most common reg class size	10–19 students
Most common lab size	20–29 students

MOST POPULAR MAJORS
bioengineering/biomedical engineering,
biology, psychology

STUDENTS SAY ". . ."

Academics

With more than half its students in the labor-intensive disciplines of engineering and the sciences, it's no wonder students tell us that "Case is about hard work." Undergrads here tell us that "a nine-to-five job will be exceptionally easy after a Case undergraduate education (which is nine-to-five classes, then five-to-two homework)." While some complain that Case Western "is designed to beat students down [and they] attempt to compete with better schools by giving more homework," others counter, "You can choose to complain about it all the time or you can take advantage of everything that's offered here—enjoy yourself and get a great education." For those who know where to look, Case offers "great means for student development outside of the classroom. The Emerging Leaders Program for first-year students…holds leadership conferences—largely planned and organized by students for students—every semester." It's also "incredibly easy to get involved" in the "groundbreaking research" that occurs on this campus daily. Some here acknowledge that Case "could improve on diversifying its non-engineering and non-science offerings," a matter of significance to all since the school introduced mandatory interdisciplinary seminars (called the SAGES program, which students tell us "is still a work in progress"). Most agree that while the administration "has done a better job at getting to know the students," most would like to see an increase in "their willingness to cater to students' interests, especially when these differ from the beaten path."

Life

"Many students feel that Case Western students do much more work than a typical student and thus miss out on more chances for socializing, even during the weekend," but others tell us that despite the "ton of hard work," there's "still plenty of time in the day for extracurricular activities." "Actually, that's part of the reason why people are so busy in the first place," says one student. Case offers "a wide range of on- and off-campus activities to choose from. Events such as Drag Ball, a local sorority's Mr. CWRU, and our university program board's major concerts pull hundreds of students out to bond and have a great time. Smaller events are always going on through one of our officially recognized student organizations, be they guest lecturers brought in by the Case Democrats, choral showcases featuring one or many of our a cappella groups, or simply smaller events." Cleveland provides further diversion; the school is located in University Circle, home to "a number of museums, the Cleveland Orchestra, the Botanical Gardens, and much more. This is a great resource of our school, which we are encouraged to take advantage of." The party scene here is "more mellow" than other colleges. "If you want to party, you can." If you would rather stay away from that scene, you can. "There's no pressure."

Student Body

A typical Case student is "heartily dedicated to classes and tries to figure out what else can fit into his/her schedule." Because the school is "so academically focused, there are plenty of the overstressing premedical students" along with similarly disposed engineers ("mostly male") and nursing students ("mostly female"). While "many Case students are primarily gamers" who "may not leave their rooms" very often, students "who are incredibly involved and busy joining and leading numerous organizations" are "increasingly more common" on campus. There's also "a vibrant musical community" as well as an active group of intramural sports enthusiasts. One student sums it up, "The greatest strengths of Case are the diversity of the student body, the studious character of the student body, the professors, and the tolerance students have toward different students."

CASE WESTERN RESERVE UNIVERSITY

FINANCIAL AID: 216-368-4530 • E-MAIL: ADMISSION@CASE.EDU • WEBSITE: WWW.CASE.EDU

THE PRINCETON REVIEW SAYS

Admissions

Very important factors considered include: Academic GPA, class rank, rigor of secondary school record, standardized test scores, extracurricular activities. *Important factors considered include:* Application essay, recommendation(s), character/personal qualities, interview, level of applicant's interest, talent/ ability, volunteer work, work experience. *Other factors considered include:* Alumni/ae relation, first generation, racial/ethnic status. SAT or ACT required; ACT with writing component required. TOEFL required of all international applicants. High school diploma is required, and GED is accepted. *Academic units required:* 4 English, 3 mathematics, 3 science (2 science labs), 2 foreign language, 3 social studies. *Academic units recommended:* 4 mathematics, (3 science labs), 3 foreign language, 4 social studies.

Financial Aid

Students should submit: FAFSA, institution's own financial aid form. The Princeton Review suggests that all financial aid forms be submitted as soon as possible after January 1. *Need-based scholarships/grants offered:* Federal Pell, SEOG, state scholarships/grants, private scholarships, school scholarship or grant aid from institutional funds. *Loan aid offered:* Federal Perkins, Federal Nursing Loans, state loans, university loans from institutional funds. Applicants will be notified of awards on a rolling basis beginning March 15. Federal Work-Study Program available. Off-campus job opportunities are excellent.

The Inside Word

Case faces tough competition from similar schools and handles it well as both the number of overall applications and out-of-state applications has increased substantially over the past decade, indicating an improving national profile. As a result, Case grows ever more selective. Case uses a "single-door" admissions policy, meaning that once you're admitted you can change your intended major without having to reapply, even if it means switching schools (for example, switching from the School of Engineering to the School of Management).

THE SCHOOL SAYS "..."

From the Admissions Office

"Challenging and innovative academic programs, next-level technology, experiential learning, real-world environments, and faculty mentors are at the core of the Case Western Reserve University experience. Case's faculty challenges and supports motivated students, and its partnerships with world-class cultural, educational, and scientific institutions ensure that your education extends beyond the classroom. Case offers more than seventy-five majors and minors and a single-door admission policy; once admitted to Case, you can major in any of our programs, or double and even triple major in several of them. Our student/faculty ratio, among the best in the nation, allows students to have close interaction with professors. Co-ops, internships, study abroad, and other opportunities bring theory to life in amazing settings, and sixty-six percent of students participate in research and independent study. SAGES, Case's four-year undergraduate core curriculum, connects students with faculty, peers and the community through small seminars that explore effective communication and analytical skills, and culminates in a Senior Capstone project. With eighty-five percent of students living on campus, Case has a residential feel unique to urban universities. First-year students live together in one of three themed residential colleges that involve resources from across Northeast Ohio: Cedar (arts), Juniper (world culture), and Mistletoe (leadership through service). Admission Counselors consider all sections of the SAT, taking the best score for each section from multiple dates. The SAT (or ACT with writing) is used for evaluating applications for admission (and not used for course placement purposes)."

SELECTIVITY

Admissions Rating	90
# of applicants	9,472
% of applicants accepted	67
% of acceptees attending	16
# accepting a place on wait list	307
% admitted from wait list	1

FRESHMAN PROFILE

Range SAT Critical Reading	600–700
Range SAT Math	650–750
Range SAT Writing	590–700
Range ACT Composite	28–32
Minimum paper TOEFL	550
Minimum computer TOEFL	213
Minimum web-based TOEFL	80
% graduated top 10% of class	67
% graduated top 25% of class	93
% graduated top 50% of class	99

DEADLINES

Early action	
Deadline	11/1
Notification	12/15
Regular	
Deadline	1/15
Nonfall registration?	yes

APPLICANTS ALSO LOOK AT AND OFTEN PREFER

Northwestern University, Washington University in St. Louis

AND SOMETIMES PREFER

Carnegie Mellon University, The Ohio State University, University of Pittsburgh—Pittsburgh Campus

FINANCIAL FACTS

Financial Aid Rating	93
Annual tuition	$37,300
Room and board	$15,440
% frosh rec. need-based scholarship or grant aid	65
% UG rec. need-based scholarship or grant aid	62
% frosh rec. non-need-based scholarship or grant aid	63
% UG rec. non-need-based scholarship or grant aid	61
% frosh rec. need-based self-help aid	56
% UG rec. need-based self-help aid	57
% frosh rec. any financial aid	90
% UG rec. any financial aid	86
% UG borrow to pay for school	60
Average cumulative indebtedness	$39,239

CATAWBA COLLEGE

2300 WEST INNES STREET, SALISBURY, NC 28144 • ADMISSIONS: 704-637-4402 • FAX: 704-637-4222

CAMPUS LIFE
Quality of Life Rating	81
Fire Safety Rating	83
Green Rating	87
Type of school	private
Affiliation	United Church of Christ
Environment	town

STUDENTS
Total undergrad enrollment	1,291
% male/female	44/56
% from out of state	18
% from public high school	80
% live on campus	49
# of countries represented	11

SURVEY SAYS . . .
Students are friendly
Students get along with local community
Students are happy
Everyone loves the Catawba Indians
Theater is popular
Student government is popular

ACADEMICS
Academic Rating	77
% students graduating within 4 years	43
% students graduating within 6 years	54
Calendar	semester
Student/faculty ratio	15:1
Profs interesting rating	90
Profs accessible rating	85
Most common reg class size	10–19 students
Most common lab size	fewer than 10 students

MOST POPULAR MAJORS
business/commerce, drama and dramatics/theatre arts, elementary education and teaching

STUDENTS SAY ". . ."

Academics
Catawba College sports "a small, close-knit community where you can really get to know your professors and your fellow classmates." The school is known especially for its "high-ranking theater program and the hugely growing music program" as well as its athletics. Don't let its small size fool you, as "big things come in small packages." "Class sizes are small in order for you to receive as much of a personalized education as possible." "Excellent financial aid" attracts many students, although some feel the university isn't doing enough to "increase scholarships to match rising tuition." Catawba is particularly strong for "highly focused programs (theater [and] music in particular)." The honors program also gets high marks among students. "I can get whatever educational experience I make for myself here, especially because of the diversity of the honors program courses." Some students feel that the facilities could be improved. "While our computer labs are good, I feel like that Catawba's computer centers and facilities are not as advanced and developed as [at] other schools." "Most of the professors here really care about the students" and "know your name as well as your interests." As "a melting pot with many opportunities if you reach out for them," Catawba is "a place where you can truly discover who you are through exposure to a variety of thoughts and perspectives."

Life
Life on Catawba campus is driven by the school's strong athletics, theater, and music programs. Students tend to be "busy, busy, busy. Everyone is active. Campus clubs are huge, and there is a school-sponsored event every weekend." There are frequent sporting events, "theater and music performances," and other activities sponsored by the school or clubs. "The students focus a lot on their activities," one student says. "For instance, my life centers around rehearsal for the many performances by the Catawba Singers. The same goes for the theater department as well as athletics." Another student describes life: "My life at school? Class, work in the theater, homework, sleep, rinse, repeat," but also notes that "other students have more free time." "There are usually campus-wide events on the weekends that generally have very high turnouts." When asked what the school could improve on, the chorus responds unanimously: "Food! The food is pretty bad. We pay a lot of money to be here, and our food is sometimes not edible." Consequently, many students leave campus to "go to downtown Salisbury or Charlotte for shopping, restaurants, and clubbing." Note that Catawba does impose an age limit for students to live off campus, although it was recently "lowered to twenty-one."

Student Body
The student body is divided clearly into "three types of students. The athletes are a large make up of the student population. The theater and music students make up the next largest population. Then there is the other category." "We all identify with a category," one student explains, "but that does not mean that we are always divided this way." Others see the campus fairly divided, with the three sections busy in their own work. "Athletes don't go to theater, and theater students don't go to sporting events" although "generally everyone mixes because of our general education classes, so no one really stands out." Students "are either athletes, all about education, or theater/music kids. They all do their own thing, and it works." Most students are from the area, but "thirty-three percent of Catawba students are from out of state." Otherwise, it's "difficult to describe the typical student, because there is such diversity at Catawba College." "Catawba has almost anyone you can imagine, it's a wide array of different cultures of people that go here."

FINANCIAL AID: 704-637-4416 • E-MAIL: ADMISSION@CATAWBA.EDU • WEBSITE: WWW.CATAWBA.EDU

THE PRINCETON REVIEW SAYS

Admissions

Very important factors considered include: Academic GPA, application essay, recommendation(s), standardized test scores. *Important factors considered include:* Class rank, rigor of secondary school record, character/personal qualities, extracurricular activities, interview, level of applicant's interest, talent/ability. *Other factors considered include:* Volunteer work. SAT or ACT required; ACT with writing component recommended. TOEFL required of all international applicants. High school diploma is required, and GED is accepted. *Academic units recommended:* 4 English, 3 mathematics, 3 science (3 science labs), 2 foreign language, 3 social studies.

Financial Aid

Students should submit: FAFSA. The Princeton Review suggests that all financial aid forms be submitted as soon as possible after January 1. *Need-based scholarships/grants offered:* Federal Pell, SEOG, state scholarships/grants, private scholarships, school scholarship or grant aid from institutional funds. *Loan aid offered:* Federal Perkins, university loans from institutional funds. Applicants will be notified of awards on a rolling basis beginning February 15. Federal Work-Study Program available. Off-campus job opportunities are good.

The Inside Word

Since Catawba competes for students with several top regional schools, it's willing to take a chance on students who may not make the cut at Davidson, Chapel Hill, or Duke. Students who may not have been the highest achievers in high school but are ready to excel at the college level should put Catawba on their list. For students of all stripes with an interest in theater or music, Catawba demands consideration.

THE SCHOOL SAYS "..."

From the Admissions Office

"Catawba College prepares students for rewarding lives and careers in the liberal arts tradition. This attractive campus is centrally located in Salisbury, North Carolina, a short drive away from the mountains and Atlantic beaches. The community possesses a rich past and commitment to preserving its cultural and historic charm. In contrast, just forty-five minutes away is the much faster pace of Charlotte, North Carolina where shopping, transportation, and entertainment of all kinds are readily available.

"On campus, students study and socialize in a small college setting that offers strong traditions, excellent facilities, and beautiful surroundings. The high standards of quality set by Catawba's academic programs are matched by equally demanding sports and co-curricular programs. Students describe the community as caring and personable. They also exhibit a high rate of involvement in campus activities ranging form the performing arts to homecoming and travel abroad. Faculty and staff are described by students as being important mentors. Whether in a state-of-the-art environmental science facility, attractive music and theatrical performance center, classroom, or one of the college's first-class athletic facilities, students report they feel as if they are among family when on campus.

"Perhaps the most important testimony to the attractiveness of Catawba is found in the words of its graduates who report numerous successful careers and rich memories of their time at school.

"Students applying for admissions to Catawba College are required submit to scores from the SAT, including the writing portion of the test. In lieu of SAT scores, Catawba will accept student scores on the ACT when they include scores on the ACT writing portion of the test. Catawba will use the student's best scores from either test in making admissions decisions."

SELECTIVITY

Admissions Rating	77
# of applicants	1,398
% of applicants accepted	55
% of acceptees attending	34

FRESHMAN PROFILE

Range SAT Critical Reading	420–540
Range SAT Math	450–560
Minimum paper TOEFL	525
Minimum computer TOEFL	197
Average HS GPA	3.41
% graduated top 10% of class	14
% graduated top 25% of class	38
% graduated top 50% of class	67

DEADLINES

Regular	
Notification	10/1
Nonfall registration?	yes

APPLICANTS ALSO LOOK AT AND SOMETIMES PREFER
Appalachian State University,
University of North Carolina—Charlotte

AND RARELY PREFER
University of North Carolina Greensboro

FINANCIAL FACTS

Financial Aid Rating	80
Annual tuition	$25,160
Room and board	$8,700
Books and supplies	$1,400
% frosh rec. need-based scholarship or grant aid	56
% UG rec. need-based scholarship or grant aid	49
% frosh rec. non-need-based scholarship or grant aid	79
% UG rec. non-need-based scholarship or grant aid	70
% frosh rec. need-based self-help aid	59
% UG rec. need-based self-help aid	52
% frosh rec. any financial aid	99
% UG rec. any financial aid	99
% UG borrow to pay for school	63
Average cumulative indebtedness	$27,907

THE CATHOLIC UNIVERSITY OF AMERICA

OFFICE OF ENROLLMENT SERVICES, WASHINGTON, D.C. 20064 • ADMISSIONS: 202-319-5305 • FAX: 202-319-6533

STUDENTS SAY "..."

Academics

At The Catholic University of America, strong academic programs are infused with "the values and traditions of conservative Catholicism, including service to the community, family, and Catholic morality." For students seeking a spiritual atmosphere, CUA is a "great learning environment where your faith can grow exponentially." However, "Contrary to popular belief, students do not attend this school based on its religious affiliation." Instead, the "intimate class sizes," generous scholarship packages, and fantastic location lure many top students to this small school. At CUA, academic opportunities (such as overseas studies) are plentiful, and courses are tough but manageable. A current student shares, "I am challenged, and will leave college feeling empowered with the skills needed to succeed in whatever career path I choose." No matter what your major, there are "required religion courses" woven into the curriculum. Students tell us, "The emphasis on classical philosophy for all majors really teaches students how to think in complex ways." While not every professor is unilaterally adored, most "are well-organized and truly knowledgeable about the subject…they teach." Instructors "really care about the individual, and you are definitely not just a number to them." Depending on your perspective, you might describe the school's administration as "an oppressive regime that allows no fun," or you might characterize them as a friendly group of student-oriented individuals who are "strict but fair." Either way, things tend to "run smoothly" on the CUA campus, despite the fact that there are some "communication issues" between administrative departments.

Life

Offering a range of clubs and activities, an active campus ministry, varied social events, and varsity sports, life at CUA is a "good mix of spirituality and fun." "There is a huge spirit [of] community service and giving back" at CUA, and many students are involved in volunteer work with Catholic charities. In fact, "CUA is located in a section of D.C. dubbed 'Little Vatican.' The large number of Catholic organizations in the immediate area provides ample opportunities for spiritual development and self-discovery." In addition to faith-based activities, the surrounding city is a great jumping-off point for culture and recreation. In their spare time, students "go to concerts, museums, parks, [and] political rallies" in surrounding D.C., or they enjoy eating in some of the "amazing restaurants in the area." Given the propitious location, it's not surprising that "a lot of students are interested in politics and become active in political groups." Come the weekend, CUA is a "bit of a party school," and "most people go out to the bars at night on Thursdays, Fridays, and Saturdays for fun." More than sixty percent of undergraduates live on campus, which they describe as a "quiet oasis located amidst a bustling metropolis."

Student Body

With its distinctive personality and cosmopolitan location in Washington, D.C., CUA tends to attract students from a similar background. On this small campus, undergraduates are predominately "white, upper-middle-class, [and] Catholic," and almost "every student is either from New York, Massachusetts, or ROP (right outside Philly)." Most characterize the community as lacking diversity, telling us, "Aside from drama and architecture students, the majority of the undergrads do not stick out." CUA has a "strong Catholic identity" and a good portion of students are "extremely religious." At the same time, "There are a decent number of non-Catholics at the school, as well as kids from other countries and cultures." With academics, as with religion, some students are more committed to their studies than others. A current student elaborates, "Half the students are very religious or academic, while the other half are less interested in academics and more interested in fun activities."

FINANCIAL AID: 202-319-5307 • E-MAIL: CUA-ADMISSIONS@CUA.EDU • WEBSITE: WWW.CUA.EDU

THE PRINCETON REVIEW SAYS

Admissions

Very important factors considered include: Academic GPA, recommendation(s), rigor of secondary school record, standardized test scores, character/personal qualities, level of applicant's interest, volunteer work. *Important factors considered include:* Application essay, extracurricular activities, first generation, interview, talent/ability. *Other factors considered include:* Class rank, alumni/ae relation, geographical residence, racial/ethnic status, work experience. SAT or ACT required; ACT with writing component required. TOEFL required of all international applicants. High school diploma is required, and GED is accepted. *Academic units recommended:* 4 English, 3 mathematics, 3 science (1 science lab), 2 foreign language, 4 social studies.

Financial Aid

Students should submit: FAFSA. Regular filing deadline is April 10. The Princeton Review suggests that all financial aid forms be submitted as soon as possible after January 1. *Need-based scholarships/grants offered:* Federal Pell, SEOG, state scholarships/grants, private scholarships, school scholarship or grant aid from institutional funds. *Loan aid offered:* Direct Subsidized Stafford, Direct Unsubsidized Stafford, Direct PLUS, Federal Nursing Loans. Applicants will be notified of awards on a rolling basis beginning April 1. Federal Work-Study Program available. Off-campus job opportunities are good.

The Inside Word

CUA offers a nonbinding early action program, as well as regular admission. A student's academic record and test scores are important elements in an admissions decision, as is a history of service in his or her school or community. If it sounds like a fit, prospective students can get a feel for life at CUA during an "open house" day, when they're invited to attend mass, meet with the deans, take a tour, and eat lunch on campus.

THE SCHOOL SAYS " . . ."

From the Admissions Office

"The Catholic University of America's friendly atmosphere, rigorous academic programs, and emphasis on time-honored values attract students from all fifty states and more than eighty foreign countries. Its 193-acre, tree-lined campus is only ten minutes from the Capitol building. Distinguished as the national university of the Catholic Church in the United States, CUA is the only institution of higher education established by the U.S. Catholic bishops; however, students from all religious traditions are welcome. CUA offers undergraduate degrees in more than eighty major areas in eight schools of study. Students enroll into the School of Arts and Sciences, Social Work, Architecture, Nursing, Engineering, Music, Philosophy or Professional Studies. Additionally, CUA students can concentrate in areas of preprofessional study including law, dentistry, medicine, or veterinary studies.

"With Capitol Hill, the Smithsonian Institution, NASA, the Kennedy Center, and the National Institutes of Health among the places students obtain internships, firsthand experience is a valuable piece of the experience that CUA offers.

Numerous students also take the opportunity in their junior year to study abroad at one of Catholic's thirty-eight different semester programs. Political science majors even have the opportunity to do a Parliamentary Internship in either England or Ireland. With the campus just minutes away from downtown via the Metrorail rapid transit system, students enjoy a residential campus in an exciting city of historical monuments, theaters, festivals, ethnic restaurants, and parks.

"Matriculating students should submit the SAT Subject Test: Foreign Language exam if they plan to continue studying that language at CUA."

SELECTIVITY

Admissions Rating	75
# of applicants	6,207
% of applicants accepted	87
% of acceptees attending	18

FRESHMAN PROFILE

Range SAT Critical Reading	500–610
Range SAT Math	500–610
Range ACT Composite	22–27
Minimum paper TOEFL	550
Minimum computer TOEFL	213
Minimum web-based TOEFL	80
Average HS GPA	3.29

DEADLINES

Early action	
Deadline	11/15
Notification	12/15
Regular	
Deadline	2/15
Notification	3/15
Nonfall registration?	yes

APPLICANTS ALSO LOOK AT AND OFTEN PREFER
Boston College, University of Maryland

AND RARELY PREFER
American University, The George Washington University

FINANCIAL FACTS

Financial Aid Rating	84
Annual tuition	$35,260
Room and board	$13,824
Required fees	$200
Books and supplies	$1,400
% frosh rec. need-based scholarship or grant aid	63
% UG rec. need-based scholarship or grant aid	57
% frosh rec. non-need-based scholarship or grant aid	29
% UG rec. non-need-based scholarship or grant aid	29
% frosh rec. need-based self-help aid	57
% UG rec. need-based self-help aid	53
% frosh rec. any financial aid	92
% UG rec. any financial aid	87

CENTENARY COLLEGE OF LOUISIANA

2911 CENTENARY BOULEVARD, SHREVEPORT, LA 71104 • ADMISSIONS: 318-869-5131 • FAX: 318-869-5005

CAMPUS LIFE

Quality of Life Rating	68
Fire Safety Rating	82
Green Rating	60*
Type of school	private
Affiliation	Methodist
Environment	metropolis

STUDENTS

Total undergrad enrollment	891
% male/female	41/59
% from out of state	43
% from public high school	70
% live on campus	66
# of fraternities	5
# of sororities	2
% African American	8
% Asian	2
% Caucasian	82
% Hispanic	4
% international	2
# of countries represented	12

SURVEY SAYS . . .

*Registration is a breeze
Students are friendly
Students get along with local community
Musical organizations are popular
Student publications are popular
Student government is popular*

ACADEMICS

Academic Rating	83
% students graduating within 4 years	43
% students graduating within 6 years	57
Calendar	semester
Student/faculty ratio	12:1
Profs interesting rating	89
Profs accessible rating	87
Most common reg class size	10–19 students

MOST POPULAR MAJORS
biology, business/commerce, mass communication/media studies

STUDENTS SAY ". . ."

Academics

With fewer than 1,000 undergraduates, Centenary College of Louisiana certainly qualifies as a small school. In fact, there are only a handful of elite undergraduate institutions smaller. That said, smallness has its virtues. As one student notes, "The small size of the student body gives students the opportunity to receive individual attention in class, be involved in many organizations and hold leadership positions outside of class." It also fosters "a community atmosphere" in which "professors really care about you emotionally and academically," along with providing "a lot of one-on-one help and projects." Premedical sciences are said to be excellent (nearly twenty percent of all students major in life sciences), as are business studies, music, and communications. Academics are "extremely rigorous and thorough," so much so that "no one graduates without expanding their knowledge base." As at many small schools, "the professors are absolutely wonderful. They're engaging, knowledgeable, and really care about what they're teaching and about their students." The school places a premium on such high-caliber teaching skill. "Bad teachers do not last long around here," one undergrad assures us. The downside of a small school, of course, is that certain limitations are an unavoidable fact of life. Some "miss the perks a bigger school [has to offer] like more classes and a better cafeteria."

Life

"Campus life centers around athletics, clubs, and Greek life" at Centenary, where "the real trick is finding that one thing that you love (be it sororities, radio, theater, whatever) and excelling at it. The school has a lot of opportunities for responsible individuals." There's the "awesome" radio station, for one, and lots of lectures, internships, and mentoring opportunities. And while "There are occasional events on weekdays, including sports games," when it comes time for fun "life at Centenary revolves around the weekend" and "includes going to some of the local attractions, to a movie, to dinner, or to either one of the sport teams' house or a fraternity house." Because the campus is officially dry, "those unwilling to hide their contraband alcohol...normally just hang out in residence hall lobbies and watch movies" or they "go down to the fraternity houses (which allow alcohol)." Hometown Shreveport "doesn't offer many options for students, especially students under twenty-one. It's definitely not a 'college town.'" Another student explains, "There is not a lot to do in Shreveport besides shopping, but there are many opportunities to do so in the surrounding area. There not too many local music shows, but the Shreveport Opera and community theaters are worth the time."

Student Body

For such a small school, Centenary does a good job of drawing a diverse mix of interests and backgrounds. Here "You can find everything from far right-wing ministry majors to highly liberal individuals actively involved in campus organizations promoting gay rights" as well as "a large and diverse number of international students, most notably from Europe and Hong Kong." What you won't find is a lot of minority students; "There are very few minorities on this campus," one student observes. Most students here "are overachievers or hard workers, whether it is in an academic sense or in an extracurricular sense." Though many note that the student body is "generally white, middle-class, and religious," they are also quick to point out that it also accommodates "a lot of gay and lesbian students, and overall, the campus is very accepting and supportive of these students."

CENTENARY COLLEGE OF LOUISIANA

FINANCIAL AID: 318-869-5137 • E-MAIL: ADMISSIONS@CENTENARY.EDU • WEBSITE: WWW.CENTENARY.EDU

THE PRINCETON REVIEW SAYS

Admissions

Very important factors considered include: Academic GPA, rigor of secondary school record. *Important factors considered include:* Application essay, class rank, recommendation(s), standardized test scores, alumni/ae relation, character/personal qualities, extracurricular activities, interview, level of applicant's interest, talent/ability, volunteer work, work experience. *Other factors considered include:* First generation, geographical residence, racial/ethnic status, religious affiliation/commitment. SAT or ACT required; ACT with or without writing component accepted. TOEFL required of all international applicants. High school diploma is required, and GED is accepted. *Academic units recommended:* 4 English, 3 mathematics, 3 science (2 science labs), 2 foreign language, 3 social studies.

Financial Aid

Students should submit: FAFSA, institution's own financial aid form. The Princeton Review suggests that all financial aid forms be submitted as soon as possible after January 1. *Need-based scholarships/grants offered:* Federal Pell, SEOG, state scholarships/grants, private scholarships, school scholarship or grant aid from institutional funds. *Loan aid offered:* Direct Subsidized Stafford, Direct Unsubsidized Stafford, Direct PLUS, Federal Perkins. Federal Work-Study Program available. Off-campus job opportunities are good.

The Inside Word

Centenary's applicant pool has grown substantially over the past decade, allowing the school to become more selective in its admissions process. The school's reputation, though regional, is quite solid, and the college does a good job of enrolling those it admits—a sign that the school is tops on more than a few applicants' lists. No doubt a very friendly and efficient admissions office also contributes to this success.

THE SCHOOL SAYS "..."

From the Admissions Office

"Just as a student's four-year experience at Centenary will be very personalized, so too is the application process. We pride ourselves on treating each applicant as an individual. We encourage all interested students to visit us—not only so they can see our campus and get a sense of the atmosphere, but also to provide us the opportunity to meet and get to know them.

"Consider Centenary for a life-changing experience. Our professors value your ideas and contributions and are passionate about teaching. We consider the Centenary Experience to be more than just a degree. You will live in a comprehensive learning environment that features connections to your academic, social, personal, and residential lives.

"Our students work and live within a strong community to create personalized, distinctive experiences, and enjoy a vibrant college life and graduate from Centenary prepared for their professional and personal lives.

"First-year applicants must submit either ACT or SAT scores. We recommend, but do not require, the ACT writing component."

SELECTIVITY

Admissions Rating	79
# of applicants	1,076
% of applicants accepted	69
% of acceptees attending	33

FRESHMAN PROFILE

Range SAT Critical Reading	520–630
Range SAT Math	520–620
Range ACT Composite	24–28
Minimum paper TOEFL	550
Minimum computer TOEFL	213
% graduated top 10% of class	33
% graduated top 25% of class	63
% graduated top 50% of class	85

DEADLINES

Early action	
Deadline	12/15
Notification	12/15
Regular	
Priority	2/15
Deadline	8/1
Notification	10/1
Nonfall registration?	yes

FINANCIAL FACTS

Financial Aid Rating	85
Annual tuition	$22,880
Room and board	$7,590
Required fees	$1,200
Books and supplies	$1,200
% frosh rec. need-based scholarship or grant aid	67
% UG rec. need-based scholarship or grant aid	56
% frosh rec. non-need-based scholarship or grant aid	15
% UG rec. non-need-based scholarship or grant aid	16
% frosh rec. need-based self-help aid	46
% UG rec. need-based self-help aid	34
% frosh rec. any financial aid	98
% UG rec. any financial aid	93
% UG borrow to pay for school	64
Average cumulative indebtedness	$19,206

CENTRE COLLEGE

600 WEST WALNUT STREET, DANVILLE, KY 40422 • ADMISSIONS: 800-423-6236 • FAX: 859-238-5373

CAMPUS LIFE

Quality of Life Rating	85
Fire Safety Rating	60*
Green Rating	82
Type of school	private
Affiliation	Presbyterian
Environment	village

STUDENTS

Total undergrad enrollment	1,214
% male/female	44/55
% from out of state	39
% from public high school	79
% live on campus	99
# of fraternities	4
# of sororities	4
% African American	4
% Asian	3
% Caucasian	88
% Hispanic	2
% international	2
# of countries represented	12

SURVEY SAYS . . .
No one cheats
Athletic facilities are great
School is well-run
Campus feels safe
Low cost of living
Very little drug use

ACADEMICS

Academic Rating	94
% students graduating within 4 years	79
% students graduating within 6 years	81
Calendar	4-1-4
Student/faculty ratio	11:1
Profs interesting rating	97
Profs accessible rating	98
Most common reg class size	10–19 students
Most common lab size	10–19 students

MOST POPULAR MAJORS
economics, English language and
literature, history

STUDENTS SAY "..."

Academics

Centre College offers "a genuine, personal, practical education in all areas of life." Its "small classes" are focused and challenging, "and students definitely spend a lot of time studying, reading, and writing papers." An international studies student comments, "I find myself working harder than I ever thought possible...I feel so accomplished at the end of each semester." Students are taught by "extremely passionate and dedicated professors." Teachers are "kind, supportive, caring, and are always available for help outside the classroom," and they make "an effort to work one-on-one with you if necessary." One of Centre's goals is "preparing students to be actively engaged global citizens," and there's "a big movement on getting out of the classroom with the community-based learning." "If a professor doesn't require that kind of learning," a student explains, "then they almost always will still make connections outside the classroom whether to real life or to other classes." Centre has an impressively strong study abroad program, and about eighty-five percent of their students take advantage of it. One student says, "You are guaranteed the chance to have an internship and study abroad." Students love this combination of global, local, and personal learning. One proudly says that Centre "looks toward the future...of our world and the need for students to be prepared for it...Centre has and will continue to prepare me for what comes next in my journey."

Life

Centre College has an active campus life. Fraternities and sororities have a big presence and host a lot of parties. One student says, "There are a lot of students who are involved in Greek life, but there are a fair amount who are not involved in any way." Another adds, "There has been a significant development in alternative organizations, such as the Art House for drama, music, and art majors." There's also the "philanthropic co-ed fraternity Alpha Phi Omega," which "provides a very different, positive experience for...students who prefer to focus on service and forming strong friendships rather than partying." The Student Activities Council also organizes a lot of events, including "midnight movies." The small, picturesque town of Danville is "very much a college town." "New restaurants and bars have been opening, which is making Danville a little more exciting," but students admit that overall "there isn't much to do off campus." However, "There is so much going on at campus" that students "don't ever want to leave."

Student Body

Centre College's small student body and rural setting lend it a "welcoming atmosphere" and help create a "close-knit community." Students are "kind, respectful, and friendly to peers, professors, and administrators alike." Students are "hyper-involved," either in athletics, Greek life, the many "clubs and organizations," or all three. Students may "work hard all week," but they still find time to "attend club meetings, support their friends in sporting events, relax in the campus center...attend sorority/fraternity activities, and attend events." The stereotype of the Centre student is one who is "white," "Southern," and "middle- or upper-class," but many insist that Centre's student body has "changed dramatically." One student says, "I believe that Centre has lived up to its mission of improving racial diversity on campus." They add, "The number of African American, international, and Hispanic students has increased dramatically." Students admit, "Centre is quite cliquish," but say, "People always find their own place." One student explains, "During the week people tend to stick to their groups," but "barriers break down on weekends."

FINANCIAL AID: 859-238-5365 • E-MAIL: ADMISSION@CENTRE.EDU • WEBSITE: WWW.CENTRE.EDU

THE PRINCETON REVIEW SAYS

Admissions

Very important factors considered include: Academic GPA, rigor of secondary school record. *Important factors considered include:* Application essay, class rank, recommendation(s), standardized test scores. *Other factors considered include:* Alumni/ae relation, character/personal qualities, extracurricular activities, first generation, geographical residence, interview, racial/ethnic status, talent/ability, volunteer work, work experience. SAT or ACT required; ACT with writing component recommended. TOEFL required of all international applicants. High school diploma or equivalent isn't required. *Academic units required:* 4 English, 3 mathematics, 2 science (2 science labs), 2 foreign language, 1 social studies, 1 history. *Academic units recommended:* 4 mathematics, 4 science, 4 foreign language, 2 social studies, 2 history, 1 visual/performing arts.

Financial Aid

Students should submit: FAFSA, institution's own financial aid form. Regular filing deadline is March 1. The Princeton Review suggests that all financial aid forms be submitted as soon as possible after January 1. *Need-based scholarships/grants offered:* Federal Pell, SEOG, state scholarships/grants, private scholarships, school scholarship or grant aid from institutional funds. *Loan aid offered:* Direct Subsidized Stafford, Direct Unsubsidized Stafford, Direct PLUS, Federal Perkins, university loans from institutional funds. Applicants will be notified of awards on a rolling basis beginning mid-March. Federal Work-Study Program available. Off-campus job opportunities are fair.

The Inside Word

Centre's small but very capable student body reflects solid academic preparation from high school. If you're ranked in the top quarter of your graduating class and have taken challenging courses throughout your high school career, you should have smooth sailing through the admissions process. Those who rank below the top quarter or who have inconsistent academic transcripts will find entrance here more difficult and may benefit from an interview.

THE SCHOOL SAYS "..."

From the Admissions Office

"Centre provides its students with a personal education that enables them to achieve extraordinary success in advanced study and their careers. Centre professors, virtually all of whom hold the highest degree available in their fields, challenge their students and give them the individual attention and support they need to meet those challenges. The end result is highly capable graduates with a can-do attitude and the ability to accomplish their goals.

"Centre offers a multitude of advantages, such as a national top fifty academic reputation (ranked number one institution of higher education in the South for the second year in a row), majors options, and exposure to internationally known artists and scholars; benefits like these produce extraordinary success. For example, entrance to top graduate and professional schools; the most prestigious postgraduate scholarships (Rhodes, Fulbright, Goldwater); interesting, rewarding jobs (ninety-seven percent of graduates are either employed or engaged in advance study within ten months of graduation).

"How do alumni respond? They have expressed their customer satisfaction by leading the United States in their percentage of annual financial support over the past twenty-five years. How much does all this cost? Because of our nation-leading alumni support, Centre is the most affordable of America's top fifty national liberal arts colleges and has been ranked as the number one value among all U.S. colleges.

SELECTIVITY

Admissions Rating	92
# of applicants	2,056
% of applicants accepted	69
% of acceptees attending	23
# accepting a place on wait list	69
% admitted from wait list	41

FRESHMAN PROFILE

Range SAT Critical Reading	550–670
Range SAT Math	570–670
Range SAT Writing	530–670
Range ACT Composite	26–30
Minimum paper TOEFL	580
Average HS GPA	3.58
% graduated top 10% of class	59
% graduated top 25% of class	84
% graduated top 50% of class	98

DEADLINES

Early action	
Deadline	12/1
Notification	1/15
Regular	
Deadline	1/15
Notification	3/15
Nonfall registration?	no

**APPLICANTS ALSO LOOK AT
AND SOMETIMES PREFER**
Furman University, Rhodes College

AND RARELY PREFER
Transylvania University,
University of Kentucky

FINANCIAL FACTS

Financial Aid Rating	85
Annual comprehensive tuition	$39,000
Books and supplies	$1,200
% frosh rec. need-based scholarship or grant aid	64
% UG rec. need-based scholarship or grant aid	59
% frosh rec. need-based self-help aid	39
% UG rec. need-based self-help aid	42
% UG borrow to pay for school	53
Average cumulative indebtedness	$17,190

CHAMPLAIN COLLEGE

163 SOUTH WILLARD STREET BOX 670, PO BOX 670, BURLINGTON, VT 05402-0670 • ADMISSIONS: 802-860-2727 • FAX: 802-860-2767

CAMPUS LIFE

Quality of Life Rating	95
Fire Safety Rating	96
Green Rating	92
Type of school	private
Environment	town

STUDENTS

Total undergrad enrollment	2,067
% male/female	59/41
% from out of state	70
% from public high school	80
% live on campus	50
% African American	2
% Asian	2
% Caucasian	69
% Hispanic	2
# of countries represented	23

SURVEY SAYS . . .
Students are happy
Great library
Career services are great
Students are friendly
Different types of students interact
Great off-campus food

ACADEMICS

Academic Rating	79
% students graduating within 4 years	52
% students graduating within 6 years	65
Calendar	semester
Student/faculty ratio	14:1
Profs interesting rating	95
Profs accessible rating	89
Most common reg class size	10–19 students
Most common lab size	fewer than 10 students

MOST POPULAR MAJORS
business, marketing, game design, professional writing, psychology, education, computer networking

STUDENTS SAY ". . ."

Academics

With highly ranked programs in professional majors such as game design and digital forensics, Champlain College "is a hands-on, professionally focused college aimed at creating well-rounded global citizens that excel in critical, interdisciplinary thinking." The school offers "one of the best, most innovative systems around to prepare students for the real-world after college by implementing requirements throughout the program that help shape college students into professional 'job hunters.'" It also has campuses in Montreal and Dublin, and studying abroad is popular. Students love the "Upside-Down Curriculum in which students take major-related classes in their first year." Major classes are complemented by the LEAD program, which helps students develop community-building skills and awareness, and the Core program, which emphasizes interdisciplinary studies and critical thinking. The classes are small—"a class of thirty is rare and considered large"—and this "allows the students and teachers to get to know one another exceptionally well." "The relationship between students and professors is more like a partnership. The professors at Champlain believe the process of learning never stops and that students have just as much to offer as they do." At a school with such strong digital and design programs, it's no surprise that "professors and their class materials [and] structures are constantly updated and mirror many current real-life situations."

Life

Students "absolutely love the Burlington area. It is the perfect college town." "The Champlain College Campus and the city itself are breathtaking," "so many Champlain students spend a good amount of time outside when weather permits." "There is so much to do," and the campus is located in the heart of it all—"only about a five-minute walk from the Church Street Market Place." "It is a great biking and walking town, which makes it easy to get around without a car." In the winter, Champlainers hit one of several nearby mountains to ski and snowboard, and North Beach on the college's namesake lake is a popular destination during warmer months. There are plenty of hiking trails and national forests nearby as well. On campus, Victorian mansions serve as dorms, and student activities abound, "such as rock-climbing... equestrian club, rugby, [and] photography." Campus events include "movie nights, special events in the cafeteria, a semiformal dance in the winter, and stress-relieving activities around exam times (such as massages and henna tattoos)." Downtown Burlington is home to a lot of live music venues and bars, and students partake of the local nightlife, "but it's always a very safe and comfortable environment."

Student Body

Students at Champlain categorize themselves in three groups: gamers, skiers/snowboarders, and everyone else: "There are hippies, photographers, writers, comedians, environmental do-gooders, adventurers, academics, and everything in between." The student body has a strong artsy streak—"hipsters are common" here. But just about everyone is "open-minded, laid-back, tech-savvy, professional," "and serious about their educations." "Many have jobs in addition to school." "The typical student is passionate about their major and is seen with a strong group of friends both in and outside of that major." The small campus and structure of the Core program encourage bonding: "Everyone knows everyone...and it's a very comfortable place to live." "The community feels like a family. We all know each other." As at most small, Northeastern, private colleges, a large portion of the student body is white, middle-class, and from the Northeast; as one student puts it, the school "could be more diverse, but it is in Vermont," and "there are no cookie-cutter students at this school."

CHAMPLAIN COLLEGE

FINANCIAL AID: 802-860-2730 • E-MAIL: ADMISSION@CHAMPLAIN.EDU • WEBSITE: WWW.CHAMPLAIN.EDU

THE PRINCETON REVIEW SAYS

Admissions

Very important factors considered include: Recalculated academic GPA, application essay, rigor of secondary school record, talent/ability. *Important factors considered include:* Class rank, recommendation(s), standardized test scores, character/personal qualities, extracurricular activities. *Other factors considered include:* Interview, volunteer work, work experience. SAT or ACT required; ACT with or without writing component accepted. TOEFL required of all international applicants. High school diploma is required, and GED is accepted. *Academic units required:* 4 English, 3 mathematics, 3 science (2 science labs), 4 history, 4 academic elective. *Academic units recommended:* 4 mathematics, 4 science (3 science labs), 2 foreign language, 2 social studies.

Financial Aid

Students should submit: FAFSA. Regular filing deadline is March 1. The Princeton Review suggests that all financial aid forms be submitted as soon as possible after January 1. *Need-based scholarships/grants offered:* Federal Pell, SEOG, state scholarships/grants, private scholarships, school scholarship or grant aid from institutional funds. *Loan aid offered:* Direct Subsidized Stafford, Direct Unsubsidized Stafford, Direct PLUS, Federal Perkins. Applicants will be notified of awards on a rolling basis beginning March 1. Federal Work-Study Program available. Off-campus job opportunities are good.

The Inside Word

Students interested in attending Champlain College should pursue a rigorous secondary school course load and make sure their career goals are a match with Champlain's major offerings. The school's supplement to the Common Application gives students an opportunity to describe their strengths and achievements—applicants should approach this as a chance to emphasize what they can contribute to the Champlain community. Students applying to the Graphic Design (BFA), Game Design, Digital Filmmaking (BFA), Professional Writing, Game Art and Animation (BFA), and Creative Media (BFA) programs will need to submit a portfolio of creative work.

THE SCHOOL SAYS "..."

From the Admissions Office

"Preparing students for the opportunities and challenges of an increasingly competitive world is not negotiable for us. When a student graduates from Champlain College, they can be confident that they are not only career-ready, but also life-ready.

"Students at Champlain College are immediately immersed in their prospective major and real-life internships via the Upside-Down Curriculum; they are challenged to think critically and further develop communication and writing abilities from the nationally acclaimed liberal arts core; and they will gain important skills such as financial sophistication, career management, and other life-building knowledge. It is an academic experience that is unparalleled, and our graduates are experiencing the benefits the day after graduation.

"However, in addition to academic preparation, going to college is about experiences, and there is no better college town in the East than Burlington, Vermont. Whether your interests are snowboarding and skiing, art and culture, music and expression, volunteering and community-building, or anything else, Burlington, Vermont, and our amazing campus have it covered. Champlain College students reside in historic Victorian mansions that overlook one of the country's most amazing natural vistas and are only steps from downtown Burlington.

"A Champlain College student is a student that feels optimistic about the future because she is taking control of it. It is a college environment of enrichment, support, and activity, and continually asks the question, what do you need to be successful upon graduation?

"We hope you can visit us soon and get a taste of the Champlain experience."

SELECTIVITY

Admissions Rating	72
# of applicants	3,077
% of applicants accepted	85
% of acceptees attending	25
# accepting a place on wait list	14
% admitted from wait list	79
# of early decision applicants	321
% accepted early decision	77

FRESHMAN PROFILE

Range SAT Critical Reading	500–610
Range SAT Math	490–590
Range ACT Composite	20–25
Minimum paper TOEFL	500
Minimum computer TOEFL	173
Minimum web-based TOEFL	61
% graduated top 10% of class	11
% graduated top 25% of class	35
% graduated top 50% of class	70

DEADLINES

Early decision	
Deadline	11/15
Notification	12/31
Early action	
Deadline	12/15
Notification	1/15
Regular	
Priority	2/1
Deadline	3/15
Nonfall registration?	yes

FINANCIAL FACTS

Financial Aid Rating	73
Annual tuition	$28,350
Room and board	$12,520
Required fees	$240
Books and supplies	$600
% frosh rec. need-based scholarship or grant aid	64
% UG rec. need-based scholarship or grant aid	59
% frosh rec. non-need-based scholarship or grant aid	30
% UG rec. non-need-based scholarship or grant aid	30
% frosh rec. need-based self-help aid	60
% UG rec. need-based self-help aid	55
% frosh rec. any financial aid	90
% UG rec. any financial aid	83
Average cumulative indebtedness	$20,000

CHAPMAN UNIVERSITY

ONE UNIVERSITY DRIVE, ORANGE, CA 92866 • ADMISSIONS: 714-997-6711 • FAX: 714-997-6713

STUDENTS SAY ". . ."

Academics

Chapman University is "a wealthy private institution" "in the heart of Orange County" that is "just the right size." There are "a lot of great facilities" here. Film production is "Chapman's most celebrated department." Resources are "totally state of the art." Students have access to "equipment that even the best studios will never have." The music conservatory is world class. Other notable majors include accounting, business administration, theater, dance, and public relations and advertising. Chapman offers a bevy of opportunities to study abroad in the summer and between semesters. "The travel courses are awesome," rejoices a political science major. International internships are also available. "Small class sizes" (typically about twenty students) are a plus. A broad yet flexible set of general education requirements ensures that everybody gets a firm grounding in the liberal arts. The administration isn't very popular. The top brass is "very ambitious" but "more focused on the school's image than its students." The registration process, which "can be a nightmare sometimes for everyone except for freshmen," "could be better," and higher-ups are "insanely difficult to contact," particularly for a smaller school. The faculty is generally "outstanding," though. "There is the occasional bad seed" who "should be avoided at all costs." "On the whole, though, the professors are very good and very accommodating," relates a computer science major. "They will always work with you for whatever you need, and you don't have to deal with any teaching assistants, period." You can talk to professors "about anything," adds a public relations major.

Life

Students here enjoy an "immaculate" and "truly beautiful campus." "The amenities are wonderful." "Chapman spends a ridiculous amount of money keeping the grounds nice." "We love sitting around the fountains in the sun between classes," says a sophomore. "It is such a nice place to spend four years," reflects a wistful senior. The food is "overpriced," though, and the cafeteria hours aren't long enough. "Get me some chain restaurants!" demands a ravenous first-year student. The social atmosphere is "lively." "It's not a hardcore party school," explains a sophomore, "but there [are] definitely parties every weekend if that's your scene." Many students participate in an intercollegiate sport. There is "a good variety of awesome clubs." "Greek life is huge" as well, and students who pledge tend to get "very, very involved" in their fraternities and sororities. Off campus, the town of Orange is "cute and historic" but "sleepy" and "sort of boring." However, "the beach is super close, like fifteen minutes," and Disneyland is "just up the street." Annual passes are reportedly "a good investment." "It's fun to go on random weekdays when it's not crowded." For more urban fare, Los Angeles is only about thirty miles north. Students often "go there for weekend visits and such."

Student Body

"If you're looking for a big, diverse school, keep looking," advises a junior. At Chapman, "the typical student would be an upper-class white kid from a relatively sheltered background." To be sure, there is a healthy percentage of "down-to-earth kids" "on loans" and scholarships. "I know I wouldn't be able to attend this school if I didn't have such an awesome financial aid package," notes a senior. There are also plenty of "rich Orange County children." "Three-outfits-a-day sorority types" who "wear Uggs with shorts" and "look like they've just walked out of a reality TV show" are not unusual. Students predominantly come from Southern California, and they describe themselves as "tan," "athletic," and "attractive." "I would say ninety-eight percent of students are ridiculously good looking," estimates a captivated first-year student. The campus is also "very cliquey." However, "there are plenty of sub-groups," giving Chapman "a very distinct, melting-pot sort of flair." There are the "liberal, tree-hugging vegans." There are the "surfers," the "stoners," the "crazy frat boys," the "oblivious pleasure-seekers," "the quiet types, the rockers, and the preppy people." "There are also a lot of creative types," primarily "eccentric" "film geeks" who "love movies and enjoy watching, making, and talking about movies."

FINANCIAL AID: 714-997-6741 • E-MAIL: ADMIT@CHAPMAN.EDU • WEBSITE: WWW.CHAPMAN.EDU

THE PRINCETON REVIEW SAYS

Admissions

Very important factors considered include: Academic GPA, application essay, class rank, rigor of secondary school record, standardized test scores, character/personal qualities. *Important factors considered include:* Extracurricular activities, talent/ability, volunteer work. *Other factors considered include:* Recommendation(s), alumni/ae relation, first generation, geographical residence, interview, racial/ethnic status, state residency, work experience. SAT or ACT required; ACT with writing component required. TOEFL required of all international applicants. High school diploma is required, and GED is accepted. *Academic units required:* 2 English, 2 mathematics, 2 science (1 science lab), 2 foreign language, 3 social studies. *Academic units recommended:* 4 English, 4 mathematics, 2 science (1 science lab), 4 foreign language, 4 social studies.

Financial Aid

Students should submit: FAFSA. The Princeton Review suggests that all financial aid forms be submitted as soon as possible after January 1. *Need-based scholarships/grants offered:* Federal Pell, SEOG, state scholarships/grants, private scholarships, school scholarship or grant aid from institutional funds. *Loan aid offered:* Federal Perkins. Applicants will be notified of awards on a rolling basis beginning March 15. Federal Work-Study Program available. Off-campus job opportunities are good.

Inside Word

Despite a plethora of California schools, Chapman continues to receive a steady stream of applications. Rather than work with formulas or cut-offs, admissions officers here prefer to take many factors into account. Well-rounded students are likely to make the most impact. Applicants who are service-oriented are also apt to do well, particularly given Chapman's "global responsibility" program.

THE SCHOOL SAYS ". . ."

From the Admissions Office

"During our 150-year history, Chapman has evolved from a small, church-related liberal arts college into a vibrant and comprehensive midsized liberal arts and sciences university distinguished for an eclectic group of nationally recognized programs including athletic training, film and television production, business and economics, dance, music, theater, writing, and teacher education. Our Orange County, California location was recently rated by *Places Rated Almanac* as "the number-one place to live in North America" citing superior climate, cultural, recreational, educational, and career entry opportunities.

"Chapman's environment is involving, and we seek students who are willing to enter an atmosphere of healthy competition where their talents will be nurtured and manifest to the fullest—whether in the classroom, on the stage, or on the athletic field. We challenge prospective students to thoroughly investigate our fine balance of liberal and professional learning so they may make a fully informed decision about 'fit' with regard to their personalities and that of the university.

"Chapman is a member of the Common Application group. Applicants for freshman admission to Chapman University will be required to submit scores from either the SAT or the ACT including the ACT writing section."

SELECTIVITY

Admissions Rating	93
# of applicants	8,056
% of applicants accepted	50
% of acceptees attending	29
# accepting a place on wait list	153
% admitted from wait list	8

FRESHMAN PROFILE

Range SAT Critical Reading	540–640
Range SAT Math	550–660
Range SAT Writing	560–650
Range ACT Composite	25–29
Minimum paper TOEFL	550
Minimum computer TOEFL	213
Average HS GPA	3.66
% graduated top 10% of class	47
% graduated top 25% of class	91
% graduated top 50% of class	98

DEADLINES

Early action	
Deadline	11/15
Notification	1/10
Regular	
Deadline	1/15
Notification	3/15
Nonfall registration?	yes

APPLICANTS ALSO LOOK AT
AND OFTEN PREFER
Loyola Marymount University, New York University, University of San Diego, University of Southern California

AND SOMETIMES PREFER
Pepperdine University

FINANCIAL FACTS

Financial Aid Rating	96
Annual tuition	$39,200
Room and board	$13,000
Required fees	$1,034
Books and supplies	$1,200
% frosh rec. need-based scholarship or grant aid	55
% UG rec. need-based scholarship or grant aid	61
% frosh rec. need-based self-help aid	47
% UG rec. need-based self-help aid	54
% UG borrow to pay for school	64
Average cumulative indebtedness	$23,917

CHRISTOPHER NEWPORT UNIVERSITY

1 UNIVERSITY PLACE, NEWPORT NEWS, VA 23606-2998 • ADMISSIONS: 757-594-7015 • FAX: 757-594-7333

CAMPUS LIFE

Quality of Life Rating	81
Fire Safety Rating	87
Green Rating	80
Type of school	public
Environment	city

STUDENTS

Total undergrad enrollment	4,768
% male/female	43/57
% from out of state	7
% live on campus	61
# of fraternities	7
# of sororities	7
% African American	9
% Asian	3
% Caucasian	79
% Hispanic	4
# of countries represented	40

SURVEY SAYS . . .
Students are friendly
Dorms are like palaces
Very little drug use
Great library

ACADEMICS

Academic Rating	79
% students graduating within 4 years	42
% students graduating within 6 years	60
Calendar	semester
Student/faculty ratio	17:1
Profs interesting rating	86
Profs accessible rating	88
Most common reg class size	20–29 students
Most common lab size	23 students

MOST POPULAR MAJORS
biology, business administration and management, psychology

STUDENTS SAY ". . ."

Academics

Named for an English seaman, Christopher Newport University (located in the Hamptons Roads area of Virginia) is a liberal arts college that runs on a "determination for student success." The small school's "modern outlook on education" is matched by its modern facilities (CNU is averaging one new building every year through 2015), and "It does not lack any of the resources of larger schools." Coupled with a well-run honors program, CNU's "growing prestige" means that "the future holds great things for this little school." While teaching methods of the "absolutely fabulous" faculty may vary, quality rarely does, and most professors "make even my least favorite subjects at least interesting." Though there are a few droning bad apples, for the most part, teachers "really [push students] to engage students in the lesson, other than just read to them," and "professors are ready to help any time you need." "The majority of my professors bring both a sense of expertise and uniqueness to their teaching styles…keeping a sense of personality in their teaching to keep students involved," says a student. Many classes are structured like workshops, and even the "few" lecture hall classes are capped at seventy-five students, so "you'll never find yourself drowning in a 500-person classroom here at CNU." Though many students abhor the buggy and complicated registration process, the administration (especially the well-liked president) "cares to listen to students' concerns," and the "free tutoring is amazing here." There's a palpable excitement for this relatively new school among its students, and though "it isn't well known across the nation, perhaps not even in Virginia…this allows those currently associated (students, faculty, administration, etc.) to help put CNU on the map for generations to come."

Life

With a campus right in the heart of the bustling city of Newport News, there are plenty of entertainment options, and "When the weather is warm, we are not too far from Virginia Beach." Almost everyone takes academics pretty seriously, but this "very socially oriented" bunch is still "able to unwind on the weekends." The campus activities board (CAB) provides free activities every weekend, such as ice skating or movie nights, which "are posted every Friday at the front desk of every resident building." The school's Ferguson Center puts on a great deal of shows and events, and anywhere you go "there are people ready to play Frisbee or talk about the deep universal truths and last night's reality show." Much like the academic buildings, the residential halls and campus are "breathtaking." "I feel like I am living in a luxury hotel," says one student. However, this dry campus has an incredibly strict alcohol policy that many students wish the administration would "lighten up" on; says one, "As someone who doesn't drink, it even makes me uncomfortable." This doesn't mean that (off-campus) parties aren't a popular pastime, and "Many students think about how to find the next party, which sometimes can be a difficult task." CNU students take their sports very seriously; or, as one student says, "Even though we are a [Division] III school, we have more school spirit than some [Division] I schools." Sundays are notorious for being "homework and housekeeping days."

Student Body

CNU prides itself on its sense of community, and the students within band together to create "a family-like atmosphere." This "incredibly friendly" group is typically the "middle-class, nice," "healthy, all-American sort." Everyone is open-minded and fairly outgoing, and "just a few weeks into classes…you feel like you know half the student body." "We pride ourselves on being a community of 'door holders,'" says a student. There are "very few socially deviant individuals, such as gang members, hardcore punks, goths, skinheads, etc.," but "nobody, regardless of race or background, sticks out like a sore thumb." Though there's a certain devotion to academics, the average student "is able to balance school work and play."

CHRISTOPHER NEWPORT UNIVERSITY

FINANCIAL AID: 757-594-7170 • E-MAIL: ADMIT@CNU.EDU • WEBSITE: WWW.CNU.EDU

THE PRINCETON REVIEW SAYS

Admissions

Very important factors considered include: Academic GPA, rigor of secondary school record. *Important factors considered include:* Application essay, class rank, recommendation(s), standardized test scores, character/personal qualities, extracurricular activities, interview, talent/ability. *Other factors considered include:* Alumni/ae relation, first generation, geographical residence, level of applicant's interest, state residency, volunteer work, work experience. SAT or ACT reccommended; ACT with or without writing component accepted. TOEFL required of all international applicants. High school diploma is required, and GED is accepted. *Academic units recommended:* 4 English, 4 mathematics, 4 science (3 science labs), 3 foreign language, 4 social studies.

Financial Aid

Students should submit: FAFSA. Priority filing deadline is February 1. The Princeton Review suggests that all financial aid forms be submitted as soon as possible after January 1. *Need-based scholarships/grants offered:* Federal Pell, SEOG, state scholarships/grants, private scholarships, school scholarship or grant aid from institutional funds. *Loan aid offered:* Direct Subsidized Stafford, Direct Unsubsidized Stafford, Direct PLUS. Applicants will be notified of awards on a rolling basis beginning February 21. Federal Work-Study Program available. Off-campus job opportunities are good.

The Inside Word

As universities go in Virginia, CNU is right up there in selectivity. The admissions people definitely play close attention to your academic success in high school, especially the strength of the curriculum and any honors or AP courses. The school looks for leaders and students with diverse experiences. Interviews are required for the President's Leadership Program and Honors Program and strongly recommended for all other applicants.

THE SCHOOL SAYS "..."

From the Admissions Office

"Christopher Newport University wants you to thrive academically. Even more so, we want you to lead a life of significance. That's why our undergraduate experience—one that combines cutting-edge academics, stellar leadership opportunities, and high-impact service initiatives—inspires great leaders for the twenty-first century.

"Honoring the best of the liberal arts and sciences, our curriculum shapes hearts and minds for a lifetime of service. We seek students of honor who will make the world a better place. Fifty percent of our students score between 1140 and 1200 on the SAT (critical reading and math), and all freshmen through juniors must live on campus. Our contemporary, state-of-the-art residential facilities win rave reviews from students and parents alike.

"Here you will study alongside distinguished professors, and over the last five years, we have added more than 100 tenure-track PhDs to our faculty. Outside the classroom, you will gain hands-on experience through internships with top organizations like NASA and the Thomas Jefferson National Laboratory.

"At CNU, you will enjoy countless opportunities to develop leadership skills. Make an impact through the President's Leadership Program; design a challenging curriculum in the Honors Program; team with faculty on groundbreaking research; take your studies overseas by studying abroad; and share your talents through 100-plus student organizations. We are also home to one of the most successful NCAA Division III programs with student-athletes who excel both in the classroom and on the field of play.

"Explore our campus further to discover opportunities as rich as your imagination."

SELECTIVITY

Admissions Rating	84
# of applicants	8,010
% of applicants accepted	53
% of acceptees attending	28
# accepting a place on wait list	260
% admitted from wait list	32
# of early decision applicants	303
% accepted early decision	70

FRESHMAN PROFILE

Range SAT Critical Reading	560–640
Range SAT Math	560–640
Range ACT Composite	22–27
Minimum paper TOEFL	530
Minimum computer TOEFL	197
Minimum web-based TOEFL	71
Average HS GPA	3.64
% graduated top 10% of class	19
% graduated top 25% of class	57
% graduated top 50% of class	94

DEADLINES

Early decision	
Deadline	11/15
Notification	12/15
Early action	
Deadline	12/1
Notification	1/15
Regular	
Deadline	2/1
Notification	3/15
Nonfall registration?	yes

APPLICANTS ALSO LOOK AT AND OFTEN PREFER
James Madison University, Virginia Tech
AND SOMETIMES PREFER
Old Dominion University, University of Mary Washington, University of Virginia
AND RARELY PREFER

FINANCIAL FACTS

Financial Aid Rating	72
Annual in-state tuition	$9,250
Annual out-of-state tuition	$17,992
Room and board	$9,540
Books and supplies	$1,000
% frosh rec. need-based scholarship or grant aid	35
% UG rec. need-based scholarship or grant aid	32
% frosh rec. non-need-based scholarship or grant aid	22
% UG rec. non-need-based scholarship or grant aid	11
% frosh rec. need-based self-help aid	38
% UG rec. need-based self-help aid	37
% frosh rec. any financial aid	75
% UG rec. any financial aid	70
% UG borrow to pay for school	51
Average cumulative indebtedness	$20,879

CITY UNIVERSITY OF NEW YORK—BARUCH COLLEGE

ONE BERNARD BARUCH WAY, NEW YORK, NY 10010 • ADMISSIONS: 646-312-1400 • FAX: 646-312-1361

CAMPUS LIFE

Quality of Life Rating	68
Fire Safety Rating	60*
Green Rating	62
Type of school	public
Environment	metropolis

STUDENTS

Total undergrad enrollment	13,120
% male/female	50/50
% from out of state	3
% from public high school	87
% live on campus	1
# of fraternities	9
# of sororities	7
% African American	10
% Asian	33
% Caucasian	30
% Hispanic	15
% international	12
# of countries represented	166

SURVEY SAYS . . .
Great computer facilities
Great library
Diverse student types on campus
Students love New York, NY
Student publications are popular
Very little drug use

ACADEMICS

Academic Rating	72
% students graduating within 4 years	34
% students graduating within 6 years	61
Calendar	semester
Student/faculty ratio	16:1
Profs interesting rating	69
Profs accessible rating	67
Most common reg class size	20–29 students
Most common lab size	20–29 students

MOST POPULAR MAJORS
accounting, finance

STUDENTS SAY ". . ."

Academics
Baruch College consists of three schools, and although its School of Arts and Sciences and School of Public Affairs are both fine, it's the Zicklin School of Business that garners nearly all the attention here (as well over three-quarters of the student body). Zicklin offers a "very demanding business-oriented program that provides a great education in an overcrowded environment" where "it's very easy to get lost," but just as easy for go-getters to access "unparalleled internships, career, and networking opportunities to major global companies' headquarters." Because New York City is a worldwide finance capital, Baruch's connections and internships provide "a gateway to the world of finance," and it is for this reason—as well as for the fact that "tuition is about one-fourth what it is at NYU," making it "the best college value in New York City"—that students flock to Baruch. Students warn that you must be willing to "put 110 percent into your studies and take advantage of the NYC network and Starr Career Development Center" to reap all available benefits here. Those who make the effort will discover a career office that "works tirelessly to prepare its students for the working world. Not only do they offer workshops on how to make yourself an attractive candidate, they also offer counseling and even resumé reviews to make sure your resume is perfect, as well as mock interviews that help you analyze your strengths and weaknesses as an interviewer."

Life
Baruch has no campus, just a collection of six buildings scattered over four city blocks. Most of the action centers around the seventeen-story Newman Vertical Campus facility, which is "beautiful" but "does not offer a lot of things to do" between classes. Furthermore, the mostly residential area surrounding the school offers "few places you can hang out at, especially when you have huge breaks between classes." Although the building is fairly new, "the escalators almost never work," and the elevators "are always as packed as the commute on the train." Many here grumpily opt for the stairway. School-related extracurriculars are hampered by the lack of a "real campus" and by the fact that many students are commuters who work part time. Some get involved in community service and/or major-related clubs and organizations, but anyone coming here for a traditional college experience will be sorely disappointed. However access to New York City, for most, more than compensates for this drawback.

Student Body
The "hardworking" student body at Baruch could well be "the most diverse university in the country." It's the sort of place where "You can eat samosas on Tuesday, mooncakes on Wednesday, and falafel on Thursdays for free because of all the cultural events that are held." Students brag that "hundreds of countries are represented in our student body" and note that "The one common thread would be we are mostly business-oriented and have jobs/internships outside of school." While students get along well in class, outside the classroom they can be "very cliquey." One student explains, "If you know people from your high school, you stick with them; if you're a foreign student you stick with others from your home country. Otherwise you get the cold shoulder." Because "the school puts tremendous pressure on grades," most students are "extremely stressed."

CITY UNIVERSITY OF NEW YORK—BARUCH COLLEGE

FINANCIAL AID: 646-312-1360 • E-MAIL: ADMISSIONS@BARUCH.CUNY.EDU • WEBSITE: WWW.BARUCH.CUNY.EDU

THE PRINCETON REVIEW SAYS

Admissions

Very important factors considered include: Academic GPA, rigor of secondary school record, standardized test scores. *Important factors considered include*: Application essay, recommendation(s). *Other factors considered include*: Class rank, alumni/ae relation, character/personal qualities, extracurricular activities, interview, talent/ability, work experience. SAT or ACT required; ACT with or without writing component accepted. TOEFL required of all international applicants. High school diploma is required, and GED is accepted. *Academic units required*: 4 English, 3 mathematics, 2 science (2 science labs), 2 foreign language, 4 social studies. *Academic units recommended*: 4 English, 4 mathematics, 2 science (2 science labs), 2 foreign language, 4 social studies, 1 academic elective.

Financial Aid

Students should submit: FAFSA. Regular filing deadline is April 30. The Princeton Review suggests that all financial aid forms be submitted as soon as possible after January 1. *Need-based scholarships/grants offered*: Federal Pell, SEOG, state scholarships/grants, school scholarship or grant aid from institutional funds. *Loan aid offered*: Direct Subsidized Stafford, Direct Unsubsidized Stafford, Direct PLUS, Federal Perkins. Applicants will be notified of awards on a rolling basis beginning April 1. Federal Work-Study Program available. Off-campus job opportunities are excellent.

The Inside Word

Baruch's business school greatly upgrades the school's profile in its hallmark academic field. Admissions have grown steadily more competitive since, especially for students seeking undergraduate business degrees. Today, Baruch receives nearly ten applications for every slot in its freshman class. Your math scores on standardized tests count more heavily here than verbal scores.

THE SCHOOL SAYS "..."

From the Admissions Office

"Baruch College is in the heart of New York City. As an undergraduate, you will join a vibrant learning community of students and scholars in the middle of an exhilarating city full of possibilities. Baruch is a place where theory meets practice. You can network with city leaders; secure business, cultural, and nonprofit internships; access the music, art, and business scene; and meet experts who visit our campus. You will take classes that bridge business, arts, science, and social policy, learning from professors who are among the best in their fields.

"Baruch offers thirty-five majors and sixty-two minors in three schools: the School of Public Affairs, the Weissman School of Arts and Science, and the Zicklin School of Business. Highly qualified undergraduates may apply to the Baruch College Honors program, which offers scholarships, small seminars and honors courses. Students may also study abroad through programs in more than thirty countries.

"Our seventeen-floor Newman Vertical Campus serves as the college's hub. Here you will find the atmosphere and resources of a traditional college campus, but in a lively urban setting. Our classrooms have state-of-the-art technology, and our library was named the top college library in the nation. Baruch also has a simulated trading floor for students who are interested in Wall Street. You can also enjoy a three-level athletics and recreation complex, which features a twenty-five-meter indoor pool as well as a performing arts complex. The College just introduced a residence hall opportunity for undergraduates on Manhattan's vibrant Lower East Side in a newly built building at 101 Ludlow Street. The first residents will move in this August, before classes begin.

"Baruch's selective admission standards, strong academic programs, top national honors, as well as its internship and job-placement opportunities make it an exceptional educational value."

SELECTIVITY

Admissions Rating	91
# of applicants	18,716
% of applicants accepted	23
% of acceptees attending	30

FRESHMAN PROFILE

Range SAT Critical Reading	510–610
Range SAT Math	580–680
Minimum paper TOEFL	620
Minimum computer TOEFL	260
Minimum web-based TOEFL	105
Average HS GPA	3.16
% graduated top 10% of class	37
% graduated top 25% of class	64
% graduated top 50% of class	90

DEADLINES

Regular	
Priority	2/1
Deadline	2/1
Notification	2/1
Nonfall registration?	yes

APPLICANTS ALSO LOOK AT AND SOMETIMES PREFER

City University of New York—Hunter College

FINANCIAL FACTS

Financial Aid Rating	65
Annual in-state tuition	$4,830
Annual out-of-state tuition	$13,050
Room and board	$11,891
Required fees	$420
Books and supplies	$1,146

CITY UNIVERSITY OF NEW YORK—BROOKLYN COLLEGE

2900 BEDFORD AVENUE, BROOKLYN, NY 11210-2889 • ADMISSIONS: 718-951-5001 • FAX: 718-951-4506

CAMPUS LIFE

Quality of Life Rating	64
Fire Safety Rating	60*
Green Rating	91
Type of school	public
Environment	metropolis

STUDENTS

Total undergrad enrollment	11,740
% male/female	40/60
% from out of state	2
% from public high school	80
# of fraternities	7
# of sororities	9
% African American	24
% Asian	17
% Caucasian	41
% Hispanic	12
% international	5

SURVEY SAYS . . .
Great computer facilities
Great library
Diverse student types on campus
Very little drug use

ACADEMICS

Academic Rating	65
% students graduating within 4 years	23
% students graduating within 6 years	48
Calendar	semester
Student/faculty ratio	15:1
Profs interesting rating	68
Profs accessible rating	67
Most common reg class size	20–29 students

MOST POPULAR MAJORS
accounting, business administration and management, psychology, film, TV/radio

STUDENTS SAY ". . ."

Academics

Brooklyn College "is the perfect representative of Brooklyn as a borough and [of] success in the community," an institution that, like its home borough, "educates its students in an environment that reflects diversity, opportunity (study abroad, research, athletics, employment), and support." "Lauded as one of the best senior colleges in CUNY" and boasting "a beautiful campus," Brooklyn College entices a lot of bright students looking for an affordable, quality, undergraduate experience as well as some attracted by the school's relatively charitable admissions standards. It's easier to get in here than to stay in; Brooklyn College is "an academically challenging and rigorous school" that "feels a lot more competitive than one would anticipate." Professors "are fabulous" and "really passionate about the subjects that they teach and their students' career paths," although there are some "grumpy and nasty professors" that might best be avoided. Students are especially sanguine about special programs here, such as the various honors programs, in which "you will meet tons of highly intelligent people. Honors classes boast very good in-class discussions and highly vibrant, enthusiastic students. Non-honors classes are more run-of-the-mill but still very good academically." The school also works hard to provide "constant and innumerable job opportunities available to students and the Magner Center, which helps students find jobs and internships, and [to] help them prepare for the real world through resume writing workshops [and] job interview workshops." There are also "many financial awards available."

Life

"Apart from all the clubs and athletics on campus, most people come for class and then leave" at Brooklyn College because "we are a commuter school, so it has to be this way. All social activities happen off campus." There are "pretty nice places to hang out around campus for the occasional coffee," and "there are a lot of student organization and a lot of activities done to help enhance student life on campus," but the "immediate surroundings of the Brooklyn College campus are generally not where you would want to stay for hours," and "on weekends the campus usually is dead." That said, "The campus is quite beautiful, and the quad during spring time is usually a nice place to sit and relax." Furthermore, "New York City hotspots are a twenty- to forty-minute [subway] ride away," and Brooklyn itself is "a great place to live" where "there are always fun things happening."

Student Body

"The typical student at Brooklyn College is hardworking, from the NY metro area, and a commuter." Many "hold part-time jobs and pay at least part of their own tuition, so they are usually in a rush because they have a lot more responsibility on their shoulders than the average college student." Like Brooklyn itself, "The student body is very diversified," with everyone from "an aspiring opera singer to quirky film majors to single mothers looking for a better life for their children," and so "no student can be described as being typical. Everyone blends in as normal, and little segregation is noticed (if it exists)." Students here represent more than 100 nations and speak nearly as many languages. There are even students "that come from Long Island to North Carolina, from Connecticut to even Hong Kong."

CITY UNIVERSITY OF NEW YORK—BROOKLYN COLLEGE

FINANCIAL AID: 718-951-5051 • E-MAIL: ADMINQRY@BROOKLYN.CUNY.EDU • WEBSITE: WWW.BROOKLYN.CUNY.EDU

THE PRINCETON REVIEW SAYS

Admissions

Very important factors considered include: Academic GPA, rigor of secondary school record, standardized test scores. SAT or ACT required; ACT with or without writing component accepted. TOEFL required of all international applicants. High school diploma is required, and GED is accepted. *Academic units recommended:* 4 English, 3 mathematics, 3 science, 3 foreign language, 4 social studies, 4 academic elective.

Financial Aid

Students should submit: FAFSA. The Princeton Review suggests that all financial aid forms be submitted as soon as possible after January 1. *Need-based scholarships/grants offered:* Federal Pell, SEOG, state scholarships/grants, private scholarships, school scholarship or grant aid from institutional funds. *Loan aid offered:* Direct Subsidized Stafford, Direct Unsubsidized Stafford, Direct PLUS, Federal Perkins. Applicants will be notified of awards on a rolling basis beginning May 1. Federal Work-Study Program available. Off-campus job opportunities are excellent.

The Inside Word

Brooklyn College doesn't set the bar inordinately high; students with less-than-stellar high school records can receive a chance to prove themselves here. Once they get in, though, they had better be prepared to work; Brooklyn College typically loses about twenty percent of its freshman class each year, and six-year graduation rates rarely exceed fifty percent. Getting into Brooklyn College is one thing; surviving its academic challenges is a whole other thing entirely.

THE SCHOOL SAYS ". . ."

From the Admissions Office

"Brooklyn College is a premier public liberal arts college. For the last five years it has been consistently designated as one of America's Best Value Colleges by The Princeton Review and, in 2009, was cited as one of the top fifty Best Value Public Colleges in the nation.

"Respected nationally for its rigorous academic standards, the college has increased both the size and academic quality of its student body. It takes pride in such innovative programs as its award-winning Freshman Year College; the Honors Academy, which houses six programs for high achievers; and its nationally recognized core curriculum. Its School of Education is ranked among the top twenty in the country for graduates who go on to be considered among the best teachers in New York City. Brooklyn College's strong academic reputation has attracted an outstanding faculty of nationally renowned teachers and scholars. Among the awards they have won are Pulitzers, Guggenheims, Fulbrights, and many National Institutes of Health grants.

"The student body consists of more than 16,000 undergraduate and graduate students who represent the ethnic and cultural diversity of the borough. The college's accessibility by subway or bus allows students to further enrich their educational experience through New York City's many cultural events and institutions. In recent years, student achievements have been acknowledged with Fulbright and Truman Scholarships and an Emmy Award. This year we received our third Rhodes Scholarship in eleven years.

"The Brooklyn College campus, considered to be among the most beautiful in the nation, is in the midst of an ambitious program of expansion and renewal. A new residence hall has opened two blocks from the campus. It includes such amenities as single, as well as shared, rooms, Wi-Fi throughout, community lounges, a fitness center, and kitchenettes in every room. The dazzling library is the most technologically advanced educational and research facility in the CUNY system. Opened in 2009, the West Quad Building has state-of-the-art student services and is home to the physical education department. A separate fitness center, basketball and handball courts, and a competition pool is open for use by students and staff. Ground will be broken soon for a new performing arts center, followed in the coming years with a new science complex."

SELECTIVITY
Admissions Rating	88
# of applicants	18,455
% of applicants accepted	30
% of acceptees attending	21

FRESHMAN PROFILE
Range SAT Critical Reading	490–580
Range SAT Math	520–610
Minimum paper TOEFL	500
Minimum computer TOEFL	173
Average HS GPA	3.30
% graduated top 10% of class	18
% graduated top 25% of class	52
% graduated top 50% of class	83

DEADLINES
Regular	
Priority	2/1
Notification	2/1
Nonfall registration?	yes

FINANCIAL FACTS
Financial Aid Rating	94
Annual in-state tuition	$4,830
Annual out-of-state tuition	$13,050
Required fees	$454
% frosh rec. need-based scholarship or grant aid	61
% UG rec. need-based scholarship or grant aid	67
% frosh rec. non-need-based scholarship or grant aid	25
% UG rec. non-need-based scholarship or grant aid	24
% frosh rec. need-based self-help aid	52
% UG rec. need-based self-help aid	66
% frosh rec. any financial aid	77
% UG borrow to pay for school	48
Average cumulative indebtedness	$9,500

CITY UNIVERSITY OF NEW YORK—HUNTER COLLEGE

695 PARK AVENUE, NEW YORK, NY 10021 • ADMISSIONS: 212-772-4490 • FAX: 212-650-3336

CAMPUS LIFE

Quality of Life Rating	75
Fire Safety Rating	88
Green Rating	84
Type of school	public
Environment	metropolis

STUDENTS

Total undergrad enrollment	14,609
% male/female	33/67
% from out of state	4
% from public high school	70
# of fraternities	2
# of sororities	2
% African American	11
% Asian	22
% Caucasian	39
% Hispanic	19
% international	8

SURVEY SAYS . . .

Diverse student types on campus
Different types of students interact
Students get along with local community
Students love New York, NY
Political activism is popular
Very little drug use

ACADEMICS

Academic Rating	64
% students graduating within 4 years	17
% students graduating within 6 years	46
Calendar	semester
Student/faculty ratio	14:1
Profs interesting rating	66
Profs accessible rating	84
Most common reg class size	20–29 students

MOST POPULAR MAJORS
accounting, psychology

STUDENTS SAY " . . . "

Academics

New Yorkers seeking "a superb learning environment for the independent and self-motivated" should check out Hunter College, a school that offers "a great education at an affordable price." A "serious academic environment" where "learning is taken very seriously" and "most people know exactly what they want and are going for it with full determination" create "an amazing energy" at Hunter, an energy that feeds off the diverse New York student body. "Hunter is all about bringing people from all different parts of the world together in one place to learn from one another and to be exposed to almost every subject imaginable to help one find their true calling in life," one student reports. The New York location also gives Hunter access to many top academics; many professors here "teach at other, more expensive, universities. Throughout my Hunter career, I have had professors who also teach at NYU, Hofstra, Cooper Union, and Yale! So it really is quite the bargain." "Crowded" classes mean students need to "take matters in their own hands" if they "want to succeed and graduate in four years," but those who seek connections tell us that "despite the heavy loads they take on, professors are always available for individual attention, and they help you through anything you ask." Tight budget constraints leave students wishing they "had more resources in terms of books, facilities, and more technology in the classrooms, but that has less to do with the school than it does with state funding." Accounting, education, media production, and psychology all earn high marks at Hunter.

Life

Hunter College "is mostly a commuter school," and as a result "students interact mostly on campus in between classes." "Making friends can be difficult, but definitely not impossible," one student explains. The school "encourages student interaction through student government-run parties and other student-run activities," and undergraduates "have our favorite spots on campus where we know we'll always run into someone. Usually we will go out for coffee or food before, in between, or after classes." The school facility is compact with no outdoor campus to speak of, but there are still "a lot of places for students to hang out: outside, on the bridges, in the cafeteria. We make the most of the space we have." Undergraduates typically "do their own thing and don't really judge or think about others," which makes for a copacetic campus but also means "it is difficult to have a real college experience." Most students don't mind because "off campus is New York City, so there is always tons to be done," including "going out to eat, walking around Manhattan, shopping," and taking in "the best nightlife in the world."

Student Body

Hunter College is "extremely diverse in almost every sense of the word." Ethnic, religious, gender preference, and political diversity are all in evidence. "Our population is as diverse as New York," one student aptly observes. Undergraduates are even diverse in age; as one undergraduate observes, "The average age for a Hunter student is, I believe, twenty-five. That alone opens up the spectrum of atypical students." What they share in common is that so many have "something to contribute, an experience that can be shared somewhere where others can learn from it. Everyone exchanges their experiences, allowing Hunter students to be some of the most open-minded, understanding people I believe New York City, and even the rest of the country, has to offer." Students tend to be "very liberal and outspoken." Women outnumber men by a two-to-one margin.

CITY UNIVERSITY OF NEW YORK—HUNTER COLLEGE

FINANCIAL AID: 212-772-4820 • E-MAIL: ADMISSIONS@HUNTER.CUNY.EDU • WEBSITE: WWW.HUNTER.CUNY.EDU

THE PRINCETON REVIEW SAYS

Admissions

Very important factors considered include: Academic GPA, application essay, rigor of secondary school record, standardized test scores. SAT or ACT required. TOEFL required of all international applicants. High school diploma is required, and GED is accepted. *Academic units required:* 2 English, 2 mathematics, 1 science (1 science lab). *Academic units recommended:* 4 English, 3 mathematics, 2 science, 2 foreign language, 4 social studies, 1 visual/performing arts, 1 academic elective.

Financial Aid

Students should submit: FAFSA. The Princeton Review suggests that all financial aid forms be submitted as soon as possible after January 1. *Need-based scholarships/grants offered:* Federal Pell, state scholarships/grants, school scholarship or grant aid from institutional funds. *Loan aid offered:* Direct Subsidized Stafford, Direct Unsubsidized Stafford, Direct PLUS, Federal Perkins, state loans, university loans from institutional funds. Applicants will be notified of awards on a rolling basis beginning May 15. Federal Work-Study Program available. Off-campus job opportunities are fair.

The Inside Word

Hunter admissions officers are inundated with more than 30,000 applications each year. There's no way the admissions office can get through all those applications without applying some cutoffs and formulas; although these aren't made public, a look at the stats for the most recent incoming class will give you some idea of what grades and test scores you'll need to be admitted here. Rolling admissions mean early application is pretty much a must here; programs fill up fast as a result of Hunter's solid reputation and bargain-basement tuition. Applications to the Macaulay Honors College must be submitted by December 1.

THE SCHOOL SAYS "..."

From the Admissions Office

"Located in the heart of Manhattan, Hunter offers students the stimulating learning environment and career-building opportunities you might expect from a college that's been a part of the world's most exciting city since 1870. The largest college in the City University of New York, Hunter pulses with energy. Hunter's vitality stems from a large, highly diverse faculty and student body. Its schools—Arts and Sciences, Education, Nursing and the CUNY Schoolf of Public Health, and Social Work—provide an affordable first-rate education. Undergraduates have extraordinary opportunities to conduct high-level research under renowned faculty, and many opt for credit-bearing internships in such exciting fields as media, the arts, and government. The college's high standards and special programs ensure a challenging education. The Block Program for first-year students keeps classmates together as they pursue courses in the liberal arts, pre–health science, pre-nursing, premed, or honors. A range of honors programs is available for students with strong academic records, including the highly competitive tuition-free Macaulay Honors College for entering freshmen and the Thomas Hunter Honors Program, which emphasizes small classes with personalized mentoring by outstanding faculty. Qualified students also benefit from Hunter's participation in minority science research and training programs, the prestigious Andrew W. Mellon Minority Undergraduate Program, and many other passports to professional success.

"Applicants for the entering class are required to take either the SAT or the ACT."

SELECTIVITY

Admissions Rating	72
# of applicants	30,256
% of applicants accepted	25
% of acceptees attending	24

FRESHMAN PROFILE

Range SAT Critical Reading	520–620
Range SAT Math	530–630
Minimum paper TOEFL	500
Minimum computer TOEFL	173

DEADLINES

Regular	
Deadline	2/1
Notification	rolling
Nonfall registration?	yes

FINANCIAL FACTS

Financial Aid Rating	85
Annual in-state tuition	$4,830
Annual out-of-state tuition	$13,050
Required fees	$399
% frosh rec. need-based scholarship or grant aid	52
% UG rec. need-based scholarship or grant aid	54
% frosh rec. non-need-based scholarship or grant aid	43
% UG rec. non-need-based scholarship or grant aid	20
% frosh rec. need-based self-help aid	7
% UG rec. need-based self-help aid	17
% frosh rec. any financial aid	91
% UG rec. any financial aid	94
% UG borrow to pay for school	53
Average cumulative indebtedness	$7,500

CITY UNIVERSITY OF NEW YORK—QUEENS COLLEGE

65-30 KISSENA BOULEVARD, FLUSHING, NY 11367 • ADMISSIONS: 718-997-5000 • FAX: 718-997-5617

CAMPUS LIFE

Quality of Life Rating	82
Fire Safety Rating	84
Green Rating	83
Type of school	public
Environment	metropolis

STUDENTS

Total undergrad enrollment	15,337
% male/female	42/58
% from out of state	1
% from public high school	85
% live on campus	3
# of fraternities	4
# of sororities	3
% African American	8
% Asian	24
% Caucasian	45
% Hispanic	18
% international	5
# of countries represented	140

SURVEY SAYS . . .

Diverse student types on campus
Students get along with local
community
Students love Flushing, NY
Dorms are like dungeons
Students are happy
Musical organizations are popular
Very little beer drinking
Very little drug use

ACADEMICS

Academic Rating	69
% students graduating within 4 years	26
% students graduating within 6 years	51
Calendar	semester
Student/faculty ratio	16:1
Profs interesting rating	71
Profs accessible rating	70
Most common reg class size	20–29 students
Most common lab size	17 students

MOST POPULAR MAJORS
accounting, economics, psychology

STUDENTS SAY ". . ."

Academics

"A great education at an affordable price" could easily be the mantra of Queens College. A stalwart of New York City's university system, Queens offers "an amazingly diverse campus" and a "warm, welcoming" atmosphere. Largely a "commuter" school, undergrads here can choose from "a wide variety of classes," although, as one psych major warns, "They can close out quickly." Despite the fact that "the workload can be quite heavy at times," undergrads speak glowingly of their "understanding" professors who constantly "push you to reach your full potential." They are "extremely intelligent and personable," and they are always "willing to meet with students outside of the classroom to discuss anything and everything." One ecstatic senior goes as far as saying, "I feel like I am around close relatives." However, other students do fret over "the high turnover" among faculty and worry that this can "make it difficult to form meaningful academic connections." Praise also extends to administrators who "always make an effort to connect with students and are always very open and willing to talk." Indeed, even though there's "a lot of bureaucracy," undergrads still find them to be "very down-to-earth" and "approachable." As a media studies major expounds, "Students and administrators host town hall meetings numerous times throughout the semester in order to exchange ideas on how to make the campus a better place."

Life

Some undergrads at Queens College lament that, because of the commuter culture, "There isn't much interaction between the students on campus." They simply "go to class and then go home." However, one content freshman insists, "There are so many activities to attend and clubs to join. You just need to get involved." Indeed, the college offers everything from "literary magazines, newspapers, and radio [to] student government." There are also plenty of opportunities for the altruistically inclined. As a media studies major shares, "I am deeply involved in a growing movement of students that are getting active in the community. We host charity drives, distribute food and clothes to the homeless, and [advocate for] a greener campus." The college also recently opened its first dormitory, which has been a definite boon to campus life. One happy resident tells us, "The Summit is amazing. It's fun to hang around there or sit on the Quad on a nice day and do homework/talk with friends." Fortunately, "There is a nice atmosphere on campus, and it feels safe and comfortable for both commuters and residents." The surrounding area offers plenty of great dining options, especially "Chinese food and Kosher restaurants, depending on which way you walk." And of course, Manhattan is "very close and easily accessible." Students frequently head into the city "to go clubbing, out to eat, or hit the bars and museums."

Student Body

As a finance major shares, "Flushing is one of the most ethnically diverse cities in the United States and the demographics of the school reflect that." Certainly, diversity is a buzzword around the Queens campus, and the college attracts many "Jewish, Asian, and Hispanics students." An impressed sophomore goes further, "There is no typical student at Queens College. If you can name a language, it's spoken here. If you name a country, someone has ethnic ties to it. There are students of all races, sexual orientations, ethnicities, and genders at Queens who live together in harmony." A speech pathology major observes, "Every time I walk through campus, I feel as if I am trekking through the seven continents." Most of these "easygoing," "unassuming," and "liberal" undergrads find common ground in their desire "to get a good education" with an "inexpensive" price tag. As one media studies major sums up, "The school has so many clubs that everyone finds a way to fit in with their own niche groups."

CITY UNIVERSITY OF NEW YORK—QUEENS COLLEGE

FINANCIAL AID: 718-997-5101 • E-MAIL: ADMISSIONS@QC.EDU • WEBSITE: WWW.QC.EDU

THE PRINCETON REVIEW SAYS

Admissions

Very important factors considered include: Academic GPA, rigor of secondary school record, standardized test scores. SAT or ACT required; ACT with or without writing component accepted. TOEFL required of all international applicants. High school diploma is required, and GED is accepted. *Academic units required:* 4 English, 3 mathematics, 2 science (2 science labs), 3 foreign language, 4 social studies. *Academic units recommended:* 3 science (3 science labs).

Financial Aid

Students should submit: FAFSA, institution's own financial aid form. Regular filing deadline is June 30, 2012 by midnight. The Princeton Review suggests that all financial aid forms be submitted as soon as possible after January 1. *Need-based scholarships/grants offered:* Federal Pell, SEOG, state scholarships/grants, private scholarships, school scholarship or grant aid from institutional funds. *Loan aid offered:* Direct Subsidized Stafford, Direct Unsubsidized Stafford, Direct PLUS, Federal Perkins. Applicants will be notified of awards on a rolling basis beginning March 1. Federal Work-Study Program available. Off-campus job opportunities are good.

The Inside Word

Minority enrollment has declined at CUNY in the past several years, partially as a result of changes to admissions criteria and stiffer competition for minority applicants. The school would love to boost its numbers, meaning that qualified minority students could be able to finagle a pretty nice financial aid package here, making an already economical situation even more affordable.

THE SCHOOL SAYS ". . ."

From the Admissions Office

"At Queens College, you will engage the world of ideas with faculty and students from the world over, prepare for your career, and enjoy the many activities our beautiful, seventy-seven-acre campus has to offer. And with the August 2009 opening of The Summit—our first residence hall—you'll find a place to enjoy everything that comes with a college residential experience.

"Since 1937, we've provided a premier liberal arts education to talented students. From graduate and undergraduate degrees, a variety of honors and pre-professional programs to research and real work internship opportunities, you'll find countless ways to realize your potential under the guidance of our award-winning, dedicated faculty. We offer nationally recognized programs—such as our Aaron Copland School of Music—in many fields. And we're also the ideal choice for aspiring teachers, preparing more future educators than any college in the tristate area.

"Located only minutes from Manhattan, our campus boasts a traditional quad overlooking the skyline. You'll find a stimulating and welcoming environment here, with a bustling student union, an impressive arts center, and opportunities to participate in dozens of clubs and sports. (We're the only City University of New York college to participate in Division II.) Campus-wide Wi-Fi, computer kiosks, and cybercafes keep you informed and in touch. And best of all, as part of CUNY, we can offer all this at an affordable cost. To apply for fall 2012, submit your application online along with your SATs comprising critical reading, writing, and math."

SELECTIVITY

Admissions Rating	71
# of applicants	18,453
% of applicants accepted	30
% of acceptees attending	27

FRESHMAN PROFILE

Range SAT Critical Reading	490–590
Range SAT Math	530–610
Minimum paper TOEFL	500
Minimum computer TOEFL	173
Minimum web-based TOEFL	62
% graduated top 10% of class	18
% graduated top 25% of class	45
% graduated top 50% of class	92

DEADLINES

Regular	
Priority	2/1
Notification	2/1
Nonfall registration?	yes

FINANCIAL FACTS

Financial Aid Rating	80
Annual in-state tuition	$4,830
Annual out-of-state tuition	$10,440
Required fees	$477
Books and supplies	$1,179
% frosh rec. need-based scholarship or grant aid	71
% UG rec. need-based scholarship or grant aid	63
% frosh rec. non-need-based scholarship or grant aid	31
% UG rec. non-need-based scholarship or grant aid	13
% frosh rec. need-based self-help aid	22
% UG rec. need-based self-help aid	28
% frosh rec. any financial aid	22
% UG rec. any financial aid	58
% UG borrow to pay for school	24
Average cumulative indebtedness	$14,000

CLAREMONT MCKENNA COLLEGE

890 COLUMBIA AVENUE, CLAREMONT, CA 91711 • ADMISSIONS: 909-621-8088 • FAX: 909-621-8516

CAMPUS LIFE
Quality of Life Rating	99
Fire Safety Rating	92
Green Rating	84
Type of school	private
Environment	town

STUDENTS
Total undergrad enrollment	1,210
% male/female	55/45
% from out of state	56
% from public high school	70
% live on campus	98
% African American	3
% Asian	12
% Caucasian	49
% Hispanic	9
% international	6
# of countries represented	24

SURVEY SAYS . . .
School is well-run
Great food on campus
Dorms are like palaces
Frats and sororities are unpopular
or nonexistent
Student government is popular
Political activism is popular

ACADEMICS
Academic Rating	97
% students graduating within 4 years	87
% students graduating within 6 years	93
Calendar	semester
Student/faculty ratio	9:1
Profs interesting rating	99
Profs accessible rating	99
Most common reg class size	10–19 students

MOST POPULAR MAJORS
economics, international relations,
political science

STUDENTS SAY ". . ."

Academics

Students at Claremont McKenna really love their school. With its "phenomenal academics, "brilliant professors," "amazing career services center," and "perfect weather," it's no wonder CMC students are "the happiest students in America." Claremont McKenna is known for its government and economics majors, but philosophy, international relations, and the joint sciences program also get high marks. Claremont is a part of the College Consortium, so if students are looking for something that Claremont doesn't have, they can probably find it at one of the four affiliated schools. Students rave about Claremont's emphasis on "professionalism" and all of the "great research and internship opportunities." The workload is heavy, and professors set "high expectations," so "students spend their weeks slaving over their papers, books, readings, research projects, problem sets, etc." Despite the intense workload, students love their professors. "Professors are absolute geniuses in their field," one student gushes. They're "helpful and encouraging," "incredibly accessible," and even "willing to Skype on the weekends to answer questions." "This sounds corny," one student admits; "This really is a place where professors become like family." Students spend a "good deal of out-of-classroom time" with their teachers. "Professors and students are so close that it might be considered creepy to outsiders," but students aren't too worried about creeping anyone out because they know how good they've got it. "When you take both academics and quality of life into account," a cognitive neuroscience major says, "I can't believe I almost went to an Ivy over this place."

Life

Life is good at Claremont McKenna. The "constantly beaming California sun and the close vicinity to both mountains and beaches" means students spend their time outdoors when they can. But even when students are lounging in the sun or playing Frisbee, they're not really taking a break. The "conversation doesn't end in the classroom," a student explains, and the "intellectual culture… really allows for twenty-four-hour learning." While Claremont McKenna has the campus and "community-life and identity of a small school" it "still [has] the resources of the other 4 C's." Even without the other schools students feel "completely pampered" because "the school cares about its students so much." A Spanish major says, "The relationship between the students and the administration is excellent here," and the "student government and Dean of Students Office…subsidize incredible off-campus trips and on-campus parties." One of the best things about Claremont McKenna is the Atheneum, which hosts prestigious guest lecturers three to four nights a week. One student wisely asks, "Where else could you have dinner with Jesse Jackson, Mitt Romney, etc.?" Partying is definitely a part of life here, and a student admits that if you don't drink, it could be "easy to feel left out." However, students agree, "There's a niche for everyone, and the welcoming, accepting atmosphere makes fitting in easy."

Student Body

"Claremont McKenna doesn't accept students who aren't amazing." "Amazing" means a "really smart and very physically fit," person who's "incredibly motivated and career-driven" and "loves drinking and partying." It's "a tight-knit community of driven, competitive, and intelligent people who know how to be successful and have a great time." "A lot of kids are political and well-informed"; most are "active on campus," very into sports, and involved with internships or clubs. But even though the environment is "academically strict, the students… rarely fit the 'nerdy' stereotype." Students are extremely well-rounded; they "know how to lead a discussion…clock hours in the library, play a varsity or club sport, and hold a leadership position in a club or organization," and they also know how to throw "a great party on Saturday night."

CLAREMONT MCKENNA COLLEGE

FINANCIAL AID: 909-621-8356 • E-MAIL: ADMISSION@CLAREMONTMCKENNA.EDU • WEBSITE: WWW.CLAREMONTMCKENNA.EDU

THE PRINCETON REVIEW SAYS

Admissions

Very important factors considered include: Rigor of secondary school record, standardized test scores, extracurricular activities. *Important factors considered include:* Application essay, recommendation(s). *Other factors considered include:* Academic GPA, alumni/ae relation, character/personal qualities, first generation, geographical residence, interview, racial/ethnic status, talent/ability, volunteer work, work experience. SAT or ACT required; ACT with writing component required. TOEFL required of all international applicants. High school diploma is required, and GED is accepted. *Academic units required:* 4 English, 3 mathematics, 2 science (2 science labs), 3 foreign language, 1 social studies, 1 history. *Academic units recommended:* 4 mathematics, 3 science.

Financial Aid

Students should submit: FAFSA, CSS/Financial Aid PROFILE. Regular filing deadline is February 1. The Princeton Review suggests that all financial aid forms be submitted as soon as possible after January 1. *Need-based scholarships/grants offered:* Federal Pell, SEOG, state scholarships/grants, private scholarships, school scholarship or grant aid from institutional funds, United Negro College Fund. *Loan aid offered:* Direct Subsidized Stafford, Direct Unsubsidized Stafford, Direct PLUS, Federal Perkins, university loans from institutional funds. Federal Work-Study Program available. Off-campus job opportunities are excellent.

The Inside Word

Although applicants have to possess exemplary academic qualifications to gain admission to Claremont McKenna, the importance of making a good match shouldn't be underestimated. Colleges of such small size and selectivity devote much more energy to determining whether the candidate as an individual fits instead of whether a candidate has the appropriate test scores.

THE SCHOOL SAYS "..."

From the Admissions Office

"CMC's mission is clear: To educate students for meaningful lives and responsible leadership in business, government, and many other professions. While many other colleges champion either a traditional liberal arts education with emphasis on intellectual breadth or training that stresses acquisition of technical skills, CMC offers a clear alternative. Instead of dividing the liberal arts and working world into separate realms, education at CMC is rooted in the interplay between the world of ideas and the world of events. By combining the intellectual breadth of liberal arts with the more pragmatic concerns of public affairs, CMC students gain the vision, skills, and values necessary for leadership in all sectors of society.

"Applicants must take the SAT Reasoning Test or ACT with writing. We will use the highest scores from the SAT or ACT. SAT Subject Tests are recommended but not required."

SELECTIVITY

Admissions Rating	96
# of applicants	3,856
% of applicants accepted	18
% of acceptees attending	40
# accepting a place on wait list	303
% admitted from wait list	8

FRESHMAN PROFILE

Range SAT Critical Reading	630–730
Range SAT Math	660–750
Minimum paper TOEFL	600
Minimum computer TOEFL	250
Minimum web-based TOEFL	100
% graduated top 10% of class	85
% graduated top 25% of class	98
% graduated top 50% of class	100

DEADLINES

Early action	
Deadline	11/15
Notification	12/15
Regular	
Deadline	1/2
Nonfall registration?	no

APPLICANTS ALSO LOOK AT AND OFTEN PREFER
Harvard College, Princeton University, Stanford University

AND SOMETIMES PREFER
Georgetown University, Pomona College, University of Pennsylvania, Washington University in St. Louis, Williams College

AND RARELY PREFER
Pitzer College, Tufts University, University of Southern California

FINANCIAL FACTS

Financial Aid Rating	99
Annual tuition	$40,230
Room and board	$12,998
Books and supplies	$2,000
% frosh rec. need-based scholarship or grant aid	42
% UG rec. need-based scholarship or grant aid	44
% frosh rec. non-need-based scholarship or grant aid	6
% UG rec. non-need-based scholarship or grant aid	15
% frosh rec. need-based self-help aid	42
% UG rec. need-based self-help aid	44
% frosh rec. any financial aid	45
% UG rec. any financial aid	51
% UG borrow to pay for school	30
Average cumulative indebtedness	$9,779

CLARK UNIVERSITY

950 MAIN STREET, WORCESTER, MA 01610-1477 • ADMISSIONS: 508-793-7431 • FAX: 508-793-8821

STUDENTS SAY ". . ."

Academics

Clark University is "an academically rich, research-oriented," small liberal arts school. Despite its size, "The research opportunities here are endless." A psychology major says, "Clark goes out of its way to provide students with as many opportunities as possible to be involved with their field." Additionally, "The professors are always involved in their fields, and they know where to direct the students." A physics student adds, "Professors are always willing to have students from the field come in to help with [their] research and put in some input about it." "Many of them [use] their own research as modern examples, which really helps to explain things." Overall, Clark professors are "extremely impressive." They're "always there for reassurance and support." One student says, "These relationships opened my eyes to all sorts of academic and professional options." Coursework is "hard but manageable," so there's "academic intensity without undue pressure." A student double-majoring in history and theater sums it up by saying that Clark "is a warm environment where the student's education is paramount, and the professors here are devoted to what they research as well as how they teach."

Life

"Community involvement is huge" at Clark. "Clubs provide a common interest point for students to get to know one another and to participate in shared activities," and since "everyone is involved in something on-campus, we all feel immense pride and ownership over the events that take place." One of the more popular campus activities is community service. A global environmental studies student says that community service "gives…students an opportunity to interact with the community," which in turn, "leads to town-gown relations that are better than most other schools in the city." Students are sharply divided on Worcester. Some say it's "depressing and gloomy" and that it's the "poor man's" "microcosm of Boston." Though Worcester does struggle with social and economic problems, it's possible that students are down on it because they "haven't given the city a chance." "Worcester has an incredibly diverse selection of restaurants, live music, and people." Students who don't venture out into the city hang out in their dorms or go to house parties. Currently, "The administration is focused on revamping Clark's image," and "The buildings…are all being renovated, and there is a lot of construction and planning for new things in the upcoming year." Already, some buildings have "undergone dramatic transformations," such as the library, the gym, and two freshman dorms that "have brand new beautiful additions."

Student Body

Clark offers a "great community" full of "friendly, witty, approachable, very conscious, and active" students. Most seem convinced that the student body is made up of "everyone who was a little awkward or uncool in high school," which includes "cool nerds, hipsters, artist/musicians," "hippies," and "jocks." There's also a significant amount of international students. Clark students are "highly optimistic" and "want to save the world." "This is a college that attracts students who want to do things in this world," one student explains, "whether it's change lives or challenge convention." Students are "very open," but the campus leans heavily to the left, and one student says they've "known people to hide their conservative beliefs for fear of being chastised." That said, "Everyone fits in, in their own way," at Clark, and though students do fall into their groups, "The groups are very fluid," and within groups of students "there is a range of ethnic, racial, religious, and academic diversity." "There is," however, "a disconnect between the athletes at Clark and everyone else." One student complains, "While jocks are in the minority, they still seem to think they rule the school." Athletes would like to have more support, which is understandable, because "no one shows up to the games." Though students might not be the strongest sports fans, "Community involvement is huge." "Most of us are involved in some club or community service through the school," and "Clubs turn into small communities themselves."

FINANCIAL AID: 508-793-7478 • E-MAIL: ADMISSIONS@CLARKU.EDU • WEBSITE: WWW.CLARKU.EDU

THE PRINCETON REVIEW SAYS
Admissions
Very important factors considered include: Academic GPA, recommendation(s), rigor of secondary school record, standardized test scores. *Important factors considered include:* Application essay, character/personal qualities, extracurricular activities, talent/ability, volunteer work. *Other factors considered include:* Class rank, alumni/ae relation, first generation, geographical residence, interview, level of applicant's interest, racial/ethnic status, work experience. SAT or ACT required; ACT with or without writing component accepted. TOEFL required of all international applicants. High school diploma is required, and GED is accepted. *Academic units recommended:* 4 English, 3 mathematics, 3 science (2 science labs), 2 foreign language, 2 social studies, 2 history.

Financial Aid
Students should submit: FAFSA, CSS/Financial Aid PROFILE. Regular filing deadline is February 1. The Princeton Review suggests that all financial aid forms be submitted as soon as possible after January 1. *Need-based scholarships/grants offered:* Federal Pell, SEOG, state scholarships/grants, school scholarship or grant aid from institutional funds. *Loan aid offered:* Direct Subsidized Stafford, Direct Unsubsidized Stafford, Direct PLUS, Federal Perkins, state loans. Federal Work-Study Program available. Off-campus job opportunities are good.

The Inside Word
Clark is surrounded by formidable competitors, and its selectivity suffers because of it. Most B students will encounter little difficulty gaining admission. Given the university's solid academic environment and access to other member colleges in the Worcester Consortium, it can be a terrific choice for students who aren't up to the ultra-competitive admissions expectations of top-tier universities.

THE SCHOOL SAYS ". . ."
From the Admissions Office
"Clark University prepares students to make a meaningful difference in a world hungry for change.

"We are a small liberal arts–based research university founded in 1887 and located in the heart of New England. At Clark, students find a dynamic learning environment that encourages them to move beyond the boundaries of traditional academics and prepares them to create positive change in our community and our world.

"Our vibrant intellectual life is an outgrowth of a dedicated faculty who are as passionate about teaching and mentoring as they are about generating new knowledge. As undergraduates, Clark students have an array of opportunities not only to study with award-winning researchers, but also to work at their side in pursuit of innovative solutions to real-world problems.

"The educational experience at Clark is characterized by rigorous academic coursework, independent and collaborative research, internships, study abroad experiences, and service opportunities that are found both locally and globally. Clark University offers a unique opportunity for access to graduate study. Our nationally recognized Accelerated Degree Program allows qualified students to begin graduate level coursework in their senior year and to complete the requirements of a master's degree in a fifth year that is tuition-free.

"Clark's admission standards are selective and focused on identifying students who are most likely to thrive in the collaborative learning environment. Among the considerations taken into account are rigor of the high school program, record of performance in core academic coursework, standardized test scores, teacher/counselor recommendations, quality of extracurricular involvement, and student writing skills."

SELECTIVITY
Admissions Rating	90
# of applicants	4,038
% of applicants accepted	69
% of acceptees attending	29
# accepting a place on wait list	0

FRESHMAN PROFILE
Range SAT Critical Reading	540–660
Range SAT Math	530–640
Range SAT Writing	550–650
Range ACT Composite	25–31
Minimum paper TOEFL	550
Minimum computer TOEFL	213
Average HS GPA	3.46
% graduated top 10% of class	32
% graduated top 25% of class	71
% graduated top 50% of class	95

DEADLINES
Early action	
Deadline	11/15
Notification	12/23
Regular	
Deadline	1/15
Nonfall registration?	yes

APPLICANTS ALSO LOOK AT
AND OFTEN PREFER
Boston College, Boston University, Brandeis University
AND SOMETIMES PREFER
Northeastern University, Skidmore College
AND RARELY PREFER
University of Massachusetts Amherst, Wheaton College (MA)

FINANCIAL FACTS
Financial Aid Rating	91
Annual tuition	$37,000
Room and board	$7,100
Required fees	$600
Books and supplies	$800
% frosh rec. need-based scholarship or grant aid	62
% UG rec. need-based scholarship or grant aid	62
% frosh rec. non-need-based scholarship or grant aid	28
% UG rec. non-need-based scholarship or grant aid	28
% frosh rec. need-based self-help aid	54
% UG rec. need-based self-help aid	54
% frosh rec. any financial aid	82
% UG rec. any financial aid	79
% UG borrow to pay for school	92
Average cumulative indebtedness	$24,000

CLARKSON UNIVERSITY

PO Box 5605, Potsdam, NY 13699 • Admissions: 315-268-6479 • Fax: 315-268-7647

STUDENTS SAY ". . ."

Academics

Clarkson University in upstate New York is a science- and technology-focused school with an "excellent" and "innovative" engineering program. Students say "Clarkson...wants you to succeed and has many resources to help you." It "places a high importance on...preparing [students] to be a professionals" and has a "wonderful job-placement rate." An electrical engineering student says, "The career center has many workshops to help you land a job, from resume help, to appropriate interview dress, to business dining etiquette." "You feel very prepared by the time you are a senior," a student adds, no doubt because of Clarkson's "high academic intensity" and "challenging coursework." Unfortunately, "Professors are all over the place." Most students report, however, "Professors are all interested in helping their students," and "If you need help there is no question that you will receive it." Professors are "passionate and engaging" and "go above and beyond to make sure students can achieve academic excellence." Others find professors care "more about their research than anything else" and are hard to understand because they're non-native English speakers. For students who need academic support, Clarkson offers "free tutoring sessions for those students who are struggling" and a "very professional" writing center. Ultimately, most students find that "Clarkson University is a great environment that helps students develop hands-on experience that is greatly valued in any industry."

Life

Clarkson is working on improving its campus. There's a lot of construction going on, and the school recently completed "a new student center with a huge movie theater, forum, open bar, free pool tables, and a virtual game room." However, "the facilities need to be upgraded." "The dorms are aging and the on-campus apartments are falling apart"; the library is "pitiful," and the "Internet connection is abysmal." Food also gets low marks. The quaint town of Potsdam "may be a small town, but there is always something happening," though it might seem that way only to someone "who is used to living in a small town," because many students think "there isn't much to do at all" in town. "There are so many clubs and activities" at Clarkson, that "no matter what type of person you are, there are multiple places that you will fit in." There's a particularly strong outdoors club. Even though students find aspects of Clarkson life frustrating, a biology major wants you to know that though students complain about "the concrete buildings, food, sex ratio, and weather," they "do it out of love," and that "the campus is a tight-knit community with a 'we're in this together' feel."

Student Body

Clarkson's heavy emphasis on engineering and the sciences has resulted in a student body full of "lots of nerdy kids," particularly "nerdy white males." There are a lot of "socially awkward people" at Clarkson, but a student explains, "If you like to be alone and stay in your room then you will meet other awkward kids who like to hang out in their room." However, "If you attempt to go out and meet people then you will meet a variety of people." Clarkson students "really want to succeed," and many students "study hard during the day and into the night," but on "the weekends they still manage to find time to socialize and have a great time." There are a lot of "frat boys" who appreciate that the "good" Greek life "offers a haven [where] people who aren't socially awkward can congregate." Clarkson's proximity to the beautiful Adirondack Mountains means it attracts students who have "an affinity for the outdoors" and take advantage of the abundant opportunities to go hiking, canoeing, skiing, and ice climbing. Students complain about the male/female ratio even though it's "improving" and is "not as bad as [it] used to be." There's also "plenty of girls at SUNY Potsdam." One student says that one of the best things about Clarkson is that "everyone seems to get along well," and "Most people are more than willing to blur the lines between groups, so sects do not form nearly as often as one might think."

CLARKSON UNIVERSITY

FINANCIAL AID: 315-268-7699 • E-MAIL: ADMISSION@CLARKSON.EDU • WEBSITE: WWW.CLARKSON.EDU

THE PRINCETON REVIEW SAYS

Admissions

Very important factors considered include: Academic GPA, rigor of secondary school record. *Important factors considered include:* Class rank, recommendation(s), standardized test scores, extracurricular activities, volunteer work. *Other factors considered include:* Application essay, alumni/ae relation, character/personal qualities, first generation, level of applicant's interest, talent/ability, work experience. SAT or ACT required; ACT with or without writing component accepted. TOEFL required of all international applicants. High school diploma is required, and GED is accepted. *Academic units required:* 4 English, 3 mathematics, 3 science. *Academic units recommended:* 4 mathematics, 4 science.

Financial Aid

Students should submit: FAFSA. Regular filing deadline is March 1. The Princeton Review suggests that all financial aid forms be submitted as soon as possible after January 1. *Need-based scholarships/grants offered:* Federal Pell, SEOG, state scholarships/grants, private scholarships, school scholarship or grant aid from institutional funds. *Loan aid offered:* Direct Subsidized Stafford, Direct Unsubsidized Stafford, Direct PLUS, Federal Perkins, university loans from institutional funds. Applicants will be notified of awards on a rolling basis beginning March 19. Federal Work-Study Program available. Off-campus job opportunities are excellent.

The Inside Word

Clarkson wants students with a strong science and math background who also have a curiosity for applying technology and science in the real world. Show them that you're interested in being involved outside the classroom. Clarkson's acceptance rate is too high for solid applicants to lose much sleep about gaining admission. Serious candidates should interview anyway. If you're particularly solid and really want to come here, it could help you get some scholarship money.

THE SCHOOL SAYS ". . ."

From the Admissions Office

"Clarkson University is New York State's highest ranked, small research institution. Clarkson is the institution of choice for 3,000 enterprising students from diverse backgrounds who embrace challenge and thrive in a rigorous, highly collaborative learning environment. Our 640-wooded-acre campus is adjacent to the six-million-acre Adirondack Park, which offers exceptional outdoor recreation and a living laboratory for field research and environmental studies.

"Clarkson's programs in engineering, business, the sciences, liberal arts, and health sciences emphasize team-based learning as well as creative problem solving and leadership skills. Clarkson is also on the leading edge of today's emerging technologies and fields of study offering innovative, boundary-spanning degree programs in engineering and management, digital arts and sciences, and environmental science and policy, among others.

"At Clarkson, students and faculty work closely together in a supportive, friendly environment. Students are encouraged to participate in faculty-mentored research projects from their first year, and to take advantage of co-ops and study abroad programs. Our collaborative approach to education translates into graduates in high demand; our placement rates are among the highest in the country. Alumni experience accelerated career growth. One in seven alumni are already a CEO, president, or vice president of a company.

"Applicants are required to take the ACT with writing section optional or the SAT. We will use the student's best scores from either test. SAT Subject Tests are recommended but not required."

SELECTIVITY

Admissions Rating	86
# of applicants	4,241
% of applicants accepted	80
% of acceptees attending	21
# accepting a place on wait list	15
% admitted from wait list	33
# of early decision applicants	151
% accepted early decision	70

FRESHMAN PROFILE

Range SAT Critical Reading	500–610
Range SAT Math	560–660
Range SAT Writing	480–590
Range ACT Composite	23–29
Minimum paper TOEFL	550
Minimum computer TOEFL	213
Minimum web-based TOEFL	80
Average HS GPA	3.47
% graduated top 10% of class	35
% graduated top 25% of class	70
% graduated top 50% of class	93

DEADLINES

Early action	
Deadline	12/1
Notification	1/1
Regular	
Deadline	1/15
Notification	2/1
Nonfall registration?	yes

APPLICANTS ALSO LOOK AT

AND OFTEN PREFER
Rensselaer Polytechnic Institute,
Rochester Institute of Technology

AND SOMETIMES PREFER
Lehigh University, University of Rochester, Worcester
Polytechnic Institute

AND RARELY PREFER
Syracuse University

FINANCIAL FACTS

Financial Aid Rating	82
Annual tuition	$35,940
Room and board	$12,050
Required fees	$840
Books and supplies	$1,100
% frosh rec. need-based scholarship or grant aid	86
% UG rec. need-based scholarship or grant aid	84
% frosh rec. non-need-based scholarship or grant aid	11
% UG rec. non-need-based scholarship or grant aid	10
% frosh rec. need-based self-help aid	73
% UG rec. need-based self-help aid	72
% frosh rec. any financial aid	97
% UG rec. any financial aid	96
% UG borrow to pay for school	84
Average cumulative indebtedness	$36,142

CLEMSON UNIVERSITY

106 SIKES HALL, BOX 345124, CLEMSON, SC 29634-5124 • ADMISSIONS: 864-656-2287 • FAX: 864-656-2464

STUDENTS SAY "..."

Academics

Located in sunny South Carolina, Clemson University is "the total package: challenging academics, beautiful campus, sports, a thriving Greek life, Southern edge, and that extra something that just makes me excited to be here every morning when I wake up." "Nowhere else feels more like home," says another student. Clemson students are especially bullish on the scholarships the university offers. "The value is unbeatable." However, students do note that the strong Greek life at the school can be "overwhelming" and that parking services and transportation can be "a nightmare." Students have high opinions of the Clemson faculty. "I feel like my academic experience is extremely dynamic, and I truly enjoy going to class." "Even the two or three [professors who] are not effective teachers still do their best to make sure the students get the information they need to be successful." "Forget Walt Disney World. This is the happiest place on earth," one student brags. "Clemson's greatest strength lies in the sense of community it fosters and the opportunities for development that it offers to its students." A finance major sums up his experience: "At Clemson, I'm earning a respected degree working alongside the leading researcher in my field, gaining valuable leadership experience while serving the community, and having the time of my life with my best friends. What's not to love?"

Life

"We bleed orange!" a sociology major says, referring not to any kind of bizarre skin condition, but rather to the student body's "Tiger pride" in Clemson athletics. "Sports are king" at Clemson, and much of student life revolves around attending and tailgating at sporting events, especially football. "I never anticipated how much people love their Clemson football," one impressed student notes. This atmosphere can be slightly off-putting to students less interested in athletics. "I think Clemson isn't the most cultured school," one student laments. "The general students would prefer to tailgate and watch football than attend an orchestra concert." However, watching sports isn't the only thing Clemson students do. Like at any school, "people hang out with their friends... party, and have fun." Students "love the fact that our school is located on one of the state's biggest freshwater lakes, minutes from the mountains, and not far from the beach. It's the ideal place to live." "Clemson has more than 300 organizations," one student notes, "meaning that nearly everyone is involved in something." Clemson is known as something of a party school, and "Greek life...has a lot of influence." The laid-back Southern atmosphere pervades Clemson, and "everyone is so happy and friendly!" "The town of Clemson is not very big and is very much a college town," with all the pros and cons that entails.

Student Body

"Clemson students have a bond," a happy student notes. "I have made so many connections with others because we both attended Clemson." Clemson is "not a hot spot of diversity by any means," and "your typical student is Southern, Christian, and somewhat preppy." That doesn't mean that students from different backgrounds can't fit in. "Although Clemson is a 'jock school' with a somewhat homogeneous student body, most people are pleasant, and you can easily enjoy your college experience." Another student relates that, while most students are Southern and religiously conservative, "as a non-religious student from the North, I've felt welcome here and have loved every minute of my experience." With the school's large Greek life, "there is a definitive line between Greeks and non-Greeks." The dominant student fashion is "preppy, preppy, preppy! With camo." "Honestly, as long as you wear orange on Fridays and love your Tigers, you'll fit in just fine." Students at the school take both their social and academic life seriously. "For the most part, Clemson students go out looking preppy on Saturday night, dress up for church on Sunday, and roll into class wearing sweats on Monday morning."

FINANCIAL AID: 864-656-2280 • E-MAIL: CUADMISSIONS@CLEMSON.EDU • WEBSITE: WWW.CLEMSON.EDU

THE PRINCETON REVIEW SAYS

Admissions

Very important factors considered include: Academic GPA, class rank, rigor of secondary school record, standardized test scores, state residency. *Important factors considered include:* Alumni/ae relation. *Other factors considered include:* Application essay, recommendation(s), extracurricular activities, talent/ability. SAT or ACT required; ACT with writing component required. TOEFL required of all international applicants. High school diploma is required, and GED is accepted. *Academic units required:* 4 English, 3 mathematics, 3 science (3 science labs), 3 foreign language, 3 social studies, 1 history, 2 academic elective. *Academic units recommended:* 4 mathematics, (4 science labs).

Financial Aid

Students should submit: FAFSA. The Princeton Review suggests that all financial aid forms be submitted as soon as possible after January 1. *Need-based scholarships/grants offered:* Federal Pell, SEOG, state scholarships/grants, private scholarships, school scholarship or grant aid from institutional funds, Federal Nursing Scholarships. *Loan aid offered:* Direct Subsidized Stafford, Direct Unsubsidized Stafford, Direct PLUS, Federal Perkins, state loans, university loans from institutional funds. Applicants will be notified of awards on a rolling basis beginning April 1.

The Inside Word

With its Southern charm, competitive Division I athletics, and Greek life, Clemson will be an ideal fit for many types of students. But don't think that Clemson doesn't take its academics seriously. It's one of the top thirty public universities in the country and has been moving up the rankings every year. Admissions are competitive, and a good GPA and test scores will be needed for all who apply.

THE SCHOOL SAYS "..."

From the Admissions Office

"One of the country's most selective public research universities, Clemson University was founded with a mission to be a high seminary of learning dedicated to teaching, research, and service. Nearly 120 years later, these three concepts remain at the heart of this university and provide the framework for an exceptional educational experience for Clemson students.

"At Clemson, professors take the time to get to know students and to explore innovative ways of teaching. Exceptional teaching is one reason Clemson's retention and graduation rates rank among the highest in the country among public universities. Exceptional teaching is also why Clemson continues to attract an increasingly talented student body. The class rank and SAT scores of Clemson's incoming freshman are among the highest of the nation's public research universities.

"Clemson offers over 250 student clubs and organizations; the spirit that students show for this university is unparalleled.

"Midway between Charlotte, North Carolina, and Atlanta, Georgia, Clemson University is located on 1,400 acres of beautiful rolling hills within the foothills of the Blue Ridge Mountains and along the shores of Lake Hartwell.

"Applicants are required to take the SAT or the ACT with the writing section. The best combined scores from SAT test will be used in the admissions process. We do not, however, combine sub scores from the ACT in order to create a new composite score."

SELECTIVITY

Admissions Rating	89
# of applicants	16,865
% of applicants accepted	58
% of acceptees attending	31
# accepting a place on wait list	638
% admitted from wait list	17

FRESHMAN PROFILE

Range SAT Critical Reading	550–650
Range SAT Math	590–680
Range SAT Writing	540–640
Range ACT Composite	26–30
Minimum paper TOEFL	550
Minimum computer TOEFL	213
Average HS GPA	4.16
% graduated top 10% of class	51
% graduated top 25% of class	83
% graduated top 50% of class	98

DEADLINES

Regular	
Priority	12/1
Deadline	5/1
Notification	2/15
Nonfall registration?	yes

APPLICANTS ALSO LOOK AT AND SOMETIMES PREFER

Georgia Institute of Technology, University of Georgia, University of Virginia

AND RARELY PREFER

Auburn University, College of Charleston, Florida State University, North Carolina State University, University of Maryland—College Park, University of South Carolina—Columbia

FINANCIAL FACTS

Financial Aid Rating	70
Annual in-state tuition	$12,346
Annual out-of-state tuition	$27,858
Room and board	$7,034
Required fees	$500
Books and supplies	$940
% frosh rec. need-based scholarship or grant aid	15
% UG rec. need-based scholarship or grant aid	18
% frosh rec. non-need-based scholarship or grant aid	77
% UG rec. non-need-based scholarship or grant aid	59
% frosh rec. need-based self-help aid	24
% UG rec. need-based self-help aid	28
% frosh rec. any financial aid	87
% UG rec. any financial aid	71
% UG borrow to pay for school	44
Average cumulative indebtedness	$17,882

COE COLLEGE

1220 FIRST AVENUE NORTHEAST, CEDAR RAPIDS, IA 52402 • ADMISSIONS: 319-399-8500 • FAX: 319-399-8816

CAMPUS LIFE

Quality of Life Rating	81
Fire Safety Rating	61
Green Rating	60*
Type of school	private
Affiliation	Presbyterian
Environment	city

STUDENTS

Total undergrad enrollment	1,330
% male/female	46/54
% from out of state	33
% from public high school	90
% live on campus	84
# of fraternities	5
# of sororities	3
% African American	3
% Asian	2
% Caucasian	84
% Hispanic	2
% international	1
# of countries represented	18

SURVEY SAYS . . .

Career services are great
Students are friendly
Student government is popular

ACADEMICS

Academic Rating	86
% students graduating within 4 years	61
% students graduating within 6 years	70
Calendar	semester
Student/faculty ratio	11:1
Profs interesting rating	84
Profs accessible rating	87
Most common reg class size	10–19 students
Most common lab size	10–19 students

MOST POPULAR MAJORS

biology, business administration and management, psychology

STUDENTS SAY ". . ."

Academics

Located in Cedar Rapids, Iowa, Coe College is a small school with a "tight-knit community feel" that provides "something different for everyone." "Coe has a very warm and friendly atmosphere" that works for "the betterment of each individual Kohawk through experiences, in and out of the classroom, as well as creating a mature adult prepared for the 'real-world.'" Students who need financial help shouldn't worry, because the "financial aid rocks!" Students love "the small class sizes that allow you to have a personable experience with each of your professors." The "small teacher/student ratio" also comes with "excellent, intelligent, helpful, and caring professors" who "all have great abundances of knowledge and all teach in different ways." "I honestly have not had a bad instructor," a chemistry major tells us. "They give you their home phone and cell phone numbers and invite you to call them. No teaching assistants here." A sociology student boasts of "relationships with my professors, and [I] feel that they invest in me and want me to succeed." Although the students rate their professors highly, they didn't feel the same way about the classrooms the professors teach in. "Our academic buildings and dorms are really run down," one student says. Others claimed the college "needs faster Internet." For many, the school is "an ideal size." "Big without being too big." One student lists Coe's strengths up as "the small class sizes, the community atmosphere, the involvement of students, study abroad programs, physics, and athletics." Coe has "the ability [to make] literally anyone feel comfortable."

Life

Although Coe is located in Iowa's second largest city, "people often fall victim to the 'Coe bubble,'" one student warns. "A lot of people are not familiar with the city and refuse to venture out. Most people I know enjoy alcohol on the weekends." While Coe isn't located "in the best neighborhood to go out in, we do have bars that are within blocks from our campus [and that] are attended a lot on the weekends by students." Like many colleges, drinking is a common social activity. "In all honesty, Coe's students typically do drink alcohol—both on campus and off campus at the Cedar Rapids bars." However, other students see a variety of activities available. "There are parties, lots of video games, people playing intramural sports, Friday after class events… something for everyone." "For fun students go to SAC events like free midnight movies, tie-dying, dance socials in the pub, quarter bowling night, ice skating." When asked what the school could improve on, the students were unanimous in their complaint: "The food is something we all wish would improve." To compound matters, "Students are required to have a meal plan," and there aren't many options for "alternative diets such as vegan and vegetarian." The school hosts a regular talent show, Blindspot, which is so named because it's "open for students to perform without judgment."

Student Body

"About one-third of [Coe's] student body is athletes," but "there really isn't a particular social group or type of personality that this school is known for, so it's easy to fit in with one—or any—group on campus." "The average students are exactly that: average," a student explains. "It is a very typical representation of the Midwest. There are very few students (I'd say less than ten people in the entire population on campus) [who] do not truly fit in anywhere." "While Greek organizations maintain a significant presence in numbers," Greek life doesn't dominate the school: "They don't organize for significant events or provide any clear distinction from other students." Students at Coe "are friendly," a trait helped by an "orientation [that] creates a forced interaction [and] gets people mingling." "There is not a typical student at Coe," one student says, "because each student is treated uniquely and takes a unique set of classes."

FINANCIAL AID: 319-399-8540 • E-MAIL: ADMISSION@COE.EDU • WEBSITE: WWW.COE.EDU

THE PRINCETON REVIEW SAYS

Admissions

Very important factors considered include: Academic GPA, standardized test scores. *Important factors considered include:* Application essay, class rank, recommendation(s). *Other factors considered include:* Rigor of secondary school record, alumni/ae relation, character/personal qualities, extracurricular activities, first generation, interview, level of applicant's interest, racial/ethnic status, talent/ability, volunteer work. SAT or ACT required; ACT with or without writing component accepted. TOEFL required of all international applicants. High school diploma is required, and GED is accepted. *Academic units recommended:* 4 English, 3 mathematics, 3 science (1 science lab), 2 foreign language, 3 social studies, 2 academic elective.

Financial Aid

Students should submit: FAFSA. The Princeton Review suggests that all financial aid forms be submitted as soon as possible after January 1. *Need-based scholarships/grants offered:* Federal Pell, SEOG, state scholarships/grants, private scholarships, school scholarship or grant aid from institutional funds. *Loan aid offered:* Direct Subsidized Stafford, Direct Unsubsidized Stafford, Direct PLUS, Federal Perkins, university loans from institutional funds. Applicants will be notified of awards on a rolling basis beginning March 15. Federal Work-Study Program available. Off-campus job opportunities are excellent.

The Inside Word

About 400 new students begin their college journey at Coe College each fall, and classes average a mere sixteen students. Despite its small size, Coe has the largest undergraduate writing center in the country, and many students enjoy its help. If you're seeking an intimate college experience with quality academics—Coe is one of the smallest universities to contain a Phi Beta Kappa chapter—you would do well to consider Coe.

THE SCHOOL SAYS ". . ."

From the Admissions Office

"A Coe education begins to pay off right away. In fact, ninety-eight percent of last year's graduating class was either working or in graduate school within six months of graduation. One reason our graduates do so well is the Coe Plan—a step-by-step sequence of activities designed to prepare our students for life after Coe. This required sequence stretches from the first-year seminar to community service, issue dinners, career planning seminars, and the required hands-on experience. The hands-on component may be satisfied through an internship, research, practicum, or study abroad. One student lived with a Costa Rican family while she studied the effects of selective logging on rain forest organisms. Others have interned at places like Warner Brothers in Los Angeles and the Chicago Board of Trade. Still others combine travel with an internship or student teaching for an unforgettable off-campus experience. Coe College is one of the few liberal arts institutions in the country to require hands-on learning for graduation."

SELECTIVITY

Admissions Rating	88
# of applicants	2,400
% of applicants accepted	61
% of acceptees attending	24

FRESHMAN PROFILE

Range SAT Critical Reading	570–670
Range SAT Math	510–640
Range SAT Writing	540–650
Range ACT Composite	23–28
Minimum paper TOEFL	500
Minimum computer TOEFL	173
Average HS GPA	3.67
% graduated top 10% of class	26
% graduated top 25% of class	64
% graduated top 50% of class	95

DEADLINES

Early action	
Deadline	12/10
Notification	1/20
Regular	
Priority	12/10
Deadline	3/1
Notification	10/1
Nonfall registration?	yes

APPLICANTS ALSO LOOK AT AND SOMETIMES PREFER
Cornell College, University of Iowa

FINANCIAL FACTS

Financial Aid Rating	85
Annual tuition	$32,060
Room and board	$7,570
Required fees	$320
Books and supplies	$1,000
% frosh rec. need-based scholarship or grant aid	81
% UG rec. need-based scholarship or grant aid	80
% frosh rec. non-need-based scholarship or grant aid	17
% UG rec. non-need-based scholarship or grant aid	13
% frosh rec. need-based self-help aid	61
% UG rec. need-based self-help aid	63
% frosh rec. any financial aid	99
% UG rec. any financial aid	94
% UG borrow to pay for school	80
Average cumulative indebtedness	$32,260

COLBY COLLEGE

4000 MAYFLOWER HILL, WATERVILLE, ME 04901-8848 • ADMISSIONS: 800-723-3032 • FAX: 207-859-4828

CAMPUS LIFE

Quality of Life Rating	86
Fire Safety Rating	90
Green Rating	84
Type of school	private
Environment	village

STUDENTS

Total undergrad enrollment	1,825
% male/female	46/54
% from out of state	88
% from public high school	54
% live on campus	93
% African American	4
% Asian	8
% Caucasian	57
% Hispanic	4
% Native American	1
% international	5
# of countries represented	62

SURVEY SAYS . . .
Great food on campus
Dorms are like palaces
Frats and sororities are unpopular
or nonexistent

ACADEMICS

Academic Rating	96
% students graduating within 4 years	86
% students graduating within 6 years	90
Calendar	4-1-4
Student/faculty ratio	10:1
Profs interesting rating	92
Profs accessible rating	88
Most common reg class size	10–19 students
Most common lab size	10–19 students

MOST POPULAR MAJORS
biology, economics, international/
global studies

STUDENTS SAY "..."

Academics
This small, close-knit liberal arts college draws praise from students for its rigorous but caring approach to academics. It's a place where devoted professors "invite students to dinner" and learning happens "for learning's sake." Small classes are one of Colby's biggest draws. "Professors are always willing to go the extra mile," one student says. A senior adds, "Over the course of my time at Colby I've been to at least six different professors' houses for departmental events, class dinners, and group discussions." Professors get high grades for their teaching and accessibility, which together foster a "love for learning" in undergraduates. As one student dryly notes, "Waterville, Maine is not the country's academic capital, so the professors that choose to be at Colby are here to teach, not to use the facilities." This dedication to academics can make Colby an intense place to go to school, and students here aren't "afraid to work hard and study." In addition, students must not only complete their major requirements but also fulfill a hefty load of distribution requirements to graduate. The popular "Jan Plan" allows students to pursue focused course work, independent study or internships during an intensive four-week term in January. While the administration "works hard to keep students happy and entertained," some feel that their needs are "occasionally ignored in favor of the everlasting quest to turn Colby into a small Ivy."

Life
"Friends and a sense of community drive life at Colby," one senior writes. Students live together in coed, mixed-class dorms. Everything centers around the campus, which is "constructed on a gorgeous wooded hill near the Kennebec River in central Maine." Since "there isn't a ridiculous amount to do" in these self-contained environs, "Colby works hard to fill the day with countless events, lectures, discussions, and concerts. People can study hard, party, take advantage of the beautiful outdoors, and most do all three." A student notes, "The size of the school is perfect: On any given day, I could see five friends or acquaintances (and countless familiar faces!) on my way to class." This makes for a friendly atmosphere as "it's easy to start up a conversation with pretty much anyone. When the great outdoors beckons, students answer the call by hiking in autumn and spring, skiing in winter, and participating in traditional outdoor sports like football. A senior explains, "People like to unwind after our incredibly stressful weeks with movies, skiing, and partying." The "alcohol-centered social scene" usually takes place at small dorm parties or at the few local pubs.

Student Body
While the prototypical Colby student may be "white and from twenty minutes outside of Boston," undergrads are quick to point out that their "campus is very open to diversity and ready to embrace it." Students single out the administration for "doing a great job of bringing in a more diverse student population." One student explains, "More and more international students and urban kids are coming through programs like the Posse Scholarship." A junior adds, "We have students here that dress in business suits and bow ties while others walk around in capes." Most students, however, settle for the more general description of "preppy students who enjoy the outdoors and enjoy having a good time." That said, students report, "There's pretty much a place for everyone somewhere at Colby; chances are you'll find people both very similar to you in interests, background, etc. and people who are completely the opposite." One student elaborates, explaining that despite all differences, "The one word I'd use to describe a Colby student is friendly."

FINANCIAL AID: 800-723-3032 • E-MAIL: ADMISSIONS@COLBY.EDU • WEBSITE: WWW.COLBY.EDU

THE PRINCETON REVIEW SAYS

Admissions

Very important factors considered include: Rigor of secondary school record, character/personal qualities. *Important factors considered include:* Academic GPA, application essay, class rank, recommendation(s), standardized test scores, extracurricular activities, racial/ethnic status, talent/ability. *Other factors considered include:* Alumni/ae relation, first generation, geographical residence, interview, level of applicant's interest, state residency, volunteer work, work experience. ACT with or without writing component accepted. TOEFL required of all international applicants. High school diploma or equivalent isn't required. *Academic units recommended:* 4 English, 3 mathematics, 2 science (2 science labs), 3 foreign language.

Financial Aid

Students should submit: FAFSA, CSS/Financial Aid PROFILE, parents 2011 year-end paystubs. Regular filing deadline is January 15. The Princeton Review suggests that all financial aid forms be submitted as soon as possible after January 1. *Need-based scholarships/grants offered:* Federal Pell, SEOG, state scholarships/grants, private scholarships, school scholarship or grant aid from institutional funds. *Loan aid offered:* Direct Subsidized Stafford, Direct Unsubsidized Stafford, Direct PLUS, Federal Perkins, state loans, university loans from institutional funds, and Colby-funded student employment. Federal Work-Study Program available. Off-campus job opportunities are poor.

The Inside Word

Colby continues to be both very selective and successful in converting admits to enrollees, which makes for a perpetually challenging admissions process. Currently, only thirty-four percent of applicants are accepted, so hit those books and ace those exams to stand a fighting chance. One thing that could set you apart from the pack? An interest in travel. Two-thirds of Colby students study abroad—in fact, for some degrees it's required.

THE SCHOOL SAYS "..."

From the Admissions Office

"Colby is one of only a handful of liberal arts colleges that offer world-class academic programs, leadership in internationalism, an active community life, and rich opportunities after graduation. Set in Maine on one of the nation's most beautiful campuses, Colby provides students a host of opportunities for active engagement, in Waterville or around the world. The Goldfarb Center for Public Affairs and Civic Engagement connects teaching and research with current political, economic, and social issues at home and abroad. Recently Colby replaced loans in its financial aid packages with grants, which don't have to be repaid, making it possible for students to graduate without college-loan debt. Students' access to Colby's outstanding faculty is extraordinary, and the college is a leader in undergraduate research and project-based learning. The college has won awards for sustainable environmental practices as well as one of the first Senator Paul Simon Awards for Internationalizing the Campus.

"The challenging academic experience at the heart of Colby's programs is complemented by a vibrant community life and campus atmosphere featuring more than 100 student-run organizations, more than fifty athletic and recreational choices, and numerous leadership and volunteer opportunities.

"Colby graduates succeed. They find their places at the best medical schools and research universities, the finest law and business programs, top financial firms, in the arts, government service, social service, education, and nonprofit organizations, and they are inspired leaders in their communities.

"Applicants must submit scores from the SAT, ACT, or SAT Subject Tests in three different subject areas. The choice of which test(s) to take is entirely up to each applicant. The optional ACT writing test is recommended."

SELECTIVITY

Admissions Rating	94
# of applicants	4,213
% of applicants accepted	34
% of acceptees attending	34
# accepting a place on wait list	507
% admitted from wait list	2
# of early decision applicants	418
% accepted early decision	52

FRESHMAN PROFILE

Range SAT Critical Reading	630–710
Range SAT Math	620–710
Range SAT Writing	620–715
Range ACT Composite	28–31
Minimum web-based TOEFL	100
% graduated top 10% of class	70
% graduated top 25% of class	91
% graduated top 50% of class	98

DEADLINES

Early decision	
Deadline	11/15
Notification	12/15
Regular	
Deadline	1/1
Nonfall registration?	yes

APPLICANTS ALSO LOOK AT AND OFTEN PREFER

Amherst College, Bowdoin College, Dartmouth College, Middlebury College, Williams College

AND SOMETIMES PREFER

Bates College, Boston College, Colgate University

AND RARELY PREFER

Hamilton College, Skidmore College, University of Vermont

FINANCIAL FACTS

Financial Aid Rating	97
Annual comprehensive tuition	$51,990
Books and supplies	$700
% frosh rec. need-based scholarship or grant aid	40
% UG rec. need-based scholarship or grant aid	42
% frosh rec. non-need-based scholarship or grant aid	1
% UG rec. non-need-based scholarship or grant aid	1
% frosh rec. need-based self-help aid	30
% UG rec. need-based self-help aid	33
% frosh rec. any financial aid	46
% UG rec. any financial aid	47
% UG borrow to pay for school	37
Average cumulative indebtedness	$24,600

COLGATE UNIVERSITY

13 OAK DRIVE, HAMILTON, NY 13346 • ADMISSIONS: 315-228-7401 • FAX: 315-228-7544

CAMPUS LIFE

Quality of Life Rating	84
Fire Safety Rating	78
Green Rating	85
Type of school	private
Environment	rural

STUDENTS

Total undergrad enrollment	2,868
% male/female	47/53
% from out of state	74
% from public high school	61
% live on campus	91
# of fraternities	6
# of sororities	3
% African American	4
% Asian	4
% Caucasian	72
% Hispanic	7
% international	6
# of countries represented	36

SURVEY SAYS . . .

Lab facilities are great
Great computer facilities
Great library
School is well-run
Dorms are like palaces
Students are happy
Lots of beer drinking
Hard liquor is popular

ACADEMICS

Academic Rating	96
% students graduating within 4 years	83
% students graduating within 6 years	88
Calendar	semester
Student/faculty ratio	10:1
Profs interesting rating	91
Profs accessible rating	95
Most common reg class size	10–19 students
Most common lab size	10–19 students

MOST POPULAR MAJORS

economics, English language and literature, sociology and anthropology

STUDENTS SAY ". . ."

Academics

Colgate University is known for its "very rigorous academic curriculum" and "invaluable" professors who "are the glue that hold the university together." Many students say they chose Colgate because of "the opportunity to be a part of a small community where students can genuinely interact with their professors" and "the academic prestige" combined with an alumni network that "makes the Colgate connection a truly valuable resource." All agree that, at Colgate, you're "more than just a number" and say, "The faculty are very interested in helping their students develop as scholars." Although there's the rare "dud," professors get high marks for being "incredibly enthusiastic" and wanting "to support [students] to the fullest." A psychology major says, "I have been to at least one professor's house each semester. Professors sincerely want all of their students to succeed academically," and a junior adds, "One of the wonderful things about Colgate is that these relationships start as early as freshman year. Students do not have to wait until their senior year to build fantastic relationships with the faculty." However, another student grumbles, "Course selection is very stressful, and freshmen often get slighted." Overall, Colgate is "a challenging school, but at the end of the day, the challenge is all about the student's development."

Life

Colgate University "has an amazing campus with people who work hard and have goals but also know how to have a really fun time." Students say the campus is "breathtaking," and they value "its small size and intimate nature." A philosophy major says, "Colgate is great because you can't walk 200 feet without a professor, student, or faculty member acknowledging you by name, yet you're constantly meeting new people and having new experiences. There is never a dull moment at Colgate." Students say, "Colgate strives for the perfect combination of academics and extracurriculars," and they feel the university "does a great job at helping us balance those and gives us opportunities to get involved in all the groups and events around campus." In addition to a plethora of clubs, students are actively involved in Greek life and Division I athletics. A junior says, "I loved how Colgate was located in the middle of nowhere" because "everything revolved around the campus," but in case you're worried about isolation, another student adds, "Colgate brings a lot of interesting speakers to the campus, which helps provide for a more rounded liberal arts experience." Students praise the administration, saying, "It is easy for students to contact the administration and thus have their voices directly heard by the community. The president holds drop-in office hours for students every week and takes notes on what students say during the session."

Student Body

Colgate boasts a "happy and enthusiastic student body" that "follows the motto 'work hard, play hard.'" Many say a typical student is "white, very well-rounded, a hard partier," and "rich and preppy." A sophomore says, "Imagine J. Crew models. Now give them brains, and that is who is walking around Colgate's campus." Fraternities and sororities are popular: "Greek life does have a huge presence in the social life at Colgate," but "it is not exclusive to just those who are members." An English major says, "I wouldn't describe the party scene as being [full of] peer pressure, but there are few alternatives, so if it's not your preferred pastime you may find yourself very bored." There are students who wish the university would be "a little tighter with alcohol control." Some students wish the administration would work harder to "break down huge social barriers that exist between people of different races," and say, "The campus is striving to make the campus more diverse, but unfortunately the diverse groups like to keep…[to] themselves." However, despite the "country club atmosphere," a computer science major says, "When you're stranded in Hamilton, New York, for four years you'll inevitably end up fitting in regardless whether you are the typical student or not."

FINANCIAL AID: 315-228-7431 • E-MAIL: ADMISSION@COLGATE.EDU • WEBSITE: WWW.COLGATE.EDU

THE PRINCETON REVIEW SAYS

Admissions

Very important factors considered include: Academic GPA, class rank, rigor of secondary school record. *Important factors considered include:* Application essay, recommendation(s), standardized test scores, character/personal qualities, extracurricular activities, talent/ability. *Other factors considered include:* Alumni/ae relation, first generation, geographical residence, racial/ethnic status, volunteer work, work experience. SAT or ACT required; ACT with or without writing component accepted. TOEFL required of all international applicants. High school diploma is required, and GED is accepted. Students have until March 1 to convert their application from Regular to Early Decision II and will be notified of their decision within four weeks of completing their Early Decision II application. *Academic units required:* 4 English, 3 mathematics, 3 science (2 science labs), 3 foreign language, 3 social studies. *Academic units recommended:* 4 English, 4 mathematics, 4 science (4 science labs), 4 foreign language, 4 social studies.

Financial Aid

Students should submit: CSS/Financial Aid PROFILE. Regular filing deadline is January 15. The Princeton Review suggests that all financial aid forms be submitted as soon as possible after January 1. *Need-based scholarships/grants offered:* Federal Pell, SEOG, state scholarships/grants, private scholarships, school scholarship or grant aid from institutional funds. *Loan aid offered:* Direct Subsidized Stafford, Direct Unsubsidized Stafford, Direct PLUS, Federal Perkins. Applicants will be notified of awards on a rolling basis beginning April 1. Federal Work-Study Program available. Off-campus job opportunities are good.

The Inside Word

Admission to the university is selective, and Colgate places the most value on previous academic achievement, evaluating both the level of courses taken in high school and the success reached in those courses. Applications undergo individual review by the admissions staff, who look for a record of "substantive involvement in extracurricular and community activities." Additionally, the admissions office is committed to the "recruitment and retention" of a diverse student body.

THE SCHOOL SAYS " . . . "

From the Admissions Office

"Colgate provides an environment where students can appreciate, celebrate, and learn about their own cultures as well as those of the people around them. The class of 2014 is the most diverse class ever, with 26.2 percent of students claiming a multicultural background and 8.5 percent international students. Students and faculty alike are drawn to Colgate by the quality of its academic programs. Faculty initiative has given the university a rich mix of learning opportunities that includes a liberal arts core, fifty-one academic concentrations, and a wealth of Colgate faculty-led, off-campus study programs in the United States and abroad. But there is more to Colgate than academic life, including a full complement of living options set within a campus described as one of the most beautiful in the country. The new Trudy Fitness Center is an integral component of Colgate's Wellness Initiative, which encourages healthy, purposeful, and balanced lifestyles within the community. A center for community service builds upon the tradition of Colgate students interacting with the surrounding community in meaningful ways. Colgate students become extraordinarily devoted alumni, contributing significantly to career networking and exploration programs on and off campus. For students in search of a busy and varied campus life, Colgate is a place to learn and grow."

SELECTIVITY

Admissions Rating	97
# of applicants	7,872
% of applicants accepted	33
% of acceptees attending	33
# accepting a place on wait list	671
% admitted from wait list	0
# of early decision applicants	651
% accepted early decision	58

FRESHMAN PROFILE

Range SAT Critical Reading	630–720
Range SAT Math	640–740
Range ACT Composite	29–32
Average HS GPA	3.60
% graduated top 10% of class	64
% graduated top 25% of class	90
% graduated top 50% of class	98

DEADLINES

Early decision I	
Deadline	11/15
Notification	12/15
Early decision II	
Deadline	1/15
Regular	
Deadline	1/15
Nonfall registration?	no

APPLICANTS ALSO LOOK AT AND OFTEN PREFER
Boston College, Cornell University, Dartmouth College, Tufts University

AND SOMETIMES PREFER
Bowdoin College, Middlebury College

AND RARELY PREFER
Boston University, Bucknell University, Colby College, Hamilton College, Lehigh University, University of Richmond, University of Rochester, University of Vermont, Villanova University

FINANCIAL FACTS

Financial Aid Rating	98
Annual tuition	$42,625
% frosh rec. need-based scholarship or grant aid	32
% UG rec. need-based scholarship or grant aid	33
% frosh rec. need-based self-help aid	25
% UG rec. need-based self-help aid	26
% frosh rec. any financial aid	33
% UG rec. any financial aid	34
% UG borrow to pay for school	33
Average cumulative indebtedness	$18,629

COLLEGE OF THE ATLANTIC

105 EDEN STREET, BAR HARBOR, ME 04609 • ADMISSIONS: 207-288-5015 • FAX: 207-288-4126

STUDENTS SAY ". . ."

Academics

The College of the Atlantic takes a unique approach to academics. All undergrads "major in Human Ecology," an interdisciplinary philosophy that addresses environmental and social issues. While there are distribution requirements, a sophomore ensures us that "those are easy to fulfill" and asserts that "all other classes are elective." Unfortunately, due to COA's small size, "most classes are [only] offered every other year." Therefore, if a particular course sparks your interest, you "need to jump on the [opportunity]." The intimate size does have plenty of advantages however. Undergrads here seem to unanimously agree that "COA is a very close-knit community" where "interpersonal relationships with staff, faculty, and administration" flourish. Students eagerly sing the praises of their professors: "an eclectic and brilliant group of people" who are "extremely accessible." And this availability isn't limited to normal workday hours. One junior told us that it's quite common for professors "to give out their home phone numbers." Though friendly and supportive, professors don't let their students slack off. While the workload "varies from class to class" it's most definitely "not light." Luckily, these "self-motivated" undergrads happily embrace their assignments. As one impressed freshman sums up, "For students in search of a school that will challenge them, [COA] is an excellent place."

Life

Though COA students are often "swamped with reading and homework" there is always "time to have fun." Hometown Bar Harbor is a place "that is booming with tourists in the summer and pretty much dead in the winter." While undergrads frequent a few local hangouts, they mostly "make our own fun." Students can often be found playing "hockey on the pond" or "pick-up games of soccer," hosting "spontaneous midnight poetry readings," "tobogganing at the golf course," or throwing "dance parties in the art gallery." There's even the occasional "sword fight in the library." COA's location is an outdoor enthusiast's dream, and students are quick to take advantage of the school's proximity to Acadia National Park. Opportunities abound to "hike, bike [and] go out on the ocean" and "snowshoe/ski in the winter." The small population helps to ensure a "strong sense of community," and undergrads are always content with attending a potluck and simply enjoying "philosophical conversations that last until early morning." There's a party scene, but "Alcohol does not dominate social life at all." Finally, the school also hosts a variety of activities "such as concerts, open mics, and hiking trips."

Student Body

Undergrads at the COA readily acknowledge that many people assume they're "all tree-hugging hippies" who always wear "Birkenstocks and tie dye." And while there are plenty of "outdoorsy" types, students are quick to assert that many of their peers shatter this stereotype. Though the majority might categorize themselves as "atypical," most everyone is "compassionate, kind, and aware." Passion is another common attribute, and one freshman gushes, "Everyone is incredibly cool and into something, whether it be poetry, fighting climate change, dance, whales [or] organic farming...everyone wants to improve the lives of others." With such a politically aware student body, COA is a bastion for liberal, left-leaning undergrads. Indeed, this sentiment is punctuated by a sophomore who exclaims, "I think there are about two Republicans in the whole school." That being said, "The college [has] a very egalitarian outlook, [and] everyone is equal and equally valued." While the majority of COA undergrads are "white [and] middle-class," the college manages to attract "a lot of international students through the Davis Scholarship Program," ensuring a diversity of experience and opinion.

FINANCIAL AID: 207-288-5015 • E-MAIL: INQUIRY@ECOLOGY.COA.EDU • WEBSITE: WWW.COA.EDU

THE PRINCETON REVIEW SAYS

Admissions

Very important factors considered include: Application essay, recommendation(s), rigor of secondary school record. *Important factors considered include:* Academic GPA, class rank, character/personal qualities, extracurricular activities, interview, talent/ability, volunteer work, work experience. *Other factors considered include:* Standardized test scores, alumni/ae relation, first generation, geographical residence, level of applicant's interest, racial/ethnic status, state residency. ACT with or without writing component accepted. TOEFL required of all international applicants. High school diploma is required, and GED is accepted. *Academic units required:* 4 English, 3 mathematics, 2 science (2 science labs), 2 social studies. *Academic units recommended:* 4 mathematics, 3 science, 2 foreign language, 2 history, 1 academic elective.

Financial Aid

Students should submit: FAFSA, institution's own financial aid form. Regular filing deadline is February 15. The Princeton Review suggests that all financial aid forms be submitted as soon as possible after January 1. *Need-based scholarships/grants offered:* Federal Pell, SEOG, state scholarships/grants, private scholarships, school scholarship or grant aid from institutional funds. *Loan aid offered:* Federal Perkins. Federal Work-Study Program not available. Off-campus job opportunities are good.

The Inside Word

As applicants might expect, admissions standards at COA are somewhat atypical. The school covets students who carve their own intellectual courses rather than follow a conventional academic path. Students at COA are expected to bring strong ideas and values to the classroom, and applicants are assessed accordingly. Essays and interviews are where you can make your mark. Of course, the college's integrated approach also means you should have a well-rounded secondary school record. Candidates should also demonstrate a kinship with the philosophy of human ecology.

THE SCHOOL SAYS ". . ."

From the Admissions Office

"College of the Atlantic is a small, intellectually challenging college on Mount Desert Island, Maine. We look for students seeking a rigorous, hands-on, self-directed academic experience. Come for a visit, and you will begin to understand that COA's unique approach to education, governance and community life extends throughout its structure. Resolutely value centered and interdisciplinary—there are no departments and no majors, COA sees its mission as preparing people to become independent thinkers, to challenge conventional wisdom, to deal with pressing global change—both environmental and social—and to be passionately engaged in transforming the world around them into a better place.

"College of the Atlantic does not require standardized testing as part of the application process. Learning and intelligence can be gauged in many ways; standardized test scores are just one of many measures. If an applicant chooses to submit standardized test scores for consideration, the SAT, SAT Subject Tests, or ACT scores are all acceptable."

SELECTIVITY

Admissions Rating	89
# of applicants	390
% of applicants accepted	64
% of acceptees attending	34
# accepting a place on wait list	17
% admitted from wait list	35
# of early decision applicants	41
% accepted early decision	71

FRESHMAN PROFILE

Range SAT Critical Reading	570–690
Range SAT Math	520–650
Range SAT Writing	570–670
Range ACT Composite	24–29
Minimum paper TOEFL	567
Minimum computer TOEFL	227
Minimum web-based TOEFL	86
Average HS GPA	3.56
% graduated top 10% of class	43
% graduated top 25% of class	65
% graduated top 50% of class	92

DEADLINES

Early decision	
Deadline	12/1
Notification	12/15
Regular	
Deadline	2/15
Nonfall registration?	yes

APPLICANTS ALSO LOOK AT
AND OFTEN PREFER
Bowdoin College, Colby College
AND SOMETIMES PREFER
Bard College, Hampshire College
AND RARELY PREFER
Green Mountain College, University of Maine, Warren Wilson College

FINANCIAL FACTS

Financial Aid Rating	90
Annual tuition	$35,532
Room and board	$8,250
Required fees	$531
Books and supplies	$600
% frosh rec. need-based scholarship or grant aid	87
% UG rec. need-based scholarship or grant aid	84
% frosh rec. need-based self-help aid	82
% UG rec. need-based self-help aid	82
% frosh rec. any financial aid	88
% UG rec. any financial aid	85
% UG borrow to pay for school	66
Average cumulative indebtedness	$20,125

COLLEGE OF CHARLESTON

66 GEORGE STREET, CHARLESTON, SC 29424 • ADMISSIONS: 843-953-5670 • FAX: 843-953-6322

STUDENTS SAY ". . ."

Academics

The College of Charleston provides "huge university opportunities with a small college, personalized atmosphere." "It's actually a fairly large school (10,000 students), but it feels much smaller in the historic Charleston setting," explains one student. Even though it's not the smallest university, it "offers great classes in a smaller, one-on-one environment." Located "right in the heart of downtown Charleston," the university is "a Southern secret that welcomes diversity with warm arms." Students can't say enough good things about the location. "The city of Charleston is fun and inviting, the weather is a million times better than the North, and the beach is close by!" Since the "College of Charleston is very old" and was "founded in 1770," many of the facilities "are getting older" and could really "use some work." College of Charleston "exemplifies 'progressive traditionalism'" and "is all about liberal arts; the education is well-rounded and intriguing." The "professors really do care about you." "The professors I've encountered in the history department truly love their field and have greatly shaped my own research," one student testifies. "I'm from Charleston, and I couldn't imagine living anywhere else!" one student boasts. "The weather is great, the city is beautiful, you get a great education for a reasonable price, and of course the people from here are amazing…why not choose College of Charleston?" "I'll use one word [to describe College of Charleston]," a physics student tells us, "underrated."

Life

"It's the city of Charleston that defines the student body and joins them together." Charleston is "one of the most beautiful cities in the South," and students experience "the perfect blend of social life between the university and the city." "Ask any student about Charleston as a city and they'll excitedly tell you about their favorite place to eat or how they went to a wonderful play last week." "Southern hospitality" pervades the campus. Students "love to go the beach, the movies, the park, the theater, the mall, museums, and to the great selections of bars and restaurants." Charleston is known for an active party scene, much of which revolves around Greek life. "Although actual Greek…membership numbers are low, it provides the social life for campus," one student explains. "Most independents spend their time attending [fraternity] parties off campus." Students love "the beach when the weather is nice," which is about a "fifteen- to twenty-minute drive" from campus. "Charleston has become huge in the music scene," and bands such as "Phish, Widespread Panic, StS9, Pat Green, Rebelution, Slightly Stoopid, Yonder Mountain String Band, and Umphrey's fill up the dates." In general, students in Charleston "[live] life to its fullest while preparing for the rest!"

Student Body

The student body is more than sixty percent female—a fact that some love while others wish for "a better girl-to-guy ratio" as well as "more ethnic diversity." "The typical student is Caucasian, female, and wealthy," and "very preppy/Southern. Not too many Northerners." That doesn't mean that the students aren't "friendly" and "accepting." "Students fit in pretty well because there are many groups and clubs on campus where you can meet people." Although an out-of-state student cautions that "it can be difficult for students from out of state to fit in because sixty-four percent of the students are either local or in-state and already know each other." "There are three types of students at this school," one student claims. "1) Preppy Southerners clad in Vera Bradley and Ralph Lauren. 2) Disaffected hipsters/artists who clearly are not the starving type seeing as their entire wardrobe comes from Urban Outfitters and American Apparel. 3) Everyone else." "Most are the 'prep' or 'hipster' type," another student confirms. "There is a barely a counterculture." However, others see a wider variety in the student body. "There are hippies, sorority girls, fratastic guys, feminists, surfers, preppy Southern gentlemen, people from the Jersey shore, international students, Christians, atheists, pagans, vegans, Republicans, Democrats, Libertarians…it is hard to sum up just one 'typical' student here."

FINANCIAL AID: 843-953-5540 • E-MAIL: ADMISSIONS@COFC.EDU • WEBSITE: WWW.COFC.EDU

THE PRINCETON REVIEW SAYS

Admissions

Very important factors considered include: Academic GPA, rigor of secondary school record, standardized test scores, state residency. *Important factors considered include:* Class rank, character/personal qualities, first generation, talent/ability. *Other factors considered include:* Application essay, recommendation(s), extracurricular activities, level of applicant's interest, racial/ethnic status, volunteer work, work experience. SAT or ACT required; ACT with or without writing component accepted. TOEFL required of all international applicants. High school diploma is required, and GED is accepted. *Academic units required:* 4 English, 4 mathematics, 3 science (3 science labs), 3 foreign language, 2 social studies, 1 history, 3 academic elective. *Academic units recommended:* 4 English, 4 mathematics, 2 history, 1 computer science.

Financial Aid

Students should submit: FAFSA. The Princeton Review suggests that all financial aid forms be submitted as soon as possible after January 1. *Need-based scholarships/grants offered:* Federal Pell, SEOG, state scholarships/grants, private scholarships, school scholarship or grant aid from institutional funds. *Loan aid offered:* Direct Subsidized Stafford, Direct Unsubsidized Stafford, Direct PLUS, Federal Perkins. Applicants will be notified of awards on a rolling basis beginning April 10. Federal Work-Study Program available. Off-campus job opportunities are fair.

The Inside Word

The College of Charleston is the thirteenth oldest university in the country, and its location in historic Charleston provides a truly unique Southern experience with strong liberal arts and sciences academics. Students absolutely rave about the weather, the beaches, the city, and the social life the campus and the city combine to provide.

THE SCHOOL SAYS "..."

From the Admissions Office

"To succeed in our increasingly complex world, college graduates must be able to think creatively, explore new ideas, compete, collaborate, and meet the challenges of our global society. At the College of Charleston, students find out about themselves, their lives and the lives of others. They discover how to shape their future, and they prepare to create change and opportunity.

"Founded in 1770, the College of Charleston's mission is to provide students with a first-class education in the arts and sciences, education and business. Students have 118 majors and minors from which to choose—and they often choose to combine several—and complement their academic courses with overseas study, research and internships for a truly customized education.

"Nearly 10,000 undergraduates choose the College for its small-college feel blended with the advantages and diversity of an urban, mid-sized university. The College, home to students from fifty states and sixty-seven countries, provides a creative and intellectually stimulating environment where students are challenged and guided by a committed and caring full-time faculty of 500 distinguished teacher-scholars, all in an incomparable historic setting.

"The city of Charleston serves as a living and learning laboratory for student experiences in business, science, teaching, the humanities, languages and the arts. At the same time, students and faculty are engaged with the community in partnerships to improve education, enhance the business community and enrich the overall quality of life in the region.

"In the great liberal arts tradition, a College of Charleston education focuses on discovery and personal growth, as well as preparation for life, work and service to our society."

SELECTIVITY

Admissions Rating	88
# of applicants	11,280
% of applicants accepted	70
% of acceptees attending	25

FRESHMAN PROFILE

Range SAT Critical Reading	570–650
Range SAT Math	570–640
Range ACT Composite	23–27
Minimum paper TOEFL	570
Minimum computer TOEFL	230
Minimum web-based TOEFL	88
Average HS GPA	3.87
% graduated top 10% of class	31
% graduated top 25% of class	68
% graduated top 50% of class	94

DEADLINES

Early action	
Deadline	11/1
Regular	
Priority	2/1
Deadline	4/1
Nonfall registration?	yes

APPLICANTS ALSO LOOK AT AND OFTEN PREFER

University of Georgia, University of North Carolina at Chapel Hill, University of Virginia

AND SOMETIMES PREFER

Clemson University, Furman University, James Madison University, Tulane University, University of South Carolina—Columbia

AND RARELY PREFER

Appalachian State University, Auburn University, Coastal Carolina University, Winthrop University

FINANCIAL FACTS

Financial Aid Rating	77
Annual in-state tuition	$9,965
Annual out-of-state tuition	$23,172
Room and board	$9,843
Books and supplies	$1,204
% frosh rec. need-based scholarship or grant aid	31
% UG rec. need-based scholarship or grant aid	28
% frosh rec. non-need-based scholarship or grant aid	33
% UG rec. non-need-based scholarship or grant aid	19
% frosh rec. need-based self-help aid	33
% UG rec. need-based self-help aid	35
% frosh rec. any financial aid	43
% UG rec. any financial aid	42
% UG borrow to pay for school	44
Average cumulative indebtedness	$19,875

COLLEGE OF THE HOLY CROSS

ADMISSIONS OFFICE, ONE COLLEGE STREET, WORCESTER, MA 01610-2395 • ADMISSIONS: 508-793-2443 • FAX: 508-793-3888

CAMPUS LIFE

Quality of Life Rating	65
Fire Safety Rating	95
Green Rating	93
Type of school	private
Affiliation	Roman Catholic
Environment	city

STUDENTS

Total undergrad enrollment	2,862
% male/female	46/54
% from out of state	63
% from public high school	50
% live on campus	89
% African American	5
% Asian	5
% Caucasian	66
% Hispanic	9
% international	1
# of countries represented	19

SURVEY SAYS . . .

*Frats and sororities are unpopular
or nonexistent
Student government is popular
Lots of beer drinking
Hard liquor is popular*

ACADEMICS

Academic Rating	95
% students graduating within 4 years	90
% students graduating within 6 years	93
Calendar	semester
Student/faculty ratio	11:1
Profs interesting rating	93
Profs accessible rating	93
Most common reg class size	10–19 students
Most common lab size	fewer than 10 students

MOST POPULAR MAJORS
economics, English language and
literature, political science

STUDENTS SAY ". . ."

Academics

The College of the Holy Cross is a smallish, "rigorous" Jesuit school "that does an incredible job of giving its students a very broad education [and] preparing them with the tools for the real world." Every student must complete a broad liberal arts curriculum. Regardless of your major, you'll take courses in history, literature, religion, philosophy, foreign language, math, science, and art. In additional, all first-year students take part in full-year seminars that are heavy on intellectual development. There's an array of exciting and often exotic study abroad options. The semester in Washington, D.C., receives a lot of praise. Internship programs are also abundant, and students also have access to a "large and strong alumni network." "Holy Cross alums are insane" about their old alma mater, and they love to hire the latest batch of graduates. "The emphasis here is on teaching and learning, not research," and the academic atmosphere is intense. "At Holy Cross, the professors will keep you busy throughout the week." "Classes are hard," warns a biology major. Good grades are hard to come by. "You have to work your tail off to just get an A–." At the same time, students love their "caring" and "amazing" professors, and they point out that small class sizes provide opportunities for meaningful faculty-student interaction. Profs are "very accessible outside the classroom," too. In fact, they "almost force you to get to know them." "If you show interest and work hard, you will do well," concludes an English major.

Life

There's "a lively social scene" on this "beautiful" hilltop campus. There are more than eighty clubs and organizations, and virtually everyone is "active in something, whether it be a varsity team, intramurals, student government, clubs, the newspaper, theater, or music." Studying is also an exceedingly common pastime. "The libraries and study rooms are often packed with students at night." On the weekends, however, "Holy Cross is a very big party school." "Although I would not consider Holy Cross to be the most outrageously fun school," relates a senior, "the student body at Holy Cross likes to drink." "People work hard during the week, and they like to let loose and have fun." Parties generally occur "in dorm rooms or at nearby off-campus housing." "Bars are popular," too, and usually "cheap." Students are also quick to call our attention to the fact that there is plenty to do on the weekends besides drinking. "If that's not your scene, there are so many other things to do," reports one student. There is everything "from going to plays, to sporting events, dances, karaoke, and stand-up comedians—all right here on campus." The food is probably the biggest complaint we hear. "Stick to the pasta," recommends a senior. The surrounding city of Worcester is home to "great" grub, but it's kind of sketchy otherwise. Luckily, "trips to Boston and Providence are extremely feasible, and the school has free buses to these locations on the weekends."

Student Body

Holy Cross is a "remarkably" welcoming campus. "This is the most friendly campus you will ever step foot on," claims a senior. You can find students from just about every state, but the majority tends to come from New England and the mid-Atlantic states. Students tend to be Catholic, though there are certainly plenty of people with different religions and with no religion at all. "Religion is not a major issue" here, really. Atypical students exist, and they "fit in just fine," but most of the undergraduate population at Holy Cross does kind of fit a certain mold. "The typical student is upper-middle-class, white, somewhat preppy, and athletic." That student is "smart," "hardworking," and probably "from the suburbs." "If you dress really preppy all the time, party hard on the weekends, and study in the rest of your remaining time, this is the school for you."

FINANCIAL AID: 508-793-2265 • E-MAIL: ADMISSIONS@HOLYCROSS.EDU • WEBSITE: WWW.HOLYCROSS.EDU

THE PRINCETON REVIEW SAYS

Admissions

Very important factors considered include: Academic GPA, class rank, recommendation(s), rigor of secondary school record, interview. *Important factors considered include:* Application essay, character/personal qualities, extra-curricular activities, level of applicant's interest. *Other factors considered include:* Standardized test scores, alumni/ae relation, first generation, geographical residence, racial/ethnic status, talent/ability, volunteer work, work experience. ACT with or without writing component accepted. TOEFL required of all international applicants. High school diploma is required, and GED is accepted. *Academic units recommended:* 4 English, 4 mathematics, 4 science (2 science labs), 4 foreign language, 2 social studies, 2 history.

Financial Aid

Students should submit: FAFSA, CSS/Financial Aid PROFILE. Regular filing deadline is February 1. The Princeton Review suggests that all financial aid forms be submitted as soon as possible after January 1. *Need-based scholarships/grants offered:* Federal Pell, SEOG, state scholarships/grants, private scholarships, school scholarship or grant aid from institutional funds. *Loan aid offered:* Direct Subsidized Stafford, Direct Unsubsidized Stafford, Direct PLUS, Federal Perkins. Federal Work-Study Program available. Off-campus job opportunities are fair.

The Inside Word

Admission to Holy Cross is competitive; therefore, a demanding high school course load is required to be a viable candidate. The college values effective communication skills—it thoroughly evaluates each applicant's personal statement and short essay responses. Interviews are important, especially for those applying early decision. Students who graduate from a Jesuit high school might find themselves at a slight advantage.

THE SCHOOL SAYS "..."

From the Admissions Office

"When applying to Holy Cross, two areas deserve particular attention. First, the essay should be developed thoughtfully, with correct language and syntax in mind. That essay reflects for the Board of Admissions how you think and how you can express yourself. Second, activity beyond the classroom should be clearly defined. Since Holy Cross [has only] 2,800 students, the chance for involvement/participation is exceptional. The board reviews many applications for academically qualified students. A key difference in being accepted is the extent to which a candidate participates in-depth beyond the classroom—don't be modest; define who you are.

"Standardized test scores (i.e., SAT, SAT Subject Tests, and ACT) are optional. Students may submit their scores if they believe the results paint a fuller picture of their achievements and potential, but those students who don't submit scores will not be at a disadvantage in admissions decisions."

SELECTIVITY

Admissions Rating	96
# of applicants	6,911
% of applicants accepted	35
% of acceptees attending	30
# accepting a place on wait list	538
% admitted from wait list	4
# of early decision applicants	454
% accepted early decision	73

FRESHMAN PROFILE

Range SAT Critical Reading	590–680
Range SAT Math	600–690
Range SAT Writing	600–690
Range ACT Composite	27–31
Minimum paper TOEFL	550
Minimum computer TOEFL	213
Minimum web-based TOEFL	79
Average HS GPA	3.77
% graduated top 10% of class	64
% graduated top 25% of class	91
% graduated top 50% of class	100

DEADLINES

Early decision	
Deadline	12/15
Regular	
Deadline	1/15
Nonfall registration?	no

APPLICANTS ALSO LOOK AT AND OFTEN PREFER
Boston College, Georgetown University, University of Notre Dame

AND SOMETIMES PREFER
Villanova University

AND RARELY PREFER
Providence College

FINANCIAL FACTS

Financial Aid Rating	92
Annual tuition	$40,910
Room and board	$11,270
Required fees	$578
Books and supplies	$700
% frosh rec. need-based scholarship or grant aid	47
% UG rec. need-based scholarship or grant aid	44
% frosh rec. non-need-based scholarship or grant aid	1
% UG rec. non-need-based scholarship or grant aid	2
% frosh rec. need-based self-help aid	43
% UG rec. need-based self-help aid	45
% frosh rec. any financial aid	58
% UG rec. any financial aid	55
% UG borrow to pay for school	58
Average cumulative indebtedness	$23,662

THE COLLEGE OF IDAHO

2112 CLEVELAND BOULEVARD, CALDWELL, ID 83605 • ADMISSIONS: 208-459-5305 • FAX: 208-459-5757

CAMPUS LIFE

Quality of Life Rating	85
Fire Safety Rating	73
Green Rating	77
Type of school	private
Environment	town

STUDENTS

Total undergrad enrollment	1,025
% male/female	42/58
% from out of state	21
# of fraternities	3
# of sororities	4
% Asian	1
% Caucasian	30
% Hispanic	5
% international	9
% unknown	55
# of countries represented	40

SURVEY SAYS . . .
Students are friendly
Different types of students interact
Campus feels safe
Low cost of living

ACADEMICS

Academic Rating	83
% students graduating within 4 years	48
% students graduating within 6 years	58
Calendar	semester
Student/faculty ratio	12:1
Profs interesting rating	93
Profs accessible rating	93
Most common reg class size	10–19 students
Most common lab size	20–29 students

MOST POPULAR MAJORS
biology, business administration and management, psychology

STUDENTS SAY ". . ."

Academics
A small liberal arts school, The College of Idaho is "like a diamond in the rough." Students tell us, "You'd be surprised at the very high quality this little school offers!" The small class sizes and low student-to-teacher ratio promote the school's emphasis on "individual learning" and a "personalized education plan." The academic experience at The College of Idaho is "incredibly rigorous but also very rewarding." Though the school has a "well-developed" liberal arts core, students also describe the biology and premed programs as "fantastic." Courses are "challenging," "fascinating," and "great preparation for both graduate school and the professional world." The small school environment provides a "sense of community" and allows students to develop "strong working relationships" with their professors. Students tell us their professors are "attentive," "very accessible," and "passionate about what they teach." One graduating senior described the school as "an academic gold mine of some of the most published and highly regarded professors and researchers in the field." The "personal teaching" approach the professors at The College of Idaho take makes them "consistently recognized nationally and internationally for their contributions to the academic community and to their students." The administration is "involved with the students" and "effective" though "the professors are what make The College of Idaho great." Also great is the fact that the school is "cost competitive" and offers "generous scholarships." As one freshman tells us, "My school is way more than a place for me to learn. My teachers have become more like guardians for my education, and my peers…my second family."

Life
Life in Caldwell can be "pretty quiet" but Boise, the capital, is only about a thirty-minute drive away, and the school regularly hosts trips into the city. However, the campus "strives" and "mostly succeeds" in making up for the town by sponsoring many activities on campus. A student tells us, "On campus there is always something going on…I rarely have a night where there isn't something that I could do for fun." The College of Idaho offers a variety of extracurricular activities. The school's Program Council "puts on great events all year long." Such events as movie and bowling nights are open to all students and are often offered free of charge. Students at The College of Idaho also tend to be very interested in clubs and club-sponsored events. With a multitude of clubs to join, there is a club "for all personality types." One student tells us, "Whether it is attending a theater or band concert, an athletic event, or a club meeting, there are plenty of ways to get involved." Students describe their school life as "great overall," and because the school is so small, "any major campus-sponsored activity brings us all together as one, giant, friendly social club."

Student Body
Students tell us, The College of Idaho has "students from many walks of life" and a "student body full of individuals." While a majority of the student body is "white, middle-class, and right out of high school," students at The College of Idaho promote an "atmosphere of learning from others no matter their background." Many students tell us that there really isn't a "typical student," which isn't so surprising given its large international student population. Each student at The College of Idaho is "an active participant in the campus community." One junior tells us students are, "overly involved" and "extremely busy with clubs, campus activities, athletics, and academics." Students are "hardworking but social," "intelligent," and "well-rounded." According to one sophomore, "though [we are all] different, the commonality of going to C of I brings us together."

FINANCIAL AID: 208-459-5308 • E-MAIL: ADMISSION@COLLEGEOFIDAHO.EDU • WEBSITE: WWW.COLLEGEOFIDAHO.EDU

THE PRINCETON REVIEW SAYS

Admissions

Very important factors considered include: Academic GPA, recommendation(s), rigor of secondary school record, standardized test scores, character/personal qualities, level of applicant's interest. *Important factors considered include:* Application essay, class rank, extracurricular activities, interview. *Other factors considered include:* Alumni/ae relation, first generation, talent/ability, volunteer work. SAT or ACT required; ACT with writing component required. TOEFL or IELTS required of all international applicants. High school diploma is required, and GED is accepted. *Academic units recommended:* 4 English, 4 mathematics, 3 science, 3 foreign language, 4 history.

Financial Aid

Students should submit: FAFSA, institution's own financial aid form. The Princeton Review suggests that all financial aid forms be submitted as soon as possible after January 1. *Need-based scholarships/grants offered:* Federal Pell, SEOG, state scholarships/grants, private scholarships, school scholarship or grant aid from institutional funds. *Loan aid offered:* Direct Subsidized Stafford, Direct Unsubsidized Stafford, Direct PLUS, Federal Perkins. Applicants will be notified of awards on a rolling basis beginning February 1. Federal Work-Study Program available. Off-campus job opportunities are good.

The Inside Word

The admissions committee at The College of Idaho is looking for students who have taken high school seriously. Candidates who demonstrate reasonable academic success and a variety of extracurricular activities will be handed the keys to a quality academic program and a unique college experience, one that stresses self-confidence and social responsibility.

THE SCHOOL SAYS ". . ."

From the Admissions Office

"While the mission of The College of Idaho is traditional in that it remains committed to the teaching of the liberal arts, many of the approaches to accomplishing this goal are unique. Within the campus community is the opportunity to create classroom opportunities for students that span the globe—both technologically and geographically. Here, students are just as apt to attend a biology class on campus as they are to hike in the nearby Owyhee or Sawtooth Mountains to carry out field research. During the college's six-week winter term, more than thirty percent of the students are emailing friends and family from such locales as Australia, Israel, France, Ireland, England, Peru, and or Mexico while taking part in faculty-led, multidisciplinary trips. International students from forty-five different countries comprise nine percent of the student body. Students are invited to visit the campus and the admissions counselors, either in person or online.

"C of I requires all admission candidates (who have not reached sophomore status in college) to submit either the SAT or the ACT with the writing component. The College of Idaho will consider all scores. There is no SAT Subject Test requirement, but scores will be considered as part of a holistic evaluation."

SELECTIVITY

Admissions Rating	84
# of applicants	919
% of applicants accepted	92
% of acceptees attending	33

FRESHMAN PROFILE

Range SAT Critical Reading	500–633
Range SAT Math	478–610
Range SAT Writing	460–590
Range ACT Composite	22–28
Minimum paper TOEFL	550
Minimum computer TOEFL	213
Minimum web-based TOEFL	79
Average HS GPA	3.62
% graduated top 10% of class	36
% graduated top 25% of class	64
% graduated top 50% of class	92

DEADLINES

Early action	
Deadline	11/15
Notification	12/15
Regular	
Priority	2/15
Deadline	8/1
Notification	10/15
Nonfall registration?	yes

APPLICANTS ALSO LOOK AT AND OFTEN PREFER

Boise State University, Brigham Young University (UT), Gonzaga University, Idaho State University, Northwest Nazarene University, University of Idaho

FINANCIAL FACTS

Financial Aid Rating	83
Annual tuition	$21,940
Room and board	$7,769
Required fees	$755
Books and supplies	$1,200
% frosh rec. need-based scholarship or grant aid	57
% UG rec. need-based scholarship or grant aid	48
% frosh rec. non-need-based scholarship or grant aid	77
% UG rec. non-need-based scholarship or grant aid	68
% frosh rec. need-based self-help aid	60
% UG rec. need-based self-help aid	52
% frosh rec. any financial aid	99
% UG rec. any financial aid	98
% UG borrow to pay for school	62
Average cumulative indebtedness	$23,404

THE COLLEGE OF NEW JERSEY

PO BOX 7718, EWING, NJ 08628-0718 • ADMISSIONS: 609-771-2131 • FAX: 609-637-5174

CAMPUS LIFE

Quality of Life Rating	90
Fire Safety Rating	95
Green Rating	85
Type of school	public
Environment	village

STUDENTS

Total undergrad enrollment	6,410
% male/female	42/58
% from out of state	6
% from public high school	70
% live on campus	62
# of fraternities	13
# of sororities	13
% African American	6
% Asian	6
% Caucasian	66
% Hispanic	9
# of countries represented	30

SURVEY SAYS . . .
Lab facilities are great
Great library
School is well-run
Students are friendly
Low cost of living
Students are happy
Student publications are popular

ACADEMICS

Academic Rating	89
% students graduating within 4 years	71
% students graduating within 6 years	86
Calendar	semester
Student/faculty ratio	13:1
Profs interesting rating	90
Profs accessible rating	90
Most common reg class size	20–29 students
Most common lab size	20–29 students

MOST POPULAR MAJORS
biology, business administration and management, psychology

STUDENTS SAY ". . ."

Academics

The College of New Jersey, "a small, liberal arts, state school that offers, to the best of its abilities, everything that a private school offers," earns plaudits from a student body that understands just what a great deal the school represents. "Many of my friends had well above 1300 SAT scores and got into very prestigious schools such as Georgetown, NYU, Columbia, and Villanova, but chose TCNJ because of its unbeatable cost," explains one student, who warns that the school is "no joke" academically and notes that even those aforementioned friends "are constantly studying and find no cake-walk when it comes to classes." Students benefit from "up-to-date facilities" including "an amazing library" and solid career services. Most impressive, however, is the small-school service students here receive; professors "clearly have their students' best interests in mind," and the administration is not only "amazingly helpful" but also solicitous of student opinion; "Whenever a position opens up in a department, the students are encouraged to attend lectures by prospective candidates and offer their input," one student writes. No wonder undergrads insist that TCNJ is "a smaller school that is a bargain for its quality of education."

Life

With "a beautiful campus, great location, top-notch faculty, the newest technology, an interested student body, and competitive sports teams," TCNJ really "is the total package." There "are a lot of things going on on-campus for people to get involved in," including "clubs and intramural sports that people commonly do for fun." The student center "offers games, and there are always performances going on," and "There are tons of student organizations and club teams." Although "people are generally the Abercrombie or Hollister type" here, "You don't have to be athletic or involved at all to be popular at TCNJ. It's completely acceptable to just hang out with people doing nothing constructive." The off-campus party scene "is fine," and many people "attend the fraternity parties offered on Tuesdays, Fridays, and Saturdays," but "There is not much to do once you leave campus unless you have a car," and one student notes, "Some of the surrounding areas are a little sketchy." Further afield things get better, as "our school is a fifteen-minute drive from Princeton and forty-five minutes outside of Philly."

Student Body

"You can find any personality type at TCNJ," students tell us, from "your typical jocks who love to party," to "extremely conservative kids who haven't missed a Sunday mass since getting here," and "a few hippie types and everything in between. Whatever your social circle, you're bound to fit in." What they share in common is that most are "smart, dedicated people who care about their education very much," "were in the top fifteen percent of their high school class," and "are willing to push themselves to do better in school." While "everyone has different interests, inside the classroom there is never an intellectual differentiation between those in the Medieval Club and those in Greek life. I think everyone is atypical in his own way, and this is a great place for everyone to be able to find a niche." And while "the typical student at TCNJ is white and middle-upper-class to upper-class," the school also hosts a solid population of students of "different faiths and ethnicities."

THE COLLEGE OF NEW JERSEY

FINANCIAL AID: 609-771-2211 • E-MAIL: TCNJINFO@TCNJ.EDU • WEBSITE: WWW.TCNJ.EDU

THE PRINCETON REVIEW SAYS

Admissions

Very important factors considered include: Class rank, rigor of secondary school record, academic major, standardized test scores, extracurricular activities, geographical residence, leadership experience, volunteer work. *Important factors considered include:* Application essay, recommendation(s), character/personal qualities, geographical residence, state residency, talent/ability. *Other factors considered include:* Academic GPA, alumni/ae relation, first generation, level of applicant's interest, racial/ethnic status, work experience. SAT or ACT required. TOEFL required of all international applicants. High school diploma is required, and GED is accepted. *Academic units required:* 4 English. *Academic units recommended:* 4 English, 3 mathematics, 3 science (3 science labs), 3 foreign language, 3 social studies.

Financial Aid

Students should submit: FAFSA. Priority filing deadline is March 1. The Princeton Review suggests that all financial aid forms be submitted as soon as possible after January 1. *Need-based scholarships/grants offered:* Federal Pell, SEOG, state scholarships/grants, private scholarships, school scholarship or grant aid from institutional funds. *Loan aid offered:* Direct Subsidized Stafford, Direct Unsubsidized Stafford, Direct PLUS, Federal Perkins, Federal Nursing Loans. Applicants will be notified of awards on a rolling basis beginning June 1. Federal Work-Study Program available. Off-campus job opportunities are excellent.

The Inside Word

TCNJ accepts nearly half of all applicants, but that figure is deceiving; this is a self-selecting applicant pool; those with no chance of acceptance simply don't bother. Admissions are as competitive as you would expect at a school that offers state residents a small-college experience and a highly respected degree for bargain-basement prices. Competition among biology applicants has grown especially fierce.

THE SCHOOL SAYS " . . ."

From the Admissions Office

"The College of New Jersey is one of the United States' great higher education success stories. With a long history as New Jersey's preeminent teacher of teachers, the college has grown into a new role as educator of the nation's best students in a wide range of fields. The College of New Jersey has created a culture of constant questioning—a place where knowledge is not merely received but reconfigured. In small classes, students and faculty members collaborate in a rewarding process: As they seek to understand fundamental principles, apply key concepts, reveal new problems, and pursue new lines of inquiry, students gain a fluency of thought in their disciplines. The college's 289-acre tree-lined campus is a union of vision, engineering, beauty, and functionality. Neoclassical Georgian Colonial architecture, meticulous landscaping, and thoughtful design merge in a dynamic system, constantly evolving to meet the needs of TCNJ students. About half of TCNJ's entering class will be academic scholars, with large numbers of National Merit finalists and semifinalists. The College of New Jersey is bringing together the best ideas from around the nation and building a new model for public undergraduate education on one campus."

SELECTIVITY

Admissions Rating	90
# of applicants	9,956
% of applicants accepted	47
% of acceptees attending	30
# accepting a place on wait list	549
% admitted from wait list	21
# of early decision applicants	609
% accepted early decision	55

FRESHMAN PROFILE

Range SAT Critical Reading	560–670
Range SAT Math	590–680
Range SAT Writing	560–670
Minimum paper TOEFL	550
Minimum web-based TOEFL	90
% graduated top 10% of class	60
% graduated top 25% of class	91
% graduated top 50% of class	100

DEADLINES

Early decision	
Deadline	11/15
Notification	12/15
Regular	
Deadline	1/15
Notification	1/15
Nonfall registration?	yes

APPLICANTS ALSO LOOK AT AND OFTEN PREFER

Boston College, Cornell University, New York University, Rutgers, The State University of New Jersey, University of Delaware, Villanova University

AND SOMETIMES PREFER

Boston University, Drexel University, Lehigh University, Northeastern University, Penn State—University Park, Rowan University, Stevens Institute of Technology

FINANCIAL FACTS

Financial Aid Rating	66
Annual in-state tuition	$9,340
Annual out-of-state tuition	$18,726
Room and board	$10,358
Required fees	$3,953
Books and supplies	$1,000
% frosh rec. need-based scholarship or grant aid	23
% UG rec. need-based scholarship or grant aid	20
% frosh rec. non-need-based scholarship or grant aid	38
% UG rec. non-need-based scholarship or grant aid	22
% frosh rec. need-based self-help aid	34
% UG rec. need-based self-help aid	36
% frosh rec. any financial aid	80
% UG rec. any financial aid	70
% UG borrow to pay for school	56
Average cumulative indebtedness	$27,057

COLLEGE OF THE OZARKS

OFFICE OF ADMISSIONS, POINT LOOKOUT, MO 65726 • ADMISSIONS: 417-334-6411 • FAX: 417-335-2618

CAMPUS LIFE

Quality of Life Rating	88
Fire Safety Rating	80
Green Rating	75
Type of school	private
Environment	rural

STUDENTS

Total undergrad enrollment	1,367
% male/female	43/57
% from out of state	18
% from public high school	88
% live on campus	80
% African American	1
% Caucasian	92
% Hispanic	2
% international	1
# of countries represented	14

SURVEY SAYS . . .

Students are very religious
Students get along with local community
Frats and sororities are unpopular or nonexistent
Theater is popular
Very little beer drinking

ACADEMICS

Academic Rating	80
Calendar	semester
Student/faculty ratio	13:1
Profs interesting rating	81
Profs accessible rating	83
Most common reg class size	10–19 students
Most common lab size	10–19 students

MOST POPULAR MAJORS

business administration and management, elementary education and teaching, speech communication and rhetoric

STUDENTS SAY ". . ."

Academics

Students describe the academic experience at this tuition-free, Christian college as "very challenging and very rewarding." "Time management is very important at C of O," where it's vital to find a balance "between classes, work, and homework." College of the Ozarks places strong emphasis on "high moral value, hard work, and academic integrity," and the school is "dedicated to the growth and maturity of its students." Many students cite "the work-study program and the core values of the school" as "two of the college's greatest strengths." Those values are detailed in the school's mission, which lists its goals in five principle categories: academic, vocational, Christian, patriotic, and cultural. The professors are an integral part of making "character development...a key value of this college," and many "have an open-door policy to all students." Students praise their faculty as "amazing," "second-to-none," and most often as "passionate." One student sums it up by saying, "My professors are amazing. I know that I can go up to any of them and they are more than willing to help me with my academic pursuits and personal issues as well." Though a few students grumble that they "don't always enjoy general education courses," which are "mostly" lectures, the vast majority are very happy with the courses within their chosen areas of study. "Small class sizes provide for easy one-on-one interaction with the professors" and encourage students to "become involved in active classroom learning."

Life

"Life at College of the Ozarks is pretty unique because we support ourselves." All students at C of O participate in a work program in exchange for free tuition, which helps the school live up to its nickname, Hard Work U. "Between the sixteen to eighteen credit hours of classes, fifteen hours of work on campus, and studying, students here are kept pretty dang busy." As on many Christian campuses, "Partying is almost nonexistent," but students don't seem to mind. They're happy "creating lasting friendships while getting not only knowledge in the classroom setting but also working skills for future jobs." "There are groups and organizations for everyone," and "various organizations hold events for the whole campus like Senate Movie Night, and there are plenty of interesting speakers for convocations." "The cafeteria is a cozy place to have a meal with several different selections for all meals," and the campus offers plenty of activities: "swimming, weight lifting, basketball, movies, dances, coffee nights, ballgames, etc." Off campus, "There is always something to do in this area," "whether you hang out with your friends, go to shows in Branson, go to campus-sponsored events, or just go play ping-pong." The college provides a weekly shuttle to Wal-Mart, and nearby Branson is a popular destination, and "many of the attractions give discounts for students," including theme park Silver Dollar City.

Student Body

C of O students describe themselves as "friendly," "hardworking," "down-to-earth," and "very religious, but not pushy." The nature of the school places a strong emphasis on community, and first-year students bond during a week-long orientation called Character Camp. Most students are from Christian backgrounds, and they're "somewhat conservative." Many "are from the local Ozark region." Despite the similarities, students describe their school as "very diverse" and say that everyone is "welcomed into the community" and "always eager to help and support you in any type of situation." "There are the 'aggies,' the 'jocks,' the 'nerds,' and other types of students," like "the prep, the homeschooler...the indie...[and] the geek," but many students happily note the lack of exclusive cliques and say "social barriers are easily crossed."

FINANCIAL AID: 417-334-6411 • E-MAIL: ADMISS4@COFO.EDU • WEBSITE: WWW.COFO.EDU

THE PRINCETON REVIEW SAYS

Admissions

Very important factors considered include: Financial need, class rank, rigor of secondary school record, character/personal qualities, geographical residence, interview. *Important factors considered include:* Academic GPA, recommendation(s), standardized test scores, geographical residence, level of applicant's interest, volunteer work, work experience. *Other factors considered include:* Alumni/ae relation, extracurricular activities, first generation, religious affiliation/commitment, state residency, talent/ability. SAT or ACT required; ACT with or without writing component accepted. TOEFL required of all international applicants. High school diploma is required, and GED is accepted. *Academic units required:* 4 English, 3 mathematics, 2 science (1 science lab), 3 history. *Academic units recommended:* 4 English, 3 mathematics, 2 science (1 science lab), 2 foreign language, 3 social studies.

Financial Aid

Students should submit: FAFSA. The Princeton Review suggests that all financial aid forms be submitted as soon as possible after January 1. *Need-based scholarships/grants offered:* Federal Pell, SEOG, state scholarships/grants, private scholarships, school scholarship or grant aid from institutional funds. Federal Work-Study Program not available. Off-campus job opportunities are excellent.

The Inside Word

The unusual nature of the C of O translates directly into its admissions process. Because a significant aspect of the school's mission statement is to provide educational opportunities to those in need of financial aid, candidates for admission must demonstrate that need. C of O's free tuition and unique philosophy attract strong interest, and the admissions process is competitive. That said, it's more important to be a good fit with the school philosophically and financially than to have a sky-high GPA. Oh yeah, a serious work ethic is a must!

THE SCHOOL SAYS " . . ."

From the Admissions Office

"College of the Ozarks is unique because of its no-tuition, work-study program, but also because it strives to educate the head, the heart, and the hands. At C of O, there are high expectations of students—the college stresses character development as well as study and work. An education from 'Hard Work U.' offers many opportunities, not the least of which is the chance to graduate debt-free. Life at C of O isn't all hard work and no play, however. There are many opportunities for fun. The nearby resort town of Branson, Missouri, offers ample opportunities for recreation and summer employment, and Table Rock Lake, only a few miles away, is a terrific spot to swim, sun, and relax. Numerous on-campus activities such as Mudfest, Luau Night, dances, and holiday parties give students lots of chances for fun without leaving the college. At 'Hard Work U.,' we work hard, but we know how to have fun, too.

"Applicants are required to submit scores from the ACT or the SAT. We will use the student's best scores from either test. writing scores are not required."

SELECTIVITY

Admissions Rating	91
# of applicants	2,975
% of applicants accepted	10
% of acceptees attending	90
# accepting a place on wait list	800
% admitted from wait list	7

FRESHMAN PROFILE

Range ACT Composite	20–25
Minimum paper TOEFL	550
Minimum computer TOEFL	213
Minimum web-based TOEFL	79
Average HS GPA	3.53
% graduated top 10% of class	30
% graduated top 25% of class	64
% graduated top 50% of class	94

DEADLINES

Regular	
Priority	2/15
Notification	3/1
Nonfall registration?	no

APPLICANTS ALSO LOOK AT
AND OFTEN PREFER
Missouri State University
AND SOMETIMES PREFER
Southwest Baptist University

FINANCIAL FACTS

Financial Aid Rating	89
Annual tuition	$0
Room and board	$5,600
Required fees	$430
Books and supplies	$800
% frosh rec. need-based scholarship or grant aid	86
% UG rec. need-based scholarship or grant aid	93
% frosh rec. non-need-based scholarship or grant aid	8
% UG rec. non-need-based scholarship or grant aid	13
% frosh rec. need-based self-help aid	78
% UG rec. need-based self-help aid	79
% frosh rec. any financial aid	100
% UG rec. any financial aid	100
% UG borrow to pay for school	11
Average cumulative indebtedness	$5,389

THE COLLEGE OF WILLIAM & MARY

PO BOX 8795, WILLIAMSBURG, VA 23187-8795 • ADMISSIONS: 757-221-4223 • FAX: 757-221-1242

CAMPUS LIFE

Quality of Life Rating	89
Fire Safety Rating	78
Green Rating	92
Type of school	public
Environment	village

STUDENTS

Total undergrad enrollment	5,836
% male/female	45/55
% from out of state	32
% from public high school	79
% live on campus	75
# of fraternities	20
# of sororities	11
% African American	7
% Asian	8
% Caucasian	55
% Hispanic	7
% Native American	1
% international	3
# of countries represented	47

SURVEY SAYS . . .
No one cheats
Great library
Athletic facilities are great
Students are friendly
Campus feels safe
Students are happy
Student publications are popular
Student government is popular

ACADEMICS

Academic Rating	90
% students graduating within 4 years	83
% students graduating within 6 years	91
Calendar	semester
Student/faculty ratio	12:1
Profs interesting rating	93
Profs accessible rating	92
Most common reg class size	10–19 students
Most common lab size	10–19 students

MOST POPULAR MAJORS
business, English, government,
history, biology

STUDENTS SAY "..."

Academics

Students at The College of William & Mary are extraordinarily happy with their overall experience and with their academics in particular. One student sums up the school's vibe by saying, "William & Mary achieves a remarkable balance between the dynamic, progressive academics of a liberal arts college and the strong sense of history and tradition one would expect from America's second-oldest school." "There are endless and amazing" opportunities here, with an emphasis on undergraduate research that makes W&M unique among small liberal arts schools. "Professors will engage you outside of the classroom and give you the opportunity to conduct your own research project, even in a non-science curriculum." Many "are often in newspapers and magazines and have relevant and copious work experience in the subjects they're teaching." Across the board, "professors are one of the best things about W&M." They "are always accessible for extra help," and "they also really take the time to get to know their students outside of the classroom." In the classroom, "William & Mary professors truly know how to balance lecture with discussion. Especially in traditionally lecture-based subjects, like history, professors devote a lot of class time to discussion to understand what students think." Slackers take note: "Professors expect a lot of work outside of class," and "classes usually require a good amount of reading, especially for the humanities." All this hard work is very rewarding, though, with many upperclassmen and graduating seniors expressing how well-prepared they feel for the "real-world," and one student says that the professors "have upended the way I thought about their subject, opening completely new veins of inquiry."

Life

When students describe campus life at W&M, the word community comes up—a lot. And this community "is made up of incredibly involved, dedicated, and supportive students who have big dreams and big fun," who say: "We study hard, but we know how to have fun, too." Alma Mater Productions (AMP), the college programming board, "sponsors a lot of different events that are well-attended, including...comedians, music artists, movies, etc." Student organizations are also very strong, from intramural sports, some form of which "almost everyone plays," to arts organizations such as "the William & Mary Symphony Orchestra, three university choirs, the Arabic Music Ensemble, an Early Music Ensemble, an Appalachian string band, a small chamber orchestra, eleven a cappella groups and...two all-student theater companies." "On the weekends, there is always a party to go to" and "the Greek community is very inclusive." Off campus, students enjoy the charms of Colonial Williamsburg, theme park Busch Gardens, Jamestown Beach on the James River, and "great outlet shopping!" Despite a few gripes about parking (which are common on a small campus), students are generally happy with their facilities, with the library and the business school receiving special mention.

Student Body

Students are quick to note that there's a generalization that the "T.W.A.M.P., or Typical William & Mary Person...is the person [who] does all their reading, shows up to class every day, and is a nerd," but most are equally quick to cast this stereotype aside. The real T.W.A.M.P., they tell us, is "open-minded, outgoing, charismatic, driven, dedicated, caring, and unique." The school is full of "well-rounded people who are in touch with their inner nerd," and "intellectual people who care about the world find the zaniest ways to have fun." "Students fit in many social circles," and students credit the close bonding that happens in freshmen dorms for this inclusivity. "You will often see the members of the football team in the library as much as any other student," and "everyone is involved with at least one other thing outside of class, and often...about ten other things." "Students are an eclectic bunch united by our thirst for knowledge and overwhelming Tribe Pride."

THE COLLEGE OF WILLIAM & MARY

FINANCIAL AID: 757-221-2420 • E-MAIL: ADMISS@WM.EDU • WEBSITE: WWW.WM.EDU

THE PRINCETON REVIEW SAYS

Admissions

Very important factors considered include: Academic GPA, application essay, class rank, recommendation(s), rigor of secondary school record, standardized test scores, character/personal qualities, extracurricular activities, state residency, talent/ability, volunteer work, work experience. *Other factors considered include:* Alumni/ae relation, first generation, geographical residence, interview, racial/ethnic status. SAT or ACT required; ACT with or without writing component accepted. TOEFL strongly recommended. High school diploma or equivalent isn't required. *Academic units recommended:* 4 English, 4 mathematics, 4 science (3 science labs), 4 foreign language, 4 social studies.

Financial Aid

Students should submit: FAFSA. Regular filing deadline is March 15. The Princeton Review suggests that all financial aid forms be submitted as soon as possible after January 1. *Need-based scholarships/grants offered:* Federal Pell, SEOG, state scholarships/grants, private scholarships, school scholarship or grant aid from institutional funds. *Loan aid offered:* Direct Subsidized Stafford, Direct Unsubsidized Stafford, Direct PLUS, Federal Perkins. Applicants will be notified of awards on a rolling basis beginning March 15. Federal Work-Study Program available. Off-campus job opportunities are excellent.

The Inside Word

The volume of applications at W&M is extremely high; thus, admission is ultra-competitive. Only very strong students from out of state should apply. The large applicant pool necessitates a labor-intensive candidate evaluation process; each admissions officer reads roughly 150 application folders per week during the peak review season. But this is one admissions committee that moves fast without sacrificing a thorough review. There probably isn't a tougher public college admissions committee in the country.

THE SCHOOL SAYS "..."

From the Admissions Office

"William & Mary is the nation's second-oldest college and preeminent small public university. Yes, we have one of the lowest student/faculty ratio (twelve to one) of any public university. We're also known for having one of the most successful undergraduate business programs in the United States, a model United Nations team that perennially vies for the world championship, and extensive opportunities for undergraduate research. Students at William & Mary follow in the footsteps of alumni ranging from Thomas Jefferson, James Monroe, and John Tyler to Comedy Central's Jon Stewart, President Obama's Chair of the Council of Economic Advisers Christina Romer, and Super-Bowl-winning Pittsburg Steeler's coach Mike Tomlin. In short, William & Mary offers a top-rated educational experience at a comparatively low cost and in the company of interesting people from a broad variety of backgrounds. If you are an academically strong, involved student looking for a challenge in a great campus community, William & Mary may well be the place for you."

SELECTIVITY

Admissions Rating	97
# of applicants	12,539
% of applicants accepted	32
% of acceptees attending	35
# accepting a place on wait list	1,446
% admitted from wait list	17
# of early decision applicants	1,081
% accepted early decision	49

FRESHMAN PROFILE

Range SAT Critical Reading	640–730
Range SAT Math	620–710
Range SAT Writing	620–720
Range ACT Composite	28–32
Minimum paper TOEFL	600
Minimum computer TOEFL	250
Minimum web-based TOEFL	100
Average HS GPA	4.05
% graduated top 10% of class	79
% graduated top 25% of class	96
% graduated top 50% of class	99

DEADLINES

Early decision	
Deadline	11/1
Notification	12/1
Regular	
Deadline	1/1
Nonfall registration?	no

APPLICANTS ALSO LOOK AT AND SOMETIMES PREFER

Cornell University, Dartmouth College, Duke University, Georgetown University, Notre Dame College, Princeton University, University of North Carolina at Chapel Hill, University of Virginia, Vanderbilt University

FINANCIAL FACTS

Financial Aid Rating	76
Annual in-state tuition	$7,523
Annual out-of-state tuition	$28,546
Room and board	$8,600
Required fees, in-state	$4,665
Required fees, out-of-state	$5,217
Books and supplies	$1,375
% frosh rec. need-based scholarship or grant aid	23
% UG rec. need-based scholarship or grant aid	25
% frosh rec. non-need-based scholarship or grant aid	14
% UG rec. non-need-based scholarship or grant aid	12
% frosh rec. need-based self-help aid	20
% UG rec. need-based self-help aid	21
% frosh rec. any financial aid	67
% UG rec. any financial aid	60
% UG borrow to pay for school	38
Average cumulative indebtedness	$18,410

THE COLLEGE OF WOOSTER

847 COLLEGE AVENUE, WOOSTER, OH 44691 • ADMISSIONS: 800-877-9905 • FAX: 330-263-2621

CAMPUS LIFE

Quality of Life Rating	83
Fire Safety Rating	73
Green Rating	73
Type of school	private
Affiliation	historically affiliated with Presbyterian
Environment	town

STUDENTS

Total undergrad enrollment	2,003
% male/female	46/54
% from out of state	56
% from public high school	65
% live on campus	98
# of fraternities	5
# of sororities	6
% African American	7
% Asian	3
% Caucasian	70
% Hispanic	3
% international	5
# of countries represented	33

SURVEY SAYS . . .
No one cheats
Lab facilities are great
Great computer facilities
Great library
Students are friendly
Low cost of living
Students are happy
Musical organizations are popular
Lots of beer drinking

ACADEMICS

Academic Rating	93
% students graduating within 4 years	71
% students graduating within 6 years	76
Calendar	semester
Student/faculty ratio	12:1
Profs interesting rating	95
Profs accessible rating	94
Most common reg class size	10–19 students
Most common lab size	10–19 students

MOST POPULAR MAJORS
biology, English language and literature, psychology

STUDENTS SAY ". . ."

Academics

The College of Wooster is "a small liberal arts school" in northeastern Ohio "with strong academics and a great campus community." Students enjoy tons of undergraduate research opportunities, and "small class sizes" are another big plus. "I have never been in a class [where] the professor did not know my name," reflects a physics major. "The biggest strength of this school," according to more than one student, is Wooster's unique Independent Study program. Under the guidance of a faculty adviser, "every senior" "engages in an independent research project that spans the entire senior year." Students love the concept. They say these projects are comparable "to graduate-level work," and they promise that the experience will do wonders for your "writing and research skills." There are some "unnecessary bureaucratic processes" here but the "very responsive" administration "does a good job of running the school and keeping the students up to date with what is going on." "Overall, the professors at Wooster are great," says an international relations major. There are "only a few lousy ones." Students appreciate the fact that faculty members are "always available" and "will do anything—as long as you're trying—to help you pass classes." "The level of interest and caring in students' lives and concerns is pretty outstanding." As far as academic complaints, limited course offerings can be a problem depending on your major. "Some of the departments barely even exist." "The smaller departments obviously have a harder time getting a good variety of classes," explains an art history major, "but the quality of the professors more than makes up for it."

Life

Studying takes up "a lot of time" but students are also "very involved on campus." "Most people who attend Wooster are in many groups and clubs." Students attend intercollegiate sporting events, theatrical and musical productions, and art exhibitions. They also participate in "a variety of other activities that over 100 student-led groups schedule over the course of the semester." Though Greek life definitely doesn't dictate Wooster's social scene, "sorority and fraternity parties are often popular destinations on the weekends." "Many people go out to parties and drink," "but a lot of people also don't." "Some people think that they are huge partiers," pronounces a sophomore, "but compared to bigger schools, they aren't." Wooster "might seem boring if you can't just sit down with your friends and hang out for hours on end," counsels a sophomore. "It's a small school in a small town, and unless you're creative you can run out of things to do. However, the people that you'll meet will make it so easy to just sit around for hours until you go to dinner, or decide to have a snowball fight." Students generally agree that their campus is "beautiful." The residence halls aren't the greatest, though. "Some of them are old and small," warns a junior. "Others are new but they are still small." "The athletic facilities are not in the best shape," either. Off campus, the surrounding town is "in the cornfields" and doesn't offer much in the way of entertainment. There's "nowhere to go shopping" and "local residents can be unfriendly." If you have a car, Cleveland and Columbus are about an hour away.

Student Body

Wooster "is surprisingly diverse given its size." The population here tends to be "studious and usually moderate to left-leaning politically." Beyond that, there's not much of a Wooster type. It's "an awesome mix of people who are jocks, hippies, musicians, preps, artists," and "people with no style at all." Virtually everyone is "eccentric in one way or another." "There is a niche for everybody and those who would commonly be considered atypical seem to find theirs." Students swear that you'll feel welcome here because "anyone feels welcome on campus." "Everyone seems to have a group of friends and every friend group seems to overlap," explains a sophomore. "It may sound empty and too simple but you will really love how people are so close and nice to each other," guarantees a wistful senior. "Emotionally, you will be happy."

FINANCIAL AID: 800-877-3688 • E-MAIL: ADMISSIONS@WOOSTER.EDU • WEBSITE: WWW.WOOSTER.EDU

THE PRINCETON REVIEW SAYS

Admissions

Very important factors considered include: Academic GPA, class rank, rigor of secondary school record. *Important factors considered include:* Application essay, recommendation(s), standardized test scores, character/personal qualities, talent/ability. *Other factors considered include:* Alumni/ae relation, extracurricular activities, geographical residence, interview, level of applicant's interest, racial/ethnic status, state residency, volunteer work, work experience. SAT or ACT required; ACT with writing component required. TOEFL required of all international applicants. High school diploma is required, and GED is accepted. *Academic units recommended:* 4 English, 4 mathematics, 4 social science and history, 4 science, 2 foreign language, 2 academic elective.

Financial Aid

Students should submit: FAFSA, institution's own financial aid form, CSS/Financial Aid PROFILE. Suggested filing deadline is February 15. The Princeton Review suggests that all financial aid forms be submitted as soon as possible after January 1. *Need-based scholarships/grants offered:* Federal Pell, SEOG, state scholarships/grants, private scholarships, school scholarship or grant aid from institutional funds. *Loan aid offered:* Direct Subsidized Stafford, Direct Unsubsidized Stafford, Direct PLUS, Federal Perkins. Federal Work-Study Program available. Off-campus job opportunities are good.

The Inside Word

The College of Wooster is a small, selective liberal arts school in a region of the country where there are quite a few small, selective liberal arts schools. For the most part, only solid students get past the gatekeepers here, and you should expect a thorough review of your application. Nevertheless, the admit rate is high. Stiff competition from similar institutions means the school will occasionally admit students who don't have stellar academic records.

THE SCHOOL SAYS "..."

From the Admissions Office

"The College of Wooster is America's premier college for mentored undergraduate research. Our mission is to graduate educated, not merely trained, people; to produce responsible, independent thinkers, rather than specialists in any given field. Our commitment to independence is especially evident in IS, the college's distinctive program in which every senior works one-to-one with a faculty mentor to complete a project in the major. IS comes from 'independent study,' but, in reality, it is an intellectual collaboration of the highest order and permits every student the freedom to pursue something in which he or she is passionately interested. IS is the centerpiece of an innovative curriculum. More than just the project itself, the culture that sustains IS—and, in turn, is sustained by IS—is an extraordinary college culture. The same attitudes of student initiative, openness, flexibility, and individual support enrich every aspect of Wooster's vital residential college life."

SELECTIVITY
Admissions Rating	90
# of applicants	4,635
% of applicants accepted	67
% of acceptees attending	20
# of early decision applicants	64
% accepted early decision	92

FRESHMAN PROFILE
Range SAT Critical Reading	560–670
Range SAT Math	550–670
Range SAT Writing	550–660
Range ACT Composite	24–29
Minimum paper TOEFL	550
Minimum computer TOEFL	213
Minimum web-based TOEFL	80
Average HS GPA	3.60
% graduated top 10% of class	39
% graduated top 25% of class	69
% graduated top 50% of class	93

DEADLINES
Early decision	
Deadline	11/15
Notification	12/15
Early action	
Deadline	12/15
Notification	1/15
Regular	
Deadline	2/15
Nonfall registration?	yes

FINANCIAL FACTS
Financial Aid Rating	88
Annual tuition	$38,000
Room and board	$9,310
Required fees	$290
Books and supplies	$1,000
% frosh rec. need-based scholarship or grant aid	60
% UG rec. need-based scholarship or grant aid	58
% frosh rec. non-need-based scholarship or grant aid	49
% UG rec. non-need-based scholarship or grant aid	47
% frosh rec. need-based self-help aid	46
% UG rec. need-based self-help aid	48
% frosh rec. any financial aid	98
% UG rec. any financial aid	98
% UG borrow to pay for school	58
Average cumulative indebtedness	$25,252

COLORADO COLLEGE

14 EAST CACHE LA POUDRE STREET, COLORADO SPRINGS, CO 80903 • ADMISSIONS: 719-389-6344 • FAX: 719-389-6816

STUDENTS SAY ". . ."

Academics

The unique thing about small, "intimate" and "intensive" Colorado College is the Block Plan. The school year here is broken into eight three-and-a-half-week chunks. Students take just one course during each block. "Taking one class at a time allows you to devote all of your time to it," explains an English major. Classes average about fifteen students and typically last for three hours each morning, though "there are some classes with labs in the afternoon." Students love the "personalized" nature of the program and the flexibility it offers. Double majors are frequent, almost normal. Internships are profuse. Studying abroad is very easy. "Many students" spend time abroad for a single block or for consecutive blocks in places such as China, Costa Rica, India, and Russia. There are also semesters in Washington, D.C., and Chicago. However, the Block Plan is also a pressure-packed situation. Work piles up quickly in every class. "Sciences are very tough." "Forget about getting sick, even for a day." The "super-duper" administration at CC is "very interested in student input." The full-time faculty is generally stellar. "Your professors know you by name and remember you." They "genuinely care about each of their students," and they're "always available" outside of class. Visiting professors can be another story, though. They often "don't seem to understand how the system works and tend to either give way too much work or hardly any at all."

Life

Colorado College is located in "a cute little town." The beautiful campus "makes life feel like a resort." Social life is bountiful. "My favorite thing about CC is that there is always something going on," declares a happy junior, "from readings by famous poets to porn debates, internationally known advocates to lacrosse games, protests to plays, music festivals to dances, techno raves to campus political debates, and fencing club to midnight pancake breakfasts." "There is a drug and alcohol scene," and students who participate "party pretty hard." Intramural and intercollegiate sports are also popular, especially hockey. The fabled men's team here is a "perennial contender" at the Division I level. The Block Plan gives life an unusual tempo. "The beginning of the block is really fun," explains one student. "You're not bogged down with tons of work yet, so we go out and party a lot." Toward the end of each block, papers come due, finals loom, and life becomes very hectic. Then, after "cramming a semester's work in three and a half weeks," students get a four-day vacation. Some students take advantage of the countless outdoor activities in the area. "skiing is very popular." Others students take part in activities sponsored by the school. You can take a bicycle trip to Aspen, just for example, or raft the Colorado River. Still other students "fill breaks with crazy adventures" or just enjoy "hardcore relaxation before being violently thrown into an entirely new and different world for the next block."

Student Body

"The population is not so diverse" at Colorado College according to some students. "Most students are white" and "from affluent families." The "trusta-farian" is a pretty common creature. Otherwise, students describe themselves as "intellectual, easygoing, and active." They're "environmentally aware," "idealistic," and "enthusiastic about trying new things." They have "many creative interests." They are "very liberal," too. "It is rare to find a conservative on campus." Other students tell us that Colorado College is "eclectic" and filled with every sort of student. There are two main groups: "hippies and preps." There are also plenty of "outdoor enthusiasts" "dressed in fancy outdoor gear." However, CC is small enough and students are open enough that there is quite a bit of overlap among cliques. "You can have an athlete who is the president of her sorority or a really outdoorsy person who plays in the school orchestra."

FINANCIAL AID: 719-389-6651 • E-MAIL: ADMISSION@COLORADOCOLLEGE.EDU • WEBSITE: WWW.COLORADOCOLLEGE.EDU

THE PRINCETON REVIEW SAYS

Admissions

Very important factors considered include: Rigor of secondary school record. *Important factors considered include:* Academic GPA, application essay, class rank, recommendation(s), standardized test scores, extracurricular activities, interview. *Other factors considered include:* Alumni/ae relation, character/personal qualities, first generation, level of applicant's interest, racial/ethnic status, religious affiliation/commitment, talent/ability, volunteer work, work experience. ACT with or without writing component accepted. High school diploma or equivalent isn't required. *Academic units required:* 4 English. *Academic units recommended:* 4 English.

Financial Aid

Students should submit: FAFSA, CSS/Financial Aid PROFILE. Regular filing deadline is February 15. The Princeton Review suggests that all financial aid forms be submitted as soon as possible after January 1. *Need-based scholarships/ grants offered:* Federal Pell, SEOG, state scholarships/grants, private scholarships. *Loan aid offered:* Direct Subsidized Stafford, Direct Unsubsidized Stafford, Direct PLUS, Federal Perkins. Federal Work-Study Program available. Off-campus job opportunities are fair.

The Inside Word

Colorado College works to identify those students who will most benefit from its distinct academic environment. Because the Block Program requires focus and demands that students become active participants in their educations, admissions officers value applicants who take on a rigorous course load in high school and engage in activities that complement their intellectual achievements. All candidates should take the application essay seriously—strong writing skills are seen as critical to success at CC.

THE SCHOOL SAYS "..."

From the Admissions Office

"Students enter Colorado College for the opportunity to study intensely in small learning communities. Groups of students work closely with one another and faculty in discussion-based classes and hands-on labs. CC encourages a well-rounded education, combining the academic rigor of an honors college with rich programs in athletics, community service, student government, the arts, and more. The college encourages students to push themselves academically, and many continue their studies at the best graduate and professional schools in the nation. CC is a great choice for field study and for international study. (CC ranks fourth nationally in the number of students studying abroad.) CC also takes advantage of its location, using its Baca campus in the San Luis Valley and the mountain cabin for a variety of classes. Its location at the base of the Rockies makes CC a great choice for students who enjoy backpacking, hiking, climbing, and skiing.

"Colorado College requires students to submit either the SAT or ACT. Scores are accepted for both. CC uses the highest sub score on the SAT and the highest ACT composite. SAT Subject Tests are accepted for review."

SELECTIVITY

Admissions Rating	93
# of applicants	4,466
% of applicants accepted	34
% of acceptees attending	36
# accepting a place on wait list	248
% admitted from wait list	0
# of early decision applicants	288
% accepted early decision	52

FRESHMAN PROFILE

Range SAT Critical Reading	610–710
Range SAT Math	610–700
Range SAT Writing	620–700
Range ACT Composite	28–32
% graduated top 10% of class	59
% graduated top 25% of class	89
% graduated top 50% of class	98

DEADLINES

Early decision	
Deadline	11/15
Notification	12/15
Early action	
Deadline	11/15
Notification	12/20
Regular	
Priority	1/15
Deadline	1/15
Nonfall registration?	yes

FINANCIAL FACTS

Financial Aid Rating	89
Annual tuition	$38,748
Room and board	$9,416
Books and supplies	$1,116
% frosh rec. need-based scholarship or grant aid	33
% UG rec. need-based scholarship or grant aid	36
% frosh rec. non-need-based scholarship or grant aid	10
% UG rec. non-need-based scholarship or grant aid	11
% frosh rec. need-based self-help aid	23
% UG rec. need-based self-help aid	24
% frosh rec. any financial aid	52
% UG rec. any financial aid	56
% UG borrow to pay for school	35
Average cumulative indebtedness	$16,172

COLORADO STATE UNIVERSITY

AMMONS HALL, FORT COLLINS, CO 80523 • ADMISSIONS: 970-491-6909 • FAX: 970-491-7799

CAMPUS LIFE
Quality of Life Rating	84
Fire Safety Rating	81
Green Rating	98
Type of school	public
Environment	city

STUDENTS
Total undergrad enrollment	21,953
% male/female	49/51
% from out of state	16
% live on campus	96
# of fraternities	23
# of sororities	15
% African American	2
% Asian	2
% Caucasian	79
% Hispanic	7
% international	2
# of countries represented	84

SURVEY SAYS . . .
Students love Fort Collins, CO
Great off-campus food
Low cost of living
Student publications are popular

ACADEMICS
Academic Rating	70
% students graduating within 4 years	37
% students graduating within 6 years	64
Calendar	semester
Student/faculty ratio	17:1
Profs interesting rating	80
Profs accessible rating	73
Most common reg class size	20–29 students
Most common lab size	20–29 students

MOST POPULAR MAJORS
biology, kinesiology and exercise science, psychology

STUDENTS SAY ". . ."

Academics
Colorado State University offers a breadth and depth of quality academics, especially in career-specific disciplines. Students here heap praise on the university's programs in such diverse fields as engineering, social work, math, business, interior design, health and exercise science, and music therapy. Topping many students' lists are agricultural and other natural sciences; one student explains, "Science-oriented classes are definitely quite challenging and a huge strength of our school, considering we have the second-highest-ranked veterinary college in the nation." Given its size and research mission, CSU surprisingly satisfies many students with the level of one-on-one service; many here insist that CSU "is big enough that people have heard of it but small enough that you don't get lost in the numbers" and that it "has a small-school feel because professors are always available and not everything is taught by TAs." This sense strengthens considerably once students clear the hurdles of underclassman requirements. Students warn, "Entry-level courses have very large class sizes and not many opportunities for personal interactions academically in class or out of it," but add, "As you progress through your field of study, class size becomes a lot smaller and more intimate."

Life
The CSU campus and surrounding area offer a lot of distractions, so "life at Colorado State can be challenging. It can be difficult to keep your focus on school when the mountains are right there" to tantalize students with snowboarding, skiing, hiking, and mountain biking. There's also Horsetooth Reservoir, a popular spot for swimming and hanging out during the warm season, and road trips to Laramie, Boulder, and Denver. Closer to home, "There is always something fun going on at campus like free movie showings, dance recitals, and choir concerts. CSU does a good job of bringing in guests like Barack Obama, Eva Longoria, Zach Braff, Matt Roloff, and Holocaust survivors." College football draws a raucous and devoted crowd; "Students usually come about an hour early to tailgate and enjoy one another's company. People wear crazy outfits and scream at the top of their lungs, cheering on their favorite players." CSU also offers "intramural and club sports," "plenty of organizations," and, of course, the requisite party scene. "People around here love beer," and with "four microbreweries serving world-class beer" nearby students can indulge in quality brew when the mood strikes. Hometown Fort Collins "is also a great place" that's "very safe with lots of places to eat and a good downtown. It has everything you need, but it still has somewhat of a small-town atmosphere," making it "a great college town" in the eyes of many.

Student Body
"The typical student at CSU is a Colorado resident, although there are plenty of people from outside the state," with students representing every state and eighty-five foreign nations. Undergrads are generally "committed to academics but also enjoy having fun when they aren't studying. Outdoor recreation is really important on this campus," and for many the school's access to the mountains is one of its chief allures. The school "does not draw huge minority populations…despite its efforts to increase diversity," but "there is a great focus on making minority students feel welcome and a part of the campus," so those who do come should find a solid support network. The typical undergrad is "very down-to-earth and environmentally friendly" and "politically conservative," although "the campus has shifted somewhat," and "there aren't as many conservative students here as there once were."

COLORADO STATE UNIVERSITY

FINANCIAL AID: 970-491-6321 • E-MAIL: ADMISSIONS@COLOSTATE.EDU • WEBSITE: WWW.COLOSTATE.EDU

THE PRINCETON REVIEW SAYS

Admissions

Very important factors considered include: Academic GPA, class rank, rigor of secondary school record, standardized test scores. *Important factors considered include:* Application essay, recommendation(s), character/personal qualities, extracurricular activities, talent/ability, volunteer work. *Other factors considered include:* Alumni/ae relation, first generation, geographical residence, state residency, work experience. SAT or ACT required; ACT with or without writing component accepted. TOEFL required of all international applicants. High school diploma is required, and GED is accepted. *Academic units required:* 4 English, 4 mathematics, 3 science (2 science labs), 1 foreign language, 2 social studies, 1 history, 2 academic elective. *Academic units recommended:* 4 English, 4 mathematics, 3 science (2 science labs), 2 foreign language, 2 social studies, 1 history, 2 academic elective.

Financial Aid

The Princeton Review suggests that all financial aid forms be submitted as soon as possible after January 1. *Need-based scholarships/grants offered:* Federal Pell, SEOG, state scholarships/grants, private scholarships, school scholarship or grant aid from institutional funds. *Loan aid offered:* Direct Subsidized Stafford, Direct Unsubsidized Stafford, Direct PLUS, Federal Perkins. Applicants will be notified of awards on a rolling basis beginning March 1. Federal Work-Study Program available. Off-campus job opportunities are excellent.

The Inside Word

CSU admits about nine out of ten applicants; the primary task of its admissions office is to determine who not to admit. Certain majors and programs are more competitive and impose additional admissions qualifications. Art and design programs, for example, require a portfolio review; programs in art, biomedical sciences, business, computer science, engineering, and technical journalism impose higher GPA and standardized test score floors than the school's other programs.

THE SCHOOL SAYS ". . ."

From the Admissions Office

"As one of the nation's premier research universities, Colorado State offers more than 150 undergraduate programs of study in eight colleges. Students come here from fifty states and eighty-five countries, and they appreciate the quality and breadth of the university's academic offerings. But Colorado State is more than just a place where students can take their scholarship to the highest level. It's also a place where they can gain invaluable experience in the fields of their choice, whether they're immersing themselves in professional internships, studying on the other side of the globe or teaming up with faculty on groundbreaking research projects. In addition to an outstanding experiential learning environment, Colorado State students enjoy a sense of community that's unusual for a large university. They develop meaningful relationships with faculty members who bring out their best work, and they live and learn with diverse peers who value their ideas and expand their perspectives. These types of connections lead to countless opportunities for social networking and professional accomplishments. By the time our students graduate from Colorado State, they have the knowledge, practical experience, and interpersonal skills they need to make a significant contribution to their world.

"Although academic performance is a primary factor in admissions decisions, Colorado State's holistic review process also recognizes personal qualities and experiences that have the potential to enrich the university and the Fort Collins community. To apply, students may submit the Common Application or the Colorado State University application for admission."

SELECTIVITY

Admissions Rating	81
# of applicants	14,680
% of applicants accepted	81
% of acceptees attending	38

FRESHMAN PROFILE

Range SAT Critical Reading	510–620
Range SAT Math	510–630
Range ACT Composite	22–27
Minimum paper TOEFL	450
Minimum web-based TOEFL	45
Average HS GPA	3.56
% graduated top 10% of class	23
% graduated top 25% of class	53
% graduated top 50% of class	88

DEADLINES

Regular	
Priority	2/1
Deadline	7/1
Notification	10/15
Nonfall registration?	yes

APPLICANTS ALSO LOOK AT AND OFTEN PREFER

Arizona State University at the Tempe campus, Colorado School of Mines, Cornell University, University of Colorado—Boulder, University of Denver

FINANCIAL FACTS

Financial Aid Rating	81
Annual in-state tuition	$5,256
Annual out-of-state tuition	$21,366
Room and board	$8,744
Required fees	$1,729
Books and supplies	$1,126
% frosh rec. need-based scholarship or grant aid	37
% UG rec. need-based scholarship or grant aid	36
% frosh rec. need-based self-help aid	31
% UG rec. need-based self-help aid	36
% frosh rec. any financial aid	72
% UG rec. any financial aid	69
% UG borrow to pay for school	60
Average cumulative indebtedness	$21,224

COLUMBIA UNIVERSITY

212 HAMILTON HALL MC 2807, 1130 AMSTERDAM AVENUE, NY, NY 10027 • ADMISSIONS: 212-854-2522 • FAX: 212-894-1209

STUDENTS SAY ". . ."

Academics

Nestled in Manhattan's upper west side neighborhood and "at the crossroads of the world," Columbia's campus "itself is an inspiration and a motivation to push and to excel academically." While being "one of the world's great research universities," the school still manages to feel "closer to a liberal arts college than a gigantic mega-school." Students are drawn to this "first rate intellectual oasis" for its "holistic education" and "rich, historic Columbia core curriculum," which "surveys the humanities and the sciences" and "serves as a knowledge base as well as the connecting thread to all Columbia students." Another boon is the "high quality" of "thought-provoking" and "brilliant and successful" professors who are "truly invested in teaching the things they love to their students" but who "will not hold your hand or check up on you." "It is very, very difficult to get an A here, but it's difficult to do too much worse as well." Using a "tough love" approach, Columbia "believes in treating its students like adults" and pushes them toward "independence and self sufficiency" while providing "amazing resources in fields of networking, research, and internships" that will make everyone "a better citizen of the world." Although students acknowledge that Columbia's administration "truly cares about its students and the health of the school," many wish to improve the school's bureaucracy, which is "notoriously difficult to deal with."

Life

"Columbia is as cosmopolitan and entertaining as New York City," sums up one satisfied student. Provided with "the best of both worlds," students often take advantage of their "secluded and idyllic green" campus' prime location, which gives them "unparalleled access to all the resources of the greatest city in the world." Another student boasts that attending Columbia gives you an "easy pass to the city, whether you are visiting museums for free with a flash of your ID or seeing your application pushed to the front when applying for amazing internships." The majority of students "venture downtown at least once a week to see a Broadway show, go to a concert or museum, or just explore." For those who are not tempted by the "free admission to over thirty museums in New York" or "a meal or dessert in Chinatown or Little Italy," there are plenty of "campus clubs and activities, including the fraternity and sorority scenes or on-campus parties." With a campus that "caters to every single person that comes through its doors," Columbia is "like being in a really rich agar" where students can pursue whatever they are interested in from "engaging in intellectual conversation" to "getting involved in politics through student groups on campus to continuing (or discovering) a love for the arts by being a part of a musical ensemble."

Student Body

A "diverse community of serious thinkers who also know how to have fun," Columbia students describe themselves as "bookworms" who are "cynical but enthusiastic" as well as "very politically active and liberal." With "driven" people "from distinct backgrounds, distinct ideologies, distinct everything," Columbia students list the school's diversity as one of its strengths, but one student cautions that "the diversity could use less of a leftist bias." "Extremely smart and interested in learning for its own sake," a "typical" Columbia student "has strong views but is willing to discuss and change them." Columbia students are also "more intense than those you might find at other schools," points out one student. Indeed, during exam season it's not uncommon to see students "bring sleeping bags and cases of Red Bull to the library." Despite this intensity, there is "a minimal amount of ill-intended competition," and "nobody is scrutinized for being different or pressured to be anything they are not."

FINANCIAL AID: 212-854-3711 • WEBSITE: WWW.STUDENTAFFAIRS.COLUMBIA.EDU/ADMISSIONS

THE PRINCETON REVIEW SAYS

Admissions

Very important factors considered include: Academic GPA, application essay, class rank, recommendation(s), rigor of secondary school record, standardized test scores, character/personal qualities. *Important factors considered include:* Extracurricular activities, talent/ability. *Other factors considered include:* Alumni/ae relation, geographical residence, interview, racial/ethnic status, volunteer work, work experience. ACT with writing component required. TOEFL required of all international applicants. High school diploma is required, and GED is accepted. *Academic units recommended:* 4 English, 4 mathematics, 4 science (4 science labs), 4 foreign language, 4 history, 4 academic elective.

Financial Aid

Students should submit: FAFSA, CSS/Financial Aid PROFILE, tax returns. Regular Decision filing deadline is March 1. The Princeton Review suggests that all financial aid forms be submitted as soon as possible after January 1. *Need-based scholarships/grants offered:* Federal Pell, SEOG, state scholarships/grants, private scholarships, school scholarship or grant aid from institutional funds. Students aren't packaged with loans, just institutional grants. *Federal loan aid offered:* Federal Perkins, FFEL Subsidized and Unsubsidized Direct Student Loans, FFEL Parent Plus Loans. Applicants will be notified of awards on a rolling basis beginning when they're admitted. Federal Work-Study Program available. Off-campus job opportunities are excellent.

The Inside Word

Earning an acceptance letter from Columbia is no easy feat. Applications to the university continue to rise, and many great candidates are rejected each year. Admissions officers take a holistic approach to evaluating applications; there's no magic formula or pattern to guide students seeking admission. One common denominator among applicants is stellar grades in rigorous classes and personal accomplishments in non-academic activities. Admissions officers are looking to build a diverse class that will greatly contribute to the university.

THE SCHOOL SAYS "..."

From the Admissions Office

"Columbia maintains an intimate college campus within one of the world's most vibrant cities. After a day exploring New York City you come home to a traditional college campus within an intimate neighborhood. Nobel Prize–winning professors will challenge you in class discussions and meet one-on-one afterward. The core curriculum attracts intensely free-minded scholars, and connects all undergraduates. Science and engineering students pursue cutting-edge research in world-class laboratories with faculty members at the forefront of scientific discovery. Classroom discussions are only the beginning of your education. Ideas spill out from the classrooms, electrifying the campus and Morningside Heights. Friendships formed in the residence halls solidify during a game of Frisbee on the South Lawn or over bagels on the steps of Low Library. From your first day on campus, you will be part of our diverse community.

"Columbia offers extensive need-based financial aid and meets the full need of every student admitted as a first-year with grants instead of loans. Parents with calculated incomes below $60,000 are not expected to contribute any income or assets to tuition, room, board and mandatory fees and families with calculated incomes between $60,000 and $100,000 and with typical assets have a significantly reduced contribution. Parents earning over $100,000 can still qualify for significant financial aid. To support students pursuing study abroad, research, internships and community service opportunities, Columbia offers the opportunity to apply for additional funding and exemptions from academic year and summer work expectations. A commitment to diversity—of every kind—is a long-standing Columbia hallmark. We believe cost should not be a barrier to pursuing your educational dreams."

SELECTIVITY

Admissions Rating	99
# of applicants	26,179
% of applicants accepted	9
% of acceptees attending	59
# of early decision applicants	2,921

FRESHMAN PROFILE

Range SAT Critical Reading	690–780
Range SAT Math	700–790
Range SAT Writing	690–780
Range ACT Composite	31–34
Minimum paper TOEFL	600
Minimum computer TOEFL	50
% graduated top 10% of class	97

DEADLINES

Early decision	
Deadline	11/1
Notification	12/15
Regular	
Deadline	1/1
Nonfall registration?	no

APPLICANTS ALSO LOOK AT AND OFTEN PREFER

Harvard College, Massachusetts Institute of Technology, Stanford University, Yale University

AND SOMETIMES PREFER

Princeton University, University of Pennsylvania

FINANCIAL FACTS

Financial Aid Rating	99
Annual tuition	$41,160
Room and board	$10,570
Required fees	$2,655
Books and supplies	$1,020
% frosh rec. need-based scholarship or grant aid	52
% UG rec. need-based scholarship or grant aid	50
% frosh rec. need-based self-help aid	40
% UG rec. need-based self-help aid	43
% frosh rec. any financial aid	54
% UG rec. any financial aid	60

CONNECTICUT COLLEGE

270 MOHEGAN AVENUE, NEW LONDON, CT 06320 • ADMISSIONS: 860-439-2200 • FAX: 860-439-4301

STUDENTS SAY ". . ."

Academics

"Warm environment" doesn't always refer to the weather at Connecticut College, a close-knit school in eastern Connecticut. It refers to an environment that encourages students "to get out and experience the world," and "prepares them for life in the 'real-world' as a grad." The school's relatively small size allows students to get to know one another well and affords "a large variety of academic opportunities" to each one—a far cry from the waiting-list mentality that often overtakes larger universities. Numerous resources are provided to help with academics, such as a writing center, language lab, a career services office, internship and study abroad programs, and the school's unique certificate programs. Students also all adhere to the school's Honor Code, which "instills a sense of self-awareness and self-governance among the student body." The student government garners a high level of respect from the body at large, and there's a feeling that it "really enacts change on campus and in the New London community."

Classes are "engaging and interesting," which makes for a smooth transition from high school to college, and "professors are available inside and outside of the classroom." Indeed, professors' personal touches are the most highly sung aspect of Conn College life, and students rave over having "more than just a teacher-student relationship, but rather a person-person relationship" with their teachers. Most professors go by their first names, and are "down-to-earth people who place themselves at the same level as their students." "I am constantly learning and enthralled in class," says a senior art history major.

Life

Students without cars have trouble getting off campus, which doesn't matter as "there is basically nothing to do in New London." However, the city does have a few distractions like museums and restaurants and happens to be "perfectly located right in between New York City and Boston," with a train station conveniently located downtown. The vast majority of people live on campus, so dorms are "great social houses" in which people leave their doors open and are interested in getting to know their neighbors. When the weather is nice, going to the beach and hanging out on the green is very popular, and when it's not, students are given free-rein to start their own clubs and to volunteer with local organizations. People work hard during the week, but Thursdays and Saturdays are the big days to let loose. Everyone stays on campus on the weekends, and the school organizes plenty of things to do, such as theme dances, movies, a capella shows, and "Friday Night Lives" where up-and-coming bands come and play a concert for students.

Student Body

"People are just nice" at Conn College, and friends aren't hard to come by." Most people here are highly involved in the social and academic atmosphere of the school, play a sport, and are "open-minded and involved in a variety of activities." "For better or worse, people are unapologetically themselves…it is a unique quality about Conn that makes it both wonderful and unbearable at times," says one student. The typical student is from "right outside of Boston, New York, Connecticut, or any other New England state." There "is not a particularly diverse student body at Conn," though life experiences and interests of the students make it so that the perceived diversity is "truly immense." "Generally, students are wealthy" and "uncommonly good-looking." There "are a few academic superstars but, for the most part, students are on the same page academically." The school has many international students and study abroad options to promote academic and personal diversity.

FINANCIAL AID: 860-439-2200 • E-MAIL: ADMISSION@CONNCOLL.EDU • WEBSITE: WWW.CONNCOLL.EDU

THE PRINCETON REVIEW SAYS

Admissions

Very important factors considered include: Academic GPA, class rank, rigor of secondary school record, character/personal qualities. *Important factors considered include:* Application essay, recommendation(s), extracurricular activities, interview, racial/ethnic status, talent/ability, volunteer work, work experience. *Other factors considered include:* Standardized test scores, alumni/ae relation, first generation, geographical residence, level of applicant's interest, religious affiliation/commitment, state residency. Submission of standardized test scores (SAT, SAT Subject Tests, ACT) is optional. ACT with or without writing component accepted. TOEFL required of all international applicants. High school diploma is required, and GED is accepted.

Financial Aid

Students should submit: FAFSA, CSS/Financial Aid PROFILE. Regular filing deadline is February 1. The Princeton Review suggests that all financial aid forms be submitted as soon as possible after January 1. *Need-based scholarships/grants offered:* Federal Pell, SEOG, state scholarships/grants, school scholarship or grant aid from institutional funds. *Loan aid offered:* Direct Subsidized Stafford, Direct Unsubsidized Stafford, Direct PLUS, Federal Perkins. Federal Work-Study Program available. Off-campus job opportunities are good.

The Inside Word

Connecticut College is the archetypal selective New England college, and admissions officers are judicious in their decisions. Competitive applicants will have pursued a demanding course load in high school. Admissions officers look for students who are curious and who thrive in challenging academic environments. Since Connecticut College has a close-knit community, personal qualities are also closely evaluated, and interviews are important.

THE SCHOOL SAYS ". . ."

From the Admissions Office

"Chartered in 1911, Connecticut College was founded in the spirit of political and social equality, self-determination, and shared governance. The college seeks students who are not only smart and intellectually curious, but who also bring a wide range of life experiences and perspectives that enable this spirit to endure within the college community. The college's near century-old Honor Code defines campus life and is observed by all students, faculty, and staff. The Honor Code inspires students to challenge themselves and their peers to see the world from diverse perspectives, to remain receptive to new ideas and experiences, and, by instilling a sense of mutual respect, to consider how their actions and education may ultimately better the common good. Ninety-nine percent of students live on campus. There is no Greek system. Dozens of clubs represent the students' numerous activist, volunteer, spiritual, creative, or athletic interests.

"The college offers more than fifty majors and minors and a series of interdisciplinary learning centers. All classes and labs are taught by professors. Students participate in the NCAA Division III New England Small College Athletic Conference (NESCAC). The college is nationally known for pioneering environmental initiatives, including commitments to renewable energy, and career and internship placement. The college has been called a "college with a conscience" by the Princeton Review for fostering social responsibility and public service and is one of the top sending schools for both Teach for America and The Peace Corps. In the past four years, eighteen Connecticut College students have been awarded Fulbright Scholarships and three students have been awarded Goldwater Scholarships."

SELECTIVITY

Admissions Rating	93
# of applicants	5,301
% of applicants accepted	32
% of acceptees attending	29
# accepting a place on wait list	442
% admitted from wait list	13
# of early decision applicants	393
% accepted early decision	61

FRESHMAN PROFILE

Range SAT Critical Reading	630–710
Range SAT Math	610–690
Range SAT Writing	630–720
Range ACT Composite	27–31
Minimum paper TOEFL	600
Minimum computer TOEFL	250
Minimum web-based TOEFL	100
% graduated top 10% of class	57
% graduated top 25% of class	91
% graduated top 50% of class	99

DEADLINES

Early decision	
Deadline	11/15
Notification	12/15
Regular	
Deadline	1/1
Nonfall registration?	no

APPLICANTS ALSO LOOK AT AND OFTEN PREFER

Bates College, Bowdoin College, Colby College, Hamilton College, Middlebury College, Tufts University, Vassar College, Wesleyan University

AND SOMETIMES PREFER
Trinity College (CT)

AND RARELY PREFER
Brown University, Skidmore College

FINANCIAL FACTS

Financial Aid Rating	94
Annual tuition	$54,970
Books and supplies	$1,000
% frosh rec. need-based scholarship or grant aid	44
% UG rec. need-based scholarship or grant aid	43
% frosh rec. need-based self-help aid	41
% UG rec. need-based self-help aid	42
% frosh rec. any financial aid	46
% UG borrow to pay for school	39
Average cumulative indebtedness	$26,545

THE COOPER UNION FOR THE ADVANCEMENT OF SCIENCE AND ART

30 COOPER SQUARE, NEW YORK, NY 10003 • ADMISSIONS: 212-353-4120 • FAX: 212-353-4342

STUDENTS SAY ". . ."

Academics

Believe it or not, "free tuition" isn't the only reason gifted students clamor for a spot at The Cooper Union for the Advancement of Science and Art. Of course, the universal "full-tuition scholarships" are one of the school's major selling points. However, the rigorous and "very reputable" academic programs are the main reason to attend this unique New York City college. "An institution of the highest caliber," Cooper Union has a narrow academic focus, conferring degrees only in fine arts, architecture, and engineering. Cooper Union's "engineering program is considered one of the best in the nation"; there are "plenty of opportunities for independent study in your field," and "lab facilities are incredible." Individual learning is emphasized, and the student-to-teacher ratio is excellent: "The freshman year courses have about twenty to twenty-five students in each, while the courses in later years have as few as five students in a class." When it comes to the teaching staff, adjunct faculty gets mixed reviews, while "full-time professors are really great. They have great experience, like what they do, like the students, [and] are really accessible and happy to help." "Professors vary widely in their teaching methods"; yet most are "very accessible, friendly, [and] expect a high level of quality for work." Unfortunately, if you don't like your instructor, you're out of luck because "there are only a few professors in each department, meaning students have the same professor over and over again." Not surprisingly, academic excellence doesn't come without its share of challenges. In all departments, Cooper Union professors "really make you work hard to earn your grade," and even "extremely intelligent, hardworking students are not necessarily going to do well" in the school's competitive classes.

Life

Located in New York City's East Village, Cooper Union offers "an opportunity to live in one of the most energetic and dynamic cities in the world." Unfortunately, "There isn't time for anything other than your classes" at Cooper Union. To meet the school's high academic demands and "spine-breaking workload," "The typical schedule for any Cooper student who hopes to survive is go to class, study and do homework, sleep for a few hours, and repeat." At Cooper Union, there are few Greek organizations, no dormitories for upperclassmen, and "no recreational facilities or cafeterias on campus." Students are the first to admit that "the social life is rather limited" and "weekends are more often spent in the lab or library than at parties." However, those who make time for a little recreation say, "There are plenty of parties happening in the Village and at NYU that students can attend"— not to mention, plenty of "comedy clubs, movies, bowling, lounges, and bars" throughout New York City. Art students, though also self-professed workaholics, may also make time to "go to art openings of fellow students, professors, and friends, party, [or] play a lot of music." However, most students say that when they "sacrifice a few hours of sleep to do something enjoyable, it usually includes just hanging out with friends."

Student Body

Cooper Union's campus is largely comprised of "three distinct types of students," each delineated by major field: art, architecture, and engineering. Typical art students are "alternative kids" with the "just-rolled-out-of-bed look" while future architects are "very sleek" and fashionable, but "never leave their studio." The more "socially awkward" engineers are also largely like minds. One says, "If you have some obscure technological passion, someone in the engineering school is guaranteed to be as passionate." According to some, "Artists hang out with artists, engineers with engineers, architects with architects." However, most Cooper Union students laugh off stereotypes, telling us the school is filled with "very unique, interesting people," eager to learn and cross-pollinate between departments. A current student reassures us, "Of course, the odds are high that a group of electrical engineers will end up talking about video games, but there seems to be a broad spectrum of personalities present here." Across the board, students in every major are serious about their studies, and most of Cooper's selective admits are "super intelligent, super creative, and/or just super hardworking."

THE COOPER UNION FOR THE ADVANCEMENT OF SCIENCE AND ART

FINANCIAL AID: 212-353-4130 • E-MAIL: ADMISSIONS@COOPER.EDU • WEBSITE: WWW.COOPER.EDU

THE PRINCETON REVIEW SAYS

Admissions

Very important factors considered include: Academic GPA, rigor of secondary school record, standardized test scores, level of applicant's interest, talent/ability. *Important factors considered include:* Application essay, character/personal qualities, extracurricular activities. *Other factors considered include:* Class rank, recommendation(s), first generation, interview, racial/ethnic status, volunteer work, work experience. SAT or ACT required; ACT with writing component recommended. TOEFL required of all international applicants. High school diploma is required, and GED is accepted. *Academic units required:* 4 English, 1 mathematics, 1 science, 1 social studies, 1 history, 8 academic elective. *Academic units recommended:* 4 English, 4 mathematics, 4 science (3 science labs), 2 foreign language, 4 social studies.

Financial Aid

Students should submit: FAFSA, CSS/Financial Aid PROFILE. Regular filing deadline is June 1. The Princeton Review suggests that all financial aid forms be submitted as soon as possible after January 1. *Need-based scholarships/grants offered:* Federal Pell, SEOG, state scholarships/grants, private scholarships, school scholarship or grant aid from institutional funds. *Loan aid offered:* Direct Subsidized Stafford, Direct Unsubsidized Stafford, Direct PLUS, Federal Perkins, university loans from institutional funds. Federal Work-Study Program available. Off-campus job opportunities are excellent.

The Inside Word

The admission rate to Cooper Union is extremely competitive. In recent years, only about eight percent of applicants have been accepted to the undergraduate program. The fine arts (BFA) program is usually the most competitive of Cooper's three schools, though all admits must be academically accomplished and top of their high school class. Depending on if you plan to pursue engineering, art, or architecture, admissions requirements and applications deadlines vary.

THE SCHOOL SAYS ". . ."

From the Admissions Office

"Each of Cooper Union's three schools, architecture, art, and engineering, adheres strongly to preparation for its profession and is committed to a problem-solving philosophy of education in a unique, scholarly environment. A rigorous curriculum and group projects reinforce this unique atmosphere in higher education and contribute to a strong sense of community and identity in each school. With McSorley's Ale House and the Joseph Papp Public Theatre nearby, Cooper Union remains at the heart of the city's tradition of free speech, enlightenment, and entertainment. Cooper's Great Hall has hosted national leaders, from Abraham Lincoln to Booker T. Washington, from Mark Twain to Samuel Gompers, from Susan B. Anthony to Betty Friedan, and more recently, President Bill Clinton and President Barack Obama.

"In fall of 2009, we opened the doors of our new academic building. Designed by Pritzker Prize–winning architect, Thom Mayne, the new building was designed to enhance and encourage more interaction between students in all three schools.

"We're seeking students who have a passion to study our professional programs. Cooper Union students are independent thinkers, following the beat of their own drum. Many of our graduates become world-class leaders in the disciplines of architecture, fine arts, design, and engineering.

"For art and architecture applicants, SAT scores are considered after the home test and portfolio work. For engineering applicants, high school grades and the SAT and SAT Subject Test scores are the most important factors considered in admissions decisions. Currently, we do not use the writing section of the SAT to assist in making admissions decisions. We expect to revisit that policy as more data is available in the near future."

SELECTIVITY

Admissions Rating	99
# of applicants	3,354
% of applicants accepted	8
% of acceptees attending	76
# accepting a place on wait list	70
% admitted from wait list	7
# of early decision applicants	820
% accepted early decision	9

FRESHMAN PROFILE

Range SAT Critical Reading	610–730
Range SAT Math	610–780
Range SAT Writing	620–640
Range ACT Composite	29–33
Minimum paper TOEFL	600
Minimum computer TOEFL	250
Minimum web-based TOEFL	100
Average HS GPA	3.60
% graduated top 10% of class	93
% graduated top 25% of class	98
% graduated top 50% of class	99

DEADLINES

Early decision	
Deadline	12/1
Notification	12/23
Regular	
Priority	12/1
Deadline	1/1
Nonfall registration?	no

APPLICANTS ALSO LOOK AT AND OFTEN PREFER
Columbia University, Cornell University, Harvard College, Massachusetts Institute of Technology, Princeton University

AND SOMETIMES PREFER
Carnegie Mellon University, Duke University, Franklin W. Olin College of Engineering

FINANCIAL FACTS

Financial Aid Rating	91
Annual tuition	$35,000
Room and board	$13,700
Required fees	$1,650
Books and supplies	$1,800
% frosh rec. need-based scholarship or grant aid	25
% UG rec. need-based scholarship or grant aid	27
% frosh rec. non-need-based scholarship or grant aid	100
% UG rec. non-need-based scholarship or grant aid	100
% frosh rec. need-based self-help aid	16
% UG rec. need-based self-help aid	20
% frosh rec. any financial aid	100
% UG rec. any financial aid	100
% UG borrow to pay for school	27
Average cumulative indebtedness	$11,414

CORNELL COLLEGE

600 FIRST STREET WEST, MOUNT VERNON, IA 52314-1098 • ADMISSIONS: 319-895-4477 • FAX: 319-895-4451

STUDENTS SAY ". . ."
Academics
Cornell College, a small liberal arts school in Iowa, employs a unique one-course-at-a-time program, allowing students to focus on just one course (or "block") each month, providing an "intense, thorough, and complete immersion." Though students agree that this "series of experiences" "doesn't give you any time to think about anything but the class you're in right then," it allows for personalized curricula design, and areas like the humanities "work perfectly with the block plan." Students also "always know when to find people," which makes it easy to get together. Some classes may not be the most challenging, but "upper-level courses are very engaging and fulfilling." "You could have hours and hours of homework one block and practically none the next," says a student. The block plan makes it very easy to gain off-campus field experience or do international study, and it's "easier to try off-campus opportunities." Administration is generally "excellent at taking a personal interest in each student," though some note, "There is not much transparency at the administrative level," which can be "out of touch" at times. The registrar is "the most dreaded office on campus," with residence life a close second. On the classroom side, professors "know how to motivate and encourage their students," and though "you may get a bad apple maybe once a year," they're "not only knowledgeable but dedicated." "The personal attention you can receive from any given professor, given that you seek them out, is especially rewarding," says a student. All in all, students love the block structure and the sense of community it creates, as "no matter what it is you may want to do, you can find someone to do it with you." One student claims he "cannot imagine learning any other way."

Life
Since Cornell is very campus-focused (you "rarely see students venture past the edge of campus"), the school makes sure there's a large variety of campus organizations and "many events going on almost every weekend." Though there's definitely a "small-town quiet," Cedar Rapids and Iowa City are both only a twenty-minute drive away, and "ice climbing, rock-climbing, paddling, and hiking" are popular outdoor pastimes. It's also "fairly easy to start up a new club or group." In addition, the school provides seven "block breaks," which last four and a half days and give students the opportunity to travel, go skiing or camping, and so on. The cold weather can cause problems here, in both a locked-in feel and the possibility for accidents, and students are encouraged to "bring snow boots!" Many here tend to have a love-hate relationship with sports; while athletics are a huge boon, "The athletes and the non-athletes are seldom friends." Much like the curriculum, lunchtimes are pretty unique, and students all eat in a common cafeteria, naturally falling into a somewhat "high school" habit of eating at the same tables every day. The meals themselves are another matter. One student sums up the feelings of all: "Cornell needs to work on the food. There, I said it." Most people stay on campus for entertainment and socializing, "creating a cohesive community." Parties do take place on weekends, and "Drinking is popular on campus but never forced," but in general, "People are more interested in just having a good conversation with their peers."

Student Body
There's "a great diversity of interests" in people who attend Cornell, and the "super busy" students have a hard time defining a more common characteristic than the fact that almost all are driven and involved. Some division into typical groups does occur—"the cafeteria design and Greek life are very conducive to this problem"—but "even group to group there is always mingling because you never know who will be in your next class." Since the classes are so small and "you see the same people four hours a day for three and a half weeks," people are generally accepting, and "You have to be really, really strange here to stick out." As one freshman says, "The only intolerance I've seen is toward the consistently indolent."

CORNELL COLLEGE

FINANCIAL AID: 319-895-4216 • E-MAIL: ADMISSIONS@CORNELLCOLLEGE.EDU • WEBSITE: WWW.CORNELLCOLLEGE.EDU

THE PRINCETON REVIEW SAYS

Admissions

Very important factors considered include: Academic GPA, application essay, recommendation(s), rigor of secondary school record. *Important factors considered include:* Class rank, standardized test scores, character/personal qualities, extracurricular activities, background, interview, level of applicant's interest, talent/ability, volunteer work, work experience. *Other factors considered include:* Alumni/ae relation, geographical residence, racial/ethnic status, state residency. SAT or ACT required; ACT with or without writing component accepted. TOEFL required of all international applicants. High school diploma is required, and GED is accepted. *Academic units recommended:* 4 English, 3–4 mathematics, 3–4 science, 2–4 foreign language, 3–4 social studies.

Financial Aid

Students should submit: FAFSA, institution's own financial aid form. Regular filing deadline is March 1. The Princeton Review suggests that all financial aid forms be submitted as soon as possible after January 1. *Need-based scholarships/grants offered:* Federal Pell, SEOG, state scholarships/grants, private scholarships, school scholarship or grant aid from institutional funds. *Loan aid offered:* Direct Subsidized Stafford, Direct Unsubsidized Stafford, Direct PLUS. Applicants will be notified of awards on a rolling basis beginning March 1. Federal Work-Study Program available. Off-campus job opportunities are fair.

The Inside Word

Given Cornell's relatively unique approach to study, it's no surprise that the admissions committee here focuses attention on both academic and personal strengths. Cornell's small, highly self-selected applicant pool is chock-full of students with solid self-awareness, motivation, and discipline. Pay particular attention to offering evidence of challenging academic course work and solid achievement on your high school record. Strong writers can do much for themselves under admissions circumstances such as these.

THE SCHOOL SAYS "..."

From the Admissions Office

"Very few colleges are truly distinctive like Cornell College. Founded in 1853, Cornell is recognized as one of the nation's finest colleges of the liberal arts and sciences. It is Cornell's combination of special features, however, that distinguishes it. An attractively diverse, caring residential college, Cornell places special emphasis on service and leadership. Foremost, it is a place where theory and practice are brought together in exciting ways through the college's one-course-at-a-time academic calendar. Here, students enjoy learning as they immerse themselves in a single subject for a 3.5-week term. They and their professor devote all of their efforts to that course in an engagingly interactive learning environment. This academic system also offers wonderful enrichment experiences through field-based study, travel abroad, student research, and meaningful internship opportunities. Eight terms are offered each year; thirty-two course credits are required for graduation with each course equal to four credit hours. Since all classes are on a standard schedule, students are able to pursue their extracurricular interests, whether in the performing arts, athletics, or interest groups, with the same passion with which they pursue their course work. Typically, each year applicants from all fifty states and more than forty countries apply for admission. Cornell graduates are in demand, with more than two-thirds eventually earning advanced degrees. The college's beautiful hilltop campus is one of only two campuses nationwide listed on the National Register of Historic Places. Located in the charming town of Mount Vernon, Cornell is also within commuting distance of Iowa City (home of the University of Iowa) and Cedar Rapids (the second largest city in the state). Freshman applicants are required to submit their SAT Reasoning or ACT results (the writing component is optional for the ACT, as students are required to submit an essay as part of the application for admission). In addition, for students submitting multiple score reports their best scores from either exam will be used in the application review process. SAT Subject Tests are not required."

SELECTIVITY

Admissions Rating	92
# of applicants	3,791
% of applicants accepted	39
% of acceptees attending	24
# accepting a place on wait list	75
% admitted from wait list	55
# of early decision applicants	178
% accepted early decision	19

FRESHMAN PROFILE

Range SAT Critical Reading	540–680
Range SAT Math	530–680
Range SAT Writing	530–640
Range ACT Composite	24–29
Minimum paper TOEFL	550
Minimum computer TOEFL	213
Average HS GPA	3.50
% graduated top 10% of class	33
% graduated top 25% of class	62
% graduated top 50% of class	88

DEADLINES

Early decision	
Deadline	11/1
Notification	12/15
Early action	
Deadline	12/1
Notification	2/1
Regular	
Priority	2/1
Deadline	2/1
Nonfall registration?	yes

APPLICANTS ALSO LOOK AT AND SOMETIMES PREFER

Beloit College, Coe College, Colorado College, Kalamazoo College, Knox College

FINANCIAL FACTS

Financial Aid Rating	90
Annual tuition	$32,720
Room and board	$7,730
Required fees	$200
Books and supplies	$810
% frosh rec. need-based scholarship or grant aid	75
% UG rec. need-based scholarship or grant aid	74
% frosh rec. non-need-based scholarship or grant aid	67
% UG rec. non-need-based scholarship or grant aid	63
% frosh rec. need-based self-help aid	63
% UG rec. need-based self-help aid	62
% frosh rec. any financial aid	94
% UG rec. any financial aid	95
% UG borrow to pay for school	73
Average cumulative indebtedness	$22,455

CORNELL UNIVERSITY

UNDERGRADUATE ADMISSIONS, 410 THURSTON AVENUE, ITHACA, NY 14850 • ADMISSIONS: 607-255-5241 • FAX: 607-255-0659

CAMPUS LIFE

Quality of Life Rating	90
Fire Safety Rating	78
Green Rating	97
Type of school	private
Environment	town

STUDENTS

Total undergrad enrollment	13,935
% male/female	50/50
% from out of state	64
% from public high school	70
% live on campus	57
# of fraternities	47
# of sororities	19
% African American	5
% Asian	16
% Caucasian	46
% Hispanic	8
% international	9
# of countries represented	120

SURVEY SAYS . . .
Great computer facilities
Great library
Great food on campus
Student publications are popular

ACADEMICS

Academic Rating	92
% students graduating within 4 years	86
% students graduating within 6 years	93
Calendar	semester
Student/faculty ratio	9:1
Profs interesting rating	77
Profs accessible rating	77
Most common reg class size	10–19 students
Most common lab size	10–19 students

MOST POPULAR MAJORS
engineering, business/marketing, biology, agriculture, social sciences

STUDENTS SAY ". . ."

Academics

"Any person, any study." Thus goes the motto of Cornell University, located in rural, cold upstate New York. The school consists of seven different undergraduate colleges, all of which have "differing focuses and missions that are somehow unified and work together pretty cohesively." These smaller schools, including the well-known Hotel School and College of Agricultural and Life Sciences, allow students to "receive all the benefits of a smaller college with the access, excitement, and opportunity provided by a large university." However, "You have to strongly believe in what you're studying and why you're studying it so as not to be freaked out by others who are in different majors and colleges." Though Cornell "may seem awfully large," students say it makes finding a close-knit community incredibly easy and "constantly challenges you to do better." No matter what major you choose, Cornell offers "rigorous" academics, where "it takes a lot of hard work to succeed, but the resources are there for you to do so." The administration "makes huge attempts to be transparent," often using student panels for advice, though there's still some red tape clinging to a few processes (such as class registration). Class sizes range from small to large, but professors remain "incredible" and attentive across the board, though the size of the school (about 14,000 undergrads) often means you have to be proactive in seeking out help. "If you show genuine interest, [faculty] are more than excited to help you." Many are also focused on their research, which can be distracting, but it also provides students with plenty of opportunities to work with the academic bigwigs themselves. "Just the other day in one of my biology classes, my professor was going over a very important topic and just added in, 'Yeah, I came up with this,'" says a student.

Life

"Cornell is about studying hard, being involved in many activities, and always doing more than the average person can handle, all while still having a social life and partying hard," says a senior. "Work hard, work harder, stress hard, play hard," says another senior about the resounding ethos that makes for a "nice balance" of life. There's also a natural progression for students as they become upperclassmen—living in the dorms and drinking at parties or frat houses is quite popular for freshmen and sophomores, while upperclassmen often find apartments and outside venues for weekend entertainment. There are always "a variety of activities that do not include drinking" on offer, including "a capella concerts, movie nights, special speakers and discussions, and sports games." Hometown Ithaca offers a farmers' market, restaurants, bars, and a movie theater. On campus, extracurricular offerings abound, and "it's not too hard to find something that interests everyone"—there's even an origami club—and the majority of students choose to join multiple organizations. On top of all that Ithaca offers, the school's northeast location also allows for "access to great weekend and break destinations like New York City and Washington, D.C."

Student Body

With such a large student body, "there is always a niche that any individual can fall into." Sure enough, the school's size and Ivy League status make it "a largely diverse and exciting bubble" where there is an abundance of "athletes or frat/sorority people," but at the same time, "you have a large group of students who do other activities." "We have our nerdy engineers, our outgoing hoteliers, our hipster art students, [and] our hardcore dairy farmers," brags one proud student. A "strong work ethic" seems to be the unifying thread among Cornell's diverse student body, as all students are "very focused on performing well in the classroom." "Most everyone has a secret nerdiness inside them that actually adds to their 'coolness,'" explains one. The different schools tend to naturally group together more frequently, so that each quad "has its own vibe," but "everyone is very friendly and approachable." Basically, "when you come here, you become the typical Cornellian."

CORNELL UNIVERSITY

FINANCIAL AID: 607-255-5145 • E-MAIL: ADMISSIONS@CORNELL.EDU • WEBSITE: WWW.CORNELL.EDU

THE PRINCETON REVIEW SAYS

Admissions

Very important factors considered include: Academic GPA, application essay, recommendation(s), rigor of secondary school record, standardized test scores, extracurricular activities, talent/ability. *Important factors considered include:* Class rank. *Other factors considered include:* Alumni/ae relation, character/personal qualities, first generation, geographical residence, interview, racial/ethnic status, state residency, volunteer work, work experience. SAT or ACT required; ACT with writing component required. TOEFL required of all international applicants. High school diploma or equivalent isn't required. *Academic units required:* 4 English, 3 mathematics. *Academic units recommended:* 3 science (3 science labs), 3 foreign language, 3 social studies, 3 history.

Financial Aid

Students should submit: FAFSA, institution's own financial aid form, CSS/Financial Aid PROFILE. Regular filing deadline is January 2. The Princeton Review suggests that all financial aid forms be submitted as soon as possible after January 1. *Need-based scholarships/grants offered:* Federal Pell, SEOG, state scholarships/grants, private scholarships, school scholarship or grant aid from institutional funds. *Loan aid offered:* Direct Subsidized Stafford, Direct Unsubsidized Stafford, Direct PLUS, Federal Perkins, university loans from institutional funds. Federal Work-Study Program available. Off-campus job opportunities are fair.

The Inside Word

Gaining admission to Cornell is a tough coup regardless of your intended field of study, but some of the university's seven schools are more competitive than others. If you're thinking of trying to "backdoor" your way into one of the most competitive schools—by gaining admission to a less competitive one, then transferring after one year—be aware that you will have to resubmit the entire application and provide a statement outlining your academic plans. It's not impossible to accomplish, but Cornell works hard to discourage this sort of maneuvering.

THE SCHOOL SAYS "..."

From the Admissions Office

"Cornell University, an Ivy League school and land-grant college located in the scenic Finger Lakes region of central New York, provides an outstanding education to students in seven small to midsize undergraduate colleges: Agriculture and Life Sciences; Architecture, Art, and Planning; Arts and Sciences; Engineering; Hotel Administration; Human Ecology; and Industrial and Labor Relations. Cornellians come from all fifty states and more than 120 countries, and they pursue their academic goals in more than 100 departments. The College of Arts and Sciences, one of the smallest liberal arts schools in the Ivy League, offers more than forty majors, most of which rank near the top nationwide. Applied programs in the other six colleges also rank among the best in the world. "Other special features of the university include a world-renowned faculty; over 4,000 courses available to all students; an extensive undergraduate research program; superb research, teaching, and library facilities; a large, diverse study abroad program; and more than 800 student organizations and thirty-four varsity sports. Cornell's campus is one of the most beautiful in the country; students pass streams, rocky gorges, and waterfalls on their way to class. First-year students make their home on North Campus, a living-learning community that features a special advising center, faculty-in-residence, a fitness center, and traditional residence halls as well as theme-centered buildings such as Ecology House. Cornell University invites applications from all interested students and uses the Common Application exclusively with a short required Cornell Supplement. Students applying for admissions will submit scores from the SAT or ACT (with writing). We also require SAT Subject Tests. Subject test requirements are college-specific."

SELECTIVITY	
Admissions Rating	96
# of applicants	36,392
% of applicants accepted	18
% of acceptees attending	48
# accepting a place on wait list	1,483
% admitted from wait list	0
# of early decision applicants	3,480
% accepted early decision	35

FRESHMAN PROFILE	
Range SAT Critical Reading	640–730
Range SAT Math	670–770
Range ACT Composite	29–33
Minimum paper TOEFL	600
Minimum web-based TOEFL	100
% graduated top 10% of class	90
% graduated top 25% of class	99
% graduated top 50% of class	100

DEADLINES	
Early decision	
Deadline	11/1
Notification	mid-December
Regular	
Deadline	1/3
Notification	early April
Nonfall registration?	no

FINANCIAL FACTS	
Financial Aid Rating	95
Annual tuition	$41,325
Room and board	$13,154
Required fees	$216
Books and supplies	$800
% frosh rec. need-based scholarship or grant aid	50
% UG rec. need-based scholarship or grant aid	48
% frosh rec. need-based self-help aid	44
% UG rec. need-based self-help aid	44
% UG borrow to pay for school	52
Average cumulative indebtedness	$20,648

CREIGHTON UNIVERSITY

2500 CALIFORNIA PLAZA, OMAHA, NE 68178 • ADMISSIONS: 402-280-2703 • FAX: 402-280-2685

STUDENTS SAY ". . ."

Academics

The voices echoing from this Omaha school are resoundingly pleased with their choice to attend "a great Jesuit university focused on academics and creating well-rounded students." Students are also active outside the classroom, getting "involved" in the campus and local community, and the school makes sure it churns a student out as a complete package: "academically, socially, culturally, faith-filled, and service-oriented." Creighton wants to form students who are driven inside the classroom but "want to find deeper meanings in all that they do to enact change in the world." Though classes are tough, the typical class size is small, which "makes discussion possible in nearly every class." Likewise, professors are extraordinarily helpful and "know how to present material in an interesting manner for the most part." Professors are all "exceptional" and really run the gamut "from quirky nerds to outspoken rebels to hilarious Jesuit priests." Many students come here for medical school, allied health, or business school. There are also a variety of services offered, such as a tutoring program called "The Study," where students get help from other students on a one-on-one basis. "Students at Creighton learn to enjoy the process, rather than just the product," says one. Both the teaching staff and administration are highly accessible; office hours don't seem to stop, and every Wednesday morning the much-loved president has breakfast with a different group of students to listen to their concerns and to talk about how life at Creighton is going. "At Creighton students come first, and it is as simple as that!" chirps a happy junior.

Life

"While academics are a huge part of our schooling, they are not all-encompassing," says a student. Community service happily takes up a lot of students' time, and there are fall break and spring break service trips all over the United States. Sports, both intercollegiate and intramural, are huge on and off campus; Omaha and the Old Market have plenty of music venues, bowling, shopping, and restaurants (a good thing, because the food at Creighton is universally despised and "needs to be improved drastically"). Students would like to see some more options for getting off campus, though; the difficulty and cost of living off campus means on-campus housing is in high demand. The Greek community at Creighton "is not as intense as at state schools," but students in sorority or fraternities hold many leadership positions on campus. Weeknights are mainly for studying, but house parties are available on weekends, and "the bar scene is where many students spend their nights off." The school and student government do an excellent job of providing plenty of activities that are enjoyed by all, such as ice skating, weekly movies, and "mock TV shows like the 'Price is Right,'" and no one has any problem with peer pressure. "It is very easy to be productive and involved but still be able to find time for fun," says a biology and Spanish major.

Student Body

The typical student is white and from the Midwest, and most are "outgoing and friendly," which is probably why atypical students have no problems fitting in. And the "old brick road that runs down the middle of campus (called the mall) provides excellent opportunities to meet new people." "It doesn't matter where you came from or why you're here" as "most students have the same values, which allows the community to feel connected." "Everyone is interconnected through someone; there are very few degrees of separation between individuals," says one student, though others claim that there's no shortage of cliques. Creighton students are incredibly balanced in their work and play and are "over-the-top involved" with activities and community service while maintaining full academic loads. The school is very involved in study abroad programs, so there are a fair number of international students in each class. "I've never been in a place where so many people will hold the door open for me to walk through, if that gives any indication of the type of student here," says a student.

FINANCIAL AID: 402-280-2731 • E-MAIL: ADMISSIONS@CREIGHTON.EDU • WEBSITE: WWW.ADMISSION.CREIGHTON.EDU

THE PRINCETON REVIEW SAYS

Admissions

Very important factors considered include: Academic GPA, rigor of secondary school record. *Important factors considered include:* Application essay, standardized test scores. *Other factors considered include:* Class rank, recommendation(s), character/personal qualities, extracurricular activities, first generation, level of applicant's interest, racial/ethnic status, talent/ability, volunteer work. SAT or ACT required; ACT with or without writing component accepted. TOEFL required of all international applicants. High school diploma is required, and GED is accepted. *Academic units required:* 4 English, 3 mathematics, 2 science, 2 foreign language, 2 social studies, 3 academic elective. *Academic units recommended:* 4 English, 4 mathematics, 3 science, 3 foreign language, 3 social studies, 1 history, 3 academic elective.

Financial Aid

Students should submit: FAFSA, institution's own financial aid form. The Princeton Review suggests that all financial aid forms be submitted as soon as possible after January 1. *Need-based scholarships/grants offered:* Federal Pell, SEOG, state scholarships/grants, private scholarships, school scholarship or grant aid from institutional funds. *Loan aid offered:* Federal Perkins, Federal Nursing Loans. Applicants will be notified of awards on a rolling basis beginning March 15. Federal Work-Study Program available. Off-campus job opportunities are excellent.

The Inside Word

Creighton's lack of name recognition and its location can handicap its search for quality students, occasionally forcing the school to lower the bar to fill its incoming classes, so the school's loss could well be your gain. For those comfortable in a Jesuit school, Creighton offers bright, hardworking students a great opportunity at a quality education.

THE SCHOOL SAYS "..."

From the Admissions Office

"Creighton is a leading national Jesuit Catholic university, offering sophisticated academic opportunities found normally at schools twice its size. Our reputation for diversity and educational excellence draws students from across the nation and around the world. Students find balance in rigorous academics, strong focus on leadership skills, abundant opportunities for internships and undergraduate research, and life-changing community service experiences. Creighton is committed to providing intellectual challenge, promoting critical thinking, and inspiring leadership and service to others with a faith-filled view of the world.

"With about 7,500 students (4,000 undergraduates); more than fifty undergraduate majors and twenty graduate and professional programs; our small, personal classes; accomplished faculty mentors; a wealth of internship opportunities; and a ninety-four percent job-placement rate within eight months of graduation, Creighton provides a perfect learning environment. With recognition from prestigious organizations such as the Fulbright Fellows and Goldwater Scholars and synergy among undergraduate, graduate, and professional faculty, it's not surprising that Creighton launches about half of its graduates into medical, dental, pharmacy, physical or occupational therapy, graduate, or law school—one of the highest rates in the country.

"Creighton's cutting-edge and highly ranked programs allow students to excel in a wide variety of areas both in and outside the classroom. From our location— within walking distance of five Fortune 500 company headquarters, providing more business internships than we have students to fill them—to our commitment to alternative energy through our Energy Technology major, to our direct entry top-ranked Nursing School, Creighton students succeed personally as well as professionally."

SELECTIVITY

Admissions Rating	88
# of applicants	4,752
% of applicants accepted	82
% of acceptees attending	27
# accepting a place on wait list	60
% admitted from wait list	30

FRESHMAN PROFILE

Range SAT Critical Reading	520–640
Range SAT Math	550–660
Range SAT Writing	510–630
Range ACT Composite	24–29
Minimum paper TOEFL	550
Minimum computer TOEFL	213
Average HS GPA	3.76
% graduated top 10% of class	44
% graduated top 25% of class	73
% graduated top 50% of class	95

DEADLINES

Regular	
Priority	12/1
Deadline	2/15
Notification	12/15
Nonfall registration?	yes

APPLICANTS ALSO LOOK AT

AND OFTEN PREFER
University of Missouri—Columbia, University of Notre Dame

AND SOMETIMES PREFER
Gonzaga University, Kansas State University, Marquette University, Saint Louis University, University of Colorado—Boulder, University of Kansas, University of Nebraska at Omaha

AND RARELY PREFER
Drake University, Iowa State University, University of Iowa, University of Minnesota—Twin Cities, University of Nebraska-Lincoln, University of Saint Thomas (MN)

FINANCIAL FACTS

Financial Aid Rating	87
Annual tuition	$29,226
Room and board	$9,164
% frosh rec. need-based scholarship or grant aid	67
% UG rec. need-based scholarship or grant aid	51
% frosh rec. non-need-based scholarship or grant aid	92
% UG rec. non-need-based scholarship or grant aid	87
% frosh rec. need-based self-help aid	51
% UG rec. need-based self-help aid	42
% frosh rec. any financial aid	96
% UG rec. any financial aid	82
% UG borrow to pay for school	67
Average cumulative indebtedness	$32,152

DARTMOUTH COLLEGE

6016 McNUTT HALL, HANOVER, NH 03755 • ADMISSIONS: 603-646-2875 • FAX: 603-646-1216

CAMPUS LIFE

Quality of Life Rating	98
Fire Safety Rating	60*
Green Rating	94
Type of school	private
Environment	village

STUDENTS

Total undergrad enrollment	4,135
% male/female	50/50
% from out of state	95
% from public high school	62
% live on campus	87
# of fraternities	14
# of sororities	6
% African American	8
% Asian	15
% Caucasian	50
% Hispanic	8
% Native American	3
% international	7
# of countries represented	78

SURVEY SAYS . . .

Great computer facilities
School is well-run
Campus feels safe
Frats and sororities dominate
social scene
Student publications are popular
Lots of beer drinking

ACADEMICS

Academic Rating	96
% students graduating within 4 years	88
% students graduating within 6 years	95
Calendar	quarter
Student/faculty ratio	8:1
Profs interesting rating	86
Profs accessible rating	90
Most common reg class size	10–19 students

MOST POPULAR MAJORS

economics, political science, psychology

STUDENTS SAY ". . ."

Academics

Dartmouth College is an intellectual amusement park, a place where academic and extracurricular life intertwine to create "a tight-knit community dedicated to scholarship, creativity, intellectualism, and the well-rounded individual." While "academic interests vary widely" across campus, the school's "interdisciplinary approach...allows students from all different majors to be able to engage in analytical discussions on issues from the depiction of women and gender roles in science fiction, to the marginalization of the bottom billion in the international political economy, to nostalgia resulting from rural to urban relocation in the age of globalization." Central to this approach is the D-Plan, Dartmouth's quarterly academic calendar "where students take about three classes at a time for ten weeks." Students love it, telling us, "It gives you great flexibility to go abroad and secure fantastic off-term internships and volunteer opportunities." Students typically take advantage of the opportunities; as one explains, "Dartmouth is really big on the 'Dartmouth experience,' which basically means trying to do the most awesome things that you can fit into four years as an undergrad. This means that about two-thirds of undergrads, regardless of major, study abroad at least once. Everyone uses their 'off terms' to either try to save the world by volunteering or doing research if they're not doing some high-profile internship."

Life

Life at Dartmouth "is always busy...after attending classes in the morning, we run from meetings to debates to the library and finally to Frat Row. It is a relentless, fast-paced cycle, but it is so unbelievably fun and rewarding." "Greek life dominates" the Dartmouth campus, where student involvement in the Greek system approaches a whopping fifty percent, although one student notes that "once you get to know the Greek scene, it becomes apparent that it's unique and very welcoming and much more low key than at other schools." For those wondering, "Yes, Dartmouth is the school upon which Animal House was based... we do party a lot, but the mentality is definitely work hard, play hard." Dartmouth has an active drama and dance scene, and "a capella is particularly popular." Students like to stay active: "We throw a Frisbee on the green, hike through the mountains, play hockey on Occom Pond, play tennis, ski at the Skiway," and "sled on cafeteria trays" to burn off extra energy. "A strong sense of school spirit" is fueled by the college's "rich traditions," like "running around a giant bonfire hundreds of times." No matter what they're into, "no one leaves campus on weekends because no one wants to miss a weekend at Dartmouth."

Student Body

The quintessential Dartmouth undergraduate is "athletic, sociable, and very active within the community inside and outside of Dartmouth." "The binding element of the typical Dartmouth student is passion," one student tells us. "Whether it is academics or the environment, students are committed to an area of interest and try to contribute to that field." "There is a ton of diversity," one undergrad reports. "Through my friends I can interact and get a taste of Ghana, Trinidad, and Japan; what it means to be a Sikh, Jew, Buddhist, or Christian; how it feels to be a homosexual or transsexual; what it's like to live below the poverty line or miles above it." Wonder what they all share in common? "Everyone here is exceptional."

FINANCIAL AID: 603-646-2451 • E-MAIL: ADMISSIONS.OFFICE@DARTMOUTH.EDU • WEBSITE: WWW.DARTMOUTH.EDU

THE PRINCETON REVIEW SAYS

Admissions

Very important factors considered include: Academic GPA, application essay, class rank, recommendation(s), rigor of secondary school record, standardized test scores, character/personal qualities, extracurricular activities. *Important factors considered include:* Talent/ability, volunteer work. *Other factors considered include:* Alumni/ae relation, first generation, geographical residence, interview, racial/ethnic status. SAT or ACT required; ACT with writing component required. TOEFL required of all international applicants. High school diploma or equivalent isn't required. *Academic units recommended:* 4 English, 4 mathematics, 4 science, 3 social studies, 3 history.

Financial Aid

Students should submit: FAFSA, CSS/Financial Aid PROFILE. Regular filing deadline is February 1. The Princeton Review suggests that all financial aid forms be submitted as soon as possible after January 1. *Need-based scholarships/grants offered:* Federal Pell, SEOG, state scholarships/grants, private scholarships, school scholarship or grant aid from institutional funds. *Loan aid offered:* Direct Subsidized Stafford, Direct Unsubsidized Stafford, Direct PLUS, Federal Perkins, university loans from institutional funds. Applicants will be notified of awards on a rolling basis beginning when admission decisions are issued. Federal Work-Study Program available. Off-campus job opportunities are excellent.

The Inside Word

Dartmouth doesn't have any problem attracting qualified applicants. On the contrary, this elite institution receives many, many more applications from fully qualified hopefuls than the school can possibly accommodate. As a result, many students who meet all the qualifications to attend Dartmouth are turned away every year because there simply isn't room for them. Dartmouth reviews applications holistically, meaning your best shot is to compile an application that paints a compelling portrait. Some special talent, life experience, or personal trait may be your ticket in, if Dartmouth thinks it will enhance the education of your classmates.

THE SCHOOL SAYS "..."

From the Admissions Office

"'Do something great, be ambitious, and aspire to change the world.' This advice comes from Dr. Jim Yong Kim, who is the President of Dartmouth College and also an internationally recognized physician and humanitarian who founded Partners in Health and served as the Director of the Department of HIV/AIDS at the World Health Organization.

"With its focus on undergraduate education and a flexible year-round academic calendar that encourages travel and research, Dartmouth is uniquely positioned to help students pursue their interests, prepare for a career and make an impact on the world. All classes are taught by members of the faculty, over 1,000 students per year pursue independent study for credit, and almost two-thirds of students participate in study abroad programs. On campus, students participate in nearly 400 student organizations, including thirty-four intercollegiate varsity teams, over forty different community service projects, and more than fifty performing groups. Dartmouth's hometown of Hanover offers an active political scene, a vibrant arts community, and unparalleled outdoors and recreational opportunities (including our own ski mountain!).

"To help all Dartmouth students take advantage of the Dartmouth Experience, the college practices need-blind admission for all applicants, meets the full demonstrated need for all admitted students, and offers free tuition and no loan requirements for all students whose annual family incomes are below $75,000.

"Dartmouth's admissions process is designed to identify students who will thrive in a challenging and flexible academic environment, who value community, and who will take advantage of the college's undergraduate focus."

SELECTIVITY

Admissions Rating	96
# of applicants	18,778
% of applicants accepted	12
% of acceptees attending	52
# accepting a place on wait list	1,027
% admitted from wait list	23
# of early decision applicants	1,574
% accepted early decision	29

FRESHMAN PROFILE

Range SAT Critical Reading	670–780
Range SAT Math	690–790
Range SAT Writing	690–790
Range ACT Composite	30–34
Minimum paper TOEFL	550
Minimum computer TOEFL	213
Minimum web-based TOEFL	79
% graduated top 10% of class	90
% graduated top 50% of class	100

DEADLINES

Early decision	
Deadline	11/1
Notification	12/15
Regular	
Deadline	1/1
Nonfall registration?	no

FINANCIAL FACTS

Financial Aid Rating	96
Annual tuition	$38,445
Room and board	$11,295
Required fees	$344
Books and supplies	$1,618
% frosh rec. need-based scholarship or grant aid	48
% UG rec. need-based scholarship or grant aid	51
% frosh rec. need-based self-help aid	40
% UG rec. need-based self-help aid	47
% frosh rec. any financial aid	50
% UG rec. any financial aid	52
% UG borrow to pay for school	48
Average cumulative indebtedness	$19,051

DAVIDSON COLLEGE

PO Box 7156, Davidson, NC 28035-7156 • Admissions: 704-894-2230 • Fax: 704-894-2016

CAMPUS LIFE

Quality of Life Rating	99
Fire Safety Rating	60*
Green Rating	60*
Type of school	private
Affiliation	Presbyterian
Environment	village

STUDENTS

Total undergrad enrollment	1,738
% male/female	50/50
% from out of state	74
% from public high school	51
% live on campus	91
# of fraternities	8
% African American	7
% Asian	5
% Caucasian	72
% Hispanic	5
% international	4
# of countries represented	36

SURVEY SAYS . . .

No one cheats
Lab facilities are great
Great computer facilities
School is well-run
Students are friendly
Students get along with local
community
Campus feels safe

ACADEMICS

Academic Rating	98
% students graduating within 4 years	89
% students graduating within 6 years	91
Calendar	semester
Student/faculty ratio	10:1
Profs interesting rating	96
Profs accessible rating	99
Most common reg class size	10–19 students
Most common lab size	10–19 students

MOST POPULAR MAJORS
biology, English language and
literature, history

STUDENTS SAY ". . ."

Academics
This small school north of Charlotte, North Carolina, cultivates an environment "that is very open to change and improvement" and empowers students to "be better people and make a difference in the world." The administration works hard to create an on-campus community and constantly makes efforts "to support and improve Davidson," all while keeping students happy and minds full. "I have never witnessed people so eager to come do their job every day. [Professors] are almost too willing to help," says a student. There is also a trickle-down effect because even the student body is supportive and "eager to watch you succeed." The school offers a classic liberal arts education, encouraging students to take classes in all areas, and "all of these people come out smarter than they came in." "If I could spend twenty years being educated by this administration and these professors, I would," says a very happy junior. School is the number one priority for all of the students here, and while academics are all-consuming, time-wise, they are also "fascinating and rewarding." Without a doubt, Davidson is a tough school—"ninety-nine percent of us left our 4.0 GPAs back in high school," claims a student—and professors don't believe in grade inflation or curving grades, but they do readily make themselves available outside of class for help or discussion. There is a lot of work, but it "is accompanied by even more resources with which it can be successfully managed." One student testimonial: "My calculus teacher last semester has office hours in the student union, and he invited the whole class over to his house for chicken dinner—twice!" The dedication of the staff is contagious, and "though the work is rigorous, time spent in school never feels wasted."

Life
Davidson "possesses an intense study culture, and people hit the books regularly; it's cool to be smart." One of the many wonderful things about Davidson "is that academics voluntarily leave the classroom." "It's not uncommon to hear people discussing their current academic topics at lunch or in the gym." Basketball is a huge common ground for the student body at large; "Everyone enjoys being a part of the underdog/Cinderella story." Weeks are devoted to study, as well as extracurricular activities—"you see your friends because you are doing homework together or eating meals together, not because you're vegging out." Of course, even Davidson students need to kick back, and there are always plenty of parties to be found on the weekends. Fraternities and eating houses (the Davidson version of sororities) are popular. Fortunately, "There really is no pressure to drink. You can go out and dance and have a great time or have movie nights with friends," says a student. The combination of the idyllic atmosphere and the workload "can make it hard to stay up-to-date on current events, yet most students remain well-informed."

Student Body
Davidson is "an amalgamation of all types of people, religiously, ethnically, politically, economically, etc.," all "united under the umbrella of intellectual curiosity" and their devotion to the school as a community. The typical Davidson student is "probably white," but in the past few years, admissions has been making progress in racially diversifying the campus, which students agree upon as necessary. Though there are plenty of Southern, preppy, athletic types to fit the brochure examples, there are many niches for every type of "atypical" student. "There are enough people that one can find a similar group to connect with, and there are few enough people that one ends up connecting with dissimilar [people] anyway," says a student. Everyone here is smart and well-rounded; admissions "does a good job...so if you're in you'll probably make the cut all the way through the four years." Most students have several extracurriculars to round out their free time, and they have a healthy desire to enjoy themselves when the books shut. "During the week we work hard. On the weekends we play hard. We don't do anything halfway," says a senior. Though the majority of students lean to the left, there's a strong conservative contingent, and there are no real problems between the two.

FINANCIAL AID: 704-894-2232 • E-MAIL: ADMISSION@DAVIDSON.EDU • WEBSITE: WWW.DAVIDSON.EDU

THE PRINCETON REVIEW SAYS

Admissions

Very important factors considered include: Recommendation(s), rigor of secondary school record, character/personal qualities, volunteer work. *Important factors considered include:* Application essay, standardized test scores, extracurricular activities, interview, talent/ability. *Other factors considered include:* Academic GPA, class rank, alumni/ae relation. SAT or ACT required; ACT with or without writing component accepted. TOEFL required of all international applicants. *Academic units required:* 4 English, 3 mathematics, 2 science, 2 foreign language. *Academic units recommended:* 4 mathematics, 4 science, 4 foreign language.

Financial Aid

Students should submit: FAFSA, CSS/Financial Aid PROFILE. Regular filing deadline is February 15. The Princeton Review suggests that all financial aid forms be submitted as soon as possible after January 1. *Need-based scholarships/grants offered:* Federal Pell, SEOG, state scholarships/grants, private scholarships, school scholarship or grant aid from institutional funds. *Loan aid offered:* Direct Subsidized Stafford, Direct Unsubsidized Stafford, Direct PLUS. Federal Work-Study Program available. Off-campus job opportunities are excellent.

The Inside Word

The combination of Davidson's low acceptance rate and high yield really packs a punch. Prospective applicants beware: Securing admission at this prestigious school is no easy feat. Admitted students are typically at the top of their high school classes and have strong standardized test scores. Candidates with leadership experience generally garner the favor of admissions officers. The college takes its honor code seriously and, as a result, seeks out students of demonstrated reputable character.

THE SCHOOL SAYS "..."

From the Admissions Office

"Davidson College is one of the nation's premier academic institutions, a college of the liberal arts and sciences respected for its intellectual vigor, the high quality of its faculty and students, and the achievements of its alumni. Davidson is distinguished by its strong honor code, close collaboration between professors and students, an environment that encourages both intellectual growth and community service, and a commitment to international education. Davidson places great value on student participation in extracurricular activities, intercollegiate athletics, and intramural sports. The college has a strong regional identity, grounded in traditions of civility and mutual respect, and has historic ties to the Presbyterian Church. The college has a strong commitment to making a Davidson education affordable. The college doesn't include student loans in its financial aid packages. Through the Davidson Trust, 100 percent of demonstrated financial need will be met with a combination of grants and student employment.

"Applicants are required to complete and submit scores from the SAT and/or the ACT. SAT Subject Tests (mathematics and one of your choice) are recommended. Davidson will utilize the scores that place the student in the greatest possible light."

SELECTIVITY
Admissions Rating	98
# of applicants	4,088
% of applicants accepted	29
% of acceptees attending	41
# of early decision applicants	425
% accepted early decision	58

FRESHMAN PROFILE
Range SAT Critical Reading	630–720
Range SAT Math	630–710
Range SAT Writing	620–720
Range ACT Composite	28–32
Minimum paper TOEFL	600
Minimum computer TOEFL	250
Average HS GPA	4.00
% graduated top 10% of class	78
% graduated top 25% of class	95
% graduated top 50% of class	100

DEADLINES
Early decision	
Deadline	11/15
Notification	12/15
Regular	
Deadline	1/2
Nonfall registration?	no

FINANCIAL FACTS
Financial Aid Rating	98
Annual tuition	$38,866
Room and board	$10,917
% frosh rec. need-based scholarship or grant aid	42
% UG rec. need-based scholarship or grant aid	41
% frosh rec. non-need-based scholarship or grant aid	18
% UG rec. non-need-based scholarship or grant aid	17
% frosh rec. need-based self-help aid	23
% UG rec. need-based self-help aid	21
% frosh rec. any financial aid	35
% UG rec. any financial aid	35
% UG borrow to pay for school	32
Average cumulative indebtedness	$23,233

DEEP SPRINGS COLLEGE

HC 72 Box 45001, Deep Springs, CA via Dyer, NV 89010-9803 • Admissions: 760-872-2000 • Fax: 760-872-4466

CAMPUS LIFE

Quality of Life Rating	93
Fire Safety Rating	82
Green Rating	60*
Type of school	private
Environment	rural

STUDENTS

Total undergrad enrollment	26
% male/female	100/0
% from out of state	80
% from public high school	50
% live on campus	100
# of countries represented	3

SURVEY SAYS . . .

Lots of liberal students
Class discussions encouraged
Great food on campus
Dorms are like palaces
Low cost of living
Intercollegiate sports are unpopular
or nonexistent
Frats and sororities are unpopular
or nonexistent
Very little beer drinking
Very little hard liquor
Very little drug use

ACADEMICS

Academic Rating	99
Calendar	semester
Student/faculty ratio	14:1
Profs interesting rating	93
Profs accessible rating	99
Most common	
reg class size	fewer than 10 students

MOST POPULAR MAJORS
liberal arts and sciences

STUDENTS SAY ". . ."

Academics

The "three pillars" of a Deep Springs education—"labor, academics, and self-governance"—combine to produce "unparalleled challenges" that run the gamut "from fixing a hay baler in the middle of the night to puzzling over a particularly difficult passage of Hegel." That's what the twenty-six men who attend Deep Springs tell us. These unique undergraduates basically run their own school, work the ranch where it is located, and complete a rigorous curriculum, an itinerary that "creates an environment of intense growth and responsibility." Class work occurs in a seminar format in which "the distinction between teacher and student becomes fuzzy [because] everyone is equally invested, thoughtful, and engaged." Composition and public speaking are the only required courses; all others are chosen by the student body and taught by a faculty of three long-term professors (one each in the humanities, social sciences, and natural sciences) and three visiting scholars or artists. The system relies on a commitment to self-determination, which means "the smoothness with which many programs run depends largely on the kind of responsibility students take. Sometimes students do a good job taking care of administrative tasks, sometimes a worse job. It's all part of the educational experience." While the size of the school inevitably means that "lab and library facilities are not what they might be," students tell us that the overall Deep Springs experience compensates for any shortcomings. As one student explains, "through intense academics and running the college administratively and practically, we receive an unprecedented education in citizenship of a conscious human being."

Life

Deep Springs is totally unlike other colleges in terms of the everyday life of a student," because "no one drinks, everyone helps run the ranch in some way, and no one can be totally self-absorbed (unless he's out hiking in the desert)." Instead, students immerse themselves in the Deep Springs way. As one student explains, "The Deep Springs program is our whole life. The intellectual questions we're asking and the labor we're doing is all bound up with our identity." Students spend their free time "thinking about intellectual things: moral issues, politics, and the community. 'Fun' is hard to come by, and one has to learn how to enjoy people, work, and engagement." Students do occasionally take a break, however; "On weekends in the rumpus room of the dorm, you can find a group of motley adventurers engaged in a Dungeons & Dragon's quest or a pack of students watching 'Gossip Girl.' You'll find even more people scoffing at such pedantry and watching arty French movies," and "communal soccer is excellent…we even play in the snow." Also, occasionally "We have dance parties called 'boojies,'" and "We do some other strange things for fun, like sledding naked down 800-foot-tall sand dunes in neighboring Eureka Valley." Undergrads concede that Deep Springs "life can be intense. Students usually are utterly exhausted. But most of the time we know that something good is coming out of this," and that keeps undergrads energized and motivated.

Student Body

"Having only twenty-six students makes it even harder to characterize the 'typical' Deep Springer," students understandably warn, but they add that "we're all very able and driven, but in our own ways, not in the way that most Ivy League students are. Deep Springs isn't a stepping stone to the world of white-collar work but an end in itself that we all pursue with all our hearts. So I guess the typical student has a healthy disgust for the pedagogy of most other universities." Undergrads are also predictably "intelligent, motivated, and responsible," as they "must demonstrate depth of thought to be accepted" to the school. As one student puts it, "The typical student at Deep Springs is committed to the life of the intellect and committed to finding education in our labor program. Most of the students here believe that a life of service, informed by discourse and labor, is a necessary notion to understand in today's world."

DEEP SPRINGS COLLEGE

FINANCIAL AID: 760-872-2000 • E-MAIL: APCOM@DEEPSPRING.EDU • WEBSITE: WWW.DEEPSPRINGS.EDU

THE PRINCETON REVIEW SAYS

Admissions

Very important factors considered include: Application essay, character/personal qualities, interview, level of applicant's interest. *Important factors considered include:* Academic GPA, rigor of secondary school record, extracurricular activities, volunteer work, work experience. *Other factors considered include:* Class rank, recommendation(s), standardized test scores, racial/ethnic status, talent/ability. SAT or ACT required. High school diploma or equivalent isn't required.

Financial Aid

The Princeton Review suggests that all financial aid forms be submitted as soon as possible after January 1. All students receive a full scholarship worth more than $50,000. Federal Work-Study Program not available.

The Inside Word

Students will be hard-pressed to find a school with a more personal or thorough application process than Deep Springs. Given the intimate and collegial atmosphere of the school, matchmaking is the top priority. Candidates are evaluated by a body composed of students, faculty, and staff members. The application is writing intensive; finalists are expected to spend several days on campus, during which they will undergo a lengthy interview.

THE SCHOOL SAYS "..."

From the Admissions Office

"Founded in 1917, Deep Springs College lies isolated in a high desert valley of eastern California, thirty miles from the nearest town. Its enrollment is limited to twenty-six students, each of whom receives a full scholarship that covers tuition and room and board, and is valued at more than $50,000 per year. Students engage in rigorous academics, govern themselves, and participate in the operation of our cattle and alfalfa ranch. After two years, students generally transfer to other schools to complete their studies. Students regularly transfer to Harvard, The University of Chicago, and Brown, but also choose Cornell, Columbia, Stanford, Swarthmore, University of California—Berkeley, and Yale.

In the past five years Deep Springers have won the following national scholarship competitions:

- The Jack Kent Cooke Scholarship (2)

- The Barry M. Goldwater Scholarship (1)

- The Rhodes Scholarship (1)

- The Harry S. Truman Scholarship (5)

- The Morris Udall Scholarship (1)"

SELECTIVITY

Admissions Rating	99
# of applicants	170
% of applicants accepted	7
% of acceptees attending	92
# accepting a place on wait list	3
% admitted from wait list	0

FRESHMAN PROFILE

Range SAT Critical Reading	750–800
Range SAT Math	700–800
% graduated top 10% of class	86
% graduated top 25% of class	93
% graduated top 50% of class	100

DEADLINES

Regular	
Deadline	11/15
Nonfall registration?	no

APPLICANTS ALSO LOOK AT AND RARELY PREFER

Harvard College, Swarthmore College, University of Chicago

FINANCIAL FACTS

Financial Aid Rating	60*
Annual comprehensive tuition	$50,000
Books and supplies	$1,200
% frosh rec. any financial aid	100
% UG rec. any financial aid	100

DENISON UNIVERSITY

BOX 740, GRANVILLE, OH 43023 • ADMISSIONS: 740-587-6276 • FAX: 740-587-6306

STUDENTS SAY ". . ."

Academics
Students describe Denison University as "a mecca of top-notch academics" located "in the seclusion of rural Ohio." By necessity Denison University may be "huge on community," but regardless of the impetus, students, faculty, and administrators here "become like a big family where everyone takes care of one another." Students agree that that's a good thing, as this environment provides "academically motivated students a chance to excel in their respective studies through a supportive student population and dedicated faculty, while also providing many social opportunities." Denison is "all about educating the whole student, whether it be through classes, speakers, sports, clubs, or even Greek life." Academically, Denison can be "challenging." "It is possible to spend an entire semester stressed out to the extreme with twenty-plus academic credits and no time to do the readings for every class. But it is also very possible to manage your time well and get everything done in a mannerly fashion, without overexerting yourself, but still having a successful and productive semester." Students who find themselves in over their heads can count on "professors who are willing to go the extra mile with their students." Professors "have organized study groups before exams and extend their office hours so that you can meet with them about a paper or project." As one student observes, "It's your own fault if you do poorly, because there are so many ways for you to get help through teachers, study groups, tutoring, etc."

Life
"What is nice about Denison is that most people stay on campus during the weekends, so there is always something to do," students here report. The school and the Student Activities Committee "always sponsor concerts, speakers, and events around campus," and, of course, there is always a party or two available on the weekends. "There is so much to do all week, every week," which "is somewhat necessary, as the town of Granville is quite small and offers few diversions." A party scene "is available if that's what you want," and quite a few students do, telling us that "go-out-and-party nights" are Fridays and Saturdays and "Mondays and Wednesdays also, since some students have fewer classes on Tuesdays and Thursdays." Greek life encompasses about thirty percent of the student body. Denison has "a number of sports teams that are nationally ranked," but students are just as likely to follow OSU as Denison. While hometown Granville is "small" and "very quiet," Columbus "is only thirty minutes away, which allows [students] to visit other restaurants, bars, concerts, and, of course, big sister OSU." Easton "is just twenty-five minutes away and has a huge shopping center."

Student Body
While "There are not a lot of atypical students on the extreme ends of 'different'" at Denison, students hasten to point out that "Denison does not solely consist of popped collars and Uggs. Those students just like to make themselves known." There are "a lot of athletes on campus, and fraternities and sororities are pretty big." "Kids are hardworking and usually friendly." Also, Denison is not without its "internationals, artsy types, and [even] the socially awkward." There's "even a small counterculture made up of environmentalists and hippies who live at the Homestead and hang out at Bandersnatch." These people "are the minority, but there's a niche for them." As one student explains, "It's pretty easy to find a core group of friends."

DENISON UNIVERSITY

FINANCIAL AID: 740-587-6279 • E-MAIL: ADMISSIONS@DENISON.EDU • WEBSITE: WWW.DENISON.EDU

THE PRINCETON REVIEW SAYS

Admissions

Very important factors considered include: Academic GPA, application essay, recommendation(s), rigor of secondary school record. *Important factors considered include:* Extracurricular activities, interview, level of applicant's interest, talent/ability. *Other factors considered include:* Class rank, standardized test scores, alumni/ae relation, character/personal qualities, first generation, geographical residence, racial/ethnic status, state residency, volunteer work, work experience. ACT with or without writing component accepted. TOEFL required of all international applicants. High school diploma is required, and GED is accepted. *Academic units required:* 4 English, 4 mathematics, 4 science, 3 foreign language, 2 social studies, 1 history, 1 academic elective.

Financial Aid

Students should submit: FAFSA. The Princeton Review suggests that all financial aid forms be submitted as soon as possible after January 1. *Need-based scholarships/grants offered:* Federal Pell, SEOG, state scholarships/grants, private scholarships, school scholarship or grant aid from institutional funds. *Loan aid offered:* Direct Subsidized Stafford, Direct Unsubsidized Stafford, Direct PLUS, Federal Perkins, university loans from institutional funds. Federal Work-Study Program available. Off-campus job opportunities are fair.

The Inside Word

Admission to Denison is pretty straightforward. The school "suggests" an interview, meaning you should do one if at all possible. It's a great way to demonstrate your interest in the school, which improves your chances of admission, especially if your grades, test scores, and overall profile put you on the admit/reject borderline.

THE SCHOOL SAYS "..."

From the Admissions Office

"Denison is a college that can point with pride to its success in enrolling and retaining intellectually motivated, diverse, and well-balanced students who are being taught to become effective leaders in the twenty-first century. This year, over fifty percent of our first-year students were in the top ten percent of their high school graduating class; their SAT scores average 1300, twenty-five percent of the incoming class is students of color or international; and a large percentage of our student body is receiving some type of financial assistance. Our First-Year Program focuses on helping students make a successful transition from high school to college, and the small classes and accessibility of faculty assure students the opportunity to interact closely with their professors and fellow students. We care about our students, and the loyalty of our 28,000 alumni proves that the Denison experience is one that lasts for a lifetime.

"Denison operates under a 'test optional' admissions policy."

SELECTIVITY

Admissions Rating	94
# of applicants	4,723
% of applicants accepted	49
% of acceptees attending	27
# accepting a place on wait list	306
% admitted from wait list	11
# of early decision applicants	164
% accepted early decision	83

FRESHMAN PROFILE

Range SAT Critical Reading	600–700
Range SAT Math	590–680
Range ACT Composite	27–30
Minimum paper TOEFL	550
Minimum computer TOEFL	213
Average HS GPA	3.50
% graduated top 10% of class	49
% graduated top 25% of class	90
% graduated top 50% of class	100

DEADLINES

Early decision I	
Deadline	11/15
Notification	rolling
Early decision II	
Deadline	1/15
Notification	rolling
Regular	
Deadline	1/15
Nonfall registration?	no

APPLICANTS ALSO LOOK AT

AND OFTEN PREFER
Oberlin College, University of Richmond

AND SOMETIMES PREFER
College of Wooster, DePauw University, Eion University, Hobart William Smith Colleges, Miami University—Ohio

AND RARELY PREFER
Allegheny College, Case Western Reserve University, DePauw University, Dickinson College, Franklin & Marshall College, Ohio Wesleyan University, The Ohio State University—Columbus, University of Vermont

FINANCIAL FACTS

Financial Aid Rating	89
Annual tuition	$39,330
Room and board	$9,960
Required fees	$880
% frosh rec. need-based scholarship or grant aid	53
% UG rec. need-based scholarship or grant aid	49
% frosh rec. non-need-based scholarship or grant aid	48
% UG rec. non-need-based scholarship or grant aid	40
% frosh rec. need-based self-help aid	40
% UG rec. need-based self-help aid	38
% frosh rec. any financial aid	95
% UG rec. any financial aid	94
% UG borrow to pay for school	42
Average cumulative indebtedness	$16,258

DePaul University

ONE EAST JACKSON BOULEVARD, CHICAGO, IL 60604-2287 • ADMISSIONS: 312-362-8300 • FAX: 312-362-5749

CAMPUS LIFE

Quality of Life Rating	94
Fire Safety Rating	98
Green Rating	88
Type of school	private
Affiliation	Roman Catholic
Environment	metropolis

STUDENTS

Total undergrad enrollment	15,801
% male/female	45/55
% from out of state	16
% from public high school	89
% live on campus	16
# of fraternities	9
# of sororities	13
% African American	9
% Asian	8
% Caucasian	55
% Hispanic	15
% international	1
# of countries represented	101

SURVEY SAYS . . .
Athletic facilities are great
Diverse student types on campus
Students love Chicago, IL
Great off-campus food
Low cost of living

ACADEMICS

Academic Rating	78
% students graduating within 4 years	48
% students graduating within 6 years	68
Calendar	quarter
Student/faculty ratio	17:1
Profs interesting rating	83
Profs accessible rating	84
Most common reg class size	20–29 students
Most common lab size	10–19 students

MOST POPULAR MAJORS
accounting, humanities, psychology

STUDENTS SAY ". . ."

Academics
The mission at this "very city-school structured" university located in Chicago is about Vincentian values in an urban setting. Whether encouraging its students to help those less fortunate (there's a strong "commitment to social justice and community service") or cheering on its always-solid basketball team, DePaul University is "about diversity and real-world experience" instead of books and tests. This message is even further carried out by the leanings of the teachers, the majority of whom "are not strictly academics—they have a great deal of applicable experience." Though students report a few bad apples in the teaching lot, most students enjoy their classes (many account for student discussion as part of the grade) and teachers on the whole and say it "is easy to get in touch with professors outside of the classroom." "Professors not only have open-door policies but do everything but make candy trails into their offices," says a student.

There are multiple colleges within the university, so there are plenty of opportunities for student leadership for studies within your field, but students do cite red tape issues when trying to maneuver between colleges. The administration here is "sometimes annoying," and it is "very slow to solve problems and not empathetic when registration errors are made." Still, "the study spectrum is huge," so "you'll find what you want to do here." "All of my classes are challenging and force me to work harder than I may want to, but they are never overbearing to the point where I give up," says a sophomore. Music education and the honors programs are some of the school's stronger programs.

Life
Just like the school itself, the students embrace Chicago for all it's worth and actively try to both help and patronize the community. "There are so many plays, galleries, museums, restaurants, clubs, bars, and stores that life is always interesting," says a student, adding to a list that already includes "improv/comedy shows, Broadway in Chicago, the beach, and Wrigley & Lakeside." Life at DePaul can differ depending on what campus you use—The Loop or Lincoln Park. The LPC provides "a more classical college environment and sense of community," while The Loop gives more of "a city-school feel." DePaul itself hosts many events for students, and though students are pleased overall with the variety of extracurriculars offered, they say that "more advertising for clubs, sports, organizations, etc., would be helpful," especially for the commuters. The food on campus may be "atrocious," but the nightlife is "great" at DePaul; many students go out to the bars in Lincoln Park, but are careful to avoid the school's feared "three-strike rule." There are also many students who choose" to just hang out and watch movies, go for dinner, and don't drink." "There is always something happening in this city," says a student. Depaul also offers a good chance to get a job on campus, which not only allows students to make money, but "you can often find something that relates to your major and would look good on your resume."

Student Body
Students here "know how to balance a social life with their academic life," which is generally a difficult thing to do in a big city. Beyond that commonality, students really span the spectrum of personal and ethnic diversity. "There are your frat boys who live to party and your book worms who never leave the dorm," but everyone eventually settles into their own and "seems to be able to find at least one other person they can start a conversation with." The school is "definitely very open-minded and liberal, despite being religiously affiliated." Many students live off campus; a fair number are from the suburbs, so a lot of them go home each weekend. There's a large LBGT population at DePaul, which is very well accepted, and people are "very aware of domestic and foreign affairs."

FINANCIAL AID: 312-362-8091 • E-MAIL: ADMITDPU@DEPAUL.EDU • WEBSITE: WWW.DEPAUL.EDU

THE PRINCETON REVIEW SAYS

Admissions

Very important factors considered include: Academic GPA, application essay, rigor of secondary school record, standardized test scores. *Important factors considered include:* Class rank, recommendation(s), character/personal qualities, extracurricular activities, level of applicant's interest, talent/ability, volunteer work, work experience. *Other factors considered include:* Alumni/ae relation, first generation, geographical residence, interview, racial/ethnic status, religious affiliation/commitment, state residency. SAT or ACT required; ACT with or without writing component accepted. TOEFL required of all international applicants. High school diploma is required, and GED is accepted. *Academic units required:* 4 English, 3 mathematics, 3 science (2 science labs). *Academic units recommended:* 2 foreign language.

Financial Aid

Students should submit: FAFSA. The Princeton Review suggests that all financial aid forms be submitted as soon as possible after January 1. *Need-based scholarships/grants offered:* Federal Pell, SEOG, state scholarships/grants, private scholarships, school scholarship or grant aid from institutional funds. *Loan aid offered:* Direct Subsidized Stafford, Direct Unsubsidized Stafford, Direct PLUS, Federal Perkins. Applicants will be notified of awards on a rolling basis beginning March 15. Federal Work-Study Program available. Off-campus job opportunities are excellent.

The Inside Word

DePaul has earned its reputation as one of the most diverse campuses in the United States. The school courts minority students not only as freshmen but also as transfers. It recognizes that its tuition is beyond the means of many (even with financial aid), so it works with area community colleges to allow students to fulfill requirements at a lower cost before completing their degrees at DePaul.

THE SCHOOL SAYS "..."

From the Admissions Office

"The nation's largest Catholic university, DePaul University is nationally recognized for its innovative academic programs that embrace a comprehensive learn-by-doing approach. DePaul has two residential campuses and four commuter campuses in the suburbs. The Lincoln Park campus is located in one of Chicago's most exciting neighborhoods, filled with theaters, cafés, clubs, and shops. It is home to DePaul's College of Liberal Arts and Sciences, the School of Education, the Theater School, and the School of Music. New buildings on the thirty-six-acre campus include residence halls, a science building, a student recreational facility, and the student center, which features a café where students can gather with friends. The Loop campus, located in Chicago's downtown—a world-class center for business, government, law, and culture—is home to DePaul's College of Commerce; College of Law; School of Computer Science, Telecommunications, and Information Systems; School for New Learning; and School of Accountancy and Management Information Systems.

"Applicants are required to take either the ACT or the SAT. The writing test on the ACT and the writing section on the SAT are not required for admission consideration."

SELECTIVITY

Admissions Rating	81
# of applicants	12,031
% of applicants accepted	69
% of acceptees attending	27
# accepting a place on wait list	0

FRESHMAN PROFILE

Range SAT Critical Reading	530–650
Range SAT Math	520–620
Range SAT Writing	520–630
Range ACT Composite	22–27
Minimum paper TOEFL	550
Minimum computer TOEFL	213
Minimum web-based TOEFL	80
Average HS GPA	3.46
% graduated top 10% of class	24
% graduated top 25% of class	55
% graduated top 50% of class	87

DEADLINES

Early action	
Deadline	11/15
Notification	1/15
Regular	
Priority	11/15
Deadline	2/1
Nonfall registration?	yes

FINANCIAL FACTS

Financial Aid Rating	67
Annual tuition	$28,240
Room and board	$10,955
Required fees	$618
Books and supplies	$1,134
% frosh rec. need-based scholarship or grant aid	64
% UG rec. need-based scholarship or grant aid	56
% frosh rec. non-need-based scholarship or grant aid	45
% UG rec. non-need-based scholarship or grant aid	27
% frosh rec. need-based self-help aid	54
% UG rec. need-based self-help aid	54
% frosh rec. any financial aid	90
% UG rec. any financial aid	76
% UG borrow to pay for school	65
Average cumulative indebtedness	$26,190

DePauw University

101 East Seminary, Greencastle, IN 46135 • Admissions: 765-658-4006 • Fax: 765-658-4007

STUDENTS SAY " . . . "

Academics

Serious-minded students are drawn to DePauw University for its "small classes," "encouraging" professors, and the "individual academic attention" they can expect to receive. Academically, DePauw is "demanding but rewarding," and "requires a lot of outside studying and discipline" in order to keep up. Professors' "expectations are very high," which means "you can't slack off and get good grades." Be prepared to pull your "fair share of all-nighters." Fortunately, DePauw professors are more than just stern taskmasters. Though they pile on the work, they "are always helpful and available" to students in need. When things get overwhelming, "They are very understanding and will cut you a break if you really deserve" it. As a result, students come to know their professors "on a personal level," making DePauw the kind of school where it is "common [for students] to have dinner at a professor's house." Beyond stellar professors, DePauw's other academic draws include "extraordinary" study abroad opportunities and a "wonderful" alumni network great for "connections and networking opportunities." Alums also "keep our endowment pretty high, making it easy for the school to give out merit scholarships," which undergraduates appreciate. Student opinion regarding the administration ranges from ambivalent to slightly negative. One especially thorny issue is class registration; you "rarely" get into all the classes you want.

Life

Few schools are as Greek as DePauw, but students are quick to point out that "it is by no means *Animal House*." The Greek system here is more holistic than that. It "promotes not only social activities but also philanthropic events." That's not to say there aren't lots of frat parties here. There are. But "the administration has cracked down big time" on the larger frat parties, and "now there are just small parties in apartments and dorms." One recently issued rule is that freshmen "will not be allowed on Greek property until after rush, which is the first week of second semester." In addition to administrative regulation, students exercise their own self-restraint; for the typical undergraduate, "the week is mostly reserved for studying." Beyond the frats and sororities, "there is always a theater production, athletic event, or organization-sponsored event going on," and popular bands occasionally perform on campus. It's a good thing so much is happening at the school because off-campus entertainment options are scarce: "If there is really any fun to be had, it's not in Greencastle." The situation could be greatly improved if there were just a few "more restaurants and stores in the town or a nearby town." As things stand, however, students "have to go to Indianapolis (forty-five miles) to go shopping, watch a good movie, eat at a good restaurant, etc."

Student Body

The typical DePauw student is "upper-middle-class," "a little preppy, a little athletic," and "hardworking;" "parties hard on weekend," and "usually become involved with the Greek system." Students describe their peers as "driven" and wearing "polos and pearls." They "have all had multiple internships, international experience, and [have held] some type of leadership position." Though these folks may seem "overcommitted," they "always get their work done." For those who don't fit this mold, don't fret; most students seem to be "accepting of the different types" of people on campus. Diversity on campus is augmented through the school's partnership with the Posse Foundation, which brings in urban (though not necessarily minority) "students from Chicago and NYC every year." These students are described as "leaders on campus" and "take real initiative to hold their communities together."

FINANCIAL AID: 765-658-4030 • E-MAIL: ADMISSION@DEPAUW.EDU • WEBSITE: WWW.DEPAUW.EDU

THE PRINCETON REVIEW SAYS

Admissions

Very important factors considered include: Academic GPA, rigor of secondary school record, standardized test scores. *Important factors considered include:* Application essay, class rank, recommendation(s). *Other factors considered include:* Alumni/ae relation, character/personal qualities, extracurricular activities, first generation, geographical residence, interview, level of applicant's interest, state residency, talent/ability, volunteer work, work experience. SAT or ACT required; ACT with or without writing component accepted. TOEFL required of all international applicants. High school diploma is required, and GED is accepted. *Academic units recommended:* 4 English, 4 mathematics, (2 science labs).

Financial Aid

Students should submit: FAFSA, institution's own financial aid form. The Princeton Review suggests that all financial aid forms be submitted as soon as possible after January 1. *Need-based scholarships/grants offered:* Federal Pell, SEOG, state scholarships/grants, private scholarships, school scholarship or grant aid from institutional funds, United Negro College Fund. *Loan aid offered:* Direct Subsidized Stafford, Direct Unsubsidized Stafford, Direct PLUS, Federal Perkins, state loans, university loans from institutional funds. Federal Work-Study Program available. Off-campus job opportunities are fair.

The Inside Word

Prospective applicants should not be deceived by DePauw's high acceptance rate. The students who are accepted and choose to enroll here have the academic goods to justify their admission. Many of them are accepted by more "competitive" schools and still choose DePauw. DePauw's generous merit scholarships have a lot to do with students' choice to enroll.

THE SCHOOL SAYS ". . ."

From the Admissions Office

"DePauw University is nationally recognized for intellectual and experiential challenge that links liberal arts education with life's work, preparing graduates for uncommon professional success, service to others, and personal fulfillment. DePauw graduates count among their ranks a Nobel Laureate, a vice president and U.S. congressman, Pulitzer Prize winning and Newbery Award winning authors, and a number of CEOs and humanitarian leaders. Our students demonstrate a love for learning, a willingness to serve others, the reason and judgment to lead, an interest in engaging worlds and cultures unknown to them, the courage to question their assumptions, and a strong commitment to community. Pre-professional and career exploration are encouraged through winter term, when more than 700 students pursue their own off-campus internships. This represents more students in experiential learning opportunities than at any other liberal arts college in the nation. Other innovative programs include Honor Scholars, Information Technology Associates Program, Management Fellows, Media Fellows, and Science Research Fellows, affording selected students additional seminar and internship opportunities.

"Freshman applicants are required to submit scores of the writing section of the SAT or the ACT."

SELECTIVITY
Admissions Rating	92
# of applicants	5,206
% of applicants accepted	57
% of acceptees attending	21
# accepting a place on wait list	39
% admitted from wait list	15
# of early decision applicants	68
% accepted early decision	82

FRESHMAN PROFILE
Range SAT Critical Reading	530–640
Range SAT Math	550–670
Range SAT Writing	530–640
Range ACT Composite	24–29
Minimum paper TOEFL	560
Minimum computer TOEFL	225
Average HS GPA	3.56
% graduated top 10% of class	53
% graduated top 25% of class	83
% graduated top 50% of class	97

DEADLINES
Early decision	
Deadline	11/1
Notification	1/1
Early action	
Deadline	12/1
Notification	2/15
Regular	
Deadline	2/1
Nonfall registration?	yes

APPLICANTS ALSO LOOK AT
AND OFTEN PREFER
Indiana University at Bloomington, University of Notre Dame, Vanderbilt University

AND SOMETIMES PREFER
Denison University, Miami University, Purdue University—West Lafayette, University of Illinois at Urbana-Champaign, Washington University in St. Louis

AND RARELY PREFER
Hanover College

FINANCIAL FACTS
Financial Aid Rating	89
Annual tuition	$34,440
Room and board	$9,180
Required fees	$465
Books and supplies	$750
% frosh rec. need-based scholarship or grant aid	57
% UG rec. need-based scholarship or grant aid	53
% frosh rec. non-need-based scholarship or grant aid	13
% UG rec. non-need-based scholarship or grant aid	11
% frosh rec. need-based self-help aid	43
% UG rec. need-based self-help aid	41
% UG borrow to pay for school	48
Average cumulative indebtedness	$24,210

DICKINSON COLLEGE

PO Box 1773, Carlisle, PA 17013-2896 • Admissions: 717-245-1231 • Fax: 717-245-1442

STUDENTS SAY ". . ."

Academics

Many students cite Dickinson's unique combination of being a small liberal arts institution with a global perspective as their reason for coming here. There's a host of study abroad options, and "it's assumed that most juniors will go abroad." Students who have attended large universities while studying abroad come to appreciate Dickinson's "small class sizes," which "allow professors to get to know their students." "Professors are tremendously accessible" and are "always willing to find a way to help students achieve their goals and meet their potential." "They come with all sorts of life experiences and connections in their respective fields to get students to interact with people in the areas they are studying." Classes are often "discussion-based, and [they] really give you an opportunity to engage and grow into the topic," though a few students wish lab science classes were more accessible to non-majors. "Class materials are very well-chosen, and professors are always passionate about their subjects." While some students gripe about the administration's "superficial changes" and "red tape," many more praise it as accessible and "forward-thinking"—this praise tends to come from students who chose Dickinson in part for its recently adopted emphasis on "promoting sustainable and green lifestyles."

Life

Descriptions of student life at Dickinson vary widely—suggesting a lot of options. While many students subscribe to the "work hard, play hard" philosophy, "the campus has a pretty good social life that does not involve alcohol." "The college's Event Advisory Board makes the plans readily available through e-mail and paper posts for every weekend. These lists are typically pretty extensive as there are many options to do for fun around campus." Sports are very popular, and many students note that participation in a campus group, whether it's a team, club, or Greek organization, is integral to social life. Some feel there's a bit of pressure for men to go Greek, but those who have chosen non-Greek life are generally happy, and for fun they "participate in Dickinson-sponsored dances and events and hang out with friends." Students are satisfied overall with their campus and facilities, and note that the library and cafeteria can be social hotbeds, though many wish for more meal options (one student suggests "the cafeteria should give up cooking fish."). Though small hometown Carlisle "isn't for everyone," "there are quite a few good restaurants within easy walking distance of campus," and the Carlisle Theater "brings in independent films and those sponsored by community groups and offers excellent discounts to students." "There is also a shuttle service that takes students anywhere in the town of Carlisle from 9:00 P.M. to 3:00 A.M."

Student Body

"The typical Dickinson student is outgoing, balanced, and engaged," and "because it's such a small community most people find their niche or group fairly easily." "While some report "most students are pretty preppy," "upper-middle-class," from the Northeast, and "are really fit, go to the gym a lot, [and] play a lot of sports," we also hear that "the beauty of Dickinson is that there is no 'typical' student. Everyone is here to become more globally aware and educated." Dickinson's emphasis on global perspectives and a strong international studies program draw "a lot of international [students], so there is good cultural diversity." "There are different crowds. There is a faction that parties all the time, and there is a faction that is heavily involved in academics, extra-curriculars, and community service." "Involved" and "engaged" are two words that come up a lot: "Joining clubs and extracurricular activities is a great way to meet people, and there are plenty of them!"

DICKINSON COLLEGE

FINANCIAL AID: 717-245-1308 • E-MAIL: ADMIT@DICKINSON.EDU • WEBSITE: WWW.DICKINSON.EDU

THE PRINCETON REVIEW SAYS

Admissions

Very important factors considered include: Academic GPA, rigor of secondary school record, extracurricular activities, talent/ability, volunteer work. *Important factors considered include:* Class rank, recommendation(s), standardized test scores, alumni/ae relation, work experience. *Other factors considered include:* Application essay, character/personal qualities, first generation, geographical residence, interview, level of applicant's interest, racial/ethnic status, state residency. SAT or ACT reccommended; ACT with or without writing component accepted. TOEFL required of all international applicants. High school diploma is required, and GED is accepted. *Academic units required:* 4 English, 3 mathematics, 3 science (2 science labs), 2 foreign language, 2 social studies, 2 academic elective. *Academic units recommended:* 3 foreign language.

Financial Aid

Students should submit: FAFSA, CSS/Financial Aid PROFILE. Regular filing deadline is February 1. The Princeton Review suggests that all financial aid forms be submitted as soon as possible after January 1. *Need-based scholarships/grants offered:* Federal Pell, SEOG, state scholarships/grants, private scholarships, school scholarship or grant aid from institutional funds. *Loan aid offered:* Direct Subsidized Stafford, Direct Unsubsidized Stafford, Direct PLUS, Federal Perkins, university loans from institutional funds. Applicants will be notified of awards on or about March 20. Federal Work-Study Program available. Off-campus job opportunities are good.

The Inside Word

The applicant pool for small liberal arts colleges has become increasingly competitive in recent years, and Dickinson is no exception. For admission here, you'll want to be the stereotypical well-rounded student, with a solid GPA in challenging classes, and broad extracurricular involvement.

THE SCHOOL SAYS ". . ."

From the Admissions Office

"College is more than a collection of courses. It is about crossing traditional boundaries, about seeing the interrelationships among different subjects, about learning a paradigm for solving problems, about developing critical thinking and communication skills, and about speaking out on issues that matter. Dickinson was intended as an alternative to the fifteen colleges that existed in the U.S. at the time of its founding; its aim, then as now, was to provide a useful education whereby students would 'learn by doing' through hands-on experience and engagement with the community, the region, the nation, and the world. And this is truer today than ever, with workshop science courses replacing traditional lectures, fieldwork experiences in community studies in which students take oral histories, and thirteen study centers abroad in nontourist cities where students, under the guidance of a Dickinson faculty director, experience a true international culture. Almost fifty-eight percent of the student body study abroad, and a total of sixty-one percent study off campus, preparing them to compete and succeed in a complex global world.

"Applicants wishing to be considered for academic scholarships are required to submit scores from either the SAT or ACT, but Dickinson does not require results from either test for admission."

SELECTIVITY
Admissions Rating	89
# of applicants	5,033
% of applicants accepted	48
% of acceptees attending	27
# accepting a place on wait list	425
% admitted from wait list	3
# of early decision applicants	405
% accepted early decision	73

FRESHMAN PROFILE
Range SAT Critical Reading	600–680
Range SAT Math	600–688
Range SAT Writing	590–690
Range ACT Composite	27–30
Minimum paper TOEFL	600
Minimum computer TOEFL	250
Minimum web-based TOEFL	100
% graduated top 10% of class	54
% graduated top 25% of class	80
% graduated top 50% of class	97

DEADLINES
Early decision	
Deadline	11/15
Notification	12/15
Early action	
Deadline	12/1
Notification	2/1
Regular	
Deadline	2/1
Notification	3/20
Nonfall registration?	no

APPLICANTS ALSO LOOK AT
AND OFTEN PREFER
Brown University, College of William and Mary, Franklin & Marshall College, Middlebury College

AND SOMETIMES PREFER
Bucknell University, Colby College, Colgate University, Connecticut College, Hamilton College, Kenyon College, Lafayette College

AND RARELY PREFER
American University, Gettysburg College, Skidmore College

FINANCIAL FACTS
Financial Aid Rating	92
Annual tuition	$42,610
Room and board	$10,800
Required fees	$475
Books and supplies	$1,000
% frosh rec. need-based scholarship or grant aid	57
% UG rec. need-based scholarship or grant aid	52
% frosh rec. non-need-based scholarship or grant aid	6
% UG rec. non-need-based scholarship or grant aid	3
% frosh rec. need-based self-help aid	54
% UG rec. need-based self-help aid	50
% frosh rec. any financial aid	59
% UG rec. any financial aid	54
% UG borrow to pay for school	51
Average cumulative indebtedness	$22,451

DREW UNIVERSITY

OFFICE OF COLLEGE ADMISSIONS, MADISON, NJ 07940-1493 • ADMISSIONS: 973-408-3739 • FAX: 973-408-3068

CAMPUS LIFE

Quality of Life Rating	72
Fire Safety Rating	96
Green Rating	84
Type of school	private
Affiliation	Methodist
Environment	village

STUDENTS

Total undergrad enrollment	1,715
% male/female	40/60
% from out of state	40
% from public high school	66
% live on campus	84
% African American	9
% Asian	5
% Caucasian	55
% Hispanic	13
% international	2
# of countries represented	21

SURVEY SAYS . . .

*Frats and sororities are unpopular
or nonexistent
Theater is popular
Student publications are popular
Political activism is popular*

ACADEMICS

Academic Rating	84
Calendar	semester
Student/faculty ratio	11:1
Profs interesting rating	85
Profs accessible rating	85
Most common reg class size	10–19 students
Most common lab size	10–19 students

MOST POPULAR MAJORS
economics, political science,
psychology

STUDENTS SAY ". . ."

Academics

Drew University features three major draws, according to current students: a gorgeous campus, a prime location (an hour from New York City by train), and strong academics. As at many schools, "some majors...are stronger than others," and introductory classes tend to be large lectures, but "class sizes, especially in upper-level courses, are generally small," which allows for "meaningful discussions." Though some say the administration "tends to be aloof," this obviously isn't a problem with the faculty. Students say professors are "very approachable, accommodating, and enthusiastic about what they teach." "They are quite engaging...have PhDs in the field that they teach, and...seem genuinely interested in helping us improve." "They're always there when students want extra help and are very understanding." One happy English major tells us, "My professors have really encouraged me to pursue the most out of my education here. One provided me with the opportunity to read my original poetry in NYC with distinguished poets. Another has influenced my decision to write a senior thesis. Within my major, I feel like part of a family. All of my professors know me, and I think they truly care about my performance." A neuroscience major raves, "Science professors will be acting out the material or showing demos of the material." Study abroad opportunities also abound, and the proximity to New York City gives students amazing internship opportunities.

Life

Life at Drew is typical of life on other small, Northeastern campuses, with a balanced blend of school-sponsored events, student clubs, and "of course, like any other college, students drink and party once the weekend comes, but it's not the only focus here." Students also enjoy heading off campus to nearby Morristown, and "trips to NYC are funded to go to museums, the outlet mall, basketball games, etc." Also on campus is the Shakespeare Theatre of New Jersey, and students are happy to take advantage of work-study opportunities there, as well as performances. On campus, there are a lot of "activities—at least one every night," and "facilities and living councils are constantly making improvements." "Students tend to try and get their money's worth by participating in as many opportunities as they can," and whether it's "environmental film screenings, a lecture by Anderson Cooper, or free food from the Polish Culture Club, there is always something you can become involved in." "There are lots of alcohol-free events planned for the weekends," "for example, sometimes performers like musicians or comedians come and perform, or sometimes there are guests." "The campus coffeehouse, The Other End, holds open mic nights or jazz nights on the weekend. It's a really fun place to hang out or do homework." Club Drew, "a club [night] once a month on campus with a DJ," is well-attended.

Student Body

"A typical student at Drew is smart, driven," and "hardworking, but still parties at least once a week." "Talkative," "outgoing," and "social" also come up a lot when Drew students describe themselves. While some say "the typical Drew student is white, American, [and] from the East Coast," "we have an abundance of students from diverse ethnic backgrounds," and "there's a lot of different types of people, from jocks to hipsters." "There are jocks, theater junkies, musicians, premed students, international students, political science enthusiasts, and everything else." "It's mind-boggling how different the 1,700 undergraduates are," but "with an outstanding number of clubs and other social groups, literally any student can find a group of people to click with," and students suggest "to get the best experience out of Drew...you need to get involved."

DREW UNIVERSITY

FINANCIAL AID: 973-408-3112 • E-MAIL: CADM@DREW.EDU • WEBSITE: WWW.DREW.EDU

THE PRINCETON REVIEW SAYS

Admissions

Very important factors considered include: Academic GPA, rigor of secondary school record. *Important factors considered include:* Application essay, recommendation(s), extracurricular activities. *Other factors considered include:* Class rank, standardized test scores, character/personal qualities, interview, level of applicant's interest, talent/ability, volunteer work, work experience. ACT with or without writing component accepted. TOEFL required of all international applicants. High school diploma is required, and GED is accepted. *Academic units recommended:* 4 English, 3 mathematics, 2 science, 2 foreign language, 2 social studies, 2 history, 3 academic elective.

Financial Aid

Students should submit: FAFSA. Regular filing deadline is February 15. The Princeton Review suggests that all financial aid forms be submitted as soon as possible after January 1. *Need-based scholarships/grants offered:* Federal Pell, SEOG, state scholarships/grants, private scholarships, school scholarship or grant aid from institutional funds. *Loan aid offered:* Direct Subsidized Stafford, Direct Unsubsidized Stafford, Direct PLUS, Federal Perkins, state loans. Federal Work-Study Program available. Off-campus job opportunities are fair.

The Inside Word

Drew takes a holistic approach to evaluating applications, so you definitely want to showcase more than just your GPA (though that's important, too). In line with this, applicants have the option of submitting a graded analytical writing sample in place of SAT scores. Drew's applicant pool has grown significantly in recent years, so presenting yourself as not only a great student but also a great fit with the school will help you stand out from the pack.

THE SCHOOL SAYS "..."

From the Admissions Office

"At Drew, great teachers in small classes are transforming the undergraduate learning experience. With a commitment to civic engagement, nurturing leadership skills and mentoring, Drew professors make educating undergraduates their top priority. With a spirit of innovation, they bring the most distinctive modes of experiential learning into and beyond the Drew classroom. The result is a stimulating and a challenging education that connects the traditional liberal arts and sciences to the community, to the workplace, and to the world. New programs in Business, Public Health, Environmental Science, and new Honors and Civic Scholar Programs complement innovative programs like the Drew International Seminars and NYC semesters focused on Wall Street, the UN, museums, and theaters.

"Drew University is a test optional school; it accepts the SAT, the ACT or, a graded high school research paper. The Selection Committee will consider the highest verbal, math, and writing scores individually in its evaluation of candidates for admission. A student's transcript is considered to be the most important factor during the application process."

SELECTIVITY

Admissions Rating	85
# of applicants	5,531
% of applicants accepted	80
% of acceptees attending	11
# of early decision applicants	29
% accepted early decision	90

FRESHMAN PROFILE

Range SAT Critical Reading	510–630
Range SAT Math	490–610
Range SAT Writing	510–630
Range ACT Composite	22–26
Minimum paper TOEFL	550
Minimum computer TOEFL	213
Average HS GPA	3.34
% graduated top 10% of class	36
% graduated top 25% of class	64
% graduated top 50% of class	93

DEADLINES

Early decision	
Deadline	11/1
Notification	1/15
Early action	
Deadline	1/15
Regular	
Deadline	2/15
Notification	11/15
Nonfall registration?	yes

FINANCIAL FACTS

Financial Aid Rating	81
Annual tuition	$40,122
Room and board	$11,150
Required fees	$582
Books and supplies	$1,228
% UG rec. need-based scholarship or grant aid	58
% UG rec. non-need-based scholarship or grant aid	8
% UG rec. need-based self-help aid	48
% frosh rec. any financial aid	98
% UG rec. any financial aid	85
% UG borrow to pay for school	62
Average cumulative indebtedness	$19,634

DREXEL UNIVERSITY

3141 CHESTNUT STREET, PHILADELPHIA, PA 19104 • ADMISSIONS: 215-895-2400 • FAX: 215-895-5939

STUDENTS SAY "..."

Academics

By far the biggest draw for students seems to be Drexel University's cooperative education program that "gives students the opportunity to gain hands-on experience and develop professionally in their field of study." The co-op program is "an amazing experience" and "really sets [Drexel] apart." The program "offers real-world work experience and contacts at up to three local and/or national companies before graduation—and in this economy, it's all in who you know!" The co-op really helps students get "an excellent job after graduation." "Drexel University has diversified from its roots," and the school is "no longer being about just engineering. [Drexel] has set out to educate students to prepare them for careers in all industries." Students enjoy a "great campus location" in Philadelphia and "prides itself on innovative technologies that value sustainability, progressive learning that encourages constant change, and opportunities for invaluable experience." Although most of the professors "are very knowledgeable in their field" and offer "hands-on learning combined with direct application," many students say that "too many professors speak English as a second language" and "have difficulty communicating to their students." "Some professors need to retake an English language course," one student says bluntly. Students also pinpoint the "red tape" and "bureaucracy" as frustrating, saying that it bogs down the school. "Drexel is unfortunately run too much like a business sometimes," one student explains. "It can be difficult to get through the red tape that ties up departments." Some students also see the tuition as "outrageous." Although "some facilities are old and need work," Drexel is good about "dumping money into improving facilities" and most are "top-quality." One student proudly says, "Drexel is a great school," and it "is only going upward from here."

Life

Drexel University is located "right in the heart" of Philadelphia, one of the country's largest and most vibrant cities. Consequently, much of student life involves exploring this unique city. "It is so easy to learn how to use the subway and go into the heart of the city. It's so much fun to check out new locations, go shopping, and try out some of the best restaurants in town." Students love "the comedy club in center city [and] the bars in Olde City," and they often head to a "Phillies, Flyers, or 76ers game." "The music scene in Philadelphia is great," and "the Philadelphia Museum of Art is just a twenty-minute walk from campus." In addition to having the entire city of Philadelphia at your disposal, the University of Pennsylvania is "right across the street." "If you're into partying, there's always a party going on, if not, head over to UPenn or Temple," one student advises. On campus, "Greek life is a big part of Drexel's community." If there's a downside to Drexel life, it's that there's "very little school spirit." "The basketball team is all the school spirit that exists; there isn't any besides that," a student explains. But as soon as you step off campus, "there are countless other things to do too, like museums, operas, and musicals."

Student Body

"There is no such thing as a typical Drexel student," one student declares. "Our campus is incredibly diverse in every way." "Drexel is a mixing bowl" and "very multicultural." "Everyone is different, and we all interact with each other and fit in [with] all different groups." "There are so many different people from everywhere, and it's amazing. Black, white, gay, straight: it just makes the college life here diverse and exciting." "Most students get involved in one or more student organizations" to fit in. Students are also very hardworking and "busy with classes and studies." "Everyone is focused on careers after college, but people still like to have fun on the weekends." "We're generally pretty mellow people," a chemical engineering student explains. "[We] work hard, but don't get too uptight about grades and classes."

DREXEL UNIVERSITY

FINANCIAL AID: 215-895-2535 • E-MAIL: ENROLL@DREXEL.EDU • WEBSITE: WWW.DREXEL.EDU

THE PRINCETON REVIEW SAYS

Admissions

Very important factors considered include: Academic GPA, class rank, rigor of secondary school record, standardized test scores. *Important factors considered include:* Application essay, recommendation(s), character/personal qualities. *Other factors considered include:* Alumni/ae relation, extracurricular activities, first generation, interview, level of applicant's interest, talent/ability, volunteer work, work experience. SAT or ACT required; ACT with or without writing component accepted. TOEFL required of all international applicants. High school diploma is required, and GED is accepted. *Academic units required:* 3 mathematics, 1 science (1 science lab). *Academic units recommended:* 1 foreign language.

Financial Aid

Students should submit: FAFSA. The Princeton Review suggests that all financial aid forms be submitted as soon as possible after January 1. *Need-based scholarships/grants offered:* Federal Pell, SEOG, state scholarships/grants, private scholarships, school scholarship or grant aid from institutional funds, United Negro College Fund. *Loan aid offered:* Direct Subsidized Stafford, Direct Unsubsidized Stafford, Direct PLUS, Federal Perkins, Federal Nursing Loans, university loans from institutional funds. Applicants will be notified of awards on a rolling basis beginning March 15.

The Inside Word

Drexel University's nationally recognized co-op program provides unique hands-on experience for students with companies in and around Philadelphia to help them in their post-college employment. Given the current state of the economy, that's a huge boost for prospective applicants, especially in the engineering fields that Drexel still specializes in.

THE SCHOOL SAYS "..."

From the Admissions Office

"Drexel has gained a reputation for academic excellence since its founding in 1891. In 2006, Drexel became the first top-ranked doctoral university in more than twenty-five years to open a law school. Its main campus is a ten-minute walk from Center City Philadelphia. More than sixty percent of undergraduate students prepare for successful careers through Drexel's prestigious five-year experiential education program—The Drexel Co-op. Alternating periods of full-time, professional employment with periods of classroom study, students can earn an average of $14,000 per six-month co-op. At any one time, about 2,000 full-time undergraduates are on co-op assignments. Drexel integrates science and technology into all seventy undergraduate majors. Students looking for a special challenge can apply to one of fourteen accelerated degree programs including the BS/MBA in business, BA/BS/MD in medicine, BA/BS/TD in law, BS/MS or BS/PhD in engineering, BS/MS in information technology, and BS/DPT in physical therapy.

"Pennoni Honors College offers high achievers unique opportunities. Students Tackling Advanced Research (STAR) allows qualified undergraduates to participate in a paid summer research project, and the Center for Civic Engagement matches students with community service opportunities. Students in any major can take dance, music, and theater classes offered through Drexel's performing arts programs.

"Drexel's study abroad program allows students to spend a term or more earning credits while gaining international experience. Adventurous students can also enjoy co-op abroad. Locations include London, Costa Rica, Prague, Rome, and Paris. The admissions office invites prospective students to schedule a campus visit for a first-hand look at all Drexel offers."

SELECTIVITY

Admissions Rating	82
# of applicants	48,715
% of applicants accepted	55
% of acceptees attending	10

FRESHMAN PROFILE

Range SAT Critical Reading	540–640
Range SAT Math	570–670
Range SAT Writing	520–630
Range ACT Composite	23–28
Minimum paper TOEFL	550
Minimum computer TOEFL	213
% graduated top 10% of class	32
% graduated top 25% of class	64
% graduated top 50% of class	89

DEADLINES

Regular	
Deadline	3/1
Nonfall registration?	yes

FINANCIAL FACTS

Financial Aid Rating	76
Annual tuition	$32,000
Room and board	$13,635
Required fees	$2,205
Books and supplies	$1,950
% frosh rec. need-based scholarship or grant aid	64
% UG rec. need-based scholarship or grant aid	61
% frosh rec. non-need-based scholarship or grant aid	10
% UG rec. non-need-based scholarship or grant aid	5
% frosh rec. need-based self-help aid	52
% UG rec. need-based self-help aid	59
% frosh rec. any financial aid	99
% UG rec. any financial aid	89
% UG borrow to pay for school	73
Average cumulative indebtedness	$35,082

DUKE UNIVERSITY

2138 CAMPUS DRIVE, DURHAM, NC 27708 • ADMISSIONS: 919-684-3214 • FAX: 919-681-8941

STUDENTS SAY ". . ."

Academics

Duke University is "all about academic excellence complemented by highly competitive Division I sports and an enriching array of extracurricular activities," making the university "an exciting, challenging, and enjoyable place to be." Undergraduates choose Duke because they "are passionate about a wide range of things, including academics, sports, community service, research, and fun." And because the school seems equally committed to accommodating all of those pursuits; as one student puts it, "Duke is for the Ivy League candidate who is a little bit more laid-back about school and overachieving (but just a bit) and a lot more into the party scene." Academics "are very difficult in the quantitative majors (engineering, math, statistics, economics, premed)" and "much easier in the non-quantitative majors," but there's an "across-the-board excellence in all departments from humanities to engineering." In all areas, there's a "supportive environment in which the faculty, staff, and students are willing to look out for the other person and help them succeed." It's the norm to have large study groups, and "The review sessions, peer tutoring system, writing center, and academic support center are always helpful when students are struggling with anything from math homework to creating a resume." Professors' "number-one priority is teaching undergraduates," and their love of discussion means they "would rather that the students lead the class as opposed to them leading the class." "There are a few who make me want to stay at Duke forever," says a student. Because "the school has a lot of confidence in its students," it offers them "seemingly limitless opportunities."

Life

Life at Duke "is very relaxed," and "You can either be a part of nothing, or you can be so over-committed that it's not even funny." Because "the student union and other organizations provide entertainment all the time, from movies to shows to campus-wide parties," there's "a wealth of on-campus opportunities to get involved." Indeed, weekends are for relaxing, and "People usually stay on campus for fun," because hometown Durham "has a few quirky streets and squares with restaurants, shops, clubs, etc., but to really do much you have to go to Raleigh or Chapel Hill," each twenty to thirty minutes away by car. The perception that "Durham is pretty dangerous" further dampens students' enthusiasm for the city. Undergrads' fervor for Blue Devils sports, on the other hand, can be boundless; sports, "especially basketball, are a huge deal here," and undergrads "will paint themselves completely blue and wait in line on the sidewalk in K-ville for three days to jump up and down in Cameron Indoor Stadium." Greek life "plays a big role in the social scene here," but "Almost all the parties are open, so it definitely isn't hard to get into a party." Though it's a "very party-heavy school," a lot of people "just do their own thing—have a movie night, go exploring, go skiing or to the beach for a weekend." Still, the social scene can be "a little too intense" at times.

Student Body

The typical Duke student "is someone who cares a lot about his or her education but at the same time won't sacrifice a social life for it." Life involves "getting a ton of work done first and then finding time to play and have fun." The typical student here is studious but social, athletic but can never be seen in the gym, job hunting but not worrying, and so on and so forth." Everyone is "incredibly focused," but "That includes social success as well." Students tend to be "focused on graduating and obtaining a lucrative and prosperous career," and although they "go out two to three times a week," they're "always looking polished." An "overwhelming number" are athletes, "not just varsity athletes…but athletes in high school or generally active people. Duke's athletic pride attracts this kind of person." The student body "is surprisingly ethnically diverse, with a number of students of Asian, African, and Hispanic descent," and "Every type of person finds a welcoming group where he or she fits in."

FINANCIAL AID: 919-684-6225 • E-MAIL: UNDERGRAD-ADMISSIONS@DUKE.EDU • WEBSITE: WWW.DUKE.EDU

THE PRINCETON REVIEW SAYS

Admissions

Very important factors considered include: Application essay, recommendation(s), rigor of secondary school record, standardized test scores, extracurricular activities, talent/ability. *Important factors considered include:* Character/personal qualities. *Other factors considered include:* Academic GPA, class rank, alumni/ae relation, geographical residence, interview, racial/ethnic status, state residency, volunteer work, work experience. SAT and SAT Subject Tests or ACT required. *Academic units recommended:* 4 English, 4 mathematics, 4 science, 4 foreign language, 4 social studies.

Financial Aid

Students should submit: FAFSA, CSS/Financial Aid PROFILE. Regular filing deadline is March 1. The Princeton Review suggests that all financial aid forms be submitted as soon as possible after January 1. *Need-based scholarships/grants offered:* Federal Pell, SEOG, state scholarships/grants, private scholarships, school scholarship or grant aid from institutional funds. *Loan aid offered:* Direct Subsidized Stafford, Direct Unsubsidized Stafford, Direct PLUS, Federal Perkins, university loans from institutional funds. Federal Work-Study Program available. Off-campus job opportunities are good.

The Inside Word

Duke is an extremely selective undergraduate institution, which affords the school the luxury of rejecting many qualified applicants. You'll have to present an exceptional record just to be considered; to make the cut, you'll have to impress the admissions office that you can contribute something unique and valuable to the incoming class. Being one of the best basketball players in the nation (male or female) helps a lot, but even athletes have to show academic excellence to get in the door here.

THE SCHOOL SAYS "..."

From the Admissions Office

"Duke University offers an interesting mix of tradition and innovation, undergraduate college and major research university, Southern hospitality and international presence, and athletic prowess and academic excellence. Students come to Duke from all over the United States and the world and from a range of racial, ethnic, and socioeconomic backgrounds. They enjoy contact with a world-class faculty through small classes and independent study. More than forty majors are available in the arts and sciences and engineering; arts and sciences students may also design their own curriculum through Program II. Certificate programs are available in a number of interdisciplinary areas. Special academic opportunities include the Focus Program and seminars for first-year students, study abroad, study at the Duke Marine Laboratory and Duke Primate Center, the Duke in New York and Duke in Los Angeles arts programs, and several international exchange programs. While admission to Duke is highly selective, applications of U.S. citizens and permanent residents are evaluated without regard to financial need and the university pledges to meet 100 percent of the demonstrated need of all admitted U.S. students and permanent residents. A limited amount of financial aid is also available for foreign citizens, and the university will meet the full demonstrated financial need for those admitted students as well.

"Applicants must take either the ACT with the writing exam, or the SAT plus two SAT Subject Tests (mathematics Subject Test required for applicants to the Pratt School of Engineering)."

SELECTIVITY

Admissions Rating	97
# of applicants	18,090
% of applicants accepted	22
% of acceptees attending	43
# accepting a place on wait list	1,026
% admitted from wait list	10
# of early decision applicants	1,482
% accepted early decision	32

FRESHMAN PROFILE

Range SAT Critical Reading	690–770
Range SAT Math	690–800
Range ACT Composite	29–34
% graduated top 10% of class	90
% graduated top 25% of class	98
% graduated top 50% of class	100

DEADLINES

Early decision	
Deadline	11/1
Notification	12/15
Regular	
Deadline	1/2
Nonfall registration?	no

FINANCIAL FACTS

Financial Aid Rating	94
Annual tuition	$31,420
Room and board	$8,950
Required fees	$1,180
Books and supplies	$970
% frosh rec. need-based scholarship or grant aid	38
% UG rec. need-based scholarship or grant aid	37
% frosh rec. non-need-based scholarship or grant aid	1
% UG rec. non-need-based scholarship or grant aid	1
% frosh rec. need-based self-help aid	35
% UG rec. need-based self-help aid	35
% UG borrow to pay for school	40
Average cumulative indebtedness	$16,502

DUQUESNE UNIVERSITY

600 FORBES AVENUE, PITTSBURGH, PA 15282 • ADMISSIONS: 412-396-2222 • FAX: 412-396-5644

STUDENTS SAY ". . ."

Academics

Cosmopolitan yet caring, you get the best of both worlds at Duquesne University. Located in the heart of downtown Pittsburgh, this Catholic school unites "the diversity and opportunities of an urban university with the community and comfort of a small liberal arts college." "Well-respected in the Pittsburgh area," health fields are particularly strong at Duquesne. "The physician assistant program is world-renowned and selective," while pharmacy students say it's unique to find such a "good pharmacy program [at] a smaller university." The music school also receives ample praise and benefits from studio teachers who are "some of the best in the world." Regardless of the specific program, "Professors are eager to really engage with students and are available for extra support whenever you need it." Course work can be challenging, yet "The school wants [its] students to do well, and it offers many different services to aid in this." In fact, "Every department offers free tutors" to help students make the grade. On the flip side, the school's academic advisors often fall short, and many students struggle to schedule classes and meet graduation requirements. A music student admits, "One semester, I was not even a full-time student because my advisor failed to schedule three of my classes!" Fortunately, the majority of the school's staff is accessible, visible, and friendly; "The administrators, the professors, and the school ministers can be seen walking around campus. All of them have been known to stop and talk to groups of students around the school."

Life

Located "on a very pretty, secluded campus in the middle of downtown Pittsburgh," students at Duquesne love their school's location, just steps outside a city with "a rich cultural district and an even better nightlife." During the week, "Life at school consists of going to classes, spending many hours at the library, and going to Starbucks for social interactions." During the weekend, things get more exciting. Thanks to "the free campus buses that shuttle students to the Oakland and South Side areas on Friday and Saturday nights," students enjoy "bars, movie theaters, concerts (big names and locals), and tons of restaurants." While the Duquesne campus is dry, "Many people go out on the weekends, typically to parties on the south side or at the University of Pittsburgh." In addition, "Students also attend a lot of sporting events, including the Pittsburgh Steelers and Penguins, Duquesne games and Pitt games." If you don't feel like straying too far from home, the school manages a campus club called Nite Spot, "where they show movies that haven't come out on DVD yet, have bizarre activities like pillow-making that actually turn out to be really fun, and dance lessons." Another popular hangout is the Power Center—the "nicest facility on campus"—where "the exercise equipment is new and the classes are free."

Student Body

From Greek organizations to the table tennis club, "Many of the students at Duquesne are very involved in campus organizations and service-oriented activities." At the same time, students are "driven to succeed" academically, and "show up to every class with his or her work complete." "Well-mannered and well-dressed," Duquesne students don their best duds to go to lecture, and "The majority of people look like they just walked out a fashion catalog." Students admit the school isn't particularly diverse, and "the typical student at Duquesne is white, from the Pittsburgh area (or at least Pennsylvania), and Catholic." However, "Not all of the student body has Catholic values, and I have found that the student body doesn't push their own values onto anyone else." With 5,800 undergraduates, "The school is big enough that you can meet a lot of different people, but small enough that you have a sense of community by being able to see people you know anywhere you go on campus." Still, most students divide into smaller cliques, and "unless you join a frat or sorority, making a large networked group of friends is difficult."

FINANCIAL AID: 412-396-6607 • E-MAIL: ADMISSIONS@DUQ.EDU • WEBSITE: WWW.DUQ.EDU

THE PRINCETON REVIEW SAYS

Admissions

Very important factors considered include: Academic GPA, application essay, recommendation(s), rigor of secondary school record, standardized test scores. *Important factors considered include:* Class rank, character/personal qualities, extracurricular activities, interview, talent/ability, volunteer work. *Other factors considered include:* Alumni/ae relation, first generation, level of applicant's interest, racial/ethnic status, work experience. SAT or ACT required; ACT with writing component required. High school diploma is required, and GED is accepted. *Academic units recommended:* 4 English, 2 mathematics, 2 science, 2 foreign language, 2 social studies, 4 academic elective.

Financial Aid

Students should submit: FAFSA, institution's own financial aid form. Regular filing deadline is May 1. The Princeton Review suggests that all financial aid forms be submitted as soon as possible after January 1. *Need-based scholarships/grants offered:* Federal Pell, SEOG, state scholarships/grants, private scholarships, school scholarship or grant aid from institutional funds, United Negro College Fund. *Loan aid offered:* Direct Subsidized Stafford, Direct Unsubsidized Stafford, Direct PLUS, Federal Perkins, Federal Nursing Loans. Applicants will be notified of awards on a rolling basis beginning March 1. Federal Work-Study Program available. Off-campus job opportunities are good.

The Inside Word

Duquesne requires all prospective students to complete a college preparatory curriculum in high school; however, there is no minimum GPA required for admission, nor minimum test scores. Nonetheless, a student's academic record and test scores are the only two factors considered in awarding merit scholarships.

THE SCHOOL SAYS "..."

From the Admissions Office

"Duquesne University was founded in 1878 by the Holy Ghost Fathers. Although it is a private, Roman Catholic institution, Duquesne is proud of its ecumenical reputation. Duquesne University's attractive and secluded campus is set on a forty-nine-acre hilltop ('the bluff') overlooking the large corporate metropolis of Pittsburgh's Golden Triangle. It offers a wide variety of educational opportunities, from the liberal arts to modern professional training. Duquesne is a medium-sized university striving to offer personal attention to its students in addition to the versatility and opportunities of a true university. A deep sense of tradition is combined with innovation and flexibility to make the Duquesne experience both challenging and rewarding. The Palumbo Convocation/Recreation Complex features a 6,300-seat arena, home court to the university's Division I basketball team; racquetball and handball courts; weight rooms; and saunas. Extracurricular activities are recognized as an essential part of college life, complementing academics in the process of total student development. Students are involved in nearly 100 university-sponsored activities, and Duquesne's location gives students the opportunity to enjoy sports and cultural events both on campus and in the city. There are six residence halls with the capacity to house 3,538 students."

SELECTIVITY

Admissions Rating	82
# of applicants	6,502
% of applicants accepted	77
% of acceptees attending	28
# of early decision applicants	242
% accepted early decision	69

FRESHMAN PROFILE

Range SAT Critical Reading	510–600
Range SAT Math	520–610
Range SAT Writing	500–600
Range ACT Composite	22–26
Minimum paper TOEFL	575
Minimum computer TOEFL	233
Minimum web-based TOEFL	90
Average HS GPA	3.63
% graduated top 10% of class	23
% graduated top 25% of class	56
% graduated top 50% of class	88

DEADLINES

Early decision	
Deadline	11/1
Notification	12/15
Early action	
Deadline	12/1
Notification	1/15
Regular	
Priority	11/1
Deadline	7/1
Notification	10/1
Nonfall registration?	yes

APPLICANTS ALSO LOOK AT AND OFTEN PREFER

Penn State—University Park,
University of Pittsburgh—Pittsburgh Campus,
Washington & Jefferson College

AND SOMETIMES PREFER

Gannon University, Robert Morris University, Saint
Vincent College, West Virginia University

FINANCIAL FACTS

Financial Aid Rating	79
Annual tuition	$26,413
Room and board	$9,806
Required fees	$2,258
Books and supplies	$1,000
% frosh rec. need-based scholarship or grant aid	73
% UG rec. need-based scholarship or grant aid	68
% frosh rec. non-need-based scholarship or grant aid	72
% UG rec. non-need-based scholarship or grant aid	63
% frosh rec. need-based self-help aid	64
% UG rec. need-based self-help aid	60
% frosh rec. any financial aid	100
% UG rec. any financial aid	98

ECKERD COLLEGE

4200 FIFTY-FOURTH AVENUE SOUTH, ST. PETERSBURG, FL 33711 • ADMISSIONS: 727-864-8331 • FAX: 727-866-2304

CAMPUS LIFE

Quality of Life Rating	76
Fire Safety Rating	79
Green Rating	60*
Type of school	private
Environment	city

STUDENTS

Total undergrad enrollment	1,819
% male/female	42/58
% from out of state	73
% live on campus	81
% African American	4
% Asian	1
% Caucasian	80
% Hispanic	6
% international	3
# of countries represented	33

SURVEY SAYS . . .
Great library
Career services are great
Frats and sororities are unpopular
or nonexistent
Lots of beer drinking
Hard liquor is popular

ACADEMICS

Academic Rating	77
% students graduating within 6 years	69
Calendar	4-1-4
Student/faculty ratio	13:1
Profs interesting rating	86
Profs accessible rating	88
Most common reg class size	20–29 students
Most common lab size	10–19 students

MOST POPULAR MAJORS
marine science, environmental studies,
communication

STUDENTS SAY ". . ."

Academics
Eckerd College "in sunny Florida" is "a small, personable college with beach bum flare" that offers a "well-rounded," "excellent liberal arts education" and a "beautiful beachfront environment." Standouts include a "great" marine science program—"one of the best in the country" according to scores of students—and "many opportunities for" "freakin' awesome internships." "We also have a really good study abroad program," notes a sophomore. Eckerd really emphasizes international travel and you can study in a host of far-flung locales during your career here. The academic environment is "challenging but not too rough." In addition to your basic two semesters each year, Eckerd has a fairly unique winter term that allows students to focus on one course intensively. You'll find "some horrid teachers" but most classes are "extremely interesting." Professors tend to "encourage discussion," and "you can build very close relationships" with them. "I enjoy that I am not in a room filled with 300 students," relates a human development major. "I get one-on-one help when I need it. The professors seem to love their jobs and love helping students." "Professors are almost always accessible outside of the classroom and love to see you succeed in classes," adds an environmental studies major.

Life
The food on campus is "not so good," and "the older dorms need some work." Also, the campus is "fairly secluded from St. Petersburg, so getting anywhere without a car is difficult." Otherwise, though, life here is grand. "We call it Camp Eckerd," relates a sophomore. Students say the campus is "very easy to get around." The weather is perpetually warm. "You never have to wear shoes." The atmosphere is "laid-back." At the same time, "There is always some type of school- or organization-sponsored event going on." Students are also "very active in the outdoors," not least because the campus is "surrounded by water on three sides." The "really awesome" waterfront program allows students to check out kayaks and boats. You can also take sailing and windsurfing classes. The party scene here is by all accounts outstanding. "Weekends are pretty crazy," explains a senior. "Thursday through Saturday it is not hard to find…some kind of themed party in upper-class dorms." "A lot of beer is consumed on the weekends," observes an awed first-year student. When you feel the urge to get away, two gorgeous beaches are very nearby. Downtown Tampa is only a half-hour from campus, and Busch Gardens and Disney World are within a reasonable drive as well.

Student Body
"Picture what would happen if you combined the school stoner, the class president, the jock, and the funny guy," depicts a first-year student. "Now, subtract the shoes and add a perfect tan." That, in a nutshell, is the typical undergrad at Eckerd. "Students here have a lot of self-confidence" and they are "surprisingly friendly." Most are "pretty physically fit and outdoorsy." It's hard to generalize about this place, though. Many students don't fit that profile at all. "There is a hodgepodge of people." Students "range from complete hippies, to alternative, to party girls," to "pale-skinned gamers," to "artsy marine science people." There's also the jock, the "indie-rocker," and "the math nerd." Cliques happen, especially among athletes, but "everyone can hang out with everyone with 100 percent comfort." "People smile at each other and say hey," describes a senior. "It is a pretty relaxed and friendly atmosphere."

ECKERD COLLEGE

FINANCIAL AID: 727-864-8334 • E-MAIL: ADMISSIONS@ECKERD.EDU • WEBSITE: WWW.ECKERD.EDU

THE PRINCETON REVIEW SAYS

Admissions

Very important factors considered include: Academic GPA, rigor of secondary school record. *Important factors considered include:* Application essay, recommendation(s), standardized test scores, character/personal qualities, extracurricular activities, interview, talent/ability. *Other factors considered include:* Class rank, alumni/ae relation, first generation, level of applicant's interest, volunteer work, work experience. SAT or ACT required; ACT with or without writing component accepted. High school diploma is required, and GED is accepted. *Academic units recommended:* 4 English, 3 mathematics, 3 science (2 science labs), 2 foreign language, 2 social studies, 1 history, 3 academic elective.

Financial Aid

Students should submit: FAFSA. Regular filing deadline is March 1. The Princeton Review suggests that all financial aid forms be submitted as soon as possible after January 1. *Need-based scholarships/grants offered:* Federal Pell, SEOG, state scholarships/grants, private scholarships, school scholarship or grant aid from institutional funds. *Loan aid offered:* Direct Subsidized Stafford, Direct Unsubsidized Stafford, Direct PLUS, Federal Perkins, university loans from institutional funds. Applicants will be notified of awards on a rolling basis beginning February 15.

The Inside Word

Most of the applicants Eckerd admits come from the top quarter of their high school classes. However, competition from other small liberal arts schools of roughly the same caliber or better is stiff. As a result, Eckerd is a relatively easy admit for B-plus students with decent standardized test scores. The admissions process here is rolling, which means that applying early will help your chances. Eckerd can afford to be more selective later on in the admissions cycle, especially for candidates who profess an interest in its most esteemed programs (for example, marine science).

THE SCHOOL SAYS "..."

From the Admissions Office

"Eckerd's diverse student body comes from forty-eight states and thirty-three countries. In this international setting, the majors of international relations and international business are very popular. Close to seventy percent of our graduates spend at least one term studying abroad. The beautiful waterfront campus is a perfect location for the study of marine science and environmental studies. We characterize Eckerd students as competent givers because of their extensive involvement in the life of the campus and their many volunteer service contributions to the local environment and the St. Petersburg community. The Academy of Senior Professionals draws to campus distinguished persons who have retired from fields our students aspire to enter. Academy members, such as the late novelist James Michener, Nobel Prize–winner Elie Wiesel, and the late black historian John Hope Franklin, enrich classes and offer valuable counsel for career and life planning.

"Students applying for admission are allowed to submit SAT or ACT examination results, and Eckerd will use the best scores from either test."

SELECTIVITY
Admissions Rating	82
# of applicants	3,252
% of applicants accepted	71
% of acceptees attending	22

FRESHMAN PROFILE
Range SAT Critical Reading	510–620
Range SAT Math	495–610
Range SAT Writing	495–600
Range ACT Composite	23–27
Minimum computer TOEFL	550
Minimum web-based TOEFL	79
Average HS GPA	3.26

DEADLINES
Regular Notification	10/1
Nonfall registration?	yes

FINANCIAL FACTS
Financial Aid Rating	83
Annual tuition	$34,250
Room and board	$9,652
Required fees	$296
Books and supplies	$1,200
% frosh rec. any financial aid	60
% UG rec. any financial aid	59
Average cumulative indebtedness	$30,881

ELON UNIVERSITY

2700 CAMPUS BOX, ELON, NC 27244-2010 • ADMISSIONS: 336-278-3566 • FAX: 336-278-7699

STUDENTS SAY ". . ."

Academics

Elon University works hard to "broaden students' horizons in all aspects of life, both in and out of the classroom" by "embracing the idea that student involvement is a key tool to developing a strong future." Central to this mission is the school's emphasis on experiential learning. "You will work your butt off in the classroom," students assure us, "but that is not where your day ends—you get involved outside the classroom and gain more knowledge" through "extensive undergraduate research, service learning, study abroad, and internship opportunities." Of these, students are most vocal about the "amazing study abroad program," through which Elon seeks to transform a student into a "world citizen rather than just another American with a college degree." Undergrads report approvingly that the school "fully prepares you for your [study abroad] experience and tries to ensure that every student gets to go somewhere." The school's strengths trend toward the professions—business, communications, education, and biology are all considered among the best departments here—but Elon also boasts "one of the very best performing arts schools with a liberal arts education," including "a great dance department." In all departments, "The class sizes are small, and professors take an interest in student achievement both inside and outside of academics." "The class size and teacher/student ratio, I'm convinced, are the main reasons I am succeeding at this school," one student believes. "If it weren't for the teachers knowing me personally, I probably wouldn't care at all."

Life

"Any individual can fit in at Elon, so long as they take the time to find what they are interested in," because "Elon offers a wide variety in its student population and activities. Going to sporting events, attending schools plays, and getting involved in community service organizations are all major factors of Elon life," and "if Elon does not have exactly what you want, you can start it up." That said, students who love the Greek scene will have an easier time fitting in than those who don't; Even though "there are a ton of other things to get involved with so long as students try to get involved," many here still believe "in order to have fun at Elon, students should get involved in Greek life." Students report "the campus is absolutely gorgeous," contributing to "a definite aspect of southern comfort." Burlington, the nearest city, "is the fast food capital of North Carolina, so there is always somewhere to go out and eat, but in terms of entertainment we have a bowling alley, parks, the mall, and a movie theater—which isn't much. But, we're also thirty minutes from Chapel Hill and fifteen minutes from Greensboro, so we're within traveling distance of other areas with a more varied choice of activities."

Student Body

The Elon student body is sometimes criticized "for being too preppy or not diverse enough, but these are just generalizations," students tell us. "Sure, there are a lot of preppy people here, but there are a lot of different types of people as well. Not everyone here is rich, Southern, and dresses like an Easter egg." They are hardly your stereotypical selfish, rich kids, as "the majority of students at Elon simply want to make a difference in one way or another. We are a very community-service based school and constantly have fundraisers and drives for a variety of causes." "The typical student is in a sorority of fraternity, and the Greeks have a very large presence on campus. There is a lack of 'atypical' students as most people tend to fit the Elon 'mold.' If you are interested in Greek life, this is a great place to be, but if you aren't, don't bother."

FINANCIAL AID: 800-334-8448 • E-MAIL: ADMISSIONS@ELON.EDU • WEBSITE: WWW.ELON.EDU

THE PRINCETON REVIEW SAYS

Admissions

Very important factors considered include: Academic GPA, rigor of secondary school record, standardized test scores. *Important factors considered include:* Application essay, recommendation(s), alumni/ae relation, extracurricular activities, talent/ability, volunteer work, work experience. *Other factors considered include:* Class rank, character/personal qualities, first generation, geographical residence, level of applicant's interest, racial/ethnic status, state residency. SAT or ACT required; ACT with writing component required. TOEFL required of all international applicants. High school diploma is required, and GED is accepted. *Academic units required:* 4 English, 3 mathematics, 3 science (1 science lab), 2 foreign language, 1 social studies, 2 history. *Academic units recommended:* 4 English, 4 mathematics, 3 science (1 science lab), 3 foreign language, 1 social studies, 2 history.

Financial Aid

Students should submit: FAFSA, institution's own financial aid form, CSS/Financial Aid PROFILE. Recommended filing deadline is February 15. The Princeton Review suggests that all financial aid forms be submitted as soon as possible after January 1. *Need-based scholarships/grants offered:* Federal Pell, SEOG, state scholarships/grants, private scholarships, school scholarship or grant aid from institutional funds. *Loan aid offered:* Direct Subsidized Stafford, Direct Unsubsidized Stafford, Direct PLUS, Federal Perkins, state loans. Applicants will be notified of awards on a rolling basis beginning February 28. Federal Work-Study Program available. Off-campus job opportunities are good.

The Inside Word

Elon has worked hard to elevate its national profile, and admissions standards have risen with the school's reputation. Today, Elon has more than enough solid performers to fill its incoming class with accomplished, capable students; there are no seats left over for slackers. That said, Elon considers the entire application and will use evidence of academic promise (for example, excellent writing and glowing recommendations) to mitigate weaknesses in test scores or, occasionally, even high school grades.

THE SCHOOL SAYS "..."

From the Admissions Office

"Elon offers the resources of a university in a close-knit community atmosphere. The university's 5,032 undergraduates choose from more than fifty majors in the arts and sciences, business, communications, and education. Graduate programs are offered in business administration, law, education, interactive media, and physical therapy. The National Survey of Student Engagement recognizes Elon among the nation's most effective universities in promoting hands-on learning. Academic and co-curricular activities are seamlessly blended, especially in the Elon Experiences: study abroad, internships, service, leadership, and undergraduate research. Participation is among the highest in the nation. Seventy per cent of graduating seniors have studied abroad, seventy-eight percent have internship experiences, and eighty-three percent have participated in service. Elon's 4-1-4 academic calendar allows students to devote January to international study or to explore innovative on-campus courses. Elon's historic 600-acre campus is recognized as one of the most beautiful in the country. New additions include the $10 million Ernest A. Koury, Sr., Business Center; the 30,000-square-foot Alumni Field House; Lindner Hall, the 'greenest' building on campus and anchor for the Academic Village, a quad dedicated to the arts and sciences; and the Colonnades Dining Hall, a two-story dining facility featuring a full-service restaurant, an organic market, and a fire stone oven for pizzas. Elon's NCAA Division I Phoenix athletics programs compete in the Southern Conference. Freshman applicants are required to take the SAT (or the ACT with the writing section). The best critical reading, math, and writing scores from either test will be used."

SELECTIVITY
Admissions Rating	93
# of applicants	9,771
% of applicants accepted	49
% of acceptees attending	29
# accepting a place on wait list	1,379
% admitted from wait list	12
# of early decision applicants	408
% accepted early decision	86

FRESHMAN PROFILE
Range SAT Critical Reading	560–650
Range SAT Math	560–660
Range SAT Writing	560–660
Range ACT Composite	25–28
Minimum paper TOEFL	550
Minimum computer TOEFL	213
Minimum web-based TOEFL	79
Average HS GPA	3.94
% graduated top 10% of class	32
% graduated top 25% of class	67
% graduated top 50% of class	91

DEADLINES
Early decision	
Deadline	11/1
Notification	12/1
Early action	
Deadline	11/10
Notification	12/20
Regular	
Priority	11/1
Deadline	1/10
Nonfall registration?	no

APPLICANTS ALSO LOOK AT
AND OFTEN PREFER
University of North Carolina at Chapel Hill, Wake Forest University

AND SOMETIMES PREFER
Boston College, University of Maryland—College Park, University of Richmond

FINANCIAL FACTS
Financial Aid Rating	77
Annual tuition	$26,480
Required fees	$347
Books and supplies	$900
% frosh rec. need-based scholarship or grant aid	33
% UG rec. need-based scholarship or grant aid	33
% frosh rec. non-need-based scholarship or grant aid	3
% UG rec. non-need-based scholarship or grant aid	3
% frosh rec. need-based self-help aid	32
% UG rec. need-based self-help aid	30
% frosh rec. any financial aid	65
% UG rec. any financial aid	74
% UG borrow to pay for school	46
Average cumulative indebtedness	$27,163

EMERSON COLLEGE

120 BOYLSTON STREET, BOSTON, MA 02116-4624 • ADMISSIONS: 617-824-8600 • FAX: 617-824-8609

STUDENTS SAY ". . ."

Academics

Emerson College provides "is a microcosm of professionalism, talent, passion, and skill." "Emerson College is a place where creative individuals can flourish while studying the communication arts and sciences." Among its strengths are "one of the most well-respected theater education programs in the country" and "an *amazing* communications school." Located in Boston, the school is "extremely career-oriented," "provides worthwhile opportunities," and "allows for *lots* of extracurricular involvement." Students who embrace the "environment of motivation" will excel, while those "who are unmotivated or unsure of what they want to do have a hard time." The "faculty and staff are knowledgeable and helpful, and the entire campus is gorgeous, high-tech, modern, and very clean with the most up-to-date resources." Emerson can even be a little too high-tech for some. "Sometimes important notices from the college are tweeted as opposed to e-mailed. It gets very confusing," one student laments. "Ninety percent of the time, professors at Emerson are working professionals who are passionate and extremely knowledgeable in their fields" and "extremely accessible." "Most of [the professors] are part-time," but this can be a benefit because "they're working in their fields while teaching us. That means they're great networking connections and are always learning new things to teach us!" One thing to note: "The school does not have 'typical' college feel, so things like traditions are a lacking." "Anything is possible here, all you need is imagination and motivation," one student explains. "Most importantly, the student body is mainly comprised of driven, independent people who can be mature and professional when working but youthful and adventurous during free time."

Life

Students at Emerson "live and breathe their majors." They are "highly motivated" and know "exactly what they want and come to a school that will guide them in a direction to get exactly that." Much of student life revolves around the artistic fields that students study. "On weekends, most kids are doing projects or film shoots during the day and drinking at night." "Most students participate in clubs or activities that involve what they are studying." Some see Emerson as a "hipster nation where your level of involvement is up to you." "Athletics are not a huge thing except for the people who play them," and Emerson doesn't have much of a Greek presence. "However, during the weekends students often gather around in small, student-owned homes…and have crowded parties." "Emerson is definitely not known for its fabulous social/night life," and "Boston isn't as great until you're twenty-one, but there's a lot to do after—bars, clubs, concerts, theaters, etc." "There's just such an amazing energy at Emerson," one happy student says. "Everyone is busy, doing what they love, and there's all this awesome creative, passionate energy that's just bouncing around."

Student Body

"The students at Emerson are the ones who were outcasts at their high schools in some way…but that's a good thing" because "everyone is very creative [and] driven." Students here are busy bees that "just jump onto the speedway of Emerson and press the gas." Everyone "is outspoken, opinionated, passionate, and a little weird—to different degrees." "Yes, we are hipsters," one student admits, "and yes a lot of people like black-and-white movies with cigarettes in hand, but it also means that if you are a little odd, or you were picked on in high school, we're your people." "I just want to point out that Emerson is an extremely accepting school when it comes to gender identity," one student notes. "Almost any type of person can fit in here (except science buffs), because it is a very open and welcoming campus." One student does caution that "because Emerson is such a goal-specific school, you have a lot of students here who are willing to step on others to make it to the top. But you also have a good share of students who work together and build relationships and connections to help each other out." All in all, Emersonians are creative people who work together and have "so much pride in their school" and "the pride continues after graduation. The Emerson mafia is no joke!"

EMERSON COLLEGE

FINANCIAL AID: 617-824-8655 • E-MAIL: ADMISSION@EMERSON.EDU • WEBSITE: WWW.EMERSON.EDU

THE PRINCETON REVIEW SAYS

Admissions

Very important factors considered include: Academic GPA, standardized test scores. *Important factors considered include:* Application essay, class rank, recommendation(s), rigor of secondary school record, character/personal qualities, extracurricular activities, talent/ability. *Other factors considered include:* Alumni/ae relation, first generation, geographical residence, racial/ethnic status, volunteer work, work experience. SAT or ACT required; ACT with writing component required. TOEFL required of all international applicants. High school diploma is required, and GED is accepted. *Academic units required:* 4 English, 3 mathematics, 3 science, 3 foreign language, 3 social studies. *Academic units recommended:* 4 English, 3 mathematics, 3 science, 3 foreign language, 3 social studies, 4 academic elective.

Financial Aid

Students should submit: FAFSA, CSS/Financial Aid PROFILE. The Princeton Review suggests that all financial aid forms be submitted as soon as possible after January 1. *Need-based scholarships/grants offered:* Federal Pell, SEOG, state scholarships/grants, private scholarships, school scholarship or grant aid from institutional funds. *Loan aid offered:* Direct Subsidized Stafford, Direct Unsubsidized Stafford, Direct PLUS, Federal Perkins, state loans. Federal Work-Study Program available. Off-campus job opportunities are excellent.

The Inside Word

Located in the Boston Theatre District, Emerson is one of the premier colleges for students interesting in theater and other artistic fields. That's not to say it's not a high-quality university in other fields as well; Emerson offers hands-on work in creative industries as well as a vibrant and motivated community.

THE SCHOOL SAYS "..."

From the Admissions Office

"Founded in 1880, Emerson is one of the premier colleges in the country for communication and the arts. Students may choose from more than two-dozen undergraduate and graduate programs supported by state-of-the-art facilities and a nationally renowned faculty. The campus is home to WERS-FM, the oldest noncommercial radio station in Boston; the historic 1,200-seat Cutler Majestic Theatre; and *Ploughshares*, the award winning literary journal for new writing.

"Located on Boston Common in the heart of the city's Theatre District, the campus is walking distance from the Massachusetts State House, Chinatown, and historic Freedom Trail. More than half the students reside on-campus, some in special learning communities such as the Writers' Block and Digital Culture Floor. There is also a fitness center, athletic field, and new gymnasium and campus center.

"Emerson has nearly eighty student organizations and performance groups as well as fifteen NCAA teams, student publications, and honor societies. The College also sponsors programs in Los Angeles and Washington, D.C.; study abroad in the Netherlands, Taiwan, and Czech Republic; and course cross-registration with the six-member Boston ProArts Consortium.

"Students have access to outstanding facilities, including sound treated television studios, digital editing and audio post-production suites. An eleven-story performance and production center houses a theatre design/technology center, makeup lab, and costume shop. There are seven programs to observe speech and hearing therapy, a professional marketing focus group room, and digital newsroom, and new performance development center with a sound stage, scene shop, black box, and film screening room."

SELECTIVITY	
Admissions Rating	94
# of applicants	6,943
% of applicants accepted	42
% of acceptees attending	26
# accepting a place on wait list	798
% admitted from wait list	13

FRESHMAN PROFILE	
Range SAT Critical Reading	570–670
Range SAT Math	540–640
Range SAT Writing	580–670
Range ACT Composite	24–29
Minimum paper TOEFL	550
Minimum computer TOEFL	213
Minimum web-based TOEFL	80
Average HS GPA	3.59
% graduated top 10% of class	42
% graduated top 25% of class	77
% graduated top 50% of class	98

DEADLINES	
Early action	
Deadline	11/1
Notification	12/15
Regular	
Deadline	1/5
Nonfall registration?	yes

**APPLICANTS ALSO LOOK AT
AND OFTEN PREFER**
New York University
AND SOMETIMES PREFER
Ithaca College, University of Southern California
AND RARELY PREFER
Boston University, Syracuse University

FINANCIAL FACTS	
Financial Aid Rating	85
Annual tuition	$29,408
Room and board	$12,280
Required fees	$672
Books and supplies	$800
% frosh rec. need-based scholarship or grant aid	53
% UG rec. need-based scholarship or grant aid	43
% frosh rec. non-need-based scholarship or grant aid	3
% UG rec. non-need-based scholarship or grant aid	1
% frosh rec. need-based self-help aid	53
% UG rec. need-based self-help aid	52
% frosh rec. any financial aid	63
% UG rec. any financial aid	61
% UG borrow to pay for school	59
Average cumulative indebtedness	$15,262

EMORY UNIVERSITY

OFFICE OF UNDERGRADUATE ADMISSION, ATLANTA, GA 30322 • ADMISSIONS: 404-727-6036 • FAX: 404-727-4303

CAMPUS LIFE

Quality of Life Rating	98
Fire Safety Rating	70
Green Rating	94
Type of school	private
Affiliation	Methodist
Environment	town

STUDENTS

Total undergrad enrollment	7,140
% male/female	45/55
% from out of state	73
% from public high school	62
% live on campus	68
# of fraternities	14
# of sororities	12
% African American	10
% Asian	16
% Caucasian	47
% Hispanic	4
% international	13
# of countries represented	101

SURVEY SAYS . . .

Lab facilities are great
Great computer facilities
Great library
Students love Atlanta, GA
Great off-campus food
Campus feels safe
Student publications are popular

ACADEMICS

Academic Rating	94
% students graduating within 4 years	82
% students graduating within 6 years	88
Calendar	semester
Student/faculty ratio	7:1
Profs interesting rating	89
Profs accessible rating	88
Most common reg class size	10–19 students
Most common lab size	fewer than 10 students

MOST POPULAR MAJORS

business, economics,
biology, psychology

STUDENTS SAY ". . ."

Academics

As one of the South's premier universities, Emory University "provides a warm, challenging environment where everyone is willing to make you feel a part of the Emory family." The university offers a "huge variety of classes to choose from" and fortunately it's "relatively easy to get [into the ones] you want." Though classes can be "tough," Emory does its best to ensure that "resources are readily available to help those who need it." Undergrads do warn, however, that science classes are often "weed-out courses." While courses taught by grad students receive mixed reviews, undergrads are nearly unanimous in their praise for their professors. In addition to being "intelligent [and] engaging," the faculty "wants to help you do well and achieve your goals." And their love for their subject matter is contagious. A freshman notes, "the passion my professors have…encourages me to engage in classroom discussions and makes me excited about the material covered in class." Many undergrads also stress that professors are very "accessible." As one neuro-science major explains, "I have actually been able to get e-mail replies from my organic chemistry professor at 2:00 A.M. the night before a test." Overall, students are also happy with the administration. Although on occasion it can "take some prodding" to get things done, most find that they are very "attentive and responsive to student concerns."

Life

As one content sophomore shares, life at Emory is "never boring." Though students are "very conscious of what they want to do with themselves once they graduate," there's definitely a work hard, play hard mentality. And when students want to break out of the dorms or the library, they have a plethora of activities to choose from. "There is always something going on, whether it's a sporting event, an a capella performance, a community service project or a fraternity or sorority event." Undergrads can participate in anything from "tango lessons from Tangueros Emory [to the] Hindu Students Association's Diwali celebration." Additionally, "frat parties are pretty popular, as well as house parties near campus." Those who tire of the Emory scene can easily explore all that bustling Atlanta has to offer. A knowledgeable senior offers, "There's a lot to do in [the city] at night to take a break from school when you need to, and places like Piedmont Park make for a great escape on the weekend. Once you get to know the area, there are some great little neighborhood restaurants, shops and bars in places like Decatur, Little Five Points, and Virginia Highlands." Those without a car fear not, as "Emory also runs free shuttles to various locations all over Atlanta at night on the weekends and many underclassmen make use of these."

Student Body

Emory undergrads are a "hardworking" lot and the typical student is "extremely committed to their academics." Most have "high aspirations" and a "large chunk of the student body is very pre-professional (premed, pre-law, business, etc.)." Luckily, they're "not afraid to have fun," and many are "involved in extracurricular activities and do some community service." Importantly, they also view their peers as "friendly, outgoing, and personable." To some students, it seems as though Emory attracts a large number of "white, wealthy, Northeastern, prep-school kids." And it sometimes feels like "every other person you meet is from Long Island." However, others insist that the university is rather diverse, proclaiming that there are "people from all types of lifestyles, cultures, and backgrounds." As one satisfied international studies undergrad boasts, "All students bring unique perspectives to the Emory campus, which is part of what makes Emory an interesting place." Overall, it's an "easygoing" and "pretty accepting" student body here. A happy freshman sums up, "Everyone gets along, and religion and origin are definitely not defining characteristics."

FINANCIAL AID: 800-727-6039 • E-MAIL: ADMISS@EMORY.EDU • WEBSITE: WWW.EMORY.EDU

THE PRINCETON REVIEW SAYS

Admissions

Very important factors considered include: Academic GPA, application essay, recommendation(s), rigor of secondary school record, standardized test scores, character/personal qualities, extracurricular activities. *Important factors considered include:* Level of applicant's interest, talent/ability, volunteer work, work experience. *Other factors considered include:* Class rank, alumni/ae relation, first generation, geographical residence, interview, racial/ethnic status, state residency. SAT or ACT required; ACT with writing component required. TOEFL required of all international applicants. *Academic units required:* 4 English, 3 mathematics, 2 science (2 science labs), 2 foreign language, 2 social studies, 2 history, 1 visual/performing arts, 2 academic elective. *Academic units recommended:* 4 mathematics, 3 science, 3 foreign language.

Financial Aid

Students should submit: FAFSA, CSS/Financial Aid PROFILE. Regular filing deadline is March 1. The Princeton Review suggests that all financial aid forms be submitted as soon as possible after January 1. *Need-based scholarships/grants offered:* Federal Pell, SEOG, state scholarships/grants, private scholarships, school scholarship or grant aid from institutional funds. *Loan aid offered:* Direct Subsidized Stafford, Direct Unsubsidized Stafford, Direct PLUS, Federal Perkins, Federal Nursing Loans, university loans from institutional funds. Federal Work-Study Program available. Off-campus job opportunities are good.

The Inside Word

Early decision applicants to Emory have risen drastically over the past few years, creating a quandary for aspiring Emory students: Do they join the growing crowd of early applicants and presumably increase the likelihood of admission, or do they take their chances with the regular admission date? Locking into one school early in the process can be a blessing or a curse; what if the aid package (which doesn't arrive until mid-April) isn't sufficient? Here's the good news: Emory financial aid has traditionally met 100 percent of applicants' demonstrated need.

THE SCHOOL SAYS "..."

From the Admissions Office

"Emory is an inquiry-driven, ethically engaged, and diverse community whose members work collaboratively for positive transformation in the world through courageous leadership in teaching, research scholarship, healthcare, and social action. The university is internationally recognized for its outstanding liberal arts colleges, superb professional schools, and leading health care system. Emory is noted as one of the most diverse selective universities in the country.

"Emory offers a distinctive undergraduate experience with programs in the humanities, sciences, business, and nursing allowing students to explore their interests and talents in the classroom and in the field. Entering freshman may apply to Emory College, a four-year liberal arts education within the heart of a major research university. Students may also apply to Oxford College where student spend the first two years on Emory's original campus thirty-eight miles east of Atlanta. Emory provides a rich setting for learning from excellent teaching in small classes to lectures from prominent scholars to opportunities for study abroad, research, and internships.

"Emory students balance hard work with having fun. With seventy percent of students living on campus, the community is enhanced by a close-knit living environment. The campus life thrives on constant activity, and students are encouraged to get involved, share opinions, and flourish. Emory is a dynamic place that is constantly in a state of sustainable growth and improvement. Take a look at all Emory has to offer—you'll see why Emory students feel inspired to do more with what they learn here."

SELECTIVITY

Admissions Rating	98
# of applicants	15,550
% of applicants accepted	30
% of acceptees attending	3
# accepting a place on wait list	1,091
% admitted from wait list	6
# of early decision applicants	1,208
% accepted early decision	44

FRESHMAN PROFILE

Range SAT Critical Reading	640–740
Range SAT Math	670–760
Range SAT Writing	650–750
Range ACT Composite	30–33
Minimum computer TOEFL	250
Minimum web-based TOEFL	100
Average HS GPA	3.84
% graduated top 10% of class	84
% graduated top 25% of class	98
% graduated top 50% of class	100

DEADLINES

Early decision	
Deadline	11/1
Notification	12/15
Regular	
Deadline	1/15
Nonfall registration?	no

APPLICANTS ALSO LOOK AT AND OFTEN PREFER

Duke University, Georgia Institute of Technology, University of North Carolina at Chapel Hill, Vanderbilt University, Washington University in St. Louis

AND SOMETIMES PREFER

Amherst College, Boston University, Dartmouth College, Davidson College, Wake Forest University

AND RARELY PREFER

DePauw University, Drexel University, Morehouse College, Oral Roberts University, Providence College

FINANCIAL FACTS

Financial Aid Rating	93
Annual tuition	$38,600
Room and board	$11,198
Required fees	$558
Books and supplies	$1,100
% frosh rec. need-based scholarship or grant aid	47
% UG rec. need-based scholarship or grant aid	47
% frosh rec. non-need-based scholarship or grant aid	5
% UG rec. non-need-based scholarship or grant aid	4
% frosh rec. need-based self-help aid	43
% UG rec. need-based self-help aid	42
% frosh rec. any financial aid	55
% UG rec. any financial aid	54
% UG borrow to pay for school	43
Average cumulative indebtedness	$26,311

EUGENE LANG COLLEGE THE NEW SCHOOL FOR LIBERAL ARTS

65 WEST ELEVENTH STREET, OFFICE OF ADMISSION, NEW YORK, NY 10011 • ADMISSIONS: 212-229-5665 • FAX: 212-229-5166

STUDENTS SAY ". . ."
Academics
Eugene Lang College is an "unconventional," highly urban school with few academic requirements where courses have "really long poetic titles" and professors "go by their first names." "Lang is about small classes in a big city," summarizes a writing major. There's a "rich intellectual tradition" and, no matter what your major, an "interdisciplinary curriculum." "At Eugene Lang, you have the freedom to pursue your artistic or intellectual direction with absolute freedom," says a philosophy major. However, "students who are uncomfortable in a city and who are not excited about learning for learning's sake should not come to this school." Lang's "clueless," "incredibly bureaucratic" administration is hugely unpopular. The "approachable" and monolithically "radical" faculty is a mixed bag. "Seventy-five percent of the professors are pure gold, but the twenty-five percent who are not really are awful." "Lang's greatest strength (other than location) is its seminar style of teaching," explains a first-year student. "I've yet to be in a class with more then fifteen people." Students say their class discussions are phenomenal. "The students, however, at times can be somewhat draining." "All the teachers are highly susceptible to being led off on long tangents" and some "are too gentle and not comfortable shutting down wandering or irrelevant conversation." Juniors and seniors can take classes at several schools within the larger university (including Parsons The New School for Design and Mannes College The New School for Music). "So if Lang's ultra-liberal, writing-intensive seminars are too much," notes an urban studies major, "you can always take a break." Internships all over Manhattan are common, too.

Life
There are "great talks given on campus every week by a wide variety of academics on almost every social issue imaginable." Otherwise, "Lang is the anti-college experience." "There is very little community" on this speck of a campus on the northern end of Greenwich Village. "Space and facilities are limited." "There is no safe haven in the form of a communal student space" except for "a courtyard of a million cigarette butts." Certainly, "you aren't going to have the traditional college fun" here. On the other hand, few students anywhere else enjoy this glorious level of independence. "Life at Eugene Lang is integrated completely with living in New York City," and "you have the entire city at your fingertips." When you walk out of class, "you walk out into a city of nine million people." There are dorms here, but "most students have apartments," especially after freshman year. For fun, Lang students sometimes "hang around other students' apartments and smoke pot." Many "thoroughly enjoy the club scene." Mostly though, "people band into small groups and then go out adventuring in the city" where "there is always something to do that you've never done, or even heard of, before."

Student Body
"Lang offers the kids with dreadlocks and piercings an alternative place to gather, smoke, and write pretentious essays." It's "overrun with rabid hipsters." "Cool hair" and "avant-garde" attitudes proliferate. So do "tight pants." "Every student at Lang thinks they are an atypical student." "There is a running joke that all Lang students were 'that kid' in high school," says a senior. "Shock is very popular around here," and "everyone fits in as long as they are not too mainstream." "It's the normal ones who have the trouble," suggests a sophomore. "But once they take up smoking and embrace their inner hipster, everything's cool." "There are a lot of queer students, who seem to be comfortable." "We're really not all that ethnically diverse," admits a first-year student. There are "less affluent kids due to great financial aid," and there is a strong contingent of "trust-fund babies" and "over-privileged communists from Connecticut." "Most students are wealthy but won't admit it," says a senior. "To be from a rich family and have it be apparent is a cardinal sin." "Most students are extremely liberal and on the same wavelength politically." "Conservative kids are the freaks at our school. Left is in. But having a Republican in class is so exciting," suggest a senior. "We can finally have a debate."

EUGENE LANG COLLEGE THE NEW SCHOOL FOR LIBERAL ARTS

FINANCIAL AID: 212-229-8930 • E-MAIL: LANG@NEWSCHOOL.EDU • WEBSITE: WWW.LANG.EDU

THE PRINCETON REVIEW SAYS

Admissions

Very important factors considered include: Academic GPA, application essay, character/personal qualities, level of applicant's interest, talent/ability. *Important factors considered include:* Class rank, recommendation(s), rigor of secondary school record, extracurricular activities, volunteer work. *Other factors considered include:* Standardized test scores, alumni/ae relation, first generation, interview. ACT with writing component required. TOEFL required of all international applicants. High school diploma is required, and GED is accepted. *Academic units recommended:* 4 English, 4 mathematics, 4 science, 4 foreign language, 4 social studies, 4 history, 4 academic elective.

Financial Aid

Students should submit: FAFSA. Regular filing deadline is March 1. The Princeton Review suggests that all financial aid forms be submitted as soon as possible after January 1. *Need-based scholarships/grants offered:* Federal Pell, SEOG, state scholarships/grants, private scholarships, school scholarship or grant aid from institutional funds. *Loan aid offered:* Direct Subsidized Stafford, Direct Unsubsidized Stafford, Direct PLUS, Federal Perkins. Applicants will be notified of awards on a rolling basis beginning April 1. Federal Work-Study Program available. Off-campus job opportunities are excellent.

The Inside Word

The college draws a very self-selected and intellectually curious pool. Those who demonstrate little self-motivation will find themselves denied.

THE SCHOOL SAYS "..."

From the Admissions Office

"Eugene Lang College offers students of diverse backgrounds an innovative and creative approach to a liberal arts education, combining the stimulating classroom activity of a small, intimate college with the rich resources of a dynamic, urban university—The New School. The curriculum at Lang is challenging and flexible. Small classes, limited in size to eighteen students, promote energetic and thoughtful discussions, and writing is an essential component of all classes. Students can earn a bachelor's degree in Liberal Arts by designing their own program of study within one of fourteen interdisciplinary areas in the arts, social sciences, and humanities. Lang also offers bachelor's degrees in the Arts, Culture and Media, Economics, Education Studies, Environmental Studies, History, Philosophy, and Psychology. Students have the opportunity to pursue a five-year BA/BFA or BA/MA with other programs offered at the university. Lang's Greenwich Village location puts many of the city's cultural treasures—museums, libraries, music venues, theaters, and more—at your doorstep."

SELECTIVITY

Admissions Rating	84
# of applicants	1,900
% of applicants accepted	63
% of acceptees attending	28

FRESHMAN PROFILE

Range SAT Critical Reading	530–660
Range SAT Math	470–610
Range SAT Writing	530–650
Range ACT Composite	24–28
Minimum paper TOEFL	600
Minimum computer TOEFL	250
Minimum web-based TOEFL	100
Average HS GPA	3.47
% graduated top 10% of class	16
% graduated top 25% of class	47
% graduated top 50% of class	87

DEADLINES

Early decision	
Deadline	11/1
Notification	12/1
Regular	
Deadline	1/5
Nonfall registration?	yes

APPLICANTS ALSO LOOK AT AND SOMETIMES PREFER

Emerson College, New York University, Sarah Lawrence College

FINANCIAL FACTS

Financial Aid Rating	69
Annual tuition	$18,485
% frosh rec. need-based scholarship or grant aid	66
% UG rec. need-based scholarship or grant aid	55
% frosh rec. non-need-based scholarship or grant aid	5
% UG rec. non-need-based scholarship or grant aid	1
% frosh rec. need-based self-help aid	62
% UG rec. need-based self-help aid	54
% UG borrow to pay for school	67
Average cumulative indebtedness	$30,830

THE EVERGREEN STATE COLLEGE

2700 EVERGREEN PARKWAY, NORTHWEST, OFFICE OF ADMISSIONS, OLYMPIA, WA 98505 • ADMISSIONS: 360-867-6170 • FAX: 360-867-5114

CAMPUS LIFE
Quality of Life Rating	75
Fire Safety Rating	84
Green Rating	86
Type of school	public
Environment	city

STUDENTS
Total undergrad enrollment	4,314
% male/female	46/54
% from out of state	27
% live on campus	21
% African American	4
% Asian	3
% Caucasian	70
% Hispanic	5
% Native American	3
# of countries represented	15

SURVEY SAYS . . .
Lots of liberal students
Students aren't religious
Low cost of living
Frats and sororities are unpopular
or nonexistent
Political activism is popular

ACADEMICS
Academic Rating	76
% students graduating within 4 years	39
% students graduating within 6 years	50
Calendar	quarter
Student/faculty ratio	23:1
Profs interesting rating	88
Profs accessible rating	77
Most common reg class size	20–29 students

MOST POPULAR MAJORS
humanities, interdisciplinary studies,
social sciences

STUDENTS SAY ". . ."

Academics

The Evergreen State College takes a decidedly different approach to higher education. At this small public school, students receive narrative evaluations of their academic achievements, not letter grades. Collaboration is encouraged, and coursework is entirely interdisciplinary. Each term, Evergreen students sign up for one course or "program," through which a single topic is explored by a team of teachers from a variety of different subject areas. Many students choose Evergreen precisely for this type of academic freedom, saying it's the right school for "students who want to engineer their education instead of being handed a list of requirements and sent on their way." A current student elaborates, "the interdisciplinary programs have allowed me to learn things I would never have expected—like microscopy in an art class or critical theory in a history class. It's allowed me to find what I'm truly passionate about and pursue it." On this "green" campus, the environmental studies program is very strong, and the "forest land is often utilized for learning experiences." In fact, "field trips are common" in many programs, and there is an "emphasis on group projects and on hands-on work here. At Evergreen you learn by doing, not just by reading about it." Usually addressed by their first name, "the professors at Evergreen are more than teachers; they are your partner in education and dedicate themselves to facilitating the students' learning." By the same token, students say it's important to do a little research before signing up for courses because "a personal dispute with a professor can be a big problem."

Life

There is no Greek system and no football team, but that doesn't mean the Evergreen campus lacks spirit, pride, or culture. On the contrary, "there is always something going on" at Evergreen, and, for those living on campus, "social life is very vivid." With acres of pristine forest surrounding the school grounds, "many students go walking in the woods to socialize, unwind, and appreciate its almost natural state." In addition, outdoorsy activities like "hiking, kayaking, biking, and snowboarding" are popular pastimes. On campus, "there are clubs and student organizations for pretty much anything you can imagine, from the 'Evergreen Jesus Folk' to the local SDS chapter." A student enthuses, "I've also started trying tons of new activities since I got here. Now I go to yoga twice a week; I go rock-climbing all the time; I go swimming a bunch and to the sauna; I go down to the beach and into the woods pretty frequently; [and] I do a lot more bike riding and reading." There is a modest party scene on and off campus, yet Evergreen students tend toward mellower activities. In their free time, "most people take the bus or ride their bikes downtown to see a show or have a meal at a café," and potluck dinner parties are "one of the main social outlets in Olympia." For those who like to boogie, "there are a lot of musicians on campus, and there is a thriving music scene in Olympia."

Student Life

Evergreen is a "quirky" college, and, as such, it tends to attract students looking for something other than the classic undergraduate experience. There is "no typical student" at Evergreen, but you'll definitely meet your share of "hipster, coffee-shop types" and "Earth-friendly, artsy types" at this alternative school. A sophomore jokes, "I'm not sure what you would have to wear to not fit in at Evergreen—maybe a suit and tie?" Politically and socially, "the student body definitely swings left, with a large portion of students interested in environmental conservation, organic farming, LGBT rights, and Eastern philosophy and religion." While "hiking boots, sweaters, and bicycles are everywhere," students say there is more diversity at Evergreen than meets the eye. A current student shares, "I have had classes with any type of student one can imagine. I've had seminar with WWII Navy veterans sitting next to radical freshman activists." On that note, Evergreen attracts many returning students, and undergraduates "range from young to old, experienced in life to just out of high school, living with parents to having children of their own."

THE EVERGREEN STATE COLLEGE

FINANCIAL AID: 360-867-6205 • E-MAIL: ADMISSIONS@EVERGREEN.EDU • WEBSITE: WWW.EVERGREEN.EDU

THE PRINCETON REVIEW SAYS

Admissions

Very important factors considered include: Academic GPA, application essay, rigor of secondary school record. *Important factors considered include:* Standardized test scores, first generation, level of applicant's interest. *Other factors considered include:* Recommendation(s), extracurricular activities, interview, volunteer work, work experience. SAT or ACT required; ACT with or without writing component accepted. TOEFL required of all international applicants. High school diploma is required, and GED is accepted. *Academic units required:* 4 English, 3 mathematics, 2 science (2 science labs), 2 foreign language, 3 social studies, 1 academic elective.

Financial Aid

Students should submit: FAFSA. Regular filing deadline is March 15. The Princeton Review suggests that all financial aid forms be submitted as soon as possible after January 1. *Need-based scholarships/grants offered:* Federal Pell, SEOG, state scholarships/grants, private scholarships, school scholarship or grant aid from institutional funds. *Loan aid offered:* Direct Subsidized Stafford, Direct Unsubsidized Stafford, Direct PLUS, Federal Perkins, university loans from institutional funds. Applicants will be notified of awards on a rolling basis beginning April 1. Federal Work-Study Program available. Off-campus job opportunities are good.

The Inside Word

While admissions aren't particularly selective, many students enter Evergreen with a strong academic record. Evergreen places a lot of credence in character and personal qualities when making admissions decisions. The school's atypical academic program calls for a curious and independent spirit, and admissions officers want to ensure that applicants will have the maturity to direct their own educational development.

THE SCHOOL SAYS "..."

From the Admissions Office

"Evergreen, a public college of arts and sciences, is a national leader in developing full-time interdisciplinary studies programs. Students work closely with faculty to study an issue or theme from the perspective of several academic disciplines. They apply what's learned to real world issues, complete projects in groups, and discuss concepts in seminars that typically involve a faculty member and twenty-three students. The emphasis on seminars, interdisciplinary problem solving, and collaboration means students are well prepared for graduate school and the world of work. Our students tend to be politically active, environmentally savvy, and more concerned about social justice than competition and personal gain.

"All applicants are encouraged to complete a Free Application for Federal Student Aid (FAFSA). Evergreen's priority financial aid deadline is March 15, though applicants may submit the form later and may be awarded aid if funds are still available.

"Freshman applicants are required to submit test scores from either the SAT or ACT tests. The student's best composite score will be used in the admissions process."

SELECTIVITY

Admissions Rating	72
# of applicants	1,965
% of applicants accepted	94
% of acceptees attending	34

FRESHMAN PROFILE

Range SAT Critical Reading	510–640
Range SAT Math	460–590
Range SAT Writing	480–590
Range ACT Composite	21–27
Minimum paper TOEFL	550
Minimum computer TOEFL	213
Minimum web-based TOEFL	79
Average HS GPA	3.08
% graduated top 10% of class	12
% graduated top 25% of class	27
% graduated top 50% of class	62

DEADLINES

Regular	
Deadline	3/1
Notification	11/1
Nonfall registration?	yes

APPLICANTS ALSO LOOK AT

AND OFTEN PREFER
Central Washington University, University of Washington, Western Washington University

AND SOMETIMES PREFER
Portland State University, University of Oregon, University of Puget Sound

AND RARELY PREFER
Hampshire College, University of California—Santa Cruz, Warren Wilson College

FINANCIAL FACTS

Financial Aid Rating	72
Annual in-state tuition	$6,108
Annual out-of-state tuition	$17,235
Room and board	$8,460
Required fees	$571
Books and supplies	$972
% frosh rec. need-based scholarship or grant aid	36
% UG rec. need-based scholarship or grant aid	46
% frosh rec. non-need-based scholarship or grant aid	29
% UG rec. non-need-based scholarship or grant aid	11
% frosh rec. need-based self-help aid	34
% UG rec. need-based self-help aid	44
% frosh rec. any financial aid	50
% UG rec. any financial aid	57
% UG borrow to pay for school	48
Average cumulative indebtedness	$16,065

FAIRFIELD UNIVERSITY

1073 NORTH BENSON ROAD, FAIRFIELD, CT 06824 • ADMISSIONS: 203-254-4100 • FAX: 203-254-4199

STUDENTS SAY "..."

Academics

Fairfield University, founded in 1942, is "a promising young institution short on tradition and diversity, but big on community, cross-disciplinary academics" and "educating the whole person: body, mind, and spirit." This Jesuit institution is based in "an amazing little New England town an hour outside of New York City." "It was everything I wanted in my school," a happy biology student testifies. "Small class size, beautiful campus, approachable professors—it's perfect." The school has a strong "commitment to the Jesuit values," a "friendly atmosphere," and a small size that means you'll "see so many familiar faces every day." Fairfield works hard to prepare "its students for life after college with the tools inherent in a Jesuit education." Students found the professors to be "amazingly engaging and knowledgeable." They're "experienced veterans in their fields of study" who have "actual industry, practical, real-world experience. This gives the students real insight into what a career actually is." Thanks to the small size, professors are "very accessible and tend to truly care about their students." One religious studies student sums up the Fairfield experience as being "about community—between the encouragement to get involved, living and learning communities, and its dedication to service, Fairfield is about forming and improving its own community and the greater community around it."

Life

Although some students can "get stuck in the 'Fairfield bubble,'" New Haven and "New York City [are] not that far away," and "it's easy to get on the train and go to the city if you want real fun." On campus, "students attend parties on the weekends, concerts on campus, or local concerts." The convenient location "enables students to visit other schools as well." "Townhouse parties are the biggest things for the weekend," and going to the "beach is always fun once the weather gets warmer in the spring." "FUSA (Fairfield University Student Association) plans activities for every night of the week (games, speakers, late night food, etc.)." "The extracurricular activities the school provides for its students are really a great diversion from school work when you've had a stressful day!" If there's one downside to campus life, it seems to be "the food in the cafeteria," which was frequently derided, as well as the definite "lack of school spirit." Although one student proclaimed: "We learn and live together; we are Stags!" "Overall, it's a laid-back school with night life, and I like it that way, nothing really wild."

Student Body

Fairfield students are typically "white, middle- or upper-class students," who are "usually devoted to studies as well as serving the community and others." However, many students feel the school "should improve in recruiting a more diverse student body." "Perhaps the downfall of Fairfield is that the student population seems pretty homogeneous," one student explains. "White and wealthy would be a fitting description for most. However, diversity is an initiative the university is working on." In particular, "socioeconomic differences are very clearly defined." "Although it is not very diverse, most students are open to people of different backgrounds, and joining clubs or other teams is an easy way to make friends and fit in." One student points out that, while the school isn't racially diverse, that doesn't mean the school isn't accepting: "Being a minority here, I think the openness to minorities is undervalued. Everyone here is accepting, and though there are some things that could be improved upon, it is a very good school to belong." As for fashion, Fairfield "has the 'J. Crew U.' reputation" for a reason. "The typical student owns a Northface, was really good at some sport back in high school, owns some articles of Polo, is moderately attractive, and enjoys a weekend of partying." However, while "everyone always looks put together...no one is going over the top—we do have to go to class."

FINANCIAL AID: 203-254-4125 • E-MAIL: ADMIS@MAIL.FAIRFIELD.EDU • WEBSITE: WWW.FAIRFIELD.EDU

THE PRINCETON REVIEW SAYS
Admissions

Very important factors considered include: Academic GPA, application essay, recommendation(s), rigor of secondary school record. *Important factors considered include:* Character/personal qualities, extracurricular activities, first generation, interview, talent/ability, volunteer work, work experience. *Other factors considered include:* Class rank, standardized test scores, alumni/ae relation, geographical residence, racial/ethnic status. ACT with or without writing component accepted. TOEFL required of all international applicants. *Academic units required:* 4 English, 3 mathematics, 2 science (2 science labs), 2 foreign language, 2 social studies, 2 history, 1 academic elective. *Academic units recommended:* 4 English, 4 mathematics, 3 science (2 science labs), 4 foreign language, 2 social studies, 2 history, 1 academic elective.

Financial Aid

Students should submit: FAFSA, CSS/Financial Aid PROFILE, non-custodial profile. Regular filing deadline is February 15. The Princeton Review suggests that all financial aid forms be submitted as soon as possible after January 1. *Need-based scholarships/grants offered:* Federal Pell, SEOG, state scholarships/grants, private scholarships, school scholarship or grant aid from institutional funds, Federal Nursing Scholarships. *Loan aid offered:* Direct Subsidized Stafford, Direct Unsubsidized Stafford, Direct PLUS, Federal Perkins, Federal Nursing Loans. Applicants will be notified of awards by April 1. Federal Work-Study Program available. Off-campus job opportunities are fair.

The Inside Word

Steady increases in the number of admission applications have nicely increased selectivity in recent years. Fairfield's campus and central location, combined with improvements to the library, campus center, classrooms, athletic facilities, and campus residencies, make this a campus worth seeing.

THE SCHOOL SAYS "..."
From the Admissions Office

"Fairfield University welcomes students of unique promise into a learning and living community that will give them a solid intellectual foundation and the confidence they need to reach their individual goals. Students at Fairfield benefit from the deep-rooted Jesuit commitment to education of the whole person—mind, body, and spirit, and our admission policies are consistent with that mission. When considering an applicant, Fairfield looks at measures of academic achievement, students' curricular and extracurricular activities, their life skills and accomplishments, and the degree to which they have an appreciation for Fairfield's mission and outlook. In keeping with its holistic review process, Fairfield is test optional for undergraduate students seeking admission for the fall of 2010 and beyond. Students who decide not to submit SAT or ACT scores will be required to write an additional essay and are encouraged to participate in an admission interview.

"Fairfield University students are challenged to be creative and active members of a community in which diversity is encouraged and honored. With its commitment to education for an inspired life, Fairfield has developed a unique educational model to ensure that students receive the guidance they need to reach their fullest potential. The integration of living and learning is at the heart of a Fairfield education through students' participation in living and learning communities, vocational exploration, civic engagement, and finally, discernment of how they want to put their gifts and education to work in the world. As a result of this holistic model of education, Fairfield graduates are highly successful in gaining admission to selective graduate schools, while others achieve satisfying careers. A signification achievement for the university is that fifty-five Fairfield graduates have been tapped as Fulbright scholars since 1993."

SELECTIVITY
Admissions Rating	88
# of applicants	8,420
% of applicants accepted	72
% of acceptees attending	15
# accepting a place on wait list	527
% admitted from wait list	17

FRESHMAN PROFILE
Range SAT Critical Reading	530–620
Range SAT Math	540–630
Range SAT Writing	540–630
Range ACT Composite	23–27
Minimum paper TOEFL	550
Minimum computer TOEFL	213
Minimum web-based TOEFL	80
Average HS GPA	3.34
% graduated top 10% of class	7
% graduated top 25% of class	83
% graduated top 50% of class	95

DEADLINES
Early decision	
Deadline	12/15
Notification	1/15
Early action	
Deadline	11/1
Notification	12/20
Regular	
Deadline	1/15
Nonfall registration?	no

APPLICANTS ALSO LOOK AT AND OFTEN PREFER
Boston College
AND SOMETIMES PREFER
Boston University, College of the Holy Cross, Villanova University

FINANCIAL FACTS
Financial Aid Rating	80
Annual tuition	$38,450
Room and board	$11,740
Required fees	$590
Books and supplies	$1,100
% frosh rec. need-based scholarship or grant aid	50
% UG rec. need-based scholarship or grant aid	49
% frosh rec. non-need-based scholarship or grant aid	29
% UG rec. non-need-based scholarship or grant aid	20
% frosh rec. need-based self-help aid	50
% UG rec. need-based self-help aid	48
% frosh rec. any financial aid	62
% UG rec. any financial aid	56
% UG borrow to pay for school	65
Average cumulative indebtedness	$37,015

FISK UNIVERSITY

1000 SEVENTEENTH AVENUE NORTH, NASHVILLE, TN 37208-3051 • ADMISSIONS: 615-329-8665 • FAX: 615-329-8774

STUDENTS SAY ". . ."

Academics

"Many greats have graced the gates of Fisk University," a historically black university that "produces independent and aware adults...capable of functioning in almost any capacity." Those greats include NAACP co-founder W.E.B DuBois, historian John Hope Franklin, poet Nikki Giovanni, and civil rights activist Ida B. Wells, an impressive roster of past luminaries for sure. Today, this "top HBCU excels highly in the sciences;" about one in four students majors in psychology here, and nearly as many pursue degrees in biology (business is the other big attraction, claiming about one in five students). With those strengths, it's no wonder students tell us "Fisk University is about preparing its students for careers and the real world." Students remind us that it's "about the DETAILS" here, an acronym for Diversity, Excellence, Teamwork, Accountability, Integrity, Leadership, and Service. Finally, it's about "a family atmosphere" fostered by professors who "are all passionate about their jobs" and who "really care about their students' wellbeing and education." Instructors "fully equip us to survive in today's society," while the Fisk curriculum "is challenging, but [as a result] we are guaranteed to be [among] the most competitive of our fields." Administrators, on the other hand, "lack communication skills when it comes to informing the students about what concerns them. Oftentimes students...find out through the media after major events have occurred." Students also complain that "campus housing and building quality" need to be improved.

Life

Fisk University is "a small school" where "there are very few secrets and very few males" (women outnumber men by a more than a two-to-one ratio). "Because it's surrounded by many other schools," Fisk provides "a great college atmosphere" that makes it easy to have fun when you want to but also "easy to stay focused on school." Campus life offers "many organizations," including Greek organizations and the Jubilee Singers, the school's world-famous singing group specializing in African American spirituals. Indeed, "Music is a large part of our school's history, and it is still respected today. There is usually music on the Yard on Friday nights, and this is an event that gives the students an opportunity to mix and mingle and dance with one another in a relaxed manner." College athletics are also important: "We have boys' and girls' basketball teams, and they are very popular on campus," one student explains. On-campus events such as parties, club meetings, and philanthropic programs are driven by "a core group of students [who] push and push to make life better here," including many involved in Greek life. While some students from big cities may find Nashville "pretty boring," others will enjoy the city's vibrant music scene and its eateries catering to everyone from the meat-and-three crowd to upscale epicures.

Student Body

"Studious African Americans...willing to help others" make up the majority of the Fisk student body, where undergrads describe themselves as "smart, creative, motivated, and determined individuals who are constantly learning how to make ourselves better people." The typical student "probably has a lot going on such as class, community service, and on-campus activities" and "looks nice, dresses appropriately for any occasion," and is "very outspoken but respectful" as well. Quite a few students noted the high proportion of "nerds" here; as one puts it, "Everyone at Fisk University is different in their own way. There are many people here that others may call weird, but they still fit in because of that uniqueness." The same student continues, "Although everyone at Fisk is different, we all have many things in common: for example, intellectual abilities and the love of music."

FINANCIAL AID: 615-329-8735 • E-MAIL: ADMISSIONS@FISK.EDU • WEBSITE: WWW.FISK.EDU

THE PRINCETON REVIEW SAYS

Admissions

Very important factors considered include: Rigor of secondary school record. *Important factors considered include:* Academic GPA, application essay, class rank, standardized test scores, character/personal qualities, extracurricular activities, interview. *Other factors considered include:* Recommendation(s), alumni/ae relation, geographical residence, level of applicant's interest, talent/ability, volunteer work. SAT or ACT required; ACT with writing component recommended. TOEFL required of all international applicants. High school diploma is required, and GED is accepted. *Academic units required:* 4 English, 3 mathematics, 3 science (2 science labs), 1 foreign language, 1 history. *Academic units recommended:* 4 English, 4 mathematics, 3 science (2 science labs), 2 foreign language, 1 history.

Financial Aid

The Princeton Review suggests that all financial aid forms be submitted as soon as possible after January 1.

The Inside Word

Intangibles can play a big part in the admissions decision at Fisk, especially for borderline candidates. A marked improvement in high school grades during junior and senior years, a demonstrated high level of determination, and commitment to school, community, and/or places of worship can all help create a successful application.

THE SCHOOL SAYS "..."

From the Admissions Office

"Founded in 1866, the university is coeducational, private, and one of America's premier Historically Black Universities. The first black college to be granted a chapter of Phi Beta Kappa Honor Society, Fisk serves a diverse student body with students from forty states and six foreign countries. There are residence halls for men and women. The focal point of the forty-acre campus and architectural symbol of the university is Jubilee Hall, the first permanent building for the education of blacks in the South, named for the internationally renowned Fisk Jubilee Singers, who continue their tradition of singing and sharing classic Negro spirituals along with other genres of music from African, Brazilian, African American and other diverse cultures. From its earliest days, Fisk faculty and alumni have been among America's intellectual leaders providing leadership in several fields including medicine, science, art, humanities, religion, literature, sociology and philosophy. Fisk Alumni include W.E.B. Du Bois, the first black PhD from Harvard, and co-founder of the NAACP, Nikki Giovanni, poet/writer; Dr. John Hope Franklin, historian/scholar; David Lewis, professor/recipient of the prestigious Pulitzer Prize; Hazel O'Leary, Fisk President and former U.S. Secretary of Energy; John Lewis, U.S. Representative (GA); Judith Jamison, director of the Alvin Ailey Dance Company; and Johnetta B. Cole, former President of Spelman College. In proportion to its size, Fisk continues to contribute a higher percentage of African American alumni to the ranks of scholars pursuing doctoral degrees than any other institution in the United States."

SELECTIVITY

Admissions Rating	79
# of applicants	2,700
% of applicants accepted	45
% of acceptees attending	51

FRESHMAN PROFILE

Range SAT Critical Reading	467–546
Range SAT Math	455–540
Range SAT Writing	447–547
Range ACT Composite	18–23
Minimum paper TOEFL	550
Average HS GPA	3.33
% graduated top 10% of class	10
% graduated top 25% of class	30
% graduated top 50% of class	75

DEADLINES

Early action	
Deadline	12/1
Notification	12/20
Regular	
Priority	3/1
Deadline	3/1
Notification	9/1

FINANCIAL FACTS

Financial Aid Rating	65
Annual tuition	$15,140
Room and board	$7,730
Required fees	$1,100
Books and supplies	$1,500

FLAGLER COLLEGE

74 KING STREET, PO BOX 1027, ST. AUGUSTINE, FL 32085-1027 • ADMISSIONS: 800-304-4208 • FAX: 904-826-0094

CAMPUS LIFE

Quality of Life Rating	76
Fire Safety Rating	78
Green Rating	71
Type of school	private
Environment	town

STUDENTS

Total undergrad enrollment	2,747
% male/female	42/58
% from out of state	32
% from public high school	78
% live on campus	37
% African American	2
% Caucasian	80
% Hispanic	7
% Native American	1
% international	2
# of countries represented	25

SURVEY SAYS . . .

Students love St. Augustine, FL
Low cost of living
Frats and sororities are unpopular
or nonexistent
Very little drug use

ACADEMICS

Academic Rating	79
% students graduating	
within 4 years	50
% students graduating	
within 6 years	64
Calendar	semester
Student/faculty ratio	18:1
Profs interesting rating	85
Profs accessible rating	86
Most common	
reg class size	20–29 students

MOST POPULAR MAJORS

business/commerce, communication/
journalism, elementary education and
teaching

STUDENTS SAY ". . ."

Academics

Students "like the small-school feel" of Flagler College, an intimate liberal arts school with "an excellent education program" (including "one of the best deaf education programs in the country") and a "sound business department." Programs in communication, English, and graphic design also earn students' praises. No matter what they study, Flagler undergrads "actually get the chance to have a personal relationship with professors" who "are always there to help. They take a genuine interest and concern in the students. Most have their doctorates and are very knowledgeable about the classes they teach." The faculty also boasts some impressive real-world credentials; writes one business major, "I have professors who work for the FBI teaching us about criminal justice, major CEOs giving business lessons, and a retired judge teaching me about law and society. I have the best of all worlds. I really enjoy the curriculum and the small classrooms that make learning much more accessible." On the downside, the school's administration is widely regarded as "extremely conservative. It is like living with your parents when you are on campus if they were staunch Pat Robertson supporters." The most prominent example of this paternalism is a relatively strict class attendance policy, which many regard as "repressive and demeaning to students. We are adults, and if we have not learned to manage our time appropriately by now, we have much bigger problems than missing classes." Some, however, appreciate how the policy "keeps us in check."

Life

The conservatism of Flagler's administration is most evident in the way it governs campus life. Students report, "There is a no-tolerance rule on campus for alcohol (it is not allowed in the dorms, and you cannot be on campus drunk)", and "there is a no interdorm visitation policy (no guys/girls allowed in each other's halls)," restrictions that many find "Draconian and unnecessary." Fortunately, there's a simple work-around; "We mostly just hang off-campus at other students' houses." More than half of all students, including a large majority of non-freshmen, live off campus. Hometown St. Augustine is "a tourist town" that "does not cater to the college but rather the tourist. Shops and places close at 8 P.M.," and town police tend to act quickly to discourage off-campus rowdiness, so Flagler parties tend to be "smaller get-togethers" rather than raging Bacchanalias. But here again students find acceptable alternatives; "Jacksonville is only a thirty-minute drive, and we are also very close to Daytona. And there is always the beach," one explains. Intramural sports "are really popular on campus," and "there are a ton of clubs on campus for every kind of interest." All in all, "life at Flagler is pretty easygoing," a situation that fits most students' temperaments.

Student Body

Flagler draws a lot of "artsy types with a unique style and attitude...many of whom are environmentally conscious," as well as a solid contingent of "religious types—Inter Varsity members and students [who] join local churches." Finally, "there are the surfers, who probably make up one-third of the campus. They chose to come here because they knew the school was near the beach." Most are "laid-back, easygoing individuals, although not in a lazy way." Flagler is academically rigorous, after all, so students must "work hard to achieve our goals and help each other achieve our goals," and many "have multiple majors and are academically inclined." Women substantially outnumber men here. While the majority of students are white Floridians, "the recruiters are doing excellent job of trying to diversify the student population."

FINANCIAL AID: 904-819-6225 • E-MAIL: ADMISS@FLAGLER.EDU • WEBSITE: WWW.FLAGLER.EDU

THE PRINCETON REVIEW SAYS

Admissions

Very important factors considered include: Rigor of secondary school record. *Important factors considered include:* Academic GPA, application essay, standardized test scores, alumni relation, extracurricular activities, talent/ability. *Other factors considered include:* Class rank, recommendation(s), character/personal qualities, first generation, interview, level of applicant's interest, volunteer work. SAT or ACT required; ACT with or without writing component accepted. TOEFL required of all international applicants. High school diploma is required, and GED is accepted. *Academic units required:* 4 English, 3 mathematics, 2 science (1 science lab), 3 social studies, 1 history, 2 academic elective. *Academic units recommended:* 4 English, 4 mathematics, 3 science (2 science labs), 2 foreign language, 3 social studies, 2 history, 1 visual/performing arts, 2 academic elective, 1 computer science.

Financial Aid

Students should submit: FAFSA and institution's own financial aid form. The Princeton Review suggests that all financial aid forms be submitted as soon as possible after January 1. *Need-based scholarships/grants offered:* Federal Pell, SEOG, state scholarships/grants, private scholarships, school scholarship or grant aid from institutional funds. *Loan aid offered:* Direct Subsidized Stafford, Direct Unsubsidized Stafford, Direct PLUS, Federal Perkins. Applicants will be notified of awards on a rolling basis beginning April 1. Federal Work-Study Program available. Off-campus job opportunities are excellent.

The Inside Word

Several high-profile programs, a desirable location, and a small, incoming freshman class all conspire to drive down Flagler's admissions rate. Still, Flagler is not top-tier when it comes to selectivity, and strong candidates should meet little resistance From the Admissions Office. Admission as a prospective education major requires a minimum 1010 combined SAT score; admission to the department itself occurs by the end of sophomore year and is dependent on the student's performance at Flagler during the first two years.

THE SCHOOL SAYS "..."

From the Admissions Office

"Flagler College is an independent, four-year, coeducational, residential institution located in picturesque St. Augustine. A famous historic tourist center in northeast Florida, it is located to the south of Jacksonville and north of Daytona Beach. Flagler students have ample opportunity to explore the rich cultural heritage and international flavor of St. Augustine, and there's always time for a relaxing day at the beach, about four miles from campus. The annual cost for tuition, room, and board at Flagler is about the same as state universities. The small student body helps to keep one from becoming 'just a number.' Flagler serves a predominately full-time student body and seeks to enroll students who can benefit from the type of educational experience the college offers. Because of the college's unique mission and distinctive characteristics, some students may benefit more from an educational experience at Flagler than others. The college's admission standards and procedures are designed to select from among the applicants those students most likely to succeed academically, to contribute significantly to the student life program at Flagler, and to become graduates of the college. Flagler College provides an exceptional opportunity for a private education at an extremely affordable cost.

"All applicants to Flager College must submit either their SAT or ACT scores."

SELECTIVITY

Admissions Rating	84
# of applicants	2,650
% of applicants accepted	56
% of acceptees attending	42
# accepting a place on wait list	102
% admitted from wait list	11
# of early decision applicants	577
% accepted early decision	65

FRESHMAN PROFILE

Range SAT Critical Reading	510–590
Range SAT Math	500–580
Range SAT Writing	500–580
Range ACT Composite	21–25
Minimum paper TOEFL	550
Minimum computer TOEFL	213
Average HS GPA	3.37
% graduated top 10% of class	14
% graduated top 25% of class	39
% graduated top 50% of class	78

DEADLINES

Early decision	
Deadline	12/1
Notification	12/15
Regular	
Priority	1/15
Deadline	3/1
Nonfall registration?	yes

APPLICANTS ALSO LOOK AT AND RARELY PREFER
Florida Southern College

FINANCIAL FACTS

Financial Aid Rating	75
Annual tuition	$14,510
Room and board	$7,990
Books and supplies	$1,100
% frosh rec. need-based scholarship or grant aid	52
% UG rec. need-based scholarship or grant aid	44
% frosh rec. non-need-based scholarship or grant aid	41
% UG rec. non-need-based scholarship or grant aid	41
% frosh rec. need-based self-help aid	54
% UG rec. need-based self-help aid	52
% frosh rec. any financial aid	90
% UG rec. any financial aid	90
% UG borrow to pay for school	60
Average cumulative indebtedness	$20,895

FLORIDA SOUTHERN COLLEGE

OFFICE OF ADMISSIONS, 111 LAKE HOLLINGSWORTH DRIVE, LAKELAND, FL 33801 • ADMISSIONS: 800-274-4131 • FAX: 863-680-4120

CAMPUS LIFE

Quality of Life Rating	74
Fire Safety Rating	78
Green Rating	66
Type of school	private
Affiliation	Methodist
Environment	city

STUDENTS

Total undergrad enrollment	1,984
% male/female	42/58
% from out of state	30
% from public high school	84
% live on campus	74
# of fraternities	7
# of sororities	7
% African American	7
% Asian	2
% Caucasian	77
% Hispanic	8
% Native American	1
% international	4
# of countries represented	42

SURVEY SAYS . . .

Athletic facilities are great
Students get along with local
community
Great off-campus food
Intramural sports are popular
Frats and sororities dominate
social scene
Musical organizations are popular
Student government is popular

ACADEMICS

Academic Rating	78
% students graduating within 4 years	40
% students graduating within 6 years	52
Calendar	semester
Student/faculty ratio	14:1
Profs interesting rating	83
Profs accessible rating	81
Most common reg class size	10–19 students
Most common lab size	10–19 students

MOST POPULAR MAJORS

biology, business administration and
management, nursing

STUDENTS SAY ". . ."

Academics

Expect a "personalized education" at Florida Southern College, a small school that's "the perfect size for any student that doesn't want to go unnoticed!" Indeed, students insist, "FSC gives you a great education, both academically and socially, not only because the campus is small...but [also] because the professors want to get to know you as a person, not just a number on their roll call." With "small classes where you can actually ask questions during class and participate in group discussions" and "amazing" professors who "are always available to you if you need anything (every single professor...gives you their cell phone number on their syllabus in case you need anything at all)," students certainly don't lack for attention here. The music program is a definite standout at FSC; nursing, psychology, journalism, advertising, and business all have their enthusiastic adherents among the student body. Administrators "are seen on campus all the time, and [you] can approach them pretty easily," says one student. No wonder students tell us, "FSC is about community. This small school is like a big family where you always have someone to talk to or to help you."

Life

FSC is located "right on a lake so there are all sorts of water activities" for students to enjoy. "Kayaking, canoeing, swimming, biking, jogging, and much more" keep the lakefront hopping throughout daylight hours. The lake is most certainly the main attraction of hometown Lakeland. Students complain that the town is "not too exciting." "There's not really a whole lot to do in Lakeland," one undergrad points out, but fortunately FSC is located "right between Tampa and Orlando, two bigger cities that have more attractions and are only a forty-five-minute drive away." Campus life centers on Greek organizations and events organized by the Association of Campus Entertainment (ACE). The latter is "very creative. They have had casino night, raffle ticket giveaways, comedians, and a variety of other events." Greeks throw the requisite parties but also "go on a lot of service trips, serving food at soup kitchens, gleaning in the fields of local farmers, all sorts of stuff" that "keep members busy, but it's a good busy. It's the perfect balance of work and play." Drinking occurs primarily off campus "since it's not allowed on site," and students warn, "There is little life on campus over the weekend...You are forced to go off campus to find something that's worthwhile to do."

Student Body

The "friendly," "mostly outgoing" student body of FSC is predominantly "white, preppy, and upper-middle-class." Most "are religious, involved in sports, or part of the Greek system," but "There are a few outliers, and enough people are outliers that they hang out together." Students tend to be "involved in a number of clubs and organizations on campus. Our campus is small so it's really easy to get involved." There's a notable subpopulation of "students who did not perform well at their private high school institutions" and so couldn't gain admission to more competitive schools, but most everyone does what he or she has to do to get through. "There are students who are very into their schoolwork, always studying and striving to do their best, and then there are others who are very laid-back but still get their schoolwork done," one student tells us.

FLORIDA SOUTHERN COLLEGE

FINANCIAL AID: 800-205-1600 • E-MAIL: FSCADM@FLSOUTHERN.EDU • WEBSITE: WWW.FLSOUTHERN.EDU

THE PRINCETON REVIEW SAYS

Admissions

Very important factors considered include: Academic GPA, rigor of secondary school record. *Important factors considered include:* Application essay, recommendation(s), standardized test scores, character/personal qualities, extracurricular activities, level of applicant's interest, talent/ability. *Other factors considered include:* Class rank, alumni/ae relation, first generation, interview, racial/ethnic status, religious affiliation/commitment, volunteer work, work experience. SAT or ACT required; ACT with or without writing component accepted. TOEFL required of all international applicants. High school diploma is required, and GED is accepted. *Academic units required:* 4 English, 3 mathematics, 2 science (2 science labs), 3 social studies, 3 history, 2 academic elective. *Academic units recommended:* 2 foreign language.

Financial Aid

Students should submit: FAFSA, institution's own financial aid form. Regular filing deadline is July 1. The Princeton Review suggests that all financial aid forms be submitted as soon as possible after January 1. *Need-based scholarships/ grants offered:* Federal Pell, SEOG, state scholarships/grants, private scholarships, school scholarship or grant aid from institutional funds, Federal Nursing Scholarships. *Loan aid offered:* Federal Perkins. Applicants will be notified of awards on a rolling basis beginning March 1. Federal Work-Study Program available. Off-campus job opportunities are good.

The Inside Word

Individual attention is a cornerstone of the Florida Southern experience, and the experience begins with the admissions process. Admissions officers give each application a careful review, looking for indications of latent capabilities and potential to contribute to campus life and the campus community. Focus is directed not only on grades and test scores, but also on peripherals like personal attributes and unique experiences that speak to extracurricular achievement. Candidates are encouraged to employ creativity throughout their applications and are invited to submit additional academic materials and portfolio samples.

THE SCHOOL SAYS "..."

From the Admissions Office

"Florida Southern is friendly and dynamic, offering exciting engaged learning opportunities that include guaranteed internships, student-faculty collaborative research and performance, service learning, and study abroad. An innovative new program—the Junior Journey—guarantees all entering students the opportunity to study domestically or overseas during their junior year at no cost for the trip other than minimal course credit charges. FSC offers more than fifty majors in fields such as art, biology, business, communication, education, environmental studies, music and theater performance, nursing, and psychology. Pre-professional programs include premedicine, pre-pharmacy, pre-dentistry, and pre-law. The college is known for its great professors, small classes, and personalized attention. A state-of-the-art, 24/7 technology center just opened on campus, as have contemporary residence halls with stunning views to beautiful Lake Hollingsworth. A new classroom building including a modern language lab, film studies center, and art gallery opened in Fall 2010. Our involved students enjoy rich and varied student life programming that includes championship NCAA Division II events in eighteen sports, intramurals, more than seventy clubs and organizations, a volunteer-oriented Greek system, and an awesome choice of weekend events. The college's popular lakefront program features free kayaks, canoes, and sailboats. Overlooking Lake Hollingsworth, FSC is home to the world's largest collection of buildings designed by Frank Lloyd Wright, which provides a stunning setting for living and learning. Ninety-four percent of graduates report landing jobs in their fields or continuing their studies at top-tier grad schools within three months of graduation."

SELECTIVITY
Admissions Rating	81
# of applicants	2,948
% of applicants accepted	67
% of acceptees attending	31
# of early decision applicants	75
% accepted early decision	81

FRESHMAN PROFILE
Range SAT Critical Reading	490–580
Range SAT Math	500–590
Range SAT Writing	470–570
Range ACT Composite	21–27
Minimum paper TOEFL	550
Minimum computer TOEFL	213
Average HS GPA	3.40
% graduated top 10% of class	21
% graduated top 25% of class	51
% graduated top 50% of class	81

DEADLINES
Early decision	
Deadline	12/1
Notification	12/15
Regular	
Deadline	3/1
Notification	1/15
Nonfall registration?	yes

APPLICANTS ALSO LOOK AT
AND OFTEN PREFER
University of Florida
AND SOMETIMES PREFER
Stetson University, University of Tampa
AND RARELY PREFER
Flagler College

FINANCIAL FACTS
Financial Aid Rating	78
Annual tuition	$25,529
Room and board	$8,808
Required fees	$583
% frosh rec. need-based scholarship or grant aid	66
% UG rec. need-based scholarship or grant aid	58
% frosh rec. non-need-based scholarship or grant aid	85
% UG rec. non-need-based scholarship or grant aid	72
% frosh rec. need-based self-help aid	33
% UG rec. need-based self-help aid	30
% frosh rec. any financial aid	99
% UG rec. any financial aid	97
% UG borrow to pay for school	64
Average cumulative indebtedness	$28,294

THE BEST 376 COLLEGES ■ 237

FLORIDA STATE UNIVERSITY

2500 UNIVERSITY CENTER, TALLAHASSEE, FL 32306-2400 • ADMISSIONS: 850-644-6200 • FAX: 850-644-0197

CAMPUS LIFE

Quality of Life Rating	86
Fire Safety Rating	80
Green Rating	90
Type of school	public
Environment	city

STUDENTS

Total undergrad enrollment	30,830
% male/female	45/55
% from out of state	9
% from public high school	84
% live on campus	20
# of fraternities	31
# of sororities	27
% African American	11
% Asian	4
% Caucasian	69
% Hispanic	14
% Native American	1
# of countries represented	132

SURVEY SAYS . . .

Athletic facilities are great
Everyone loves the Seminoles
Students are happy
Great library
Lots of beer drinking
Frats and sororities dominate
social scene

ACADEMICS

Academic Rating	68
% students graduating within 4 years	69
% students graduating within 6 years	74
Calendar	semester
Student/faculty ratio	22:1
Profs interesting rating	79
Profs accessible rating	81
Most common reg class size	20–29 students

MOST POPULAR MAJORS

criminal justice/safety studies, finance, political science

STUDENTS SAY ". . ."

Academics

Florida State University is "a large, sports-oriented, research-intensive state school that has a niche for everybody, as long as you are willing to search." In addition to its strong academics, students tended to choose FSU for its "sports teams"—the Florida State Seminoles—the "great weather," and the fact that it's "a place with great traditions." "Florida State is a school that is so rooted in tradition it is extremely hard not to proudly call yourself a True Seminole." FSU is also "affordable" for in-state students with "excellent scholarships." "The tight vicinity of the campus [causes] the student body to be a close-unit of individuals." "FSU's reputation as a small-school feel in a big university was what drew me in," says an accounting and finance student. Reviews of the professors are mixed, as is common at many large universities. "About one-fourth of the professors are no good at teaching, about half of them are decent or good, and about one-fourth are great," one student explains. Another attests, "I have had wonderful professors that have eyes, ears, and heart to a world beyond my own, and have shown me that anything is achievable if I try hard enough." Students do wish for "smaller class sizes" and "more discussions in class." If the students have one common complaint, it's *"parking!,"* which is "always a huge hassle." Students also wish for better sustainability, recycling, and green programs. "FSU has traditionally been all about the humanities, and it's great that we're expanding into other areas, but we shouldn't forget our main focus," says one student. An English major sums up FSU: "Florida State University is a school where students are asked to uphold the garnet and gold and to live intentionally in the direction of leadership, academics, and service."

Life

"Sports is basically your whole life here," one student claims. While a university as large as FSU—the population is 40,000 plus—has students of many types, athletics and "school spirit" are what "bring everyone together" at FSU. "Everyone likes to socialize and party, usually off campus, like at bars or houses." Greek life is also "very prominent" FSU has a reputation as a party school, and "many students go out on the weekend or even sometimes during the week. The use of alcohol and marihuana is very common." "The majority of FSU students gets rowdy almost every night of the week," confirms another. However, one student claims that "FSU is a 'recovering party school.' Since its heyday in the mid-nineties, FSU has calmed down a bit, but you can still find thriving parties and clubs any day of the week." "People go to Wakulla Springs to swim or to Bear Paw to go around the river during the weekends." Although "Tallahassee is one of the most boring cities I have ever been to," "the nightlife is…very important in Tallahassee; there are many bars and clubs to attend." "My life at Florida State is busy," one political science student explains. "I am always on the move. From class, to student government, Greek life, internships at the capital, and night life. I think people at FSU are constantly thinking about how they can better themselves and the university."

Student Body

Your average FSU student is a "football fan, partier, into academics and community service, [and] passionate." Students tend to be "extremely involved," whether it's in athletics, "Greek life or community service, or one of the other hundreds of groups and clubs here at FSU." "Greek is a huge part of campus, but you are fine if you are not in one." Although "the majority of students are Caucasians," "students of all races and religions work together here to make FSU an enjoyable environment," and "the school continues to become more diverse each year." No matter what their background, every FSU student has "a colossal amount of school spirit and loves to go out and support the team."

FINANCIAL AID: 850-644-5871 • E-MAIL: ADMISSIONS@ADMIN.FSU.EDU • WEBSITE: WWW.FSU.EDU

THE PRINCETON REVIEW SAYS

Admissions

Very important factors considered include: Academic GPA, rigor of secondary school record. *Important factors considered include:* Standardized test scores, state residency, talent/ability. *Other factors considered include:* Application essay, class rank, recommendation(s), alumni/ae relation, character/personal qualities, extracurricular activities, first generation, geographical residence, volunteer work, work experience. SAT or ACT required; ACT with writing component required. TOEFL required of all international applicants. High school diploma is required, and GED is accepted. *Academic units required:* 4 English, 4 mathematics, 3 science (2 science labs), 2 foreign language, 1 social studies, 2 history, 3 academic elective. *Academic units recommended:* 4 English, 4 mathematics, 4 science (2 science labs), 4 foreign language, 2 social studies, 2 history, 3 academic elective.

Financial Aid

Students should submit: FAFSA. The Princeton Review suggests that all financial aid forms be submitted as soon as possible after January 1. *Need-based scholarships/grants offered:* Federal Pell, SEOG, state scholarships/grants, private scholarships, school scholarship or grant aid from institutional funds. *Loan aid offered:* Direct Subsidized Stafford, Direct Unsubsidized Stafford, Direct PLUS, Federal Perkins. Applicants will be notified of awards on a rolling basis beginning March 15. Federal Work-Study Program available. Off-campus job opportunities are good.

The Inside Word

With 25,000 applications to process annually, FSU must rely on a formula-driven approach to triage its applicant pool. With the exception of applicants to special programs, only borderline candidates receive a truly thorough review; all others are either clearly in or clearly out based on grades, curriculum, and test scores. Candidates for programs in fine arts, creative arts, and performing arts must undergo a more rigorous review that includes a portfolio or audition.

THE SCHOOL SAYS " . . ."

From the Admissions Office

"The Florida State University is an internationally recognized teaching and research institution committed to preparing our students for a life that balances knowledge, creativity, leadership, and contribution. Designated as a Carnegie Research University (very high research activity), Florida State offers more than 320 undergraduate, graduate, and professional degree programs, including medicine and law. Our students have the opportunity to conduct research alongside Nobel laureates and Pulitzer Prize winners, Guggenheim Fellows, members of the National Academy of Sciences and American Academy of Arts and Sciences, and other globally recognized teachers and researchers. Through the efforts of our Office of Undergraduate Research, students partner with faculty who share their academic interests, and who encourage them to design and conduct original research projects. Through the Office of National Fellowships, Florida State has become a leader among the state's public universities by setting records in the award of national fellowships and scholarships for our students. We offer state-of-the-art teaching techniques in our technologically enhanced classrooms and wireless networking community. Our innovative student services include a comprehensive campus-wide leadership learning program, a center for community and global-based learning through service, and an award-winning career center. World-class cultural events, championship athletics, extensive recreational facilities, and a friendly, close-knit University community enrich student life and extend learning well beyond the classroom. Our diverse student body hails from all fifty states and more than 130 countries, and our numerous international programs throughout the world include year-round programs in Florence, Italy; London, England; Panama City, Panama; and Valencia, Spain."

SELECTIVITY

Admissions Rating	89
# of applicants	26,037
% of applicants accepted	60
% of acceptees attending	38

FRESHMAN PROFILE

Range SAT Critical Reading	550–640
Range SAT Math	560–650
Range SAT Writing	550–630
Range ACT Composite	24–28
Minimum paper TOEFL	550
Minimum web-based TOEFL	80
Average HS GPA	3.76
% graduated top 10% of class	39
% graduated top 25% of class	76
% graduated top 50% of class	97

DEADLINES

Regular	
Deadline	1/25
Nonfall registration?	yes

FINANCIAL FACTS

Financial Aid Rating	91
Annual in-state tuition	$3,156
Annual out-of-state tuition	$17,691
Room and board	$8,390
Required fees	$2,081
Books and supplies	$1,000
% frosh rec. need-based scholarship or grant aid	23
% UG rec. need-based scholarship or grant aid	23
% frosh rec. non-need-based scholarship or grant aid	36
% UG rec. non-need-based scholarship or grant aid	28
% frosh rec. need-based self-help aid	24
% UG rec. need-based self-help aid	27
% frosh rec. any financial aid	97
% UG rec. any financial aid	86
% UG borrow to pay for school	48
Average cumulative indebtedness	$20,993

FORDHAM UNIVERSITY

441 EAST FORDHAM ROAD, DUANE LIBRARY, NEW YORK, NY 10458 • ADMISSIONS: 718-817-4000 • FAX: 718-367-9404

CAMPUS LIFE

Quality of Life Rating	77
Fire Safety Rating	75
Green Rating	60*
Type of school	private
Affiliation	Roman Catholic
Environment	metropolis

STUDENTS

Total undergrad enrollment	7,950
% male/female	42/58
% from out of state	45
% from public high school	47
% live on campus	55
% African American	5
% Asian	8
% Caucasian	55
% Hispanic	13
% international	3
# of countries represented	58

SURVEY SAYS . . .
Great library
Great off-campus food
Campus feels safe
Students are happy
Frats and sororities are unpopular
or nonexistent
Student publications are popular
Hard liquor is popular

ACADEMICS

Academic Rating	79
% students graduating within 4 years	72
% students graduating within 6 years	79
Calendar	semester
Student/faculty ratio	13:1
Profs interesting rating	80
Profs accessible rating	82
Most common reg class size	10–19 students
Most common lab size	10–19 students

MOST POPULAR MAJORS
business/commerce, social sciences

STUDENTS SAY ". . ."

Academics
Fordham University—"the Jesuit school located in the capital of the world"—"offers a sense of community and a true college experience within the hustle and bustle" of New York City. Noteworthy majors include the performing arts and "an exceptional business program." There's also an "excellent honors program" and "a pretty good library." Students here tell us that they receive "a broad and holistic liberal arts education," thanks in large part to a "strict" and "extensive" core curriculum with a "somewhat large number of degree requirements." Classes are "small," and the "incredibly accessible" professors "love what they do." "Each of my professors has made me interested in their subject, even if I was only taking the class out of requirement," relates a finance major. "I get the impression that they are genuinely interested in what the students think." "I do not think I have ever had a really *bad* professor," adds an English major. Be warned, though: "The grade differentiation between some professors for the same class is absurd." Some students tell us that management is "friendly and approachable." "You can drop anyone an e-mail and expect a response back," proponents say. Critics pan the staff for an "overall lack of collaborative spirit" and gripe that the red tape is "fairly annoying."

Life
Fordham is two schools in one. There's the school's long-established location in Rose Hill, a "beautiful, Gothic, green" college campus complete with a "huge lawn" that is "located in an oasis in the middle of the Bronx," adjacent to "the original Little Italy" and its "amazing Italian food." There's also another, smaller campus at Lincoln Center in the heart of Manhattan. The big complaint here is the on-campus grub, which ranges from "pretty bad" to "prison-grade gruel." "Honestly," asks a mystified first-year student, "what is this stuff?" Otherwise, students are quite happy. Size-wise, Fordham is "just small enough that you'll see people you recognize whenever you walk around, but just large enough that it's always different people." "Life at Fordham is busy," explains a junior. "Obviously, we are all here for the academics, and that is a big focus for everyone but, additionally, almost all students are involved in activities on and off campus." There are "extracurriculars for every taste." "People love to play intramural sports." Fordham is big on community service as well, and "There are so many ways to get involved with volunteering." Students also spend a lot of time just soaking up all the "extensive and vibrant culture" "that New York City has to offer on any given day." "The choices of things to do here are endless." "Students often spend a lot of time in bars," and it's possible to "party four or sometimes five times a week." However, parties are usually "kept under control." Fordham students "know when to put their academic well-being before" a good time.

Student Body
"Students fit into two main groups at Fordham: East Coast prep or NYC hipster." It's generally an "upper-middle-class," "hardworking" crowd. "Dress is stylish." Fashions are especially trendy among the more artsy "urbanites" at Lincoln Center. However, "There is room here for every kind of person imaginable because, after all, this is New York." Students at Fordham "get along very well and tend to dabble in a variety of clubs and programs." Students "tend to socialize in smaller groups," but "stereotypical cliques, like you would classify in high school, don't really apply here." "The Catholic culture contributes to a willingness to suspend typical political labels in exchange for a deeper look at the moral and social issues of our day," reflects a senior. "Everyone finds their niche."

FORDHAM UNIVERSITY

FINANCIAL AID: 718-817-3800 • E-MAIL: ENROLL@FORDHAM.EDU • WEBSITE: WWW.FORDHAM.EDU

THE PRINCETON REVIEW SAYS
Admissions
Very important factors considered include: Class rank, rigor of secondary school record, standardized test scores. *Important factors considered include:* Application essay, recommendation(s), character/personal qualities, extracurricular activities, talent/ability. *Other factors considered include:* Alumni/ae relation, first generation, geographical residence, racial/ethnic status, volunteer work, work experience. SAT or ACT required; ACT with writing component recommended. TOEFL required of all international applicants. High school diploma is required, and GED is accepted. *Academic units required:* 4 English, 3 mathematics, 3 science, 2 foreign language, 2 social studies, 2 history, academic elective. *Academic units recommended:* 4 English, 4 mathematics, 4 science, 3 foreign language, 2 social studies, 2 history, 6 academic elective.

Financial Aid
Students should submit: FAFSA, CSS/Financial Aid PROFILE. Regular filing deadline is February 1. The Princeton Review suggests that all financial aid forms be submitted as soon as possible after January 1. *Need-based scholarships/grants offered:* Federal Pell, SEOG, state scholarships/grants, private scholarships, school scholarship or grant aid from institutional funds. *Loan aid offered:* Direct Subsidized Stafford, Direct Unsubsidized Stafford, Direct PLUS, Federal Perkins.

The Inside Word
Applicants to Fordham are required to indicate whether they are applying to the Rose Hill campus in the Bronx or the Lincoln Center campus in Manhattan. If you want to enroll in the Gabelli School of Business, you must specify that, too. Admission criteria vary by school, but all are very competitive. Graduation from a Catholic high school—particularly a prestigious one on the East Coast—is always a plus.

THE SCHOOL SAYS "..."
From the Admissions Office
"Fordham University offers a distinctive, values-centered educational experience that is rooted in the Jesuit tradition of intellectual rigor and personal attention. Located in New York City, Fordham offers to students the unparalleled educational, cultural and recreational advantages of one of the world's greatest cities. Fordham has two residential campuses in New York—the tree-lined, eighty-five-acre Rose Hill campus in the Bronx, and the cosmopolitan Lincoln Center campus in the heart of Manhattan's performing arts center. The University's state-of-the-art facilities and buildings include one of the most technologically advanced libraries in the country. Fordham offers a variety of majors, concentrations and programs that can be combined with an extensive career planning and placement program. More than 2,600 organizations in the New York metropolitan area offer students internships that provide hands-on experience and valuable networking opportunities in fields such as business, communications, medicine, law and education.

"Applicants are required to take SAT or the ACT with the writing section. SAT Subject Tests are recommended but not required."

SELECTIVITY
Admissions Rating	93
# of applicants	24,557
% of applicants accepted	50
% of acceptees attending	15
# accepting a place on wait list	1,490
% admitted from wait list	9

FRESHMAN PROFILE
Range SAT Critical Reading	570–670
Range SAT Math	570–670
Range SAT Writing	570–670
Range ACT Composite	26–30
Minimum paper TOEFL	575
Minimum computer TOEFL	230
Average HS GPA	3.70
% graduated top 10% of class	42
% graduated top 25% of class	78
% graduated top 50% of class	97

DEADLINES
Early action	
Deadline	11/1
Notification	12/25
Regular	
Priority	1/15
Deadline	1/15
Nonfall registration?	yes

APPLICANTS ALSO LOOK AT
AND OFTEN PREFER
Boston College, New York University, The George Washington University
AND SOMETIMES PREFER
College of the Holy Cross, Georgetown University, Loyola College in Maryland, Rutgers, The State University of New Jersey
AND RARELY PREFER
Hofstra University, Marist College, Pace University

FINANCIAL FACTS
Financial Aid Rating	77
Annual tuition	$37,545
Room and board	$14,491
Required fees	$1,057
Books and supplies	$915
% frosh rec. need-based scholarship or grant aid	66
% UG rec. need-based scholarship or grant aid	62
% frosh rec. non-need-based scholarship or grant aid	12
% UG rec. non-need-based scholarship or grant aid	9
% frosh rec. need-based self-help aid	49
% UG rec. need-based self-help aid	51
% frosh rec. any financial aid	66
% UG rec. any financial aid	65
% UG borrow to pay for school	65
Average cumulative indebtedness	$33,365

FRANKLIN & MARSHALL COLLEGE

PO BOX 3003, LANCASTER, PA 17604-3003 • ADMISSIONS: 717-291-3953 • FAX: 717-291-4381

CAMPUS LIFE

Quality of Life Rating	69
Fire Safety Rating	89
Green Rating	96
Type of school	private
Environment	town

STUDENTS

Total undergrad enrollment	2,279
% male/female	47/53
% from out of state	69
% from public high school	62
% live on campus	99
# of fraternities	8
# of sororities	3
% African American	3
% Asian	3
% Caucasian	75
% Hispanic	5
% international	9
# of countries represented	41

SURVEY SAYS . . .
No one cheats
Lab facilities are great
Great computer facilities
Great library
School is well-run
Lots of beer drinking
Hard liquor is popular

ACADEMICS

Academic Rating	88
% students graduating within 4 years	80
% students graduating within 6 years	87
Calendar	semester
Student/faculty ratio	10:1
Profs interesting rating	86
Profs accessible rating	95
Most common reg class size	20–29 students
Most common lab size	10–19 students

MOST POPULAR MAJORS
business/commerce, political science, psychology

STUDENTS SAY ". . ."

Academics

Franklin & Marshall College is "a small, focused liberal arts college dedicated to giving every student the opportunity to succeed." Known for its "extremely high academic standards" and "great faculty accessibility," the school is "about furthering academic achievement and providing superior skills and opportunities for success after graduation." Many students say, "F&M is all about good undergrad programs and tight-knit networking," and students laud the opportunity to make connections in their chosen fields. The college has "a slight emphasis on the sciences," which makes an English major grumble, "Some really fantastic humanities programs lack in administrative support whereas science programs get everything and anything they want." Nevertheless, the college's "policy of deferring major declaration until sophomore year…allows undecided students to really find a major that suits their interests." The faculty gets good marks for being available to students outside the classroom, but students acknowledge that, "as with many things, professors vary widely in style and quality." A sophomore notes, "Some are very difficult but interesting; some are very boring, etc. There are enough wonderful professors to go around, though." Many students complain about the course registration process saying it can be "competitive and difficult to get into desired classes."

Life

F&M boasts a "lush and beautiful campus" with "state-of-the-art educational and living facilities" and "a strong community feel." Students say, "Events are constantly being organized, and there's always something interesting going on if you take the time to participate." Students also point out, "If you see that there is a need for a new school group, you can definitely petition for it, and the school will back you up. F&M cares a lot about on-campus diversity." Overall, it's a, "close-knit student body," and students feel that "as an F&M student, you are not a number or a name on a class roster, you are an active contributor on campus." However, students are torn on the issue of school spirit, with some feeling it's strong and others griping that "school spirit is laughable." "There isn't enough student involvement and enthusiasm with clubs and activities." However, all students agree that "the school could stand to improve on campus dining." There are complaints about the mandatory four-year residency requirement, particularly among upperclassmen who feel it "needs to be modified" because it "makes housing far more expensive than it should be." Some feel the administration can be "hard to work with" and think the college should "streamline administrative departments" to "decrease wasteful spending."

Student Body

At F&M, the motto seems to be, "Work hard, play hard." Students say they take their academics seriously, but "because the work is so demanding, on weekends everyone gets pretty crazy." Greek life is a predominant part of the social scene, and some say, "On weekends, it's pretty much the only outlet for socializing." Many say the student body is "preppier and more Greek than you'd expect" and that "the typical student is Caucasian, upper-middle-class, from the tristate area" and looks like "a J. Crew model." However, a neuroscience major says, "While Greek life seems to dominate campus, after one or two years you come to realize that there is a lot more to do for fun," and another student adds, "It's a very laid-back lifestyle so people like to relax and enjoy time with their friends." A junior says, "in reality, everyone has their 'thing' that they're involved in," and in general "students are friendly and pleasant, but they tend to stick to themselves and their small groups of friends." However, many agree that, "For a small school, there is an enormous variety of things to do," and they say, "on any given weekend you can find people all over campus, whether it be at the artsy green room theater, the library…in the college center, in a friend's apartment, or at a frat party."

FRANKLIN & MARSHALL COLLEGE

FINANCIAL AID: 717-291-3991 • E-MAIL: ADMISSION@FANDM.EDU • WEBSITE: WWW.FANDM.EDU

THE PRINCETON REVIEW SAYS

Admissions

Very important factors considered include: Academic GPA, class rank, rigor of secondary school record, character/personal qualities. *Important factors considered include:* Application essay, recommendation(s), standardized test scores, extracurricular activities, interview, talent/ability, volunteer work. *Other factors considered include:* Alumni/ae relation, geographical residence, level of applicant's interest, racial/ethnic status, work experience. ACT with or without writing component accepted. TOEFL required of all international applicants. High school diploma is required, and GED is accepted. *Academic units required:* 4 English, 3 mathematics, 2 science (2 science labs), 2 foreign language, 1 social studies, 2 history, 1 visual/performing arts. *Academic units recommended:* 4 mathematics, 3 science (3 science labs), 4 foreign language, 3 social studies, 3 history.

Financial Aid

Students should submit: FAFSA, CSS/Financial Aid PROFILE. Regular filing deadline is February 15. The Princeton Review suggests that all financial aid forms be submitted as soon as possible after January 1. *Need-based scholarships/ grants offered:* Federal Pell, SEOG, state scholarships/grants, private scholarships, school scholarship or grant aid from institutional funds. *Loan aid offered:* Federal Perkins, university loans from institutional funds.

The Inside Word

While admission at F&M is competitive, the admissions committee does show some flexibility. The college allows students who feel that standardized test scores don't reflect their true academic capacity to submit two graded writing samples to replace the test scores. Applicants are also encouraged to include nontraditional materials, such as art portfolios or recordings of musical performances, in their applications. Finally, F&M offers a "Spring Option," in which students can elect to start classes in the spring semester after spending the fall abroad, or pursuing a "challenging program in consultation with an experienced faculty advisor at F&M."

THE SCHOOL SAYS "..."

From the Admissions Office

"Franklin & Marshall students choose from a variety of fields of study, traditional and interdisciplinary, that typify liberal learning. Professors in all of these fields are committed to a common purpose, which is to teach students to think, speak, and write with clarity and confidence. Whether the course is in theater or in physics, the class will be small, engagement will be high, and discussion will dominate over lecture. Thus, throughout their four years, beginning with the First-Year Seminar, students at Franklin & Marshall are repeatedly invited to active participation in intellectual play at high levels. Our graduates consistently testify to the high quality of an F&M education as a preparation for life."

SELECTIVITY

Admissions Rating	92
# of applicants	4,934
% of applicants accepted	45
% of acceptees attending	29
# accepting a place on wait list	709
% admitted from wait list	5
# of early decision applicants	512
% accepted early decision	76

FRESHMAN PROFILE

Range SAT Critical Reading	590–680
Range SAT Math	620–710
Range ACT Composite	28–30
Minimum paper TOEFL	600
Minimum computer TOEFL	250
% graduated top 10% of class	53
% graduated top 25% of class	82
% graduated top 50% of class	99

DEADLINES

Early decision	
Deadline	11/15
Notification	12/15
Regular	
Deadline	2/1
Nonfall registration?	yes

APPLICANTS ALSO LOOK AT AND SOMETIMES PREFER
Bucknell University, Dickinson College, Lafayette College

FINANCIAL FACTS

Financial Aid Rating	89
Annual tuition	$41,090
Room and board	$10,920
Required fees	$50
Books and supplies	$1,170
% frosh rec. need-based scholarship or grant aid	46
% UG rec. need-based scholarship or grant aid	41
% frosh rec. non-need-based scholarship or grant aid	1
% UG rec. non-need-based scholarship or grant aid	1
% frosh rec. need-based self-help aid	45
% UG rec. need-based self-help aid	43
% frosh rec. any financial aid	51
% UG rec. any financial aid	54
% UG borrow to pay for school	52
Average cumulative indebtedness	$28,451

FRANKLIN W. OLIN COLLEGE OF ENGINEERING

OLIN WAY, NEEDHAM, MA 02492-1200 • ADMISSIONS: 781-292-2222 • FAX: 781-292-2210

CAMPUS LIFE

Quality of Life Rating	98
Fire Safety Rating	87
Green Rating	67
Type of school	private
Environment	town

STUDENTS

Total undergrad enrollment	346
% male/female	55/45
% from out of state	88
% live on campus	99
% African American	1
% Asian	17
% Caucasian	57
% Hispanic	3
% international	8
# of countries represented	14

SURVEY SAYS . . .

No one cheats
Lab facilities are great
Great computer facilities
Students are friendly
Different types of students interact
Students get along with local community
Great food on campus
Dorms are like palaces
Campus feels safe
Students are happy
Student government is popular

ACADEMICS

Academic Rating	99
% students graduating within 4 years	83
% students graduating within 6 years	90
Calendar	semester
Student/faculty ratio	9:1
Profs interesting rating	99
Profs accessible rating	95
Most common reg class size	20–29 students

MOST POPULAR MAJORS
electrical and electronics engineering, engineering, mechanical engineering

STUDENTS SAY ". . ."

Academics

Revered for its "tight-knit community, rigorous academics, project-based learning, and ingenuous approach to education," Franklin W. Olin College of Engineering "bridges the gap between a traditional engineering education and [the] real world." On this campus of 300 undergraduates where "smart" and "quirky" are the norm, "Students [are] eager to be challenged academically and faculty gladly deliver that challenge." "Learning is doing" at Olin, and students laud the "innovative curriculum" for its "small classes," "hands-on approach," and "group-focused learning." "Olin believes in Renaissance engineers, " and allows "students to pursue passions beyond engineering." Though classes are "wickedly challenging," students say they "bond around the difficulty." The focus on "experiential education" and "entrepreneurial implementation" provides students with "the ability to help design the curriculum and the school culture." Professors are "one of the best—if not the best—part of Olin," and are frequently described as "always available, always knowledgeable, [and] always approachable." Students note that even the higher-ups go by a first name basis: "You can regularly chat with the president at lunch." The kicker? Every enrolled student receives a half-tuition scholarship. Students with additional demonstrated need are awarded grants.

Life

At Olin, the spirit of hands-on collaboration transcends the classroom. This "tight-knit community of eager learners and tinkerers" thrives on a spirit of "innovation and initiative." "Small, quirky, and somewhat in a bubble, but full of amazing adventures and opportunities," Olin is all about "bringing together amazing people to build twenty-first century engineers." "People work hard, but they also know how to play hard, take breaks, and have fun." Though students say that there are "boatloads of work," in general life at Olin is "intense and fun." "There's also a lot going on, like Nerf wars, tyrannosaurus dodge ball, experimental baking, pickup soccer, zombie video games, auditorium movie screenings, midnight dump raids, elevator dance parties, themed hall parties, etc." A typical day includes everything from "watching a movie" to a "midnight bike expedition." Located a stone's throw from Beantown, Olin students "go into Boston" on the weekends. Students here thrive on the spirit of "carpe diem," a phrase that has now become an "e-mail list to which almost all students subscribe." "Students send out these carpes about anything and everything that others might find interesting or fun." The facilities aren't too shabby either. Each room comes with "its own fridge, microwave, freezer, and bathroom/shower."

Student Body

"Olin is a place where intelligent, motivated students can explore their interests both in engineering and in life as a whole." "Take the nation's top engineering students, mix with awesome personalities, add a dash of amazing resources, shake vigorously." When it comes to describing the typical student, there is no status quo. "There are all sorts of people at Olin. Some of us avoid homework by discussing meta-physics and ethics. Others watch old episodes of *Firefly*...Some people read books in their spare time." The commonality? "Students care about their educations," and "everyone takes their own paths." Though students say they "may make geeky jokes," "People don't act like socially stunted nerds." "Passionate, intelligent, witty, [and] exceedingly interesting," "The typical student at Olin is atypical, whether that means having a hidden talent in unicycle fire juggling, a passion for writing musicals, an obsession with velociraptors, or a tendency to make pancakes at three in the morning every Thursday." Students say, "Every student at Olin is interesting enough that you want to sit down and talk to them for hours." "We think about pretty much everything from quantum physics to Obama's health care reform to *Speedracer* to what's for dinner." As innovative and diverse as their curriculum, Olin students "are straight, gay, Jewish, nerdy, partiers, gamers, rich, poor, and encompass all other social groups."

FRANKLIN W. OLIN COLLEGE OF ENGINEERING

FINANCIAL AID: 781-292-2222 • E-MAIL: INFO@OLIN.EDU • WEBSITE: WWW.OLIN.EDU

THE PRINCETON REVIEW SAYS

Admissions

Very important factors considered include: Academic GPA, application essay, recommendation(s), rigor of secondary school record, character/personal qualities, extracurricular activities, interview, level of applicant's interest, talent/ability. *Important factors considered include:* Standardized test scores, racial/ethnic status, volunteer work. *Other factors considered include:* Class rank, first generation, geographical residence, work experience. SAT or ACT required; ACT with or without writing component accepted. High school diploma or equivalent isn't required. *Academic units recommended:* 4 English, 4 mathematics, 3 science (3 science labs), 2 foreign language, 2 social studies, 2 history.

Financial Aid

Students should submit: FAFSA. Regular filing deadline is February 15. The Princeton Review suggests that all financial aid forms be submitted as soon as possible after January 1. *Need-based scholarships/grants offered:* Federal Pell, SEOG, private scholarships, school scholarship or grant aid from institutional funds. *Loan aid offered:* Direct Subsidized Stafford, Direct Unsubsidized Stafford, Direct PLUS. Applicants will be notified of awards on a rolling basis beginning April 1. Federal Work-Study Program available.

The Inside Word

Not many colleges can boast that they are filled with students who turned down offers from the likes of MIT, Cal Tech, and Carnegie Mellon, but Olin can. Olin is unique among engineering schools in that the admissions office really looks for more than just brains. Things like social skills and eloquence are taken extremely seriously here. Students who exhibit creativity, passion, and an entrepreneurial spirit are favored over their less adventurous peers. Reclusive geniuses seeking four years of technical monasticism will be at a disadvantage in the application pool.

THE SCHOOL SAYS ". . ."

From the Admissions Office

"Every enrolled student receives a half-tuition scholarship. Students with additional demonstrated need are awarded grants (no loans)."

"The selection process at Olin College is unique to college admission. Each year a highly self-selecting pool of approximately 900 applicants is reviewed on traditional selection criteria. Approximately 270 finalists are invited to one of three Candidates' Weekends in February and March. These candidates are grouped in to five-person teams for a weekend of design-and-build exercises, group discussions, and interviews with Olin students, faculty, and alumni. Written evaluations and recommendations for each candidate are prepared by all Olin participants and submitted to the faculty admission committee. The committee admits about 170 candidates to yield a freshman class of eight-five. The result is that the freshman class is ultimately chosen on the strength of personal attributes such as leadership, cooperation, creativity, communication, and their enthusiasm for Olin College.

"A waiting list of approximately twenty is also established. All wait-list candidates who are not offered a spot in the class may defer enrollment for one year—with the guarantee of the Olin Scholarship. Wait-list students are strongly encouraged to do something unusual, exciting, and productive during their sabbatical year.

"Students applying for admission are required to take the SAT (or the ACT with the writing section). Olin College also requires scores from two SAT Subject Tests: math (Level 1 or 2) and a science of the student's choice."

FURMAN UNIVERSITY

3300 POINSETT HIGHWAY, GREENVILLE, SC 29613 • ADMISSIONS: 864-294-2034 • FAX: 864-294-3127

STUDENTS SAY ". . ."

Academics

Students can't stop talking about Furman University's "beautiful campus" and "warm, but challenging, academic community." This combination of brains and beauty is what makes Furman "an ideal choice" for four years. "Furman is about academic excellence through engaged learning," says one undergrad. Expect to hear "engaged" used "ad nauseum" on campus, but students claim that such a term "truly describes the kind of personal education available" thanks to "small class sizes," professors "who love to teach and enjoy getting to know their students," and "numerous" academic and extracurricular opportunities. Furman's science programs are "especially" challenging. Professors here are "very qualified (sometimes overqualified), passionate about what they teach, and are not easy graders." That said, they're "very willing to help their students." Despite being described as being "far to the left of the student body politically," the "good" administration is "really accessible." In the words of one undergrad, "They work with students to solve problems and genuinely care about making Furman a better school and not just a higher-ranking institution." However, some students find that the administration can be "very conservative in their thinking about student on-campus social life." Ultimately, while "Furman is not for the academically faint-of-heart," there's pride in knowing that "You're receiving a great education that will help you after you graduate."

Life

With so many students reporting that Furman's campus is "absolutely gorgeous," it's a wonder they ever leave it. However, "The surrounding city of Greenville is great," and its "thriving, small-town feel" brings in plenty of students on the weekends. Life at school is "busy, but so much fun." Students here spend "a lot of time thinking about academics, classes, and their future," but they also "invest a lot of time in their relationships with their friends." The school's "inclusive, close-knit community" is complemented with "lots of interesting things to do on campus, from music concerts to improv shows to sports games." "Weeknights are mostly spent studying," says one undergrad, which makes the library "a popular social spot." However, once the weekend rolls around, students spend their nights "out on the town." "There are tons of bars, restaurants, and clubs for people to go to" in Greenville, while those looking for a "party" can head for "fraternity houses." While the university "is not as crazy party-wise as larger schools," students "can find a party if they want to." Mostly though, students are happy to "meet up with friends for meals, coffee, or just to hang out."

Student Body

Many find that Furman is something of a "country club" when it comes to its student body, not just "because it is private and somewhat expensive," but also because the "typical" student is "wealthy, white, conservative, and preppy." Some find that "The majority of the student body is obsessed with being as 'generic' and 'normal' as possible, so that any student who does not fit the norm, be it due to a difference in religion or clothing style, will find it harder to fit in." However, others have found that there's more to the student body than first meets the eye. As one undergrad says, "The longer I stay at Furman, the more I realize that many students don't fit the stereotype." One thing that everyone seems to agree on is that everyone is "very accepting" and "very committed to their academic pursuits." That said, some wouldn't mind seeing the school "improve by attracting a more diverse student body, as well as lowering the cost of tuition."

FINANCIAL AID: 864-294-2204 • E-MAIL: ADMISSIONS@FURMAN.EDU • WEBSITE: WWW.FURMAN.EDU

THE PRINCETON REVIEW SAYS

Admissions

Very important factors considered include: Rigor of secondary school record. *Important factors considered include:* Academic GPA, application essay, class rank, character/personal qualities, extracurricular activities. *Other factors considered include:* Recommendation(s), alumni/ae relation, first generation, level of applicant's interest, racial/ethnic status, talent/ability, volunteer work, work experience. SAT or ACT optional. If scores not submitted, then students must participate in a formal interview. TOEFL required of all international applicants. High school diploma is required, and GED is accepted. *Academic units required:* 4 English, 3 mathematics, 2 science (2 science labs), 2 foreign language, 3 social studies. *Academic units recommended:* 4 English, 4 mathematics, 3 science (2 science labs), 3 foreign language, 4 social studies.

Financial Aid

Students should submit: FAFSA, institution's own financial aid form, CSS/Financial Aid PROFILE. Regular filing deadline is March 1. The Princeton Review suggests that all financial aid forms be submitted as soon as possible after January 1. *Need-based scholarships/grants offered:* Federal Pell, SEOG, state scholarships/grants, private scholarships, school scholarship or grant aid from institutional funds. *Loan aid offered:* Direct Subsidized Stafford, Direct Unsubsidized Stafford, Direct PLUS, Federal Perkins, state loans. Applicants will be notified of awards on a rolling basis beginning April 1. Federal Work-Study Program available. Off-campus job opportunities are excellent.

The Inside Word

Chances are, if you're applying to Furman, you already have a good idea if you can get in or not. Furman's applicant pool is highly self-selected, meaning that the university's high acceptance rate doesn't equate to easy admission; in fact, it's the direct opposite, as applicants are typically very strong. Looking for a way to stand out from the crowd? Let the admissions committee know how valuable you are through your extracurriculars—sports, community service, and artistic endeavors will go a long way in making your case.

THE SCHOOL SAYS ". . ."

From the Admissions Office

"Furman University is a private liberal arts university that seeks and cultivates engaged, well-rounded, and passionate students. With 2,700 undergraduates from forty-six states and forty-seven countries, Furman's academic community prepares its students for meaningful lives of service and leadership through engaged learning, a process characterized by small classes, a close-knit community, student-faculty research, internships, and faculty-led study. With emphasis on a collaborative educational experience, Furman challenges students to put into practice the theories and methods learned from a distinguished and active faculty. Furman offers seventeen NCAA Division I men's and women's athletic teams, a nationally competitive music program, and hundreds of organizations and clubs. The stunning campus is located just minutes from vibrant downtown Greenville, noted as one of America's most livable cities, and the foothills of the Blue Ridge Mountains, where hiking and other adventure sports abound. Nearby are also some of the nation's most picturesque beaches and coastal towns. The Admission Committee believes that a student's potential for success is not determined solely by standardized test scores. Rather, it is interested in getting to know the whole student—one who seeks leadership, service, commitment to the community, and civic engagement. Therefore, Furman does not require prospective students to submit test scores unless the student determines the scores best represent academic ability and accomplishment. If a student chooses not to submit standardized test scores, then the university requires the student to participate in a formal interview as part of the application."

SELECTIVITY

Admissions Rating	94
# of applicants	4,538
% of applicants accepted	68
% of acceptees attending	21
# accepting a place on wait list	131
% admitted from wait list	29
# of early decision applicants	642
% accepted early decision	71

FRESHMAN PROFILE

Range SAT Critical Reading	580–690
Range SAT Math	600–680
Range SAT Writing	580–680
Range ACT Composite	25–30
Minimum paper TOEFL	570
Minimum computer TOEFL	230
Average HS GPA	3.83
% graduated top 10% of class	61
% graduated top 25% of class	86
% graduated top 50% of class	98

DEADLINES

Early decision	
Deadline	11/15
Notification	12/15
Regular	
Deadline	1/15
Nonfall registration?	no

APPLICANTS ALSO LOOK AT AND OFTEN PREFER
Duke University, University of North Carolina at Chapel Hill, Vanderbilt University, Wake Forest University

AND SOMETIMES PREFER
Clemson University, Davidson College, Emory University—Oxford College, University of South Carolina—Columbia

FINANCIAL FACTS

Financial Aid Rating	86
Annual tuition	$39,200
Room and board	$10,192
Required fees	$360
Books and supplies	$1,110
% frosh rec. need-based scholarship or grant aid	53
% UG rec. need-based scholarship or grant aid	47
% frosh rec. non-need-based scholarship or grant aid	48
% UG rec. non-need-based scholarship or grant aid	37
% frosh rec. need-based self-help aid	38
% UG rec. need-based self-help aid	35
% frosh rec. any financial aid	85
% UG rec. any financial aid	83
% UG borrow to pay for school	40
Average cumulative indebtedness	$27,373

GEORGE MASON UNIVERSITY

4400 UNIVERSITY DRIVE MSN 3A4, FAIRFAX, VA 22030-4444 • ADMISSIONS: 703-993-2400 • FAX: 703-993-2392

STUDENTS SAY "..."

Academics

When describing George Mason University, current students are quick to quote the school motto: This is a place "where innovation is tradition." One student expands on that, saying, "Mason provides a space for students to achieve academic excellence; expand their knowledge of the diverse cultures, practices, and beliefs that surround them; and be prepared to enter the real-world as a global citizen." Diversity of the student body and proximity to Washington, D.C., are major selling points at this large public university, so it's no surprise that government, global affairs, and communication are popular majors. The faculty is "extremely knowledgeable and experienced" here, and "most try to learn your name." The Robinson Professors program brings "distinguished" professors in the liberal arts and sciences to campus, and students highly recommend classes taught by these professors. "They are experts in their fields, know what they are talking about, and have real life experiences they bring into the classroom." As well, "adjunct professors can be a great strength" because many of them are practicing professionals in D.C., and they "bring stories and examples from the real-world into our classroom." "For example, my professor for my Conflict 300 course is one of the main peace facilitators in the Georgian/South Ossetian conflict...when she returned from this conference [between the two countries], she told us everything and we got to see how the material and techniques we were studying are actually applied in our field." Students are equally satisfied with the school's administration: "The school will take action immediately to fix any problems that arise."

Life

Students at GMU never seem to be bored. Campus life is "filled with classes, friends, and work." On campus activities are very popular, and there are many on offer, including the university's ambassador program and intramural sports, such as underwater hockey and even quidditch. Just a few of the regular events on campus include "movies playing in our Johnson Center Cinema that are in between theater and DVD release, there are local bands playing live in the Rathskeller, the HIV/AIDS Awareness Fashion Show, drag competitions, University dances and highlighter parties." Greek life is there for those who want it: "We're not a 'fratty' school by any means, but the Greek community is very active and they do party." The campus is "beautiful," and "there are new housing buildings going up and even new academic buildings" (which is good news, since the two things students want to see improve are parking and housing availability). Students love living close to D.C. without the "hassle of city living," but when they want to head downtown, "it's very easy to get into the city by taking the Mason-to-Metro shuttle to the Vienna Metro Station, hopping on the Orange Line and then taking the Metro into the heart of the city!" Many students have internships in the city, including those "on Capitol Hill." "The music scene and bars are fantastic as well!"

Student Body

"Diversity is off the charts" at GMU, and many students describe their school as "a melting pot." As one student puts it, "There are so many different nationalities represented, so many stories, so many languages spoken. At the same time, it didn't take me long to find a good group of friends that were interested in hanging out and just having a good time together." "The typical GMU student is always busy—between coursework and extracurricular activities we're very involved on campus and are also into other activities, such as having jobs or internships." "Mason students are also politically active and global citizens." While a majority of students come from Virginia, there are also "students from over 130 countries, so everyone adds their own personal flavor to our student body." In spite of all these different backgrounds and cultures, "There are many student organizations that successfully create programs and events to unite students."

FINANCIAL AID: 703-993-2353 • E-MAIL: ADMISSIONS@GMU.EDU • WEBSITE: WWW.MASONMETRO.EDU

THE PRINCETON REVIEW SAYS

Admissions

Very important factors considered include: Academic GPA, rigor of secondary school record. *Important factors considered include:* Application essay, class rank, recommendation(s), alumni/ae relation, character/personal qualities, talent/ability. *Other factors considered include:* Standardized test scores, extracurricular activities, first generation, level of applicant's interest, volunteer work, work experience. ACT with or without writing component accepted. TOEFL required of all international applicants. High school diploma is required, and GED is accepted. *Academic units required:* 4 English, 3 mathematics, (2 science labs), 2 foreign language, 3 social studies, 3 academic elective. *Academic units recommended:* 4 English, 4 mathematics, (3 science labs), 3 foreign language, 4 social studies, 5 academic elective.

Financial Aid

Students should submit: FAFSA. The Princeton Review suggests that all financial aid forms be submitted as soon as possible after January 1. *Need-based scholarships/grants offered:* Federal Pell, SEOG, state scholarships/grants, private scholarships, school scholarship or grant aid from institutional funds. *Loan aid offered:* Direct Subsidized Stafford, Direct Unsubsidized Stafford, Direct PLUS, Federal Perkins, Federal Nursing Loans. Applicants will be notified of awards on a rolling basis beginning April 1. Federal Work-Study Program available. Off-campus job opportunities are excellent.

The Inside Word

GMU is a popular college choice for two key reasons: Its proximity to Washington, D.C., and the fact that its applicant pool isn't as competitive as those of University of Virginia and The College of William & Mary, the two flagships of the Virginia state system. GMU's quality faculty and impressive facilities make it worth consideration, especially if you're looking for a school in the D.C. area and affordability is a factor.

THE SCHOOL SAYS " . . . "

From the Admissions Office

"George Mason University enjoys the best location in the world. Our connections to the D.C. area result in faculty members who are engaged in the top research in their fields. We have professors who are regular contributors on all of the major news networks, and you can hardly listen to a program on National Public Radio without hearing from one of our scholars. This connectivity extends to our students, who take internships and get jobs at some of the best organizations and companies in the world. We have students at AOL/Time Warner, the National Institutes of Health, the Kennedy Center, the World Bank, the White House, and the National Zoo. We have all the advantages of the excitement of our nation's Capital combined with the comfort and security of this beautiful suburban campus. At Mason, we pride ourselves on being among the most innovative universities in the world. Many of our degree programs are the first of their kinds, including the first PhD program in biodefense, the first D.C.-based undergraduate program in conflict resolution, the first integrated school of information technology and engineering based on computer related programs, and one of the most innovative performing arts management programs in the United States. As a result, George Mason University is at the forefront of the emerging field of biotechnology, is a natural leader in the performing arts, and holds a preeminent position in the fields of economics, electronic journalism, and history, just to name a few. George Mason University will accept the ACT and the SAT. Scores from the writing section will not be considered in our admission decisions, as our faculty does not feel the writing section reflects quality or methodology of our award-winning writing across the curriculum program. Mason has the largest score-optional program in the U.S."

SELECTIVITY

Admissions Rating	85
# of applicants	17,228
% of applicants accepted	52
% of acceptees attending	29
# accepting a place on wait list	657
% admitted from wait list	17

FRESHMAN PROFILE

Range SAT Critical Reading	520–620
Range SAT Math	530–620
Range ACT Composite	23–28
Minimum paper TOEFL	570
Minimum computer TOEFL	230
Minimum web-based TOEFL	88
Average HS GPA	3.59
% graduated top 10% of class	21
% graduated top 25% of class	58
% graduated top 50% of class	94

DEADLINES

Early action	
Deadline	11/1
Notification	12/17
Regular	
Priority	12/1
Deadline	1/15
Nonfall registration?	yes

APPLICANTS ALSO LOOK AT AND SOMETIMES PREFER

James Madison University, The George Washington University, University of Virginia, Virginia Tech

FINANCIAL FACTS

Financial Aid Rating	74
Annual in-state tuition	$6,320
Annual out-of-state tuition	$23,084
Room and board	$8,220
Required fees	$2,364
Books and supplies	$900
% frosh rec. need-based scholarship or grant aid	40
% UG rec. need-based scholarship or grant aid	36
% frosh rec. non-need-based scholarship or grant aid	14
% UG rec. non-need-based scholarship or grant aid	7
% frosh rec. need-based self-help aid	38
% UG rec. need-based self-help aid	38
% frosh rec. any financial aid	68
% UG rec. any financial aid	57
% UG borrow to pay for school	54
Average cumulative indebtedness	$22,219

THE GEORGE WASHINGTON UNIVERSITY

2121 I STREET NORTHWEST, SUITE 201, WASHINGTON, D.C. 20052 • ADMISSIONS: 202-994-6040 • FAX: 202-994-0325

CAMPUS LIFE

Quality of Life Rating	91
Fire Safety Rating	60*
Green Rating	92
Type of school	private
Environment	metropolis

STUDENTS

Total undergrad enrollment	10,055
% male/female	45/55
% from out of state	98
% from public high school	70
% live on campus	70
# of fraternities	12
# of sororities	9
% African American	7
% Asian	10
% Caucasian	55
% Hispanic	7
% international	7
# of countries represented	134

SURVEY SAYS . . .
*Athletic facilities are great
Students love Washington, D.C.
Great off-campus food
Dorms are like palaces
Campus feels safe
Students are happy
Student publications are popular
Student government is popular
Political activism is popular*

ACADEMICS

Academic Rating	82
% students graduating within 4 years	75
% students graduating within 6 years	81
Calendar	semester
Student/faculty ratio	13:1
Profs interesting rating	79
Profs accessible rating	83
Most common reg class size	10–19 students
Most common lab size	20–29 students

MOST POPULAR MAJORS
business administration and management, international relations, psychology

STUDENTS SAY ". . ."

Academics

Get ready for "hands-on learning in an environment unlike any other" at George Washington University, where a location "four blocks away from the White House, down the street from the State Department, and near nearly all world headquarters" means "connections and opportunity" for undergraduates. Students call it "the perfect place to study international affairs" and praise the "amazing journalism program," the excellent political communications major, the political science program ("What political science major would pass up the chance to go toe-to-toe with protestors every week at the rallies outside the White House and Congress?"), the sciences (benefiting from the region's many research operations), and other departments too numerous to name. As one student puts it, "GW is a place where everyone can find their niche. Whether you are a politically active campaign volunteer, a hip-hop dancer, or a future Broadway actor, there is a place for you at GW." The school places a premium on hiring "professors of practice," teachers who "are either currently working in their field or just retired to teach." The faculty includes "former ambassadors, governors on the Federal Reserve Board, and CNN correspondents." These instructors emphasize "a balance between theory and practice that provides a foundation of knowledge and pragmatism from which students can feel prepared to enter any sector of work after school." The resulting education "gets students prepared for post-college life through an emphasis on internships and career-focused classes," putting "a lot of emphasis on acclimation to the real world."

Life

"Life at GW is about independence," students report. "There are no real cafeterias" on campus, "You have to rely on your own feet for transportation, and there is very little regulation in dorms." As a result, "There is little school spirit, but that fact alone seems to tie everyone together." The campus isn't entirely dead; there are frat parties ("which are hard to attend for non-member males and easy to attend for women"), the "occasional dorm-room party, which is usually small," and "apartment parties off campus" for upperclassmen. Campus organizations offer all sorts of events, and the school hosts a veritable who's who of guest speakers on a regular basis. Students love the school's Midnight Monument Tour, held "during the warmer parts of the year," during which "students walk the five blocks to the National Mall at 2:00 A.M. and tour the monuments. It is an awesome experience." Still, most students prefer to spend free time exploring D.C. on their own. The city provides "so much to do…it's overwhelming: monuments, free museums, fairs, every major sports franchise, and lots of student specials on the above things." D.C.'s upscale Georgetown neighborhood is nearby for "shopping, dining, seeing movies, etc.," while culturally diverse Adams Morgan is great for shopping, ethnic dining, and live music.

Student Body

"GW students are often stereotyped as spoiled and wealthy Northeastern kids," and while quite a few students here concede that there's some basis for the stereotype, most would also add that "white, preppy, fraternity/sorority members" who "like nice labels on their clothing" neither define nor dominate the campus population. "The reality is that there's tremendous diversity here of all stripes—geographic, religious, political, racial, and intellectual," with "students from dozens of countries and all fifty states." "GW is truly a national and even international school," one student writes. "I love walking out of the library and hearing conversations happening in a half-dozen languages." The school has always been a popular destination for Jewish students. There is also "a huge LGBT group on campus, with very little discrimination." Nearly everyone here is "incredibly driven," "combining classes with an internship, maybe a sport, and usually a few extracurriculars."

THE GEORGE WASHINGTON UNIVERSITY

FINANCIAL AID: 202-994-6620 • E-MAIL: GWADM@GWU.EDU • WEBSITE: WWW.GWU.EDU

THE PRINCETON REVIEW SAYS

Admissions

Very important factors considered include: Academic GPA, rigor of secondary school record. *Important factors considered include:* Application essay, class rank, recommendation(s), standardized test scores, extracurricular activities, interview, talent/ability, volunteer work. *Other factors considered include:* Alumni/ae relation, character/personal qualities, first generation, geographical residence, level of applicant's interest, racial/ethnic status, work experience. SAT or ACT required; ACT with or without writing component accepted. TOEFL required of all international applicants. *Academic units required:* 4 English, 2 mathematics, 2 science (1 science lab), 2 foreign language, 2 social studies. *Academic units recommended:* 4 English, 4 mathematics, 4 science, 4 foreign language, 4 social studies.

Financial Aid

Students should submit: FAFSA, CSS/Financial Aid PROFILE. Regular filing deadline is February 1. The Princeton Review suggests that all financial aid forms be submitted as soon as possible after January 1. *Need-based scholarships/grants offered:* Federal Pell, SEOG, state scholarships/grants, school scholarship or grant aid from institutional funds. *Loan aid offered:* Direct Subsidized Stafford, Direct Unsubsidized Stafford, Direct Plus, Federal Perkins. Applicants will be notified of awards on a rolling basis beginning April 1. Federal Work-Study Program available. Off-campus job opportunities are excellent.

The Inside Word

With more than 21,000 applications to process annually, GW could be forgiven if it gave student essays only a perfunctory glance. The school insists, however, that essays are carefully reviewed. Take note and proceed accordingly. If you thought the economic downturn would diminish interest in this pricey institution, think again: In 2009–2010, applications were up three percent over the previous year. That's part of a larger trend at GW, where application rates have surged throughout the past decade. This school is only getting more popular, so applicants should be prepared to bring their A-game.

THE SCHOOL SAYS "..."

From the Admissions Office

"At GW, we welcome students who show a measure of impatience with the limitations of traditional education. At many universities, the edge of campus is the real world, but not at GW, where our campus and Washington, D.C. are seamless. We look for bold, bright students who are ambitious, energetic, and self-motivated. Here, where we are so close to the centers of thought and action in every field we offer, we easily integrate our outstanding academic tradition and faculty connections with the best internship and job opportunities of Washington, D.C. A generous scholarship and financial assistance program attracts top students from all parts of the country and the world."

SELECTIVITY

Admissions Rating	95
# of applicants	21,433
% of applicants accepted	32
% of acceptees attending	35
# of early decision applicants	2,271
% accepted early decision	38

FRESHMAN PROFILE

Range SAT Critical Reading	600–690
Range SAT Math	610–700
Range SAT Writing	620–700
Range ACT Composite	27–31
Minimum paper TOEFL	550
Minimum computer TOEFL	213
Minimum web-based TOEFL	80
% graduated top 10% of class	74
% graduated top 25% of class	96
% graduated top 50% of class	100

DEADLINES

Early decision	
Deadline	11/10
Notification	12/15
Regular	
Priority	12/1
Deadline	1/10
Notification	4/1
Nonfall registration?	yes

APPLICANTS ALSO LOOK AT AND OFTEN PREFER
Boston University, Georgetown University, New York University

FINANCIAL FACTS

Financial Aid Rating	87
Annual tuition	$44,103
% frosh rec. need-based scholarship or grant aid	45
% UG rec. need-based scholarship or grant aid	42
% frosh rec. non-need-based scholarship or grant aid	5
% UG rec. non-need-based scholarship or grant aid	8
% frosh rec. need-based self-help aid	36
% UG rec. need-based self-help aid	36
Average cumulative indebtedness	$32,547

GEORGETOWN UNIVERSITY

THIRTY-SEVENTH AND P STREETS, NORTHWEST, WASHINGTON, D.C. 20057 • ADMISSIONS: 202-687-3600 • FAX: 202-687-5084

CAMPUS LIFE

Quality of Life Rating	80
Fire Safety Rating	82
Green Rating	87
Type of school	private
Affiliation	Roman Catholic
Environment	metropolis

STUDENTS

Total undergrad enrollment	7,092
% male/female	45/55
% from out of state	99
% from public high school	46
% live on campus	70
% African American	7
% Asian	9
% Caucasian	65
% Hispanic	6
% international	7
# of countries represented	138

SURVEY SAYS . . .
Students love Washington, D.C.
Great off-campus food
Students are happy
Frats and sororities are unpopular
or nonexistent
Student publications are popular
Political activism is popular
Lots of beer drinking

ACADEMICS

Academic Rating	87
% students graduating within 4 years	85
% students graduating within 6 years	93
Calendar	semester
Student/faculty ratio	10:1
Profs interesting rating	84
Profs accessible rating	81

MOST POPULAR MAJORS
English language and literature,
international relations, political science

STUDENTS SAY ". . ."

Academics

This moderately sized elite academic establishment stays true to its Jesuit foundations by educating its students with the idea of "cura personalis," or "care for the whole person." The "well-informed" student body perpetuates upon itself, creating an atmosphere full of vibrant intellectual life, that is "also balanced with extracurricular learning and development." "Georgetown is...a place where people work very, very hard without feeling like they are in direct competition," says an international politics major. Located in Washington, D.C., there's a noted School of Foreign Service here, and the access to internships is a huge perk for those in political or government programs. In addition, the proximity to the nation's capital fetches "high-profile guest speakers," with many of the most powerful people in global politics speaking regularly, as well as a large number of adjunct professors who, either are currently working in government, or have retired from high-level positions.

Georgetown offers a "great selection of very knowledgeable professors, split with a good proportion of those who are experienced in realms outside of academia (such as former government officials) and career academics," though there are a few superstars who might be "somewhat less than totally collegial." Professors tend to be "fantastic scholars and teachers" and are "generally available to students," as well as often being "interested in getting to know you as a person (if you put forth the effort to talk to them and go to office hours)." Though Georgetown has a policy of grade deflation, meaning "A's are hard to come by," there are "a ton of interesting courses available," and TAs are used only for optional discussion sessions and help with grading. The academics "can be challenging or they can be not so much (not that they are ever really easy, just easier);" it all depends on the courses you choose and how much you actually do the work. The school administration is well-meaning and "usually willing to talk and compromise with students," but the process of planning activities can be full of headaches and bureaucracy, and the administration itself "sometimes is overstretched or has trouble transmitting its message." Nevertheless, "a motivated student can get done what he or she wants."

Life

Students are "extremely well aware of the world around them," from government to environment, social to economic, and "Georgetown is the only place where an argument over politics, history, or philosophy is preceded by a keg stand." Hoyas like to have a good time on weekends, and parties at campus and off-campus apartments and townhouses "are generally open to all comers and tend to have a somewhat networking atmosphere; meeting people you don't know is a constant theme." With such a motivated group on such a high-energy campus, "people are always headed somewhere, it seems—to rehearsal, athletic practice, a guest speaker, [or] the gym." Community service and political activism are particularly popular, as is basketball. Everything near Georgetown is in walking distance, including the world of D.C.'s museums, restaurants, and stores, and "grabbing or ordering late night food is a popular option."

Student Body

There are "a lot of wealthy students on campus," and preppy-casual is the fashion de rigueur; this is "definitely not a 'granola' school," but students from diverse backgrounds are typically welcomed by people wanting to learn about different experiences. Indeed, everyone here is well-traveled and well-educated, and there are "a ton of international students." "You better have at least some interest in politics or you will feel out-of-place," says a student. The school can also be "a bit cliquish, with athletes at the top," but there are "plenty of groups for everybody to fit into and find their niche," and "there is much crossover between groups."

FINANCIAL AID: 202-687-4547 • WEBSITE: WWW.GEORGETOWN.EDU

THE PRINCETON REVIEW SAYS

Admissions

Very important factors considered include: Academic GPA, application essay, class rank, recommendation(s), rigor of secondary school record, standardized test scores, character/personal qualities,talent/ability. *Important factors considered include:* Extracurricular activities, interview, volunteer work. *Other factors considered include:* Alumni/ae relation, geographical residence, racial/ethnic status, state residency, work experience. SAT or ACT required; ACT with or without writing component accepted. TOEFL required of all international applicants. High school diploma is required, and GED is accepted. *Academic units recommended:* 4 English, 2 mathematics, 1 science, 2 foreign language, 2 social studies, 2 history.

Financial Aid

Students should submit: FAFSA, CSS/Financial Aid PROFILE. Regular filing deadline is February 1. The Princeton Review suggests that all financial aid forms be submitted as soon as possible after January 1. *Need-based scholarships/ grants offered:* Federal Pell, SEOG, state scholarships/grants, private scholarships, school scholarship or grant aid from institutional funds. *Loan aid offered:* Direct Subsidized Stafford, Direct Unsubsidized Stafford, Direct PLUS, Federal Perkins, Federal Nursing Loans. Federal Work-Study Program available. Off-campus job opportunities are excellent.

The Inside Word

It was always tough to get admitted to Georgetown, but in the early 1980s Patrick Ewing and the Hoyas created a basketball sensation that catapulted the place into position as one of the most selective universities in the nation. There has been no turning back since. GU gets almost ten applications for every space in the entering class, and the academic strength of the pool is impressive. Virtually fifty percent of the entire student body took AP courses in high school. Candidates who are wait-listed should hold little hope for an offer of admission; over the past several years Georgetown has taken very few off their lists.

THE SCHOOL SAYS ". . ."

From the Admissions Office

"Georgetown was founded in 1789 by John Carroll, who concurred with his contemporaries Benjamin Franklin and Thomas Jefferson in believing that the success of the young democracy depended upon an educated and virtuous citizenry. Carroll founded the school with the dynamic Jesuit tradition of education, characterized by humanism and committed to the assumption of responsibility and action. Georgetown is a national and international university, enrolling students from all fifty states and over 100 foreign countries. Undergraduate students are enrolled in one of four undergraduate schools: the College of Arts and Sciences, School of Foreign Service, Georgetown School of Business, and Georgetown School of Nursing and Health Studies. All students share a common liberal arts core and have access to the entire university curriculum.

"Applicants must submit scores from SAT or the ACT. SAT Subject Tests can also be recommended."

SELECTIVITY

Admissions Rating	95
# of applicants	18,916
% of applicants accepted	19
% of acceptees attending	42
# accepting a place on wait list	1,362
% admitted from wait list	12

FRESHMAN PROFILE

Range SAT Critical Reading	650–750
Range SAT Math	660–750
Range ACT Composite	27–33
Minimum paper TOEFL	200

DEADLINES

Early action	
Deadline	11/1
Notification	12/15
Regular	
Deadline	1/10
Nonfall registration?	no

APPLICANTS ALSO LOOK AT

AND OFTEN PREFER
Duke University, University of Pennsylvania

AND SOMETIMES PREFER
Cornell University, Northwestern University, University of Notre Dame, University of Virginia

AND RARELY PREFER
Boston College, New York University, The George Washington University, Tufts University

FINANCIAL FACTS

Financial Aid Rating	95
Annual tuition	$38,616
Room and board	$13,125
Required fees	$420
Books and supplies	$1,060
% frosh rec. need-based scholarship or grant aid	40
% UG rec. need-based scholarship or grant aid	37
% frosh rec. non-need-based scholarship or grant aid	8
% UG rec. non-need-based scholarship or grant aid	7
% frosh rec. need-based self-help aid	38
% UG rec. need-based self-help aid	36
% UG borrow to pay for school	44
Average cumulative indebtedness	$23,333

GEORGIA INSTITUTE OF TECHNOLOGY

219 UNCLE HEINE WAY, ATLANTA, GA 30332-0320 • ADMISSIONS: 404-894-4154 • FAX: 404-894-9511

CAMPUS LIFE

Quality of Life Rating	81
Fire Safety Rating	89
Green Rating	99
Type of school	public
Environment	metropolis

STUDENTS

Total undergrad enrollment	13,160
% male/female	69/31
% from out of state	26
% from public high school	86
% live on campus	59
# of fraternities	39
# of sororities	16
% African American	6
% Asian	17
% Caucasian	62
% Hispanic	5
% international	7
# of countries represented	73

SURVEY SAYS . . .

Great computer facilities
Athletic facilities are great
Diverse student types on campus
Students love Atlanta, GA
Great off-campus food
Everyone loves the Yellow Jackets
Student publications are popular

ACADEMICS

Academic Rating	72
% students graduating within 4 years	33
% students graduating within 6 years	80
Calendar	semester
Student/faculty ratio	20:1
Profs interesting rating	61
Profs accessible rating	63
Most common reg class size	10–19 students
Most common lab size	20–29 students

MOST POPULAR MAJORS

business administration and
management, industrial engineering,
mechanical engineering

STUDENTS SAY ". . ."

Academics

The Georgia Institute of Technology—Georgia Tech for short—"challenges its students academically while providing a culturally diverse environment; all culminating in preparation for life after college." Students warn that the school "is extremely challenging, academically. If you don't like learning it's probably not for you." They also point out that "since Georgia Tech is a research school, most professors are more concerned about their own research than the quality of their teaching. You're basically teaching yourself the entire subject in order to prepare for an almost impossible exam," although students also add that "while many of the professors at Georgia Tech are focused on their research, there are teachers who truly care about their students and the learning process." As one student advises, "a lot of classes seem to be more about getting the right professor: Some are bad teachers, some are inaccessible, but some are so good that their classes fill up seconds after registration opens." And while "classes are challenging," they're also "interesting" so all of that hard work is "not too bad. If you're organized and get help when you need it, you'll be okay, because we have tons of free tutoring on campus…If you need help with anything, there are countless different places that offer tutoring. The best resource is usually fellow students. Because everyone knows how tough of a school it is, there is a spirit of camaraderie here that you don't find anywhere else." Students also appreciate that Tech "is one of the only schools in the country that offers the BS distinction for liberal arts majors because we [get] such a rigorous grounding in math and science." Finally, students note that "career services are outstanding."

Life

One Georgia Tech engineer sums up the typical student itinerary this way: "Study, study, drink. Repeat." As another student puts it, "there is a saying here that between good grades, a social life, and sleep, you can only have two." That's why "basically people bust their [butts] during the week, and when the weekends arrive they're prepared to let loose a bit." Fortunately, "Georgia Tech has a little something for everyone. Salsa club on weekends, musical groups, intramural sports—even a skydiving club!" Other options include "a 'good enough' NCAA Division I sports program, a good social scene," a welcoming Greek community, "and for everyone else, there's the city of Atlanta right at your doorstep. You're just a short ride away from movies, shopping, the Fox Theatre, the High Museum of Art, Piedmont Park, and one of the best club and bar scenes in the South," centered mainly in the neighborhoods of Buckhead and Midtown. For those without cars in this driving city, transportation comes in the form of "a 'Tech Trolley' that takes a route around midtown, and a 'Stinger Shuttle' that goes to the MARTA [Atlanta's subway] station, giving students access to the airport, downtown (although that is walkable), and Lenox Square Mall." With more than "300 organizations already on campus," students seeking leadership experience can most likely find it, and they can find other students with like-minded interests.

Student Body

"The greatest strength of Georgia Tech is its diversity," undergrads report. "Students, activities, opportunities, teachers—all are diverse." One observes that the school hosts "the full range of stereotypes, from the fraternity boys with their croackies and boat shoes to the socially challenged nerds who stay in their rooms 24/7 programming computers. But no matter what, you know everyone is highly intelligent. Many times it is the students who have the best grades who are the drunkest." One student explains, "Unlike at high school, no one looks down upon you if you know the entire periodic table, if you can do differential equations, or you can speak three languages; rather, you are respected." One sore spot: Men outnumber women here by greater than a two to one ratio. The situation is most pronounced in engineering (three to one) and computer (more than four to one) disciplines. Women actually outnumber men in the liberal arts and science colleges.

GEORGIA INSTITUTE OF TECHNOLOGY

FINANCIAL AID: 404-894-4160 • E-MAIL: ADMISSION@GATECH.EDU • WEBSITE: WWW.GATECH.EDU

THE PRINCETON REVIEW SAYS

Admissions

Very important factors considered include: Academic GPA, rigor of secondary school record, extracurricular activities, geographical residence. *Important factors considered include:* Application essay, standardized test scores, character/personal qualities, geographical residence, state residency, talent/ability, volunteer work, work experience. *Other factors considered include:* Alumni/ae relation, racial/ethnic status. SAT or ACT required; ACT with writing component required. High school diploma is required, and GED is accepted. *Academic units required:* 4 English, 4 mathematics, 3 science (3 science labs), 2 foreign language, 3 social studies.

Financial Aid

Students should submit: FAFSA, institution's own financial aid form. Regular filing deadline is March 1. The Princeton Review suggests that all financial aid forms be submitted as soon as possible after January 1. *Need-based scholarships/grants offered:* Federal Pell, SEOG, state scholarships/grants, private scholarships, school scholarship or grant aid from institutional funds. *Loan aid offered:* Direct Subsidized Stafford, Direct Unsubsidized Stafford, Direct PLUS, Federal Perkins, university loans from institutional funds. Federal Work-Study Program available. Off-campus job opportunities are excellent.

The Inside Word

Students considering Georgia Tech shouldn't be deceived by the relatively high acceptance rate. Georgia Tech is a demanding school, and its applicant pool is largely self-selecting. While admissions counselors have begun to implement a more well-rounded approach to the admissions process, grades and test scores are still where candidates make their mark. Requirements vary depending on the school one applies to at Georgia Tech—applicants are advised to inquire in advance.

THE SCHOOL SAYS "..."

From the Admissions Office

"Georgia Tech consistently ranks among the nation's top public universities producing leaders in engineering, computing, management, architecture, and the sciences while remaining one of the best college buys in the country. The 330-acre campus is nestled in the heart of the fun, dynamic and progressive city of Atlanta. During the past decade, over $400 million invested in campus improvements has yielded new state-of-the-art academic and research buildings, apartment-style housing, phenomenal social and recreational facilities, and the most extension fiber-optic cable system on any college campus.

"Georgia Tech has a great academic reputation, and our graduates are well-prepared to meet today's challenges. A unique advantage many students find is Georgia Tech's strong emphasis on undergraduate students. Undergraduates can gain practical work experience through our co-op and internship programs and can begin doing research as early as their freshman year. Students can also gain an international perspective through study abroad, work abroad, or the international plan.

"With a Division I ACC sports program and access to Atlanta's music, theater, and other cultural venues, Georgia Tech offers its diverse and passionate student body a unique combination of top academics in a thriving and vibrant setting. We encourage you to come visit campus and see why Georgia Tech continues to attract the nation's most motivated, interesting, and creative students."

SELECTIVITY
Admissions Rating	96
# of applicants	13,495
% of applicants accepted	52
% of acceptees attending	39
# accepting a place on wait list	621
% admitted from wait list	42

FRESHMAN PROFILE
Range SAT Critical Reading	590–690
Range SAT Math	650–740
Range SAT Writing	590–690
Range ACT Composite	27–32
Average HS GPA	3.87
% graduated top 10% of class	89
% graduated top 25% of class	98
% graduated top 50% of class	100

DEADLINES
Early action	
Deadline	10/1
Notification	11/20
Regular	
Deadline	1/15
Nonfall registration?	yes

APPLICANTS ALSO LOOK AT AND OFTEN PREFER
Duke University, Emory University, Massachusetts Institute of Technology, University of Florida, University of Georgia, University of Michigan—Ann Arbor, Virginia Tech

AND SOMETIMES PREFER
Cornell University, The University of Texas at Austin, University of California—Berkeley, University of Illinois at Urbana-Champaign, University of North Carolina at Chapel Hill, University of Virginia

AND RARELY PREFER
Purdue University—West Lafayette, Rensselaer Polytechnic Institute, Rice University, University of Maryland—College Park

FINANCIAL FACTS
Financial Aid Rating	80
Annual in-state tuition	$7,070
Annual out-of-state tuition	$25,280
Room and board	$8,746
Required fees	$1,646
Books and supplies	$1,000
% frosh rec. need-based scholarship or grant aid	36
% UG rec. need-based scholarship or grant aid	32
% frosh rec. non-need-based scholarship or grant aid	25
% UG rec. non-need-based scholarship or grant aid	19
% frosh rec. need-based self-help aid	19
% UG rec. need-based self-help aid	24
% frosh rec. any financial aid	79
% UG rec. any financial aid	73
% UG borrow to pay for school	51
Average cumulative indebtedness	$21,838

GETTYSBURG COLLEGE

ADMISSIONS OFFICE, EISENHOWER HOUSE, GETTYSBURG, PA 17325-1484 • ADMISSIONS: 717-337-6100 • FAX: 717-337-6145

CAMPUS LIFE

Quality of Life Rating	85
Fire Safety Rating	88
Green Rating	83
Type of school	private
Affiliation	Lutheran
Environment	village

STUDENTS

Total undergrad enrollment	2,484
% male/female	47/53
% from out of state	75
% from public high school	70
% live on campus	94
# of fraternities	12
# of sororities	6
% African American	4
% Asian	2
% Caucasian	81
% Hispanic	4
% international	2
# of countries represented	38

SURVEY SAYS . . .

Lab facilities are great
Great computer facilities
Great food on campus
Dorms are like palaces
Campus feels safe
Students are happy
Frats and sororities dominate social scene
Lots of beer drinking

ACADEMICS

Academic Rating	95
% students graduating within 4 years	82
% students graduating within 6 years	85
Calendar	semester
Student/faculty ratio	10:1
Profs interesting rating	91
Profs accessible rating	94
Most common reg class size	10–19 students
Most common lab size	10–19 students

MOST POPULAR MAJORS
business/commerce, political science, psychology

STUDENTS SAY ". . ."

Academics

Personal and intellectual growth is at the heart of the Gettysburg College experience. Students eagerly praise the school's "friendly, community-oriented atmosphere," and competent, caring professors. "The faculty takes a developed interest in the students' academics and successes, [and] the campus offers countless opportunities for leadership, self-discovery, and the like." In fact, first-year students are surprised to find that "by the first day, the professor knows each student by name and why they're taking the class." With uniformly small class sizes and an emphasis on discussion in the classroom, "Professors at Gettysburg make sure that students understand why they are learning the things that they are, and there is a lot of emphasis put on putting 'theory into practice' outside of the classroom." "Many professors go above and beyond, making themselves available to aid students." A current student shares, "My Intro to Chemistry professor would be at the Science Center until 11 P.M. before an exam, helping everyone study." Academic opportunities—such as the "amazing study abroad program"—are ample at Gettysburg. Plus, as an exclusively undergraduate institution, Gettysburg "allows for opportunities (i.e., research, publications) that many do not get" at larger universities. In this "nurturing environment," the "administration knows students by name" and even the "registrar, transportation services, off-campus studies, and library staff are lovely and do everything they can to help you." In particular, "President Riggs (a Gettysburg alum and former faculty member) is a phenomenal community leader and makes a sincere effort to connect with students, faculty, and staff."

Life

Enthusiastic and overcommitted, most students at Gettysburg are pursuing "a major and a minor or a double-major, and a majority are involved in at least several college organizations (whether it's a community service group, sports team, or Greek organization)." With so much on their plate, it is no surprise that "the students at Gettysburg buckle down and work hard" during the week. Socially, "Life at Gettysburg is very Greek-oriented," and, come the weekend, "frat hopping" is "popular on this campus." Not your style? No worries: Greek life may be "huge" on campus; "However, that does not mean that that is the only thing to do." For students looking for alternate activities, the school hosts "movie nights, plays, and musical performances." Many students also "love going to our theme parties and Happy Hours at the Attic, our on-campus nightclub," while others "get together with friends and watch movies or go out for coffee." For a relaxing respite, "The surrounding area and town is beautiful, so one of my favorite things to do is just walk around out on the battlefields or through town." In addition, "People also like to get off campus traveling to bigger city areas like Baltimore, Harrisburg, D.C., and even Philly and New York City."

Student Body

Academics come first at Gettysburg, where "The student body is extremely intelligent and motivated and serious about their work." When they're not studying, "Gettysburg's student body is very involved" in the school and local community, and "Volunteering is very popular." "Each student—in one way or another—takes part in community service during their time at Gettysburg." Demographically, "Most of the student body is…middle class, white, and from the Northeast." And, lest we forget, the Gettysburg student body is also well known for its uniform "tendency to wear preppy clothes." A current student elaborates, "Open up a J. Crew magazine and find the most attractive models in it and you have a typical Gettysburg College student." While some say the student body has a "cookie-cutter" feel to it, others remind us that "While Gettysburg has a reputation for being mostly white, upper-class students, there is diversity all around if you are willing to open up your eyes and see it."

FINANCIAL AID: 717-337-6611 • E-MAIL: ADMISS@GETTYSBURG.EDU • WEBSITE: WWW.GETTYSBURG.EDU

THE PRINCETON REVIEW SAYS

Admissions

Very important factors considered include: Academic GPA, class rank, recommendation(s), rigor of secondary school record. *Important factors considered include:* Application essay, standardized test scores, character/personal qualities, extracurricular activities, interview, talent/ability, volunteer work. *Other factors considered include:* Alumni/ae relation, first generation, geographical residence, level of applicant's interest, racial/ethnic status, work experience. SAT or ACT reccommended; ACT with or without writing component accepted. TOEFL required of all international applicants. High school diploma is required, and GED is accepted. *Academic units required:* 4 English, 3 mathematics, 3 science (3 science labs), 3 foreign language, 3 social studies, 3 history. *Academic units recommended:* 4 English, 4 mathematics, 4 science (4 science labs), 4 foreign language, 4 social studies, 4 history.

Financial Aid

Students should submit: FAFSA, CSS/Financial Aid PROFILE. Regular filing deadline is February 15. The Princeton Review suggests that all financial aid forms be submitted as soon as possible after January 1. *Need-based scholarships/grants offered:* Federal Pell, SEOG, state scholarships/grants, private scholarships, school scholarship or grant aid from institutional funds. *Loan aid offered:* Direct Subsidized Stafford, Direct Unsubsidized Stafford, Direct PLUS, Federal Perkins, university loans from institutional funds. Federal Work-Study Program available. Off-campus job opportunities are excellent.

The Inside Word

Prospective Gettysburg students can register for an account on the school's website to view Gettysburg events in their area or connect with students on campus. To really get a feel for Gettysburg, however, many students say a campus visit is a must. If you're lucky enough to gain admission to this competitive liberal arts school, a campus visit might be just the thing to seal the deal.

THE SCHOOL SAYS "..."

From the Admissions Office

"Four major goals of Gettysburg College to best prepare students to enter the real world, include, first, to accelerate the intellectual development of our first-year students by integrating them more quickly into the intellectual life of the campus; second, to use interdisciplinary courses combining the intellectual approaches of various fields; third, to encourage students to develop an international perspective through course work, study abroad, association with international faculty, and a variety of extracurricular activities; and fourth, to encourage students to develop (1) a capacity for independent study by ensuring that all students work closely with individual faculty members on an extensive project during their undergraduate years and (2) the ability to work with their peers by making the small group a central feature in college life.

"Gettysburg College strongly recommends that freshman applicants submit scores from the SAT. Students may also choose to submit scores from the ACT (with or without the writing component) in lieu of the SAT."

SELECTIVITY

Admissions Rating	93
# of applicants	5,392
% of applicants accepted	40
% of acceptees attending	33
# accepting a place on wait list	588
% admitted from wait list	0
# of early decision applicants	486
% accepted early decision	66

FRESHMAN PROFILE

Range SAT Critical Reading	610–690
Range SAT Math	620–680
% graduated top 10% of class	68
% graduated top 25% of class	86
% graduated top 50% of class	99

DEADLINES

Early decision	
Deadline	11/15
Notification	12/15
Regular	
Priority	2/1
Deadline	2/1
Nonfall registration?	yes

APPLICANTS ALSO LOOK AT

AND OFTEN PREFER
Colgate University
AND SOMETIMES PREFER
Bucknell University
AND RARELY PREFER
Muhlenberg College

FINANCIAL FACTS

Financial Aid Rating	95
Annual tuition	$41,070
Room and board	$9,810
Books and supplies	$1,100
% frosh rec. need-based scholarship or grant aid	55
% UG rec. need-based scholarship or grant aid	53
% frosh rec. non-need-based scholarship or grant aid	31
% UG rec. non-need-based scholarship or grant aid	27
% frosh rec. need-based self-help aid	51
% UG rec. need-based self-help aid	50
% frosh rec. any financial aid	70
% UG rec. any financial aid	68
% UG borrow to pay for school	60
Average cumulative indebtedness	$24,981

GONZAGA UNIVERSITY

502 EAST BOONE AVENUE, SPOKANE, WA 99258 • ADMISSIONS: 509-313-6572 • FAX: 509-313-5780

STUDENTS SAY ". . ."

Academics

Gonzaga University "has a strong Jesuit Catholic tradition and has sustained an environment of academic excellence." By far, the two most commonly cited strengths are the basketball team and the "awesome community!" Gonzaga is a "close-knit community." "At Gonzaga, we are one big family," one student says. "Everyone is incredibly friendly," and there's "a great sense of school spirit and a family-like environment." "Not to mention being able to cheer in of the most intimidating basketball stadiums in the United States." "It is a family here, and you really get to know your professors," one student explains. "Everyone here is interconnected, and basketball is wonderful too! It's a way we all come together." Students also believe "the Jesuit mission of Gonzaga sets it apart from other schools." Gonzaga "is a socially competent, caring institution" where you'll "be constantly challenged to be your best, make lifelong relationships, and develop a critical understanding of the world around you." The professors get mixed reviews: "It is about a fifty percent chance of getting a good professor." "Professors are good in general, but adjunct faculty is typically hired at the last minute and not good," one student explains. "Many of the professors for the core requirements are very religious and not especially open to new ideas." "Gonzaga tries to get students to think about the world in a holistic way—understanding how everything is interrelated—and finding our purpose in that." Students think the "registration processes" and "cafeteria food" could "use some improvement," and "because Gonzaga is a smaller school, it is at times difficult to arrange your schedule due to limited availability of classes and time constraints."

Life

Students at Gonzaga are "devoted equally to...academics and social life." "People generally just want to socialize," one student explains. "Everyone for the most part does do their work, but there is definitely an emphasis on developing relationships." "The party scene is lively" at Gonzaga although students caution "we're not *that* big of a party school." During basketball season, Gonzaga basketball becomes "a way of life," and "basketball games and waiting in line for tickets are the largest social experience on campus." "*Everyone* goes to the basketball games. It's practically required to graduate." This leads some students to wish there was "less focus on men's basketball." Because the school is located in rainy Spokane, Washington, "the worst thing about Gonzaga is the weather, which the school can't really do anything about." Still, many students "stay active through sports" and enjoy the outdoors, "whether that's skiing, hiking, rafting, climbing, wake boarding, or just soaking up some rays." "People often snowboard at Mount Spokane, or if they are feeling adventurous, they drive the hour to Canada or hour to Montana." At Gonzaga, students "Read, Rage, Repent, Repeat. We wake up, work out, eat, and make memories."

Student Body

Although Gonzaga students stress the college's tight-knit community, many feel that while "the university claims to be accepting of all beliefs, opinions, and life-styles," "in reality that's just not the case." "It is a community for sure, but really only if you're white and upper-middle-class, and the Jesuit Catholic mission can sometimes be troublesome for those of us with liberal and non-mainstream Catholic beliefs," explains one student. "Even feminism is kind of seen as taboo here." Others insist that "everyone here seems to blend well together," and "no matter your background, you are accepted here." Students study "hard through the week" but have "a lot of fun on weekends." Students describe themselves as "friendly, very open," "mostly preppy," "conventionally minded," "well-mannered," "religious," and tending to come "from a good family." Gonzaga has "a mostly Caucasian population," and "diversity is a huge issue, and Gonzaga could definitely improve how it treats students of diverse backgrounds." It should be no shock that "the typical student is a huge basketball fan" with "extreme school spirit."

GONZAGA UNIVERSITY

FINANCIAL AID: 800-793-1716 • E-MAIL: ADMISSIONS@GONZAGA.EDU • WEBSITE: WWW.GONZAGA.EDU

THE PRINCETON REVIEW SAYS

Admissions

Very important factors considered include: Academic GPA, rigor of secondary school record, character/personal qualities, first generation. *Important factors considered include:* Application essay, recommendation(s), standardized test scores, extracurricular activities, talent/ability. *Other factors considered include:* Class rank, alumni/ae relation, interview, level of applicant's interest, racial/ethnic status, volunteer work, work experience. SAT or ACT required; ACT with or without writing component accepted. TOEFL required of all international applicants. *Academic units required:* 4 English, 3 mathematics, 3 science (3 science labs), 2 foreign language, 2 social studies, 2 history, 2 academic elective. *Academic units recommended:* 4 English, 4 mathematics, 4 science (4 science labs), 4 foreign language, 3 social studies, 3 history, 3 academic elective.

Financial Aid

Students should submit: FAFSA. Regular filing deadline is February 1. The Princeton Review suggests that all financial aid forms be submitted as soon as possible after January 1. *Need-based scholarships/grants offered:* Federal Pell, SEOG, state scholarships/grants, private scholarships, school scholarship or grant aid from institutional funds, Federal Nursing Scholarships. *Loan aid offered:* Federal Direct Stafford Loans, Federal Perkins, Federal Nursing Loans, university loans from institutional funds. Applicants will be notified of awards on a rolling basis beginning March 15. Federal Work-Study Program available. Off-campus job opportunities are excellent.

The Inside Word

Gonzaga is a great example of how a high-profile athletic program can transform a competitive school into a highly competitive one. During the past decade, Gonzaga's admit rate has decreased substantially while class rank, standardized test scores, and high school GPA have all increased measurably. Perhaps the only substandard students admitted here these days are those who can consistently drain three pointers.

THE SCHOOL SAYS "..."

From the Admissions Office

"Education at Gonzaga is not comparable to an academic 'assembly line'; rather, it is person-to-person and face-to-face. This personal quality is also true of our admission and financial aid processes. Therefore, allow us to know you beyond the boundaries of your college application. Visit campus, phone us, e-mail us—let us see the person behind the data. Good luck with your college search and your applications. Go Zags!

"All sections of the SAT will be accepted, but the written portion will not receive universal consideration. The written score will be considered in cases where more information specific to writing ability would be helpful in decision making."

SELECTIVITY

Admissions Rating	89
# of applicants	6,258
% of applicants accepted	64
% of acceptees attending	28
# accepting a place on wait list	207
% admitted from wait list	22

FRESHMAN PROFILE

Range SAT Critical Reading	530–640
Range SAT Math	560–660
Range ACT Composite	25–29
Minimum paper TOEFL	550
Minimum computer TOEFL	213
Average HS GPA	3.72
% graduated top 10% of class	40
% graduated top 25% of class	73
% graduated top 50% of class	92

DEADLINES

Early action	
Deadline	11/15
Notification	1/15
Regular	
Priority	2/1
Deadline	2/1
Nonfall registration?	yes

APPLICANTS ALSO LOOK AT AND SOMETIMES PREFER
Santa Clara University, University of Washington
AND RARELY PREFER
Washington State University

FINANCIAL FACTS

Financial Aid Rating	85
Annual tuition	$30,440
Room and board	$8,300
Required fees	$498
Books and supplies	$1,000
% frosh rec. need-based scholarship or grant aid	73
% UG rec. need-based scholarship or grant aid	71
% frosh rec. non-need-based scholarship or grant aid	94
% UG rec. non-need-based scholarship or grant aid	90
% frosh rec. need-based self-help aid	39
% UG rec. need-based self-help aid	46
% frosh rec. any financial aid	98
% UG rec. any financial aid	95
% UG borrow to pay for school	68
Average cumulative indebtedness	$20,178

GOUCHER COLLEGE

1021 DULANEY VALLEY ROAD, BALTIMORE, MD 21204-2794 • ADMISSIONS: 410-337-6100 • FAX: 410-337-6354

STUDENTS SAY ". . ."

Academics

A "small, East Coast, liberal arts school, with a tremendous history," Goucher College provides a "global education" best embodied in the motto "Learn for yourself, learn to be yourself, enjoy yourself, respect everyone else and you will succeed." Located on a "beautiful campus right outside a big city," students say the "intimate size is what is apparent about Goucher through and through." With a "socially informed" student body of self-motivated learners and thinkers, academics at Goucher are about "owning your education." As one student notes, "What you get out of your Goucher experience is directly related to what you put into it." Innovative thinkers flock here for "the openness of the student body, political nature of the institution, and the required study abroad program." Students say Goucher is a "very creative place" where "importance is placed on academics as well as the arts." "Easily accessible and ready to talk about anything and everything, while providing incredible insight and tools for students to investigate their own questions," professors "are what make Goucher great." As one student observes, academics at Goucher are all about "pushing myself beyond my old boundaries and really discovering what I am capable of and who I am." Assignments tend to focus on "challenging you to make your own opinions on a topic and testing them." Though some students feel they "could get rid of the administration for the most part," others note that while "The administration can be a little hands-off, you can access who you need to when it comes down to it." In principle, Goucher is "a place where one feels comfortable to talk to anyone, even the president of the college." "The professors are always available. Many will give you their home phone numbers or eat lunch with you."

Life

"Goucher is about living to learn and having fun in the process." An "eclectic yet tight-knit community," with a focus on "activism and global citizenship," "Goucher strives to represent, explore, and respect all aspects of humanity." Not typically known as a party school, parties on campus "tend to be low key, in people's rooms or apartments." Students say that the absence of fraternities and sororities "really helps to minimize [the] pressure of drinking." As studying abroad is required, it is "a major topic of conversation and a major source of student unity." In addition, there are "lots of school-sponsored events, such as speakers, plays, [and] small-name bands." As one student notes, "We've had everyone from [Karl Rove] to Tuvan Throat Singers to Paul Rusesabagina (the man Hotel Rwanda was based on), to an amazing group of poets called the Elephant Engine High Dive Revival, just this year alone. " On campus, "There's a kind of coffee house/pub/general hang out spot called the Gopher Hole where there are often dance parties, poetry slams, and other...fun activities always happening." Hometown Towson boasts "terrific restaurants, a concert venue, a movie theater, art galleries, quirky shops," [and] a large and modern mall. "When campus starts to feel a little small...there is a free shuttle that runs into Baltimore."

Student Body

A haven for liberal-minded, independent thinkers with a flair for unique hobbies and interests, students jokingly say that Goucher is "a place where students who never 'fit in' in high school come and find each other," "zombies and pirates included." The typical Goucher student is "socially, politically, emotionally, and internationally aware." "Everyone's a little weird, and most of them [are] very intelligent." When asked to give a composite picture, students paint the average Goucher student as "eighteen to twenty years old, female, liberal-minded, and very strong-headed." "We're a group of feminists, hippies, oddballs, geeks, HvZ players, and intellectuals, with the occasional soccer player thrown in." Another notes, "I can walk down Van Meter highway at any given time and see a group of lacrosse boys on the way to the SRC, the Pirate Club selling cupcakes in front of Pearlstone, or kids hanging out in front of the library." "There's a group for everyone at Goucher."

GOUCHER COLLEGE

FINANCIAL AID: 410-337-6141 • E-MAIL: ADMISSION@GOUCHER.EDU • WEBSITE: WWW.GOUCHER.EDU

THE PRINCETON REVIEW SAYS

Admissions

Very important factors considered include: Academic GPA, rigor of secondary school record. *Important factors considered include:* Application essay, recommendation(s), talent/ability. *Other factors considered include:* Standardized test scores, alumni/ae relation, character/personal qualities, extracurricular activities, first generation, geographical residence, interview, level of applicant's interest, racial/ethnic status, state residency, volunteer work, work experience. ACT with writing component required. TOEFL required of all international applicants. High school diploma is required, and GED is accepted. *Academic units required:* 4 English, 3 mathematics, 2 science, 2 foreign language, 3 social studies, 2 academic elective. *Academic units recommended:* 4 English, 4 mathematics, 3 science, 4 foreign language, 3 social studies, 2 academic elective.

Financial Aid

Students should submit: FAFSA, CSS/Financial Aid PROFILE. Regular filing deadline is February 1. The Princeton Review suggests that all financial aid forms be submitted as soon as possible after January 1. *Need-based scholarships/grants offered:* Federal Pell, SEOG, state scholarships/grants, private scholarships, school scholarship or grant aid from institutional funds. *Loan aid offered:* Direct Subsidized Stafford, Direct Unsubsidized Stafford, Direct PLUS, Federal Perkins, university loans from institutional funds. Federal Work-Study Program available. Off-campus job opportunities are excellent.

The Inside Word

Although there is a test-optional admissions policy, Goucher accepts the ACT with Writing in lieu of the SAT, and SAT Subject Tests are required for an applicant to be considered for merit funding. Goucher's high admit rate masks a self-selecting applicant pool; you cannot gain acceptance here without a solid high school transcript and test scores.

THE SCHOOL SAYS "..."

From the Admissions Office

"Through a broad-based arts and sciences curriculum and a groundbreaking approach to study abroad, Goucher College gives students a sweeping view of the world. Goucher is an independent, coeducational institution dedicated to both the interdisciplinary traditions of the liberal arts and a truly international perspective on education. The first college in the nation to pair required study abroad with a special travel stipend of $1,200 for every undergraduate, Goucher believes in complementing its strong majors and rigorous curriculum with abundant opportunities for hands-on experience. In addition to participating in the college's many study abroad programs (including innovative three-week intensive courses abroad alongside traditional semester and academic year offerings), many students also complete internships and service-learning projects that further enhance their learning.

"The college's almost 1,500 undergraduate students live and learn on a tree-lined campus of 287 acres just north of Baltimore, Maryland. Goucher boasts a student/faculty ratio of just nine to one, and professors routinely collaborate with students on major research projects—often for publication, and sometimes as early as students' first or second years. The curriculum emphasizes international and intercultural awareness throughout, and students are encouraged to explore their academic interests from a variety of perspectives beyond their major disciplines.

"A Goucher College education encompasses a multitude of experiences that ultimately converge into one cohesive academic program that can truly change lives. Students grow in dramatic and surprising ways here. They graduate with a strong sense of direction and self-confidence, ready to engage the world—and succeed—as true global citizens."

SELECTIVITY

Admissions Rating	85
# of applicants	3,587
% of applicants accepted	73
% of acceptees attending	15
# accepting a place on wait list	108
% admitted from wait list	21
# of early decision applicants	69
% accepted early decision	74

FRESHMAN PROFILE

Range SAT Critical Reading	530–650
Range SAT Math	500–620
Range SAT Writing	530–650
Range ACT Composite	23–28
Minimum paper TOEFL	550
Minimum computer TOEFL	213
Average HS GPA	3.13
% graduated top 10% of class	28
% graduated top 25% of class	58
% graduated top 50% of class	91

DEADLINES

Early decision	
Deadline	11/15
Notification	12/15
Early action	
Deadline	12/1
Notification	2/15
Regular	
Deadline	2/1
Nonfall registration?	yes

FINANCIAL FACTS

Financial Aid Rating	77
Annual tuition	$36,011
Room and board	$10,569
Required fees	$542
% frosh rec. need-based scholarship or grant aid	57
% UG rec. need-based scholarship or grant aid	57
% frosh rec. non-need-based scholarship or grant aid	5
% UG rec. non-need-based scholarship or grant aid	4
% frosh rec. need-based self-help aid	53
% UG rec. need-based self-help aid	53
% frosh rec. any financial aid	81
% UG rec. any financial aid	80
% UG borrow to pay for school	75
Average cumulative indebtedness	$23,859

GREEN MOUNTAIN COLLEGE

One Brennan Circle, Poultney, VT 05764-1199 • Admissions: 802-287-8000 • Fax: 802-287-8099

CAMPUS LIFE

Quality of Life Rating	75
Fire Safety Rating	61
Green Rating	97
Type of school	private
Affiliation	Methodist
Environment	rural

STUDENTS

Total undergrad enrollment	759
% male/female	52/48
% from out of state	87
% from public high school	86
% live on campus	84
% African American	3
% Asian	1
% Caucasian	72
% Hispanic	2
% Native American	1
# of countries represented	44

SURVEY SAYS . . .
Students are friendly
Low cost of living
Frats and sororities are unpopular
or nonexistent

ACADEMICS

Academic Rating	83
% students graduating within 4 years	33
% students graduating within 6 years	10
Calendar	semester
Student/faculty ratio	14:1
Profs interesting rating	89
Profs accessible rating	87
Most common reg class size	10–19 students
Most common lab size	10–19 students

MOST POPULAR MAJORS
adventure education, biology,
fine arts, environmental studies,
sustainable agriculture

STUDENTS SAY ". . ."

Academics

"Small," "incredibly progressive" Green Mountain College in rural Vermont "does the environmental, green thing" throughout its academic programs. "A strong liberal arts program" includes four core courses that relate in way or another to the environment. GMC gets more than half of its electricity from Vermont dairy farms. The pride and joy of the campus is a "fossil fuel-free" and generally "kick-ass" farm that "gives students firsthand experience in sustainable agriculture and subsistent farming." There's a barn "packed with animals." "We grow delicious, organic produce," notes an environmental studies major. Reviews of the academic experience here are generally positive. There is a wealth of opportunities for "hands-on learning," internships, and studying abroad. Unique majors include adventure education and resort management. There's also the progressive program, which allows students to chart their own academic course. "Professors go by their first names." A few are "absolutely awful," but most are "a joy to have in class." They're "very approachable" and active in the larger community. "I love going to a bluegrass concert and seeing my stats professor playing banjo," gushes a happy first-year student.

Life

"Green Mountain is all about environmentalism, skiing, the outdoors, and the Grateful Dead." Maple trees "cover the campus." There are several "very pretty buildings," too. In keeping with its environmentally sustainable ethos, a LEED Gold Certified residence hall was completed in fall of 2009. Socially, "life is laid-back." "Everybody pretty much knows everybody." "During the winter, the weather is harsh," but both fall and spring are pleasant. "It is amazing to go outside when it is nice out to see rugby, Frisbee, volleyball, music circles, and music coming from all different dorms," observes a junior. "There is a river right behind the college, and it's a popular hangout spot," adds a senior. "People swim during the day and have bonfires at night." "There is a lot of partying" as well. Campus activities include "concerts, contra-dances, dinners, parties, and much more." The "isolated" hamlet of Poultney has "little to offer beyond small-town New England charm." "The closest city, Rutland, isn't that big and is a half hour away." The area is "scenic," though, and it's a nature lover's paradise. "There are ski hills in every direction," and the College "runs trips almost every weekend to do outdoor activities such as kayaking, rock-climbing, hiking, etc."

Student Body

The typical Green Mountain student is a "tree-loving" "outdoors type." Individuality is "deeply embraced" here. "Our school population consists mainly of people who would be atypical at other schools," explains a senior. Most students are "left-wing liberals" who are "environmentally aware." "If you have a different point of view, it can be overwhelming." "Future activists" proliferate. There are "many vegetarians and vegans." On the whole, Green Mountain's student population is "a conglomeration of hippies and ski bums." Students are "sixties-oriented in fashion, lifestyle, food choices, and personality." Even the rare preppy students "seem to be able to embrace their inner hippie." "At times, it's like a time warp."

FINANCIAL AID: 802-287-8210 • E-MAIL: ADMISS@GREENMTN.EDU • WEBSITE: WWW.GREENMTN.EDU

THE PRINCETON REVIEW SAYS

Admissions

Very important factors considered include: Academic GPA, application essay, rigor of secondary school record, character/personal qualities. *Important factors considered include:* Class rank, recommendation(s), extracurricular activities, interview, volunteer work. *Other factors considered include:* Standardized test scores, level of applicant's interest, talent/ability, work experience. Green Mountain is a test optional school. Applicants who choose not to submit SAT or ACT scores must complete an Insight Portfolio. TOEFL required of all international applicants. High school diploma is required, and GED is accepted. *Academic units required:* 4 English, 3 mathematics, 3 science (2 science labs), 2 foreign language, 3 social studies, 1 history, 5 academic elective. *Academic units recommended:* 4 mathematics, 4 science, 3 foreign language, 3 social studies, 2 history.

Financial Aid

Students should submit: FAFSA. Priority filing deadline is January 15. (FAFSA forms are accepted on a rolling basis after the priority filing date.) The Princeton Review suggests that all financial aid forms be submitted as soon as possible after January 1. *Need-based scholarships/grants offered:* Federal Pell, SEOG, state scholarships/grants, private scholarships, school scholarship or grant aid from institutional funds. *Loan aid offered:* Direct Subsidized Stafford, Direct Unsubsidized Stafford, Direct PLUS. Applicants will be notified of awards on a rolling basis beginning January 1. Federal Work-Study Program available. On-campus job opportunities are available. Campus employment available for international students. All campus employment is through the GMC Green Job Corps.

The Inside Word

It's a holistic process here, which is fabulous news if your academic record thus far is less than stellar. Standardized test scores are optional. Only send yours if they are good. Don't miss the interview. Pay meticulous attention to the essay. Take advantage of the opportunity to supplement your application with additional materials. Also, note that financial aid is ample.

THE SCHOOL SAYS "..."

From the Admissions Office

"Green Mountain College was named the number one "Coolest School" by Sierra magazine. GMC is a liberal arts college that is on the forefront of sustainability education.

"While we are proud of our national recognition for sustainability, three-quarters of our students do not major in environmental studies, but rather select a liberal arts major that they are passionate about—education, business, art, psychology, biology, etc. The student body is united by a sense of social responsibility and penchant for service. Diversity thrives at Green Mountain College. The academic community thrives on opposing views and provides a truthful and authentic scholarly environment.

"GMC's working farm is a special attraction for students from all majors. It provides a visible model of sustainability and produces a significant quantity of food for the college community. Students can also major in Sustainable Agriculture and Food Production and/or earn twelve credits over the summer in Farm Life Ecology, a 'field and table' intensive.

"We award scholarships for academic merit, service, leadership, creative arts, and environmental advancement at the time of admission, so students should submit evidence of these activities with their application for admission. The college is committed to and guarantees graduation in four years for students who meet academic requirements. An entrepreneurial spirit carries throughout the entire community resulting in a one of kind preparation for career and or graduate/professional school upon graduation."

SELECTIVITY

Admissions Rating	75
# of applicants	1,290
% of applicants accepted	79
% of acceptees attending	25

FRESHMAN PROFILE

Range SAT Critical Reading	470–600
Range SAT Math	450–560
Range SAT Writing	460–580
Range ACT Composite	17–23
Minimum paper TOEFL	500
Minimum computer TOEFL	173
Minimum IELTS	5.0
Average HS GPA	3.10
% graduated top 10% of class	11
% graduated top 25% of class	25
% graduated top 50% of class	58

DEADLINES

Regular	
Priority	12/1
Notification	rolling
Nonfall registration?	yes

FINANCIAL FACTS

Financial Aid Rating	75
Annual tuition	$26,920
Required fees	$1,278
Books and supplies	$1,100
% frosh rec. need-based scholarship or grant aid	84
% UG rec. need-based scholarship or grant aid	71
% frosh rec. non-need-based scholarship or grant aid	16
% UG rec. non-need-based scholarship or grant aid	15
% frosh rec. need-based self-help aid	69
% UG rec. need-based self-help aid	63
% frosh rec. any financial aid	95
% UG rec. any financial aid	86
% UG borrow to pay for school	79

GRINNELL COLLEGE

OFFICE OF ADMISSION, 1103 PARK STREET, 2ND FLOOR, GRINNELL, IA 50112-1690 • ADMISSIONS: 641-269-3600 • FAX: 641-269-4800

CAMPUS LIFE

Quality of Life Rating	82
Fire Safety Rating	83
Green Rating	83
Type of school	private
Environment	village

STUDENTS

Total undergrad enrollment	1,603
% male/female	45/55
% from out of state	87
% from public high school	70
% live on campus	88
% African American	5
% Asian	6
% Caucasian	59
% Hispanic	7
% international	12
# of countries represented	54

SURVEY SAYS . . .
No one cheats
Frats and sororities are unpopular or nonexistent
Student government is popular
Political activism is popular

ACADEMICS

Academic Rating	96
% students graduating within 4 years	84
% students graduating within 6 years	87
Calendar	semester
Student/faculty ratio	9:1
Profs interesting rating	92
Profs accessible rating	95
Most common reg class size	10–19 students
Most common lab size	10–19 students

MOST POPULAR MAJORS
economics, English, psychology

STUDENTS SAY ". . ."

Academics

Offering "a great mix of serious academics and a fun community," Grinnell College "is a crazy, unique, busy, caffeinated cornfield of geniuses" whose "hard work, critical thinking, and social consciousness" define the Grinnell experience. The school "is challenging academically," so "you have to work very hard, and it's not always easy. It can be stressful at times, but the pressure all comes from yourself. It's not a competitive atmosphere. And the academics here are extremely effective." An open curriculum ("no requirements other than the freshman tutorial") and a self-governance policy mean that "students feel at home here because we are independent," operating "without stringent rules about how to live our lives and what choices to make." A low teacher-student ratio allows for close relationships, meaning students aren't entirely without guidance. "I have never heard of an inaccessible professor," one student reports. "They are very willing to help and genuinely care about us and our performance in class. In addition, I have never heard of a class with more than thirty people in it: They just don't exist." That commitment to having small classes "ensures group discussion and personal attention: There are no straight lecture classes." Thanks to a "huge endowment," students have tremendous latitude in plotting their studies. One undergrad observes, "Money never really seems to be an issue here. If you can dream it, Grinnell can pay for it." The school is "full of resources! Students needing to do research in museums, archives, and libraries for thesis-level research projects can easily get funding from the college. Also, the arts and science facilities are top-of-the-line."

Life

The academic rigors at Grinnell are substantial. You "won't have to worry about surviving the Midwest winter" here, because "being buried in books and papers and paper revisions and articles and essays and book reviews and to-do lists keeps you surprisingly warm." The environment can be stressful, and many are inclined toward traditional collegiate stress-relieving activities. "That being said, there is no pressure to try things if one is not interested," and there are in fact "many substance-free students, some of whom choose to live in sub-free housing." "The administration, as part of self governance, does not police drinking/drugs," but it does encourage students to act responsibly. "Student security is present at school-sponsored parties." Students agree that "extracurricular activities are highly popular," running the gamut from "artists the college brings in" to "lectures, movies, concerts, even therapy dogs during mid-semester exams" to "just hanging out with some cards or 'How I Met Your Mother' DVDs." Hometown Grinnell is "isolated," but not without its charms. One student explains, "I love the town of Grinnell and think Midwest-nice is a great asset, but that's my personal taste. I like recognizing the lady who walks her dog by our house every day and the kid who bags our groceries. And I love going to the farmer's market and things like the 4-H tractor show that took place this summer."

Student Body

Grinnell undergrads describe themselves and their classmates as "students interested in social justice and having a good time." They tend to be "highly intelligent, motivated, and inquisitive" students who constantly challenge one another "to examine topics from different perspectives. This constant thinking outside of the box is a primary aspect of a true liberal arts education." Grinnellians "are frequently left-leaning, but there's not a typical Grinnell student. All the students are different, so there are few issues with fitting in." Intellect and intensity are the most frequent common denominators; as one student explains, "I've heard that every single student is a nerd about something. Perhaps that is what unites us—our passion, whether that be for a sport, academic subject, Joss Whedon, foam-sword fighting, or politics. We all respect that we have different interests but bond because we are interested rather than apathetic, therefore interesting and unique."

GRINNELL COLLEGE

FINANCIAL AID: 641-269-3250 • E-MAIL: ASKGRIN@GRINNELL.EDU • WEBSITE: WWW.GRINNELL.EDU

THE PRINCETON REVIEW SAYS

Admissions

Very important factors considered include: Academic GPA, class rank, recommendation(s), rigor of secondary school record, standardized test scores, extracurricular activities, talent/ability. *Important factors considered include:* Application essay, interview, racial/ethnic status. *Other factors considered include:* Alumni/ae relation, character/personal qualities, first generation, geographical residence, level of applicant's interest, state residency, volunteer work, work experience. SAT or ACT required; ACT with or without writing component accepted. TOEFL required of all international applicants. High school diploma is required, and GED is accepted. *Academic units recommended:* 4 English, 4 mathematics, 4 social studies.

Financial Aid

Students should submit: FAFSA, institution's own financial aid form. Regular filing deadline is February 1. The Princeton Review suggests that all financial aid forms be submitted as soon as possible after January 1. *Need-based scholarships/grants offered:* Federal Pell, SEOG, state scholarships/grants, private scholarships, school scholarship or grant aid from institutional funds. *Loan aid offered:* Direct Subsidized Stafford, Direct Unsubsidized Stafford, Direct PLUS, Federal Perkins, university loans from institutional funds.

The Inside Word

Grinnell's admissions process is refreshingly straightforward. According to the school's website, the school bases fifty percent of its decision on high school performance, including quality of curriculum, and twenty-five percent depends on standardized test scores. The remaining twenty-five percent is based on the school's assessment of each candidate's potential contributions in the classroom and to the Grinnell campus community. Grinnell is extremely selective, so you'll have to give it your all. An interview isn't required here, but do it anyway.

THE SCHOOL SAYS " . . ."

From the Admissions Office

"Grinnell College is a place where independence of thought and social conscience are instilled. Grinnell is a college with the resources of a school ten times its size, a faculty that reads like a Who's Who of Teaching, and a learning environment where debate does not end in the classroom and often begins in the Campus Center.

"Grinnellians are committed to learning, respect for themselves and others, contributing to global social good, willing collaboration, and the courage to try.

"We look for students who show strong potential, have the courage to try new things, demonstrate a willingness to speak out and share their opinions, and bring different perspectives to our international campus in the middle of Iowa. Grinnell College is filled with students who are serious about learning but are not always serious."

SELECTIVITY

Admissions Rating	93
# of applicants	2,845
% of applicants accepted	43
% of acceptees attending	34
# accepting a place on wait list	356
% admitted from wait list	4
# of early decision applicants	300
% accepted early decision	46

FRESHMAN PROFILE

Range SAT Critical Reading	610–740
Range SAT Math	610–730
Range ACT Composite	28–32
% graduated top 10% of class	62
% graduated top 25% of class	88
% graduated top 50% of class	98

DEADLINES

Early decision I	
Deadline	11/15
Notification	12/15
Early decision II	
Deadline	1/1
Notification	2/1
Regular	
Deadline	1/15
Nonfall registration?	no

FINANCIAL FACTS

Financial Aid Rating	98
Annual tuition	$39,250
Room and board	$9,334
Required fees	$560
Books and supplies	$900
% frosh rec. need-based scholarship or grant aid	72
% UG rec. need-based scholarship or grant aid	67
% frosh rec. non-need-based scholarship or grant aid	14
% UG rec. non-need-based scholarship or grant aid	19
% frosh rec. need-based self-help aid	65
% UG rec. need-based self-help aid	60
% frosh rec. any financial aid	90
% UG rec. any financial aid	87
% UG borrow to pay for school	53
Average cumulative indebtedness	$18,578

GROVE CITY COLLEGE

100 CAMPUS DRIVE, GROVE CITY, PA 16127-2104 • ADMISSIONS: 724-458-2100 • FAX: 724-458-3395

STUDENTS SAY ". . ."

Academics

Students see the world from a "Christian viewpoint in a safe atmosphere" at Grove City, a college in Pennsylvania that offers "conservative libertarian Christianity applied to a serious Western liberal arts curriculum." As one student puts it, "we are a school that celebrates the trinity of Jesus, C.S. Lewis, and Ronald Reagan." Students here "serve God while working their butts off" in academically rigorous classes designed to give "a good education based on biblical values" through the integration of faith in both the curriculum and college life. Administration makes it a point to be available to the students; the president of the college has weekly time set apart when students can personally talk with him. Still, campus living can sometimes get complicated, as "rules at Grove City are not always enforced as they say, and some rules exist that are not written anywhere." Class registration is "one of the most stressful things *ever*!" The campus itself is beautiful, and the school "does a great job with keeping it up," but parking is both expensive and far away. Since the average class size at GCC is relatively small, the classroom is "definitely a student-friendly setting." Though many have a couple of teachers they've been unhappy with, all are very satisfied with both what the professors give them and ask of them. Professors have extremely high expectations for their students and "have challenging tests and a lot of work," but they "truly care about you and are open to students asking questions and talking to them about work or anything else outside of class." "They are committed to learning and mastering all areas of human endeavor for the glory of God," says a student. The school's excellent job placement rate and "reasonable price" are just a few more of the many reasons students choose to come here.

Life

Activities abound at Grove City, with "excellent" intramurals topping the popularity list, and "a million and one" clubs. "I am involved in Clowns for Christ, Life Advocates (a pro-life group), and the Grove City Democrats," says a busy student. A favorite activity on campus is Warriors, which is an hour of worship once a week. This dry campus is "not exactly a party school or one where weekend life is traditionally 'hopping.'" On weekends, students typically hang out in their friends' rooms and watch movies or go to dances. The rules here are quite strict—there are "inter-visitation rules proscribing which hours males and females may be on male and female halls"—so students do "fun but non-illegal things" in their spare time. Many agree that the school could stand to "[rein] in campus safety." No one is a big fan of the town itself, but Pittsburgh is only an hour or so away. There are also, thankfully, "good restaurants within fifteen or twenty minutes," since the school "could improve drastically in quality of food provided." All students live on campus and must have meal plans. "I'd have to say that the most fun is making up your own fun," says a student. One "could stop and have a deep conversation with a perfect stranger, and it would be normal," and indeed, "you hear many conversations about religious issues."

Student Body

No doubt about it—the typical student here is "white, middle- to upper-class, and very religious." Many of these "Grovers" were homeschooled. As for atypical students and minorities, well, "there aren't a lot," but they do manage to find each other. Diversity here could definitely use some TLC—a large number of students wish that the school would "[bring] in people who are not all the same." Still, most people are "friendly and helpful," and "there is rarely an interpersonal conflict." Studies tend to be a center of focus here, and the "library is constantly crowded with students working hard to keep up." They all "work together in order to achieve a diploma instead of believing they have to compete with each other." "Everyone on campus is over-committed. Coming to Grove City, you basically admit to and crave being stressed beyond belief," says an elementary education major.

FINANCIAL AID: 724-458-2163 • E-MAIL: ADMISSIONS@GCC.EDU • WEBSITE: WWW.GCC.EDU/PR

THE PRINCETON REVIEW SAYS

Admissions

Very important factors considered include: Academic GPA, application essay, rigor of secondary school record, standardized test scores, character/personal qualities, geographical residence, interview, level of applicant's interest, religious affiliation/commitment. *Important factors considered include:* Recommendation(s), extracurricular activities, geographical residence. *Other factors considered include:* Class rank, alumni/ae relation, first generation, racial/ethnic status, state residency, talent/ability, volunteer work, work experience. SAT or ACT required; ACT with or without writing component accepted. TOEFL required of all international applicants. High school diploma is required, and GED is accepted. *Academic units recommended:* 4 English, 3 mathematics, 3 science (2 science labs), 3 foreign language, 2 social studies, 2 history.

Financial Aid

Students should submit: Institution's own financial aid form. Regular filing deadline is April 15. The Princeton Review suggests that all financial aid forms be submitted as soon as possible after January 1. *Need-based scholarships/grants offered:* state scholarships/grants, private scholarships, school scholarship or grant aid from institutional funds. *Loan aid offered:* State loans. Applicants will be notified of awards on a rolling basis beginning March 15. Federal Work-Study Program available. Off-campus job opportunities are good.

The Inside Word

Admission to Grove City has become very competitive, and any serious contender will need to hit the books. While a rigorous class schedule is a given, admissions officers also closely assess character and personal qualities. GCC is steeped in Christian values, and the school seeks students who will be comfortable in such an environment. As such, interviews and recommendations hold significant weight.

THE SCHOOL SAYS "..."

From the Admissions Office

"A good college education doesn't have to cost a fortune. For decades, Grove City College has offered a quality education at costs among the lowest nationally. Since the 1990s, increased national academic acclaim has come to Grove City College. Grove City College is a place where professors teach; you will not see graduate assistants or teacher's aides in the classroom. Our professors are also active in the total life of the campus. More than 100 student organizations on campus afford opportunity for a wide variety of cocurricular activities. Outstanding scholars and leaders in education, science, and international affairs visit the campus each year. The environment at GCC is friendly, secure, and dedicated to high standards. Character-building is emphasized and traditional Christian values are supported.

"There is a fresh spiritual vitality on campus that touches every aspect of your college life. In the classroom, we don't shy away from discussing all points of view, however we adhere to Christ's teaching as relevant guidance for living. Come and visit and learn more."

SELECTIVITY

Admissions Rating	92
# of applicants	1,660
% of applicants accepted	74
% of acceptees attending	53
# accepting a place on wait list	88
% admitted from wait list	14
# of early decision applicants	451
% accepted early decision	78

FRESHMAN PROFILE

Range SAT Critical Reading	560–690
Range SAT Math	570–680
Range ACT Composite	25–30
Minimum paper TOEFL	550
Minimum computer TOEFL	213
Minimum web-based TOEFL	79
Average HS GPA	3.71
% graduated top 10% of class	47
% graduated top 25% of class	75
% graduated top 50% of class	97

DEADLINES

Early decision	
Deadline	11/15
Notification	12/15
Regular	
Deadline	2/1
Nonfall registration?	yes

APPLICANTS ALSO LOOK AT
AND OFTEN PREFER
Hillsdale College, Penn State—University Park, Wheaton College (IL)

AND SOMETIMES PREFER
Geneva College, Gordon College, Houghton College

FINANCIAL FACTS

Financial Aid Rating	64
Annual tuition	$13,598
Room and board	$7,410
Books and supplies	$1,000
% frosh rec. need-based scholarship or grant aid	40
% UG rec. need-based scholarship or grant aid	38
% frosh rec. non-need-based scholarship or grant aid	4
% UG rec. non-need-based scholarship or grant aid	3
% frosh rec. need-based self-help aid	23
% UG rec. need-based self-help aid	25
% frosh rec. any financial aid	40
% UG rec. any financial aid	40
% UG borrow to pay for school	58
Average cumulative indebtedness	$25,773

GUILFORD COLLEGE

5800 WEST FRIENDLY AVENUE, GREENSBORO, NC 27410 • ADMISSIONS: 336-316-2100 • FAX: 336-316-2954

STUDENTS SAY ". . ."

Academics

Nestled in beautiful Greensboro, North Carolina, Guilford College is a school that places an "emphasis on community." Indeed, as one junior gushes, "When I visited, everyone stopped what they were doing and welcomed me to [the] college. It was such a different atmosphere than anywhere I had ever seen, and I immediately wanted to be a part of it." This convivial environment can likely be attributed to the school's Quaker roots and value system, which continue to permeate the campus. Most importantly, the warmth and openness extends into the classroom. As another junior raves, "The professors here are incredible. We all go on a first-name basis (Quakers love equality), and they go out of their way to make sure everyone is getting the material." Slackers beware! An English major warns, "We are extremely writing intensive; I've done more writing for an intro physics course than I've done for some English courses." Fortunately, the "teachers are available to offer advice and make sure we succeed." Student approval also extends to the college's administration. As one impressed psych major tells us, "The administration works very hard to address all of the school's issues. They even sit and have discussions with students about how they feel things need to be changed and what it is they see as needing to be done for the overall well-being of the school and students."

Life

Though most Guilford undergrads "spend the daytime doing homework," there are plenty of opportunities for students to kick back and take a breather from academics. On this socially conscious campus, many students "join clubs like Pride and Blacks Unifying Society, or participate in politics/community service." One sophomore concurs, adding that "Everywhere you walk you will find some sort of flyer posted about speakers coming to talk and share their beliefs or meetings that students have put together to discuss issues on campus. People love sharing their thoughts about what they want done." Many also praise the efforts of the Campus Activities Board which sponsors a number of "dances, movies, game nights, and biggest of all Serendipity [an annual music festival]." Considering Guilford's "beautiful" setting, it's no wonder that most undergrads also "love to be outside." As one English major shares, "We try to get off campus [during] the weekend with day trips like hiking, apple picking, swimming, etc." The campus is surrounded by a "ton of woods" and "Most people like to be out there when they can. People camp out for weeks and hike in for classes." Though there are "no fraternities or sororities," there's a "goofy party scene—lots of bonfires in the woods, lots of themed parties (i.e., '80s Aerobics)" which, as one junior assures us, "*Everyone* is welcome to attend."

Student Body

A number of undergrads are quick to assert that "It's hard to describe the typical Guilford student." As one sophomore brags, "I have met and befriended people from many social classes, sexual orientations, religious and spiritual beliefs, interests and backgrounds." That being said, "Most students have liberal tendencies and the conservatives are definitely in the minority." Indeed, "Guilford seems to breed a second hippie generation." A French major explains, "I think the typical student is very carefree and laid-back and they care a lot about sustainability, local produce, and issues like that." Students do warn that "There is a great divide between the athletes and the [rest of the] student body." However, a junior assures us, "There really is a place for any kind of person to fit in." As one English explains, "We are all a little odd [so] we fit in together just fine." "If a kid is sitting alone or is just walking by him/herself someone will talk to them, join them, befriend them. No matter what, Guilford College students take care of one another."

FINANCIAL AID: 336-316-2354 • E-MAIL: ADMISSION@GUILFORD.EDU • WEBSITE: WWW.GUILFORD.EDU

THE PRINCETON REVIEW SAYS

Admissions

Very important factors considered include: Academic GPA, application essay, rigor of secondary school record, character/personal qualities. *Important factors considered include:* Class rank, recommendation(s), standardized test scores, extracurricular activities, interview, level of applicant's interest, talent/ability, volunteer work, work experience. *Other factors considered include:* Alumni/ae relation, first generation, geographical residence, racial/ethnic status, state residency. ACT with or without writing component accepted. TOEFL required of all international applicants. High school diploma is required, and GED is accepted. *Academic units recommended:* 4 English, 3 mathematics, 3 science, 2 foreign language, 3 social studies, 3 history.

Financial Aid

Students should submit: FAFSA. The Princeton Review suggests that all financial aid forms be submitted as soon as possible after January 1. *Need-based scholarships/grants offered:* Federal Pell, SEOG, state scholarships/grants, private scholarships, school scholarship or grant aid from institutional funds. *Loan aid offered:* Direct Subsidized Stafford, Direct Unsubsidized Stafford, Direct PLUS, Federal Perkins, university loans from institutional funds. Applicants will be notified of awards on a rolling basis beginning February 15. Federal Work-Study Program available. Off-campus job opportunities are fair.

The Inside Word

Getting into Guilford College goes beyond the numbers. Guilford is looking for students who demonstrate strong drive and personal motivation. Applicants to the school should have a solid high school record and good extracurricular activities (preferably of the tree-hugging and/or varsity sports variety.) While a Quaker connection couldn't hurt, the school is more interested in your character and personal qualities and level of interest in the school. The admissions essay is your chance to make your case.

THE SCHOOL SAYS "..."

From the Admissions Office

"Guilford is proud to be included for the eighteenth consecutive year in The Princeton Review's 'Best College' edition. Guilford can best be described by its academic rigor, preparation for graduate school, and its commitment to service in a caring, socially aware and supportive community.

"Comments from a small sample of Guilford students do not adequately convey the richness of the campus experience. Guilford is building a community that honors traditional as well as alternative lifestyles and viewpoints. No one lifestyle or thought predominates the campus. Regardless of your background, if you are open-minded and willing to interact with others, the Guilford experience can be transformational. If you enroll at Guilford, there will be others like you.

"There is no stereotypical Guilford student. Our students have many passions including athletics and intramurals, community service, social justice and multiculturalism. However the bond that ties them together is the academic curriculum that prepares them for life and a career."

SELECTIVITY

Admissions Rating	79
# of applicants	4,245
% of applicants accepted	53
% of acceptees attending	17
# accepting a place on wait list	33
% admitted from wait list	9

FRESHMAN PROFILE

Range SAT Critical Reading	460–620
Range SAT Math	480–600
Range SAT Writing	450–590
Range ACT Composite	20–27
Minimum paper TOEFL	550
Minimum computer TOEFL	213
Average HS GPA	3.15
% graduated top 10% of class	15
% graduated top 25% of class	46
% graduated top 50% of class	84

DEADLINES

Early action	
Deadline	1/15
Regular	
Priority	2/15
Deadline	8/10
Notification	10/1
Nonfall registration?	yes

APPLICANTS ALSO LOOK AT AND SOMETIMES PREFER
Earlham College, Elon University, University of North Carolina at Chapel Hill

FINANCIAL FACTS

Financial Aid Rating	73
Annual tuition	$28,470
Room and board	$7,950
Required fees	$330
Books and supplies	$1,150
% frosh rec. need-based scholarship or grant aid	83
% UG rec. need-based scholarship or grant aid	75
% frosh rec. non-need-based scholarship or grant aid	82
% UG rec. non-need-based scholarship or grant aid	72
% frosh rec. need-based self-help aid	55
% UG rec. need-based self-help aid	60
% frosh rec. any financial aid	91
% UG rec. any financial aid	89
% UG borrow to pay for school	60
Average cumulative indebtedness	$23,050

GUSTAVUS ADOLPHUS COLLEGE

800 WEST COLLEGE AVENUE, SAINT PETER, MN 56082 • ADMISSIONS: 507-933-7676 • FAX: 507-933-7474

CAMPUS LIFE

Quality of Life Rating	97
Fire Safety Rating	92
Green Rating	91
Type of school	private
Affiliation	Lutheran
Environment	village

STUDENTS

Total undergrad enrollment	2,515
% male/female	44/57
% from out of state	18
% from public high school	92
% live on campus	81
# of fraternities	5
# of sororities	5
# of countries represented	15

SURVEY SAYS . . .

Athletic facilities are great
Great food on campus
Musical organizations are popular

ACADEMICS

Academic Rating	95
% students graduating within 4 years	79
% students graduating within 6 years	81
Calendar	4-1-4
Student/faculty ratio	12:1
Profs interesting rating	99
Profs accessible rating	99
Most common reg class size	10–19 students
Most common lab size	10–19 students

MOST POPULAR MAJORS

biology, business/commerce, psychology

STUDENTS SAY ". . ."

Academics

Gustavus Adolphus College, "a school that fosters a close community between the students, staff, and faculty and strives to prepare the students academically and vocationally for the post-college world," gets high marks from undergrads for its "demanding, yet encouraging" professors who are "there to help you learn, not just to give you a grade." As one student explains, "Each year, I become more and more impressed with how devoted members of the faculty and administration are to the students. My professors always bend over backward to meet with students who have questions and work with them on problems related and unrelated to course material." Although professors have "high expectations," the "extra guidance" that is offered helps students achieve "far beyond graduation." Expect to be challenged by classes that are "rigorous and discussion-based." Small class sizes allow for "great interaction with professors" but will leave your "empty chair sticking out like a neon sign" if you are absent. Unique opportunities here include the Curriculum II general-education program, an integrated series of courses that, together, provide a survey of Western civilization, with supplemental study of non-Western cultures for context and comparison. Enrollment is limited to sixty students and typically attracts some of the college's brightest undergrads.

Life

Gustavus boasts "a very academically strong student body" that is also "known for our athletics, specifically tennis, hockey, and soccer." Students "attend a lot of sporting events" as well as "parties and social events on campus and off" over the weekends, when campus is "a great place to be…because very few people go home. We are certainly not a suitcase college." Besides the aforementioned activities, "shows, concerts, and basketball games" are "especially popular," as are the "free movies on Fridays and Saturdays" and the "on-campus student dance club 'The Dive.'" Most students choose to unwind with "a good amount of partying and drinking," but while alcohol and parties are easy to find on campus, abstaining students "never feel any pressure to do either." Being located in a small town is no problem for most; students tell us that "the town is supportive of Gustavus and thankful to have the college in town" and explain that "there are always things going on at school," so the lack of big-city fun isn't that much of a drawback. Students who get cabin fever can head to nearby Mankato and its "excellent mall and restaurants" for entertainment. Although the Minnesotan winter may be long, things heat up during the January "Interim Experience" when a light course load gives students a "chance to take a class outside their major" or just "hang out with friends." When students really want a thrill, they'll "borrow a tray from the cafeteria and sled down the many hills behind the dorms" in a Gustavus tradition called "traying."

Student Body

Gustavus "is known to have a very [close-knit campus] consisting of students who not only achieve academically but are [also] very involved in their community and school. There are more than 140 student organizations on campus. For a student population [of] approximately 2,600, that is a lot." "Virtually everyone here is white and of Scandinavian descent," and "of these, roughly half seem to come from small rural towns in Minnesota or surrounding Midwest states (Iowa, Wisconsin, North and South Dakota, etc.), and the other half from well-off suburbs of Minneapolis–St. Paul…Most tend to have some Christian affiliation, but not necessarily a strong one, and there are a fair amount of non-religious students, which is refreshing." Students are polite in a way that seems unusual on the coasts but less so in the Midwest; it has been said that if students visit the campus, "They don't have to hold any doors because the students are so friendly and welcoming," one student reports.

GUSTAVUS ADOLPHUS COLLEGE

FINANCIAL AID: 507-933-7527 • E-MAIL: ADMISSION@GUSTAVUS.EDU • WEBSITE: WWW.GUSTAVUS.EDU

THE PRINCETON REVIEW SAYS

Admissions

Very important factors considered include: Rigor of secondary school record. *Important factors considered include:* Academic GPA, application essay, recommendation(s), standardized test scores. *Other factors considered include:* Alumni/ae relation, extracurricular activities, first generation, geographical residence, interview, level of applicant's interest, racial/ethnic status, religious affiliation/commitment, state residency, talent/ability, volunteer work, work experience. SAT or ACT reccommended; ACT with or without writing component accepted. TOEFL required of all international applicants. High school diploma is required, and GED is accepted. *Academic units required:* 4 English, 3 mathematics, 2 science (2 science labs), 2 foreign language, 2 social studies, 2 history. *Academic units recommended:* 4 mathematics, 3 science (3 science labs), 3 foreign language, 2 academic elective.

Financial Aid

Students should submit: FAFSA, CSS/Financial Aid PROFILE. Regular filing deadline is April 15. The Princeton Review suggests that all financial aid forms be submitted as soon as possible after January 1. *Need-based scholarships/grants offered:* Federal Pell, SEOG, state scholarships/grants, private scholarships, school scholarship or grant aid from institutional funds. *Loan aid offered:* Direct Subsidized Stafford, Direct Unsubsidized Stafford, Direct PLUS, Federal Perkins, state loans. Applicants will be notified of awards on a rolling basis beginning January 20. Federal Work-Study Program available. Off-campus job opportunities are good.

The Inside Word

Gustavus Adolphus considers a variety of factors when making admissions decisions. Students should display motivation for tackling challenging courses and a desire to be active participants in their community. The majority of applicants are from local areas—those who can provide some geographic diversity are welcome. The school has a rolling admissions policy, so interested students should think about sending in their applications early. All available slots are usually filled by early spring.

THE SCHOOL SAYS ". . ."

From the Admissions Office

"Gustavus Adolphus College is all about helping you make your life count-in the classroom, on the field, here in St. Peter, and wherever you go after college. Our college is built on a powerful sense of community and the will to enhance the common good. Everyone is active and involved, doing meaningful things—whether it's service or political action, playing basketball or making music, studying biology or writing a paper. We're part of a great team. We support and respect each other. Ideas are exchanged openly. Everyone's opinion matters. Gustavus students, faculty and alumni lead lives of uncommon passion and purpose, guided by the College's heritage and core values. Founded in 1862 by Swedish Lutheran immigrants, the College is affiliated with the Evangelical Lutheran Church in America and we host the Nobel Conference®, which brings the world's greatest minds to campus every October to discuss the most important scientific issues of the day. Gustavus's 340-acre campus sits on a hill overlooking St. Peter, a classic college town of 10,000 residents in the Minnesota River Valley. You should visit. And, we want you to apply. Make the decision to make your life count. Be a Gustie."

SELECTIVITY

Admissions Rating	82
# of applicants	3,128
% of applicants accepted	75
% of acceptees attending	27
# accepting a place on wait list	0

FRESHMAN PROFILE

Range SAT Math	580–690
Range ACT Composite	24–29
Minimum paper TOEFL	550
Minimum computer TOEFL	213
Minimum web-based TOEFL	80
Average HS GPA	3.64
% graduated top 10% of class	34
% graduated top 25% of class	69
% graduated top 50% of class	97

DEADLINES

Early action	
Deadline	11/1
Notification	11/20
Regular	
Notification	11/20
Nonfall registration?	yes

FINANCIAL FACTS

Financial Aid Rating	85
Annual tuition	$29,990
Room and board	$7,460
Required fees	$430
Books and supplies	$750
% frosh rec. need-based scholarship or grant aid	70
% UG rec. need-based scholarship or grant aid	65
% frosh rec. non-need-based scholarship or grant aid	35
% UG rec. non-need-based scholarship or grant aid	39
% frosh rec. need-based self-help aid	70
% UG rec. need-based self-help aid	65
% frosh rec. any financial aid	96
% UG rec. any financial aid	95
% UG borrow to pay for school	70
Average cumulative indebtedness	$24,297

HAMILTON COLLEGE

198 COLLEGE HILL ROAD, CLINTON, NY 13323 • ADMISSIONS: 315-859-4421 • FAX: 315-859-4457

CAMPUS LIFE

Quality of Life Rating	85
Fire Safety Rating	85
Green Rating	90
Type of school	private
Environment	rural

STUDENTS

Total undergrad enrollment	1,843
% male/female	47/53
% from out of state	67
% from public high school	64
% live on campus	98
# of fraternities	9
# of sororities	7
% African American	4
% Asian	8
% Caucasian	67
% Hispanic	5
% Native American	1
% international	5
# of countries represented	37

SURVEY SAYS . . .
Lab facilities are great
Great computer facilities
Athletic facilities are great
School is well-run
Low cost of living

ACADEMICS

Academic Rating	96
% students graduating within 4 years	84
% students graduating within 6 years	88
Calendar	semester
Student/faculty ratio	9:1
Profs interesting rating	98
Profs accessible rating	96
Most common reg class size	10–19 students
Most common lab size	10–19 students

MOST POPULAR MAJORS
economics, political science, psychology

STUDENTS SAY ". . ."

Academics

A small, liberal arts school, Hamilton College "runs smoothly" with "top-notch" professors who are "very committed, passionate, and genuinely caring." The close student-faculty relationships are a distinguishing characteristic of Hamilton. One junior who chose Hamilton for its "small class size and opportunity to really establish a relationship with the professors" described the accessibility of the professors as *"amazing."* A graduating senior tells us, "My professors have inspired me to take on my education as a truly personal and important aspect of my life, even after I complete my formal education." One student comments on how Hamilton is a leader in teaching effective writing and persuasive speaking: "Hamilton challenges me to improve my writing each and every day, regardless of the class…writing is a central aspect." Though the "extraordinary focus on writing" is paramount at Hamilton, the school also offers a "strong science program." The science curriculum emphasizes "undergraduate research" and a recently built, state-of-the-art science facility provides students with ample "research opportunities." Students also love Hamilton's distinct open curriculum. The "lack of distribution requirements" gives students the freedom to make their own educational choices and to select classes that reflect their unique interests. With "no required curriculum…it's nice to know that you're not wasting any time and are taking the classes that you really want [and] need to."

Life

A "picturesque oasis of academia" Hamilton makes students feel like the fact that they are "isolated away from city noise and bustle, but close enough to an urban area to be connected." The closest major city is Syracuse, located about an hour's drive from campus, and the school "organizes trips to New York City regularly." Hamilton is a "small town," but students agree that though Hamilton "is in the middle of nowhere" it doesn't mean it is lacking in things to do. In fact, says one student, "That's far from the truth." During the week, "the pressure is on," and life at Hamilton is "academically oriented" with everyone working hard and "little time to play." At week's end, students are ready to "have as much fun as possible," and the focus turns to "various fraternity or sorority parties and any athletic events going on." Students tell us, "Greek life is popular but not threatening" and "provides much of the party life on-campus." Most Greek events are "open to the campus" but foster a "very inclusive social environment." The campus "accommodates students so that everyone is able to get together and have fun." Students agree that there is "something to do for everyone." Hamilton boasts a long list of student-run clubs and teams, active intramural leagues, "incredible athletic and workout facilities," a "pretty decent" nine-hole golf course, and "miles of trails for skiing, snow-shoeing, and jogging." Winters tend to be quite long, "so curling up with a blanket and a movie in a dorm room is always popular."

Student Body

If you are looking for a school "where you hold doors for people" and "greet friends, acquaintances, and even professors" while walking around campus, Hamilton may be just the place for you. Students are enthusiastic about the "tight-knit community" of students and professors on campus. One student tells us, "There's such a great sense of community. Everyone is friendly, intelligent, and driven without being overly competitive." Students find that Hamilton provides a great opportunity to attend an "elite liberal arts school" where "students will want to help you instead of compete against you." One freshman tells us that the student body at Hamilton was "frighteningly friendly." While Hamilton "doesn't exactly have a wealth of diversity," the "student body is very inclusive." The majority of Hamilton students are "very preppy, white, and upper-class," but "everyone and anyone can find their niche" and still be "respected as an individual by the community at large." Overall, students at Hamilton have "diverse interests" and are often involved on campus in a variety of ways. When it comes to the environment, politics, or any other current events, students tell us, "It's the most aware group of people I've ever met."

FINANCIAL AID: 800-859-4413 • E-MAIL: ADMISSION@HAMILTON.EDU • WEBSITE: WWW.HAMILTON.EDU

THE PRINCETON REVIEW SAYS

Admissions

Very important factors considered include: Academic GPA, class rank, rigor of secondary school record. *Important factors considered include:* Application essay, recommendation(s), standardized test scores, character/personal qualities, extracurricular activities, interview. *Other factors considered include:* Alumni/ae relation, first generation, geographical residence, level of applicant's interest, racial/ethnic status, talent/ability, volunteer work, work experience. ACT with or without writing component accepted. TOEFL required of all international applicants. High school diploma is required, and GED is accepted. *Academic units recommended:* 4 English, 3 mathematics, 3 science, 3 foreign language, 3 social studies.

Financial Aid

Students should submit: FAFSA, institution's own financial aid form, CSS/Financial Aid PROFILE. Regular filing deadline is February 8. The Princeton Review suggests that all financial aid forms be submitted as soon as possible after January 1. *Need-based scholarships/grants offered:* Federal Pell, SEOG, state scholarships/grants, private scholarships, school scholarship or grant aid from institutional funds. *Loan aid offered:* Direct Subsidized Stafford, Direct Unsubsidized Stafford, Direct PLUS, Federal Perkins, university loans from institutional funds. Federal Work-Study Program available.

The Inside Word

Similar to any prestigious liberal arts schools, Hamilton takes a well-rounded, personal approach to admissions. They rely heavily on academic achievement and intellectual promise, but in a mission to create a talented and diverse incoming class, admissions officers also strive to attain a complete, accurate profile of each candidate. The admissions team at Hamilton is adamant about interviews either on or off campus with alumni volunteers.

THE SCHOOL SAYS "..."

From the Admissions Office

"As a national leader for teaching students to write effectively, learn from one another, and think for themselves, Hamilton produces graduates who have the knowledge, skills, and confidence to make their own voices heard on issues of importance to them and their communities.

"A key component of the Hamilton experience is the college's open, yet rigorous, liberal arts curriculum. In place of distribution requirements that are common at most colleges, Hamilton gives its students freedom to choose the courses that reflect their unique interests and plans. Faculty advisors assist students in planning a coherent and highly individualized academic program. In fact, close student-faculty relationships at Hamilton are a distinguishing characteristic of the college, but ultimately students at Hamilton take responsibility for their own future. Part of that future includes a lifelong relationship with the college. Hamilton alumni are exceptionally loyal and passionate supporters of their alma mater. That support manifests itself through internships, speaking engagements, job-shadowing opportunities, and financial donations.

"The intellectual maturity that distinguishes a Hamilton education extends to the application process. Students are free to choose which standardized tests to submit, based on a specified set of options, so that those who do not test well on the SAT or ACT may decide to submit the results of their AP or SAT Subject Tests. The approach allows students the freedom to decide how to present themselves best to the Committee on Admission."

SELECTIVITY

Admissions Rating	96
# of applicants	4,857
% of applicants accepted	29
% of acceptees attending	33
# accepting a place on wait list	532
% admitted from wait list	5
# of early decision applicants	553
% accepted early decision	44

FRESHMAN PROFILE

Range SAT Critical Reading	650–740
Range SAT Math	650–730
Range SAT Writing	650–730
Range ACT Composite	27–31
% graduated top 10% of class	73
% graduated top 25% of class	97
% graduated top 50% of class	99

DEADLINES

Early decision	
Deadline	11/15
Notification	12/15
Regular	
Deadline	1/1
Nonfall registration?	yes

APPLICANTS ALSO LOOK AT
AND OFTEN PREFER
Amherst College, Bowdoin College, Brown University, Dartmouth College, Middlebury College, Princeton University, Williams College

AND SOMETIMES PREFER
Colby College, Colgate University, Wesleyan University

FINANCIAL FACTS

Financial Aid Rating	97
Annual tuition	$42,220
Room and board	$10,830
Books and supplies	$1,300
% frosh rec. need-based scholarship or grant aid	51
% UG rec. need-based scholarship or grant aid	42
% frosh rec. need-based self-help aid	45
% UG rec. need-based self-help aid	37
% frosh rec. any financial aid	62
% UG rec. any financial aid	53
% UG borrow to pay for school	41
Average cumulative indebtedness	$16,982

HAMPDEN-SYDNEY COLLEGE

PO BOX 667, HAMPDEN-SYDNEY, VA 23943 • ADMISSIONS: 434-223-6120 • FAX: 434-223-6346

CAMPUS LIFE

Quality of Life Rating	80
Fire Safety Rating	79
Green Rating	73
Type of school	private
Affiliation	Presbyterian
Environment	rural

STUDENTS

Total undergrad enrollment	1,058
% male/female	100/0
% from out of state	31
% from public high school	62
% live on campus	95
# of fraternities	10
% African American	6
% Asian	1
% Caucasian	85
% Hispanic	2
% Native American	1
% international	2
# of countries represented	17

SURVEY SAYS . . .
No one cheats
Career services are great
Students are happy
Student government is popular
Lots of beer drinking

ACADEMICS

Academic Rating	84
% students graduating within 4 years	66
% students graduating within 6 years	68
Calendar	semester
Student/faculty ratio	10:1
Profs interesting rating	98
Profs accessible rating	98
Most common reg class size	10–19 students

MOST POPULAR MAJORS
economics, history, government
and foreign affairs

STUDENTS SAY ". . ."

Academics
Hampden-Sydney is "an all-male institution that promotes a community of brotherhood and has a strong liberal arts education." Students enjoy Hampden-Sydney's "rich history and sense of brotherhood," which has been "forming good men and good citizens since 1775." A "Southern tradition in the heart of Virginia," Hampden-Sydney boasts a "small size," good "student/teacher ratio," and a strong "honor code." "Because it's small and is all-male, you don't get the distractions you would at a large college," one student explains. "Hampden-Sydney is all about community" and has "this distinct ability of this place to make you feel at home." There's an "intense" rhetoric program that students are required to complete, and most seem pleased with it. Since the college was founded before the American Revolution, "some facilities are old and historic. This means that some modern-day luxuries are absent." Hampden-Sydney students think of themselves as "gentlemen," and one of the school's primary appeals its old-boy alumni network that "recruits gentlemen upon graduation and helps to guide them on a path of successful endeavors." Students and professors aren't just homogenous in regards to gender, they have a "generally shared perspective on politics" that's strongly conservative. The professors are a strong draw at Hampden-Sydney. "They have a unique way of making you think for yourself," and "many have some very valuable real-world experience that they are able to translate into the classroom." As one student points out, "small classrooms with brilliant professors = outstanding learning opportunity."

Life
Hampden-Sydney students are about "honor and brotherhood. Also beer." Drinking is a huge part of campus life, which is located in the "small town" of Farmville and "about an hour away from anything that could be considered a major city." The "social life [is] anchored in the fraternities." "Our school's social life is based off of Greek life," another student confirms. "We are also an all-guys school, so during the week it's a lot of video games and studying, but during the weekend there are girls all over campus, and we become a huge party school." Even during the weekdays many party, although without women on campus it becomes "mostly just guys hanging out." There's also "high attendance at sporting events, especially football and basketball." If there's one common complaint, it's the "food, food, food," which is "sub-par" even though "for the amount of money we pay it could be loads better."

Student Body
The average Hampden-Sydney student is an "all-American, preppy, white guy from a wealthy middle- or upper-class family." Most students are "very Southern" and "come from usually a high socioeconomic background." "Athletes make up twenty percent of the student population (football about ten percent), and fraternities make up a large portion as well." "Students here are very friendly because we like to promote an environment of gentlemanliness," one student explains, "that is, as a traditional Southern school, we are in touch with the concept that politeness and manners make a better man." However, this politeness seems to extend only to heterosexual and conservative white males. The school needs to "work on discrimination…but the discrimination comes from the other students, not professors," one student says. Another advises: "If you are gay or a liberal don't come here." One student estimates that "ninety-five percent of students are conservative." "There is an informal and unwritten dress code with social consequences if it is not followed; the students are informally expected to dress nicely in an outfit consisting of khaki pants and a button-up shirt or polo shirt." The way to fit in is "by being 'fratty,'" and "students who live alternative lifestyles (nerds, gays, socially awkward people) are hard-pressed to find friends."

HAMPDEN-SYDNEY COLLEGE

FINANCIAL AID: 804-223-6119 • E-MAIL: ADMISSIONS@HSC.EDU • WEBSITE: WWW.HSC.EDU

THE PRINCETON REVIEW SAYS
Admissions
Very important factors considered include: Academic GPA, application essay, recommendation(s), rigor of secondary school record, standardized test scores, character/personal qualities. *Important factors considered include:* Class rank, extracurricular activities. *Other factors considered include:* First generation, interview, level of applicant's interest, talent/ability, volunteer work, work experience. SAT or ACT required; ACT with or without writing component accepted. TOEFL required of all international applicants. High school diploma is required, and GED is accepted. *Academic units required:* 4 English, 3 mathematics, 2 science (1 science lab), 2 foreign language, 1 social studies, 1 history, 3 academic elective. *Academic units recommended:* 4 mathematics, 3 science, 3 foreign language.

Financial Aid
Students should submit: FFAFSA, CSS/Financial Aid PROFILE. Regular filing deadline is March 1. The Princeton Review suggests that all financial aid forms be submitted as soon as possible after January 1. *Need-based scholarships/grants offered:* Federal Pell, SEOG, state scholarships/grants, private scholarships, school scholarship or grant aid from institutional funds. *Loan aid offered:* Direct Subsidized Stafford, Direct Unsubsidized Stafford, Direct PLUS, Federal Perkins, university loans from institutional funds. Federal Work-Study Program available. Off-campus job opportunities are fair.

The Inside Word
Hampden-Sydney is one of the last of its kind. Understandably, the applicant pool is heavily self-selected, and a fairly significant percentage of those who are admitted choose to enroll. This enables the admissions committee to be more selective, which in turn requires candidates to take the process more seriously than might otherwise be necessary. Students with consistently sound academic records should have little to worry about nonetheless.

THE SCHOOL SAYS "..."
From the Admissions Office
"The spirit of Hampden-Sydney is its sense of community. As one of only 1,120 students, you will be in small classes and find it easy to get extra help or inspiration from professors when you want it. Many of our professors live on campus and enjoy being with students in the snack bar as well as in the classroom. They give you the best, most personal education as possible. A big bonus of small-college life is that everybody is invited to go out for everything, and you can be as much of a leader as you want to be. From athletics to debating to publications to fraternity life, this is part of the process that produces a well-rounded Hampden-Sydney graduate.

"Hampden-Sydney College requires either the SAT or ACT standardized test with essay."

SELECTIVITY
Admissions Rating	75
# of applicants	2,528
% of applicants accepted	54
% of acceptees attending	23
# of early decision applicants	140
% accepted early decision	31

FRESHMAN PROFILE
Range SAT Critical Reading	500–610
Range SAT Math	510–620
Range SAT Writing	480–580
Range ACT Composite	24–27
Minimum paper TOEFL	600
Minimum computer TOEFL	250
Minimum web-based TOEFL	100
Average HS GPA	3.40
% graduated top 10% of class	12
% graduated top 25% of class	22
% graduated top 50% of class	57

DEADLINES
Early decision	
Deadline	11/15
Notification	12/15
Early action	
Deadline	1/15
Notification	2/15
Regular	
Deadline	3/1
Nonfall registration?	yes

APPLICANTS ALSO LOOK AT
AND OFTEN PREFER
University of Virginia, Virginia Tech
AND SOMETIMES PREFER
James Madison University, Sewanee—The University of the South, University of Georgia, University of North Carolina at Chapel Hill, University of South Carolina—Columbia
AND RARELY PREFER
Randolph-Macon College

FINANCIAL FACTS
Financial Aid Rating	83
Annual tuition	$30,944
Room and board	$10,126
Required fees	$1,170
Books and supplies	$1,200
% frosh rec. need-based scholarship or grant aid	60
% UG rec. need-based scholarship or grant aid	56
% frosh rec. non-need-based scholarship or grant aid	12
% UG rec. non-need-based scholarship or grant aid	10
% frosh rec. need-based self-help aid	48
% UG rec. need-based self-help aid	46
% frosh rec. any financial aid	100
% UG rec. any financial aid	98
% UG borrow to pay for school	49
Average cumulative indebtedness	$25,426

HAMPSHIRE COLLEGE

ADMISSIONS OFFICE, 893 WEST STREET, AMHERST, MA 01002 • ADMISSIONS: 413-559-5471 • FAX: 413-559-5631

STUDENTS SAY ". . ."

Academics

Undergrads come to Hampshire College "seduced by the prospect of designing [their] own program of study." The school offers students "a self-designed curriculum" facilitated by "close relationships with professors, small classes, and the great combination of communal living and individualism that a true Hampshire student embodies." A "divisional system," with a student's academic career consisting of three divisions, imposes some sense of order. Division I "is first-year requirements and such," while "Divisions II and III constitute the core of your time. That's when you focus down upon the areas that interest you more than the rest of the school." Undergrads explain that "in class, students learn as a group in discussions or hands-on activities (few lectures, no tests), while outside of class one focuses on independent projects (research, reading, writing, art-making)." The experience culminates in a 'Division III,' an all-consuming year-long senior thesis project "that allows students to become excited and completely invested" while "producing a unique product at the end of the year." Students "receive evaluations instead of grades, which we feel is a much more productive system." While Hampshire "is very small," which might limit students' choices, "it belongs to the Five Colleges consortium," a group that includes the massive University of Massachusetts—Amherst. With the course offerings of five colleges available to them, Hampshire students can "take any course we could dream of."

Life

"Life at Hampshire seems extremely spontaneous," so "while one minute we may be complaining of boredom, the next we may start doing something fun and exciting. We are normally very good at entertaining ourselves." "Usually what people do is just hang out with a small group of friends," and "there is partying on the weekends," although "parties here consist generally of fifty people or less, never the roaring, dangerously wild parties that are often found at colleges." Parties often take place in the "mods," apartment-style housing favored by upperclassmen, where students "throw a lot of sweaty dance parties where hippies, scenesters, and geeks all grind up against each other." Also, "live music is very common" on and around campus, "drum circles and random games of Frisbee are unavoidable," and "going to the nearby towns of Amherst or Northampton isn't bad." Students can also choose from "tons of clubs, from Spinsters Unite! to the Red Scare Ultimate Frisbee Team, [or] Students for a Free Tibet to Excalibur, which is the sci-fi and fantasy club. You can even take yoga, karate, or tai chi classes. There are parties all the time for those who like that kind of thing, and movies, video games, clubs, and playing in the forest or on the farm for those who don't." There are also "five colleges in the area to hang out at. Enough said."

Student Body

"Picture all the various groups of misfits in high school" and you'll have a picture of the students at Hampshire, a place where "Nonconformity is so normal it's almost conformist to be nonconformist. You can't say 'the kid with the dreadlocks' because the person would reply with 'Which one?'" Undergrads assure us that "Hampshire is really open to any type of student." Though there many different types of students on campus, all students have "at least one serious and one kitschy academic or extracurricular pursuit. Those who identify as male are usually bearded and wear plaid." The common threads among students: "They are all interesting. They all have talents, stories, and are just plain interesting to be around. They are full of creativity and life and seem to really enjoy where they are." They also tend to be "socially conscious, left-wing, and artistic. We are fond of do-it-yourself philosophies, from [magazines] to music and film production to designing ecologically sustainable communities." One student warns, "this is not a good school for fundamentalist Christians."

FINANCIAL AID: 413-559-5484 • E-MAIL: ADMISSIONS@HAMPSHIRE.EDU • WEBSITE: WWW.HAMPSHIRE.EDU

THE PRINCETON REVIEW SAYS

Admissions

Very important factors considered include: Application essay, character/personal qualities. *Important factors considered include:* Recommendation(s), rigor of secondary school record, extracurricular activities, level of applicant's interest, talent/ability. *Other factors considered include:* Academic GPA, class rank, standardized test scores, alumni/ae relation, interview, racial/ethnic status, volunteer work, work experience. ACT with or without writing component accepted. TOEFL required of all international applicants. High school diploma is required, and GED is accepted. *Academic units required:* 4 English, 3 mathematics, 3 science (2 science labs), 3 foreign language, 3 history. *Academic units recommended:* 4 English, 4 mathematics, 4 science (2 science labs), 4 foreign language, 4 history.

Financial Aid

Students should submit: FAFSA, CSS/Financial Aid PROFILE. Regular filing deadline is February 1. The Princeton Review suggests that all financial aid forms be submitted as soon as possible after January 1. *Need-based scholarships/grants offered:* Federal Pell, SEOG, state scholarships/grants, private scholarships, school scholarship or grant aid from institutional funds. *Loan aid offered:* Direct Subsidized Stafford, Direct Unsubsidized Stafford, Direct PLUS, Federal Perkins.

The Inside Word

Hampshire's admissions policies are the antithesis of formula-based practices. Officers want to know the individual behind the transcript, and personal characteristics hold substantial weight in the admissions decision. Demonstrating discipline and an independent and inquisitive spirit may just carry more weight than a perfect 4.0. Writing is pivotal to a Hampshire education, and applicants must put considerable thought into their personal statements. They will be read carefully.

THE SCHOOL SAYS "..."

From the Admissions Office

"The Admissions Committee focuses its selection process on fit over formula. Because all majors at Hampshire are personalized, it is important that you have the passion and ambition requisite to negotiate your education with faculty advisors. Hampshire seeks students who have elected to challenge themselves in high school and demonstrate a genuine passion for learning."

"In addition to the Common Application, Hampshire's supplement asks questions that are meant to reveal more about you as a thinker, learner, and community member. An analytical essay gives the Admissions Committee a sense of your ability to ask complex questions, think critically, synthesize information, and formulate original conclusions. The Admissions Committee welcomes examples of work, whether that be scientific or creative. Personal interviews are valued and strongly encouraged."

"At Hampshire, you will personalize your major. You will gain a strong foundation in the liberal arts and learn the skills to create new knowledge in virtually any chosen field of study. The process of personalizing majors requires a highly personalized, intensive connection with faculty advisors; faculty begin as teachers and mentors and become colleagues and collaborators. As a Hampshire student, you will be able to take courses at four other neighboring colleges for free—and you will have a limitless range of opportunities to engage in outside-the-classroom real-world experiences. Hampshire's program will give you the skills and confidence to create knowledge and accomplish great things as a graduate."

SELECTIVITY

Admissions Rating	89
# of applicants	2,606
% of applicants accepted	71
% of acceptees attending	23
# accepting a place on wait list	96
% admitted from wait list	41
# of early decision applicants	59
% accepted early decision	78

FRESHMAN PROFILE

Range SAT Critical Reading	600–700
Range SAT Math	550–660
Range SAT Writing	580–680
Range ACT Composite	25–29
Minimum paper TOEFL	577
Minimum computer TOEFL	233
Minimum web-based TOEFL	91
Average HS GPA	3.68
% graduated top 10% of class	27
% graduated top 25% of class	58
% graduated top 50% of class	91

DEADLINES

Early decision	
Deadline	11/15
Notification	12/15
Early action	
Deadline	12/1
Notification	2/1
Regular	
Priority	11/15
Deadline	1/1
Nonfall registration?	yes

APPLICANTS ALSO LOOK AT AND OFTEN PREFER
Bard College, Sarah Lawrence College

FINANCIAL FACTS

Financial Aid Rating	90
Annual tuition	$41,900
Room and board	$11,180
Books and supplies	$700
% frosh rec. need-based scholarship or grant aid	62
% UG rec. need-based scholarship or grant aid	61
% frosh rec. non-need-based scholarship or grant aid	49
% UG rec. non-need-based scholarship or grant aid	37
% frosh rec. need-based self-help aid	62
% UG rec. need-based self-help aid	61
% frosh rec. any financial aid	85
% UG rec. any financial aid	79
% UG borrow to pay for school	58
Average cumulative indebtedness	$21,673

HAMPTON UNIVERSITY

OFFICE OF ADMISSIONS, HAMPTON UNIVERSITY, HAMPTON, VA 23668 • ADMISSIONS: 757-727-5328 • FAX: 757-727-5095

CAMPUS LIFE

Quality of Life Rating	61
Fire Safety Rating	65
Green Rating	60*
Type of school	private
Environment	city

STUDENTS

Total undergrad enrollment	5,056
% male/female	36/64
% from out of state	69
% from public high school	90
% live on campus	59
# of fraternities	6
# of sororities	3
% African American	86
% Asian	1
% Caucasian	12
% Hispanic	1
# of countries represented	33

SURVEY SAYS . . .
Great library
Campus feels safe
Everyone loves the Pirates
Frats and sororities dominate social scene
Musical organizations are popular
Student publications are popular
Student government is popular

ACADEMICS

Academic Rating	71
Calendar	semester
Student/faculty ratio	16:1
Profs interesting rating	68
Profs accessible rating	65
Most common reg class size	20–29 students
Most common lab size	10–19 students

MOST POPULAR MAJORS
business/commerce, psychology

STUDENTS SAY "..."

Academics

Hampton University, "one of the premier Historically Black Colleges and Universities in the country," is "perfect for students who desire to be around other intelligent and focused black students who have a future and are making plans to achieve their goals. Our students are making changes in this world and will always continue to." With popular programs in business and management, psychology, pharmacy, nursing, sociology, the hard sciences, and communication, Hampton "is about producing successful, bright, and talented professionals." The school has made a special commitment to journalism and communication, opening a state-of-the-art facility a few years back that includes a full working studio with editing facilities, a student-run radio station, and five computer labs. Throughout its many departments, Hampton stresses the importance of experiential learning, "presenting a host of opportunities for students to get internships and jobs." One student reports, "I have had three internships and have been on the campus radio station for my entire career at HU." Professors here earn good marks for dedication and teaching skills; "The administration tries," and "overall, they care," but students say some are "not very punctual" and can "act uppity." Most agree the inconvenience is worth it for "the connections and networking" Hampton provides. As one student notes, "Everyone here is important, related to, or knows someone important, and everyone will become successful and important."

Life

"Hampton is not the typical party school," students agree. One student writes, "Life at Hampton is pretty boring compared to where I'm from." Undergrads report, "Most events take place off campus, so you really have to find your own fun." Fortunately the area provides some diversion, including "malls, fine dining, and parties…Also, Hampton is surrounded by cities that are no more than fifteen to twenty minutes away," including Norfolk, Newport News, and Virginia Beach. "Nearby amusement parks are also great attractions for the spring and summer." On campus, "there is a really nice student center that turns into a virtual party every day from noon to 2:00 P.M. The student center is tri-level and has everything from a theater to [a] bowling ally and a fitness center." Hampton's Greek system is very popular; the most popular ones "are highly competitive and selective, and the whole process is crazy and oh-so-hard to get into." Some here complain that restrictive regulations dampen campus life. One student writes, Students are not allowed to have refrigerators apparently due to outdated wiring in the dorms… Administration, faculty, and staff do not respect students as adults."

Student Body

Hampton "is a Historically Black [College and] University, but the range of black students here is amazing. There is a niche for everyone, and I mean everyone, and most are universally accepted." Many are "very outgoing and professional," "are well-off, and come from a nice home." Some "tend to be very materialistic and… care a lot about social matters. They all dress well, spend plenty of money on clothes, and drive very nice cars (even better cars than teachers)," but "There are many different types of students." Atypical students here "mesh well with the others," because Hampton students are a part of a family. "We are called Hamptonians, symbolizing our unity. Here we have a bond that is very strong—we all fit in—and it is not to be broken."

FINANCIAL AID: 800-624-3341 • E-MAIL: ADMIT@HAMPTONU.EDU • WEBSITE: WWW.HAMPTONU.EDU

THE PRINCETON REVIEW SAYS

Admissions

Very important factors considered include: Application essay, rigor of secondary school record, standardized test scores, character/personal qualities. *Important factors considered include:* Class rank, recommendation(s). *Other factors considered include:* Alumni/ae relation, extracurricular activities, talent/ability, volunteer work. SAT or ACT required. TOEFL required of all international applicants. High school diploma is required, and GED is accepted. *Academic units required:* 4 English, 3 mathematics, 2 science (2 science labs), 2 social studies, academic elective. *Academic units recommended:* 2 foreign language.

Financial Aid

Students should submit: FAFSA. The Princeton Review suggests that all financial aid forms be submitted as soon as possible after January 1. *Need-based scholarships/grants offered:* Federal Pell, SEOG, state scholarships/grants, private scholarships, school scholarship or grant aid from institutional funds, Federal Nursing Scholarships. *Loan aid offered:* Direct Subsidized Stafford, Direct Unsubsidized Stafford, Direct PLUS, Federal Perkins. Applicants will be notified of awards on a rolling basis beginning April 15. Federal Work-Study Program not available. Off-campus job opportunities are excellent.

The Inside Word

Hampton University allows for early action admissions, meaning that students can receive an early decision without having to commit to attending the school. Well more than half of HU's applicant pool pursues this option. You would be wise to follow suit; the school is bound to be more lenient early in the process than later, when it has already admitted many qualified students. Don't be fooled by the fact that the number of applicants to HU has dropped in recent years; that's the result of more stringent admission standards, not a drop in the school's cachet.

THE SCHOOL SAYS "..."

From the Admissions Office

"Hampton attempts to provide the environment and structures most conducive to the intellectual, emotional, and aesthetic enlargement of the lives of its members. The university gives priority to effective teaching and scholarly research while placing the student at the center of its planning. Hampton will ask you to look inwardly at your own history and culture and examine your relationship to the aspirations and development of the world."

SELECTIVITY
Admissions Rating	86
# of applicants	7,120
% of applicants accepted	37
% of acceptees attending	43

FRESHMAN PROFILE
Range SAT Critical Reading	481–552
Range SAT Math	464–606
Range ACT Composite	17–26
Minimum paper TOEFL	550
Minimum computer TOEFL	214
Average HS GPA	3.20
% graduated top 10% of class	20
% graduated top 25% of class	45
% graduated top 50% of class	90

DEADLINES
Early action	
Deadline	12/1
Notification	12/15
Regular	
Priority	3/1
Nonfall registration?	yes

FINANCIAL FACTS
Financial Aid Rating	64
Annual tuition	$13,358
Room and board	$6,746
Required fees	$1,460
Books and supplies	$750
% frosh rec. need-based scholarship or grant aid	96
% UG rec. need-based scholarship or grant aid	44
% frosh rec. non-need-based scholarship or grant aid	23
% UG rec. non-need-based scholarship or grant aid	13
% frosh rec. need-based self-help aid	79
% UG rec. need-based self-help aid	44
% frosh rec. any financial aid	44
% UG rec. any financial aid	100
% UG borrow to pay for school	51
Average cumulative indebtedness	$17,125

HANOVER COLLEGE

PO Box 108, Hanover, IN 47243-0108 • Admissions: 812-866-7021 • Fax: 812-866-7098

CAMPUS LIFE

Quality of Life Rating	69
Fire Safety Rating	78
Green Rating	75
Type of school	private
Affiliation	Presbyterian
Environment	rural

STUDENTS

Total undergrad enrollment	1,004
% male/female	44/56
% from out of state	34
% from public high school	82
% live on campus	95
# of fraternities	5
# of sororities	5
% African American	4
% Asian	1
% Caucasian	85
% Hispanic	2
% international	3
# of countries represented	13

SURVEY SAYS . . .

Lab facilities are great
Athletic facilities are great
Students are friendly
Campus feels safe
Low cost of living
Frats and sororities dominate
social scene
Lots of beer drinking
Hard liquor is popular

ACADEMICS

Academic Rating	92
% students graduating within 4 years	62
% students graduating within 6 years	66
Calendar	4-4-1
Student/faculty ratio	11:1
Profs interesting rating	93
Profs accessible rating	90
Most common reg class size	10–19 students

MOST POPULAR MAJORS

biology, history, speech communication and rhetoric

STUDENTS SAY ". . ."

Academics

A "gem in the Midwest," Hanover College is a rigorous liberal arts school with an impressive focus on the individual learner. Students absolutely love Hanover's "small but engaging classes," led by professors who "show a high level of dedication to the students, and a great affinity for the subjects they teach." Personalized education is the name of the game at Hanover, where professors "take a personal interest in your education and interests, and strive to make every class engaging for every student, even if it means catering to and adapting to a different learning style than the one they're used to." Hanover's "discussion-led classes are great for those who are interested in real-world applications," and the curriculum is successful in building "essential life skills such as problem-solving and organizational skills." Despite the friendliness of the faculty, a Hanover education is no walk in the park: "The academics are rigorous and students are pushed to levels outside of their comfort zone." A current student tells us, "It has been extremely challenging at points, but with the help and understanding of my professors and peers, it has been very enriching." Fortunately, not every moment at Hanover is all stress and study. An oasis of relaxation, the school's unique Spring Term is a "four-week period in May where you only take one class. The rest of the time is devoted to intramurals, parties, and enjoying the weather." On this friendly campus, "The administration is very available" and "very in touch with the students," but students say there's always room for improvement, especially when it comes to "communication."

Life

Large and well-kept, Hanover's "gorgeous campus" provides "the perfect setting for learning." Located in a little town on the Ohio River, students warn us that, "Even if you have a great group of friends, there is not a whole lot to do. So getting involved is a huge key to being happy here." Fortunately, on and around campus, "There are 165 student organizations," including "intramural sports…club-sponsored outings and a massive wooded area to go hiking in." In addition to organized activities, students like to hang out at the "student-run restaurant on campus called the Shoebox, which has great food and entertainment." Parties are another popular way to wile away the weekend hours. A student explains, "although the administration publishes an annual booklet entitled '164 Things to Do at Hanover College,' it seems that drinking is still a particularly common pastime, especially on Friday and Saturday nights." However, "Students generally are smart and responsible when drinking," and parties are "fairly safe." In addition to the Greek scene, there are "large groups of people who are happy to simply hang out, talk, watch movies, that kind of thing." In addition, "Most people go off campus at least one day of the weekend, just to break routine a little bit." To enjoy more cosmopolitan environs, "Louisville is about forty minutes away," and nearby Madison is "a great town [in which] to experience community connections and a festive atmosphere."

Student Body

At Hanover College, "The typical student is studious, involved in campus activities, and enjoys spending free time with friends." Among the school's 1,000 undergraduates, "The majority of students are white, but there are many other ethnic groups," as well as "a variety of people of different religious backgrounds, sexualities, political views, and personality types." "Students are split about evenly from large suburban high schools and smaller rural schools," though most come from "Indiana, Kentucky, Illinois, or Ohio." There are "definitely social divisions at Hanover," which tend to form around certain clubs and social groups. If you aren't interested in going Greek, "There is an active 'geek' population that is waiting to be tapped if you search for it (Sci-fi Club, Anime Club)." "Most people are friendly and don't mind crossing-over into a variety of circles of friends."

FINANCIAL AID: 812-866-7030 • E-MAIL: ADMISSION@HANOVER.EDU • WEBSITE: WWW.HANOVER.EDU

THE PRINCETON REVIEW SAYS

Admissions

Very important factors considered include: Academic GPA, class rank, rigor of secondary school record. *Important factors considered include:* Recommendation(s), standardized test scores, talent/ability. *Other factors considered include:* Application essay, alumni/ae relation, character/personal qualities, extracurricular activities, first generation, geographical residence, interview, level of applicant's interest, racial/ethnic status, state residency, volunteer work, work experience. SAT or ACT required; ACT with writing component recommended. TOEFL required of all international applicants. *Academic units required:* 4 English, 3 mathematics, 3 science (2 science labs), 2 foreign language, 2 social studies, 2 history, 2 academic elective. *Academic units recommended:* 4 English, 4 mathematics, 4 science (3 science labs), 4 foreign language, 3 social studies, 3 history, 1 visual/performing arts, 3 academic elective.

Financial Aid

Students should submit: FAFSA. The Princeton Review suggests that all financial aid forms be submitted as soon as possible after January 1. *Need-based scholarships/grants offered:* Federal Pell, SEOG, state scholarships/grants, private scholarships, school scholarship or grant aid from institutional funds. *Loan aid offered:* University loans from institutional funds. Applicants will be notified of awards on a rolling basis beginning March 1. Federal Work-Study Program available. Off-campus job opportunities are fair.

The Inside Word

There are five main criteria that the Hanover admissions committee uses to evaluate applicants: academic record, personal excellence, respect for others, community responsibility, and accountability. If you think you're a good fit, the school will help arrange an overnight visit to campus, which gives you the opportunity to stay in a dorm, attend classes, and interview with the admissions department.

THE SCHOOL SAYS ". . ."

From the Admissions Office

"Since our founding in 1827, we have been committed to providing students with a personal, rigorous, and well-rounded liberal arts education. Part of the college search process is finding that school that proves to be a good match. For those who see the value in an education that demands engagement and who see college as a time for exploration and involvement, they will find that Hanover is all they could hope for and more.

"The admission process serves as an introduction to the personal education that students receive at Hanover College. Every application is considered individually with emphasis being placed on a student's high school curriculum and the student's academic performance in that curriculum. While we realize that not every high school has the same course offerings, we expect students to have selected a college preparatory curriculum as challenging as possible within his or her particular high school or academic setting.

"Hanover College accepts both the SAT and ACT. Students taking the ACT are required to take the optional writing section. For students who have taken one or both of the tests multiple times, we will use the highest sub scores when calculating a student's score on either test for admission and scholarship purposes."

SELECTIVITY

Admissions Rating	87
# of applicants	2,964
% of applicants accepted	67
% of acceptees attending	16
# accepting a place on wait list	0

FRESHMAN PROFILE

Range SAT Critical Reading	510–610
Range SAT Math	500–600
Range SAT Writing	480–590
Range ACT Composite	22–28
Minimum paper TOEFL	550
Minimum computer TOEFL	213
Minimum web-based TOEFL	120
Average HS GPA	3.64
% graduated top 10% of class	31
% graduated top 25% of class	65
% graduated top 50% of class	92

DEADLINES

Early action	
Deadline	12/1
Notification	12/20
Regular	
Deadline	3/1
Notification	9/1
Nonfall registration?	yes

APPLICANTS ALSO LOOK AT AND OFTEN PREFER
Butler University, DePauw University

AND SOMETIMES PREFER
Centre College, Indiana University at Bloomington, Miami University, University of Evansville, Wabash College

FINANCIAL FACTS

Financial Aid Rating	87
Annual tuition	$26,950
Room and board	$8,300
Required fees	$550
Books and supplies	$900
% frosh rec. need-based scholarship or grant aid	70
% UG rec. need-based scholarship or grant aid	77
% frosh rec. non-need-based scholarship or grant aid	12
% UG rec. non-need-based scholarship or grant aid	11
% frosh rec. need-based self-help aid	58
% UG rec. need-based self-help aid	66
% frosh rec. any financial aid	99
% UG rec. any financial aid	98
% UG borrow to pay for school	66
Average cumulative indebtedness	$28,185

HARVARD COLLEGE

BYERLY HALL, EIGHT GARDEN STREET, CAMBRIDGE, MA 02138 • ADMISSIONS: 617-495-1551 • FAX: 617-495-8821

CAMPUS LIFE

Quality of Life Rating	82
Fire Safety Rating	60*
Green Rating	99
Type of school	private
Environment	city

STUDENTS

Total undergrad enrollment	6,641
% male/female	50/50
% from out of state	74
% African American	7
% Asian	16
% Caucasian	43
% Hispanic	8
% international	10
# of countries represented	110

SURVEY SAYS . . .

Lab facilities are great
Great computer facilities
Great library
Diverse student types on campus
Musical organizations are popular
Student publications are popular
Political activism is popular

ACADEMICS

Academic Rating	99
% students graduating within 4 years	87
% students graduating within 6 years	97
Calendar	semester
Student/faculty ratio	7:1
Profs interesting rating	71
Profs accessible rating	69
Most common reg class size	fewer than 10 students

MOST POPULAR MAJORS

economics, political science, sociology

STUDENTS SAY ". . ."

Academics

Bully to those who get the chance to be a part of the "dynamic universe" that is Harvard College, who find themselves in an "amazing irresistible hell" that pushes them to the extremes of their intellect and ability. Unsurprisingly, the legendarily "very difficult" school attracts some of the country's most promising youth, who rise to the occasion in almost every aspect of their life on campus, not just the classroom. Harvard's recent financial aid enhancements have increased the number of applications by a landslide, but even after getting past the admissions hurdle, "People find ways to make everything (especially clubs and even partying) competitive." Happily, this streak is more of a "latent competition," as there are more than enough opportunity and resources to go around. "It is impossible to 'get the most out of Harvard' because Harvard offers so much," says one student. Much like the students, the professors at this "beautiful, fun, historic, and academically alive place" in Cambridge, Massachusetts, are among "the brightest minds in the world," and "The level of achievement is unbelievable." Some of the larger introductory classes are taught by teaching fellows (TFs), meaning "you do have to go to office hours to get to know your big lecture class professors on a personal level," but once your figurative underclass dues are paid, the access to "incredible" and "every so often, fantastic" professors is perfectly within reach. Top it off with Grade-A internship and employment opportunities, a good old alumni network, and a crimson pedigree for your resume, and you may just end up agreeing with the Harvard student who refers to his experience as "rewarding beyond anything else I've ever done." Though the administration can be "waaaaay out of touch with students" and "reticent to change," it at least "does a good job of watching over its freshmen through extensive advising programs," and students all have faith that their best interests are being kept in mind.

Life

Cambridge and Boston are nothing if not college towns, and students never lack for options if they just want to "go see a play, a concert, hit up a party, go to the movies, or dine out." Students quickly learn when to hit the books and when to hit the streets, so "studying becomes routine." "There is a vibrant social atmosphere on campus and between students and the local community." As one student puts it, "Boredom does not exist here. There are endless opportunities and endless passionate people to do them with." "Basically, if you want to do it, Harvard either has it or has the money to give to you so you can start it." "Partying in a more traditional setting is available at Harvard, but is not a prevalent aspect of the school's social life. While there is a pub on campus that provides an excellent venue to hang out and play a game of pool or have a reasonably priced drink," and parties happen on weekends at Harvard's finals clubs, there's no real pressure for students to partake if they're not interested.

Student Body

Much as you might expect, ambition and achievement are the ties that bind at Harvard, and "Everyone is great for one reason or another," says a student. Most every student can be summed up with the same statement: "Works really hard. Doesn't sleep. Involved in a million extracurriculars." Diversity is found in all aspects of life, from ethnicities to religion to ideology, and "there is a lot of tolerance and acceptance at Harvard for individuals of all races, religions, socioeconomic backgrounds, life styles, etc."

FINANCIAL AID: 617-495-1581 • E-MAIL: COLLEGE@FAS.HARVARD.EDU • WEBSITE: WWW.FAS.HARVARD.EDU

THE PRINCETON REVIEW SAYS

Admissions

Factors considered include: Academic GPA, application essay, recommendation(s), rigor of secondary school record, standardized test scores, alumni/ae relation, character/personal qualities, extracurricular activities, first generation, geographical residence, interview, racial/ethnic status. SAT or ACT required; ACT with writing component required. High school diploma or equivalent isn't required. *Academic units recommended:* 4 English, 4 mathematics, 4 science, 4 foreign language, 3 social studies, 2 history.

Financial Aid

Students should submit: FAFSA, CSS/Financial Aid PROFILE. Regular filing deadline is February 1. The Princeton Review suggests that all financial aid forms be submitted as soon as possible after January 1. *Need-based scholarships/ grants offered:* Federal Pell, SEOG, state scholarships/grants, private scholarships, school scholarship or grant aid from institutional funds. *Loan aid offered:* Direct Subsidized Stafford, Direct Unsubsidized Stafford, Direct PLUS, Federal Perkins, university loans from institutional funds. Federal Work-Study Program available. Off-campus job opportunities are excellent.

The Inside Word

It just doesn't get any tougher than this. Candidates to Harvard face dual obstacles—an awe-inspiring applicant pool and, as a result, admissions standards that defy explanation in quantifiable terms. Harvard denies admission to the vast majority, and virtually all of them are top students. It all boils down to splitting hairs, which is quite hard to explain and even harder for candidates to understand. Rather than being as detailed and direct as possible about the selection process and criteria, Harvard keeps things close to the vest—before, during, and after. They even refuse to admit that being from lesser populated states like South Dakota is an advantage. Thus the admissions process does more to intimidate candidates than to empower them. Moving to a common application seemed to be a small step in the right direction, but with the current explosion of early decision applicants and a super-high yield of enrollees, things aren't likely to change dramatically.

THE SCHOOL SAYS "..."

From the Admissions Office

"The admissions committee looks for energy, ambition, and the capacity to make the most of opportunities. Academic ability and preparation are important, and so is intellectual curiosity—but many of the strongest applicants have significant, non-academic interests and accomplishments, as well. There is no formula for admission, and applicants are considered carefully, with attention to future promise.

"Freshman applicants may submit the SAT. The ACT with writing component is also accepted. All students must also submit three SAT Subject Tests of their choosing."

SELECTIVITY	
Admissions Rating	99
# of applicants	30,489
% of applicants accepted	7
% of acceptees attending	75
# accepting a place on wait list	0

FRESHMAN PROFILE	
Range SAT Critical Reading	690–800
Range SAT Math	700–790
Range SAT Writing	710–800
Range ACT Composite	31–34

DEADLINES	
Regular	
Deadline	2/1
Nonfall registration?	no

FINANCIAL FACTS	
Financial Aid Rating	96
Annual tuition	$34,976
Room and board	$12,308
Required fees	$3,440
Books and supplies	$1,000
% frosh rec. need-based scholarship or grant aid	63
% UG rec. need-based scholarship or grant aid	61
% frosh rec. need-based self-help aid	38
% UG rec. need-based self-help aid	50
% UG borrow to pay for school	34
Average cumulative indebtedness	$10,102

HARVEY MUDD COLLEGE

301 PLATT BOULEVARD, CLAREMONT, CA 91711-5990 • ADMISSIONS: 909-621-8011 • FAX: 909-607-7046

CAMPUS LIFE
Quality of Life Rating	90
Fire Safety Rating	77
Green Rating	78
Type of school	private
Environment	town

STUDENTS
Total undergrad enrollment	773
% male/female	59/41
% from out of state	60
% from public high school	69
% live on campus	99
% African American	1
% Asian	19
% Caucasian	58
% Hispanic	7
% international	5
# of countries represented	23

SURVEY SAYS . . .
No one cheats
Lab facilities are great
Great computer facilities
School is well-run
Students are friendly
Dorms are like palaces
Low cost of living
Frats and sororities are unpopular
or nonexistent

ACADEMICS
Academic Rating	96
% students graduating within 4 years	80
% students graduating within 6 years	87
Calendar	semester
Student/faculty ratio	9:1
Profs interesting rating	98
Profs accessible rating	98
Most common reg class size	10–19 students
Most common lab size	10–19 students

MOST POPULAR MAJORS
computer and information sciences,
engineering, mathematics

STUDENTS SAY "..."

Academics
Harvey Mudd College, one of the five Claremont Colleges in Southern California's Inland Empire, "is a small science and math school with a quirky community that is the perfect fit for those who are serious about both their technical studies and having an indefinably strange yet amazing time." With "an excellent program in the sciences and engineering," strong undergraduate research opportunities, and "a very high percentage of students [who] go to graduate school," Harvey Mudd "is unique and offers a personalized education that you can't get at a larger technical university." While the rigorous academics "can be very stressful for some," most students are quick to emphasize the support provided by professors and the student body. "The academic experience is heightened by the students...who act cooperatively rather than competitively to conquer the material rather than each other." This collaborative atmosphere is created in large part by the respected honor code, which students say "defines us and allows us to have take-home finals [and] unproctored tests." "The trust the faculty has for the students gives us a sense of responsibility, and thus everyone lives up to expectations." Students trust the faculty, as well. "I love the professors here," one student says (echoing the sentiments of many). "They are all brilliant and extremely accessible. Most of them know my name and will stop to talk any time." "Lectures and office hours are both amazing! Professors really want you to understand the material." Overall, students say their lives at Harvey Mudd are "tons of work, but really fun."

Life
Because "Harvey Mudd is a highly academic school, a lot of time is spent doing homework and studying." Students manage to find time for fun, though, even at the expense of some shut-eye: "Many people are sleep-deprived but happy in general." "Community is such a big part of Harvey Mudd, people spend a lot of time with each other," and there are many niches within the larger community. "Every dorm has a unique personality, and what people do for fun is different for each person." "Some are devoted to video games and the more classic 'nerd' activities. Some groups are devoted to drinking and partying a ton. There is a wide spectrum of unique dorm communities represented." "One can easily find groups to play sports or video games with, take on carpentry or other independent construction or engineering projects, start an afternoon game of bocce ball or croquet, compete in the fiercely competitive CMS intramural water polo league, and of course, help in the construction of the campus-wide Rube Goldberg Machine, to name a few popular activities." "CAP (Committee for Activities Planning) subsidizes concert tickets, sporting event tickets, ski trips, and other events" if at least eight Mudders plan to attend. "Dorms throw some kick-ass parties," "taking great care to make them fun for people who don't drink as well." Favorites include "Casemas," when "we import five tons of snow to celebrate winter," and "Slippery When Wet" when students "construct decks to support hundreds of dancing people" and then invite the other Claremont Colleges to test their strength over a flooded courtyard.

Student Body
"We are nerds," Mudders tell us, "and we embrace it." They also describe themselves as "outgoing, quirky, and fun but very studious." Students are united by "a brimming passion for science and a love of knowledge for its own sake." "All students are exceptionally intelligent and are able to perform their work in a professional manner." Beyond that, there's "a really diverse group of personalities" at Mudd, who are "not afraid to show their true colors" and who all have "a unique sense of humor." Students say they "are all friendly, smart, and talented, which brings us together. Upperclassmen look out for underclassmen, and students tend to bond together easily over difficult homework." In such a welcoming community, "students primarily fit in by not fitting in—wearing pink pirate hats or skateboarding while playing harmonica or practicing unicycle jousting are all good ways to fit in perfectly."

FINANCIAL AID: 909-621-8055 • E-MAIL: ADMISSION@HMC.EDU • WEBSITE: WWW.HMC.EDU

THE PRINCETON REVIEW SAYS

Admissions

Very important factors considered include: Academic GPA, application essay, recommendation(s), rigor of secondary school record, character/personal qualities, talent/ability. *Important factors considered include:* Class rank, standardized test scores, extracurricular activities. *Other factors considered include:* Alumni/ae relation, first generation, geographical residence, interview, level of applicant's interest, racial/ethnic status, state residency, volunteer work, work experience. SAT or ACT required; ACT with writing component required. TOEFL required of all international applicants. High school diploma or equivalent isn't required. *Academic units required:* 4 English, 3 mathematics, 3 science, 1 history. *Academic units recommended:* 4 mathematics, 4 science (2 science labs), 2 foreign language, 2 social studies, 2 history.

Financial Aid

Students should submit: FAFSA, CSS/Financial Aid PROFILE. Regular filing deadline is February 1. The Princeton Review suggests that all financial aid forms be submitted as soon as possible after January 1. *Need-based scholarships/grants offered:* Federal Pell, SEOG, state scholarships/grants, private scholarships, school scholarship or grant aid from institutional funds. *Loan aid offered:* Direct Subsidized Stafford, Direct Unsubsidized Stafford, Direct PLUS, Federal Perkins, university loans from institutional funds. Federal Work-Study Program available. Off-campus job opportunities are excellent.

The Inside Word

There's little mystery to the admissions process at Harvey Mudd College, but there's a lot of competition. Like most top-tier science, math, and engineering schools, Harvey Mudd considers far more qualified applicants than it can accommodate in its incoming class. Load up on science classes, don't neglect your extracurriculars, give the application everything you've got, and accept the fact that being perfectly qualified to attend this school is no guarantee of admission.

THE SCHOOL SAYS "..."

From the Admissions Office

"HMC is a wonderfully unusual combination of a liberal arts college and research institute. Our students love math and science, want to live and learn deeply in an intimate climate of cooperation and trust, thrive on innovation and discovery, and enjoy rigorous coursework in arts, humanities, and social sciences in addition to a technical curriculum. At least a year of research or our innovative clinic program is required (or guaranteed, if you prefer). The resources at HMC are astounding, and all are accessible to undergraduates: labs, shops, work areas, and most importantly, faculty. You'll find the professors and student body stimulating and supportive—they'll challenge you inside and outside the classroom, and share your love of learning and collaboration. They'll also share your love of fun and sense of humor (math jokes and all). In addition, we benefit from the unique consortium that is the Claremont Colleges.

"While we may not take ourselves too seriously, employers and graduate schools do. We enjoy a powerful reputation for preparing our graduates for all kinds of career paths. A wide range of companies are eager to hire our seniors, and HMC sends the highest proportion of graduates to PhD programs of any undergraduate college in the country."

SELECTIVITY

Admissions Rating	97
# of applicants	2,508
% of applicants accepted	25
% of acceptees attending	31
# accepting a place on wait list	272
% admitted from wait list	0
# of early decision applicants	212
% accepted early decision	28

FRESHMAN PROFILE

Range SAT Critical Reading	670–760
Range SAT Math	740–800
Range SAT Writing	668–760
Range ACT Composite	32–35
Minimum paper TOEFL	600
Minimum computer TOEFL	250
Minimum web-based TOEFL	100
% graduated top 10% of class	89
% graduated top 25% of class	99
% graduated top 50% of class	100

DEADLINES

Early decision	
Deadline	11/15
Notification	12/15
Regular	
Deadline	1/2
Notification	4/1
Nonfall registration?	no

APPLICANTS ALSO LOOK AT
AND OFTEN PREFER
California Institute of Technology, Massachusetts Institute of Technology, Stanford University

AND SOMETIMES PREFER
Cornell University, University of California—Berkeley, University of California—Los Angeles

AND RARELY PREFER
Franklin W. Olin College of Engineering, University of California—San Diego

FINANCIAL FACTS

Financial Aid Rating	97
Annual tuition	$40,133
Room and board	$13,198
Required fees	$257
Books and supplies	$800
% frosh rec. need-based scholarship or grant aid	49
% UG rec. need-based scholarship or grant aid	52
% frosh rec. non-need-based scholarship or grant aid	18
% UG rec. non-need-based scholarship or grant aid	24
% frosh rec. need-based self-help aid	34
% UG rec. need-based self-help aid	39
% frosh rec. any financial aid	77
% UG rec. any financial aid	82
% UG borrow to pay for school	57
Average cumulative indebtedness	$19,169

HAVERFORD COLLEGE

370 WEST LANCASTER AVENUE, HAVERFORD, PA 19041 • ADMISSIONS: 610-896-1350 • FAX: 610-896-1338

STUDENTS SAY ". . ."

Academics

"The academic experience is nothing less than stellar" at Haverford. "The classroom is an incredible place where I have been intellectually pushed beyond what I believed possible." The work load can be "intense," but "professors are always available and willing to help," and there is "a support system to help you…composed of students and faculty." Everyone raves about the accessibility of professors. "I have the cell phone number or house number of all my professors. An incredible number of professors live on or within a block of campus and regularly invite students over for tea or dinner." Some students note the lack of research opportunities, but most "love how we have access to Bryn Mawr, Penn, and Swarthmore. The schools really work together to provide a wide range of courses." Haverford is known for its honor code, which "really works, and we actually do have things like closed-book, timed, take-home tests. I honestly don't know of anyone that who ever cheated." The administration also receives high marks. "There is a lot of discourse between the administration and the students," and "the deans…are pretty receptive to student opinions." Though a few students feel "the degree of transparency between the administration and students has dropped in recent years," the "administration does a good job of keeping us informed about important news," and the president holds weekly office hours.

Life

The academic demands of Haverford keep its students focused. "In general, students go to class, participate in extracurriculars, and do homework all day Monday through Thursday." "Students are very active on campus," "with classes, work, on-campus jobs, volunteering, running clubs, and acting on administrative committees." "People are very oriented toward social justice, and overall, our student body is very aware." "Conversations at meals consist of discussions on political issues, scientific breakthroughs, etc." "But that doesn't mean people don't know how to have fun," students assure us. "There are a ton of concerts, a capella shows, student theater, movies, dinners, dances, sponsored events in Philly." "While students here do party," many note and there's no pressure to drink, and plenty of students don't. There is easy access to public transportation, and students say "it's nice to have Philadelphia so close—the music scene is amazing." At the same time, "a lot of people never leave campus because there is so much to do there." Thursday and Saturday are the nights to party, owing to the athletic teams' schedules, and there's not much of a bar scene. Most socializing is on campus, and school-sponsored events are well-attended. "Every weekend night there are at least three options—a music show, an improv show, a movie, or games." It seems Haverford students never really disengage from the classroom, though "Don't be surprised if you witness a discussion about someone's senior thesis next to a keg-stand."

Student Body

Many students describe themselves as a little "nerdy" or "quirky," but in the best possible way. "For the most part, Haverfordians are socially awkward, open to new friends, and looking for moral, political, [or] scholarly debate." The honor code draws a particular type of student—"don't choose to go here if you're not dedicated to the ideas of trust, concern, and respect and to making sure we are a well-run community." Most are "liberal-minded" and "intellectual" and "want to save the world after they graduate."

HAVERFORD COLLEGE

FINANCIAL AID: 610-896-1350 • E-MAIL: ADMITME@HAVERFORD.EDU • WEBSITE: WWW.HAVERFORD.EDU

THE PRINCETON REVIEW SAYS

Admissions

Very important factors considered include: Academic GPA, application essay, recommendation(s), rigor of secondary school record, character/personal qualities, extracurricular activities. *Important factors considered include:* Class rank, standardized test scores, talent/ability, volunteer work, work experience. *Other factors considered include:* Alumni/ae relation, first generation, geographical residence, interview, level of applicant's interest, racial/ethnic status. SAT or ACT required; ACT with writing component recommended. TOEFL required of all international applicants. High school diploma or equivalent isn't required. *Academic units recommended:* 4 English, 3 mathematics, 3 science, 2 foreign language, 2 social studies, 3 history.

Financial Aid

Students should submit: FAFSA, CSS/Financial Aid PROFILE. Regular filing deadline is January 31. The Princeton Review suggests that all financial aid forms be submitted as soon as possible after January 1. *Need-based scholarships/grants offered:* Federal Pell, SEOG, state scholarships/grants, school scholarship or grant aid from institutional funds. *Loan aid offered:* Direct Subsidized Stafford, Direct Unsubsidized Stafford, Direct PLUS, Federal Perkins. Federal Work-Study Program available. Off-campus job opportunities are good.

The Inside Word

Haverford's applicant pool is an impressive and competitive lot. Intellectual curiosity is paramount, and applicants are expected to keep a demanding academic schedule in high school. Additionally, the college places a high value on ethics, as evidenced by its honor code. The admissions office seeks students who will reflect and promote Haverford's ideals.

THE SCHOOL SAYS "..."

From the Admissions Office

"Haverford strives to be a college in which integrity, honesty, and concern for others are dominant forces. The college does not have many formal rules; rather, it offers an opportunity for students to govern their affairs and conduct themselves with respect and concern for others. Each student is expected to adhere to the honor code as it is adopted each year by the Students' Association. Haverford's Quaker roots show most clearly in the relationship of faculty and students, in the emphasis on integrity, in the interaction of the individual and the community, and through the college's concern for the uses to which its students put their expanding knowledge. Haverford's 1,100 students represent a wide diversity of interests, backgrounds, and talents. They come from public, parochial, and independent schools across the United States, Puerto Rico, and thirty-eight foreign countries. Students of color are an important part of the Haverford community.

"Haverford College requires that all applicants submit the results of the SAT exam or the ACT with the optional writing test. Two SAT Subject Tests are required."

SELECTIVITY

Admissions Rating	97
# of applicants	3,312
% of applicants accepted	26
% of acceptees attending	38
# accepting a place on wait list	375
% admitted from wait list	0
# of early decision applicants	232
% accepted early decision	54

FRESHMAN PROFILE

Range SAT Critical Reading	650–740
Range SAT Math	650–750
Range SAT Writing	660–750
Minimum paper TOEFL	600
Minimum computer TOEFL	250
% graduated top 10% of class	94
% graduated top 25% of class	99
% graduated top 50% of class	100

DEADLINES

Early decision	
Deadline	11/15
Notification	12/15
Regular	
Deadline	1/15
Nonfall registration?	no

FINANCIAL FACTS

Financial Aid Rating	95
Annual tuition	$41,830
Room and board	$12,842
Books and supplies	$1,194
% frosh rec. need-based scholarship or grant aid	51
% UG rec. need-based scholarship or grant aid	50
% frosh rec. need-based self-help aid	48
% UG rec. need-based self-help aid	48
% frosh rec. any financial aid	61
% UG rec. any financial aid	60
% UG borrow to pay for school	34
Average cumulative indebtedness	$16,238

HENDRIX COLLEGE

1600 WASHINGTON AVENUE, CONWAY, AR 72032 • ADMISSIONS: 501-450-1362 • FAX: 501-450-3843

STUDENTS SAY ". . ."

Academics

"Generous" financial aid and "a strong reputation for science" are two hallmarks of Hendrix College, "a progressive liberal arts school filled with Southern hospitality." Another perk is Hendrix's unique Odyssey Program, which allows students to "explore all sorts of things" in a hands-on way. You can learn printmaking, just for example, or maybe jet off to Prague to observe ballroom dancing. Class sizes are "small" here, and the academic atmosphere is "exceptionally rigorous." "There is a *ton* of writing." "A lot of time must be devoted to studying." "Unmotivated students do not last long." "It's sink or swim," contemplates a philosophy major. "If you swim, you're in for a really great experience." Professors are tough, but they're also "unwaveringly genial and helpful." Faculty members "love what they do and are very good at it." "They make the subjects really interesting," swears a religious studies major. They're "passionate about their fields and very accessible in and out of the classroom." Students do have some academic complaints. "The registration process could be better." The level of academic satisfaction is pretty high overall, though, and the fact that about one-third of all newly minted Hendrix grads proceed directly to graduate and professional school is evidence that all the hard work pays off.

Life

Social life here is extremely "campus-centric," and Hendrix is "small enough to evoke a sense of familiarity without feeling boring." "Hendrix is its own little world where you can't help but get caught up in something." "We have everything from sword club, Frisbee team, volunteer committee, to full orchestra," enthuses one student. "There is always something to do." "A lot of kids play intramural sports and stay pretty athletic." "People are very involved in the act of hanging out" as well, and "There are really interesting conversations going on all over campus." "During the week, Hendrix is quiet because everybody is studying or working on something school related." On the weekends, however, "Hendrix definitely has an active party scene." The revelry is "easy to avoid if you want to" but most students embrace it. "The lack of Greek life makes parties much more open and universal." "Super-fun parties" reportedly abound. "Almost every weekend has been predesignated for some sort of ongoing annual event." Off campus, some feel Conway, Arkansas, boasts little to do, but relatively urbane Little Rock is a short drive and "a common destination for Hendrix students wanting to break away from the routine." Students say the campus here is "absolutely gorgeous." However, some note that housing isn't uniformly objectionable, but some of the dorms "have issues." Students have few other gripes about their lives here, though. The food: always "digestible" and occasionally "fantastic."

Student Body

Some students tell us that Hendrix is "a cross between" a hippie school and a nerd school. Others call this place "more preppy than hippie." More often than not, students have left-leaning political views. "Hendrix is the liberal mecca of Arkansas." A fairly high percentage of students smoke—sometimes "heavily." Students describe themselves as "hardworking," "very ambitious," "pretty free-spirited," and "eclectic" "intellectual misfits" who tend to have "lots of interests and hidden abilities." "People with particularly odd or strange quirks fit right in" at Hendrix because "everybody is weird in one way or another." "While I can't say we are ethnically diverse," promises one student, "I can say that everyone is wholeheartedly welcome." In the cafeteria, "you'll see a jock, a gay drama kid, and a hippie all sitting together having a good time together." "People form groups quickly and really just stick to those groups," though.

HENDRIX COLLEGE

FINANCIAL AID: 501-450-1368 • E-MAIL: ADM@HENDRIX.EDU • WEBSITE: WWW.HENDRIX.EDU

THE PRINCETON REVIEW SAYS

Admissions

Very important factors considered include: Academic GPA, application essay, rigor of secondary school record, standardized test scores. *Important factors considered include:* Class rank, recommendation(s), extracurricular activities. *Other factors considered include:* Interview, talent/ability, volunteer work. SAT or ACT required; ACT with or without writing component accepted. TOEFL required of all international applicants. High school diploma is required, and GED is accepted. *Academic units recommended:* 4 English, 3 mathematics, 2 science, 2 foreign language, 3 social studies.

Financial Aid

Students should submit: FAFSA. Priority filing date is February 15. The Princeton Review suggests that all financial aid forms be submitted as soon as possible after January 1. Application for admission serves as primary merit-based scholarship application. *Need-based scholarships/grants offered:* Federal Pell, SEOG, state scholarships/grants, private scholarships, school scholarship or grant aid from institutional funds. *Loan aid offered:* Direct Subsidized Stafford, Direct Unsubsidized Stafford, Direct PLUS, Federal Perkins. Applicants will be notified of awards on a rolling basis beginning February 15. Federal Work-Study Program available and Hendrix also funds a companion Hendrix work program. Off-campus job opportunities are good.

The Inside Word

Don't be fooled by the high acceptance rate; Hendrix is an academically demanding place. The applicant pool here is both very self-selecting and very well-qualified. This school remains a great destination for applicants who have stellar grades but relatively lower standardized test scores.

THE SCHOOL SAYS "..."

From the Admissions Office

"Hendrix students are participants, not spectators. They like to be involved, and they like to know that what they do makes a difference. Hendrix students are voting members of almost every campus committee, which gives them an important voice in college governance. They are very hands-on about their education as well. Internships, study abroad, research projects, service projects, expressive arts projects, and leadership development—these are all areas that Hendrix students find attractive. The Hendrix curriculum is demanding, but the environment is one of support and cooperation—not competition. Hendrix students form a close-knit, inclusive community. They build lifetime connections and close friendships, the kind of relationships that grow in a residential college where learning is a 24/7 kind of thing. It doesn't hurt that the campus is beautifully maintained and that Hendrix graduates are admitted to top graduate schools and recruited for good jobs around the world.

"Hendrix believes that you learn best when you can integrate what you learn in your courses with a variety of hands-on learning experiences. In over a century of educating bright, innovative students, Hendrix has perfected the art of seamlessly integrating a traditional liberal arts education with active learning experiences. It's a way of learning that reflects Hendrix's motto: "Unto the whole person." The College recently introduced Your Hendrix Odyssey: Engaging in Active Learning—the ultimate expression of its unique approach to learning. The Odyssey Program guarantees that every Hendrix student will participate in at least three hands-on learning opportunities chosen from six different categories. Students receive transcript credit for their Odyssey experiences. Since the program's inception in 2005, students and faculty have engaged in more than 5,000 Odyssey experiences and been awarded nearly $1.75 million in Odyssey grants for projects that merited special funding."

SELECTIVITY

Admissions Rating	91
# of applicants	1,554
% of applicants accepted	83
% of acceptees attending	31
# accepting a place on wait list	0

FRESHMAN PROFILE

Range SAT Critical Reading	600–700
Range SAT Math	580–680
Range ACT Composite	27–32
Minimum paper TOEFL	550
Minimum computer TOEFL	213
Minimum web-based TOEFL	79
Average HS GPA	3.89
% graduated top 10% of class	53
% graduated top 25% of class	81
% graduated top 50% of class	95

DEADLINES

Early action I	
Deadline	11/15
Notification	12/15
Early action II	
Deadline	2/1
Notification	3/1
Regular	
Deadline	3/1
Notification	4/1
Nonfall registration?	yes

APPLICANTS ALSO LOOK AT AND OFTEN PREFER
Rhodes College, The University of Arkansas—Fayettville, University of Central Arkansas, The University of Tulsa, Trinity University

AND SOMETIMES PREFER
Austin College, Southwestern University, Tulane University, Washington University in St. Louis

FINANCIAL FACTS

Financial Aid Rating	82
Annual tuition	$31,740
Room and board	$9,086
Required fees	$300
Books and supplies	$900
% frosh rec. need-based scholarship or grant aid	66
% UG rec. need-based scholarship or grant aid	64
% frosh rec. non-need-based scholarship or grant aid	29
% UG rec. non-need-based scholarship or grant aid	20
% frosh rec. need-based self-help aid	37
% UG rec. need-based self-help aid	44
% frosh rec. any financial aid	100
% UG rec. any financial aid	100
% UG borrow to pay for school	89
Average cumulative indebtedness	$21,170

HILLSDALE COLLEGE

33 EAST COLLEGE STREET, HILLSDALE, MI 49242 • ADMISSIONS: 517-607-2327 • FAX: 517-607-2223

CAMPUS LIFE

Quality of Life Rating	84
Fire Safety Rating	87
Green Rating	60*
Type of school	private
Environment	village

STUDENTS

Total undergrad enrollment	1,326
% male/female	48/52
% from out of state	60
% from public high school	48
% live on campus	88
# of fraternities	4
# of sororities	3
% international	2
# of countries represented	8

SURVEY SAYS . . .
No one cheats
Great computer facilities
Students are friendly
Students are very religious
Campus feels safe
Low cost of living
Students are happy
Musical organizations are popular
Student publications are popular
Political activism is popular
Very little drug use

ACADEMICS

Academic Rating	95
% students graduating within 4 years	72
% students graduating within 6 years	76
Calendar	semester
Student/faculty ratio	10:1
Profs interesting rating	98
Profs accessible rating	95
Most common reg class size	10–19 students
Most common lab size	20–29 students

MOST POPULAR MAJORS
biology, business administration and management, education, history, politics, English

STUDENTS SAY ". . ."

Academics

"Tiny" Hillsdale College "provides a classic liberal arts education" "deeply rooted in our country's Greco-Roman and Christian Heritage." Students spend their time "reading dead guys," grappling with "timeless ideas," and "constantly fighting change." A "rigorous classical liberal arts education" includes mandatory courses on the Constitution, Western civilization, and the "great books" (stuff like *The Odyssey* and Dante's *Inferno*). "Writing skills are heavily addressed," and Hillsdale operates on the idea that "some things are worthy to be studied for their own sake, as beneficial for the formation of the complete human being, and not for the sake of what they produce." There's "no grade inflation" whatsoever, cautions a Spanish major, and there certainly "aren't any fluff classes at Hillsdale." While professors "demand a lot," they "have a genuine love for the things they study and the students they teach," and students have nothing but praise for the academic experience. The "extremely accessible" faculty is reportedly full of "profoundly enlightening, deep thinkers" who have "made the Hillsdale experience what it is, period." The administration is "well-organized" despite "periodic quirks"; many rules are severe. Management has "no qualms about keeping a close eye on the students." Also, you should be aware that "Hillsdale refuses to accept government money," making it "free from government control." Every scholarship and financial aid dime is privately funded. Don't worry, though, the average aid package is more than $12,000, thanks to "an expansive and highly dedicated donor base."

Life

Hillsdale's "rural" and "boring" location "almost makes it seem like a secret intellectual getaway," but mostly there's a lot to be desired. Consequently, the "beautiful" campus here "is the hub of social life." At Hillsdale, you have to live in a dormitory as a freshman and sophomore, but there are no coed dorms, and visitation hours are "strict." During the week, students tend to "take responsibility for their studies; we tend to place academics above other things," so free time is at a premium. "Virtually everyone is studying like mad." Nevertheless, students are "involved in many organizations" or often "make their own fun." Greek houses "are not only the best places to find parties on the weekends, but they house our campus leaders," and "are more focused on the core values of Greek life than many Greek organizations today." Religious groups are "prominent" as well. "Everyone goes out to support the athletes" in varsity sports, but "intramural sports are always popular" as well; there's also self-made fun like "campus-wide snowball fights, water balloon fights, dances, ping-pong tournaments, etc." "Everyone loves ideas and good debate." "Imagine a place where people name their dogs after economists [and] freshman have four-hour-long conversations about Kant and deontology." "We are not one of those evangelical schools that forbids alcohol," declares a junior. "Kegs and drinking games" are occasionally available, but most all hedonism "is done in moderation." For road trips, student often head about seventy miles northeast to the "real college town" of Ann Arbor.

Student Body

"Hillsdale prides itself on being one of the first colleges to openly accept anyone irrespective of nation, color, or sex." All the same, the population here is almost entirely composed of "white, upper-middle-class" students, and "most of our 'minority' students are actually from other countries." There are "leftish students" and plenty of people who don't go to church, but the "majority of our campus calls itself Christian" and "hold strong moral values." "There's a good libertarian crowd," too. However, Christianity, and right-wing politics dominate. "The typical student is religious and conservative," relates a sophomore. "That's the nature of the college." Students describe themselves as "well-mannered" "hard workers" who "are passionate about learning." Ten to twelve percent of students are home-schooled, so it's not hard to find "your homeschoolers who spend Friday night swing-dancing in the dorm." Greeks, athletes, and thespians constitute the other main cliques; though all of these groups may appear dramatically different on the surface, "There a general feeling of respect and friendship between all students."

FINANCIAL AID: 517-437-7341 • E-MAIL: ADMISSIONS@HILLSDALE.EDU/ADMISSIONS • WEBSITE: WWW.HILLSDALE.EDU

THE PRINCETON REVIEW SAYS

Admissions

Very important factors considered include: Academic GPA, rigor of secondary school record, standardized test scores, character/personal qualities, interview. *Important factors considered include:* Application essay, class rank, recommendation(s), extracurricular activities, level of applicant's interest, volunteer work, work experience. *Other factors considered include:* Alumni/ae relation, talent/ability. SAT or ACT required; ACT with writing component recommended. TOEFL required of all international applicants. High school diploma is required, and GED is accepted. *Academic units recommended:* 4 English, 4 mathematics, 3 science (1 science lab), 2 foreign language, 1 social studies, 2 history.

Financial Aid

Students should submit: Institution's own financial aid form. Regular filing deadline is March 15. The Princeton Review suggests that all financial aid forms be submitted as soon as possible after January 1. *Need-based scholarships/grants offered:* Private scholarships, school scholarship or grant aid from institutional funds. *Loan aid offered:* University loans from institutional funds. Applicants will be notified of awards on a rolling basis beginning February 15. Federal Work-Study Program available. Off-campus job opportunities are good.

Inside Word

Don't be fooled by Hillsdale's high acceptance rate. Only serious, solid candidates bother applying here and the academic profile of incoming freshmen is tremendous. While you don't have to be politically conservative to get in, a passionate and well-reasoned essay defending traditional values or singing the praises of free-market economics certainly can't hurt you.

THE SCHOOL SAYS " . . ."

From the Admissions Office

"Personal attention is a hallmark at Hillsdale. Small classes are combined with teaching professors who make their students a priority. The academic environment at Hillsdale will actively engage you as a student. Extracurricular activities abound at Hillsdale with the more than 100 clubs and organizations that offer excellent leadership opportunities. From athletics and the fine arts, to Greek life and community volunteer programs, you will find it difficult not to be involved in our thriving campus community. In addition, numerous study abroad programs, a conservation research venture in South Africa, a professional sales internship program with national placements and the Washington-Hillsdale Internship Program (WHIP) are just a few of the unique off-campus opportunities available to you at Hillsdale.

"Our strength as a college is found in our mission and in our curriculum. The core curriculum at Hillsdale contains the essence of the classical liberal arts education. Through it you are introduced to the history, the philosophical and theological ideas, the works of literature, and the scientific discoveries that set Western Civilization apart. As explained in our mission statement, 'the college considers itself a trustee of modern man's intellectual and spiritual inheritance from the Judeo-Christian faith and Greco-Roman culture, a heritage finding its clearest expression in the American experiment of self-government under law.'

"We seek students who are ambitious, intellectually active and who are ready to become leaders worthy of this heritage in their personal as well as professional lives.

"Applicants can meet admissions requirements by submitting the results of the SAT, or the ACT (writing section optional). We will use the student's best composite/combined score in the evaluation process. The SAT Subject Tests in literature and U.S. history are also recommended."

SELECTIVITY

Admissions Rating	93
# of applicants	1,865
% of applicants accepted	57
% of acceptees attending	39
# accepting a place on wait list	50
% admitted from wait list	10
# of early decision applicants	120
% accepted early decision	80

FRESHMAN PROFILE

Range SAT Critical Reading	630–740
Range SAT Math	570–700
Range SAT Writing	590–720
Range ACT Composite	26–31
Minimum paper TOEFL	570
Minimum computer TOEFL	210
Average HS GPA	3.75
% graduated top 10% of class	48
% graduated top 25% of class	77
% graduated top 50% of class	98

DEADLINES

Early decision	
Deadline	11/15
Notification	12/1
Early action	
Deadline	12/15
Notification	2/15
Regular	
Priority	2/15
Deadline	4/1
Nonfall registration?	yes

APPLICANTS ALSO LOOK AT

AND OFTEN PREFER
Grove City College, Hope College, Northwestern University, University of Dallas, University of Michigan—Ann Arbor, University of Notre Dame, Wheaton College (IL)

AND SOMETIMES PREFER
Albion College, Davidson College, Pepperdine University, Purdue University—West Lafayette, Taylor University, University of Nebraska at Omaha, University of North Carolina at Chapel Hill

AND RARELY PREFER
Colorado College, Kenyon College, Knox College, Pitzer College, University of California, Santa Barbara, Washington and Lee University, Wittenberg University

FINANCIAL FACTS

Financial Aid Rating	84
Annual tuition	$20,760
Room and board	$8,310
Required fees	$540
Books and supplies	$1,000
% frosh rec. need-based scholarship or grant aid	27
% UG rec. need-based scholarship or grant aid	29
% frosh rec. non-need-based scholarship or grant aid	76
% UG rec. non-need-based scholarship or grant aid	87
% frosh rec. need-based self-help aid	34
% UG rec. need-based self-help aid	33
% frosh rec. any financial aid	93
% UG rec. any financial aid	95
% UG borrow to pay for school	42
Average cumulative indebtedness	$15,570

HIRAM COLLEGE

PO Box 67, Hiram, OH 44234 • Admissions: 800-362-5280 • Fax: 330-569-5944

STUDENTS SAY ". . ."

Academics

Students come to Hiram College seeking "a very community-based environment" that provides "not only a feeling of immediate comfort but also the appeal of being in close relationship with my professors," and few leave disappointed. Undergrads here "love how involved all of the professors are into guiding the students through not just classes and majors, but future plans and career paths" and praise the "big-school opportunities in a small-school environment." As one student points out, "Undergrads can work in research with professors here, which is an invaluable skill and great for resumes." Students tell us Hiram boasts "a great biology program that does well getting its students into veterinary and medical school," a "great education program," and strong offerings in environmental science. Throughout the school "small classes of no more than thirty students and the intimate nature of the learning [environment] keep us from feeling lost in a sea of students." A "unique semester system splits terms into a twelve-week main session followed by a three-week intensive class. It gives you fewer classes to have to take all at once, and the three-week is a great opportunity for electives or study abroad trips that I couldn't do for a whole semester for financial reasons or because I can't spare that time away from my major."

Life

Most students concede that Hiram is "in the middle of nowhere," but not all see this as an insurmountable negative. On the contrary, many appreciate how the location "allows for us to meet together and create our own fun, make new friends, and enjoy the simplest pleasures in life. Hiram is especially fun in the winter, as we get tons of snow and have so many hills you [can] sled off. Everyone goes out at night and sleds together." Others "find unique things to do—stargazing, making our own apple cider, going to local square dances…we learn lots of cool things." Furthermore, "The school is excellent for providing the students with gatherings multiple times a week. Each club on campus is required to sponsor a campus-wide event each semester, and the student-run club, KCPB, is devoted to organizing as many on-campus and off-campus events as possible. Examples include movie nights in town, Destressfests before midterms and finals," Bowler First Fridays, talent shows, and game shows. While "drinking is prohibited in rooms where the resident is not twenty-one, and [the rule] is enforced," those looking to party usually can find the opportunity. Undergrads report "for the most part everyone is respectful. The students usually regulate each other and take care of issues when someone gets out of control."

Student Body

Hiram is "a gentle mix of athletes, artists, and scientists, and…Everyone gets along and respects what the others are capable of doing." The school "gets the rap of having 'weird' kids," which most here wear as a badge of honor. As one puts it, "The jocks can be philosophy majors, and the band geeks can be the people to hang out with on a Friday night…This place doesn't respect stereotypes." Though proud "each individual brings something unique and interesting to the community here," students are also quick to point out their commonalities. "All students do have a dedication to serving others, in varying degrees and…attempt to include themselves in the community in a variety of different ways (social groups, athletics, community service or social activism groups, student government, etc.)."

HIRAM COLLEGE

FINANCIAL AID: 330-569-5107 • E-MAIL: ADMISSION@HIRAM.EDU • WEBSITE: ADMISSION.HIRAM.EDU

THE PRINCETON REVIEW SAYS

Admissions
TOEFL required of all international applicants.

Financial Aid
Students should submit: FAFSA. The Princeton Review suggests that all financial aid forms be submitted as soon as possible after January 1. *Need-based scholarships/grants offered:* Federal Pell, SEOG, state scholarships/grants, private scholarships, school scholarship or grant aid from institutional funds, United Negro College Fund. *Loan aid offered:* Direct Subsidized Stafford, Direct Unsubsidized Stafford, Direct PLUS, Federal Perkins, university loans from institutional funds. Applicants will be notified of awards on a rolling basis beginning March 1.

The Inside Word
The typical Hiram admit performed solidly but not spectacularly in a college preparatory high school curriculum and earned above average but not stellar standardized test scores. Applicants seem to know whether they fit the Hiram profile, explaining the school's high admissions rate as few who don't stand a decent chance of getting in bother to apply. A thorough application review process allows hopefuls to make up for academic deficiencies with solid essays and/or strong recommendations. Admissions are rolling, a process that favors early applicants.

THE SCHOOL SAYS " . . . "

From the Admissions Office
"Hiram College offers distinctive programs that set us apart from other small, private liberal arts colleges. About half of Hiram's students study abroad at some point during their four years. In 2010, a group of students led by two faculty members traveled around the world to study climate change, stopping in nine different locations. Common study abroad destinations include France, China, Mexico, Guatemala, Costa Rica, the Galapagos Islands, and several African countries. Because Hiram students receive credits for the courses taught by Hiram faculty on these trips, studying abroad will not impede progress in their majors or delay graduation.

"Another unique aspect of a Hiram education is our academic calendar, known as the Hiram Plan. Our semesters are divided into twelve-week and three-week periods. Students usually enroll in three courses during each twelve-week, and one intensive course during the three-week. Many students spend the three-week on study abroad trips or taking unusual courses not typically offered during the twelve-week. Our small classes encourage interaction between students and their professors. Students can work with professors on original research projects and often participate in musical groups and intramural sports teams alongside faculty members.

"The Hiram College Tuition Guarantee ensures that the annual cost for tuition will not increase between the first year a student is enrolled and the student's senior year."

SELECTIVITY
Admissions Rating	76
# of applicants	1,513
% of applicants accepted	75
% of acceptees attending	29

FRESHMAN PROFILE
Range SAT Critical Reading	480–610
Range SAT Math	470–590
Range ACT Composite	20–26
Minimum paper TOEFL	550
Average HS GPA	3.30
% graduated top 10% of class	18
% graduated top 25% of class	42
% graduated top 50% of class	79

DEADLINES
Regular	
Deadline	12/20

APPLICANTS ALSO LOOK AT
AND SOMETIMES PREFER
John Carroll University, The College of Wooster

AND RARELY PREFER
Kent State University—Kent Campus

FINANCIAL FACTS
Financial Aid Rating	60*
Annual tuition	$26,435
Room and board	$9,010
Required fees	$700
Books and supplies	$700
Average cumulative indebtedness	$21,247

HOBART AND WILLIAM SMITH COLLEGES

629 SOUTH MAIN STREET, GENEVA, NY 14456 • ADMISSIONS: 315-781-3472 • FAX: 315-781-3471

CAMPUS LIFE

Quality of Life Rating	66
Fire Safety Rating	87
Green Rating	90
Type of school	private
Environment	village

STUDENTS

Total undergrad enrollment	2,138
% male/female	45/55
% from out of state	56
% from public high school	60
% live on campus	90
# of fraternities	5
% African American	4
% Asian	2
% Caucasian	63
% Hispanic	4
% international	4
# of countries represented	18

SURVEY SAYS . . .
No one cheats
Great computer facilities
Career services are great
Dorms are like palaces
Students are happy
Everyone loves the Statesmen
Lots of beer drinking
Hard liquor is popular

ACADEMICS

Academic Rating	86
% students graduating within 4 years	70
% students graduating within 6 years	75
Calendar	semester
Student/faculty ratio	11:1
Profs interesting rating	86
Profs accessible rating	88
Most common reg class size	10–19 students
Most common lab size	10–19 students

MOST POPULAR MAJORS
economics, political science, psychology

STUDENTS SAY "..."

Academics

Hobart and William Smith Colleges together are "a college that is large enough to provide a wide variety of majors, yet small enough that your professors are able to know you by your name." Students enjoy "small class sizes, [the] feel of community," a "unique liberal arts curriculum, gorgeous campus...[and] one of the country's best study abroad programs." "Everyone knows everyone" at this very small school located right on central New York's Seneca Lake. "Hobart and William Smith College has the most incredible campus community I've ever seen," one student boasts, although beware of the "cold winters!" "There are countless opportunities for involvement [at HWS] such as internships, study abroad, athletics, clubs, and student activities." Because of the small size, the "absolutely fantastic faculty" "knows, remembers, and cares about all their students." "The best thing about the professors here is that they are always accessible outside of class, either with office hours or constant e-mail communication." However, some students caution that while many professors are "amazing," others are "awful and really should not be teaching." Students did feel the school "needs to work on really trying to make environmental sustainability an actual issue on campus." In summary, HWS is "a small, liberal arts college where the professors' first priority is their students," and there's a *gorgeous lake* outside [your] window!"

Life

"Life at HWS is very comfortable," and "Students fit in by being friendly and spending a lot of money on partying." "People either love HWS or they hate it," one psychology student explains. "Life here is centered almost entirely around the social aspects of the college experience, which is fine, to a point, but it doesn't allow for deeper intellectual rigor." "People think about partying a lot, and on this campus it happens a lot" especially "at frats (there are no sororities) and at on-campus houses." On the weekends, there are "wild woods parties, house parties, frats, a quiet movie night, stargazing, jazz...you can find it all on a Saturday night." Another student laments, "There isn't much to do on weekends. The Campus Activities Board is good at the occasional big event...but there should be more events throughout the year," although the "school-sponsored events are actually enjoyable" when they do occur. Although many students complain about the campus food options, luckily "there are places to [get] good off-campus food and movies in walking distance." Make sure to bring your thickest winter coats, because HWS life slows down during the "endless winter" that "sometimes starts as early as October and can yield snow as late as mid-May."

Student Body

"The males here tend to be 'bros' for the most part, and the women are referred to as 'smithies,'" which means that "they carry expensive bags and wear big sunglasses, and are usually pretty skinny (or at least dress like they think they are)." "'Ho Bros,' the typical Hobart student, will join one of the six frats, own at least one pair of pants in the color 'Nantucket Red,' and probably drive a nicer car than most faculty." However, students caution that "there are always exceptions to the rule" "who don't fit these stereotypes and actually enjoy mocking them." Most students are "WASPs" or "preppy" and "white," and students feel that HWS needs to do more to create a more diverse student body from America and bring in more international students as well. Students in different populations "hardly mingle," and students "tend to stay in separate circles." "North Face and Uggs are far more rampant among the student body now than [the traditional HWS look of] Polo, Lily Pulitzer, and Lacoste."

HOBART AND WILLIAM SMITH COLLEGES

FINANCIAL AID: 315-781-3315 • E-MAIL: ADMISSIONS@HWS.EDU • WEBSITE: WWW.HWS.EDU

THE PRINCETON REVIEW SAYS

Admissions

Very important factors considered include: Rigor of secondary school record. *Important factors considered include:* Academic GPA, application essay, recommendation(s), character/personal qualities, interview, volunteer work, work experience. *Other factors considered include:* Class rank, standardized test scores, alumni/ae relation, extracurricular activities, first generation, geographical residence, level of applicant's interest, racial/ethnic status, talent/ability. ACT with or without writing component accepted. TOEFL required of all international applicants. High school diploma is required, and GED is accepted. *Academic units required:* 4 English, 3 mathematics, 3 science (2 science labs), 2 foreign language, 2 social studies, 2 academic elective. *Academic units recommended:* 3 foreign language, 3 social studies, 4 academic elective.

Financial Aid

Students should submit: FAFSA, CSS/Financial Aid PROFILE. Regular filing deadline is March 1. The Princeton Review suggests that all financial aid forms be submitted as soon as possible after January 1. *Need-based scholarships/grants offered:* Federal Pell, SEOG, state scholarships/grants, private scholarships, school scholarship or grant aid from institutional funds. *Loan aid offered:* Direct Subsidized Stafford, Direct Unsubsidized Stafford, Direct PLUS, Federal Perkins, state loans, university loans from institutional funds. Federal Work-Study Program available. Off-campus job opportunities are good.

The Inside Word

Applicants to the academic side of Seneca Lake's scene shores should know that HWS likes to see a student who embraces a challenge. They recommend that hopefuls prepare for a rigorous college curriculum by taking at least two years of a foreign language and a couple of AP courses for good measure.

THE SCHOOL SAYS " . . ."

From the Admissions Office

"Hobart and William Smith Colleges seek students with a sense of adventure and a commitment to the life of the mind. Inside the classroom, students find the academic climate to be rigorous, with a faculty that is deeply involved in teaching and working with them. Outside, they discover a supportive community that helps to cultivate a balance and hopes to foster an integration among academics, extracurricular activities, and social life. Hobart and William Smith, as coordinate colleges, have an awareness of gender differences and equality and are committed to respect and a celebration of diversity.

"Freshman applicants are required to take either the ACT with or without the optional writing portion or the SAT. Their highest composite score will be used in admissions decisions. Students are encouraged to submit results of any SAT Subject Test they have taken."

SELECTIVITY

Admissions Rating	84
# of applicants	4,682
% of applicants accepted	62
% of acceptees attending	21
# accepting a place on wait list	96
% admitted from wait list	4
# of early decision applicants	251
% accepted early decision	85

FRESHMAN PROFILE

Range SAT Critical Reading	560–650
Range SAT Math	560–640
Range ACT Composite	25–28
Minimum paper TOEFL	550
Minimum computer TOEFL	220
Minimum web-based TOEFL	80
% graduated top 10% of class	43
% graduated top 25% of class	78
% graduated top 50% of class	97

DEADLINES

Early decision	
Deadline	11/15
Notification	12/15
Regular	
Deadline	2/1
Nonfall registration?	no

APPLICANTS ALSO LOOK AT AND OFTEN PREFER
Colgate University

AND SOMETIMES PREFER
Dickinson College, Gettysburg College, Skidmore College, St. Lawrence University

AND RARELY PREFER
University of Vermont

FINANCIAL FACTS

Financial Aid Rating	91
Annual tuition	$40,592
Room and board	$10,458
Required fees	$1,118
Books and supplies	$1,300
% frosh rec. need-based scholarship or grant aid	73
% UG rec. need-based scholarship or grant aid	72
% frosh rec. non-need-based scholarship or grant aid	1
% UG rec. non-need-based scholarship or grant aid	1
% frosh rec. need-based self-help aid	61
% UG rec. need-based self-help aid	61
% frosh rec. any financial aid	80
% UG rec. any financial aid	76
% UG borrow to pay for school	82
Average cumulative indebtedness	$29,932

HOFSTRA UNIVERSITY

ADMISSIONS CENTER, BERNON HALL, HEMPSTEAD, NY 11549 • ADMISSIONS: 516-463-6700 • FAX: 516-463-5100

STUDENTS SAY ". . ."

Academics

Hofstra University, "the most prestigious private university on Long Island," according to students, is "large enough to feel part of something big but small enough to feel a sense of community." Students say the size is just right, providing "admirable" class sizes that "are perfect for nurturing relationships with professors." Hofstra undergraduates are especially bullish on the undergraduate business program and the communications and broadcast journalism programs. The latter are "anchored by [an]…award-winning radio station" and numerous other "opportunities to get hands-on experience in various aspects of broadcast [journalism]." All programs benefit from the school's proximity to New York City, which affords not only "top-notch…guest speakers and lecturers to the university" but also abundant "career-making connections to [your chosen] profession through internships and opportunities." Students also love Hofstra's music and theater programs, but most students look toward more reliably remunerative professions. As one student puts it, "This school is about successfully preparing its students for their professional careers as effectively and efficiently as possible." The rewards here are especially great for go-getters. One student explains, "Hofstra provides all of the opportunities that a college student can ask for," but "Many students don't take advantage of them, so it allows relatively easy access to some amazing programs if you have the drive."

Life

Hofstra "is generally considered a party school," students concede, "but it is easy to avoid that if you want to." Many students "go to the bars and pubs that are around college campus" to blow off steam, or "if not, they make parties at their dorms when their RA is away and invite people over to play beer pong." Greek organizations on campus are "really enjoyable," hosting "fundraisers and activities," not to mention the occasional house party. For those seeking alternatives, "There are several malls and movie theaters nearby, the train station is ten minutes away, and it's only about a half hour ride into NYC, and Nassau Coliseum is also right next door so there are always concerts and events. Jones Beach is also very close and popular when [the weather] is nice." The Student Center Theater shows "popular films that are out of the theaters but not yet released on DVD almost every weekend." College sporting events are less popular—"Our teams aren't great," one student concedes—and the school recently dropped its football program to save money. Hometown Hempstead "is a bit of a bust." Not only is there "nothing to do" in town, but students perceive it as "an area of depression and crime…The campus itself is generally quite safe, but that safety does not extend very far past the limits of the campus." Fortunately, safer destinations are nearby and easily accessible by car or public transportation.

Student Body

You will certainly find examples of the Long Island stereotype here, kids who are into "buying expensive brands that display their logo on their clothing," sport "fake tans, fake hair, and fake personalities," and are "primarily concerned with drinking, getting laid, and finishing their business degrees." But while these may be the most conspicuous students on campus at Hofstra, they hardly make up the entire student body. Opinions differ on whether they are "only a slight majority" or an even smaller percentage, but most here agree that there's plenty of room for everyone. One student explains that "As Hofstra positions itself as a national institution, geographic diversity as well as nontraditional student populations have grown." Another adds, "There is a sizable group of atypical students who hang out with the other atypical students like themselves." Their ranks include "the free-spirited hippies, the metal heads, the guys who just like sports but don't play, and the people who are actually here to study. They fit in because this minority (albeit it's a big one) all acts similarly."

FINANCIAL AID: 516-463-6680 • E-MAIL: ADMITME@HOFSTRA.EDU • WEBSITE: WWW.HOFSTRA.EDU

THE PRINCETON REVIEW SAYS

Admissions

Very important factors considered include: Academic GPA, application essay, class rank, recommendation(s), rigor of secondary school record, standardized test scores. *Important factors considered include:* Character/personal qualities, extracurricular activities, interview, talent/ability. *Other factors considered include:* Alumni/ae relation, geographical residence, level of applicant's interest, racial/ethnic status, volunteer work, work experience. ACT with writing component required. TOEFL required of all international applicants. High school diploma is required, and GED is accepted. *Academic units required:* 4 English, 3 mathematics, 3 science (1 science lab), 2 foreign language, 3 social studies. *Academic units recommended:* 4 mathematics, 4 science (2 science labs), 3 foreign language, 4 social studies.

Financial Aid

Students should submit: FAFSA and state aid form. Filing deadline is rolling. The Princeton Review suggests that all financial aid forms be submitted as soon as possible after January 1. *Need-based scholarships/grants offered:* Federal Pell, SEOG, state scholarships/grants, private scholarships, school scholarship or grant aid from institutional funds. *Loan aid offered:* Direct Subsidized Stafford, Direct Unsubsidized Stafford, Direct PLUS, Federal Perkins, state loans, university loans from institutional funds. Applicants will be notified of awards on a rolling basis beginning March 1. Federal Work-Study Program available. Off-campus job opportunities are excellent.

The Inside Word

Hofstra is aggressive about filling its incoming class as quickly as possible, offering two rounds of early action and rolling admissions. This is a process that favors those who apply early, so you'd do well to get your application in here as soon as possible.

THE SCHOOL SAYS " . . ."

From the Admissions Office

"Hofstra is a university on the rise. When you step onto campus you feel the energy and sense the momentum of a university building a national reputation as a center for academic excellence.

"At Hofstra, you'll find an outstanding faculty dedicated to teaching, and small classes, averaging just fewer than twenty students. Outside the classroom, you'll find a multitude of study abroad options, a vibrant extracurricular life, and amazing internship opportunities and cultural experiences in nearby New York City.

"The Hofstra campus—so beautiful it is recognized as an arboretum—features new and cutting-edge teaching facilities. At Hofstra, you will share your classrooms and residence halls with students from nearly every U.S. state and more than seventy countries.

"Students applying for admission may submit either SAT or ACT scores, and an essay is required. The admission team at Hofstra realizes that each applicant is unique and gives each one individual attention."

SELECTIVITY

Admissions Rating	87
# of applicants	18,909
% of applicants accepted	59
% of acceptees attending	13
# accepting a place on wait list	339
% admitted from wait list	32

FRESHMAN PROFILE

Range SAT Critical Reading	530–620
Range SAT Math	540–630
Range ACT Composite	24–27
Minimum paper TOEFL	550
Minimum computer TOEFL	213
Minimum web-based TOEFL	80
Average HS GPA	3.46
% graduated top 10% of class	27
% graduated top 25% of class	59
% graduated top 50% of class	84

DEADLINES

Early action	
Deadline	11/15
Notification	12/15
Regular	
Notification	rolling
Nonfall registration?	yes

APPLICANTS ALSO LOOK AT

AND OFTEN PREFER
Boston University, New York University, Syracuse University

AND SOMETIMES PREFER
Fordham University, Penn State—University Park, Quinnipiac University, State University of New York—Stony Brook

AND RARELY PREFER
Rutgers, The State University of New Jersey, St. John's University, University of Massachusetts Amherst

FINANCIAL FACTS

Financial Aid Rating	68
Annual tuition	$30,750
Room and board	$11,710
Required fees	$1,050
Books and supplies	$1,000
% frosh rec. need-based scholarship or grant aid	61
% UG rec. need-based scholarship or grant aid	53
% frosh rec. non-need-based scholarship or grant aid	9
% UG rec. non-need-based scholarship or grant aid	6
% frosh rec. need-based self-help aid	52
% UG rec. need-based self-help aid	50
% frosh rec. any financial aid	93
% UG rec. any financial aid	85
% UG borrow to pay for school	68

HOLLINS UNIVERSITY

PO Box 9707, Roanoke, VA 24020-1707 • Admissions: 800-456-9595 • Fax: 540-362-6218

CAMPUS LIFE

Quality of Life Rating	79
Fire Safety Rating	76
Green Rating	83
Type of school	private
Environment	city

STUDENTS

Total undergrad enrollment	759
% male/female	0/100
% from out of state	43
% from public high school	79
% live on campus	78
% African American	1
% Asian	1
% Caucasian	76
% Hispanic	4
% Native American	1
% international	4
# of countries represented	14

SURVEY SAYS . . .
No one cheats
Great library
Low cost of living
Frats and sororities are unpopular
or nonexistent
Student government is popular

ACADEMICS

Academic Rating	87
% students graduating within 4 years	58
% students graduating within 6 years	63
Calendar	4-1-4
Student/faculty ratio	11:1
Profs interesting rating	91
Profs accessible rating	86
Most common reg class size	10–19 students
Most common lab size	fewer than 10 students

MOST POPULAR MAJORS
English language and literature, psychology, studio art, business, biology

STUDENTS SAY ". . ."

Academics
"Tiny," all-female Hollins University "drips in" "unique traditions" and offers "an intimate atmosphere" that "feels like a community or family, not an institution." Students assure us that "a Hollins education is inspiring and nothing short of life-changing." There are fabulous opportunities to study abroad. Double-majors are mundane. Among the thirty or so majors available here, the "strong English program" is especially notable. The creative writing program in particular is "one of the nation's best." Classes are small and extremely "interactive." "The discussions in class will start slowly," observes an English major, "but they'll suddenly be out of the teacher's control the next minute." "Don't go if you didn't do the readings," adds a physics major. "Professors pour so much time into their students," relates a studio art major. They "want to hear from their students" and "are always more than willing to help." The staff in the financial aid office, on the other hand, can sometimes be "unwilling to help."

Life
Students at Hollins "adore the school." Life on this "gorgeous" and "peaceful" campus is "a unique amalgam of individualistic zaniness and required academic hustle and bustle." "People are very concerned about homework." "Sleepless nights during weekdays" aren't uncommon. At the same time, the student community is "hugely strong." "Hollins really embodies the concept of sisterhood." "Everyone comes together for" a throng of "crazy and not-so-crazy traditions." "It isn't uncommon to put on odd costumes or break into songs or see seniors in decorated robes. It's hard to explain these things other than to say, 'it's a Hollins thing.'" In the fall, the school president cancels morning classes and declares Tinker Day. "Everyone dresses up in wacky costumes, everything from a wetsuit to a prom dress, and hikes Tinker Mountain." Ring Night ("the best weekend of your life") and faculty Christmas caroling are a couple other noteworthy traditions. Hollins is also home to "amazing extracurriculars" including "a great horseback riding program." "There is a high level of student involvement" across the board, and "there is always something happening on campus." Lectures, concerts, and recitals are abundant. The theater program "is excellent, and the shows are always worth going to." "There are several sub-cultures people can fit into"—everything from intercollegiate athletics to a surprisingly strong anime contingent. "If you want to attend frat parties and keggers, it is very easy with the number of coed universities nearby," but "this isn't the typical 'party school.'" "Life at Hollins is walking down the dorm hall with all the dorm doors open and girls running down the hall to each other's rooms to talk and have fun or do homework together," explains one student. "The friends we make here are still going to be our sisters long after we have gone out into the world to accomplish what our experience at Hollins gave us the courage to do." "The dorms are hospitable but old." "Every now and then, the food is great and wonderful" but, for the gourmand, meals here general have some room for improvement.

Student Body
The women of Hollins describe themselves as "empowered, enthusiastic," "worldly, aware," "strong, and confident." "There are all sorts at Hollins: horse girls, anime girls, art majors, writers, filmmakers, bio students, dancers, feminists, scientists." The gay and transgender population is "large." "The glory of Hollins is that there is seldom a stereotype," agrees another student. "There is no mold that any student must fit, regardless of what activities and groups you are involved in. It is a place to be yourself." "Odd ducks" proliferate. "You name it; you see it (minus males, that is)." "Everyone is so different, and everyone is so amazingly tolerant of everyone's differences." However, some students can be "clique-y and exclusive." "Most people are involved in several clubs and organizations so it's easy to have a very diverse group of friends," describes one student.

FINANCIAL AID: 540-362-6332 • E-MAIL: HUADM@HOLLINS.EDU • WEBSITE: WWW.HOLLINS.EDU

THE PRINCETON REVIEW SAYS

Admissions

Very important factors considered include: Academic GPA, standardized test scores. *Important factors considered include:* Application essay, recommendation(s), talent/ability. *Other factors considered include:* Class rank, rigor of secondary school record, alumni/ae relation, character/personal qualities, extracurricular activities, first generation, interview, level of applicant's interest, volunteer work, work experience. SAT or ACT required; ACT with or without writing component accepted. TOEFL required of all international applicants. High school diploma is required, and GED is accepted. *Academic units required:* 4 English, 3 mathematics, 3 science, 3 foreign language, 3 social studies.

Financial Aid

Students should submit: FAFSA. The Princeton Review suggests that all financial aid forms be submitted as soon as possible after January 1. *Need-based scholarships/grants offered:* Federal Pell, SEOG, state scholarships/grants, private scholarships, school scholarship or grant aid from institutional funds. *Loan aid offered:* Direct Subsidized Stafford, Direct Unsubsidized Stafford, Direct PLUS, Federal Perkins, university loans from institutional funds. Applicants will be notified of awards on a rolling basis beginning March 1. Federal Work-Study Program available. Off-campus job opportunities are good.

The Inside Word

While the overall stats at Hollins are solid, the admit rate is high, and gaining admission won't be terrifically difficult if you have decent test scores and above-average grades. Keep in mind, though, that the applicants here are a highly self-selecting group and the admissions staff is able to take a long look at everyone who applies. Consequently, your best bet is to demonstrate a sincere desire to be a part of the unique milieu on this campus.

THE SCHOOL SAYS "..."

From the Admissions Office

"Hollins University's slogan, 'Women who are going places start at Hollins,' endures because it captures what this independent liberal arts institution means to its students. Hollins has been a motivating force for women to go places creatively, intellectually, and geographically since it was founded over 165 years ago. As Hollins graduate and Pulitzer Prize–winner Annie Dillard said, Hollins is a place 'where friendships thrive, minds catch fire, careers begin, and hearts open to a world of possibility.'

"Hollins offers majors in twenty-seven fields. While perhaps best known for its creative writing discipline, the university features strong programs in the visual and performing arts (especially dance) and the social and physical sciences. Hollins also has an innovative general education program called Education Through Skills and Perspectives (ESP). In ESP, students acquire knowledge across the curriculum. One of the most sought-after programs at Hollins is the Batten Leadership Institute, a comprehensive curricular program designed to maximize each student's leadership style and potential and teach her skills she will use both now and in the future. It is the only program of its kind in the nation.

"Hollins was among the first colleges in the nation to offer an international study abroad program. Today, almost half of Hollins' students—many times the national average—study abroad. Internship opportunities are another of Hollins' distinctions. Thanks to an active, dedicated network of alumnae and friends of the university, sixty-five percent of Hollins seniors put their education to work with a diverse group of organizations.

"Hollins' slogan underscores the most important question each student is asked from the moment she arrives until the day she leaves, and it is asked by her professors, her peers, and especially by herself: 'Where do you want to go?'"

SELECTIVITY

Admissions Rating	79
# of applicants	687
% of applicants accepted	89
% of acceptees attending	30
# accepting a place on wait list	2
% admitted from wait list	0
# of early decision applicants	65
% accepted early decision	68

FRESHMAN PROFILE

Range SAT Critical Reading	500–640
Range SAT Math	470–590
Range SAT Writing	480–620
Range ACT Composite	21–27
Minimum paper TOEFL	550
Minimum computer TOEFL	213
Minimum web-based TOEFL	79
Average HS GPA	3.45
% graduated top 10% of class	24
% graduated top 25% of class	54
% graduated top 50% of class	76

DEADLINES

Early decision	
Deadline	12/1
Notification	12/15
Regular	
Priority	2/1
Notification	12/15
Nonfall registration?	yes

FINANCIAL FACTS

Financial Aid Rating	79
Annual tuition	$30,220
Room and board	$10,670
Required fees	$575
% frosh rec. need-based scholarship or grant aid	83
% UG rec. need-based scholarship or grant aid	80
% frosh rec. non-need-based scholarship or grant aid	72
% UG rec. non-need-based scholarship or grant aid	40
% frosh rec. need-based self-help aid	81
% UG rec. need-based self-help aid	73
% frosh rec. any financial aid	99
% UG rec. any financial aid	96
% UG borrow to pay for school	80
Average cumulative indebtedness	$19,982

HOWARD UNIVERSITY

2400 Sixth Street Northwest, Washington, D.C. 20059 • Admissions: 202-806-2755 • Fax: 202-806-4465

CAMPUS LIFE
Quality of Life Rating	62
Fire Safety Rating	94
Green Rating	60*
Type of school	private
Environment	metropolis

STUDENTS
Total undergrad enrollment	7,086
% male/female	34/66
% from out of state	97
% from public high school	80
% live on campus	56
# of fraternities	10
# of sororities	8
% African American	49
% Hispanic	1
% international	4
# of countries represented	86

SURVEY SAYS . . .
Students are happy
Frats and sororities dominate social scene
Musical organizations are popular
College radio is popular
Student publications are popular
Student government is popular
Political activism is popular

ACADEMICS
Academic Rating	73
% students graduating within 4 years	46
% students graduating within 6 years	65
Calendar	semester
Student/faculty ratio	8:1
Profs interesting rating	63
Profs accessible rating	61
Most common reg class size	fewer than 10 students
Most common lab size	10–19 students

MOST POPULAR MAJORS
biology

STUDENTS SAY ". . ."

Academics

Howard University, which students proclaim as "the Mecca of black education," has a storied history and an excellent location (ideal for students seeking internships and post-graduation job placements) to "prepare students for the future through academic integrity and social enterprise." Recruiters flock to the Howard campus, in part because "academically, Howard is very strong" and in part because "the university has connections all across the country. Howard does a great job of bringing those connections to campus." Undergrads here report, "The academic experience largely depends on what you major in. If you're going for African-American studies, business, or dentistry, you'll get what you've paid for." The presence of a college of medicine (and its affiliated hospital) bolsters offerings in life sciences and premedical studies as well. Students caution, "Facilities are outdated and need a major technological and physical update," and "The administration needs some work." Though students say, "There are great, qualified people in places of high authority," many feel that the administration at large is "not transparent in the decision making process." Some add, they can be "very disorganized, and you must be extremely patient to deal with the entire financial aid process." However, students universally agree, "The professors at Howard are the best! They truly care about their students, and they want everyone to succeed."

Life

"We always, always, always have something going on" on the "very active" Howard campus. There are "hundreds of organizations that tailor to any needs you can think of," and students are "very active politically and socially, so there are rallies and there are parties. Each and every extreme is met with its opposite here." There's "always somewhere to go" on campus, "whether it be the Punchout Cafe to hang with your friends, Power Hall to relax, study and work with your friends, to 'the yard' to chill and people watch, [or] to the gym to work out. If you are isolated on Howard's campus it is because you choose to be." The world awaiting off campus is even more active. As one student explains, "There is so much to do in the Washington, D.C., area that there is rarely any room for boredom. Georgetown, Chinatown, and Pentagon City are just a few of the places that students go." Adams Morgan is another popular destination. No need to bring a car here. "Everything we would want to go to is Metro-accessible so there's no problem moving about D.C. as if we've lived here our whole lives." Fun is typically confined to weekends, as "Many of us work very hard during the week. Sunday through Thursday, we stay on campus and focus on getting schoolwork done and attending any organizational meetings or events."

Student Body

The typical Howard student "is African American with a deep desire toward success." Undergrads are "extremely serious about their career goals and their academic achievement," and "very involved in political activism, campus organizations, and community." Although nearly all black, the student population "is extremely diverse. I sit in classes with people from Spain, England, Trinidad and Tobago, South Africa, Nigeria, Alaska, etc." Students "come from all walks of life. You can find people with different religious beliefs, ethnic origins, and sexual preferences. There are students with interests in every field imaginable. Howard represents the black world."

HOWARD UNIVERSITY

FINANCIAL AID: 202-806-2820 • E-MAIL: ADMISSION@HOWARD.EDU • WEBSITE: WWW.HOWARD.EDU

THE PRINCETON REVIEW SAYS

Admissions

Very important factors considered include: Class rank, rigor of secondary school record, standardized test scores. *Important factors considered include:* Recommendation(s), character/personal qualities. *Other factors considered include:* Application essay, alumni/ae relation, extracurricular activities, talent/ability, volunteer work, work experience. SAT or ACT required; ACT with writing component required. TOEFL required of all international applicants. High school diploma is required, and GED is accepted. *Academic units required:* 4 English, 2 mathematics, 2 science, 2 foreign language, 2 social studies, 2 history. *Academic units recommended:* 4 English, 3 mathematics, 4 science (2 science labs), 2 foreign language, 2 social studies, 2 history.

Financial Aid

Students should submit: FAFSA. Regular filing deadline is August 15. The Princeton Review suggests that all financial aid forms be submitted as soon as possible after January 1. *Need-based scholarships/grants offered:* Federal Pell, SEOG, state scholarships/grants, private scholarships, school scholarship or grant aid from institutional funds, Federal Nursing Scholarships. *Loan aid offered:* Direct Subsidized Stafford, Direct Unsubsidized Stafford, Direct PLUS, Federal Perkins, Federal Nursing Loans. Applicants will be notified of awards on a rolling basis beginning April 1. Federal Work-Study Program available. Off-campus job opportunities are excellent.

The Inside Word

A large applicant pool and graduation rate of those who enroll is a combination that adds up to selectivity at Howard. The school is willing to give applicants a pass on standardized test scores if their high school records indicate seriousness about, and the ability to handle, advanced study.

THE SCHOOL SAYS ". . ."

From the Admissions Office

"Since its founding, Howard has stood among the few institutions of higher learning where blacks and other minorities have participated freely in a truly comprehensive university experience. Thus, Howard has assumed a special responsibility in preparing its students to exercise leadership wherever their interests and commitments take them. Howard has issued approximately 111,233 degrees, diplomas, and certificates to men and women in the professions, the arts and sciences, and the humanities. The university has produced and continues to produce a high percentage of the nation's African American professionals in the fields of medicine, dentistry, pharmacy, engineering, nursing, architecture, religion, law, music, social work, education, and business. There are more than 10,036 students from across the nation and approximately eighty-five countries and territories attending the university. Their varied customs, cultures, ideas, and interests contribute to Howard's international character and vitality. More than 1,598 faculty members represent the largest concentration of black scholars in any single institution of higher education.

"All applicants who have never been to college are required to submit scores from either the SAT or the ACT (with the writing component)."

SELECTIVITY

Admissions Rating	89
# of applicants	9,750
% of applicants accepted	49
% of acceptees attending	31

FRESHMAN PROFILE

Range SAT Critical Reading	470–670
Range SAT Math	460–680
Range SAT Writing	430–670
Range ACT Composite	19–29
Minimum paper TOEFL	550
Minimum computer TOEFL	213
Average HS GPA	3.20
% graduated top 10% of class	26
% graduated top 25% of class	55
% graduated top 50% of class	84

DEADLINES

Early decision	
Deadline	11/1
Notification	12/24
Early action	
Deadline	11/1
Notification	12/24
Regular	
Priority	11/1
Deadline	2/15
Nonfall registration?	yes

APPLICANTS ALSO LOOK AT
AND OFTEN PREFER
Hampton University, Morehouse College, Spelman College

AND SOMETIMES PREFER
Florida A&M University, University of Maryland—College Park

FINANCIAL FACTS

Financial Aid Rating	63
Annual tuition	$15,270
Room and board	$7,966
Required fees	$805
Books and supplies	$2,000
% frosh rec. need-based scholarship or grant aid	32
% UG rec. need-based scholarship or grant aid	38
% frosh rec. non-need-based scholarship or grant aid	4
% UG rec. non-need-based scholarship or grant aid	15
% frosh rec. need-based self-help aid	24
% UG rec. need-based self-help aid	21
% frosh rec. any financial aid	96
% UG rec. any financial aid	96
% UG borrow to pay for school	80
Average cumulative indebtedness	$16,473

ILLINOIS INSTITUTE OF TECHNOLOGY

10 WEST THIRTY-THIRD STREET, CHICAGO, IL 60616 • ADMISSIONS: 312-567-3025 • FAX: 312-567-6939

STUDENTS SAY ". . ."

Academics

Known for its "rigorous academics," "small student-to-teacher ratio," plentiful "research opportunities," and "great financial aid," Illinois Institute of Technology draws students interested in engineering, business, architecture, and the sciences. The curriculum here is focused on "developing technically oriented, yet well-rounded professionals." In addition to its "reputation as a premier engineering school," IIT boasts "one of the best architecture schools in the nation." Designed by Mies Van der Rohe, "The campus has an amazing architectural heritage and continues to foster the growth of cutting-edge, contemporary practice." "Studying architecture in Chicago [is]…a really big incentive," and the program prepares students for the "'real world,' giving not only an aesthetic education in design, but also a technical understanding of structure." The computer engineering program at IIT is also "very good," and "Finding research opportunities is not difficult (even as a freshman)," says one. For the most part, professors are lauded as "very accessible, easy to talk to," and "very knowledgeable"; "My teachers all know me by name, [and] I have the confidence to ask questions in class," one student tells us. "We have recently had many changes in our administration, including a new president, new provost, new chairman of the board of trustees, and three new deans to various colleges/departments. Overall, these changes have been incredibly positive. We have a female Dean of Engineering, and our new president cares passionately about students."

Life

"Life" at IIT "is busy, [and] homework comes first." As one student points out, "The college experience, no matter where you are, is what *you* make of it yourself." Says another, "You can spend all your time not doing anything and being unhappy with life, but with IIT there are so many opportunities to get involved… from programming events such as homecoming, to fundraising for Habitat for Humanity trips to Haiti and even relief efforts in the United States." "There is usually something to do, whether a planned event or random excursion to the city." Students take advantage of nearby Chicago, where they enjoy "the parks, the pier, Michigan Ave., ethnic restaurants, orchestra hall, etc." A serious-minded group of burgeoning engineers, "Occasionally we drink…and go out for parties, but not [so] much." For a more relaxed night of socializing, students congregate at the "BOG, a place inside the school where there are shows and different activities like bowling." In addition, "The Student Activities Center always has discounted movie tickets, and every weekend they try to have some planned event, including group tickets to musicals, plays, and shows." For sports fans, "There are intramural tournaments that are sponsored by the school, programs such as yoga and Pilates also sponsored by the school, a gym with hours that are suitable for a typical student's schedule, and clubs for tennis and other sports." Students' biggest complaint is the food. Though the "large cafeteria has many food options," "they are all always mediocre at best."

Student Body

At IIT the student body is "focused, smart, and quirky." Says one student, IIT is comprised of "geeky tech people who are always crazy busy, never sleep, but still find time to party." "The typical student spends a lot of time in class, and even more time studying." IIT offers "a very diverse population not just ethnically but when it comes to different interests." "There are many international students from various parts of the world, many architect students who are very different from the engineers and computer science majors, plus students from the Vandercook School of Music, making [for an] unbelievably diverse student body." Despite the fact that "students are the most diverse in the entire United States," "Everyone gets along and fits in." One student jokes, "We all share common ground in that we're nerdy."

FINANCIAL AID: 312-567-7219 • E-MAIL: ADMISSION@IIT.EDU • WEBSITE: WWW.IIT.EDU

THE PRINCETON REVIEW SAYS

Admissions

Very important factors considered include: Academic GPA, rigor of secondary school record. *Important factors considered include:* Application essay, class rank, recommendation(s), standardized test scores. *Other factors considered include:* Alumni/ae relation, character/personal qualities, extracurricular activities, first generation, interview, level of applicant's interest, talent/ability, volunteer work, work experience. ACT with writing component recommended. TOEFL required of all international applicants. High school diploma is required, and GED is accepted. *Academic units required:* 4 English, 4 mathematics, 3 science (2 science labs), 2 foreign language, 2 social studies. *Academic units recommended:* 4 English, 4 mathematics, 3 science (2 science labs), 2 foreign language, 2 social studies, 2 history, 1 visual/performing arts, 1 computer science.

Financial Aid

Students should submit: FAFSA. The Princeton Review suggests that all financial aid forms be submitted as soon as possible after January 1. *Need-based scholarships/grants offered:* Federal Pell, SEOG, state scholarships/grants, private scholarships, school scholarship or grant aid from institutional funds. *Loan aid offered:* Federal Perkins, university loans from institutional funds. Applicants will be notified of awards on a rolling basis beginning March 15. Federal Work-Study Program available. Off-campus job opportunities are good.

The Inside Word

Students at IIT say it's "easy to get in, tough to get out," but the term "easy" is deceptive in this case. With applicants concurrently looking to MIT and CalTech, IIT remains highly competitive in relation to the vast majority of undergraduate institutions. Few bother applying here unless they suspect they can handle the demanding curriculum. In essence, the admissions pool is somewhat self-selecting. Only the extremely bright and/or extremely ambitious apply. According to the admissions office, "All students are evaluated for significant merit-based scholarships upon admission."

THE SCHOOL SAYS ". . ."

From the Admissions Office

"IIT is committed to providing students a distinctive and relevant education through hands-on learning, dedicated teachers, small class sizes, and under-graduate research opportunities. Classes are taught by senior faculty—not teaching assistants—who foster our culture of innovation with their own firsthand research experience.

"Students are immersed in our interdisciplinary approach to learning through the team-based, creative problem-solving experience of the Interprofessional Projects Program (IPROs). The Office of Undergraduate Research provides mentored collaborative research experiences for undergraduates. Our entre-preneurship program challenges students to develop start-up technology companies. University Technology Park at IIT, a business incubator located on campus, supports this challenge by providing numerous opportunities to work with companies at every stage of growth, from conception to sophistica-tion. The Leadership Academy teaches leadership skills that advance students in their personal and professional development. "IIT's location in the world-class city of Chicago gives students priceless access to the professional world through internships and employment. The university's own diverse student population mirrors the global work environment faced by all graduates.

"First year students applying for admission into the entering class are required to submit an SAT or ACT score. We will use the student's best scores from either test. Subject tests are accepted, but not required. "It is highly recommended that trans-fer applicants have completed thirty credit hours and have taken calculus and/or physics. Both first-year and transfer students are evaluated for significant merit based scholarships upon admission."

SELECTIVITY

Admissions Rating	90
# of applicants	2,295
% of applicants accepted	64
% of acceptees attending	27
# of early decision applicants	57
% accepted early decision	75

FRESHMAN PROFILE

Range SAT Critical Reading	520–670
Range SAT Math	610–740
Range SAT Writing	520–650
Range ACT Composite	25–31
Minimum paper TOEFL	550
Minimum computer TOEFL	213
Minimum web-based TOEFL	80
Average HS GPA	3.92
% graduated top 10% of class	43
% graduated top 25% of class	74
% graduated top 50% of class	96

DEADLINES

Early decision	
Deadline	11/1
Notification	12/1
Early action	
Deadline	2/1
Notification	2/1
Regular	
Priority	2/10
Notification	10/1
Nonfall registration?	yes

APPLICANTS ALSO LOOK AT

AND OFTEN PREFER
Northwestern University, University of Illinois at Urbana-Champaign

AND SOMETIMES PREFER
Purdue University—West Lafayette, University of Illinois at Chicago, University of Minnesota—Twin Cities

AND RARELY PREFER
Loyola University of Chicago, Milwaukee School of Engineering

FINANCIAL FACTS

Financial Aid Rating	78
Annual tuition	$33,800
Room and board	$10,338
Required fees	$1,080
Books and supplies	$1,000
% frosh rec. need-based scholarship or grant aid	66
% UG rec. need-based scholarship or grant aid	61
% frosh rec. non-need-based scholarship or grant aid	12
% UG rec. non-need-based scholarship or grant aid	6
% frosh rec. need-based self-help aid	47
% UG rec. need-based self-help aid	48
% frosh rec. any financial aid	100
% UG rec. any financial aid	99

ILLINOIS WESLEYAN UNIVERSITY

PO Box 2900, Bloomington, IL 61702-2900 • Admissions: 309-556-3031 • Fax: 309-556-3820

CAMPUS LIFE

Quality of Life Rating	76
Fire Safety Rating	78
Green Rating	75
Type of school	private
Environment	city

STUDENTS

Total undergrad enrollment	2,088
% male/female	42/58
% from out of state	12
% from public high school	81
% live on campus	75
# of fraternities	6
# of sororities	5
% African American	5
% Asian	4
% Caucasian	75
% Hispanic	3
% international	4
# of countries represented	23

SURVEY SAYS . . .

Lab facilities are great
Great computer facilities
Great library
Athletic facilities are great
Low cost of living
Musical organizations are popular

ACADEMICS

Academic Rating	88
% students graduating within 4 years	77
% students graduating within 6 years	81
Calendar	4-1-4
Student/faculty ratio	11:1
Profs interesting rating	86
Profs accessible rating	87
Most common reg class size	10–19 students
Most common lab size	10–19 students

MOST POPULAR MAJORS

business/commerce, English language and literature, psychology

STUDENTS SAY ". . ."

Academics

Illinois Wesleyan, a "small school...with the prestige and academic diversity of a larger institution," is "extremely intense academically," students warn. Some—especially those in the sciences—go so far as to bemoan the "unreasonably hard classes," but most "love that at the end of the day you always have dozens of peers to support you and remind you that you'll get through it." Supportive professors "genuinely care about each student's success," which also helps, as do the "almost limitless resources" that allow undergraduates "to do anything and everything that interests them, both in and out of the classroom." Because "there are no graduate students" here, undergraduates are "given many opportunities that wouldn't exist at a larger university." One student reports, "As a sophomore psychology major, I'm gaining valuable lab experience that will prepare me for a career in research. Academic and leadership opportunities are abundant here." The school's relatively small size doesn't hamper its ability to excel in numerous disciplines. Students lavish praise on the "very competitive and very reputable biology program," the "great science program," the "prestigious" accounting program, a "reputable" nursing program, a "stellar music program," and a "highly acclaimed" theater department. Smaller academic departments utilize "adjunct professors from Illinois State" to deliver program requirements. "The anthropology department, for example, has only two full-time professors, but it is still able to tailor classes to specific student requests via ISU adjuncts."

Life

Life at IWU is workload-driven. Students with good time-management skills (or less challenging majors) "involve themselves in extracurricular activities while developing a strong academic background both inside and out[side] of their major's subject area," but others immerse themselves in academics and "only see the light of day when walking between classes. Studying is like breathing to [some] students here, they can't even imagine what it would be like to be able to stop for more than a few minutes." Many here tell us that "Greek life is very strong at this school," as are athletics. "Sports events are big here," one student writes. "This town is literally full of...people that live for Wesleyan athletics, which gives it a good homegrown feel when you are there." Hometown Bloomington, which IWU shares with Illinois State University, "is not exactly a hot spot" but it does have "a lot of bars that are popular with the upperclassmen." On campus, "Music and theater productions are extremely popular...and for a good reason: They're really good!" When all else fails, "Conversation is never lacking, and even on the nights when people can't find entertainment, late night discussions about anything—the Cold War, hypothetical zombie apocalypse, what matters most in life, or simply favorite meals—can be some of the most memorable moments of your college experience."

Student Body

"It's hard to describe a typical Wesleyan student," students tell us, observing "we are all so different. I suppose we are all dedicated to academic success, but you really have everything from bookworms to typical sorority girls to artsy people and athletes. Everyone fits in well together, however, regardless of being so different from one another." If there is a prevailing demographic, it is "an impressive student from...the Chicago suburbs." The number of international students here "is increasing almost exponentially," one undergraduate tells us, "and these students manage to fit in very well, although sometimes [they form a] cohort with fellow international students (which happens everywhere, it seems)."

ILLINOIS WESLEYAN UNIVERSITY

FINANCIAL AID: 309-556-3096 • E-MAIL: IWUADMIT@TITAN.IWU.EDU • WEBSITE: WWW.IWU.EDU

THE PRINCETON REVIEW SAYS

Admissions

Very important factors considered include: Academic GPA, rigor of secondary school record, interview. *Important factors considered include:* Application essay, class rank, standardized test scores, character/personal qualities, extracurricular activities, talent/ability. *Other factors considered include:* Recommendation(s), alumni/ae relation, first generation, geographical residence, level of applicant's interest, racial/ethnic status, state residency, volunteer work, work experience. SAT or ACT required; ACT with or without writing component accepted. TOEFL required of all international applicants. High school diploma is required, and GED is accepted. *Academic units recommended:* 4 English, 3 mathematics, 3 science (2 science labs), 3 foreign language, 2 social studies.

Financial Aid

Students should submit: FAFSA, institution's own financial aid form. The Princeton Review suggests that all financial aid forms be submitted as soon as possible after January 1. *Need-based scholarships/grants offered:* Federal Pell, SEOG, state scholarships/grants, private scholarships, school scholarship or grant aid from institutional funds. *Loan aid offered:* Direct Subsidized Stafford, Direct Unsubsidized Stafford, Direct PLUS, Federal Perkins, Federal Nursing Loans, university loans from institutional funds. Applicants will be notified of awards on a rolling basis beginning March 1. Federal Work-Study Program available. Off-campus job opportunities are good.

The Inside Word

There's no application fee at IWU, and the school accepts the Common Application (with the IWU Common Application Supplement, which asks for your intended major and includes an essay question about your reasons for wanting to attend IWU), so there are few reasons to not apply to IWU if you're even slightly interested in attending. Don't expect to breeze through, though. You won't get into this highly selective college without a solid academic profile or a compelling story.

THE SCHOOL SAYS ". . ."

From the Admissions Office

"Illinois Wesleyan University attracts a wide variety of students who are interested in pursuing diverse fields such as vocal performance, biology, psychology, German, physics, or business administration. At IWU, students are not forced into either/or choices. Rather, they are encouraged to pursue multiple interests simultaneously—a philosophy that is in keeping with the spirit and value of a liberal arts education. The distinctive 4-4-1 calendar allows students to follow their interests each school year in two semesters followed by an optional month-long class in May. May term opportunities include classes on campus; research collaboration with faculty; travel and study in such places as Australia, China, South Africa, and Europe; as well as local, national, and international internships. Study abroad is very popular, with one out of every two students enjoying a travel experience.

"The IWU mission statement reads in part: 'A liberal education at Illinois Wesleyan fosters creativity, critical thinking, effective communication, strength of character, and a spirit of inquiry; it deepens the specialized knowledge of a discipline with a comprehensive world view. It affords the greatest possibilities for realizing individual potential while preparing students for democratic citizenship and life in a global society…The university, through its policies, programs, and practices, is committed to diversity, social justice, and environmental sustainability. A tightly knit, supportive university community, together with a variety of opportunities for close interaction with excellent faculty, both challenges and supports students in their personal and intellectual development.'"

SELECTIVITY

Admissions Rating	92
# of applicants	3,395
% of applicants accepted	62
% of acceptees attending	28
# accepting a place on wait list	59
% admitted from wait list	17

FRESHMAN PROFILE

Range SAT Critical Reading	570–695
Range SAT Math	575–695
Range ACT Composite	26–31
Minimum paper TOEFL	550
Minimum computer TOEFL	213
Average HS GPA	3.82
% graduated top 10% of class	44
% graduated top 25% of class	80
% graduated top 50% of class	99

DEADLINES

Early action	
Deadline	11/15
Notification	1/15
Regular	
Notification	1/15
Nonfall registration?	yes

APPLICANTS ALSO LOOK AT
AND OFTEN PREFER
Northwestern University, University of Notre Dame
AND SOMETIMES PREFER
University of Illinois at Urbana-Champaign, Washington University in St. Louis
AND RARELY PREFER
Augustana College (IL)

FINANCIAL FACTS

Financial Aid Rating	89
Annual tuition	$35,076
Room and board	$8,106
Required fees	$180
Books and supplies	$780
% frosh rec. need-based scholarship or grant aid	71
% UG rec. need-based scholarship or grant aid	68
% frosh rec. non-need-based scholarship or grant aid	10
% UG rec. non-need-based scholarship or grant aid	9
% frosh rec. need-based self-help aid	57
% UG rec. need-based self-help aid	56
% frosh rec. any financial aid	98
% UG rec. any financial aid	94
% UG borrow to pay for school	68
Average cumulative indebtedness	$31,904

INDIANA UNIVERSITY—BLOOMINGTON

300 NORTH JORDAN AVENUE, BLOOMINGTON, IN 47405-1106 • ADMISSIONS: 812-855-0661 • FAX: 812-855-5102

CAMPUS LIFE
Quality of Life Rating	90
Fire Safety Rating	83
Green Rating	96
Type of school	public
Environment	city

STUDENTS
Total undergrad enrollment	31,892
% male/female	50/50
% from out of state	31
% live on campus	36
# of fraternities	38
# of sororities	25
% African American	4
% Asian	4
% Caucasian	78
% Hispanic	3
% international	7
# of countries represented	137

SURVEY SAYS . . .
Great computer facilities
Great off-campus food
Students are happy
Everyone loves the Hoosiers
Student publications are popular
Hard liquor is popular

ACADEMICS
Academic Rating	73
% students graduating within 4 years	49
% students graduating within 6 years	71
Calendar	semester
Student/faculty ratio	19:1
Profs interesting rating	78
Profs accessible rating	83
Most common reg class size	20–29 students
Most common lab size	20–29 students

MOST POPULAR MAJORS
business, exploratory biology,
journalism, psychology

STUDENTS SAY ". . ."

Academics
Indiana University is a "Big Ten research university that offers a huge variety of classes and majors (even allowing students to create their own) with a surprisingly diverse student body that allows anybody to fit in regardless of whether they enjoy partying or are interested in the Greek system. " Although some think of IU as "a party school with an active Greek population"—an image students reinforce when they insist that IU is "about going to massive parties...and getting the job done, but not being defined by schoolwork"— most students appreciate both the academic and social aspects of the school, telling us that IU offers "the best combination of academics and extracurriculars one could ask for in a school." IU's "world renowned" business school is taught by professors who "are at the top of their respective fields of expertise. They have a lot to teach us, and they are almost universally excellent at doing so." An equally acclaimed music school and a language department that "has everything from the romance languages to Urdu, Haitian Creole, and Tibetan" also draw students' attention. Many majors require students to hold an internship before graduating, so "you really have to be self-motivated, since IUB is one hour away from a metropolitan area. Although being in this town has its social benefits, it definitely makes it tougher as you prepare for life after college."

Life
"Every day is a new and exciting experience at Indiana University," where "there is too much going on all of the time." The campus is alive with lectures, art exhibits, theatrical and musical shows, and the school's beloved intercollegiate athletics. "We spend a lot of time thinking about basketball and football, depending obviously on the season," students tell us. You don't have to look hard to find a party here, and "a lot of people tend to get drunk as entertainment," but that's hardly the only option, and many pass four happy years here outside the party scene. Undergrads love hometown Bloomington, "a great city to live in" with "amazing cultural events, such as the Lotus World Music Festival and Chocolate Fest" along with "lots of little stores demonstrating their own niches and a wide range of different authentic-ish ethnic restaurants." Campuswide traditions such as Little 500, a party "at the end of the year when the whole campus stops what they're doing to attend concerts, parties, and the men's and women's bike races," help cement a strong sense of school spirit.

Student Body
While "most IU students are white and come from a middle-class background," the school's "international and minority student populations are growing, and there are a lot of services available to help minority students feel comfortable on campus." Those who aren't native Hoosiers are most often Chicagoans or East Coasters from New York and New Jersey, although IU attracts students from all fifty states and 137 countries. The school is big enough to accommodate many personality types: "some Greeks, some who are academically oriented, some who enjoy and actively pursue the arts, and others who enjoy sports such as IU basketball...small cultures exist within the larger IU culture." There are "a lot of students who come to IU with the intention of partying all the time, and rarely studying," but most don't last long; those who "work hard all week and worship the weekends," on the other hand, can and often do thrive here.

FINANCIAL AID: 812-855-0321 • E-MAIL: IUADMIT@INDIANA.EDU • WEBSITE: WWW.IUB.EDU

THE PRINCETON REVIEW SAYS

Admissions

Very important factors considered include: Academic GPA, class rank, rigor of secondary school record. *Important factors considered include:* Standardized test scores. *Other factors considered include:* Application essay, recommendation(s), alumni/ae relation, character/personal qualities, extracurricular activities, first generation, geographical residence, interview, level of applicant's interest, racial/ethnic status, state residency, talent/ability. SAT or ACT required; ACT with writing component required. High school diploma is required, and GED is accepted. *Academic units required:* 4 English, 3 science (2 science labs), 2 foreign language, 3 social studies, 3.5 math (with trigonometry, pre-calculus, or calculus required). *Academic units recommended:* Please see the IU website.

Financial Aid

Students should submit: FAFSA. Regular filing deadline is March 10. The Princeton Review suggests that all financial aid forms be submitted as soon as possible after January 1. *Need-based scholarships/grants offered:* Federal Pell, SEOG, state scholarships/grants, private scholarships, school scholarship or grant aid from institutional funds. *Loan aid offered:* Direct Subsidized Stafford, Direct Unsubsidized Stafford, Direct PLUS, Federal Perkins, university loans from institutional funds. Applicants will be notified of awards on a rolling basis beginning April 1. Federal Work-Study Program available. Off-campus job opportunities are good.

The Inside Word

Above-average high school performers (defined by both grade point average and test scores) should meet little resistance from the IU admissions office. Students will have the opportunity to meet admissions representatives at numerous recruiting events held in many locations throughout the country or during a campus visit. Rolling admissions favor those who apply early in the process. IU's music program is highly competitive; admission hinges upon a successful audition.

THE SCHOOL SAYS " . . ."

From the Admissions Office

"Indiana University—Bloomington, one of America's great teaching and research universities, extends learning and teaching beyond the walls of the traditional classroom. When visiting campus, students and parents typically describe IU as 'what a college should look and feel like.' Students bring their diverse experiences, beliefs, and backgrounds from all fifty states and 137 countries, which adds a richness and diversity to life at IU—a campus often cited as one of the most beautiful in the nation. Indiana University—Bloomington truly offers a quintessential college town, campus, and overall experience. Students enjoy all of the advantages, opportunities, and resources that a larger school can offer, while still receiving personal attention and support. Because of the variety of outstanding academic and cultural resources, students at IU have the best of both worlds.

"Indiana offers more than 5,000 courses and 183 undergraduate majors, of which many are known nationally and internationally. IU—Bloomington is known worldwide for outstanding programs in the arts, sciences, humanities, and social sciences as well as for highly rated Schools of Business, Music, Education, Journalism, Optometry; Public and Environmental Affairs; and Health, Physical Education, and Recreation. Students can customize academic programs with double and individualized majors, internships, and research opportunities, while utilizing state-of-the-art technology. Representatives from more than 1,000 businesses, government agencies, and not-for-profit organizations come to campus each year to recruit IU students.

"IUB requires the SAT the ACT with writing component. The university will use the writing sections to determine possible credit, placement, or exemption from writing requirements. All application materials for admission must be submitted online or postmarked by November 1 for Automatic Academic Scholarship consideration."

SELECTIVITY

Admissions Rating	88
# of applicants	36,719
% of applicants accepted	69
% of acceptees attending	28
# accepting a place on wait list	0

FRESHMAN PROFILE

Range SAT Critical Reading	520–630
Range SAT Math	540–650
Range ACT Composite	24–29
Average HS GPA	3.61
% graduated top 10% of class	38
% graduated top 25% of class	74
% graduated top 50% of class	97

DEADLINES

Regular	
Priority	4/1
Notification	rolling
Nonfall registration?	yes

FINANCIAL FACTS

Financial Aid Rating	80
Annual in-state tuition	$8,124
Annual out-of-state tuition	$26,785
Room and board	$7,918
Required fees	$904
Books and supplies	$812
% frosh rec. need-based scholarship or grant aid	37
% UG rec. need-based scholarship or grant aid	32
% frosh rec. non-need-based scholarship or grant aid	7
% UG rec. non-need-based scholarship or grant aid	4
% frosh rec. need-based self-help aid	27
% UG rec. need-based self-help aid	3
% UG borrow to pay for school	55
Average cumulative indebtedness	$27,752

INDIANA UNIVERSITY OF PENNSYLVANIA

117 SUTTON HALL, INDIANA, PA 15705 • ADMISSIONS: 724-357-2230 • FAX: 724-357-6281

CAMPUS LIFE

Quality of Life Rating	63
Fire Safety Rating	88
Green Rating	62
Type of school	public
Environment	village

STUDENTS

Total undergrad enrollment	12,827
% male/female	44/56
% from out of state	6
% live on campus	34
# of fraternities	15
# of sororities	14
% African American	10
% Asian	1
% Caucasian	79
% Hispanic	2
% international	3
# of countries represented	71

SURVEY SAYS . . .
Great computer facilities
Frats and sororities dominate
social scene
Student publications are popular
Lots of beer drinking
Hard liquor is popular

ACADEMICS

Academic Rating	62
Calendar	semester
Student/faculty ratio	18:1
Profs interesting rating	76
Profs accessible rating	75
Most common	
reg class size	20–29 students
Most common	
lab size	10–19 students

MOST POPULAR MAJORS
criminology, nursing, psychology,
communication media

STUDENTS SAY

Academics

"An affordable school that has something to offer everyone," Indiana University of Pennsylvania serves up "excellent academic programs" that are "academically challenging but not impossible if you make an honest effort." "Music, nursing, and education are the school's greatest strengths," one student says. Others laud the "fantastic fine arts program"; IUP's "very good College of Business;" and solid programs in theater, mathematics, chemistry, criminology, and English. Students here enjoy "awesome professors" who are "concerned with [students'] welfare and academic growth," and the students find their teachers "ridiculously easy to get into contact with—no need to make an appointment." The vast majority of students here are firmly focused on their post-graduation earning potential; they tell us that the school "is about learning to be the best at your career in the future." Students with higher intellectual and academic ambitions usually find their way into the Robert E. Cook Honors College, which "teaches students to think critically, participate in cultural events, and take active roles in the global community." The program has "fewer than 100 students in the freshman class, which means that we can have very small classes. Our professors know who we are and are able to give us more individual attention than would be possible with a larger group."

Life

Indiana, Pennsylvania, is the kind of town John Mellencamp would sing about—small, working-class, but not without its charms or bars. In fact, some claim the town "has a lot to offer kids to do. Malls, skating rinks, restaurants, movie theaters, ice hockey rinks, sports events, and campus events keep most of the students busy." Others aren't so sure; one writes, "Indiana is a small town with little to do, especially in the winter, when we get a lot of snow," which is why "people drink," and "when we aren't drinking, we think about the next time we will be drinking." Students concede that "Sometimes IUP gets a bad rap being known as a party school," but they point out that "college is all what you make it. The academic programs are exceptional," and those students "who want no alcohol/drugs involved in their college life whatsoever" will find options available to them, including trips to town, "movies and games," and "outdoor activities when the weather is nice." The school also boasts a "good selection of clubs" that provide a quick way "to meet people." If you need a taste of city life, "Pittsburgh is an hour away by car" and has "lots to do."

Student Body

Most IUP undergrads "are from the surrounding small towns," which are "predominantly white," but the school remains "more diverse" than the region (although "less diverse than U.S. Census percentage numbers") by drawing from other areas, including the city of Pittsburgh. Students describe the population as "very mixed," affording "the opportunity to interact with more people" than they would at "many other colleges." "No matter what your interest is, it wouldn't be too hard to find someone that you can share this interest with," one student tells us. Students view themselves as "down-to-earth" and pragmatic; as one explains, "This is the kind of school where intellectual growth is not the primary concern; it seems as if people are interested in getting a degree to get a better job...The few that are here for intellectual growth and enlightenment suffer from an apathetic community."

INDIANA UNIVERSITY OF PENNSYLVANIA

FINANCIAL AID: 724-357-2218 • E-MAIL: ADMISSIONS-INQUIRY@IUP.EDU • WEBSITE: WWW.IUP.EDU

THE PRINCETON REVIEW SAYS

Admissions

Very important factors considered include: Academic GPA, standardized test scores. *Important factors considered include:* Rigor of secondary school record. *Other factors considered include:* Application essay, class rank, recommendation(s), extracurricular activities. SAT or ACT required; ACT with or without writing component accepted. TOEFL required of all international applicants. High school diploma is required, and GED is accepted. *Academic units recommended:* 3 English, 3 mathematics, 3 science, 2 foreign language, 3 social studies.

Financial Aid

Students should submit: FAFSA. The Princeton Review suggests that all financial aid forms be submitted as soon as possible after January 1. *Need-based scholarships/grants offered:* Federal Pell, SEOG, state scholarships/grants, private scholarships, school scholarship or grant aid from institutional funds, United Negro College Fund. *Loan aid offered:* Direct Subsidized Stafford, Direct Unsubsidized Stafford, Direct PLUS, Federal Perkins. Applicants will be notified of awards on a rolling basis beginning March 15. Federal Work-Study Program available. Off-campus job opportunities are good.

The Inside Word

IUP serves a dual mission: to provide low-cost higher education to as broad a range of students as possible and to maintain rigorous academic standards. Accordingly, admissions aren't as competitive here as they are at other top schools; students with above-average secondary school records and average or better standardized test scores are likely admits here. Once in, middling students better be prepared to step up their game, or they will soon find themselves on their way out the door.

THE SCHOOL SAYS " . . ."

From the Admissions Office

"At IUP, we look at each applicant as an individual, not as a number. That means we'll review your application materials very carefully. When reviewing applications, the admissions committee's primary focus is on the student's high school record and SAT scores. In addition, the committee often reviews the optional personal essay and letters of recommendations submitted by the student to help aid in the decision-making process. We're always happy to speak with prospective students. Call us toll-free at 800-422-6830 or 724-357-2230, or e-mail us at admissions-inquiry@iup.edu.

"Students applying for admission are required to take the SAT or ACT."

SELECTIVITY

Admissions Rating	69
# of applicants	12,114
% of applicants accepted	60
% of acceptees attending	25

FRESHMAN PROFILE

Range SAT Critical Reading	440–530
Range SAT Math	450–540
Range SAT Writing	420–520
Minimum paper TOEFL	500
Minimum computer TOEFL	173
% graduated top 10% of class	9
% graduated top 25% of class	26
% graduated top 50% of class	59

DEADLINES

Regular	
Notification	9/15
Nonfall registration?	yes

FINANCIAL FACTS

Financial Aid Rating	67
Annual in-state tuition	$5,804
Annual out-of-state tuition	$14,510
Room and board	$9,300
Required fees	$1,767
Books and supplies	$1,100
% frosh rec. need-based scholarship or grant aid	52
% UG rec. need-based scholarship or grant aid	51
% frosh rec. non-need-based scholarship or grant aid	25
% UG rec. non-need-based scholarship or grant aid	15
% frosh rec. need-based self-help aid	69
% UG rec. need-based self-help aid	65
% frosh rec. any financial aid	75
% UG rec. any financial aid	78
% UG borrow to pay for school	83
Average cumulative indebtedness	$27,477

IOWA STATE UNIVERSITY

100 ENROLLMENT SERVICES, AMES, IA 50011-2011 • ADMISSIONS: 515-294-5836 • FAX: 515-294-2592

CAMPUS LIFE

Quality of Life Rating	91
Fire Safety Rating	80
Green Rating	88
Type of school	public
Environment	town

STUDENTS

Total undergrad enrollment	23,104
% male/female	56/44
% from out of state	25
% from public high school	91
% live on campus	46
# of fraternities	33
# of sororities	19
% African American	2
% Asian	3
% Caucasian	79
% Hispanic	3
% international	8
# of countries represented	103

SURVEY SAYS . . .
Low cost of living
Student publications are popular

ACADEMICS

Academic Rating	71
% students graduating within 4 years	39
% students graduating within 6 years	70
Calendar	semester
Student/faculty ratio	18:1
Profs interesting rating	69
Profs accessible rating	72
Most common reg class size	20–29 students
Most common lab size	20–29 students

MOST POPULAR MAJORS
finance, marketing, mechanical engineering

STUDENTS SAY ". . ."

Academics

Iowa State University holds true to its initial mission of providing affordable, practical education with a special focus on agriculture. Today, the school remains "a great agriculture school" with "a great food science program" and a strong pre-veterinary program. Students also proudly tout its status as "one of the top engineering schools" in the region (offering noteworthy support for women engineers) and the home to a "strong architecture program." Students praise this "large university with a small-town feel," telling us that "I felt like I could find a home here and be exposed to almost limitless opportunities." Throughout the curriculum, "There are a lot of opportunities for student research and 'hands on' learning;" so many, in fact, that some students claim ISU is "the best 'outside of class' university in the nation." Undergrads also appreciate a strong support network; one explains, "There are so many services on campus to help students, it is almost unreal. From tutoring to study sessions and counseling to mock interviews and resumé building, ISU offers a wide variety of services to students." The faculty "is one of ISU's strengths. If students take a chance and get to know their professors and other staff members, they make a great professional connection [with someone who] will bend over backwards, whether it be as a professional reference or helping fund a trip. The faculty really is here for students." Likewise, career services "are excellent" and offer such pluses as "one of the largest engineering career fairs."

Life

"Life at Iowa State can be as great as you want to make it," with more than "600 clubs and organizations" plus "a large intramural program, great crowds at athletic events, various free events, and many ways to get involved in leadership positions." Intercollegiate athletics are quite popular; "There's always a great turnout for big events," and "oftentimes the discussions around campus are [about] football or other sports. Very rarely do you find a group of people discussing world issues." Just for fun students enjoy recreational and surrounding community activities."Hometown Ames is no bustling metropolis; the population "doubles with students around, and the city has adapted to this increase. That said, there is always plenty to do throughout the year. Many students take advantage of the dollar theater (which is actually $1.50) or attend events on campus." Ames also has some "unique restaurants," and Cyride (the bus system that is operated by the city and university) offers students free transportation to mostly everywhere in Ames." Students agree that "the campus is really beautiful."

Student Body

As at many big schools, "It is hard to describe a typical student at Iowa State because there are many styles of students." "Every stereotype is here; sorority girl/frat boy, farmer kid, international student, nerd, computer geek, socially awkward, [and] goth. Iowa State has every kind of person." Iowa is a conservative state, and ISU has a large agricultural student population. The "population of out-of-state students seems to be growing," and "there is a diversity of international students" filling out the ranks as well, so most students can find a niche at ISU, and fortunately "Everyone here is laid-back and easygoing," so the overall vibe is live-and-let-live.

FINANCIAL AID: 515-294-2223 • E-MAIL: ADMISSIONS@IASTATE.EDU • WEBSITE: WWW.IASTATE.EDU

THE PRINCETON REVIEW SAYS

Admissions

Very important factors considered include: Academic GPA, class rank, rigor of secondary school record, standardized test scores. *Other factors considered include:* Application essay, recommendation(s), character/personal qualities, extracurricular activities, geographical residence, interview, state residency, talent/ability, volunteer work, work experience. SAT or ACT required; ACT with or without writing component accepted. TOEFL required of all international applicants. High school diploma is required, and GED is accepted. *Academic units required:* 4 English, 3 mathematics, 3 science (2 science labs), 2 foreign language, 2 social studies. *Academic units recommended:* 4 English, 4 mathematics, 4 science (3 science labs), 3 foreign language, 4 social studies.

Financial Aid

Students should submit: FAFSA. Regular filing deadline is March 1. The Princeton Review suggests that all financial aid forms be submitted as soon as possible after January 1. *Need-based scholarships/grants offered:* Federal Pell, SEOG, TEACH, state scholarships/grants, school scholarship or grant aid from institutional funds. *Loan aid offered:* Federal Direct Subsidized Stafford, Direct Unsubsidized Stafford, Direct PLUS, Federal Perkins, university loans from institutional funds. Applicants will be notified of awards on a rolling basis beginning April 1. Federal Work-Study Program available. Off-campus job opportunities are excellent.

The Inside Word

Admission to ISU is formula-driven and based on: ACT composite score; high school GPA; high school percentile rank; and number of high school courses completed in the core subject areas. The formula, known as the Regent Admission Index (RAI), is as follows: RAI = (2 × ACT composite score) + (1 × percentile high school rank) + (20 × high school grade point average) + (5 × number of years of high school courses completed in the core subject areas). Anyone earning an RAI score of at least 245 is automatically admitted; the admissions office reviews applicants scoring below 245 individually to determine which will also be admitted.

THE SCHOOL SAYS "..."

From the Admissions Office

"Iowa State University offers all the advantages of a major university along with the friendliness and warmth of a residential campus. There are more than 100 undergraduate programs of study in the Colleges of Agriculture and Life Sciences, Business, Design, Human Sciences, Engineering, Liberal Arts and Sciences, and Veterinary Medicine. Our 1,700 faculty members include Rhodes Scholars, Fulbright Scholars, and National Academy of Sciences and National Academy of Engineering members. Recognized for its high quality of life, Iowa State has taken practical steps to make the university a place where students feel like they belong. Iowa State has been recognized for the high quality of campus life and the exemplary out-of-class experiences offered to its students. Along with a strong academic experience, students also have opportunities for further developing their leadership skills and interpersonal relationships through any of the more than 700 student organizations, sixty intramural sports, and a multitude of arts and recreational activities."

SELECTIVITY
Admissions Rating	83
# of applicants	15,066
% of applicants accepted	81
% of acceptees attending	38

FRESHMAN PROFILE
Range SAT Critical Reading	460–640
Range SAT Math	530–670
Range ACT Composite	22–28
Minimum paper TOEFL	530
Minimum web-based TOEFL	71
Average HS GPA	3.54
% graduated top 10% of class	29
% graduated top 25% of class	61
% graduated top 50% of class	92

DEADLINES
Regular	
Deadline	7/1
Notification	rolling
Nonfall registration?	yes

APPLICANTS ALSO LOOK AT AND OFTEN PREFER
Purdue University—West Lafayette, University of Illinois at Urbana-Champaign, University of Minnesota—Twin Cities, University of Wisconsin—Madison

FINANCIAL FACTS
Financial Aid Rating	82
Annual in-state tuition	$6,102
Annual out-of-state tuition	$17,668
Room and board	$7,472
Required fees	$895
Books and supplies	$1,014
% frosh rec. need-based scholarship or grant aid	54
% UG rec. need-based scholarship or grant aid	54
% frosh rec. non-need-based scholarship or grant aid	27
% UG rec. non-need-based scholarship or grant aid	26
% frosh rec. need-based self-help aid	40
% UG rec. need-based self-help aid	45
% frosh rec. any financial aid	87
% UG rec. any financial aid	79
% UG borrow to pay for school	69
Average cumulative indebtedness	$30,062

ITHACA COLLEGE

953 Danby Road, Ithaca, NY 14850-7002 • Admissions: 607-274-3124 • Fax: 607-274-1900

CAMPUS LIFE

Quality of Life Rating	80
Fire Safety Rating	81
Green Rating	97
Type of school	private
Environment	town

STUDENTS

Total undergrad enrollment	6,382
% male/female	44/56
% from out of state	56
% from public high school	83
# of fraternities	3
# of sororities	1
% African American	3
% Asian	3
% Caucasian	73
% Hispanic	5
% international	2
# of countries represented	77

SURVEY SAYS . . .

Great off-campus food
Frats and sororities are unpopular or nonexistent
Musical organizations are popular
College radio is popular
Theater is popular
Student publications are popular
Lots of beer drinking
Hard liquor is popular

ACADEMICS

Academic Rating	75
% students graduating within 4 years	69
% students graduating within 6 years	77
Calendar	semester
Student/faculty ratio	12:1
Profs interesting rating	83
Profs accessible rating	87
Most common reg class size	10–19 students

MOST POPULAR MAJORS

business/commerce, music, radio and television

STUDENTS SAY ". . ."

Academics

"Small class sizes" that afford plenty of "personal attention," "outstanding" scholarships, and cross-registration with nearby Cornell University are a few great reasons to choose Ithaca College, a smallish school in central New York that offers many of the resources you would expect to find at a much larger university. "You are able to be a part of a community and get the chance to pursue interests that are not necessarily a part of your chosen course of study," relates an English major. "We have loads of opportunities to do and try a wide variety of things." The vast multitude of academic offerings includes "one of the best communication schools in the country." Also notable are "strong" majors in music, business, and drama; a "highly competitive" six-year doctorate program in physical therapy; and the cinema and photography program. Professors are "really engaging and understand how to present the material so that it is relevant and meaningful." On the whole, faculty members are "really passionate about their fields and have a genuine interest in getting students excited about their passions." By far, the most common academic complaint about academics at Ithaca concerns registration, which can be trying. Some say, "the buildings—inside and out—are a bit outdated." Overall the campus is known for its picturesque beauty. "People aren't kidding when they say 'Ithaca is Gorges (gorgeous),'" promises one student.

Life

The number of extracurricular choices is "considerable" at Ithaca College. At the same time, "the school is small enough for anyone to get involved." There are "speakers and events offered on campus." There's also a pretty much professional-quality college radio station. Many students "are part of an athletic team or participate in intramural athletics." For relaxation, students often "hang out on the quad," throwing Frisbees or "playing music on the lawns on tie-dye sheets." The social situation at Ithaca is "nothing like the party scene you'd find at a larger university," but "there are some good parties" now and then. While the campus is a little "isolated," students also frequently manage to attend frat parties at Cornell and generally "enjoy the social scene" the nearby Ivy offers. "The town of Ithaca is quaint but lively." There's "a good music scene and a lot of cool stores." When the weather is nice, "There's always some festival," or at least it seems that way. "If you're an outdoorsy person," the wooded and rocky surrounding area is a wonderland of activity. "The hiking here is unbelievable," and few other schools offer the opportunity to "go cliff jumping on a hot Saturday." On the negative side, winters are cold as a matter of course, and "the cold and rain do hinder activities." Students joke, be prepared to get your exercise walking between classes, "the hills here will kill you."

Student Body

The typical undergrad here is "genuine," "easygoing," "always busy," "well-dressed," and has a "sunny disposition despite the gray skies." Beyond those qualities, the population is "a wide mix of hipsters, jocks, theater kids, music students," and "crunchy granola hippies." "People of all kinds fit in here." "Everyone finds their niche." Cliques are often based loosely on academics. "Ithaca is not so much one community as a whole," explains one student. "Instead, each school (music, communications, business, etc.) is its own community." Ethnic diversity and other kinds of diversity are "not entirely unheard of." However, people are "usually from the Northeast," and "The population of students that fit into the typical suburban, upper-middle-class family is definitely significant." Politically, "students at Ithaca tend to be liberal." Some students tell us that you'll find "a lot of people are environmentally and socially conscious" here who want "to change the world."

FINANCIAL AID: 607-274-3131 • E-MAIL: ADMISSION@ITHACA.EDU • WEBSITE: WWW.ITHACA.EDU

THE PRINCETON REVIEW SAYS

Admissions

Very important factors considered include: Academic GPA, rigor of secondary school record. *Important factors considered include:* Application essay, class rank, recommendation(s), standardized test scores, character/personal qualities, extracurricular activities, talent/ability. *Other factors considered include:* Alumni/ae relation, first generation, interview, level of applicant's interest, racial/ethnic status, volunteer work, work experience. SAT or ACT required; ACT with writing component required. TOEFL required of all international applicants. High school diploma is required, and GED is accepted. *Academic units required:* 4 English, 3 mathematics, 3 science, 2 foreign language, 3 social studies, 1 academic elective. *Academic units recommended:* 4 English, 4 mathematics, 4 science, 2 foreign language, 4 social studies, 1 academic elective.

Financial Aid

Students should submit: FAFSA, CSS/Financial Aid PROFILE. Regular filing deadline is February 1. The Princeton Review suggests that all financial aid forms be submitted as soon as possible after January 1. *Need-based scholarships/grants offered:* Federal Pell, SEOG, private scholarships, school scholarship or grant aid from institutional funds. *Loan aid offered:* Direct Subsidized Stafford, Direct Unsubsidized Stafford, Direct PLUS, Federal Perkins. Applicants will be notified of awards on a rolling basis beginning February 15. Federal Work-Study Program available. Off-campus job opportunities are good.

The Inside Word

Ithaca's admissions profile continues to be on the rise with a good deal of highly competitive applicants. Programs requiring an audition (for example, music) or portfolio review (for example, art) are among Ithaca's most demanding for admission. If you want to pursue the six-year clinical doctorate in physical therapy, focus on completing substantial math and science coursework in high school.

THE SCHOOL SAYS " . . ."

From the Admissions Office

"Ithaca College was founded in 1892 as a music conservatory, and it continues that commitment to performance and excellence. Its modern, residential 750-acre campus, equipped with state-of-the-art facilities, is home to the Schools of Business, Communications, Health Sciences and Human Performance, Humanities and Sciences, and Music. With more than 100 majors—from biochemistry to business administration, journalism to jazz, philosophy to physical therapy, and special programs in Washington, D.C.; Los Angeles; and London—students enjoy the curricular choices of a large campus in a personalized, smaller school environment. And Ithaca's students benefit from an education that emphasizes active learning, small classes, collaborative student-faculty research, and development of the whole student. Located in central New York's spectacular Finger Lakes region in what many consider the classic college town, the college has twenty-five highly competitive varsity teams, more than 130 campus clubs, two radio stations, and a television station, as well as hundreds of concerts, recitals, and theater performances annually.

"Students applying for admission must have official scores from either the SAT or the ACT with the writing section sent to Ithaca College by the testing agency. The college will also consider results of SAT Subject Tests, if submitted."

SELECTIVITY
Admissions Rating	78
# of applicants	13,191
% of applicants accepted	69
% of acceptees attending	18
# accepting a place on wait list	411
% admitted from wait list	31

FRESHMAN PROFILE
Range SAT Critical Reading	530–640
Range SAT Math	530–630
Range SAT Writing	530–630
Minimum paper TOEFL	550
Minimum computer TOEFL	213
Minimum web-based TOEFL	80
% graduated top 10% of class	29
% graduated top 25% of class	65
% graduated top 50% of class	91

DEADLINES
Early decision	
Deadline	11/1
Notification	12/15
Regular	
Deadline	2/1
Notification	11/15
Nonfall registration?	yes

APPLICANTS ALSO LOOK AT
AND OFTEN PREFER
Boston University, New York University, Northeastern University, Syracuse University

AND SOMETIMES PREFER
Cornell University, Penn State—University Park, University of Vermont

AND RARELY PREFER
American University, Fordham University, State University of New York at Albany

FINANCIAL FACTS
Financial Aid Rating	88
Annual tuition	$33,630
Room and board	$12,314
Books and supplies	$1,275
% frosh rec. need-based scholarship or grant aid	69
% UG rec. need-based scholarship or grant aid	67
% frosh rec. non-need-based scholarship or grant aid	19
% UG rec. non-need-based scholarship or grant aid	16
% frosh rec. need-based self-help aid	67
% UG rec. need-based self-help aid	65
% frosh rec. any financial aid	93
% UG rec. any financial aid	91

JAMES MADISON UNIVERSITY

SONNER HALL, MSC 0101, HARRISONBURG, VA 22807 • ADMISSIONS: 540-568-5681 • FAX: 540-568-3332

STUDENTS SAY "..."

Academics

James Madison University has a reputation as "a school that values education, respect, and integrity." The university boasts "one of the best BA programs for musical theater on the East Coast," and an "amazing" business school. A communication major says, "James Madison offered a positive, enriching, and supportive learning environment," and most students agree that JMU is an "inspiring environment filled with students striving to be productive members of society." A senior says, "I found the JMU environment to be comfortable and conducive to learning," and it seems clear that "JMU is all about taking your academics seriously." Professors get consistently high marks for being "available to help" and "interested in student achievement." Although they're often described as "challenging," students say professors are "willing to facilitate your education in any way possible" and "are very down to earth, approachable, and huge supporters of discussion based classes." Like any large university, there are "some professors you want to avoid," and students grumble that "registering for classes, if you don't have priority is a pain." It's worth noting, however, that "classrooms and facilities are always well kept and very up-to-date with all the best teaching technology."

Life

Located in Virginia's Shenandoah Valley, JMU is known for its "beautiful" campus, and students rave about the "benefits of walking in the mountains." An English major says, "The moment I walked on campus I was captured by the student spirit and how beautiful it is." School spirit is generally high and students say, "There's a huge sense of JMU pride, everyone loves the Dukes!" A senior adds, "We have so much pride for our school. There is a friendly, collaborative ambiance here that is unparalleled anywhere else." The university is known for its Southern hospitality, and one student describes the student body as "the 'door-holding freaks of America' because even when people are several feet away, we stand there to hold the door for them." There are numerous ways to get involved on campus, and the "sheer number of student activities is stellar." Students rave about the "personal involvement that JMU offer(s)," and say, "They make you feel like a part of the campus, not just another number." Food services and facilities get high marks across the board, and most agree that the "administration and faculty are always willing to talk to students and point them in the right direction," noting that one of "the greatest strengths of the school is the ability to get any sort of assistance when needed." Regardless, there are complaints about traffic on campus, and many feel, "The school could improve on parking, by a long shot."

Student Body

At JMU, "The typical student is friendly, smart, open-minded, and fun." Students describe themselves as "excellent [at] maintaining a round, balanced life," and say, "everyone seems relaxed and knows how to have fun but keep their school work a priority." One student jokes that the typical student is "probably a girl considering our ratio seems like eighty to twenty at times," and another concurs, "more males would be nice." Students tend to be "white from the upper to middle class," and an International Affairs major says, "Although we do have all types here, most people consist of your typical prep wearing Uggs and a North Face." Some complain, "There is party atmosphere here that can seem dominating," and "If you do not go out and party you stand out." Others note, however, "Greek life is small," and parties "are usually open to everyone," adding that partying isn't "all students here think about. People will get together and drink for fun, but it isn't a necessity." A sophomore says, "On the weekends, students can go to downtown Harrisonburg to the various restaurants and shops," or enjoy on-campus movies at a reduced rate. Still others take advantage of the "great places to hike and spend time outdoors" and JMU's easy accessibility to nearby ski resorts.

JAMES MADISON UNIVERSITY

FINANCIAL AID: 540-568-7820 • E-MAIL: GOTOJMU@JMU.EDU • WEBSITE: WWW.JMU.EDU

THE PRINCETON REVIEW SAYS

Admissions

Very important factors considered include: Academic GPA, rigor of secondary school record, standardized test scores. *Other factors considered include:* Application essay, recommendation(s), alumni/ae relation, extracurricular activities, first generation, geographical residence, racial/ethnic status, state residency, talent/ability, volunteer work, work experience. SAT or ACT required; ACT with or without writing component accepted. TOEFL required of all international applicants. High school diploma is required, and GED is accepted. *Academic units required:* 4 English, 4 mathematics, 3 science (3 science labs), 3 foreign language, 2 social studies, 2 history.

Financial Aid

Students should submit: FAFSA. The Princeton Review suggests that all financial aid forms be submitted as soon as possible after January 1. *Need-based scholarships/grants offered:* Federal Pell, SEOG, state scholarships/grants, private scholarships, school scholarship or grant aid from institutional funds. *Loan aid offered:* Direct Subsidized Stafford, Direct Unsubsidized Stafford, Direct PLUS, Federal Perkins, Federal Nursing Loans. Applicants will be notified of awards on a rolling basis beginning April 1. Federal Work-Study Program available. Off-campus job opportunities are good.

The Inside Word

At JMU admissions are competitive, but the admissions staff insists that they're not searching for a "magic combination" of test scores and GPA. Admissions officers review each application individually and are most interested in the quality of an applicant's secondary school education, followed by performance and test scores. The personal statement is a vehicle for conveying information an applicant deems important but that doesn't appear elsewhere in the application, as such it's optional.

THE SCHOOL SAYS "..."

From the Admissions Office

"James Madison University's philosophy of inclusiveness—known as 'all together one'—means that students become a part of a real community that nurtures its own to learn, grow, and succeed. Our professors, many of whom have a wealth of real-world experience, pride themselves on making teaching their top priority. We take seriously the responsibility to maintain an environment that fosters learning and encourages students to excel in and out of the classroom. Our rich variety of educational, social, and extracurricular activities include more than 100 innovative and traditional undergraduate majors and programs, a well-established study abroad program, a cutting-edge information security program, more than 350 student clubs and organizations, and a 147,000-square-foot, state-of-the-art recreation center. The university's picturesque, self-contained campus is located in the heart of the Shenandoah Valley, a four-season area that's easy to call home. Great food, fun times, exciting intercollegiate athletics, and rigorous academics all combine to create the unique James Madison experience. From the library to the residence halls and from our outstanding honors program to our highly successful career placement program, the university is committed to equipping our students with the tools they need to achieve their dreams."

SELECTIVITY

Admissions Rating	89
# of applicants	22,221
% of applicants accepted	60
% of acceptees attending	30
# accepting a place on wait list	1,200
% admitted from wait list	38

FRESHMAN PROFILE

Range SAT Critical Reading	540–640
Range SAT Math	550–650
Range SAT Writing	540–640
Range ACT Composite	23–27
Minimum paper TOEFL	550
Minimum computer TOEFL	213
Average HS GPA	3.84
% graduated top 10% of class	27
% graduated top 25% of class	72
% graduated top 50% of class	98

DEADLINES

Early action	
Deadline	11/1
Notification	1/15
Regular	
Priority	11/1
Deadline	1/15
Nonfall registration?	no

APPLICANTS ALSO LOOK AT
AND OFTEN PREFER
University of Virginia, Virginia Tech
AND SOMETIMES PREFER
George Mason University, University of Delaware

FINANCIAL FACTS

Financial Aid Rating	75
Annual in-state tuition	$4,182
Annual out-of-state tuition	$16,946
Room and board	$8,020
Required fees	$3,678
Books and supplies	$876
% frosh rec. need-based scholarship or grant aid	22
% UG rec. need-based scholarship or grant aid	18
% frosh rec. non-need-based scholarship or grant aid	80
% UG rec. non-need-based scholarship or grant aid	27
% frosh rec. need-based self-help aid	36
% UG rec. need-based self-help aid	30
% frosh rec. any financial aid	61
% UG rec. any financial aid	57
% UG borrow to pay for school	50
Average cumulative indebtedness	$20,417

THE BEST 376 COLLEGES ■ 315

JOHNS HOPKINS UNIVERSITY

3400 NORTH CHARLES STREET/MASON HALL, BALTIMORE, MD 21218 • ADMISSIONS: 410-516-8171 • FAX: 410-516-6025

CAMPUS LIFE

Quality of Life Rating	78
Fire Safety Rating	81
Green Rating	95
Type of school	private
Environment	metropolis

STUDENTS

Total undergrad enrollment	4,980
% male/female	52/48
% from out of state	87
% from public high school	69
% live on campus	55
# of fraternities	13
# of sororities	9
% African American	5
% Asian	21
% Caucasian	52
% Hispanic	8
% international	8
# of countries represented	71

SURVEY SAYS . . .

Lab facilities are great
Great computer facilities
Great library
Athletic facilities are great

ACADEMICS

Academic Rating	86
% students graduating within 4 years	84
% students graduating within 6 years	92
Calendar	4-1-4
Student/faculty ratio	12:1
Profs interesting rating	72
Profs accessible rating	75
Most common reg class size	10–19 students
Most common lab size	20–29 students

MOST POPULAR MAJORS

international studies, biomedical engineering, public health

STUDENTS SAY "..."

Academics

Johns Hopkins University has a reputation as an academic powerhouse, one that its undergrads wholeheartedly affirm. Although the university offers "a pretty intense environment" with "really rigorous" classes, all of this is made bearable by professors who are "concerned with the individual student" and "extremely approachable, even in [an] organic chemistry class of 300 students." Indeed, "They enjoy being in the classroom and sharing what they know. Each is passionate about their area of study and eager to share it with students who are equally as enthusiastic." A satisfied senior echoes these praises, saying, "All the professors that I've encountered at Hopkins recognize that learning should be fun and thought-provoking. Their lectures or discussions engage students to think about the materials in a different way and pursue further outside study." "Engage" is the operative word here, as undergrads are "treated as though they are participants in their respective academic fields, not just 'students'." However, as one senior cautions, "There's very little grade inflation, and you work hard for the grade you get." Praise also extends to the administration, which students describe as "caring to a fault, willing to help, and generally highly interested in the undergraduate experience." As one junior sums up, "It's clear that our professors and deans genuinely care about the students, as evidenced by their attendance at student fundraisers, fraternity scholarship events, and even plays and a cappella concerts. They want students to learn about anything that interests them, but they want students to grow as people too, and it's astonishing how high their success rate is in that regard."

Life

Life at Hopkins is "certainly based around work." Indeed, most undergrads are diligent students "who put work over everything else." This is a school where "people care about what they study" and it's not uncommon to see fellow students "stay up all night debating philosophy, politics or the theory of evolution." Sound a little intense? No worries: One junior assures us that "there's never a dull moment at Johns Hopkins: You just have to step outside your room and look for five seconds." Another senior confirms, "There's always something cool going on around campus, whether it's from the world of entertainment (like Will Ferrell coming to speak) or academia." There are numerous "free on-campus movies, plays, dance, and a cappella performances" to take in along with "the *best* lacrosse team in America" and "incredibly competitive [Division III] sports like soccer and water polo." And with roughly a quarter of the student body involved in fraternities and sororities, Greek life offers a "tremendous social outlet." Fortunately, when students get bored on campus, they can always explore hometown Baltimore for entertainment options. The city offers "movie theaters, malls, shopping centers, a *ton* of restaurants, a good music scene, and proximity to D.C., clubs, and other colleges. Many undergrads can frequently be found hanging out by the Inner Harbor or the nearby Towson Mall.

Student Body

While it might be difficult to define the typical Hopkins undergrad, the vast majority are "hardworking and care about their GPAs, and will do what they can to get the grades they want." Thankfully, many are also "balance artists; they are able to balance schoolwork, extracurricular activities, jobs, and a social life without getting too bogged down or stressed." Though students "are competitive in the sense that they all want to do well," that competitiveness is never adversarial. One junior declares, "I have found that there is an incredible mutual respect that permeates the student body, one that allows engineers to discuss poetry with English majors, sees historians present at astronomy lectures, and gets linguists to help lacrosse players study for French tests, all while reserving judgment upon each other." A sophomore continues, "I've never been someplace where there are so many diverse interests. As clichéd as it may sound, there truly is a niche for everyone."

JOHNS HOPKINS UNIVERSITY

FINANCIAL AID: 410-516-8028 • E-MAIL: GOTOJHU@JHU.EDU • WEBSITE: WWW.JHU.EDU

THE PRINCETON REVIEW SAYS

Admissions

Very important factors considered include: Academic GPA, recommendation(s), rigor of secondary school record, character/personal qualities. *Important factors considered include:* Application essays, class rank, standardized test scores, extracurricular activities, talent/ability, volunteer work, work experience. *Other factors considered include:* Alumni/ae relation, first generation, geographical residence, interview, racial/ethnic status. SAT or ACT with writing component required. TOEFL required of international applicants. *Academic units recommended:* 4 English, 4 mathematics, 4 science, 4 foreign language, 2 social studies, 2 history.

Financial Aid

Students should submit: FAFSA. Regular filing deadline is March 1. The Princeton Review suggests that all financial aid forms be submitted as soon as possible after January 1. *Need-based scholarships/grants offered:* Federal Pell, SEOG, state scholarships/grants, private scholarships, school scholarship or grant aid from institutional funds. *Loan aid offered:* Direct Subsidized Stafford, Direct Unsubsidized Stafford, Direct PLUS, Federal Perkins, university loans from institutional funds. Federal Work-Study Program available. Off-campus job opportunities are good.

The Inside Word

Top schools like Hopkins receive more and more applications every year and, as a result, grow harder and harder to get into. With more than 18,000 applicants, Hopkins has to reject numerous applicants who are thoroughly qualified. Give your application everything you've got, and don't take it personally if you don't get a fat envelope in the mail.

THE SCHOOL SAYS "..."

From the Admissions Office

"The Johns Hopkins tradition of preeminent academic excellence naturally attracts the very best students in the nation and from around the world. The admissions committee carefully examines each application for evidence of compelling intellectual interest and academic performance as well as strong personal recommendations and meaningful extracurricular contributions. Every applicant who matriculates to Johns Hopkins University was found qualified by the admissions committee through a 'whole person' assessment, and every applicant accepted for admission is fully expected to graduate. The admissions committee determines whom they believe will take full advantage of the exceptional opportunities offered at Hopkins, contribute the most to the educational process of the institution, and be the most successful in using what they have learned and experienced for the benefit of society."

SELECTIVITY
Admissions Rating	99
# of applicants	18,459
% of applicants accepted	21
% of acceptees attending	33
# accepting a place on wait list	3,256
% admitted from wait list	1
# of early decision applicants	1,097
% accepted early decision	44

FRESHMAN PROFILE
Range SAT Critical Reading	630–740
Range SAT Math	660–770
Range SAT Writing	640–740
Range ACT Composite	29–33
Minimum paper TOEFL	600
Average HS GPA	3.72
% graduated top 10% of class	87
% graduated top 25% of class	98
% graduated top 50% of class	99

DEADLINES
Early decision	
Deadline	11/1
Notification	12/15
Regular	
Deadline	1/1
Nonfall registration?	no

APPLICANTS ALSO LOOK AT
AND OFTEN PREFER
Harvard College, Princeton University, University of Pennsylvania, Yale University

AND SOMETIMES PREFER
Cornell University, Northwestern University

AND RARELY PREFER
Rice University, Washington University in St. Louis

FINANCIAL FACTS
Financial Aid Rating	94
Annual tuition	$42,280
Room and board	$12,962
Books and supplies	$1,000
% frosh rec. need-based scholarship or grant aid	44
% UG rec. need-based scholarship or grant aid	41
% frosh rec. non-need-based scholarship or grant aid	6
% UG rec. non-need-based scholarship or grant aid	5
% frosh rec. need-based self-help aid	44
% UG rec. need-based self-help aid	42
% frosh rec. any financial aid	52
% UG rec. any financial aid	49
% UG borrow to pay for school	48
Average cumulative indebtedness	$25,307

JUNIATA COLLEGE

1700 MOORE STREET, HUNTINGDON, PA 16652 • ADMISSIONS: 814-641-3420 • FAX: 814-641-3100

CAMPUS LIFE

Quality of Life Rating	77
Fire Safety Rating	81
Green Rating	69
Type of school	private
Environment	village

STUDENTS

Total undergrad enrollment	1,593
% male/female	43/57
% from out of state	32
% from public high school	82
% live on campus	80
% African American	2
% Asian	2
% Caucasian	85
% Hispanic	3
% international	5
# of countries represented	38

SURVEY SAYS . . .
Lab facilities are great
Students are friendly
Campus feels safe
Low cost of living
Frats and sororities are unpopular
or nonexistent

ACADEMICS

Academic Rating	86
% students graduating within 4 years	67
% students graduating within 6 years	72
Calendar	semester
Student/faculty ratio	13:1
Profs interesting rating	84
Profs accessible rating	89
Most common reg class size	10–19 students
Most common lab size	10–19 students

MOST POPULAR MAJORS
biology, business/commerce, education

STUDENTS SAY ". . ."

Academics

Juniata College has catapulted from regional to national status in the past decade on the strength of its great natural science programs, housed in the 88,000-square-foot, state-of-the-art von Liebig Center for Science (VLCS). Students tell us while Juniata "is centered around a very tough but rewarding science program," science is hardly the only game in town. The "business, theatre, and education departments are strong, too." Another student explains, "Other departments are beginning to receive support from trustees and alumni now that VLCS is complete. Several buildings will be undergoing renovations to allow for the expansion of the humanities and social sciences." Business, in particular, seems likely to receive a lot of attention as it is among the school's most popular disciplines. Undergrads tout JC's "great entrepreneurial program…where all students are encouraged to start their own businesses and some are given start-up cash." Education is also popular. Students appreciate that they're "given a practicum their first semester freshman year," meaning "if they don't like being in the classroom, they can change their major right away." "At most other schools, you have to wait until your junior year to get some classroom experience, [in your major]" says a student. Other perks of a Juniata education include the prominence of the study abroad program and the program of emphasis where, "students are afforded the option to create their own major which allows us to explore many possibilities that would otherwise be restricted by a designated major."

Life

Juniata "is located in Huntingdon, Pennsylvania, which is a tiny town in the middle of nowhere, thirty minutes south of State College," so "needless to say, there is not a lot to do off campus." Fortunately, "the Juniata Activities Board (JAB) brings numerous acts to campus including comedians, musicians, hypnotists, [and] magicians." The campus also hosts "various weekend parties, but they normally don't happen until Saturday nights because a large population of the student body is active in athletics with games either Friday night or Saturday afternoon." Since Juniata "doesn't have any Greek societies," students compensate by being "active in many clubs, including the Agriculture Club, Health Occupations Students of America, student government, the Equine club, and the Student Alumni Association." Otherwise, quiet fun ("video games and movie watching are very popular") dominates. One student explains, "The people who are dissatisfied with Juniata were definitely expecting something else, usually something more along the lines of Penn State."

Student Body

Juniata "is notoriously middle-class and Caucasian" with "very few minority students." Diversity arrives in the form of "a vast number of international students, both in semester and year-long exchange programs. The international presence at Juniata does a lot for class debate, and often opens the eyes of otherwise typically American students to the perspectives of those from other nations." Undergrads here "work hard for their grades. They want to excel. Basically, they're motivated and determined to succeed in the real world," to the point they often "choose to do homework and study above most other activities." Ultimately, "a typical student is really studious and really cares about their education. Everyone is able to find their own clique in which they fit into and feel comfortable."

FINANCIAL AID: 814-641-3142 • E-MAIL: INFO@JUNIATA.EDU • WEBSITE: WWW.JUNIATA.EDU

THE PRINCETON REVIEW SAYS

Admissions

Very important factors considered include: Academic GPA, application essay, recommendation(s), rigor of secondary school record, standardized test scores, character/personal qualities. *Important factors considered include:* Extracurricular activities, interview, talent/ability, volunteer work. *Other factors considered include:* Alumni/ae relation, geographical residence, level of applicant's interest, racial/ethnic status. SAT or ACT recommended; ACT with or without writing component accepted. TOEFL required of all international applicants. High school diploma is required, and GED is accepted. *Academic units required:* 4 English, 3 mathematics, 3 science (2 science labs), 2 foreign language, 1 social studies, 3 history. *Academic units recommended:* 4 English, 4 mathematics, 4 science, 2 foreign language, 1 social studies, 3 history.

Financial Aid

Students should submit: FAFSA. Regular filing deadline is March 1. The Princeton Review suggests that all financial aid forms be submitted as soon as possible after January 1. *Need-based scholarships/grants offered:* Federal Pell, SEOG, state scholarships/grants, private scholarships, school scholarship or grant aid from institutional funds. *Loan aid offered:* Direct Subsidized Stafford, Direct Unsubsidized Stafford, Direct PLUS, Federal Perkins, university loans from institutional funds. Applicants will be notified of awards on a rolling basis beginning February 28. Federal Work-Study Program available. Off-campus job opportunities are good.

The Inside Word

As at many traditional liberal arts schools, the admissions process at Juniata is a personal one. Applications are scoured for evidence the student is committed to attending Juniata and to remaining there for the full four years. The school is best known for its premedical programs, meaning applicants to these programs will have the highest hurdles to clear.

THE SCHOOL SAYS "..."

From the Admissions Office

"Juniata's unique approach to learning has a flexible, student-centered focus. With the help of two advisors, more than half of Juniata's students design their own majors (called the "Program of Emphasis" or "POE"). Those who choose a more traditional academic journey still benefit from the assistance of two faculty advisors and interdisciplinary collaboration between multiple academic departments.

"In addition, all students benefit from the recent, significant investments in academic facilities that help students actively learn by doing. For example, the new Halbritter Center for the Performing Arts houses an innovative theater program where theater professionals work side-by-side with students. The Sill Business Incubator provides $5,000 in seed capital to students with a desire to start their own business. The LEED-certified Raystown Environmental Studies Field Station, located on nearby Raystown Lake, gives unparalleled, hands-on study opportunities to students. And the von Liebig Center for Science provides opportunities for student/faculty research surpassing those available at even large universities.

"As the 2003 Middle States Accreditation Team noted, 'Juniata is truly a student-centered college. There is a remarkable cohesiveness in this commitment—faculty, students, trustees, staff, and alumni, each from their own vantage point, describe a community in which the growth of the student is central.' This cohesiveness creates a dynamic learning environment that enables students to think and grow intellectually, to evolve in their academic careers, and to graduate as active, successful participants in the global community.

"Freshman applicants may submit the SAT (or the ACT with or without the writing component). We will use their best scores from either test. "

SELECTIVITY

Admissions Rating	89
# of applicants	2,198
% of applicants accepted	72
% of acceptees attending	26
# of early decision applicants	63
% accepted early decision	87

FRESHMAN PROFILE

Range SAT Critical Reading	530–640
Range SAT Math	530–640
Minimum paper TOEFL	550
Minimum web-based TOEFL	79
Average HS GPA	3.75
% graduated top 10% of class	38
% graduated top 25% of class	74
% graduated top 50% of class	95

DEADLINES

Early decision	
Deadline	12/1
Notification	12/31
Early action	
Deadline	1/1
Notification	1/30
Regular	
Priority	12/1
Deadline	3/15
Notification	2/28
Nonfall registration?	yes

APPLICANTS ALSO LOOK AT

AND OFTEN PREFER
Franklin & Marshall College

AND SOMETIMES PREFER
Allegheny College, Dickinson College, Elizabethtown College, Susquehanna University

AND RARELY PREFER
McDaniel College, Penn State—University Park, Ursinus College

FINANCIAL FACTS

Financial Aid Rating	88
Annual comprehensive tuition	$43,420
Books and supplies	$600
% frosh rec. need-based scholarship or grant aid	74
% UG rec. need-based scholarship or grant aid	72
% frosh rec. non-need-based scholarship or grant aid	14
% UG rec. non-need-based scholarship or grant aid	11
% frosh rec. need-based self-help aid	61
% UG rec. need-based self-help aid	61
% frosh rec. any financial aid	100
% UG rec. any financial aid	100
% UG borrow to pay for school	87
Average cumulative indebtedness	$23,637

KALAMAZOO COLLEGE

1200 ACADEMY STREET, KALAMAZOO, MI 49006 • ADMISSIONS: 269-337-7166 • FAX: 269-337-7390

CAMPUS LIFE

Quality of Life Rating	80
Fire Safety Rating	69
Green Rating	81
Type of school	private
Environment	city

STUDENTS

Total undergrad enrollment	1,369
% male/female	43/57
% from out of state	39
% from public high school	75
% live on campus	75
% African American	6
% Asian	5
% Caucasian	69
% Hispanic	6
% Native American	1
% international	7
# of countries represented	20

SURVEY SAYS . . .

No one cheats
Great library
Frats and sororities are unpopular
or nonexistent
Political activism is popular

ACADEMICS

Academic Rating	92
% students graduating within 4 years	78
% students graduating within 6 years	80
Calendar	trimester
Student/faculty ratio	14:1
Profs interesting rating	96
Profs accessible rating	89
Most common reg class size	10–19 students
Most common lab size	fewer than 10 students

MOST POPULAR MAJORS
economics, English language and
literature, psychology

STUDENTS SAY ". . ."

Academics

Study at Kalamazoo College is built around the K-Plan, "a solid liberal arts education combined with study abroad and internships and externships" and "the SIP, a senior individualized project, [which is] a senior thesis with a fun and much-used acronym." Students tell us that all aspects of the K-Plan "emphasize the importance of applying what you've learned in the classroom to other areas of life," allowing students to "see the whole picture and understand what [we] want to do with [our] degrees." A plan like this is only as good as its execution. Fortunately, by nearly all accounts Kalamazoo delivers with well-supported "study abroad, internship, externship, and domestic study-away opportunities" that are "endless" in variety. Students here once complained that demanding general education requirements impeded independent study. The school apparently was listening, as it recently introduced a new curriculum that "gives ultimate flexibility...allowing us to explore new disciplines and classes. We can even double major and still spend a quarter [term] abroad!" Kalamazoo's cozy size creates an "intimate setting [that] fosters community unlike any other school I've ever visited." A faculty that's "out of this world...attentive, engaged, and always available after class, usually for as much help as one needs" further strengthens those bonds. In the end, students leave feeling prepared for the real world. As one explains, "Students graduate completely ready to pursue a career in what they are passionate about or to continue their education on the next level."

Life

"Life goes by fast at K College," where, thanks to the trimester system, "You're in class for just a few weeks, and you already have your first round of exams." While "everyone is busy with classes and their clubs," students "will always somehow find time to help each other out." Most here "tend to take on a lot more classes/activities than they probably should," which "stresses everyone out," but students find creative ways to release the pressure. The Childish Games Commission, for example, which "meets every Friday at midnight to play games like tag, hide and seek, four-square, and Duck Duck Goose" is a popular option for relieving stress. Those seeking the sort of fun more characteristic of big schools can head over to Western Michigan University, where "there are upwards of 20,000 students," which allows K kids to "experience the social aspects of a large school while still enjoying a liberal arts education." Hometown Kalamazoo "is an overgrown artists' commune in a lot of ways," with "a monthly arts festival" and "plenty of shops, museums, and a nice park with concert events." Many here recommend regular trips downtown to escape "the K bubble." As one student explains, "It is sometimes...difficult to get off campus or get away from the people here. Everyone needs that time, and it's difficult to find, especially in winter quarter when there's five feet of snow outside."

Student Body

"Most students are very studious and care a lot about their grades but still know how to have fun," the "book smart, worldly, aware, passionate, argumentative, dedicated, hardworking, opinionated, [and] friendly" undergrads at Kalamazoo assure us. The school "has traditionally drawn a lot of strange students, but this has been changing lately." Across the board, students tend to be "very liberal-minded and idealistic, from a fairly well-off background...There is a lack of ideological diversity, but most students are too busy stressing out about their classes to spend much time focusing on radicalism." Most "are from Michigan or the Midwest, although that percentage decreases every year."

FINANCIAL AID: 269-337-7192 • E-MAIL: ADMISSION@KZOO.EDU • WEBSITE: WWW.KZOO.EDU

THE PRINCETON REVIEW SAYS

Admissions

Very important factors considered include: Academic GPA, rigor of secondary school record, extracurricular activities, volunteer work, work experience. *Important factors considered include:* Application essay, recommendation(s), standardized test scores. *Other factors considered include:* Alumni/ae relation, character/personal qualities, first generation, geographical residence, interview, level of applicant's interest, racial/ethnic status, talent/ability. SAT or ACT required; ACT with writing component required. TOEFL required of all international applicants. High school diploma is required, and GED is accepted. *Academic units required:* 4 English, 3 mathematics, 3 science, 3 foreign language, 2 social studies, 2 history. *Academic units recommended:* 4 English, 4 mathematics, 4 science, 4 foreign language, 2 social studies, 2 history.

Financial Aid

Students should submit: FAFSA, institution's own financial aid form. Regular filing deadline is February 15. The Princeton Review suggests that all financial aid forms be submitted as soon as possible after January 1. *Need-based scholarships/grants offered:* Federal Pell, SEOG, state scholarships/grants, private scholarships, school scholarship or grant aid from institutional funds. *Loan aid offered:* Direct Subsidized Stafford, Direct Unsubsidized Stafford, Direct PLUS, Federal Perkins. Applicants will be notified of awards on a rolling basis beginning March 21. Federal Work-Study Program available. Off-campus job opportunities are good.

The Inside Word

Kalamazoo admissions officers work hard to find good matches for the school's unique K-Plan. Applicants who demonstrate creativity, the ability to self-motivate, and ambition fit the bill. Solid academics and strong standardized test scores are also pretty much required; admissions are very competitive here. The arts play a central role on the Kalamazoo campus, so if you have special talent in art, theater, music, or writing, by all means submit a portfolio along with your application.

THE SCHOOL SAYS " . . ."

From the Admissions Office

"Anyone can pursue any component of the K-Plan at any college, but it is rare to see the purposeful integration and high participation rate found at Kalamazoo. During the past fifty years, 85 percent of our graduates have formally studied in another country while 80 percent have completed an internship or externship, and 100 percent complete a senior project. Our students often pursue international internships and senior project experiences, in addition to their planned study abroad terms. Also, Kalamazoo is one of the few selective liberal arts colleges to be found in a city—the Kalamazoo metro area has a population of approximately 225,000 with the advantage of being near a university of nearly 30,000 students. It is a diverse and vibrant community with wonderful access to the arts, athletics, service-learning, and community-service opportunities. We are a small and personal college with bigger opportunities.

"An SAT or ACT score is required for admission; SAT Subject Tests are not. Students taking only the ACT must take the writing portion."

SELECTIVITY

Admissions Rating	90
# of applicants	1,945
% of applicants accepted	75
% of acceptees attending	29
# accepting a place on wait list	61
% admitted from wait list	45
# of early decision applicants	34
% accepted early decision	88

FRESHMAN PROFILE

Range SAT Critical Reading	570–690
Range SAT Math	560–680
Range SAT Writing	560–680
Range ACT Composite	26–30
Minimum paper TOEFL	550
Minimum computer TOEFL	213
Minimum web-based TOEFL	80
Average HS GPA	3.60
% graduated top 10% of class	46
% graduated top 25% of class	79
% graduated top 50% of class	96

DEADLINES

Early decision	
Deadline	11/10
Notification	11/20
Early action	
Deadline	11/20
Notification	12/20
Regular	
Priority	11/20
Deadline	2/1
Nonfall registration?	no

APPLICANTS ALSO LOOK AT

AND OFTEN PREFER
University of Michigan—Ann Arbor

AND SOMETIMES PREFER
Macalester College, Oberlin College

AND RARELY PREFER
Albion College, Alma College, Hope College

FINANCIAL FACTS

Financial Aid Rating	78
Annual tuition	$35,508
Room and board	$8,079
Required fees	$312
% frosh rec. need-based scholarship or grant aid	67
% frosh rec. non-need-based scholarship or grant aid	93
% frosh rec. need-based self-help aid	46
% UG rec. need-based self-help aid	47
% frosh rec. any financial aid	95
% UG rec. any financial aid	98

KANSAS STATE UNIVERSITY

119 ANDERSON HALL, MANHATTAN, KS 66506 • ADMISSIONS: 800-432-8270 OR 785-532-6250 • FAX: 785-532-6393

CAMPUS LIFE

Quality of Life Rating	98
Fire Safety Rating	65
Green Rating	83
Type of school	public
Environment	town

STUDENTS

Total undergrad enrollment	18,753
% male/female	52/48
% from out of state	15
% from public high school	81
% live on campus	17
# of fraternities	28
# of sororities	16
% African American	4
% Asian	1
% Caucasian	82
% Hispanic	5
% international	5
# of countries represented	102

SURVEY SAYS . . .
Students are friendly
Students get along with local community
Everyone loves the Wildcats

ACADEMICS

Academic Rating	77
% students graduating within 4 years	26
% students graduating within 6 years	60
Calendar	semester
Student/faculty ratio	21:1
Profs interesting rating	74
Profs accessible rating	76
Most common reg class size	10–19 students

MOST POPULAR MAJORS
animal sciences, business administration and management, elementary education and teaching

STUDENTS SAY ". . ."

Academics
"Underrated" and tremendously affordable Kansas State University is "a big school with a small-school feel." Agriculture will always be prevalent here, but there are nine colleges and "more than 250 majors and options." Other "marquee programs" include engineering, the hard sciences, and a "grueling" architecture program. The library is "amazing." The faculty is "a mixed bag." "Some instructors you'll love and some you won't be able to stand," says a microbiology major. Intro and general education courses can be on the large side. They're "awkward and usually just rehash information from the textbook." "We struggle with graduate teaching assistants, especially those whose first language is not English," notes a political science major. In upper level courses, "it becomes easier to cultivate a relationship with your professor." Administratively, "the school is a pretty well-oiled machine." Management is full of "gifted people who genuinely love K-State;" and "students have a large say in everything the university does." Also, the top brass is ultra-accessible for such a large institution. In some areas, though, red tape is unavoidable. "If you change your major here," cautions a junior, "you're pretty much screwed as far as trying to graduate on time."

Life
The residence halls could use some sprucing up and some buildings "are about to crumble" but this "very compact" campus is "easy to navigate" and "beautiful in every season." KSU offers a "laid-back atmosphere" and "an extensive variety of clubs." "Movies on the lawn are fun." "Greek life is also huge and is responsible for a multitude of events." Hordes of students are "sports crazy." Intramurals are popular and "cheering on the 'Cats is a must.' In the fall, "people are obsessed with K-State football." "During game day weekends, the whole town is dressed in purple." "I do get tired of hearing about the football team 24/7," admits a senior, "but whatever." Beyond campus, Manhattan is a "great college town." It's "just big enough and everything you need for college life is available" including "a decent party scene." House parties and frat parties are common but most students head to Aggieville, the Little Apple's "famous" bar district. K-Staters call it "four square blocks of fun" and "one of the greatest places on Earth." Watering holes are "usually full on the weekends" and, "a lot of times, a weeknight at the bars can be even more fun." "Every college student should experience Aggieville," recommends one proud junior.

Student Body
The "hardworking and honest" students at K-State tell us they bask in "country hospitality." "The students are the friendliest in the country," asserts a senior. "You cannot walk through campus without people smiling or acknowledging you"—"not in that creepy, stalker way, but the way that makes you feel warm and fuzzy inside." The "typical Midwestern" population here mostly comes in two varieties. There are the "yokels" and "farm boys from small towns in Kansas." There are also the kids from "suburban white neighborhoods" in Kansas City and Wichita. You'll see "punk rock kids," "cowboys in Wranglers," and "the occasional hippie," but "they form their own weird groups." For the most part, the vibe is "very homogeneous" and "hopelessly vanilla." "The vast majority of the students look, dress, and act the same." Politically, K-State "tends towards conservatism." On the whole, though, these students "generally represent the middle of the road in nearly every American way of thought." As for minority enrollment, it's pretty low, and many K-Staters lament "the lack of diversity."

KANSAS STATE UNIVERSITY

FINANCIAL AID: 877-817-2287 OR 785-532-6420 • E-MAIL: K-STATE@K-STATE.EDU • WEBSITE: CONSIDER.K-STATE.EDU

THE PRINCETON REVIEW SAYS

Admissions

Very important factors considered include: Academic GPA, class rank, rigor of secondary school record, standardized test scores. *Other factors considered include:* Recommendation(s). SAT or ACT reccommended; ACT with or without writing component accepted. High school diploma is required, and GED is accepted. Accepts admissions applications all year. Apply before November 1 to be considered for all scholarships available. Recommended that transfer students apply nine months to one year in advance. Priority date for freshman is November 1. Deadline for College of Architecture, Planning, and Design; priority deadline for the interior design program in the College of Human Ecology; priority deadline for the wildlife and outdoor enterprise management program in the College of Agriculture is February 1. *Academic units recommended:* 4 English, 3 mathematics, 3 science, 3 social studies.

Financial Aid

Students should submit: FAFSA. The Princeton Review suggests that all financial aid forms be submitted as soon as possible after January 1. *Need-based scholarships/grants offered:* Federal Pell, SEOG, state scholarships/grants, private scholarships, school scholarship or grant aid from institutional funds. *Loan aid offered:* Direct Subsidized Stafford, Direct Unsubsidized Stafford, Direct PLUS, Federal Perkins, university loans from institutional funds. Applicants will be notified of awards on a rolling basis beginning April 1. Federal Work-Study Program available. Off-campus job opportunities are good.

The Inside Word

Though K-State is chock full of strong students, admission is very undemanding. The process here is also refreshingly straightforward. Basically, get a 21 on the ACT or graduate in the top third of your high school class, and you're in. If you're a Kansas resident, a third way to get accepted is to complete a college-bound curriculum with a 2.0 GPA. Non-residents need at least a 2.5.

THE SCHOOL SAYS "..."

From the Admissions Office

"Kansas State University offers strong academic programs, a lively intellectual atmosphere, a friendly campus community, and an environment where students achieve: K-State's total of Rhodes, Marshall, Truman, Goldwater, and Udall scholars in the past twenty-five years ranks first in the nation among state universities. In the Goldwater competition, only Princeton, Harvard, and Duke have produced more winners. K-State's Student Governing Association has been recognized several times as one of the nation's top student governments. As part of K-State's shared governance, they allocate $15 million a year for programs and services for K-State students. K-State's Black Student Union was named the Best in the Big 12 by the Big 12 Council on Black Student Government in 2009. Research facilities include the Konza Prairie, the world's largest tall grass prairie preserve, and the Biosecurity Research Institute. K-State is the research hub for the world's top scientists in animal health and food safety.

"Open House, held each spring, is a great way to explore K-State's more than 250 majors and options and 400 student organizations.

"Kansas State University requires ACT or SAT scores to complete a freshman applicant file. The SAT or ACT writing score is not considered for admission to the university. Students may submit scores from any or all test dates. The best score from any one test date is used."

SELECTIVITY
Admissions Rating	79
# of applicants	8,268
% of applicants accepted	99
% of acceptees attending	44

FRESHMAN PROFILE
Range ACT Composite	21–27
Average HS GPA	3.45
% graduated top 10% of class	20
% graduated top 25% of class	45
% graduated top 50% of class	76

DEADLINES
Regular	
Priority	11/1
Nonfall registration?	yes

FINANCIAL FACTS
Financial Aid Rating	79
Annual in-state tuition	$6,672
Annual out-of-state tuition	$17,700
Room and board	$6,954
Required fees	$704
Books and supplies	$1,100
% frosh rec. need-based scholarship or grant aid	33
% UG rec. need-based scholarship or grant aid	31
% frosh rec. non-need-based scholarship or grant aid	37
% UG rec. non-need-based scholarship or grant aid	24
% frosh rec. need-based self-help aid	38
% UG rec. need-based self-help aid	42
% frosh rec. any financial aid	47
% UG rec. any financial aid	49
% UG borrow to pay for school	54
Average cumulative indebtedness	$22,633

KENYON COLLEGE

ADMISSIONS OFFICE, RANSOM HALL, GAMBIER, OH 43022-9623 • ADMISSIONS: 740-427-5776 • FAX: 740-427-5770

CAMPUS LIFE

Quality of Life Rating	83
Fire Safety Rating	67
Green Rating	92
Type of school	private
Affiliation	Episcopal, but nondenominational in practice
Environment	rural

STUDENTS

Total undergrad enrollment	1,632
% male/female	48/52
% from out of state	86
% from public high school	51
% live on campus	99
# of fraternities	7
# of sororities	4
% African American	4
% Asian	6
% Caucasian	79
% Hispanic	3
% Native American	1
% international	4
# of countries represented	57

SURVEY SAYS . . .
No one cheats
Lab facilities are great
Athletic facilities are great
Students are friendly
Campus feels safe
Students are happy
Musical organizations are popular
Lots of beer drinking

ACADEMICS

Academic Rating	97
% students graduating within 4 years	85
% students graduating within 6 years	89
Calendar	semester
Student/faculty ratio	10:1
Profs interesting rating	98
Profs accessible rating	96
Most common reg class size	10–19 students
Most common lab size	12 students

MOST POPULAR MAJORS
English language and literature, political science, psychology

STUDENTS SAY ". . ."

Academics
A Kenyon education provides undergraduates with an "opportunity to learn in a creative and caring atmosphere" and encourages students "to think about things in different, innovative, and sometimes daring ways." The college has "an interesting combination of competitive academics and down-to-earth, relaxed students." One of Kenyon's strengths is "interdisciplinary concentration programs, which allow you to create a meaningful synthesis of knowledge across different fields quite effectively." A math major concurs, adding, "Almost every class has challenged me to think about things from a different perspective and has opened my mind to subjects in all aspects of life." Though the workload is "fairly substantial," it's not so "overwhelming so that you can't do anything [aside from] work." Perhaps most importantly, the professors are "intelligent and stimulating, encourage discussion, and constantly [ask] provoking questions." Moreover, they "really go that extra mile" and often "invite [students] over for dinner, bring snacks to class, plan extracurricular departmental events, and are always willing to help with schoolwork." Simply put, "The professors are what make Kenyon so great." And though some undergrads grumble that the administration is "for the most part anti-Greek," most students give them high marks as well. They are "friendly," "visible on campus," and often "seek the opinions of students when making [administrative] decisions."

Life
Since hometown Gambier doesn't provide much "besides corn fields," life at Kenyon really does revolve around the campus. Fortunately, there are always a myriad of events of which to take advantage, from "Kenyon Film Society movie screenings" to "various theater productions, a cappella concerts, and speakers." For those interested in the social scene, "The Greek system facilitates most of the parties on campus, but that doesn't mean that Kenyon has a typical frat culture; you don't ever have to worry about 'getting in' to a party." A psych major agrees, adding, "The social environment is inclusive and fun—most parties have different student bands playing a wide variety of music (from electronic music to Motown) and everyone is invited." Of course, should the typical fare start getting old, Kenyon students are more than happy to find creative ways to have fun. As one pleased junior shares, "We've had midnight sledding parties, swims in the river when it's warm, 'Project Runway' design challenges, movie nights, bike rides through farm country to the local farmers', market [and] fort-building parties." When students do feel the urge to get off campus, they often "go to Wal-Mart," "restaurants in [nearby] Mt. Vernon" or head to Columbus (roughly forty-five minutes away) for "some shopping and culture."

Student Body
On the surface, it appears as though Kenyon students can be divided into two categories: "a North Face, L.L. Bean–wearing, outdoorsy type, or a hipster in skinny jeans, flannel, and boots." "Of course," a classics major assures us, "there are plenty of others who don't fit distinctly into these groups." Indeed, "We have many 'alpha-males' who play rugby by day and are in musicals by night." All of this is indicative of a campus where "everyone finds a comfortable place to fit in." Or, as one English and Spanish double-major bluntly states, "We all get along—we're in the middle of nowhere so we kinda have to." One common trait these "hardworking, intelligent" students do possess is "a love of learning about new things." As a sophomore expounds, "I love classics and Socrates, and I can discuss with my best friend why I think Athens is better than Rome, and she'll argue back." Yes, many undergrads here are self-professed "nerds" and proud of it. As one student sums up, Kenyon manages to attract "all of the quirky, cool smart kids from your high school."

FINANCIAL AID: 740-427-5430 • E-MAIL: ADMISSIONS@KENYON.EDU • WEBSITE: WWW.KENYON.EDU

THE PRINCETON REVIEW SAYS

Admissions

Very important factors considered include: Academic GPA, application essay, recommendation(s), rigor of secondary school record, character/personal qualities. *Important factors considered include:* Class rank, standardized test scores, extracurricular activities, interview, level of applicant's interest, talent/ability. *Other factors considered include:* Alumni/ae relation, first generation, geographical residence, racial/ethnic status, state residency, volunteer work, work experience. SAT or ACT required; ACT with or without writing component accepted. TOEFL required of all international applicants. High school diploma is required, and GED is accepted. *Academic units required:* 4 English, 3–4 mathematics, 3 science (3 science labs), 3 foreign language, 3 social studies, 2 history, 3 academic elective, 1 fine arts. *Academic units recommended:* 4 English, 4 mathematics, 4 science (3 science labs), 4 foreign language, 1 social studies, 3 history, 3 academic elective.

Financial Aid

Students should submit: FAFSA, CSS/Financial Aid PROFILE. Regular filing deadline is February 15. The Princeton Review suggests that all financial aid forms be submitted as soon as possible after January 1. *Need-based scholarships/grants offered:* Federal Pell, SEOG, state scholarships/grants, private scholarships, school scholarship or grant aid from institutional funds. *Loan aid offered:* Direct Subsidized Stafford, Direct Unsubsidized Stafford, Direct PLUS, Federal Perkins, university loans from institutional funds. Federal Work-Study Program available. Off-campus job opportunities are poor.

The Inside Word

In terms of admissions selectivity, Kenyon is of the first order of selective, small, Midwestern, liberal arts schools. Kenyon shares a lot of application and admit overlap with other schools in this niche, and the choice for many students comes down to "best fit." As Kenyon is a writing-intensive institution, applicants should expect that all written material submitted to the school in the admissions process will be scrutinized. Revise and proofread accordingly.

THE SCHOOL SAYS " . . ."

From the Admissions Office

"Students and alumni alike think of Kenyon as a place that fosters 'learning in the company of friends.' While faculty expectations are rigorous and the work challenging, the academic atmosphere is cooperative, not competitive. Indications of intellectual curiosity and passion for learning, more than just high grades and test scores, are what we look for in applications. Important as well are demonstrated interests in non-academic pursuits, whether in athletics, the arts, writing, or another passion. Life in this small college community is fueled by the talents and enthusiasm of our students, so the admission staff seeks students who have a range of talents and interests.

"The high school transcript, recommendations, the personal statement, and answers on the supplement are of primary importance in reviewing preparedness and fit. Standardized tests (SAT or ACT) are of secondary importance."

SELECTIVITY

Admissions Rating	96
# of applicants	4,272
% of applicants accepted	33
% of acceptees attending	30
# accepting a place on wait list	216
% admitted from wait list	6
# of early decision applicants	406
% accepted early decision	59

FRESHMAN PROFILE

Range SAT Critical Reading	640–740
Range SAT Math	610–690
Range SAT Writing	630–730
Range ACT Composite	28–32
Minimum paper TOEFL	600
Minimum web-based TOEFL	100
Average HS GPA	3.85
% graduated top 10% of class	63
% graduated top 25% of class	88
% graduated top 50% of class	98

DEADLINES

Early decision	
Deadline	11/15
Notification	12/15
Regular	
Deadline	1/15
Nonfall registration?	no

APPLICANTS ALSO LOOK AT

AND OFTEN PREFER
Amherst College, Brown University, Middlebury College, Vassar College

AND SOMETIMES PREFER
Bowdoin College, Carleton College, Oberlin College, Wesleyan University

AND RARELY PREFER
College of Wooster, Denison University, Dickinson College, Skidmore College

FINANCIAL FACTS

Financial Aid Rating	90
Annual tuition	$44,090
Room and board	$10,200
Required fees	$1,540
Books and supplies	$1,800
% frosh rec. need-based scholarship or grant aid	40
% UG rec. need-based scholarship or grant aid	39
% frosh rec. non-need-based scholarship or grant aid	10
% UG rec. non-need-based scholarship or grant aid	9
% frosh rec. need-based self-help aid	37
% UG rec. need-based self-help aid	39
% UG borrow to pay for school	56
Average cumulative indebtedness	$20,492

KNOX COLLEGE

BOX K-148, GALESBURG, IL 61401 • ADMISSIONS: 309-341-7100 • FAX: 309-341-7070

STUDENTS SAY ". . ."

Academics

You can choose your own educational adventure at Knox College, a small school that offers the resources, support, and creative atmosphere students need to get the most out of their college experience. Many students come to Knox for its lauded creative writing major, as well as its "strong premedical program." For those still looking for their calling, the good thing about Knox is there are "very minimal requirements for graduation," and students are encouraged to explore a variety of fields. A freshman says, "Even as a science major preparing for medical school, I'm able to take a ton of electives." In this and every way, students can take an active role in planning and executing their educations. At Knox, "If you have an idea or the inkling of an idea, advisers are quick to help your dreams come true," and eighty percent of undergraduates work on independent study projects during college. In a classroom setting, "Professors are incredibly informed and enthusiastic about their subject matter," and coursework is rigorous. Of particular note, the academic calendar is divided into three 10-week terms so, in challenging classes like organic chemistry, you may end up "locking yourself in your room and only emerging for food, showers, and class." The upshot is that, "although most classes are pretty challenging academically, it is very easy, and encouraged, to just drop in and ask questions" of your professors. Administrators are likewise available and ready to attend to student concerns. When you've got a question or problem, "There's no shortage of help and making an appointment with anyone in any office is a breeze."

Life

Academics are top priority for most Knox undergraduates, but there's much more to life than holing up in the library. A junior explains, "While the academics are very demanding and the expectations are high, it is the life outside of the classroom that truly defines the challenges of a Knox education." With more than 100 student clubs and plenty of administrative support, Knox gives students "the opportunity to create their own atmosphere—everything from creating new clubs and courses to doing independent research and putting up art exhibits." Hometown Galesburg gets a universal thumbs down, so "Students usually don't go far outside of the college borders." On the weekends, "Most fun consists of attending parties and hanging out with friends on campus." In general, "Parties tend to revolve around the frats (sororities don't have their own houses)," and drinking is a popular pastime, though certainly not the only one. A student shares, "As a person who chooses not to drink at Knox, I very rarely feel excluded from activities. I can easily go to a party and refuse alcohol without pressure." For a mellow evening, "Knox is always bringing in political speakers, comedians, performing groups, or individuals to present seminars." To add to the charms, living facilities are top-notch, and "The dorms and suite-style living do wonders for comfort and residential satisfaction."

Student Body

On this small campus, you'll find an "entertaining and diverse" student body, represented by a range of styles, pastimes, and interests, as well as "great socioeconomic diversity." Students lovingly describe their classmates as "Knox Awkward," and most students aren't "overly concerned with appearance or name brands." A sophomore says, "It is easy to make friends at Knox, because nobody is pretentious. That's something I really valued when I visited, and what continues to make me happy [now] I am here." Students "are very politically and socially liberal." A student tells us, "Conservative students can have a hard time fitting in here when political tensions are high, but I have friends on both ends of the spectrum, and they get along fine when not talking politics." Aside from political predilections, "Students tend to be very open-minded and accepting of all things—religion, gender, race, sexuality."

FINANCIAL AID: 309-341-7149 • E-MAIL: ADMISSION@KNOX.EDU • WEBSITE: WWW.KNOX.EDU

THE PRINCETON REVIEW SAYS

Admissions

Very important factors considered include: Academic GPA, application essay, rigor of secondary school record. *Important factors considered include:* Class rank, recommendation(s), character/personal qualities, interview. *Other factors considered include:* Standardized test scores, alumni/ae relation, extracurricular activities, first generation, geographical residence, level of applicant's interest, racial/ethnic status, talent/ability, volunteer work. ACT with or without writing component accepted. TOEFL required of all international applicants. High school diploma is required, and GED is accepted. *Academic units recommended:* 4 English, 4 mathematics, 4 science (2 science labs), 3 foreign language, 2 social studies, 2 history.

Financial Aid

Students should submit: FAFSA, institution's own financial aid form. The Princeton Review suggests that all financial aid forms be submitted as soon as possible after January 1. *Need-based scholarships/grants offered:* Federal Pell, SEOG, state scholarships/grants, private scholarships, school scholarship or grant aid from institutional funds. *Loan aid offered:* Direct Subsidized Stafford, Direct Unsubsidized Stafford, Direct PLUS, Federal Perkins, university loans from institutional funds. Applicants will be notified of awards on a rolling basis beginning March 15. Federal Work-Study Program available. Off-campus job opportunities are good.

The Inside Word

With just fewer than 1,400 students, Knox makes diversity a priority, attracting students from forty-seven states and forty-eight countries. Both qualitative and quantitative factors are important to Knox, and admissions are competitive. Seventy-six percent of incoming freshman rank in the top quarter of their high school class.

THE SCHOOL SAYS "..."

From the Admissions Office

"Knox was founded on the idea that education has the power to confer a kind of freedom—what we've come to call 'freedom to flourish.' On the surface, 'freedom to flourish' is a simple and powerful concept—it is the knowledge and skills one needs to live a rewarding personal, professional, and civic life. But 'freedom to flourish' also has more subtle meaning that touches on how education happens at Knox.

"Most schools ask what you want to study and give you a checklist of courses needed for that degree. Knox asks, 'What do you want to know, and what do you want to do with that knowledge?' Within the context of the goals and milestones of one of our many majors, you and your advisor will develop a personalized educational plan of classes, internships, off-campus study, and independent research projects that meet the agenda you set for yourself. In this sense, a Knox education is an act of imagination, an act of entrepreneurship, an act of freedom.'

"That self-direction doesn't end in advising sessions and course selection. You'll be encouraged to bring your own interests and perspective to every class you take, and you'll be challenged to apply what you learn to the world around you. In the end you will learn how to set goals, how to figure out what you need to know to achieve those goals, and how to identify and collaborate with mentors who can help you along the way. That is 'freedom to flourish.'

"At Knox, you'll never be a number. Knox reviews each application holistically, fully considering a student's academic record, course selection, and performance (grades), as well as essays, recommendations, interviews, and other accomplishments. As a result, the submission of SAT or ACT scores is optional for most applicants."

SELECTIVITY

Admissions Rating	89
# of applicants	2,395
% of applicants accepted	75
% of acceptees attending	20
# accepting a place on wait list	17
% admitted from wait list	41

FRESHMAN PROFILE

Range SAT Critical Reading	590–720
Range SAT Math	560–690
Range SAT Writing	600–700
Range ACT Composite	26–31
Minimum paper TOEFL	550
Minimum web-based TOEFL	80
Average HS GPA	3.35
% graduated top 10% of class	42
% graduated top 25% of class	75
% graduated top 50% of class	96

DEADLINES

Early action	
Deadline	12/1
Notification	12/31
Regular	
Deadline	2/1
Nonfall registration?	no

APPLICANTS ALSO LOOK AT

AND OFTEN PREFER

AND SOMETIMES PREFER
Beloit College, Earlham College, Illinois Wesleyan University, University of Illinois at Urbana-Champaign

AND RARELY PREFER
Augustana College (IL), Grinnell College, Lawrence University, Macalester College, Washington University in St. Louis

FINANCIAL FACTS

Financial Aid Rating	87
Annual tuition	$34,110
Room and board	$7,488
Required fees	$354
Books and supplies	$900
% frosh rec. need-based scholarship or grant aid	68
% UG rec. need-based scholarship or grant aid	72
% frosh rec. non-need-based scholarship or grant aid	7
% UG rec. non-need-based scholarship or grant aid	8
% frosh rec. need-based self-help aid	62
% UG rec. need-based self-help aid	65
% frosh rec. any financial aid	98
% UG rec. any financial aid	97
% UG borrow to pay for school	69
Average cumulative indebtedness	$26,506

LAFAYETTE COLLEGE

118 MARKLE HALL, EASTON, PA 18042 • ADMISSIONS: 610-330-5100 • FAX: 610-330-5355

STUDENTS SAY ". . ."

Academics

Lafayette College is "a small, prestigious liberal arts school" that offers "a welcoming community that embraces a rigorous and well-respected education." Thanks to the "top-quality engineering education," many students say, "Lafayette is your classic liberal arts college with a twist" and point to the "vast array of research opportunities" available to undergrads. The college "prides itself on student/faculty relationships," and students say, "Each student is provided with the resources he or she needs to really shine and be recognized for his or her achievements and talents." An international affairs major says, "Whether you're an engineer, a premed student, or an art major, there is a great academic program and an embracing group of people waiting for you at Lafayette." Overall the professors get high marks because "their office doors are always open," and they're "the kind of people who learn your name and never forget it." Students say, for the most part, "Professors are interesting and encourage class discussion, which is a staple of Lafayette classes," and add, "It's not very common to hear that someone doesn't like one of their professors at Lafayette." Generally, "Classes are challenging but manageable, if you put in the time," but students gripe, "The class registration system is dicey."

Life

At Lafayette, the "campus is gorgeous," and students say you feel the "close atmosphere of the school" after "immediately walking onto the campus." Overall students feel, "The campus community is very supportive," and a civil engineering major says, "The family atmosphere adds to the education and makes Lafayette feel more like home than school." With "over 200 clubs and organizations on campus," there "is something that will fit everyone's lifestyle and hobbies," and when it comes to their Division I athletics, "Students radiate school pride." Lafayette boasts a "great career center due to the close ties alumni have with the college," and career services are offered to students during all four years of their undergraduate study. A senior says, "Being a small school, students have direct access to administrative offices and deans," and the staff is described as "extremely welcoming." While some say "the facilities are first rate" and improving, others complain, "Certain dorms could use renovation," especially since students are required to live on campus for their first three years. However, all agree that the "cafeteria food could use some improvement."

Student Body

Lafayette students are "passionate and driven" and "tend to be athletic, very preppy, and serious about their education." A sophomore says, "The vast majority of students here are middle-to-upper class Caucasians from the tristate area," but another adds, "Every kind of crowd imaginable is present on campus; whether you're a hipster or a prepster, you'll find a group you're comfortable in." Regardless, some students wish for "better integration of the different cultures represented at school," and say, "More support for the LGBTQ community would be a pleasant change." Many students are "involved with Greek life," and some feel that those "not involved in Greek life or sports can be isolated"; however, an economics major notes, "There are definitely cliques, but nothing even close to the high school scale." On weekends, most students stay on campus, and it's commonly held that "there is quite a bit of drinking," even though "campus safety is very strict and off-campus housing is limited to seniors so the party scene is limited." Many feel there's a "large disconnect between [the] administration and students especially on social issues like the alcohol policy," and say, "instead of trying to keep people safe, they continually try to bust people."

FINANCIAL AID: 610-330-5055 • E-MAIL: ADMISSIONS@LAFAYETTE.EDU • WEBSITE: WWW.LAFAYETTE.EDU

THE PRINCETON REVIEW SAYS

Admissions

Very important factors considered include: Academic GPA, rigor of secondary school record. *Important factors considered include:* Application essay, class rank, recommendation(s), standardized test scores, character/personal qualities, extracurricular activities, talent/ability. *Other factors considered include:* Alumni/ae relation, first generation, geographical residence, interview, level of applicant's interest, racial/ethnic status, volunteer work, work experience. SAT or ACT required; ACT with writing component required. TOEFL required of all international applicants. High school diploma or equivalent isn't required. *Academic units recommended:* 4 English, 3 mathematics, 2 science (2 science labs), 2 foreign language, 5 academic elective.

Financial Aid

Students should submit: FAFSA, CSS/Financial Aid PROFILE. Regular filing deadline is March 1. The Princeton Review suggests that all financial aid forms be submitted as soon as possible after January 1. *Need-based scholarships/grants offered:* Federal Pell, SEOG, state scholarships/grants, private scholarships, school scholarship or grant aid from institutional funds. *Loan aid offered:* Direct Subsidized Stafford, Direct Unsubsidized Stafford, Direct PLUS, Federal Perkins, university loans from institutional funds. Federal Work-Study Program available. Off-campus job opportunities are good.

The Inside Word

Lafayette College takes into account a variety of factors when evaluating prospective students. Emphasis is placed on an applicant's performance in secondary school, the quality of that education, and the class standing. The admissions committee also values a commitment to social awareness and potential for leadership as exhibited through extracurricular activities. The results of standardized tests are recommended but not required for admission.

THE SCHOOL SAYS "..."

From the Admissions Office

"Lafayette offers academic choices as broad and diverse as universities many times our size. Students and alumni say our curriculum—with extraordinary breadth and depth for an undergraduate college—is a key strength.

"At Lafayette, education is a dynamic and engaged process—not passive. Students are encouraged to cross traditional academic boundaries to connect and integrate knowledge from different fields in the humanities, social sciences, natural sciences, and engineering and to work together to approach intellectual challenges and wider-world problems from multiple perspectives.

"Our approach is active and global, working in communities locally, nationally, and internationally. Global opportunities range from faculty-led semester programs to concentrated interim session courses to international service projects. Students who experience immersion in international settings or work in student-faculty teams to address global challenges have an advantage in advanced studies and employment after they graduate. These experiences are vital for citizenship and leadership in an increasingly interconnected, globalized world.

"Lafayette is a vibrant environment in which to explore and grow. With more than 250 clubs and activities—including the arts, Division I sports, and community service, to name just a few—students have many ways to balance work and play, develop leadership skills, and have fun. And because of our location, just seventy miles from New York City, Lafayette offers significant opportunities to connect with prominent leaders in many fields who visit campus and to take advantage of the major artistic, cultural, and financial centers of the Eastern United States."

SELECTIVITY

Admissions Rating	95
# of applicants	5,822
% of applicants accepted	42
% of acceptees attending	27
# accepting a place on wait list	534
% admitted from wait list	5
# of early decision applicants	432
% accepted early decision	69

FRESHMAN PROFILE

Range SAT Critical Reading	570–670
Range SAT Math	610–700
Range SAT Writing	590–680
Range ACT Composite	26–30
Minimum paper TOEFL	550
Average HS GPA	3.41
% graduated top 10% of class	57
% graduated top 25% of class	86
% graduated top 50% of class	99

DEADLINES

Early decision	
Deadline	2/1
Notification	12/15
Regular	
Deadline	1/1
Nonfall registration?	yes

APPLICANTS ALSO LOOK AT
AND OFTEN PREFER
Cornell University

AND SOMETIMES PREFER
Bucknell University, Colgate University, Lehigh University

FINANCIAL FACTS

Financial Aid Rating	93
Annual tuition	$38,810
Room and board	$11,959
Required fees	$1,005
Books and supplies	$1,000
% frosh rec. need-based scholarship or grant aid	37
% UG rec. need-based scholarship or grant aid	43
% frosh rec. non-need-based scholarship or grant aid	11
% UG rec. non-need-based scholarship or grant aid	12
% frosh rec. need-based self-help aid	34
% UG rec. need-based self-help aid	39
% UG borrow to pay for school	52
Average cumulative indebtedness	$20,687

LAKE FOREST COLLEGE

555 NORTH SHERIDAN ROAD, LAKE FOREST, IL 60045 • ADMISSIONS: 847-735-5000 • FAX: 847-735-6291

STUDENTS SAY ". . ."

Academics

Students at Lake Forest College rave about "an extraordinary educational environment where students share a close bond with their professors while living and studying in an intimate college community among an enriching Chicago background." A broad-ranging general education curriculum "emphasizes giving each student an individual and well-rounded education in the liberal arts," one that many pursue in their majors; you also have to love to write, because "this is a writing-intensive school. If you only want to take exams, this school isn't for you." The academic breadth at Lake Forest College is "both challenging and inspiring," and the class sizes and teachers "won't let anyone hide or get away with spotty work. Rest assured they will push you beyond what you believe you are capable of each semester till you nearly break." Quite a few students at Lake Forest are looking to go on to grad school, and students tell us, "There are endless opportunities here if a person actively seeks them out." The school isn't as well-known as it might be if it were located in the Northeast, leading some to describe it as "an undercover gem," and a popular perception is that "Lake Forest is a solid college with great financial aid." The small school size means "administration can help you, and they actually do"; however, the college is planning to expand enrollment over the next few years.

Life

The area surrounding Lake Forest College "is an extremely wealthy community, so many of the businesses that are there are too expensive for the average student. There is just one bar, and everything shuts down very early," but the town is trying to attract more college students by expanding hours. Students do avail themselves of "the basics: a couple of good restaurants (The Lantern, Burger King, Egg Harbor), a grocery store and pharmacy, and a post office," but "Students really have to leave the city to have fun." Vernon Hills, "with a large mall and lots of restaurants, "is about twenty minutes away," but most students are more than happy to head to Chicago, which is only an hour and a five-dollar (weekend) roundtrip ticket away. "We use Chicago as an asset," says one student. "Chicago is ever-changing and does not get dull." "Life varies by which campus you live on:" "North Campus has most of the quiet dorms" while "Middle and South are the center of party life at Lake Forest, and there's a ninety-nine percent chance you'll hear stereos pulsing on Friday and Saturday nights." Clubs and organizations are "highly attended," and there's usually "an ACP (all campus party) being hosted by an organization, or a residence hall activity night."

Student Body

The typical Lake Forest student "is an intelligent kid who doesn't want to completely devote his life to studying [and] likes to party." Students report that most students are "upper-middle-class" and "very preppy" (although more than three-quarters of Lake Forest undergraduates receive some form of need-based aid), lending itself to "an East Coast atmosphere." Regardless of their economic background, "everyone is generally quite friendly, and if they aren't, they are at least civil." The school "is very cliquey," and "Students stick to groups of friends that either play the same sport, are in the same fraternity or sorority, or are the same race," but at least there's "a healthy mix" of students from which those cliques originate. The school boasts a fair number of commuters, as well as "a large LGB community, and Greek life but no houses." Minorities are most often represented among the large population of international students, who "give the campus a more diverse feeling."

LAKE FOREST COLLEGE

FINANCIAL AID: 847-735-5103 • E-MAIL: ADMISSIONS@LAKEFOREST.EDU • WEBSITE: WWW.LAKEFOREST.EDU

THE PRINCETON REVIEW SAYS
Admissions
Very important factors considered include: Academic GPA, recommendation(s), rigor of secondary school record, interview. *Important factors considered include:* Application essay, character/personal qualities, extracurricular activities, level of applicant's interest, talent/ability. *Other factors considered include:* Class rank, standardized test scores, alumni/ae relation, first generation, geographical residence, volunteer work, work experience. ACT with or without writing component accepted. TOEFL required of all international applicants. High school diploma is required, and GED is accepted. *Academic units required:* 4 English, 3 mathematics, 3 science (3 science labs), 2 foreign language, 2 social studies, 2 history, 3 academic elective. *Academic units recommended:* 4 English, 4 mathematics, 4 science (4 science labs), 4 foreign language, 2 social studies, 2 history, 3 academic elective.

Financial Aid
Students should submit: FAFSA, institution's own financial aid form. Regular filing deadline is May 1. The Princeton Review suggests that all financial aid forms be submitted as soon as possible after January 1. *Need-based scholarships/grants offered:* Federal Pell, SEOG, state scholarships/grants, private scholarships, school scholarship or grant aid from institutional funds. *Loan aid offered:* Direct Subsidized Stafford, Direct Unsubsidized Stafford, Direct PLUS, Federal Perkins. Applicants will be notified of awards on a rolling basis beginning February 1. Federal Work-Study Program available. Off-campus job opportunities are good.

The Inside Word
Lake Forest is small enough to give each application it receives close and careful consideration. Solid high school performers should have little difficulty gaining admission, but keep in mind that Lake Forest has a prep-school-at-the-college-level feel and likes to assess the whole candidate, not just grades and test scores. In fact, test scores are optional. The school will look closely at the graded essay you submit with your application, so choose carefully.

THE SCHOOL SAYS "..."
From the Admissions Office
"Lake Forest College's beautiful 107-acre campus is located thirty miles north of downtown Chicago along the shore of Lake Michigan. Lake Forest has a long tradition of academic excellence and is known for its innovative curriculum. In addition to majors in the humanities, social sciences, and natural sciences, the college features programs of study in pre-law, premedicine, communication, business, finance, computer science, and still other practical areas. Abundant internships, research opportunities, personal guidance from professors, and connections to nearby Chicago also set Lake Forest apart. Students learn in a rigorous academic environment in small class settings where professors do all the teaching and also serve as advisors and mentors. Professors are accomplished scholars, published authors, and recipients of prestigious grants.

"Students represent nearly every state and seventy-one countries around the world and international and ethnic minorities make up more than twenty-five percent of the student body. Together they comprise a learning community that prepares them to succeed in a global society. Just an hour's train ride away, Chicago offers students unique experiential learning opportunities, and professors regularly use the city's resources to complement coursework. The college's Center for Chicago Programs facilitates internships at chicago institutions as well as plans trips to the city's dozens of ethnic neighborhoods. More than sixty student groups provide a host of opportunities that develop leadership skills and enhance students' campus experience and post-college prospects. The college offers recreational music, art, and theater programs, as well as seventeen varsity sports and intramural and club sports."

SELECTIVITY	
Admissions Rating	88
# of applicants	2,398
% of applicants accepted	60
% of acceptees attending	17
# accepting a place on wait list	25
% admitted from wait list	72

FRESHMAN PROFILE	
Range SAT Critical Reading	540–640
Range SAT Math	530–640
Range SAT Writing	490–640
Range ACT Composite	23–28
Minimum paper TOEFL	550
Minimum computer TOEFL	220
Average HS GPA	3.56
% graduated top 10% of class	33
% graduated top 25% of class	64
% graduated top 50% of class	92

DEADLINES	
Early decision	
Deadline	12/1
Notification	12/20
Early action	
Deadline	12/1
Notification	1/20
Regular	
Priority	2/15
Nonfall registration?	yes

FINANCIAL FACTS	
Financial Aid Rating	94
Annual tuition	$34,885
Room and board	$8,327
Required fees	$640
Books and supplies	$1,000
% frosh rec. need-based scholarship or grant aid	79
% UG rec. need-based scholarship or grant aid	76
% frosh rec. need-based self-help aid	65
% UG rec. need-based self-help aid	44
% frosh rec. any financial aid	94
% UG rec. any financial aid	94
% UG borrow to pay for school	74
Average cumulative indebtedness	$29,279

LAWRENCE UNIVERSITY

711 E. BOLDT WAY, APPLETON, WI 54911 • ADMISSIONS: 920-832-6500 • FAX: 920-832-6782

STUDENTS SAY "..."

Academics

Lawrence University boasts "excellence in both the liberal arts and the fine arts" and "offers small class sizes with top-notch professors" in a "welcoming environment." The university is known for its "prestigious music conservatory" and "individualized and well-rounded approach to learning." Many students take advantage of "interdisciplinary options where departments work together to create specialized majors," and say, "Lawrence is extremely accommodating; they want you to succeed and be happy." Students say, "The people at Lawrence as a whole are very passionate about their studies and seriously want to learn," and the consensus is that there's a general "attitude" of "mutual learning and personal improvement." Professors are "brilliant, passionate about their work and teaching, and...totally engaging in the classroom," and a music education major says, "They really care about their students as people and want to support their education as much as possible and in every way they can!" A senior adds, "If you get the opportunity to have a tutorial with a prof (which is common here), it only gets better." Although "academics at Lawrence are rigorous," students say, "Class size is kept to a minimum" and the "competition between students is not cutthroat but very healthy."

Life

Lawrence University is known for its "student-oriented environment" on an "amazing campus" that's "beautiful yet nicely urban." Students say, "Lawrence is a small, but tight-knit community" and that the university "cares that we are engaged both inside and outside the classroom." Another student adds, "It is unusual to meet students who are not involved in one [or] more extracurricular activities or student groups." The community is one that "promotes open-mindedness and intellectual and individual growth," and a biology major says, "Not only is Lawrence more ethnically diverse than many other liberal arts schools, there is also a lot of diversity in interests." Many students are thankful for having "the Con" on campus because, "there is always great, free music," although the flipside is that "funding for some of the sports teams could be improved." At Lawrence, students are "required to live on campus all four years," which results in "a very strong campus environment," but many students feel the "residence halls are fairly outdated." There are complaints that the "student health center is lacking."

Student Body

At Lawrence, "The typical student has interests and passions all across the map and can usually find ways to express all those interests." A senior says, "A hockey player might be working on an intensive honors thesis in biochemistry." Regardless, some feel, "The conservatory of music students and bachelor of art students are quite segregated" and acknowledge "a friendly rivalry between the two halves of the university, but [say] it's not serious." Most students are "Midwestern, laid-back, open-minded, proud but not pretentious" and "madly in love with music." The student body is "an eclectic blend of musicians, athletes, student government junkies, writers, poets, and wallflowers," and "Students find their niches incredibly easily here." A junior says, "Nerdiness is a bonus," and a theater arts major agrees, "Don't be surprised if a choir or orchestra concert has more attendees than a football game on your average weekend." One student says, "Though there are parties, I think most students are pretty low-key (*not* boring, just not huge partiers)," and another adds, "Various theme houses, frats, and clubs have their own party at least once a term and all parties are open to everyone." Overall, Lawrentians say they're "hardworking and dedicated, but love to chill out and have fun," and that "the school's small size promotes a positive community that isn't difficult to find a place in."

FINANCIAL AID: 920-832-6583 • E-MAIL: ADMISSIONS@LAWRENCE.EDU • WEBSITE: WWW.LAWRENCE.EDU

THE PRINCETON REVIEW SAYS

Admissions

Very important factors considered include: Academic GPA, class rank, rigor of secondary school record. *Important factors considered include:* Application essay, recommendation(s), character/personal qualities, extracurricular activities, talent/ability. *Other factors considered include:* Standardized test scores, alumni/ae relation, first generation, interview, racial/ethnic status, volunteer work, work experience. ACT with or without writing component accepted. TOEFL required of all international applicants. *Academic units required:* 4 English. *Academic units recommended:* 3 mathematics, 3 science, 2 foreign language, 2 social studies, 2 history.

Financial Aid

Students should submit: FAFSA, institution's own financial aid form. The Princeton Review suggests that all financial aid forms be submitted as soon as possible after January 1. *Need-based scholarships/grants offered:* Federal Pell, SEOG, state scholarships/grants, private scholarships, school scholarship or grant aid from institutional funds. *Loan aid offered:* Direct Subsidized Stafford, Direct Unsubsidized Stafford, Direct PLUS, Federal Perkins. Applicants will be notified of awards on a rolling basis beginning March 1. Federal Work-Study Program available. Off-campus job opportunities are fair.

The Inside Word

Students interested in applying to Lawrence University's Conservatory are required to schedule an audition and submit a music resume detailing their experiences as a musician, in addition to the traditional application. Furthermore, prospective Conservatory students must submit an additional recommendation from a music teacher qualified to evaluate their musical abilities.

THE SCHOOL SAYS "..."

From the Admissions Office

"Lawrence believes college should not be a one-size-fits-all experience, and that you'll learn best when you're educated as a unique individual. Within our college of liberal arts and sciences and our conservatory of music—both devoted exclusively to undergraduate education—you'll have unparalleled opportunities to collaborate closely with your professors in small classes (ninety percent have fewer than twenty students in them; sixty-five percent have total enrollments of one). Our 1,433 students come from nearly every state and about fifty countries to enjoy the distinctive benefits of this engaged—and engaging—community. It's a close-knit, residential, 24/7 campus filled with smart and talented people who are pursuing an astonishing variety of academic and extracurricular interests. Our picturesque, residential campus is nestled on the banks of the Fox River in Appleton, Wisconsin, (metro population: 200,000), one of the fastest growing metropolitan areas in the Midwest. Björklunden, our 425-acre estate on more than one mile of pristine Lake Michigan shoreline (two hours north of campus), provides educational and recreational opportunities for students to enhance their on-campus learning experiences.

"We seek students who are intellectual, imaginative, and innovative: qualities best quantified from a thorough review of your curriculum, academic performance, essay, activities, and recommendations. Accordingly, Lawrence considers—but does not require—the ACT and the SAT in our review of applications for admission and scholarship."

SELECTIVITY

Admissions Rating	91
# of applicants	2,625
% of applicants accepted	66
% of acceptees attending	26
# accepting a place on wait list	85
% admitted from wait list	6
# of early decision applicants	43
% accepted early decision	95

FRESHMAN PROFILE

Range SAT Critical Reading	580–710
Range SAT Math	590–700
Range SAT Writing	580–680
Range ACT Composite	27–31
Minimum paper TOEFL	577
Minimum computer TOEFL	233
Minimum web-based TOEFL	90
Average HS GPA	3.66
% graduated top 10% of class	43
% graduated top 25% of class	73
% graduated top 50% of class	95

DEADLINES

Early decision	
Deadline	11/15
Notification	12/1
Early action	
Deadline	12/1
Notification	1/31
Regular	
Deadline	1/15
Notification	4/1
Nonfall registration?	no

APPLICANTS ALSO LOOK AT AND OFTEN PREFER

Beloit College, Carleton University, Macalester College, Saint Olaf College, University of Wisconsin—Madison

AND SOMETIMES PREFER

Grinnell College, Illinois Wesleyan University, Knox College, Northwestern University, Oberlin College

FINANCIAL FACTS

Financial Aid Rating	89
Annual tuition	$38,205
Room and board	$7,890
Required fees	$276
Books and supplies	$1,800
% frosh rec. need-based scholarship or grant aid	57
% UG rec. need-based scholarship or grant aid	58
% frosh rec. non-need-based scholarship or grant aid	50
% UG rec. non-need-based scholarship or grant aid	42
% frosh rec. need-based self-help aid	47
% UG rec. need-based self-help aid	50
% frosh rec. any financial aid	93
% UG rec. any financial aid	92
% UG borrow to pay for school	75
Average cumulative indebtedness	$30,224

LEHIGH UNIVERSITY

27 MEMORIAL DRIVE WEST, BETHLEHEM, PA 18015 • ADMISSIONS: 610-758-3100 • FAX: 610-758-4361

STUDENTS SAY ". . ."

Academics

Lehigh University is a "prestigious," "small- to medium-sized school" that "offers great programs" and the "resources of a large university." It "boasts a strong engineering program," and students say it truly "lives up to its academic reputation." Students "genuinely care about their education" and have "an incredible work ethic." A psychology major says, "People want to learn and want to do well, which creates a really good college environment," and a junior adds, "Students are driven, but not competitive with one another"; instead, "Lehigh expects a lot out of you, which in turn allows you to push and challenge yourself." Students are grateful for the "strong connection with alumni, which is great for prospective employment," and say, "The career opportunities post graduation are excellent for both engineer and business students." Professors get generally high marks, with students saying they're "extremely qualified in their fields" and "do all they can to assure that they succeed." Academics are considered "extremely rigorous and rewarding," leading a freshman to say, "Professors expect a lot from their students, but they do everything they can to help us." It's worth noting, however, that although "professors are extremely qualified in their fields...that does not always qualify them to be effective teachers," and some are "very hard to understand." Students also complain that "registration for courses is a mess."

Life

Lehigh offers "a friendly, community oriented atmosphere" on a hilly campus that is "beyond beautiful." Overall, there's "a vibrant, active student body, and a gorgeous campus, which combines to form a tremendously rich and invigorating experience." Students say, "There's a lot of school spirit," particularly during Lehigh-Laf week when they compete against local rival, Lafayette College, and that's considered "one of the best traditions Lehigh has." At Lehigh, "You always feel like you are part of something," and a junior says, "I've been blown away by the Lehigh community's loyalty to and love for all that is Lehigh." An engineering majors says, "Lehigh's sense of community stretches far past just the years a student spends on campus," noting lasting friendships and successful networking. Students partake in "more than 100 clubs and organizations," and say they "have many opportunities to join groups," adding, "Starting new clubs is also widely supported." Despite this, students wish for "better interaction between the student body and the administration in a way that involves the students in the decisions that the school makes," and say, "The food at the dining halls is often sub-par."

Student Body

Lehigh is "big on Greek life," with roughly one-third of the student body involved in a fraternity and sorority, and students say, "Greek life is huge everyday of the week." Some feel "it's a great way to get involved and meet new people," and say, "Partying on the 'hill' is definitely the most popular activity throughout the year." Yet others feel, "The heavy influence and importance of Greek life" is a "problem," and the university "could work more to integrate Greek life with the rest of the student body." Regardless, students say, "Enough goes on on-campus that if you don't want to go to parties you don't have to to have fun," and say, "It's easy to have fun without alcohol," adding, "There are substance-free halls and dorms as well as school-run activities during weeknights and weekends." Although some gripe, "There isn't much to do locally," the university provides "a free shuttle [that] takes students to the mall and movie theaters on weekends." Students are typically "from the east coast," "white," "pretty wealthy," and, "children of alumni [who] have [a] legacy." There are complaints that "Lehigh lacks a sense of diversity," and a marketing major says, "While there are numerous programs set up to help increase the racial, socioeconomic diversity here, it still remains a problem."

FINANCIAL AID: 610-758-3181 • E-MAIL: ADMISSIONS@LEHIGH.EDU • WEBSITE: WWW.LEHIGH.EDU

THE PRINCETON REVIEW SAYS

Admissions

Very important factors considered include: Recommendation(s), rigor of secondary school record, academic GPA. *Important factors considered include:* Application essay, standardized test scores, character/personal qualities, extracurricular activities, level of applicant's interest, talent/ability, volunteer work. *Other factors considered include:* Class rank, alumni/ae relation, first generation, geographical residence, interview, racial/ethnic status, work experience. SAT or ACT required; ACT with writing component required. TOEFL required of all international applicants. High school diploma or equivalent isn't required. *Academic units required:* 4 English, 3 mathematics, 2 science (2 science labs), 2 foreign language, 2 social studies, 3 academic elective.

Financial Aid

Students should submit: FAFSA, CSS/Financial Aid PROFILE. Regular filing deadline is February 15. The Princeton Review suggests that all financial aid forms be submitted as soon as possible after January 1. *Need-based scholarships/grants offered:* Federal Pell, SEOG, state scholarships/grants, private scholarships, school scholarship or grant aid from institutional funds, United Negro College Fund. *Loan aid offered:* Direct Subsidized Stafford, Direct Unsubsidized Stafford, Direct PLUS, Federal Perkins, university loans from institutional funds. Applicants will be notified of awards on or around March 30. Federal Work-Study Program available. Off-campus job opportunities are good.

The Inside Word

Admission to Lehigh University is competitive and the admissions committee suggests starting process the early and paying careful attention to deadlines and required supplemental materials. For the class of 2014, the university received more than 10,000 applications for a class size that's just over 1,200. Prospective students are strongly encouraged to visit campus to experience Lehigh firsthand and speak to the admissions staff.

THE SCHOOL SAYS "..."

From the Admissions Office

"Lehigh University is located fifty miles north of Philadelphia and seventy-five miles southwest of New York City in Bethlehem, Pennsylvania. We are a premier residential research university, ranked in the top tier of national research universities each year. Lehigh combines the learning opportunities of a large research university with the personal attention of a small, private college. We take an innovative approach to learning, discovery, and teaching by fusing traditionally separate majors to create a richer, fuller, more meaningful experience for you. Learning is connected to real-world applications and reinforced with cutting-edge academic research and hands-on experiences. You can customize your experience by tailoring majors and academic programs across four colleges and dozens of fields of study. Investigation, innovation, and global exposure will drive your educational experience at Lehigh. You'll learn and work alongside faculty who are leaders in their fields and bring the latest knowledge and newest discoveries to the classrooms, laboratories, and workshops to enhance you educational experience and give you real-world exposure. Here, we share a common set of core values: integrity and honesty, equitable community, academic freedom, intellectual curiosity, and leadership. A vibrant campus life offers many social activities from more than 150 clubs and organizations, twenty-five intercollegiate sports, and intramural sports and club programs. Campus Square, a residential and retail complex, integrates the campus with the surrounding community.

"Lehigh requires students to submit scores from the SAT or the ACT. Students submitting the ACT must also include with the writing portion. SAT Subject Tests are recommended but not required."

SELECTIVITY
Admissions Rating	96
# of applicants	10,328
% of applicants accepted	38
% of acceptees attending	31
# accepting a place on wait list	1,206
% admitted from wait list	1
# of early decision applicants	792
% accepted early decision	69

FRESHMAN PROFILE
Range SAT Critical Reading	580–670
Range SAT Math	640–720
Range ACT Composite	27–31
Minimum paper TOEFL	570
Minimum web-based TOEFL	90
% graduated top 10% of class	95
% graduated top 25% of class	99
% graduated top 50% of class	100

DEADLINES
Early decision	
Deadline	11/15
Notification	12/15
Regular	
Deadline	1/1
Nonfall registration?	yes

APPLICANTS ALSO LOOK AT
AND OFTEN PREFER
Boston College, Carnegie Mellon University, Cornell University, University of Maryland—College Park, University of Virginia

AND SOMETIMES PREFER
Bucknell University, Penn State—University Park, Rensselaer Polytechnic Institute, The George Washington University, Villanova University

AND RARELY PREFER
Boston University, Drexel University, Lafayette College, Rutgers, The State University of New Jersey, University of Delaware

FINANCIAL FACTS
Financial Aid Rating	93
Annual tuition	$40,660
Room and board	$10,840
Required fees	$300
Books and supplies	$1,000
% frosh rec. need-based scholarship or grant aid	45
% UG rec. need-based scholarship or grant aid	44
% frosh rec. non-need-based scholarship or grant aid	4
% UG rec. non-need-based scholarship or grant aid	5
% frosh rec. need-based self-help aid	42
% UG rec. need-based self-help aid	42
% frosh rec. any financial aid	60
% UG rec. any financial aid	60
% UG borrow to pay for school	57
Average cumulative indebtedness	$31,922

LEWIS & CLARK COLLEGE

0615 SOUTHWEST PALATINE HILL ROAD, PORTLAND, OR 97219-7899 • ADMISSIONS: 503-768-7040 • FAX: 503-768-7055

CAMPUS LIFE

Quality of Life Rating	84
Fire Safety Rating	97
Green Rating	78
Type of school	private
Environment	city

STUDENTS

Total undergrad enrollment	1,905
% male/female	40/60
% from out of state	82
% from public high school	75
% live on campus	67
% African American	2
% Asian	7
% Caucasian	57
% Hispanic	5
% Native American	1
% international	6

SURVEY SAYS . . .

Lots of liberal students
Students aren't religious
Students love Portland, OR
Frats and sororities are unpopular
or nonexistent
Political activism is popular

ACADEMICS

Academic Rating	89
% students graduating within 4 years	69
% students graduating within 6 years	76
Calendar	semester
Student/faculty ratio	12:1
Profs interesting rating	90
Profs accessible rating	87
Most common reg class size	10–19 students
Most common lab size	20–29 students

MOST POPULAR MAJORS
biology, international relations, psychology

STUDENTS SAY ". . ."

Academics

Lewis & Clark is a unique liberal arts college with a distinctively progressive personality. Academics at this small school emphasize "leadership, civic engagement, and education that impacts the world." Across disciplines, students are "pushed to grow, to be creative, [and] to go beyond your expectations for yourself." "The course catalogue is pretty expansive, while still retaining small class sizes." "The low student-professor ratio is amazing," and coursework is generally "much more discussion-based than lecture-oriented." There are myriad special programs to augment the traditional academic experience, including the school's "great overseas program," the "engaging" arts environment (including a campus art gallery and resident poets), and unique opportunities for extracurricular exploration and study. A case in point, a student tells us, "My most recent physics professor taught a particle physics mini-course for free every other Monday." Within the faculty and staff, "The focus is primarily on academics, but the mental and physical health of the students is also taken very seriously." As such, "Professors really make an effort to get to know their students," and personal relationship help to "generate thoughtful discussions in class and better engagement with the class material." Even so, L&C doesn't sacrifice quality for kindness. When it comes to professors, students are "impressed by their credentials and experience, especially at such a small college."

Life

Students appreciate the "relaxed but studious atmosphere" at L&C. In the classroom, there's "absolutely zero academic competition, which is wonderful and lets the focus be on every individual student's learning experience." Outside the classroom, there are tons of "awesome, student-run clubs on campus," which "range from intensive sport clubs, like soccer or Frisbee, to fun extracurriculars like gaming or Hawaii club." L&C has "a great athletics department for such a small school," and outdoorsy groups "organize trips for students to go backpacking, snowshoeing, [and] kayaking" in the beautiful Oregon wilderness. Students can't say enough good things about the "gorgeous campus" in suburban Portland, a peaceful backdrop for work and play. Rain keeps the campus pleasantly green, though "When it's sunny, it's fun to study on the grass and hang out outside." "There is a bus that goes from campus to downtown pretty regularly" so students can take advantage of the great cultural scene in surrounding Portland. Though not your typical college town, "There is a ton of stuff to do downtown and a lot of very cool, small, and unique (weird) neighbors in the greater Portland area." Back on campus, "Partying happens on the weekends, though in a more laid-back way than at many schools."

Student Body

"The typical Lewis & Clark student is liberal, intelligent, cares about their school work, and is a little quirky." Most students are "well-acquainted with current issues impacting our community, the nation, and the world at large." The typical undergraduate is the "hipster type, who eats at vegan food carts, goes to indie music concerts, gets [his or her] clothes from 'the bins' (a second-hand place), drinks copious amounts of yerba mate or black coffee, and is very, very politically correct." Another student adds that "drum/guitar playing, shoeless, dancing, yoga-doing students" are pretty much the norm in the L&C community. Students insist, "We may look like a bunch of Birkenstock-wearing, tree-hugging hippies, but there's a surprising amount of ideological diversity here that fosters critical thinking from many different perspectives." Cliques do form, but "There is no outright rejection of difference—just voluntary clumping together of similar people." A current student attests, "The typical student at L&C is a very liberal, non-religious, hipster...However, as a blue-collar girl from a farming town, they're pretty nice to everyone." If anything, students notice a "slight division between the athletic side of campus and people who do not participate in athletics."

LEWIS & CLARK COLLEGE

FINANCIAL AID: 503-768-7090 • E-MAIL: ADMISSIONS@LCLARK.EDU • WEBSITE: WWW.LCLARK.EDU

THE PRINCETON REVIEW SAYS

Admissions

Very important factors considered include: Academic GPA, rigor of secondary school record, racial/ethnic status. *Important factors considered include:* Application essay, class rank, recommendation(s), standardized test scores, alumni/ae relation, character/personal qualities, extracurricular activities, first generation, talent/ability, volunteer work. *Other factors considered include:* Geographical residence, interview, level of applicant's interest, state residency, work experience. ACT with or without writing component accepted. TOEFL required of all international applicants. High school diploma is required, and GED is accepted. *Academic units recommended:* 4 English, 4 mathematics, 3 science (2 science labs).

Financial Aid

Students should submit: FAFSA, CSS/Financial Aid PROFILE. The Princeton Review suggests that all financial aid forms be submitted as soon as possible after January 1. *Need-based scholarships/grants offered:* Federal Pell, SEOG, state scholarships/grants, private scholarships, school scholarship or grant aid from institutional funds. *Loan aid offered:* Direct Subsidized Stafford, Direct Unsubsidized Stafford, Direct PLUS, Federal Perkins. Applicants will be notified of awards on a rolling basis beginning March 1. Federal Work-Study Program available. Off-campus job opportunities are fair.

The Inside Word

While grades and SAT scores are certainly important to the college, L&C is also interested in students who will take advantage of the school's unique philosophy and educational environment. Successful applicants show the admissions committee why L&C is the right fit.

THE SCHOOL SAYS "..."

From the Admissions Office

"The record number of applicants in recent years cited a variety of reasons they were drawn to Lewis & Clark. Many had to do with the multiple environments experienced by our students, including a small arts and sciences college with a twelve to one student/faculty ratio; a location only six miles from downtown Portland (metropolitan population 1.9 million); a setting in the heart of the Pacific Northwest, making more than eighty trips per year possible for our College Outdoors Program; and the rest of the world—almost sixty percent of our graduates included an overseas program in their curriculum. Since 1962, more than 9,600 students and 212 faculty members have participated in 598 programs in sixty-six countries on six continents. Our international curriculum has undergone a total review to better prepare graduates going into the twenty-first century.

"At Lewis & Clark College, SAT Subject Test scores are not required."

SELECTIVITY

Admissions Rating	93
# of applicants	5,343
% of applicants accepted	65
% of acceptees attending	14
# accepting a place on wait list	234
% admitted from wait list	19

FRESHMAN PROFILE

Range SAT Critical Reading	610–710
Range SAT Math	610–680
Range SAT Writing	590–690
Range ACT Composite	27–30
Minimum paper TOEFL	550
Minimum computer TOEFL	213
Average HS GPA	3.69
% graduated top 10% of class	46
% graduated top 25% of class	81
% graduated top 50% of class	98

DEADLINES

Early action	
Deadline	11/1
Notification	1/15
Regular	
Priority	2/1
Deadline	2/1
Nonfall registration?	yes

APPLICANTS ALSO LOOK AT

AND OFTEN PREFER
University of California—Santa Cruz

AND SOMETIMES PREFER
University of Puget Sound, Whitman College

AND RARELY PREFER
University of Oregon

FINANCIAL FACTS

Financial Aid Rating	86
Annual tuition	$36,394
Room and board	$9,648
Required fees	$238
Books and supplies	$1,050
% frosh rec. need-based scholarship or grant aid	55
% UG rec. need-based scholarship or grant aid	54
% frosh rec. non-need-based scholarship or grant aid	2
% UG rec. non-need-based scholarship or grant aid	2
% frosh rec. need-based self-help aid	40
% UG rec. need-based self-help aid	41
% frosh rec. any financial aid	79
% UG rec. any financial aid	70
% UG borrow to pay for school	58
Average cumulative indebtedness	$17,084

LOUISIANA STATE UNIVERSITY

1146 PLEASANT HALL, BATON ROUGE, LA 70803 • ADMISSIONS: 225-578-1175 • FAX: 225-575-4433

CAMPUS LIFE

Quality of Life Rating	76
Fire Safety Rating	86
Green Rating	90
Type of school	public
Environment	metropolis

STUDENTS

Total undergrad enrollment	22,625
% male/female	49/51
% from out of state	17
% from public high school	54
% live on campus	25
# of fraternities	23
# of sororities	15
% African American	9
% Asian	3
% Caucasian	79
% Hispanic	3
% international	2
# of countries represented	108

SURVEY SAYS . . .

Athletic facilities are great
Great off-campus food
Everyone loves the Tigers
Frats and sororities dominate
social scene
Student publications are popular
Lots of beer drinking
Hard liquor is popular

ACADEMICS

Academic Rating	65
% students graduating within 4 years	28
% students graduating within 6 years	61
Calendar	semester
Student/faculty ratio	20:1
Profs interesting rating	96
Profs accessible rating	68
Most common reg class size	10–19 students
Most common lab size	20–29 students

MOST POPULAR MAJORS
biology, mass communication/media
studies, physical education teaching
and coaching

STUDENTS SAY ". . ."

Academics

At Louisiana State University's flagship campus, you'll find "outstanding academics combined with a great college life." Some students here opt for only the latter as for many, "LSU is about football and partying." "Those who wish to apply themselves," however, "have ample opportunity and resources," and they can learn almost anything, since "the greatest strength of LSU by far is its diversity. [You] can come to LSU for sports, music…science, economics, or nearly any sort of humanities discipline you are interested in." Areas of strength include programs in premedical science, engineering, agriculture, and mass communications. The school is huge, which means "somewhere within that huge number is someone that you can get along with," but also it is easy to "get lost in the crowd," especially in intro-level classes. However, "once you get into classes that are smaller and more geared toward your chosen major, you are able to develop more of a one-on-one relationship with your professors." Fortunately "many administrative tasks" (such as "bills and registration") "can be completed online, and computers are available all across campus for students who don't have personal computers," making the bureaucracy somewhat easier to navigate. The school also offers academic lifelines such as "free tutoring all day long. The tutors are students who have already taken [the] courses."

Life

LSU is a big enough school to offer something for everyone, and undergrads here enjoy countless activities within a variety of subcultures. Most divisions, however, dissolve on game day, when tailgating is raised to the level of "an art form." A freshman reports, "On Saturdays during football season everyone is on campus before the game with friends, beer, and barbeque." Fans "come from all over and stay out all day. It's the one day when it doesn't matter who you are, as long as you're wearing purple and gold." Other entertainment options (for those of age) include Thursday nights at the bars of Tigerland, "a street with three popular college bars right next to each other," and parties wherever and whenever possible. The Greek system here is "highly influential," but students note, "This isn't the kind of school where a student doesn't have a social life if he or she isn't Greek." For the more aesthetically inclined, "LSU has an amazing art center—The Shaw Center—complete with a theater and fancy sushi bar on the top floor, which looks over the Mississippi River." Undergrads report "the beauty of our campus is amazing. The 100-plus-year-old oaks and the Italian Renaissance architecture wow any visitor to LSU's campus."

Student Body

The typical student at LSU "studies moderately—enough to get the grade he or she desires in a class"—and "frequently spends time with friends, possibly going to parties or places that serve alcohol." Mixed in is "a good number of atypical students who study more and do not go partying over the weekends. These students find fulfillment in their own interests regardless of what others think." While "conservative frat boys and sorority girls dominate the campus," the school is home to a diverse population including "many from foreign countries and other ethnic groups." There are even a few who "don't give a damn about LSU football"—hey, at a school this big, anything's possible. The student body also includes a substantial population of legacies.

LOUISIANA STATE UNIVERSITY

FINANCIAL AID: 225-578-3103 • E-MAIL: ADMISSIONS@LSU.EDU • WEBSITE: WWW.LSU.EDU

THE PRINCETON REVIEW SAYS

Admissions

Very important factors considered include: Academic GPA, rigor of secondary school record, standardized test scores. *Important factors considered include:* Class rank, talent/ability. *Other factors considered include:* Application essay, recommendation(s), alumni/ae relation, extracurricular activities, first generation. SAT or ACT required; ACT with writing component recommended. TOEFL required of all international applicants. High school diploma is required, and GED is accepted. *Academic units required:* 4 English, 3 mathematics, 3 science, 2 foreign language, 1 social studies, 2 history. *Academic units recommended:* 4 mathematics.

Financial Aid

Students should submit: FAFSA. The Princeton Review suggests that all financial aid forms be submitted as soon as possible after January 1. *Need-based scholarships/grants offered:* Federal Pell, SEOG, state scholarships/grants, private scholarships, school scholarship or grant aid from institutional funds. *Loan aid offered:* Direct Subsidized Stafford, Direct Unsubsidized Stafford, Direct PLUS, Federal Perkins, university loans from institutional funds. Applicants will be notified of awards on a rolling basis beginning April 1. Federal Work-Study Program available. Off-campus job opportunities are excellent.

The Inside Word

If you've got the right numbers, getting in to LSU is 1-2-3. Guaranteed admission requirements include completion of eighteen core units, 1030 SAT or 22 ACT, and a 3.0 GPA. Students who don't meet these requirements should submit supporting documentation and a letter outlining their qualifications for admission with their initial application. Check LSU's website to see which combinations of GPA, class rank, and test scores qualify you for admission.

THE SCHOOL SAYS "..."

From the Admissions Office

"LSU holds a prominent position in U.S. higher education and is committed to meeting the challenge of pursuing intellectual development for its students, expanding the bounds of knowledge through research, and creating economic opportunities for Louisiana. LSU, one of only twenty-five universities nationwide designated as both a land-grant and sea-grant institution, also holds the Carnegie Foundation's doctoral research, extensive designation.

"LSU's instructional programs include 200 undergraduate and graduate or professional degrees. Outside of the classroom, residential colleges, service-learning opportunites, and more than 350 registered student organizations contribute to an exciting and meaningful college experience.

"Louisiana State University offers the Southern hospitality of a small community while providing the benefits of a large, technologically advanced institution.

"Freshman applicants are required to take the SAT or ACT; ACT with writing component required for Honors College applicants. LSU will use the best scores from either SAT or ACT, when making admission decisions."

SELECTIVITY
Admissions Rating	83
# of applicants	15,917
% of applicants accepted	69
% of acceptees attending	43

FRESHMAN PROFILE
Range SAT Critical Reading	510–630
Range SAT Math	540–650
Range ACT Composite	23–28
Minimum paper TOEFL	550
Minimum computer TOEFL	213
Minimum web-based TOEFL	79
Average HS GPA	3.49
% graduated top 10% of class	25
% graduated top 25% of class	53
% graduated top 50% of class	83

DEADLINES
Regular	
Priority	11/15
Deadline	4/15
Nonfall registration?	yes

FINANCIAL FACTS
Financial Aid Rating	75
Annual in-state tuition	$3,968
Annual out-of-state tuition	$14,753
Room and board	$8,210
Required fees	$1,796
Books and supplies	$1,500
% frosh rec. need-based scholarship or grant aid	33
% UG rec. need-based scholarship or grant aid	28
% frosh rec. non-need-based scholarship or grant aid	2
% UG rec. non-need-based scholarship or grant aid	1
% frosh rec. need-based self-help aid	20
% UG rec. need-based self-help aid	23
% frosh rec. any financial aid	96
% UG rec. any financial aid	78
% UG borrow to pay for school	41
Average cumulative indebtedness	$18,118

LOYOLA MARYMOUNT UNIVERSITY

ONE LMU DRIVE, SUITE 100, LOS ANGELES, CA 90045 • ADMISSIONS: 310-338-2750 • FAX: 310-338-2797

STUDENTS SAY "..."

Academics

Loyola Marymount University is a "fun, beautiful, Jesuit institution," with a top-tier teaching staff and "fabulous location" in sunny Los Angeles, California. The school emphasizes a well-rounded education, which balances academics with spiritual life and community involvement. Every student must complete a core curriculum, which introduces them to the liberal arts within the context of the "Ignation and Marymount traditions of social responsibility and education of the whole person." LMU has more than fifty major fields and almost 6,000 undergraduates; however, individual classes are often "between ten and twelve students and are highly dependent on discussion or the practice of material in the classroom." Within every major, there's a mix of "easy classes and very challenging classes." Fortunately, "professors are approachable and passionate," and always "willing to meet with students outside of class for discussion and help." Beyond academics, "The faculty and staff are concerned about the student's well-being" and "want to create an environment that will successfully facilitate healthy learning." A civil engineering student adds, "I attribute my success at LMU to my professors taking a personal interest in me, which inspired me to work harder for them." Thanks to LMU's "powerful networks of alums" and enviable urban location, many students are able to score "internships at top accounting firms, movie studios, television networks" and other Southern California industries. Through this and other channels, "LMU strives to make this campus a place where students can discover their passion and pursue whatever they want."

Life

"Located on the beautiful Southern California coast," LMU is a "gorgeous place to learn." At this well-polished and well-endowed university, "The facilities, housing, amenities, landscaping, and location are all excellent." Even the "Library is beautiful and functional...and classrooms are large and stocked with all the necessities." Clubs, events, and "community service opportunities" abound on LMU's active campus, and students tend to be joyously juggling a hectic schedule of schoolwork and extracurricular pursuits. The school definitely "brings out the busy bee in students," so "If you want to fit in at LMU, find something you love and join, join, join!" When it's time to relax, "Most of the fun activities revolve around Greek life, such as sorority and fraternity formals and exchanges," although it should be noted that Greek life doesn't include any residential component. However, "Being in Los Angeles also has many perks for off-campus life," like "hanging out with friends at the beach or going out to eat" at restaurants around Hollywood and Santa Monica. Taking advantage of the diverse urban environment, "People go into the city to nightclubs, restaurants, movie theaters, hookah bars, comedy clubs...this is Los Angeles! You can find something that fits your personality in this city." A medium-sized campus, LMU is "not so big that you don't know anyone, but it's not small enough that you see the same people every day."

Student Body

"The typical LMU student is laid-back and friendly, but also hardworking and involved in the many, many aspects of LMU, from service work to Greek life to athletics." "There are a lot of sorority girls and frat guys" on campus, and most students are "socially active," enjoying a good party or a romp around Los Angeles on the weekends. "Students tend to be from California" and, in the true Los Angeles spirit, many are "physically fit," as well as "very fashion-forward and trendy." Most agree, "Everyone is very accepting and chill" at LMU. In fact, "Most people are smart, focused, and engaging young adults," whether or not they don designer duds. Many students also note, "The student body is becoming more and more diverse," and there's a "high degree of tolerance and respect here for people of different cultures, sexual orientations, and religions." On the whole, "students seem to interact quite well together in and outside the classroom."

LOYOLA MARYMOUNT UNIVERSITY

FINANCIAL AID: 310-338-2753 • E-MAIL: ADMISSIONS@LMU.EDU • WEBSITE: WWW.LMU.EDU

THE PRINCETON REVIEW SAYS

Admissions

Very important factors considered include: Academic GPA. *Important factors considered include:* Application essay, rigor of secondary school record, standardized test scores, character/personal qualities, talent/ability. *Other factors considered include:* Class rank, recommendation(s), alumni/ae relation, extracurricular activities, first generation. SAT or ACT required; ACT with writing component recommended. TOEFL required of all international applicants. High school diploma is required, and GED is accepted. *Academic units recommended:* 4 English, 3 mathematics, 2 science (2 science labs), 3 foreign language, 3 social studies, 1 academic elective.

Financial Aid

Students should submit: FAFSA. The Princeton Review suggests that all financial aid forms be submitted as soon as possible after January 1. *Need-based scholarships/grants offered:* Federal Pell, SEOG, state scholarships/grants, private scholarships, school scholarship or grant aid from institutional funds. *Loan aid offered:* Direct Subsidized Stafford, Direct Unsubsidized Stafford, Direct PLUS, Federal Perkins, university loans from institutional funds. Applicants will be notified of awards on a rolling basis beginning March 15. Federal Work-Study Program available. Off-campus job opportunities are excellent.

The Inside Word

LMU's admission staff reviews each application individually. There's no minimum GPA or minimum test scores required for admission, and the school strives to consider the student's range of experiences and character. Nonetheless, the academic record is the single most important factor in an admissions decision. For interested students, the school offers an early action program, though students admitted through this program aren't required to attend.

THE SCHOOL SAYS ". . ."

From the Admissions Office

"Loyola Marymount University is a dynamic, student-centered university. We are medium-sized (5,800 undergraduates), and we are the only Jesuit university in the southwestern United States.

"Our campus is located in Westchester, a friendly, residential neighborhood that is removed from the hustle and bustle of Los Angeles, yet offers easy access to all the richness of our most cosmopolitan environment. One mile from the ocean, our students enjoy ocean and mountain vistas as well as the moderate climate and crisp breezes characteristic of a coastal location.

"Loyola Marymount is committed to the ideals of Jesuit and Marymount education. We are a student-centered university, dedicated to the education of the whole person and to the preparation of our students for lives of service to their families, communities, and professions. Breadth and rigor are the hallmarks of the curriculum.

"Taken together, our academic program, our Jesuit and Marymount heritage, and our terrific campus environment afford our students unparalleled opportunity to prepare for life and leadership in the twenty-first century."

SELECTIVITY
Admissions Rating	90
# of applicants	10,192
% of applicants accepted	54
% of acceptees attending	25
# accepting a place on wait list	363
% admitted from wait list	23

FRESHMAN PROFILE
Range SAT Critical Reading	550–640
Range SAT Math	560–660
Range SAT Writing	560–660
Range ACT Composite	25–29
Minimum paper TOEFL	550
Minimum computer TOEFL	213
Minimum web-based TOEFL	80
Average HS GPA	3.74
% graduated top 10% of class	37
% graduated top 25% of class	69
% graduated top 50% of class	94

DEADLINES
Early action	
Deadline	11/1
Notification	12/21
Regular	
Deadline	1/15
Notification	4/1
Nonfall registration?	yes

APPLICANTS ALSO LOOK AT
AND OFTEN PREFER
University of California—Berkeley, University of California—Los Angeles, University of Southern California
AND SOMETIMES PREFER
Santa Clara University, University of California, Santa Barbara, University of California—San Diego
AND RARELY PREFER
Chapman University, Pepperdine University, University of California—Irvine, University of San Diego

FINANCIAL FACTS
Financial Aid Rating	76
Annual tuition	$36,912
Room and board	$12,722
Required fees	$693
Books and supplies	$1,656
% frosh rec. need-based scholarship or grant aid	51
% UG rec. need-based scholarship or grant aid	50
% frosh rec. non-need-based scholarship or grant aid	7
% UG rec. non-need-based scholarship or grant aid	5
% frosh rec. need-based self-help aid	43
% UG rec. need-based self-help aid	48
% frosh rec. any financial aid	86
% UG rec. any financial aid	79
% UG borrow to pay for school	60
Average cumulative indebtedness	$29,906

LOYOLA UNIVERSITY—CHICAGO

1032 W. SHERIDAN RD., CHICAGO, IL 60660 • ADMISSIONS: 773-508-3075 • FAX: 312-915-7216

STUDENTS SAY ". . ."

Academics

Standing tall alongside the shore of Lake Michigan eight miles north of Chicago, Loyola University benefits from an optimal location (so long as you don't mind cold winters). "The location, Chicago, is key in providing a unique educational experience," one student explains. "The neighborhoods, restaurants, parks, and museums of Chicago provide just as much information as a classroom setting would." A "strong Jesuit tradition" "encourages creative thinking and allows students to explore the complexities of the world in and out of the classroom," which, of course, includes its closest city. Students also appreciate the school's "really strong emphasis on preparing the individual to leave college and start a career. There are plenty of internship opportunities," and the school makes "it relatively easy to get in touch with employers. We have many career fairs." Professors are "amazing overall." Students say they are "very approachable and really care about their students in terms of their academic performance as well as their mental and physical health. They treat students with respect and are passionate about their subjects." "Small class sizes" further help students "feel comfortable asking questions," and professors' "expertise" and "passion" make it "much easier to learn." Students brag of the nursing program's "great reputation" and add that "the history and philosophy departments are really good." Many, however, express disappointment with the administration citing "red tape" and "layers of bureaucracy," which make many offices "a bit inaccessible."

Life

Loyola "has the aspects of a 'normal' campus," but "it has a different twist because it is located in Chicago. Students frequently use the city's attractions as opposed to college activities" for extracurricular diversion. Living in Chicago, "students tend to have plenty of options in terms of what to do for fun." There's an active "local bar scene," as well as "concerts, museums, plays, and almost anything else one can think of doing." Getting around town is really easy: "There is a [CTA] station dedicated to the campus, which makes it extremely easy to travel anywhere within the city. Each student is also given a U-pass, which provides unlimited rides on any Chicago public transportation." Getting from campus to campus is another matter; students complain that "the school needs better transportation from the two campuses. They have one shuttle run every fifteen to twenty minutes, but time is of the essence, and if you miss one, it is hard to get from one to the other quickly. This affects classes, meetings, and jobs." Students who prefer to stay on campus for fun will find "plenty of other activities" to capture their attention, including "intramural sports, clubs, and Division I basketball games." "If you're not a drinker, there is still plenty to do" on campus "such as concerts, comedians, or even smaller venues like drag shows or improv." Serious sports fans should be warned, however, as "Sports teams do not rule this school," even though the city itself is pretty well known for its enthusiasm for athletics.

Student Body

"When first coming to a Jesuit school, I feared a conservative rule that would be in order," writes one student. "To my surprise, quite the opposite was here in Chicago. The school is very liberal, and the body is incredibly diverse." Indeed, while many undergrads here are "white and from the Chicago suburbs," many others are "of all different races, ethnicities, religions, and sexual orientations." "There is a very high gay population on campus, and very little discrimination," one undergrad observes. The university supports diversity through its on-campus "ethnic and cultural groups" so that students "rarely feel alone or ostracized." As one student explains, Loyola is a "good place to be surrounded by such a diverse student body" as "there's definitely room for different people." Many here "have a service-oriented mindset and tend to be aware of current events and global issues that need to be dealt with."

FINANCIAL AID: 773-508-3155 • E-MAIL: ADMISSION@LUC.EDU • WEBSITE: WWW.LUC.EDU

THE PRINCETON REVIEW SAYS

Admissions

Very important factors considered include: Academic GPA, rigor of secondary school record, standardized test scores. *Important factors considered include:* Application essay, recommendation(s), character/personal qualities, extracurricular activities, level of applicant's interest, volunteer work. *Other factors considered include:* Class rank, alumni/ae relation, first generation, geographical residence, interview, state residency, talent/ability, work experience. SAT or ACT required; ACT with or without writing component accepted. TOEFL required of all international applicants. High school diploma is required, and GED is accepted. *Academic units required:* 4 English, 3 mathematics, 3 science, 2 foreign language, 2 social studies, 1 history. *Academic units recommended:* 4 English, 4 mathematics, 3 science, 2 foreign language, 2 social studies, 2 history, 3 academic elective.

Financial Aid

Students should submit: FAFSA. The Princeton Review suggests that all financial aid forms be submitted as soon as possible after January 1. *Need-based scholarships/ grants offered:* Federal Pell, SEOG, state scholarships/grants, private scholarships, school scholarship or grant aid from institutional funds. *Loan aid offered:* Direct Subsidized Stafford, Direct Unsubsidized Stafford, Direct PLUS, Federal Perkins, Federal Nursing Loans. Applicants will be notified of awards on a rolling basis beginning February 15. Federal Work-Study Program available. Off-campus job opportunities are good.

The Inside Word

Loyola is fairly conventional when it comes to admissions policies. Successful candidates usually have a combination of strong grades, success in a tough college preparatory curriculum, and solid extracurricular activities. The school adheres to Jesuit teaching, so applicants with significant volunteer work should impress admissions officers.

THE SCHOOL SAYS "..."

From the Admissions Office

"Loyola University Chicago continues to open new facilities and renovate existing buildings. Loyola is investing $100 million into reimagine, a campaign to revolutionize the student community at Loyola. This campaign is an ambitious, five-phased building project that will touch every facet of life at the Lake Shore Campus. Expected to be completed in 2015, reimagine will benefit the entire Loyola community. As a result of the campaign, Loyola has already gained a three-story, state-of-the-art athletics facility, a true sports arena, and will gain a new student union, an updated sports center, and a new Centennial Forum, with room for large-scale conferences and a new face for Loyola. In addition, the School of Communication recently opened a new convergence studio at the Water Tower Campus, which includes television and radio production equipment. Loyola's Information Commons is a high-tech lakefront library featuring large group study spaces, more than 250 computers, wireless Internet connections, and a lakefront café. Loyola frequently enhances its undergraduate academic programs and adds new majors in emerging fields. The Core Curriculum enhances student credentials by emphasizing lifelong skills and values, and giving students the opportunity to easily complete a second major or add a minor. Nationally recognized researchers and scholars continue to teach freshman-level and advanced courses. Loyola's two main campuses enable students to experience both traditional residential campus life, and a vibrant urban environment. With more than 200 campus organizations offering numerous activities and events, as well as cultural, recreational, and internship opportunities throughout the world-class city of Chicago, undergraduate education at Loyola extends well beyond the classroom. For more information about undergraduate academics, housing, student life, financial assistance, and more, please visit www.luc.edu/undergrad. Please note that students whose native language is not English and/or if the primary language of instruction has not been English will be required to take the TOEFL or IELTS."

SELECTIVITY

Admissions Rating	88
# of applicants	17,671
% of applicants accepted	60
% of acceptees attending	20
# accepting a place on wait list	0

FRESHMAN PROFILE

Range SAT Critical Reading	540–650
Range SAT Math	540–640
Range SAT Writing	540–650
Range ACT Composite	25–29
Minimum paper TOEFL	550
Minimum web-based TOEFL	79
Average HS GPA	3.72
% graduated top 10% of class	34
% graduated top 25% of class	67
% graduated top 50% of class	95

DEADLINES

Regular	
Priority	12/1
Notification	10/15
Nonfall registration?	yes

APPLICANTS ALSO LOOK AT

AND OFTEN PREFER
DePaul University, Fordham University, Illinois State University, Indiana University at Bloomington, Marquette University, Michigan State University, Northwestern University, Saint Louis University, University of Chicago, University of Illinois at Chicago

AND SOMETIMES PREFER
Boston College, Boston University, Bradley University, Illinois Wesleyan University, Miami University, New York University, Northern Illinois University, Purdue University—West Lafayette, Saint Xavier University, The Ohio State University—Columbus

AND RARELY PREFER
American University, Augustana College (IL), Benedictine University, Butler University, Creighton University, Dominican University, Drake University, Elmhurst College, Georgetown University, Northeastern University, Santa Clara University, Tulane University

FINANCIAL FACTS

Financial Aid Rating	75
Annual tuition	$32,200
Room and board	$11,570
Required fees	$1,094
Books and supplies	$1,200
% frosh rec. need-based scholarship or grant aid	74
% UG rec. need-based scholarship or grant aid	72
% frosh rec. non-need-based scholarship or grant aid	7
% UG rec. non-need-based scholarship or grant aid	5
% frosh rec. need-based self-help aid	65
% UG rec. need-based self-help aid	66
% frosh rec. any financial aid	97
% UG rec. any financial aid	92
% UG borrow to pay for school	72

LOYOLA UNIVERSITY MARYLAND

4501 NORTH CHARLES STREET, BALTIMORE, MD 21210 • ADMISSIONS: 410-617-5012 • FAX: 410-617-2176

CAMPUS LIFE

Quality of Life Rating	91
Fire Safety Rating	89
Green Rating	85
Type of school	private
Affiliation	Roman Catholic
Environment	metropolis

STUDENTS

Total undergrad enrollment	3,807
% male/female	40/60
% from out of state	81
% from public high school	46
% live on campus	81
% African American	4
% Asian	3
% Caucasian	84
% Hispanic	5
% international	1
# of countries represented	64

SURVEY SAYS . . .
Athletic facilities are great
School is well-run
Dorms are like palaces
Frats and sororities are unpopular
or nonexistent
Student government is popular

ACADEMICS

Academic Rating	90
% students graduating within 4 years	79
% students graduating within 6 years	82
Calendar	semester
Student/faculty ratio	13:1
Profs interesting rating	93
Profs accessible rating	90
Most common reg class size	20–29 students
Most common lab size	20–29 students

MOST POPULAR MAJORS
general business, communication, biology

STUDENTS SAY "..."

Academics
The Jesuits have a long history of excellence in higher education, and that tradition is richly reflected in the academic programs at Loyola University Maryland. The undergraduate experience is built around Loyola's "fantastic core curriculum," which ensures "a solid foundation in the natural sciences, English, history, philosophy and theology." Through the core, students across disciplines "take some awesome classes that will completely change your perspective on the world." Jesuit values and philosophy are emphasized in the coursework, yet the school strikes the "right balance between religion, spirituality, and the everyday life of college students." No matter what field you choose to study, "The academics are outstanding and the coursework is challenging." A true teaching university, Loyola professors use "different learning techniques to cater to everyone's different learning styles." With small "classes capped at thirty-five," professors "actually know each of their students by name." Serving as both personal and academic mentors, Loyola professors "get to know you personally, take time out of their office hours to have intellectual discussions, show you how to learn and how to teach, and help you out when you are having difficulties." The relationship can even extend off campus, as it's "fairly common for professors to give out their personal cell phone numbers or to even invite the class to their home for dinner." There's extensive "academic support" and tutoring for students in every discipline, and the "Career Center is open for students starting at day one." Though some would like to see a "larger variety of classes" for undergraduates, many praise the "excellent study abroad program," which offers the opportunity to spend a year in one of fourteen countries.

Life
Loyola students juggle school, service, spirituality, and social life with extraordinary flair. Monday through Friday, most undergraduates are "insanely busy doing loads of homework, projects, reading, community service, clubs, lectures, [and] sports." Of particular note, Loyola offers "amazing opportunities to get involved in the Baltimore community through service." In fact, the school uses "Baltimore city as an extension of the classroom," where students learn about real life, rather than living in a college bubble. On the weekends, things slow down around campus, though students can partake of the "numerous speakers, movies, events, or sporting events" hosted by the university. In addition, "A lot of people go out to bars on Fridays and Saturdays," because "there is no Greek life" on campus and Loyola's strict alcohol policies make it difficult to throw parties. Loyola students can be found out and about in Baltimore, "going out to eat, catching an Orioles game, attending a concert at the BSO, [or] walking around the harbor." "Most students live on campus" during the school year, enjoying a surprisingly comfortable lifestyle in Loyola's cushy dormitories. If you score a spot in one of the suites, you and your roommates will "have full kitchens in your dorm by sophomore year."

Student Body
In addition to being predominantly Catholic, "Many of the students are white, from New York or New Jersey, and come from private high schools." You'll see plenty of "Uggs, North Face, pearls, and J. Crew" around campus. Although "the student body may appear homogenous," students insist that, "Everyone can fit in well if you get past the initial stereotypes and immerse yourself in the opportunities Loyola has to offer." On that note, students "try to live out the core values of the university and enjoy being a contributing member of school community." Here, students "care about their academics and do well in school, but they also try to balance that with extracurriculars and their spiritual life." On the whole, the campus "really welcoming and trustworthy," with a "great sense of community." With so many ways to get involved, most students "find their niche at Loyola very quickly."

LOYOLA UNIVERSITY MARYLAND

FINANCIAL AID: 410-617-2576 • WEBSITE: WWW.LOYOLA.EDU

THE PRINCETON REVIEW SAYS

Admissions

Very important factors considered include: Application essay, recommendation(s), rigor of secondary school record, character/personal qualities. *Important factors considered include:* Class rank, alumni/ae relation, extracurricular activities, first generation, talent/ability, volunteer work. *Other factors considered include:* Academic GPA, geographical residence, interview, level of applicant's interest, racial/ethnic status, work experience. ACT with or without writing component accepted. TOEFL required of all international applicants. High school diploma is required, and GED is accepted. *Academic units required:* 4 English, 3 mathematics, 3 science, 3 foreign language, 2 social studies, 2 history. *Academic units recommended:* 4 English, 4 mathematics, 4 science, 4 foreign language, 3 social studies, 3 history, 1 visual/performing arts, 1 computer science.

Financial Aid

Students should submit: FAFSA, CSS/Financial Aid PROFILE. Regular filing deadline is February 15. The Princeton Review suggests that all financial aid forms be submitted as soon as possible after January 1. *Need-based scholarships/grants offered:* Federal Pell, SEOG, state scholarships/grants, private scholarships, school scholarship or grant aid from institutional funds. *Loan aid offered:* Direct Subsidized Stafford, Direct Unsubsidized Stafford, Direct PLUS, Federal Perkins, university loans from institutional funds. Federal Work-Study Program available. Off-campus job opportunities are good.

The Inside Word

Loyola University Maryland considers a student's academic record to be among the most important factors in an admissions decision. Successful students usually rank in the top quarter of their classes. Although Loyola will consider standardized test scores if you submit them, the SAT or ACT are optional for all first-year applicants. If you decide to apply without taking the SAT, Loyola asks that you submit an additional personal essay or recommendation.

THE SCHOOL SAYS "..."

From the Admissions Office

"To make a wise choice about your college plans, you will need to find out more. We extend to you these invitations. Question-and-answer periods with an admissions counselor are helpful to prospective students. An appointment should be made in advance. Admission office hours are 9:00 A.M. to 5:00 P.M., Monday through Friday. College day programs and Saturday information programs are scheduled during the academic year. These programs include a video about Loyola, a general information session, a discussion of various majors, a campus tour, and lunch. Summer information programs can help high school juniors to get a head start on investigating colleges. These programs feature an introductory presentation about the college and a campus tour."

SELECTIVITY
Admissions Rating	88
# of applicants	10,901
% of applicants accepted	55
% of acceptees attending	17
# accepting a place on wait list	1,100
% admitted from wait list	18

FRESHMAN PROFILE
Range SAT Critical Reading	545–640
Range SAT Math	560–650
Range ACT Composite	24–28
Minimum paper TOEFL	550
Minimum computer TOEFL	213
Average HS GPA	3.48
% graduated top 10% of class	31
% graduated top 25% of class	84
% graduated top 50% of class	91

DEADLINES
Early action	
Deadline	11/1
Notification	1/15
Regular	
Priority	11/1
Deadline	6/1
Nonfall registration?	yes

APPLICANTS ALSO LOOK AT
AND OFTEN PREFER
Boston College
AND SOMETIMES PREFER
College of the Holy Cross, Villanova University
AND RARELY PREFER
Fairfield University, Fordham University, Providence College

FINANCIAL FACTS
Financial Aid Rating	96
Annual tuition	$37,950
Room and board	$10,650
Books and supplies	$1,130
% frosh rec. need-based scholarship or grant aid	51
% UG rec. need-based scholarship or grant aid	46
% frosh rec. non-need-based scholarship or grant aid	10
% UG rec. non-need-based scholarship or grant aid	11
% frosh rec. need-based self-help aid	52
% UG rec. need-based self-help aid	46
% frosh rec. any financial aid	58
% UG rec. any financial aid	53
% UG borrow to pay for school	73
Average cumulative indebtedness	$26,740

LOYOLA UNIVERSITY—NEW ORLEANS

6363 ST. CHARLES AVENUE, BOX 18, NEW ORLEANS, LA 70118 • ADMISSIONS: 504-865-3240 • FAX: 504-865-3383

STUDENTS SAY ". . ."

Academics
Loyola University New Orleans provides undergraduates with an education deeply rooted in the Jesuit tradition. The school aims to produce "well-rounded students" who strive "to serve the world around them." Undergraduates are seen "as individuals" and encouraged to "discover their passions." Loyola offers "small classes," which helps to foster strong relationships between students and professors. Indeed, "personal attention" is a hallmark of the academic experience here, and the faculty is eager "to see you succeed." Undergrads are quick to praise their "intelligent, helpful, and kind" professors who "take a genuine interest in every student" and "make a firm decision to learn your name and what type of person you are." By and large, their doors are always open, and most professors make themselves "readily available to answer any and all questions you may have both inside and outside the classroom." The small class size also means that "discussions are frequently encouraged" and, as one political science major divulges, "challenging a professor's ideas [is] completely welcome." Impressively, "Loyola does a great job of encouraging students to apply their knowledge outside of the classroom, through internships as well as service-learning opportunities." The "friendly and very approachable" administration also wins kudos from the undergrads. They are "very open to students and their suggestions," and "you can see them working to make our school a better place."

Life
As one English lit major confidently declares, "Going to school in New Orleans means that you will never be bored. Ever. There is never a shortage of good food, good times, or good music." Yes, these Loyola students bask in the fact that they have New Orleans as their playground. The city offers "great opportunities for theater, music, and art," and many undergrads "go out and listen to live music on the weekends." They also enjoy the "great shopping on Magazine Street" and love to "explore the French Quarter." Students can also frequently be found "riding their bikes through Audubon Park and having a picnic on the Mississippi River." And naturally, "Mardi Gras is definitely the social highlight of the spring semester, closely followed by Jazz Fest." Of course, there's always plenty of activity at the university itself. "Whether [there's] a speaker, movie night, [or] free food, students are up at all hours of the day and night enjoying the campus." A satisfied senior goes further sharing, "Residential life offers some good floor and hall programs [such as] Third Friday quad parties and laser tag." As a music education major succinctly puts it, "There is never a dull day at Loyola."

Student Body
Loyola University undergrads are a "laid-back and friendly" lot who often "greet one another with a smile." Most students view their peers as "creative," "imaginative," and "really down-to-earth." Further, they are a "driven" group, motivated "to do well academically" and "participate in a wide range of activities." Of course, many "also want to let loose and have fun during the weekends." Additionally, "most Loyola students have an interest in music or an interest in service and rebuilding the city." Perhaps most notably, Loyola manages to attract students from a wide variety of backgrounds. As one political science major brags, "We consist of such a diverse group of people that I couldn't put my finger on just one type of person. But then again, that's one of my favorite things about being here. You can be anyone and do anything you want. Everyone fits in here. I have made friends with such a vast variety of people and that is something I never thought possible for me until I came here." Ultimately, as a biology major shares, "we all just mesh well."

LOYOLA UNIVERSITY—NEW ORLEANS

FINANCIAL AID: 504-865-3231 • E-MAIL: ADMIT@LOYNO.EDU • WEBSITE: WWW.LOYNO.EDU

THE PRINCETON REVIEW SAYS
Admissions
Very important factors considered include: Academic GPA, rigor of secondary school record, standardized test scores. *Important factors considered include:* Application essay, recommendation(s), extracurricular activities, talent/ability. *Other factors considered include:* Class rank, alumni/ae relation, character/personal qualities, geographical residence, interview, level of applicant's interest, state residency, volunteer work, work experience. SAT or ACT required; ACT with or without writing component accepted. TOEFL required of all international applicants. High school diploma is required, and GED is accepted. *Academic units required:* 4 English, 2 mathematics, 2 science, 2 social studies. *Academic units recommended:* 4 English, 3 mathematics, 3 science (1 science lab), 2 foreign language, 2 social studies.

Financial Aid
Students should submit: FAFSA. Regular filing deadline is June 1. The Princeton Review suggests that all financial aid forms be submitted as soon as possible after January 1. *Need-based scholarships/grants offered:* Federal Pell, SEOG, private scholarships, school scholarship or grant aid from institutional funds. *Loan aid offered:* Federal Perkins. Applicants will be notified of awards on a rolling basis beginning March 1. Federal Work-Study Program available. Off-campus job opportunities are excellent.

The Inside Word
Volunteer work and community service will serve your application to any school well, but they're especially helpful at this Jesuit institution. Post-Katrina New Orleans has spooked some prospective applicants, but the school has made great strides in rebuilding undergraduate enrollment, attracting new faculty members, and keeping alive the spirit of the school.

THE SCHOOL SAYS "..."
From the Admissions Office
"Chartered in 1912, Loyola University New Orleans is one of America's twenty-eight Jesuit institutions of higher learning. Its rich history dates back to the early eighteenth century when the Jesuits first arrived in New Orleans. As a Catholic university, Loyola has continued to emphasize the valuable Jesuit tradition of educating the whole person. Our more than 37,000 graduates have excelled in innumerable areas for ninety-seven years; their influence is felt around the world.

"Loyola's growth has increased the diversity of education available, all delivered within the educational values traditionally associated with our Jesuit heritage. This unique, nationally acclaimed institution—the crown jewel for a Jesuit education in the Southern United States—offers a welcoming and festive campus atmosphere and an emphasis on a liberal arts and sciences education, emphasizing self-discovery, exploration of values, while fostering personal initiative and critical thinking. Undergraduates enjoy individual attention in a university that strives to educate not only intellectually, but also spiritually, socially, and athletically. Undergraduate experience is broadened through special programs such as the First-Year Experience, learning communities, research, service learning, study abroad, and internships.

"Students applying for admission are required to take the SAT (or the ACT with the writing section). The highest composite scores will be used in admissions decisions."

SELECTIVITY
Admissions Rating	89
# of applicants	5,399
% of applicants accepted	57
% of acceptees attending	26

FRESHMAN PROFILE
Range SAT Critical Reading	570–670
Range SAT Math	540–650
Range SAT Writing	550–660
Range ACT Composite	24–29
Minimum paper TOEFL	550
Minimum computer TOEFL	213
Average HS GPA	3.77
% graduated top 10% of class	26
% graduated top 25% of class	57
% graduated top 50% of class	88

DEADLINES
Regular	
Priority	12/1
Notification	10/20
Nonfall registration?	yes

APPLICANTS ALSO LOOK AT
AND OFTEN PREFER
Boston University, Fordham University, Saint Louis University, University of Miami

AND SOMETIMES PREFER
Louisiana State University, Loyola University of Chicago, Tulane University, Xavier University of Louisiana

FINANCIAL FACTS
Financial Aid Rating	79
Annual tuition	$32,266
Room and board	$10,990
Required fees	$1,036
Books and supplies	$1,200
% frosh rec. need-based scholarship or grant aid	70
% UG rec. need-based scholarship or grant aid	66
% frosh rec. non-need-based scholarship or grant aid	10
% UG rec. non-need-based scholarship or grant aid	9
% frosh rec. need-based self-help aid	56
% UG rec. need-based self-help aid	50
% frosh rec. any financial aid	98
% UG rec. any financial aid	99
% UG borrow to pay for school	64
Average cumulative indebtedness	$22,320

LYNCHBURG COLLEGE

1501 LAKESIDE DRIVE, LYNCHBURG, VA 24501 • ADMISSIONS: 434-544-8300 • FAX: 434-544-8653

STUDENTS SAY ". . ."

Academics

This small, "welcoming" school in central Virginia focuses on "preparing students for life's big challenges" through a supportive environment, small class sizes, and ample academic resources. "Classes are small and generally discussion-based." In most Lynchburg classrooms, "Desks are normally arranged in a circular position to allow for easy communication and debating." Lynchburg professors "know how to capture our attention, even during the most boring topics." As at any college, "Some of the professors are better than others," and "Certain teachers do not cater well to certain learning styles." However, almost every professor will "make an effort to connect on a personal level with students, inside and outside the classroom." According to many satisfied undergraduates, "The ability to create personal relationships with classmates and professors" is one of the school's greatest strengths. "People really care about you and your future" at Lynchburg, and the school "provides students with countless resources and tools for success." Students note the "different learning facilities" available on campus, from peer tutoring and the writing center to "breakout study rooms, computer labs, and the library." With so much to offer and a student body of just 2,000, "Lynchburg College is a very nurturing place" that "promotes individual personal growth."

Life

There's strong sense of community on the Lynchburg campus. Right off the bat, first-year programming succeeds at "helping freshmen adjust to college life" and "break the ice" with classmates. Most students agree that it's "really easy to make friends" at Lynchburg, where "Students are not afraid to express their individuality, and no one is criticized for who they are." A current undergrad enthuses, "I enjoy feeling like a part of a family, instead of going through the weeks seeing hundreds or even thousands of new faces." For many, cheering on the school's "excellent athletic teams" is a highlight of the experience. In addition, "Greek life plays a huge role" in the school community, and not just through parties. Here, "Greeks on campus are highly involved in service projects," as are many non-Greek members of the Lynchburg community. On campus, "There is always something going on, from sports, to movies, to game night, to awareness programs." If you feel like getting off campus, "There are a ton of places to eat and hang out at in the vicinity." Though students love to convene for a few drinks on Friday night, "The school cracks down on parties." Therefore, many undergraduates prefer to simply relax or watch movies in the dorms. Living facilities aren't particularly posh, and students admit that academic "facilities are old and could use a facelift." However, the "Campus is beautiful," and many students say it feels like a "home away from home."

Student Body

Lynchburg students are "laid-back but studious," with a shared love of sports. Many undergraduates were "star athletes in high school," and, because of the school's top-ranked athletics, "Most of the kids that go here either do varsity or club sports." The "campus is not that diverse," principally comprised of "nice, middle- to upper-class kids" from Virginia. However, you don't have to fit a mold to be accepted at Lynchburg. No matter their background, "Most students fit in quite well," and "It is not hard to make friends here regardless of sex, age, or anything else." As one student puts it, "The only way someone cannot fit in here at Lynchburg College, is if they blockade themselves in their room and refuse to eat, shower, or attend class." From theater groups to field hockey, "Everyone quickly becomes involved with different organizations" on campus. Although "Students do have their own group of friends," everyone agrees, "There really aren't a lot of cliques" at Lynchburg.

FINANCIAL AID: 434-544-8228 • E-MAIL: ADMISSIONS@LYNCHBURG.EDU • WEBSITE: WWW.LYNCHBURG.EDU

THE PRINCETON REVIEW SAYS

Admissions

Very important factors considered include: Academic GPA, rigor of secondary school record, standardized test scores. *Important factors considered include:* Class rank, interview. *Other factors considered include:* Application essay, recommendation(s), extracurricular activities, level of applicant's interest, talent/ability, volunteer work, work experience. SAT or ACT required; ACT with or without writing component accepted. TOEFL required of all international applicants. High school diploma is required, and GED is accepted. *Academic units required:* 4 English, 3 mathematics, 3 science (2 science labs), 2 foreign language, 2 social studies, 2 history. *Academic units recommended:* 4 English, 4 mathematics, 4 science (2 science labs), 3 foreign language, 2 social studies, 2 history, 1 academic elective.

Financial Aid

Students should submit: FAFSA. Regular preferred filing deadline is March 1. The Princeton Review suggests that all financial aid forms be submitted as soon as possible after January 1. *Need-based scholarships/grants offered:* Federal Pell, SEOG, state scholarships/grants, private scholarships, school scholarship or grant aid from institutional funds. *Loan aid offered:* Direct Subsidized Stafford, Direct Unsubsidized Stafford, Direct PLUS, Federal Perkins. Applicants will be notified of awards on a rolling basis beginning March 5. Federal Work-Study Program available. Off-campus job opportunities are good.

Inside Word

You need to submit an application form, high school transcripts, and standardized test scores to apply to Lynchburg College. The school also suggests that you include a letter of recommendation and a personal essay or graded writing sample in your application packet. Regular admissions decisions are made on a rolling basis, but the college also offers both early action and early decision deadlines.

THE SCHOOL SAYS " . . . "

From the Admissions Office

"Lynchburg College is a nationally recognized private college in Virginia that goes above and beyond to challenge, engage, and inspire students to succeed in a global society. From the moment that prospective students step onto the spectacular campus, they are aware that LC is a place where they will have opportunities to grow intellectually, morally, and spiritually, and that there are faculty, staff, and peer mentors waiting to support them in their quest to achieve their personal goals.

"One of only forty higher education institutions included in the popular college guide *Colleges That Change Lives*, Lynchburg College emphasizes the development of the whole person, as evidenced by the low student/faculty ratio and an abundance of student organizations, athletic teams, intramural and club sports, and experiential learning opportunities, including service learning, internships, study abroad, and faculty student collaborative research.

"Lynchburg College seeks to enroll students who wish to take advantage of all that the school has to offer and who want to be part of a caring community. LC welcomes and encourages interested high school students to visit the campus to see for themselves why the college has received record numbers of applications and multiple national honors in recent years. The Admissions Office sponsors open houses and other events for prospective students throughout the year. For more information visit our website at www.lynchburg.edu.

"We allow students to submit scores from either the SAT or the ACT, and we will use the student's best score from these tests. In regard to the SAT, the critical reading and math scores will be the primary SAT scores used for admission decisions."

SELECTIVITY

Admissions Rating	77
# of applicants	4,574
% of applicants accepted	67
% of acceptees attending	19
# of early decision applicants	295
% accepted early decision	1

FRESHMAN PROFILE

Range SAT Critical Reading	450–550
Range SAT Math	450–560
Range SAT Writing	440–540
Range ACT Composite	19–24
Minimum paper TOEFL	525
Minimum computer TOEFL	197
Average HS GPA	3.14
% graduated top 10% of class	10
% graduated top 25% of class	35
% graduated top 50% of class	72

DEADLINES

Early decision	
Deadline	11/15
Notification	12/15
Regular	
Notification	rolling
Nonfall registration?	yes

FINANCIAL FACTS

Financial Aid Rating	83
Annual tuition	$29,860
Room and board	$8,380
Required fees	$945
Books and supplies	$1,000
% frosh rec. need-based scholarship or grant aid	76
% UG rec. need-based scholarship or grant aid	73
% frosh rec. non-need-based scholarship or grant aid	18
% UG rec. non-need-based scholarship or grant aid	24
% frosh rec. need-based self-help aid	58
% UG rec. need-based self-help aid	15
% frosh rec. any financial aid	94
% UG rec. any financial aid	96
% UG borrow to pay for school	76
Average cumulative indebtedness	$32,130

MACALESTER COLLEGE

1600 GRAND AVENUE, ST. PAUL, MN 55105 • ADMISSIONS: 651-696-6357 • FAX: 651-696-6724

STUDENTS SAY "..."

Academics

"Globalism, liberalism, social justice, and environmentalism rule the day" at Macalester College, a small, Minnesota liberal arts school where "academics are taken very seriously," and students "really have to work" for good grades. Academic offerings "are top-notch" here, "particularly chemistry, economics, and international studies," and faculty "understand that students learn from other students" and encourage discussion on all fronts. Most professors are "vibrantly enthusiastic about what they're teaching and supportive of [one's] own studies." Students warn that because of Macalester's small size, some other departments "are extremely understaffed," but even these departments do a good job of integrating "internships and volunteering into the syllabus." Professors truly "help students connect course work to real-life situations." Students report, "In true liberal arts style, every department is somehow inter-connected to seemingly opposite departments: Numerous inter-disciplinary majors exist, and even within individual classes, professors approach teaching their given subject from numerous angles." The school excels at "giving students a balance of direction and free reign" on everything from academics to housing to study abroad, but it's "very easy to get guidance on the classes I should be taking." Most students do an internship and/or participate in some kind of civic engagement during their time at Macalester, as "apathy doesn't exist here."

Life

Life at Mac is "ruled by randomness." "I've gone sledding in full-body trash bag 'sleds,' held election night viewing parties in the dorm lounges, and sat around talking until 3:30 in the morning about different religions," says one student. The Macalester campus is situated right in the middle of one of the oldest (not to mention "charming and appealing") neighborhoods in the Twin Cities, and "There are rarely large parties. Instead, people will drink and hang out in the dorms (if underclassmen) or friends' houses (if juniors or seniors)" where they tend to discuss big ideas. However, it's not all deconstruction and theorizing: "A typical conversation at lunch might start with the weather, then touch briefly on physics, then classical opera, then study abroad options in Africa, then world politics, then Sherlock Holmes, then that TV show we all saw last night, and finish with 'Guess who's going to the Super Bowl, guys!'" The school provides the perfect atmosphere for "finding the sweet spot between academics and things you enjoy." There are always things to do on campus throughout the week, such as "dances, movie showings, improv shows, poetry slams, concerts, and guest speakers," as well as "plays, musicals, and other things." And "when Mac lets us down, there are two cities (Minneapolis and St. Paul) for us to go play in," as "the location of campus makes bus travel a breeze." Other urban options include "football or basketball games...some people go clubbing or out to eat. Lots go to the museums or just out shopping."

Student Body

Macalester "has a very diverse population as far as ethnicity and origin go, but as a whole it is very politically liberal." It's "very easy to fall into a niche at Mac," and while there are the usual cliques—"hipsters, jocks, nerds, hippies"—many students "have the same interests and passions, regardless of their social groups." Undergrads tend to be "fairly relaxed and easy going," "free-thinking," "high-achieving, hardworking, and unpretentious;" and most of all, "bizarrely unique." Many describe themselves as "awkward," adding, "We are nerds and proud of it." "I never feel threatened or unwanted here, even when I'm at my oddest," says one student. Jocks that are "only interested in playing football and partying" are atypical, "but they seem to have fun among themselves, too."

FINANCIAL AID: 651-696-6214 • E-MAIL: ADMISSIONS@MACALESTER.EDU • WEBSITE: WWW.MACALESTER.EDU

THE PRINCETON REVIEW SAYS

Admissions

Very important factors considered include: Academic GPA, rigor of secondary school record. *Important factors considered include:* Application essay, recommendation(s), standardized test scores, character/personal qualities, extracurricular activities. *Other factors considered include:* Class rank, alumni/ae relation, first generation, interview, racial/ethnic status, talent/ability, volunteer work, work experience. SAT or ACT required; ACT with or without writing component accepted. TOEFL required of all international applicants. *Academic units recommended:* 4 English, 3 mathematics, 3 science (3 science labs), 3 foreign language, 3 social studies.

Financial Aid

Students should submit: FAFSA, CSS/Financial Aid PROFILE. Regular filing deadline is March 1. The Princeton Review suggests that all financial aid forms be submitted as soon as possible after January 1. *Need-based scholarships/grants offered:* Federal Pell, SEOG, state scholarships/grants, private scholarships, school scholarship or grant aid from institutional funds. *Loan aid offered:* Direct Subsidized Stafford, Direct Unsubsidized Stafford, Direct PLUS, Federal Perkins, state loans, university loans from institutional funds. Applicants will be notified of awards shortly after admission. Federal Work-Study Program available. Off-campus job opportunities are excellent.

The Inside Word

To say that Macalester's star is on the rise is to put it very mildly. The number of applicants to the school continues to increase. The freshman class has grown slightly in that time but not at anything approaching the growth rate of the applicant pool. Accordingly, it has grown substantially more difficult to gain admission here within a very short period of time. Candidates need to put their best foot forward in their applications.

THE SCHOOL SAYS "..."

From the Admissions Office

"Macalester has been preparing students for world citizenship and providing an integrated international education for over six decades. The United Nations flag has flown on campus since 1950 and eighteen percent of the students are citizens of another country, with over ninety countries represented on campus. Over sixty percent of Mac students study abroad, going to nearly fifty countries all over the world each year. Graduates enter the workforce or graduate school with respected scholarship and real experience in a global community, prepared to succeed in their chosen fields. Mac students thrive in a rigorous academic environment, supported by accomplished faculty who love to teach. Located in a friendly residential neighborhood in the heart of a vibrant metropolitan area, Macalester offers unusually broad, easily accessible internship opportunities to add valuable experience, connections and practice at getting things done, often leading to job opportunities after graduation. Two out of three Mac students complete an internship at a Twin Cities business, law firm, hospital, financial institution, museum, theater, state government, research lab, environmental agency, or nonprofit group (and more), all within a few miles of campus. Students rave about the food at Mac, which includes vegetarian fare, food for meat lovers, plenty of variety and entrées from around the world. A new athletic and recreation center opened in the fall of 2009, including a large fitness center, indoor track, gymnasium, natatorium, field house, gathering spaces, juice bar, atrium and more. Athletic teams frequently earn the highest cumulative GPA in the nation. Macalester meets the full demonstrated need for every admitted student, providing broad socioeconomic representation in the student body."

SELECTIVITY

Admissions Rating	94
# of applicants	4,317
% of applicants accepted	43
% of acceptees attending	28
# accepting a place on wait list	243
% admitted from wait list	0
# of early decision applicants	241
% accepted early decision	53

FRESHMAN PROFILE

Range SAT Critical Reading	640–740
Range SAT Math	620–720
Range SAT Writing	630–730
Range ACT Composite	28–32
Minimum paper TOEFL	600
Minimum web-based TOEFL	100
% graduated top 10% of class	69
% graduated top 25% of class	92
% graduated top 50% of class	100

DEADLINES

Early decision	
Deadline	11/15
Notification	12/15
Regular	
Deadline	1/15
Notification	3/30
Nonfall registration?	no

APPLICANTS ALSO LOOK AT
AND OFTEN PREFER
Brown University, Swarthmore College

AND SOMETIMES PREFER
Carleton College, Middlebury College, Pomona College, University of Chicago, Vassar College, Wesleyan University

AND RARELY PREFER
Colorado College, Kenyon College, Oberlin College

FINANCIAL FACTS

Financial Aid Rating	98
Annual tuition	$41,800
Room and board	$9,396
Required fees	$221
Books and supplies	$990
% frosh rec. need-based scholarship or grant aid	75
% UG rec. need-based scholarship or grant aid	69
% frosh rec. non-need-based scholarship or grant aid	7
% UG rec. non-need-based scholarship or grant aid	4
% frosh rec. need-based self-help aid	67
% UG rec. need-based self-help aid	65
% frosh rec. any financial aid	80
% UG rec. any financial aid	73

MANHATTANVILLE COLLEGE

2900 PURCHASE STREET, ADMISSIONS OFFICE, PURCHASE, NY 10577 • ADMISSIONS: 914-323-5124 • FAX: 914-694-1732

CAMPUS LIFE

Quality of Life Rating	89
Fire Safety Rating	97
Green Rating	84
Type of school	private
Environment	town

STUDENTS

Total undergrad enrollment	1,692
% male/female	34/66
% from out of state	40
% live on campus	80
% African American	8
% Asian	2
% Caucasian	42
% Hispanic	17
% international	12
# of countries represented	53

SURVEY SAYS . . .

Diverse student types on campus
Different types of students interact
Frats and sororities are unpopular
or nonexistent

ACADEMICS

Academic Rating	73
% students graduating within 4 years	58
% students graduating within 6 years	63
Calendar	semester
Student/faculty ratio	11:1
Profs interesting rating	84
Profs accessible rating	86
Most common reg class size	10–19 students

MOST POPULAR MAJORS

business/commerce, psychology, visual and performing arts

STUDENTS SAY ". . ."

Academics

"Helpful and easy-to-reach" professors and "close proximity to New York City" all contribute to the "close and supportive community" that is Manhattanville College. Students here have the "unbelievable" opportunity to "exchange ideas" with professors who have "studied in the best universities in the world. There are so many distinguished professors here, ranging from experts in world religions, to former ambassadors in the United Nations. Almost all of them are well-known in their areas of study." Better still, nearly all "are approachable" and "offer office hours and are always there when they are supposed to be." Further help is available through "the Supplemental Instructor Program, which provides free extra help in math, history, and science courses." Mville (as it is affectionately called by its students) places a lot of emphasis on experiential learning, and the school's location is an asset in that regard. Not only is Mville close to the myriad of internship opportunities of the megalopolis next door, but "We [also] have tons of corporations literally in our neighborhood, like MasterCard, IBM, MBIA, [and] JPMorgan" that bring "plenty of internships." A "good education program" and "strong programs in psychology and marketing" are among the standouts here. Many undergrads appreciate the fact that "Manhattanville College reaches out to people with no money to pay for school."

Life

"There is not too much to do on campus" at Manhattanville, "and the school's campus is pretty small so you cannot really explore the grounds too much," students warn. "Many people commute, so the campus is basically dead at night and on weekends," and what socializing might occur is at least in some instances hampered by "the very strict residence assistants and residence directors" who battle on-campus partying. As a result, most students seek fun "in nearby White Plains, a small city filled with different restaurants, malls, Wal-Mart-type places, and a huge movie theater. People also go into New York City for fun, as our Valiant Express bus takes people into the city every weekend, and shuttles go to and from White Plains every day." On-campus options include "lots of interest groups and activities that one can join," and "a game room with different things like billiards and ping-pong." Finally, "the students here have a lot of school spirit, so there is always a great turnout for games." Men's and women's basketball and men's hockey are among the popular draws.

Student Body

"The diversity at Manhattanville is enormous," students report. "Although the school is fairly small, there are people from all over the world." One student observes, "Sometimes I feel like I'm in the minority as a non-Spanish speaker, which is interesting." Undergrads tend to hang with their own; "Dominicans sit with Dominicans, Puerto Ricans with Puerto Ricans, misfits with misfits, artists with artists, jocks with jocks. At Manhattanville the stereotypical personalities are clumped together by habit and for the most part tend to gravitate toward one another, with minor glimpses of interaction with other groups." Regardless of any cliques, "all of the students at the school are extremely cordial. Since it is such a small school, you get to know everyone's face." Undergrads here generally "are not the type of people who are very academically competitive with one another, want to change the world, or have super-high goals for their future. What they may lack in ambition they make up for in kindness. There are a few students here who work very hard and want to go to a great graduate school, or have a great job, and do everything they can to get all A's. They fit in just as well as everyone else because almost all the students here are very accepting and good-natured."

FINANCIAL AID: 914-323-5357 • E-MAIL: ADMISSIONS@MVILLE.EDU • WEBSITE: WWW.MVILLE.EDU

THE PRINCETON REVIEW SAYS

Admissions

Very important factors considered include: Rigor of secondary school record. *Important factors considered include:* Application essay, recommendation(s), extracurricular activities, interview. *Other factors considered include:* Alumni/ae relation, character/personal qualities, geographical residence, talent/ability, volunteer work, work experience. SAT or ACT reccommended. TOEFL required of all international applicants. High school diploma is required, and GED is accepted. *Academic units required:* 4 English, 3 mathematics, 2 science, 2 social studies, 5 academic elective.

Financial Aid

Students should submit: FAFSA. Regular filing deadline is March 1. The Princeton Review suggests that all financial aid forms be submitted as soon as possible after January 1. *Need-based scholarships/grants offered:* Federal Pell, SEOG, state scholarships/grants, private scholarships, school scholarship or grant aid from institutional funds. *Loan aid offered:* Direct Subsidized Stafford, Direct Unsubsidized Stafford, Direct PLUS. Applicants will be notified of awards on a rolling basis beginning March 1. Federal Work-Study Program available. Off-campus job opportunities are excellent.

The Inside Word

Applicants demonstrating middle-of-the-road academic achievement will most likely find themselves with an acceptance letter from Manhattanville. The school does seek "good fits," however and frequently attempts to assess compatibility with a candidate interview. The college still seeks to achieve greater gender balance, so male candidates enjoy a slightly higher admission rate than female candidates. In addition to meeting regular admissions requirements, students who wish to pursue a degree in fine arts or performing arts must present a portfolio or audition, respectively.

THE SCHOOL SAYS "..."

From the Admissions Office

"Manhattanville's mission—to educate ethically and socially responsible leaders for the global community—is evident throughout the college, from academics to athletics to social and extracurricular activities. With almost 1,700 undergraduates from fifty-nine nations and thirty-nine states, our diversity spans geographic, cultural, ethnic, religious, socioeconomic, and academic backgrounds. Students are free to express their views in this tight-knit community, where we value the personal as well as the global. Any six students with similar interest can start a club, and most participate in a variety of campus wide programs. Last year, students engaged in more than 23,380 hours of community service and social justice activity. Study abroad opportunities include not only the most desirable international locations, but also a semester-long immersion for living, studying, and working in New York City. In the true liberal arts tradition, students are encouraged to think for themselves and develop new skills—in music, the studio arts, on stage, in the sciences, or on the playing field. With more than fifty areas of study and a popular self-designed major, there is no limit to our academic scope. Our Westchester County location, just thirty-five miles north of New York City, gives students an edge for jobs and internships. Last year, the men's and women's ice hockey teams were ranked number one in the nation for Division III."

SELECTIVITY

Admissions Rating	71
# of applicants	4,099
% of applicants accepted	60
% of acceptees attending	17

FRESHMAN PROFILE

Minimum paper TOEFL	550
Minimum computer TOEFL	217

DEADLINES

Early decision	
Deadline	12/1
Notification	12/31
Regular	
Priority	3/1
Deadline	3/1
Notification	1/5
Nonfall registration?	yes

APPLICANTS ALSO LOOK AT

AND OFTEN PREFER
New York University

AND SOMETIMES PREFER
Fordham University

AND RARELY PREFER
Pace University, White Plains

FINANCIAL FACTS

Financial Aid Rating	79
Annual tuition	$33,030
Room and board	$13,920
Books and supplies	$800
% frosh rec. need-based scholarship or grant aid	72
% UG rec. need-based scholarship or grant aid	66
% frosh rec. non-need-based scholarship or grant aid	59
% UG rec. non-need-based scholarship or grant aid	54
% frosh rec. need-based self-help aid	69
% UG rec. need-based self-help aid	61
% frosh rec. any financial aid	75
% UG rec. any financial aid	70
% UG borrow to pay for school	53
Average cumulative indebtedness	$23,138

MARIST COLLEGE

3399 NORTH ROAD, POUGHKEEPSIE, NY 12601-1387 • ADMISSIONS: 845-575-3226 • FAX: 845-575-3215

STUDENTS SAY ". . ."

Academics

Marist College, "a smaller private school in a nice area with a great campus life," offers a surprising range of options to its largely career-minded student population. The school is home to "a very good business school;" "a good criminal justice department;" "a reputable teacher education program;" and "great concentrations in teaching, communication, and fashion." All departments benefit from the school's "unique partnership with IBM," which translates into "very advanced computer technology and Web services. Our online library is very extensive and extremely helpful for research papers and projects." Similarly, students appreciate the school's vigorous efforts to place them in meaningful internships. One student explains: "The internship departments have directors in each major, and a great many opportunities are made available to students for internships during both the academic year and the summer months. There is even staff on campus to go over your resume with you and make sure it is properly formatted and has all of the necessary information in it for potential employers to review when you apply for an internship." The school's location, "about an hour and a half from New York City," is key to the success of the internship program. Students also love the "intensive study abroad program," through which they "can go almost anywhere in the world for the same price as a semester at Marist."

Life

With "breathtaking views of the Hudson River" and "a great campus complete with nature trails and a riverfront park," Marist College offers an idyllic setting in which to pursue a college degree. Students tell us that campus life "pretty much has something for everyone: campus organizations based around race/heritage, Greek organizations, service, sports, performing arts, and co-curricular organizations. Students have many opportunities to build their social networks." Many here "are extremely concerned with life after college, and therefore many engage in activities and internships that will give them more experience in their careers." They still find time for fun, though. Campus-based diversions include "comedians, bands, hypnotists, singers, and speakers [who] come every week to give performances for the students," while off-campus life includes forays into hometown Poughkeepsie ("the school is about seven minutes from the Galleria Mall, which has a big selection of stores") or nearby historic Hyde Park; trips to New York City are most likely to occur on the weekend, since the city is about ninety minutes away (the trip, however, only requires "an extremely easy train ride to the middle of the city"). Poughkeepsie has an active nightclub and bar scene, students tell us.

Student Body

"A typical Marist student is from New York, New Jersey, or Connecticut;" is "middle- to upper-middle-class;" and has "a good background education and social skills." Undergrads here "display a hard work ethic in class while taking the initiative to become involved with student-run clubs, activities, and sports," but students aren't especially driven by academics for their own sake; they simply want to "get their work done and have a good time while getting great grades." Many here "tend to be politically conservative, but a lot of students just don't have an interest in politics. Also, Marist does not have the hipster crowd." The school was once a Catholic school, and although it is now officially non-denominational, vestiges of its old identity are evident in the student body; "Most students are Catholic," one student reports, "but religious diversity is increasing bit by bit" as the years pass.

FINANCIAL AID: 845-575-3230 • E-MAIL: ADMISSIONS@MARIST.EDU • WEBSITE: WWW.MARIST.EDU

THE PRINCETON REVIEW SAYS

Admissions

Very important factors considered include: Academic GPA, rigor of secondary school record, standardized test scores, geographical residence. *Important factors considered include:* Application essay, class rank, recommendation(s), character/ personal qualities, extracurricular activities, geographical residence, state residency, talent/ability, volunteer work, work experience. *Other factors considered include:* Alumni/ae relation, level of applicant's interest, racial/ethnic status. Standardized tests are optional but considered if submitted. ACT with or without writing component accepted. TOEFL required of all international applicants. High school diploma is required, and GED is accepted. *Academic units required:* 4 English, 3 mathematics, 3 science (2 science labs), 2 foreign language, 2 social studies, 1 history, 2 academic elective. *Academic units recommended:* 4 mathematics, 4 science (3 science labs).

Financial Aid

Students should submit: FAFSA, institution's own financial aid form. Regular filing deadline is May 1. The Princeton Review suggests that all financial aid forms be submitted as soon as possible after January 1. *Need-based scholarships/ grants offered:* Federal Pell, SEOG, state scholarships/grants, private scholarships, school scholarship or grant aid from institutional funds. *Loan aid offered:* Direct Subsidized Stafford, Direct Unsubsidized Stafford, Direct PLUS, Federal Perkins. Applicants will be notified of awards on a rolling basis beginning April 1. Federal Work-Study Program available. Off-campus job opportunities are excellent.

The Inside Word

About one-quarter of its most recent incoming class graduated outside the top twenty-five percent of their high school class. Those lacking academic bona fides will have to make it up in other areas, however; evidence of leadership, ability to contribute to the life of the campus (for example, artistic or athletic skill), an interesting background that will add diversity to classroom discussion, or a similar distinguishing trait will be needed to make up for a middling academic record.

THE SCHOOL SAYS "..."

From the Admissions Office

"Marist is a 'hot school' among prospective students. We are seeing a record number of applications each year. But the number of seats available for the freshman class remains the same, about 1,000. Therefore, becoming an accepted applicant is an increasingly competitive process. Our recommendations: keep your grades up, participate in community service both in and out of school, and exercise leadership in the classroom, athletics, extracurricular activities, and your place of worship. We encourage a campus visit. When prospective students see Marist—our beautiful location on a scenic stretch of the Hudson River, the quality of our facilities, the interaction between students and faculty, and the fact that everyone really enjoys their time here—they want to become a part of the Marist College community. We'll help you in the transition from high school to college through an innovative first-year program that provides mentors for every student. You'll also learn how to use technology in whatever field you choose. We emphasize three aspects of a true Marist experience: excellence in education, community, and service to others. At Marist, you'll get a premium education, develop your skills, have fun and make lifelong friends, be given the opportunity to gain valuable experience through our great internship and study abroad programs, including our branch campus in Florence, Italy, and be ahead of the competition for graduate school or work."

SELECTIVITY

Admissions Rating	90
# of applicants	9,547
% of applicants accepted	40
% of acceptees attending	29
# accepting a place on wait list	619
% admitted from wait list	3
# of early decision applicants	172
% accepted early decision	92

FRESHMAN PROFILE

Range SAT Critical Reading	530–620
Range SAT Math	540–630
Range SAT Writing	540–630
Range ACT Composite	23–27
Minimum paper TOEFL	550
Minimum computer TOEFL	213
Minimum web-based TOEFL	80
Average HS GPA	3.30
% graduated top 10% of class	28
% graduated top 25% of class	70
% graduated top 50% of class	91

DEADLINES

Early decision	
Deadline	11/15
Notification	12/15
Early action	
Deadline	12/1
Notification	1/30
Regular	
Deadline	2/15
Nonfall registration?	yes

APPLICANTS ALSO LOOK AT
AND OFTEN PREFER
Boston College, Villanova University

AND SOMETIMES PREFER
Fairfield University, Loyola University in Maryland, Providence College, University of Delaware

AND RARELY PREFER
Iona College, Quinnipiac University, Siena College, State University of New York—University at Albany

FINANCIAL FACTS

Financial Aid Rating	73
Annual tuition	$27,150
Room and board	$11,676
Required fees	$590
Books and supplies	$1,600
% frosh rec. need-based scholarship or grant aid	43
% UG rec. need-based scholarship or grant aid	39
% frosh rec. non-need-based scholarship or grant aid	47
% UG rec. non-need-based scholarship or grant aid	39
% frosh rec. need-based self-help aid	49
% UG rec. need-based self-help aid	52
% frosh rec. any financial aid	85
% UG rec. any financial aid	76
% UG borrow to pay for school	68
Average cumulative indebtedness	$25,135

MARLBORO COLLEGE

PO BOX A, SOUTH ROAD, MARLBORO, VT 05344-0300 • ADMISSIONS: 802-258-9236 • FAX: 802-451-7555

CAMPUS LIFE

Quality of Life Rating	76
Fire Safety Rating	74
Green Rating	73
Type of school	private
Environment	rural

STUDENTS

Total undergrad enrollment	278
% male/female	51/49
% from out of state	88
% from public high school	70
% live on campus	80
% African American	1
% Asian	2
% Caucasian	68
% Hispanic	3
% international	1
# of countries represented	4

SURVEY SAYS . . .
Lots of liberal students
Class discussions encouraged
No one cheats
Campus feels safe
Frats and sororities are unpopular
or nonexistent
Student government is popular

ACADEMICS

Academic Rating	99
% students graduating within 4 years	35
% students graduating within 6 years	45
Calendar	semester
Student/faculty ratio	6:1
Profs interesting rating	97
Profs accessible rating	92
Most common reg class size	fewer than 10 students

MOST POPULAR MAJORS
English language and literature, social sciences, visual and performing arts

STUDENTS SAY ". . ."

Academics
Marlboro College is all about giving students "the freedom to pursue their own interests and study what they want." Here, undergrads design their own junior and senior curricula, then pursue them in one-on-one tutorials with professors. The process, known here simply as "The Plan," culminates in a substantial senior thesis. The goal is to "learn how to think critically and find the resources you need in the course of completing a dissertation-level project," and undergrads here "wouldn't settle for anything less in their academic pursuits." Freshmen and sophomores complete more traditional-style courses, albeit in smaller classrooms and with a greater-than-usual focus on writing and discussion. The size of the school—just more than 300 undergraduates attend—is sometimes a hindrance. One student observes that, "Since there is generally only one professor per field, it is a bit disappointing to realize that there can only be a limited number of classes offered per semester." "Too often a student will reach the final year when his/her Plan sponsor goes on sabbatical. This presents a problem: Does the student leave the college until their professor returns, or does the student switch Plan sponsors, potentially altering the focus of their work so much they dislike what they're doing?" Despite these issues, "professors are very receptive and try to accommodate individual interests as best they can." Most here feel these are reasonable costs to bear in order to pursue "independent, difficult, intellectually stimulating work inside a student-centered and directed curriculum."

Life
Marlboro is "a little school on top of a hill" with Brattleboro, the closest town, "about a half hour away," so "Life is pretty intensely focused on the campus." "While we do make the trip to Brattleboro fairly often, most of our time is spent 'on the hill,'" says one student. Students "study a lot, but there is also a lot of hanging out, mainly in small impromptu ways." They "like to debate about philosophy, politics, and religion." Fun "is found in the 300 acres that surround the college: skiing, hiking, long walks in an apple orchard, broomball (a hippie version of hockey), soccer, etc." Trips to Brattleboro are pleasant because it's "an arts town." Students occasionally travel to Massachusetts college towns Amherst and Northampton for concerts or shopping and "frequently classes take field trips to NYC or Boston." Many get involved in grassroots political organization, both on campus and off.

Student Body
The typical Marlboro student "wouldn't fit quite right anywhere else: academically driven, maybe a little nerdy, politically vocal, and looking for a laid-back environment. There is no atypical student at Marlboro, because we all would have been atypical someplace else." Personality types run the gamut, including "hippie environmentalists, geeks and gamers, theater kids, artists, and so on and so forth and every combination thereof. We're underrepresented in the jock and beauty queen categories, but that doesn't seem to bother anybody." Everyone here, we're told, "is extremely passionate about their own little academic niche, and furthermore each person is one of the smartest people you will ever meet." The school is home to "a large gay population and a few transgender students," but "There is a lack of minority students, [and] Republicans."

FINANCIAL AID: 800-343-0049 • E-MAIL: ADMISSIONS@MARLBORO.EDU • WEBSITE: WWW.MARLBORO.EDU

THE PRINCETON REVIEW SAYS

Admissions

Very important factors considered include: Academic GPA, application essay, rigor of secondary school record, character/personal qualities. *Important factors considered include:* Extracurricular activities, interview. *Other factors considered include:* Class rank, recommendation(s), standardized test scores, alumni/ae relation, first generation, geographical residence, level of applicant's interest, state residency, talent/ability, volunteer work, work experience. ACT with or without writing component accepted. TOEFL required of all international applicants. High school diploma is required, and GED is accepted. *Academic units recommended:* 4 English, 3 mathematics, 3 science (1 science lab), 3 foreign language, 3 social studies, 3 history, 3 academic elective.

Financial Aid

Students should submit: FAFSA. Regular filing deadline is March 1. The Princeton Review suggests that all financial aid forms be submitted as soon as possible after January 1. *Need-based scholarships/grants offered:* Federal Pell, SEOG, state scholarships/grants, private scholarships, school scholarship or grant aid from institutional funds. Applicants will be notified of awards on a rolling basis beginning March 15. Federal Work-Study Program available. Off-campus job opportunities are fair.

The Inside Word

Don't be misled by Marlboro's acceptance rate—this isn't the type of school that attracts many applications from students unsure of whether they belong at Marlboro. Most applicants are qualified both in terms of academic achievement and sincere intellectual curiosity. The school seeks candidates "with intellectual promise, a high degree of self-motivation, self-discipline, personal stability, social concern, and the ability and desire to contribute to the college community." These are the qualities you should stress on your application.

THE SCHOOL SAYS ". . ."

From the Admissions Office

"Marlboro College is distinguished by its curriculum, praised in higher education circles as unique; it is known for its self-governing philosophy, in which each student, faculty, and staff has an equal vote on many issues affecting the community; and it is recognized for its sixty-year history of offering a rigorous, exciting, self-designed course of study taught in very small classes and individualized study with faculty. Marlboro's size also distinguishes it from most other schools. With 300 students and a student/faculty ratio of eight to one, it is one of the nation's smallest liberal arts colleges. Few other schools offer a program where students have such close interaction with faculty, and where community life is inseparable from academic life. The result, the self-designed, self-directed Plan of Concentration, allows students to develop their own unique academic work by defining a problem, setting clear limits on an area of inquiry, and analyzing, evaluating, and reporting on the outcome of a significant project. A Marlboro education teaches you to think for yourself, articulate your thoughts, express your ideas, believe in yourself, and do it all with the clarity, confidence, and self-reliance necessary for later success, no matter what postgraduate path you take."

SELECTIVITY

Admissions Rating	91
# of applicants	318
% of applicants accepted	76
% of acceptees attending	21
# of early decision applicants	10
% accepted early decision	90

FRESHMAN PROFILE

Range SAT Critical Reading	610–690
Range SAT Math	510–650
Range SAT Writing	570–680
Range ACT Composite	24–32
Minimum paper TOEFL	550
Minimum computer TOEFL	213
Minimum web-based TOEFL	80
Average HS GPA	3.20
% graduated top 10% of class	40
% graduated top 25% of class	60
% graduated top 50% of class	80

DEADLINES

Early decision	
Deadline	11/15
Notification	12/15
Early action	
Deadline	1/15
Notification	2/15
Regular	
Deadline	3/1
Notification	12/1
Nonfall registration?	yes

APPLICANTS ALSO LOOK AT

AND OFTEN PREFER
Reed College

AND SOMETIMES PREFER
Bard College, College of the Atlantic,
The Evergreen State College

AND RARELY PREFER
Bennington College, Green Mountain College,
Hampshire College, University of Vermont

FINANCIAL FACTS

Financial Aid Rating	84
Annual comprehensive tuition	$46,200
Books and supplies	$1,000
% frosh rec. need-based scholarship or grant aid	75
% UG rec. need-based scholarship or grant aid	69
% frosh rec. non-need-based scholarship or grant aid	75
% UG rec. non-need-based scholarship or grant aid	70
% frosh rec. need-based self-help aid	73
% UG rec. need-based self-help aid	71
% frosh rec. any financial aid	75
% UG rec. any financial aid	72
% UG borrow to pay for school	86
Average cumulative indebtedness	$22,456

MARQUETTE UNIVERSITY

PO Box 1881, Milwaukee, WI 53201-1881 • Admissions: 414-288-7302 • Fax: 414-288-3764

CAMPUS LIFE

Quality of Life Rating	78
Fire Safety Rating	81
Green Rating	91
Type of school	private
Affiliation	Roman Catholic-Jesuit
Environment	metropolis

STUDENTS

Total undergrad enrollment	7,912
% male/female	47/53
% from out of state	59
% from public high school	56
% live on campus	55
# of fraternities	11
# of sororities	11
% African American	5
% Asian	4
% Caucasian	80
% Hispanic	7
% international	2
# of countries represented	70

SURVEY SAYS . . .
Great library
Low cost of living
Everyone loves the Golden Eagles
Very little drug use

ACADEMICS

Academic Rating	75
% students graduating within 4 years	62
% students graduating within 6 years	81
Calendar	semester
Student/faculty ratio	14:1
Profs interesting rating	83
Profs accessible rating	86
Most common reg class size	10–19 students
Most common lab size	20–29 students

MOST POPULAR MAJORS
biomedical sciences, marketing, nursing

STUDENTS SAY ". . ."

Academics

Looking for a school with a "dedication to academic excellence," and an "involved and intelligent" student body an "open-minded attitude?" Then the Jesuit ideals at Marquette where "people are dedicated to helping others, are incredibly motivated to do well, and hopefully one day, change the world," may be for you. This medium-sized Milwaukee school manages to be "pretty well-run," and students rave about their professors. One junior tells us, "The professors strive to know you personally and to help you achieve your goals," while one communication major "*loves, loves, loves* every professor" in her college. One student goes as far as to say, "I haven't had much of an experience with the administration, but it is clear that professors here work because they are committed to the Jesuit way of education and are truly willing to help students in any way possible." However, great professors will only get you so far, "the education you receive at Marquette is what you put into it. The resources are available to you...You just have to reach out and take personal responsibility." Though the school seems to run fairly smoothly, "if you do not get a decent registration slot, prepare for extra years of college." But barring a few minor complaints, students seem to agree "the teachers and administrators work to challenge you so that accomplishment is truly your own and learning is at its highest standard."

Life

As you might expect from a school located in a major city, Marquette students' social lives tend to lead them downtown where they "usually head out to eat and hang out. The city is so big people can actually do anything and are rarely restricted to some activities." Students do know how to let loose. "The lifestyle at Marquette is drinking alcohol on the weekends," and "Milwaukee is known for making good beer, and thus students take advantage of the city." For those who prefer to stay on campus "in the evening, there is almost always something going on or to do with friends. To a program sponsored by the university or a campus organization or a pick-up game of Frisbee." But keep in mind the bright students at Marquette like to exercise their intellect with "discussions ranging from a variety of topics, from politics, religion, issues of social justice, or the economy classes." "Our men's basketball program is a pretty big deal on campus," and students are psyched about new head coach Buzz Williams and the team's three straight NCAA tournament appearances. Some students also participate in Greek life, "intramural sports, student organizations," and "the school's radio station."

Student Body

The majority of Marquette students are "white, upper-middle" and "from the Chicago suburbs," but "it seems as if everyone fits in." Says another, "I haven't seen one single person not fit in; doesn't matter what race, gender, or sexual orientation, everyone hangs out with everyone." "The motto of Marquette is Curas Personalis, which means 'care for the whole person.' This is a saying by which our students live." One student says, "The typical student wears jeans, a Marquette t-shirt, and gym shoes." Sounds about right—school spirit definitely thrives here. Many student's cite the athletics as their favorite part of attending Marquette, and "everyone comes together to support our sports teams." Many others enjoy the school's Jesuit values and its focus on "emphasizing community service, and many are involved in making the city a better place." "Marquette lives up to its promise in promoting Jesuit values in and outside of the classroom."

MARQUETTE UNIVERSITY

FINANCIAL AID: 414-288-7390 • E-MAIL: ADMISSIONS@MARQUETTE.EDU • WEBSITE: WWW.MARQUETTE.EDU

THE PRINCETON REVIEW SAYS

Admissions

Very important factors considered include: Academic GPA, rigor of secondary school record. *Important factors considered include:* Application essay, class rank, recommendation(s), standardized test scores. *Other factors considered include:* Alumni/ae relation, character/personal qualities, extracurricular activities, first generation, geographical residence, racial/ethnic status, state residency, talent/ability, volunteer work. SAT or ACT required; ACT with writing component recommended. TOEFL required of all international applicants. High school diploma is required, and GED is accepted. *Academic units required:* 4 English, 2 mathematics, 2 science (2 science labs), 2 social studies, 2 academic elective. *Academic units recommended:* 4 English, 4 mathematics, 3 science (3 science labs), 2 foreign language, 3 social studies, 5 academic elective.

Financial Aid

Students should submit: FAFSA. The Princeton Review suggests that all financial aid forms be submitted as soon as possible after January 1. *Need-based scholarships/grants offered:* Federal Pell, SEOG, state scholarships/grants, private scholarships, school scholarship or grant aid from institutional funds. *Loan aid offered:* Direct Subsidized Stafford, Direct Unsubsidized Stafford, Direct PLUS, Federal Perkins, Federal Nursing Loans, state loans, university loans from institutional funds. Applicants will be notified of awards on a rolling basis beginning March 20. Federal Work-Study Program available. Off-campus job opportunities are excellent.

The Inside Word

Despite the number of applications Marquette receives, at least two admissions counselors look at each one. Admissions are increasingly selective, and applicants should have solid grades and a respectable course record. Nearly all Marquette students finished in the top half of their graduating class. The admissions department pays close attention to student essays and values writing skills in its candidates.

THE SCHOOL SAYS "..."

From the Admissions Office

"Since 1881, Marquette has been noted for its commitment to educational excellence in the 450-year-old Catholic/Jesuit tradition. Marquette embraces the philosophy that true education should be more than an acquisition of knowledge; it should develop your intellect as well as your moral and spiritual character. This all-encompassing education will challenge you to develop the goals and values that will shape the rest of your life. Each of Marquette's 8,100 undergraduates is admitted as a freshman to one of seven colleges: Arts and Sciences, Business Administration, Communication, Education, Engineering, Health Sciences, or Nursing. The faculty within these colleges are prolific writers and researchers, but more importantly, they all teach and advise students.

"Marquette is nestled in the financial center of Milwaukee, the nation's eighteenth-largest city, allowing you to take full advantage of the city's cultural, professional, and governmental opportunities. Marquette's urban experience is unique; a ninety-three-acre campus, an outdoor athletic complex, and an internationally diverse student body (ninety percent of which live on or near campus) all make Marquette a close-knit community in which you can learn and live.

"Marquette applicants must submit scores from either the SAT or the ACT with writing component. The highest composite score will be used in admissions decisions."

SELECTIVITY

Admissions Rating	81
# of applicants	19,930
% of applicants accepted	62
% of acceptees attending	16
# accepting a place on wait list	949
% admitted from wait list	73

FRESHMAN PROFILE

Range SAT Critical Reading	540–640
Range SAT Math	545–660
Range SAT Writing	530–630
Range ACT Composite	24–29
Minimum paper TOEFL	520
Minimum computer TOEFL	190
Minimum web-based TOEFL	76
% graduated top 10% of class	34
% graduated top 25% of class	62
% graduated top 50% of class	92

DEADLINES

Regular	
Priority	12/1
Deadline	12/1
Nonfall registration?	yes

FINANCIAL FACTS

Financial Aid Rating	78
Annual tuition	$31,400
Room and board	$10,340
Required fees	$422
Books and supplies	$960
% frosh rec. need-based scholarship or grant aid	63
% UG rec. need-based scholarship or grant aid	60
% frosh rec. non-need-based scholarship or grant aid	8
% UG rec. non-need-based scholarship or grant aid	6
% frosh rec. need-based self-help aid	53
% UG rec. need-based self-help aid	54
% frosh rec. any financial aid	99
% UG rec. any financial aid	93
% UG borrow to pay for school	65
Average cumulative indebtedness	$32,824

MARYWOOD UNIVERSITY

OFFICE OF ADMISSIONS, 2300 ADAMS AVENUE, SCRANTON, PA 18509 • ADMISSIONS: 570-348-6234 • FAX: 570-961-4763

CAMPUS LIFE

Quality of Life Rating	72
Fire Safety Rating	95
Green Rating	97
Type of school	private
Affiliation	Roman Catholic
Environment	city

STUDENTS

Total undergrad enrollment	2,267
% male/female	30/70
% from out of state	27
% from public high school	89
% live on campus	45
# of sororities	1
% African American	1
% Asian	2
% Caucasian	86
% Hispanic	3
% international	1
# of countries represented	20

SURVEY SAYS . . .
Athletic facilities are great
Low cost of living
Musical organizations are popular
Very little drug use

ACADEMICS

Academic Rating	75
% students graduating within 4 years	55
Calendar	semester
Student/faculty ratio	13:1
Profs interesting rating	74
Profs accessible rating	72
Most common reg class size	10–19 students

MOST POPULAR MAJORS
dietics, elementary education and teaching, psychology

STUDENTS SAY ". . ."

Academics

Marywood University is a small Catholic university that offers a wide range of undergraduate majors and pre-professional programs, from art therapy and music performance to physician assistant and interior design. Marywood University consists of four colleges and a School of Architecture. No matter what you choose to study, the intimate classroom environment is the strength of a Marywood education. A freshman explains, "Through class discussions, I feel that I am truly learning and absorbing the material, as opposed to other schools where teachers dictate or lecture for hours." Academic programs are "challenging but not overwhelming," and "The professors do everything in their power to help their students learn and be able to apply that knowledge to real life." At the same time, personal accountability is vital. Teachers know you by name, and "Small class sizes get you extra attention but also make it obvious if you skip class." If you're looking to take a wide range of classes, Marywood isn't the best option, as most majors have extensive course requirements, and it can be difficult to get a spot in classes outside your declared department. On the other hand, "Marywood is awesome if you know exactly what you want to do. It has some excellent programs and combines them with general humanities classes."

Life

When they're not in the library, Marywood students enjoy college life through "on-campus events, movies, bowling, house parties, and just hanging out in the lounges." School spirit surges during the school's sporting events, and "Students get excited about the basketball games as well as the women's soccer games." Even though Marywood is a dry campus, you can always take "a trip down to Scranton University for party life (if that's what you're into)." When it comes to the surrounding city, "A lot of people complain that there is nothing to do around Scranton, but you just have to know where to look." In fact, "There is a lot of good shopping, movie theaters, restaurants, bars, and clubs" in Scranton, and some nightclubs permit entry to age eighteen and up. If you're willing to take a trip outside the city, "The spring and fall are a great time to go on hikes or enjoy the outdoor attractions," and in the winter, "There is a ski resort close by."

Student Body

Well-rounded, friendly, and studious, the typical Marywood undergraduate "does well in class, works out at the gym, is involved with clubs, and is surrounded by many friends." Most undergraduates at Marywood are "young, white, middle-class" students from New York, New Jersey, and Pennsylvania, though the campus also attracts "students from all over the world, all different religions." Within the college community, you'll find "art lovers in our art field and sport lovers in our new gym, movie watchers in the Madonna Hall Movie Theater, and dancers in our new dance studio. There are sorority girls always looking to add new girls to the Zeta Phi Delta and coffee drinkers at the many coffee spots on campus." Fortunately, all students "fit in as one big friendly community." A freshman shares, "Life at college is very safe and relaxing. People are free to make their own choices and [are] encouraged to have their own opinions."

FINANCIAL AID: 866-279-9663 • E-MAIL: YOURFUTURE@MARYWOOD.EDU • WEBSITE: WWW.MARYWOOD.EDU

THE PRINCETON REVIEW SAYS

Admissions

Very important factors considered include: Academic GPA, class rank, rigor of secondary school record, standardized test scores, character/personal qualities. *Important factors considered include:* Application essay, recommendation(s), interview, talent/ability. *Other factors considered include:* Extracurricular activities, level of applicant's interest, volunteer work. SAT or ACT required; ACT with or without writing component accepted. TOEFL required of all international applicants. High school diploma is required, and GED is accepted. *Academic units required:* 4 English, 2 mathematics, 1 science (1 science lab), 3 social studies, academic elective.

Financial Aid

The complete FAFSA application needs to be submitted by incoming students by February 15. The deadline for other students is April 15. However, The Princeton Review suggests that all financial aid forms be submitted as soon as possible after January 1. Applicants will be notified of awards on a rolling basis beginning February 15. Work-study funds available.

The Inside Word

After you have applied to Marywood, you can participate in their "College for a Day" program, which gives prospective students an inside look at university life, from the classroom to the cafeteria. Marywood reviews applications on a rolling basis, and therefore, you should apply as early as possible. Once a prospective student has submitted all of the application materials, the admissions department will usually make a decision within two or three weeks.

THE SCHOOL SAYS ". . ."

From the Admissions Office

"Marywood University is a comprehensive, Catholic university with just over 2,267 full-time and part-time men and women undergraduates and 1,212 graduate students on campus. There are over ninety undergraduate programs to choose from, many offering graduate components or even doctoral degree programs, if desired. Established in 1915, the university today houses 1,000 undergraduate resident students on a national award-winning campus considered one of the most beautiful in the northeast. In recent years, the university has made $100 million in improvements to campus, including new athletics, residence hall and dining facilities, and one of the finest studio arts facilities in the northeast. Marywood offered the first doctoral degree programs in the Northeastern Pennsylvania region. Of our full-time faculty members, eighty-five percent hold the most advanced degrees in their field. Our faculty members are grounded in professional practice and skilled in the art of teaching, and are highly respected practitioners, industry professionals, and visionary educators.

"Marywood operates on a rolling admissions basis. High school seniors are encouraged to submit their application for admission before March 1. Students applying for federal and state financial aid should submit the Free Application for Federal Student Aid (FAFSA) by February 15. At Marywood, you will discover that a top-notch private college experience is more affordable than you ever dreamed. In fact, ninety-eight percent of our first-time students receive financial assistance in the form of scholarships, grants, loans, and work-study programs."

SELECTIVITY

Admissions Rating	80
# of applicants	2,062
% of applicants accepted	72
% of acceptees attending	34

FRESHMAN PROFILE

Range SAT Critical Reading	480–570
Range SAT Math	480–570
Range SAT Writing	470–570
Range ACT Composite	20–23
Minimum paper TOEFL	530
Minimum computer TOEFL	197
Minimum web-based TOEFL	71
Average HS GPA	3.21
% graduated top 10% of class	18
% graduated top 25% of class	48
% graduated top 50% of class	88

DEADLINES

Regular	
Notification	10/1
Nonfall registration?	yes

FINANCIAL FACTS

Financial Aid Rating	79
Annual tuition	$27,000
Room and board	$12,520
Required fees	$1,175
Books and supplies	$1,200
% frosh rec. need-based scholarship or grant aid	86
% UG rec. need-based scholarship or grant aid	85
% frosh rec. non-need-based scholarship or grant aid	15
% UG rec. non-need-based scholarship or grant aid	17
% frosh rec. need-based self-help aid	75
% UG rec. need-based self-help aid	69
% frosh rec. any financial aid	92
% UG rec. any financial aid	93
% UG borrow to pay for school	87
Average cumulative indebtedness	$27,736

MASSACHUSETTS INSTITUTE OF TECHNOLOGY

MIT ADMISSIONS OFFICE, ROOM 10-100, 77 MASSACHUSETTS AVENUE, CAMBRIDGE, MA 02139 • ADMISSIONS: 617-253-3400

CAMPUS LIFE

Quality of Life Rating	81
Fire Safety Rating	78
Green Rating	91
Type of school	private
Environment	city

STUDENTS

Total undergrad enrollment	4,285
% male/female	55/45
% from out of state	90
% from public high school	65
% live on campus	93
# of fraternities	27
# of sororities	6
% African American	8
% Asian	24
% Caucasian	37
% Hispanic	13
% Native American	1
% international	9
# of countries represented	92

SURVEY SAYS . . .
Registration is a breeze
Lab facilities are great
Great computer facilities
Athletic facilities are great
School is well-run
Diverse student types on campus
Students love Cambridge, MA

ACADEMICS

Academic Rating	97
% students graduating within 4 years	84
% students graduating within 6 years	93
Calendar	4-1-4
Student/faculty ratio	8:1
Profs interesting rating	70
Profs accessible rating	76
Most common reg class size	fewer than 10 students
Most common lab size	10–19 students

MOST POPULAR MAJORS
computer science, mathematics, mechanical engineering

STUDENTS SAY ". . ."

Academics

Massachusetts Institute of Technology, the East Coast mecca of engineering, science, and mathematics, "is the ultimate place for information overload, endless possibilities, and expanding your horizons." The "amazing collection of creative minds" includes enough Nobel laureates to fill a jury box as well as brilliant students who are given substantial control of their educations; one explains, "The administration's attitude toward students is one of respect. As soon as you come on campus, you are bombarded with choices." Students need to be able to manage a workload that "definitely push[es you] beyond your comfort level." A chemical engineering major elaborates: "MIT is different from many schools in that its goal is not to teach you specific facts in each subject. MIT teaches you how to think, not about opinions but about problem solving. Facts and memorization are useless unless you know how to approach a tough problem." Professors here range from "excellent teachers who make lectures fun and exciting" to "dull and soporific" ones, but most "make a serious effort to make the material they teach interesting by throwing in jokes and cool demonstrations." "Access to an amazing number of resources, both academic and recreational," "research opportunities for undergrads with some of the nation's leading professors," and a rock-solid alumni network complete the picture. If you ask "MIT alumni where they went to college, most will immediately stick out their hand and show you their 'brass rat' (the MIT ring, the second most recognized ring in the world)."

Life

At MIT, "It may seem…like there's no life outside problem sets and studying for exams," but "There's always time for extracurricular activities or just relaxing" for those "with good time-management skills" or the "ability to survive on [a] lack of sleep." Options range from "building rides" (recent projects have included a motorized couch and a human-sized hamster wheel) "to partying at fraternities to enjoying the largest collection of science fiction novels in the United States at the MIT Science Fiction Library." Students occasionally find time to "pull a hack," which is an ethical prank, "like the life-size Wright brothers' plane that appeared on top of the Great Dome for the one-hundredth anniversary of flight." Undergrads tell us, "MIT has great parties—a lot of Wellesley, Harvard, and BU students come to them," but also that "there are tons of things to do other than party" here. "Movies, shopping, museums, and plays are all possible with our location near Boston. There are great restaurants only [blocks] away from campus, too…From what I can tell, MIT students have way more fun on the weekends than their Cambridge counterparts [at] Harvard."

Student Body

"There actually isn't one typical student at MIT," students here assure us, explaining that "hobbies range from building robots and hacking to getting wasted and partying every weekend. The one thing students all have in common is that they are insanely smart and love to learn. Pretty much anyone can find the perfect group of friends to hang out with at MIT." "Most students do have some form of 'nerdiness'" (like telling nerdy jokes, being an avid fan of *Star Wars*, etc.), but "Contrary to MIT's stereotype, most MIT students are not geeks who study all the time and have no social skills. The majority of the students here are actually quite 'normal.'" The "stereotypical student [who] looks techy and unkempt…only represents about twenty-five percent of the school." The rest include "multiple-sport standouts, political activists, fraternity and sorority members, hippies, clean-cut business types, LARPers, hackers, musicians, and artisans. There are people who look like they stepped out of an Abercrombie & Fitch catalog and people who dress in all black and carry flashlights and multi-tools. Not everyone relates to everyone else, but most people get along, and it's almost a guarantee that you'll fit in somewhere."

MASSACHUSETTS INSTITUTE OF TECHNOLOGY

FINANCIAL AID: 617-258-8600 • WEBSITE: WEB.MIT.EDU

THE PRINCETON REVIEW SAYS

Admissions

Very important factors considered include: Character/personal qualities. *Important factors considered include:* Academic GPA, application essay, recommendation(s), rigor of secondary school record, standardized test scores, extracurricular activities, interview, talent/ability. *Other factors considered include:* Class rank, first generation, geographical residence, racial/ethnic status, volunteer work, work experience. SAT or ACT required; ACT with writing component required. High school diploma or equivalent isn't required. *Academic units recommended:* 4 English, 4 mathematics, 4 science, 2 foreign language, 2 social studies.

Financial Aid

Students should submit: FAFSA, CSS/Financial Aid PROFILE. Regular filing deadline is February 15. The Princeton Review suggests that all financial aid forms be submitted as soon as possible after January 1. *Need-based scholarships/grants offered:* Federal Pell, SEOG, state scholarships/grants, private scholarships, school scholarship or grant aid from institutional funds. Loan aid offered: Direct Subsidized Stafford, Direct Unsubsidized Stafford, Direct PLUS, Federal Perkins, university loans from institutional funds. Federal Work-Study Program available. Off-campus job opportunities are excellent.

The Inside Word

MIT has one of the nation's most competitive admissions processes. The school's applicant pool is so rich it turns away numerous qualified candidates each year. Put your best foot forward and take consolation in the fact that rejection doesn't necessarily mean that you don't belong at MIT, but only that there wasn't enough room for you the year you applied. Your best chance to get an edge: Find ways to stress your creativity, a quality that MIT's admissions director told *USA TODAY* is lacking in many prospective college students.

THE SCHOOL SAYS ". . ."

From the Admissions Office

"The students who come to the Massachusetts Institute of Technology are some of America's—and the world's—best and most creative. As graduates, they leave here to make real contributions—in science, technology, business, education, politics, architecture, and the arts. From any class, many will go on to do work that is historically significant. These young men and women are leaders, achievers, and producers. Helping such students make the most of their talents and dreams would challenge any educational institution. MIT gives them its best advantages: a world-class faculty, unparalleled facilities, and remarkable opportunities. In turn, these students help to make the institute the vital place it is. They bring fresh viewpoints to faculty research: More than three-quarters participate in the Undergraduate Research Opportunities Program, developing solutions for the world's problems in areas such as energy, the environment, cancer, and poverty. They play on MIT's thirty-three intercollegiate teams as well as in its fifty-plus music, theatre, and dance groups. To their classes and to their out-of-class activities, they bring enthusiasm, energy, and individual style."

SELECTIVITY

Admissions Rating	99
# of applicants	16,632
% of applicants accepted	10
% of acceptees attending	64
# accepting a place on wait list	573
% admitted from wait list	11

FRESHMAN PROFILE

Range SAT Critical Reading	670–760
Range SAT Math	740–800
Range SAT Writing	670–770
Range ACT Composite	32–35
Minimum paper TOEFL	577
Minimum computer TOEFL	233
Minimum web-based TOEFL	90
% graduated top 10% of class	98
% graduated top 25% of class	100
% graduated top 50% of class	100

DEADLINES

Early action	
Deadline	11/1
Notification	12/20
Regular	
Deadline	1/1
Nonfall registration?	no

APPLICANTS ALSO LOOK AT

AND OFTEN PREFER
Harvard College

AND SOMETIMES PREFER
Princeton University, Stanford University, Yale University

AND RARELY PREFER
California Institute of Technology, Columbia University, Cornell University, Duke University, University of Pennsylvania

FINANCIAL FACTS

Financial Aid Rating	93
Annual tuition	$38,940
Room and board	$11,234
Required fees	$272
Books and supplies	$1,050
% frosh rec. need-based scholarship or grant aid	65
% UG rec. need-based scholarship or grant aid	63
% frosh rec. non-need-based scholarship or grant aid	5
% UG rec. non-need-based scholarship or grant aid	2
% frosh rec. need-based self-help aid	39
% UG rec. need-based self-help aid	43
% frosh rec. any financial aid	88
% UG rec. any financial aid	87
% UG borrow to pay for school	44
Average cumulative indebtedness	$15,228

McGill University

845 Sherbrooke Street West, Montreal, QC H3A 2T5, Canada • Admissions: 514-398-3910 • Fax: 514-398-3683

STUDENTS SAY ". . ."

Academics

McGill University is "one of Canada's top-rated universities," boasting "prestigious academics" and "high international standing" at a "fraction of the price" of U.S. universities. The university is known for offering an "excellent quality of education in the sciences" and "amazing research opportunities," but students note the lack of humanities funding. Students say, "McGill is a school where you will work hard" and that "McGill is a large university that requires its students take on independence and self-responsibility," adding there's "no hand-holding." It's clear that the university offers "access to a wealth of information," but students say, "Professors at McGill are hit or miss." A biochemistry major says, "My professors are top-notch researchers… but you also have to expect that your questions might be deferred by the prof to the TA," and a junior adds, "Classes definitely get more interesting as they get smaller, but there aren't a lot of small classes because of the size of the university." The consensus seems to be that "the best experiences with profs come in the upper-year courses."

Life

Located in Montreal, McGill University offers "challenging academics in a great urban location," that is, "in the heart of a culturally infused, vibrant city." Students say, "Montreal is a great city. There is anything and everything to do," and a political science adds, "The fact that McGill is one of the best universities in the world merely complements my experience." Most students say they have two lives: "one on campus and one outside"; a sophomore adds, "Once we're done with classes and all, we walk out of campus into the center of an amazing cosmopolitan city." Because of this, some note an absence of campus culture, but students insist, "The school environment is very accepting and peaceful," saying "extracurriculars are abundant." Students grumble about the administration, saying that it's "very bureaucratic," that at times "it's difficult to find the information that you need," and that "all the red tape is kind of like a running joke around campus." It's commonly held that the "registration process, website, [or] anything online really" can be confusing and difficult. Undergrads, particularly freshman, wish for "better support…academically, facilities-wise, and emotionally." Lastly, students say the university "could improve in the areas of offering a better and wider variety of meals throughout the campus," noting "some places are really crowded or really expensive."

Student Body

McGill University has a "large international student body," and students say, "A huge cultural diversity means a pot-luck of students from different backgrounds" and that, "since everyone is different, everyone is accepted." A senior says, "You can just as easily meet someone from the area as someone from outside," and another adds, "Local students tend to be bilingual and will interact with others easily and comfortably." Students are known for being "socially quite liberal," "well-traveled, and culturally aware," and alternative lifestyles find acceptance. A political science major says, "It is a progressive environment where students [from] different backgrounds live and grow together." As a whole, the student body tends to be "focused, hardworking, passionate," and "a typical student is outgoing, likes to party, but also studies a fair amount." An information systems major says, "The reason McGill is popular is also because of Montreal—an incredible city." "Montreal is a party city. Therefore, entertainment at night is great," but students note, "There is a lack of McGill-only events."

FINANCIAL AID: 514-398-6013 • E-MAIL: ADMISSIONS@MCGILL.CA • WEBSITE: WWW.MCGILL.CA

THE PRINCETON REVIEW SAYS

Admissions

Very important factors considered include: Academic GPA, rigor of secondary school record, standardized test scores. *Important factors considered include:* Class rank. *Other factors considered include:* Recommendation(s). ACT with writing component required. TOEFL required of all international applicants. *Academic units recommended:* 4 English, 4 mathematics, 3 science (3 science labs), 3 foreign language, 2 social studies, 2 history.

Financial Aid

Students should submit: Institution's own financial aid form. Regular filing deadline is June 30. The Princeton Review suggests that all financial aid forms be submitted as soon as possible after January 1. *Need-based scholarships/grants offered:* private scholarships, school scholarship or grant aid from institutional funds. *Loan aid offered:* Direct Subsidized Stafford, Direct Unsubsidized Stafford, Direct PLUS, university loans from institutional funds. Applicants will be notified of awards on a rolling basis beginning March 1. Federal Work-Study Program available. Off-campus job opportunities are fair.

The Inside Word

Admission to McGill is highly competitive and decisions are based on an applicant's academic record. Extracurricular activities aren't significant in the admissions decision but may pertain to entrance scholarships. Applicants from the United States are required to submit standardized test scores, and minimum test score requirements are published on the McGill website.

THE SCHOOL SAYS "..."

From the Admissions Office

"McGill processes more than 30,000 online applications a year. Very few programs are available to non-Quebec students for January admission; consult the website for details.

"Applicants may submit results from of the SAT (plus at least two appropriate SAT Subject Tests). The ACT is accepted in lieu of the SAT and SAT Subject Test combination. Please note that certain programs can require specific SAT Subject Tests."

SELECTIVITY

Admissions Rating	84
# of applicants	22,847
% of applicants accepted	54
% of acceptees attending	44

FRESHMAN PROFILE

Range SAT Critical Reading	640–740
Range SAT Math	650–720
Range SAT Writing	650–730
Range ACT Composite	29–32
Minimum paper TOEFL	577
Minimum computer TOEFL	233
Minimum web-based TOEFL	90
Average HS GPA	3.52

DEADLINES

Regular	
Deadline	1/15
Notification	1/30
Nonfall registration?	yes

APPLICANTS ALSO LOOK AT
AND OFTEN PREFER
Concordia University (QC), New York University, Queen's University, The University of British Columbia, Universite de Montreal, University of Toronto

AND SOMETIMES PREFER
Columbia University, Harvard College, The University of Western Ontario, University of California—Berkeley, University of Ottowa, University of Waterloo

FINANCIAL FACTS

Financial Aid Rating	63
Annual out-of-state tuition	$5,500
Room and board	$11,000
Required fees	$1,500
Books and supplies	$1,000
% UG rec. need-based scholarship or grant aid	18
% UG rec. non-need-based scholarship or grant aid	9
% UG rec. need-based self-help aid	25
% UG rec. any financial aid	28
% UG borrow to pay for school	24

MERCER UNIVERSITY—MACON

ADMISSIONS OFFICE, 1400 COLEMAN AVENUE, MACON, GA 31207-0001 • ADMISSIONS: 478-301-2650 • FAX: 478-301-2828

CAMPUS LIFE

Quality of Life Rating	75
Fire Safety Rating	81
Green Rating	79
Type of school	private
Affiliation	Baptist
Environment	city

STUDENTS

Total undergrad enrollment	2,325
% male/female	48/52
% from out of state	17
% live on campus	68
# of fraternities	9
# of sororities	7
% African American	19
% Asian	7
% Caucasian	61
% Hispanic	3
% international	3
# of countries represented	37

SURVEY SAYS . . .

Athletic facilities are great
Low cost of living
Frats and sororities dominate
social scene
Very little drug use

ACADEMICS

Academic Rating	87
% students graduating within 4 years	44
% students graduating within 6 years	61
Calendar	semester
Student/faculty ratio	13:1
Profs interesting rating	86
Profs accessible rating	86
Most common reg class size	10–19 students
Most common lab size	20–29 students

MOST POPULAR MAJORS

biology, business/commerce,
engineering

STUDENTS SAY "..."

Academics

Mercer University is a school on the rise, students tell us. Its administration "is moving toward a nationally recognized name" for the school and seems to be taking some critical steps in that direction, by building a reputation for several standout programs, imposing academic rigor throughout the curriculum, and inspiring the sort of student loyalty that translates into alumni donations down the line. Solid offerings in business, pre-pharmacy, engineering, and music lead the way here. All are supported by a solid liberal arts curriculum grounded in the classics; indeed, the school offers an eight-course great books program, "which allows students to read the 'great' books of the accepted literary canon instead of taking general courses." All this takes place in "a small-school atmosphere" that encourages competition with "a strong push for academic success" and nurtures students' development "with a comforting feeling of belonging." "The professors and staff offer exceptional outreach to students, and the relationship between professors and students is unparalleled," students report. Another adds, "The administration is very much in touch with the student body and makes itself available to those" who wish to discuss "developing and improving faculties and programs. Student suggestions are taken seriously, and some have even been implemented campus-wide." The combined effect of all of the above is some pretty happy students of the type who insist Mercer creates "the perfect college experience complete with friendly professors, helpful staff, easy accessibility, and student activities to maintain interest."

Life

"There seem to be two main groups who sets the tone for campus life at Mercer: the religious group and the Greek-life group," with some overlap between the two. The difference is fairly simple. "Those who are more interested in religious organizations focus more on social gatherings without alcohol, while sororities and fraternities also focus on social gatherings, but alcohol is present," one student explains. Quadworks, the school's campus activities board, is another major player in the social scene. It "sponsors events from tailgating at basketball games to movies on the lawn, etc." "Quadworks, sponsors so many on-campus activities that there's often little reason to leave," one undergrad writes, "although students are becoming increasingly involved in mixing with the Macon community, especially at the restaurants and shops near to the college." Macon's downtown club scene is popular with some students (easily and safely accessible thanks to the student-government run trolley), but many here complain "there aren't a lot of things to do on the weekends, even around the city of Macon," which explains why "mostly everyone goes home or off campus" when the school week is over.

Student Body

"Many students here are religious, mostly Baptist or other Protestants, though you will also find unapologetic atheists and deists mixed in with a small population of Catholics, Orthodox Christians, and various other religious groups. Any student who doesn't happen to have a passionate social or academic interest or a strong commitment to a Christian faith tends to have a hard time belonging, so they leave or fly under the radar for their years here." Some caution, "Upon first glance it seems that the entire campus is Greek, when in fact only about thirty percent is. This is because the Greeks hold most high positions in student organizations on campus." Don't come here looking for an alternative community; "There are not many extremely different students, i.e., emo, Gothic, etc."

FINANCIAL AID: 478-301-2670 • E-MAIL: ADMISSIONS@MERCER.EDU • WEBSITE: WWW.MERCER.EDU

THE PRINCETON REVIEW SAYS

Admissions

Very important factors considered include: Academic GPA, rigor of secondary school record, standardized test scores, level of applicant's interest. *Important factors considered include:* Character/personal qualities, extracurricular activities, talent/ability, volunteer work. *Other factors considered include:* Class rank, recommendation(s), alumni/ae relation, interview, work experience. SAT or ACT required; ACT with or without writing component accepted. TOEFL required of all international applicants. High school diploma is required, and GED is accepted. *Academic units required:* 4 English, 4 mathematics, 3 science (2 science labs), 2 foreign language, 1 social studies, 2 history.

Financial Aid

Students should submit: FAFSA. Regular filing deadline is February 1. The Princeton Review suggests that all financial aid forms be submitted as soon as possible after January 1. *Need-based scholarships/grants offered:* Federal Pell, SEOG, state scholarships/grants, school scholarship or grant aid from institutional funds, Federal Nursing Scholarships. *Loan aid offered:* Direct Subsidized Stafford, Direct Unsubsidized Stafford, Direct PLUS, Federal Perkins, Federal Nursing Loans, university loans from institutional funds. Applicants will be notified of awards on a rolling basis beginning March 15. Federal Work-Study Program available. Off-campus job opportunities are good.

The Inside Word

One student warns that Mercer, "while somewhat lenient in its admission's policy, will give you an excellent education," so "don't come here thinking it will be easy. Plenty of transfer students from major universities have not lasted a semester here." Make sure you're ready to put in the hard work before applying here; getting in is one thing, staying through graduation is another. The school works with a small but growing number of homeschooled applicants.

THE SCHOOL SAYS " . . ."

From the Admissions Office

"The mission of the Mercer University office of admissions is to attract, admit, and enroll qualified and talented students who will ultimately become happy, successful alumni. We do this by becoming personally involved with each admitted student and family during the admissions process. Mercer admissions staff takes time to know each admitted applicant on a personal level and are concerned about the family's questions regarding financial assistance, campus life, and academic affairs. High school and campus visits, regional receptions, and programs are all conducted by admissions staff who are knowledgeable about the high schools and two-year colleges in a particular region. This makes for a truly enjoyable and productive admissions experience for all involved.

"Freshman applicants must take the SAT or the ACT with writing component."

SELECTIVITY

Admissions Rating	89
# of applicants	3,734
% of applicants accepted	64
% of acceptees attending	25

FRESHMAN PROFILE

Range SAT Critical Reading	540–640
Range SAT Math	540–640
Range SAT Writing	510–620
Range ACT Composite	23–29
Minimum paper TOEFL	550
Minimum computer TOEFL	213
Average HS GPA	3.62
% graduated top 10% of class	40
% graduated top 25% of class	72
% graduated top 50% of class	92

DEADLINES

Early action	
Deadline	11/1
Notification	11/15
Regular	
Priority	4/1
Deadline	7/1
Notification	9/1
Nonfall registration?	yes

APPLICANTS ALSO LOOK AT AND OFTEN PREFER
Emory University, Oxford College, Georgia Institute of Technology, Samford University, University of Georgia

AND SOMETIMES PREFER
Auburn University, Florida State University, Furman University

AND RARELY PREFER
Clemson University, Georgia Southern University

FINANCIAL FACTS

Financial Aid Rating	87
Annual tuition	$30,560
Room and board	$9,338
Required fees	$200
Books and supplies	$1,200
% frosh rec. need-based scholarship or grant aid	78
% UG rec. need-based scholarship or grant aid	72
% frosh rec. non-need-based scholarship or grant aid	21
% UG rec. non-need-based scholarship or grant aid	17
% frosh rec. need-based self-help aid	51
% UG rec. need-based self-help aid	49
% frosh rec. any financial aid	100
% UG rec. any financial aid	98
% UG borrow to pay for school	66
Average cumulative indebtedness	$30,460

MIAMI UNIVERSITY

301 SOUTH CAMPUS AVENUE, OXFORD, OH 45056 • ADMISSIONS: 513-529-2531 • FAX: 513-529-1550

CAMPUS LIFE

Quality of Life Rating	76
Fire Safety Rating	76
Green Rating	76
Type of school	public
Environment	village

STUDENTS

Total undergrad enrollment	14,741
% male/female	47/53
% from out of state	29
% from public high school	73
% live on campus	49
# of fraternities	31
# of sororities	20
% African American	4
% Asian	3
% Caucasian	84
% Hispanic	2
% international	3
# of countries represented	54

SURVEY SAYS . . .

Athletic facilities are great
Great food on campus
Low cost of living
Frats and sororities dominate
social scene

ACADEMICS

Academic Rating	78
% students graduating within 4 years	68
% students graduating within 6 years	80
Calendar	semester
Student/faculty ratio	17:1
Profs interesting rating	79
Profs accessible rating	82
Most common reg class size	20–29 students
Most common lab size	20–29 students

MOST POPULAR MAJORS

accounting, finance, marketing,
zoology, psychology

STUDENTS SAY ". . ."

Academics

Nestled within a vast expanse of rural Ohio, Miami University is a medium-sized public school offering diverse academic programs and a surprisingly close-knit atmosphere. With more than 100 majors, choice is central to the Miami experience. Whether majoring in humanities or sciences, "students have broad discretion when selecting courses. It is truly up to the individual to decide how far to push oneself academically." In most departments, the workload is sizable; fortunately, "professors at Miami are extremely personable and are always willing to lend an extra hand." A junior tells us, "I've never run into a professor that was not approachable when needing help, and most of them are very passionate about sharing their knowledge with the students." You'll definitely wind up in a number of lecture courses during your first two years (luckily, "most of them are actually pretty good at keeping you awake"). At the same time, many students praise the school's required liberal education courses. A junior shares, "I certainly didn't expect a freshman English class to leave an impact on me. However, the professor awoke so much passion for writing in me that now I work at the writing center on campus." Even so, the academic experience is best during junior and senior year, when upper division courses include "lots of class discussion, projects, no tests, and competent teachers." Not all of the school's administration is known to be as easily accessible or caring as the teaching staff. However, the school's president has made an effort to get personally involved in the student community, and "it is not uncommon to receive a well-developed response from the president if you send him an e-mail."

Life

Offering "countless social, academic, political, and career opportunities," Miami University will offer you a "great college experience" inside and outside the classroom. Academics are definitely taken seriously, and "during the weekdays most people spend their time studying either in their dorms or at the library." When they aren't hitting the books, theatrical or musical performances, movies, parties, speakers, ice hockey games, and campus events create "a good mix of social life and academic life." While academic programs definitely prepare you for the real world, the social life won't. Located in rural Southwest Ohio, "many people refer to life at Miami as living in the 'Miami bubble.' It's hard to imagine life outside of Oxford." On that note, Oxford is "a town built for college life," with "wonderful food and activities," that cater specifically to college students. For the socially inclined, "the party scene at Miami is top-notch. There are the ever-present frat parties, but the small size of the town also leaves us with tons of bars and off-campus houses devoted solely to us." With about a quarter of undergraduates joining fraternities and sororities, "Greek life is enormous, but, with so many students, it doesn't dominate the campus."

Student Body

Stepping onto the Miami University campus, you may not immediately see astounding diversity within the student body. Demographically, the majority of undergraduates hail from a "suburban, generally Mid-Western community," and "There is not much racial diversity on campus." However, students reassure us that the school is working to recruit a more diverse student body, and "Each student is very open to diversity and welcomes it with open arms." Due to the overwhelming preference for preppy attire, the "nickname for Miami is J. Crew U," and students admit there are "not many alternative students like you would find in the big city schools." However, the school's predominant dress code doesn't necessarily translate into a totally uniform student body. A sophomore explains, "A lot of the students at Miami are preppy and may seem snobby at first, but once you experience it for yourself, you find all types of people." In fact, "fashion aside, the students here are typically friendly and intelligent, and all seem to apply to the "work hard, play hard" mentality." Ambitious and well-rounded, most Miami students are "passionate, driven, very career-oriented, involved around campus, and very social."

FINANCIAL AID: 513-529-8734 • E-MAIL: ADMISSION@MUOHIO.EDU • WEBSITE: WWW.MUOHIO.EDU

THE PRINCETON REVIEW SAYS

Admissions

Very important factors considered include: Academic GPA, application essay, class rank, recommendation(s), rigor of secondary school record, standardized test scores, character/personal qualities, talent/ability. *Other factors considered include:* Alumni/ae relation, extracurricular activities, first generation, geographical residence, state residency, volunteer work, work experience. SAT or ACT required. TOEFL required of all international applicants. High school diploma is required, and GED is accepted. *Academic units recommended:* 4 English, 3 mathematics, 3 science, 2 foreign language, 2 social studies, 1 history, 1 visual/performing arts.

Financial Aid

Students should submit: FAFSA. The Princeton Review suggests that all financial aid forms be submitted as soon as possible after January 1. *Need-based scholarships/grants offered:* Federal Pell, SEOG, state scholarships/grants, private scholarships, school scholarship or grant aid from institutional funds. *Loan aid offered:* Direct Subsidized Stafford, Direct Unsubsidized Stafford, Direct PLUS, Federal Perkins, Federal Nursing Loans, university loans from institutional funds. Applicants will be notified of awards on a rolling basis beginning March 20. Federal Work-Study Program available. Off-campus job opportunities are good.

The Inside Word

Admission to Miami University is competitive. In addition to high grades and test scores (forty-one percent of incoming students at Miami had SAT scores above 1200), Miami University admits students who are active in their schools and communities. Last year, ninety-seven percent of incoming students had volunteered in their communities during high school, and seventy-four percent participated in varsity sports.

THE SCHOOL SAYS " . . ."

From the Admissions Office

"At Miami, you'll find a level of involvement—in your classes, in your research, in your extracurricular activities—that you won't find at other schools. What sets Miami apart is the ability to give students a personalized small-college experience within the excitement and opportunities of a midsize university, all at a public school cost. With more than 100 majors to choose from, and a liberal arts foundation that allows students to explore different areas of interest, finding your true passion—in and out of the classroom—is at the heart of what the MU experience is all about. This deep level of engagement is reflected in the ninety percent freshman to sophomore retention rate and Miami's graduation rate, which is among the top for public universities across the country. Miami's reputation for producing outstanding leaders with real-world experience makes us a target school for top national firms, and our graduates' acceptance rate into law and medical school are far above the national average. Students also benefit from small class sizes—ninety percent of undergraduate classes have fewer than fifty students—and personal attention from faculty members in the classroom, through research opportunities, and through faculty mentoring programs. Outside of the classroom, students can participate in more than 300 student organizations, attend social and cultural events, or get involved with one of the most extensive intramural and club sports program in the country."

SELECTIVITY

Admissions Rating	87
# of applicants	16,960
% of applicants accepted	79
% of acceptees attending	27
# accepting a place on wait list	352
% admitted from wait list	0
# of early decision applicants	494
% accepted early decision	85

FRESHMAN PROFILE

Range SAT Critical Reading	520–630
Range SAT Math	550–650
Range ACT Composite	24–29
Minimum paper TOEFL	533
Minimum computer TOEFL	200
Minimum web-based TOEFL	72
Average HS GPA	3.62
% graduated top 10% of class	33
% graduated top 25% of class	69
% graduated top 50% of class	95

DEADLINES

Early decision	
Deadline	11/1
Notification	12/15
Early action	
Deadline	12/1
Notification	2/1
Regular	
Deadline	2/1
Notification	3/15
Nonfall registration?	yes

APPLICANTS ALSO LOOK AT

AND OFTEN PREFER
Northwestern University, University of Michigan—Ann Arbor, University of Notre Dame, Vanderbilt University

AND SOMETIMES PREFER
Boston College, Indiana University at Bloomington, Purdue University—West Lafayette, The Ohio State University—Columbus, University of Illinois at Urbana-Champaign, University of Wisconsin—Madison

AND RARELY PREFER
Ohio University—Athens, University of Cincinnati, University of Dayton, Xavier University (OH)

FINANCIAL FACTS

Financial Aid Rating	68
Annual in-state tuition	$12,198
Annual out-of-state tuition	$26,988
Room and board	$9,786
Required fees	$588
Books and supplies	$1,460
% frosh rec. need-based scholarship or grant aid	41
% UG rec. need-based scholarship or grant aid	25
% frosh rec. non-need-based scholarship or grant aid	27
% UG rec. non-need-based scholarship or grant aid	23
% frosh rec. need-based self-help aid	38
% UG rec. need-based self-help aid	35
% frosh rec. any financial aid	46
% UG rec. any financial aid	43
% UG borrow to pay for school	53
Average cumulative indebtedness	$26,582

MICHIGAN STATE UNIVERSITY

250 ADMINISTRATION BUILDING, EAST LANSING, MI 48824-1046 • ADMISSIONS: 517-355-8332 • FAX: 517-353-1647

CAMPUS LIFE

Quality of Life Rating	80
Fire Safety Rating	60*
Green Rating	89
Type of school	public
Environment	city

STUDENTS

Total undergrad enrollment	35,765
% male/female	48/52
% from out of state	9
% live on campus	40
# of fraternities	31
# of sororities	19
% African American	7
% Asian	4
% Caucasian	74
% Hispanic	3
% international	8
# of countries represented	130

SURVEY SAYS . . .
Students are friendly
Everyone loves the Spartans
Student publications are popular

ACADEMICS

Academic Rating	69
% students graduating within 4 years	48
% students graduating within 6 years	77
Calendar	semester
Student/faculty ratio	16:1
Profs interesting rating	71
Profs accessible rating	74
Most common reg class size	20–29 students
Most common lab size	20–29 students

STUDENTS SAY ". . ."

Academics
The size of Michigan State University "scares some people," students tell us, but for those comfortable in crowds it's "one of the strongest advantages. Where else do you cut through the Cereal Wing of the Human Nutrition Building to get to a Navigating the Universe class (a class on the parallels between art, philosophy, and physics)?" One student sees it this way: "The size of MSU makes it like training wheels for the real world. Every type of person, value, and belief is here, so you learn just as many street smarts as academic smarts, which is what sets it apart from so many other schools." There are more than "200 majors to choose from" here, including "good engineering and science programs," an "amazing communications program," "the best political science program in Michigan," "the only agriculture school in the state," and "an absolutely amazing school of Hospitality Business." Economies of scale also allow MSU to offer "great study abroad programs," "a lot of helpful free tutoring in math and other subjects," and "great Web programs that make it very easy to download class materials and view assignments. You can also e-mail the whole class questions or just your professor, through our Angel system." As far as possible downsides to the school's size, MSU students find you have to "fend for yourself." That means potential peril for students who aren't self-motivated. One undergrad explains, "There are two roads you can follow when at MSU. You can study hard and earn a degree in a reputable, challenging setting; or you can soak your brain cells with alcohol instead of academia."

Life
"It requires a lot of studying to keep up with classes" in most disciplines at MSU, but that doesn't mean students bury their heads in the books 24/7. On the contrary, "Michigan State is great because everyone is there to learn but also to have a good time, which is important for any college to flow smoothly." When the weekend arrives, "everyone likes to go out, usually to frats, and have a good time. We do our share of partying, but we know when and how hard to hit the books. We keep our heads very level," except, perhaps, when attending sporting events. Life on campus "generally revolves around the weekend and the basketball or football game. You get through the week looking forward to one of the two." Indeed, "Sports are huge, and nothing beats football Saturdays or basketball nights. Tailgating is a religion." And if neither sports appeal to you, don't sweat it. "If there's something you want to do, someone else does too. You'll be hard pressed to find an activity that doesn't have its own organization and social network." Hometown East Lansing has its own allures; a student explains, "Walking downtown on Grand River is awesome when it gets warmer out," and there are "decent stores and restaurants. Also, in the warm weather you are bound to see people sitting out on their porches. Many of them are having parties or just hanging out, and a lot of times they'll invite you to come on up!" Or you can just enjoy the "breathtaking beauty of the campus," with its "old buildings and beautiful trees and plants that make every walk to class a great one."

Student Body
MSU's size ensures that "this is a fairly diverse campus, especially considering that it is located in the northern Midwest." One student observes, "You can completely immerse yourself among different people in different situations knowing that you have the comfort of your own dorm, and somewhere there is a group just like you." Because "study abroad is emphasized at MSU," there are "a lot of foreign students, and they seem to fit right into the general population." If anything unites students—besides their love of MSU sports—it is that most "are extremely friendly. Random people in classes ask you if you need a ride home, and, even better, random people offer you a seat on the bus."

MICHIGAN STATE UNIVERSITY

FINANCIAL AID: 517-353-5940 • E-MAIL: ADMIS@MSU.EDU • WEBSITE: WWW.MSU.EDU

THE PRINCETON REVIEW SAYS

Admissions

Very important factors considered include: Academic GPA, standardized test scores. *Important factors considered include:* Application essay, rigor of secondary school record. *Other factors considered include:* Class rank, recommendation(s), character/personal qualities, extracurricular activities, first generation, geographical residence, interview, level of applicant's interest, talent/ability, volunteer work, work experience. SAT or ACT required; ACT with writing component required. TOEFL required of all international applicants. High school diploma is required, and GED is accepted. *Academic units required:* 3 mathematics, (2 science labs). *Academic units recommended:* 4 English, 4 mathematics, 2 science, 2 foreign language, 3 social studies.

Financial Aid

Students should submit: FAFSA. The Princeton Review suggests that all financial aid forms be submitted as soon as possible after January 1. *Need-based scholarships/grants offered:* Federal Pell, SEOG, state scholarships/grants, private scholarships, school scholarship or grant aid from institutional funds, United Negro College Fund. *Loan aid offered:* Direct Subsidized Stafford, Direct Unsubsidized Stafford, Direct PLUS, Federal Perkins, university loans from institutional funds. Applicants will be notified of awards on a rolling basis beginning March 15. Federal Work-Study Program available. Off-campus job opportunities are excellent.

The Inside Word

Given the extraordinary volume of applications the admissions office receives, it's no wonder that Michigan State relies primarily on numbers. Decisions typically come down to grades, class rank, and test scores. Applicants who have proven to be capable students in college prep courses are relatively likely to find themselves the proud addressees of fat admissions envelopes. Applications are processed on a rolling basis, a process that typically favors early applicants.

THE SCHOOL SAYS " . . ."

From the Admissions Office

"Although Michigan State University is a graduate and research institution of international stature and acclaim, your undergraduate education is a high priority. More than 2,600 instructional faculty members (ninety percent of whom hold a terminal degree) are dedicated to providing academic instruction, guidance, and assistance to our undergraduate students. Our 35,000 undergraduate students are a select group of academically motivated men and women. The diversity of ethnic, racial, religious, and socioeconomic heritage makes the student body a microcosm of the state, national, and international community.

"Students applying for admission to Michigan State University are required to take the new version of the SAT or the ACT exam with the Writing section. The Writing assessment will be considered in the holistic review of the application for admission. SAT Subject Tests are not required."

SELECTIVITY
Admissions Rating	85
# of applicants	26,907
% of applicants accepted	70
% of acceptees attending	40

FRESHMAN PROFILE
Range SAT Critical Reading	450–610
Range SAT Math	530–670
Range SAT Writing	460–600
Range ACT Composite	23–28
Minimum paper TOEFL	550
Minimum computer TOEFL	213
Minimum web-based TOEFL	79
Average HS GPA	3.60
% graduated top 10% of class	29
% graduated top 25% of class	69
% graduated top 50% of class	96

DEADLINES
Regular	
Priority	11/1
Notification	10/1
Nonfall registration?	yes

APPLICANTS ALSO LOOK AT AND OFTEN PREFER
Central Michigan University, University of Michigan—Ann Arbor, Western Michigan University

AND SOMETIMES PREFER
Indiana University at Bloomington

FINANCIAL FACTS
Financial Aid Rating	67
Annual in-state tuition	$11,153
Annual out-of-state tuition	$29,108
Room and board	$7,770
Books and supplies	$980
% frosh rec. need-based scholarship or grant aid	30
% UG rec. need-based scholarship or grant aid	30
% frosh rec. non-need-based scholarship or grant aid	20
% UG rec. non-need-based scholarship or grant aid	13
% frosh rec. need-based self-help aid	46
% UG rec. need-based self-help aid	46
% frosh rec. any financial aid	51
% UG rec. any financial aid	50
% UG borrow to pay for school	45
Average cumulative indebtedness	$21,818

THE BEST 376 COLLEGES ■ 371

MICHIGAN TECHNOLOGICAL UNIVERSITY

1400 TOWNSEND DRIVE, HOUGHTON, MI 49931 • ADMISSIONS: 906-487-2335 • FAX: 906-487-2125

CAMPUS LIFE

Quality of Life Rating	80
Fire Safety Rating	97
Green Rating	74
Type of school	public
Environment	village

STUDENTS

Total undergrad enrollment	5,620
% male/female	75/25
% from out of state	22
% from public high school	90
% live on campus	44
# of fraternities	13
# of sororities	8
% African American	2
% Asian	1
% Caucasian	82
% Hispanic	2
% Native American	1
% international	8
# of countries represented	69

SURVEY SAYS . . .

Great computer facilities
Athletic facilities are great
Career services are great
Students get along with local
community
Campus feels safe
Lots of beer drinking

ACADEMICS

Academic Rating	73
% students graduating within 4 years	28
% students graduating within 6 years	66
Calendar	semester
Student/faculty ratio	14:1
Profs interesting rating	68
Profs accessible rating	71
Most common reg class size	10–19 students
Most common lab size	10–19 students

MOST POPULAR MAJORS

civil engineering, electrical and
electronics engineering, mechanical
engineering

STUDENTS SAY ". . ."

Academics

Michigan Technological University has "very high standards when it comes to education" and offers "serious study in a beautiful (often snowy) environment." It boasts a "really good reputation as an engineering school," and it's no secret that "engineering is a part of everybody's life." All agree, "Michigan Tech provides an atmosphere that nurtures learning" and "puts students first when it comes to their learning experience by providing hands-on experience." The university offers "lots of internship and co-op opportunities" and "pathways for career development and professional advancement." Students say that the courses are "challenging" and that the university "pushes students to excel academically." Professors are "generally interesting and helpful," but some can be "dull." A junior says, "Concentrated courses are great, but Gen Eds are huge, impersonal, and just plain awful," and another student adds, "The experience gets better with more time you put into your program, the professors become more interactive, and the experience becomes more meaningful."

Life

Michigan Tech "is in a small town in the middle of the deep North woods," which makes "the sense of community remarkable." Students say that campus is "incredibly safe," that "the atmosphere is very friendly," and that "there are a lot of opportunities to get involved." A physics major notes, "You start to see people you know everywhere on campus. It is really easy to find a friend and talk to someone." Enhancing the "strong student community" are "over 200 clubs" and a variety of "winter activities to be a part of." Many students take advantage of "free access to Mount Ripley," the university's own ski hill and the oldest one in Michigan. A freshman says, "We have broomball, Winter Carnival, and lots of campus-wide events!" Many students say, "The administration in every department works hard to answer questions and help out as much as possible, which is really great when you're a freshman," but some feel there's a "gap between [the] administration and students," particularly when it comes to spending. There are complaints about dorm food, leading a junior to say, "I would like to see some more selection and variation between dining halls," and students feel there's a need for "more parking spots close to campus." While "the library is a great place to study," some "of the classrooms are dated" and could use technological updating.

Student Body

At Michigan Tech, the typical student "is smart and a little more introspective than average," but still "great at balancing school and hanging out." Most students "are looking to get a good education and are fairly laid-back," and the student body consists of "down-to-earth friendly people," who "work hard during the week and look forward to relaxing and having fun on the weekends." It's no secret that "the ratio is a little guy-heavy" and that, because of this, "girls get doors opened for them across campus." Students tend to be "white and male," and a junior acknowledges, "There's little diversity ethnically, but everyone feels welcome." A chemical engineering major says, "You have to be a little bit of a nerd to fit in," and another student agrees, "I think most people think about classes first, hanging out second." It's common for students to "stay in and play video games," but there's also a large contingent of "outdoorsy people." A sophomore says, "Winters are long and cold up here," and students take advantage of the plentiful snow by "hiking, biking, four-wheeling, skiing, [and] snowmobiling." Students look forward to Winter Carnival, "a long weekend off from classes where students build giant, impressive snow sculptures, play broomball, [and] stay out all night," and for fun they enjoy "house parties and moderate drinking/merrymaking [to] warm up the cold winters."

FINANCIAL AID: 906-487-2622 • E-MAIL: MTU4U@MTU.EDU • WEBSITE: WWW.MTU.EDU

THE PRINCETON REVIEW SAYS

Admissions

Very important factors considered include: Academic GPA, rigor of secondary school record, standardized test scores. *Important factors considered include:* Class rank. *Other factors considered include:* Application essay, recommendation(s), alumni/ae relation, character/personal qualities, extracurricular activities, interview, talent/ability, volunteer work, work experience. SAT or ACT required; ACT with or without writing component accepted. TOEFL required of all international applicants. High school diploma is required, and GED is accepted. *Academic units required:* 3 English, 3 mathematics, 2 science. *Academic units recommended:* 4 English, 4 mathematics, 3 science, 2 foreign language, 3 social studies, 1 history, 2 academic elective, 1 computer science.

Financial Aid

Students should submit: FAFSA. The Princeton Review suggests that all financial aid forms be submitted as soon as possible after January 1. *Need-based scholarships/grants offered:* Federal Pell, SEOG, state scholarships/grants, private scholarships, school scholarship or grant aid from institutional funds. *Loan aid offered:* Direct Subsidized Stafford, Direct Unsubsidized Stafford, Direct PLUS, Federal Perkins, university loans from institutional funds. Applicants will be notified of awards on a rolling basis beginning March 15. Federal Work-Study Program available. Off-campus job opportunities are excellent.

The Inside Word

Michigan Tech strives to enroll bright, adventurous students. Students aren't required to submit recommendations from teachers, although they may submit a "High School Counselor Information Page" if they would like their counselor to share information regarding their high school performance. Applicants to the Visual and Performing Arts Department degree programs are required to submit supplemental materials, including an essay.

THE SCHOOL SAYS ". . ."

From the Admissions Office

"At Michigan Tech, our students create the future. Our unique Enterprise Program lets students work on real industry problems such as bicycle design, alternative fuels, groundwater analysis, and video production. Through student groups like Engineers without Borders and the campus-wide Make a Difference Day, our students impact lives in our community and around the world. Students can choose from 130 degree programs in engineering; forest resources; computing; technology; business; economics; natural, physical and environmental sciences; arts; humanities; and social sciences. We offer exciting degree programs in growing fields including biomedical engineering, applied ecology and environmental science, and pre-health studies.

"Outside of the classrooms and labs, students enjoy our golf course, ski hill, trails and recreational forest, and friendly, small-town atmosphere in beautiful Upper Michigan. Located on Portage Waterway, the campus is only minutes from Lake Superior. During Winter Carnival, students build huge snow statues and play broomball, the biggest game on campus, among many other activities.

"We recommend that students applying for admission take the SAT (or the ACT with the writing section)."

SELECTIVITY

Admissions Rating	85
# of applicants	4,548
% of applicants accepted	74
% of acceptees attending	33

FRESHMAN PROFILE

Range SAT Critical Reading	520–650
Range SAT Math	560–590
Range SAT Writing	510–620
Range ACT Composite	23–29
Minimum paper TOEFL	550
Minimum computer TOEFL	213
Minimum web-based TOEFL	79
Average HS GPA	3.58
% graduated top 10% of class	30
% graduated top 25% of class	62
% graduated top 50% of class	90

DEADLINES

Regular	
Notification	7/1
Nonfall registration?	yes

APPLICANTS ALSO LOOK AT AND SOMETIMES PREFER

Michigan State University, Milwaukee School of Engineering, University of Michigan—Ann Arbor, University of Minnesota—Twin Cities, University of Wisconsin—Madison, Western Michigan University

FINANCIAL FACTS

Financial Aid Rating	74
Annual in-state tuition	$11,175
Annual out-of-state tuition	$23,685
Room and board	$8,462
Required fees	$842
Books and supplies	$1,200
% frosh rec. need-based scholarship or grant aid	56
% UG rec. need-based scholarship or grant aid	49
% frosh rec. non-need-based scholarship or grant aid	59
% UG rec. non-need-based scholarship or grant aid	46
% frosh rec. need-based self-help aid	57
% UG rec. need-based self-help aid	55
% frosh rec. any financial aid	95
% UG rec. any financial aid	88
% UG borrow to pay for school	68
Average cumulative indebtedness	$26,764

MIDDLEBURY COLLEGE

THE EMMA WILLARD HOUSE, MIDDLEBURY, VT 05753-6002 • ADMISSIONS: 802-443-3000 • FAX: 802-443-2056

STUDENTS SAY ". . ."

Academics

Home to "smart people who enjoy Aristotelian ethics and quantum physics, but aren't too stuck up to go sledding in front of Mead Chapel at midnight," Middlebury College is a small, exclusive liberal arts school with "excellent foreign language programs" as well as standout offerings in environmental studies, the sciences, theater, and writing. Distribution requirements and other general requirements ensure that a Middlebury education "is all about providing students with a complete college experience including excellent teaching, exposure to many other cultures, endless opportunities for growth and success, and a challenging (yet relaxed) environment." Its "small class size and friendly yet competitive atmosphere make for the perfect college experience," as do "the best facilities of a small liberal arts college in the country. The new library, science center, athletic complex, arts center, and a number of the dining halls and dorms have been built in the past ten years." Expect to work hard; "It's tough, but this is a mini-Ivy, so what should one expect? There is plenty of time to socialize, and due to the collaborative atmosphere here, studying and socializing can often come hand in hand. The goal of many students here is not to get high grades" but rather "learning in its purest form, and that is perhaps this college's most brightly shining aspect." The collaborative atmosphere is abetted by the fact that "admissions doesn't just bring in geniuses, they bring in people who are leaders and community servants. Think of the guy or girl in your high school whom everybody describes as 'so nice'...that's your typical Middlebury student."

Life

"This high level of involvement in everything translates into an amazing campus atmosphere" at Middlebury, where "most people are very involved. There is a club for just about everything you can imagine, and if you can imagine one that hasn't yet been created, you go ahead and create it yourself." With great skiing and outdoor activity close by, "Almost everyone is athletic in some way. This can translate into anything from varsity sports to intramural hockey (an extremely popular winter pastime!). People are enthusiastic about being active and having fun." Because the school "is set in a very small town, there aren't too many (if any) problems with violence, drugs, [or] crime. It's the ideal college town because of its rural setting, in that there are no real distractions other than those that are provided within the college campus." Of course, the small-town setting also means that "the only real off-campus activity is going out to eat at the town's quaint restaurants or going to the one bar in town," but fortunately "when it comes to on-campus activities, Middlebury provides the student population with tons of great events. Everything from classy music concerts to late-night movies and dance parties can be found as a Midd-supported activity. The student activity board does a fabulous job with entertaining the students virtually every day."

Student Body

"The typical [Middlebury] student is athletic, outdoorsy, and very intelligent." The two most prominent demographics are "very preppy students (popped collars)" and "extreme hippies." One undergrad explains: "The typical students are one of two types: either 'Polo, Nantucket red, pearls, and summers on the Cape,' or 'Birks, wool socks, granola, and suspicious smells about them.' A lot of people break these two molds, but they often fall somewhere on the spectrum between them." There's also "a huge international student population, which is awesome," but some international students, "tend to separate out and end up living in language houses." There's also "a really strong theater/artsy community" here. One student notes, "Other than a few groups, everyone mingles pretty well."

MIDDLEBURY COLLEGE

FINANCIAL AID: 802-443-5158 • E-MAIL: ADMISSIONS@MIDDLEBURY.EDU • WEBSITE: WWW.MIDDLEBURY.EDU

THE PRINCETON REVIEW SAYS

Admissions

Very important factors considered include: Academic GPA, class rank, rigor of secondary school record, character/personal qualities, extracurricular activities, talent/ability. *Important factors considered include:* Application essay, recommendation(s), standardized test scores, racial/ethnic status. *Other factors considered include:* Alumni/ae relation, first generation, geographical residence, interview, level of applicant's interest, volunteer work, work experience. ACT with or without writing component accepted. High school diploma or equivalent isn't required. *Academic units recommended:* 4 English, 4 mathematics, 3 science (3 science labs), 4 foreign language, 3 social studies, 2 history, 1 academic elective.

Financial Aid

Students should submit: FAFSA, CSS/Financial Aid PROFILE. Regular filing deadline is February 1. The Princeton Review suggests that all financial aid forms be submitted as soon as possible after January 1. *Need-based scholarships/ grants offered:* Federal Pell, SEOG, state scholarships/grants, private scholarships, school scholarship or grant aid from institutional funds. *Loan aid offered:* Federal Perkins, university loans from institutional funds.

The Inside Word

Middlebury gives you options in standardized testing. The school will accept either the SAT or the ACT or three SAT Subject Tests. (The three must be in different subject areas, however.) Middlebury is extremely competitive; improve your chances of admission by crafting a standardized test profile that shows you in the best possible light.

THE SCHOOL SAYS "..."

From the Admissions Office

"The successful Middlebury candidate excels in a variety of areas including academics, athletics, the arts, leadership, and service to others. These strengths and interests permit students to grow beyond their traditional 'comfort zones' and conventional limits. Our classrooms are as varied as the Green Mountains, the Metropolitan Museum of Art, or the great cities of Russia and Japan. Outside the classroom, students informally interact with professors in activities such as intramural basketball games and community service. At Middlebury, students develop critical-thinking skills, enduring bonds of friendship, and the ability to challenge themselves.

"Middlebury offers majors and programs in forty-five different fields, with particular strengths in languages, international studies, environmental studies, literature and creative writing, and the sciences. Opportunities for engaging in individual research with faculty abound at Middlebury."

SELECTIVITY

Admissions Rating	97
# of applicants	7,984
% of applicants accepted	17
% of acceptees attending	42
# accepting a place on wait list	865
% admitted from wait list	15
# of early decision applicants	913
% accepted early decision	36

FRESHMAN PROFILE

Range SAT Critical Reading	640–740
Range SAT Math	650–740
Range SAT Writing	650–750
Range ACT Composite	30–33
% graduated top 10% of class	86
% graduated top 25% of class	90
% graduated top 50% of class	100

DEADLINES

Early decision	
Deadline	11/1
Notification	12/15
Regular	
Deadline	11/1
Nonfall registration?	yes

APPLICANTS ALSO LOOK AT AND OFTEN PREFER

Amherst College, Dartmouth College, Harvard College, Williams College

AND SOMETIMES PREFER

Brown University, Duke University, Pomona College, Stanford University, Yale University

FINANCIAL FACTS

Financial Aid Rating	95
Annual comprehensive tuition	$52,500
Books and supplies	$1,000
% frosh rec. need-based scholarship or grant aid	41
% UG rec. need-based scholarship or grant aid	47
% frosh rec. need-based self-help aid	36
% UG rec. need-based self-help aid	43
% frosh rec. any financial aid	41
% UG rec. any financial aid	47
% UG borrow to pay for school	42
Average cumulative indebtedness	$21,520

MILLS COLLEGE

5000 MacArthur Boulevard, Oakland, CA 94613 • Admissions: 510-430-2135 • Fax: 510-430-3298

CAMPUS LIFE

Quality of Life Rating	71
Fire Safety Rating	71
Green Rating	98
Type of school	private
Environment	metropolis

STUDENTS

Total undergrad enrollment	957
% male/female	0/100
% from out of state	20
% from public high school	80
% live on campus	58
% African American	8
% Asian	8
% Caucasian	39
% Hispanic	18
% Native American	1
% international	2
# of countries represented	9

SURVEY SAYS . . .

Lots of liberal students
Great computer facilities
Low cost of living
Frats and sororities are unpopular
or nonexistent
Political activism is popular

ACADEMICS

Academic Rating	88
% students graduating within 4 years	53
% students graduating within 6 years	63
Calendar	semester
Student/faculty ratio	11:1
Profs interesting rating	90
Profs accessible rating	84
Most common reg class size	10–19 students
Most common lab size	fewer than 10 students

MOST POPULAR MAJORS

English, psychology, ethnic studies,
political, legal, and economic analysis,
studio art

STUDENTS SAY ". . ."

Academics

Mills College is a "socially aware, progressive, academically serious, community-based, and diverse" women's institution, located in Oakland, California. This small school offers forty major programs to fewer than 1,000 undergraduates, distinguished by uniformly "small class sizes and caring professors." Across the board, students say that "academics are exceptional" at Mills, with passionate instructors, ample class discussion, and plenty of homework. Despite the challenges, "all academic expectations are reasonable and clearly stated, and professors or TAs are available to help with any questions." In complement to their academic programs, Mills "is a school dedicated to social justice and environmental awareness." These concerns are incorporated into the classroom and curriculum; "race, class, sexuality, and gender issues are brought up in almost all classes by students and professors alike, regardless of the discipline." In addition, the school's extensive sustainability initiatives make Mills one of the most "green" campuses in the United States. While a majority of students feel right at home in Mills' unique environment, it is important for prospective students to take note of the school's distinctive flavor, which leans toward the left politically and values quirkiness and experimentation. A senior explains, "Mills may not be for everyone, but if it's the right place for you, you'll know." When it comes to the nuts and bolts, students report occasional administrative glitches, but, for the most part, "the administration is surprisingly organized, and the mechanics all flow well."

Life

A pretty oasis in the middle of urban Oakland, the Mills campus is a relaxing, quiet, and studious environment that will make a good fit for serious students. Mills' dorms are quiet environments where "people's personal space and peace are respected." The school dining halls offer "many options for both vegans and vegetarians." Plus, the campus grounds are "good for taking relaxing walks, and the fitness center is inviting." Mills is definitely "not a party school," and students warn us, "There is nothing within walking distance of the campus." Therefore, weekends tend to be mellow affairs, with many residential students hanging out in the dorms or studying. To combat the Friday night blues, "many students venture beyond campus, utilizing the rich surroundings in the Bay Area to work in the community, attend events to raise awareness for nonprofits, and for entertainment and shopping." If they want a night out, "girls go to the UC Berkeley frat parties" or head to San Francisco for dancing. For those without a car, "the Mills shuttle bus will stop by Telegraph Avenue, where many girls go to have fun."

Student Body

At Mills College, students hail from "very diverse cultural and class backgrounds, age ranges from seventeen to seventy-five, and life experiences from Cairo to Compton." It might seem like a "culture shock for some at first, but the atmosphere is one of acceptance and personal growth." Mills students describe their classmates as studious, serious, quirky, diverse, and atypical, and many mention that Mills has "a large population of lesbian, queer, bisexual, gender-curious, and transgender students." Acceptance is the rule. As one senior testifies, "I have yet to see any kind of prejudice or intolerance of another person's beliefs. Everyone is polite and courteous when faced with another's points of view." A freshman gushes, "Mills is the most vibrant and diverse community that I have ever been a part of, and from what I can tell, everybody that chooses to be at Mills, fits in at Mills." Reflecting the prevailing perspective in the San Francisco Bay Area, "the student body as a whole is very liberal, socially and politically." In fact, social awareness and political activism is practically a prerequisite among the student population, which principally consists of "environmentally aware, intelligent women who enjoy learning and making a difference."

FINANCIAL AID: 510-430-2000 • E-MAIL: ADMISSION@MILLS.EDU • WEBSITE: WWW.MILLS.EDU

THE PRINCETON REVIEW SAYS

Admissions

Very important factors considered include: Rigor of secondary school record. *Important factors considered include:* Academic GPA, application essay, class rank, recommendation(s), standardized test scores, character/personal qualities, extracurricular activities. *Other factors considered include:* Alumni/ae relation, first generation, geographical residence, interview, level of applicant's interest, racial/ethnic status, talent/ability, volunteer work, work experience. SAT or ACT required; ACT with or without writing component accepted. TOEFL required of all international applicants. High school diploma is required, and GED is accepted. *Academic units required:* 4 English, 3 mathematics, 2 science (2 science labs), 2 foreign language, 2 social studies, 2 history. *Academic units recommended:* 4 English, 4 mathematics, 4 science (2 science labs), 4 foreign language, 4 social studies, 4 history, 2 visual/performing arts.

Financial Aid

Students should submit: FAFSA, institution's own financial aid form. The Princeton Review suggests that all financial aid forms be submitted as soon as possible after January 1. *Need-based scholarships/grants offered:* Federal Pell, SEOG, state scholarships/grants, private scholarships, school scholarship or grant aid from institutional funds. Loan aid offered: Direct Subsidized Stafford, Direct Unsubsidized Stafford, Direct PLUS, Federal Perkins, university loans from institutional funds. Applicants will be notified of awards on a rolling basis beginning March 1. Federal Work-Study Program available.

Inside Word

Mills strives to create a diverse community of students and welcomes older, non-traditional undergraduates. In fact, twenty percent of the Mills undergraduate population is older than twenty-three. In addition to the application, test scores, and transcripts, Mills requests that all first-year applicants submit a graded writing sample. Admissions interviews, though not required, are highly encouraged.

THE SCHOOL SAYS "..."

From the Admissions Office

"For more than 150 years, Mills College has shaped women's lives. Offering a progressive liberal arts and sciences curriculum taught by nationally renowned faculty, Mills gives students the personal attention that leads to extraordinary learning. Through intensive, collaborative study in a community of forward-thinking individuals, students gain the ability to make their voices heard, the strength to risk bold visions, an eagerness to experiment, and a desire to change the world.

"Nestled on 135 lush acres in the heart of the San Francisco Bay Area, Mills draws energy from the college's dynamic location. Mills students connect with centers of learning, business, and technology; pursue research and internship opportunities; and explore the Bay Area's many sources of cultural, social, and recreational enrichment.

"Ranked fourth among top colleges in the West, Mills offers a renowned education for students who are seeking an intimate, collaborative college experience. You'll learn from distinguished professors who are truly dedicated to teaching. You'll interact with dynamic women of different backgrounds, ethnicities, cultures, ages, and mindsets, making your learning rich and inspiring.

"With more than forty different majors to choose from at Mills, you'll have a wide variety of education options. Mills also offers seven unique programs that enable undergraduates with clear career goals in certain fields to streamline their college and graduate school programs. At Mills, the classroom debate will be your intellectual catalyst, but you'll find plenty of opportunities to express yourself, both inside and outside of the classroom."

SELECTIVITY

Admissions Rating	89
# of applicants	2,129
% of applicants accepted	57
% of acceptees attending	17
# accepting a place on wait list	0

FRESHMAN PROFILE

Range SAT Critical Reading	520–650
Range SAT Math	490–600
Range SAT Writing	510–620
Range ACT Composite	21–27
Minimum paper TOEFL	550
Minimum computer TOEFL	213
Average HS GPA	3.54
% graduated top 10% of class	40
% graduated top 25% of class	75
% graduated top 50% of class	99

DEADLINES

Early action	
Deadline	11/15
Notification	12/1
Regular	
Priority	2/1
Deadline	8/1
Notification	12/1
Nonfall registration?	yes

APPLICANTS ALSO LOOK AT

AND OFTEN PREFER
Pitzer College, San Francisco State University, Santa Clara University, Stanford University, University of California, Santa Barbara, University of California—Riverside, University of California—Berkeley, University of California—Davis, University of California

AND SOMETIMES PREFER
Bryn Mawr College, Chapman University, Mount Holyoke College, Mount St. Mary's University, New York University, Occidental College, Saint Mary's College of California, Smith College, University of Puget Sound, University of San Francisco

AND RARELY PREFER
California State University—Sacramento, Colby College, Hampshire College, University of Redlands, University of Southern California, Whitman College, Willamette University

FINANCIAL FACTS

Financial Aid Rating	88
Annual tuition	$36,428
Room and board	$11,644
Required fees	$1,157
Books and supplies	$1,400
% frosh rec. need-based scholarship or grant aid	86
% UG rec. need-based scholarship or grant aid	88
% frosh rec. non-need-based scholarship or grant aid	76
% UG rec. non-need-based scholarship or grant aid	74
% frosh rec. need-based self-help aid	81
% UG rec. need-based self-help aid	80
% frosh rec. any financial aid	97
% UG rec. any financial aid	97
% UG borrow to pay for school	80
Average cumulative indebtedness	$25,795

MILLSAPS COLLEGE

1701 NORTH STATE STREET, JACKSON, MS 39210-0001 • ADMISSIONS: 601-974-1050 • FAX: 601-974-1059

CAMPUS LIFE
Quality of Life Rating	81
Fire Safety Rating	86
Green Rating	65
Type of school	private
Affiliation	Methodist
Environment	metropolis

STUDENTS
Total undergrad enrollment	948
% male/female	49/51
% from out of state	54
% from public high school	62
% live on campus	86
# of fraternities	6
# of sororities	6
% African American	9
% Asian	5
% Caucasian	76
% Hispanic	3
% Native American	1
% international	3
# of countries represented	19

SURVEY SAYS . . .
No one cheats
Low cost of living
Frats and sororities dominate
social scene
Student publications are popular

ACADEMICS
Academic Rating	90
% students graduating within 4 years	61
% students graduating within 6 years	68
Calendar	semester
Student/faculty ratio	9:1
Profs interesting rating	99
Profs accessible rating	92
Most common reg class size	10–19 students
Most common lab size	fewer than 10 students

MOST POPULAR MAJORS
biology, business administration and management, English language and literature

STUDENTS SAY "..."

Academics
You'll get a rigorous undergraduate education at Millsaps College, complimented by a patently student-oriented atmosphere and a satisfying dose of Southern charm. Offering thirty-four major programs, Millsaps' curriculum distinguishes itself through its "emphasis on writing and discussion-based classrooms." Get ready to burn the midnight oil: Preparing for class is indispensable, and life "revolves around doing papers." Fortunately, students say their academic experience is well worth the extra effort. A sophomore tells us that Millsaps is "all about creating an atmosphere in which students are excited to not only learn, but [to also] think." In addition, Millsaps is a highly student-oriented atmosphere. "Professors are extremely impressive with their knowledge and abilities" and their dedication to their students. Small class sizes ensure individual attention. For those who need an extra hand, Millsaps offers "great academic resources such as the writing center; subject tutors; and numerous opportunities to broaden our horizons through forums, concerts, enrichment programs, and speakers." Academics extend well beyond the classroom, and real-world opportunities abound. A senior shares, "I've worked at a school for the blind in India, studied Mayan ruins in Mexico, written federal grants at a transitional housing facility for people with HIV/AIDS...and worked with a local independent newspaper. I wouldn't have had the chance or the initiative to do any of those things before I came here." Down-to-earth and friendly, administrators, faculty, and staff are "frequently spotted in the cafeteria, the bleachers of a ball game, or the front row of the latest players (theater) production." Even if there is a problem, students feel involved in the campus community. A student explains, "Some of the decisions made by the administration at Millsaps have been questioned, but several of the deans are very accessible and constantly seek student input."

Life
Life at Millsaps is busy, fulfilling, fun, and well-rounded. Firing on all pistons, the typical Millsaps undergraduate is "over-committed to various clubs and organizations, hyper-productive in school work, ready to serve the community, and ready to have a good time when the weekend rolls around." On campus, there are more than eighty student clubs and organizations, including "a fencing club, an anime club, and a ballroom dancing club!" In addition, "the majority of the students at Millsaps participate in intercollegiate or intramural sports." During the weekends, it is easy to find a bit of diversion from your schoolwork; "Whether it is concerts at local pizza joints or bars, fraternity parties, or simply scary movie nights with popcorn in the residence halls, the students find ways to relax and enjoy this unique period of life known as college." Socially, "the Greek system is huge at Millsaps;" however, students insist that the Millsaps Greeks are very different from what you'd find at most schools. With their firm commitment to community service, "everyone can find a place in the Millsaps Greek system, even if you would never have pictured yourself in a fraternity or sorority."

Student Body
Millsaps attracts "intelligent, open-minded, and proactive" students, who might be best described as "over-involved, overachievers who wouldn't have it any other way." One quality that really distinguishes Millsaps students is their "strong desire to serve the community and be good neighbors to the Jackson area." In fact, "most students work hard at their school work and put academics first, but nearly everyone is involved in service in spite of the heavy workload." While most students hail from the Southern states, the student body represents students from twenty-eight states and twenty-four countries with a majority coming from Mississippi, Louisiana, and Texas. Students "vary in race, socioeconomic background, religious traditions and beliefs, and political perspective." Even on such a small campus, "There is enough variety that everyone can find their niche." Friendliness is also a common denominator, as "Millsaps students are very accepting of everyone—real Southern hospitality is evident on campus!"

FINANCIAL AID: 601-974-1220 • E-MAIL: ADMISSIONS@MILLSAPS.EDU • WEBSITE: WWW.MILLSAPS.EDU

THE PRINCETON REVIEW SAYS

Admissions

Very important factors considered include: Academic GPA, rigor of secondary school record, standardized test scores, character/personal qualities. *Important factors considered include:* Application essay, class rank, recommendation(s), extracurricular activities, talent/ability. *Other factors considered include:* Interview, volunteer work, work experience. SAT or ACT required; ACT with or without writing component accepted. TOEFL required of all international applicants. High school diploma is required, and GED is accepted. *Academic units required:* 4 English, 3 mathematics, 3 science (2 science labs), 1 foreign language, 2 social studies, 2 history, 1 academic elective. *Academic units recommended:* 4 English, 4 mathematics, 4 science (2 science labs), 2 foreign language, 2 social studies, 2 history, 2 academic elective.

Financial Aid

Students should submit: FAFSA. For early decision admission, priority deadline is November 15. For early action decision admission, priority deadline is December 1. Priority filing deadline is March 1. The Princeton Review suggests that all financial aid forms be submitted as soon as possible after January 1. *Need-based scholarships/grants offered:* Federal Pell, SEOG, state scholarships/grants, private scholarships, school scholarship or grant aid from institutional funds. *Loan aid offered:* Direct Subsidized Stafford, Direct Unsubsidized Stafford, Direct PLUS, Federal Perkins, university loans from institutional funds. Applicants will be notified of awards on a rolling basis beginning March 15. Federal Work-Study Program available. Off-campus job opportunities are good.

The Inside Word

Millsaps' trademark friendliness begins during the admissions process. The school encourages prospective students to get in touch with an admissions counselor to ask questions, arrange a visit, or connect you with a current student. For early action admission or scholarships, students need to apply in January. After that, the school admits students on a rolling basis.

THE SCHOOL SAYS "..."

From the Admissions Office

"Millsaps offers outstanding value in nationally ranked liberal arts education. Your academic journey begins with Critical Thinking and Academic Literacy, a comprehensive freshman experience that develops reasoning, communication, quantitative thinking, historical consciousness, aesthetic judgment, global, and multicultural awareness, and valuing and decision making. Throughout your Millsaps years you'll be encouraged to think differently; learn critical, analytical skills; embrace independence of thought; and prepare for study in your chosen major. We offer unique opportunities such as study abroad and in the field at our Yucatán Program; an exploration of your personal and professional future in relation to issues of ethics, values, faith, and the common good through our Faith and Work Initiative; highly respected pre-professional programs in law, medicine, and social work; and a five-year business track leading to an MBA or master's in accountancy with a liberal arts perspective that is accredited by the Association to Advance Collegiate Schools of Business. Our student body included Mississippi's 2003–2004 Rhodes scholar, a 2008–2009 Fulbright Scholar, and the faculty included the Carnegie Foundation's 2006, 2007, 2008 and 2009 Mississippi Professor of the Year. Our courses are taught without graduate assistants and our intimate student-faculty-community relationship is a hallmark of a Millsaps education. The emerging cultural climate in Jackson, Mississippi's capital city, provides unique artistic, athletic, and social opportunities in the modern south. We encourage you to look at Millsaps College. You'll appreciate the quality of our educational experience in comparison to the costs you'll discover at other national liberal arts institutions."

SELECTIVITY
Admissions Rating	86
# of applicants	1,186
% of applicants accepted	77
% of acceptees attending	24
# of early decision applicants	0

FRESHMAN PROFILE
Range SAT Critical Reading	520–640
Range SAT Math	540–650
Range ACT Composite	24–29
Minimum paper TOEFL	550
Minimum computer TOEFL	220
Minimum web-based TOEFL	80
Average HS GPA	3.61
% graduated top 10% of class	40
% graduated top 25% of class	71
% graduated top 50% of class	90

DEADLINES
Early decision	
Deadline	11/15
Notification	12/1
Early action	
Deadline	12/1
Regular	
Notification	10/15
Nonfall registration?	yes

APPLICANTS ALSO LOOK AT
AND OFTEN PREFER
Birmingham-Southern College
AND SOMETIMES PREFER
Rhodes College

FINANCIAL FACTS
Financial Aid Rating	87
Annual tuition	$27,650
Room and board	$10,312
% frosh rec. need-based scholarship or grant aid	63
% UG rec. need-based scholarship or grant aid	59
% frosh rec. non-need-based scholarship or grant aid	20
% UG rec. non-need-based scholarship or grant aid	14
% frosh rec. need-based self-help aid	41
% UG rec. need-based self-help aid	41
% frosh rec. any financial aid	100
% UG rec. any financial aid	96
% UG borrow to pay for school	52
Average cumulative indebtedness	$28,745

MISSOURI UNIVERSITY OF SCIENCE AND TECHNOLOGY

106 PARKER HALL, ROLLA, MO 65409 • ADMISSIONS: 573-341-4165 • FAX: 573-341-4082

STUDENTS SAY ". . ."

Academics

Formerly known as University of Missouri—Rolla, Missouri University of Science and Technology has undergone a name change, but its "reputation for academic excellence" has remained the same. Its focus on "challenging" academics ensures "the classes are tough," so "don't expect to walk right on through, but be glad that you aren't able to." Luckily, the school offers a "large number of assets" to students, including "lots of opportunities for students to lead" and professors who "really want the students to understand the material." Most students describe the professors as "very knowledgeable" and "willing to help students whenever they are in need of assistance." Some find them "varied," noting that "you have a good chance of getting an excellent professor, but then again some have thick accents, some have thick heads, and some just make you wonder if they really know and believe in what they're talking about." One thing nearly all students agree on is that the "extensive and very strong engineering and science programs" are the school's "biggest strength." "Missouri S&T does a lot of research and funds a lot of experiments and expeditions that give it an edge over other colleges," says one undergrad. They also appreciate Missouri S&T's "cheaper cost" than comparable colleges, as well as the fact their "tuition goes toward academics, not athletics." Opinions on the administration are mixed. Some find they "do a very good job at keeping the students informed about what is going on throughout the school" and "listen heavily to the students." Others aren't so positive, noting "administrators are completely unreachable."

Life

"Classes, studying, and homework dominate the weeks" at Missouri S&T, "so the weekends are when the campus comes alive." But "alive" can be a relative term. Some find life on campus is "great." "Most people get together in large groups and play outside sports for fun, work out together, or play video games in large groups," says one undergrad. "There is a great sense of community." On the other hand, when students are working so hard during the week, sometimes all they want to do with their free time is rest. "What I do for fun is sleep," explains one student, "because I'm always losing it." Either way the wind blows, "there's an organization for everyone" at Missouri S&T, with "fraternities and sororities being a very prominent part of residential life." There are also "a lot of social events that Residential Life puts on." Most agree the town of Rolla "doesn't offer a lot of entertainment." As one student puts it, "It's Rolla. Quarter Bowling night is the most fun thing to do." Many students "leave on the weekends," but most agree "part of that is that there are many different places to go within a three-hour drive." For those who stay, most "have fun with what they learn." While "pranking isn't as prevalent as it was in the past, it still happens." So expect the "normal college pastimes" of "potato cannons" and "siege machines" to take on a "more competitive level when students design equations or create programs to improve their designs."

Student Body

The typical student here is described as "a Midwestern white boy" or, as one student puts it, "a white male, nerdy, who never sees the sun." Either way, one thing is clear, women are "very much in the minority" here. This is reflected on both sides of the gender coin, with guys noting "there aren't many girls here, which stinks," and girls sometimes feeling that they're being "treated differently" by their peers. That said, some say "what once was a huge gap in gender population is now becoming a more respectable margin" and "the ethnic makeup of the student population is quite diverse." Fundamentally, students here are "smart," "welcoming," and "open-minded." They "make their own fun," and a good deal of bonding is done with video games: *Rock Band, Guitar Hero,* and *World of Warcraft* are "hugely popular" here.

MISSOURI UNIVERSITY OF SCIENCE AND TECHNOLOGY

FINANCIAL AID: 800-522-0938 • E-MAIL: ADMISSIONS@MST.EDU • WEBSITE: WWW.MST.EDU

THE PRINCETON REVIEW SAYS

Admissions

Very important factors considered include: Academic GPA, class rank, rigor of secondary school record, standardized test scores. *Important factors considered include:* Recommendation(s). *Other factors considered include:* Application essay, character/personal qualities, extracurricular activities, interview, talent/ability, volunteer work, work experience. SAT or ACT required; ACT with or without writing component accepted. TOEFL required of all international applicants. High school diploma is required, and GED is accepted. *Academic units required:* 4 English, 4 mathematics, 3 science (1 science lab), 2 foreign language, 3 social studies, 1 visual/performing arts.

Financial Aid

Students should submit: FAFSA. The Princeton Review suggests that all financial aid forms be submitted as soon as possible after January 1. *Need-based scholarships/grants offered:* Federal Pell, state scholarships/grants, private scholarships, school scholarship or grant aid from institutional funds. *Loan aid offered:* Direct Subsidized Stafford, Direct Unsubsidized Stafford, Direct PLUS, Federal Perkins. Federal Work-Study Program available. Off-campus job opportunities are good.

The Inside Word

In line with other leading public universities, gaining entrance to Missouri S&T is largely a numbers game. Applicants who meet class rank and standardized test cut-offs, as well as distribution requirements, will be granted admission. But don't rest on your laurels if you have them—the university draws a competitive, self-selecting pool of applicants, meaning the earlier you apply, the better the advantage you'll have.

THE SCHOOL SAYS "..."

From the Admissions Office

"Widely recognized as one of our nation's best universities for engineering, sciences, computer science, and technology, Missouri University of Science and Technology also offers programs in information science, business, and liberal arts. Personal attention, access to leadership opportunities, research projects, and co-ops and internships mean students are well-prepared for the future. Across all majors, ninety percent of students report 'firm plans' (either career, grad school, or military) at graduation. This plus a seventy-five percent placement rate to medical, law, and other professional schools tell the tale: Missouri S&T offers a terrific undergraduate experience and value for your money. In addition, our graduates enjoy one of the highest average starting salaries in the nation among public universities right out of school at $57,300.

"Missouri University of Science and Technology makes individual admission decisions based primarily on each applicant's standardized test scores and class rank or GPA. In the case of borderline admission situations, additional factors may be considered."

SELECTIVITY

Admissions Rating	86
# of applicants	2,620
% of applicants accepted	93
% of acceptees attending	46

FRESHMAN PROFILE

Range SAT Critical Reading	550–670
Range SAT Math	610–700
Range ACT Composite	25–31
Minimum paper TOEFL	550
Minimum computer TOEFL	213
Minimum web-based TOEFL	79
Average HS GPA	3.63
% graduated top 10% of class	43
% graduated top 25% of class	71
% graduated top 50% of class	94

DEADLINES

Regular	
Priority	12/1
Deadline	7/1
Nonfall registration?	yes

FINANCIAL FACTS

Financial Aid Rating	80
Annual in-state tuition	$7,848
Annual out-of-state tuition	$20,643
Room and board	$8,342
Required fees	$2,504
Books and supplies	$948
% frosh rec. need-based scholarship or grant aid	42
% UG rec. need-based scholarship or grant aid	42
% frosh rec. non-need-based scholarship or grant aid	60
% UG rec. non-need-based scholarship or grant aid	57
% frosh rec. need-based self-help aid	46
% UG rec. need-based self-help aid	45
% frosh rec. any financial aid	70
% UG rec. any financial aid	83
% UG borrow to pay for school	81
Average cumulative indebtedness	$24,235

MONMOUTH UNIVERSITY (NJ)

400 CEDAR AVENUE, WEST LONG BRANCH, NJ 07764-1898 • ADMISSIONS: 732-571-3456 • FAX: 732-263-5166

STUDENTS SAY ". . ."

Academics

Monmouth University "is a small school that…provides an excellent community-like atmosphere," where you "can really get to know your instructors" "because of the small class size," which is twenty-two students on average. Professors are "very accomplished and have impressive backgrounds," and students feel that they're learning from "professionals in their fields [who] know exactly what they are talking about" and are willing to "share their career experiences." Monmouth offers thirty-one undergraduate majors: business administration, general communication studies/speech communication, education, music, criminal justice, premedical sciences, and psychology are among the most popular and have a "good reputation." One confident English major says that the university is interested in "creating leaders and looking toward the future." Monmouth also has a "very good" honors school with "excellent teachers," though professors throughout the school "seem to love their jobs" and "truly care about helping their students succeed." One student speaks for many when he says, "I know many Monmouth University alumni, and all have loved their experience. They say MU prepared them for their careers."

Life

At Monmouth University, "everyone is able to find something fun to do." While "academics are the top priority" for many, the school "is dedicated to ensuring that students have fun when class isn't in session." Students enjoy the "free weekend movies" or intramural sports such as "flag football, dodgeball, and volleyball" and report that "clubs are always planning and executing charity events [and] drives." Of course, Monmouth's "beautiful campus" and close proximity to the ocean mean students spend a lot of time outdoors, and it's a given that students "love to relax at the beach." Greek life is "very popular on campus," so "there are always frat parties," though students complain they "usually get busted extremely early" because local police are "very strict." This means that "people don't usually party in the dorms," either, and instead hit local bars, leading some to complain that if you're "under twenty-one, it is extremely difficult to find activities to do in the community." A political science major notes that "You can't get around without a car, and many kids go home for the weekend." Those who don't often have cars take advantage of the school's location and take day trips to "New York City and Philadelphia." Those who do have cars may have an advantage, but they also must contend with one big problem: "limited parking."

Student Body

At Monmouth, "the typical student…is an outgoing, friendly, easygoing individual who is ready to experience everything Monmouth has to offer," and many students seem to find that "making friends is quite easy." Students tend to be from "affluent" or "upper-middle-class" families, and drive "BMWs [and] Mercedes" and carry "Louis Vuitton bags," which leads some to say the student body can be "snobby." Many students are in fraternities or sororities, and athletes have a big presence on campus. While "there is little diversity," "the school is becoming more diverse" and "there have been no conflicts with diversity." The majority of students are "homegrown," from New Jersey or New York, and some students feel that local and commuter students "don't bother making new friends." At Monmouth, there are plenty of "laid-back" beach kids, but most students agree that Monmouth students "know when to hit the books hard."

MONMOUTH UNIVERSITY (NJ)

FINANCIAL AID: 732-571-3463 • E-MAIL: ADMISSION@MONMOUTH.EDU • WEBSITE: WWW.MONMOUTH.EDU

THE PRINCETON REVIEW SAYS

Admissions

Very important factors considered include: Academic GPA, rigor of secondary school record, standardized test scores. *Important factors considered include:* Extracurricular activities, volunteer work, work experience. *Other factors considered include:* Application essay, recommendation(s), alumni/ae relation, character/personal qualities. SAT or ACT required; ACT with writing component required. TOEFL required of all international applicants. High school diploma is required, and GED is accepted. *Academic units required:* 4 English, 3 mathematics, 2 science (1 science lab), 2 history, 5 academic elective. *Academic units recommended:* 2 foreign language, 2 social studies.

Financial Aid

Students should submit: FAFSA. Regular filing deadline is June 30. The Princeton Review suggests that all financial aid forms be submitted as soon as possible after January 1. *Need-based scholarships/grants offered:* Federal Pell, SEOG, state scholarships/grants, private scholarships, school scholarship or grant aid from institutional funds, Federal Nursing Scholarships. *Loan aid offered:* Direct Subsidized Stafford, Direct Unsubsidized Stafford, Direct PLUS, Federal Perkins, state loans, university loans from institutional funds. Applicants will be notified of awards on a rolling basis beginning February 15. Federal Work-Study Program available. Off-campus job opportunities are good.

Inside Word

B students with slightly above-average SAT or ACT scores should find little impediment to gaining admission to Monmouth. The school's national stature is on the rise, resulting in more competitive applicant base, but Monmouth must still compete with a lot of heavy hitters for top regional students.

THE SCHOOL SAYS "..."

From the Admissions Office

"Monmouth University, a first-tier, dynamic private university, empowers students to reach their full potential as leaders who make significant contributions to their community and society. Small classes, allowing for individual attention and student-faculty dialogue, are hallmarks of a Monmouth education. A ratio of fifteen students to each professor ensures active and engaged learning. At Monmouth, students and faculty connect. In and out of the classroom, ideas are nurtured and then become real, hands-on experiences.

"Experiential education, which includes study abroad, select service learning projects, dedicated experiential coursework, internships, or cooperative learning experiences, is a required part of the curriculum. Before graduation, more than seventy percent of Monmouth students have completed a 'real-world' experience; only forty-six percent of graduating students at comparable institutions have done this according to the 2010 National Survey of Student Engagement.

"Monmouth University is located in the New York metropolitan area, home to many prominent firms that are leaders in the technology, media, and financial industries. This allows students access to exceptional hands-on learning opportunities.

"Monmouth's student life, including cultural events, festivals, and active student clubs and organizations, reflect the school's spirit. Monmouth's twenty NCAA Division I athletic teams attract lively support from students and other members of the Monmouth and local community.

"Monmouth's President, Paul G. Gaffney II, believes the reputation of the university starts with the achievements and successes of its students. Monmouth provides students with a value-added education, personalized experience, and the support and guidance needed to move forward and make their mark."

SELECTIVITY

Admissions Rating	80
# of applicants	6,561
% of applicants accepted	60
% of acceptees attending	25

FRESHMAN PROFILE

Range SAT Critical Reading	490–570
Range SAT Math	500–590
Range SAT Writing	490–580
Range ACT Composite	22–26
Minimum paper TOEFL	550
Minimum computer TOEFL	213
Minimum web-based TOEFL	79
Average HS GPA	3.37
% graduated top 10% of class	18
% graduated top 25% of class	51
% graduated top 50% of class	88

DEADLINES

Early action	
Deadline	12/1
Notification	1/15
Regular	
Priority	12/1
Deadline	3/1
Nonfall registration?	yes

FINANCIAL FACTS

Financial Aid Rating	71
Annual tuition	$25,728
Room and board	$9,936
Required fees	$628
Books and supplies	$1,200
% frosh rec. need-based scholarship or grant aid	30
% UG rec. need-based scholarship or grant aid	28
% frosh rec. non-need-based scholarship or grant aid	68
% UG rec. non-need-based scholarship or grant aid	63
% frosh rec. need-based self-help aid	62
% UG rec. need-based self-help aid	58
% frosh rec. any financial aid	99
% UG rec. any financial aid	94
% UG borrow to pay for school	72
Average cumulative indebtedness	$29,921

MONTANA TECH OF THE UNIVERSITY OF MONTANA

1300 WEST PARK STREET, BUTTE, MT 59701 • ADMISSIONS: 406-496-4256 • FAX: 406-496-4710

STUDENTS SAY ". . ."

Academics
Montana Tech is a small state school that's "all about giving students a high-quality education and getting students successful careers in the work force." Though the school emphasizes the sciences, and has particularly strong engineering, science, and technology majors, Montana Tech also offers degrees in nursing and liberal studies. Classes at Montana Tech are small, "which gives opportunity for one-on-one learning," and students really get "to know their professors on a personal level." Course loads are very "challenging" and students are aware of the "high level" at which they have to perform. However, they find their professors "are well-trained and offer good guidance," and "bring real life experience into the classroom," which "makes understanding the applicability of theory interesting." Additionally, professors "go above and beyond" to help students "reach [their] educational and professional goals." A mechanical engineering student says professors "are very willing to help and will meet with you even if it isn't their office hours." Getting a job after graduation is huge priority here, and with a job-placement rate of ninety-seven percent, students rightfully feel that "the majors here deliver when it comes to work after graduation." Professional placement is helped by the "hands-on practical lab experience and the number of internships a student can complete by the time they graduate." The ultimate combination of class size and support makes one student feel that Montana Tech is a "college built entirely for students."

Life
Students at Montana Tech say "there is always lots of school work to be done," and that most students "are very dedicated to their school work and have to be." However, though they work hard, they "play hard as well." An engineering student explains that the rigorous curriculum means "students are…very good at time management," and that they "try to get all of their work done in a way that leaves them time to do other things." With its enviable location halfway between Yellowstone and Glacier National Parks, those other things often include "fishing, snowboarding, skiing, hiking, [and] mountain biking." One student brags that "you can literally take a five-minute drive off campus into the countryside," which is great, because "being outdoors helps ease stress." In addition to blowing off steam outdoors, the school has "many activities to get people involved, especially when you live in the dorms, such as movie nights or intramural sports." Students "get e-mails from the school all the time about different stuff going on," such as "trips to concerts, trips to swimming hot springs, different contests, games, dances, parties," and more. Drinking can be part of life at Montana Tech for those students who seek it out. As one student notes, parties can get "a little rowdy." In addition, Butte is small but has "lots of bars to socialize in." However, though "most love a good time," "when it's time to study/hit the books, there is an extreme amount of dedication."

Student Body
Students at Montana Tech are "driven" but "nice" and "very friendly." While the school has "tons of little niches," such as "groups of cowboys, goths, athletes," and so on, everyone is generally united by their desire to succeed. As one student says, "It is hard to find students here that aren't nerds." Though students are devoted to their work, they don't mention a competitive atmosphere. In fact, many believe they "get along great together because they depend on each other" and they'll "help each other out" anytime. The school is predominantly male, and most are from Montana. It attracts a sizable portion of older, "nontraditional" students, so there's "a greater diversity of learning styles and experiences." There are also lots of international students, particularly from the Middle East, and though "there is a wide variety of cultures and beliefs," most people feel that "everybody gets along with everybody."

Montana Tech of the University of Montana

Financial Aid: 406-496-4256 • E-mail: Enrollment@mtech.edu • Website: www.mtech.edu

THE PRINCETON REVIEW SAYS

Admissions

Factors considered include: Academic GPA, class rank, standardized test scores. SAT or ACT required; ACT with writing component required. TOEFL required of all international applicants. High school diploma is required, and GED is accepted. *Academic units required:* 4 English, 3 mathematics, 2 science (2 science labs), 3 social studies. *Academic units recommended:* 4 English, 4 mathematics, 4 science (2 science labs), 2 foreign language.

Financial Aid

Students should submit: FAFSA, institution's own financial aid form. The Princeton Review suggests that all financial aid forms be submitted as soon as possible after January 1. *Need-based scholarships/grants offered:* Federal Pell, SEOG, state scholarships/grants, private scholarships, school scholarship or grant aid from institutional funds. *Loan aid offered:* Direct Subsidized Stafford, Direct Unsubsidized Stafford, Direct PLUS, Federal Perkins, university loans from institutional funds. Applicants will be notified of awards on a rolling basis beginning March 15. Federal Work-Study Program available. Off-campus job opportunities are good.

The Inside Word

Montana Tech is a godsend for students who are strong academically but not likely to be offered admission to nationally renowned technical institutes. In fact, because of its small size and relatively remote location, Montana Tech is a good choice for anyone leaning toward a technical career. You would be hard-pressed to find many other places as low-key and personal in the realm of academia.

THE SCHOOL SAYS "..."

From the Admissions Office

"Characterize Montana Tech by listening to what employers say. They tell us Tech graduates stand out with an incredible work ethic and top-notch technical skills. Last year, 164 companies held on-campus interviews and attended Montana Tech's career fairs competing for our students and graduates. The beneficiaries: the students! Montana Tech has had a ten-year annual average placement rate of ninety-six percent with exceptional starting salaries. Learning takes place in a personalized environment, in first-class academic facilities, and in the heart of the Rocky Mountains. Students at Tech work hard and play hard. Outdoor recreation provides a great balance to the rigors of the course work at Montana Tech. It's not a large, multifaceted university with lots of frills, but our students get a terrific education, and in the end, great jobs! The SAT (or the ACT with the writing section) is recommended for all students applying for admission. Students who do not take the tests with the writing component may be required to take an additional English placement test from the college before they enroll."

SELECTIVITY

Admissions Rating	73
# of applicants	831
% of applicants accepted	90
% of acceptees attending	66

FRESHMAN PROFILE

Range SAT Critical Reading	470–580
Range SAT Math	515–630
Range SAT Writing	450–560
Range ACT Composite	21–26
Minimum paper TOEFL	525
Minimum computer TOEFL	195
Minimum web-based TOEFL	71
Average HS GPA	3.38
% graduated top 10% of class	23
% graduated top 25% of class	49
% graduated top 50% of class	78

DEADLINES

Regular	
Priority	2/1
Notification	rolling
Nonfall registration?	yes

APPLICANTS ALSO LOOK AT AND SOMETIMES PREFER
Montana State University—Bozeman, The University of Montana

AND RARELY PREFER
Carroll College (MT)

FINANCIAL FACTS

Financial Aid Rating	64
Annual in-state tuition	$6,094
Annual out-of-state tuition	$17,284
Room and board	$6,162
Books and supplies	$1,000
% frosh rec. need-based scholarship or grant aid	58
% UG rec. need-based scholarship or grant aid	49
% frosh rec. non-need-based scholarship or grant aid	16
% UG rec. non-need-based scholarship or grant aid	14
% frosh rec. need-based self-help aid	45
% UG rec. need-based self-help aid	44
% frosh rec. any financial aid	63
% UG rec. any financial aid	55
% UG borrow to pay for school	87
Average cumulative indebtedness	$23,000

MORAVIAN COLLEGE

1200 MAIN STREET, BETHLEHEM, PA 18018 • ADMISSIONS: 610-861-1320 • FAX: 610-625-7930

CAMPUS LIFE

Quality of Life Rating	79
Fire Safety Rating	82
Green Rating	74
Type of school	private
Affiliation	Moravian
Environment	city

STUDENTS

Total undergrad enrollment	1,599
% male/female	42/58
% from out of state	36
% from public high school	62
% live on campus	76
# of fraternities	3
# of sororities	4
% African American	3
% Asian	2
% Caucasian	84
% Hispanic	7
% international	1
# of countries represented	9

SURVEY SAYS . . .
Great computer facilities
Low cost of living
Students are happy
Musical organizations are popular

ACADEMICS

Academic Rating	85
% students graduating within 4 years	68
% students graduating within 6 years	71
Calendar	semester
Student/faculty ratio	11:1
Profs interesting rating	84
Profs accessible rating	88
Most common reg class size	10–19 students
Most common lab size	10–19 students

MOST POPULAR MAJORS
business administration and management, nursing, psychology

STUDENTS SAY "..."

Academics
Moravian College "challenges students academically" in a "small environment," where "professors know their students on a personal level." The college is known for its "strong faculty and academic programs," and students say, "Moravian College bends over backward to accommodate its students." Students are exposed to "a good education" through "Learning in Common, which is a set of courses in multidisciplinary categories that interconnect different fields of study." Students boast about "personal attention and genuine enthusiasm from professors," and say, "Moravian College is dedicated to the education of its students as well as building a community between students and faculty." Professors are "accessible, approachable, helpful, and always willing to spend that extra time making sure you understand the material," and students attribute this to "the small student population" and the "mentoring relationship" that develops as a result. A chemistry major says, "The student-professor interactions improve the speed with which students understand course materials." However, a freshman says, "Like any school, there are the great professors and there are the not so great," adding, "You take the bad with the excellent and it makes you a better student."

Life
Moravian College is known for being a "small school with a friendly atmosphere" that fosters a "supportive environment" for "students to learn and grow." A sophomore says, "I love the atmosphere of the campus," and another student adds, "I love the kindness and genuine concern that people have for others." Students say, "The campus itself is beautiful," and "you always run into someone you know," which creates a "sense of community and pride." A psychology major says, "Even though it's a relatively small school, there are so many things to do," and another student concurs that Moravian is "all about engaging students in real life experiences outside of the classroom using campus speakers, internships, and field study experiences." Students participate in "clubs, organizations, Greek life, and sports teams," and say, "Moravian College provides many opportunities to exceed above and beyond," noting being small allows "opportunities to get involved in different organizations and take leadership roles." Students speak highly of the staff, saying it's "a very personal experience overall" and that the "maintenance of facilities is outstanding." However, some gripe, "Communication between administration and students" could be improved in regards to "decisions [about the] use of funds." There are complaints about the requirement that students live on campus all four years, particularly because many feel "housing could be greatly improved upon."

Student Body
The typical Moravian student is "fun and hardworking," "very laid-back and sociable," and "dedicated to their education during the weekday, but able to relax and have fun on the weekends." A sophomore says, "The greatest quality is the school's diversity and acceptance of all backgrounds, religions, lifestyles," and another student adds, "You not only meet students who are like you, but students who are different in a positive way." However, others feel there's still much to be desired in terms of diversity and say most students are "middle class [and] white," although they note, "There are [more] students of color, especially in recent years" and say generally "these individuals are not at all excluded from any aspects of campus life." When "the weekend comes, students tend to let loose and enjoy themselves while they spend time with friends," and "Much of the campus population attends some sort of party over the weekend." However, because "off campus housing was taken away…it makes it easier for campus safety to bust the parties on campus during the weekends." A music education major says, "There is also a large part of the school that does not party and participates in many school events," and another student adds, "Moravian always has something to do. On weekends they offer alternatives to drinking such as movies and bingo." The small town of Bethlehem also "offers many places to eat, take a stroll, shop, or hang out."

FINANCIAL AID: 610-861-1330 • E-MAIL: ADMISSIONS@MORAVIAN.EDU • WEBSITE: WWW.MORAVIAN.EDU

THE PRINCETON REVIEW SAYS

Admissions

Very important factors considered include: Academic GPA, class rank, rigor of secondary school record, alumni/ae relation, character/personal qualities. *Important factors considered include:* Application essay, recommendation(s), standardized test scores, extracurricular activities, first generation, level of applicant's interest, racial/ethnic status, talent/ability, volunteer work. *Other factors considered include:* Geographical residence, interview, work experience. SAT or ACT optional (required for consideration for most merit scholarships). TOEFL required of all international applicants. High school diploma is required, and GED is accepted. *Academic units required:* 4 English, 3 mathematics, 3 science (2 science labs), 2 foreign language, 4 social studies. *Academic units recommended:* 4 mathematics, (3 science labs).

Financial Aid

Students should submit: FAFSA, institution's own financial aid form. Priority filing deadline is February 14. The Princeton Review suggests that all financial aid forms be submitted as soon as possible after January 1. *Need-based scholarships/grants offered:* Federal Pell, SEOG, state scholarships/grants, private scholarships, school scholarship or grant aid from institutional funds. *Loan aid offered: Federal Direct Stafford Loans, Federal Direct Parent PLUS Loans,* Federal Perkins. Federal Work-Study Program available.

The Inside Word

Admissions officers at Moravian College base admissions decisions primarily on an applicant's secondary school career. Course selection and performance are crucial elements and outweigh standardized test scores. Recommendations and community activism are also weighed heavily. The admissions staff strongly encourages a campus visit and although interviews aren't required they're recommended.

THE SCHOOL SAYS "..."

From the Admissions Office

"Moravian partners with students to build a foundation for their future. In today's challenging and highly competitive work environment, college graduates need more than a college degree to succeed in the world. Students today require in-depth knowledge of their subject, real-world experience, and leadership and social skills. Moravian College puts students first. We're committed to providing students with the well-rounded, strong foundation they need to succeed.

"With more than 250 years of experience in providing equal access to education for all, Moravian promises to partner with students to build a strong foundation for their personal and professional future. Moravian College students are challenged to reach their full potential as individuals while they benefit from our supportive learning community.

"Moravian challenges students with a strong, personalized academic major. Students grow intellectually from programs that develop from our faculty's innovative teaching, from the intellectual relationships between faculty and students, and from the broad range of opportunities for personalized learning.

"At Moravian, students also experience hands-on learning. They participate in collaborative research and scholarship such as the SOAR and honors programs, internships, study abroad, leadership, work study, and community service opportunities.

"Students live and learn in an environment that promotes the development of a deeper enjoyment of life. They develop personally through co-curricular activities such as athletics and recreation, music and the arts, and opportunities for an active social life.

"Students leave Moravian with the skills, knowledge, and support necessary to more deeply enjoy life, work, and their role in the world."

SELECTIVITY	
Admissions Rating	78
# of applicants	2,004
% of applicants accepted	79
% of acceptees attending	23
# of early decision applicants	197
% accepted early decision	81

FRESHMAN PROFILE	
Range SAT Critical Reading	470–590
Range SAT Math	480–590
Range SAT Writing	480–590
Range ACT Composite	20–22
Minimum paper TOEFL	550
Minimum computer TOEFL	213
Average HS GPA	3.33
% graduated top 10% of class	28
% graduated top 25% of class	56
% graduated top 50% of class	82

DEADLINES	
Early decision	
Deadline	2/1
Notification	12/15
Early action	
Deadline	12/1
Notification	12/15
Regular	
Priority	3/1
Deadline	3/1
Nonfall registration?	yes

**APPLICANTS ALSO LOOK AT
AND OFTEN PREFER**
Lafayette College, Muhlenberg College

AND SOMETIMES PREFER
Gettysburg College, Susquehanna University,
Ursinus College

FINANCIAL FACTS	
Financial Aid Rating	77
Annual tuition	$31,662
Room and board	$9,164
Required fees	$515
Books and supplies	$1,000
% frosh rec. need-based scholarship or grant aid	82
% UG rec. need-based scholarship or grant aid	81
% frosh rec. non-need-based scholarship or grant aid	9
% UG rec. non-need-based scholarship or grant aid	7
% frosh rec. need-based self-help aid	74
% UG rec. need-based self-help aid	74
% frosh rec. any financial aid	98
% UG rec. any financial aid	96
% UG borrow to pay for school	80

MOUNT HOLYOKE COLLEGE

OFFICE OF ADMISSIONS, NEWHALL CENTER, SOUTH HADLEY, MA 01075 • ADMISSIONS: 413-538-2023 • FAX: 413-538-2409

CAMPUS LIFE

Quality of Life Rating	91
Fire Safety Rating	79
Green Rating	76
Type of school	private
Environment	town

STUDENTS

Total undergrad enrollment	2,287
% male/female	0/100
% from out of state	74
% from public high school	58
% live on campus	94
% African American	4
% Asian	7
% Caucasian	48
% Hispanic	7
% international	21
# of countries represented	74

SURVEY SAYS . . .
Lab facilities are great
Great computer facilities
Diverse student types on campus
Campus feels safe
Frats and sororities are unpopular
or nonexistent
Musical organizations are popular
Political activism is popular

ACADEMICS

Academic Rating	98
% students graduating within 4 years	74
% students graduating within 6 years	82
Calendar	semester
Student/faculty ratio	9:1
Profs interesting rating	97
Profs accessible rating	96
Most common reg class size	10–19 students
Most common lab size	10–19 students

MOST POPULAR MAJORS
biology, international relations,
political science

STUDENTS SAY ". . ."

Academics
Mount Holyoke is a "small student-focused liberal arts college," "specializing in the higher education of women." Students say it's "an amazing school with a strong history of producing remarkable and intelligent young women who go on to achieve great things" and rave about the "supportive all-women environment and the excellent academics." A freshman says, "It's a traditional yet modern school with brilliant alumni and top-notch academics." Mount Holyoke is known for its "academic rigor" and "consortium opportunities," with the other schools in the Five College consortium. The school "provides a fantastic learning environment where students value their education" and offers a "balance between the sciences and a liberal arts education." A history major says, "Mount Holyoke College provides an incredible academic experience with outstanding faculty [and] engaged classmates," and professors are deemed "incredibly motivated and interesting." Students say, "Mount Holyoke professors are brilliant, but human and accessible," and "From your first year to senior year, you feel very supported by the faculty" who are "interested in getting to know students on a personal level."

Life
Mount Holyoke is known for its "beautiful campus" that provides a "plethora of opportunities beyond the classroom in terms of extracurricular activities." Students say, "It's a wonderful, inviting and challenging environment," where "smart, passionate, diverse women come together…in a beautiful campus setting"…"to form a strong community and to pursue their educational goals." A freshman says the college "makes sure its students are involved, proactive, and learning the rest of the time that they're on campus," and another student adds, "I'm consistently impressed with the involvement of the students here." Students says, "The support system here is great," and "I feel like I can really count on my peers," adding "the Alumnae Association does a wonderful job at helping current students connect in terms of careers, internships, or just common interest." Most feel, "The administration listens to the students and does its best to provide for us," although some disagree saying, "Communication between the administration and the student body is not always prompt or clear." There are complaints about being "forced to live in on campus," with students saying, "Residential life could use some work," and "some of the dorms need more maintenance." Despite the "warm, loving, and open," community, a psychology major says, "The school-sponsored events are poorly attended, and there isn't much of a social life on campus for heterosexual students."

Student Body
At Mount Holyoke, "The students are happy, intelligent women dedicated to making a real difference in the world." Typical students are "poised, eloquent, passionate, and doing interesting things both inside and outside the classroom" and "down-to-earth and laid-back but also willing to have complex conversations over breakfast." It's clear most are "very into being left-wing and excited about political awareness," and a sophomore says, "Mt. Holyoke is full of geeky feminists," who are "at least socially engaged if not activists." There is "a very strong gay community and much of the party scene is queer-based social networks," and students say, "Sexual orientation is often flexible." However, there are also those who complain, "There aren't any men around, which is less than ideal," and say, "Despite the percentages touting great racial/ethnic diversity, much improvement is needed." Most agree, "The typical student is incredibly smart, a tad quirky, and above all passionate," and say "There's definitely a niche for everyone, regardless of sexual orientation or gender expression." Students are "studious, ambitious, and determined," and "able to laugh and enjoy camaraderie."

MOUNT HOLYOKE COLLEGE

FINANCIAL AID: 413-538-2291 • E-MAIL: ADMISSION@MTHOLYOKE.EDU • WEBSITE: WWW.MTHOLYOKE.EDU

THE PRINCETON REVIEW SAYS

Admissions

Very important factors considered include: Academic GPA, application essay, class rank, recommendation(s), rigor of secondary school record. *Important factors considered include:* Character/personal qualities, extracurricular activities, first generation, interview, talent/ability, volunteer work, work experience. *Other factors considered include:* Standardized test scores, alumni/ae relation, geographical residence, level of applicant's interest, racial/ethnic status. ACT with or without writing component accepted. TOEFL required of all international applicants. High school diploma is required, and GED is accepted. *Academic units recommended:* 4 English, (3 science labs), 3 history, 1 academic elective.

Financial Aid

Students should submit: FAFSA, CSS/Financial Aid PROFILE. The Princeton Review suggests that all financial aid forms be submitted as soon as possible after January 1. *Need-based scholarships/grants offered:* Federal Pell, SEOG, state scholarships/grants, private scholarships, school scholarship or grant aid from institutional funds. *Loan aid offered:* Direct Subsidized Stafford, Direct Unsubsidized Stafford, Direct PLUS, Federal Perkins, state loans, university loans from institutional funds. Federal Work-Study Program available. Off-campus job opportunities are fair.

The Inside Word

Mount Holyoke follows traditional admissions requirements, but encourages applicants to submit supplemental materials exhibiting artistic or athletic talents. The admission committee is happy to receive portfolios, slides, and so on, that showcase an applicant's talents. In addition, interviews are strongly encouraged as way for the admission staff to learn more about a prospective student's academic goals and personal experiences.

THE SCHOOL SAYS " . . ."

From the Admissions Office

"The majority of students who choose Mount Holyoke do so simply because it is an outstanding liberal arts college. After a semester or two, they start to appreciate the fact that Mount Holyoke is a women's college, even though most Mount Holyoke students never thought they'd go to a women's college when they started their college search. Students talk of having 'space' to figure out who they really are. They speak about feeling empowered to excel in traditionally male subjects such as science and technology. They appreciate the remarkable array of opportunities—for academic achievement, career exploration, and leadership—and the impressive, creative accomplishments of their peers. If you're looking for a college that will challenge you to be your best, most powerful self and to fulfill your potential, Mount Holyoke should be at the top of your list.

"Submission of standardized test scores is optional for most applicants to Mount Holyoke College. However, the TOEFL is required of students for whom English is not their primary language, and the SAT Subject Tests are required for homeschooled students."

SELECTIVITY

Admissions Rating	95
# of applicants	3,359
% of applicants accepted	52
% of acceptees attending	31
# accepting a place on wait list	515
% admitted from wait list	15
# of early decision applicants	211
% accepted early decision	61

FRESHMAN PROFILE

Range SAT Critical Reading	610–700
Range SAT Math	580–690
Range SAT Writing	620–710
Range ACT Composite	27–31
Average HS GPA	3.70
% graduated top 10% of class	58
% graduated top 25% of class	82
% graduated top 50% of class	98

DEADLINES

Early decision	
Deadline	11/15
Notification	1/1
Regular	
Deadline	1/15
Nonfall registration?	yes

APPLICANTS ALSO LOOK AT
AND OFTEN PREFER
Amherst College, Barnard College, Brown University, Dartmouth College, Harvard College, Vassar College, Wellesley College, Williams College, Yale University

AND SOMETIMES PREFER
Bryn Mawr College, Columbia University, Middlebury College, Smith College, Tufts University

AND RARELY PREFER
Boston University, Skidmore College, University of Massachusetts Amherst

FINANCIAL FACTS

Financial Aid Rating	96
Annual tuition	$41,270
Room and board	$12,140
Required fees	$186
Books and supplies	$950
% frosh rec. need-based scholarship or grant aid	70
% UG rec. need-based scholarship or grant aid	68
% frosh rec. non-need-based scholarship or grant aid	12
% UG rec. non-need-based scholarship or grant aid	9
% frosh rec. need-based self-help aid	62
% UG rec. need-based self-help aid	67
% frosh rec. any financial aid	82
% UG rec. any financial aid	79
% UG borrow to pay for school	66
Average cumulative indebtedness	$22,499

MUHLENBERG COLLEGE

2400 WEST CHEW STREET, ALLENTOWN, PA 18104-5596 • ADMISSIONS: 484-664-3200 • FAX: 484-664-3234

STUDENTS SAY ". . ."

Academics
A small, liberal arts school with a decidedly friendly touch, Muhlenberg College encourages a spirit of community between students, faculty, and staff. Muhlenberg professors are "warm, willing to talk, and really nice," giving students the confidence, resources, and opportunities they seek in an undergraduate education. A senior enthuses, "If you take advantage of it, you can get close with your professors, do independent work, and pave your own way in preparation for whatever you want to eventually do or become." A student in the pre-medical program adds, "The science classes are very difficult, but there are a lot of resources, such as workshops, tutoring, recitations, and meeting with the professor personally." While academics are challenging, they aren't so rigorous student don't have time for a well-balanced lifestyle. A junior explains, "Muhlenberg allows me to take a full course load each semester while still giving me time to have a job, have a social life, and be connected with the organizations with which I want to be affiliated, in a comfortable and close-knit setting." Things tend to run smoothly, and "the administrators have reached a balanced approach where they are not visible in everyday activities but are clearly in control." At the same time, many students say they've had the opportunity to brush elbows with the school's top administrators. A freshman remembers, "I couldn't believe it when, during the first week of classes, President Helm sat down with my friends and me at brunch and asked us how our first week was going."

Life
Academics are taken seriously, but personal life and extracurricular activities are also an important part of the experience at Muhlenberg College. A sophomore explains, "Academically, Muhlenberg can be rigorous at times, depending on what you place on yourself, but activities outside the classroom are also given a lot of emphasis, so it's not like all you're ever doing is studying." On campus, students participate in intramural sports, attend campus events, or join student clubs. In addition, "all of the sports teams have games nonstop." In dorms, in the suites, in the fraternity houses, or off-campus, "parties are commonplace on the weekends." At the same time, students reassure us "partying happens very often on and off campus, but it is rarely out of control like on bigger campuses." A senior adds, "People definitely work hard here, but then we let loose on the weekends. Saturdays aren't big study days, but Sunday nights in the library are packed." Although first-year students are not allowed to have cars, "there's a shopping center within walking distance," as well as "a shuttle service that will drive students to any place in Allentown, such as the bowling alley, movies, mall, ice skating rink, mini golf, and restaurants." At the same time, students remind us Allentown doesn't offer a multitude of social options for college students. For more cosmopolitan options, the school's location between New York and Philadelphia is unbeatable.

Student Body
Muhlenberg is a patently "friendly campus" where everyone finds a niche and "people smile at you as you walk by them." The overwhelming majority of undergraduates hail from middle-class, suburban families in New Jersey, Long Island, or Pennsylvania, creating a "fairly homogeneous" student body. Preppy is the dominant dress code, though there is also a big group of "artsy, theater-type students" who come to participate in the school's excellent theater program. Fortunately, "the Muhlenberg community is extremely accommodating to all types of students," and varying interests and lifestyles are represented and accepted. A student attests, "Typical students are usually white and middle-class, however, there is a great amount of diversity with people of different religious backgrounds, social backgrounds, and sexual orientations." Adds another, "At first glance we appear to be a very homogeneous campus, but upon closer inspection and by personal experience, it is clear the student body is diverse and is very accepting of that diversity."

FINANCIAL AID: 484-664-3175 • E-MAIL: ADMISSION@MUHLENBERG.EDU • WEBSITE: WWW.MUHLENBERG.EDU

THE PRINCETON REVIEW SAYS

Admissions

Very important factors considered include: Academic GPA, rigor of secondary school record. *Important factors considered include:* Application essay, class rank, recommendation(s), standardized test scores, character/personal qualities, extracurricular activities, interview, talent/ability, volunteer work. *Other factors considered include:* Alumni/ae relation, first generation, geographical residence, level of applicant's interest, racial/ethnic status, work experience. ACT with writing component recommended. TOEFL required of all international applicants. High school diploma is required, and GED is accepted. *Academic units required:* 4 English, 3 mathematics, 2 science (2 science labs), 2 foreign language, 2 history, 3 academic elective. *Academic units recommended:* 4 English, 4 mathematics, 3 science (3 science labs), 4 foreign language, 2 social studies, 2 history, 1 academic elective.

Financial Aid

Students should submit: FAFSA, institution's own financial aid form, CSS/Financial Aid PROFILE. Regular filing deadline is February 15. The Princeton Review suggests that all financial aid forms be submitted as soon as possible after January 1. *Need-based scholarships/grants offered:* Federal Pell, SEOG, state scholarships/grants, private scholarships, school scholarship or grant aid from institutional funds, United Negro College Fund. *Loan aid offered:* Direct Subsidized Stafford, Direct Unsubsidized Stafford, Direct PLUS, Federal Perkins. Applicants will be notified of awards on a rolling basis beginning in late March. Federal Work-Study Program available. Off-campus job opportunities are excellent.

The Inside Word

Muhlenberg College accepts only the Common Application and doesn't require any supplemental essays, unless you're applying early decision. Muhlenberg is also part of a growing group of colleges that don't require SAT scores or other standardized tests for admission. Students who don't submit test scores are required to appear for an admissions interview and to submit a graded essay from their junior or senior year in high school.

THE SCHOOL SAYS "..."

From the Admissions Office

"Listening to our own students, we've learned that most picked Muhlenberg mainly because it has a long-standing reputation for being academically demanding on one hand but personally supportive on the other. We expect a lot from our students, but we also expect a lot from ourselves in providing the challenge and support they need to stretch, grow, and succeed. It's not unusual for professors to put their home phone numbers on the course syllabus and encourage students to call them at home with questions. Upperclassmen are helpful to underclassmen. 'We really know about collegiality here,' says an alumna who now works at Muhlenberg. 'It's that kind of place.' The supportive atmosphere and strong work ethic produce lots of successes. The premed and pre-law programs are very strong, as are programs in theater arts, English, psychology, the sciences, business, and accounting. 'When I was a student here,' recalls Dr. Walter Loy, now a professor emeritus of physics, 'we were encouraged to live life to its fullest, to do our best, to be honest, to deal openly with others, and to treat everyone as an individual. Those are important things, and they haven't changed at Muhlenberg.'

"Students have the option of submitting SAT or ACT scores (including the writing sections) or submitting a graded paper with teacher's comments and grade on it from junior or senior year and interviewing with a member of the admissions staff."

SELECTIVITY

Admissions Rating	91
# of applicants	4,568
% of applicants accepted	48
% of acceptees attending	27
# accepting a place on wait list	374
% admitted from wait list	16
# of early decision applicants	392
% accepted early decision	79

FRESHMAN PROFILE

Range SAT Critical Reading	560–670
Range SAT Math	560–670
Range SAT Writing	560–670
Range ACT Composite	24–30
Minimum paper TOEFL	550
Minimum computer TOEFL	213
Minimum web-based TOEFL	79
Average HS GPA	3.30
% graduated top 10% of class	47
% graduated top 25% of class	80
% graduated top 50% of class	95

DEADLINES

Early decision	
Deadline	2/15
Notification	12/1
Regular	
Priority	2/15
Deadline	2/15
Notification	3/15
Nonfall registration?	yes

APPLICANTS ALSO LOOK AT

AND OFTEN PREFER
Bucknell University, Lafayette College, Lehigh University, Villanova University

AND SOMETIMES PREFER
Dickinson College, Franklin & Marshall College, Gettysburg College, Skidmore College, The College of New Jersey, University of Delaware, Ursinus College

AND RARELY PREFER
Drew University, Goucher College, Ithaca College, Penn State—University Park, Susquehanna University

FINANCIAL FACTS

Financial Aid Rating	92
Annual tuition	$38,380
Room and board	$9,185
% frosh rec. need-based scholarship or grant aid	49
% UG rec. need-based scholarship or grant aid	47
% frosh rec. non-need-based scholarship or grant aid	23
% UG rec. non-need-based scholarship or grant aid	22
% frosh rec. need-based self-help aid	32
% UG rec. need-based self-help aid	36
% frosh rec. any financial aid	80
% UG rec. any financial aid	79
% UG borrow to pay for school	63
Average cumulative indebtedness	$23,004

NATIONAL UNIVERSITY OF IRELAND MAYNOOTH

NATIONAL UNIVERSITY OF IRELAND, MAYNOOTH, CO. KILDARE, IRELAND • ADMISSIONS: +353-1-7086000 • FAX: +353-1-6289063

CAMPUS LIFE

Quality of Life Rating	89
Fire Safety Rating	60*
Green Rating	60*
Type of school	international
Environment	town

STUDENTS

Total undergrad enrollment	8,400
% male/female	50/50
% live on campus	11
# clubs and societies	>150
% international	9
# of countries represented	>50

SURVEY SAYS . . .

Students are happy
Lab facilities are great
Great library
Students are friendly
Great off-campus food
Campus feels safe
Athletic facilities are great
Lots of beer drinking

ACADEMICS

Academic Rating	60*
% students graduating	
within 4 years	90
Calendar	semester
Student/faculty ratio	25:1
Profs interesting rating	83
Profs accessible rating	80
Most common	
reg class size	20–29 students
Most common	
lab size	10–19 students

MOST POPULAR MAJORS

business, accounting and finance,
biology and biomedical sciences,
psychology, social science, music
technology, media studies

STUDENTS SAY ". . ."

Academics

In emerald Ireland, just outside of Dublin, there lies the country's second-oldest and fastest growing university, the National University of Ireland Maynooth. The school's town location and its relatively small size give off a "community atmosphere," and "modern and up-to-date" facilities and a "beautiful campus" make it "a nice environment to study in" with a "great history" to back it up. "The academic standard at Maynooth is impeccable, with lecturers, lecture halls, tutors, and labs of the finest stature," says a science major. There's a wide selection of classes available at Maynooth, and course content "is generally well-explained, with tutorials and support centers available." Professors "are without exception experts in their field" and "continually encouraging us to engage in discussions, to ask questions, and to develop not only a well-informed but independent way of thinking." "Almost all my lecturers are great orators that bring their subjects to life, creating a genuine interest among their students," says a Spanish major. Add to that the fact that they're "very, very, very approachable outside of class" ("There is always someone that you can approach for help and guidance"), and students are happy to receive "the best learning experience possible." Administration is responsive to student concerns, and there's a "friendliness of everyone on campus, from the president right down to the cleaners." The services the school provides are all "brilliant," from the library to the residence services. People also all love the "great" online class system, Moodle, which allows you to upload assignments and download class notes. "You are given every little or big piece of help you require or request to ensure you can achieve your highest grades," says a student. "In my six months here, I have yet to hear a disgruntled word aimed at the campus or the staff."

Life

Maynooth is a "very vibrant town" that "has all facilities needed by third-level students (including clubs, pubs, and pizzerias)." The student body "isn't too big," and the majority "keep on top of college work, participate in a club or society or two, and enjoy a night in the pub with their friends." There's a "vast amount" of clubs and societies, which means "there's always somewhere for you to go, whether it's the Play-Doh society or the Harry Potter appreciation society—we got it all!" The student union also "hosts concerts and social events regularly," and everyone enjoys the "good mood" of their compatriots. "For fun, the nightlife is key," and "every Wednesday and Thursday [are] party nights," when people go to the nightclubs or bars, play card games, drink beers, and "hang out with…mates." The school consists of two connected campuses, which "combine the old with the new." "South campus covered in snow is like a scene from Hogwarts in Harry Potter, [and] then "the north campus is modern." For those who live on campus, "Everything is just at your fingertips," including a free gym. Though there are "few facilities in the university for simply sitting and studying," there are plenty of computers for students, and a new cafeteria is under construction.

Student Body

Look around Maynooth, and for the most part you'll just see a whole bunch of "your normal average twenty-year-old Irish girl [or] boy," though there's "a great mix of both city students and those from a rural background," as well as international, traditional, and "mature" students. "Individuality is very much encouraged" here, and in the midst of this "bubbly," "friendly" group is "a good place to make new friends." "Being Irish, we all like to have the 'craic' with people, meaning have fun," says a student. This group is also very "trustworthy," and "You can leave your laptop in the library for hours, and no one would ever take it."

NATIONAL UNIVERSITY OF IRELAND, MAYNOOTH

E-MAIL: ADMISSIONS@NUIM.IE • WEBSITE: WWW.NUIM.IE

THE PRINCETON REVIEW SAYS

Admissions

Very important factors considered include: Academic GPA, rigor of secondary school record, standardized test scores, character/personal qualities, talent/ability. *Important factors considered include:* Extracurricular activities, volunteer work, work experience. *Other factors considered include:* Level of applicant's interest, recommendation(s). High school diploma is required, and GED is accepted. SAT or ACT results are required from all U.S. applicants. Evidence of classes/tests taken in subject area relevant to chosen major is recommended. *Academic units required:* Depends on the student's chosen degree program. Academic requirements for each course can be found at www.nuim.ie/courses/. The deadline for application is August 1 of the year of entry. Early action students can apply up to one year in advance of entry. Notification of acceptance is on a rolling basis beginning November 1 of the year before entry.

Financial Aid

Students should submit: FAFSA. Regular filing deadline is June 1. The Princeton Review suggests that all financial aid forms be submitted as soon as possible after January 1. *Need-based scholarships/grants offered:* Private scholarships, school scholarship or grant aid from institutional funds. *Loan aid offered:* Direct Subsidized Stafford, Direct Unsubsidized Stafford, Direct PLUS. Applicants will be notified of awards on a rolling basis beginning March 1, with the condition that the student has received an offer of a place at the university.

THE SCHOOL SAYS "..."

From the Admissions Office

"National University of Ireland Maynooth is pleased to be one of the few international universities to be included in The Princeton Review Best Colleges series. You do not require a visa to study in Ireland if you are a U.S. citizen, and the fees for National University of Ireland Maynooth are comparable to most in-state tuition fees in the U.S. So, for the price of your flights, you could get an international university experience for nearly the same price as staying at home!

"Degrees awarded by Irish Universities are internationally recognized as being of high quality. Irish universities do not have a general education requirement, which means that students begin studying their chosen major immediately. Due to this, degrees in the Arts and Humanities will be completed in three years, while Science and Engineering degrees will be completed in four years. Students registered on undergraduate degrees at NUIM can also apply to study abroad in their third year, in Europe, Asia, South America, or Australia. This extends your degree by one year, and you will earn a Bachelor (International) degree.

"The International Office offers full support to all international students during the application process and once you arrive on campus. National University of Ireland Maynooth is very popular with U.S. students studying in Ireland and the campus is known as one of the friendliest in Ireland, so you will receive a warm welcome. If you have questions about studying at NUIM, contact the International Office at any time."

SELECTIVITY

Admissions Rating	60*
# of applicants	3,712
% of applicants accepted	54
% of acceptees attending	49

FRESHMAN PROFILE

Minimum SAT Composite	2400
Minimum IELTS	6
Minimum computer TOEFL	220
Minimum web-based TOEFL	80
Average HS GPA	3.50
Minimum HS GPA	3.00

DEADLINES

Regular	
Deadline	8/1
Notification	rolling
Nonfall registration?	no

FINANCIAL FACTS

Financial Aid Rating	60*
Annual tuition	
Arts and Humanities	€11,500/
	$16,300*
Social Sciences	€12,500/
	$17,700
Science and Engineering	€14,500/
	$20,600*
Room	€3,500–€4,200/
	$5,000–$6,000*
Average cumulative indebtedness	$12,297

* Fees and room rates are guidelines. Dollar amounts are subject to currency exchange rate fluctuation. To obtain an accurate quote for specific course fees, visit www.nuim.ie/international. Room rates don't include any meal plans. All on-campus accommodation is in the format of apartments. Each apartment contains four to five private/twin bedrooms with shared kitchen facilities and living space.

NAZARETH COLLEGE

4245 EAST AVENUE, ROCHESTER NY 14618 • ADMISSIONS: 800-462-3944 OR 585-389-2860• FAX: 585-389-2826

CAMPUS LIFE

Quality of Life Rating	90
Fire Safety Rating	61
Green Rating	60*
Type of school	private
Environment	village

STUDENTS

Total undergrad enrollment	2,144
% male/female	24/76
% from out of state	6
% from public high school	90
% live on campus	53
% African American	5
% Asian	2
% Caucasian	83
% Hispanic	3
% international	1
# of countries represented	13

SURVEY SAYS . . .

Students are friendly
Students get along with local community
Students love Rochester, NY
Great off-campus food
Frats and sororities are unpopular or nonexistent
Musical organizations are popular
Theater is popular

ACADEMICS

Academic Rating	84
% students graduating within 4 years	60
% students graduating within 6 years	72
Calendar	semester
Student/faculty ratio	12:1
Profs interesting rating	89
Profs accessible rating	86
Most common reg class size	10–19 students
Most common lab size	10–19 students

MOST POPULAR MAJORS
business, education, physical therapy

STUDENTS SAY ". . ."

Academics

Nazareth College "is a small liberal arts school located in a great suburb of Rochester" that offers "a great atmosphere to learn and grow as an individual and as a professional." The college has "a high focus on education," is known for an "outstanding" music program, and is made up of "a community full of ambitious and serious learners." Students say, "Nazareth is a close community of students and faculty working together to pursue positive educational experiences," and "Class sizes are small, which helps students to get the attention [they] need." Professors get high marks for being "very flexible and understanding," and students say they "The professors know their material, and they all want you to succeed so they give you all the tools necessary to do so." A social work major says, "The professors at Naz are great. They take the time to help you in and outside of class," and another student adds, "The professors here are passionate, interested, funny, and accessible. The lack of pretension is palpable." However, a sophomore notes, "Professors are people too, and they are allowed to be as varied and diverse as we students are," and another concurs: "My professors, just like professors from any other college, vary drastically in my book."

Life

Nazareth College offers "a small close-knit community" on an "intimate campus," where "there is a general tone of friendliness and politeness amongst students, faculty, and staff." Students say, "Nazareth is a beautiful school with many opportunities," and "The greatest strength is the sense of community. Everyone looks out for everyone else." There are "many activities on campus and a wide range of clubs," and students say, "There is always something happening on campus whether it's a program by an RA or an event in the Arts Center open to the community." Nazareth is good at "reaching out to the student population," and students say, "The students are full of school spirit and the campus is a very safe environment to be living in." A junior says, "The school provides a ton of extracurricular activities to participate in," and another student adds, "Student life is wonderful and service opportunities are always available." Students are grateful for the "underground tunnels" during the cold winter months, and "Security is great." Some complain, "Technology programs could be improved to work more efficiently and reliably," and "The residential facilities and faculties could improve on the efficiency and quality of services provided." Almost everyone gripes that the "food could use some improvement," but raves that "free parking and free laundry are great."

Student Body

At Nazareth, "The student body is friendly and spirited" and "dedicated to balancing work and play." Students say they "care about their education, but are not overly studious—they want to have fun as well." Most students are "middle-class white women," and a sophomore says, "I think I speak for the majority of the girls on campus when I say: men. We need more men on campus." There's an active community of gay men, and a sophomore says, "Everyone has their groups: There are jocks, music majors, etc., but people mingle between groups a lot." Students say they know "when it's time to study and when it's time to relax or have fun," and "people like to go to mixers and hang out." A music education major says, "There are two types of people on campus: partiers and non-partiers," but another adds, "I like how at Nazareth if you are into partying/drinking or if you are not there is always someone to hang out with or something to do on the weekend." Students say, "Weekends at Nazareth are always the same, but with Rochester being so close it is easy to find something to do," and "There are also many activities such as mixers and movie nights on weekends for people who are not into partying."

FINANCIAL AID: 585-389-2310 • E-MAIL: ADMISSIONS@NAZ.EDU • WEBSITE: WWW.NAZ.EDU

THE PRINCETON REVIEW SAYS
Admissions
Very important factors considered include: Academic GPA, application essay, class rank, recommendation(s), rigor of secondary school record, geographical residence. *Important factors considered include:* Character/personal qualities, extra-curricular activities, geographical residence, interview, level of applicant's interest, racial/ethnic status, state residency, talent/ability, volunteer work, work experience. *Other factors considered include:* Standardized test scores, alumni/ae relation, first generation. ACT with or without writing component accepted. TOEFL required of all international applicants. High school diploma is required, and GED is accepted. *Academic units required:* 4 English, 3 mathematics, 3 science (2 science labs), 3 foreign language, 3 social studies. *Academic units recommended:* 4 English, 4 mathematics, 4 science, 4 foreign language, 4 social studies.

Financial Aid
Students should submit: FAFSA. Regular filing deadline is May 1. The Princeton Review suggests that all financial aid forms be submitted as soon as possible after January 1. *Need-based scholarships/grants offered:* Federal Pell, SEOG, state scholarships/grants, private scholarships, school scholarship or grant aid from institutional funds. *Loan aid offered:* Direct Subsidized Stafford, Direct Unsubsidized Stafford, Direct PLUS, Federal Perkins. Applicants will be notified of awards on a rolling basis beginning February 20. Federal Work-Study Program available. Off-campus job opportunities are excellent.

The Inside Word
The admissions staff at Nazareth College gives primary consideration to secondary school academic achievement but also sees talent in the arts and co-curricular activities as enhancements to an application. Applicants to the art, theater, and music programs are required to schedule and an audition or portfolio review. Prospective students aren't required to submit standardized test scores.

THE SCHOOL SAYS "..."
From the Admissions Office
"Growing interest in Nazareth—applications have grown twenty-five percent in five years—is a result of many factors. New facilities have increased and improved academic, performing arts, residential, and athletic spaces. Major offerings now include music/business, international business, communication and rhetoric, and music theatre. Nazareth has worked diligently to keep tuition at $5,000 less than the New York State average for private colleges. Our track record is strong—retention and graduation rates exceed national averages; seventy-five percent of our students participate in a career-related internship with ninety-three percent of them citing this a very worthwhile experience; and ninety-three percent of our students are employed or in graduate school within one year of graduation. The College has produced twelve Fulbright scholars and six faculty Fulbrights, in the past decade alone, along with two Thomas R. Pickering Graduate Foreign Affairs Fellowships. The Center for International Education has developed more opportunities for our students to study abroad and for international students to study at Nazareth. With civic engagement and service learning as hallmarks of the Nazareth experience, ninety-one percent of undergrads participate in community service while at Nazareth. A proactive approach to campus security and state-of-the-art emergency notification system places Nazareth ahead of the curve regarding student safety. Student athletes, veterans of conference and national championships, have one of the highest graduation rates among NCAA Division III institutions. The Nazareth College Arts Center brings an international roster of performing art companies to campus, and provides high-quality facilities for student productions."

SELECTIVITY
Admissions Rating	84
# of applicants	2,181
% of applicants accepted	74
% of acceptees attending	29
# accepting a place on wait list	28
% admitted from wait list	82
# of early decision applicants	45
% accepted early decision	91

FRESHMAN PROFILE
Range SAT Critical Reading	530–630
Range SAT Math	530–630
Range SAT Writing	510–610
Range ACT Composite	23–27
Minimum paper TOEFL	550
Minimum computer TOEFL	213
Minimum web-based TOEFL	79
Average HS GPA	3.30
% graduated top 10% of class	30
% graduated top 25% of class	67
% graduated top 50% of class	91

DEADLINES
Early decision	
Deadline	11/15
Notification	12/15
Early action	
Deadline	12/15
Notification	1/15
Regular	
Priority	12/15
Deadline	2/15
Nonfall registration?	yes

FINANCIAL FACTS
Financial Aid Rating	77
Annual tuition	$25,046
Room and board	$9,800
Required fees	$1,000
% frosh rec. need-based scholarship or grant aid	78
% UG rec. need-based scholarship or grant aid	79
% frosh rec. non-need-based scholarship or grant aid	10
% UG rec. non-need-based scholarship or grant aid	9
% frosh rec. need-based self-help aid	66
% UG rec. need-based self-help aid	67
% UG borrow to pay for school	78
Average cumulative indebtedness	$26,711

NEW COLLEGE OF FLORIDA

5800 BAY SHORE ROAD, SARASOTA, FL 34243-2109 • ADMISSIONS: 941-487-5000 • FAX: 941-487-5010

CAMPUS LIFE

Quality of Life Rating	80
Fire Safety Rating	82
Green Rating	74
Type of school	public
Environment	town

STUDENTS

Total undergrad enrollment	801
% male/female	40/60
% from out of state	20
% from public high school	80
% live on campus	76
% African American	1
% Asian	3
% Caucasian	76
% Hispanic	13
# of countries represented	22

SURVEY SAYS . . .

Lots of liberal students
No one cheats
Students are friendly
Students aren't religious
Dorms are like palaces
Campus feels safe
Intercollegiate sports are unpopular
or nonexistent
Frats and sororities are unpopular
or nonexistent
Student government is popular
Political activism is popular

ACADEMICS

Academic Rating	94
% students graduating within 4 years	57
% students graduating within 6 years	68
Calendar	4-1-4
Student/faculty ratio	10:1
Profs interesting rating	98
Profs accessible rating	89
Most common reg class size	10–19 students

MOST POPULAR MAJORS
biology, economics, psychology

STUDENTS SAY "..."

Academics

New College of Florida, a uniquely small and unconventional public institution, "provides challenging courses for highly self-motivated students who want a large amount of control over their academic choices." It's all about "self-directed learning" here ("the student decides what she is going to learn and how she is going to learn it") that leaves undergrads "free to do what they please—with their bodies, their studies, their behavior—but while also being held to high academic standards." Those who can balance the intellectual freedom NCF offers with the academic accountability it demands, wind up with "a rounded education that enables them to critically and pragmatically examine and understand the world in which we live…and weird parties." The academics "are undeniably awesome" at NCF, while the small-school setting and the student body "encourage a love of learning, whether it be academic, political, or hobby-related." It's the sort of school where "it is very popular for groups of students to get together to talk about class readings outside of the classroom, usually at the college coffee shop, as a means of socializing." NCF undergrads receive "narrative evaluations instead of grades. These evaluations give advice and help us to become better students." Many here "love having written evaluations in which our process and progress are documented, not only the final outcome. The evaluations force students to fully participate and the professors to pay close attention." All students must write a senior thesis to graduate; reports one undergrad, "recently we had a survey…on which one of the sections dealt with the possibility of making the senior thesis optional. There was an overwhelming response that this was unacceptable. I think that says a lot about how proud we are of our academic standards."

Life

Having fun "in a glorified retirement community requires ingenuity of the New College student population," but "thankfully, most grew up in suburban Florida" and so are used to a slower pace It helps that the campus is near Lido Beach, "where [students] enjoy unlimited swimming, sunning, and Frisbee playing," and that "downtown Sarasota isn't that bad either," since it's home to a number of "ethnic eateries. Thai food, in particular, seems to have a strange cult following on campus—constant debate as to which restaurant is the best or most authentic and student events that advertise Thai food are bound to pull in dozens of followers." On campus, students enjoy everything "from club meetings to public speakers to 'hip' bands playing shows. There's usually something to do and usually free food to be found!" There are also "school-wide parties every Friday and Saturday night in a courtyard outside of the dorms. Different students get to decide the theme of each dance party and the music to be played. Most on-campus students never leave campus during the weekend because of these dance parties."

Student Body

New College students share "a few things in common: Most…are friendly, passionate about the things they believe in, very hard workers, liberal, and most of all, try to be open to new experiences." They're "largely middle-class, white, and liberal. There are of course exceptions, but the school is rather small,'" there is "a fairly strong queer community here, and many transgendered people who have decided to make New College their coming-out grounds. The student body is generally aware of gender issues and respectful of queer people of all types." There are even "some Republicans on campus. Maybe four. I'm not sure. We're not the type of school that generally attracts heavy right-wingers."

FINANCIAL AID: 941-487-5001 • E-MAIL: ADMISSIONS@NCF.EDU • WEBSITE: WWW.NCF.EDU

THE PRINCETON REVIEW SAYS

Admissions

Very important factors considered include: Academic GPA, application essay, rigor of secondary school record. *Important factors considered include:* Recommendation(s), standardized test scores, character/personal qualities. *Other factors considered include:* Class rank, alumni/ae relation, extracurricular activities, first generation, geographical residence, interview, level of applicant's interest, state residency, talent/ability, volunteer work, work experience. SAT or ACT required; ACT with writing component required. TOEFL required of all international applicants. High school diploma is required, and GED is accepted. *Academic units required:* 4 English, 4 mathematics, 3 science (2 science labs), 2 foreign language, 3 social studies, 2 academic elective. *Academic units recommended:* 4 English, 4 mathematics, 4 science (2 science labs), 4 foreign language, 4 social studies, 4 academic elective.

Financial Aid

Students should submit: FAFSA. Regular filing deadline is March 1. The Princeton Review suggests that all financial aid forms be submitted as soon as possible after January 1. *Need-based scholarships/grants offered:* Federal Pell, SEOG, state scholarships/grants, private scholarships, school scholarship or grant aid from institutional funds. *Loan aid offered:* Direct Subsidized Stafford, Direct Unsubsidized Stafford, Direct PLUS. Applicants will be notified of awards on a rolling basis beginning October 1. Federal Work-Study Program available. Off-campus job opportunities are good.

The Inside Word

New College isn't your typical public school. The tiny student body allows admissions officers here to review each application carefully; expect a thorough going over of your essays, recommendations, and extracurricular activities. Iconoclastic students tend to thrive here, and the admissions staff knows that. Don't be afraid to let your freak flag fly; it won't get you in here if your academics aren't top flight, but it certainly won't hurt you either.

THE SCHOOL SAYS " . . ."

From the Admissions Office

"Inspired individualism, with a dash of quirkiness, best describes New College of Florida and its students. At New College, you participate directly in your education by collaborating with faculty to develop an individualized program of classes, seminars, independent research projects, and off-campus experiences designed to meet your personal academic interests and needs. As a result, you receive the high-quality, personalized education of a top-tier private college yet at the affordable cost of a public university. If you are independent, open-minded, and welcome the challenge of a rigorous academic program matched with a relaxed social environment, then New College may be the perfect fit for you.

"Students applying must submit scores from the SAT (or ACT) with the writing section). We will use the student's best scores from either test."

SELECTIVITY

Admissions Rating	94
# of applicants	1,414
% of applicants accepted	53
% of acceptees attending	24
# accepting a place on wait list	56
% admitted from wait list	39

FRESHMAN PROFILE

Range SAT Critical Reading	640–740
Range SAT Math	580–670
Range SAT Writing	600–690
Range ACT Composite	27–31
Minimum paper TOEFL	560
Minimum computer TOEFL	220
Minimum web-based TOEFL	83
Average HS GPA	4.03
% graduated top 10% of class	50
% graduated top 25% of class	80
% graduated top 50% of class	94

DEADLINES

Regular	
Priority	2/15
Deadline	4/15
Nonfall registration?	yes

APPLICANTS ALSO LOOK AT
AND OFTEN PREFER
Lewis & Clark College, Smith College, University of Central Florida, University of Miami, University of South Florida, Vanderbilt University, Wellesley College

AND SOMETIMES PREFER
Columbia University, Oberlin College, Pitzer College, Reed College, University of North Carolina at Chapel Hill, University of Tampa

AND RARELY PREFER
Vassar College, Warren Wilson College, Yale University

FINANCIAL FACTS

Financial Aid Rating	92
Annual in-state tuition	$6,032
Annual out-of-state tuition	$28,949
Room and board	$8,472
Books and supplies	$800
% frosh rec. need-based scholarship or grant aid	51
% UG rec. need-based scholarship or grant aid	51
% frosh rec. non-need-based scholarship or grant aid	8
% UG rec. non-need-based scholarship or grant aid	4
% frosh rec. need-based self-help aid	43
% UG rec. need-based self-help aid	45
% frosh rec. any financial aid	100
% UG rec. any financial aid	97
% UG borrow to pay for school	36
Average cumulative indebtedness	$11,458

NEW JERSEY INSTITUTE OF TECHNOLOGY

UNIVERSITY HEIGHTS, NEWARK, NJ 07102 • ADMISSIONS: 973-596-3300 • FAX: 973-596-3461

CAMPUS LIFE

Quality of Life Rating	62
Fire Safety Rating	93
Green Rating	80
Type of school	public
Environment	metropolis

STUDENTS

Total undergrad enrollment	5,737
% male/female	79/21
% from out of state	6
% from public high school	85
% live on campus	25
# of fraternities	15
# of sororities	7
% African American	1
% Asian	15
% Caucasian	37
% Hispanic	8
% Native American	1
% international	19
# of countries represented	83

SURVEY SAYS . . .
Diverse student types on campus
Low cost of living
Very little drug use

ACADEMICS

Academic Rating	70
% students graduating within 4 years	19
% students graduating within 6 years	55
Calendar	semester
Student/faculty ratio	15:1
Profs interesting rating	67
Profs accessible rating	66
Most common reg class size	20–29 students

MOST POPULAR MAJORS
civil engineering, mechanical engineering

STUDENTS SAY ". . ."

Academics
Mathematics, science, technology, and architecture offerings all shine at New Jersey Institute of Technology. The school is a "leader in the field of technology in the tristate area" whose public school pricing allows students to "graduate without the bank owning our first-borns, which is a definite plus," says a student. As is the case at many prestigious tech-oriented schools, "The professors are generally hired for research rather than teaching ability, [so] there are some who cannot teach, and they aren't that great at grading assignments or handing back papers either." The demanding undergraduate curriculum means "you have to be serious about studies if you are choosing NJIT. There is no time for fun and games." Students groan about the demands made on them but also recognize the benefits. "NJIT is an intense academic university that allows students to be prepared for the working world," explains one architect. Another plus of studying at NJIT is "how well the students interact, especially during exam time. Seniors help juniors, who help sophomores, who help freshman. It's helpful when someone who has taken the courses you're taking at the moment can put things into perspective and give you hints about what may be on the test."

Life
NJIT is "not the best school socially, but few engineering schools are," students concede. Since "a lot of classes give amazing amounts of homework, it is hard to have a normal social life. Most nights are spent doing homework late, then getting a few hours of fun before passing out." Extracurricular life has improved recently with the addition of new recreation facilities; one student notes, "The game room has been improved, with pool tables, bowling, and arcades, and a much-needed pub on campus." NJIT also boasts "a pretty good gym to work out in, and a brand-new soccer field." Undergrads note optimistically that "our team sports are all performing better, and the students are starting to feel a sense of competition building. There are plenty of parties on Thursday nights on campus, organized by frats or clubs," and, of course, "possibilities are endless because New York City is minutes away." Affordable public transportation opens the door to "major league sports, world-class museums, and theater." Hometown Newark, although much maligned by students and locals, offers "great food and restaurants less than half a mile away from campus, in the Ironbound section." Students do appreciate how the "small classes and campus make a 'small-town' atmosphere during the semester," though offset against the school's urban environs.

Student Body
"There are two types of students at NJIT," writes one undergrad, elaborating: "The first are the ones who are involved with athletics, clubs, organizations, and other things. The others are the antisocial ones. These people stay in their dorms and play computer games all day." How many of each category populate this campus? One student offers some pertinent data: "Class attendance dropped thirty-two percent the day *Halo 2* came out." Like the region surrounding it, "NJIT is a total melting pot; the mix of ethnic backgrounds of students is diverse." Because of curricular demands, "Everyone is pretty smart. But you also have the very smart people." When asked in what ways his school could stand to improve, one succinct information technology student wrote "girls!" reflecting a sentiment running through much of the student body. The male/female ratio is about four to one.

NEW JERSEY INSTITUTE OF TECHNOLOGY

FINANCIAL AID: 973-596-3480 • E-MAIL: ADMISSIONS@NJIT.EDU • WEBSITE: WWW.NJIT.EDU

THE PRINCETON REVIEW SAYS

Admissions

Very important factors considered include: Class rank, rigor of secondary school record, standardized test scores. *Important factors considered include:* Academic GPA. *Other factors considered include:* Application essay, recommendation(s), alumni/ae relation, character/personal qualities, extracurricular activities, geographical residence, interview, level of applicant's interest, racial/ethnic status, religious affiliation/commitment, state residence. SAT or ACT required. TOEFL required of all international applicants. High school diploma is required, and GED is accepted. *Academic units required:* 4 English, 4 mathematics, 2 science (2 science labs). *Academic units recommended:* 2 foreign language, 1 social studies, 1 history, 2 academic elective.

Financial Aid

The Princeton Review suggests that all financial aid forms be submitted as soon as possible after January 1. Federal Work-Study Program available. Off-campus job opportunities are good.

The Inside Word

NJIT is a great choice for students who aspire to technical careers but don't meet the requirements for better known and more selective universities. To top it off, it's a pretty good buy.

THE SCHOOL SAYS ". . ."

From the Admissions Office

"Talented high school graduates from across the nation come to NJIT to prepare for leadership roles in architecture, business, engineering, medical, legal, science, and technological fields. Students experience a public research university conducting nearly $90 million in research that maintains a small-college atmosphere at a modest cost. Our attractive forty-five-acre campus is just minutes from New York City and less than an hour from the Jersey shore. Students find an outstanding faculty and a safe, diverse, and caring learning and residential community. NJIT's academic environment challenges and prepares students for rewarding careers and full-time advanced study after graduation. The campus is computing-intensive. NJIT is a Top 50 Best Value College, according to The Princeton Review

"Students applying for admission to NJIT may provide scores from either the SAT or the ACT. writing sample scores will not be used for admission purposes, but are used for placement in first-year courses. SAT Subject Test scores are not required for any major."

SELECTIVITY

Admissions Rating	74
# of applicants	4,398
% of applicants accepted	67
% of acceptees attending	32
# accepting a place on wait list	220
% admitted from wait list	27

FRESHMAN PROFILE

Range SAT Critical Reading	470–590
Range SAT Math	540–650
Range SAT Writing	460–570
Minimum paper TOEFL	550
Minimum computer TOEFL	213
Minimum web-based TOEFL	79
% graduated top 10% of class	27
% graduated top 25% of class	55
% graduated top 50% of class	84

DEADLINES

Regular	
Deadline	4/1
Notification	11/15
Nonfall registration?	yes

APPLICANTS ALSO LOOK AT AND OFTEN PREFER

Drexel University, Rensselaer Polytechnic Institute, Rutgers, The State University of New Jersey, The College of New Jersey

AND SOMETIMES PREFER

Penn State—University Park, Stevens Institute of Technology, Virginia Tech, Worcester Polytechnic Institute

FINANCIAL FACTS

Financial Aid Rating	72
Annual in-state tuition	$11,248
Annual out-of-state tuition	$21,800
Books and supplies	$2,700

NEW YORK UNIVERSITY

50 WEST 4TH ST., NEW YORK, NY 10012 • ADMISSIONS: 212-998-4500 • FAX: 212-995-4902

CAMPUS LIFE

Quality of Life Rating	83
Fire Safety Rating	89
Green Rating	96
Type of school	private
Environment	metropolis

STUDENTS

Total undergrad enrollment	22,097
% male/female	39/61
% from out of state	65
% from public high school	65
% live on campus	48
# of fraternities	16
# of sororities	9
% African American	4
% Asian	20
% Caucasian	44
% Hispanic	8
% international	9
# of countries represented	129

SURVEY SAYS . . .
Lots of liberal students
Students love New York, NY
Great off-campus food
*Intercollegiate sports are unpopular
or nonexistent*
*Frats and sororities are unpopular
or nonexistent*

ACADEMICS

Academic Rating	77
% students graduating within 4 years	78
% students graduating within 6 years	85
Calendar	semester
Student/faculty ratio	11:1
Profs interesting rating	78
Profs accessible rating	71
Most common reg class size	10–19 students
Most common lab size	10–19 students

MOST POPULAR MAJORS
drama and dramatics/theatre arts,
finance, liberal arts and sciences

STUDENTS SAY ". . ."

Academics
"Location, location, location" in "the most amazing city on earth," along with "great facilities" and "top-notch faculty," makes New York University an excellent choice for those seeking "an untraditional college experience" in "a paradise for the independent and motivated." With more than 20,000 students and eleven distinct schools offering more than 230 areas of study, NYU "is about diversity. Students are from all over the world; they come from different cultures, and they have different talents and interests. Similarly, NYU offers endless opportunities for students, no matter what their interests or ambitions are." The school offers voluminous opportunities to participate in research, pursue an internship, or begin a career in the arts (although "you have to be active and willing to find these opportunities"). Given the school's size, many students are "actually quite surprised by the accessibility of both the faculty and administration." Although "this is not the kind of school where students really get to know all of their teachers, as it is unlikely that a student will have a professor more than once," those who make the effort report that "It is so easy to meet with [professors] outside of class, and I still get e-mails from professors about internships, jobs, and scholarship recommendations." Many here also tout the "great study abroad programs."

Life
"Living in New York City is the biggest part of going to school at New York University," NYU students agree. The school's New York City campus is located in the heart of Greenwich Village, one of the city's major nightlife destinations, so "there is always something to do at any hour of the day," usually within walking distance of the school. One student reports, "Every weekend there are tons of things to do, both at NYU and in New York City. NYU really takes advantage of its location, so a lot of the programming provided by residence life or the student resource center is engaging you in the city that has become your new home." Living in the Big Apple means that "On any given day you can go to a museum, concert, sporting event, or theater performance…and a lot of the times, NYU will foot the bill if you go to an event in the city with your RA or with a club." The location also provides plenty of internship opportunities, which is good because "The vast majority of students at NYU are interested in interning and finding jobs through that gateway." The school has no campus per se; it surrounds Washington Square Park, a busy public square where students love to relax when the weather is accommodating.

Student Body
"There is no typical student at NYU," where an undergraduate student body of more than 20,000 and a broad range of academic interests ensure a broad demographic. "Each school at NYU attracts a different group," students tell us. "The Tisch School of the Arts attracts a very out-there group of actors and the like," while the Stern Business School "has a massive population of Asians and Indians." "Hipsters are pretty pervasive throghout all schools except Stern," although "every school has people who break those stereotypes. [Even so,] few students can find ways to not fit in because of the huge number of students" at the university. Throughout NYU, "Students tend to be incredibly motivated and ambitious." Students insist that "it is also important to note that NYU students are very accepting of each other's differences," an important factor at a school that brings together "students of all different backgrounds, ethnicities, and gender identities and makes them coexist within the university."

NEW YORK UNIVERSITY

FINANCIAL AID: 212-998-4444 • WEBSITE: WWW.NYU.EDU

THE PRINCETON REVIEW SAYS

Admissions

Very important factors considered include: Academic GPA, class rank, rigor of secondary school record, standardized test scores, talent/ability. *Important factors considered include:* Application essay, recommendation(s), character/personal qualities, extracurricular activities, volunteer work, work experience. *Other factors considered include:* Alumni/ae relation, first generation, geographical residence, racial/ethnic status. SAT or ACT flexible. All students must submit some form of standardized testing (SAT, ACT, or AP). TOEFL required of all non-native English speakers. High school diploma or GED is required. *Academic units required:* 4 English, 3 mathematics, 3 science, 2 foreign language, 4 history. *Academic units recommended:* 4 English, 4 mathematics, 4 physical science, 3 foreign language, 4 social science/history.

Financial Aid

Students should submit: FAFSA. Regular filing deadline is February 15. The Princeton Review suggests that all financial aid forms be submitted as soon as possible after January 1. *Need-based scholarships/grants offered:* Federal Pell, SEOG, state scholarships/grants, private scholarships, school scholarship or grant aid from institutional funds. *Loan aid offered:* Direct Subsidized Stafford, Direct Unsubsidized Stafford, Direct PLUS, Federal Perkins, Federal Nursing Loans. Applicants will be notified of awards on a rolling basis beginning April 1. Federal Work-Study Program available. Off-campus job opportunities are excellent.

The Inside Word

Undergraduates must apply to one of NYU's undergraduate schools and colleges: the College of Arts and Science; the Liberal Studies Program; the Stern School of Business; the College of Nursing; the Gallatin School of Individualized Study; the Silver School of Social Work; the Steinhardt School of Culture, Education, and Human Development; the Tisch School of the Arts; or the Preston Robert Tisch Center for Hospitality, Tourism, and Sports. This is different from the application process at some universities and obviously requires some forethought. Remember that this is a highly competitive university; if your application doesn't reflect a serious interest in your intended area of study, your chances of gaining admission will be diminished.

THE SCHOOL SAYS ". . ."

From the Admissions Office

"NYU is unlike any other institution of higher edu cation in the world. It is a university of micro-communities within a larger global network university with three portals of entry. The energy and resources of New York City serve as an exten sion of our Washington Square campus in the heart of Greenwich Village. NYU welcomed students to its new honors college in Abu Dhabi in fall 2010 and will open a new portal campus in Shanghai in 2012. With a staggering 4,300 course offerings and over 230 areas of study from which to choose, you can explore and develop your academic and professional interests from your first semester. NYU's intellectual climate is fostered by a faculty of world-famous scholars, researchers, and artists who teach both undergradu ate and graduate courses. To fuel its reputation as the world's first truly global network university, NYU offers ten global academic centers for study abroad—Berlin, Buenos Aires, Florence, Ghana, London, Madrid, Paris, Prague, Shanghai, and Tel Aviv, with plans for two more—in Washington, D.C., and Sydney. As a result, NYU sends more students abroad than any other American college or university."

SELECTIVITY
Admissions Rating	96
# of applicants	37,464
% of applicants accepted	38
% of acceptees attending	35
# accepting a place on wait list	1,513
% admitted from wait list	8
# of early decision applicants	2,854
% accepted early decision	39

FRESHMAN PROFILE
Range SAT Critical Reading	610–710
Range SAT Math	630–740
Range SAT Writing	620–720
Range ACT Composite	28–31
Average HS GPA	3.60
% graduated top 10% of class	61
% graduated top 25% of class	92
% graduated top 50% of class	99

DEADLINES
Early decision I	
Deadline	11/1
Notification	12/15
Early decision II	
Deadline	1/1
Notification	2/15
Regular	
Deadline	1/1
Notification	4/1
Nonfall registration?	no

FINANCIAL FACTS
Financial Aid Rating	76
Annual tuition	$37,866
Room and board	$14,668
Required fees	$2,211
% frosh rec. need-based scholarship or grant aid	54
% UG rec. need-based scholarship or grant aid	51
% UG rec. non-need-based scholarship or grant aid	1
% frosh rec. need-based self-help aid	53
% UG rec. need-based self-help aid	48
% frosh rec. any financial aid	56
% UG rec. any financial aid	53
% UG borrow to pay for school	55
Average cumulative indebtedness	$41,300

THE BEST 376 COLLEGES ■ 401

NORTH CAROLINA STATE UNIVERSITY

BOX 7103, RALEIGH, NC 27695 • ADMISSIONS: 919-515-2434 • FAX: 919-515-5039

CAMPUS LIFE

Quality of Life Rating	95
Fire Safety Rating	98
Green Rating	97
Type of school	public
Environment	metropolis

STUDENTS

Total undergrad enrollment	23,500
% male/female	57/43
% from out of state	7
% from public high school	80
% live on campus	32
# of fraternities	32
# of sororities	17
% African American	8
% Asian	5
% Caucasian	77
% Hispanic	3
% international	1
# of countries represented	117

SURVEY SAYS . . .
Lab facilities are great
Great computer facilities
Everyone loves the Wolfpack
Student publications are popular

ACADEMICS

Academic Rating	77
Calendar	semester
Student/faculty ratio	18:1
Profs interesting rating	83
Profs accessible rating	84
Most common reg class size	20–29 students
Most common lab size	20–29 students

MOST POPULAR MAJORS
biology, business administration and management, mechanical engineering

STUDENTS SAY "..."

Academics

Blending a close-knit community with a prestigious name, North Carolina State University offers "big-school opportunity with a small-school feel." The sheer number of academic options is impressive—the engineering department alone offers eighteen different majors. With "plenty of opportunities to study abroad or get an internship," as well extensive opportunities to conduct research as an undergraduate, students say "NCSU is all about developing skills in school that will help you throughout your professional career." A biochemistry student adds, "Professors are often active in research, and there are tons of opportunities for students to get involved in the exciting research that is going on here." Resources are plentiful: "If you need a computer, they've got them everywhere. If you need a camera, you can rent one." Despite the sizable student population, "The way the school is split up into colleges makes it seem less intimidating." Within the colleges, "each department is pretty tight." As one student explains, "With the 33,000-plus students who attend [the school], you wonder where they all are." NCSU professors "are smart, they are funny, and they are accessible. Above all, they love what they teach, and it shows." While "there are lots of students in most freshman lectures," students say that "Even in the larger classes, [professors] strive to engage students and keep classes interesting." More importantly, "most of the professors genuinely care about their students," and "Even the professors whose teaching abilities [are] questionable are still very approachable, friendly, and readily available to the students." Despite recent shake-ups in the administration, "Everything at North Carolina State seems to run pretty efficiently."

Life

On NCSU's outgoing and lively campus, students balance academic work with an active social calendar. While they may suffer some sleepless nights, "Everyone has their own way of making academic and social life work." From Greek life to honor societies to "tons of intramural sports," "There are multitudes of organizations and activities to participate in on campus." Boredom is not an issue: "Between theater, music, cultural events, and athletics, there's no point when the campus feels 'dead' or inactive." "Students at NCSU are really into sports," and the whole campus comes out to tailgate before football games. Students also love the "great recreational facilities and gyms on campus," which boast multiple racquetball courts and pools, among other amenities. Socially, "NCSU is a very friendly, social campus," and on the weekends "going to nightclubs is popular, as are parties," while other students like to "just hang out with friends." A cosmopolitan, medium-sized city, "Downtown Raleigh has a lot to offer, from local bands, to Broadway musicals, to art nights, and amazing food." "There are a few independent movie theaters in town, like the Rialto, which plays independent movies or local documentaries." Many students also mention the local music scene, pointing out that "Raleigh is a hoppin' and boppin' place, and there [are] always shows and concerts of every kind in the area."

Student Body

NCSU "students have a reputation for being very practical," and most are "very driven" academically. "The students [on campus] vary from Southern-born-and-raised crop science majors, to devout Muslims, to 4.0 Columbia-bound premeds, to partying fraternity boys...and sometimes all of these are combined into one." "The city student is typically a Democrat, not particularly religious, [and] very friendly. The smaller-town student is typically a religious Republican and is also very friendly." Fortunately, "people of all ethnicities and backgrounds interact seamlessly," though on the whole, "The student body is somewhat conservative compared to other schools in the area." If there's any uniting factor on campus, it's that "Everyone loves the Wolfpack...everyone is very loyal and very passionate about the school's athletic program, no matter how successful or unsuccessful it might be that year."

FINANCIAL AID: 919-515-2421 • E-MAIL: UNDERGRAD_ADMISSIONS@NCSU.EDU • WEBSITE: WWW.NCSU.EDU

THE PRINCETON REVIEW SAYS

Admissions

Very important factors considered include: Academic GPA, class rank, rigor of secondary school record, standardized test scores. *Other factors considered include:* Application essay, recommendation(s), alumni/ae relation, character/personal qualities, extracurricular activities, first generation, geographical residence, level of applicant's interest, racial/ethnic status, religious affiliation/commitment. SAT or ACT required; ACT with writing component required. TOEFL required of all international applicants. *Academic units required:* 4 English, 4 mathematics, 3 science (1 science lab), 2 foreign language, 1 social studies, 1 history, 1 academic elective. *Academic units recommended:* 4 English, 4 mathematics, 4 science (2 science labs), 2 foreign language, 1 social studies, 1 history, 4 academic elective.

Financial Aid

Students should submit: FAFSA, institution's own financial aid form. The Princeton Review suggests that all financial aid forms be submitted as soon as possible after January 1. *Need-based scholarships/grants offered:* Federal Pell, SEOG, state scholarships/grants, private scholarships, school scholarship or grant aid from institutional funds, United Negro College Fund. *Loan aid offered:* Federal Perkins, state loans, university loans from institutional funds. Applicants will be notified of awards on a rolling basis beginning April 1. Federal Work-Study Program available. Off-campus job opportunities are excellent.

The Inside Word

At North Carolina State University, the most important factor in the admissions decision is a student's high school record. Competitive applicants will have at least a B-plus average in a college preparatory curriculum. SAT or ACT scores are also considered, though the school puts more emphasis on a student's coursework, grade point average, and class rank than on test scores.

THE SCHOOL SAYS ". . ."

From the Admissions Office

"NC State is arguably the most popular university in the state, with more NC students seeking admission than at any other college or university. More than 17,000 students from across the nation seek one of the 3,600 available freshman spaces. Students choose NC State for its strong and varied academic programs (approximately ninety), national reputation for excellence, low cost, location in Raleigh and the Research Triangle Park area, and very friendly atmosphere. Our students like the excitement of a large campus and the many opportunities it offers, such as Cooperative Education, Study Abroad, extensive honors programming, and theme residence halls. Each year, hundreds of NC State graduates are accepted into medical or law schools or other areas of advanced professional study. More corporate and government entities recruit graduates from NC State than from any other university in the United States.

"Freshman applicants must take either the SAT, the ACT with the writing component."

SELECTIVITY

Admissions Rating	92
# of applicants	19,503
% of applicants accepted	54
% of acceptees attending	43
# accepting a place on wait list	0

FRESHMAN PROFILE

Range SAT Critical Reading	530–620
Range SAT Math	560–660
Range SAT Writing	510–610
Range ACT Composite	23–28
Minimum paper TOEFL	550
Minimum computer TOEFL	213
Minimum web-based TOEFL	80
Average HS GPA	4.24
% graduated top 10% of class	42
% graduated top 25% of class	81
% graduated top 50% of class	99

DEADLINES

Early action	
Deadline	11/1
Notification	1/30
Regular	
Priority	11/1
Deadline	2/1
Notification	10/15
Nonfall registration?	yes

APPLICANTS ALSO LOOK AT
AND OFTEN PREFER
University of North Carolina at Chapel Hill

AND SOMETIMES PREFER
University of North Carolina—Charlotte

AND RARELY PREFER
Virginia Tech

FINANCIAL FACTS

Financial Aid Rating	87
Annual in-state tuition	$4,853
Annual out-of-state tuition	$17,388
Room and board	$8,154
Required fees	$1,676
Books and supplies	$1,000
% frosh rec. need-based scholarship or grant aid	49
% UG rec. need-based scholarship or grant aid	45
% frosh rec. non-need-based scholarship or grant aid	4
% UG rec. non-need-based scholarship or grant aid	3
% frosh rec. need-based self-help aid	37
% UG rec. need-based self-help aid	38
% frosh rec. any financial aid	72
% UG rec. any financial aid	67
% UG borrow to pay for school	47
Average cumulative indebtedness	$19,988

NORTHEASTERN UNIVERSITY

360 HUNTINGTON AVENUE, 150 RICHARDS HALL, BOSTON, MA 02115 • ADMISSIONS: 617-373-2200 • FAX: 617-373-8780

STUDENTS SAY "..."

Academics
Northeastern University is renowned for its "unique cooperative programming," which "integrates real-world experience and academics to form experiential learning." Students say Northeastern is an "institution that is dedicated to real-world experiences coupled with classroom guidance," and many students list "cooperative learning" opportunities as main reason for choosing the school. Additionally, the students boast about the school's "stellar academic reputation," and a junior says, "Northeastern is about equipping students with the academic prowess to have successful careers and dynamic, multifaceted lives." A political science major says, "Professors come from a wide array of fields and bring their expertise from the outside world to the classroom and then challenge us to do the same." Professors are generally "educated, engaging, [and] enthusiastic," but students say, "There's a range"—some "aren't as exciting," and a sophomore says, "I've had a good mix of mediocre and fantastic professors." Regardless, "They all expect a high level of dedication and hard work on [the] student's part to their classes," and they're "always looking to help us connect and apply our learning to our lives outside of the classroom."

Life
Northeastern University offers "the campus feel in an urban setting," "providing [an] outstanding campus life in the great city of Boston." A sophomore says, "It's a city school, but our campus has so much green space," and another student adds, "It's a closed-in campus in the middle of a city filled with opportunities." Students say, "We've got awesome facilities, and we're always building and improving them," and "The student population is very passionate about a wide variety of things, and that's manifested through student life and activities." Students say, "Getting involved in campus clubs and organizations is the best way to meet people and make lasting friendships," and "A good amount of students are involved in leadership activities and student organizations." A communication studies major adds, "If students want to get involved and fit in, just join any of the 250 clubs on campus." Despite the high level of student involvement, there are complaints that "school spirit and athletics are not as strong as at other colleges." Students also lament the notorious "NU shuffle," which means, "You'll get tossed from one office to another just to get a single question answered." A sophomore says, "We're a big school, but the bureaucracy is the number one complaint of students."

Student Body
At Northeastern, "The typical student is driven, ambitious, extremely practical," and "career-oriented." Northeastern students are "more mature than most college students earlier in their careers because of the city environment and the co-op program." "The majority [of students] are from the East Coast," and students say, "Boston is just one giant college town—anything you want, it has." The typical student "works hard in school, but definitely knows how to fit a raucous hockey game or obscenely crowded off-campus party," and "People do work hard and study hard, but there is somewhat of a relaxing and partying culture." A criminal justice majors says, "There is always a party (or ten) off campus and never far, but it is easy to avoid them if you choose." However, a sophomore describes other weekend activities: "It could mean shopping in the Prudential Center...or participating in one of Boston's many college-friendly events." In general, students feel, "There's a ton to do on and off campus, and it's really easy to get around town on the weekends." When it comes to diversity, some complain that the campus is "not a very diverse place even though they make it sound like it is." Although others contradict that, saying, "Students come from every corner of the world, and you can't walk through a quad without hearing at least three languages being spoken."

NORTHEASTERN UNIVERSITY

FINANCIAL AID: 617-373-3190 • E-MAIL: ADMISSIONS@NEU.EDU • WEBSITE: WWW.NORTHEASTERN.EDU

THE PRINCETON REVIEW SAYS

Admissions

Very important factors considered include: Academic GPA, application essay, recommendation(s), rigor of secondary school record, standardized test scores. *Important factors considered include:* Character/personal qualities, extracurricular activities, first generation, geographical residence, talent/ability, volunteer work, work experience. *Other factors considered include:* Class rank, alumni/ae relation, interview, racial/ethnic status, state residency. SAT or ACT required; ACT with writing component required. TOEFL required of all international applicants. High school diploma is required, and GED is accepted. *Academic units required:* 4 English, 3 mathematics, 3 science (2 science labs), 2 foreign language, 3 social studies, 2 history. *Academic units recommended:* 4 mathematics, 4 science (3 science labs), 3 foreign language.

Financial Aid

Students should submit: FAFSA, CSS/Financial Aid PROFILE, non-custodial profile. The Princeton Review suggests that all financial aid forms be submitted as soon as possible after January 1. *Need-based scholarships/grants offered:* Federal Pell, SEOG, state scholarships/grants, private scholarships, school scholarship or grant aid from institutional funds. *Loan aid offered:* Direct Subsidized Stafford, Direct Unsubsidized Stafford, Direct PLUS, Federal Perkins, Federal Nursing Loans, state loans, university loans from institutional funds. Applicants will be notified of awards on or about April 1. Federal Work-Study Program available. Off-campus job opportunities are excellent.

The Inside Word

Applicants to Northeastern are evaluated based on their secondary school performance, with the difficulty of courses given emphasis, and you should go beyond minimum graduation requirements for high school to show broad intellectual curiosity. The committee recommends having strong standardized test scores and does consider the writing section of the SAT in its decision.

THE SCHOOL SAYS " . . ."

From the Admissions Office

"Northeastern students take charge of their education in a way you'll find nowhere else, because a Northeastern education is like no other. Our students don't just take class: They take class further, integrating their course work with real-world experiences—professional co-op placements, research, study abroad, and community service. Northeastern's dynamic of academic excellence and experience means that our students are better prepared to succeed in the lives they choose. On top of that, they experience all of this on a beautifully landscaped, seventy-three-acre campus in the heart of Boston, where culture, commerce, civic pride, and college students from around the globe are all a part of the mix."

SELECTIVITY

Admissions Rating	91
# of applicants	37,688
% of applicants accepted	38
% of acceptees attending	20

FRESHMAN PROFILE

Range SAT Critical Reading	600–680
Range SAT Math	630–710
Range SAT Writing	590–680
Range ACT Composite	28–31
Minimum paper TOEFL	563
Minimum computer TOEFL	223
Minimum web-based TOEFL	84
% graduated top 10% of class	51
% graduated top 25% of class	82
% graduated top 50% of class	97

DEADLINES

Early action	
Deadline	11/1
Notification	12/31
Regular	
Deadline	1/15
Notification	4/1
Nonfall registration?	yes

FINANCIAL FACTS

Financial Aid Rating	70
Annual tuition	$36,380
Room and board	$12,760
Required fees	$762
Books and supplies	$1,000
% frosh rec. need-based scholarship or grant aid	50
% UG rec. need-based scholarship or grant aid	50
% frosh rec. non-need-based scholarship or grant aid	9
% UG rec. non-need-based scholarship or grant aid	5
% frosh rec. need-based self-help aid	45
% UG rec. need-based self-help aid	49

NORTHWESTERN UNIVERSITY

PO BOX 3060, 1801 HINMAN AVENUE, EVANSTON, IL 60208-3060 • ADMISSIONS: 847-491-7271

CAMPUS LIFE

Quality of Life Rating	73
Fire Safety Rating	73
Green Rating	78
Type of school	private
Environment	town

STUDENTS

Total undergrad enrollment	8,364
% male/female	48/52
% from out of state	75
% from public high school	65
% live on campus	65
# of fraternities	17
# of sororities	19
% African American	5
% Asian	18
% Caucasian	58
% Hispanic	7
% international	5
# of countries represented	42

SURVEY SAYS . . .

Athletic facilities are great
Great off-campus food
Frats and sororities dominate
social scene
Musical organizations are popular
Student publications are popular

ACADEMICS

Academic Rating	89
% students graduating	
within 4 years	86
% students graduating	
within 6 years	93
Calendar	quarter
Student/faculty ratio	7:1
Profs interesting rating	75
Profs accessible rating	76
Most common	
reg class size	fewer than
	10 students
Most common	
lab size	10–19 students

MOST POPULAR MAJORS

economics, engineering, journalism

STUDENTS SAY ". . ."

Academics

"The strength of the school is its range." Northwestern students agree, vowing their school "has everything": "Intelligent but laid-back students, excel[lence] in academic fields," "great extracurriculars and good parties," "strong [Big Ten] sports spirit," and "so many connections and opportunities during and after graduation." Undergrads here brag of "nationally acclaimed programs for almost anything anyone could be interested in, from engineering to theater to journalism to music," and report "everything is given fairly equal weight. Northwestern students and faculty do not show a considerable bias" toward specific fields. The school accomplishes all this while maintaining a manageable scale. While its relatively small size allows for good student-professor interaction, it has "all the perks" of a big school, including "many opportunities" for research and internships. Be aware, however, "Northwestern is not an easy school. It takes hard work to be average here." If you "learn from your failures quickly and love to learn for the sake of learning rather than the grade," students say it is quite possible to stay afloat and even to excel. Helping matters are numerous resources established by administrators and professors, including tutoring programs such as Northwestern's Gateway Science Workshop. Those who take advantage of these opportunities find the going much easier than those who don't.

Life

There are two distinct sections of the Northwestern campus. The North Campus is where "you can find a party every night of the week" and "the Greek scene is strong." The South Campus, about a one-mile trek from the action to the north, is "more artsy and has minimal partying on weeknights," but is closer to town so "it is easy" to "buy dinner, see a show at the movies, and go shopping. People who live on North Campus have a harder time getting motivated to go into Evanston and tap into all that is offered." As one South Campus resident puts it, "South Campus is nice and quiet in its own way. I enjoy reading and watching movies here, and the quietude is appreciated when study time rolls around. But for more exciting fun, a trip north is a must." Regardless of where students live, extracurriculars are "incredible here. There is a group for every interest, and the groups are amazingly well-managed by students alone. This goes hand-in-hand with how passionate students at Northwestern are about what they love." Many students "are involved in plays, a cappella groups, comedy troupes, and other organizations geared toward the performing arts. Activism is also very popular, with many involved in political groups, human-rights activism, and volunteering." In addition, Northwestern's membership in the Big Ten means students "attend some of the best sporting events in the country." Chicago, of course, "is a wonderful resource. People go into the city for a wide variety of things—daily excursions, jobs, internships, nights out, parties, etc."

Student Body

The typical Northwestern student "was high school class president with a 4.0, swim team captain, and on the chess team." So it makes sense everyone here "is an excellent student who works hard" and "has a leadership position in at least two clubs, plus an on-campus job." Students also tell us "there's [a] great separation between North Campus (think: fraternities, engineering, state school mentality) and South Campus (think: closer to Chicago and its culture, arts and letters, liberal arts school mentality). Students segregate themselves depending on background and interests, and it's rare for these two groups to interact beyond a superficial level." The student body here includes sizeable Jewish, Indian, and East-Asian populations.

FINANCIAL AID: 847-491-7400 • E-MAIL: UG-ADMISSION@NORTHWESTERN.EDU • WEBSITE: WWW.NORTHWESTERN.EDU

THE PRINCETON REVIEW SAYS

Admissions

Very important factors considered include: Academic GPA, application essay, class rank, rigor of secondary school record, standardized test scores. *Important factors considered include:* Recommendation(s), character/personal qualities, extracurricular activities, talent/ability. *Other factors considered include:* Alumni/ae relation, first generation, interview, level of applicant's interest, racial/ethnic status, volunteer work, work experience. SAT or ACT required; ACT with writing component required. TOEFL required of all international applicants. High school diploma or equivalent isn't required. *Academic units recommended:* 4 English, 3 mathematics, 2 science (2 science labs), 2 foreign language, 2 social studies, 1 academic elective.

Financial Aid

Students should submit: FAFSA, CSS/Financial Aid PROFILE. Regular filing deadline is February 15. The Princeton Review suggests that all financial aid forms be submitted as soon as possible after January 1. *Need-based scholarships/grants offered:* Federal Pell, SEOG, state scholarships/grants, private scholarships, school scholarship or grant aid from institutional funds, United Negro College Fund. *Loan aid offered:* Direct Subsidized Stafford, Direct Unsubsidized Stafford, Direct PLUS, Federal Perkins, university loans from institutional funds. Federal Work-Study Program available. Off-campus job opportunities are excellent.

The Inside Word

Northwestern is among the nation's most expensive undergraduate institutions, a fact that dissuades some qualified students from applying. The school is working to attract more low-income applicants by increasing the number of full scholarships available for students whose family income is less than $45,000. Low-income students who score well on the ACT may receive a letter from the school encouraging them to apply. Even if you don't receive this letter, you should consider applying if you've got the goods—you may be pleasantly surprised by the offer you receive from the financial aid office.

THE SCHOOL SAYS "..."

From the Admissions Office

"Consistent with its dedication to excellence, Northwestern provides both an educational and an extracurricular environment that enables its undergraduate students to become accomplished individuals and informed and responsible citizens. To the students in all its undergraduate schools, Northwestern offers liberal learning and professional education to help them gain the depth of knowledge that will empower them to become leaders in their professions and communities. Furthermore, Northwestern fosters in its students a broad understanding of the world in which we live as well as excellence in the competencies that transcend any particular field of study: writing and oral communication, analytical and creative thinking and expression, and quantitative and qualitative methods of thinking.

"Applicants are required to take the SAT or the ACT with the writing section."

SELECTIVITY

Admissions Rating	97
# of applicants	25,013
% of applicants accepted	26
% of acceptees attending	32
# accepting a place on wait list	1,307
% admitted from wait list	12
# of early decision applicants	1,395
% accepted early decision	40

FRESHMAN PROFILE

Range SAT Critical Reading	670–750
Range SAT Math	690–780
Range SAT Writing	670–750
Range ACT Composite	30–33
Minimum paper TOEFL	600
Minimum computer TOEFL	250
% graduated top 10% of class	85
% graduated top 25% of class	96
% graduated top 50% of class	99

DEADLINES

Early decision	
Deadline	11/1
Notification	12/15
Regular	
Deadline	1/1
Nonfall registration?	yes

APPLICANTS ALSO LOOK AT

AND OFTEN PREFER
Harvard College, Yale University

AND SOMETIMES PREFER
Stanford University, University of Chicago

FINANCIAL FACTS

Financial Aid Rating	93
Annual tuition	$38,088
Room and board	$11,703
Required fees	$373
Books and supplies	$1,686
% frosh rec. need-based scholarship or grant aid	38
% UG rec. need-based scholarship or grant aid	40
% frosh rec. need-based self-help aid	34
% UG rec. need-based self-help aid	36
% frosh rec. any financial aid	60
% UG rec. any financial aid	60
% UG borrow to pay for school	49
Average cumulative indebtedness	$19,908

OBERLIN COLLEGE

101 NORTH PROFESSOR STREET, OBERLIN, OH 44074 • ADMISSIONS: 440-775-8411 • FAX: 440-775-6905

CAMPUS LIFE

Quality of Life Rating	69
Fire Safety Rating	71
Green Rating	89
Type of school	private
Environment	rural

STUDENTS

Total undergrad enrollment	2,948
% male/female	45/55
% from out of state	91
% from public high school	60
% live on campus	89
% African American	8
% Asian	7
% Caucasian	72
% Hispanic	6
% Native American	1
% international	6
# of countries represented	46

SURVEY SAYS . . .

Lots of liberal students
No one cheats
Low cost of living
Frats and sororities are unpopular
or nonexistent
Musical organizations are popular
Political activism is popular

ACADEMICS

Academic Rating	96
% students graduating within 4 years	73
% students graduating within 6 years	87
Calendar	4-1-4
Student/faculty ratio	9:1
Profs interesting rating	94
Profs accessible rating	96
Most common reg class size	10–19 students
Most common lab size	fewer than 10 students

MOST POPULAR MAJORS

English language and literature, history

STUDENTS SAY "..."

Academics

Oberlin College, a school "for laid-back people who enjoy learning and expanding social norms, allows each and every student to have the undergrad experience for which he or she is looking, all the while challenging the students to change themselves and the world for the better." Oberlin is a place where students "focus on learning for learning's sake rather than making money in a career." As one student explains, "I didn't plan on becoming a scholar when I entered Oberlin....As fate would have it, I ended up loving my college classes and professors. Now I hope to be a professor of religion." At Oberlin, "academics are very highly valued, but balanced with a strong interest in the arts and a commitment to society." Some might suggest Oberlin puts the "liberal" in "liberal arts," and the school's staunchest supporters agree, stressing the school's emphasis on open-mindedness and the belief that "one person can change the world." Among the school's offerings, "the sciences, English, politics, religion, music, environmental studies, and East-Asian studies are particularly noteworthy." The presence of a prestigious music school imbues the entire campus community. One undergrad writes, "Oberlin's greatest strength is the combination of the college and the conservatory. They are not separated, so students mix with each other all the time." Professors here—the "heart and soul of the school"—are dedicated teachers who "treat you more like collaborators and realize that even with their PhDs, they can learn and grow from you, as well as you from them." They are "excellent instructors and fantastic people" who are "focused on learning instead of deadlines." Undergrads also appreciate "a cooperative learning environment" in which "Students bond over studying together for difficult exams."

Life

Life during the week at Oberlin can be "pretty bland," as "almost everyone has to crack the books and study it up." It's not always bland, though. Some here manage to find time for the many "events [going on] each weekend—operas, plays, organ pumps, etc.," or "rally to stage to help the oppressed." Thursday afternoons at Oberlin means "Classical Thursdays," an event during which "you get free beer from the college if you bring a professor to the on-campus pub." Another feature of campus life is "the musical scene, which has its heart in the conservatory. All of the other arts—performing, studio, whatever—are intertwined with the talent in the conservatory." On weekends, "people let loose and drink beer. Not everyone does this every weekend. Some don't do it at all," and "there is absolutely no pressure on those who don't." There are also "tons of student-produced social events like parties, fundraisers, concerts, dances, etc.," keeping students "very connected to each other and to what's going on in the community." Hometown Oberlin "is a small town, and about all there is to do there is go out for pizza or Chinese, see a movie for $2 or $3 at the Apollo, or go to the Feve, the bar in town."

Student Body

"If you're a liberal, artsy, indie loner who likes to throw around the phrase 'heteronormative white privilege,'" then Oberlin might be the place for you. "We're like the Island of Misfit Toys, but together we make a great toy chest." "We're all different and unusual, which creates a common bond between students." "Musicians, jocks, science geeks, creative writing majors, straight, bi, questioning, queer, and trans [students]," all have their place here, alongside "straight-edge, international, local, and joker students." Oberlin has a reputation for a left-leaning and active student body. One undergrad observes, "They are less active politically than they would like to think, but still more active than most people elsewhere." Another adds, "Most students are very liberal, but the moderates and (few) Republicans have a fine time of it. Every student has different interests and isn't afraid to talk about them." Some here worry "Oberlin's student body is becoming more and more mainstream each year."

FINANCIAL AID: 440-775-8142 • E-MAIL: COLLEGE.ADMISSIONS@OBERLIN.EDU • WEBSITE: WWW.OBERLIN.EDU

THE PRINCETON REVIEW SAYS

Admissions

Very important factors considered include: Academic GPA, class rank, rigor of secondary school record, standardized test scores. *Important factors considered include:* Application essay, recommendation(s), character/personal qualities, extracurricular activities, first generation, talent/ability. *Other factors considered include:* Alumni/ae relation, interview, level of applicant's interest, racial/ethnic status, volunteer work, work experience. SAT or ACT required; ACT with writing component required. TOEFL required of all international applicants. High school diploma is required, and GED is accepted. *Academic units required:* 4 English, 4 mathematics, 3 science, 3 foreign language, 3 social studies.

Financial Aid

Students should submit: FAFSA, institution's own financial aid form, CSS/Financial Aid PROFILE. Regular filing deadline is February 1. The Princeton Review suggests that all financial aid forms be submitted as soon as possible after January 1. *Need-based scholarships/grants offered:* Federal Pell, SEOG, state scholarships/grants, private scholarships, school scholarship or grant aid from institutional funds. *Loan aid offered:* Direct Subsidized Stafford, Direct Unsubsidized Stafford, Direct PLUS, Federal Perkins, university loans from institutional funds.

The Inside Word

Oberlin's music conservatory is one of the most elite programs in the nation. Aspiring music students should expect stiff competition for one of the 600 available slots. Other applicants won't have a much easier time of it. Oberlin is a highly selective institution that attracts a highly competitive applicant pool. Your personal statement could be the make-or-break factor here.

THE SCHOOL SAYS "..."

From the Admissions Office

"Oberlin College is an independent, coeducational, liberal arts college. It comprises two divisions, the College of Arts and Sciences, with roughly 2,800 students enrolled, and the Conservatory of Music, with about 600 students. Students in both divisions share one campus; they also share residence and dining halls as part of one academic community. Many students take courses in both divisions. Oberlin awards the Bachelor of Arts and the Bachelor of Music degrees; a five-year program leads to both degrees. Selected master's degrees are offered in the conservatory. Oberlin is located thirty-five miles southwest of Cleveland. Founded in 1833, Oberlin College is highly selective and dedicated to recruiting students from diverse backgrounds. Oberlin was the first coeducational college in the United States, as well as a historic leader in educating African Americans. Oberlin's 440-acre campus provides outstanding facilities, modern scientific laboratories, a large computing center, a library unexcelled by other college libraries for the depth and range of its resources, and one of the top-five college- or university-based art museums in the country.

"Freshman applicants must take the SAT the ACT with writing component."

SELECTIVITY

Admissions Rating	98
# of applicants	7,222
% of applicants accepted	31
% of acceptees attending	35
# accepting a place on wait list	942
% admitted from wait list	3
# of early decision applicants	385
% accepted early decision	61

FRESHMAN PROFILE

Range SAT Critical Reading	650–740
Range SAT Math	630–710
Range SAT Writing	650–740
Range ACT Composite	28–32
Minimum paper TOEFL	600
Minimum computer TOEFL	200
Minimum web-based TOEFL	100
Average HS GPA	3.60
% graduated top 10% of class	69
% graduated top 25% of class	91
% graduated top 50% of class	99

DEADLINES

Early decision	
Deadline	11/15
Notification	12/20
Regular	
Deadline	1/15
Nonfall registration?	no

APPLICANTS ALSO LOOK AT
AND OFTEN PREFER
Brown University, Swarthmore College, Wesleyan University

AND SOMETIMES PREFER
Vassar College

FINANCIAL FACTS

Financial Aid Rating	93
Annual tuition	$41,234
Room and board	$11,010
Required fees	$343
Books and supplies	$1,808
% frosh rec. need-based scholarship or grant aid	55
% UG rec. need-based scholarship or grant aid	56
% frosh rec. non-need-based scholarship or grant aid	31
% UG rec. non-need-based scholarship or grant aid	38
% frosh rec. need-based self-help aid	43
% UG rec. need-based self-help aid	45
% frosh rec. any financial aid	61
% UG rec. any financial aid	60
Average cumulative indebtedness	$17,085

OCCIDENTAL COLLEGE

1600 CAMPUS ROAD, LOS ANGELES, CA 90041 • ADMISSIONS: 800-825-5262 • FAX: 323-341-4875

CAMPUS LIFE

Quality of Life Rating	82
Fire Safety Rating	72
Green Rating	80
Type of school	private
Environment	metropolis

STUDENTS

Total undergrad enrollment	2,073
% male/female	44/56
% from out of state	54
% from public high school	58
% live on campus	80
# of fraternities	3
# of sororities	4
% African American	6
% Asian	16
% Caucasian	57
% Hispanic	14
% Native American	2
% international	3
# of countries represented	26

SURVEY SAYS . . .
No one cheats
Students are friendly
Diverse student types on campus
Great food on campus

ACADEMICS

Academic Rating	90
% students graduating within 4 years	80
% students graduating within 6 years	85
Calendar	semester
Student/faculty ratio	10:1
Profs interesting rating	84
Profs accessible rating	84
Most common reg class size	10–19 students
Most common lab size	10–19 students

MOST POPULAR MAJORS
economics, international relations,
English language and literature

STUDENTS SAY ". . ."

Academics
"Combine sunny weather with big-city opportunities, amazing professors, a gorgeous campus, and an emphasis on diversity, and you get Oxy!" That's how Occidental College is affectionately known by its "happy, outgoing, and bright" students. Located "just over the hill from bustling Los Angeles," Oxy is "a small school that provides the opportunity to develop one's intellect in a safe, friendly, and mentally challenging environment." This "very prestigious school" is "tough academically. The work is hard, and there's a high level of work expected of all students. But the benefits of getting an education here are worth all the work." Strong instruction is a big part of the equation; Oxy profs "are the absolute best because they are extremely personable toward and available for the students. They have a great desire for all their students to succeed, especially those who are on the premedicine track." Profs here don't exist to "publish or perish"; "they actually are at Oxy to teach—and not to teach so they can research." That said, Oxy is no slacker when it comes to research either. Students say it is "really easy" to get "independent study, internships, and grants" that would "not be offered anywhere else to undergraduates." Students love "class sizes [that] are small for the most part" and the school's Center for Academic Excellence, "which provides free tutoring for many academic subjects."

Life
Los Angeles "is an amazing town to learn in," and Oxy exploits this asset. "Every week the school offers trips around Southern California." Extracurricular diversions are copious, but most require access to an automobile. "Everyone who doesn't have a car wishes they did and hangs out with people who do," undergrads warn. For those with wheels, "there's so much to do" in Los Angeles "that you can always find something to do on weekends. Old Town Pasadena is only ten minutes away, and it's a great place to spend a Saturday night." Students also sojourn "to Chinatown, Disneyland, the beach, the movies, plays, museums, the Glendale Galleria, [and] the Santa Monica Promenade. The location definitely has advantages," and so does the Oxy campus, where "there is always something fun going on," such as "a thematic party or just a cool social gathering," more than one "speaker series hosted by departments, movies projected on the dining hall wall, and many other things." Students "stay connected to what's going through our very effective 'daily digest e-mail.'" While most students are "fairly social," Oxy is "not what I would call a party school." Most of the parties "are all just off campus," and "drinks are easy to obtain but also easy to refuse."

Student Body
The typical Oxy undergrad "is politically and globally aware, is passionate about more than one interest, and loves to speak up about any and every issue (both related to the school and outside of it)." Most are "very liberal, studious, hardworking, and playful." Atypical students "are usually conservative or party animals. The conservative students have a bit of a hard time since the college and its students are typically very left-winged, yet they manage. The party animals fit in very well, although [they are] not necessarily liked in all situations, such as group projects, since they are a bit less hardworking." In terms of personality types, "we range from kids who are proud of being hicks to the artsy hipsters to some Goth kids to just your average run-of-the-mill sandwich-eating college kid." Common threads are "intelligence and desire to discuss issues, whatever they may be" and "the laid-back groove of California," which most here embody.

FINANCIAL AID: 323-259-2548 • E-MAIL: ADMISSION@OXY.EDU • WEBSITE: WWW.OXY.EDU

THE PRINCETON REVIEW SAYS

Admissions

Very important factors considered include: Rigor of secondary school record, extracurricular activities, volunteer work, work experience. *Important factors considered include:* Academic GPA, application essay, class rank, recommendation(s), standardized test scores. *Other factors considered include:* Alumni/ae relation, character/personal qualities, first generation, geographical residence, interview, level of applicant's interest, racial/ethnic status, talent/ability. SAT or ACT required; ACT with writing component required. TOEFL required of all international applicants. High school diploma is required, and GED is accepted. *Academic units recommended:* 4 English, 4 mathematics, 3 science (2 science labs), 3 foreign language, 2 social studies, 2 history, 2 academic elective.

Financial Aid

Students should submit: FAFSA, CSS/Financial Aid PROFILE. Regular filing deadline is February 1. The Princeton Review suggests that all financial aid forms be submitted as soon as possible after January 1. *Need-based scholarships/grants offered:* Federal Pell, SEOG, state scholarships/grants, private scholarships, school scholarship or grant aid from institutional funds. *Loan aid offered:* Direct Subsidized Stafford, Direct Unsubsidized Stafford, Direct PLUS, Federal Perkins, university loans from institutional funds. Applicants will be notified of awards on a rolling basis beginning April 1. Federal Work-Study Program available. Off-campus job opportunities are good.

The Inside Word

The admissions team at Occidental is adamant about not adhering to formulas. They rely heavily on essays and recommendations in their mission to create a talented and diverse incoming class. The college attracts some excellent students, so a demanding course load in high school is essential for the most competitive candidates. Successful applicants tend to be creative and academically motivated.

THE SCHOOL SAYS "..."

From the Admissions Office

"Here's what our students tell us:

'The professors have all been just amazing. They're all very willing to coordinate times to meet and discuss how you feel about a class and what you want to get out of it.'

'I realize the caliber of discussion that occurs at Oxy is not easily matched. I've developed very strong relationships with many professors, and that's something I believe is unique to Oxy.'

'The program has been awesome. Whether you want to go to med school or grad school, it's a great experience. The professors really want you to succeed.'

'I've been working with postdoctoral researchers as an undergraduate. It's very rewarding. Oxy challenges me both inside and outside the classroom.'

'Occidental opened my eyes to different beliefs, values, and ideas. Discussions in class are much more interesting, because you consider things you might not have thought about before.'

'Oxy's close-knit community and its size make me feel this is a place I can call home.'

'Oxy instills curiosity and makes students want to go out and learn a subject on their own. I've gotten a broader sense of self and have been able to fulfill my learning goals.'

Occidental requires all applicants (including international students) to take either the SAT or ACT with the writing component. SAT subject tests are recommended but not required."

SELECTIVITY

Admissions Rating	95
# of applicants	5,882
% of applicants accepted	42
% of acceptees attending	23
# accepting a place on wait list	352
% admitted from wait list	8
# of early decision applicants	156
% accepted early decision	39

FRESHMAN PROFILE

Range SAT Critical Reading	600–690
Range SAT Math	600–690
Range SAT Writing	610–690
Range ACT Composite	26–30
Minimum paper TOEFL	600
Minimum computer TOEFL	250
Average HS GPA	3.60
% graduated top 10% of class	62
% graduated top 25% of class	93
% graduated top 50% of class	100

DEADLINES

Early decision	
Deadline	11/15
Notification	12/15
Regular	
Deadline	1/10
Nonfall registration?	no

APPLICANTS ALSO LOOK AT AND OFTEN PREFER

Pomona College, University of California—Berkeley, University of California—Los Angeles, University of Southern California

AND SOMETIMES PREFER

Claremont McKenna College

FINANCIAL FACTS

Financial Aid Rating	97
Annual comprehensive tuition	$53,850
Books and supplies	$1,180
% frosh rec. need-based scholarship or grant aid	59
% UG rec. need-based scholarship or grant aid	54
% frosh rec. non-need-based scholarship or grant aid	9
% UG rec. non-need-based scholarship or grant aid	5
% frosh rec. need-based self-help aid	49
% UG rec. need-based self-help aid	50
% frosh rec. any financial aid	77
% UG rec. any financial aid	79
% UG borrow to pay for school	67
Average cumulative indebtedness	$17,561

OGLETHORPE UNIVERSITY

4484 PEACHTREE ROAD, NORTHEAST, ATLANTA, GA 30319 • ADMISSIONS: 404-364-8307 • FAX: 404-364-8491

CAMPUS LIFE

Quality of Life Rating	83
Fire Safety Rating	76
Green Rating	70
Type of school	private
Environment	metropolis

STUDENTS

Total undergrad enrollment	1,054
% male/female	40/60
% from out of state	28
% from public high school	79
% live on campus	62
# of fraternities	4
# of sororities	3
% African American	24
% Asian	4
% Caucasian	45
% Hispanic	6
% international	3
# of countries represented	24

SURVEY SAYS . . .

Students are friendly
Diverse student types on campus
Different types of students interact
Students get along with local
community
Students love Atlanta, GA
Great off-campus food
Dorms are like palaces
Theater is popular

ACADEMICS

Academic Rating	86
% students graduating within 4 years	47
% students graduating within 6 years	58
Calendar	semester
Student/faculty ratio	16:1
Profs interesting rating	93
Profs accessible rating	87
Most common reg class size	10–19 students
Most common lab size	8 students

MOST POPULAR MAJORS
business/commerce, English language
and literature, psychology

STUDENTS SAY ". . ."

Academics

Oglethorpe University offers "an exceptional, well-rounded education in a close-knit community," with "dedicated professors." Students say, "The core curriculum is incredible," because it brings together "different disciplines and has so much variety that all students end up being very able to discuss many subjects." Students value the "strong focus on a liberal arts education," and, "a small class student/teacher ratio." The university is known for its, "great English and Theatre departments," and, "individualized education." Professors are, "dedicated," "are highly qualified and are very personable." A junior says, "I have had really knowledgeable, engaging, and accessible professors. They all know me on a personal level and are very helpful both in and outside of class." Most agree that, "The classroom experience is unsurpassed," and say you are, "expected to actively participate in class," adding that, "writing is imperative." Some acknowledge, "There are also some professors that are awful," and many say, "The registration process is quite outdated and could stand to be reworked," and, "OU could improve on the amount of class[es] offer[ed] per semester." Regardless, a psychology student says Oglethorpe is a "community that cares about a high standard of academia and excellence."

Life

Oglethorpe is a "very open-minded community," "nestled in Atlanta," which "sets you up for success." A sophomore says, "Oglethorpe has small rural city feel on campus but outside of campus you can enjoy the big city," and another adds, "It's such a beautiful school, you can't help but be in a good mood when you enter the campus." Students say, "This school is all about community and preparing the students to go as far as they can," and rave about the "emphasis on service" and level of "student involvement." Students feel that they "have a lot of power on our campus" and that "the staff is very willing to help you pursue your goals and will aid you in every way possible." In general, "The students are very immersed in sports and clubs" and "involved in both their campus and the community." A freshman says, "Everyone is part of something, which connects us together in a very special way," and a communication major says, "Everyone is pretty much respectful of one another on campus and crime is nonexistent." There are complaints that "Oglethorpe is lacking in facilities, due to its small size," and most gripe, "It doesn't have the exercise or dining facilities of schools with bigger endowments."

Student Body

At Oglethorpe University, "The typical student is intelligent, capable, and willing to put forth effort into what they are doing." Students say, "It is extremely diverse," and add, "OU students are all different: white, black, brown, gay, straight, conservative, liberal, etc." A senior says, "Because of the small population, is it very easy to meet people," and another agrees, "Students are all very accepting of other lifestyles and interests, and to be honest, many of us are huge nerds." Oglethorpe is a community of "laid-back smart kids," who "know how to enjoy their time in college." One student says, "There is a lot of partying at our school but it is not expected of you," and another agrees, "Of course drinking is popular, but [it's] not considered important." For fun, "People party at Greek Row or explore the Atlanta area," and many say they "leave campus a lot and go into downtown Atlanta either to go out to eat, to the movies, or go to clubs." Even though, "The fraternities and sororities host many fun events," a communication major says, "Campus life can be pretty dull for students who come expecting huge parties." A freshman sums it up, saying, "Life here can be just as busy or slow and peaceful as you'd like it."

OGLETHORPE UNIVERSITY

FINANCIAL AID: 404-364-8356 • E-MAIL: ADMISSION@OGLETHORPE.EDU • WEBSITE: WWW.OGLETHORPE.EDU

THE PRINCETON REVIEW SAYS

Admissions

Very important factors considered include: Academic GPA, rigor of secondary school record, standardized test scores. *Important factors considered include:* Application essay, class rank, recommendation(s), extracurricular activities, interview, level of applicant's interest, volunteer work. *Other factors considered include:* Alumni/ae relation, character/personal qualities, first generation, talent/ability, work experience. SAT or ACT with writing component required. 2 SAT Subject Tests recommended. TOEFL required of all international applicants. High school diploma is required, and GED is accepted. *Academic units required:* 4 English, 3 mathematics, 2 science, 3 social studies. *Academic units recommended:* 2 foreign language.

Financial Aid

Students should submit: FAFSA, institution's own financial aid form. The Princeton Review suggests that all financial aid forms be submitted as soon as possible after January 1. *Need-based scholarships/grants offered:* Federal Pell, SEOG, state scholarships/grants, private scholarships, school scholarship or grant aid from institutional funds. *Loan aid offered:* Direct Subsidized Stafford, Direct Unsubsidized Stafford, Direct PLUS, Federal Perkins. Applicants will be notified of awards on a rolling basis beginning December 1. Federal Work-Study Program available. Off-campus job opportunities are excellent.

The Inside Word

With rising national interest in the South, it won't be long before the academic strength found at Oglethorpe attracts wider attention and more applicants. At present, it's much easier to gain admission here than at many universities of similar quality. Go to Atlanta for a campus interview—you'll leave impressed.

THE SCHOOL SAYS ". . ."

From the Admissions Office

"Promising students and outstanding teachers come together at Oglethorpe University in an acclaimed program of liberal arts and sciences. Here you'll find an active intellectual community on a beautiful English Gothic campus just ten miles from the center of Atlanta, capital of the Southeast, site of the 1996 Summer Olympics, and home to four million people. If you want challenging academics, the opportunity to work closely with your professors, and the stimulation of a great metropolitan area, consider Oglethorpe, a national liberal arts college in a world-class city."

SELECTIVITY

Admissions Rating	85
# of applicants	2,443
% of applicants accepted	86
% of acceptees attending	11

FRESHMAN PROFILE

Range SAT Critical Reading	530–640
Range SAT Math	510–610
Range SAT Writing	510–610
Range ACT Composite	22–28
Minimum paper TOEFL	550
Minimum computer TOEFL	200
Average HS GPA	3.53
% graduated top 10% of class	23
% graduated top 25% of class	58
% graduated top 50% of class	85

DEADLINES

Early action	
Deadline	12/15
Notification	12/20
Regular	
Priority	12/5
Nonfall registration?	yes

FINANCIAL FACTS

Financial Aid Rating	78
Annual tuition	$27,700
Room and board	$9,990
Required fees	$250
Books and supplies	$900
% frosh rec. need-based scholarship or grant aid	79
% UG rec. need-based scholarship or grant aid	73
% frosh rec. non-need-based scholarship or grant aid	9
% UG rec. non-need-based scholarship or grant aid	8
% frosh rec. need-based self-help aid	58
% UG rec. need-based self-help aid	57
% frosh rec. any financial aid	95
% UG rec. any financial aid	95
% UG borrow to pay for school	72

OHIO NORTHERN UNIVERSITY

525 SOUTH MAIN STREET, ADA, OH 45810 • ADMISSIONS: 419-772-2260 • FAX: 419-772-2313

CAMPUS LIFE

Quality of Life Rating	72
Fire Safety Rating	60*
Green Rating	60*
Type of school	private
Affiliation	Methodist
Environment	village

STUDENTS

Total undergrad enrollment	2,610
% male/female	52/48
% from out of state	15
% live on campus	64
# of fraternities	6
# of sororities	4
% African American	4
% Asian	1
% Caucasian	88
% Hispanic	1
% international	4
# of countries represented	17

SURVEY SAYS . . .

Students are friendly
Campus feels safe
Low cost of living

ACADEMICS

Academic Rating	78
% students graduating within 4 years	47
% students graduating within 6 years	66
Calendar	quarter
Student/faculty ratio	11:1
Profs interesting rating	76
Profs accessible rating	84
Most common reg class size	10–19 students
Most common lab size	20–29 students

MOST POPULAR MAJORS

biology, mechanical engineering, nursing, pharmacy

STUDENTS SAY ". . ."

Academics

At Ohio Northern University in tiny Ada, Ohio, there is a very strong "focus on academics and helping students excel." ONU's premier attraction is its Raabe College of Pharmacy; the school, which enrolls about one-third of all undergraduates here, offers a six-year PharmD option as well as a dual major in pharmacy/biology. Students in the program warn that "the academics can be tough," but they say they're always "prepared for what awaits them when they get into the job market," and the school's "good reputation for applying for jobs" and the plethora of internship opportunities justifies the work required to succeed. Less prestigious but equally popular (and, according to students, nearly as excellent) are the James F. Dicke College of Business Administration and the T.J. Smull College of Engineering, each claiming between fifteen and twenty percent of the student body. "High academic standards" are encouraged across all five schools at this small university, where students report that they "get involved in major-related activities as soon as they arrive on campus." The favorable faculty-to-student ratio means "you are not a number; you are a name." There's no slacking here; decent students find that ONU is entirely easy to get into but more difficult to excel at, as "the school does a good job of weeding out the social-scene-centered students, and by second year most students are overall very academically motivated." Indeed, "nobody comes to ONU as a last resort; they choose it," and this is reflected in the atmosphere on campus. Regardless of your program, professors are "very interested in their lecture material it shows in their classroom" and "make the material easier to learn with real-life references."

Life

Ohio Northern is "not located in a metropolis," that's for sure, and Ada is an hour and a half's drive northwest of Columbus. "There may not be much to do around campus...but we get creative and make our own fun." For those with cars, the cities of Lima and Findlay are a half-hour off and "provide lots of eating and shopping places." Many choose to get involved with campus activities, and students tell us that "almost all students are involved in athletics, Greek life or theater/music" and that there are more than "150 student organizations at Ohio Northern, so there always seems to be something going on that you can attend," such as "movie nights, comedians and the hypnotists." Snow football and skiing in the winter are both common, as are "volleyball and cornhole when it's nice out." Many indulge in the party scene, explaining that "if students aren't studying they tend to go out and drink," though "mostly on campus, since there are only two bars in Ada)." "Parties on the weekend are a regular occurrence, but at the same time so is community involvement," says a sophomore. However, "There is a sizeable population of students that keep their fun clean with cards, board games, movies, etc." Housing at Ohio Northern is also "much nicer than other schools."

Student Body

ONU students are "always working hard and studying," and all have a passion for some sort of side project. Minority students are in short supply; nearly everyone is "white, middle-class, and fairly smart," but remain "open-minded toward different sexual orientations, cultures, etc." Most of these "well-rounded" students graduated at "the top portion of their high schools" and remain just as active now as they did then; everyone is "usually involved in at least two campus clubs or organizations. "Cliques do tend to form, but it's a friendly group, and "Each student is a part of several different group of friends."

FINANCIAL AID: 419-772-2272 • E-MAIL: ADMISSIONS-UG@ONU.EDU • WEBSITE: WWW.ONU.EDU

THE PRINCETON REVIEW SAYS

Admissions

Very important factors considered include: Academic GPA, rigor of secondary school record, standardized test scores. *Important factors considered include:* Application essay, class rank, recommendation(s), extracurricular activities, interview. *Other factors considered include:* Alumni/ae relation, character/personal qualities, first generation, level of applicant's interest, talent/ability, volunteer work. SAT or ACT required; ACT with or without writing component accepted. TOEFL required of all international applicants. High school diploma is required, and GED is accepted. *Academic units required:* 4 English, 2 mathematics, 2 science (2 science labs), 2 social studies, 2 history, 4 academic elective. *Academic units recommended:* 4 English, 4 mathematics, 3 science (2 science labs), 2 foreign language, 3 social studies, 2 history, 1 visual/performing arts, 4 academic elective, 1 computer science.

Financial Aid

Students should submit: FAFSA. Regular filing deadline is April 15. The Princeton Review suggests that all financial aid forms be submitted as soon as possible after January 1. *Need-based scholarships/grants offered:* Federal Pell, SEOG, state scholarships/grants, private scholarships, school scholarship or grant aid from institutional funds. *Loan aid offered:* Direct Subsidized Stafford, Direct Unsubsidized Stafford, Direct PLUS, Federal Perkins, university loans from institutional funds. Applicants will be notified of awards on a rolling basis beginning March 1. Federal Work-Study Program available. Off-campus job opportunities are good.

The Inside Word

Solid high school grades and above-average standardized test scores will pretty much punch your ticket to Ohio Northern. Admissions standards for the pharmacy school are considerably more stringent. Applicants may qualify for substantial merit-based scholarships based on standardized test scores and high school GPA; see the school's website for details.

THE SCHOOL SAYS ". . ."

From the Admissions Office

"The purpose of Ohio Northern is to help students develop into self-reliant, mature men and women capable of clear and logical thinking and sensitive to the higher values of truth, beauty, and goodness. ONU selects its student body from among those students possessing characteristics congruent with the institution's objectives. Generally, a student must be prepared to use the resources of the institution to achieve personal and educational goals.

"Students applying for admission are urged to submit scores for the SAT or the ACT with the writing section. The student's best composite scores will be used for scholarship purposes.

"The Office of Admissions highly encourages a campus visit. To schedule a visit, please visit www.onu.edu/visit or call 888-408-4668."

SELECTIVITY
Admissions Rating	86
# of applicants	3,147
% of applicants accepted	81
% of acceptees attending	24

FRESHMAN PROFILE
Range SAT Critical Reading	520–630
Range SAT Math	560–670
Range SAT Writing	510–620
Range ACT Composite	24–29
Minimum paper TOEFL	480
Minimum computer TOEFL	157
Minimum web-based TOEFL	54
Average HS GPA	3.73
% graduated top 10% of class	50
% graduated top 25% of class	74
% graduated top 50% of class	91

DEADLINES
Early action I	
Deadline	11/1
Notification	1/10
Early action II	
Deadline	12/1
Notification	12/31
Regular	
Deadline	2/1
Notification	3/1
Nonfall registration?	yes

APPLICANTS ALSO LOOK AT AND SOMETIMES PREFER
Bowling Green State University, Miami University, The Ohio State University—Columbus, University of Toledo, Wittenberg University

FINANCIAL FACTS
Financial Aid Rating	78
Annual tuition	$34,140
Room and board	$9,476
Required fees	$240
% frosh rec. need-based scholarship or grant aid	84
% UG rec. need-based scholarship or grant aid	83
% frosh rec. non-need-based scholarship or grant aid	12
% UG rec. non-need-based scholarship or grant aid	6
% frosh rec. need-based self-help aid	68
% UG rec. need-based self-help aid	71
% frosh rec. any financial aid	84
% UG rec. any financial aid	83
% UG borrow to pay for school	83
Average cumulative indebtedness	$45,753

THE OHIO STATE UNIVERSITY—COLUMBUS

110 ENARSON HALL, 54 WEST TWELFTH AVENUE, COLUMBUS, OH 43210 • ADMISSIONS: 614-292-3980 • FAX: 614-292-4818

CAMPUS LIFE

Quality of Life Rating	85
Fire Safety Rating	80
Green Rating	95
Type of school	public
Environment	metropolis

STUDENTS

Total undergrad enrollment	40,851
% male/female	53/47
% from out of state	11
% from public high school	87
% live on campus	25
# of fraternities	42
# of sororities	25
% African American	6
% Asian	5
% Caucasian	78
% Hispanic	3
% international	5
# of countries represented	106

SURVEY SAYS . . .

Athletic facilities are great
Great off-campus food
Everyone loves the Buckeyes
Student publications are popular

ACADEMICS

Academic Rating	70
% students graduating within 4 years	49
% students graduating within 6 years	78
Calendar	quarter
Student/faculty ratio	19:1
Profs interesting rating	65
Profs accessible rating	70
Most common reg class size	20–29 students
Most common lab size	20–29 students

MOST POPULAR MAJORS
biology, finance, psychology

STUDENTS SAY ". . ."

Academics

The Ohio State University in Columbus is "a great blend of academics, opportunity, and fun." This is one of the largest universities in the country, and as such, you'll find "every resource you could possibly need" and "unlimited" academic opportunities. "Everything from music to biochemical engineering and anything and everything in between" is available. "You name it and we've got it," guarantees an English major. "The size of campus can be in some ways intimidating," though. It's a "cattle call" here. Classes are often enormous, and it can be hard to get the ones you want. Also, while "the administration seems to run the school fairly smoothly," "red tape" is a problem. "If you want to do anything out of the ordinary, such as apply a scholarship to the summer quarter, or take a leave of absence, it is very difficult." "You have to kind of fend for yourself to figure out how the school works." "OSU is not a school which holds your hand though planning and logistical matters," cautions a business major. The general education curriculum is unpopular with many students, but Ohio State is on a quarter system and coursework moves pretty fast. Any class you don't like will be over relatively quickly. Some professors are "incredibly eager to work with students" and are "as interesting and entertaining as they can be when lecturing." "There are a lot of mediocre professors," too. Still other faculty members are "too wrapped up in their research" and "don't pay attention to whether the students are learning or not." Also, just like at any big state school, there are plenty of teaching assistants here, and they're "sometimes sub-par."

Life

For many students, life at Ohio State comes down to "drinking and sports." The entire campus is fulled up with "a ton of Buckeye spirit." "Attending the varsity sports events is popular." "Everyone is obsessed with Buckeye football." It's a little bit "like a religion," and the team is "idolized." Students also "party a lot in general." "It's hard to tell exactly how many people really are partying," explains a senior. "It just seems like a lot." For many students, "awesome" house parties "are the preferred medium" for social activity, but there's "always a party, always a bar" "Thursday through Saturday." "There are other scenes than just the party scene," of course. The "great" recreation center here is absolutely gargantuan. "There is always an interesting event, conference, or performance," and OSU brings in plenty of "big entertainment acts." There are more than 900 student organizations as well. "Greek life here isn't dominant" but it's noticeable, and a few thousand students are involved. "It's impossible to not find something that fits you," promises a senior. "You're never bored." Off campus, "Columbus boasts a population of more than one million souls." Many students "gallery hop in the art district" or regularly take advantage of the area's "great shopping."

Student Body

"It's hard to categorize students here," says a sophomore. The vibe is "middle class" and "very Midwestern," and just about everyone is either "from small Ohio towns" or from "from a suburban-type setting" around Columbus, Toledo, Cincinnati, or Cleveland. Otherwise, "Ohio State is a melting pot," and "it easy to blend into the crowd." "There is no real homogenous, average student." Several ethnic minorities are solidly represented. Many students dress "like they shopped in a department store, albeit a nice department store," observes a senior. "There is a lot of style and fashion walking around campus," too. There are also hordes of students clad in "OSU clothing." A huge contingent of students is "smart, outgoing, athletic, and involved," but "the stereotypical weird kids at other universities have several hundred like-minded classmates at OSU." There are "drunks, nerds, overachievers, underachievers," "artists," outcasts, and hippies. Many students are "working a job or two." "The large community provides diversity," relates a senior. "However, we have our own smaller communities to help campus feel like home."

THE OHIO STATE UNIVERSITY—COLUMBUS

FINANCIAL AID: 614-292-0300 • E-MAIL: ASKABUCKEYE@OSU.EDU (FRESHMEN AND TRANSFER)• WEBSITE: WWW.OSU.EDU

THE PRINCETON REVIEW SAYS

Admissions

Very important factors considered include: Academic GPA, class rank, rigor of secondary school record, standardized test scores. *Important factors considered include:* Application essay, extracurricular activities, first generation, talent/ability, volunteer work, work experience. *Other factors considered include:* Recommendation(s), character/personal qualities, geographical residence, racial/ethnic status, state residency. SAT or ACT required; ACT with writing component required. TOEFL required of all international applicants. High school diploma is required, and GED is accepted. *Academic units required:* 4 English, 3 mathematics, 3 science (with labs), 2 foreign language, 2 social studies, 1 visual/performing arts, 1 academic elective. *Academic units recommended:* 4 English, 4 mathematics, 3 science (with labs), 3 foreign language, 3 social studies, 1 visual/performing arts, 1 academic elective.

Financial Aid

Students should submit: FAFSA. Regular filing deadline is February 15. The Princeton Review suggests that all financial aid forms be submitted as soon as possible after January 1. *Need-based scholarships/grants offered:* Federal Pell, SEOG, state scholarships/grants, private scholarships, school scholarship or grant aid from institutional funds. *Loan aid offered:* Direct Subsidized Stafford, Direct Unsubsidized Stafford, Direct PLUS, Federal Perkins, Federal Nursing Loans, university loans from institutional funds. Federal Work-Study Program available. Off-campus job opportunities are good.

The Inside Word

Though the sheer number of applicants to OSU each year is sizeable, applications are read with more than a cursory glance toward grades and class rank. Standards are high, but OSU is certainly worth a shot for the average student. The university's great reputation and affordable cost make it a good choice for anyone looking at large schools.

THE SCHOOL SAYS " . . ."

From the Admissions Office

"The Ohio State University has changed dramatically in the last decade, and, as a result, has seen its academic reputation thrive. A strong focus on helping first-year students make a successful transition to the university, competitive admissions, and a physical transformation (amazing new and renovated facilities across campus) are changes that have increased Ohio State's ability to draw students and faculty of exceptional scholarly talent."

"Once you're on campus, "big school" translates to depth, diversity, and opportunity. Ohio State prides itself on offering about any academic or extra-curricular opportunity a student could dream of: 175-plus majors; 1,000-plus student organizations; 100 study abroad programs; internship, research, and service-learning opportunities in every college; multiple Honors and Scholars programs; and nearly forty learning communities. Professional and faculty advisors assigned to each student help identify the opportunities that meet the student's interests and goals.

"Ohio State consistently boasts an impressive first-year retention rate over ninety percent; the national average is around seventy-five percent. Ohio State's focus on the first year is campus-wide, including strong orientation and first-year programs."

SELECTIVITY
Admissions Rating	84
# of applicants	24,302
% of applicants accepted	68
% of acceptees attending	40
# accepting a place on wait list	247
% admitted from wait list	83

FRESHMAN PROFILE
Range SAT Critical Reading	540–650
Range SAT Math	590–700
Range SAT Writing	540–640
Range ACT Composite	26–30
Minimum paper TOEFL	527
Minimum computer TOEFL	197
Minimum web-based TOEFL	71
% graduated top 10% of class	54
% graduated top 25% of class	89
% graduated top 50% of class	98

DEADLINES
Regular	
Deadline	2/1
Notification	11/15
Nonfall registration?	yes

APPLICANTS ALSO LOOK AT
AND SOMETIMES PREFER
Case Western Reserve University, Miami University, Purdue University—West Lafayette
AND RARELY PREFER
Ohio University—Athens, University of Cincinnati

FINANCIAL FACTS
Financial Aid Rating	70
Annual in-state tuition	$8,994
Annual out-of-state tuition	$23,178
Room and board	$9,180
Required fees	$426
Books and supplies	$1,554
% frosh rec. need-based scholarship or grant aid	46
% UG rec. need-based scholarship or grant aid	40
% frosh rec. non-need-based scholarship or grant aid	3
% UG rec. non-need-based scholarship or grant aid	1
% frosh rec. need-based self-help aid	47
% UG rec. need-based self-help aid	51
% frosh rec. any financial aid	98
% UG rec. any financial aid	83
% UG borrow to pay for school	59
Average cumulative indebtedness	$22,830

OHIO UNIVERSITY—ATHENS

120 CHUBB HALL, ATHENS, OH 45701 • ADMISSIONS: 740-593-4100 • FAX: 740-593-0560

STUDENTS SAY ". . ."

Academics

"Academically, Ohio University has something for everyone, from astrophysics to the history of rock and roll," students at this large state-run university boast. And students have an equally wide range of choices when it comes to committing themselves to academics; "You can take advantage of the vast amount of knowledge and resources directly available, or you can forget studies and party," students tell us. Those seeking a challenge will have no trouble finding it here, however; OU boasts "a strong engineering faculty," a noteworthy aviation program offered within the university's demanding school of engineering and technology, an "excellent and very selective early childhood education program," and "one of the best journalism schools in the country"—the E.W. Scripps School of Journalism—which offers "frequent opportunities to learn and grow outside the classroom with guest speakers and special events." Scripps houses "a great communications school" offering great hands-on experience; one student informs us that "Southeast Ohio depends on our college television and radio station for their news, weather, and high school sports." As at any large university, unassertive students are in danger of getting lost in the crowd, but those who make the effort to seek out faculty and administrators assure us that "The school is very supportive of the students. I have close relationships with multiple professors, and I think that they generally take a strong interest in the students."

Life

"Ohio University has a beautiful campus with lots of character, both in academia and nightlife," students here report. Greek organizations play a major role in the life of the campus, providing service to the community and serving as a social catalyst. Undergraduates assure us that the school "truly lives up to its reputation as a party school. It is never hard to find a party on any given night, whether in the dorms or off campus." One undergrad writes "a nationwide reputation as a party school is not something I'm proud of," but most accept things as they are, noting that "Ohio University is a school where everyone can find a group of people doing whatever they're particularly interested in," which is to say that partying is hardly the only option here. College athletics are a big draw (especially football, men's basketball, and women's volleyball), as are such annual events as Homecoming and Halloween celebrations, and the school is host to literally hundreds of student clubs and organizations serving interests of every variety. Hometown Athens is a typical small college town with access to a wide variety of outdoor activities. The closest cities of note—Columbus; Ohio and Charleston, West Virginia—are each about a ninety-minute drive from the OU campus.

Student Body

The OU student body "is pretty homogenous," with a large contingent of undergrads who are "white, middle- to upper-class, and from Ohio." "We have a small minority population, especially in the undergraduate programs," one student concedes, "but it's easy to interact with other cultures if you seek them out." Students here "try to get involved in community service, especially those involved in Greek life," and they are "generally friendly." Most work hard enough to get by but rarely harder; one student observes that "students totally devoted to their schoolwork are atypical here."

OHIO UNIVERSITY—ATHENS

FINANCIAL AID: 740-593-4141 • E-MAIL: ADMISSIONS.FRESHMEN@OHIOU.EDU • WEBSITE: WWW.OHIOU.EDU

THE PRINCETON REVIEW SAYS

Admissions

Very important factors considered include: Academic GPA, rigor of secondary school record. *Important factors considered include:* Class rank, standardized test scores. *Other factors considered include:* Application essay, recommendation(s), alumni/ae relation, character/personal qualities, extracurricular activities, talent/ability, volunteer work, work experience. SAT or ACT required; ACT with writing component recommended. High school diploma is required, and GED is accepted. *Academic units required:* 4 English, 3 mathematics, 3 science, 2 foreign language, 3 social studies.

Financial Aid

Students should submit: FAFSA. Regular filing deadline is March 15. The Princeton Review suggests that all financial aid forms be submitted as soon as possible after January 1. *Need-based scholarships/grants offered:* Federal Pell, SEOG, state scholarships/grants, private scholarships, school scholarship or grant aid from institutional funds. *Loan aid offered:* Direct Subsidized Stafford, Direct Unsubsidized Stafford, Direct PLUS, Federal Perkins. Federal Work-Study Program available. Off-campus job opportunities are fair.

The Inside Word

Admissions requirements vary from school to school at Ohio University. The Honors Tutorial is most selective (you should be in the top ten percent of your graduating class and earn at least a 30/1300 on your ACT/SAT), followed by the journalism school (top fifteen percent, 25/1140), the business school (top twenty percent, 24/1100), media arts and visual studies, engineering, and visual communication. Admissions decisions are numbers-driven; those on the cusp should get in if they've demonstrated academic improvement during their junior and senior years.

THE SCHOOL SAYS "..."

From the Admissions Office

"Ohio University offers limitless opportunities for students to fulfill their promise and effect positive change. We do this through an accessible, engaging, and transforming student experience; through the breadth and excellence of our degree programs and facilities; and through the documented academic success and career accomplishments of our students, faculty, and alumni.

"Education at Ohio University extends beyond the classroom. Students study abroad, participate in research and internship programs, and get involved in community service as well as in 323 student organizations. Ohio is an incubator for research, exploration, creativity, innovation, and collaboration, enabling students to develop leadership skills, form new ideas, and reach potential they did not know they had. Our high graduation rate, welcoming residential living campus—rated as one of the country's most beautiful—and successful learning communities make Ohio a unique place to live and learn. Ohio values the importance of citizenship and educating students for success in their careers and their lives. Our nationally ranked colleges and degree programs, such as the Scripps College of Communication, Centers of Excellence in energy/environment and biomedicine/health care, and our unique Honors Tutorial College, make a degree from Ohio an instant advantage.

"Students, faculty, and alumni are consistently recognized for their contributions across campus and around the globe. Our students' success in winning many of the nation's most prestigious and competitive academic awards remains at a record high. Our total number of Fulbright winners, for example, consistently ranks us first in Ohio and has placed us in elite company nationally with schools such as Boston College, Princeton, and UCLA. Faculty members are engaged in renowned, world-class research in energy, biological sciences, health care, avionics, and more. For over 200 years, more than 200,000 alumni have enjoyed leadership positions in all walks of life through the path to promise they followed as proud Ohio students."

SELECTIVITY

Admissions Rating	76
# of applicants	13,366
% of applicants accepted	85
% of acceptees attending	35
# accepting a place on wait list	82
% admitted from wait list	5

FRESHMAN PROFILE

Range SAT Critical Reading	490–610
Range SAT Math	490–610
Range SAT Writing	480–590
Range ACT Composite	21–26
Average HS GPA	3.38
% graduated top 10% of class	14
% graduated top 25% of class	41
% graduated top 50% of class	80

DEADLINES

Regular	
Deadline	2/1
Notification	9/15
Nonfall registration?	yes

APPLICANTS ALSO LOOK AT AND OFTEN PREFER

Bowling Green State University, Kent State University—Kent Campus, Miami University, The Ohio State University—Columbus

FINANCIAL FACTS

Financial Aid Rating	67
Annual in-state tuition	$9,603
Annual out-of-state tuition	$18,567
Room and board	$9,621
Books and supplies	$873
% frosh rec. need-based scholarship or grant aid	58
% UG rec. need-based scholarship or grant aid	54
% frosh rec. non-need-based scholarship or grant aid	34
% UG rec. non-need-based scholarship or grant aid	22
% frosh rec. need-based self-help aid	55
% UG rec. need-based self-help aid	51
% frosh rec. any financial aid	64
% UG rec. any financial aid	58
% UG borrow to pay for school	68
Average cumulative indebtedness	$25,330

OHIO WESLEYAN UNIVERSITY

ADMISSIONS OFFICE, 61 SOUTH SANDUSKY STREET, DELAWARE, OH 43015 • ADMISSIONS: 740-368-3020 • FAX: 740-368-3314

CAMPUS LIFE

Quality of Life Rating	84
Fire Safety Rating	61
Green Rating	60*
Type of school	private
Affiliation	Methodist
Environment	town

STUDENTS

Total undergrad enrollment	1,960
% male/female	48/52
% from out of state	41
% from public high school	77
% live on campus	82
# of fraternities	11
# of sororities	7
% African American	5
% Asian	2
% Caucasian	79
% Hispanic	1
% international	9
# of countries represented	41

SURVEY SAYS . . .
Lab facilities are great
Students are friendly
*Frats and sororities dominate
social scene*
Lots of beer drinking

ACADEMICS

Academic Rating	89
% students graduating within 4 years	60
% students graduating within 6 years	68
Calendar	semester
Student/faculty ratio	12:1
Profs interesting rating	91
Profs accessible rating	93
Most common reg class size	10–19 students
Most common lab size	10–19 students

MOST POPULAR MAJORS
economics, premedicine, psychology

STUDENTS SAY ". . ."

Academics

With just 550 students in each entering class, it is easy to feel a part of the intimate and friendly Ohio Wesleyan community. Personal attention is key to the OWU experience, and "The eleven to one student-to-faculty ratio allows a great deal of communication, which fosters a better learning environment for each individual." Outside of class, "most professors have an open-door policy and are even willing to come in on the weekends for review sessions." In fact, OWU professors "are very interested in spending time getting to know students personally, which definitely adds a positive experience to academic life." With world-class facilities, small class sizes, and ample one-on-one time with their professors, students have a surprising number of opportunities at this small college. A sophomore tells us, "My coursework often involves hands-on lab experience, and, in the chemistry department, I have even had the opportunity to use equipment that is often only used by graduate students at larger institutions." In this student-oriented environment, OWU undergraduates feel well-prepared the meet their educational goals, as well as their dreams for post-college life. A sophomore explains, "OWU fosters the pursuit of each student's interests and goals through various forms of support, including financial support, academic support through our academic skills center, mental support through our counseling program, and help with internships and long-term goals through career services." From the dorms to the dining hall, learning spills out of the classroom; you'll often find students engaged in "some kind of intellectual discussion during lunch." A freshman marvels, "The intellectual atmosphere here exceeds anything I could have dreamed of."

Life

Life at Ohio Wesleyan "is a fantastic combination of academics and extracurriculars, which allows the students to participate in whatever events interest them." When it comes to clubs and activities, OWU has it all: "From the Ultimate Frisbee club to the Medieval Sword Fighting Club, there is just about anything here you can imagine to do." In an unstructured moment, OWU students might "start a pickup game of Frisbee, play piano, go into town to cruise the local mall, [or] take a walk to the park." Students also enjoy the surrounding town Delaware, Ohio, "a cute place to be with fun shops and an old-fashioned movie theater." On the weekends, "the school's campus program board brings in entertainment such as comedians, hypnotists, magicians, and musicians/bands." In addition, fraternities and sororities play a fairly important role in the campus social scene (not to mention, serve as popular watering holes on the weekend); however, students insist that Greek life appeals to people who "cherish the idea of brotherhood and sisterhood and believe in community service," rather than those who simply want to party. Another special part of OWU residential life are the Small Living Units, theme-based houses in which every resident is required to "complete a house project based upon the theme of the house." Themes vary from creative arts to ethnic cultures.

Student Body

Ohio Wesleyan undergrads have "different backgrounds and history." OWU doesn't attract any single type of person, and you'll rub elbows with "shy kids, outgoing kids, creative types, scientific types, people [who] dye their hair, people who have tattoos, [and] people that don't do either." A sophomore adds, "I have friends from China, Japan, Vietnam, Taiwan, and Russia. To be able to hear their perspectives on the world is valuable to me." Despite the diversity, there are some "common threads" throughout the campus, including a general interest in "environmental preservation, community service, [and] political awareness." According to most students, the typical OWU undergraduate participates "in some kind of club or organization" and "cares about their academics and the community." A freshman says, "I really enjoy the balance between academics and having fun. People respect and understand when someone needs to study, but it is never so stressful that you cannot go out and have fun on the weekends."

OHIO WESLEYAN UNIVERSITY

FINANCIAL AID: 740-368-3050 • E-MAIL: OWUADMIT@OWU.EDU • WEBSITE: WWW.OWU.EDU

THE PRINCETON REVIEW SAYS

Admissions

Very important factors considered include: Academic GPA, application essay, recommendation(s), rigor of secondary school record, character/personal qualities, interview. *Important factors considered include:* Class rank, standardized test scores, extracurricular activities, talent/ability. *Other factors considered include:* Alumni/ae relation, first generation, geographical residence, level of applicant's interest, racial/ethnic status, volunteer work, work experience. SAT or ACT required; ACT with or without writing component accepted. TOEFL required of all international applicants. High school diploma is required, and GED is accepted. *Academic units required:* 4 English, 3 mathematics, 3 science, 2 foreign language, 3 social studies. *Academic units recommended:* 4 mathematics, 4 science, 3 foreign language, 4 social studies.

Financial Aid

Students should submit: FAFSA, institution's own financial aid form. Regular filing deadline is May 1. The Princeton Review suggests that all financial aid forms be submitted as soon as possible after January 1. *Need-based scholarships/grants offered:* Federal Pell, SEOG, state scholarships/grants, private scholarships, school scholarship or grant aid from institutional funds. *Loan aid offered:* Direct Subsidized Stafford, Direct Unsubsidized Stafford, Direct PLUS, Federal Perkins, university loans from institutional funds. Applicants will be notified of awards on a rolling basis beginning February 15. Federal Work-Study Program available. Off-campus job opportunities are excellent.

The Inside Word

In addition to offering loads of information about the school, Ohio Wesleyan's admissions page offers loads of expert advice to high school seniors. Each year, Ohio Wesleyan University receives about 4,200 applications for just 560 spots in the entering class. The average first-year student ranked in the top thirty percent of his or her high school class, with an average GPA of 3.4.

THE SCHOOL SAYS "..."

From the Admissions Office

"Ohio Wesleyan is a small university that offers more than ninety majors, sequences, and courses of study, far more than usually are found in an institution of this size. The university's focus is on a rigorous liberal arts curriculum supplemented by abundant opportunities to unite theory and practice in a global context. A new program of competitive research grants allows students and faculty to study off-campus, both domestically and abroad; the new Sagan Fellows classes offer similar opportunities for larger, interdisciplinary groups of students, working directly with a faculty member designated as a Sagan Fellow.

"In 2009, a major was added in planetary science. The Economics Management Fellows program, offered by the Economics Department and the Woltemade Center for Economics, Business & Entrepreneurship, provides special seminars, classes, networking opportunities, and a study trip to New York City for highly qualified first-year students interested in careers in economics disciplines.

"Ohio Wesleyan has embarked upon a campaign of renewal of the University's built environment, with three completely remodeled residences available for senior men and women. One of the campus's historic residence halls buildings also is slated for complete renovation, and in Fall 2010, the university will open the new, "green" Meek Aquatics and Recreation Center.

"In 2010, Ohio Wesleyan was one of only three colleges nationwide to win the 2009 Presidential Award for Excellence in General Community Service. Applicants may submit the SAT or ACT. Best scores from either test will be considered in the application review."

SELECTIVITY

Admissions Rating	86
# of applicants	3,814
% of applicants accepted	66
% of acceptees attending	23
# accepting a place on wait list	12
% admitted from wait list	50
# of early decision applicants	53
% accepted early decision	32

FRESHMAN PROFILE

Range SAT Critical Reading	520–640
Range SAT Math	520–650
Range ACT Composite	22–28
Minimum paper TOEFL	550
Minimum computer TOEFL	213
Average HS GPA	3.43
% graduated top 10% of class	30
% graduated top 25% of class	59
% graduated top 50% of class	87

DEADLINES

Early decision	
Deadline	12/1
Notification	12/15
Early action	
Deadline	12/15
Notification	1/15
Regular	
Priority	3/1
Notification	10/1
Nonfall registration?	yes

APPLICANTS ALSO LOOK AT
AND OFTEN PREFER
Denison University, Miami University, The College of Wooster

AND SOMETIMES PREFER
Allegheny College, Rhodes College

FINANCIAL FACTS

Financial Aid Rating	84
Annual tuition	$34,570
Room and board	$8,030
Required fees	$460
Books and supplies	$2,402
% frosh rec. need-based scholarship or grant aid	60
% UG rec. need-based scholarship or grant aid	56
% frosh rec. non-need-based scholarship or grant aid	11
% UG rec. non-need-based scholarship or grant aid	9
% frosh rec. need-based self-help aid	50
% UG rec. need-based self-help aid	47
% frosh rec. any financial aid	99
% UG rec. any financial aid	98
% UG borrow to pay for school	76
Average cumulative indebtedness	$25,627

PENNSYLVANIA STATE UNIVERSITY—UNIVERSITY PARK

201 SHIELDS BUILDING, BOX 3000, UNIVERSITY PARK, PA 16802-3000 • ADMISSIONS: 814-865-5471 • FAX: 814-863-7590

CAMPUS LIFE

Quality of Life Rating	97
Fire Safety Rating	95
Green Rating	89
Type of school	public
Environment	town

STUDENTS

Total undergrad enrollment	37,855
% male/female	55/45
% from out of state	25
% live on campus	37
# of fraternities	58
# of sororities	32
% African American	4
% Asian	5
% Caucasian	78
% Hispanic	4
# of countries represented	119

SURVEY SAYS . . .
Athletic facilities are great
Everyone loves the Nittany Lions
Student publications are popular
Hard liquor is popular

ACADEMICS

Academic Rating	72
% students graduating within 4 years	62
% students graduating within 6 years	85
Calendar	semester
Student/faculty ratio	17:1
Profs interesting rating	76
Profs accessible rating	85
Most common reg class size	20–29 students
Most common lab size	20–29 students

STUDENTS SAY ". . ."

Academics
Pennsylvania State University "offers an amazing education [and] a sense of community, family, and pride," its students tell us, and while students appreciate the "hundreds of classes to choose from (you can literally take any class you could ever dream of)" and the "endless opportunities for academic and personal growth," it's the "amazing sense of pride and tradition" that truly captivates most. As one student explains, "It's about…the feeling you get even when you come back to visit twenty years later. Once you're a Penn Stater, you're always a Penn Stater. You don't get the same feeling anywhere else. Believe me, I've looked." With "strong academics in the sciences, engineering, and business," PSU has the means to educate the go-getters of tomorrow, then help them find jobs through "a very strong alumni base" that students tell us is "the largest dues-paying alumni association in the world." Academics are "incredible," with "innumerable opportunities to connect with administrators and professors, although it is up to the student to take advantage of them." Online course management services "make keeping up to date in your classes really easy." All these options and opportunities have students bragging that PSU is "a Public Ivy." One with way better football.

Life
"Once the weekend arrives it's either party time or rest-up time" at Penn State, and students tell us that "it's usually party time." "Fraternities are very popular at Penn State for first-year students, and apartments and house parties go well with the upperclassmen." Students also tout University Park's "many places to go out to dinner" ("people go out to eat a lot!"), and close proximity to "Target, Wal-Mart, and movie theaters that can all be accessed by cheap buses that run on campus." In addition, students can attend "a ton of concerts that come through State College because the Bryce Jordan Center is the biggest arena between Pittsburgh and Philadelphia" and "free events sponsored by the Student Programming Association." "Almost every weekend there is a student group performing on campus, whether it be comedy, singing, or acting," one student reports. And then there's Nittany Lion football. As one student puts it, "Football is a way of life here." Many students are also active in philanthropy; THON, the school's annual dance marathon, is "the largest student-run philanthropy in the world, raising money for pediatric cancer research."

Student Body
PSU is a big school with lots of different types of students, but there is definitely a predominant look on campus, which is "sweatpants and t-shirts. We like to be comfortable, relaxed, but always school spirited." Indeed, your typical PSU undergrad is "a diehard football fan" with "a plethora of pride for the school and lion." About one-quarter of the student body originates from outside Pennsylvania ("there's a large number of students from New Jersey"), with the majority of Keystone State natives coming "usually from either the Philadelphia or Pittsburgh area" as well as representing "middle-class white kids from central Pennsylvania." Whatever their geographical roots, the typical PSU undergrad "is someone who works hard during the week [and] is involved in activities on campus, but definitely wants to have a good time once the weekend comes." As one student puts it, "The libraries and study areas on campus are always packed but so are the streets downtown on weekends."

PENNSYLVANIA STATE UNIVERSITY—UNIVERSITY PARK

FINANCIAL AID: 814-865-6301 • E-MAIL: ADMISSIONS@PSU.EDU • WEBSITE: WWW.PSU.EDU

THE PRINCETON REVIEW SAYS

Admissions

Very important factors considered include: Academic GPA, standardized test scores. *Important factors considered include:* Rigor of secondary school record. *Other factors considered include:* Application essay, class rank, recommendation(s), alumni/ae relation, character/personal qualities, extracurricular activities, talent/ability, volunteer work, work experience. SAT or ACT required; ACT with writing component required. TOEFL required of all international applicants. High school diploma is required, and GED is accepted. *Academic units required:* 4 English, 3 mathematics, 3 science, 2 foreign language, 3 social studies.

Financial Aid

Students should submit: FAFSA. The Princeton Review suggests that all financial aid forms be submitted as soon as possible after January 1. *Need-based scholarships/grants offered:* Federal Pell, SEOG, state scholarships/grants, private scholarships, school scholarship or grant aid from institutional funds. *Loan aid offered:* Direct Subsidized Stafford, Direct Unsubsidized Stafford, Direct PLUS, Federal Perkins, university loans from institutional funds. Applicants will be notified of awards on a rolling basis beginning March 1. Federal Work-Study Program available. Off-campus job opportunities are good.

The Inside Word

High school GPA is by far the most important factor in PSU admissions. According to the school's website, high school grades account for two-thirds of the final admissions decision. Standardized test scores, class rank, extracurricular activities, and other factors make up the remaining one-third. PSU admits on a rolling basis. Given this school's popularity with Pennsylvania residents, applicants would do well to get their applications in as early as possible.

THE SCHOOL SAYS " . . ."

From the Admissions Office

"Unique among large public universities, Penn State combines the almost 38,000-student setting of its University Park campus with twenty academically and administratively integrated undergraduate locations—small-college settings ranging in size from 600 to 3,400 students. Each year, more than sixty percent of incoming freshmen begin their studies at these residential and commuter campuses, while nearly forty percent begin at the University Park campus. The smaller locations focus on the needs of new students by offering the first two years of most Penn State baccalaureate degrees in settings that stress close interaction with faculty. Depending on the major selected, students may choose to complete their degree at University Park or one of the smaller locations. Your application to Penn State qualifies you for review for any of our campuses. Your two choices of location are reviewed in the order given. Entrance difficulty is based, in part, on the demand. Due to its popularity, the University Park campus is the most competitive for admission.

"Freshman applicants may submit the results from the SAT or the ACT with the writing component. The writing portions of these tests will not necessarily be factored into admission decisions."

SELECTIVITY

Admissions Rating	93
# of applicants	40,714
% of applicants accepted	52
% of acceptees attending	31
# accepting a place on wait list	1,456
% admitted from wait list	100

FRESHMAN PROFILE

Range SAT Critical Reading	530–630
Range SAT Math	560–670
Range SAT Writing	540–640
Minimum paper TOEFL	550
Minimum computer TOEFL	213
Minimum web-based TOEFL	80
Average HS GPA	3.55
% graduated top 10% of class	50
% graduated top 25% of class	86
% graduated top 50% of class	98

DEADLINES

Regular	
Priority	11/30
Notification	11/1
Nonfall registration?	yes

FINANCIAL FACTS

Financial Aid Rating	66
Annual in-state tuition	$14,412
Annual out-of-state tuition	$26,276
Room and board	$9,030
Required fees	$838
Books and supplies	$1,456
% frosh rec. need-based scholarship or grant aid	21
% UG rec. need-based scholarship or grant aid	27
% frosh rec. non-need-based scholarship or grant aid	20
% UG rec. non-need-based scholarship or grant aid	16
% frosh rec. need-based self-help aid	37
% UG rec. need-based self-help aid	42
% frosh rec. any financial aid	71
% UG rec. any financial aid	72
% UG borrow to pay for school	68
Average cumulative indebtedness	$28,680

PEPPERDINE UNIVERSITY

24255 PACIFIC COAST HIGHWAY, MALIBU, CA 90263-4392 • ADMISSIONS: 310-456-4861 • FAX: 310-506-4861

STUDENTS SAY ". . ."

Academics

A small private college overlooking the Pacific Ocean, Pepperdine is an "amazingly beautiful" place to get an education. With about 3,000 undergraduates and an excellent teacher/student ratio, Pepperdine and its "smaller class sizes make it beyond easy to form personal yet academic relationships with your professors." Although "academics are quite challenging," professors "take their role as a mentor seriously. They invite classes over for meals, meet students for coffee, and are eager to help you move in the direction of your dreams." While universally supportive, professors get mixed reviews regarding the ability to keep your attention: Some professors "are very lively and exciting, while some are boring and you would rather take a nap." Career and internship opportunities naturally grow out of the school's prime location, strong alumni network, and regional ties. "Professors are well-connected with both corporations and the surrounding community," and there are "endless internship and volunteer opportunities" in the region. Plus, "Pepperdine's International Program is consistently ranked as one of the best," offering "programs in Florence, London, Shanghai, Buenos Aires…the list goes on! Anyone who is looking forward to studying abroad should definitely look into our programs." Pepperdine is affiliated with the Church of Christ, and Christian values are "prevalent but not overwhelming" in academic curriculum; all students, regardless of their background, are required to attend the "mandatory Convocation program"—a series of chapels, Bible studies, and speakers, designed to promote spirituality. While there's a conservative slant among the higher-ups, Pepperdine's administration is "much more moderate than what you would find at other small, Christian schools."

Life

Pepperdine students gloat about their school's perfect location in Malibu, California, where "there is a 360 view of the Pacific Ocean, and students can walk to the beach." The "campus is surrounded by national parks and beach," so nature lovers enjoy "countless opportunities for hiking, swimming, running, waterfall jumping, camping, [and] rock-climbing." "The close proximity to LA, Santa Monica, Hollywood, and the Pacific Coast Highway make it easy for students to find things to do." Students say that a car is a necessity. Fortunately, "There are enough students with cars to hitch a ride," if you don't have your own set of wheels. Alcohol is prohibited at Pepperdine, and "the dry campus policy is strictly enforced." Therefore, "People have to go off campus to drink and party." "The people who party can do so without it affecting the people who don't at all." While the campus is undeniably dreamy, students would like to see the school "improve is the student health facilities and workout facilities"—as well as provide more student parking.

Student Body

"Academics, service, athletics, and social events are all a big part of the life of a typical student." During college, "The typical Pepperdine student is involved in two service projects, spends their spring break building homes in Central America, has huge career goals, is involved in a performing arts group, looks forward to new student orientation all year, and studies abroad as a sophomore." Pepperdine students are also good about "being healthy and eating well and exercising right." It can feel "as if all the popular kids across all the different high schools across America convened in Malibu." However, students tell us "there is a lot more diversity" at Pepperdine today. You get a nice mix of "art majors to the science kids to the surfers to the hardcore studiers to the philosophy majors." Most students come from "a Christian background whether or not they are religious now," and some students are strongly religious and conservative. "Finding alternative viewpoints may be tough," but most students are "fairly open-minded" and "extremely nice."

PEPPERDINE UNIVERSITY

FINANCIAL AID: 310-506-4301 • E-MAIL: ADMISSION-SEAVER@PEPPERDINE.EDU • WEBSITE: WWW.PEPPERDINE.EDU

THE PRINCETON REVIEW SAYS

Admissions

Very important factors considered include: Academic GPA, application essay, recommendation(s), rigor of secondary school record, standardized test scores, character/personal qualities, extracurricular activities, talent/ability. *Important factors considered include:* Religious affiliation/commitment, volunteer work. *Other factors considered include:* Alumni/ae relation, first generation, racial/ethnic status, work experience. SAT or ACT required; ACT with writing component required. TOEFL required of all international applicants. High school diploma is required, and GED is accepted. *Academic units recommended:* 4 English, 4 mathematics, 4 science (3 science labs), 3 foreign language, 3 social studies, 3 history, 3 academic elective.

Financial Aid

Students should submit: FAFSA. Regular filing deadline is February 15. The Princeton Review suggests that all financial aid forms be submitted as soon as possible after January 1. *Need-based scholarships/grants offered:* Federal Pell, SEOG, state scholarships/grants, private scholarships, school scholarship or grant aid from institutional funds, United Negro College Fund. *Loan aid offered:* Direct Subsidized Stafford, Direct Unsubsidized Stafford, Federal Perkins, university loans from institutional funds. Federal Work-Study Program available. Off-campus job opportunities are good.

The Inside Word

Admission to Pepperdine is highly selective. The school generally receives almost 8,000 applications for the incoming class of fewer than 1,000 students. Decisions are made based on a student's academic record, standardized test scores, and two letters of recommendation—one personal and the other academic. Students affiliated with the Church of Christ are eligible for special Church of Christ scholarships; to be considered, applicants must submit a letter of recommendation from a church leader.

THE SCHOOL SAYS " . . ."

From the Admissions Office

"As a selective university, Pepperdine seeks students who show promise of academic achievement at the collegiate level. However, we also seek students who are committed to serving the university community, as well as others with whom they come into contact. We look for community-service activities, volunteer efforts, and strong leadership qualities, as well as a demonstrated commitment to academic studies and an interest in the liberal arts.

"Seaver College of Pepperdine University requires freshman applicants to submit scores from either the SAT Reasoning Test (including the writing portion) or the ACT (including the writing test). The scores are evaluated in conjunction with the grade point average in specific courses completed."

SELECTIVITY

Admissions Rating	94
# of applicants	7,949
% of applicants accepted	31
% of acceptees attending	26

FRESHMAN PROFILE

Range SAT Critical Reading	550–670
Range SAT Math	560–680
Range SAT Writing	550–660
Range ACT Composite	25–30
Minimum paper TOEFL	550
Minimum computer TOEFL	220
Minimum web-based TOEFL	80
Average HS GPA	3.65
% graduated top 10% of class	42
% graduated top 25% of class	79
% graduated top 50% of class	97

DEADLINES

Regular	
Priority	11/15
Deadline	1/15
Nonfall registration?	yes

APPLICANTS ALSO LOOK AT
AND OFTEN PREFER
Loyola Marymount University, University of California—Los Angeles, University of California—San Diego, University of San Diego, University of Southern California

AND SOMETIMES PREFER
New York University, Vanderbilt University

AND RARELY PREFER
Biola University, Occidental College

FINANCIAL FACTS

Financial Aid Rating	83
Annual tuition	$39,080
Books and supplies	$1,200
% frosh rec. need-based scholarship or grant aid	56
% UG rec. need-based scholarship or grant aid	47
% frosh rec. non-need-based scholarship or grant aid	54
% UG rec. non-need-based scholarship or grant aid	46
% frosh rec. need-based self-help aid	47
% UG rec. need-based self-help aid	36
% UG borrow to pay for school	57
Average cumulative indebtedness	$35,747

PITZER COLLEGE

1050 NORTH MILLS AVENUE, CLAREMONT, CA 91711-6101 • ADMISSIONS: 909-621-8129 • FAX: 909-621-8770

CAMPUS LIFE
Quality of Life Rating	92
Fire Safety Rating	82
Green Rating	92
Type of school	private
Environment	town

STUDENTS
Total undergrad enrollment	1,080
% male/female	41/59
% from out of state	46
% live on campus	74
% African American	6
% Asian	9
% Caucasian	41
% Hispanic	16
% Native American	1
% international	3
# of countries represented	15

SURVEY SAYS . . .
Lots of liberal students
Students are friendly
Different types of students interact
Students aren't religious
Frats and sororities are unpopular
or nonexistent
Student government is popular
Political activism is popular

ACADEMICS
Academic Rating	96
% students graduating within 4 years	80
% students graduating within 6 years	79
Calendar	semester
Student/faculty ratio	11:1
Profs interesting rating	92
Profs accessible rating	94
Most common reg class size	10–19 students

MOST POPULAR MAJORS
film/cinema/video studies, psychology, sociology

STUDENTS SAY ". . ."

Academics
Pitzer College is "small, personal, and unique," but because students have access to the classes and "excellent resources" at four other local colleges through the Claremont Consortium, "you can choose to make your college experience as large or as small as you want!" Pitzer doesn't have a lot of requirements, so there's a high degree of academic freedom and flexibility, including the opportunity to create your own major. Students gush about the level of "student autonomy," calling Pitzer "a challenging school that allows students to become effective leaders." Emphasis is on "social responsibility" and "intercultural understanding," and classes "are constantly being connected to present society and how you can pursue social issues through your field of study." "Professors are as zesty and zany as they are brilliant and intriguing" and they "encourage respectful dialogue inside and outside the classroom." Generally, "emphasis [is] on discussion; besides intro courses you won't find many lecture classes." "Pitzer is all about analytical thinking and learning to think beyond the material in front of you. Professors won't settle for summary; be prepared to form and argue your own opinions." Students are very positive about their professors, calling them "life changing" and "dedicated and enthusiastic." A history major says professors "demand a lot from their students," and a political science major adds that "they want to know each of their students individually and help them out as much as they can."

Life
Pitzer's location means great weather, which means "year-round outdoor activities." "Everyday walking through campus you'll see classes being held outside on the grass, students lying in hammocks reading, students studying while laying out by the pool, or students fixing old bikes at the Green Bike Program (a student-run club, promoting green transportation by providing bikes for the community)." Pitzer students love the "very laid-back and easygoing environment," but find the school is still able to enforce "a serious education." The College Consortium means there's always something going on, whether it's a "speaker series, dances, parties, or concerts," and there's "no shortage of things to do." Students report an "average" amount of drinking and drug use, and a few noted that though there's "a lot of pot smoking" they "never felt pressured" to take part. The five colleges "sponsor parties…with kegs, deejays, etc.," though the big parties usually take place at the other colleges, or off campus. Pitzer is "close enough to Los Angeles to head in for concerts, museums, shopping, etc., [and] many students do camping trips in Southern California [or] head to the beach." There's also a campus organization, Pitzer Outdoor Adventures (POA), that "funds students each week to basically go out on epic adventures. Want gas money for surfing? Okay! Want some funds for a back packing trip? Done!" A leader of POA admits with the school funding adventures, it "doesn't get much better."

Student Body
"The one thing all Pitzer students do have in common is awareness and community involvement. Every student on this campus has a strong voice." Pitzer students are hard workers and "passionate thinkers," "intelligent, chill, accepting, and friendly." Though Pitzer is small, "there is such a wide variety of people [that] you'll find a place where you fit in," and a sociology student adds that, "You only really don't fit in if you're unfriendly and mean." "At Pitzer, there are countless ways to meet people…and if you can't find something at Pitzer you can definitely find it at one of the other Claremont Colleges." Pitzer has a reputation as a "hippie" (and sometimes "hipster") school, but students say the "diversity among personalities is growing rapidly." One student says that Pitzer students "are a collection of creative people who, in their different ways, like to think outside of the box."

PITZER COLLEGE

FINANCIAL AID: 909-621-8208 • E-MAIL: ADMISSION@PITZER.EDU • WEBSITE: WWW.PITZER.EDU

THE PRINCETON REVIEW SAYS

Admissions
Very important factors considered include: Academic GPA, application essay, class rank, recommendation(s), rigor of secondary school record, character/personal qualities, extracurricular activities, geographical residence, racial/ethnic status. *Important factors considered include:* First generation, geographical residence, interview, level of applicant's interest, talent/ability, volunteer work. *Other factors considered include:* Standardized test scores, alumni/ae relation, work experience. ACT with writing component recommended. TOEFL required of all international applicants. High school diploma is required, and GED is accepted. *Academic units required:* 4 English, 3 mathematics, 3 science (3 science labs), 3 foreign language, 3 social studies, 1 history, 1 visual/performing arts.

Financial Aid
Students should submit: FAFSA, CSS/Financial Aid PROFILE. Regular filing deadline is February 1. The Princeton Review suggests that all financial aid forms be submitted as soon as possible after January 1. *Need-based scholarships/grants offered:* Federal Pell, SEOG, state scholarships/grants, private scholarships, school scholarship or grant aid from institutional funds. *Loan aid offered:* Direct Subsidized Stafford, Direct Unsubsidized Stafford, Direct PLUS, Federal Perkins, university loans from institutional funds. Federal Work-Study Program available. Off-campus job opportunities are good.

The Inside Word
This is a place where applicants can feel confident in letting their thoughts flow freely on admissions essays. Not only does the committee read them (a circumstance more rare in college admissions that one is led to believe), but they've also set up the process to emphasize them! Thus, what you have to say for yourself will go much further than numbers in determining your suitability for Pitzer.

THE SCHOOL SAYS "..."

From the Admissions Office
"Pitzer is about opportunities. It's about possibilities. The students who come here are looking for something different from the usual 'take two courses from column A, two courses from column B, and two courses from column C.' That kind of arbitrary selection doesn't make a satisfying education at Pitzer. So we look for students who want to have an impact on their own education, who want the chief responsibility—with help from their faculty advisors—in designing their own futures.

"Pitzer's admission policy uses a test-optional policy. Students in the top ten percent of their class or those who have an unweighted academic GPA of 3.5 or higher are not required to submit test scores. Others are allowed to choose from a variety of choices, including standardized tests (i.e., the SAT and ACT with the writing component)."

SELECTIVITY
Admissions Rating	97
# of applicants	3,812
% of applicants accepted	26
% of acceptees attending	27

FRESHMAN PROFILE
Range SAT Critical Reading	600–680
Range SAT Math	590–670
Range ACT Composite	26–30
Minimum paper TOEFL	520
Minimum web-based TOEFL	70
Average HS GPA	3.84
% graduated top 10% of class	47
% graduated top 25% of class	89
% graduated top 50% of class	100

DEADLINES
Early decision	
Deadline	11/15
Notification	1/1
Regular	
Deadline	1/1
Nonfall registration?	no

APPLICANTS ALSO LOOK AT AND OFTEN PREFER
Claremont McKenna College, Occidental College, Pomona College, Scripps College, University of California—Berkeley, University of California—Los Angeles, University of Southern California

FINANCIAL FACTS
Financial Aid Rating	98
Annual tuition	$37,520
Room and board	$11,950
Required fees	$3,610
Books and supplies	$1,200
% frosh rec. need-based scholarship or grant aid	42
% UG rec. need-based scholarship or grant aid	37
% frosh rec. need-based self-help aid	40
% UG rec. need-based self-help aid	39
% frosh rec. any financial aid	45
% UG rec. any financial aid	45
% UG borrow to pay for school	45
Average cumulative indebtedness	$20,448

THE BEST 376 COLLEGES ■ 427

POMONA COLLEGE

333 NORTH COLLEGE WAY, CLAREMONT, CA 91711-6312 • ADMISSIONS: 909-621-8134 • FAX: 909-621-8952

CAMPUS LIFE
Quality of Life Rating	97
Fire Safety Rating	90
Green Rating	94
Type of school	private
Environment	town

STUDENTS
Total undergrad enrollment	1,546
% male/female	49/51
% from out of state	68
% from public high school	75
% live on campus	98
# of fraternities	3
% African American	7
% Asian	11
% Caucasian	46
% Hispanic	11
% international	6
# of countries represented	21

SURVEY SAYS . . .
No one cheats
School is well-run
Students are friendly
Students aren't religious
Dorms are like palaces
Low cost of living
Students are happy
Musical organizations are popular

ACADEMICS
Academic Rating	97
% students graduating within 4 years	91
% students graduating within 6 years	94
Calendar	semester
Student/faculty ratio	7:1
Profs interesting rating	93
Profs accessible rating	97
Most common reg class size	10–19 students
Most common lab size	10–19 students

MOST POPULAR MAJORS
economics, environmental analysis, neuroscience, politics

STUDENTS SAY ". . ."

Academics

At Pomona College in Claremont, you can get "an academically rigorous education" in a "low-stress California atmosphere." At this prestigious liberal arts school, "The professors are, for the most part, fantastic—engaging, creative, and sharp," and "All classes are taught by professors, not grad students or TAs." With small class sizes in every department, "There is an emphasis on collaborative learning," and "Many professors are great discussion leaders and really motivate students to get involved in class." Students have the advantage of "getting to know professors outside the classroom, in any setting, from office hours, to Thanksgiving dinner at their homes." Illustrating how personal the experience can be, a student tells us, "Today, I had a class with seven people in it, then lunch with a physics professor, and then a personal tutorial with a philosophy professor." Another student adds, "Between department barbecues, parties, and weekend retreats, by the time you're an upperclassman, you will know most of the professors in your major department quite well." In complement to the intimate academic atmosphere, Pomona "offers the resources of a large university" through the Claremont Consortium, which offers joint events and cross-registration with four adjoining colleges. Among other programs, "Pomona pays for students to take otherwise unpaid internship positions." Students praise Pomona's "efficiency in taking care of administrative tasks such as financial aid and registration," adding that the administration "is very good at responding to what students want."

Life

Pomona students are "ridiculously happy" about their lot in life, and why shouldn't they be? They're living in a "perfect world full of intelligent, engaging, and open individuals, amazing academics, brilliant opportunities to get involved in, and enough sunshine to make anyone happy to be alive." The weather is a key aspect of the experience, and "On a nice day, everyone heads outside in shorts and t-shirts to do their class work." On any given day, "You'll see people setting up telescopes outside the dorms at night to try to get a glimpse of the stars, you'll find people practicing ukulele on our quad, you'll see students filming for a project in the dining halls, [or] you'll see someone riding around campus on a bamboo bike." "Many people are involved in intramural sports," and students love "hiking, skiing, and going to the beach year round." There are many beautiful beaches in the area, and "Joshua Tree is only an hour and a half away, so there are camping trips there just about every weekend." Though the school is small, there are four other colleges in the Claremont Consortium, and Pomona students can "take their classes, eat at their dining halls, go to their parties, swim in their pools, and generally share in a great experience." When its time to blow off steam, "There are large 5C-sponsored parties that people go to and enjoy."

Student Body

At Pomona, "Only a third or so of students are from California," yet the California attitude reigns supreme. Here, you'll find a number of "tree-hugging, rock-climbing, Tom's shoes–wearing" undergraduates, with most students generally falling within the "liberal, upper-middle-class, hipster-athlete" continuum. Students report a "decent level of diversity and a strong international community." Studious and talented, Pomona undergraduates "excel in the classroom and usually have some sort of passion that they pursue outside of the classroom." "Underneath our sundresses and rainbow flip-flops, we're all closet nerds—everybody is really passionate about something or other." At Pomona, "You will meet the football player who got a perfect score on his SAT or the dreadlocked hippie who took multivariable calculus when he was sixteen." Dress code is uniformly casual, and "flip-flops, polo, or tank tops and shorts" are the unofficial uniform.

FINANCIAL AID: 909-621-8205 • E-MAIL: ADMISSIONS@POMONA.EDU • WEBSITE: WWW.POMONA.EDU

THE PRINCETON REVIEW SAYS

Admissions

Very important factors considered include: Academic GPA, application essay, class rank, recommendation(s), rigor of secondary school record, standardized test scores, character/personal qualities, extracurricular activities, talent/ability. *Important factors considered include:* Interview. *Other factors considered include:* Alumni/ae relation, first generation, geographical residence, racial/ethnic status, volunteer work, work experience. ACT with writing component recommended. TOEFL required of all international applicants. High school diploma or equivalent isn't required. *Academic units required:* 4 English, 3 mathematics, 3 science (2 science labs), 2 foreign language, 2 social studies, 3 history. *Academic units recommended:* 4 English, 4 mathematics, 4 science (3 science labs), 3 foreign language, 2 social studies, 3 history.

Financial Aid

Students should submit: FAFSA, CSS/Financial Aid PROFILE. Regular filing deadline is February 1. The Princeton Review suggests that all financial aid forms be submitted as soon as possible after January 1. *Need-based scholarships/ grants offered:* Federal Pell, SEOG, state scholarships/grants, private scholarships, school scholarship or grant aid from institutional funds. Pomona meets full financial aid need without requiring loans. *Loan aid offered:* Direct Subsidized Stafford, Direct Unsubsidized Stafford, Direct PLUS, Federal Perkins, university loans from institutional funds. Federal Work-Study Program available. Off-campus job opportunities are good.

The Inside Word

For first-year applicants, Pomona College offers regular decision admissions, as well as a binding early decision program. Admissions officials evaluate a student's academic record carefully, examining the rigor of high school coursework, class rank, and grade point average. Ninety percent of Pomona admits rank in the top ten percent of their class. If you live in Southern California, Pomona expects you to interview on campus; students in other regions are strongly encouraged to visit campus and meet with admissions staff, though it's not required.

THE SCHOOL SAYS "..."

From the Admissions Office

"Perhaps the most important thing to know about Pomona College is that we are what we say we are. There is enormous integrity between the statements of mission and philosophy governing the college and the reality that students, faculty, and administrators experience. The balance in the curriculum is unusual. Sciences, social sciences, humanities, and the arts receive equal attention, support, and emphasis. Most importantly, the commitment to undergraduate education is absolute. Teaching awards remain the highest honor the trustees can bestow upon faculty. The typical method of instruction is the seminar and the average class size of fifteen offers students the opportunity to become full partners in the learning process. Our location in the Los Angeles basin and in Claremont, with four other colleges, provides a remarkable community.

"Pomona College requires the SAT plus two SAT Subject Tests (in different fields) or the ACT with the writing component."

SELECTIVITY

Admissions Rating	98
# of applicants	6,764
% of applicants accepted	15
% of acceptees attending	40
# accepting a place on wait list	300
# of early decision applicants	513
% accepted early decision	23

FRESHMAN PROFILE

Range SAT Critical Reading	690–780
Range SAT Math	700–780
Range SAT Writing	690–770
Range ACT Composite	31–34
Minimum paper TOEFL	600
Minimum computer TOEFL	250
Minimum web-based TOEFL	100
% graduated top 10% of class	91
% graduated top 25% of class	100
% graduated top 50% of class	100

DEADLINES

Early decision	
Deadline	11/1
Notification	12/15
Regular	
Deadline	1/2
Notification	4/1
Nonfall registration?	yes

APPLICANTS ALSO LOOK AT AND OFTEN PREFER
Harvard College, Princeton University, Stanford University, University of California—Berkeley, Yale University

AND SOMETIMES PREFER
Brown University, University of California— Los Angeles, Williams College

FINANCIAL FACTS

Financial Aid Rating	99
Annual tuition	$38,087
Room and board	$13,096
Required fees	$307
Books and supplies	$1,000
% frosh rec. need-based scholarship or grant aid	51
% UG rec. need-based scholarship or grant aid	52
% frosh rec. need-based self-help aid	51
% UG rec. need-based self-help aid	52
% frosh rec. any financial aid	50
% UG rec. any financial aid	53
% UG borrow to pay for school	47
Average cumulative indebtedness	$8,776

PORTLAND STATE UNIVERSITY

OFFICE OF ADMISSIONS AND RECORDS, PO BOX 751, PORTLAND, OR 97207-0751 • ADMISSIONS: 503-725-3511 • FAX: 503-725-5525

CAMPUS LIFE

Quality of Life Rating	75
Fire Safety Rating	66
Green Rating	88
Type of school	public
Environment	metropolis

STUDENTS

Total undergrad enrollment	21,816
% male/female	47/53
% from out of state	12
% from public high school	85
% live on campus	12
# of fraternities	1
# of sororities	1
% African American	3
% Asian	9
% Caucasian	64
% Hispanic	6
% Native American	1
% international	5
# of countries represented	94

SURVEY SAYS . . .

Athletic facilities are great
Students love Portland, OR
Great off-campus food
Great library

ACADEMICS

Academic Rating	67
% students graduating within 4 years	11
% students graduating within 6 years	34
Calendar	quarter
Student/faculty ratio	18:1
Profs interesting rating	73
Profs accessible rating	70
Most common reg class size	20–29 students
Most common lab size	10–19 students

MOST POPULAR MAJORS

business/commerce, psychology, social sciences

STUDENTS SAY ". . ."

Academics

Portland State University's motto is "let knowledge serve the city," and students echo this philosophy, saying their school "has a strong focus on civic engagement and sustainability." "PSU is a great learning environment in the heart of the city" and a "good value" for your tuition dollars. It's also "a green-minded urban school" that's "training students to be good community members." "There is a wealth of courses" on offer here, with degrees in social work, a range of business majors, and the hard sciences all receiving praise. "Classes are usually pretty small," and professors "promote lots of in-class discussion and are readily available to meet outside of class as well." "They really care about the student's success, and they really help broaden our scope of learning [and] thinking critically." Adjunct professors are "very connected to the community and their particular areas of expertise." Overall, students are happy with their instructors, saying, "Most professors are engaging and truly want to challenge you and help you succeed." They "are well-educated [and] well-versed in current issues and research." There's "the occasional dud thrown into the mix," though. Generally, "They are prepared and are passionate about the classes they teach. They have a wealth of experiences to bring to classroom," and they're "easily accessible for questions or further assistance," "students just need to reach out."

Life

The city of Portland is a big draw for PSU students. "The campus is extraordinarily beautiful and ideally located." Outdoor activities are big here: "There's skiing, hiking, camping, [and] fishing." "The downtown area has plenty of microbrew pubs, nightlife, eateries, and theaters." "The people are friendly, and the city is gorgeous and easy to navigate. You can go to the beach or to the mountain in about two hours, and there are many things to do outdoors. There are great parks throughout the city." "The public transportation is outstanding." It's bike- and vegan-friendly. "There are lots of activist and awareness-raising events going on all the time, and lots of students are involved in volunteering (on and off campus)." Because PSU has a large nontraditional undergraduate population and the majority of students live off campus, the sense of community extends beyond the school and into the city. "There are a lot of things to do on campus, and there are different groups on campus that promote going out into the community at large and helping out." "Because the student body is so big and really diverse, PSU has tons of programs/clubs/groups that help make you feel more involved with your school. PSU is also committed to sustainability: Any new buildings are made with the latest green technology, and recycling is a big deal."

Student Body

"It is difficult to define the typical PSU student, because there are so many of us from so many different backgrounds," one student says, and diversity does indeed seem to be the name of the game at PSU. Students describe themselves as "environmentally aware, hip," and "very liberal." Overall, people at PSU are "invested in their education and are friendly." There's a large population of nontraditional undergraduates, so students are "either typical college-age…or people in their thirties and forties with kids and full-time job trying to juggle everything." Even within this large, diverse student body, "everyone finds a niche pretty quickly." "It's easy to find people you get along with, but it's also easy to find people who are completely different from you, which makes school a lot more interesting."

FINANCIAL AID: 800-547-8887 • E-MAIL: ADMISSIONS@PDX.EDU • WEBSITE: WWW.PDX.EDU

THE PRINCETON REVIEW SAYS

Admissions

Very important factors considered include: Academic GPA, rigor of secondary school record. *Important factors considered include:* Standardized test scores. SAT or ACT required; ACT with writing component required. TOEFL required of all international applicants. High school diploma is required, and GED is accepted. *Academic units required:* 4 English, 3 mathematics, 2 science, 2 foreign language, 3 social studies. *Academic units recommended:* (1 science lab).

Financial Aid

Students should submit: FAFSA. The Princeton Review suggests that all financial aid forms be submitted as soon as possible after January 1. *Need-based scholarships/grants offered:* Federal Pell, SEOG, state scholarships/grants, private scholarships, school scholarship or grant aid from institutional funds, United Negro College Fund. *Loan aid offered:* Direct Subsidized Stafford, Direct Unsubsidized Stafford, Direct PLUS, Federal Perkins, state loans. Federal Work-Study Program available. Off-campus job opportunities are excellent.

The Inside Word

PSU offers a range of admission options for new freshmen, transfers, students enrolled at local community colleges, continuing students, and those with nontraditional high school backgrounds. Regardless of an applicant's status, admissions officers look for a secondary school GPA of at least 3.0, though high test scores can make up for a lower average.

THE SCHOOL SAYS "..."

From the Admissions Office

"Portland State University is Oregon's largest and most diverse public university located in the heart of one of America's most progressive cities. It offers more than sixty undergraduate and forty graduate programs in fine and performing arts, liberal arts and sciences, business administration, education, urban and public affairs, social work, engineering, and computer science. PSU offers more than 120 bachelor's, master's, and doctoral degrees.

"The forty-nine-acre downtown campus—whose motto is "Let Knowledge Serve the City"—places students in a vibrant center of culture, business, and technology. Portland State's urban mission offers opportunities for every student to participate in internships and community-based projects in business, education, social services, government, technology, and the arts and sciences.

"The award-winning University Studies curriculum provides small class sizes and mentoring for undergraduates and culminates in Senior Capstone, which takes students out of the classroom and into the field, where they utilize their knowledge and skills to develop community projects.

"Portland State has taken aggressive steps to enhance the student experience and campus life, with new student housing and a comprehensive recreation complex and remodeled science and performing arts facilities. The university also has hired more academic and career advisers and created new programs to support students. Sustainability—initiatives that balance environmental, economic, and social concerns—is incorporated throughout the curriculum and across the campus."

SELECTIVITY

Admissions Rating	72
# of applicants	4,924
% of applicants accepted	71
% of acceptees attending	41

FRESHMAN PROFILE

Range SAT Critical Reading	460–590
Range SAT Math	460–570
Range SAT Writing	430–560
Range ACT Composite	19–36
Minimum paper TOEFL	525
Minimum computer TOEFL	197
Minimum web-based TOEFL	71
Average HS GPA	3.34

DEADLINES

Early action	
Deadline	12/1
Regular	
Notification	1/1
Nonfall registration?	yes

FINANCIAL FACTS

Financial Aid Rating	77
Annual in-state tuition	$7,100
Annual out-of-state tuition	$21,600
Room and board	$9,000
Required fees	$1,482
Books and supplies	$1,968
% frosh rec. need-based scholarship or grant aid	48
% UG rec. need-based scholarship or grant aid	40
% frosh rec. non-need-based scholarship or grant aid	1
% frosh rec. need-based self-help aid	56
% UG rec. need-based self-help aid	52
% frosh rec. any financial aid	65
% UG rec. any financial aid	56
% UG borrow to pay for school	64
Average cumulative indebtedness	$26,287

PRESCOTT COLLEGE

220 GROVE AVENUE, PRESCOTT, AZ 86301 • ADMISSIONS: 877-350-2100 • FAX: 928-776-5242

STUDENTS SAY ". . ."

Academics
Prescott College, a small, progressive school, "encourages critical and forward thinking around issues of social justice and sustainability." The school shines in interdisciplinary fields, such as environmental studies, human development and psychology, outdoor adventure education, and arts-based fields such as photography and creative writing. Prescott "is about taking learning out of the classroom," and true to its word, classes, according to the university, "take place in field sites throughout the Southwest, in art galleries, wilderness areas, along the U.S./Mexico border and in local schools, to name a few." Students see their education as "experiential, hands-on, real-world, and self-directed," and consider it to be a "journey, not a destination." Prescott's academic calendar is a unique "block and quarter system," which is "very effective at immersing students in their studies." Students take only one course for three four-week blocks before entering a ten-week semester. The quality of teaching "really varies. Some teachers are excellent and experienced and work well with the majority of the student body," and are "engaging and committed to their students." However, many students feel that "visiting" and "adjunct" professors "tend to be not so good." All the freedom at Prescott means that "academics are what you make them," and while some students find Prescott to be "academically stimulating but not very challenging," others think "there are plenty of opportunities for a rigorous academic experience."

Life
Prescott's emphasis on outdoor education and its ideal location near 1.4 million acres of National Forest mean that most students "live and play outside." One student says, "The majority of students rock climb, mountain bike, ski, snowboard, surf, raft, kayak, skydive, or ice climb." "If you want to go on an adventure, have no fear, you'll have an accomplice in less than an hour." The laid-back, artsy town of Prescott has a few bars that host "some good live music," which lots of students see whenever possible, though "sometimes you have to go to a larger city for that." Most students at Prescott are community-minded individuals, so it makes sense that one of the most popular social activities is to go to, or host, a potluck. As one student enthuses, "students also love potlucks; cooking is huge here." Others confirm that "potlucks are a huge part of student life," and that "much revolves around food." These gatherings can be "really fun and sometimes is crazy and sometimes really low-key." At potlucks and other gatherings, students "really enjoy each other's company." Generally, students do "not drink to get drunk, but drink as a part of a great evening out with friends," and most students seem to think people at Prescott "have good heads on their shoulders" and don't indulge in out-of-control partying.

Student Body
Prescott's emphasis on individual education, the environment, and sustainability means students are "environmentally and politically conscious" and "committed to their learning and creating a better community." Students are there because "they want to better themselves and have a positive impact on the world at large," and they're "motivated, empowered, and feisty." Additionally, students are very invested in social activism. Prescott's location means it attracts "athletic nerds" and "typical students love spending time outdoors." Yes, you'll probably see a lot of "hippies, hippies, hippies," but many students "wouldn't identify themselves that way." Though the school is predominantly white, students feel the community is "from a wide variety of cultural backgrounds" and that there's "a colorful array of people." As one student put it, the school "is made up of hundreds of different individuals who all bring their unique aspects to classes and social settings." Though students at Prescott tend to lean left, they say "any student fits in here. Everyone talks to everyone."

E-MAIL: ADMISSIONS@PRESCOTT.EDU • WEBSITE: WWW.PRESCOTT.EDU

THE PRINCETON REVIEW SAYS

Admissions

Very important factors considered include: Application essay, recommendation(s), rigor of secondary school record. *Important factors considered include:* Academic GPA, standardized test scores, extracurricular activities, interview, level of applicant's interest, talent/ability, volunteer work, work experience. *Other factors considered include:* Character/personal qualities. SAT or ACT required; ACT with or without writing component accepted. TOEFL required of all international applicants. High school diploma is required, and GED is accepted. *Academic units recommended:* 4 English, 3 mathematics, 2 science, 1 foreign language, 3 social studies, 2 history, 1 visual/performing arts.

Financial Aid

Students should submit: FAFSA. The Princeton Review suggests that all financial aid forms be submitted as soon as possible after January 1. *Need-based scholarships/grants offered:* Federal Pell, SEOG, state scholarships/grants, private scholarships, school scholarship or grant aid from institutional funds. Applicants will be notified of awards on a rolling basis beginning March 15. Federal Work-Study Program available. Off-campus job opportunities are excellent.

The Inside Word

The acceptance rate at Prescott is high, but the applicant pool is very self-selecting, and Prescott is the kind of place where you have to want to be. For example, while many colleges have fun-filled, low-pressure orientation programs for incoming students, Prescott students spend their first four weeks engaged in an immersion orientation experience in the Arizona wilderness that builds student's experiential education skills and integrates them into the Prescott academic community.

THE SCHOOL SAYS "..."

From the Admissions Office

"Prescott College highlights the dramatic educational return on investment when experience is at the center of learning. Tucked into a corner of the town in central Arizona of the same name, Prescott College is an evolving experiment in rejecting hierarchical thinking for collaboration and teamwork as the cornerstone of learning. This is an educational institution that puts students at the center in everything it does and is. Optional Grades. Narrative Evaluations. No barriers. Limited bureaucracy. No summa or magna or 'best in show' ribbons. Just a peripatetic community of lively intellects and fearless explorers whose connecting threads are a passion for social responsibility and the environment, and a keen sense of adventure.

"At Prescott College, our goal is to fuel your passion and give you a deeper understanding of the world around you through collaborative learning and personal experience. We don't settle for the mundane college experience. Instead, we take learning outside the classroom and into the real world through experiential and field-based learning. From field studies, internships, and independent studies to community service and study abroad opportunities, our students are challenged to think critically, explore the world up close, and form solutions through collaborative efforts.

"If you're looking for a college experience unlike any other—the kind that enables you to take control of your education and truly make a positive impact in your community and in the world—then Prescott College is the ideal college for you."

SELECTIVITY

Admissions Rating	74
# of applicants	363
% of applicants accepted	99
% of acceptees attending	21
# of early decision applicants	6
% accepted early decision	67

FRESHMAN PROFILE

Range SAT Critical Reading	510–670
Range SAT Math	480–570
Range SAT Writing	500–620
Range ACT Composite	20–28
Minimum paper TOEFL	550
Minimum computer TOEFL	213
Minimum web-based TOEFL	61
Average HS GPA	2.90
% graduated top 10% of class	17
% graduated top 25% of class	17
% graduated top 50% of class	66

DEADLINES

Early decision	
Deadline	12/1
Notification	12/15
Regular	
Priority	3/1
Deadline	8/15
Notification	4/1
Nonfall registration?	yes

APPLICANTS ALSO LOOK AT
AND OFTEN PREFER
College of the Atlantic, Earlham College, Mills College
AND SOMETIMES PREFER
Whitman College
AND RARELY PREFER
Hendrix College, Reed College, Sarah Lawrence College, The Evergreen State College, University of Arizona

FINANCIAL FACTS

Financial Aid Rating	70
Annual tuition	$26,235
Room and board	$6,000
Books and supplies	$624
% frosh rec. need-based scholarship or grant aid	70
% UG rec. need-based scholarship or grant aid	69
% frosh rec. non-need-based scholarship or grant aid	74
% UG rec. non-need-based scholarship or grant aid	59
% frosh rec. need-based self-help aid	66
% UG rec. need-based self-help aid	68
% frosh rec. any financial aid	93
% UG rec. any financial aid	88
% UG borrow to pay for school	67
Average cumulative indebtedness	$15,182

PRINCETON UNIVERSITY

PO Box 430, ADMISSION OFFICE, PRINCETON, NJ 08542-0430 • ADMISSIONS: 609-258-3060 • FAX: 609-258-6743

STUDENTS SAY ". . ."

Academics

As a member of the grand old Ivy League, Princeton University has long maintained a "sterling reputation" for quality academics; however, students say Princeton's "unique focus on the undergraduate experience" is what makes their school stand out among institutions. It attracts "really experienced and big-name professors, who actually want to teach undergraduate." Introductory lecture classes can be rather large, but "Once you take upper-level courses, you'll have a lot of chances to work closely with professors and study what you are most interested in." A current undergrad enthuses, "The discussions I have in seminar are the reason I get out of bed in the morning; after a great class, I feel incredibly invigorated." Though all Princeton professors are "leading scholars in their field," students admit that some classes can be "dry." Fortunately, "The overwhelming majority of professors are wonderful, captivating lecturers" who are "dedicated to their students." While you may be taking a class from a Nobel laureate, "The humility and accessibility of world-famous researchers and public figures is always remarkable." At Princeton, "There are so many chances to meet writers, performers, and professionals you admire." A student details, "The two years I've been here, I've been in discussions with Frank Gehry, David Sedaris, Peter Hessler, John McPhee, Jeff Koons, Chang-Rae Lee, Joyce Carol Oates, W.S. Merwin, and on and on." No matter what you study, Princeton is an "intellectually challenging place," and the student experience is "intense in almost every way." Hard work pays off, though "the academic caliber of the school is unparalleled," and a Princeton education is "magnificently rewarding."

Life

Princeton students "tend to participate in a lot of different activities, from varsity sports (recruits), intramural sports (high school athletes), and more academically restricted activities like autonomous vehicle design club, Engineers Without Borders, and the literary magazine." In and out of the classroom, there are a "billion opportunities to do what you know you love" on the Princeton campus, from performance to sports to research. "Princeton offers a lot of different opportunities to relax and de-stress," including "sporting events, concerts, recreational facilities," "a movie theater that frequently screens current films for free," and "arts and crafts at the student center." For some, social life is centered along Prospect Avenue, where "Princeton's eating clubs are lined up like ten booze-soaked ducklings in a row." These eating clubs—private houses that serve as social clubs and cafeterias for upperclassmen—"play a large role in the social scene at the university." On the weekends, "The eating clubs are extremely popular for partying, chatting, drinking, and dancing"—not to mention, "free beer." "The campus is gorgeous year-round;" however, when students need a break from the college atmosphere, "There's NJ Transit if you want to go to New York, Philly, or even just the local mall."

Student Body

It's not surprising that most undergraduates are "driven, competitive, and obsessed with perfection." "Academics come first," and Princeton students are typified by dedication to their studies and "a tendency to overwork." "Almost everyone at Princeton is involved with something other than school about which they are extremely passionate," and most have "at least one distinct, remarkable talent." "It's fairly easy for most people to find a good group of friends with whom they have something in common," and many students get involved in one of the "infinite number of clubs" on campus. Superficially, "The preppy Ivy League stereotype" is reflected in the student population, and many students are "well-spoken," "dress nicely," and stay in shape. A student jokes, "Going to Princeton is like being in a contest to see who can be the biggest nerd while simultaneously appearing least nerdy."

PRINCETON UNIVERSITY

FINANCIAL AID: 609-258-3330 • E-MAIL: UAOFFICE@PRINCETON.EDU • WEBSITE: WWW.PRINCETON.EDU

THE PRINCETON REVIEW SAYS

Admissions

Very important factors considered include: Academic GPA, application essay, class rank, recommendation(s), rigor of secondary school record, standardized test scores, character/personal qualities, talent/ability. *Important factors considered include:* Extracurricular activities. *Other factors considered include:* Alumni/ae relation, first generation, geographical residence, interview, level of applicant's interest, racial/ethnic status, volunteer work, work experience. SAT or ACT required; ACT with writing component required. TOEFL required of all international applicants. High school diploma or equivalent isn't required. *Academic units recommended:* 4 English, 4 mathematics, 4 science (2 science labs), 4 foreign language, 2 social studies, 2 history, 1 visual/performing arts.

Financial Aid

Students should submit: FAFSA, institution's own financial aid form. Regular filing deadline is February 1. The Princeton Review suggests that all financial aid forms be submitted as soon as possible after January 1. *Need-based scholarships/grants offered:* Federal Pell, SEOG, state scholarships/grants, private scholarships, school scholarship or grant aid from institutional funds. *Loan aid offered:* Direct Subsidized Stafford, Direct Unsubsidized Stafford, Direct PLUS, Federal Perkins, university loans from institutional funds. Applicants will be notified of awards on a rolling basis at the end of March. Federal Work-Study Program available. Off-campus job opportunities are good.

The Inside Word

Not surprisingly, admission to Princeton is highly selective. Only about nine percent of applicants are accepted, and these students usually rank at the top of their high school class. Prospective students should prepare for Princeton by excelling in honors, AP, and upper-level coursework during high school. The application materials and personal essays are carefully read and evaluated, so students should also allocate time to prepare their applications. Admission to Princeton comes with a great deal of prestige, and to make the deal even sweeter, Princeton's remarkable no-loan financial aid program means that every student has 100 percent of their financial need met, without student loans.

THE SCHOOL SAYS "..."

From the Admissions Office

"Methods of instruction [at Princeton] vary widely, but common to all areas is a strong emphasis on individual responsibility and the free interchange of ideas. This is displayed most notably in the wide use of preceptorials and seminars, in the provision of independent study for all upperclass students and qualified underclass students, and in the availability of a series of special programs to meet a range of individual interests. The undergraduate college encourages the student to be an independent seeker of information and to assume responsibility for gaining both knowledge and judgment that will strengthen later contributions to society. Two hallmarks of the academic experience are the junior paper and senior thesis, which allow students the opportunity to pursue original research and scholarship in a field of their choosing.

"Princeton offers a distinctive financial aid program that provides grants, which do not have to be repaid, rather than loans. Princeton meets the full demonstrated financial need of all students—domestic and international—offered admission. About sixty percent of Princeton's undergraduates receive financial aid.

"All applicants must submit results for both the SAT as well as SAT Subject Tests in two different subject areas."

SELECTIVITY

Admissions Rating	99
# of applicants	26,247
% of applicants accepted	9
% of acceptees attending	57
# accepting a place on wait list	1,002
% admitted from wait list	16

FRESHMAN PROFILE

Range SAT Critical Reading	690–790
Range SAT Math	710–790
Range SAT Writing	700–790
Range ACT Composite	31–35
Average HS GPA	3.89
% graduated top 10% of class	99
% graduated top 25% of class	100
% graduated top 50% of class	100

DEADLINES

Early action	
Deadline	11/1
Notification	12/15
Regular	
Deadline	1/1
Notification	3/31
Nonfall registration?	no

APPLICANTS ALSO LOOK AT AND SOMETIMES PREFER

Harvard College, Massachusetts Institute of Technology, Stanford College, Yale University

FINANCIAL FACTS

Financial Aid Rating	99
Annual tuition	$37,000
Room and board	$12,069
Books and supplies	$1,269
% frosh rec. need-based scholarship or grant aid	60
% UG rec. need-based scholarship or grant aid	60
% frosh rec. need-based self-help aid	60
% UG rec. need-based self-help aid	60
% frosh rec. any financial aid	60
% UG rec. any financial aid	60
% UG borrow to pay for school	23
Average cumulative indebtedness	$5,225

PROVIDENCE COLLEGE

RIVER AVENUE AND EATON STREET, PROVIDENCE, RI 02918 • ADMISSIONS: 401-865-2535 • FAX: 401-865-2826

CAMPUS LIFE

Quality of Life Rating	66
Fire Safety Rating	98
Green Rating	73
Type of school	private
Affiliation	Roman Catholic
Environment	city

STUDENTS

Total undergrad enrollment	3,892
% male/female	43/57
% from out of state	92
% from public high school	57
% live on campus	80
% African American	3
% Asian	2
% Caucasian	76
% Hispanic	4
% international	1

SURVEY SAYS . . .

Diversity lacking on campus
Everyone loves the Friars
Intramural sports are popular
Frats and sororities are unpopular
or nonexistent
Student government is popular
Lots of beer drinking
Hard liquor is popular

ACADEMICS

Academic Rating	81
% students graduating within 4 years	83
% students graduating within 6 years	86
Calendar	semester
Student/faculty ratio	12:1
Profs interesting rating	71
Profs accessible rating	76
Most common reg class size	20–29 students
Most common lab size	20–29 students

MOST POPULAR MAJORS
biology, business administration and management, marketing

STUDENTS SAY ". . ."

Academics

"Governed by the thought of St. Thomas Aquinas," Providence College is "a tight-knit community of well-rounded, charismatic, and intelligent kids" benefiting from "a definite emphasis on a Catholic intellectual approach to the world." Nowhere is that approach more evident then in PC's "well-rounded core curriculum," one student writes. The cornerstone of the curriculum is the Development of Western Civilization course sequence, "a great asset to the school" that "produces students who have an awareness of the West's cultural heritage." Outside of the core, students flock to business and marketing, pre-medical studies, and education programs; a "great political science program" is also popular among students. Students report that "PC is full of wonderful professors, very genuine people who want to share their knowledge…and help their students to become thoughtful and conscientious adults." Likewise, their classmates "are caring individuals who are…willing to go the extra-mile for their peers." The result is a "sense of community—the smaller campus and student body mean that you see familiar faces every day, definitely something that comforts new students" and encourages them to participate in the life of the campus. As one student sums up, "PC in a nutshell is thinking about Kant, Hegel, or Dostoevsky, listening to Taylor Swift, making lifelong relationships and getting involved in student-run clubs."

Life

Life at PC can get a bit "monotonous during the week" when students "are engrossed in their work," but campus life "changes dramatically when the weekend arrives." "Most everyone likes to party Thursday, Friday, and Saturday night (and some even during the week)," with a typical night starting at a bar. Seniors usually "go to McPhail's, the on-campus bar") and ending at a party in off-campus houses "after the bars close." Basketball and hockey games "are big school events," and many students are "very involved in clubs, some of the most popular being Student Congress, Friars Club, Board of Programmers, and Board of Multicultural Student Affairs." Intramurals are also "very popular at PC." Students love venturing out into hometown Providence, "a great city with so many options." "There is a great mall about ten minutes from campus with a movie theater and an Imax," as well as "great restaurants" and "a lot of other colleges in the area." Getting to these places is "easy," "as PC students can take the RIPTA bus for free with their student ID card." While most here like to have fun, most also know when to stop. "Whenever I visit the library it is full, and I hardly find a place to sit, and this is not because the library is too small," one student warns.

Student Body

The Providence College population is largely "white and Catholic from New England, New York, or New Jersey." There is "not a great amount of diversity" in this "preppy," "sheltered" crowd of kids. "Everyone is the same," one student cautions. "Girls all have Vera Bradley bags, [and] every student has a North Face jacket." Students tend to be "very focused on their academics while remaining highly involved in extracurricular activities and volunteerism" and very career-minded; most "will probably work in the business world upon graduation." The number of international students here "is quite small," but they "fit in perfectly with the rest of the American students," according to one international student.

PROVIDENCE COLLEGE

FINANCIAL AID: 401-865-2286 • E-MAIL: PCADMISS@PROVIDENCE.EDU • WEBSITE: WWW.PROVIDENCE.EDU

THE PRINCETON REVIEW SAYS

Admissions

Very important factors considered include: Academic GPA, application essay, rigor of secondary school record. *Important factors considered include:* Recommendation(s), character/personal qualities, extracurricular activities. *Other factors considered include:* Class rank, standardized test scores, alumni/ae relation, first generation, geographical residence, level of applicant's interest, racial/ethnic status, talent/ability, volunteer work, work experience. ACT with or without writing component accepted. TOEFL required of all international applicants. *Academic units required:* 4 English, 4 mathematics, 3 science (2 science labs), 3 foreign language, 2 social studies, 2 history. *Academic units recommended:* 4 English, 4 mathematics, 4 science (2 science labs), 3 foreign language, 2 social studies, 2 history.

Financial Aid

Students should submit: FAFSA, CSS/Financial Aid PROFILE. Regular filing deadline is February 1. The Princeton Review suggests that all financial aid forms be submitted as soon as possible after January 1. *Need-based scholarships/grants offered:* Federal Pell, SEOG, state scholarships/grants, private scholarships, school scholarship or grant aid from institutional funds. *Loan aid offered:* Direct Subsidized Stafford, Direct Unsubsidized Stafford, Direct PLUS, Federal Perkins. Federal Work-Study Program available. Off-campus job opportunities are good.

The Inside Word

Few schools can claim a more transparent admissions process than Providence College. The admissions section of the school's website includes a voluminous blog authored by the assistant dean of admissions. Surf on over to http://blogs. targetx.com/providence/ScottSeseske/ and learn everything you could possibly want to know about the how, what, when, and why of Providence admissions. Providence has a test-optional policy, meaning applicants aren't required to submit standardized test scores.

THE SCHOOL SAYS "..."

From the Admissions Office

"Infused with the history, tradition, and learning of a 700-year-old Catholic teaching order, the Dominican Friars, Providence College offers a value-affirming environment where students are challenged on every level—body, mind, heart, and soul. Providence College offers forty-nine majors leading to baccalaureate degrees in business, education, the sciences, arts, and humanities. Our faculty is noted for a strong commitment to teaching. A close student/faculty relationship allows for in-depth classwork, independent research projects, and detailed career exploration. While noted for the physical facilities and academic opportunities associated with larger universities, Providence also fosters personal growth through a small, spirited, family-like atmosphere that encourages involvement in student activities and athletics.

"Submission of standardized test scores is optional for students applying for admission. This policy change allows each student to decide whether they wish to have their standardized test results considered as part of their application for admission. Students who choose not to submit SAT or ACT test scores will not be penalized in the review for admission. Additional details about the test-optional policy can be found on our website at Providence.edu/ testoptionalpolicy."

SELECTIVITY
Admissions Rating	90
# of applicants	8,398
% of applicants accepted	67
% of acceptees attending	20
# accepting a place on wait list	690
% admitted from wait list	62

FRESHMAN PROFILE
Range SAT Critical Reading	520–630
Range SAT Math	530–640
Range SAT Writing	530–650
Range ACT Composite	23–28
Minimum paper TOEFL	550
Minimum computer TOEFL	215
Minimum web-based TOEFL	80
Average HS GPA	3.37
% graduated top 10% of class	37
% graduated top 25% of class	66
% graduated top 50% of class	95

DEADLINES
Early action	
Deadline	11/1
Notification	1/1
Regular	
Deadline	1/15
Nonfall registration?	yes

APPLICANTS ALSO LOOK AT
AND OFTEN PREFER
Boston College, College of the Holy Cross
AND SOMETIMES PREFER
Boston University, Loyola College in Maryland, Villanova University
AND RARELY PREFER
Fairfield University, Fordham University, Stonehill College, University of Connecticut, University of Massachusetts Amherst

FINANCIAL FACTS
Financial Aid Rating	79
Annual tuition	$38,610
Room and board	$11,780
Required fees	$825
Books and supplies	$900
% frosh rec. need-based scholarship or grant aid	57
% UG rec. need-based scholarship or grant aid	57
% frosh rec. non-need-based scholarship or grant aid	5
% UG rec. non-need-based scholarship or grant aid	5
% frosh rec. need-based self-help aid	56
% UG rec. need-based self-help aid	51
% frosh rec. any financial aid	81
% UG rec. any financial aid	85
% UG borrow to pay for school	74
Average cumulative indebtedness	$32,850

THE BEST 376 COLLEGES ■ 437

PURDUE UNIVERSITY—WEST LAFAYETTE

475 STADIUM MALL DR., SCHLEMAN HALL, WEST LAFAYETTE, IN 47907 • ADMISSIONS: 765-494-1776 • FAX: 765-494-0544

CAMPUS LIFE

Quality of Life Rating	86
Fire Safety Rating	84
Green Rating	85
Type of school	public
Environment	town

STUDENTS

Total undergrad enrollment	30,836
% male/female	58/42
% from out of state	37
% live on campus	30
# of fraternities	48
# of sororities	33
% African American	3
% Asian	5
% Caucasian	74
% Hispanic	3
% international	11
# of countries represented	127

SURVEY SAYS . . .

Great computer facilities
Great food on campus
Students are happy
Everyone loves the Boilermakers
Student publications are popular

ACADEMICS

Academic Rating	71
% students graduating within 4 years	40
% students graduating within 6 years	70
Calendar	semester
Student/faculty ratio	14:1
Profs interesting rating	73
Profs accessible rating	80
Most common reg class size	20–29 students
Most common lab size	20–29 students

MOST POPULAR MAJORS

mechanical engineering, biology, management, consumer science retail, civil engineering

STUDENTS SAY ". . ."

Academics

When people think of Purdue University, what usually comes to mind is its "outstanding" engineering and agricultural programs, but students pursuing other degrees want you to know there are "many other prestigious majors." There are "an abundance of professors and programs…in areas other than engineering that are top-notch," such as liberal arts, education, nursing, business, and hotel management. Regardless of your major, "Purdue prepares students to be leaders by helping them grow personally and professionally during their collegiate years through a combination of strong academic programs, leadership opportunities, and social activities." It provides "one-of-a-kind experiences in research, professors, and organizations." The registration process has improved recently, but many students still voice frustration about some of the professors, calling them "hit or miss." A computer graphics technology major says, "There are enough foreign professors who are hard to understand that it sometimes makes things harder, but most professors are knowledgeable, passionate, fun, and easy to work with." One student says that while "the first year, the professors are a little harder to contact," in the upper years, "the professors are surprisingly engaged with the students and encourage them to succeed not only academically but in obtaining experiences (lab and intern) as well." Ultimately, many students think Purdue prepares them "to be leaders by helping them grow personally and professionally…through a combination of strong academic programs, leadership opportunities, and social activities."

Life

With its large student body, life at Purdue is "whatever you want to make it… There are art galleries, concerts, plays, community service, sports, etc." More than a few students say that though people "study during the week, once Thursday comes people are pretty into partying." There's "a large Greek population on campus, and it is a huge school, so parties are fairly prevalent on weekends and sometimes even during the week. A lot of people drink, but certainly not everyone. There are plenty of organized nonalcoholic events on campus as well as off." "Boilermaker pride" runs deep, and "Big Ten sports are huge…but not so huge that those who are uninterested in sports feel left out." Tailgating parties are popular, as well as "breakfast club where students dress up in costumes before a home football game and go out to the bars around 7:00 A.M.!" An agricultural economics student says she participates in "a wide variety of activities from concerts to international food festivals," and another notes that "a lot of musical performances and Broadway shows," come to the area. Lafayette, "has plenty of restaurants, movie theaters, bowling, and shopping," but those who find it "kind of boring" appreciate that "Chicago and Indianapolis are also near enough for day trips!"

Student Body

Students are "very relaxed and friendly," despite always being "aware of their obligations, be it for school or one of the student organizations that they may be involved with." The majority of students come from Indiana, and are "conservative, but not radically conservative. They are what you expect from twenty-somethings in the Midwest." Happily, students think Purdue's size means "that no matter who you are or where your interests may lie, you will be able to find another group of students that share similar interests." "The Greek System is pretty big here, but by no means is that necessary for someone to fit in," and the same goes for sports. Some say that "it is true that science and engineering majors sometimes look down on other students," a growing number of others say "The technical majors do not think that other majors are less intelligent. Campus life affords a mutual respect, and though there is joking around, everyone understands that having a Purdue degree is prestigious, no matter what their major is titled."

PURDUE UNIVERSITY—WEST LAFAYETTE

FINANCIAL AID: 765-494-5050 • E-MAIL: ADMISSIONS@PURDUE.EDU • WEBSITE: WWW.PURDUE.EDU

THE PRINCETON REVIEW SAYS

Admissions

Very important factors considered include: Rigor of secondary school record. *Important factors considered include:* Academic GPA, application essay, standardized test scores. *Other factors considered include:* Class rank, recommendation(s), character/personal qualities, extracurricular activities, first generation, geographical residence, level of applicant's interest, racial/ethnic status, state residency, talent/ability, volunteer work, SAT or ACT required; if taking ACT only, must have writing component. TOEFL required of all international applicants. High school diploma is required, and GED is accepted. *Academic units required:* 4 English, 4 mathematics, 3 science (3 science labs), 2 foreign language, 3 social studies.

Financial Aid

Students should submit: FAFSA. Regular filing deadline is March 1. The Princeton Review suggests that all financial aid forms be submitted as soon as possible after January 1. *Need- and merit-based scholarships/grants offered:* Federal Pell, SEOG, state scholarships/grants, private scholarships, school scholarship or grant aid from institutional funds. *Loan aid offered:* Direct Subsidized Stafford, Direct Unsubsidized Stafford, Direct PLUS, Federal Perkins, university loans from institutional funds. Applicants will be notified of awards on a rolling basis. Federal Work-Study Program available. Off-campus job opportunities are good.

The Inside Word

Purdue will consider your class rank when reviewing your application (along with your grades, test scores, and application essay, of course). Don't panic if you're not valedictorian—admissions officers look at your rank in the context of your class choices as well as your high school's size and rigor.

THE SCHOOL SAYS ". . ."

From the Admissions Office

"Although it is one of America's largest universities, Purdue does not 'feel' big to its students. The campus is very compact when compared to universities with similar enrollment. Purdue is a comprehensive university with an international reputation in a wide range of academic fields. A strong work ethic prevails at Purdue. As a member of the Big Ten, Purdue has a strong and diverse athletic program. Purdue offers more than 850 clubs and organizations. The residence halls and Greek community offer many participatory activities for students. Numerous convocations and lectures are presented each year. Purdue is all about people, and allowing students to grow academically as well as socially, preparing them for the real world.

"Applicants seeking admission are required to have their SAT or ACT test score sent from the testing agency. Purdue accepts either test, will use the best score, and requires a writing score."

SELECTIVITY
Admissions Rating	88
# of applicants	30.707
% of applicants accepted	65
% of acceptees attending	32
# accepting a place on wait list	250
% admitted from wait list	0

FRESHMAN PROFILE
Range SAT Critical Reading	500–610
Range SAT Math	540–680
Range SAT Writing	490–610
Range ACT Composite	23–29
Minimum paper TOEFL	550
Minimum computer TOEFL	213
Minimum web-based TOEFL	79
Average HS GPA	3.60
% graduated top 10% of class	37
% graduated top 25% of class	71
% graduated top 50% of class	95

DEADLINES
Regular	
Priority	11/15
Deadline	3/1
Notification	12/10
Nonfall registration?	yes

APPLICANTS ALSO LOOK AT AND SOMETIMES PREFER
Indiana University at Bloomington, University of Illinois at Urbana-Champaign, Valparaiso University

FINANCIAL FACTS
Financial Aid Rating	86
Annual in-state tuition	$8,592
Annual out-of-state tuition	$26,144
Room and board	$9,120
Required fees	$478
Books and supplies	$1,270
% frosh rec. need-based scholarship or grant aid	39
% UG rec. need-based scholarship or grant aid	35
% frosh rec. non-need-based scholarship or grant aid	29
% UG rec. non-need-based scholarship or grant aid	17
% frosh rec. need-based self-help aid	46
% UG rec. need-based self-help aid	44
% frosh rec. any financial aid	53
% UG rec. any financial aid	46
% UG borrow to pay for school	52
Average cumulative indebtedness	$26,360

QUINNIPIAC UNIVERSITY

275 MOUNT CARMEL AVENUE, HAMDEN, CT 06518 • ADMISSIONS: 203-582-8600 • FAX: 203-582-8906

STUDENTS SAY ". . ."

Academics

Quinnipiac University, "a professional school with the goal of educating its students to succeed in the future," boasts excellent programs in business, communications, and the health sciences, especially in those for nursing, physician's assistant, and physical and occupational therapy. Undergrads insist that QU's physical therapy program "is the best in the region." "The structure of the PT program is so well thought out that each class is working off the other in helping me get a education and actually learn the material," one student reports. Students in all health science fields appreciate QU's regional cache, especially when it comes time to apply to graduate school or to find a job. Communications and journalism majors get plenty of hands-on experience in the school's "full green-screen room as well as editing, media production, and journalist rooms." The departments produce "lively student television programming (news, sports, a game show, a travel show, and soon a cooking show), an excellent student newspaper, and an eclectic student radio station." Future teachers also find a happy home at QU; the school offers "a great five-year teaching program" that confers both a BA and a masters. "It's excellent preparation for teachers," one student tells us. By developing a number of hallmark programs, QU has elevated its national profile considerably, and students approvingly observe that the school "is focused on growing and becoming a school on the rise. There have been a lot of improvements on campus and [administrators] actually are interested in the students' opinions."

Life

According to most students, QU is your prototypical 'work-hard, play-hard' school. As one undergrad explains, "I spend Monday through Thursday doing loads of homework/studying, and as soon as Friday comes, it's time to party. Almost everyone on campus drinks, and a lot of people take the shuttles to bars and clubs." But while "drinking is definitely the students' most popular activity," it's hardly the only option. "When there is a men's ice hockey game, a lot of people get tickets and attend," students report, and basketball is also popular (both teams play in "a beautiful new arena"). QU offers a number of dry options, and "A lot of students stay sober and still have a great time with their friends or at school-sponsored events." Those looking "for quieter activities" can avail themselves of "the movie theater, bowling allies, and a ton of restaurants in Hamden, North Haven, and New Haven." The campus itself "is consistently described as a country club, and it's not far from the truth. The dorms as well as the campus are gorgeous."

Student Body

"The typical 'Quinnipiac Girl' (yes we say that here)," according to one student, "is very fashion-forward and is from Long Island. She is always in designer clothing, and in the winter she wears Uggs, tight leggings, and a North Face jacket carrying either a really nice, leather Coach bag or a Vera Bradley bag. The typical boy is also from Long Island and is Italian. He also wears fashion clothing." It's easy to dismiss these students as "mostly spoiled [and] rich" at first glace, but students caution against doing that. Says one, "Once you realize that's not everyone, and you actually get involved in the school, you realize the people at QU are amazing! It's a great place to be." Though some say, "Students tend to be naive about other ethnicities because the majority of people at Quinnipiac are Caucasian," the school's chief diversity officer has broadened outreach in recent years.

FINANCIAL AID: 203-582-8750 • E-MAIL: ADMISSIONS@QUINNIPIAC.EDU • WEBSITE: WWW.QUINNIPIAC.EDU

THE PRINCETON REVIEW SAYS

Admissions

Very important factors considered include: Academic GPA, rigor of secondary school record. *Important factors considered include:* Application essay, class rank, standardized test scores. *Other factors considered include:* Recommendation(s), alumni/ae relation, character/personal qualities, extracurricular activities, interview, level of applicant's interest, racial/ethnic status, talent/ability, volunteer work, work experience. SAT or ACT required; ACT with writing component recommended. TOEFL required of all international applicants. High school diploma is required, and GED is accepted. *Academic units required:* 4 English, 3 mathematics, 3 science (2 science labs), 2 foreign language, 2 social studies. *Academic units recommended:* 4 English, 4 mathematics, 4 science (3 science labs), 2 foreign language, 3 social studies.

Financial Aid

Students should submit: FAFSA, CSS/Financial Aid PROFILE. The Princeton Review suggests that all financial aid forms be submitted as soon as possible after January 1. *Need-based scholarships/grants offered:* Federal Pell, SEOG, state scholarships/grants, private scholarships, school scholarship or grant aid from institutional funds, Federal Nursing Scholarships. *Loan aid offered:* Direct Subsidized Stafford, Direct Unsubsidized Stafford, Direct PLUS, Federal Perkins, Federal Nursing Loans, state loans. Applicants will be notified of awards on a rolling basis beginning February 15. Federal Work-Study Program available. Off-campus job opportunities are excellent.

The Inside Word

Quinnipiac admits students on a rolling basis, a process that favors those who get their applications in early. Programs in physical therapy, nursing, and physician assistant are quite competitive. The school strongly recommends that those seeking spots in these programs apply no later than early November.

THE SCHOOL SAYS "..."

From the Admissions Office

"Quinnipiac today is 'three settings, one university', with an undergraduate population growing to 6,500, many of whom remain at QU for the ever expanding graduate programs, and a continuing focus on our core values: academic excellence, a student oriented environment and a strong sense of community.

"The Mount Carmel campus, the academic home to all undergraduates with traditional, suite and apartment housing for freshmen and sophomores, is 250 acres in a stunning setting adjacent to Sleeping Giant state park. The nearby 250 acre York Hill campus is home to juniors and seniors in apartments with breathtaking views, a lodge style student center, covered parking, and the TD Bank sports center with twin arenas for hockey and basketball. The 100 acre North Haven campus, just four miles distant, is the home to graduate programs in Health Sciences, and Education, and a soon to be developed Medical School (est. opening 2013/2014).

"Academic initiatives such as the honors program, 'writing across the curriculum', QU seminar series, extensive internship experiences, study abroad opportunities and a highly regarded emerging leaders student-life program form the foundation for excellence in business, communication, health sciences, nursing, education, liberal arts, and law.

"State of the art facilities include the Financial Technology Center, HD fully digital production studio, extensive health science labs, recreation and sports fields and arenas. More than ninety student organizations, twenty-one Division I teams, community service, student publications, and a strong student government offer a variety of outside-of-class experiences. "

SELECTIVITY

Admissions Rating	87
# of applicants	13,847
% of applicants accepted	69
% of acceptees attending	17
# accepting a place on wait list	980
% admitted from wait list	22

FRESHMAN PROFILE

Range SAT Critical Reading	540–610
Range SAT Math	560–630
Range ACT Composite	23–27
Minimum paper TOEFL	550
Minimum computer TOEFL	213
Minimum web-based TOEFL	77
Average HS GPA	3.40
% graduated top 10% of class	25
% graduated top 25% of class	66
% graduated top 50% of class	95

DEADLINES

Regular	
Priority	2/1
Notification	12/15
Nonfall registration?	yes

APPLICANTS ALSO LOOK AT
AND OFTEN PREFER
Boston University, University of Connecticut

AND SOMETIMES PREFER
Fairfield University, Northeastern University, University of Delaware

AND RARELY PREFER
Ithaca College, Sacred Heart University

FINANCIAL FACTS

Financial Aid Rating	68
Annual tuition	$32,850
Room and board	$12,730
Required fees	$1,400
Books and supplies	$800
% frosh rec. need-based scholarship or grant aid	68
% UG rec. need-based scholarship or grant aid	57
% frosh rec. non-need-based scholarship or grant aid	36
% UG rec. non-need-based scholarship or grant aid	29
% frosh rec. need-based self-help aid	50
% UG rec. need-based self-help aid	50
% frosh rec. any financial aid	72
% UG rec. any financial aid	68
% UG borrow to pay for school	69
Average cumulative indebtedness	$34,621

RANDOLPH COLLEGE

2500 RIVERMONT AVENUE, LYNCHBURG, VA 24503-1555 • ADMISSIONS: 800-745-7692 • FAX: 434-947-8996

STUDENTS SAY ". . ."

Academics

Randolph College offers "a combination of great academics, cultural integrity, individuality, and tradition" to its several hundred students on a "small, yet beautiful" campus. Many chose the school based on "its location," "its reputation," and "the quality of its academics." As one undergrad explains, "I decided to attend Randolph because I wanted a school that melded fun, wacky traditions; strong academics; small classes with teachers who really get to know you well; a family-like community; and a school that makes you feel at home." Expect to "work" here thanks to "rigorous" classes. The school's small size allows students and faculty to "take the time to have conversations." (Some here boast that certain classes have "as few as three students"). In addition to small class sizes, "the professors are excellent, exceptionally so." Though praise for the "fantastic" professors is virtually unanimous, student opinion regarding the administration is decidedly mixed. Some undergrads are quick to assert that the administration is "very caring and helpful with any student they encounter." And one content sophomore highlights that The Dean of College Offices is "accessible…and offers great advice about tackling problems." However, others feel that the school administration sometimes makes decisions "without considering the view point of the rest of the college community."

Life

Thanks to Randolph's "rigorous" coursework, many here note that "there really isn't much time for things other than studying." But you won't find any complaints regarding that here. "My life at school is usually stressful but rewarding," says one undergrad. "I'm in a number of clubs and organizations while still trying to find the time to finish my homework and study for exams." Randolph "is all about being a strong familial community that works hard and has fun traditions that make your life here a little extraordinary." These traditions provide for "a great experience and a lot of fun." For most undergrads, there's "a lot of reading," "hanging out with friends," "attending sporting events," and "trips to other schools on the weekends." Mostly, you get out of your social life what you put into it. "It's entirely up to the individual," explains a student, "unless you proactively go out to do something, it's not going to happen." With that in mind, if you're willing to put the time in, there are plenty of "activities and groups" and a "very diverse social life" to discover.

Student Body

As a rule, students at Randolph "are academically motivated and open to other ideas and cultures." In line with that, "Those that are not serious about academics or that are very close minded will most likely quickly find that this school is not the correct fit for them." This is due to the "great diversity of students" on campus that makes for some "extraordinarily unique" individuals who, despite differences, manage to "fit together perfectly." "There's enough diversity here for everyone to be different," says one undergrad, "but enough conformity for groups of friends to develop and interact with each other." Students are "serious but not very nerdy," "liberal," and "more informed than most." Despite academics being "the number one priority for students," most here are "very involved in a number of clubs and extracurricular activities." There are also "very few cliques," though "a few do exist." Some feel that "after the switch to coeducation…a disproportionate number of athletes" were admitted though the student body's passion for "equality, the environment, and education still prevails." Most students agree that Randolph's "close-knit community" is "a place where everybody really does know your name and everyone smiles at each other."

RANDOLPH COLLEGE

FINANCIAL AID: 434-947-8128 • E-MAIL: ADMISSIONS@RANDOLPHCOLLEGE.EDU • WEBSITE: WWW.RANDOLPHCOLLEGE.EDU

THE PRINCETON REVIEW SAYS

Admissions

Very important factors considered include: Academic GPA, rigor of secondary school record, character/personal qualities. *Important factors considered include:* Application essay, class rank, recommendation(s), interview, standardized test scores, extracurricular activities. *Other factors considered include:* Alumni/ae relation, level of applicant's interest, talent/ability, volunteer work, work experience. SAT or ACT required; ACT with or without writing component accepted. TOEFL required of all international applicants. High school diploma is required, and GED is accepted. *Academic units required:* 4 English, 3 mathematics, 2 science (2 science labs), 3 foreign language, 2 history, 2 academic elective. *Academic units recommended:* 20 honors, AP, and IB courses if available.

Financial Aid

Students should submit: FAFSA. Regular filing deadline is February 15. The Princeton Review suggests that all financial aid forms be submitted as soon as possible after January 1. *Need-based scholarships/grants offered:* Federal Pell, SEOG, state scholarships/grants, private scholarships, school scholarship or grant aid from institutional funds. *Loan aid offered:* Direct Subsidized Stafford, Direct Unsubsidized Stafford, Direct PLUS, Federal Perkins, university loans from institutional funds. Applicants will be notified of awards on a rolling basis beginning March 1. Federal Work-Study Program available. Off-campus job opportunities are good. Yellow Ribbon program participant.

The Inside Word

Admitting highly qualified and well-matched students is a top priority at Randolph, and applicants can rest assured that their applications will be given due consideration (something guaranteed by the school's small size). There's no minimum GPA or standardized test score requirements, but be aware that most successful candidates have impressive classroom credentials. Character also plays an important role in admissions decisions; Randolph is looking for independent, confident students who place a premium on their educations.

THE SCHOOL SAYS "..."

From the Admissions Office

"Students who thrive in a close-knit community that values original thinking and research will enjoy the educational and cultural environment at Randolph College where they may earn a BA, BS, or BFA degree.

"Nationally ranked for both its academic programs and affordability, Randolph College offers students the best features of an honors education with a wide range of majors and an emphasis on developing intercultural competence. Embedded within the strong, liberal arts foundation are ample opportunities for study abroad, leadership roles, working closely with faculty on research, and real-world experience through internships and service learning. All students are encouraged to pursue and achieve goals with personal meaning.

"A graduate of Randolph College understands the intellectual foundations of the arts, sciences, and humanities and has developed critical skills to learn, adapt, and succeed in a rapidly changing global environment. The college's strong emphasis on writing enables students to communicate clearly and persuasively, and the diverse student population and study abroad programs enable students to see and live through the eyes of another culture. The long-standing and distinctive honor system is a central part of daily life at Randolph and adds to the already close-knit community feel.

"A member of the Old Dominion Athletic Conference and IHSA (Randolph has a 100-acre riding center), Randolph enables scholar-athletes to excel and participate in a variety of sports while focusing on academics. Located in the heart of Virginia near the Blue Ridge Mountains, Randolph College's campus is part of the growing college town of Lynchburg with its abundant cultural, entertainment, and recreational opportunities."

SELECTIVITY
Admissions Rating	79
# of applicants	734
% of applicants accepted	90
% of acceptees attending	25

FRESHMAN PROFILE
Range SAT Critical Reading	500–600
Range SAT Math	500–610
Range ACT Composite	23–27
Minimum paper TOEFL	550
Minimum computer TOEFL	213
Minimum web-based TOEFL	79
Average HS GPA	3.40
% graduated top 10% of class	20
% graduated top 25% of class	60
% graduated top 50% of class	90

DEADLINES
Early action	
Deadline	12/1
Notification	12/15
Regular	
Priority	2/1
Deadline	4/1
Nonfall registration?	yes

APPLICANTS ALSO LOOK AT
AND OFTEN PREFER
James Madison University, University of Virginia
AND SOMETIMES PREFER
College of William and Mary, Sweet Briar College
AND RARELY PREFER
Hollins University, Randolph-Macon College, Virginia Tech

FINANCIAL FACTS
Financial Aid Rating	85
Annual tuition	$25,350
Room and board	$9,000
Required fees	$510
Books and supplies	$800
% frosh rec. need-based scholarship or grant aid	74
% UG rec. need-based scholarship or grant aid	66
% frosh rec. non-need-based scholarship or grant aid	22
% UG rec. non-need-based scholarship or grant aid	18
% frosh rec. need-based self-help aid	66
% UG rec. need-based self-help aid	58
% frosh rec. any financial aid	99
% UG rec. any financial aid	96
% UG borrow to pay for school	75
Average cumulative indebtedness	$27,218

REED COLLEGE

3203 SOUTHEAST WOODSTOCK BOULEVARD, PORTLAND, OR 97202-8199 • ADMISSIONS: 503-777-7511 • FAX: 503-777-7553

STUDENTS SAY ". . ."

Academics

Reed College, "offers a serious liberal-arts education in a small, creative, community" where "intellectualism is highly respected" and students pursue "learning for learning's sake" in "a challenging academic atmosphere." "We are a collection of those weird kids in high school who had a passionate interest in learning about something and made that interest academic, even if it wasn't beforehand," one student explains. They're the sort of students who seek out an "academic rigor that definitely prepares us for graduate school and scholarly work." "Small, discussion based classes, frequent interaction with professors, and general intellectual curiosity override all other aspects of the life at Reed," where "studying and going to classes is not somehow the price to pay for staying here (with the ultimate goal being the weekend and, eventually, a diploma); rather, it is the core joy of being at Reed." Unsurprisingly, "students work incredibly hard," but "the school is there for us every step of the way. As freshmen, students meet with their humanities professors after every paper one-on-one for paper conferences." Seniors must complete a thesis project; "When writing one's senior thesis, students meet with professors one-on-one for an hour every week." It's exactly the right sort of place for students who "want to be excited about school again," says one student. "I wanted to be around other people who were both excited about academics and excited about being at a place where academics excited them. I wanted to be in a place where people didn't take themselves too seriously but took their work seriously." Welcome to Reed.

Life

Reed is an academically intense school, so "a great amount of time is spent on academics, even on the weekends" here. "Late at night, it is not uncommon to see Reedies debating the merits of Thucydides and Herodotus or discussing the financial bailout package in the library lobby, dorm common rooms, and at the hotcake house (a nearby twenty-four-hour pancake joint)," one student reports. But although "people are very involved in their studies, especially seniors and their individual theses…everyone keeps his or her own passions alive with student government, various hobbies (baking, knitting, singing, dancing), sports (rugby, ultimate Frisbee, and basketball), and often trips around the multiple neighborhoods of Portland." The city justly is celebrated for its coffee shops, restaurants, and bookstores. Annual campus traditions include Renn Fayre, "a three-day party at the end of the year at which students celebrate the completion of senior theses. Renn Fayre begins with Thesis Parade, in which seniors burn their thesis drafts in a bonfire in front of the library and then march in costume, covered in champagne and confetti through the library across the lawn to the registrar's office to turn in their [completed] theses."

Student Body

Reed students tend to be "smart, intellectually curious, and a little quirky." Politics tilt strongly to the left. One student reports, "There is virtually no political dialogue. The student body is so liberal the only dialogue is really between socialists and communists. For students who regard themselves as liberal and, consequentially, open-minded, there is very little acceptance of people who don't identify themselves as liberal or who simply like political dialogue." The student body is also "overwhelmingly Caucasian" and affluent, although students note there is "a growing population of minority students (minority in various senses) and they are making efforts constantly to establish themselves as a social presence on campus. Student groups like the Latino, Asian, and Black and African Student Unions and places like the Multicultural Resource Center offer places for support."

FINANCIAL AID: 800-547-4750 • E-MAIL: ADMISSION@REED.EDU • WEBSITE: WWW.REED.EDU

THE PRINCETON REVIEW SAYS

Admissions

Very important factors considered include: Academic GPA, application essay, rigor of secondary school record. *Important factors considered include:* Class rank, recommendation(s), standardized test scores, interview, level of applicant's interest. *Other factors considered include:* Alumni/ae relation, character/personal qualities, extracurricular activities, first generation, geographical residence, racial/ethnic status, talent/ability, volunteer work, work experience. SAT or ACT required; ACT with or without writing component accepted. TOEFL required of all international applicants. High school diploma is required, and GED is accepted. *Academic units recommended:* 4 English, 4 mathematics, 3 science, 3 foreign language, 1 social studies, 3 history.

Financial Aid

Students should submit: FAFSA, CSS/Financial Aid PROFILE. Regular filing deadline is February 1. The Princeton Review suggests that all financial aid forms be submitted as soon as possible after January 1. *Need-based scholarships/ grants offered:* Federal Pell, SEOG, state scholarships/grants, private scholarships, school scholarship or grant aid from institutional funds. *Loan aid offered:* Direct Subsidized Stafford, Direct Unsubsidized Stafford, Direct PLUS, Federal Perkins, university loans from institutional funds. Federal Work-Study Program available.

The Inside Word

Reed admissions officers know exactly what type of student will thrive here, and that's who they seek. Being smart isn't enough to get in here. Reedies are fiercely intellectual and more concerned with academic pursuits for their own sake than for any financial rewards their educations will produce. Successful applicants demonstrate genuine intellectual curiosity as well as the aptitude to handle a demanding curriculum.

THE SCHOOL SAYS ". . ."

From the Admissions Office

"Reed is animated and energized by its seemingly paradoxical features. Reed has, for example: (1) a traditional, classical, highly structured curriculum—yet, at the same time, a progressive, free-thinking, decidedly unstructured community culture; (2) a powerful emphasis on intellectuality, serious study, and the very highest standards of academic achievement—yet, at the same time, a rich and rewarding program of recreational and extracurricular activity, including a physical education requirement; (3) a refusal to overemphasize grades—yet, third in the nation in the production of future PhDs; (4) a faculty culture absolutely dedicated to superb undergraduate teaching—yet, at the same time, a faculty culture that supports and celebrates high-level research and scholarship at the cutting edge of each academic discipline.

"Reed is not a simple place. It's a complex amalgam of diverse elements. But those elements have been chosen and developed over the years with great care. The result is an intricate—even ornate—but utterly coherent and clearly articulated architecture that has been called by at least one outside observer 'exquisite' and by another 'the most intellectual college in the country.' Reed is not for everyone. But for students who are interested both in exploring great ideas and in developing personal autonomy, it makes very good sense indeed.

"Reed accepts either the ACT or SAT and does not require SAT Subject Tests or the ACT writing exam."

SELECTIVITY

Admissions Rating	98
# of applicants	3,075
% of applicants accepted	43
% of acceptees attending	28
# accepting a place on wait list	616
% admitted from wait list	1
# of early decision applicants	179
% accepted early decision	53

FRESHMAN PROFILE

Range SAT Critical Reading	670–750
Range SAT Math	640–710
Range SAT Writing	660–730
Range ACT Composite	30–33
Minimum paper TOEFL	600
Minimum web-based TOEFL	100
Average HS GPA	3.90
% graduated top 10% of class	63
% graduated top 25% of class	90
% graduated top 50% of class	99

DEADLINES

Early decision	
Deadline	11/15
Notification	12/15
Regular	
Deadline	1/15
Nonfall registration?	no

APPLICANTS ALSO LOOK AT

AND OFTEN PREFER
University of California—Berkeley,
University of Chicago

AND SOMETIMES PREFER
Oberlin College, Swarthmore College

AND RARELY PREFER
Lewis & Clark College

FINANCIAL FACTS

Financial Aid Rating	96
Annual tuition	$40,940
Room and board	$10,650
Required fees	$260
Books and supplies	$950
% frosh rec. need-based scholarship or grant aid	46
% UG rec. need-based scholarship or grant aid	48
% frosh rec. need-based self-help aid	49
% UG rec. need-based self-help aid	50
% frosh rec. any financial aid	53
% UG rec. any financial aid	54
% UG borrow to pay for school	53
Average cumulative indebtedness	$16,910

RENSSELAER POLYTECHNIC INSTITUTE

110 EIGHTH STREET, TROY, NY 12180-3590 • ADMISSIONS: 518-276-6216 • FAX: 518-276-4072

STUDENTS SAY ". . ."

Academics

Rensselaer Polytechnic Institute, which proud students declare as "a small research institute making a large impact on the world" is "essentially a hardcore technical school oriented toward engineering and the sciences." Although the school is trying to expand its offerings in the humanities and arts (and boasts strong architecture and management programs), even those "are very technology- and science-based." Still, the school makes no secret of its strengths, and students in all disciplines face "a very tough four years with a very bright future after." Professors "act more like mentors than teachers," and most programs incorporate "a hands-on studio-based method" supplemented by "top-of-the-line facilities… and numerous resources for all students to use." RPI's identity as a research center helps here; according to one undergrad, "RPI is all about ensuring every student gets legitimate experience in his/her field of study as soon as possible and equipping each student with the skills needed to be a valuable member of any research team or company." The school excels in this, and "Any RPI student who wants a research position can usually find one." RPI's co-op program and Career Development Center "are also outstanding, leading to a high placement rate in excellent jobs," although of the latter, some warn, "Many engineering firms are familiar with Rensselaer, but employers in other fields still have yet to learn of the students available." However, students flock to RPI for "the name and the reputation that stands behind it. We have the programs and experience that other schools only dream about."

Life

"The academics are challenging" at RPI, making life "stressful, but in a good way. Time management is a key to success here." A few students have trouble walking away from the books, but there are various clubs and "many intramural sports" that are available to all. "If there's anything that you enjoy doing, you can most likely find it as a club," says a student. The Greek scene is popular, but it's not your stereotypical *Animal House* variety; sure, "There are definitely a bunch of parties every weekend if you're into that," but "they're all pretty much very responsible with sober bartenders and sober drivers." RPI's Greek organizations also "do a lot of community service in the area and philanthropy events on campus." Greek or not, all here agree that the Division I men's hockey team is "excellent" and "especially big," as is the student union, where "you can always find friends…even late at night, it's pretty crowded." So much is happening that most students stay here over the weekends, "even those who are local," and students often "split up the weekend with some homework and pick and choose which events to attend." The dorms are "open and friendly but never too loud," but hometown Troy "is not the best town to live in, although it has a few cool things to do." But, Albany is only a twenty-minute drive away (the bus is free), and "There's always something to do there." "We work hard and really do care about doing well in our classes, but we still find time to just hang out with friends and have fun," says a student.

Student Body

"The typical student may be considered 'nerdy' by the liberal arts world, but being a nerd is totally cool here," says a senior, and right he is. Nerds abound, but "There are a large number of 'normal' people as well, and each year, the percent of females in each incoming class increases." While the three-to-one guy-to-girl gender gap may be narrowing, it's still pretty wide, meaning that the typical student at RPI remains "a white male. They might be into sports, video games, drinking, Greek life, computers, RPG, or whatever, but they're an overwhelming aspect of campus." Girls seem pretty fine with the student body makeup: "I do not find the ratio overwhelming at all," says one. The growing minority population includes "many Asian and Indian students." One benefit of the student body being on the small side is that it allows "tight-knit relationships among students…to be established."

RENSSELAER POLYTECHNIC INSTITUTE

FINANCIAL AID: 518-276-6813 • E-MAIL: ADMISSIONS@RPI.EDU • WEBSITE: WWW.RPI.EDU

THE PRINCETON REVIEW SAYS

Admissions

Very important factors considered include: Academic GPA, class rank, rigor of secondary school record, standardized test scores. *Important factors considered include:* Application essay, recommendation(s), character/personal qualities, extracurricular activities, level of applicant's interest. *Other factors considered include:* Alumni/ae relation, geographical residence, interview, racial/ethnic status, talent/ability, volunteer work, work experience. SAT or ACT required; ACT with writing component required. TOEFL required of all international applicants. High school diploma is required, and GED is accepted. *Academic units required:* 4 English, 4 mathematics, 3 science, 2 social studies. *Academic units recommended:* 4 science, 3 social studies.

Financial Aid

Students should submit: FAFSA, CSS/Financial Aid PROFILE. The Princeton Review suggests that all financial aid forms be submitted as soon as possible after January 1. *Need-based scholarships/grants offered:* Federal Pell, SEOG, state scholarships/grants, private scholarships, school scholarship or grant aid from institutional funds. *Loan aid offered:* Direct Subsidized Stafford, Direct Unsubsidized Stafford, Direct PLUS, Federal Perkins, state loans, university loans from institutional funds. Federal Work-Study Program available. Off-campus job opportunities are good.

The Inside Word

Outstanding test scores and grades are pretty much a must for any applicant hopeful of impressing the RPI admissions committee. Underrepresented minorities and women—two demographics the school would like to augment—will get a little more leeway than others, but in all cases, the school is unlikely to admit anyone who lacks the skills and background to survive here. RPI offers many students January admission in order to allow them to pursue productive activities (work, travel, volunteering) in the fall semester following high school graduation.

THE SCHOOL SAYS ". . ."

From the Admissions Office

"The oldest degree-granting technological research university in North America, RPI or Rensselaer was founded in 1824 to instruct students to apply 'science to the common purposes of life.' Rensselaer offers more than 100 programs and 1,000 courses leading to bachelor's, master's, and doctoral degrees. Undergraduates pursue studies in architecture, engineering, humanities, arts, and social sciences, management and technology, science, and information technology (IT). A pioneer in interactive learning, Rensselaer provides real-world, hands-on educational opportunities that cut across academic disciplines. Students have ready access to laboratories and attend classes involving lively discussion, problem solving, and faculty mentoring. The Office of First-Year Experience provides programs for students and their primary support persons that begin even before students arrive on campus. Students are able to take full advantage of Rensselaer's three unique research platforms: the $80 million state-of-the-art Center for Biotechnology and Interdisciplinary Studies (CBIS); one of the world's most powerful academic supercomputers, the Computational Center for Nanotechnology Innovations (CCNI); and the newly opened Experimental Media and Performing Arts Center (EMPAC), which encourages students to explore the intersection of science, technology, and the arts. Newly renovated residence halls, wireless computing network, and studio classrooms create a fertile environment for study and learning. Rensselaer offers recreational and fitness facilities plus numerous student-run organizations and activities, including fraternities and sororities, a newspaper, a radio station, drama and musical groups, and more than 160 clubs. In addition to intramural sports, NCAA varsity sports include Division I men's and women's ice hockey teams and twenty-one Division III men's and women's teams in thirteen sports. The new East Campus Athletic Village, opened in 2009, raises the bar for student athletic facilities for varsity and non-varsity athletes alike, and includes a new football arena, basketball stadium, and sports medicine complex."

SELECTIVITY

Admissions Rating	93
# of applicants	13,465
% of applicants accepted	40
% of acceptees attending	21
# accepting a place on wait list	1,871
% admitted from wait list	5
# of early decision applicants	1,218
% accepted early decision	26

FRESHMAN PROFILE

Range SAT Critical Reading	610–700
Range SAT Math	670–750
Range SAT Writing	580–685
Range ACT Composite	26–30
Minimum paper TOEFL	570
Minimum computer TOEFL	230
Minimum web-based TOEFL	88
% graduated top 10% of class	65
% graduated top 25% of class	92
% graduated top 50% of class	99

DEADLINES

Early decision	
Deadline	11/1
Notification	12/10
Regular	
Deadline	1/15
Notification	3/12
Nonfall registration?	yes

APPLICANTS ALSO LOOK AT
AND OFTEN PREFER
Cornell University, Massachusetts Institute of Technology

AND SOMETIMES PREFER
Boston University, Carnegie Mellon University, University of Rochester

AND RARELY PREFER
Rochester Institute of Technology, Syracuse University, Worcester Polytechnic Institute

FINANCIAL FACTS

Financial Aid Rating	86
Annual tuition	$39,600
Room and board	$11,465
Required fees	$1,080
Books and supplies	$1,890
% frosh rec. need-based scholarship or grant aid	71
% UG rec. need-based scholarship or grant aid	66
% frosh rec. non-need-based scholarship or grant aid	18
% UG rec. non-need-based scholarship or grant aid	12
% frosh rec. need-based self-help aid	55
% UG rec. need-based self-help aid	25
% frosh rec. any financial aid	96
% UG rec. any financial aid	97
% UG borrow to pay for school	70
Average cumulative indebtedness	$30,125

RHODES COLLEGE

OFFICE OF ADMISSIONS, 2000 NORTH PARKWAY, MEMPHIS, TN 38112 • ADMISSIONS: 901-843-3700 • FAX: 901-843-3631

CAMPUS LIFE

Quality of Life Rating	81
Fire Safety Rating	79
Green Rating	80
Type of school	private
Affiliation	Presbyterian
Environment	metropolis

STUDENTS

Total undergrad enrollment	1,712
% male/female	42/58
% from out of state	73
% from public high school	50
% live on campus	73
# of fraternities	7
# of sororities	6
% African American	7
% Asian	6
% Caucasian	81
% Hispanic	3
% Native American	1
% international	3
# of countries represented	15

SURVEY SAYS . . .
No one cheats
Great computer facilities
School is well-run
Great off-campus food
Low cost of living

ACADEMICS

Academic Rating	97
% students graduating within 4 years	76
% students graduating within 6 years	80
Calendar	semester
Student/faculty ratio	10:1
Profs interesting rating	96
Profs accessible rating	95
Most common reg class size	10–19 students
Most common lab size	20–29 students

MOST POPULAR MAJORS
biology, business/commerce, English, history, psychology

STUDENTS SAY ". . ."

Academics

A "beautiful" campus located in the heart of Memphis, Tennessee, the "tight-knit community" of Rhodes College offers "individual study in a liberal arts mold," which involves exposing students to "as many different disciplines as possible in order to gain a broader understanding of the world." Academics here are extremely challenging, "but nothing that hard work and study time can't handle." "I have been pushed (in a good way) to the outer limits of my academic capabilities," says a sophomore. Professors are undoubtedly "one of Rhodes' best assets"—invitations to faculty members' houses for dinner are par for the course—and "truly care about our achievement, grasping the right concepts, and progressing in our education." "Professors don't just care about passing the tests, they want students to be able to take what they have learned and apply it to real life," beams a student. The "small classes" and "comprehensive honor code" only help to further students' love of the Rhodes' classroom experience. The concerned individuals making up the Rhodes administration are "not just doing a job," they are "dedicated to the mission of this college and committed to the students they serve." Though some students have had some bad experiences with administrators, most are content, and it doesn't hurt that the school just "took all of the different offices that were spread throughout campus and consolidated them into one newly-renovated building that makes any form or process/meeting much simpler."

Life

With "gothic architecture [that] will make you feel like you live in a fantasy world," the Rhodes campus is "easy on the eyes," while the food is tough on the gut ("mediocre at best" says one of the less harsh critics, of which there are many). There is a huge Greek contingent here—"frat parties on campus are always fun and wild"—and all students are sure to find their fratastic niche since "each fraternity is different." Generally speaking, the typical student schedule breaks down like this: "weekdays and nights in the library (which is beautiful, so it's not as bad as it could be), and starting Thursdays, partying." Don't be fooled, though: "Most people here work hard and see it academically pay off." "Students focus on getting their school work done before going out and hold their friends accountable so not many get behind," says another student. The school itself offers tons of service activities, cultural events, speakers, and intramurals, and people like to get off campus and have fun in Memphis, which is "surrounded by fun sports teams" to which the school provides cheap tickets. The library can also be a social place, especially during exams, "because so many people spend their time there."

Student Body

Rhodes has its fair share of "white, upper-middle-class" students, but "no one is elitist," and the overall student body itself is diverse on many fronts. Many students here are from the South and "preppy," and you can spot many "polos and khakis around campus." "Everyone is well accepted regardless of socioeconomic status," and the few atypical student groups "mix freely" and "interact with few problems." The school is full of hard workers ("academic but not full of nerds") and the school's honor code is taken very seriously. "People rarely ever cheat or steal"—most students live on campus and "a large percentage don't ever lock their doom rooms." One thing is for certain, though—students here are "busy" in all areas of their life: studying, taking advantage of the "countless service opportunities," arts/athletics, and Greek life. The typical student is generally an "overachiever" while still "[liking] to have fun and enjoy him or herself." "Rhodes is filled with the types of students that are any high school counselor's...dream," sums up a student.

FINANCIAL AID: 901-843-3810 • E-MAIL: ADMINFO@RHODES.EDU • WEBSITE: WWW.RHODES.EDU

THE PRINCETON REVIEW SAYS

Admissions

Very important factors considered include: Academic GPA, class rank, rigor of secondary school record. *Important factors considered include:* Application essay, recommendation(s), standardized test scores, alumni/ae relation, character/ personal qualities, racial/ethnic status. *Other factors considered include:* Extracurricular activities, first generation, geographical residence, interview, level of applicant's interest, state residency, talent/ability, volunteer work, work experience. SAT or ACT required; ACT with or without writing component accepted. TOEFL required of all international applicants. High school diploma is required, and GED is accepted. *Academic units required:* 4 English, 3 mathematics, 2 science (2 science labs), 2 foreign language, 2 social studies, 3 academic elective. *Academic units recommended:* 4 years of each academic area.

Financial Aid

Students should submit: FAFSA, CSS/Financial Aid PROFILE. Regular filing deadline is March 1. The Princeton Review suggests that all financial aid forms be submitted as soon as possible after January 1. *Need-based scholarships/grants offered:* Federal Pell, SEOG, state scholarships/grants, private scholarships, school scholarship or grant aid from institutional funds. *Loan aid offered:* Direct PLUS, Federal Perkins. Federal Work-Study Program available. Off-campus job opportunities are good.

The Inside Word

Rhodes' national profile is growing. Even though the majority of students come from Tennessee and nearby states, students from farther-flung points of origin will enjoy a leg up because they add to the geographic diversity. As with all small, selective schools, applicants are advised to schedule a campus visit and to interview to demonstrate their interest in attending.

THE SCHOOL SAYS "..."

From the Admissions Office

"Your journey at Rhodes begins with the breathtaking beauty of the campus. You quickly become part of the culture: our love of academic discovery is matched by the depth of respect we have for each other. You experience a new sense of freedom—to wonder aloud, to get immersed in new interests, to create a community that reflects everything that's important to you. Rhodes faculty create a classroom culture free of pretense and posturing where students are encouraged to dig deeper and think harder. Faculty mentors become truly invested in students' trajectory over four years—and beyond. We're located right where we need to be—Memphis is a city with soul, with people of all ages, races, and perspectives. We couldn't be Rhodes College anywhere else. And we wouldn't want to be. Our students love the rush of discovery and carry it throughout the city into their extracurricular lives. They immerse themselves in research, service and internships. They don't see a divide between studies and the rest of their life— it's all part of a total experience and they want to do it all."

SELECTIVITY

Admissions Rating	95
# of applicants	5,598
% of applicants accepted	45
% of acceptees attending	20
# of early decision applicants	110
% accepted early decision	5

FRESHMAN PROFILE

Range SAT Critical Reading	590–700
Range SAT Math	590–690
Range ACT Composite	26–30
Minimum paper TOEFL	550
Minimum computer TOEFL	213
Minimum web-based TOEFL	80
Average HS GPA	3.78
% graduated top 10% of class	53
% graduated top 25% of class	85
% graduated top 50% of class	97

DEADLINES

Early decision	
Deadline	11/1
Notification	12/1
Early action	
Deadline	11/15
Notification	1/15
Regular	
Priority	1/15
Notification	4/1
Nonfall registration?	yes

APPLICANTS ALSO LOOK AT
AND OFTEN PREFER
Davidson College

AND SOMETIMES PREFER
Furman University, Sewanee—The University of the South, Trinity University, Vanderbilt University

AND RARELY PREFER
Birmingham-Southern College, The University of Memphis

FINANCIAL FACTS

Financial Aid Rating	85
Annual tuition	$34,270
Room and board	$8,480
Required fees	$310
Books and supplies	$1,071
% frosh rec. need-based scholarship or grant aid	56
% UG rec. need-based scholarship or grant aid	51
% frosh rec. non-need-based scholarship or grant aid	16
% UG rec. non-need-based scholarship or grant aid	9
% frosh rec. need-based self-help aid	42
% UG rec. need-based self-help aid	40
% frosh rec. any financial aid	85
% UG rec. any financial aid	85
% UG borrow to pay for school	47
Average cumulative indebtedness	$24,946

RICE UNIVERSITY

OFFICE OF ADMISSION MS 17, PO BOX 1892, HOUSTON, TX 77251-1892 • ADMISSIONS: 713-348-7423 • FAX: 713-348-5952

CAMPUS LIFE

Quality of Life Rating	99
Fire Safety Rating	88
Green Rating	79
Type of school	private
Environment	metropolis

STUDENTS

Total undergrad enrollment	3,529
% male/female	52/48
% from out of state	55
% from public high school	70
% live on campus	77
% African American	7
% Asian	21
% Caucasian	43
% Hispanic	11
% international	10
# of countries represented	47

SURVEY SAYS . . .
Students are friendly
Great off-campus food
Dorms are like palaces
Students are happy
*Frats and sororities are unpopular
or nonexistent*

ACADEMICS

Academic Rating	93
% students graduating within 4 years	79
% students graduating within 6 years	92
Calendar	semester
Student/faculty ratio	6:1
Profs interesting rating	84
Profs accessible rating	90
Most common reg class size	fewer than 10 students

MOST POPULAR MAJORS
biology, economics, psychology, engineering

STUDENTS SAY ". . ."

Academics

A sunny and social place to get a prestigious degree, Rice University is Houston's answer to the Ivy League. Consistently ranked as "one of the top universities of the nation," Rice maintains a stellar faculty, a "vibrant research program," and a "diverse selection of courses and departments." "Professors of big intro classes don't do a lot of discussion." Fortunately, "Classes are more interactive and small as you progress to the upper level," and students often develop a strong rapport with their instructors. A student details, "Most Rice professors love what they're doing, and you can tell that they are truly passionate about the material. They may show this by literally dancing around in the front of the classroom or by simply being available at any time to help students." Another student adds affectionately, "I want to adopt my bio-chem professor as my surrogate grandpa." Beyond traditional academics, Rice excels at offering "strong research opportunities for undergraduate students," including mentored lab work, independent projects, and "internships in the social sciences." There is also a "great engineering program" at Rice, and future doctors point out that the campus is located "next to the largest medical center in the world." Maybe it's all that Texan sunshine, but students say Rice is "not cutthroat academically, in spite of its very good academic reputation." Instead, "Academics are very challenging, but working hard will take you a long way." "Academic advising is amazing," and professors are an important source of support, "inviting students to join them for coffee in the student center or visit them in office hours to discuss class material, research, papers, or even what's going on in our lives!"

Life

Rice University offers "the most amazing balance of serious education and an unbelievably rewarding personal life." According to most undergraduates, "The college system is the key to life at Rice University," through which students are assigned to residential communities for all four years of study. The cornerstone of the Rice community, "The 'Hogwarts style' housing system creates an intimate place to create lasting friendships, as well as friendly competition between different dorms." "From the minute you walk onto Rice campus, you have upperclassmen advisors, peer academic advisors, Rice health advisors, the masters, resident associates, the counseling center, the wellness center, and many more campus groups that help you navigate your way through freshman year." "Most Friday and Saturday nights, there are parties open to the entire university, sponsored by a residential college," and everyone comes out for the annual campus-wide shindig, Beer Bike. Surrounding Houston is a big city and great college town, and students "love exploring new restaurants, going to Chinatown, volunteering, spending a lot of time at the swimming pool, shopping at thrift stores, [and] going on trips to Austin and Dallas." "The weather is fantastic."

Student Body

While they look like a bunch of "outgoing, down-to-earth kids," students reveal, "Everyone at Rice is, in some way, a nerd." At this "geek chic" school, "Regardless of your interest and no matter how nerdy it might be now, you'll definitely find someone else who shares your passion." "There is something unique about every Rice student," and career goals and intellectual interests run the gamut. A current undergraduate details, "Among my best friends, I have one who is working for Google next year, one who will be training for the Olympic trials over summer, and one who is currently working at a station in Antarctica." "Rice genuinely has a diverse community that accepts people of all backgrounds." Nonetheless, Rice students do share some common traits, generally described as "liberal for Texas," low-key, and "good natured." While most undergraduates are "studious," they're not overly serious. The typical student "rolls out of bed in a t-shirt" and is "willing to help you out in times of need."

450 ■ THE BEST 376 COLLEGES

FINANCIAL AID: 713-348-4958 • E-MAIL: ADMISSION@RICE.EDU • WEBSITE: WWW.RICE.EDU

THE PRINCETON REVIEW SAYS

Admissions

Very important factors considered include: Academic GPA, application essay, class rank, recommendation(s), rigor of secondary school record, standardized test scores, character/personal qualities, extracurricular activities, talent/ability. *Other factors considered include:* Alumni/ae relation, first generation, geographical residence, interview, level of applicant's interest, racial/ethnic status, state residency, volunteer work, work experience. SAT or ACT required; ACT with writing component required. TOEFL required of all international applicants. High school diploma or equivalent isn't required. *Academic units required:* 4 English, 3 mathematics, 2 science (2 science labs), 2 foreign language, 2 social studies, 3 academic elective. *Academic units recommended:* 4 English, 4 mathematics, 4 science (3 science labs), 4 foreign language, 2 social studies, 3 academic elective.

Financial Aid

Students should submit: FAFSA, CSS/Financial Aid PROFILE. The Princeton Review suggests that all financial aid forms be submitted as soon as possible after January 1. *Need-based scholarships/grants offered:* Federal Pell, SEOG, state scholarships/grants, private scholarships, school scholarship or grant aid from institutional funds. *Loan aid offered:* Direct Subsidized Stafford, Direct Unsubsidized Stafford, Direct PLUS, Federal Perkins, state loans. Federal Work-Study Program available. Off-campus job opportunities are excellent.

The Inside Word

Rice is a competitive university and admission is granted only to top students. In recent years, less than eighteen percent of regular decision applicants were offered a spot in the incoming class. (For a variety of reasons, early decision applicants are accepted at a slightly higher rate.) Though not required, students are encouraged to interview with an admissions counselor on the Rice campus or arrange to meet with alumni in their area. Students applying to the school of architecture must accompany their application with a portfolio of creative work, while music students must audition on the Rice campus.

THE SCHOOL SAYS "..."

From the Admissions Office

"We seek students of keen intellect and diverse backgrounds who show potential to succeed at Rice and will also contribute to the educational environment of those around them.

"Student applications are reviewed within the context of the division to which they apply. Admission committee decisions are based not only on high school grades and test scores but also on such qualities as leadership, participation in extracurricular activities, and personal creativity. Admission is extremely competitive. Rice attempts to seek out and identify those students who have demonstrated exceptional ability and the potential for personal and intellectual growth.

"Our individualized, holistic evaluation process employs many different means to identify these qualities in applicants.

"Required admission testing includes the SAT and two Subject tests, or ACT with writing. All test scores must be sent to Rice directly from the official testing agency."

SELECTIVITY
Admissions Rating	97
# of applicants	13,804
% of applicants accepted	19
% of acceptees attending	36
# accepting a place on wait list	1,444
% admitted from wait list	9
# of early decision applicants	1,214
% accepted early decision	25

FRESHMAN PROFILE
Range SAT Critical Reading	650–750
Range SAT Math	690–790
Range SAT Writing	660–760
Range ACT Composite	31–34
Minimum paper TOEFL	600
Minimum computer TOEFL	250
Minimum web-based TOEFL	100
% graduated top 10% of class	85
% graduated top 25% of class	96
% graduated top 50% of class	99

DEADLINES
Early decision	
Deadline	11/1
Notification	12/15
Regular	
Deadline	1/1
Nonfall registration?	no

APPLICANTS ALSO LOOK AT
AND OFTEN PREFER
Harvard College, Stanford University, Yale University

AND SOMETIMES PREFER
Cornell University, Duke University

AND RARELY PREFER
The University of Texas at Austin, Washington University in St. Louis

FINANCIAL FACTS
Financial Aid Rating	98
Annual tuition	$34,900
Room and board	$12,270
Required fees	$651
Books and supplies	$800
% frosh rec. need-based scholarship or grant aid	42
% UG rec. need-based scholarship or grant aid	40
% frosh rec. non-need-based scholarship or grant aid	7
% UG rec. non-need-based scholarship or grant aid	5
% frosh rec. need-based self-help aid	42
% UG rec. need-based self-help aid	36
% frosh rec. any financial aid	53
% UG rec. any financial aid	62
% UG borrow to pay for school	26
Average cumulative indebtedness	$13,944

RIDER UNIVERSITY

2083 LAWRENCEVILLE ROAD, LAWRENCEVILLE, NJ 08648 • ADMISSIONS: 609-896-5042 • FAX: 609-895-6645

STUDENTS SAY ". . ."

Academics

A private co-ed institution in Lawrenceville, New Jersey, Rider University offers a friendly and intimate college experience to a largely local crowd. In addition to dozens of majors in the liberal arts and sciences, Rider operates a "highly respected business school" and an accounting program that's "the best in the state of New Jersey." Rider "prepares you for all facets of life after college," fostering "interpersonal relationships between successful alumni and under-graduates" and offering great services like "tutoring for every class, writing labs, career services, internships, and co-ops." A current student attests, "The science professors have been really helpful with helping me achieve my goals by introducing me to opportunities for grants, internships, and other experien-tial learning." While coursework can be challenging, "The professors present the material in a way in which you can do well if you work hard." Teaching is emphasized, and there are "some phenomenal professors at Rider University who go out of their way to give their students a great education." At the same time, students admit, "While many professors are highly accessible, there are surely a few—mostly adjunct-professors—who are inadequate," both as men-tors and as teachers. On the whole, Rider is "very student-oriented," and the administration "goes the extra mile in making sure all students are treated equally." Even so, things don't always run smoothly, and "Dealing with finan-cial aid, administrative offices such as residence life, and career services is the hardest part about going to Rider University." While Rider is a private college, it helps students finance their education through "generous financial aid pack-age," loans, and "lots of opportunities for work study."

Life

Whether they live on campus or commute to school, students enjoy a friendly and social atmosphere at Rider. On campus, "Basketball games are always a big draw," and the university hosts "major comedians, musicians, [and] film nights" in the evenings. Even though the university's alcohol rules are rather strict, "Most students drink for fun, either on campus or off." For mellower times, the "residence advisors set up a lot events in their respective dorm," or students get together to "play video games, go to Zumba classes, hold hallway-parties (no alcohol), or movie nights." In addition, the "Student Rec Center is a great place to hang out because it's got basketball courts, a pool table, ping pong table, all the video game systems, a gym, a track, and a pool." When they want to pop off campus, "There are coffee shops, frozen yogurt places, [and] a house of cupcakes" in the nearby town of Princeton, and "New York City and Philly are only a train ride away." "On the weekends, the school empties out pretty quickly," as most students go home. While some complain that Rider is a "suitcase school," others insist, "The lifestyle on campus is what people make of it." For those who want a more traditional college experience, "Greek life is a great way to meet new people and get involved in campus."

Student Body

Many Rider students come from a "middle-class background," and most are East Coasters "from the Lawrenceville area" or greater New Jersey. However, "The student body is very diverse politically, socially, and academically," reflect-ing the "vastly varied demographics of the state of New Jersey: all races, all religions, and all levels of mental and physical abilities." "There is a good mix of jocks, brainy people who are committed to studying, and artsy hipster types," so most "students can usually find at least one group to fit in with." While some students "love to party," others "really care about how well they do in school and are involved in so many different organizations on campus." Rider also operates an evening program, which attracts "older, working, returning stu-dents," who are often very serious about their studies.

RIDER UNIVERSITY

FINANCIAL AID: 609-896-5360 • E-MAIL: ADMISSIONS@RIDER.EDU • WEBSITE: WWW.RIDER.EDU

THE PRINCETON REVIEW SAYS

Admissions

Very important factors considered include: Academic GPA, application essay, recommendation(s), rigor of secondary school record, standardized test scores. *Important factors considered include:* Level of applicant's interest. *Other factors considered include:* Class rank, alumni/ae relation, character/personal qualities, extracurricular activities, geographical residence, interview, state residency, talent/ability, volunteer work, work experience. SAT or ACT required; ACT with writing component required. TOEFL required of all international applicants. High school diploma is required, and GED is accepted. *Academic units required:* 4 English, 3 mathematics. *Academic units recommended:* 4 mathematics, 4 science (2 science labs), 2 foreign language, 2 social studies, 2 history.

Financial Aid

Students should submit: FAFSA. The Princeton Review suggests that all financial aid forms be submitted as soon as possible after January 1. *Need-based scholarships/grants offered:* Federal Pell, SEOG, state scholarships/grants, private scholarships, school scholarship or grant aid from institutional funds. *Loan aid offered:* Direct Subsidized Stafford, Direct Unsubsidized Stafford, Direct PLUS, Federal Perkins, state loans, university loans from institutional funds. Applicants will be notified of awards on a rolling basis beginning February 20. Federal Work-Study Program available. Off-campus job opportunities are good.

The Inside Word

To prepare for college, Rider University suggests that high school students follow a rigorous curriculum of college prep courses, including AP and honors classes. Students need at least four years of high school English and three years of math to be considered for admission to Rider. The most recent incoming class had an average high school GPA of 3.35 and a SAT score of 1610. Although most students major in the liberal arts and sciences, more than a quarter of undergraduates are enrolled in the business school.

THE SCHOOL SAYS "..."

From the Admissions Office

"Rider students are driven by their dreams of a fulfilling career and a desire to have an impact on the world around them. Rider is a place to apply your imagination, talents and aspirations in ways that will make a difference. A Rider education will prepare you as a leader and as a member of a team. When you graduate from Rider, you'll be a different person, confidently ready for your life's challenges and opportunities.

"We invite you to visit and experience Rider firsthand. Open houses are offered in the fall and late spring, tours are available daily and Information Sessions are offered most weekends.

"Freshmen applicants are required to submit the results of either the SAT or ACT exam. The highest scores from either test will be considered for admission."

SELECTIVITY
Admissions Rating	79
# of applicants	8,200
% of applicants accepted	71
% of acceptees attending	17

FRESHMAN PROFILE
Range SAT Critical Reading	470–570
Range SAT Math	480–590
Range SAT Writing	470–570
Range ACT Composite	20–25
Minimum paper TOEFL	550
Minimum computer TOEFL	213
Minimum web-based TOEFL	80
Average HS GPA	3.29
% graduated top 10% of class	23
% graduated top 25% of class	55
% graduated top 50% of class	86

DEADLINES
Early action	
Deadline	11/15
Notification	12/15
Regular	
Priority	1/18
Notification	12/15
Nonfall registration?	yes

FINANCIAL FACTS
Financial Aid Rating	91
Annual tuition	$29,870
Room and board	$11,200
Required fees	$600
Books and supplies	$1,500
% frosh rec. need-based scholarship or grant aid	75
% UG rec. need-based scholarship or grant aid	70
% frosh rec. non-need-based scholarship or grant aid	13
% UG rec. non-need-based scholarship or grant aid	11
% frosh rec. need-based self-help aid	58
% UG rec. need-based self-help aid	55
% frosh rec. any financial aid	76
% UG rec. any financial aid	73
% UG borrow to pay for school	71
Average cumulative indebtedness	$35,404

RIPON COLLEGE

300 SEWARD STREET, PO BOX 248, RIPON, WI 54971 • ADMISSIONS: 920-748-8337 • FAX: 920-748-8335

CAMPUS LIFE

Quality of Life Rating	92
Fire Safety Rating	66
Green Rating	71
Type of school	private
Environment	village

STUDENTS

Total undergrad enrollment	1,043
% male/female	48/52
% from out of state	26
% from public high school	75
% live on campus	90
# of fraternities	5
# of sororities	3
% African American	2
% Asian	1
% Caucasian	88
% Hispanic	4
% Native American	1
% international	3
# of countries represented	11

SURVEY SAYS . . .

Students are friendly
Students get along with local community
Low cost of living

ACADEMICS

Academic Rating	85
% students graduating within 4 years	57
% students graduating within 6 years	71
Calendar	semester
Student/faculty ratio	15:1
Profs interesting rating	95
Profs accessible rating	92
Most common reg class size	10–19 students
Most common lab size	10–19 students

MOST POPULAR MAJORS

business/commerce, history, psychology

STUDENTS SAY "..."

Academics

Looking for a school that provides "intensive preparation for grad school" but also a "small and comfortable" and "homey and welcoming" environment? Undergrads at Ripon College think their school is just the place for you. "Everything about this community is warm and open," so even when academics get "competitive and challenging," they're still "surprisingly enjoyable." As one student explains, "What sets the administration apart is the way they treat each student as a person, rather than as a pain. It's the same with the professors. Ripon has some truly amazing teachers and professors that everybody hates, like every other school anywhere. The difference is that each of those professors, love 'em or hate 'em, is willing to sit down one-on-one and treat you like a person with a problem, rather than just a number with a grade." "And most of the professors try to make classes interesting and engaging, whether they succeed or not." Students also appreciate how "opportunities are in surprising abundance here. Faculty connections in the community provide many students with real-world applications of the academic knowledge they are gaining" through internships, community projects, and research projects. Ripon boasts "a wonderful science department" that oversees "a great biology program" and "a decent environmental studies program." Political science and education are among the other top-flight disciplines here.

Life

Ripon is located in a small town that "shuts down at night," and it's "twenty minutes from the next closest town," so students "make our own fun," which includes "a lot of sledding, movies, shopping trips, and prairie walks," as well as the requisite campus parties, of course. "Drinking and partying are very common here," students say. "It's easily the most popular pastime," and "whether partying in the frat houses or going to the bars, people are always out and about." The campus also offers "plenty of organizations and extracurriculars to participate in," and "everyone on campus is involved in at least one club or organization." Likewise, "almost the entire student body participates in intramural sports." In short, students find sufficient diversion "whether they are participating in floor activities, all-campus activities, sporting events, school plays, or even just hanging out with friends. There is never a time when you feel as though you have nothing to do." For road trips, "Oshkosh and Fond du Lac are about half an hour away, so if somebody does have a car, these are common weekend activities." Trips to Madison or Milwaukee "are rarer" and are typically reserved for big concerts or major sporting events.

Student Body

There are "a few different groups of students at Ripon College," including "a large portion of athletes who spend a lot of their time dedicated to their respective sports and are thus, for the most part, not involved on campus." There is also a "solid group of intelligent, motivated, involved, and engaged students who make up the vast majority of the clubs," and "a substantial representation of Greek that put a lot of time and effort into being involved on campus. The different Greek organizations host the majority of events around campus." Most students here "come from the areas of Wisconsin that surround Ripon" and "tend to be fairly down-to-earth and friendly. You can make some amazing friends here."

FINANCIAL AID: 920-748-8101 • E-MAIL: ADMINFO@RIPON.EDU • WEBSITE: WWW.RIPON.EDU

THE PRINCETON REVIEW SAYS

Admissions

Very important factors considered include: Rigor of secondary school record, interview. *Important factors considered include:* Academic GPA, class rank, recommendation(s), standardized test scores, character/personal qualities, extracurricular activities. *Other factors considered include:* Application essay, talent/ability, volunteer work. SAT or ACT required; ACT with or without writing component accepted. TOEFL required of all international applicants. High school diploma is required, and GED is accepted. *Academic units required:* 4 English, 2 mathematics, 2 science, 2 social studies. *Academic units recommended:* 4 mathematics, 4 science, 2 foreign language, 4 social studies.

Financial Aid

Students should submit: FAFSA. Priority filing deadline is March 1. The Princeton Review suggests that all financial aid forms be submitted as soon as possible after January 1. *Need-based scholarships/grants offered:* Federal Pell, SEOG, state scholarships/grants, private scholarships, school scholarship or grant aid from institutional funds. *Loan aid offered:* Federal Perkins, Federal Stafford. Applicants will be notified of awards on a rolling basis beginning March 1. Federal Work-Study Program available. Off-campus job opportunities are good.

The Inside Word

Ripon seeks accomplished high school students who have challenged themselves in and out of the classroom. Solid performers—those earning a B-plus average in a college-prep curriculum and exceeding 1100 SAT/22 ACT—should find a clear path awaiting them, although the school does also consider such peripherals as potential contribution to extracurricular life and the likelihood a candidate will flourish in a small-school environment.

THE SCHOOL SAYS "..."

From the Admissions Office

"Since its founding in 1851, Ripon College has adhered to the philosophy that the liberal arts offer the richest foundation for intellectual, cultural, social, and spiritual growth. Academic strength is a 150-year tradition at Ripon. We attract excellent professors who are dedicated to their disciplines; they in turn attract bright, committed students. Together with the other members of our tightly knit learning community, students at Ripon learn more deeply, live more fully, and achieve more success. Students are surprised to discover that here there are more opportunities—to be involved, to lead, to speak out, to make a difference, to explore new interests—than at a college ten times our size. Through collaborative learning, group living, teamwork, and networking, students tap into the power of a community where we all work together to ensure success—at Ripon and beyond.

"All of the best residential liberal arts colleges strive to be true learning communities like Ripon. We succeed better than most because our enrollment of about 1,000 students is perfect for fostering connections inside and outside the classroom. Our students flourish in this environment of mutual respect, where shared values are elevated and diverse ideas are valued. If you are seeking academic challenge and want to benefit from an environment of personal attention and support—then you should take a closer look at Ripon.

"Applicants to Ripon College must submit scores from either the ACT (writing section not required) or the SAT."

SELECTIVITY
Admissions Rating	86
# of applicants	1,160
% of applicants accepted	78
% of acceptees attending	32

FRESHMAN PROFILE
Range SAT Critical Reading	430–550
Range SAT Math	460–610
Range ACT Composite	21–27
Minimum paper TOEFL	550
Minimum computer TOEFL	213
Minimum web-based TOEFL	79
Average HS GPA	3.38
% graduated top 10% of class	30
% graduated top 25% of class	61
% graduated top 50% of class	84

DEADLINES
Regular	
Priority	3/15
Notification	9/15
Nonfall registration?	yes

APPLICANTS ALSO LOOK AT
AND OFTEN PREFER
Carroll College (WI), St. Norbert College, University of Wisconsin—Stevens Point

AND SOMETIMES PREFER
University of Wisconsin—Eau Claire, University of Wisconsin—Madison, University of Wisconsin—Whitewater

AND RARELY PREFER
Beloit College, Lawrence University, University of Wisconsin—Oshkosh

FINANCIAL FACTS
Financial Aid Rating	85
Annual tuition	$26,806
Room and board	$7,770
Required fees	$275
Books and supplies	$1,000
% frosh rec. need-based scholarship or grant aid	87
% UG rec. need-based scholarship or grant aid	83
% frosh rec. non-need-based scholarship or grant aid	11
% UG rec. non-need-based scholarship or grant aid	9
% frosh rec. need-based self-help aid	74
% UG rec. need-based self-help aid	73
% frosh rec. any financial aid	87
% UG rec. any financial aid	89
% UG borrow to pay for school	84
Average cumulative indebtedness	$30,694

ROANOKE COLLEGE

221 COLLEGE LANE, SALEM, VA 24153-3794 • ADMISSIONS: 540-375-2270 • FAX: 540-375-2267

CAMPUS LIFE

Quality of Life Rating	83
Fire Safety Rating	81
Green Rating	78
Type of school	private
Affiliation	Lutheran
Environment	city

STUDENTS

Total undergrad enrollment	2,039
% male/female	44/56
% from out of state	45
% from public high school	76
% live on campus	66
# of fraternities	4
# of sororities	5
% African American	4
% Asian	1
% Caucasian	86
% Hispanic	3
% international	1
# of countries represented	22

SURVEY SAYS . . .
Students are happy
Great library
Career services are great
Students are friendly
Great off-campus food
Campus feels safe
Lots of beer drinking

ACADEMICS

Academic Rating	83
% students graduating within 4 years	65
% students graduating within 6 years	71
Calendar	semester
Student/faculty ratio	12:1
Profs interesting rating	86
Profs accessible rating	87
Most common reg class size	10–19 students
Most common lab size	10–19 students

MOST POPULAR MAJORS
business/commerce, English language
and literature, psychology

STUDENTS SAY ". . ."

Academics

Lutheran-affiliated Roanoke College "is a small school [that] allows you to stand out." With an emphasis on contemporary applications of a classic education, and a campus of green quads, red bricks, and white columns, Roanoke gives students a liberal arts curriculum in a palatial setting in the shadow of the Blue Ridge Mountains. As one student puts it, "Roanoke College is an amazing school that has given me the opportunity to challenge myself and to experience things in school and in the community that I would not have gotten anywhere else." It "provides students with an education that is challenging but at the same time rewarding for the effort you put in." As at many schools that emphasize the liberal arts and feature a low student/teacher ratio, the professors really make this place. "They are all eager to help students as much as possible, and they treat students like individuals." "They encourage students to come ask questions outside of class or just stop by for a chat." "The professors are very lively and passionate about the subjects they teach. They frequently choose interesting reading material." "They push our thinking to a new level." The English and economics departments receive high praise, as do the sciences: "I was able to do graduate level research synthesizing carbon nanotubes the very first week of school," brags one health sciences major.

Life

Life at Roanoke is, to put it simply, pretty sweet. "Because of the location in southwestern Virginia, there are many hiking and other outdoor activities available. Downtown Roanoke is only a short drive away, where there is plenty of shopping, movies, etc. Additionally, Blacksburg/Virginia Tech, James Madison University, and Natural Bridge are all close enough for a day or weekend trip." "Students go outside, hike in the mountains that surround the campus, there are water sports, [and] skiing in the winter." "There are always Outdoor Adventures activities that go on during the weekends." On campus, Roanoke features a healthy Greek scene and "a great Campus Activities Board" that "has special events every weekend that are free to students, which provides a safe and fun environment." "RC After Dark [events] are always fun, like bingo and karaoke." Concerts and theater performances are regularly held in Olin Hall, and current students note, "We just held the Virginia Gubernatorial debates and also had Sandra Day O'Connor visit our campus."

Student Body

The typical Roanoke student comes from either New England or the mid-Atlantic, and "comes from an upper-middle-class upbringing, and it shows." "They look like they can fit in at the country club." But "Roanoke has a lot more variety to it than just WASPs. There is a niche for just about everyone," and "The stereotypes of 'preppy plaid' Roanoke still lurk in Greek houses, but the majority seem to be pink- and green-free." Greek life is pervasive here, which is something to keep in mind if you don't plan on pledging, but most "students are generally happy, outgoing, fun, and well-dressed." "Students tend to find their own niche and fit into it, whether it be a club or a Greek organization." "There is not a whole lot of diversity, but the typical student is very nice and welcoming" and "very dedicated to getting the most out of their education as well as have a fun and enjoyable time at college." Athletes take note: "The school lacks a football team, making lacrosse the marquee sport here."

FINANCIAL AID: 540-375-2235 • E-MAIL: ADMISSIONS@ROANOKE.EDU • WEBSITE: WWW.ROANOKE.EDU

THE PRINCETON REVIEW SAYS

Admissions

Very important factors considered include: Academic GPA, rigor of secondary school record, standardized test scores, character/personal qualities. *Important factors considered include:* Class rank, recommendation(s), extracurricular activities, interview. *Other factors considered include:* Application essay, alumni/ae relation, level of applicant's interest, racial/ethnic status, talent/ability, volunteer work, work experience. SAT or ACT required; ACT with or without writing component accepted. TOEFL required of all international applicants. High school diploma is required, and GED is accepted. *Academic units required:* 4 English, 3 mathematics, 2 science (2 science labs), 2 social studies, 5 academic elective. *Academic units recommended:* 4 foreign language.

Financial Aid

Students should submit: FAFSA. Regular filing deadline is March 1. The Princeton Review suggests that all financial aid forms be submitted as soon as possible after January 1. *Need-based scholarships/grants offered:* Federal Pell, SEOG, state scholarships/grants, private scholarships, school scholarship or grant aid from institutional funds. *Loan aid offered:* Direct Subsidized Stafford, Direct Unsubsidized Stafford, Direct PLUS, Federal Perkins, college loans from institutional funds. Applicants will be notified of merit awards on a rolling basis beginning October 15. Federal Work-Study Program available. Off-campus job opportunities are good.

The Inside Word

Roanoke takes a holistic approach to the admissions process, so the story your whole application tells is important. While the average grades and test scores of accepted students are high, there are no formulas here, and applicants should show they're well-rounded, emphasizing their passions and extracurriculars. The optional personal statement is highly recommended; use it as an opportunity to both show off your achievements and speak to the specific reasons Roanoke appeals to you.

THE SCHOOL SAYS ". . ."

From the Admissions Office

"Roanoke College prepares students for their futures by providing a classic undergraduate liberal arts experience that is applied to modern issues. Roanoke is one of only ten percent of colleges in the U.S. that qualify academically to house a chapter of the prestigious Phi Beta Kappa honor society. Over ninety-five percent of Roanoke seniors receive job offers or continue on to graduate school within six months of graduation, and approximately forty-nine percent of Roanoke graduates attend or complete graduate school within six years.

"Roanoke is nationally recognized for its core curriculum. Unlike most colleges that require a series of introductory courses in various disciplines, all of Roanoke's core courses are topic based, and students see firsthand how fundamental concepts are applied to important issues. For example, instead of taking a generic Introduction to Chemistry course, students might choose Chemistry and Crime, where they use forensic chemistry to solve crimes. Or, instead of Statistics 101, students might choose Statistics and the Weather and discover how statistical analysis is used in weather forecasting.

"Experiential learning is a cornerstone of academics at Roanoke. While every student experiences firsthand learning, over seventy percent of Roanoke students study abroad, conduct internships, or participate in research. Ask students to describe what makes Roanoke special and they'll invariably talk about the close relationships with their professors and peers. However, there's no reason not to have fun along the way—with more than 100 clubs, it's easy for students to meet others with common interests."

SELECTIVITY

Admissions Rating	82
# of applicants	4,498
% of applicants accepted	66
% of acceptees attending	19
# accepting a place on wait list	112
% admitted from wait list	31
# of early decision applicants	62
% accepted early decision	68

FRESHMAN PROFILE

Range SAT Critical Reading	490–590
Range SAT Math	490–590
Range SAT Writing	483–570
Range ACT Composite	20–26
Minimum paper TOEFL	520
Minimum computer TOEFL	190
Minimum web-based TOEFL	68
Average HS GPA	3.39
% graduated top 10% of class	23
% graduated top 25% of class	51
% graduated top 50% of class	83

DEADLINES

Early decision	
Deadline	11/1
Notification	12/15
Early action	
Deadline	rolling
Notification	rolling
Regular	
Deadline	rolling
Notification	10/1
Nonfall registration?	yes

FINANCIAL FACTS

Financial Aid Rating	84
Annual tuition	$31,950
Room and board	$10,772
Required fees	$1,075
Books and supplies	$1,000
% frosh rec. need-based scholarship or grant aid	75
% UG rec. need-based scholarship or grant aid	70
% frosh rec. non-need-based scholarship or grant aid	72
% UG rec. non-need-based scholarship or grant aid	69
% frosh rec. need-based self-help aid	61
% UG rec. need-based self-help aid	56
% frosh rec. any financial aid	94
% UG rec. any financial aid	95
% UG borrow to pay for school	67
Average cumulative indebtedness	$27,984

ROCHESTER INSTITUTE OF TECHNOLOGY

60 LOMB MEMORIAL DRIVE, ROCHESTER, NY 14623-5604 • ADMISSIONS: 585-475-6631 • FAX: 585-475-7424

CAMPUS LIFE

Quality of Life Rating	76
Fire Safety Rating	84
Green Rating	96
Type of school	private
Environment	city

STUDENTS

Total undergrad enrollment	13,511
% male/female	67/33
% from out of state	50
% from public high school	85
% live on campus	60
# of fraternities	19
# of sororities	10
% African American	5
% Asian	5
% Caucasian	63
% Hispanic	5
% Native American	1
% international	4
# of countries represented	107

SURVEY SAYS . . .
Lab facilities are great
Great computer facilities
Great library
Athletic facilities are great
Career services are great
Diverse student types on campus

ACADEMICS

Academic Rating	76
% students graduating within 4 years	56
% students graduating within 6 years	66
Calendar	quarter
Student/faculty ratio	13:1
Profs interesting rating	74
Profs accessible rating	80
Most common reg class size	10–19 students
Most common lab size	20–29 students

MOST POPULAR MAJORS
information technology, mechanical engineering, photography

STUDENTS SAY ". . ."

Academics
Uniting creativity, innovation, and applied knowledge, Rochester Institute of Technology is the place "where the technical left and artistic right brains collide." RIT offers a range of majors in technical fields—from game design to bioinformatics—as well as programs in art, engineering, and business. Across the board, there's an "emphasis on hands-on learning," and most majors require students to complete a cooperative work experience (basically, a paid internship), designed to "give you the opportunity to make connections in [an] industry within your field." On campus, undergraduates are encouraged to pursue research. Fortunately, "Funding is everywhere if a student takes the initiative to apply." The academic calendar at RIT is built around a "rigorous and fast-paced quarter system" that allows students to take more classes annually—but also keeps them burning the midnight oil. Not everyone is up to the challenge, and "The academic rigors of the school often force people to transfer or drop out." For those willing to put in the work, RIT offers all the tools for success: "All of the teachers I have had for problem-based classes (such as calculus and computer science) set up weekly office hours," and "Free tutoring is also widely available and excellent." In the classroom, "Professors are generally good, with the occasional whack-job or stellar teacher thrown in for good measure." Thanks to the "relatively small class sizes," teachers and students often develop personal relationships, and "Even in the large lecture halls, [professors] try to get to know each student." Administrators get mixed reviews, but most students agree, "President Destler definitely shakes things up a bit (in a good way). He's all about the students and makes that very obvious."

Life
Thanks to RIT's demanding course work, "a lot of school life revolves around homework," and students are accustomed to "spending many nights in [the] lab working on an assignment." For fun, there are "huge campus events that happen once a year," and "[Division I] hockey is very popular" during the winter term. But, "For the most part, students don't really care about the clubs and organizations and simply do their own thing in their free time." In particular, students at RIT like to "play video games and drink"—though not necessarily in that order. RIT students also "go sledding in the winter, go to the movies," or make "late night diner runs." If you feel like taking a break from campus life, "There are many things to do on and off campus in the Rochester area. Museums and theaters are abundant, along with local festivals." However, not much lies within walking distance, so "a car is a necessity."

Student Body
With an unusual assortment of undergraduate majors on offer, RIT attracts a "wide variety" of people and personalities, including "art students, engineers, computer geeks, ROTC guys, deaf students, GLBTQ students, [and] foreign students." A unique addition to the student population, "There are also many deaf/hard-of-hearing students, since RIT is home to the National Technical Institute for the Deaf (NTID)." Socially, students are divided into two major categories: "Half of the students play video games all the time and the other half socialize, go to the gym, and party." No matter what camp they fall into, "There's 15,000 undergrads, so everyone has a nook somewhere" and most students "find people like them and make friends easily." Given the school's technical focus, it's no surprise that "most students are self-proclaimed computer nerds," and "even the 'cool kids' have secret passions for *Star Trek*." A fortunate perk of attending school here is that "At any time, someone within 100 feet of you can fix your computer for you." Unfortunately, to the chagrin of many students, "Women are still underrepresented on campus," ringing in at about thirty-three percent of the undergraduate population.

FINANCIAL AID: 585-475-2186 • E-MAIL: ADMISSIONS@RIT.EDU • WEBSITE: WWW.RIT.EDU

THE PRINCETON REVIEW SAYS

Admissions

Very important factors considered include: Academic GPA, rigor of secondary school record. *Important factors considered include:* Class rank, standardized test scores. *Other factors considered include:* Application essay, recommendation(s), alumni/ae relation, character/personal qualities, extracurricular activities, first generation, geographical residence, interview, level of applicant's interest, racial/ethnic status, talent/ability, volunteer work. SAT or ACT required; ACT with or without writing component accepted. TOEFL required of all international applicants. High school diploma is required, and GED is accepted. *Academic units required:* 4 English, 2 mathematics, 2 science (1 science lab), 4 social studies, 1 academic elective. *Academic units recommended:* 4 English, 3 mathematics, 3 science (2 science labs), 3 foreign language, 4 social studies, 5 academic elective.

Financial Aid

Students should submit: FAFSA, institution's own financial aid form. The Princeton Review suggests that all financial aid forms be submitted as soon as possible after January 1. *Need-based scholarships/grants offered:* Federal Pell, SEOG, state scholarships/grants, private scholarships, school scholarship or grant aid from institutional funds. *Loan aid offered:* Direct Subsidized Stafford, Direct Unsubsidized Stafford, Direct PLUS, Federal Perkins. Applicants will be notified of awards on a rolling basis beginning March 15. Federal Work-Study Program available. Off-campus job opportunities are excellent.

The Inside Word

The RIT admissions department is wired. Through their website, you can live chat with admissions or other students, follow their Twitter feed, join their Facebook community, or read blogs written by current students. When applying to RIT, prospective students must indicate their intended major (as well as a second and third choice) on their applications. Admissions requirements vary based on a student's desired field of study, though a student's academic record, test scores, personal essay, and recommendations are usually the most important factors in an admissions decision.

THE SCHOOL SAYS "..."

From the Admissions Office

"RIT is among the world's leading career-oriented, technological institutions. Ambitious, creative, diverse, and career-oriented students from every state and more than 100 foreign countries find a home in RIT's innovative, vibrant living/learning community. The university's nine colleges offer undergraduate and graduate programs areas such as engineering, computing, information technology, engineering technology, business, hospitality, science, art, design, photography, biomedical sciences, game design and development, and the liberal arts including psychology, advertising, public relations, and public policy Distinctive academic offerings include microelectronic and software engineering, imaging science, film and animation, biotechnology, physician assistant, new media, international business, telecommunications, and the programs in the School for American Crafts. In addition, students may choose from more than ninety different minors to develop personal and professional interests that complement their academic program. As home of the National Technical Institute for the Deaf (NTID), RIT is a leader in providing educational opportunities and access services for deaf and hard-of-hearing students. Experiential learning has been a hallmark of an RIT education since 1912. Every academic program at RIT offers some form of experiential education opportunity, which may include cooperative education, internships, study abroad, and undergraduate research. Students work hard, but learning is complemented with plenty of organized and spontaneous events and activities. RIT is a unique blend of rigor and fun, creativity and specialization, intellect and practice that prepares alumni for long-term career success in global society."

SELECTIVITY

Admissions Rating	81
# of applicants	14,097
% of applicants accepted	60
% of acceptees attending	31
# accepting a place on wait list	344
% admitted from wait list	22
# of early decision applicants	1,461
% accepted early decision	66

FRESHMAN PROFILE

Range SAT Critical Reading	530–640
Range SAT Math	560–670
Range SAT Writing	520–640
Range ACT Composite	25–30
Minimum paper TOEFL	550
Minimum computer TOEFL	215
Minimum web-based TOEFL	79
Average HS GPA	3.60
% graduated top 10% of class	32
% graduated top 25% of class	65
% graduated top 50% of class	93

DEADLINES

Early decision	
Deadline	12/1
Notification	1/15
Regular	
Priority	2/1
Deadline	2/1
Notification	3/15
Nonfall registration?	yes

APPLICANTS ALSO LOOK AT

AND OFTEN PREFER
Carnegie Mellon University, Cornell University

AND SOMETIMES PREFER
Rensselaer Polytechnic Institute, University of Rochester, Worcester Polytechnic Institute

AND RARELY PREFER
State University of New York—University at Buffalo

FINANCIAL FACTS

Financial Aid Rating	92
Annual tuition	$31,584
Room and board	$10,413
Required fees	$453
Books and supplies	$1,050
% frosh rec. need-based scholarship or grant aid	73
% UG rec. need-based scholarship or grant aid	66
% frosh rec. non-need-based scholarship or grant aid	21
% UG rec. non-need-based scholarship or grant aid	21
% frosh rec. need-based self-help aid	68
% UG rec. need-based self-help aid	64
% frosh rec. any financial aid	88
% UG rec. any financial aid	77
Average cumulative indebtedness	$23,800

ROLLINS COLLEGE

CAMPUS BOX 2720, WINTER PARK, FL 32789-4499 • ADMISSIONS: 407-646-2161 • FAX: 407-646-1502

CAMPUS LIFE

Quality of Life Rating	76
Fire Safety Rating	91
Green Rating	90
Type of school	private
Environment	town

STUDENTS

Total undergrad enrollment	1,730
% male/female	41/59
% from out of state	49
% from public high school	53
% live on campus	69
# of fraternities	5
# of sororities	7
% African American	4
% Asian	3
% Caucasian	75
% Hispanic	10
% international	5
# of countries represented	47

SURVEY SAYS . . .
Great computer facilities
Athletic facilities are great
Students love Winter Park, FL
Great off-campus food
*Frats and sororities dominate
social scene*
Lots of beer drinking
Hard liquor is popular

ACADEMICS

Academic Rating	88
% students graduating within 4 years	59
% students graduating within 6 years	69
Calendar	semester
Student/faculty ratio	10:1
Profs interesting rating	91
Profs accessible rating	89
Most common reg class size	10–19 students

MOST POPULAR MAJORS
economics, international business,
psychology

STUDENTS SAY ". . ."

Academics
Rollins College offers "an amazing campus with great academics surrounded by the richest students around," leading some to describe the school as "a country club for college kids." Rollins' high-end cachet means some regard it as academically low impact—even some students believe the school "is above average in regards to academics, but not top echelon since many students do not work hard"—but a strong majority here contends success here requires "a lot of work, much more than some people think. While Rollins is stereotyped for being a 'party school' we also have highly rated academic programs," and professors here "are tough. Some require a lot of reading and work, but if you have problems they are always available outside of class to help." Small classes mean students "are really forced into keeping up-to-date with the reading and with the assigned writings." Classroom work often takes the form of smaller discussion groups. One student explains, "Rollins is also a cool place to learn because many of our classes are taught around tables or in circles to stimulate discussion." The school also offers "many opportunities for studying abroad, and financial aid helps to pay for most of them." Areas of academic strength include "an impressive physics department, a great theater program with professors who are working professionals, a strong pre-law program, [and] a good education department."

Life
Rollins provides "an excellent quality of life for its students. Whether it is relaxing by our lakefront pool, jet skiing on the lake, visiting the beach, shopping, going to the theme parks, or just eating lunch on the patio, we know how to have a good time." While "life at this school can be balanced if you take full advantage of everything that is offered," many here are less interested in balance than in good times, which is why "the party scene is vibrant and dominating on many evenings." Many here concede Rollins "is a pretty big party school." Greek life "is huge," and "fraternity and sorority parties are big." Students point out that "all parties are welcoming to students" and students "may choose to attend any party regardless of their Greek affiliation." Intercollegiate athletics "are not as popular here for some reason. No one knows when games are, or who's playing." When students need to escape campus life, they find themselves fortunate enough to be "in a perfect location in Winter Park. We're close to movies, shopping, parks, museums, and nightlife in downtown Orlando. The beach is only forty-five minutes away, Disney World and Universal Studios are only twenty-five minutes away, and there are golf courses all over the place." "Close" is a relative term, of course. The campus is close to all these destinations for students who have cars, but "If you don't have a car, don't plan on going anywhere. Nothing's in walking distance except a couple of great bars that are loaded with Rollins students 24/7."

Student Body
"The typical student [at Rollins] is rich, white, and preppy," and while "there are obviously different kinds of people who attend Rollins, the above description seems to apply to the majority." As one undergrad observes, "Most students drive a BMW, Mercedes, Land Rover, etc., and only wear or carry Coach, Prada, Ralph Lauren, A&F, etc." Those outside the ranks of the economic elite "don't necessarily have trouble fitting in at school, for most everyone finds their niche." Undergrads warn, however, that while "students generally are friendly…cliques do develop," in part because "Rollins is such a small school." Through the Office of Multicultural Affairs, Rollins College has been working diligently to create and sustain a diverse community that is inclusive, welcoming, and respectful. In the past, students have noted that "there is not much diversity…particularly in social groups like sororities and fraternities. The few who do stand out find their own crowd and begin their own clubs, such as Pinehurst (for alternative lifestyles) and the Anime Club."

FINANCIAL AID: 407-646-2395 • E-MAIL: ADMISSION@ROLLINS.EDU • WEBSITE: WWW.ROLLINS.EDU

THE PRINCETON REVIEW SAYS

Admissions

Very important factors considered include: Academic GPA, rigor of secondary school record. *Important factors considered include:* Application essay, recommendation(s), standardized test scores, extracurricular activities, talent/ability. *Other factors considered include:* Class rank, alumni/ae relation, character/personal qualities, first generation, interview, level of applicant's interest, volunteer work, work experience. ACT with writing component recommended. TOEFL required of all international applicants. High school diploma is required, and GED is accepted. *Academic units required:* 4 English, 3 mathematics, 2 science, 2 foreign language, 2 social studies, 2 history, 2 academic elective. *Academic units recommended:* 4 English, 4 mathematics, 4 science, 3 foreign language, 3 social studies, 3 history, 3 academic elective.

Financial Aid

Students should submit: FAFSA, institution's own financial aid form. The Princeton Review suggests that all financial aid forms be submitted as soon as possible after January 1. *Need-based scholarships/grants offered:* Federal Pell, SEOG, state scholarships/grants, private scholarships, school scholarship or grant aid from institutional funds. *Loan aid offered:* Direct Subsidized Stafford, Direct Unsubsidized Stafford, Direct PLUS, Federal Perkins, university loans from institutional funds. Applicants will be notified of awards on a rolling basis beginning March 1. Federal Work-Study Program available. Off-campus job opportunities are good.

The Inside Word

Applicants to Rollins who don't seek academic merit scholarships have the option of including a graded paper in lieu of standardized test scores. It's the school's way of creating another opportunity for students who test poorly but otherwise excel in academics, and it's characteristic of the individualized approach taken here. Each applicant is assigned an admissions officer who acts as his or her liaison, ensuring a personalized admissions experience. Early decision applicants are given priority in admissions as well as in considerations for merit-based scholarships and need-based financial aid.

THE SCHOOL SAYS "..."

From the Admissions Office

"As you begin the college selection process, remember that you are in control of your destiny. Your academic record—course load, grades earned, test scores—are the most important part of your application credentials. But Rollins also pays close attention to your personal dimension—interests, strengths, values, and potential to contribute to college life. Don't sell yourself short in the application process. Be proud of what you've accomplished and who you are, and be honest when you describe yourself. Finally, the admission committee always likes to see candidates who express interest in the college. If we're your first choice, apply early decision. Each year we admit approximately one-third of the entering class through the early decision process. Are you unsure about your choice? If you can, schedule some visits, meet with an admission counselor, tour campus, and spend time in a class so you can see for yourself what Rollins and other colleges are all about. Take control of your destiny, and enjoy the process along the way.

"First-year applicants may submit either SAT or ACT scores for admission consideration. Candidates are strongly encouraged to complete the writing components, but results without Writing will be considered. Each candidate's best score combination will be used in the selection process; we strongly recommend that candidates consider taking both the SAT and the ACT."

SELECTIVITY

Admissions Rating	89
# of applicants	3,771
% of applicants accepted	56
% of acceptees attending	22
# accepting a place on wait list	160
% admitted from wait list	38
# of early decision applicants	219
% accepted early decision	75

FRESHMAN PROFILE

Range SAT Critical Reading	560–650
Range SAT Math	560–650
Range SAT Writing	550–650
Range ACT Composite	24–29
Minimum paper TOEFL	550
Minimum computer TOEFL	213
Minimum web-based TOEFL	80
Average HS GPA	3.60
% graduated top 10% of class	38
% graduated top 25% of class	67
% graduated top 50% of class	89

DEADLINES

Early decision	
Deadline	11/15
Notification	12/15
Regular	
Deadline	2/15
Nonfall registration?	yes

APPLICANTS ALSO LOOK AT
AND OFTEN PREFER
Emory University, University of Florida

AND SOMETIMES PREFER
College of Charleston, Florida State University, Furman University, Tulane University

AND RARELY PREFER
Eckerd College, Stetson University, University of Central Florida, University of South Florida

FINANCIAL FACTS

Financial Aid Rating	88
Annual tuition	$37,640
Room and board	$11,760
Books and supplies	$770
% frosh rec. need-based scholarship or grant aid	52
% UG rec. need-based scholarship or grant aid	48
% frosh rec. non-need-based scholarship or grant aid	3
% UG rec. non-need-based scholarship or grant aid	3
% frosh rec. need-based self-help aid	44
% UG rec. need-based self-help aid	40
% frosh rec. any financial aid	80
% UG rec. any financial aid	78
% UG borrow to pay for school	46
Average cumulative indebtedness	$25,294

ROSE-HULMAN INSTITUTE OF TECHNOLOGY

5500 WABASH AVENUE-CM 1, TERRE HAUTE, IN 47803-3999 • ADMISSIONS: 812-877-8213 • FAX: 812-877-8941

STUDENTS SAY " . . ."

Academics

Rose-Hulman earns its "reputation as an excellent undergraduate engineering school" with a combination of strong academics and "personal attention, small class sizes, and a family atmosphere" a rarity among tech schools. Sure, "The workload is fairly heavy, especially sophomore year with the engineering curriculum." Sometimes students feel "Rose is about beating you up and putting you through hell so when you graduate you'll be the only engineer who knows what it's like to be on a project that completely sucks, but you've been taught that all projects are like that so you're the only engineer who will see it all the way through." However, students enjoy an unusually strong support system, and that mitigates the strain. "The transition is made as smooth as possible from high school to college for freshmen" with "on-campus tutoring in the learning center (an excellent resource for students to get homework help)" and "professors who are always available outside of class." One student elaborates, "Our professors are personal and focus on undergraduate education. They will know your name, ask if you are okay if you miss a class or two, and even pull up a chair next to your table at the bar." Those who make it through four years here enjoy the added benefit of "a great alumni base. With almost ninety-nine percent job placement, if you get a decent GPA you're almost guaranteed a job in the field of your choice."

Life

"Life at Rose is academically demanding," but "the community here is so supportive and safe that you get through it," and while "students do a lot of homework and study a lot," they do occasionally find time to close the books and relax. "It's all work and little play Sunday through Thursday," but come Friday "we play hard.'" Students inform us "there's always something to do on campus, whether it's going to a fraternity party or attending a concert or going to a dance or just watching a movie with friends." Greek life is big, "but it's not your typical *Animal House*," and both intramural and Division III intercollegiate athletics have their supporters. There are also "tons of different groups to get involved in" on campus. Hometown Terre Haute, on the other hand, isn't so lively. "There isn't much to do" in town other than "go to the shadiest bars and check out the locals." As one student points out, "We are located in the middle of nowhere…not much they can do about it, but it is not so great."

Student Body

"The kids who attend Rose-Hulman are smart, dedicated, and consequently, nerds," but "this is not a negative thing. Within the students here, there are no outcasts, and even our athletes are most likely also math-letes." "Everyone definitely marches to the beat of his own drum," students assure us. Personality types run the gamut from "geniuses, average students, student-athletes, outspoken, quiet, etc." Demographically, undergrads are "mostly white male engineers from the Midwest" (partly a function of Rose-Hulman's location), but "we are slowly expanding the Rose-Hulman name and getting people from all over the U.S. and globe." The population "is mostly boys, although the females are catching up," albeit slowly. About half of the incoming freshman class played varsity sports in high school, which is about as many had been involved in the performing arts.

ROSE-HULMAN INSTITUTE OF TECHNOLOGY

FINANCIAL AID: 812-877-8259 • E-MAIL: ADMIS.OFC@ROSE-HULMAN.EDU • WEBSITE: WWW.ROSE-HULMAN.EDU

THE PRINCETON REVIEW SAYS

Admissions

Very important factors considered include: Class rank, rigor of secondary school record. *Important factors considered include:* Academic GPA, recommendation(s), standardized test scores, character/personal qualities. *Other factors considered include:* Application essay, alumni/ae relation, extracurricular activities, interview, talent/ability, volunteer work, work experience. SAT or ACT required; ACT with or without writing component accepted. TOEFL required of all international applicants. *Academic units required:* 4 English, 4 mathematics, 2 science (2 science labs), 2 social studies, 4 academic elective. *Academic units recommended:* 5 mathematics, 3 science.

Financial Aid

Students should submit: FAFSA. The Princeton Review suggests that all financial aid forms be submitted as soon as possible after January 1. *Need-based scholarships/grants offered:* Federal Pell, SEOG, state scholarships/grants, school scholarship or grant aid from institutional funds. *Loan aid offered:* Direct Subsidized Stafford, Direct Unsubsidized Stafford, Direct PLUS. Federal Work-Study Program available.

The Inside Word

Rose-Hulman attracts an accomplished applicant pool and counselors believe only its less-than-optimally-desirable location prevents it from attracting an even more competitive group. Grades and test scores are paramount in the review process, but the school invites applicants to submit any supporting materials they think will help their case; such as an essay explaining why you want to be an engineer. Qualified women applicants should receive an especially favorable review, as Rose-Hulman—like most engineering schools—would love to reduce its gender imbalance.

THE SCHOOL SAYS "..."

From the Admissions Office

"Rose-Hulman Institute of Technology is nationally recognized as the premier undergraduate college of engineering, science and mathematics in the country. Our emphasis on teaching is the core element to our success. At Rose-Hulman, we educate the next generation of technological leaders. The rich extracurricular life gives students the opportunity to hone their leadership and teaming skills while also making college more fun. With ninety clubs and student organizations, every student has the chance to grow as a human being as well as grow in their profession. World-class undergraduate laboratories complement the instruction."

SELECTIVITY

Admissions Rating	93
# of applicants	4,274
% of applicants accepted	61
% of acceptees attending	43

FRESHMAN PROFILE

Range SAT Critical Reading	570–670
Range SAT Math	630–740
Range SAT Writing	550–650
Range ACT Composite	27–32
Minimum paper TOEFL	550
Minimum computer TOEFL	215
Minimum web-based TOEFL	80
Average HS GPA	3.92
% graduated top 10% of class	63
% graduated top 25% of class	91
% graduated top 50% of class	100

DEADLINES

Regular	
Priority	12/1
Deadline	3/1
Notification	10/1
Nonfall registration?	no

FINANCIAL FACTS

Financial Aid Rating	76
Annual tuition	$37,297
Room and board	$10,455
Required fees	$675
Books and supplies	$1,500
% frosh rec. need-based scholarship or grant aid	74
% UG rec. need-based scholarship or grant aid	72
% frosh rec. non-need-based scholarship or grant aid	18
% UG rec. non-need-based scholarship or grant aid	6
% frosh rec. need-based self-help aid	68
% UG rec. need-based self-help aid	68
% frosh rec. any financial aid	99
% UG rec. any financial aid	98
% UG borrow to pay for school	74
Average cumulative indebtedness	$40,619

RUTGERS, THE STATE UNIVERSITY OF NEW JERSEY—NEW BRUNSWICK

65 DAVIDSON ROAD, PISCATAWAY, NJ 08854-8097 • ADMISSIONS: 732-932-4636 • FAX: 732-445-0237

CAMPUS LIFE

Quality of Life Rating	63
Fire Safety Rating	77
Green Rating	60*
Type of school	public
Environment	town

STUDENTS

Total undergrad enrollment	30,038
% male/female	52/48
% from out of state	7
# of fraternities	29
# of sororities	15
% African American	8
% Asian	24
% Caucasian	50
% Hispanic	11
% international	2
# of countries represented	117

SURVEY SAYS . . .

Class discussions are rare
Great computer facilities
Athletic facilities are great
Diverse student types on campus
Everyone loves the Scarlet Knights
Student publications are popular
Lots of beer drinking
Hard liquor is popular

ACADEMICS

Academic Rating	61
Calendar	semester
Student/faculty ratio	15:1
Profs interesting rating	61
Profs accessible rating	61
Most common	
reg class size	10–19 students
Most common	
lab size	20–29 students

MOST POPULAR MAJORS
biology, engineering

STUDENTS SAY ". . ."

Academics

Rutgers, The State University of New Jersey—New Brunswick, "is the kind of university [at which], if you make the effort to create your niche and find opportunities to succeed, you will have one of the best experiences of your life." With "a great study abroad program, solid academic departments and professors, the vast resources of a large research [school] and lots of scholarship money for honors students," Rutgers "offers boundless opportunity, both educational and professional, but you have to be willing to go out and seek it." Rutgers' immenseness is made more manageable by its subdivision into thirteen colleges, "each with its own unique community and environment, all unified under one entity that can afford all the opportunities of a large university." Even so, the university's bureaucracy is legendary. One student writes, "The school seems to take pride in its web of red tape. The famous 'RU Screw' has become so notorious that the university president had to publicly denounce it." It's a good sign that Rutgers "is progressively changing its administrative policies under the administration of its relatively new president. There is a renewed focus on student service, and the changes are evident." As at many state schools, "Good things will not happen at Rutgers by sitting in the corner and waiting for opportunity to knock. It is a big school, so the more you put yourself out and make yourself known, the more likely you'll be able to find help in academics and administration." For self-starters, the rewards can be great. One writes, "I've had the opportunity to [conduct] my own research in the Rutgers facilities." Indeed, "there is a lot of research going on at Rutgers. The topics are numerous, and there are plenty of spots to fill if you look around well enough."

Life

"Weekdays are busy, and you can find places crowded at any time of the day" on the Rutgers campus. "There's always something going on: concerts, free movies, talks. It's all about diversity and going out to find what you want to do." Student government "is huge." Students say there are "always voter registration drives, and we even have Tent State University in the spring, during which a bunch of political student groups set up tents on the main courtyard and camp out for a week handing out literature, having fun stuff (concerts, etc.), and talking to people about what they do and how they can get involved." For some, "drinking is a big thing." One student writes, "If there was no such thing as getting inebriated, there would be nothing to do here." Many refute that position, noting "there are other things you can do as well. There are lots of places to eat and drink coffee…or going to a small discussion group with Jhumpa Lahiri, the Pulitzer Prize winning writer," to name a few. While weekdays are lively, weekends are another story. One student comments, "Life at Rutgers would feel more college-y if people didn't leave on weekends and it [didn't feel] so deserted."

Student Body

Rutgers "is huge, so there is just about every type of person you could think of here." One undergrad observes, "With so many students, it's hard not to find others with whom you fit in. But the drawback to such a large student body is that you need to go out and make friends; you can't expect them to come to you." Another student adds, "To be fair, sometimes it feels a bit like high school (there are 'skaters' and 'preps' and 'thugs' and all that), but once you're an upperclassmen you kind of learn to ignore it."

FINANCIAL AID: 732-932-7057 • WEBSITE: WWW.RUTGERS.EDU

THE PRINCETON REVIEW SAYS

Admissions

Very important factors considered include: Academic GPA, class rank, rigor of secondary school record, standardized test scores. *Other factors considered include:* Application essay, recommendation(s), extracurricular activities, first generation, geographical residence, interview, racial/ethnic status, state residency, talent/ability, volunteer work, work experience. SAT or ACT required. TOEFL required of all international applicants. High school diploma is required, and GED is accepted. *Academic units required:* 4 English, 3 mathematics, 2 science, 2 foreign language, 5 academic elective. *Academic units recommended:* 4 mathematics, 2 foreign language.

Financial Aid

Students should submit: FAFSA. The Princeton Review suggests that all financial aid forms be submitted as soon as possible after January 1. *Need-based scholarships/grants offered:* Federal Pell, SEOG, state scholarships/grants, private scholarships, school scholarship or grant aid from institutional funds. *Loan aid offered:* Direct Subsidized Stafford, Direct Unsubsidized Stafford, Direct PLUS, Federal Perkins, state loans, university loans from institutional funds. Applicants will be notified of awards on a rolling basis beginning February 1.

The Inside Word

With a literal mountain of applications to process each admissions season, Rutgers doesn't have the luxury of time. The school looks at your grades, the quality of your high school curriculum, your standardized test scores, and your essay to decide whether you can make the grade at Rutgers. Although the school grows more competitive each year, solid students should still find little difficulty getting in.

THE SCHOOL SAYS " . . ."

From the Admissions Office

"Rutgers, The State University of New Jersey, one of only sixty-two members of the Association of American Universities, is a research university that attracts students from across the nation and around the world. What does it take to be accepted for admission to Rutgers University? Our primary emphasis is on your past academic performance as indicated by your high school grades (particularly in required academic subjects), your class rank or cumulative average, the strength of your academic program, your standardized test scores on the SAT or ACT, any special talents you may have, and your participation in school and community activities. We seek students with a broad diversity of talents, interests, and backgrounds. Above all else, we're looking for students who will get the most out of a Rutgers education—students with the intellect, initiative, and motivation to make full use of the opportunities we have to offer.

"First-year applicants should take the SAT or the ACT (with writing component). Test scores are not required for students who graduated high school more than two years ago or have completed more than twelve college credits since graduating."

SELECTIVITY

Admissions Rating	77
# of applicants	29,532
% of applicants accepted	59
% of acceptees attending	35
# accepting a place on wait list	0

FRESHMAN PROFILE

Range SAT Critical Reading	530–630
Range SAT Math	560–680
Range SAT Writing	540–640
Minimum paper TOEFL	550
Minimum computer TOEFL	213
% graduated top 10% of class	42
% graduated top 25% of class	38
% graduated top 50% of class	18

DEADLINES

Regular	
Priority	12/1
Nonfall registration?	yes

FINANCIAL FACTS

Financial Aid Rating	73
Annual in-state tuition	$9,926
Annual out-of-state tuition	$21,682
Room and board	$10,906
Books and supplies	$1,474
% frosh rec. need-based scholarship or grant aid	33
% UG rec. need-based scholarship or grant aid	34
% frosh rec. non-need-based scholarship or grant aid	31
% UG rec. non-need-based scholarship or grant aid	24
% frosh rec. need-based self-help aid	46
% UG rec. need-based self-help aid	43
% frosh rec. any financial aid	67
% UG rec. any financial aid	69
% UG borrow to pay for school	52
Average cumulative indebtedness	$19,760

SACRED HEART UNIVERSITY

5151 PARK AVENUE, FAIRFIELD, CT 06825 • ADMISSIONS: 203-371-7880 • FAX: 203-365-7607

STUDENTS SAY ". . ."

Academics

Business is big business at Sacred Heart University, where one-third of a recent class graduated with an undergraduate business degree. The "up-and-coming" Welch College of Business (named for former General Electric CEO Jack Welch) uses the school's proximity to New York City to "enable students majoring in business, finance, media studies, etc., with tremendous opportunities" for internships. Nursing, physical therapy, and athletic training are among the school's other strong programs. "The surrounding towns provide amazing sites for...clinical experiences," so many members of SHU's career-minded student body leave here with solid experience under their belts to go along with course knowledge. However, pre-professional preparation is only part of the picture at this "small, Catholic university that prides itself [on] religion and faith." To ensure that students gain general knowledge along with expertise in their specialization (and to reinforce the school's commitment to the liberal arts–driven Catholic Intellectual Tradition), SHU recently introduced a Common Core Curriculum focusing on such lofty topics as justice and humanity's place in the cosmos. A number of students complain about the added requirements and deem the program "a waste of time," but most prefer to focus on the positives, telling us that SHU is "full of spirit along with great academics in a well-balanced manner that allows for the best and fullest college experience one could ask for."

Life

"People are heavily involved in community service, [with] Habitat for Humanity being the largest [service organization] on campus." "If you're into community service and volunteering"—and most students here are—"you'll be in your glory with the opportunities that are available for students." SHU undergrads take the school's mission of service seriously, although that doesn't mean they don't also know how to have a good time. "During the week the school is pretty laid-back," but on weekends, "A good portion of the student population goes out to clubs to drink." One student explains, "Sacred Heart isn't a party school so much as a bar school." Weekends are spent "frivolously" by many, although those who shun the alcohol scene say, "The school does supply fun activities on campus" for them, including movie nights and concerts. Intercollegiate football, basketball, and hockey are all popular as well. Hometown Fairfield "offers shopping, good food, and the beach during warmer months" in addition to the clubs, and "The train is very close [to campus] so you can ride to New Haven or New York City for the day."

Student Body

The typical SHU undergrad "is pretty well-rounded [and is] involved in sports, community service, and clubs." She (two out of three students are female) is "preppy, friendly, and likes to have fun." The small size of the student body means that "everyone is involved in many different groups on campus" and that many "are student athletes. If they are not on one of the Division I sports teams then they are doing some type of club team." There are "a lot of people from Long Island" and an overall "strong Northeast presence (New York, New Jersey, Massachusetts in addition to Connecticut natives)." Many students (though hardly all) come from affluent families. As one student observes, "The parking lot says a lot. Lots of BMWs, Mercedes, and Audis." Other than their charitable undertakings, which are considerable, students tend not to look far beyond their daily lives and obligations. "The majority of students are not very active thinkers on world and political issues outside of their own lives," one student observes.

E-MAIL: ENROLL@SACREDHEART.EDU • WEBSITE: WWW.SACREDHEART.EDU

THE PRINCETON REVIEW SAYS

Admissions

Very important factors considered include: Academic GPA, rigor of secondary school record, interview. *Important factors considered include:* Class rank, recommendation(s), character/personal qualities, extracurricular activities, level of applicant's interest, talent/ability, volunteer work, work experience. *Other factors considered include:* Application essay, standardized test scores, alumni/ae relation, first generation, geographical residence, racial/ethnic status, religious affiliation/commitment, state residency. ACT with or without writing component accepted. TOEFL required of all international applicants. High school diploma is required, and GED is accepted. *Academic units required:* 4 English, 3 mathematics, 3 science (1 science lab), 2 foreign language, 3 social studies, 3 history, 3 academic elective. *Academic units recommended:* 4 English, 4 mathematics, 4 science (2 science labs), 4 foreign language, 4 social studies, 4 history, 4 academic elective.

Financial Aid

Students should submit: FAFSA, CSS/Financial Aid PROFILE. The Princeton Review suggests that all financial aid forms be submitted as soon as possible after January 1. *Need-based scholarships/grants offered:* Federal Pell, SEOG, state scholarships/grants, private scholarships, school scholarship or grant aid from institutional funds. *Loan aid offered:* Direct Subsidized Stafford, Direct Unsubsidized Stafford, Direct PLUS, Federal Perkins, state loans. Applicants will be notified of awards on a rolling basis beginning March 1. Federal Work-Study Program available. Off-campus job opportunities are excellent.

The Inside Word

Admissions officers at Sacred Heart take the time to consider each applicant on his or her own merits. There's no formula-crunching here; applicants have ample opportunity to make the case why they belong here on their applications. A campus visit is strongly recommended as a way of expressing your interest in the school and setting yourself apart from the crowd. SHU accepts the Common Application.

THE SCHOOL SAYS "..."

From the Admissions Office

"Sacred Heart University, distinguished by the personal attention it provides its students, is a thriving, dynamic university known for its commitment to academic excellence, cutting-edge technology, and community service. The second-largest Catholic university in New England, Sacred Heart continues to be innovative in its offerings to students; recently launched programs include Connecticut's first doctoral program in physical therapy, an MBA program for liberal arts undergraduates at the newly AACSB-accredited John F. Welch College of Business, and a campus in County Kerry, Ireland. The university's commitment to experiential learning incorporates concrete, real-life study for students in all majors. Drawing on the robust resources in New England and New York City, students are connected with research and internship opportunities ranging from co-ops at international advertising agencies to research with faculty on marine life in the Long Island Sound. These experiential learning opportunities are complemented by a rich student life program offering more than eighty student organizations including strong music programs, media clubs, and academic honor societies. Sacred Heart University is test-optional; SAT/ACT scores are not required but will be considered is submitted. For students taking the SAT more than once, the highest math score and the highest critical reading score will be evaluated by the admissions committee. No current policy exists for the use of the SAT writing component."

SELECTIVITY

Admissions Rating	82
# of applicants	7,569
% of applicants accepted	64
% of acceptees attending	20
# of early decision applicants	193
% accepted early decision	78

FRESHMAN PROFILE

Range SAT Critical Reading	480–560
Range SAT Math	490–580
Minimum paper TOEFL	570
Minimum web-based TOEFL	92
Average HS GPA	3.20
% graduated top 10% of class	15
% graduated top 25% of class	47
% graduated top 50% of class	84

DEADLINES

Early decision	
Deadline	12/1
Notification	12/15
Regular	
Priority	1/15
Deadline	rolling
Nonfall registration?	yes

APPLICANTS ALSO LOOK AT

AND OFTEN PREFER
University of Connecticut, Villanova University

AND SOMETIMES PREFER
Fairfield University, Fordham University, Loyola College in Maryland, Providence College

AND RARELY PREFER
Hofstra University, Iona College, St. John's University, University of Hartford

FINANCIAL FACTS

Financial Aid Rating	69
Annual tuition	$31,224
Room and board	$12,340
Required fees	$216
Books and supplies	$1,000
% frosh rec. need-based scholarship or grant aid	74
% UG rec. need-based scholarship or grant aid	71
% frosh rec. non-need-based scholarship or grant aid	23
% UG rec. non-need-based scholarship or grant aid	24
% frosh rec. need-based self-help aid	66
% UG rec. need-based self-help aid	64
% frosh rec. any financial aid	94
% UG rec. any financial aid	89
% UG borrow to pay for school	99
Average cumulative indebtedness	$43,969

SAINT ANSELM COLLEGE

100 SAINT ANSELM DRIVE, MANCHESTER, NH 03102-1310 • ADMISSIONS: 603-641-7500 • FAX: 603-641-7550

CAMPUS LIFE

Quality of Life Rating	80
Fire Safety Rating	80
Green Rating	60*
Type of school	private
Affiliation	Roman Catholic
Environment	city

STUDENTS

Total undergrad enrollment	1,889
% male/female	43/57
% from out of state	79
% from public high school	65
% live on campus	91
% African American	1
% Asian	1
% Caucasian	87
% Hispanic	2
% Native American	1
# of countries represented	20

SURVEY SAYS . . .
Students are friendly
Students get along with local community
Great food on campus
Student government is popular
Political activism is popular

ACADEMICS

Academic Rating	84
% students graduating within 4 years	71
% students graduating within 6 years	73
Calendar	semester
Student/faculty ratio	11:1
Profs interesting rating	89
Profs accessible rating	87
Most common reg class size	10–19 students
Most common lab size	10–19 students

STUDENTS SAY ". . ."

Academics

Saint Anselm College in Manchester, New Hampshire is best known for providing "a true liberal arts education." The college provides a liberal arts 'foundation' for all majors, but the biggest and best known programs are in nursing, business and criminal justice. In addition to comprehensive exams in every major, all students must complete courses in philosophy and theology, English courses, science courses, a foreign language, and four semesters of the college's well-known humanities program. "Some people enjoy the humanities program." Others say "the lectures can be absolute torture." Depending on who you talk to, the administration either "functions smoothly" or is "too Catholic" and "takes its time with everything." Students almost universally gush about their "passionate" professors. "I get tons of individual attention," brags a nursing major. "They are always willing to set a time with you outside of class for help." However, "Essays are numerous," and "classes are very difficult." "The library is always filled." There is something of a "crusade against grade inflation" on this campus as well. "Despite how hard you work, you may not see the results you want," warns an English major. Other students tell us "the work is not excruciatingly hard." "It's definitely not impossible," says a biochemistry major. "I'm no rocket scientist, and I'm taking in at least two A's this semester," agrees a classics major. "St. A's requires you to work very hard, but in a warm, friendly, and respectful atmosphere where there are plenty of opportunities to make your college years fantastic," reflects a business major.

Life

This "absolutely gorgeous" campus boasts "spectacular" food. A few students complain that Saint Anselm is "a suitcase school" but others say "you can be involved in numerous things." "It is a small, tight-knit school, where if you stick around on campus and get involved you will have the best time ever," declares a senior. "Community service is big." "I've never seen such a giving school," gloats a first-year student. There's mass every day (though student attendance is not required), and you'll always find a few Benedictine monks around campus. "The monks are awesome," says a junior. "For students who are interested, Saint Anselm is a haven for politics." The "really cool" New Hampshire Institute of Politics provides "a lot of speakers and political candidates," particularly when primary season rolls around. "It's a big deal to go to the hockey games." "Intramural sports are very popular," too. "The pub is a great place on campus for juniors and seniors who are twenty-one to grab a drink and relax." Various campus policies are "strict" though. First-year residence halls are not co-ed and visitation hours for members of the opposite sex are limited. "If you're looking for an intense party scene, Saint Anselm College isn't the place," advises a senior. Nevertheless, "the senior housing always has something going on" and "drinking is very prevalent" on the weekends, "though students must be sneaky." Nearby Boston is "a great option for the weekends" as well.

Student Body

The stereotype at Saint Anselm is definitely a "white, Catholic Red Sox fan." "Most students I've met here have Boston accents, and at least half are Irish and went to a private school," observes a freshman. "The student body is not the most diverse community but most people are very welcoming," adds a senior. "Social groups here tend to be well-defined and yet somehow still permeable, or at least, amiable to one another." There are "sheltered, ignorant snobs," but "The majority of students is middle-class and receives some sort of financial aid." Students at Saint A's describe themselves as "smart, hardworking, involved in community service," and "very preppy." "There are a select few who are rebellious, artsy, and try to stand out but they generally get along with the preppy kids." "Most kids are on an athletic team of some type." Many are serious about religion, "but many are not." Politically, opinions "are surprisingly varied for a campus that is pretty conservative."

FINANCIAL AID: 603-641-7110 • E-MAIL: ADMISSION@ANSELM.EDU • WEBSITE: WWW.ANSELM.EDU

THE PRINCETON REVIEW SAYS

Admissions

Very important factors considered include: Academic GPA, application essay, recommendation(s), rigor of secondary school record, standardized test scores. *Other factors considered include:* Class rank, alumni/ae relation, character/personal qualities, extracurricular activities, geographical residence, racial/ethnic status, state residency, talent/ability, volunteer work, work experience. SAT or ACT optional for all academic majors except nursing; ACT with or without writing component accepted. TOEFL required of all international applicants. High school diploma is required, and GED is accepted. *Academic units required:* 4 English, 3 mathematics, 3 science (2 science labs), 2 foreign language, 2 social studies. *Academic units recommended:* 4 mathematics, 4 science, 4 foreign language.

Financial Aid

Students should submit: FAFSA, CSS/Financial Aid PROFILE. Regular filing deadline is March 15. The Princeton Review suggests that all financial aid forms be submitted as soon as possible after January 1. *Need-based scholarships/ grants offered:* Federal Pell, SEOG, state scholarships/grants, private scholarships, school scholarship or grant aid from institutional funds. *Loan aid offered:* Direct Subsidized Stafford, Direct Unsubsidized Stafford, Direct PLUS, Federal Perkins. Applicants will be notified of awards on a rolling basis beginning March 1. Federal Work-Study Program available. On- and off-campus job opportunities are excellent.

The Inside Word

St. Anselm gets a predominately regional applicant pool, and Massachusetts is one of its biggest suppliers of students. An above-average academic record should be more than adequate to gain admission.

THE SCHOOL SAYS " . . ."

From the Admissions Office

"Saint Anselm is New England's only Benedictine College, a place where a 1,500 year tradition that values a love of learning and a balanced life is coupled with a very contemporary liberal arts education with strong professional preparation on a beautiful 400 acre campus. The college offers over sixty academic programs, but is particularly well-known for nursing, criminal justice, business, politics and psychology. Located in the first in the nation primary state, Saint Anselm is the home of the New Hampshire Institute of Politics which hosts national debates and provides countless opportunities for students of any major to engage with candidates, journalists, elected officials and scholars. A student who wants to meet the next President of the United States has a reasonably good chance of doing so here. Saint Anselm has been named a 'college with a conscience' by the Princeton Review, hailed by the Carnegie Foundation with Classification in both Curricular Engagement and Outreach and Partnerships, and has won federal grants to support its work in public advocacy and engagement with social problems. The college's Humanities Program, now in its third decade, has been hailed as a model of interdisciplinary study in philosophy, theology, science, and art. Faculty from many departments teach in the seminar-based program where students contemplate the fundamental question of what it means to be great. The college's Dana Center for the Arts and Humanities, used by both students and the public, hosts a broad and eclectic range of theater programming including contemporary dance and music. Saint Anselm's Chapel Arts Center provides an extraordinary array of art exhibitions from classic to contemporary with recent acquisitions focused on the human form in art. Eighty-five percent of the college's students participates in athletics, intramurals and club sports. New academic majors have been added over the past two years. Saint Anselm College offers more than eighty academic programs."

SELECTIVITY

Admissions Rating	76
# of applicants	3,664
% of applicants accepted	77
% of acceptees attending	19
# accepting a place on wait list	356
% admitted from wait list	49
# of early decision applicants	82
% accepted early decision	71

FRESHMAN PROFILE

Range SAT Critical Reading	500–590
Range SAT Math	510–580
Range SAT Writing	490–590
Range ACT Composite	20–26
Minimum paper TOEFL	550
Minimum computer TOEFL	213
Minimum web-based TOEFL	80
Average HS GPA	3.13

DEADLINES

Early action	
Deadline	11/15
Regular	
Deadline	2/15
Nursing majors	
deadline	11/15
Nonfall registration?	yes

APPLICANTS ALSO LOOK AT AND OFTEN PREFER
Boston College, College of the Holy Cross, Fairfield University, Providence College, Stonehill College

AND SOMETIMES PREFER
University of Massachusetts Amherst, University of New Hampshire

AND RARELY PREFER
Merrimack College

FINANCIAL FACTS

Financial Aid Rating	81
Annual tuition	$29,720
Room and board	$11,240
Required fees	$795
% frosh rec. need-based scholarship or grant aid	74
% UG rec. need-based scholarship or grant aid	72
% frosh rec. non-need-based scholarship or grant aid	7
% UG rec. non-need-based scholarship or grant aid	6
% frosh rec. need-based self-help aid	65
% UG rec. need-based self-help aid	65
% UG borrow to pay for school	75
Average cumulative indebtedness	$36,823

SAINT LOUIS UNIVERSITY

221 NORTH GRAND BOULEVARD, SAINT LOUIS, MO 63103 • ADMISSIONS: 314-977-2500 • FAX: 314-977-7136

STUDENTS SAY "..."

Academics

"The Jesuit tradition really resonates in everything that happens at SLU," a place where "service, social justice, and political awareness are stressed at every level of your education." This "medium-sized Jesuit school with solid academic programs and a campus that feels close-knit" is best known for its "great premedical programs," which include "a great direct-entry physical therapy program" and "a well-respected accelerated nursing program" as well as the school's premed tracks. Students also speak highly of SLU's offerings in business and pre-law, as well as its unique programs in aviation and "the one-of-a-kind nutrition program with a culinary emphasis." Students praise the way this curriculum "forces you to examine your worldview from the moment you step on campus and helps you discover what your beliefs really are." Academics, especially in the high-profile departments, can be rigorous. In this regard, SLU is "perfect for high achievers and scholars who strive for the best. The professors are nice and professional but are very stern about assignments being turned in on time." One student says, "When it comes to natural sciences, particularly chemistry, biology, etc., I think SLU can be very hard. I guess it works, though. A nursing degree or physical therapy degree from SLU is very highly respected in the health care profession."

Life

"SLU manages to provide everything your parents wish for your college experience and still everything you wouldn't want them to know about," undergrads here confide. Campus life includes "a lot of fun activities the student government puts on...such as outdoor movies, balls, and dances." "Dorm life is very strict and not much fun." The party scene "is decent," because "there are a lot of off-campus living opportunities that are close by and great places to live. The Lofts and Coronado are two great off-campus apartments that are extremely close by." College sports are in the mix. "With the new arena, basketball games are becoming the thing to do." Greek life "is great at SLU." The fraternities and sororities "provide many parties and events for the students and activities such as laser tag and barbecue" to help the students "become involved" and "get to know each other." Being in St. Louis means "great city life around, but most of it is for students that are twenty-one and above," and "off-campus eateries that are close by and range from Drunken Fish Sushi to Rally's Burgers." Students tell us "safety is a huge importance in SLU since we are so close to the city, [and fortunately] there is usually a DPS officer that is always close by to help students in need." "SLU's Jesuit influence encourages the student body to become active in the community. SLU's efforts to encourage community service give many students their first taste of the real world and better prepare them to venture out into it after graduation."

Student Body

SLU "has a pretty homogeneous student population of white, upper-middle-class students coming from a private high school (usually Jesuit, and single-sex) or from the suburbs of bigger Midwestern cities. The girls wear Uggs and North Face fleeces and dye their hair, while the boys live in their...American Eagle jeans." Many "have been in the Catholic school system their entire lives," although there are also "quite a few kids who went to public school and kids who are lower-middle-class." Students are generally committed to the concept of service, and they "put forth a lot of community service hours into the surrounding area, from Habitat for Humanity to the Big Brothers/Big Sisters programs. There are plenty of clubs students use to help raise money for their organizations."

FINANCIAL AID: 314-977-2350 • E-MAIL: ADMITME@SLU.EDU • WEBSITE: WWW.SLU.EDU

THE PRINCETON REVIEW SAYS

Admissions

Very important factors considered include: Academic GPA, standardized test scores. *Important factors considered include:* Application essay, rigor of secondary school record, character/personal qualities, extracurricular activities, talent/ability. *Other factors considered include:* Recommendation(s), alumni/ae relation, first generation, interview, level of applicant's interest, volunteer work. SAT or ACT required; ACT with or without writing component accepted. TOEFL required of all international applicants. High school diploma is required, and GED is accepted. *Academic units required:* 4 English, 4 mathematics, 3 science, 3 foreign language, 3 social studies, 3 academic elective. *Academic units recommended:* 4 English, 4 mathematics, 3 science, 3 foreign language, 3 social studies, 3 academic elective.

Financial Aid

Students should submit: FAFSA. The Princeton Review suggests that all financial aid forms be submitted as soon as possible after January 1. *Need-based scholarships/grants offered:* Federal Pell, SEOG, state scholarships/grants, private scholarships, school scholarship or grant aid from institutional funds, Federal Nursing Scholarships. *Loan aid offered:* Direct Subsidized Stafford, Direct Unsubsidized Stafford, Direct PLUS, Federal Perkins, Federal Nursing Loans, university loans from institutional funds. Applicants will be notified of awards on a rolling basis beginning March 1. Federal Work-Study Program available. Off-campus job opportunities are good.

The Inside Word

Saint Louis University's student body is primarily regional, but it continually expands its draw so that today nearly fifty-eight percent of all undergrads arrive from out of state. This increase in geographic diversity has brought with it elevated admissions standards. The grades and test scores that got your older brother or sister in here may not be good enough for you (although family ties to the school are a plus). Admissions officers look for students who display a commitment to both scholarship and Jesuit principles. Applicants must demonstrate success in college preparatory classes and a desire to be active participants in the community.

THE SCHOOL SAYS "..."

From the Admissions Office

"A hot Midwestern university with a growing national and international reputation, Saint Louis University gives students the knowledge, skills, and values to build a successful career and make a difference in the lives of those around them. Students live and learn in a safe and attractive campus environment. The beautiful urban, residential campus offers loads of internship, outreach, and recreational opportunities. Ranked as one of the best educational values in the country, the university welcomes students from all fifty states and seventy-five foreign countries who pursue rigorous majors that invite individualization. Accessible faculty, study abroad opportunities, and many small, interactive classes make SLU a great place to learn.

"A leading Jesuit, Catholic university, SLU's goal is to graduate men and women of competence and conscience—individuals who are not only capable of making wise decisions but who also understand why they made them. Since 1818, Saint Louis University has been dedicated to academic excellence, service to others, and preparing students to be leaders in society. Saint Louis University truly is the place where knowledge touches lives.

"For admission, Saint Louis University will accept either the SAT or the ACT with or without the writing component."

SELECTIVITY

Admissions Rating	90
# of applicants	10,962
% of applicants accepted	70
% of acceptees attending	21

FRESHMAN PROFILE

Range SAT Critical Reading	540–660
Range SAT Math	550–680
Range ACT Composite	24–31
Minimum paper TOEFL	550
Minimum computer TOEFL	213
Minimum web-based TOEFL	80
Average HS GPA	3.75
% graduated top 10% of class	41
% graduated top 25% of class	68
% graduated top 50% of class	92

DEADLINES

Regular	
Priority	12/1
Deadline	8/1
Notification	9/15
Nonfall registration?	yes

APPLICANTS ALSO LOOK AT

AND OFTEN PREFER
Marquette University, University of Illinois at Urbana-Champaign, University of Missouri—Columbia

AND SOMETIMES PREFER
Creighton University, Loyola University of Chicago, Notre Dame College, Truman State University, University of Dayton

AND RARELY PREFER
Maryville University of Saint Louis, Rockhurst University, Xavier University (OH)

FINANCIAL FACTS

Financial Aid Rating	70
Annual tuition	$32,180
Room and board	$9,170
Required fees	$476
Books and supplies	$1,660
% frosh rec. need-based scholarship or grant aid	64
% UG rec. need-based scholarship or grant aid	52
% frosh rec. non-need-based scholarship or grant aid	7
% UG rec. non-need-based scholarship or grant aid	5
% frosh rec. need-based self-help aid	50
% UG rec. need-based self-help aid	44
% frosh rec. any financial aid	89
% UG rec. any financial aid	88
% UG borrow to pay for school	64
Average cumulative indebtedness	$33,734

SAINT MARY'S COLLEGE OF CALIFORNIA

PO Box 4800, Moraga, CA 94575-4800 • Admissions: 925-631-4224 • Fax: 925-376-7193

CAMPUS LIFE

Quality of Life Rating	79
Fire Safety Rating	81
Green Rating	85
Type of school	private
Affiliation	Roman Catholic
Environment	village

STUDENTS

Total undergrad enrollment	2,621
% male/female	39/61
% from out of state	14
% from public high school	55
% live on campus	62
% African American	6
% Asian	10
% Caucasian	49
% Hispanic	23
% Native American	1
% international	2
# of countries represented	28

SURVEY SAYS . . .

Lab facilities are great
Campus feels safe
Frats and sororities are unpopular
or nonexistent
Lots of beer drinking
Hard liquor is popular

ACADEMICS

Academic Rating	82
% students graduating within 4 years	54
% students graduating within 6 years	64
Calendar	4-1-4
Student/faculty ratio	13:1
Profs interesting rating	90
Profs accessible rating	88
Most common reg class size	10–19 students

MOST POPULAR MAJORS
business administration,
communication studies, psychology

STUDENTS SAY ". . ."

Academics

A "small, Catholic college with a beautiful campus," Saint Mary's College "believes in the importance of education along with the idea that a student can gain faith, friendship, and their identity on their journey." The school's legendary Integrated Liberal Arts great books program combines a "unique liberal arts education" with a focus on "inspiring community, diversity, and intellectual thought," "as well as service work." As one student says, "Saint Mary's transforms students into modern-day philosophers. [It's] a college where questioning the truth is just as important as finding it." Adds another, "I am in a program where every single one of my classes encourages me to make opinions, form arguments, and listen. I read the roots of modern-day philosophy, science, mathematics and politics. I'm expected to grapple with the most difficult texts in Western civilization." Students universally sing the praises of the school's tight-knit community, an asset which "is truly reflected throughout the campus, from interactive class sizes to student-professor relationships." At Saint Mary's, "you are not simply a number, but a face with a story," one student assures us. Many are drawn to the school for its "personal attention to students, large scholarships, easy access to study abroad, and a large amount of student resources." In essence, "Saint Mary's is about teaching students of various backgrounds, how to effect change in the world." Many say that life here offers the perfect fusion of independent thought and guided mentorship; "SMC fosters a support network of faculty, advisors, and students that very few schools can compete with." Professors are "always there to lend a helping hand. They are the perfect mix between forcing you to grow but also being available at any moment for a question."

Life

"There was a sense of 'home' when I came on to campus for the first time," on student says. Beyond the "amazing campus," "A quick ride on BART leaves all of San Francisco at your fingertips." In addition, Oakland is "twenty minutes way" and "Berkeley is even closer!" The town itself is "small but nice." There are "infinite opportunities for outdoor activities," and "many restaurants and a big shopping center ten minutes away." Saint Mary's "is a community waiting to welcome anyone and everyone who enters." "Walking from class to class, [students] will pass many people they know. People are never hesitant to say hello." Students enjoy "the sunny weather," and "Sports games (mainly men's basketball and rugby) are one of the main highlights…bringing all students together." "Our school is a total basketball school where school spirit remains supreme." Students "take their academics seriously, while maintaining a social life." Beyond the ever-popular sporting events, the school promotes unity through "guest speakers, Poetry Slams, open mic night, etc." During the week, when they're not contemplating the complexities of western civilization, students "watch TV, go out to eat, go to the club in the city, go to parties, go bowling, [or] are involved in the intramural sports." Despite the lure of the campus's natural beauty, students say that some of the "facilities need improvement, especially [the] sports facilities."

Student Body

The typical Saint Mary's student is "active and open-minded," and "easy to get along with." In general, most are "dedicated to academics and involved in at least one club or sports team." Though many say that the "typical student is wealthy and Caucasian," and lament the fact that "most of the different ethnic groups stay together," the overall spirit of the student body "is not discriminatory towards race, religion, or gender." Saint Mary's students are "usually pretty involved, if not in community service or school senate, then in athletics." In the way of the Lasallian tradition, "They wouldn't hesitate to lend a helping hand and generally get along well with everyone."

FINANCIAL AID: 925-631-4370 • E-MAIL: SMCADMIT@STMARYS-CA.EDU • WEBSITE: WWW.STMARYS-CA.EDU

THE PRINCETON REVIEW SAYS

Admissions

Very important factors considered include: Academic GPA, rigor of secondary school record, standardized test scores. *Important factors considered include:* Application essay, recommendation(s), first generation. *Other factors considered include:* Class rank, alumni/ae relation, character/personal qualities, extracurricular activities, geographical residence, interview, level of applicant's interest, racial/ethnic status, religious affiliation/commitment, talent/ability, volunteer work, work experience. SAT or ACT required; ACT with or without writing component accepted. TOEFL required of all international applicants. High school diploma is required, and GED is accepted. *Academic units required:* 4 English, 3 mathematics, 2 science (1 science lab), 2 foreign language, 1 social studies, 1 history, 2 academic elective. *Academic units recommended:* 4 English, 4 mathematics, 3 science (1 science lab), 3 foreign language, 1 social studies, 1 history, 2 academic elective.

Financial Aid

Students should submit: FAFSA. Regular filing deadline is March 1. The Princeton Review suggests that all financial aid forms be submitted as soon as possible after January 1. *Need-based scholarships/grants offered:* Federal Pell, SEOG, state scholarships/grants, private scholarships, school scholarship or grant aid from institutional funds. *Loan aid offered:* Direct Subsidized Stafford, Direct Unsubsidized Stafford, Direct PLUS, Federal Perkins. Applicants will be notified of awards on a rolling basis beginning March 15. Federal Work-Study Program available. Off-campus job opportunities are good.

The Inside Word

Saint Mary's adheres to its Lasallian awareness of social and economic injustice. In line with this, it reserves one quarter of its undergraduate population for students from the lowest economic status. The school will continue to boost it own funding of financial aid in order to help such students attend the school. Here the commitment to serving the underprivileged provides a great opportunity for low-income students with strong academic potential.

THE SCHOOL SAYS "..."

From the Admissions Office

"Today, Saint Mary's College continues to offer a value-oriented education by providing a classical liberal arts background second to none. The emphasis is on teaching an individual how to think independently and responsibly, how to analyze information in all situations, and how to make choices based on logical thinking and rational examination. Such a program develops students' ability to ask the right questions and to formulate meaningful answers, not only within their professional careers but also for the rest of their lives. Saint Mary's College is committed to preparing young men and women for the challenge of an ever-changing world, while remaining faithful to an enduring academic and spiritual heritage. We believe the purpose of a college experience is to prepare men and women for an unlimited number of opportunities, and that this is best accomplished by educating the whole person, both intellectually and ethically. We strive to recruit, admit, enroll, and graduate students who are generous, faith-filled, and human, and we believe this is reaffirmed in our community of brothers, in our faculty, and in our personal concern for each student.

"For freshman applicants, we will accept the SAT, and the ACT is also accepted. The ACT writing assessment is optional. The highest critical reading and the highest math scores attained on the SAT will be used. SAT Subject Tests are not required."

SELECTIVITY

Admissions Rating	73
# of applicants	3,836
% of applicants accepted	75
% of acceptees attending	24
# accepting a place on wait list	373
% admitted from wait list	3

FRESHMAN PROFILE

Range SAT Critical Reading	490–600
Range SAT Math	500–610
Range ACT Composite	21–26
Minimum paper TOEFL	550
Minimum computer TOEFL	213
Minimum web-based TOEFL	79
Average HS GPA	3.42

DEADLINES

Early action	
Deadline	11/15
Notification	12/15
Regular	
Priority	2/15
Deadline	3/1
Nonfall registration?	yes

APPLICANTS ALSO LOOK AT
AND OFTEN PREFER
Gonzaga University, Loyola Marymount University, Santa Clara University, University of California—Davis

AND SOMETIMES PREFER
Dominican University of California, University of California—Merced, University of San Francisco

AND RARELY PREFER
California State University—Sacramento, San Francisco State University, San Jose State University, Sonoma State University, University of California—Santa Cruz, University of the Pacific

FINANCIAL FACTS

Financial Aid Rating	73
Annual tuition	$37,000
Room and board	$12,840
Required fees	$150
Books and supplies	$1,656
% frosh rec. need-based scholarship or grant aid	74
% UG rec. need-based scholarship or grant aid	64
% frosh rec. non-need-based scholarship or grant aid	37
% UG rec. non-need-based scholarship or grant aid	21
% frosh rec. need-based self-help aid	75
% UG rec. need-based self-help aid	67
% frosh rec. any financial aid	85
% UG rec. any financial aid	75
% UG borrow to pay for school	52
Average cumulative indebtedness	$36,745

SAINT MICHAEL'S COLLEGE

ONE WINOOSKI PARK, COLCHESTER, VT 05439 • ADMISSIONS: 802-654-3000 • FAX: 802-654-2906

CAMPUS LIFE

Quality of Life Rating	96
Fire Safety Rating	75
Green Rating	85
Type of school	private
Affiliation	Roman Catholic
Environment	city

STUDENTS

Total undergrad enrollment	1,859
% male/female	48/52
% from out of state	79
% from public high school	68
% live on campus	98
% African American	1
% Asian	1
% Caucasian	92
% Hispanic	3
% international	2
# of countries represented	47

SURVEY SAYS . . .

Students are friendly
Students get along with local community
Students love Colchester, VT
Great off-campus food
Students are happy
Frats and sororities are unpopular or nonexistent
Student publications are popular

ACADEMICS

Academic Rating	86
% students graduating within 4 years	74
% students graduating within 6 years	77
Calendar	semester
Student/faculty ratio	12:1
Profs interesting rating	87
Profs accessible rating	95
Most common reg class size	10–19 students
Most common lab size	20–29 students

MOST POPULAR MAJORS
biology, business/commerce, psychology

STUDENTS SAY ". . ."

Academics

Tucked away in "the heart of Vermont ski country," Saint Michael's College offers a "close-knit and familial atmosphere" where everyone "will always value and support you." "Small classes" help to ensure that "you are not just another number in a lecture hall." Indeed, the college "really wants to help its students realize their full potential." Many tout the "strong academics" and highlight the education, biology, and religion departments in particular. Classes are often "discussion-based" and "require a conscientious student who will actively participate in discussion." Moreover, undergrads here speak effusively about their professors. As one English and theater double-major shares, "the professors strongly encourage you to visit them during office hours and are always working hard to engage students and keep them interested in learning. It is clear that the majority of the professors at St. Mike's care about what they are teaching and seem genuinely interested in the subject matter." A history major succinctly adds, "Whether you like it or not, your professor will know your name." And another satisfied undergrad concludes that the professors "bring real life experience to the material, apply it to current events and to our lives, and are always available to talk about a paper, grade, or class in general. I've been able to push the limits of my mind and branch out during classes, exploring [in ways] that traditional textbook approaches don't [afford]."

Life

Though undergrads at St. Mike's take their academics seriously, they also love to take advantage of life beyond the library. While "partying is popular at Saint Mike's" it's certainly "not a requirement." Fortunately, "the college is great at providing alternative activities on weekends for those who choose to abstain." Indeed, "whether it's a benefit concert, a dance, or a pie-eating contest organized by residential life," one content student promises us that "there is always something to do on campus." A psych major adds to the list, exclaiming, "There are always socials to [attend], bowling, athletic events, concerts, plays, [and] guest speakers." Volunteering is also extremely popular. When students are itching to get off campus, they frequently head to nearby Burlington. "Church Street is crowded with unique shops, fantastic restaurants, and interesting people." Many also love to take advantage of Vermont's outdoor recreational options and the school counts many avid skiers, snowboarders, and hikers among it ranks. In fact, "Saint Michael's provides amazing ski pass deals and transportation to amazing ski resorts in the area." All these options help ensure that life at St. Mike's is "never boring."

Student Body

At first glance, the typical St. Mike's student appears to be a "white, middle-class New-Englander" who quickly dons "North Faces and UGGs during the cold Vermont winters." However, once you look past the surface you'll find a vibrant undergrad community where "everyone is unique and different" and even "a little quirky." And though the college is Catholic, undergrads assure us that "there are students of other [faiths and students] who do not practice [a] religion and they are not treated any differently." Undergrads define their peers as "intelligent, outgoing, and active" and quickly assert that "they're friendly and open to new perspectives and new types of people." Indeed, it's even commonplace to "hold doors open for people who are ridiculously far away." Many students are active in "social justice movements, green movements, [and] community service" and also frequently participate in "the school's wilderness program." And don't be fooled: While the average St. Mike's undergrad is "laid back," students here are "committed to their studies" and "focused on getting all they can out of their college experience." As this math and econ double-major sums up, "Every student here is passionate about something, and it shows in their education and in their actions."

SAINT MICHAEL'S COLLEGE

FINANCIAL AID: 802-654-3243 • E-MAIL: ADMISSION@SMCVT.EDU • WEBSITE: WWW.SMCVT.EDU

THE PRINCETON REVIEW SAYS

Admissions

Very important factors considered include: Academic GPA, class rank, rigor of secondary school record. *Important factors considered include:* Application essay, recommendation(s), standardized test scores, character/personal qualities, extracurricular activities, talent/ability. *Other factors considered include:* Alumni/ae relation, first generation, geographical residence, level of applicant's interest, racial/ethnic status, state residency, volunteer work, work experience. ACT with writing component required. TOEFL required of all international applicants. High school diploma is required, and GED is accepted. *Academic units required:* 4 English, 3 mathematics, 3 science (2 science labs), 3 foreign language, 3 social studies. *Academic units recommended:* 4 English, 4 mathematics, 4 science (3 science labs), 4 foreign language, 4 social studies.

Financial Aid

Students should submit: FAFSA. Regular filing deadline is February 15. The Princeton Review suggests that all financial aid forms be submitted as soon as possible after January 1. *Need-based scholarships/grants offered:* Federal Pell, SEOG, state scholarships/grants, private scholarships, school scholarship or grant aid from institutional funds. *Loan aid offered:* Direct Subsidized Stafford, Direct Unsubsidized Stafford, Direct PLUS, Federal Perkins. Applicants will be notified of awards on a rolling basis beginning January 15. Federal Work-Study Program available. Off-campus job opportunities are excellent.

Inside Word

Applicants to St. Mike's are more than just a number, and admissions officers do their utmost to consider candidates in their entirety. Officers consider everything from essays to extracurricular activities, though most weight is given to academic record. The college has recently made standardized tests optional, and applicants won't be penalized if they choose not to submit their scores.

THE SCHOOL SAYS " . . ."

From the Admissions Office

"Saint Michael's is a residential, Catholic, liberal arts college for students who want to 'Learn What Matters.'

A Saint Michael's education will prepare you for life, as each of our thirty majors is grounded in our liberal studies core. Our superb faculty is committed first and foremost to teaching and is known for really caring about students while simultaneously challenging them to reach higher than they ever thought possible. Because of our holistic approach, Saint Michael's graduates are prepared for their entire careers, not just their first jobs out of college.

"With nearly 100 percent of students living on campus, our '24/7' learning environment means exceptional teaching goes beyond the classroom and into the living areas, which include three new suite-style residences, townhouse apartments, and traditional residence halls. The remarkable sense of community encourages students to get involved, take risks, and think differently. A unique passion for social justice issues on campus reflects the heritage of the Edmundite priests who founded Saint Michael's in 1904.

"Saint Michael's is situated three minutes from Burlington, Vermont, one of America's top ten college towns. A unique Cultural Pass program allows students to see an array of music, dance, theater, and Broadway productions at the Flynn Center downtown. Students also take advantage of some of the best skiing in the East through an agreement with Smugglers' Notch ski resort—an all-access season pass is provided to any Saint Michael's student in good academic standing."

SELECTIVITY

Admissions Rating	85
# of applicants	3,363
% of applicants accepted	82
% of acceptees attending	20
# accepting a place on wait list	100
% admitted from wait list	29

FRESHMAN PROFILE

Range SAT Critical Reading	510–630
Range SAT Math	510–620
Range SAT Writing	510–610
Range ACT Composite	22–28
Minimum paper TOEFL	550
Minimum computer TOEFL	213
Average HS GPA	3.50
% graduated top 10% of class	30
% graduated top 25% of class	60
% graduated top 50% of class	87

DEADLINES

Regular	
Priority	11/1
Deadline	2/1
Nonfall registration?	yes

APPLICANTS ALSO LOOK AT

AND OFTEN PREFER
Boston College, College of the Holy Cross

AND SOMETIMES PREFER
Fairfield University, Stonehill College, University of Vermont

AND RARELY PREFER
Saint Anselm College, University of New Hampshire

FINANCIAL FACTS

Financial Aid Rating	80
Annual tuition	$35,940
Room and board	$9,030
Required fees	$300
Books and supplies	$1,200
% frosh rec. need-based scholarship or grant aid	74
% UG rec. need-based scholarship or grant aid	61
% frosh rec. non-need-based scholarship or grant aid	15
% UG rec. non-need-based scholarship or grant aid	11
% frosh rec. need-based self-help aid	57
% UG rec. need-based self-help aid	50
% frosh rec. any financial aid	99
% UG rec. any financial aid	95
% UG borrow to pay for school	78
Average cumulative indebtedness	$29,410

SALISBURY UNIVERSITY

ADMISSIONS OFFICE, 1101 CAMDEN AVENUE, SALISBURY, MD 21801 • ADMISSIONS: 410-543-6161 • FAX: 410-546-6016

CAMPUS LIFE

Quality of Life Rating	73
Fire Safety Rating	75
Green Rating	86
Type of school	public
Environment	town

STUDENTS

Total undergrad enrollment	7,527
% male/female	43/57
% from out of state	13
% live on campus	36
# of fraternities	7
# of sororities	4
% African American	11
% Asian	2
% Caucasian	80
% Hispanic	4
% Native American	1
% international	1
# of countries represented	53

SURVEY SAYS . . .

Lab facilities are great
Great computer facilities
Great food on campus
Intramural sports are popular
Lots of beer drinking
Hard liquor is popular

ACADEMICS

Academic Rating	68
% students graduating within 4 years	47
% students graduating within 6 years	70
Calendar	4-1-4
Student/faculty ratio	17:1
Profs interesting rating	76
Profs accessible rating	80
Most common reg class size	20–29 students
Most common lab size	20–29 students

MOST POPULAR MAJORS
biology, communication, arts, nursing

STUDENTS SAY ". . ."

Academics

A member of Maryland's university system, Salisbury provides undergraduates with stellar academic programs coupled with the benefit of a state school price tag. A "moderately sized" college, Salisbury is "big enough where [you] can meet new people all the time" and yet "small enough where [you are] treated as a student rather than a number." The school really works to foster a "comfortable and personalized environment in which students focus on learning and achievement." Additionally, "Salisbury strives to not only challenge students academically, but also to make them well-rounded as people." The university is an especially good option for those students interested in pursuing a major in education, exercise science, nursing, or environmental studies. For the most part, undergrads at Salisbury speak very highly of their professors. As one elementary education major shares, "The professors here are down-to-earth, friendly, and just passionate about what they are teaching." Fortunately, because most classes are relatively small, "it is easy to form close relationships with [them]." And an environmental studies and biology dual major sums up, "I have met so many amazing captivating professors while at Salisbury. They make the classes interesting and real. They are always willing to answer questions and share experiences with you. The wonderful professors are what I attribute much of my success in college to."

Life

Undergrads at Salisbury are experts at balancing work and play. Though plenty of students "party every weekend," one biology major says that "there [are] definitely other options." Indeed, "it's not uncommon for friends to just hang out on weekends, play board games, watch movies, or have a bonfire." And while some people grumble that "there's not much going on," others maintain that "Salisbury has lots of different clubs and organizations for people who want to join one." Students also get creative and make their own fun, as this happy undergrad shares: "One time we put bubble wrap down in the hall while no one was watching and then a bunch of us jumped on it and danced around." A handful of undergrads are less than enamored with hometown Salisbury and proclaim some neighborhoods a little "rough." Others enjoy taking advantage of the "movie theater, mall, bowling alleys, great restaurants, and…job opportunities" that the surrounding area offers. However, students are nearly unanimous in agreeing that "when the weather is warm, everyone tries to find time to go to Ocean City (only thirty minutes away!)" to escape academic stress and relax on the beach.

Student Body

Salisbury University appears to attract "all types of people," and most undergrads describe their peers as generally "welcoming and friendly." One student expands further, exclaiming, "Finding a group of people you agree with or get along with is rather easy and the diversity of people and things to do seem limitless at times. We each fit into the campus in our own way." A significant portion of students hail "from Maryland, New Jersey, or New York." Salisbury students are also highly active individuals and many are "involved outside of the classroom with a sports team, a club, or a student organization." A number of undergrads also keep "part-time jobs to help pay for tuition." Despite all the activity, we're told that the typical student is "fairly laid-back." Of course, he or she "will put a lot of effort into their field of study." Perhaps the one thing that truly unites these kids is the pride they feel in their school. As an earth science major coyly reveals, "The typical student…never passes up the opportunity to squawk proudly when told [to] by the president as a Salisbury Sea Gull."

SALISBURY UNIVERSITY

FINANCIAL AID: 410-543-6165 • E-MAIL: ADMISSIONS@SALISBURY.EDU • WEBSITE: WWW.SALISBURY.EDU

THE PRINCETON REVIEW SAYS
Admissions
Very important factors considered include: Academic GPA, rigor of secondary school record, extracurricular activities, geographical residence, talent/ability. *Important factors considered include:* Class rank, standardized test scores, alumni/ae relation, geographical residence, volunteer work. *Other factors considered include:* Application essay, recommendation(s), character/personal qualities, racial/ethnic status, work experience. ACT with or without writing component accepted. TOEFL required of all international applicants. High school diploma is required, and GED is accepted. *Academic units required:* 4 English, 3 mathematics, 3 science (2 science labs), 2 foreign language, 3 social studies. *Academic units recommended:* 4 English, 4 mathematics, 4 science (3 science labs), 3 foreign language, 3 social studies, 3 academic elective.

Financial Aid
Students should submit: FAFSA. Regular filing deadline is December 31. The Princeton Review suggests that all financial aid forms be submitted as soon as possible after January 1. *Need-based scholarships/grants offered:* Federal Pell, SEOG, state scholarships/grants, private scholarships, school scholarship or grant aid from institutional funds. *Loan aid offered:* Direct Subsidized Stafford, Direct Unsubsidized Stafford, Federal Perkins. Applicants will be notified of awards on a rolling basis beginning March 15. Federal Work-Study Program available. Off-campus job opportunities are fair.

The Inside Word
Admission to Salisbury is competitive, and admissions officers want to admit students who will not only succeed but also thrive. While each applicant's academic record is given the most weight, officers also consider personal traits such as leadership qualities, artistic and athletic talent, and diversity. Standardized tests are optional for those candidates who have earned a cumulative weighted GPA of 3.5 or higher (on a 4.0 scale). However, all applicants should submit test scores for scholarship consideration.

THE SCHOOL SAYS "..."
From the Admissions Office
"Friendly, convenient, safe, and beautiful are just a few of the words used to describe the campus of Salisbury University. The campus is a compact, self-contained community that offers the full range of student services. Beautiful, traditional-style architecture and impeccably landscaped grounds combine to create an atmosphere that inspires learning and fosters student pride. Located just thirty minutes from the beaches of Ocean City, Maryland, SU students enjoy a year-round resort social life as well as an inside track on summer jobs. Situated less than two hours from the urban excitement of Baltimore and Washington, D.C., greater Salisbury makes up for its lack of size—its population is about 80,000—by being strategically located. Within easy driving distance of a number of other major cities, including New York City, Philadelphia, and Norfolk, Salisbury is the hub of the Delmarva Peninsula, a mostly rural region flavored by the salty air of the Chesapeake Bay and Atlantic Ocean.

"Submission of SAT and/or ACT scores when applying would be optional to freshman applicants who present a weighted high school grade point average (GPA) of 3.5 or higher on a 4.0 scale. Any student applying with less than a 3.5 would still need to submit a standardized test score to supplement the official high school transcript. Additionally, an applicant may wish to submit a standardized test score subsequent to admission for full scholarship consideration as the majority of the university's scholarships include test scores as a requirement."

SELECTIVITY
Admissions Rating	86
# of applicants	7,739
% of applicants accepted	53
% of acceptees attending	30
# of early decision applicants	3,543
% accepted early decision	65

FRESHMAN PROFILE
Range SAT Critical Reading	520–600
Range SAT Math	530–610
Range SAT Writing	520–600
Range ACT Composite	21–25
Minimum paper TOEFL	550
Minimum computer TOEFL	213
Average HS GPA	3.65
% graduated top 10% of class	28
% graduated top 25% of class	63
% graduated top 50% of class	92

DEADLINES
Early action	
Deadline	12/1
Notification	1/15
Regular	
Priority	1/15
Notification	3/15
Nonfall registration?	yes

APPLICANTS ALSO LOOK AT
AND OFTEN PREFER
Towson University, University of Delaware, University of Maryland—College Park

AND SOMETIMES PREFER
Frostburg State University, James Madison University, Penn State University

AND RARELY PREFER
Boston University, Villanova University, York College

FINANCIAL FACTS
Financial Aid Rating	72
Annual in-state tuition	$4,960
Annual out-of-state tuition	$13,456
Room and board	$8,686
Required fees	$1,948
Books and supplies	$1,300
% frosh rec. need-based scholarship or grant aid	47
% UG rec. need-based scholarship or grant aid	40
% frosh rec. need-based self-help aid	36
% UG rec. need-based self-help aid	37
% frosh rec. any financial aid	85
% UG rec. any financial aid	76
% UG borrow to pay for school	56
Average cumulative indebtedness	$18,541

SAMFORD UNIVERSITY

800 LAKESHORE DRIVE, BIRMINGHAM, AL 35229 • ADMISSIONS: 205-726-3673 • FAX: 205-726-2171

CAMPUS LIFE

Quality of Life Rating	86
Fire Safety Rating	94
Green Rating	76
Type of school	private
Affiliation	Southern Baptist
Environment	town

STUDENTS

Total undergrad enrollment	2,918
% male/female	36/64
% from out of state	61
% from public high school	52
% live on campus	68
# of fraternities	5
# of sororities	7
% African American	7
% Asian	1
% Caucasian	87
% Hispanic	2
% international	1
# of countries represented	23

SURVEY SAYS . . .
Athletic facilities are great
School is well-run
Students are friendly
Students get along with local
community
Students love Birmingham, AL
Great off-campus food
Students are happy
Very little drug use

ACADEMICS

Academic Rating	80
% students graduating within 4 years	54
% students graduating within 6 years	73
Calendar	4-1-4
Student/faculty ratio	12:1
Profs interesting rating	85
Profs accessible rating	85
Most common reg class size	10–19 students
Most common lab size	10–19 students

MOST POPULAR MAJORS
journalism, nursing, teacher education

STUDENTS SAY "..."

Academics
Samford University, "a beautiful liberal arts college with Christian values," draws undergrads seeking "a close-knit community in which high value is placed on morality, academic excellence and communication skills." Students tell us that "Samford represents what is great about a Christian university. It provides an environment that is diverse and not typically conservative Christian." A "well-rounded, challenging curriculum" ensures that students transcend indoctrination while experiencing "some aspect of religious discussion…in classes where you would not usually encounter it." High expectations ensure that they don't coast through to an easy degree. As one student explains, "Samford professors expect a lot from their students, and in return we expect a lot from them. It's been said that academics at Samford are quite a bit harder than most universities, so when someone gets a B people see it as an A, when they get a C it's seen as a B, and so forth." Outstanding disciplines here include English, journalism, nursing, pharmacy, business, music, and theater. But perhaps Samford's most outstanding quality is its "incredibly friendly, welcoming, and genuine atmosphere that makes the transition to college life a pleasant one. The campus is positively breathtaking, the facilities are excellent, class sizes are relatively small, and professors are available and helpful…There is an overall feeling of contentment on campus."

Life
"There are people who party and those who don't" at Samford; despite the campus' official "dry" status, "there will always be those few people who break the rules," and furthermore, Birmingham offers "some fun nightlife" that can, and occasionally does, involve intoxicants. As a whole, however, "students generally are not big partiers, but like to have fun. Most weekends are spent hanging out with friends or traveling." "There is a strong Greek presence" on the Samford campus, "and many weekends include Greek parties or fundraisers and activities." Religious groups "are especially popular, and the majority of the student body is involved in at least one college ministry throughout the week." Students enjoy "at least five opportunities a week to worship" and "are very engaged in the community and local churches." These activities include "a strong awareness of global issues: fair trade, Darfur, etc." Samford's gated campus "is located in a very safe part of Birmingham," providing students a secure enclave from which to launch their explorations of the city. Students tell us the city is "awesome," "with plenty of places to eat, shop, and play. There are several movie theaters and shopping centers within a ten-mile radius, as well as a roller skating rink, plenty of gorgeous parks, and a thriving downtown."

Student Body
"The Samford stereotype is a white, wealthy, Southern, Protestant (usually Baptist) female, decked out in country club attire," but "while that accounts for maybe an (admittedly vocal) twenty percent of the school, there is a lot of diversity otherwise, especially outside the Greek system." Students who don't fit the mold "often hang out on the quad and are active in various campus organizations or other activities. There actually are hippies, druggies, minorities, political extremists of all stripes, gay people, and people from all over the world at Samford. Don't be deceived by your first glance." Quite a few respondents told us that while "a wide variety of people attend" Samford, "a large percent were raised in a very sheltered environment" and the majority are "white, upper-class, southern Christians" "with strong Christian values and beliefs." Students tend to be highly ambitious, with "a generally heavy interest in their future and…a plan for achieving their goals."

SAMFORD UNIVERSITY

FINANCIAL AID: 800-888-7245 • E-MAIL: ADMISSIONS@SAMFORD.EDU • WEBSITE: WWW.SAMFORD.EDU

THE PRINCETON REVIEW SAYS

Admissions

Very important factors considered include: Academic GPA, rigor of secondary school record, standardized test scores. *Important factors considered include:* Application essay, class rank, extracurricular activities. *Other factors considered include:* Recommendation(s), alumni/ae relation, geographical residence, level of applicant's interest, state residency, talent/ability, volunteer work, work experience. SAT or ACT required; ACT with or without writing component accepted. TOEFL required of all international applicants. High school diploma is required, and GED is accepted. *Academic units required:* 4 English, 3 mathematics, 2 science (2 science labs), 2 foreign language, 2 history.

Financial Aid

Students should submit: FAFSA. Regular filing deadline is March 1. The Princeton Review suggests that all financial aid forms be submitted as soon as possible after January 1. *Need-based scholarships/grants offered:* Federal Pell, SEOG, state scholarships/grants, private scholarships, school scholarship or grant aid from institutional funds, Federal Nursing Scholarships. *Loan aid offered:* Direct Subsidized Stafford, Direct Unsubsidized Stafford, Direct PLUS, Federal Perkins, Federal Nursing Loans, university loans from institutional funds. Federal Work-Study Program available. Off-campus job opportunities are excellent.

The Inside Word

Samford admits applicants on a rolling basis. The first acceptance letters go out as early as October. As is often the case with rolling admissions, those who apply early in the process are most likely to receive a generous review. The school strongly recommends a campus visit, meaning you ought to make one if at all possible. A campus visit is a great way of signaling your desire to attend the school, which in turn improves your chances of being admitted.

THE SCHOOL SAYS ". . ."

From the Admissions Office

"Samford University is Alabama's largest privately funded university and is the state's only private institution in the U.S. News & World Report rankings of national doctoral research universities. Samford was founded in 1841 by Alabama Baptists and continues to enjoy its historic relationship to Alabama Baptists, extending and enhancing their original commitment by developing and maintaining in the campus community an exemplary Christian ethos and culture.

"Samford offers twenty-three associate's, bachelor's, master's, and professional doctoral degrees in more than 100 major fields of study, as well as adult learning, continuing education, and various types of worthwhile, non-degree learning. Samford serves students through eight organizational units: Howard College of Arts and Sciences, School of Business, Beeson School of Divinity, Orlean Bullard Beeson School of Education and Professional Studies, Cumberland School of Law, Ida V. Moffett School of Nursing, School of Performing Arts, and McWhorter School of Pharmacy.

"The mission of Samford University is to nurture persons in their development of intellect, creativity, faith, and personhood. As a Christian university, the community fosters academic, career, and ethical competency while encouraging social and civic responsibility and service to others."

SELECTIVITY

Admissions Rating	84
# of applicants	2,435
% of applicants accepted	87
% of acceptees attending	34

FRESHMAN PROFILE

Range SAT Critical Reading	520–640
Range SAT Math	515–620
Range ACT Composite	23–29
Minimum paper TOEFL	550
Minimum computer TOEFL	213
Average HS GPA	3.66
% graduated top 10% of class	35
% graduated top 25% of class	64
% graduated top 50% of class	86

DEADLINES

Regular	
Priority	12/1
Nonfall registration?	yes

APPLICANTS ALSO LOOK AT AND OFTEN PREFER

Auburn University, University of Alabama—Tuscaloosa, University of Georgia, University of Tennessee—Knoxville

FINANCIAL FACTS

Financial Aid Rating	78
Annual tuition	$23,423
Room and board	$7,775
Required fees	$540
Books and supplies	$1,000
% frosh rec. need-based scholarship or grant aid	40
% UG rec. need-based scholarship or grant aid	33
% frosh rec. non-need-based scholarship or grant aid	13
% UG rec. non-need-based scholarship or grant aid	7
% frosh rec. need-based self-help aid	31
% UG rec. need-based self-help aid	29
% frosh rec. any financial aid	86
% UG rec. any financial aid	64
% UG borrow to pay for school	39
Average cumulative indebtedness	$20,328

SANTA CLARA UNIVERSITY

500 EL CAMINO REAL, SANTA CLARA, CA 95053 • ADMISSIONS: 408-554-4700 • FAX: 408-554-5255

STUDENTS SAY ". . ."

Academics

Santa Clara University is a small Jesuit school, distinctly influenced by its unique location in California's Silicon Valley. SCU is known for its strong programs in the liberal arts; however, the school also operates a "nationally ranked business school" and "fabulous engineering degree." No matter what your field, SCU is "exceptionally good at preparing students for the real world," and, within all academic programs, the "focus of the coursework is very application-based." In the Jesuit tradition, the school "encourages us to apply our education to our surrounding communities." As such, many "courses are based on social justice, so they think about the global application. Even math classes." Serious students recommend the university honors program, with "its small seminar styled classes led by the school's top professors." While there are "a handful of teachers that just don't make the cut," most SCU professors are "highly qualified" and "very enthusiastic about the material they teach." With a teacher to student ratio of thirteen to one, "Classes are discussion-based, with an emphasis on learning from each other instead of only from the professor." Professors consistently "take the time necessary to ensure that students understand the material discussed in class," and outside of class, "They are always available for office hours for extra help." For anyone looking to get into the software or Internet industry, you can't beat SCU's "great location in the heart of the Silicon Valley." "Santa Clara has a fantastic career center that provides numerous resources to students in their internship and job searches," and participating in a local internship can "enrich what we've learned through classroom curriculum with on-the-job experience." Though some students feel the campus could be even greener, they're happy to report that "the school is huge on sustainability and having a green mindset."

Life

For campus residents, life at SCU is largely defined by the school's system of Residential Learning Communities (RLCs), which group students in housing according to their interests. From your first day on campus, "RLC is a place where you meet most of your friends and are able to hang out and have a great time." With more than 100 student groups on campus, "Most people are involved in numerous clubs, whether that is community service or athletics." There's also a prevailing interest in current events, social responsibility, and service: "Volunteering and community service is a cool thing to do at SCU." In their free time, "Students work out together, volunteer together, get involved with clubs, go shopping, go clubbing, go out to dinner, hang out in San Francisco, hang out in Santa Cruz, and party." With "only two or three bars conveniently close by" and strict campus policies against alcohol, "SCU is mainly a house party school." In student residences near campus, "Parties are big on the weekends, and students get to let loose and have fun." Things get particularly upbeat when the sun comes out, and "You will never see more people outside boozing and partying in the sun than spring quarter at Santa Clara." Though surrounding town of SCU can be rather quiet, the campus is located "across the street from the Caltrain and bus stop, making it easy to get to Santa Cruz or San Francisco for the weekend."

Student Body

Embodying the laid-back California lifestyle, SCU "students are the flip-flop and tank-top-wearing type" and are generally "social and sun loving." "Students are concerned with sustainability, politics, and improving our nation," and "Many students spend time volunteering in support of the local community." "The typical student is middle-class," yet, "There are students of all races, shapes, and sizes." Philosophically, "The Jesuits encourage acceptance of all races, religions, and sexual orientations," and there's "a lot of support for minority groups and cultural awareness on campus." "Most students come from a Catholic background," and the prevailing personality is "amiable, culturally understanding, and welcoming of all people." "A lot of the campus population is committed to remaining fit, so you'll see a lot of people at the gym."

FINANCIAL AID: 408-554-4505 • WEBSITE: WWW.SCU.EDU

THE PRINCETON REVIEW SAYS

Admissions

Very important factors considered include: Academic GPA, application essay, recommendation(s), rigor of secondary school record. *Important factors considered include:* Standardized test scores, character/personal qualities, extracurricular activities, racial/ethnic status, talent/ability, volunteer work. *Other factors considered include:* Class rank, alumni/ae relation, first generation, geographical residence, level of applicant's interest, religious affiliation/commitment, state residency, work experience. SAT or ACT required; ACT with or without writing component accepted. TOEFL required of all international applicants. *Academic units required:* 4 English, 3 mathematics, 2 science, 2 foreign language, 3 social studies, 1 academic elective. *Academic units recommended:* 4 English, 4 mathematics, 3 science, 3 foreign language, 3 social studies, 1 visual/performing arts, 1 academic elective.

Financial Aid

Students should submit: FAFSA, CSS/Financial Aid PROFILE. The Princeton Review suggests that all financial aid forms be submitted as soon as possible after January 1. *Need-based scholarships/grants offered:* Federal Pell, SEOG, state scholarships/grants, private scholarships, school scholarship or grant aid from institutional funds. *Loan aid offered:* Direct Subsidized Stafford, Direct Unsubsidized Stafford, Direct PLUS, Direct PLUS, Federal Perkins. Federal Work-Study Program available. Off-campus job opportunities are good.

The Inside Word

SCU carefully evaluates each applicant's file, considering a student's academic record and test scores in addition to his or her personal qualities and family background. Extracurricular activities, letters of recommendation, and personal statements are all carefully reviewed. Accepted students had an average GPA of 3.4 to 3.8 on a 4.0 scale. Students can apply regular decision or through the nonbinding early action program.

THE SCHOOL SAYS ". . ."

From the Admissions Office

"Santa Clara University, located one hour south of San Francisco, offers its undergraduates an opportunity to be educated within a challenging, dynamic, and caring community. The university blends a sense of tradition and history (as the oldest college in California) with a vision that values innovation and a deep commitment to social justice. Santa Clara's faculty members are talented scholars who are demanding, supportive, and accessible. The students are serious about academics, are ethnically diverse, and enjoy a full range of athletic, social, community service, religious, and cultural activities—both on campus and through the many options presented by our northern California location. The undergraduate program includes three divisions: the College of Arts and Sciences, the School of Business, and the School of Engineering.

"Santa Clara University will accept either the SAT or the ACT. The ACT writing component is optional. The highest verbal and the highest math scores attained on the SAT will be used."

SELECTIVITY

Admissions Rating	90
# of applicants	11,787
% of applicants accepted	58
% of acceptees attending	19
# accepting a place on wait list	990
% admitted from wait list	37

FRESHMAN PROFILE

Range SAT Critical Reading	560–660
Range SAT Math	590–690
Range ACT Composite	25–30
Minimum paper TOEFL	575
Minimum computer TOEFL	230
Average HS GPA	3.60
% graduated top 10% of class	25
% graduated top 25% of class	81
% graduated top 50% of class	98

DEADLINES

Early action	
Deadline	11/1
Notification	12/31
Regular	
Deadline	1/7
Nonfall registration?	no

APPLICANTS ALSO LOOK AT

AND OFTEN PREFER
Loyola Marymount University, University of California—Berkeley, University of California—Davis

AND SOMETIMES PREFER
Stanford University, University of California—Los Angeles, University of San Francisco

AND RARELY PREFER
Saint Mary's College of California, University of California—Santa Cruz

FINANCIAL FACTS

Financial Aid Rating	67
Annual tuition	$37,368
Room and board	$11,742
Books and supplies	$1,620
% frosh rec. need-based scholarship or grant aid	32
% UG rec. need-based scholarship or grant aid	28
% frosh rec. non-need-based scholarship or grant aid	20
% UG rec. non-need-based scholarship or grant aid	13
% frosh rec. need-based self-help aid	24
% UG rec. need-based self-help aid	23
% frosh rec. any financial aid	84
% UG rec. any financial aid	77
% UG borrow to pay for school	37
Average cumulative indebtedness	$25,575

SARAH LAWRENCE COLLEGE

ONE MEAD WAY, BRONXVILLE, NY 10708-5999 • ADMISSIONS: 914-395-2510 • FAX: 914-395-2515

STUDENTS SAY ". . ."

Academics

Nestled in a picturesque suburb of New York City, Sarah Lawrence College is a breath of fresh air for intellectually curious students who would chafe within the confines of a more traditional academic setting. The college prides itself on offering "a personal education" that's "tailored to [each] student's interests and needs." Indeed, "self-directed" is the key phrase here, and students really value "the flexibility and openness" that SLC provides. There are no majors or grades at SLC, only concentrations and evaluations (grades are given by professors and recorded by the Registrar). Undergrads are unanimous in their praise for the "conference system," which allows students to conduct "one-on-one" research with professors in topics of their choosing. Students also greatly appreciate "the strong focus on truly learning versus simply preparing…for [a] career." Importantly, "small" class sizes allow for lots of "discussion" and "close teacher relations." And when it comes to describing their professors, undergrads are full of superlatives. One content student describes them as "passionate, engaging, and extremely intelligent." She goes on to explain, "They take an interest in you personally to understand your goals, and then they cater their teaching to that." Further, they "are also readily available for any questions outside of class." Another student simply concludes, "I couldn't ask for more."

Life

While undergrads at SLC are very academically oriented, they also fortunately "engage in a wide variety of social activities." The arts are huge here, and attendance is always high for "theatrical productions, burlesque shows, [and] the annual *Rocky Horror Picture Show* shadowcast on Halloween." Additionally, "concerts by local and campus bands are pretty popular, as are dances." Moreover, "student art shows, film screenings, political lectures, guest speakers, and workshops take place on campus throughout the year." Though a "party scene exists and thrives," it's more common to attend smaller get-togethers or gather with close friends. A "typical Friday night involves an overcrowded room, several bottles of wine, a variety of poets and musicians jamming, and often home-cooked food." Students also love to take advantage of SLC's proximity to New York City (roughly twenty minutes away by train). Many people "go into the city on the weekends" and take in "a Broadway show, check out the farmers market in Union Square, or have a picnic in Central Park."

Student Body

Though undergrads at SLC would debate vociferously as to whether a typical student exists, many define their peers as "artistically and musically inclined, intelligent, voraciously well-read, [and] outspoken with a biting wit." While some might assert you could roam the campus playing a game of spot the "hipster," others insist that "you can find any type of person at Sarah Lawrence." One student goes further, saying, "We're all different, and we all love that. We fit in by not fitting in." Although undergrads are "friendly," some caution that they can also be "aloof" and "reclusive." Fortunately, everyone "can find their niche" and make a "close-knit" group of friends. Additionally, "lots of students here are also in the process of figuring out their sexual orientation and/or gender identity, so most people (even those who aren't figuring that out) are pretty open-minded." Indeed, students at SLC "take risks with style and identity." Perhaps this satisfied undergrad sums his fellow students up best: "Everyone is passionate about something and often several things, be they academic subjects, creative outlets, sports, or political causes, but you will never find two of us who are exactly alike in our interests. I think that makes us the most interesting student body there is, and there's no better place to find an engaging conversation about something completely unexpected."

SARAH LAWRENCE COLLEGE

FINANCIAL AID: 914-395-2570 • E-MAIL: SLCADMIT@SLC.EDU • WEBSITE: WWW.SARAHLAWRENCE.EDU

THE PRINCETON REVIEW SAYS

Admissions

Very important factors considered include: Application essay, recommendation(s), rigor of secondary school record. *Important factors considered include:* Academic GPA, extracurricular activities, talent/ability. *Other factors considered include:* Class rank, alumni/ae relation, character/personal qualities, first generation, geographical residence, interview, level of applicant's interest, racial/ethnic status, volunteer work, work experience. TOEFL required of all international applicants. High school diploma is required, and GED is accepted. *Academic units required:* 4 English, 2 mathematics, 2 science, 2 foreign language, 2 history. *Academic units recommended:* 4 mathematics, 4 science, 4 foreign language, 4 social studies, 4 history.

Financial Aid

Students should submit: FAFSA, CSS/Financial Aid PROFILE. Regular filing deadline is February 1. The Princeton Review suggests that all financial aid forms be submitted as soon as possible after January 1. *Need-based scholarships/grants offered:* Federal Pell, SEOG, state scholarships/grants, private scholarships, school scholarship or grant aid from institutional funds. *Loan aid offered:* Direct Subsidized Stafford, Direct Unsubsidized Stafford, Direct PLUS, Federal Perkins. Federal Work-Study Program available. Off-campus job opportunities are good.

The Inside Word

Admissions officers at SLC really take the time to try and understand who each applicant is, not only as a student but also as an individual. Candidates should display an inquisitive nature, a passion for learning, and the ability to be an independent thinker. Writing skills are considered critical at SLC and heavy consideration is given to each applicant's essays and short-answer questions. To the relief of some, standardized tests are no longer required.

THE SCHOOL SAYS " . . ."

From the Admissions Office

"Students who come to Sarah Lawrence are curious about the world, and they have an ardent desire to satisfy that curiosity. Sarah Lawrence offers such students two innovative academic structures: the seminar/conference system and the arts components. Courses in the humanities, social sciences, natural sciences, and mathematics are taught in the seminar/conference style. The seminars enroll an average of eleven students and consist of lecture, discussion, readings, and assigned papers. For each seminar, students also meet one-on-one in biweekly conferences, for which they conceive of individualized projects and shape them under the direction of professors. Arts components let students combine history and theory with practice. Painters, printmakers, photographers, sculptors, filmmakers, composers, musicians, choreographers, dancers, actors, and directors work in readily available studios, editing facilities, and darkrooms, guided by accomplished professionals. The secure, wooded campus is thirty minutes from midtown Manhattan, and the diversity of people and ideas at Sarah Lawrence make it an extraordinary educational environment.

"Sarah Lawrence College no longer uses standardized test scores in the admission process. This decision reflects our conviction that overemphasis on test preparation can distort results and make the application process inordinately stressful, and that academic success is better predicted by the student's course rigor, their grades, recommendations, and writing ability."

SELECTIVITY

Admissions Rating	87
# of applicants	1,925
% of applicants accepted	62
% of acceptees attending	28
# of early decision applicants	149
% accepted early decision	56

FRESHMAN PROFILE

Minimum paper TOEFL	600
Minimum computer TOEFL	250
Average HS GPA	3.60
% graduated top 10% of class	46
% graduated top 25% of class	79
% graduated top 50% of class	97

DEADLINES

Early decision	
Deadline	11/1
Notification	12/15
Regular	
Deadline	1/1
Nonfall registration?	no

FINANCIAL FACTS

Financial Aid Rating	88
Annual tuition	$44,220
Room and board	$13,958
Required fees	$992
Books and supplies	$600
% frosh rec. need-based scholarship or grant aid	56
% UG rec. need-based scholarship or grant aid	60
% frosh rec. need-based self-help aid	52
% UG rec. need-based self-help aid	58
% frosh rec. any financial aid	59
% UG rec. any financial aid	61
% UG borrow to pay for school	55
Average cumulative indebtedness	$21,590

SCRIPPS COLLEGE

1030 COLUMBIA AVENUE, MAILBOX #1265, CLAREMONT, CA 91711 • ADMISSIONS: 909-621-8149 • FAX: 909-607-7508

STUDENTS SAY ". . ."

Academics

Scripps College is for serious female students looking "to get away from the preppy, East Coast feeling" of other "top-notch" liberal arts educations. Due to its membership in the Claremont College Consortium, Scripps provides the "intimacy of a small school" environment while boasting "the resources of a large university." With an "emphasis on analytical thinking and creativity" Scripps' unique Core program focuses on "broadening minds and teaching students how to think" while presenting "learning in a way that is socially conscious." Scripps' "humanities-based education" takes an "interdisciplinary approach to learning, which allows the mind to cultivate and [to] make connections amongst all subjects, creating strong, intellectual women" and providing them with "the skills to become leaders in their chosen fields." At Scripps "it's difficult to go 'under the radar'" because "the professors are extremely caring and attentive to their students' needs." Small class sizes are "an instant appeal." According to many students, Scripps "is the best of both worlds…intimacy of a small school with resources of a small-to-medium university, atmosphere of a women's college with the benefits of co-education (through the other Claremont Colleges), [and] small-town feel with LA an easy hour away by Metrolink." Dedicated to "turning loose generation after generation of confident, hopeful, courageous, and inspiring women," the school offers "a good variety of courses."

Life

"Scripps is a place where women are challenged to stretch themselves academically, have a strong voice, pursue their passions (whatever they may be), and love every minute of it." What natural luxuries the "warm weather" and "laid-back California atmosphere" provide, the school capitalizes upon: from its "beautiful grounds and dorms," to "the brand-new Sally Tiernan Field House, [which] makes working out fun and easy." "Devoted to creating strong female leaders," as one hardcore Scripps enthusiast proclaims, Scripps "is a playground for the mind, body, and spirit that allows you to learn, grow, and understand yourself and the world." For relaxation, students "will go into town or hang out at the Motley, the school coffeehouse." On a quiet night, students "watch movies, hang out in The Village, go to the theater on campus, and [find] many other extracurricular activates." Though the Five College Consortium offers numerous party options, "for those not interested in the party scene, residence halls often host evening soirees; there are numerous art openings." "Many students enjoy the weather and the opportunity for outdoor activities (surfing, skiing, hiking, etc.)." Others who have found their way into the city appreciate "the proximity to movie theaters and LA."

Student Body

"Inspiring, strong women out to change the world" who are united by curiosity and intellect, all Scripps students "are intelligent and have a passion." Scripps students are "feminist liberals who will go on to change the world with their elite education, but [they] will do so with fun and style." Though the "'typical' student is upper-middle-class, overachiever, from SoCal, the pacific northwest, or the East Coast," "there are many exceptions to this." The stereotypes at Scripps' tends to be 'Militant Feminist' or 'Daddy's Girl.' We all sort of laugh at that because neither of those are a majority here." Though the average student is "politically liberal [and] somewhat idealistic [and] enjoys obscure music and literature," "there are all kinds of women—outspoken lesbians, very outdoorsy types, girls who love to party, extreme intellects, etc." The bottom line is at Scripps "women support women." "I didn't intend on going to a women's college, but I am really glad that I did. It's been a great experience; it's helped me to build confidence in a world that is still male-dominated."

SCRIPPS COLLEGE

FINANCIAL AID: 909-621-8275 • E-MAIL: ADMISSION@SCRIPPSCOLLEGE.EDU • WEBSITE: WWW.SCRIPPSCOLLEGE.EDU

THE PRINCETON REVIEW SAYS

Admissions

Very important factors considered include: Academic record, rigor of secondary school record, standardized test scores, application essay, recommendations, character/personal qualities, co-curricular activities, first generation. SAT or ACT with writing required. TOEFL (IBT minimum score of 100) or IELTS (minimum score of 7) required of all international applicants. *Academic units required:* 4 English, 3 mathematics, 3 science, 3 foreign language, 3 social studies. *Academic units recommended:* 4 English, 4 mathematics, 3 science, 3 foreign language, 3 social studies.

Financial Aid

Students should submit: FAFSA, CSS/Financial Aid PROFILE. Regular filing deadline is February 1. The Princeton Review suggests that all financial aid forms be submitted as soon as possible after January 1. *Need-based scholarships/grants offered:* Federal Pell, SEOG, state scholarships/grants, private scholarships, school scholarship or grant aid from institutional funds. *Loan aid offered:* Direct Subsidized Stafford, Direct Unsubsidized Stafford, Direct PLUS, Federal Perkins, university loans from institutional funds. Applicants will be notified of awards at the time of admission. Federal Work-Study Program available. Off-campus job opportunities are good.

The Inside Word

Though academic excellence is a prerequisite, when it comes to applying to Scripps, admissions is based on more than just the usual suspects. In lieu of formulas or standardized test minimums, admissions officers aim to establish a diverse and talented first-year class and do so by evaluating a variety of factors. Serious candidates should carve out a unique personal statement while giving equal attention to each facet of their application. Strong writing skills and intellectual curiosity are viewed as essential qualities in successful applicants.

THE SCHOOL SAYS " . . ."

From the Admissions Office

"What distinguishes Scripps College from other liberal arts colleges is our interdisciplinary Core Curriculum, which emphasizes critical thinking and intellectual innovation. We believe that learning involves much more than amassing information. A truly educated person can think analytically, communicate effectively, question confidently, and create change in the world. Our curriculum balances breadth requirements in all areas of the liberal arts; a multicultural and a gender studies requirement; and major coursework in sixty different fields. With an average class size of fifteen, students are comfortable participating, challenging old assumptions, and testing new ideas. More than a quarter of all Scripps College students dual or double major, and all complete a senior thesis or performance/project. Almost half study abroad, and, on campus, they can choose from a vast range of clubs, organizations, and activities to participate in through the Claremont Colleges Consortium."

SELECTIVITY
Admissions Rating	96
# of applicants	2,097
% of applicants accepted	39
% of acceptees attending	32
# accepting a place on wait list	139
% admitted from wait list	6
# of early decision applicants	142
% accepted early decision	57

FRESHMAN PROFILE
Range SAT Critical Reading	640–740
Range SAT Math	630–710
Range SAT Writing	640–740
Range ACT Composite	28–32
Minimum paper TOEFL	600
Minimum computer TOEFL	250
Average HS GPA	4.10
% graduated top 10% of class	37
% graduated top 25% of class	62
% graduated top 50% of class	78

DEADLINES
Early decision	
Deadline	11/15
Notification	12/15
Early action	
Deadline	1/2
Notification	2/15
Regular	
Deadline	1/2
Notification	4/1
Nonfall registration?	yes

APPLICANTS ALSO LOOK AT AND OFTEN PREFER
Barnard College, Harvard College, Oberlin College, Occidental College, Pitzer College, Pomona College, Stanford University, Tufts University, University of California—Berkeley, University of California—Los Angeles, University of Southern California, Wellesley College

FINANCIAL FACTS
Financial Aid Rating	95
Annual tuition	$40,236
Room and board	$12,450
Required fees	$214
Books and supplies	$800
% frosh rec. need-based scholarship or grant aid	44
% UG rec. need-based scholarship or grant aid	37
% frosh rec. non-need-based scholarship or grant aid	4
% UG rec. non-need-based scholarship or grant aid	3
% frosh rec. need-based self-help aid	39
% UG rec. need-based self-help aid	37
% frosh rec. any financial aid	49
% UG rec. any financial aid	54
% UG borrow to pay for school	36
Average cumulative indebtedness	$9,435

SEATTLE UNIVERSITY

ADMISSIONS OFFICE, 900 BROADWAY, SEATTLE, WA 98122-4340 • ADMISSIONS: 206-296-2000 • FAX: 206-296-5656

CAMPUS LIFE

Quality of Life Rating	93
Fire Safety Rating	81
Green Rating	95
Type of school	private
Affiliation	Roman Catholic-Jesuit
Environment	metropolis

STUDENTS

Total undergrad enrollment	4,565
% male/female	39/61
% from out of state	50
% from public high school	63
% live on campus	42
% African American	6
% Asian	18
% Caucasian	52
% Hispanic	8
% Native American	1
% international	9
# of countries represented	95

SURVEY SAYS . . .

No one cheats
Great computer facilities
School is well-run
Diverse student types on campus
Students get along with local community
Students love Seattle, WA
Great off-campus food
Frats and sororities are unpopular or nonexistent

ACADEMICS

Academic Rating	87
% students graduating within 4 years	59
% students graduating within 6 years	75
Calendar	quarter
Student/faculty ratio	13:1
Profs interesting rating	90
Profs accessible rating	90
Most common reg class size	10–19 students
Most common lab size	10–19 students

MOST POPULAR MAJORS
nursing, management, psychology, English, finance

STUDENTS SAY ". . ."

Academics

Seattle University is a midsize Jesuit university that "offers a community experience in which students can learn and grow together." "Between its academic excellence, exceptional facilities, location, and social justice focus, this school offers the holistic Jesuit educational experience in a dynamic setting appropriate for the scholars of the twenty-first century." Issues of "community and social justice in a complex world" permeate the curriculum here, "pushing students to reevaluate their presuppositions about the world in a just and humane manner." Academically, SU "is very strong and very challenging," but great support networks—including a writing center, a math lab, and an encouraging faculty help students cope. According to students, professors "all respond to e-mails…leave us their cell phone numbers," and "will meet after hours to talk about an assignment." A "prestigious nursing program" tops a list of outstanding departments that also include public affairs, criminal justice, civil engineering, and business. Throughout the university, "SU believes in emphasizing the human aspect of education, and so access to faculty and administrative staff is seamless. Our president walks around and talks to students, and the entire administration is very visible on campus."

Life

SU students are "lucky enough to live in the middle of one of the most exciting cities in the country," and most take full advantage of the situation. "Being in Capitol Hill, there's more than enough restaurants, theaters, museums, concerts, parks, book stores/libraries to suit anyone's palate," while the greater city "is fun to explore, so weekends are not limited to sitting around drinking." Seattle is a music town, so "There is a lot of live music—both on campus and off—as well as movies." Students also venture into the city to perform community service, a popular vocation among SU undergrads. Traveling just a bit beyond city limits, students find an area "perfect for outdoorsy things like snowboarding/skiing in the winter or rock-climbing/hiking/camping in the fall and spring. The school usually sponsors these types of trips for easy access." On-campus options are "fun for all types of people," with events ranging from concerts, "sporting events, magicians, musical talent, speakers, and lots of different types of food to try," as well as "hundreds of events ranging from community cookie-baking to giant drag shows or cultural festivals. Residence halls have programming daily, and it's always some sort of awareness month or week. This is an active campus." There's also "a party life at Seattle U, but it's smaller than state schools." As one student puts it, "it's definitely not a party school, but those who like to party will be able to find something. There's really a place for everybody."

Student Body

SU attracts a lot of "generally nice, down-to-earth people" who "are using their college experience to launch into their post-college career and not as a four-year vacation before work starts." Students here "are very independent-minded. Everyone has plans set, and they want to succeed at what they're setting out to do. But with that said, we all get along really well, and everyone hangs out with each other. There's little separation between majors, and it helps that the residence halls aren't divided up by academics." They also tend to be the sort of folks who "want to make a difference in the world: business majors, music majors, English majors; we all want to help out." They're "pretty aware of events going on in the world—and care." Environmental awareness "is a huge part of campus community, as is community service." Students pride themselves on SU's "pretty diverse" population, which includes "a lot of international students," a "large gay population," and "quite a few nontraditional [older than twenty-five] students" in the mix.

FINANCIAL AID: 206-296-2000 • E-MAIL: ADMISSIONS@SEATTLEU.EDU • WEBSITE: WWW.SEATTLEU.EDU

THE PRINCETON REVIEW SAYS

Admissions

Very important factors considered include: Academic GPA, rigor of secondary school record, standardized test scores, character/personal qualities. *Important factors considered include:* Application essay, recommendation(s), extracurricular activities, level of applicant's interest. *Other factors considered include:* Class rank, alumni/ae relation, first generation, geographical residence, interview, racial/ethnic status, religious affiliation/commitment, state residency, talent/ability, volunteer work, work experience. SAT or ACT required; ACT with or without writing component accepted. TOEFL required of international applicants who are non-native English speakers. High school diploma is required, and GED is accepted. *Academic units required:* 4 English, 3 mathematics, 2 science (2 science labs), 2 foreign language, 2 social studies, 1 history, 2 academic elective. *Academic units recommended:* 4 English, 4 mathematics, 2 science (2 science labs), 2 foreign language, 2 social studies, 1 history, 2 academic elective.

Financial Aid

Students should submit: FAFSA. Regular filing deadline is February 1. The Princeton Review suggests that all financial aid forms be submitted as soon as possible after January 1. *Need-based scholarships/grants offered:* Federal Pell, SEOG, state scholarships/grants, private scholarships, school scholarship or grant aid from institutional funds, Federal Nursing Scholarships. *Loan aid offered:* Direct Subsidized Stafford, Direct Unsubsidized Stafford, Direct PLUS, Federal Perkins, Federal Nursing Loans. Applicants will be notified of awards on a rolling basis beginning March 21.

The Inside Word

School has more stringent test score and course work requirements for certain majors. Because this is a Jesuit school, admissions officers tend to value community service. Those who demonstrate a significant commitment to volunteering will find themselves at an advantage, as will those who convey a clear sense of their academic and career goals.

THE SCHOOL SAYS "..."

From the Admissions Office

"Seattle University provides an ideal environment for motivated students interested in self-reliance, awareness of different cultures, social justice, and the fulfillment that comes from making a difference. Our urban setting promotes the development of leadership skills and independence as well as providing a variety of opportunities for students to apply what they learn through internships, clinical experiences, and volunteer work. It is an environment that allows us to empower leaders for a just and humane world.

"Our academic offerings are designed to provide leadership opportunities as well as to develop global awareness and enable graduates to serve society through a demanding liberal arts and sciences foundation. In the Jesuit tradition, we teach our students how to think, not what to think. Professional undergraduate offerings include highly respected schools of business, nursing, and science and engineering, as well as career-oriented liberal arts programs such as creative writing, journalism, communications, and criminal justice.

"While located in the center of the city, Seattle University is a true residential campus, including students from forty-eight states and territories and ninety-five different nations. Washington State has designated the campus as an 'official backyard sanctuary' for its striking landscaping and environmentally conscious practices—several buildings enjoy official 'green' designations, and the student-run recycling program continually receives national recognition. Additionally, Seattle University is proud of its distinction as the most ethnically diverse institution in the Northwest—all students are valued and respected for their individual strengths, experiences, and worth."

SELECTIVITY

Admissions Rating	87
# of applicants	6,186
% of applicants accepted	71
% of acceptees attending	24
# accepting a place on wait list	385
% admitted from wait list	1

FRESHMAN PROFILE

Range SAT Critical Reading	530–640
Range SAT Math	520–630
Range SAT Writing	520–630
Range ACT Composite	24–29
Minimum paper TOEFL	520
Minimum computer TOEFL	190
Average HS GPA	3.58
% graduated top 10% of class	31
% graduated top 25% of class	64
% graduated top 50% of class	93

DEADLINES

Early action	
Deadline	11/15
Notification	12/23
Regular	
Priority	1/15
Notification	3/1
Nonfall registration?	yes

APPLICANTS ALSO LOOK AT
AND OFTEN PREFER
Gonzaga University, University of Portland, University of Washington

AND SOMETIMES PREFER
Santa Clara University, Washington State University

AND RARELY PREFER
Pacific Lutheran University, Western Washington University

FINANCIAL FACTS

Financial Aid Rating	81
Annual tuition	$32,400
Room and board	$4,855
Books and supplies	$1,440
% frosh rec. need-based scholarship or grant aid	68
% UG rec. need-based scholarship or grant aid	59
% frosh rec. non-need-based scholarship or grant aid	44
% UG rec. non-need-based scholarship or grant aid	27
% frosh rec. need-based self-help aid	61
% UG rec. need-based self-help aid	54
% frosh rec. any financial aid	75
% UG rec. any financial aid	66
% UG borrow to pay for school	74
Average cumulative indebtedness	$26,607

SETON HALL UNIVERSITY

ENROLLMENT SERVICES, 400 SOUTH ORANGE AVENUE, SOUTH ORANGE, NJ 07079 • ADMISSIONS: 973-761-9332 • FAX: 973-275-2040

CAMPUS LIFE

Quality of Life Rating	68
Fire Safety Rating	83
Green Rating	60*
Type of school	private
Affiliation	Roman Catholic
Environment	village

STUDENTS

Total undergrad enrollment	4,972
% male/female	42/58
% from out of state	25
% from public high school	70
% live on campus	43
% African American	14
% Asian	7
% Caucasian	53
% Hispanic	12
% international	2
# of countries represented	71

SURVEY SAYS . . .
Great computer facilities
Diverse student types on campus
College radio is popular
Student publications are popular

ACADEMICS

Academic Rating	74
% students graduating within 4 years	50
% students graduating within 6 years	63
Calendar	semester
Student/faculty ratio	14:1
Profs interesting rating	76
Profs accessible rating	72
Most common reg class size	10–19 students
Most common lab size	10–19 students

MOST POPULAR MAJORS
criminal justice/safety studies, speech communication and rhetoric

STUDENTS SAY ". . ."

Academics

"All the colleges within the university are well regarded" at Seton Hall, a prominent Catholic university just down the road from New York City, but the Stillman School of Business and the Whitehead School of Diplomacy and International Relations "are considered the best schools on campus" and thus typically garner the most attention, and understandably so. The former features "a great sports management program" and an attractive, five-year BA/Masters in accounting. Students benefit from proximity to New York, which creates the opportunity for valuable internships, especially in finance. The latter "is directly affiliated with the United Nations," a relationship that "provides students with professors who have had experience with international relations, whether it be ambassadors or foreign correspondents." SHU also excels in nursing, and the university's commitment to keeping pace with technology gives all students a leg up in the modern job market. Indeed, the school works hard "to link the academic world with the real world" through "study abroad, internships, international speakers and events." "The core curriculum gives all students a great foundation beyond their majors so that students are well-rounded individuals with a variety of experiences upon graduation," undergrads report. Students warn, "There is a lot of red tape at Seton Hall."

Life

The school is located in South Orange, "a boring town for college-age students." A much more appealing town, New York City, is "a twenty-minute train ride [from campus], so a lot of people go to the city for fun." Add to that the fact that "most of the student body lives in North Jersey, so it's easy for them to go home for the weekend," and many do just that. Greek life "is very popular," and the school's "big-time men's basketball program" is a huge draw. "Students are always attending basketball games" and "praying that the team does not suck." Intramurals "can be very competitive," "the athletic facilities are state-of-the-art."

Student Body

Seton Hall "is sort of a mishmash of different types. There are a lot of jocks who are definitely treated like stars by the administration, although not so much by the average professor," and "there are some very academic students who mostly try to ignore the actual school and focus on internships and study abroad opportunities." And then there's "the average student, who is from New Jersey, has a major in the School of Arts and Sciences or Business, parties on Thursdays, goes home on weekends, and coasts through college on loans their parents have taken out." "While Seton Hall is a Catholic university, "it is not difficult to find students of other religions," and "the school is accepting of all religious beliefs." Indeed, SHU is big enough that "there are a lot of different kinds of people," and "everyone finds his place by sophomore year."

FINANCIAL AID: 973-761-9332 • E-MAIL: THEHALL@SHU.EDU • WEBSITE: WWW.SHU.EDU

THE PRINCETON REVIEW SAYS

Admissions

Very important factors considered include: Academic GPA, application essay, recommendation(s), rigor of secondary school record, standardized test scores. *Important factors considered include:* Extracurricular activities, volunteer work, work experience. *Other factors considered include:* Class rank, character/personal qualities, interview, talent/ability. SAT or ACT required; ACT with writing component required. TOEFL required of all international applicants. High school diploma is required, and GED is accepted. *Academic units required:* 4 English, 3 mathematics, 1 science (1 science lab), 2 foreign language, 2 social studies, 4 academic elective.

Financial Aid

Students should submit: FAFSA. The Princeton Review suggests that all financial aid forms be submitted as soon as possible after January 1. *Need-based scholarships/grants offered:* Federal Pell, SEOG, state scholarships/grants, private scholarships, school scholarship or grant aid from institutional funds. *Loan aid offered:* Direct Subsidized Stafford, Direct Unsubsidized Stafford, Direct PLUS, Federal Perkins, state loans. Applicants will be notified of awards on a rolling basis beginning March 1. Federal Work-Study Program available. Off-campus job opportunities are good.

The Inside Word

Students seeking a good school with solid, Catholic roots should consider Seton Hall, whose proximity to New York City helps the school draw prestigious faculty and affords students excellent access to educational, internship, and entertainment opportunities. Applicants who show decent grades in a college preparatory curriculum coupled with strong recommendations should have little trouble gaining admission here. Top students may be pleasantly surprised by the school's financial aid offers.

THE SCHOOL SAYS ". . ."

From the Admissions Office

"For more than 150 years, Seton Hall University has been a catalyst for leadership, developing the whole student—mind, heart and spirit. As a Catholic university that embraces students of all races and religions, Seton Hall combines the resources of a large university with the personal attention of a small liberal arts college. The university's attractive suburban campus is only fourteen miles by train, bus or car to New York City, with the wealth of employment, internship, cultural, and entertainment opportunities the city offers. Outstanding faculty, a technologically advanced campus, and a values-centered curriculum challenge Seton Hall students. Students are exposed to a world of ideas from great scholars, opening their minds to the perspectives, history and achievements of many cultures. Our new core curriculum focuses on the need for our students to have common experiences and encourages them to become thinking, caring, communicative and ethically responsible leaders while emphasizing practical proficiencies and intellectual development. Our commitment to our students goes beyond textbooks and homework assignments, though. At Seton Hall, developing servant leaders who will make a difference in the world is a priority. That's why all students take classes in ethics and learn in a community informed by Catholic ideals and universal values. While Seton Hall certainly enjoys a big reputation, our campus community is close-knit and inclusive. Students, faculty and staff come from around the world, bringing with them a kaleidoscope of experiences and perspectives to create a diverse yet unified campus environment."

SELECTIVITY

Admissions Rating	81
# of applicants	10,851
% of applicants accepted	79
% of acceptees attending	13
# accepting a place on wait list	0

FRESHMAN PROFILE

Range SAT Critical Reading	470–570
Range SAT Math	470–580
Range SAT Writing	480–580
Range ACT Composite	20–25
Minimum paper TOEFL	550
Minimum computer TOEFL	213
Average HS GPA	3.13
% graduated top 10% of class	22
% graduated top 25% of class	50
% graduated top 50% of class	83

DEADLINES

Early action	
Deadline	11/15
Notification	12/31
Regular	
Priority	3/1
Notification	12/1
Nonfall registration?	yes

APPLICANTS ALSO LOOK AT

AND OFTEN PREFER
New York University, Penn State—University Park, William Patterson University

AND SOMETIMES PREFER
Fairfield University, Fordham University, Rider University, University of Connecticut

AND RARELY PREFER
Hofstra University, Monmouth University (NJ), Ramapo College of New Jersey, St. Bonaventure University

FINANCIAL FACTS

Financial Aid Rating	68
Annual tuition	$29,940
Room and board	$12,050
Required fees	$1,950
Books and supplies	$1,300
% frosh rec. need-based scholarship or grant aid	54
% UG rec. need-based scholarship or grant aid	38
% frosh rec. non-need-based scholarship or grant aid	47
% UG rec. non-need-based scholarship or grant aid	33
% frosh rec. need-based self-help aid	45
% UG rec. need-based self-help aid	45
% frosh rec. any financial aid	91
% UG rec. any financial aid	86
% UG borrow to pay for school	6
Average cumulative indebtedness	$16,160

SEWANEE—THE UNIVERSITY OF THE SOUTH

735 UNIVERSITY AVENUE, SEWANEE, TN 37383-1000 • ADMISSIONS: 931-598-1238 • FAX: 931-538-3248

CAMPUS LIFE

Quality of Life Rating	81
Fire Safety Rating	90
Green Rating	93
Type of school	private
Affiliation	Episcopal
Environment	rural

STUDENTS

Total undergrad enrollment	1,455
% male/female	47/53
% from out of state	76
% from public high school	50
% live on campus	93
# of fraternities	12
# of sororities	9
% African American	4
% Asian	2
% Caucasian	84
% Hispanic	3
% international	2
# of countries represented	23

SURVEY SAYS . . .
No one cheats
Students are friendly
Campus feels safe
Students are happy
Frats and sororities dominate
social scene
Lots of beer drinking
Hard liquor is popular

ACADEMICS

Academic Rating	92
Calendar	semester
Student/faculty ratio	11:1
Profs interesting rating	97
Profs accessible rating	94
Most common reg class size	10–19 students
Most common lab size	20–29 students

MOST POPULAR MAJORS
economics, English literature, history,
environmental studies

STUDENTS SAY " . . ."

Academics
The University of the South is a small, "very demanding" school "in the middle of rural Tennessee." Students describe it as "an oasis of perfection" "dripping with both Southern and academic tradition." "Sewanee embodies what a liberal arts education should," beams a history major. Classes are "small" and there's a "well-rounded curriculum." "The volume of work can make you want to pull your hair out," warns an economics major. "Sewanee does not inflate grades," either. "You must work hard to earn an A." "Occasionally a professor or two takes the absent-minded professor stereotype to a ridiculous level," but "it is hard to find a truly bad teacher among the whole lot." Professors here "care about their students." "Their passion for their fields and students is unparalleled." Profs are also very approachable. "We have incredible access to the faculty," gushes a religion major. "Many professors invite students to their homes for social and educational activities somewhat regularly," adds a music major. Students also love the "extremely reachable" administration. The only complaint we hear about academic life concerns the lack of course availability.

Life
Some dorms at Sewanee "really need some work." "Give me air conditioning," demands a sweaty sophomore. The school is generally "behind technologically" as well. The "secluded" town that surrounds the school is "void of any good restaurants, bars, and general distractions a city provides." The campus is "absolutely gorgeous," though. It's a "serene haven" in "an idyllic setting" atop a mountain. Also, the school owns an "incredible amount of land." "Hiking the beautiful perimeter trail" is a favorite pastime, and students can bike, kayak, and "play in the woods" to their hearts' content. Socially, "Sewanee is unique in its quirks." There's a revered honor code. Faculty members wear academic gowns when they teach, and "most Sewanee students follow the tradition of dressing up for class." You'll see men in bow ties and seersucker suits and women in "pointy heels and pearls." There's also an "ever-present" sense of community. "You can't compartmentalize your life here," and for good or ill, "everyone knows what everyone else did last night." During the week, studying is paramount. "We spend a lot of time in the library," notes a sophomore. However, alcohol policies here are "lenient" and "Sewanee is a pretty big party school." Booze is "by no means forced upon you," but "students here drink often and heavily." The frat scene is absolutely massive. "Almost everyone becomes involved in a fraternity or a sorority." "The administration requires all Greek events to be open to the entire campus," but "There is no other social network except the Greek organizations."

Student Body
Even though the administration here is "pushing the diversity card to the nth degree," Sewanee is "strikingly homogenous." "A lot more students here are liberal than you would guess," and Yankees are "not viewed as aliens," but "Sewanee is a Southern and conservative school in every sense of the word." Students are typically "laid-back," "rich, conservative, and fun" "children of the Southern aristocracy" who like to "get drunk on the weekends." Some are "heavily spoiled and coddled." "We have lots of cookie-cutter, preppy, extreme social drinkers, but then again you can also find people who wear only organic hemp, sleep outside, and have dreadlocks," explains a junior. "There are a lot of outdoorsy styles mixed in as well." While "social arrangements are very cliquish," students tell us they are "relatively peacefully coexisting." "It really is one of the friendliest communities that I have ever seen," declares a sophomore.

FINANCIAL AID: 931-598-1312 • E-MAIL: COLLEGEADMISSION@SEWANEE.EDU • WEBSITE: WWW.SEWANEE.EDU

THE PRINCETON REVIEW SAYS

Admissions

Very important factors considered include: Academic GPA, recommendation(s), rigor of secondary school record. *Important factors considered include:* Application essay, standardized test scores, character/personal qualities, extracurricular activities, volunteer work, work experience. *Other factors considered include:* Class rank, alumni/ae relation, first generation, geographical residence, interview, level of applicant's interest, racial/ethnic status, talent/ability. ACT with writing component required. TOEFL required of all international applicants. *Academic units required:* 4 English, 3 mathematics, 2 science (2 science labs), 2 foreign language, 1 social studies, 1 history. *Academic units recommended:* 4 English, 4 mathematics, 4 science (3 science labs), 4 foreign language, 2 social studies, 2 history.

Financial Aid

Students should submit: FAFSA, institution's own financial aid form. The Princeton Review suggests that all financial aid forms be submitted as soon as possible after January 1. *Need-based scholarships/grants offered:* Federal Pell, SEOG, state scholarships/grants, private scholarships, school scholarship or grant aid from institutional funds. *Loan aid offered:* Direct Subsidized Stafford, Direct Unsubsidized Stafford, Direct PLUS, Federal Perkins, state loans, university loans from institutional funds. Federal Work-Study Program available. Off-campus job opportunities are fair.

The Inside Word

The admissions office at Sewanee is very personable and accessible to students. Its staff includes some of the most well-respected admissions professionals in the South, and it shows in the way they work with students. Despite a fairly high acceptance rate, candidates who take the admissions process here lightly may find themselves disappointed. Applicant evaluation is too personal for a lackadaisical approach to succeed.

THE SCHOOL SAYS " . . ."

From the Admissions Office

"Sewanee is consistently ranked among the top tier of national liberal arts universities. Sewanee is committed to a rigorous academic curriculum that focuses on the liberal arts as the most enlightening and valuable form of undergraduate education. It offers thirty-six majors, thirty-two minors, and pre-professional programs including business, medicine, and education. Founded by leaders of the Episcopal Church in 1857, Sewanee continues to be owned by twenty-eight Episcopal dioceses in twelve states. The university is located on a 13,000-acre campus atop Tennessee's Cumberland Plateau between Chattanooga and Nashville. Largely forested, rich in biodiversity, this land is a distinctive asset offering an unparalleled outdoor laboratory and boundless recreational opportunities.

"The university has an impressive record of academic achievement—twenty-five Rhodes Scholars and twenty-seven NCAA postgraduate scholarship recipients have graduated from Sewanee. Four of the last eight Tennessee Professors of the Year have been members of Sewanee's faculty. Professors are leading scholars and researchers with a commitment to teaching, and in Sewanee's close community they develop rich and enduring relationships with their students.

"Beginning in 2009, prospective students may choose not to submit standardized test scores. Those who make that choice must instead submit a graded academic paper and complete an evaluative interview with a Sewanee representative. Other critical factors long considered in the Sewanee admission process remain, including strength of the high school curriculum, high school academic performance, extracurricular activities, and evidence of character and talent."

SELECTIVITY

Admissions Rating	92
# of applicants	2,765
% of applicants accepted	62
% of acceptees attending	23
# accepting a place on wait list	58
% admitted from wait list	31
# of early decision applicants	110
% accepted early decision	66

FRESHMAN PROFILE

Range SAT Critical Reading	580–690
Range SAT Math	580–670
Range SAT Writing	570–680
Range ACT Composite	26–30
Minimum paper TOEFL	550
Minimum computer TOEFL	213
Minimum web-based TOEFL	80
Average HS GPA	3.62
% graduated top 10% of class	50
% graduated top 25% of class	77
% graduated top 50% of class	92

DEADLINES

Early decision	
Deadline	11/15
Notification	12/17
Regular	
Deadline	2/1
Nonfall registration?	no

APPLICANTS ALSO LOOK AT AND OFTEN PREFER

Washington and Lee University

FINANCIAL FACTS

Financial Aid Rating	91
Annual comprehensive tuition	$41,518
Books and supplies	$800
% frosh rec. need-based scholarship or grant aid	33
% UG rec. need-based scholarship or grant aid	34
% frosh rec. non-need-based scholarship or grant aid	29
% UG rec. non-need-based scholarship or grant aid	17
% frosh rec. need-based self-help aid	25
% UG rec. need-based self-help aid	25
% frosh rec. any financial aid	79
% UG rec. any financial aid	74
% UG borrow to pay for school	39
Average cumulative indebtedness	$19,337

SIMMONS COLLEGE

300 THE FENWAY, BOSTON, MA 02115 • ADMISSIONS: 617-521-2051 • FAX: 617-521-3190

STUDENTS SAY ". . ."

Academics

A women's college "rich in history and achievement," Simmons College equips its undergraduates with the tools and confidence they need to succeed in the real-world. With a small student population of about 2,000, Simmons offers a surprisingly wide range of undergraduate majors, while also running one of the "top nursing schools in the state." Across academic programs, there's a "particular focus on experiential learning and leadership," and the curriculum excels at "educating women for positions of powerful and principled leadership." Simmons professors "do everything in their power to help us get an internship, to learn, to interact with the material, and to prepare us for life after college" and students get valuable hands-on experience through research, "community engagement," and "leadership opportunities" in campus groups. A chemistry major remembers, "My college has many research opportunities and connections. I have been able to do scientific research every semester since my first year at Simmons." Small discussion-based classes "really challenge you to do your best and to actually put some thought into your work," and Simmons professors are "interested in every student succeeding in the classroom, as well as in their future endeavors." Within administrative offices, there's "very little red tape," and the school succeeds at "giving students power to make decisions in the school, including policy, academics, administration, [and] events." "Resources are wonderful, from the career education center to the writing center to the technology center," and the college "takes advantage of its Boston location through class trips, job placement, and internship opportunities." However, when it comes to the all-important problem of paying for school, students admit that the "financial aid counselors could be more helpful."

Life

America's most college-friendly city, Boston makes a great backdrop for life at Simmons. Packed with culture and entertainment, "The city offers many great places to hang out like bowling places, karaoke bars, college parties at other colleges, and great scenery." In addition, Simmons is part of the Colleges of the Fenway association, so "Students get discounts at art museums and cultural events around the city such as plays or dances." "Simmons is not a party school," so those who want to carouse "venture out in the city" or head to nearby colleges. Other students prefer mellower activities, like "sitting in the common room and talking or watching a show together." Since so much social life takes place off campus, "The dorms are quiet and a great place to concentrate on school work." The peacefulness of campus is a plus for many students, who "spend a lot of time studying and preparing for labs and lecture." To blow off steam, "A lot of students here use the gym on a regular basis," and the campus athletic center offers "Zumba, kick boxing, spinning, and boot camps." "Simmons College is also very big on community service," and many students volunteer at organizations around Boston.

Student Body

Besides the fact that they're all female, Simmons students say there's a lot of diversity on their small campus. "Diversity is strongly valued," and "The community here is very accepting, regardless of race, ethnicity, economic status, religion, sexual orientation, gender expression, or disability." Politically, you'll meet students who are "very conservative to very liberal," though "most students are very supportive of the LGBTA community and women's rights in general." When it come to academics, "Students are very dedicated and take their school work seriously," though they also make time for fun. Socially, "Birds of a feather flock together," and students admit, "There are different cliques within the student body." However, "Everyone is generally accepted" on this friendly and community-oriented campus. In fact, some students say Simmons feels "like a big sorority."

SIMMONS COLLEGE

FINANCIAL AID: 617-521-2001 • E-MAIL: UGADM@SIMMONS.EDU • WEBSITE: WWW.SIMMONS.EDU

THE PRINCETON REVIEW SAYS

Admissions

Very important factors considered include: Academic GPA, rigor of secondary school record. *Important factors considered include:* Application essay, class rank, recommendation(s), standardized test scores. *Other factors considered include:* Extracurricular activities, interview, talent/ability, volunteer work, work experience. SAT or ACT required; ACT with or without writing component accepted. TOEFL required of all international applicants. High school diploma is required, and GED is accepted. *Academic units required:* 4 English, 3 mathematics, 3 science, 3 foreign language, 3 social studies, 3 history. *Academic units recommended:* 4 English, 4 mathematics, 3 science, 4 foreign language, 4 social studies, 3 history.

Financial Aid

Students should submit: FAFSA, institution's own financial aid form. Regular filing deadline is March 1. The Princeton Review suggests that all financial aid forms be submitted as soon as possible after January 1. *Need-based scholarships/grants offered:* Federal Pell, SEOG, state scholarships/grants, private scholarships, school scholarship or grant aid from institutional funds. *Loan aid offered:* Direct Subsidized Stafford, Direct Unsubsidized Stafford, Direct PLUS, state loans, university loans from institutional funds. Applicants will be notified of awards on a rolling basis beginning March 15. Federal Work-Study Program available. Off-campus job opportunities are excellent.

The Inside Word

Simmons evaluates prospective students for both academic strength and personal qualities, like community involvement or leadership. Applicants to Simmons should use their personal essays, letters of recommendation, and applications to show the admissions committee who they are as a person. Although a personal interview isn't required, it can be a great way to augment your application, as well as a chance to experience Simmons unique environment. A current student tells us, "I stepped onto campus, and instantly it felt like the right fit."

THE SCHOOL SAYS "..."

From the Admissions Office

"Founded in 1899, Simmons was the first college in the nation to offer women a liberal arts education integrated with professional preparation. Today, Simmons is known for providing transformative learning that links passion with lifelong purpose. The college is committed to preparing students for their careers, while also helping them discover who they are and what they can contribute to society over the course of their lifetimes.

"As a student-focused institution, Simmons offers a learning experience that is highly collaborative and much more personal than that of large universities. Simmons professors include distinguished researchers, published authors, Fulbright scholars, health professionals, and community leaders. More than fifty percent are women, and almost 100 percent hold doctorate degrees in their field. They advise numerous government, nonprofit, and corporate organizations in the United States and around the world—yet passionately uphold their primary obligation to teach.

"To help students succeed, career support starts as soon as students step on campus and continues as an ongoing, lifelong service. Over the past three years, more than ninety percent of Simmons graduates secured employment or entered graduate school within one year of graduation. And, of this population, more than eighty-six percent are employed at jobs in a field related or closely related to their major while at Simmons.

"At Simmons, we are committed to preparing women to be well-informed, open-minded, intellectually curious, and lifelong learners."

SELECTIVITY
Admissions Rating	84
# of applicants	3,666
% of applicants accepted	54
% of acceptees attending	19
# accepting a place on wait list	0

FRESHMAN PROFILE
Range SAT Critical Reading	500–590
Range SAT Math	490–600
Range SAT Writing	510–610
Range ACT Composite	22–26
Minimum paper TOEFL	560
Minimum web-based TOEFL	83
Average HS GPA	3.21
% graduated top 10% of class	22
% graduated top 25% of class	55
% graduated top 50% of class	94

DEADLINES
Early action	
Deadline	12/1
Notification	1/20
Regular	
Deadline	2/1
Nonfall registration?	yes

APPLICANTS ALSO LOOK AT
AND OFTEN PREFER
Boston University, Mount Holyoke College, Northeastern University, Smith College

AND SOMETIMES PREFER
Boston College, University of Connecticut, University of New Hampshire, University of Vermont, University of Massachusetts Amherst

AND RARELY PREFER
Emmanuel College, Quinnipiac University, Suffolk University, Wellesley College

FINANCIAL FACTS
Financial Aid Rating	70
Annual comprehensive tuition	$46,262
Books and supplies	$1,280

SKIDMORE COLLEGE

815 NORTH BROADWAY, SARATOGA SPRINGS, NY 12866-1632 • ADMISSIONS: 518-580-5570 • FAX: 518-580-5584

CAMPUS LIFE

Quality of Life Rating	94
Fire Safety Rating	60*
Green Rating	69
Type of school	private
Environment	town

STUDENTS

Total undergrad enrollment	2,734
% male/female	38/62
% from out of state	67
% from public high school	60
% live on campus	83
% African American	3
% Asian	6
% Caucasian	68
% Hispanic	7
% international	3
# of countries represented	48

SURVEY SAYS . . .

Students aren't religious
Students love Saratoga Springs, NY
Great off-campus food
Dorms are like palaces
Frats and sororities are unpopular
or nonexistent

ACADEMICS

Academic Rating	91
% students graduating	
within 4 years	80
% students graduating	
within 6 years	84
Calendar	semester
Student/faculty ratio	9:1
Profs interesting rating	93
Profs accessible rating	96
Most common	
reg class size	10–19 students
Most common	
lab size	10–19 students

MOST POPULAR MAJORS

business/commerce, English language
and literature, psychology

STUDENTS SAY ". . ."

Academics

Skidmore College is a "school that values independence, creativity, and passion." At this unique, small college, "Creative approaches to learning and education are infused into the curriculum and daily life." Skidmore's strong majors in the liberal arts and sciences are complemented by top-rated programs in art, theater, music, and dance. A senior tells us, "I couldn't decide between Ivy League academics or an arts conservatory, so this seemed to be the compromise." Skidmore "allows students with a variety of interests to take classes that they are interested in," and "interdisciplinary courses and work are common" here. Professors are "extremely enthusiastic about their subjects," and "All classes are really personal. You get to know everyone in the class, and the professors urge [you] to meet with them at least a few times one-on-one so that they can get to know you." A current student affirms, "I've been given many wonderful academic opportunities—I even started doing research as a first-semester freshman." Administrators are receptive to students, and "Every month or so the president will have fireside chats where students are open to discuss their issues with him."

Life

Fun, fulfilling, and a bit rowdy, life at Skidmore is "like summer camp for college students." On this busy campus, "Your typical student is a part of at least one club or extracurricular [activity], sometimes two or three or four." Thanks to the school's artistic inclinations, "Art openings, theater performances, student bands, a capella shows, and comedy shows are all really popular." In fact, a typical weekend night out would include "a performance and then the after-party." Here, "strong friendships and a great sense of community keep things interesting on campus," and students really like the fact that, "We don't have frats or sororities so there is no pressure to join or conform to anything." Students convene in the campus's central cafeteria, and "When the weather is nice out, students love to spend time outside talking, reading, playing tennis, or playing chess." You will also find "a network of hiking trails called 'Northwoods' that is a very popular place to exercise, talk, or have a bonfire on a Friday night." Described as "the perfect college town," Saratoga Springs is "extremely fun and accepting of college students" with "amazing restaurants" and tons of shops. In addition to recreational activities, "Skidmore students are very involved in the Saratoga community through everything from sustainability efforts to mentoring local children." You'll find "a mix of smaller parties on campus and larger ones in off-campus houses" on Friday and Saturday nights. "The dining hall offers freshly made food which is delicious and gives students a variety, from vegetarian to full-out carnivor[ous]."

Student Body

With strong arts and athletics programs, "Skidmore's enduring stereotype is that there are two groups of students: the jocks and the hipsters." In reality, things aren't so black and white. "Most students are white, upper-middle-class" and hail from New England; however, "there is a wide range of racial and geographic backgrounds" within the student body. Whether it's music, dance, theater, or visual arts, "Most people are artistically inclined or at least interested in art." In fact, "The typical student here seems to be the atypical student elsewhere: super-liberal and socially conscious, 'creative' or artsy, weirdly dressed." Some undergraduates even claim, "You can't be a Skid kid unless you are a little weird." "If you can carry on an intelligent or quirky conversation you will have no trouble-making friends." A student adds, "My group of friends in particular is always having discussions about what we are learning in classes, theoretical physics, political, and environmental issues."

FINANCIAL AID: 518-580-5750 • E-MAIL: ADMISSIONS@SKIDMORE.EDU • WEBSITE: WWW.SKIDMORE.EDU

THE PRINCETON REVIEW SAYS

Admissions

Very important factors considered include: Rigor of secondary school record. *Important factors considered include:* Academic GPA, application essay, class rank, recommendation(s), character/personal qualities, extracurricular activities, talent/ability, volunteer work, work experience. *Other factors considered include:* Standardized test scores, alumni/ae relation, first generation, geographical residence, interview, level of applicant's interest, racial/ethnic status. SAT or ACT required; ACT with writing component required. TOEFL required of all international applicants. High school diploma is required, and GED is accepted. *Academic units recommended:* 4 English, 4 mathematics, 4 science (3 science labs), 4 foreign language, 4 social studies.

Financial Aid

Students should submit: FAFSA, CSS/Financial Aid PROFILE. Regular filing deadline is January 15. The Princeton Review suggests that all financial aid forms be submitted as soon as possible after January 1. *Need-based scholarships/grants offered:* Federal Pell, SEOG, state scholarships/grants, private scholarships, school scholarship or grant aid from institutional funds. *Loan aid offered:* Direct Subsidized Stafford, Direct Unsubsidized Stafford, Direct PLUS, Federal Perkins, state loans. Applicants will be notified of awards upon admission. Federal Work-Study Program available. Off-campus job opportunities are fair.

The Inside Word

Admission to Skidmore is highly competitive, and the admissions staff carefully considers each applicant's academic background and standardized test scores. However, consistent with their motto—"creative thought matters"—Skidmore carefully reviews a student's extracurricular talents, achievements, and passions when making an admissions decision. While admissions interviews aren't a requirement for a Skidmore applicant, students may request a personal interview on campus or with an alumnus in their area.

THE SCHOOL SAYS ". . ."

From the Admissions Office

"At Skidmore, we believe a great education is about putting academic theory and creative expression into practice; hence, our belief that creative thought matters. It's a place where faculty and students work together, then figure out how to use what they've learned to make a difference. This often leads to multidisciplinary approaches, where students carry more than one major, student-faculty research is common, most students study abroad, and internships and community service are standard. Skidmore students develop into independent, creative problem-solvers who aren't restricted to looking at things in traditional ways.

This personal journey starts with the First-Year Experience—fifty seminars from which to choose, faculty and peer mentors, and living in close proximity to seminar classmates in residence halls. It's meant to ensure that first-year students hit the ground running on day one, connected and involved. When it comes to your major, you can choose from sixty-five offerings in the sciences, social sciences, and humanities, as well as pre-professional fields like management and business.

"Since we have no fraternities or sororities, student life centers on the nearly 100 student clubs and organizations, which range from the Environmental Action Club to a capella groups to snowboarding. Add to this the prominence of the arts, which has long set Skidmore apart. Science classes collaborate on exhibits at the Tang Museum. Hundreds of students perform, often in the new Zankel Music Center. Enroll in dance courses. Do theater performances. Most not even arts majors. At Skidmore, the arts don't dominate, they permeate.

"As for location, who wouldn't want to go to college in Saratoga Springs? A downtown brimming with shops, galleries, coffeehouses, and great restaurants. Boston, New York City, and Montreal are a three-hour car ride from campus. And the Adirondacks, Berkshires, and Green Mountains provide opportunities for skiing, mountain biking, hiking, rock-climbing, and kayaking."

SELECTIVITY

Admissions Rating	91
# of applicants	6,011
% of applicants accepted	47
% of acceptees attending	27
# accepting a place on wait list	1,113
% admitted from wait list	0
# of early decision applicants	403
% accepted early decision	79

FRESHMAN PROFILE

Range SAT Critical Reading	570–680
Range SAT Math	570–660
Range SAT Writing	580–690
Range ACT Composite	26–30
Minimum paper TOEFL	590
Minimum computer TOEFL	243
Minimum web-based TOEFL	243
% graduated top 10% of class	36
% graduated top 25% of class	74
% graduated top 50% of class	95

DEADLINES

Early decision	
Deadline	11/15
Notification	12/15
Regular	
Deadline	1/15
Nonfall registration?	no

APPLICANTS ALSO LOOK AT

AND OFTEN PREFER
Wesleyan University

AND SOMETIMES PREFER
Connecticut College, New York University

AND RARELY PREFER
University of Vermont

FINANCIAL FACTS

Financial Aid Rating	95
Annual tuition	$40,350
Room and board	$10,986
Required fees	$984
Books and supplies	$1,300
% frosh rec. need-based scholarship or grant aid	42
% UG rec. need-based scholarship or grant aid	38
% frosh rec. non-need-based scholarship or grant aid	5
% UG rec. non-need-based scholarship or grant aid	3
% frosh rec. need-based self-help aid	36
% UG rec. need-based self-help aid	34
% frosh rec. any financial aid	45
% UG rec. any financial aid	38
% UG borrow to pay for school	46
Average cumulative indebtedness	$19,850

SMITH COLLEGE

SEVEN COLLEGE LANE, NORTHAMPTON, MA 01063 • ADMISSIONS: 413-585-2500 • FAX: 413-585-2527

CAMPUS LIFE

Quality of Life Rating	98
Fire Safety Rating	74
Green Rating	96
Type of school	private
Environment	town

STUDENTS

Total undergrad enrollment	2,588
% male/female	0/100
% from out of state	78
% from public high school	62
% live on campus	95
% African American	5
% Asian	11
% Caucasian	43
% Hispanic	7
% international	9
# of countries represented	59

SURVEY SAYS . . .
Great off-campus food
Dorms are like palaces
Frats and sororities are unpopular
or nonexistent
Student government is popular
Political activism is popular

ACADEMICS

Academic Rating	97
% students graduating within 4 years	78
% students graduating within 6 years	83
Calendar	semester
Student/faculty ratio	9:1
Profs interesting rating	93
Profs accessible rating	91
Most common reg class size	10–19 students

MOST POPULAR MAJORS
economics, political science, psychology

STUDENTS SAY ". . ."

Academics

Smith College is "an incredibly prestigious, diverse, academically rigorous, socially liberal, and well-respected institution," located in the consummate college town of Northampton, Massachusetts. A Smith education is all about "finding and pursuing your passions." Offering "academic freedom," "Smith doesn't have course requirements" beyond the major, and "self-scheduled finals" allow students to take exam week at their own pace. "One of the most prominent women's colleges in the country," Smith "builds the self-confidence of smart women," and "Most classes, even in math and sciences, are very interdisciplinary and often have a feminist bias." Classes are "engaging and promote critical thought," and professors are "inspiring, dynamic, accessible, and brilliant." Smith professors "care deeply about students" and "take the time to get to know you on a first-name basis." Smith also offers fabulous academic facilities and "countless resources" to augment your education, including a "wonderful study abroad department" and ample opportunities for research. There's "a large number of undergrads doing serious scientific research" in addition to coursework. If they can't find what they need amid Smith's ample course selection, students "can take classes at the other four schools nearby (UMass Amherst, Amherst College, Hampshire College, and Mount Holyoke College)" through the Northampton Five College Consortium. When graduation approaches, Smith students benefit from the school's "excellent alumni network." "The Career Development Office will do everything in its power to help you get a job."

Life

Smith attracts hardworking and idealistic students, who are "striving to succeed in our classes, as well as make a difference in the Smith College community and the outside community." There's a decided "focus on academics" at Smith, and most students "study, write papers, rehearse, or practice the majority of the time." Students augment coursework with "lectures and symposium on campus," as well as "involvement in community service and activism for global issues, women's rights, LGBTQ rights, the environment, and pretty much anything that fights oppression." When they want to relax, Smithies can attend "free movies and concerts, plays, speakers, sports events, and dances," as well as "school-sponsored house parties almost every weekend." When they want to branch out or rub elbows with the opposite sex, students "go to other college parties at surrounding campuses," or head out in Northampton, which is "always bustling" with "concerts, restaurants, and cute shops." The "quality of life is outstanding" on campus, where "The dorms are not dorms but beautiful houses," and cafeteria food is a cut above the average.

Student Body

"Smithies are passionate about everything they do," especially academics. Throughout the semester, undergraduates are known to "study hard" and get "ridiculously stressed" about course work. "It's the nature of Smithies to be driven, but we all want to see our friends and housemates succeed at well." Smith's unique environment attracts "a great mix of nerdy, edgy, [and] traditional" students, including "hipsters, WASPs, crazy partiers, international students, and the average New Englander." Fortunately, there's a "strong sense of community," and "Students fit in easily, even if they have different interests." Despite diversity, "One thing all students have in common here is the will for women's empowerment and acceptance of any gender or sexual preference." On that note, many students "love the queer life on campus," where many students are either gay or have "a fluid perception of sexuality." Though there's some political diversity on campus, most Smithies hold "very liberal views," and many are "very conscious and aware, not only of their community but the world in general."

SMITH COLLEGE

FINANCIAL AID: 413-585-2530 • E-MAIL: ADMISSION@SMITH.EDU • WEBSITE: WWW.SMITH.EDU

THE PRINCETON REVIEW SAYS

Admissions

Very important factors considered include: Academic GPA, recommendation(s), rigor of secondary school record, character/personal qualities. *Important factors considered include:* Application essay, class rank, extracurricular activities, interview, talent/ability. *Other factors considered include:* Standardized test scores, alumni/ae relation, first generation, racial/ethnic status, volunteer work, work experience. ACT with or without writing component accepted. TOEFL required of all international applicants. High school diploma or equivalent isn't required. *Academic units recommended:* 4 English, 3 mathematics, 3 science (3 science labs), 3 foreign language, 2 history, 1 academic elective.

Financial Aid

Students should submit: FAFSA, institution's own financial aid form, CSS/Financial Aid PROFILE. Regular filing deadline is February 15. The Princeton Review suggests that all financial aid forms be submitted as soon as possible after January 1. *Need-based scholarships/grants offered:* Federal Pell, SEOG, state scholarships/grants, school scholarship or grant aid from institutional funds. *Loan aid offered:* Direct Subsidized Stafford, Direct Unsubsidized Stafford, Direct PLUS, Federal Perkins, university loans from institutional funds. Applicants will be notified of awards at the time of admission. Federal Work-Study Program available. Off-campus job opportunities are excellent.

The Inside Word

Every prospective Smithie is carefully evaluated by at least two members of the admissions staff. No hard numbers guarantee admission: Smith is looking for students who will succeed academically and socially in college, evaluating each applicant for both personal and intellectual qualities. To best prepare for admission, Smith recommends that students follow a rigorous college prep curriculum in high school. If you're feeling particularly enthused about your future at Smith, you can become a fan of the admissions department on Facebook or read student blogs on the admission page.

THE SCHOOL SAYS "..."

From the Admissions Office

"Smith students choose from 1,000 courses in more than fifty areas of study. There are no specific course requirements outside the major; students meet individually with faculty advisers to plan a balanced curriculum. Smith programs offer unique opportunities, including the chance to study abroad, or at another college in the United States, and a semester in Washington, D.C. The Ada Comstock Scholars Program encourages women beyond the traditional age to return to college and complete their undergraduate studies. Smith is located in the scenic Connecticut River valley of western Massachusetts near a number of other outstanding educational institutions. Through the Five College Consortium, Smith, Amherst, Hampshire, and Mount Holyoke colleges, and the University of Massachusetts enrich their academic, social, and cultural offerings by means of joint faculty appointments, joint courses, student and faculty exchanges, shared facilities, and other cooperative arrangements. Smith is the only women's college to offer an accredited major in engineering; it's also the only college in the country that offers a guaranteed paid internship program ("Praxis")."

SELECTIVITY
Admissions Rating	97
# of applicants	4,015
% of applicants accepted	47
% of acceptees attending	34
# accepting a place on wait list	204
% admitted from wait list	42
# of early decision applicants	317
% accepted early decision	50

FRESHMAN PROFILE
Range SAT Critical Reading	600–730
Range SAT Math	590–690
Range SAT Writing	620–720
Range ACT Composite	26–31
Minimum paper TOEFL	600
Minimum computer TOEFL	250
Minimum web-based TOEFL	90
Average HS GPA	3.87
% graduated top 10% of class	60
% graduated top 25% of class	89
% graduated top 50% of class	99

DEADLINES
Early decision	
Deadline	11/15
Notification	12/15
Regular	
Deadline	1/15
Nonfall registration?	no

APPLICANTS ALSO LOOK AT
AND OFTEN PREFER
Brown University
AND SOMETIMES PREFER
Wellesley College
AND RARELY PREFER
Mount Holyoke College

FINANCIAL FACTS
Financial Aid Rating	96
Annual tuition	$39,800
Room and board	$13,390
Required fees	$270
% frosh rec. need-based scholarship or grant aid	60
% UG rec. need-based scholarship or grant aid	60
% UG rec. non-need-based scholarship or grant aid	1
% frosh rec. need-based self-help aid	61
% UG rec. need-based self-help aid	62
% frosh rec. any financial aid	70
% UG rec. any financial aid	71
% UG borrow to pay for school	69
Average cumulative indebtedness	$20,989

SONOMA STATE UNIVERSITY

1801 EAST COTATI AVENUE, ROHNERT PARK, CA 94928 • ADMISSIONS: 707-664-2778 • FAX: 707-664-2060

CAMPUS LIFE

Quality of Life Rating	68
Fire Safety Rating	79
Green Rating	72
Type of school	public
Environment	town

STUDENTS

Total undergrad enrollment	7,390
% male/female	39/61
% from out of state	1
% from public high school	75
% live on campus	36
# of fraternities	5
# of sororities	9
% African American	2
% Asian	5
% Caucasian	68
% Hispanic	13
% Native American	1
% international	1

SURVEY SAYS . . .
Great computer facilities
Great library
Athletic facilities are great
Low cost of living
Very little drug use

ACADEMICS

Academic Rating	69
% students graduating within 4 years	30
% students graduating within 6 years	55
Calendar	semester
Student/faculty ratio	23:1
Profs interesting rating	76
Profs accessible rating	75
Most common reg class size	20–29 students

MOST POPULAR MAJORS
business/commerce, liberal arts and sciences

STUDENTS SAY " . . ."

Academics
For a state school, SSU's student body is on the smaller side, and the environment is friendly and casual. Major coursework takes a "one-on-one" approach, and, in most departments, "professors make it easy to build a relationship with them outside of the classroom." While SSU professors "enjoy teaching," students admit that class quality is "hit-or-miss," especially in lectures and general education courses. Fortunately, professors "want to see their students succeed and therefore, are willing to go above and beyond in assisting them." A student says, "Not only do my professors know my name, but they actually know my character as well, and whenever I need letters of recommendation, I can always ask actual professors instead of TAs." Students warn, "Classes can be hard to get, especially with budget cuts," making it more difficult to graduate in four years. For example, "All art classes are only available for art majors, and only drama majors are allowed to audition for plays."

Life
The school's dorms and suites are "beautiful," the gym and recreational center are state-of-the-art, and there are an "abundance of extracurricular activities that make the university setting more than just academics." In the evenings, "the Residential Student Association at SSU puts on many fantastic activities for students to attend, such as weekly movie nights, karaoke, crafts, pizza feeds, comedians, open mic nights, guest speakers, and so on." "A lot of people go to the cafe or just hang around campus" during their spare time. Although fraternities and sororities do not have housing, "the night life around Sonoma State University focuses on Greek events," and for many (though not all) students, "partying is a staple." For those looking for an alternative to the Greek system, "Sonoma State has great leadership opportunities for students on campus." Sonoma's stellar location makes the school a perfect home base for day trips in Northern California. From SSU, "The beach is less than an hour's drive from campus, as is San Francisco."

Student Body
Nestled amidst Northern California redwoods, Sonoma State attracts students from across the state. In addition to locals, "there are a significant amount of southern California students," who may initially stand out from their Bay Area counterparts. Eventually, however, everyone is "socialized to the laid-back atmosphere." "Most students are politically aware, care about the environment, and are accepting to those who are different." Students acknowledge that "there is personality diversity but not ethnic diversity." In any case, "you are bound to have an interesting conversation at least once a day," and everyone is "respectful of others with different opinions." No matter what you like to do, you'll find a niche; "People looking for a social realm can experience that, and those looking for a quiet, academic realm can experience that as well." "The typical students at Sonoma are dedicated to their studies but not afraid to go out and have some fun."

SONOMA STATE UNIVERSITY

FINANCIAL AID: 707-664-2389 • E-MAIL: ADMITME@SONOMA.EDU • WEBSITE: WWW.SONOMA.EDU

THE PRINCETON REVIEW SAYS

Admissions

Very important factors considered include: Academic GPA, rigor of secondary school record, standardized test scores. *Other factors considered include:* First generation, geographical residence, state residency. SAT or ACT required; ACT with or without writing component accepted. TOEFL required of all international applicants. High school diploma is required, and GED is accepted. *Academic units required:* 4 English, 3 mathematics, 2 science (1 science lab), 2 foreign language, 2 history, 1 visual/performing arts, 1 academic elective.

Financial Aid

Students should submit: FAFSA. The Princeton Review suggests that all financial aid forms be submitted as soon as possible after January 1. *Need-based scholarships/grants offered:* Federal Pell, SEOG, state scholarships/grants, private scholarships. *Loan aid offered:* Direct Subsidized Stafford, Direct Unsubsidized Stafford, Direct PLUS, Federal Perkins. Applicants will be notified of awards on a rolling basis beginning March 25. Federal Work-Study Program available. Off-campus job opportunities are good.

The Inside Word

To determine an applicant's eligibility for admission, SSU calculates an admissions index number based on his or her standardized test scores and GPA. Due to the school's budget problems, students applying for admission to impacted majors must submit higher GPAs and test scores than applicants to nonimpacted programs. Currently, impacted majors include communication studies, human development, liberal studies, pre-nursing and nursing, and psychology.

THE SCHOOL SAYS "..."

From the Admissions Office

"Sonoma State University occupies 275 acres in the beautiful wine country of Sonoma county, in northern California. Located at the foot of the Sonoma hills, the campus is an hour's drive north of San Francisco and centrally located between the Pacific Ocean to the west and the wine country to the north and east. SSU is deeply committed to the teaching of the liberal arts and sciences. The campus has earned a national reputation as a leader in integrating the use of technology into its curriculum. Within its thirty-two academic departments, SSU awards bachelor's degrees in forty-one areas of specialization and master's degrees in fourteen areas. In addition, the university offers a joint master's degree in mathematics with San Francisco State University. The campus ushered in the twenty-first century with the opening of a new library and technology center, the Jean and Charles Schulz Information Center.

"All freshmen applicants are required to provide SAT or ACT scores."

SELECTIVITY
Admissions Rating	71
# of applicants	12,609
% of applicants accepted	81
% of acceptees attending	15

FRESHMAN PROFILE
Range SAT Critical Reading	450–560
Range SAT Math	460–570
Range ACT Composite	19–24
Minimum paper TOEFL	500
Minimum computer TOEFL	173
Minimum web-based TOEFL	61
Average HS GPA	3.16

DEADLINES
Regular	
Priority	11/30
Deadline	11/30
Notification	11/1
Nonfall registration?	yes

FINANCIAL FACTS
Financial Aid Rating	70
Annual in-state tuition	$4,440
Annual out-of-state tuition	$11,160
Room and board	$10,418
Required fees	$5,290
Books and supplies	$1,704
% frosh rec. need-based scholarship or grant aid	10
% UG rec. need-based scholarship or grant aid	24
% frosh rec. non-need-based scholarship or grant aid	3
% UG rec. non-need-based scholarship or grant aid	6
% frosh rec. need-based self-help aid	16
% UG rec. need-based self-help aid	35
% frosh rec. any financial aid	47
% UG rec. any financial aid	57
% UG borrow to pay for school	53
Average cumulative indebtedness	$18,138

SOUTHERN METHODIST UNIVERSITY

PO Box 750181, Dallas, TX 75275-0181 • Admissions: 214-768-0103 • Fax: 214-768-2507

CAMPUS LIFE

Quality of Life Rating	80
Fire Safety Rating	71
Green Rating	87
Type of school	private
Affiliation	Methodist
Environment	metropolis

STUDENTS

Total undergrad enrollment	6,116
% male/female	47/53
% from out of state	49
% from public high school	61
% live on campus	33
# of fraternities	15
# of sororities	13
% African American	5
% Asian	6
% Caucasian	70
% Hispanic	1
% Native American	1
% international	6
# of countries represented	92

SURVEY SAYS . . .

Athletic facilities are great
School is well-run
Students love Dallas, TX
Great off-campus food
Frats and sororities dominate
social scene
Lots of beer drinking
Hard liquor is popular

ACADEMICS

Academic Rating	77
% students graduating within 4 years	60
% students graduating within 6 years	74
Calendar	semester
Student/faculty ratio	12:1
Profs interesting rating	70
Profs accessible rating	64
Most common reg class size	10–19 students
Most common lab size	30–39 students

MOST POPULAR MAJORS
economics, finance, psychology

STUDENTS SAY ". . ."

Academics

Southern Methodist University "is a place with a little bit of something for just about everyone...[preparing] its students for success in the professional world and [offering] a plethora of opportunities for those prudent enough to seek them." SMU's many students studying business and business-related subjects (including advertising, public relations, and corporate communication, all strong programs here) benefit from a faculty of "professionals," who "teach from real-world experience." All undergrads enjoy "internship and networking opportunities out of the wazoo" that facilitate "the education of tomorrow's innovators, leaders, movers, and shakers." SMU also excels in the performing arts, providing "conservatory-style arts training with a liberal arts education" thrown in. One theater student explains, "When I was looking for colleges, I very much wanted to train intensely as an actress, director, and playwright, but I did not want to miss out on a liberal arts education. I believe that being a well-rounded student is essential to being an artist, as science, politics, music, languages, history, literature, etc. are what inform and inspire the art we create. SMU offers both intensity in theater and breadth in outside studies." Students in all disciplines enjoy small class sizes that accommodate "interpersonal connections, whether it be with your professors, peers, or even administration. The opportunities are endless."

Life

"A lot of campus life is organized around the fraternity/sorority scene" at SMU. The Greek organizations "party a lot" and also organize events and philanthropic activities. "Tuesdays and Thursdays are usual party days," one student reports, adding that Greek-organized parties "have to register their party with SMU and provide transportation to the event (i.e., they rent out huge buses to get people there and back)." Greek life offers "a very strong social program...for those interested," but "By no means is everyone at the school in a fraternity or sorority." The school and student organizations present "many events such as movie screenings and dances to help [discourage] underage drinking," and "SMU hosts a ton of lectures throughout the year, so it's great to pop into a lecture and learn something new after class." And then there's hometown Dallas, with its "many things to do...from eating to sports to nightlife." Many here like to "go to Dallas Stars and Rangers games because student tickets are cheap and easy to get," while others enjoy "concerts, clubs, food, shopping, the arts district, [and] Billy Bob's in Fort Worth" (a popular nightspot). In short, "There is always something to do on campus or right off it."

Student Body

SMU's "reputation is 'Southern Millionaires University,'" a place where many "are white, preppy, and pretty well-off." The stereotypical SMU girl "wears pearls with her Tory Burch flats" while her male counterpart "wears polos in Easter egg hues." They are involved in Greek life and "are conservative but not political." But while a good portion of the SMU student body fits the stereotype to some degree, many here point out that "there are lots of atypical students" as well. The school "has done a great job of encouraging more diversity" through a "vast diversity of scholarships" that "bring in people from all backgrounds." Students assure us that those outside the mainstream are "able to integrate well with the other students, especially thanks to all the student activities offered." Regardless of economic background, most here "are the type that would have been a leader in high school and has high aspirations for their future." And they are loyal to one another; "Matriculating to SMU is like joining a family. A large family," one undergrad explains.

SOUTHERN METHODIST UNIVERSITY

FINANCIAL AID: 214-768-2058 • E-MAIL: UGADMISSION@SMU.EDU • WEBSITE: WWW.SMU.EDU/ADMISSION

THE PRINCETON REVIEW SAYS

Admissions

Very important factors considered include: Academic GPA, application essay, class rank, recommendation(s), rigor of secondary school record, standardized test scores. *Important factors considered include:* Character/personal qualities, extracurricular activities, talent/ability, volunteer work, work experience. *Other factors considered include:* Alumni/ae relation, first generation, interview, level of applicant's interest. SAT or ACT required; ACT with or without writing component accepted. TOEFL required of all international applicants. *Academic units required:* 4 English, 3 mathematics, 3 science (2 science labs), 2 foreign language, 1 social studies, 2 history. *Academic units recommended:* 4 English, 4 mathematics, 4 science (3 science labs), 3 foreign language, 2 social studies, 3 history.

Financial Aid

Students should submit: FAFSA, CSS/Financial Aid PROFILE. The Princeton Review suggests that all financial aid forms be submitted as soon as possible after January 1. *Need-based scholarships/grants offered:* Federal Pell, SEOG, state scholarships/grants, private scholarships, school scholarship or grant aid from institutional funds. *Loan aid offered:* Direct Subsidized Stafford, Direct Unsubsidized Stafford, Direct PLUS, Federal Perkins, state loans, university loans from institutional funds. Applicants will be notified of awards on a rolling basis beginning March 15. Off-campus job opportunities are good.

The Inside Word

SMU boasts a potent combination: high-caliber academics, a desirable location, and a beautiful campus. No surprise then that admissions are challenging, and growing more so all the time. Solid high school grades and a compelling list of extracurricular activities will usually do the trick. "Special talent" students—aesthetes and athletes in particular—can make up for academic deficiencies; those in the arts must undergo an audition/portfolio review, while promising athletes are scouted. Except for those in the arts, all admitted students enter as "pre-majors" in the Dedman College of Humanities and Sciences.

THE SCHOOL SAYS " . . ."

From the Admissions Office

"SMU students balance challenging academic programs with a vibrant campus experience in a vibrant city. Students receive personal attention in small classes led by professors dedicated to teaching while also pursuing research. Reflecting its student-centered focus, SMU is one of the few universities to have a voting student member on its Board of Trustees. Internships, community service, student research opportunities, and study abroad programs abound. SMU offers a thriving honors community and generous merit scholarship programs. More than 400 arts and cultural events each year add vitality to campus life. About 180 student organizations provide opportunities for leadership. Through the George W. Bush Presidential Center and the renowned Tate Lecture Series, students have access to dignitaries ranging from former presidents to Nobel laureates. Another unique resource is a mountain campus near Taos, New Mexico. SMU welcomes a diverse student body representing every state, over ninety countries and a wide array of backgrounds. More than seventy percent of SMU undergraduates receive some form of financial aid. Graduates attend some of the best graduate and professional schools in the nation and find career opportunities through SMU's close ties with the global city of Dallas.

"SMU requires either the ACT or SAT. Assessment of written communication skills remains an important component of the SMU application review process. To that end, it is recommended that applicants use every opportunity, including the ACT or SAT, to display their writing skills in the application process."

SELECTIVITY
Admissions Rating	92
# of applicants	8,239
% of applicants accepted	59
% of acceptees attending	30
# accepting a place on wait list	472
% admitted from wait list	10

FRESHMAN PROFILE
Range SAT Critical Reading	560–670
Range SAT Math	580–680
Range SAT Writing	560–660
Range ACT Composite	25–30
Minimum paper TOEFL	550
Minimum computer TOEFL	80
Minimum web-based TOEFL	80
Average HS GPA	3.36
% graduated top 10% of class	45
% graduated top 25% of class	72
% graduated top 50% of class	93

DEADLINES
Early action	
Deadline	11/1
Notification	12/31
Regular	
Priority	1/15
Deadline	3/15
Notification	12/31
Nonfall registration?	yes

APPLICANTS ALSO LOOK AT
AND SOMETIMES PREFER
The University of Texas at Austin
AND RARELY PREFER
Texas Christian University

FINANCIAL FACTS
Financial Aid Rating	74
Annual tuition	$33,040
Room and board	$12,735
Required fees	$4,190
Books and supplies	$800
% frosh rec. need-based scholarship or grant aid	34
% UG rec. need-based scholarship or grant aid	32
% frosh rec. non-need-based scholarship or grant aid	35
% UG rec. non-need-based scholarship or grant aid	25
% frosh rec. need-based self-help aid	39
% UG rec. need-based self-help aid	36
% frosh rec. any financial aid	75
% UG rec. any financial aid	71
% UG borrow to pay for school	36
Average cumulative indebtedness	$24,569

SOUTHWESTERN UNIVERSITY

ADMISSIONS OFFICE, PO BOX 770, GEORGETOWN, TX 78627-0770 • ADMISSIONS: 512-863-1200 • FAX: 512-863-9601

CAMPUS LIFE
Quality of Life Rating	86
Fire Safety Rating	83
Green Rating	71
Type of school	private
Affiliation	Methodist
Environment	town

STUDENTS
Total undergrad enrollment	1,372
% male/female	39/61
% from out of state	8
% from public high school	81
% live on campus	81
# of fraternities	4
# of sororities	4
% African American	3
% Asian	3
% Caucasian	73
% Hispanic	18
% Native American	1
% international	2
# of countries represented	9

SURVEY SAYS . . .
No one cheats
Great computer facilities
Career services are great
School is well-run
Students are friendly
Dorms are like palaces
Campus feels safe
Students are happy

ACADEMICS
Academic Rating	86
% students graduating within 4 years	62
% students graduating within 6 years	73
Calendar	semester
Student/faculty ratio	11:1
Profs interesting rating	94
Profs accessible rating	93
Most common reg class size	10–19 students
Most common lab size	10–19 students

MOST POPULAR MAJORS
business/commerce, political science, speech communication and rhetoric

STUDENTS SAY ". . ."

Academics
One of Texas' top-ranked universities, Southwestern offers students a "welcoming environment" and invites them to become part of a "close community" of scholars. "Small and rigorous," undergrads here truly appreciate that Southwestern "focuses heavily on student development and improvement." Though at times they might complain about the "huge work load," many value the fact that they're really learning "to think critically" and gaining "leadership skills." Impressively, a number of students feels that the university really imbues them with "the love for knowledge." Undergrads are quick to praise their professors, noting that they "sincerely care about their students' education" and are always "willing to help students in any way they can." For the most part, they encourage "participation, whether it is a class discussion or in the middle of a lecture, which allows you to get a feel for the real core of whatever topic you're studying." One history major does caution, "Don't expect to just show up and succeed—you're going to have to work." Fortunately, though the academics might be "challenging," professors are always ready to "meet with you whenever you need guidance or clarification on an assignment." Overall, the university provides a "very engaging learning experience" and allows undergrads to reach their "full potential." And as this supremely satisfied student shares, Southwestern is "the best liberal arts school you've never heard of."

Life
Though students at Southwestern are "very focused on their studies," many also try and take advantage of the myriad activities happening around campus. Fraternities and sororities are fairly popular here, and "Greek life provides the main entertainment for students if they're into the partying scene." However, don't fret if you fear that frat life isn't for you; they're not the only game in town. As one math and music double-major tells us, "There are plenty of opportunities to see shows put on by the theater department, concerts of all types, or recitals. The school also brings in music groups like Cake or Spoon or comedians like Eric O'Shea for Friday Night Live every week." Additionally, campus sponsored events like "movie nights" and "casino nights" are usually well-attended. Undergrads also appreciate leisure time outdoors and students can frequently be found "lounging on the academic mall or riding their bikes to the local park." Though some students find that the surrounding Georgetown area offers "little to do," others enjoy taking advantage of the local "movie theater or bowling alley." And when undergrads are anxious for a little more action, they often head to nearby Austin.

Student Body
Southwestern attracts "intelligent," academically inclined students who fortunately don't "obsess over their grades." They manage to be both "studious" and "fun-loving" and are typically "swamped with a million activities." Though it's a small school, undergrads assure us that "everybody finds their niche somewhere." Indeed, people at Southwestern are "warm," friendly," and "pretty approachable." And an English major adds, "Students are willing to make friends with just about anyone." While the majority are "white, middle- or upper-middle-class, [and] Christian" there are students "from every race, religion, and background," and many people are "open-minded." A large number of students are "in sororities/fraternities," and "liberals outnumber conservatives." Further, most "people dress fairly conservatively, but it is not unheard of to see colored hair, Disturbed t-shirts, or a random guy in a skirt." Perhaps this English and business double-major says it best: "It doesn't take long to find some people you fit in with at school, because you find so many types of people here that it is hard to feel like an outcast."

FINANCIAL AID: 512-863-1259 • E-MAIL: ADMISSION@SOUTHWESTERN.EDU • WEBSITE: WWW.SOUTHWESTERN.EDU

THE PRINCETON REVIEW SAYS

Admissions

Very important factors considered include: Academic GPA, application essay, class rank, recommendation(s), rigor of secondary school record, standardized test scores, geographical residence. *Important factors considered include:* Alumni/ae relation, character/personal qualities, extracurricular activities, first generation, geographical residence, interview, level of applicant's interest, racial/ethnic status, talent/ability, volunteer work, work experience. SAT or ACT required; ACT with writing component required. TOEFL required of all international applicants. High school diploma is required, and GED is accepted. *Academic units required:* 4 English, 4 mathematics, 3 science (2 science labs), 2 foreign language, 2 social studies, 1 history, 1 academic elective. *Academic units recommended:* 4 English, 4 mathematics, 4 science (3 science labs), 3 foreign language, 3 social studies, 2 history.

Financial Aid

Students should submit: FAFSA. Regular filing deadline is March 1. The Princeton Review suggests that all financial aid forms be submitted as soon as possible after January 1. *Need-based scholarships/grants offered:* Federal Pell, SEOG, state scholarships/grants, private scholarships, school scholarship or grant aid from institutional funds. *Loan aid offered:* Direct Subsidized Stafford, Direct Unsubsidized Stafford, Direct PLUS, Federal Perkins, state loans, university loans from institutional funds. Applicants will be notified of awards on a rolling basis beginning March 1. Federal Work-Study Program available. Off-campus job opportunities are good.

The Inside Word

Successful applicants to Southwestern demonstrate intellectual curiosity and a strong desire to participate in an active collegiate community. Students need to be well-rounded and highly motivated. The vast majority of those who receive that coveted thick envelope are in the top quarter of their class and have above-average SAT scores.

THE SCHOOL SAYS ". . ."

From the Admissions Office

"Southwestern University, the state's first institution of higher learning. On the outskirts of Texas's vibrant capital city of Austin. Southwestern is committed to helping students achieve personal and professional success as well as a passion for lifelong learning. The Paideia Program, funded in 2002 by an $8.5 million grant, is a distinctive new option for select students beginning their sophomore year that provides opportunities to compare, contrast, and integrate knowledge and skills gained in various areas of study. In addition to their regular studies, students work with the same Paideia professor over a three-year period in seminar groups of ten. They work to discover the powerful connections between Southwestern's rigorous academic experience and the dynamic programs available outside the classroom—through leadership, service, intercultural learning, and collaborative research or creative works. All Southwestern students discover that a premier liberal arts education leads to high acceptance rates into prestigious graduate and professional programs and careers right out of college. Southwestern is today what it has always been: a highly personal liberal arts experience that equips students with the strengths they need to develop fulfilling lives.

"Southwestern University will accept SAT scores. The writing component will be considered in a comprehensive manner, along with overall academic record, application essay, extracurricular activities, recommendations, and a personal interview."

SELECTIVITY

Admissions Rating	83
# of applicants	2,535
% of applicants accepted	67
% of acceptees attending	23
# accepting a place on wait list	13
% admitted from wait list	92
# of early decision applicants	32
% accepted early decision	75

FRESHMAN PROFILE

Range SAT Critical Reading	550–680
Range SAT Math	550–650
Range ACT Composite	24–30
Minimum paper TOEFL	570
Minimum computer TOEFL	230
% graduated top 10% of class	48
% graduated top 25% of class	79
% graduated top 50% of class	96

DEADLINES

Early decision	
Deadline	11/1
Notification	12/15
Early action	
Deadline	12/1
Notification	2/1
Regular	
Priority	2/1
Nonfall registration?	yes

APPLICANTS ALSO LOOK AT

AND OFTEN PREFER
Rice University, Trinity University

AND SOMETIMES PREFER
Texas A&M University—College Station,
The University of Texas at Austin

AND RARELY PREFER
Austin College, Baylor University,
Texas Christian University

FINANCIAL FACTS

Financial Aid Rating	87
Annual tuition	$31,630
Room and board	$9,240
Books and supplies	$1,000
% frosh rec. need-based scholarship or grant aid	68
% UG rec. need-based scholarship or grant aid	59
% frosh rec. non-need-based scholarship or grant aid	61
% UG rec. non-need-based scholarship or grant aid	49
% frosh rec. need-based self-help aid	49
% UG rec. need-based self-help aid	48
% UG borrow to pay for school	55
Average cumulative indebtedness	$29,548

SPELMAN COLLEGE

350 SPELMAN LANE, SOUTHWEST, ATLANTA, GA 30314 • ADMISSIONS: 404-270-5193 • FAX: 404-270-5201

CAMPUS LIFE
Quality of Life Rating	72
Fire Safety Rating	95
Green Rating	81
Type of school	private
Environment	metropolis

STUDENTS
Total undergrad enrollment	2,337
% male/female	0/100
% from out of state	69
% from public high school	84
% live on campus	48
# of sororities	4
% African American	96
% international	2
# of countries represented	18

SURVEY SAYS . . .
Lab facilities are great
Career services are great
Campus feels safe
Students are happy
Frats and sororities dominate
social scene
Musical organizations are popular
Student government is popular
Very little drug use

ACADEMICS
Academic Rating	83
% students graduating within 4 years	67
% students graduating within 6 years	79
Calendar	semester
Student/faculty ratio	12:1
Profs interesting rating	74
Profs accessible rating	71
Most common reg class size	10–19 students
Most common lab size	20–29 students

MOST POPULAR MAJORS
political science, psychology

STUDENTS SAY "..."

Academics
A historically black women's institution, Spelman College has built a strong reputation for "molding intelligent, goal-oriented young ladies into determined, successful, free-thinking women." Many prospective students are attracted to the school's "powerful history," including the "long list of successful, educated, strong, black women who have attended Spelman College" during the century since its founding. Once on campus, students are happy to report that Spelman's "professors are committed to the mission of the school," and they really "bring out the best" in their students. In the classroom, students are "encouraged to state our opinions," and professors "allow room for us to challenge and discuss what they present." You'll definitely work hard to stay afloat in this "challenging academic environment," because professors "do not allow for even a minute amount of slacking when it comes to completing assignments and being on time for class." Fortunately, there are "many academic resources available to help us, such as tutoring services and a writing center." Plus, the majority of Spelman professors "take additional time outside of instructional time to assist their students" with coursework. Of particular note, Spelman is "very focused on the sciences and improving the number of African American women in this field, and they offer many facilities, faculty, and opportunities" for advanced study. As graduation approaches, the "Career Counseling Center is extremely strong and has helped numerous students find employment and graduate school placements." While the future looks bright for Spelman grads, many say this private institution could better serve its students by freeing up "more money for scholarships and financial aid."

Life
There's a "strong sense of tradition and loyalty" on the Spelman campus, and most students are deeply involved in the community. From service groups to sororities, "There are so many organizations and clubs that you're bound to find one that fits you." There are tons of "opportunities to obtain leadership positions" outside the classroom, and many students are "very involved in campus life." A first-year student details, "In my freshman year already, I've walked in a fashion show, I was crowned Miss Glee Club, I write for the campus newspaper, and I play on the softball team." There's a constant buzz of activity on campus, and "Informational forums, career fairs, college fairs, performances, and sporting events are at the forefront of everyone's campus life." Socially, "Greek Life is quite important at Spelman College, but isn't a must." Even if you don't join a sorority, "There are a lot of social events on campus," and two other historically black colleges, Clark Atlanta and Morehouse, "are only inches away." Spelman undergrads say, "The camaraderie between the schools is great," and "Joint homecoming with Morehouse is the highlight of the entire year." Off campus, students "go skating, bowling, and to Six Flags Over Georgia, as well as to Atlanta Falcons, Hawks, Braves, and Thrasher games." Nearby, Atlantic Station is home to "a major movie theater, shopping, restaurants, and a bowling alley."

Student Body
Spelman College is "full of warm, welcoming, sisterly, and highly educated African American women." A unique environment, "Spelman College offers a chance for African American women to be the majority," and students appreciate being "surrounded and empowered by other young, intelligent, and goal-oriented women like myself." At the same time, "The institution promotes diversity within the student body," and Spelman women "come in all shapes and sizes and from all walks of life, though linked by our African descent. Anyone can find their place here." Confidence and individuality are prized at Spelman, and the typical undergraduate "speaks her mind, wears what she wants, [and] is comfortable in her own skin, yet she has empathy and a strong sense of social justice." Many students "love to do service for the community" and are involved in philanthropic projects around Atlanta. Spelman women are "hardworking and focused on academics." However, most are "excellent at balancing a full course load and an active social life."

FINANCIAL AID: 404-270-5212 • E-MAIL: ADMISS@SPELMAN.EDU • WEBSITE: WWW.SPELMAN.EDU

THE PRINCETON REVIEW SAYS

Admissions

Very important factors considered include: Academic GPA, application essay, rigor of secondary school record, standardized test scores, character/personal qualities. *Important factors considered include:* Recommendation(s), extracurricular activities. *Other factors considered include:* Class rank, alumni/ae relation, first generation, geographical residence, level of applicant's interest, volunteer work, work experience. SAT or ACT required; ACT with or without writing component accepted. TOEFL required of all international applicants. High school diploma is required, and GED is accepted. *Academic units required:* 4 English, 3 mathematics, 3 science (2 science labs), 2 foreign language, 3 social studies, 2 history, 2 academic elective. *Academic units recommended:* 4 English, 4 mathematics, 4 science (3 science labs), 4 foreign language, 4 social studies, 3 history, 2 academic elective.

Financial Aid

Students should submit: Institution's own financial aid form, CSS/Financial Aid PROFILE. The Princeton Review suggests that all financial aid forms be submitted as soon as possible after January 1. *Need-based scholarships/grants offered:* Federal Pell, SEOG, state scholarships/grants, private scholarships, school scholarship or grant aid from institutional funds, United Negro College Fund. *Loan aid offered:* Direct Subsidized Stafford, Direct Unsubsidized Stafford, Direct PLUS. Federal Work-Study Program available. Off-campus job opportunities are good.

The Inside Word

The best way to prepare for admission to Spelman is to pursue a strong, precollege academic curriculum during high school. In 2010, admitted students had an average GPA of 3.65. Students who are particularly interested in Spelman have two early application options: early decision, which is binding, and early notification, which is nonbinding, but allows students to receive a response more quickly.

THE SCHOOL SAYS "..."

From the Admissions Office

"As an outstanding Historically Black College for women, Spelman strives for academic excellence in liberal arts education. This predominantly residential private college provides students with an academic climate conducive to the full development of their intellectual and leadership potential. The college is a member of the Atlanta University Center consortium, and Spelman students enjoy the benefits of a small college while having access to the resources of the other three participating institutions. The purpose extends beyond intellectual development and professional career preparation of students. It seeks to develop the total person. The college provides an academic and social environment that strengthens those qualities that enable women to be self-confident as well as culturally and spiritually enriched. This environment attempts to instill in students both an appreciation for the multicultural communities of the world and a sense of responsibility for bringing about positive change in those communities.

"Applicants for are required to submit standardized test scores from an appropriate venue (i.e., ACT, TOEFL, SAT). The highest composite score will be used in admissions decisions. Writing scores from either the SAT or ACT will not be taken into consideration in the admission process."

SELECTIVITY

Admissions Rating	93
# of applicants	5,656
% of applicants accepted	33
% of acceptees attending	30
# accepting a place on wait list	0

FRESHMAN PROFILE

Range SAT Critical Reading	500–580
Range SAT Math	490–570
Range ACT Composite	21–25
Minimum paper TOEFL	500
Minimum computer TOEFL	250
Average HS GPA	3.59
% graduated top 10% of class	40
% graduated top 25% of class	73
% graduated top 50% of class	95

DEADLINES

Early decision	
Deadline	11/1
Notification	12/15
Early action	
Deadline	11/15
Notification	12/31
Regular	
Deadline	2/1
Nonfall registration?	no

APPLICANTS ALSO LOOK AT AND OFTEN PREFER
Georgia Institute of Technology

AND SOMETIMES PREFER
Clark Atlanta University, Florida A&M University, Hampton University, Howard University, Tuskegee University

FINANCIAL FACTS

Financial Aid Rating	70
Annual tuition	$14,470
Room and board	$8,750
Required fees	$2,535
Books and supplies	$1,150
% frosh rec. need-based scholarship or grant aid	80
% UG rec. need-based scholarship or grant aid	54
% frosh rec. non-need-based scholarship or grant aid	49
% UG rec. non-need-based scholarship or grant aid	21
% frosh rec. need-based self-help aid	11
% UG rec. need-based self-help aid	72
% frosh rec. any financial aid	82
% UG rec. any financial aid	75
% UG borrow to pay for school	75

ST. BONAVENTURE UNIVERSITY

PO BOX D, ST. BONAVENTURE, NY 14778 • ADMISSIONS: 716-375-2400 • FAX: 716-375-4005

STUDENTS SAY "..."

Academics

Uniting a liberal arts education with "Franciscan values," St. Bonaventure University is a small Catholic school that succeeds in "shaping its students into well-rounded, intelligent, and good people." Many students choose St. Bonaventure for its "nationally recognized journalism program" or for one of several prestigious "dual-admissions programs with medical, dental, physical therapy, and pharmacy schools" in the region. No matter what their major, undergrads must complete the Clare College curriculum, which provides an "overall liberal arts education" mixed with religion and philosophy. While students are encouraged to "become extraordinary" and ethics are woven into the curriculum, "Religion is by no means forced on you," despite the college's Catholic heritage. Within major departments, "Classes are no larger than thirty students per classroom" and "professors are always available if you need help." Talented instructors "make class both fun and informative," and most "do a good job at engaging the class and promoting discussion" between students. "The school is very focused on making successful graduates, and not just in the classroom;" therefore, the curriculum "puts a huge emphasis on real-world experience in a student's field, whether it is journalism, business, or education." Students are further benefited by the school's "amazing alumni network" in and around New York State. While engaging and worthwhile, "Academics are serious, no matter your major." However, "a steady effort will get you good grades" in most Bonaventure classes, and students appreciate the fact that "the school isn't super-competitive like the Ivy League schools. Students are willing to help each other out, and there's no cutthroat competition for internships or job interviews."

Life

Outgoing and social, students enjoy a classic college lifestyle in the "Bona bubble." "November to March is Bonnie's basketball season," and attending games is a universally popular pastime. There's also an active intramural sports program, and many students "love going to the fitness center on campus" to work out or take classes. "Student involvement in the radio station is huge," and many claim, "WSBU is the best college radio station in the country." Because the school is located in upstate New York, "It is ridiculously snowy about six months of the year" and there's little to do in surrounding Olean, a "very, very small town." "People drink, snowboard, or leave for Buffalo." On campus, "Nearly everyone parties every Friday and Saturday." A student elaborates, "Occasionally people will go to the movies or order in and have a quiet night in the dorm, but parties are definitely the big plans on the weekend." At the same time, "There are options for people who do not want to party and drink." In particular, "The Campus Activities Board always has something going on." By the time they graduate, most Bonas share "a lifetime bond forged over beer, basketball, and the worst weather ever."

Student Body

St. Bonaventure students describe their classmates as "hardworking, religious, fun-loving, outgoing, involved in many activities, friendly, and accepting." "Everyone loves sports, as evidenced by the huge intramural program," and "nearly all students love to party." Demographically similar, most undergraduates are "white and from the tristate area." However, the "student body is becoming increasingly diverse" and currently includes students "from all different age groups and backgrounds." Despite the school's religious affiliation, "not everyone is Catholic," and politically speaking, "There are some die-hard conservatives, but most people are pretty open-minded." When it comes to social groups, you'll meet plenty of East Coast preppies, but also "edgy kids who work at the campus radio station and listen to underground music." With extracurricular activities catering to a wide range of interests, "It's easy to make friends and find a good fit" at St. Bonaventure. There are some cliques; however, most "people tend to branch out of their comfort zone" to make friends.

St. Bonaventure University

FINANCIAL AID: 716-375-2528 • E-MAIL: ADMISSIONS@SBU.EDU • WEBSITE: WWW.SBU.EDU

THE PRINCETON REVIEW SAYS

Admissions

Very important factors considered include: Academic GPA, recommendation(s), rigor of secondary school record, character/personal qualities. *Important factors considered include:* Application essay, standardized test scores, extracurricular activities, talent/ability, volunteer work. *Other factors considered include:* Class rank, alumni/ae relation, first generation, geographical residence, interview, level of applicant's interest, state residency, work experience. SAT or ACT required; ACT with or without writing component accepted. TOEFL required of all international applicants. High school diploma is required, and GED is accepted. *Academic units recommended:* 4 English, 3 mathematics, 3 science (3 science labs), 2 foreign language, 4 social studies.

Financial Aid

Students should submit: FAFSA. The Princeton Review suggests that all financial aid forms be submitted as soon as possible after January 1. *Need-based scholarships/grants offered:* Federal Pell, SEOG, state scholarships/grants, private scholarships, school scholarship or grant aid from institutional funds. *Loan aid offered:* Direct Subsidized Stafford, Direct Unsubsidized Stafford, Direct PLUS, Federal Perkins, university loans from institutional funds. Applicants will be notified of awards on a rolling basis beginning March 1. Federal Work-Study Program available.

The Inside Word

There's no admissions formula at St. Bonaventure. Here, prospective students are evaluated individually and accepted based on their capacity for success in college. Though St. Bonaventure recommends that applicants submit academic transcripts, standardized test scores, recommendations, and a personal essay, the admissions committee will consider any other supporting materials that prove a student's overall eligibility for admission. St. Bonaventure has a rolling admissions program, so applications are reviewed as soon as they arrive at the admissions office.

THE SCHOOL SAYS "..."

From the Admissions Office

"The St. Bonaventure University family has been imparting an extraordinary Franciscan tradition to men and women of a rich diversity of backgrounds for more than 150 years. This tradition encourages all who become a part of it to face the world confidently, respect the earthly environment, and work for productive change in the world. The charm of our campus and the inspirational beauty of the surrounding hills provide a special place where growth in learning and living is abundantly realized. The Richter Student Fitness Center, which opened in 2004, provides all students with state-of-the-art facilities for athletics and wellness. Academics at St. Bonaventure are challenging. Small classes and personalized attention encourage individual growth and development. St. Bonaventure's nationally known Schools of Arts and Sciences, Business Administration, Journalism/Mass Communication, and Education offers more than forty majors. The School of Graduate Studies also offers several programs leading to the master's degree.

"Applicants can submit scores from either the SAT or the ACT. The biology Subject Test is required only for students applying to one of our dual-admission medical programs."

SELECTIVITY
Admissions Rating	73
# of applicants	2,303
% of applicants accepted	78
% of acceptees attending	28

FRESHMAN PROFILE
Range SAT Critical Reading	460–570
Range SAT Math	470–580
Range SAT Writing	450–560
Range ACT Composite	20–26
Minimum paper TOEFL	550
Minimum computer TOEFL	213
Average HS GPA	3.21
% graduated top 10% of class	13
% graduated top 25% of class	41
% graduated top 50% of class	75

DEADLINES
Regular	
Priority	2/15
Deadline	7/1
Nonfall registration?	yes

FINANCIAL FACTS
Financial Aid Rating	84
Annual tuition	$27,980
Room and board	$9,540
Required fees	$965
Books and supplies	$700
% frosh rec. need-based scholarship or grant aid	72
% UG rec. need-based scholarship or grant aid	69
% frosh rec. non-need-based scholarship or grant aid	62
% UG rec. non-need-based scholarship or grant aid	60
% frosh rec. need-based self-help aid	72
% UG rec. need-based self-help aid	58
% UG borrow to pay for school	83
Average cumulative indebtedness	$36,940

ST. JOHN'S COLLEGE (MD)

PO Box 2800, Annapolis, MD 21404 • Admissions: 1-800-727-9238 • Fax: 410-269-7916

STUDENTS SAY "..."

Academics

St. John's College is a "one of a kind" institution, which "teaches its students how to think for themselves" through a series of rigorous, discussion-based seminars. Here, every student follows the same academic curriculum, which consists entirely of "reading and discussing the great books of Western civilization." Students study "math, science, philosophy, language, history, and literature," and then, through in-class debate, are "encouraged to question everything, develop their own logical conclusions, and understand Western thought starting at the basics." The school's "brilliant" professors (known as tutors in St. John's parlance) gently oversee class discussions, though they're "more like moderators" in that they "do not lecture or 'teach' in the traditional sense." Tutors always "treat the students as equals," and "outside of class, they are available and friendly." A current undergrad relates, "The fact that tutors are always available (for lunch, coffee, or just to chat with a student) is wonderful. I have had many delightful discussions with tutors outside of class on topics ranging from Baudelaire to quantum mechanics." With tons of assigned reading and provoking in-class debates, the curriculum is "difficult and taxing, yet supremely rewarding." Tutors "don't cut you slack if you don't deserve it," and most "have high expectations" for their students throughout the semester. "Grades are sometimes based on a tutor's subjective opinion of the student's personality," which can be frustrating for those accustomed to receiving top marks. "Work is sometimes stressful, and the material is often difficult," but students reassure us that "there is always someone to work through it with you, and you can always ask for help."

Life

There's no strict division between study and social life at St. John's. "Discussions from in class spill out into the quad." While most Johnnies say their school is sublime, they also warn that, "If you don't like endlessly talking about books, you'll feel oppressed by the social scene at St. John's." While "school is intense and exhausting," students "rarely differentiate between schoolwork and lives outside of class." On this quirky campus, "Fun can be translating Greek or it can be taking a nap; it can be playing intramurals or drinking a beer and watching les sportifs run around; it can be making music or researching Appalachian folk songs." For a lighter evening, students attend "school-run dance parties" or get together for "hard liquor, film noir, classical books, cigarettes, and being off on an adventure." "Impromptu trips off campus are frequent," and students head to Annapolis for "sailing, watching tourists, bowling, [or] ice skating." In addition, "Many students participate in the excellent intramural sports program," which includes "soccer, football, Ultimate Frisbee, basketball, croquet, crew, fencing, aikido, boxing, and more." Social dance is also remarkably popular, and there are "swing dancing parties on a regular basis."

Student Body

The unusual St. John's curriculum tends to attract students who are "intellectual, very thoughtful, and inclined to discuss Aristotle, Hobbes, or Tolstoy at the dinner table." Talkative and analytical, St. John's students are "always down for a good conversation, whether one-on-one or in a group, whether the topic is personal or impersonal." "Students come from across the country and around the world, from all religious, political, and economic backgrounds," though there's a noticeable "proliferation of East Coast preppies and hipsters." "The diversity of personalities is astounding," and, exclusivity is minimized on this "friendly" campus. "Because the school is so small, and because of the universal curriculum, by your senior year you have a pretty strong bond with your entire class." Activists and pop culture junkies take note: "If you're interested in current events, or pretty much anything that happened after, say, 1925, it can sometimes be hard to find people who know what you're talking about."

ST. JOHN'S COLLEGE (MD)

FINANCIAL AID: 410-626-2502 • E-MAIL: ADMISSIONS@SJCA.EDU • WEBSITE: WWW.STJOHNSCOLLEGE.EDU

THE PRINCETON REVIEW SAYS

Admissions

Very important factors considered include: Application essay, rigor of secondary school record, interview. *Important factors considered include:* Recommendation(s). *Other factors considered include:* Class rank, alumni/ae relation, character/personal qualities, racial/ethnic status, extracurricular activities, first generation, level of applicant's interest, talent/ability, volunteer work. SAT or ACT with or without writing component accepted. TOEFL required of all international applicants. High school diploma is required, and GED is accepted. *Academic units required:* 3 mathematics, 2 foreign language. *Academic units recommended:* 4 English, 4 mathematics, 3 science (3 science labs), 4 foreign language, 2 social studies, 2 history.

Financial Aid

Students should submit: FAFSA, CSS/Financial Aid PROFILE. Regular filing deadline is March 1. The Princeton Review suggests that all financial aid forms be submitted as soon as possible after January 1. *Need-based scholarships/grants offered:* Federal Pell, SEOG, state scholarships/grants, private scholarships, school scholarship or grant aid from institutional funds. *Loan aid offered:* Direct Subsidized Stafford, Direct Unsubsidized Stafford, Direct PLUS, Federal Perkins, university loans from institutional funds. Applicants will be notified of awards on a rolling basis. Federal Work-Study Program available. Off-campus job opportunities are good.

The Inside Word

St. John's is a unique environment, best suited to students of a quirky yet serious intellectual predilection. To test the waters before you jump in, consider taking a campus tour or even sitting in on an active tutorial session with students. You can also send your questions about the school to a current student through the St. John's website. Each applicant is evaluated individually for potential success in the program. Among application materials, SAT scores are an optional component, though the school generally recommends that you submit them.

THE SCHOOL SAYS "..."

From the Admissions Office

"The purpose of the admission process is to determine whether an applicant has the necessary preparation and ability to complete the St. John's program satisfactorily. The essays are designed to enable applicants to give a full account of themselves. They can tell the committee much more than statistical records reveal. Previous academic records show whether an applicant has the habits of study necessary at St. John's. Letters of reference, particularly those of teachers, are carefully read for indications that the applicant has the maturity, self-discipline, ability, energy, and initiative to succeed in the St. John's program. St. John's attaches little importance to 'objective' test scores, and no applicant is accepted or rejected because of such scores.

"St. John's College does not require the results of standardized tests, except in the case of international students, homeschooled students, and those who will not receive a high school diploma. Results of the ACT or SAT are sufficient for these students."

SELECTIVITY

Admissions Rating	80
# of applicants	357
% of applicants accepted	81
% of acceptees attending	47

FRESHMAN PROFILE

Range SAT Critical Reading	640–740
Range SAT Math	570–690
Range ACT Composite	27–30
Minimum paper TOEFL	600
Minimum computer TOEFL	270
Minimum web-based TOEFL	100
% graduated top 10% of class	29
% graduated top 25% of class	54
% graduated top 50% of class	80

DEADLINES

Regular	
Priority	3/1
Nonfall registration?	yes

APPLICANTS ALSO LOOK AT

AND OFTEN PREFER
Swarthmore College, University of Chicago, University of Virginia

AND SOMETIMES PREFER
Kenyon College, Oberlin College, Reed College, Smith College

AND RARELY PREFER
Bard College

FINANCIAL FACTS

Financial Aid Rating	86
Annual tuition	$43,256
Room and board	$10,344
Required fees	$400
Books and supplies	$630
% frosh rec. need-based scholarship or grant aid	60
% UG rec. need-based scholarship or grant aid	61
% frosh rec. non-need-based scholarship or grant aid	5
% UG rec. non-need-based scholarship or grant aid	4
% frosh rec. need-based self-help aid	62
% UG rec. need-based self-help aid	64
% frosh rec. any financial aid	76
% UG rec. any financial aid	73
% UG borrow to pay for school	64
Average cumulative indebtedness	$29,869

ST. JOHN'S COLLEGE (NM)

1160 CAMINO CRUZ BLANCA, SANTA FE, NM 87505 • ADMISSIONS: 505-984-6060 • FAX: 505-984-6162

STUDENTS SAY ". . ."

Academics

The "mind-blowing," all-mandatory curriculum at "incredibly small" St. John's College in Santa Fe, New Mexico, includes "copious amounts" of philosophy, literature, language, math, and science. Students "read only primary texts as opposed to textbooks." "There are no majors." There are no lectures. "Every class is a discussion." There are few tests. Grades are based almost exclusively on papers and classroom participation. While students love the academic experience, they caution that it is full of "relentless intellectual duress." "The program is very difficult and you get kicked out if you can't keep up," warns a senior. "You have to be prepared to work hard without being rewarded with simple answers." Professors at St. John's are called tutors "because they are not professing anything." Instead, they guide students through a few thousand years of Western thought, starting with ancient Greece and ending in modern times, and allow you "to form your own opinions." Most faculty are "insightful, brilliant, and dedicated." Virtually all of them are "absurdly accessible" as well. "Students meet with the dean all the time." However, when difficulties arise, the administration sometimes causes "an ordeal far out of proportion to the problem." Other complaints include the "often less [than] modern" condition of the campus. There are some "shabby" classrooms, and the Internet connection "needs to be upgraded by an order of magnitude."

Life

Campus life at St. John's in Santa Fe is "a strange boot camp" where "the dating scene is a nightmare" and "the food needs improvement." The "life-consuming" curriculum here forces students to put in many hours of difficult reading. "We read the great, earthshaking books all the time, which necessarily takes a toll on our psychology," explains a junior. "You can only have your conception of the world shattered so many times before you feel emotionally drained." "Social life in general tends to be a less formal (frequently rather irreverent) extension of our classroom life," explains a junior. "A typical dining hall conversation might cycle between *Star Wars*, the Roman Empire, various video games, Socrates, world religions, and the nature and existence of divine truth." Beyond stimulating banter, "there is no universally popular activity." "There are lectures every Friday night." "Pickup sports are popular." Martial arts are reasonably big, "as is fencing." "Organized trips for skiing, hiking, rafting," and other outdoor activities are common. Many students "tend to drink now and then." There's no pressure to participate, though. "There are definitely people, like myself, who don't drink or smoke or do other drugs," asserts a senior. Surrounding Santa Fe boasts "excellent restaurants" and a nice view of the mountains.

Student Body

"This is a school for super geeks." Everyone is a "voracious reader" and "kind of neurotic." "For many students, St. John's is a funny interlude—a bizarre and startlingly wonderful place to reflect on the world around them and think about themselves and how they want to live their own lives." "People here tend to have considered the big questions," suggests a senior. "How can I be a good person? Why does the world work the way it does?" Some students suffer from "academic haughtiness." "Johnnies tend to have an underlying pretension regarding their role in the world as philosophers and avant-garde thinkers and writers." "The population is not diverse ethnically, but it is tolerant politically, religiously, and socially." There are "churchgoing Christians and radical atheists." "Every St. John's student is atypical in one way or another." "Although they might not fit in elsewhere, they feel quite comfortable at St. John's." "People here go after what they want," agrees a sophomore, even if that involves "finding a job as a ranch hand in the middle of nowhere."

ST. JOHN'S COLLEGE (NM)

FINANCIAL AID: 505-984-6058 • E-MAIL: ADMISSIONS@MAIL.SJCSF.EDU • WEBSITE: WWW.SJCSF.EDU

THE PRINCETON REVIEW SAYS

Admissions

Very important factors considered include: Application essay, rigor of secondary school record. *Important factors considered include:* Recommendation(s), character/personal qualities, level of applicant's interest. *Other factors considered include:* Class rank, standardized test scores, alumni/ae relation, extracurricular activities, first generation, interview, racial/ethnic status, talent/ability, volunteer work, work experience. ACT with or without writing component accepted. TOEFL required of all international applicants. High school diploma is required, and GED is accepted. *Academic units required:* 3 mathematics, 2 foreign language. *Academic units recommended:* 4 English, 4 mathematics, 3 science (3 science labs), 4 foreign language, 2 history.

Financial Aid

Students should submit: FAFSA, CSS/Financial Aid PROFILE. The Princeton Review suggests that all financial aid forms be submitted as soon as possible after January 1. *Need-based scholarships/grants offered:* Federal Pell, SEOG, state scholarships/grants, private scholarships, school scholarship or grant aid from institutional funds. *Loan aid offered:* Direct Subsidized Stafford, Direct Unsubsidized Stafford, Direct PLUS, Federal Perkins, university loans from institutional funds. Applicants will be notified of awards on a rolling basis beginning December 10. Federal Work-Study Program available. Off-campus job opportunities are excellent.

The Inside Word

Self-selection drives this admissions process—more than one-half of the entire applicant pool each year indicates that St. John's is their first choice, and half of those admitted send in tuition deposits. Even so, no one in admissions takes things for granted, and neither should any student considering an application. The admissions process is highly personal on both sides of the coin. Only the intellectually curious and highly motivated need apply.

THE SCHOOL SAYS "..."

From the Admissions Office

"St. John's appeals to students who value good books, love to read, and are passionate about discourse and debate. There are no lectures and virtually no tests or electives. Instead, classes of sixteen to twenty students occur around conference tables where professors are as likely to be asked to defend their points of view as are students. Great books provide the direction, context, and stimulus for conversation. The entire student body adheres to the same, all-required arts and science curriculum. Someone once said, 'A classic is a house we still live in,' and at St. John's, students and professors alike approach each reading on the list as if the ideas it holds were being expressed for the first time—questioning the logic behind a geometrical proof, challenging the premise of a scientific development, or dissecting the progression of modern political theory as it unfolds."

SELECTIVITY

Admissions Rating	82
# of applicants	269
% of applicants accepted	86
% of acceptees attending	52
# accepting a place on wait list	2
% admitted from wait list	0

FRESHMAN PROFILE

Range SAT Critical Reading	610–740
Range SAT Math	570–660
Range ACT Composite	25–32
Minimum paper TOEFL	550
Minimum computer TOEFL	213
% graduated top 10% of class	33
% graduated top 25% of class	52
% graduated top 50% of class	81

DEADLINES

Regular	
Priority	rolling
Nonfall registration?	yes

APPLICANTS ALSO LOOK AT

AND OFTEN PREFER
Deep Springs College, Stanford University

AND SOMETIMES PREFER
Bard College, Reed College, Rice University, University of Chicago

AND RARELY PREFER
Oberlin College

FINANCIAL FACTS

Financial Aid Rating	92
Annual tuition	$41,792
Room and board	$9,984
Required fees	$400
Books and supplies	$630
% frosh rec. need-based scholarship or grant aid	76
% UG rec. need-based scholarship or grant aid	64
% frosh rec. need-based self-help aid	79
% UG rec. need-based self-help aid	67
% frosh rec. any financial aid	81
% UG rec. any financial aid	75
% UG borrow to pay for school	71
Average cumulative indebtedness	$27,650

ST. JOHN'S UNIVERSITY

8000 UTOPIA PARKWAY, QUEENS, NY 11439 • ADMISSIONS: 718-990-2000 • FAX: 718-990-5728

STUDENTS SAY "..."

Academics

Like its hometown of Queens, New York, St. John's moves inexorably forward without forgetting its history and traditions. The school's administration is committed to constantly "updating the university's facilities." Recent improvements include "a state-of-the-art athletic training facility and revamped cafeterias," as well as an upgrade to science facilities, added townhouse residences for students, and a new 127,000 square foot University Center. In addition, the school distributes "brand-new laptops to all incoming students" and has "done a tremendous job of implementing technology throughout the campus," which "is completely wireless except for a few athletic fields and parking lots." On the traditions side of the balance, the school maintains "a lot of policies and politics opposed by typical college students [such as] the visitor policies in the dorms." Many praise St. John's' study abroad programs and Institute for Writing Studies, which provides writing support to all students. When it comes to classroom experience, "professors are professors. Like [at] any school, some are better than others." Students report that "the experience you have at St. John's really depends on what you do with it. Don't take a professor just because he/she is easy—chances are that means they suck! If you are self-motivated…you will find challenging professors." Big-picture people will see that St. John's offers "a quality private education" and, in many instances, a "generous" financial aid package that translates to an overall "low cost."

Life

Students say "There are a lot of opportunities to get involved on campus," at St. John's. "Our student government works very hard on student engagement, creating popular events to foster the University community." Still, "Life for most St. John's students is not centered around the campus. We have NYC as our playground, so time not spent in classes is often [spent] off campus." For those who prefer off-campus activities in their spare time, the school helps to make that possible. There are "shuttles that can take us into the city [aka Manhattan, to those outside New York City] and on weekends…to the mall." In addition, the "school runs programs to see Broadway shows for free." Even without the school's help, however, New York is at students' fingertips; almost everything the city has to offer "is just a subway ride away." "Clubs, sports events, parties, restaurants"—you name it, NYC's got it, and St. John's students sample it. The faithful will be happy to know that "St. John's makes it easy to incorporate a spiritual life with an academic one." For the altruistic, there are "community-service initiatives galore."

Student Body

Because it is "located in Queens, the most diverse place on Earth," it's no surprise that St. John's itself is "very, very diverse." Though "everyone gets along exceptionally well," getting along well doesn't equal total integration. Each "ethnic group tends [to] hang around with itself. Yet students' external differences belie less visible similarities. Many are may be the first in their family to attend college, so a strong work ethic is pervasive. Everyone "wants to achieve something greater than their parents." The second major similarity stems from the first: "Students here generally have many responsibilities outside of their schoolwork."

FINANCIAL AID: 1-888-9-STJOHNS • E-MAIL: ADMISSIONS@STJOHNS.EDU • WEBSITE: WWW.STJOHNS.EDU

THE PRINCETON REVIEW SAYS

Admissions

Very important factors considered include: Academic GPA, standardized test scores. *Important factors considered include:* Rigor of secondary school record. *Other factors considered include:* Application essay, class rank, recommendation(s), alumni/ae relation, character/personal qualities, extracurricular activities, first generation, geographical residence, state residency, talent/ability, volunteer work, work experience. SAT or ACT required; ACT with or without writing component accepted. TOEFL required of all international applicants. High school diploma is required, and GED is accepted. *Academic units required:* 4 English. *Academic units recommended:* 3 mathematics, 2 science (2 science labs), 2 foreign language, 2 history.

Financial Aid

Students should submit: FAFSA. The Princeton Review suggests that all financial aid forms be submitted as soon as possible after January 1. *Need-based scholarships/grants offered:* Federal Pell, SEOG, state scholarships/grants, private scholarships, school scholarship or grant aid from institutional funds. *Loan aid offered:* Direct Subsidized Stafford, Direct Unsubsidized Stafford, Direct PLUS, Federal Perkins. Applicants will be notified of awards on a rolling basis beginning March 15. Federal Work-Study Program available. Off-campus job opportunities are good.

The Inside Word

The admissions process at St. John's doesn't include many surprises. High school grades and standardized test scores are undoubtedly the most important factors though volunteer work and extracurricular activities are also highly regarded. What is surprising is that this Catholic university doesn't consider religious affiliation at all when making admissions decisions; there are students of every religious stripe here.

THE SCHOOL SAYS "..."

From the Admissions Office

"Founded by the Vincentian Fathers in 1870, St. John's is a major Catholic university that prepares students for ethical leadership in today's global society. St. John's offers quality academics, high-tech resources and confidence-building service activities enlivened by the vast opportunities available only in exciting New York City. Representing forty-six states and 111 foreign countries, students pursue more than 100 programs and concentrations in the arts, sciences, business, education, pharmacy, and allied health. Internationally respected scholars, more than ninety percent of St. John's professors hold a PhD or comparable degree. The nineteen to one student/faculty ratio ensures personal attention in class.

"St. John's also offers these advantages:

- The freshman Passport Program lets students study abroad in their very first year at St. John's, with two weeks at our Rome campus.
- Unique core courses like Discover New York use the city as a 'living classroom.'
- All entering students receive wireless laptop computers with access to our award-winning network.
- Reflecting our Vincentian heritage, course-related service activities provide real-world experience while serving those in need.
- Global studies programs like Discover the World allow students to earn fifteen credits while studying in three foreign cities in a single semester.

"St. John's has three residential New York City campuses—our flagship campus in Queens; the wooded Staten Island campus; and a 'vertical' campus in lower Manhattan. St. John's also has a campus in Rome, Italy, and locations in Oakdale, New York, and Paris, France."

SELECTIVITY

Admissions Rating	85
# of applicants	54,871
% of applicants accepted	46
% of acceptees attending	12

FRESHMAN PROFILE

Range SAT Critical Reading	480–590
Range SAT Math	490–620
Minimum paper TOEFL	600
Minimum computer TOEFL	250
Minimum web-based TOEFL	100
Average HS GPA	3.20
% graduated top 10% of class	20
% graduated top 25% of class	35
% graduated top 50% of class	66

DEADLINES

Regular	
Priority	2/1
Deadline	rolling
Notification	12/1
Nonfall registration?	yes

APPLICANTS ALSO LOOK AT AND OFTEN PREFER

Fordham University, Pennsylvania State University, Rutgers, The State University of New Jersey—New Brunswick, State University of New York—Stony Brook University

AND SOMETIMES PREFER

New York University, State University of New York at Binghamton, Syracuse University, Temple University, University of Connecticut

FINANCIAL FACTS

Financial Aid Rating	71
Annual tuition	$31,250
Room and board	$13,900
Required fees	$730
Books and supplies	$1,000
% frosh rec. need-based scholarship or grant aid	77
% UG rec. need-based scholarship or grant aid	71
% frosh rec. non-need-based scholarship or grant aid	71
% UG rec. non-need-based scholarship or grant aid	57
% frosh rec. need-based self-help aid	69
% UG rec. need-based self-help aid	68
% frosh rec. any financial aid	96
% UG rec. any financial aid	97
% UG borrow to pay for school	71
Average cumulative indebtedness	$32,886

ST. LAWRENCE UNIVERSITY

PAYSON HALL, CANTON, NY 13617 • ADMISSIONS: 315-229-5261 • FAX: 315-229-5818

STUDENTS SAY ". . ."

Academics

Students at St. Lawrence love their professors. "All of my professors have been extremely accessible and willing to help out if I've ever had questions. The quality of the professors is very high;" "The professors for the most part are very receptive to feedback and love teaching their students," and "if you're showing effort, they will do everything they can to help you." "Showing effort" might be the operative phrase; "one could coast through...by choosing easy classes. However, there are plenty of opportunities to really challenge yourself and succeed with the support of grants, professors, and advisors." Students rave about the small class sizes, "even lectures, and not only does this contribute to a more comfortable, discussion-based learning experience, it ensures that every professor is available and interested, at almost any time." A few students admit that "as a first-year student it can be frustrating trying to get the classes of your choice," but others say, "if you talk to the teachers beforehand, you can usually get the classes you want if they are offered that semester." Regarding the administration, some students claim it "leaves a bit to be desired" and "is not always on the same page as the students." Most are very happy with the administration, though. "If you reach out to them, they will give you as much information as they can," and they "care a lot about our safety and make sure that all of our needs are well-met." "Some deans also teach classes—I had my first-year seminar with an academic dean, and it was great. They seem like they're always available if a student has an issue."

Life

Because Canton is small and the winter is long, "all of the fun and events happen on the campus [because] there is not much to do in town." "The student center is always full of people, and it's hard to not to stay there all day." "Theme houses," in which small groups of students focused on particular issues or activities live, receive high marks both from their residents and the students who come to the dorms for events. "The Java Barn is a small music venue located on campus that is completely run by 11 students that live together in a theme house on campus" and features popular live music events almost every weekend. Hockey games are huge, as are outdoor activities. "At St. Lawrence the natural world is our playground," "and there are lots of people and groups who carpool up to Whiteface in Lake Placid and go downhill skiing. During the warm months there is always something going on on the quad, and many people go on trips to the near by Adirondack Mountains for hiking and other outdoor activities." The rope swing on the Grasse River is also a popular destination, as are Ottawa and Montreal for day trips. If it's too cold to venture outside, students hit the gym: "Our athletic facilities are amazing with an indoor track, squash courts, gym, and climbing wall." As is typical for small schools in similar locales, drinking is popular on weekends. "There are many parties at St. Lawrence, but it is not the only thing to do on campus!" "People go to sporting, singing, and comedy events on campus," and "SLU students are creative with their fun."

Student Body

"A lot of students at St. Lawrence University are athletic and from the East Coast." "There are a lot of the classic Abercrombie & Fitch types...until you take a better look around." Though "preppy" seems to describe many students at St. Lawrence, "There are multitudes of clubs that provide a social scene for all students no matter their interests." "Everyone seems happy and has found some group [to] fit in with." "Most students join an extracurricular activity like art, music, sports, community service, etc." "A typical St. Lawrence student is easygoing, approachable, and likes to have a good time." "There are always a few atypical types, but they make the school more interesting. There's a place here for everyone."

ST. LAWRENCE UNIVERSITY

FINANCIAL AID: 315-229-5265 • E-MAIL: ADMISSIONS@STLAWU.EDU • WEBSITE: WWW.STLAWU.EDU

THE PRINCETON REVIEW SAYS

Admissions

Very important factors considered include: Academic GPA, application essay, recommendation(s), character/personal qualities. *Important factors considered include:* Rigor of secondary school record, extracurricular activities, interview, racial/ethnic status. *Other factors considered include:* Class rank, standardized test scores, alumni/ae relation, first generation, geographical residence, level of applicant's interest, talent/ability, volunteer work, work experience. ACT with or without writing component accepted. TOEFL required of all international applicants for whom English is a second language. High school diploma is required, and GED is accepted. *Academic units recommended:* 4 English, 4 mathematics, 4 science, 4 foreign language, 2 social studies, 2 history.

Financial Aid

Students should submit: FAFSA, CSS/Financial Aid PROFILE. Regular filing deadline is February 1. The Princeton Review suggests that all financial aid forms be submitted as soon as possible after January 1. *Need-based scholarships/grants offered:* Federal Pell, SEOG, state scholarships/grants, private scholarships, school scholarship or grant aid from institutional funds. *Loan aid offered:* Direct Subsidized Stafford, Direct Unsubsidized Stafford, Direct PLUS, Federal Perkins. Federal Work-Study Program available. Off-campus job opportunities are fair.

The Inside Word

St. Lawrence is "test-optional," which means you're not required to submit scores from the SAT or the ACT, but that means your high school transcript and teacher recommendations better be stellar. If you're an international student seeking financial aid, or a homeschooled student, it's probably a good idea to submit some standardized test scores. Scholarship selection is based on overall academic profile, so good scores can help.

THE SCHOOL SAYS "..."

From the Admissions Office

"In an ideal location, St. Lawrence is a diverse liberal arts learning community of inspiring faculty and talented students guided by tradition and focused on the future. The students who live and learn at St. Lawrence are interesting and interested; they enroll with myriad accomplishments and talents, as well as desire to explore new challenges. Our faculty has chosen St. Lawrence intentionally because they know that there is institutional commitment to support great teaching. They are dedicated to making each student's experience challenging and rewarding. Our graduates make up one of the strongest networks of support among any alumni body and are ready, willing, and able to connect with students and help them succeed.

"Which students are happiest at St. Lawrence? Students who like to be actively involved. Students who are open-minded and interested in meeting people with backgrounds different from their own. Students who value having a voice in decisions that affect them. Students who appreciate all that is available to them and cannot wait to take advantage of both the curriculum and the co-curricular options. Students who want to enjoy their college experience and are able to find joy in working hard.

"You can learn the facts about us from this guidebook: We have about 2,200 students; we offer more than thirty majors; the average class size is sixteen students; a great new science center; close to fifty percent of our students study abroad; and we have an environmental consciousness that fits our natural setting between the Adirondack Mountains and St. Lawrence River. You must visit, meet students and faculty, and sense the energy on campus to begin to understand just how special St. Lawrence University is.

"The submission of standardized test scores (SAT or ACT) is optional. Students must indicate on the St. Lawrence Common Application supplement which scores, if any, they wish to have considered in the application process."

SELECTIVITY

Admissions Rating	94
# of applicants	4,900
% of applicants accepted	39
% of acceptees attending	32
# accepting a place on wait list	127
% admitted from wait list	39
# of early decision applicants	230
% accepted early decision	87

FRESHMAN PROFILE

Range SAT Critical Reading	560–660
Range SAT Math	570–660
Range SAT Writing	550–660
Range ACT Composite	25–29
Minimum paper TOEFL	600
Minimum web-based TOEFL	82
Average HS GPA	3.55
% graduated top 10% of class	44
% graduated top 25% of class	78
% graduated top 50% of class	95

DEADLINES

Early decision	
Deadline	11/1
Notification	rolling
Regular	
Deadline	2/1
Notification	late March
Nonfall registration?	yes

APPLICANTS ALSO LOOK AT
AND SOMETIMES PREFER
Colby College, Colgate University

AND RARELY PREFER
Ithaca College

FINANCIAL FACTS

Financial Aid Rating	87
Annual tuition	$42,420
Room and board	$11,005
Required fees	$315
% frosh rec. need-based scholarship or grant aid	68
% UG rec. need-based scholarship or grant aid	66
% frosh rec. non-need-based scholarship or grant aid	56
% UG rec. non-need-based scholarship or grant aid	49
% frosh rec. need-based self-help aid	50
% UG rec. need-based self-help aid	51
% frosh rec. any financial aid	89
% UG rec. any financial aid	85
% UG borrow to pay for school	66
Average cumulative indebtedness	$29,489

ST. MARY'S COLLEGE OF MARYLAND

ADMISSIONS OFFICE, 18952 EAST FISHER ROAD, ST. MARY'S CITY, MD 20686-3001 • ADMISSIONS: 240-895-5000 • FAX: 240-895-5001

CAMPUS LIFE

Quality of Life Rating	90
Fire Safety Rating	81
Green Rating	90
Type of school	public
Environment	rural

STUDENTS

Total undergrad enrollment	1,943
% male/female	41/59
% from out of state	15
% from public high school	60
% live on campus	86
% African American	8
% Asian	3
% Caucasian	81
% Hispanic	3
% international	2
# of countries represented	33

SURVEY SAYS . . .

Athletic facilities are great
Students are friendly
Different types of students interact
Great food on campus
Campus feels safe
Students are happy
Frats and sororities are unpopular
or nonexistent

ACADEMICS

Academic Rating	89
% students graduating within 4 years	72
% students graduating within 6 years	77
Calendar	semester
Student/faculty ratio	12:1
Profs interesting rating	93
Profs accessible rating	93
Most common reg class size	10–19 students
Most common lab size	10–19 students

MOST POPULAR MAJORS
psychology, English, biology, economics, political science

STUDENTS SAY ". . ."

Academics

Undergrads at St. Mary's College of Maryland proudly boast, from the moment you step onto campus your freshman year, "You are instantly part of a family." Indeed there's an "immense sense of community" here, and it's no surprise that a "friendly atmosphere" reverberates throughout the school. Importantly, as "a public honors college," St. Mary's is able to provide "a rigorous academic curriculum" at an affordable price. It also offers a "small and intimate learning environment" with "classes where the professors actually care about teaching and your success." Classes tend to have "a great combination of lecture, discussion, and experiential learning," which translates into "a stimulating, challenging and altogether high-quality academic experience." Additionally, students are quick to brag about their "passionate" and "approachable" professors who are "always available for discussion and clarification." As one public policy major further explains, "Most [teachers] are willing to meet outside their office hours for as long as needed to help a student and many professors are known to give out their cell phone numbers...in case a student needs to reach them at night." They truly want "students to succeed" and work hard to ensure you'll "enjoy even the hardest of classes." A content senior sums up, "At St. Mary's, you are not just a number in the classroom, but an essential part of the classroom experience."

Life

Similar to many college kids, undergrads at St. Mary's have a "work hard, play hard mentality." While they're "definitely focused on their studies," students here also make the most of their time outside of the library. One psych major shares, "There are many opportunities to get involved on campus whether by participating in club activities or taking a student position in campus affairs, or just becoming a student tutor." The school also sponsors a number of events. For example, "Every Thursday we have coffeehouse where artists perform at our local coffee shop, we have comedians Friday nights, and we also have movies showing Fridays, Saturdays, and Sundays." Further, "There are intramural events that take place every semester for almost every sport." Though St. Mary's is a "non-Greek" campus, "themed and house parties are always a hit." Fortunately, "Nobody's looked down upon if they choose not to drink." St. Mary's students also love to take advantage of their location on the water. An anthropology majors explains, "When it's nice out, *everyone* is outside, and on the weekends, the docks are crowded by 11:00 A.M. People throw Frisbees [and] footballs, run around barefoot, grill, and chill." As an added bonus, "Students can take out sail boats or kayaks whenever they want for free." With all these options, it's no wonder why one bio student exclaims that undergrads here "will never be bored."

Student Body

"Friendliness" is the hallmark of the typical St. Mary's undergrad, and many are quick to assert that there's "a very welcoming student body." Indeed, as this junior gushes, "You could sit down and have dinner with someone you have never seen before, and be completely comfortable." The average "Seahawk" is also "focused on their studies" and "involved in all sorts of activities." Students here tend to be "politically aware and left-leaning, and very concerned with the environment." While many St. Mary's undergrads do often share these attributes, another junior assures us, "There are many different types of students [here]: some preppy kids, jocks, the artsy kids, bookworms, hippies, country kids, city kids. Everyone finds their niche, but then mixes up with other people." An excited sophomore interjects, "Quirkiness is more than tolerated here; it is often the norm." And a knowledgeable senior concludes, "With every new class there is an opportunity to make new friends, which makes every semester here exciting."

FINANCIAL AID: 240-895-3000 • E-MAIL: ADMISSIONS@SMCM.EDU • WEBSITE: WWW.SMCM.EDU

THE PRINCETON REVIEW SAYS

Admissions

Very important factors considered include: Academic GPA, rigor of secondary school record. *Important factors considered include:* Application essay, recommendation(s), standardized test scores, extracurricular activities, first generation, talent/ability, volunteer work. *Other factors considered include:* Alumni/ae relation, geographical residence, interview, racial/ethnic status, state residency, work experience. SAT or ACT required; ACT with or without writing component accepted. TOEFL required of all international applicants. High school diploma is required, and GED is accepted. *Academic units required:* 4 English, 3 mathematics, 3 science (2 science labs), 2 foreign language, 2 social studies, 1 history. *Academic units recommended:* 4 mathematics, 4 foreign language, 2 history.

Financial Aid

Students should submit: FAFSA. Regular filing deadline is February 28. The Princeton Review suggests that all financial aid forms be submitted as soon as possible after January 1. *Need-based scholarships/grants offered:* Federal Pell, SEOG, state scholarships/grants, private scholarships, school scholarship or grant aid from institutional funds. *Loan aid offered:* Direct Subsidized Stafford, Direct Unsubsidized Stafford, Direct PLUS, Federal Perkins. Federal Work-Study Program available. Off-campus job opportunities are good.

The Inside Word

As Maryland's public honors college, gaining admissions to St. Mary's is competitive. Admissions officers here really strive to get to know the applicant as an individual, not just a set of numbers on a paper. While academic rigor definitely holds the most weight, admissions officers thoroughly evaluate your essays, recommendations, and extracurricular activities as well.

THE SCHOOL SAYS "..."

From the Admissions Office

"St. Mary's College of Maryland occupies a distinctive niche and represents a real value in American higher education. It is a public college, dedicated to the ideal of affordable, accessible education and committed to quality teaching and excellent programs for undergraduate students. St. Mary's is designated by law the state of Maryland's 'public honors college,' one of only two public colleges in the nation to hold that distinction. It is this mix of honors and affordability that makes St. Mary's an education for the twenty-first century."

SELECTIVITY

Admissions Rating	90
# of applicants	2,133
% of applicants accepted	65
% of acceptees attending	32
# accepting a place on wait list	95
% admitted from wait list	36
# of early decision applicants	232
% accepted early decision	56

FRESHMAN PROFILE

Range SAT Critical Reading	568–680
Range SAT Math	550–650
Range SAT Writing	558–660
Range ACT Composite	25–29
Minimum paper TOEFL	550
Minimum computer TOEFL	250
Minimum web-based TOEFL	90
Average HS GPA	3.58
% graduated top 10% of class	33
% graduated top 25% of class	71
% graduated top 50% of class	93

DEADLINES

Early decision	
Deadline	11/1
Notification	12/1
Regular	
Deadline	1/1
Nonfall registration?	yes

FINANCIAL FACTS

Financial Aid Rating	81
Annual in-state tuition	$12,005
Annual out-of-state tuition	$24,082
Room and board	$10,915
Required fees	$2,440
Books and supplies	$1,000
% frosh rec. need-based scholarship or grant aid	40
% UG rec. need-based scholarship or grant aid	42
% frosh rec. non-need-based scholarship or grant aid	26
% UG rec. non-need-based scholarship or grant aid	25
% frosh rec. need-based self-help aid	41
% UG rec. need-based self-help aid	42
% frosh rec. any financial aid	66
% UG rec. any financial aid	66
% UG borrow to pay for school	50
Average cumulative indebtedness	$17,505

St. Olaf College

1520 St. Olaf Avenue, Northfield, MN 55057 • Admissions: 507-786-3025 • Fax: 507-786-3832

CAMPUS LIFE

Quality of Life Rating	92
Fire Safety Rating	70
Green Rating	82
Type of school	private
Affiliation	Lutheran
Environment	village

STUDENTS

Total undergrad enrollment	3,156
% male/female	45/55
% from out of state	50
% from public high school	82
% live on campus	92
% African American	2
% Asian	5
% Caucasian	84
% Hispanic	2
% international	3
# of countries represented	26

SURVEY SAYS . . .

Athletic facilities are great
Students get along with local community
Great food on campus
Frats and sororities are unpopular or nonexistent
Musical organizations are popular

ACADEMICS

Academic Rating	93
% students graduating within 4 years	83
% students graduating within 6 years	85
Calendar	4-1-4
Student/faculty ratio	12:1
Profs interesting rating	87
Profs accessible rating	91
Most common reg class size	10–19 students
Most common lab size	20–29 students

MOST POPULAR MAJORS

biology, economics, mathematics

STUDENTS SAY "..."

Academics

St. Olaf, a small Lutheran liberal arts school located forty miles south of downtown Minneapolis, provides a "great liberal arts education rich with musical, academic, and social opportunities in a tight-knit, caring community." The school is renowned for its "amazing and extensive" music department (with which "most students are involved somehow"), but that's hardly the school's only asset. On the contrary, St. Olaf offers "excellent vocational training programs in nursing, social work, and education" (supplemented by "great... hands-on learning in addition to classroom learning through internships") as well as "an amazing science and math program. The new 200,000 square foot Regents Hall of Natural and Mathematical Sciences opened in 2008. One of the best things about this school is the broad range of academics and academic experiences you can have." For most here, those experiences include study abroad; the school's numerous study abroad programs mean that "almost everyone goes abroad for at least a month." Writes one student, "St. Olaf has an amazing study abroad program. I've ridden camels in Egypt, climbed the Great Wall in China, seen the ruins of the Acropolis, and gone drinking in Switzerland all in the same semester!" Many students here complete a five-course sequence called "the Great Conversation Program, which provides a rigorous introduction to college, exploring the many 'Great Books' of western culture. The liberal arts requirements make everyone somewhat knowledgeable on every field."

Life

"There isn't much to do in Northfield," so life at St. Olaf "is very centered on campus." The school and student organizations make sure that "there is always something to do on campus, despite the small size of the student body. Bands are brought in to the student nightclub; there are more than 100 concerts a year. The theater and dance programs put on frequent shows, and sports events are happening constantly. Students have the ability to participate in most of these activities, usually without too much prior experience, either." Also, undergraduates are "very focused on clubs and special interest groups. For about 3,000 students there are more than 100 clubs on campus, serving everything from religious beliefs to environmental concerns to just having fun." Undergraduates "are very progressive...Their passion for creating progressive social and political change often springs from their religious convictions." Intramural sports "are huge, so if varsity sports aren't your thing there are outside options," and because students "walk absolutely everywhere...the freshman fifteen is more like the freshman five, if that. We're very healthy." When students need some big-city diversion, the Twin Cities are only about forty-five minutes away. "Many students go up there to eat, see a play, sporting event, concert, or just to shop on weekends."

Student Body

"The stereotype that St. Olaf is completely made up of blond-haired, blue-eyed, Scandinavian Lutherans is not true," students insist, although they quickly admit that "We do have a large number of them!" As one student explains, "We joke about how it seems like every girl is five-foot-four, blond, and fair-skinned, but that isn't totally true. There is a place for more diverse students. It seems like the typical St. Olaf student's mindset is open enough to embrace different religions, races, ideas, and beliefs." The true common ground here is that most St. Olaf undergraduates are "highly motivated toward success, whether academic or vocational," and are "also likely...type-A personalities" who are "involved in many extracurricular events yet maintain good grades under a full academic load." While St. Olaf is a college of the Evangelical Lutheran Church in America, its student body is quite diverse when it comes to religious orientation. One student notes, "The population is not particularly conservative or evangelical. They are more liberal politically and ideologically."

FINANCIAL AID: 507-786-3019 • E-MAIL: ADMISSIONS@STOLAF.EDU • WEBSITE: WWW.STOLAF.EDU

THE PRINCETON REVIEW SAYS

Admissions

Very important factors considered include: Academic GPA, application essay, rigor of secondary school record. *Important factors considered include:* Class rank, recommendation(s), standardized test scores, character/personal qualities, extracurricular activities. *Other factors considered include:* Alumni/ae relation, first generation, geographical residence, interview, level of applicant's interest, racial/ethnic status, religious affiliation/commitment, state residency, talent/ability, volunteer work, work experience. SAT or ACT required; ACT with or without writing component accepted. TOEFL required of all international applicants. High school diploma is required, and GED is accepted. *Academic units recommended:* 4 English, 4 mathematics, 4 science (2 science labs), 4 foreign language, 4 social studies.

Financial Aid

Students should submit: FAFSA, CSS/Financial Aid PROFILE. Regular filing deadline is March 1. The Princeton Review suggests that all financial aid forms be submitted as soon as possible after January 1. *Need-based scholarships/grants offered:* Federal Pell, SEOG, state scholarships/grants, private scholarships, school scholarship or grant aid from institutional funds, Federal Nursing Scholarships. *Loan aid offered:* Direct Subsidized Stafford, Direct Unsubsidized Stafford, Direct PLUS, Federal Perkins, Federal Nursing Loans, state loans, university loans from institutional funds. Federal Work-Study Program not available. Off-campus job opportunities are fair.

The Inside Word

St. Olaf's national reputation is sharply on the rise. This elevated prominence means St. Olaf must compete for candidates with more prestigious schools; hence, the acceptance rate hasn't dropped as dramatically as one might expect, as these days the school loses more of its admits to the Harvards and Northwesterns of the world than it did in the past. The artificially high acceptance rate masks a highly selective, highly competitive admissions process. Bring your A game.

THE SCHOOL SAYS "..."

From the Admissions Office

"One of the nation's leading liberal arts colleges, St. Olaf College offers an academically rigorous education with a vibrant faith tradition as a college of the Evangelical Lutheran Church in America. St. Olaf prepares students to become responsible citizens by fostering the development of mind, body, and spirit. Widely known for its programs in mathematics, the natural sciences, and music, St. Olaf also provides dynamic opportunities for interdisciplinary study. Committed to global education, more than two-thirds of St. Olaf students study abroad before graduating. St. Olaf College is a leader among undergraduate colleges in Rhodes Scholars, Fulbright Fellows, and Peace Corps volunteers."

SELECTIVITY

Admissions Rating	92
# of applicants	4,024
% of applicants accepted	57
% of acceptees attending	37
# of early decision applicants	328
% accepted early decision	77

FRESHMAN PROFILE

Range SAT Critical Reading	600–720
Range SAT Math	600–710
Range SAT Writing	580–700
Range ACT Composite	20–31
Minimum paper TOEFL	520
Minimum computer TOEFL	213
Average HS GPA	3.65
% graduated top 10% of class	56
% graduated top 25% of class	84
% graduated top 50% of class	98

DEADLINES

Early decision	
Deadline	11/15
Notification	12/15
Early action	
Notification	1/15
Regular	
Deadline	3/20
Notification	9/1
Nonfall registration?	yes

APPLICANTS ALSO LOOK AT AND SOMETIMES PREFER

Carleton College, Grinnell College, Gustavus Adolphus College, Lawrence University, Macalester College, Northwestern University, University of Minnesota—Twin Cities, University of Saint Thomas (MN), University of Wisconsin—Madison

FINANCIAL FACTS

Financial Aid Rating	94
Annual tuition	$38,150
Room and board	$8,800
Required fees	$945
Books and supplies	$1,000
% frosh rec. need-based scholarship or grant aid	66
% UG rec. need-based scholarship or grant aid	68
% frosh rec. non-need-based scholarship or grant aid	42
% UG rec. non-need-based scholarship or grant aid	37
% frosh rec. need-based self-help aid	66
% UG rec. need-based self-help aid	68
% frosh rec. any financial aid	87
% UG rec. any financial aid	85
% UG borrow to pay for school	65
Average cumulative indebtedness	$26,115

STANFORD UNIVERSITY

UNDERGRAD. ADMISSION, 355 GALVEZ ST, MONTAG HALL, STANFORD, CA 94305 • ADMISSIONS: 650-723-2091 • FAX: 650-725-2846

CAMPUS LIFE

Quality of Life Rating	95
Fire Safety Rating	85
Green Rating	94
Type of school	private
Environment	city

STUDENTS

Total undergrad enrollment	6,889
% male/female	52/48
% from out of state	55
% from public high school	58
% live on campus	91
# of fraternities	15
# of sororities	13
% African American	10
% Asian	23
% Caucasian	34
% Hispanic	14
% Native American	3
% international	7
# of countries represented	90

SURVEY SAYS . . .
School is well-run
Students are friendly
Dorms are like palaces
Campus feels safe

ACADEMICS

Academic Rating	99
% students graduating within 4 years	78
% students graduating within 6 years	95
Calendar	quarter
Student/faculty ratio	6:1
Profs interesting rating	91
Profs accessible rating	86
Most common reg class size	10–19 students
Most common lab size	10–19 students

MOST POPULAR MAJORS
biology, economics, international relations

STUDENTS SAY ". . ."

Academics

The "passionate" undergrads at this academic powerhouse are enamored with the "amazing and unique" opportunities that Stanford has to offer. As a delighted sophomore explains, "Stanford has incredible resources, incredible people...and an unrivaled atmosphere of openness and collaboration." An "entrepreneurial spirit" and "intellectual curiosity" permeate the campus along with a general "irreverent and laid-back" attitude. Students boast that their professors are "some of the most well-respected experts in their field," and students truly appreciate the "opportunity to engage with them on a regular basis." "Flexible and enthusiastic," teachers here are "wonderful resources for guidance and tutoring." "They have regular office hours and focus on the needs of freshmen just as much as the needs of graduate students." Moreover, they "actively try and get students...to [conduct] research with them." And perhaps most impressive, as one junior highlights, "They make learning so interesting that I can't wait to go home and tell all my friends about whatever we're talking about in class." As one happy senior concludes, "To me, Stanford is a surreal utopia of Nobel Prize faculty, stellar academics, groundbreaking research, top-ranking athletics, passionate and distinguished classmates, and a beautiful campus where the sun is always shining."

Life

Fear not prospective students! Though Stanford's academics are rigorous and demanding, undergrads have been known to back away from the books every now and again. As a relieved political science major assures us, "Before I came to Stanford I thought I would be one of the few people who didn't want to spend my weekend nights in the library...I was wrong." Indeed, undergrads here are an active lot, and most are "involved in student organizations, particularly social justice, ethnic, Greek, or volunteer orgs, as well as student government and positions on University policy boards." When the weekend rolls around, "There are always frat parties or smaller house parties, student plays, musical performances, friends hiking up to the Stanford Dish, people floating around in one of our many fountains, [and] free new movies shown at Flicks." Students also appreciate Stanford's phenomenal athletics program. "Saturdays are dedicated to football (and other sports)," or "You can drive forty-five minutes west to the coast for some of the best surfing in the world, take the train forty-five minutes south to San Francisco for a Giants game, or you can even drive a few hours east to Lake Tahoe and find some of the best skiing in the world. Only at Stanford can you go from snowy mountains, to sunny beaches, to bustling city life all in one day."

Student Body

"It's easy to find your own niche" here. "There isn't a typical student." The university offers "immense diversity of race, religion, and sexual orientation," and most find their peers "incredibly accepting." While students are "driven," they're fortunately "not that competitive or intense." Indeed, the "preppy button-down [types]...are replaced with chilled-out" students in "shorts and flip-flops." Undergrads are "smart yet unassuming" and typically "committed to a million different things." Additionally, they're "generally pretty social and athletic," as well as "service-minded and focused on their future careers." One junior adds, "The jock is doing better than you in chemistry, [and] the cute party animal is double-majoring and president of an activist group." He concludes by saying, "I guess the thing that unites us is that we're all nerds, even if it's not the first thing you see."

FINANCIAL AID: 650-723-3058 • E-MAIL: ADMISSION@STANFORD.EDU • WEBSITE: WWW.STANFORD.EDU

THE PRINCETON REVIEW SAYS

Admissions

Very important factors considered include: Academic GPA, application essay, recommendation(s), rigor of secondary school record, standardized test scores, character/personal qualities, extracurricular activities, talent/ability. *Other factors considered include:* Alumni/ae relation, first generation, geographical residence, racial/ethnic status, volunteer work, work experience. SAT or ACT with writing component required. High school diploma is required, and GED is accepted. *Academic units recommended:* 4 English, 4 mathematics, 3 science (3 science labs), 3 foreign language, 3 history/social studies.

Financial Aid

Students should submit: FAFSA, CSS/Financial Aid PROFILE. Regular filing deadline is February 15. The Princeton Review suggests that all financial aid forms be submitted as soon as possible after January 1. *Need-based scholarships/grants offered:* Federal Pell, SEOG, state scholarships/grants, private scholarships, school scholarship or grant aid from institutional funds. *Loan aid offered:* Direct Subsidized Stafford, Direct Unsubsidized Stafford, Direct PLUS, Federal Perkins. Applicants will be notified of awards with the admissions packet. Federal Work-Study Program available. Off-campus job opportunities are good.

The Inside Word

Stanford is one of the nation's top universities, and landing that coveted acceptance is no easy feat. With record application numbers, open spots in this renowned institution are incredibly tight. Impressive grades in demanding courses and high standardized test scores will be given strong consideration. Admissions officers also want well-rounded individuals who will contribute to Stanford's storied campus. It will be important to demonstrate creativity, leadership, and intellectual curiosity.

THE SCHOOL SAYS "..."

From the Admissions Office

"Stanford looks for distinctive students who exhibit energy, personality, a sense of intellectual vitality and extraordinary impact outside the classroom. While there is no minimum grade point average, class rank, or test score one needs to be admitted to Stanford, the vast majority of successful applicants will be among the strongest students (academically) in their secondary schools. The most compelling applicants for admission will be those who have thus far achieved state, regional, national, and international recognition in their academic and extracurricular areas of interest.

"Stanford accepts the Common Application as its exclusive application for admission. In addition to the online version of the Common Application, all applicants must submit an online Stanford-specific supplement to be considered for admission. The online supplement allows candidates to detail information about an experience they find intellectually engaging; write a note to their freshman year roommate sharing a personal experience they have had; and explain why they feel Stanford is a good fit for them.

"While the SAT or ACT is required for admission, SAT subject tests are not required (and only recommended). AP scores are also not required but may be influential in admission decision and can be used for placement/credit purposes if an applicant decides to enroll."

SELECTIVITY

Admissions Rating	99
# of applicants	32,022
% of applicants accepted	7
% of acceptees attending	72
# of early decision applicants	4,860
# accepted early decision	753

FRESHMAN PROFILE

SAT Critical Reading	799–800
SAT Math	799–800
SAT Writing	799–800
ACT	30–36
Minimum paper TOEFL	600
Minimum web-based TOEFL	105
% graduated top 10% of class	90

DEADLINES

Early action	
Deadline	11/1
Notification	12/16
Regular	
Deadline	1/1
Notification	4/1
Nonfall registration?	no

APPLICANTS ALSO LOOK AT AND OFTEN PREFER
Harvard College, Princeton University, Yale University

AND SOMETIMES PREFER
Massachusetts Institute of Technology

FINANCIAL FACTS

Financial Aid Rating	96
Annual tuition	$38,700
Room and board	$11,876
Required fees	$501
Books and supplies	$7,785
% frosh rec. need-based scholarship or grant aid	53
% UG rec. need-based scholarship or grant aid	51
% frosh rec. non-need-based scholarship or grant aid	5
% UG rec. non-need-based scholarship or grant aid	8
% frosh rec. need-based self-help aid	30
% UG rec. need-based self-help aid	32
% UG rec. any financial aid	80
% UG borrow to pay for school	35
Average cumulative indebtedness	$14,058

STATE UNIVERSITY OF NEW YORK AT BINGHAMTON

PO BOX 6000, BINGHAMTON, NY 13902-6001 • ADMISSIONS: 607-777-2171 • FAX: 607-777-4445

CAMPUS LIFE

Quality of Life Rating	61
Fire Safety Rating	81
Green Rating	99
Type of school	public
Environment	city

STUDENTS

Total undergrad enrollment	11,745
% male/female	53/47
% from out of state	11
% from public high school	89
% live on campus	59
# of fraternities	34
# of sororities	20
% African American	5
% Asian	12
% Caucasian	48
% Hispanic	8
% international	10
# of countries represented	100

SURVEY SAYS . . .

Diverse student types on campus
Campus feels safe
Student publications are popular
Lots of beer drinking

ACADEMICS

Academic Rating	73
% students graduating within 4 years	66
% students graduating within 6 years	78
Calendar	semester
Student/faculty ratio	21:1
Profs interesting rating	69
Profs accessible rating	72
Most common reg class size	10–19 students
Most common lab size	20–29 students

MOST POPULAR MAJORS

biology, business administration and management, engineering

STUDENTS SAY ". . ."

Academics

Known to students as being "one of the top public universities of the region," SUNY Binghamton provides a "high-quality education at a low financial cost." Indeed, it's tough to beat Binghamton's combination of "top-tier academics" and palatable sticker price. The university strives to help students become "well-rounded individuals" who are "globally aware and environmentally conscious." Importantly, Binghamton offers an excellent "variety of majors," and students have the opportunity to study nearly any subject that piques their interest. Undergrads are especially quick to highlight the "great business program" as well as the biology, psychology, and anthropology departments. And though classes are "tough," a psych major assures that "with enough effort, you can do well." By and large, students find their professors "interesting and engaging" and "very friendly and accommodating." As one impressed freshman notes, "They really try to make the students involved even when there are 400 [under-grads in the class]." However, some grumble that a handful of professors "couldn't care less about teaching" and are there simply "to get funded for their own research projects." And others feel that some professors "rely too much on the TAs." Overall though, they genuinely "want students to succeed" and "show true enthusiasm for their subjects."

Life

While students at Binghamton definitely hit the books hard, they also manage to find plenty of time for socializing. According to one ecstatic engineering major, "There are always about a million things going on at one time or another." The only downfall is "it's impossible to do it all." The university sponsors a number of "fun events like hot dog eating competitions [and] Battle of the Bands." Further, "There are always charity events going on, like date auctions" or benefit concerts for "donating food to the needy." Entertainment can also be found very close to home. As one happy freshman shares, "My dorm…does cooking nights, where they invite us down for free pancakes at midnight or even crepes." Like most typical college kids, when the weekend rolls around, "Students often go to parties and the bars downtown." However, "If you're not someone who likes to drink or party every weekend, there is always the option of going to the Union for some Late Nite Binghamton where you can shoot pool, go bowling, sing karaoke, etc." Though the surrounding area is "pretty quiet," when undergrads do want to get off campus, they often take advantage of the "great" skiing and snowboarding that can be found "within decent driving [distance]."

Student Body

It might seem that the typical SUNY Binghamton student "looks as if they walked out of the Hollister catalogue." However, if you scratch the surface, you'll quickly find "many different types of students," and most undergrads find the campus "very diverse in terms of interests, cultures, religions, etc." Of course, geographically speaking, it often feels like "a large percentage of the school is from Long Island and Westchester." Fortunately, "Everyone here just goes out of their way to be friendly and to make you feel like part of the community." Most people "usually find their niche within their residential communities, or based on similar interests and student organizations." Many undergrads define their peers as "intelligent," and nearly everyone "takes their classes very seriously, which provides an intellectually stimulating environment." Further, Binghamton students are "always on the move. If not in class or studying, they will be off to some sort of club or team meeting, volunteer project, athletic training, or even heading out to a party whether it is a small dorm party or a bar bash." As this junior sums up, "From poor to rich, Canadian to Indian, stuck-up to completely relaxed, everyone fits in."

STATE UNIVERSITY OF NEW YORK AT BINGHAMTON

FINANCIAL AID: 607-777-2428 • E-MAIL: ADMIT@BINGHAMTON.EDU • WEBSITE: WWW.BINGHAMTON.EDU

THE PRINCETON REVIEW SAYS

Admissions

Very important factors considered include: Academic GPA, rigor of secondary school record, standardized test scores. *Important factors considered include:* Application essay, class rank, recommendation(s), extracurricular activities, first generation. *Other factors considered include:* Alumni/ae relation, character/personal qualities, geographical residence, level of applicant's interest, racial/ethnic status, state residency, talent/ability, volunteer work, work experience. SAT or ACT required; ACT with writing component required. TOEFL required of all international applicants. High school diploma is required, and GED is accepted. *Academic units required:* 4 English, 3 mathematics, 2 science, 3 foreign language, 2 social studies. *Academic units recommended:* 4 mathematics, 4 science, 4 social studies, 4 history.

Financial Aid

Students should submit: FAFSA. Suggested filing deadline is February 1. The Princeton Review suggests that all financial aid forms be submitted as soon as possible after January 1. *Need-based scholarships/grants offered:* Federal Pell, SEOG, state scholarships/grants, private scholarships, school scholarship or grant aid from institutional funds. *Loan aid offered:* Direct Subsidized Stafford, Direct Unsubsidized Stafford, Direct PLUS, Federal Perkins, Federal Nursing Loans, university loans from institutional funds. Applicants will be notified of awards on a rolling basis beginning March 4. Federal Work-Study Program available. Off-campus job opportunities are excellent.

The Inside Word

SUNY Binghamton is one of the premiere public institutions on the East Coast. There's no magic formula for gaining entrance here. You'll need to have taken a rigorous course load in high school and demonstrated academic success within advanced placement or honors courses. Application essay, SAT scores, and activities will all be analyzed and considered. If you're hoping to secure a coveted spot, don't slack in any area.

THE SCHOOL SAYS "..."

From the Admissions Office

"Binghamton has established itself as the premier public university in the Northeast, because of our outstanding undergraduate programs, vibrant campus culture, and committed faculty. Students are academically motivated, but there is a great deal of mutual help as they compete against the standard of a class rather than each other. Faculty and students work side by side in research labs or on artistic pursuits. Achievement, exploration, and leadership are hallmarks of a Binghamton education. Add to that a campus wide commitment to internationalization that includes a robust study abroad program, cultural offerings, languages and international studies, and you have a place where graduates leave prepared for success. Binghamton University graduates lead the nation in top starting salaries among public universities, demonstrating that our students are recognized by employers and recruiters for having strong abilities to be leaders, critical thinkers, decision makers, analysts, and researchers in many fields and industries."

SELECTIVITY

Admissions Rating	94
# of applicants	27,248
% of applicants accepted	39
% of acceptees attending	21
# accepting a place on wait list	500
% admitted from wait list	6

FRESHMAN PROFILE

Range SAT Critical Reading	580–670
Range SAT Math	620–700
Range SAT Writing	570–660
Range ACT Composite	26–30
Minimum paper TOEFL	550
Minimum computer TOEFL	213
Minimum web-based TOEFL	80
Average HS GPA	3.60
% graduated top 10% of class	50
% graduated top 25% of class	86
% graduated top 50% of class	98

DEADLINES

Early action	
Deadline	11/15
Notification	1/15
Regular	
Priority	1/15
Nonfall registration?	yes

APPLICANTS ALSO LOOK AT

AND OFTEN PREFER
Cornell University

AND SOMETIMES PREFER
Boston University, New York University

AND RARELY PREFER
State University of New York—Stony Brook, Syracuse University

FINANCIAL FACTS

Financial Aid Rating	76
Annual in-state tuition	$4,970
Annual out-of-state tuition	$13,380
Room and board	$11,244
Required fees	$1,911
Books and supplies	$1,000
% frosh rec. need-based scholarship or grant aid	37
% UG rec. need-based scholarship or grant aid	39
% frosh rec. non-need-based scholarship or grant aid	1
% UG rec. non-need-based scholarship or grant aid	2
% frosh rec. need-based self-help aid	45
% UG rec. need-based self-help aid	46
% frosh rec. any financial aid	78
% UG rec. any financial aid	69
% UG borrow to pay for school	50
Average cumulative indebtedness	$21,110

STATE UNIVERSITY OF NEW YORK AT GENESEO

ONE COLLEGE CIRCLE, GENESEO, NY 14454-1401 • ADMISSIONS: 585-245-5571 • FAX: 585-245-5550

CAMPUS LIFE

Quality of Life Rating	80
Fire Safety Rating	89
Green Rating	87
Type of school	public
Environment	village

STUDENTS

Total undergrad enrollment	5,488
% male/female	43/57
% from out of state	2
% from public high school	81
% live on campus	47
# of fraternities	8
# of sororities	11
% African American	2
% Asian	6
% Caucasian	75
% Hispanic	5
% Native American	3
# of countries represented	39

SURVEY SAYS . . .

Lab facilities are great
Great computer facilities
Students are friendly
Campus feels safe
Low cost of living
Students are happy
Student publications are popular
Lots of beer drinking
Hard liquor is popular

ACADEMICS

Academic Rating	84
% students graduating within 4 years	62
% students graduating within 6 years	77
Calendar	semester
Student/faculty ratio	20:1
Profs interesting rating	77
Profs accessible rating	83
Most common reg class size	20–29 students
Most common lab size	10–19 students

MOST POPULAR MAJORS
biology, business administration, psychology

STUDENTS SAY ". . ."

Academics

Undergrads at SUNY Geneseo laud their university for offering "an outstanding education [at] an affordable price." And with the combined "top-notch" academics and "small-town feel," it's no wonder so many students "feel at home" the minute they set foot on the campus. Indeed, Geneseo provides a "close-knit community," which in turn creates "a family environment." While the university has a number of great programs, students are especially quick to highlight the stellar education, business, and speech pathology departments. Importantly, "small classes" translates into highly "accessible" professors. Moreover, they're "truly dedicated to helping students succeed" and "are always open to talk...even during non-office hours." Undergrads do caution that you can't slack off here. Professors "seek to challenge" their students, and the "course load is tough" especially given that Geneseo is "doing a lot to combat grade inflation." Luckily, for the most part, students find their teachers "very engaging" and appreciate that they're able "to make classes very interesting" in large part through "personal stories that are relevant to the material." Perhaps this knowing senior says it best: "Geneseo has a great atmosphere, challenging classes, a wonderful student population, and the best price!"

Life

By and large, undergrads proclaim that "life is great" at SUNY Geneseo. Students "study hard and play hard" and are quite adept at striking a balance between the two. Fortunately, "Weekends are very lively, both on campus and off." An active lot, undergrads like to take advantage of Geneseo's "good" athletic facilities, which include "an ice rink, a swimming pool, a cardio room, and a weight room, as well as lots of intramural and club sports." Additionally, "Varsity sports competitions are extremely popular, especially hockey." There are also "many on-campus activities for students to get involved in throughout the week and especially late at night on the weekends." Indeed, there's "everything from laser tag to crafts to midnight bowling." Of course, "There are also outstanding clubs that [offer] a variety of services and activities such as Colleges Against Cancer, Figure Skating Club, Sports Medicine Club, Outing Club, Ski and Snowboard Club, and so many more." Though "many people do party on the weekend," students assure us, "You don't have to go to parties or join a Greek organization to have a good time." And for those with an itch to explore, a content sophomore shares, "The surrounding country is beautiful and provides lots of fun outdoorsy activities. Rochester and Buffalo are within reach, and Livingston County provides bus service to Rochester."

Student Body

What is one thing that unites Geneseo undergrads? Students here agree that their peers are "very good at time management." Indeed, "They know how to study, but they also know how to have a good time." Having multitasking down to an art form, "They are able to get their work done and excel in classes while still participating in social events and hanging out with their friends." Fortunately, Geneseo is "not a pressure cooker school," and most students are "pretty relaxed." While some assert that the school is "very diverse," others say that the "typical student is a white, middle-class, well-rounded, high school overachiever." Regardless of stereotype, students are very "open to meeting new people," and "making friends [is] really easy here." As one content freshman elaborates, "The students are very accepting. They come together frequently and support each other, causes, and the community." And a fellow classmate adds, "It's really hard to find anyone who doesn't fit in with at least one group on campus because there are so many with so many different interests."

STATE UNIVERSITY OF NEW YORK AT GENESEO

FINANCIAL AID: 716-245-5731 • E-MAIL: ADMISSIONS@GENESEO.EDU • WEBSITE: WWW.GENESEO.EDU

THE PRINCETON REVIEW SAYS

Admissions

Very important factors considered include: Rigor of secondary school record, standardized test scores. *Important factors considered include:* Academic GPA, application essay, class rank, recommendation(s), extracurricular activities, racial/ethnic status, talent/ability. *Other factors considered include:* Alumni/ae relation, character/personal qualities, first generation, level of applicant's interest, volunteer work, work experience. SAT or ACT required; ACT with or without writing component accepted. TOEFL required of all international applicants. High school diploma is required, and GED is accepted. *Academic units recommended:* 4 English, 4 mathematics, 4 science, 4 foreign language, 4 social studies.

Financial Aid

Students should submit: FAFSA. Regular filing deadline is February 15. The Princeton Review suggests that all financial aid forms be submitted as soon as possible after January 1. *Need-based scholarships/grants offered:* Federal Pell, SEOG, state scholarships/grants. *Loan aid offered:* Direct Subsidized Stafford, Direct Unsubsidized Stafford, Direct PLUS, Federal Perkins. Applicants will be notified of awards on a rolling basis beginning March 15. Federal Work-Study Program available. Off-campus job opportunities are poor.

The Inside Word

SUNY Geneseo increasingly receives applications from a strong candidate pool, and gaining admission is no easy feat. First and foremost, the admissions committee reviews your high school transcript and college entrance exam scores. Applicants who have excelled in honors, IB, or advanced placement courses will have a leg up. Additionally, those reviewing prospective students attempt to take a holistic approach so be sure to submit a well-crafted essay and to demonstrate extracurricular commitment.

THE SCHOOL SAYS "..."

From the Admissions Office

"Geneseo has carved a distinctive niche among the nation's premier public liberal arts colleges. Geneseo is the only undergraduate college in the state of New York system to be granted a chapter of Phi Beta Kappa. The college now competes for students with some of the nation's most selective private colleges, including Colgate, Vassar, Hamilton, and Boston College. Founded in 1871, the college occupies a 220-acre hillside campus in the historic Village of Geneseo, overlooking the scenic Genesee Valley. As a residential campus—with nearly two-thirds of the students living in college residence halls—it provides a rich and varied program of social, cultural, recreational, and scholarly activities. Geneseo is noted for its distinctive core curriculum and the extraordinary opportunities it offers undergraduates to pursue independent study and research with faculty who value close working relationships with talented students. Equally impressive is the remarkable success of its graduates, forty-nine percent of whom study at leading graduate and professional schools immediately following graduation.

"SUNY Geneseo will use either SAT or ACT test results in the admission selection process. The SAT writing test result will not be used. SAT Subject Test results are not required but will be considered if the applicant submits the test results."

SELECTIVITY

Admissions Rating	94
# of applicants	9,885
% of applicants accepted	38
% of acceptees attending	27
# accepting a place on wait list	342
% admitted from wait list	0
# of early decision applicants	339
% accepted early decision	39

FRESHMAN PROFILE

Range SAT Critical Reading	600–690
Range SAT Math	600–700
Range ACT Composite	27–30
Minimum paper TOEFL	525
Minimum computer TOEFL	197
Minimum web-based TOEFL	71
Average HS GPA	3.75
% graduated top 10% of class	52
% graduated top 25% of class	87
% graduated top 50% of class	99

DEADLINES

Early decision	
Deadline	11/15
Notification	12/15
Regular	
Deadline	1/1
Nonfall registration?	yes

APPLICANTS ALSO LOOK AT

AND OFTEN PREFER
Colgate University, Cornell University, Hamilton College, New York University

AND SOMETIMES PREFER
Boston College, Skidmore College, State University of New York at Binghamton, University of Rochester, Vassar College

FINANCIAL FACTS

Financial Aid Rating	88
Annual in-state tuition	$4,970
Annual out-of-state tuition	$13,380
Room and board	$10,436
Required fees	$1,431
Books and supplies	$950
% frosh rec. need-based scholarship or grant aid	19
% UG rec. need-based scholarship or grant aid	44
% frosh rec. non-need-based scholarship or grant aid	19
% UG rec. non-need-based scholarship or grant aid	16
% frosh rec. need-based self-help aid	23
% UG rec. need-based self-help aid	40
% frosh rec. any financial aid	60
% UG rec. any financial aid	70
% UG borrow to pay for school	65
Average cumulative indebtedness	$21,200

STATE UNIVERSITY OF NEW YORK—PURCHASE COLLEGE

ADMISSIONS OFFICE, 735 ANDERSON HILL ROAD, PURCHASE, NY 10577 • ADMISSIONS: 914-251-6300 • FAX: 914-251-6314

STUDENTS SAY ". . ."

Academics
"Think Wide Open" is the motto at Purchase College, where "an eccentric environment...helps to fuel people's creativity and open-mindedness." "Purchase is about unapologetically being yourself," a place that "teaches real-world lessons with an 'against the grain' sort of approach." This unusual environment is due primarily to a large performing and creative arts program, in which just over one-third of all undergraduates are enrolled. These programs, which include dance, theater, music, film, and creative writing, benefit greatly from the school's proximity to New York City, an international leader in the arts. But while "the conservatories are the best known part of Purchase College," they are hardly the school's only assets. Students tell us "we do in fact have an almost equally strong liberal arts program," with excellent offerings in psychology, media studies, journalism, and premedical sciences, leading undergrads to praise "an artistic atmosphere with loads of academic opportunities." As a smaller school, Purchase can provide "the attention you need from caring professors" and can accommodate more student input; undergraduates tell us that "There is always the possibility of discussion in class, and teachers are tolerant of most thought." Professors "are very engaged, enthusiastic, and simply love learning and teaching."

Life
"Purchase is located in an area that is by no means a college town," meaning students need to rely on campus life for extracurricular fun. Fortunately, "each night there are opportunities to find something to do" without leaving the campus confines. The high concentration of creative and performing artists at Purchase means that "there's always something going on," including "concerts, plays, recitals" and "art exhibits." There are "fewer 'let's drink to drink' parties here" than at most state campuses, students believe. Instead, "Parties are organized around diversity and themes. Dance parties are common, celebrating African American or Latino culture (there are two very active groups on campus: SOCA and a chapter of Latinos Unidos). Club activities such as Cheese Club or Hillel are [also] popular." In quieter moments, "Fun can range from hiking in the woods to playing video games, [to] playing music." Or just shooting the breeze, as Purchase is home to "more philosophical people than you would expect at a state school. Not pretentiously, though. Even athletes are influenced by the community and begin to think in different ways." When all else fails, "New York City is a quick half-hour express train away on the Metro North, which has anything you could imagine available."

Student Body
"As one of the few public arts colleges that also integrates...reputable science and humanities departments," Purchase provides a home to a remarkably diverse student body. "We have athletes, cheerleaders, musicians, singers, dancers, and actors; this is just some of the diversity that is present at Purchase College," one undergrad reports. One thing many here share in common: They're likely to be a bit nerdy. As one student explains, "Imagine if you will, that you're back in grade school. Remember the last four students to be chosen [for teams in gym]? Those are Purchase College students, and the four of them are majoring in music composition, dance, biology, and literature. Or sociology, or printmaking, or gender studies." It's hardly wall-to-wall nerds, though; it's just that "The anime community is just as large as the athletic community or the premed students." As on many artsy campuses, "we have a lot of drag queens, hipsters, hippies...etc." but because "It is still a state school, students wanting to study science or language or anything...else also come here, and still fit in."

STATE UNIVERSITY OF NEW YORK—PURCHASE COLLEGE

FINANCIAL AID: 914-251-6350 • E-MAIL: ADMISSIONS@PURCHASE.EDU • WEBSITE: WWW.PURCHASE.EDU

THE PRINCETON REVIEW SAYS

Admissions

Very important factors considered include: Academic GPA, application essay, talent/ability. *Important factors considered include:* Standardized test scores. *Other factors considered include:* Class rank, recommendation(s), rigor of secondary school record, character/personal qualities, extracurricular activities, interview. SAT or ACT required; ACT with or without writing component accepted. TOEFL required of all international applicants. High school diploma is required, and GED is accepted.

Financial Aid

Students should submit: FAFSA. The Princeton Review suggests that all financial aid forms be submitted as soon as possible after January 1. *Need-based scholarships/grants offered:* Federal Pell, SEOG, state scholarships/grants, private scholarships, school scholarship or grant aid from institutional funds. *Loan aid offered:* Direct Subsidized Stafford, Direct Unsubsidized Stafford, Direct PLUS, Federal Perkins. Applicants will be notified of awards on a rolling basis beginning March 1. Federal Work-Study Program available. Off-campus job opportunities are excellent.

The Inside Word

Just more than one-third of Purchase College undergraduates enroll in the School of the Arts. All must undergo either an audition or portfolio review as part of the application process; for such students, this is the most important part of the application. Traditional application components—such as high school transcript, test scores, and personal essay—are also considered, but figure less prominently. Applicants to the School of Liberal Arts and Sciences undergo a more conventional application review.

THE SCHOOL SAYS "..."

From the Admissions Office

"At Purchase College, you're encouraged to 'Think Wide Open.' The campus combines the energy and excitement of professional training in the performing and the visual arts with the intellectual traditions and spirit of discovery of the humanities and sciences. A Purchase College education emphasizes creativity, individual accomplishment, openness, and exploration. It culminates in a senior research or creative project that may focus on civic engagement or interdisciplinary work to become an excellent springboard to a career or to graduate or professional school. The Conservatories of Art and Design, Dance, Music, and Theatre Arts and Film that make up the School of the Arts deliver a cohort-based education with apprenticeships and other professional opportunities in nearby New York City.

"You'll find a unique and engaging atmosphere at Purchase, whether you are a student in the arts, humanities, natural sciences, or social sciences. You choose among a wide variety of programs, including arts management, journalism, creative writing, environmental science, new media, dramatic writing, premed, pre-law, and education. You'll attend performances by your friends, see world-renowned artists on stage at the Performing Arts Center, and experience the artworks on display in the Neuberger Museum of Art (one of the largest campus art museums in the country)—all without leaving campus. The new student services building, along with an enhanced student services website, is making Purchase a lot more user-friendly for its students.

"Admissions requirements vary with each program in the college and can include auditions, portfolio reviews, essays, writing samples, and interviews.

"In addition to individual program requirements, Purchase College requires SAT or ACT scores to complete your application."

SELECTIVITY

Admissions Rating	85
# of applicants	9,163
% of applicants accepted	31
% of acceptees attending	24

FRESHMAN PROFILE

Range SAT Critical Reading	510–620
Range SAT Math	480–580
Range SAT Writing	500–600
Range ACT Composite	22–26
Minimum paper TOEFL	550
Minimum computer TOEFL	213
Average HS GPA	3.20
% graduated top 10% of class	11
% graduated top 25% of class	36
% graduated top 50% of class	78

DEADLINES

Early decision	
Deadline	11/15
Notification	12/15
Regular	
Priority	3/1
Deadline	7/15
Nonfall registration?	yes

APPLICANTS ALSO LOOK AT AND OFTEN PREFER
New York University

FINANCIAL FACTS

Financial Aid Rating	66
Annual in-state tuition	$4,970
Annual out-of-state tuition	$13,380
Room and board	$10,815
Books and supplies	$1,122
% frosh rec. need-based scholarship or grant aid	48
% UG rec. need-based scholarship or grant aid	46
% frosh rec. non-need-based scholarship or grant aid	1
% UG rec. non-need-based scholarship or grant aid	1
% frosh rec. need-based self-help aid	59
% UG rec. need-based self-help aid	55
% UG borrow to pay for school	58
Average cumulative indebtedness	$33,125

STATE UNIVERSITY OF NEW YORK—STONY BROOK UNIVERSITY

OFFICE OF ADMISSIONS, STONY BROOK, NY 11794-1901 • ADMISSIONS: 631-632-6868 • FAX: 631-632-9898

CAMPUS LIFE

Quality of Life Rating	68
Fire Safety Rating	73
Green Rating	93
Type of school	public
Environment	town

STUDENTS

Total undergrad enrollment	16,045
% male/female	52/48
% from out of state	7
% from public high school	90
% live on campus	59
# of fraternities	15
# of sororities	14
% African American	6
% Asian	23
% Caucasian	38
% Hispanic	9
% international	7
# of countries represented	111

SURVEY SAYS . . .

Class discussions are rare
Great computer facilities
Great library
Diverse student types on campus
Low cost of living
Lots of beer drinking

ACADEMICS

Academic Rating	63
% students graduating within 4 years	43
% students graduating within 6 years	65
Calendar	semester
Student/faculty ratio	19:1
Profs interesting rating	67
Profs accessible rating	66
Most common reg class size	20–29 students
Most common lab size	20–29 students

MOST POPULAR MAJORS
biology, business/commerce,
psychology

STUDENTS SAY ". . ."

Academics
Stony Brook University combines affordability and excellence with academic prestige, offering a "great academic reputation," ample research opportunities, and the chance to learn from "world-renowned professors for a great price." Don't let Stony Brook's "best value" reputation fool you; known as a "science powerhouse," the school is also a leader in premedical preparation. With over 150 academic programs on offer, "the breadth of the school's curriculum" is impressive, including "a wide variety of classes that you can take, ranging from [topics] such as theory of dance to nuclear physics." Academics are challenging and "Everyone lives in the library." In particular, "The science courses are no joke. They are large and hard, and you will most likely learn most of the material yourself." Fortunately, students paint a generally positive picture of the faculty, describing professors as "approachable and interested in their subject, making them good educators." Stony Brook is a research university, so while "it is relatively easy to find internships and research opportunities" as an undergraduate, you should also be aware that "Many professors feel their lab work is more important than their students." With almost 16,000 undergraduates, you'll end up in plenty of big lecture courses, making it more difficult to get to know your instructors personally. However, faculty maintains "reasonable office hours," and most are "very accessible" if you seek them out. In fact, Stony Brook students tell us that their "school is about taking initiative and taking advantage of opportunities that are available," rather than having your hand held—a happy condition for those who feel they are "too old to be spoon-fed." A current student explains, "Professors and staff are more than willing to help, but you have to ask for it...I feel that the balance between independence and assistance has prepared me well for entering a profession."

Life
Nothing at Stony Brook University will be handed to you on a silver platter, yet students reassure us that, "If you are willing to seek out activities and events, you will never be bored." On campus, there are almost 300 clubs and organizations, including sports teams, environmental groups, several student-run newspaper, and fraternities and sororities. In their downtime, students "hang out with friends," play video games or intramural sports, "head over to the University Café, or watch movies in their rooms." For additional distraction, "Each dorm building has its own ping-pong table and pool table in the basement." If you want to take a break from college life, "campus buses go to places like the mall and Walmart every weekend," and the surrounding community offers "movie theaters, bowling, Dave and Buster's, [and] countless restaurants." In addition, New York City is "fairly close," while nearby Southampton boasts "one of the top beaches in the United States." While people get together socially, SUNY Stony Brook is not a major party school, and "The campus is very quiet on weekends because many students live nearby and go home."

Student Body
Drawing a large crowd from the state of New York and a smattering of international students, Stony Brook University "combines the diversity of New York City with academic excellence to create a truly unique experience." At this large school, "Every personality type is represented...and it is easy to find a group to fit in with." Politically, "there are both strong right-wing and left-wing school newspapers," though "many more people support the liberal side." No matter what your persuasion, the community is generally open and accepting of different backgrounds, opinions, and interests. A current student elaborates, "I've never seen such a heterogeneous mixture of individuals in my life. And yet, despite the vast differences amongst students, everyone seems to get along." Across the board, academics are a priority, but most students strike a balance between work and play. At Stony Brook, "A typical student will go to class, spend a lot of their time studying, and try to have some fun on Thursday nights and the weekends."

STATE UNIVERSITY OF NEW YORK—STONY BROOK UNIVERSITY

FINANCIAL AID: 631-632-6840 • E-MAIL: ENROLL@STONYBROOK.EDU • WEBSITE: WWW.STONYBROOK.EDU

THE PRINCETON REVIEW SAYS

Admissions

Very important factors considered include: Academic GPA, rigor of secondary school record, standardized test scores. *Important factors considered include:* Application essay, recommendation(s). *Other factors considered include:* Class rank, character/personal qualities, extracurricular activities, interview, level of applicant's interest, talent/ability, volunteer work, work experience. SAT or ACT with writing component required. TOEFL, IELTS, or SAT required of all international applicants. High school diploma is required, and GED is accepted. *Academic units required:* 4 English, 3 mathematics, 3 science, 2 foreign language, 4 social studies. *Academic units recommended:* 4 mathematics, 4 science, 3 foreign language.

Financial Aid

Students should submit: FAFSA. Regular filing deadline is March 1. The Princeton Review suggests that all financial aid forms be submitted as soon as possible after January 1. *Need-based scholarships/grants offered:* Federal Pell, SEOG, state scholarships/grants, private scholarships, school scholarship or grant aid from institutional funds. *Loan aid offered:* Direct Subsidized Stafford, Direct Unsubsidized Stafford, Direct PLUS, Federal Perkins. Applicants will be notified of awards on a rolling basis beginning March 15. Federal Work-Study Program available. Off-campus job opportunities are excellent.

The Inside Word

Admission to Stony Brook University is competitive. Students with a particularly strong academic record may be considered for the university's special programs, including the Honors Program, the University Scholars program, and the Scholars in Medicine program. Admits to the Scholars in Medicine program can earn a bachelor's degree and MD through an integrated, eight-year curriculum; but applicants must meet high minimum GPA and test score requirements to be considered.

THE SCHOOL SAYS "..."

From the Admissions Office

"Our graduates include Carolyn Porco, the leader of the Imaging Team for the Cassini mission to Saturn; John Hennessy, the president of Stanford University; and Scott Higham, a Pulitzer Prize-winning investigative journalist for the Washington Post who has come to speak to students at our new School of Journalism. Situated on 1,000 wooded acres on the North Shore of Long Island, Stony Brook offers more than 150 majors, minors, and combined-degree programs for undergraduates, including our Fast Track MBA program, a thriving research environment, and a dynamic first-year experience in one of six small undergraduate communities. Faculty include four members of our School of Marine and Atmospheric Sciences who are recent co-winners of the Nobel Peace Prize. Students enjoy comfortable campus housing, outstanding recreational facilities that include an 8,300 seat stadium, modern student activities center, indoor sports complex, and 85,000-square foot campus recreation center due to open in 2012. In addition, the Staller Center for the Arts offers spectacular theatrical and musical performances throughout the year. We invite students who possess both intellectual curiosity and academic ability to explore the countless exciting opportunities available at Stony Brook. Freshmen applying for admission to the university are required to take the SAT (or the ACT with the writing section). SAT Subject Test scores are recommended, but not required."

SELECTIVITY

Admissions Rating	92
# of applicants	27,822
% of applicants accepted	41
% of acceptees attending	24
# accepting a place on wait list	704
% admitted from wait list	5

FRESHMAN PROFILE

Range SAT Critical Reading	530–630
Range SAT Math	580–680
Range SAT Writing	520–630
Range ACT Composite	25–29
Minimum paper TOEFL	550
Minimum computer TOEFL	213
Minimum web-based TOEFL	80
Average HS GPA	3.60
% graduated top 10% of class	38
% graduated top 25% of class	72
% graduated top 50% of class	95

DEADLINES

Regular	
Priority	1/15
Nonfall registration?	yes

APPLICANTS ALSO LOOK AT
AND OFTEN PREFER
Cornell University, Rensselaer Polytechnic Institute, State University of New York at Binghamton

AND SOMETIMES PREFER
Penn State—University Park, Rutgers, The State University of New Jersey, State University of New York at Geneseo, University of Connecticut

AND RARELY PREFER
Adelphi University, Hofstra University, Pace University

FINANCIAL FACTS

Financial Aid Rating	73
Annual in-state tuition	$4,970
Annual out-of-state tuition	$13,380
Room and board	$10,142
Required fees	$1,610
Books and supplies	$900
% frosh rec. need-based scholarship or grant aid	51
% UG rec. need-based scholarship or grant aid	49
% frosh rec. non-need-based scholarship or grant aid	31
% UG rec. non-need-based scholarship or grant aid	16
% frosh rec. need-based self-help aid	54
% UG rec. need-based self-help aid	53
% frosh rec. any financial aid	75
% UG rec. any financial aid	66
% UG borrow to pay for school	59
Average cumulative indebtedness	$19,770

THE BEST 376 COLLEGES ■ 529

STATE UNIVERSITY OF NEW YORK—UNIVERSITY AT ALBANY

OFFICE OF UNDERGRAD ADMISSIONS, 1400 WASHINGTON AVE., ALBANY, NY 12222 • ADMISSIONS: 518-442-5435 • FAX: 518-442-5383

CAMPUS LIFE

Quality of Life Rating	61
Fire Safety Rating	80
Green Rating	89
Type of school	public
Environment	city

STUDENTS

Total undergrad enrollment	12,623
% male/female	51/49
% from out of state	5
% live on campus	57
# of fraternities	11
# of sororities	18
% African American	10
% Asian	6
% Caucasian	59
% Hispanic	10
% international	3
# of countries represented	84

SURVEY SAYS . . .

Class discussions are rare
Diverse student types on campus
Lousy food on campus
Lots of beer drinking
Hard liquor is popular

ACADEMICS

Academic Rating	65
% students graduating within 4 years	55
% students graduating within 6 years	64
Calendar	semester
Student/faculty ratio	19:1
Profs interesting rating	61
Profs accessible rating	61
Most common reg class size	20–29 students
Most common lab size	10–19 students

MOST POPULAR MAJORS

business administration and management, English language and literature, psychology

STUDENTS SAY ". . ."

Academics

Is SUNY Albany (UAlbany to those in the know) the perfect-sized school? Many here think so. Students describe it as "a big school numbers-wise that feels small." Notes one student, "It has a very broad range of quality academic programs, which is very important for an undecided senior in high school." Another adds, "If you know what you want and are motivated, the sky is the limit." The school exploits its location in the state capital to bolster programs in political science, criminal justice, and business, and it "offers internship opportunities to college students that very few schools can." Other standout departments include psychology, Japanese studies, mathematics, and many of the hard sciences. Professors here vary widely in quality, but a surprising number "are receptive, active, and engaging"—in other words, "a lot more accessible than I would have thought for a school this big." Teachers are especially willing to "go out of their way to help students who are interested in learning, come to class regularly, and care about their academic work." The administration, as at most state-run schools, "is basically an over-bloated bureaucracy. Students are sent from department to department in each of their endeavors. It is advisable to avoid [the] administration if at all possible."

Life

There are three distinct social orbits on the Albany campus. Some students take the initiative "by joining one of the many clubs or groups or getting involved with the student government." Others "party for a good time," telling us that "any night of the week you can find people to go out to the bars and clubs with you" and that "the average night ends between 2:30 and 4:00 A.M." Both of these groups are likely to tell you that "there is a lot to do in Albany and the surrounding area," including "a great arts district, tons of awesome restaurants, museums, [and] a state park." A third, sizable group primarily complains about the cold weather and asserts that "there's nothing to do in Albany." The school works to excite these students with "fun programs and entertainers who come to the campus. We have had a series of comedians, rappers/singers, guests from MTV and VH1, authors, political figures, musical performances, sporting events, spirit events, and many other things around campus." School spirit is on the rise among all groups, we're told. The reason? "A few years ago, basketball team began winning, and everyone came out of the woodwork to support them—it was really a great thing to see."

Student Body

Undergrads here believe that the student body is very diverse in terms of ethnicity and also in terms of personality type; one student observes, "You have your motivated students [who] get good grades, are involved, and get amazing jobs in NYC after college. Then you have your unmotivated kids [who] complain, don't go to class, and blame a bad grade on the professor (when really it is because they crammed the night before and didn't go to class)." Geographically, the school is less diverse. Nearly everyone is a New York State resident, with many coming from "downstate New York"—Long Island, New York City, and Westchester County. There's a fair amount of upstate kids as well, and "a lot of people have certain stereotypes in their heads when they first come to Albany. The Long Islander has his idea about the upstater and vice versa. After a few weeks, though, people see that these aren't always true. I think people from anywhere get along pretty well." The international students, who form a small but noticeable contingent, "tend to keep to themselves," perhaps "due to a culture or language barrier." About one-quarter of the campus population is Jewish.

STATE UNIVERSITY OF NEW YORK—UNIVERSITY AT ALBANY

FINANCIAL AID: 518-442-5757 • E-MAIL: UGADMISSIONS@ALBANY.EDU • WEBSITE: WWW.ALBANY.EDU

THE PRINCETON REVIEW SAYS
Admissions
Very important factors considered include: Academic GPA, class rank, recommendation(s), rigor of secondary school record, standardized test scores, character/personal qualities. *Important factors considered include:* Application essay. *Other factors considered include:* Alumni/ae relation, extracurricular activities, first generation, geographical residence, talent/ability, volunteer work, work experience. SAT or ACT required; ACT with writing component required. TOEFL required of most international applicants. High school diploma is required, and GED is accepted. *Academic units required:* 4 English, 2 mathematics, 2 science (2 science labs), 1 foreign language, 3 social studies, 2 history, 4 academic elective. *Academic units recommended:* 4 mathematics, 3 science (3 science labs), 3 foreign language.

Financial Aid
Students should submit: FAFSA. Priority filing deadline is March 15. The Princeton Review suggests that all financial aid forms be submitted as soon as possible after January 1. *Need-based scholarships/grants offered:* Federal Pell, SEOG, state scholarships/grants, private scholarships, school scholarship or grant aid from institutional funds. *Loan aid offered:* Direct Subsidized Stafford, Direct Unsubsidized Stafford, Direct PLUS, Federal Perkins. Applicants will be notified of awards on a rolling basis beginning March 20. Federal Work-Study Program available. Off-campus job opportunities are good.

The Inside Word
The Wall Street Journal has noted a growing trend among students who, in the past, had limited their postsecondary options to high-end private schools: More such students, the paper reported, have broadened their vision to include prestigious state schools such as SUNY Albany. The driving force, unsurprisingly, is economic. In the event of an unlikely decline in the cost of private education, expect admissions at schools like UAlbany to grow more competitive in coming years.

THE SCHOOL SAYS "..."
From the Admissions Office
"Increasing numbers of well-prepared students are discovering the benefits of study in UAlbany's nationally ranked programs and are taking advantage of outstanding internship and employment opportunities in upstate New York's 'Tech Valley.' The already strong undergraduate program is further enhanced by the Honors College, a university-wide program for ambitious students. The Honors College offers enhanced honors courses and co-curricular options including honors housing.

"Nine schools and colleges, including the nation's first College of Nanoscale Science and Engineering, offer bachelor's, master's, and doctoral programs to more than nearly 13,000 undergraduates and 5,000 graduate students. An award-winning advisement program helps students take advantage of all these options by customizing the undergraduate experiences. More than two-thirds of Albany graduates go on for advanced degrees, and acceptance to law and medical school is above the national average.

"Student life on campus includes 200 clubs, honor societies, and other groups, and nineteen Division I varsity teams. With twenty other colleges in the region, Albany is a great college town, adjacent to the spectacular natural and recreational centers of New York and New England.

"Freshmen are awarded more than $800,000 in merit scholarships each year and nearly three-quarters of our students receive financial aid."

SELECTIVITY
Admissions Rating	86
# of applicants	21,960
% of applicants accepted	47
% of acceptees attending	22

FRESHMAN PROFILE
Range SAT Critical Reading	500–590
Range SAT Math	530–620
Minimum paper TOEFL	550
Minimum computer TOEFL	213
Minimum web-based TOEFL	79
Average HS GPA	3.40
% graduated top 10% of class	21
% graduated top 25% of class	60
% graduated top 50% of class	94

DEADLINES
Early action	
Deadline	11/15
Notification	1/15
Regular	
Priority	3/1
Deadline	3/1
Notification	1/15
Nonfall registration?	yes

FINANCIAL FACTS
Financial Aid Rating	66
Annual in-state tuition	$4,970
Annual out-of-state tuition	$13,380
Room and board	$10,633
Required fees	$1,860
Books and supplies	$1,600
% frosh rec. need-based scholarship or grant aid	49
% UG rec. need-based scholarship or grant aid	50
% frosh rec. non-need-based scholarship or grant aid	2
% UG rec. non-need-based scholarship or grant aid	1
% frosh rec. need-based self-help aid	46
% UG rec. need-based self-help aid	46
% frosh rec. any financial aid	64
% UG rec. any financial aid	62
Average cumulative indebtedness	$22,092

STATE UNIVERSITY OF NEW YORK—UNIVERSITY AT BUFFALO

15 CAPEN HALL, BUFFALO, NY 14260-1660 • ADMISSIONS: 716-645-6900 • FAX: 716-645-6411

CAMPUS LIFE

Quality of Life Rating	72
Fire Safety Rating	60*
Green Rating	65
Type of school	public
Environment	city

STUDENTS

Total undergrad enrollment	19,199
% male/female	54/46
% from out of state	4
% live on campus	34
# of fraternities	22
# of sororities	17
% African American	7
% Asian	10
% Caucasian	57
% Hispanic	4
% Native American	1
% international	15
# of countries represented	108

SURVEY SAYS . . .
Diverse student types on campus
Student publications are popular
Lots of beer drinking
Hard liquor is popular

ACADEMICS

Academic Rating	66
% students graduating within 4 years	43
% students graduating within 6 years	67
Calendar	semester
Student/faculty ratio	16:1
Profs interesting rating	62
Profs accessible rating	67
Most common reg class size	20–29 students
Most common lab size	20–29 students

MOST POPULAR MAJORS
business/commerce, engineering, social sciences

STUDENTS SAY ". . ."

Academics
Offering "more academic programs per dollar than any other university in the state," SUNY Buffalo (UB for short) "is about choices. You can choose many different…combinations of academics and social activities with the support in place." Students brag that UB's "programs are all of the highest quality, translating [into] a best-value education for students." The School of Engineering and Applied Science in particular "is well respected" and "works with corporate partners in a variety of ways that range from joint-research ventures to continuing education to co-op work arrangements for our students." Other stand-out offerings include pharmacy, physical therapy, a popular business and management school "that is ranked highly," "a solid undergrad and grad architecture program," and "one of the top nursing programs in the state." Of course, a school with this much to offer is bound to be large, making it "easy not to attend class and fall through the cracks, so one must be self-motivated to do well." Administrative tasks are occasionally Kafkaesque, with "a lot of red tape to go through to get anything done. I feel like a pebble being kicked around when trying to get support or services," notes one student. Many students point out that support services and contact with professors improves during junior and senior years when students are pursuing their majors and forging stronger relationships within their departments.

Life
UB is divided into three campuses. Traditionally, South Campus in Northeast Buffalo has been where "the parties are," though students say, "it's much less safe than North Campus," which is located in the suburban enclave of Amherst. The school also has a downtown campus. The recent closing of several bars near South Campus has made it less of a party destination than it was in years past; these days many students report going to downtown Buffalo "to go clubbing." Students living on North Campus describe it as "its own little city. We have food services, our own bus system, a highway, even our own zip codes. If you know how to play, North Campus is just as much fun as Main Street [which runs by South Campus]; you just need to know where to go." The North Campus, which features "a lake and a nice bike path for when you want to escape from the hectic [atmosphere]" of academic life, is the more populous of the two; the intercampus bus system is "convenient," although a car is preferred. Students tell us that "between all of the clubs and organizations, the Office of Student Life, athletics, and the Student Association, there is always something to do" on campus. The school's Division I sports teams "are a big hit around here. Even if we are the worst in the division, we still cheer hard and go crazy for our guys and girls." Those who explore Buffalo extol its "amazing art and music scene."

Student Body
Because of UB's size, "You can find just about every kind of person there is here. Everyone has a place in this large and diverse student population." As one student notes, "Although the typical student is of traditional college age, there really isn't a 'typical' student—the student body is very diverse in terms of religion, ethnicity, nationality, age, gender, and orientation. 'Atypical' students fit in well because of the diversity of the student population." Another student adds, "There are a lot of foreign and minority students, to the point that the actual 'majority' is the minority here at UB." Geographically, UB draws "from urban areas, rural areas, NYC, Long Island, and most every country in the world." As a state school, "a lot of the students are from New York State, but with differing areas of the state, there are many different types of students."

Financial Aid: 866-838-7257 • E-mail: ub-admissions@buffalo.edu • Website: www.buffalo.edu

THE PRINCETON REVIEW SAYS

Admissions

Very important factors considered include: Academic GPA, rigor of secondary school record, standardized test scores. *Important factors considered include:* Class rank, recommendation(s), interview. *Other factors considered include:* Application essay, character/personal qualities, extracurricular activities, first generation, geographical residence, racial/ethnic status, talent/ability, volunteer work, work experience. SAT or ACT required. TOEFL required of all international applicants. High school diploma is required, and GED is accepted. *Academic units recommended:* 4 English, 3 mathematics, 3 science, 3 foreign language, 4 social studies.

Financial Aid

Students should submit: FAFSA. Regular filing deadline is March 1. The Princeton Review suggests that all financial aid forms be submitted as soon as possible after January 1. *Need-based scholarships/grants offered:* Federal Pell, SEOG, state scholarships/grants, private scholarships, school scholarship or grant aid from institutional funds, Federal Nursing Scholarships. *Loan aid offered:* Direct Subsidized Stafford, Direct Unsubsidized Stafford, Direct PLUS, Federal Perkins, Federal Nursing Loans, university loans from institutional funds. Applicants will be notified of awards on a rolling basis beginning February 1. Federal Work-Study Program available. Off-campus job opportunities are good.

The Inside Word

As students point out, UB "is famous for its architecture, nursing, and pharmacy schools," making those majors harder to get into. In fact, admissions standards at UB have grown more demanding across all programs in recent years. Despite the school's large applicant pool, it takes a close look at applications, searching for evidence of special talents and experiences that will enrich campus life.

THE SCHOOL SAYS ". . ."

From the Admissions Office

"The University at Buffalo (UB) is among the nation's finest public research universities—a learning community where you'll work side by side with world-renowned faculty, including Nobel, Pulitzer, National Medal of Science, and other award winners. As the largest, most comprehensive university center in the State University of New York (SUNY) system, UB offers more undergraduate majors than any public university in New York or New England. Through innovative resources like our Center for Undergraduate Research and Creative Activities, Discovery Seminars, and Undergraduate Academies, you'll be free to chart an academic course that meets your individual goals. At UB you can even design your own major. Our unique University Honors College and University Scholars Program offer an enhanced academic experience, including opportunities for independent study, advanced research, and specialized advisement. UB also places a high priority on offering an exciting campus environment. With nonstop festivals, Division I sporting events, concerts, and visiting lecturers, you'll have plenty to do outside of the classroom. We encourage you and your family to visit campus to see UB up close and in person. Our Visit UB campus tours and presentations are offered year-round.

"Freshman applicants must take the SAT (or the ACT with writing component)."

SELECTIVITY

Admissions Rating	87
# of applicants	21,985
% of applicants accepted	51
% of acceptees attending	28
# accepting a place on wait list	415
% admitted from wait list	64
# of early decision applicants	466
% accepted early decision	69

FRESHMAN PROFILE

Range SAT Critical Reading	500–610
Range SAT Math	550–650
Range ACT Composite	23–28
Minimum paper TOEFL	550
Minimum web-based TOEFL	79
Average HS GPA	3.30
% graduated top 10% of class	28
% graduated top 25% of class	65
% graduated top 50% of class	93

DEADLINES

Early decision	
Deadline	11/1
Notification	12/15
Regular	
Priority	11/1
Notification	2/1
Nonfall registration?	yes

FINANCIAL FACTS

Financial Aid Rating	80
Annual in-state tuition	$4,970
Annual out-of-state tuition	$13,380
Room and board	$11,162
Books and supplies	$1,004
% frosh rec. need-based scholarship or grant aid	41
% UG rec. need-based scholarship or grant aid	32
% frosh rec. non-need-based scholarship or grant aid	28
% UG rec. non-need-based scholarship or grant aid	8
% frosh rec. need-based self-help aid	43
% UG rec. need-based self-help aid	40
% frosh rec. any financial aid	50
% UG rec. any financial aid	52
% UG borrow to pay for school	37
Average cumulative indebtedness	$17,406

STEVENS INSTITUTE OF TECHNOLOGY

CASTLE POINT ON HUDSON, HOBOKEN, NJ 07030 • ADMISSIONS: 201-216-5194 • FAX: 201-216-8348

STUDENTS SAY ". . ."

Academics

Stevens Institute of Technology "is all about preparing scientists and engineers for a real work experience through research, co-op, and hands-on classes." "Engineering dominates" the curriculum here—"almost every major is engineering, and those that aren't, they throw 'and engineering' on the end to make it sound like it is"—and "The course load is demanding in its math, physics and engineering classes." Just less than half of Stevens' undergraduates participate in the school's cooperative education program (co-op), which students brag is "one of the best in the country." The program places students in real-world work environments that "allow [them] to learn more outside the classroom than inside it." As one undergrad sees it, "Stevens prepares students to actually work in these advanced technical fields as opposed to other colleges that focus solely on book smarts." As a "smaller school," Stevens can address student needs and concerns with "a lot less bureaucracy, a lot less red tape, and more direct communication" than other schools. Professors, similarly, tend to be more accessible than at larger schools, making the educational experience "a lot less stressful than it could be." It's not all rosy, though; as at many tech schools, "Some professors and lab assistants speak English poorly, and are consequently difficult to understand." When students graduate, the school "really does try hard to increase job placement," and its "career fairs and workshops…are worth every minute."

Life

"Academics are the main focus here at Stevens," but "there are also lots of activities available both on and off campus," and most students manage to find at least some time for them. The student-run entertainment committee "does a great job [of] bringing in a variety of shows," including "two big campus festivals offered in the fall and spring, known as Techfest and Boken respectively. There are lots of games, prizes, comedians, bands and much more…offered during this [event]." Many students "are very active in the ninety-plus RSOs (Registered Student Organizations) on campus," and "many play sports" as well ("The sports teams are very good overall in our conference and NCAA play"). "On Thursday, Friday, and Saturday nights, there are usually parties in dorm rooms and at the frats," but "if drinking and partying isn't your thing, there is still a lot for you to do," off campus as well as on. Hometown Hoboken "is a great place to walk around, go shopping, and hang out." It also has "a great social life and is filled with many bars to go to." And, "The train station is only a couple blocks away, making traveling into New York City easy and convenient." New York, of course, offers "endless possibilities for activities, no matter who the person is."

Student Body

Sure, there are "way too many people who are into anime" at Stevens, the kinds of kids who make jokes like "Stevens has 10 types of students: Those who know binary, and those who are hung over and forgot it." But students here insist that Stevens isn't all nerd, all the time. Most agree that "half of the students are obsessed with video games and are pretty nerdy," while the other half, "who are probably business and technology majors," "are so involved on campus it almost seems like they are running the entire school. Many of them have Blackberries and daily organizers to show just how busy they are." The student body includes "a huge proportion of athletes" as well as "great artists, great writers, great actors, and great singers." "There's absolutely a place for everyone to fit in. If you can't find a place, you must be doing something wrong," one student writes.

FINANCIAL AID: 201-216-5194 • E-MAIL: ADMISSIONS@STEVENS.EDU • WEBSITE: WWW.STEVENS.EDU

THE PRINCETON REVIEW SAYS

Admissions

Very important factors considered include: Academic GPA, application essay, recommendation(s), rigor of secondary school record, standardized test scores, character/personal qualities, extracurricular activities, interview, volunteer work, work experience. *Important factors considered include:* Class rank, talent/ ability. *Other factors considered include:* Alumni/ae relation. SAT or ACT required; ACT with or without writing component accepted. Stevens recommends that all students take SAT Subject Tests to show their strength in English, math, and a science of their choice. Accelerated premed and pre-dentistry applicants must take the SAT as well as two SAT Subject Tests in math (Level 1 or 2) and a biology or chemistry. Accelerated law applicants must take two SAT Subject Tests of their choice. TOEFL required of all international applicants. *Academic units required:* 4 English, 4 mathematics, 3 science (3 science labs). *Academic units recommended:* 4 science (4 science labs), 2 foreign language, 2 social studies, 2 history, 4 academic elective, 1 computer science.

Financial Aid

Students should submit: FAFSA. The College Board CSS Profile is required to be reviewed for institutional scholarships or grant aid. Regular filing deadline is February 15. The Princeton Review suggests that all financial aid forms be submitted as soon as possible after January 1. *Need-based scholarships/grants offered:* Federal Pell, SEOG, state scholarships/grants, private scholarships, school scholarship or grant aid from institutional funds. *Loan aid offered:* Direct Subsidized Stafford, Direct Unsubsidized Stafford, Direct PLUS, Federal Perkins, state loans. Applicants will be notified of awards on a rolling basis beginning March 30. Federal Work-Study Program available. Off-campus job opportunities are excellent.

The Inside Word

Stevens remains among the most desirable "second tier" engineering/science/ math schools; its location and cachet with employers guarantee it will always rank fairly high. If you can handle the grueling curriculum of a top tech school but can't make the cut at MIT or Caltech—in other words, if you're merely mortal—Stevens is a solid alternative. The school waives its application fee for those who apply online.

THE SCHOOL SAYS "..."

From the Admissions Office

"Founded in 1870 as the first college of mechanical engineering in the U.S., Stevens Institute of Technology stands today as one of the nation's premier research institutions and consistently ranks in the top ten percent of all U.S. universities in terms of the value of its educational, research, and placement outcomes. Noted for its unique academic approach, Stevens inexorably links its students to real-world innovation and entrepreneurship, distinct and exceptionally regarded research programs, and well-established partnerships in business, industry, and government. Stevens was recently ranked in the top five percent of schools in the nation for return on investment (ROI) for students by Bloomberg and number three among research universities for ROI for research by Forbes.com.

"Stevens' broad-based education leads to prestigious degrees in business, science, computer science, engineering, or humanities and provides diverse and interdisciplinary programs within four schools: the Schaefer School of Engineering and Science, the Howe School of Technology Management, the School of Systems and Enterprises, and the College of Arts and Letters. Research activities are vital to the university's educational mission, thus Stevens attracts world-renowned faculty to complement its exceptional on-campus facilities. In addition, Stevens maintains an honor system that has been in existence since 1908. Stevens' 2,369 undergraduate students come from more than forty states and twenty-five countries, creating a diverse, dynamic environment. Stevens also boasts an outstanding campus life—students will find more than 150 student clubs and organizations and twenty-six NCAA Division III athletics teams.

SELECTIVITY

Admissions Rating	95
# of applicants	3,239
% of applicants accepted	47
% of acceptees attending	36
# accepting a place on wait list	200
% admitted from wait list	18
# of early decision applicants	493
% accepted early decision	63

FRESHMAN PROFILE

Range SAT Critical Reading	560–640
Range SAT Math	620–700
Range SAT Writing	550–650
Range ACT Composite	25–30
Minimum paper TOEFL	550
Minimum computer TOEFL	213
Minimum web-based TOEFL	82
Average HS GPA	3.83
% graduated top 10% of class	58
% graduated top 25% of class	88
% graduated top 50% of class	98

DEADLINES

Early decision	
Deadline	11/15
Notification	12/15
Regular	
Priority	11/15
Deadline	2/1
Nonfall registration?	yes

APPLICANTS ALSO LOOK AT

AND OFTEN PREFER
Carnegie Mellon University, Cornell University, Massachusetts Institute of Technology

AND SOMETIMES PREFER
Lehigh University

AND RARELY PREFER
Drexel University, Rensselaer Polytechnic Institute, Worcester Polytechnic Institute

FINANCIAL FACTS

Financial Aid Rating	72
Annual tuition	$40,300
Room and board	$12,900
Required fees	$1,500
Books and supplies	$900
% frosh rec. need-based scholarship or grant aid	66
% UG rec. need-based scholarship or grant aid	54
% frosh rec. non-need-based scholarship or grant aid	62
% UG rec. non-need-based scholarship or grant aid	55
% frosh rec. need-based self-help aid	65
% UG rec. need-based self-help aid	57
% frosh rec. any financial aid	82
% UG rec. any financial aid	75
% UG borrow to pay for school	66
Average cumulative indebtedness	$35,319

STONEHILL COLLEGE

320 WASHINGTON STREET, EASTON, MA 02357-5610 • ADMISSIONS: 508-565-1373 • FAX: 508-565-1545

STUDENTS SAY ". . ."

Academics

"Stonehill is a small liberal arts college" "focused on educating the mind and soul" in the Roman Catholic tradition. "With a great small, interactive classroom experience" and "amazing" professors who "will help you no matter what," the academic experience here is distinctly "personal." "You won't be lost in the crowd at Stonehill. Professors know who you are and want to help you succeed." (Dare we say they will also notice when you are absent and may call you to find out why?) But that does not mean professors don't expect students to work hard. To the contrary, they "challenge you to question: question your readings, your professors, yourself." The whole point is to teach "how to be a critical thinker, and to look more in depth on ideas and topics." Faculty and administrators are extremely accessible."Many [faculty members] give students not only their school e-mail addresses, but their cell phone or home phone numbers as well as their AIM screen names if they have them!" Students also appreciate the learning opportunities off campus. "Stonehill has an amazing focus on internships and studying abroad and is known for having connections in the working world. The internships and opportunities given to students are pretty unique."

Life

"Being in the middle of Boston and Providence as well as having more than seventy clubs and organizations on campus that host two events a semester, there is always something to do" at Stonehill. "During the week, most people are considerate and allow you to get work done." "We have quiet hours at 10:00 P.M. on the weekdays and 1:00 A.M. on the weekends." But on the weekends, students cut loose. "For fun, people head into Boston a lot; the school has a shuttle to take us to the metro T station so it's very accessible if you don't have a car." On campus, "each night of the week there are different events sponsored by different groups on campus or by the Student Activities building. Some of the more widely attended events include our mixers (dances), which are held at various points throughout the year." "If you're looking for the frat/sorority party school, this isn't the place for you. It's much more laid-back, with drinking in the dorm rooms or in the twenty-one-plus common rooms." And it should be noted that alcohol is taken seriously here; many call the school's alcohol policy "way too strict," though it's possible to "learn the ways around it." The dorms here "are beautiful, and you get to choose your housing based on a point system. You get points for being active in the school (sports, clubs, attending lectures, etc.), so the more you participate the better housing you get. You can lose points for misbehavior, so the best housing goes to the best students, which is a huge plus!"

Student Body

"Stonehill is a pretty homogeneous place." Most students are "Caucasian and from middle-class families in New England." They tend to be "preppy" and "love to party on the weekends." However, they "also know how to crack down during the week and excel in class." "The typical student at Stonehill is kind, considerate, friendly, and smart. At Stonehill we hold doors, sometimes for an akwardly long time."

STONEHILL COLLEGE

FINANCIAL AID: 508-565-1088 • E-MAIL: ADMISSIONS@STONEHILL.EDU • WEBSITE: WWW.STONEHILL.EDU

THE PRINCETON REVIEW SAYS

Admissions

Very important factors considered include: Academic GPA, class rank, rigor of secondary school record, character/personal qualities, talent/ability. *Important factors considered include:* Application essay, recommendation(s), extracurricular activities, level of applicant's interest, volunteer work, work experience. *Other factors considered include:* Standardized test scores, alumni/ae relation, first generation, geographical residence, interview, racial/ethnic status, religious affiliation/commitment. ACT with writing component recommended. TOEFL required of all international applicants. High school diploma is required, and GED is accepted. *Academic units required:* 4 English, 3 mathematics, 1 science (1 science lab), 2 foreign language, 3 history, 3 academic elective. *Academic units recommended:* 4 English, 4 mathematics, 3 science (2 science labs), 3 foreign language, 3 history, 3 academic elective.

Financial Aid

Students should submit: FAFSA, CSS/Financial Aid PROFILE. The Princeton Review suggests that all financial aid forms be submitted as soon as possible after January 1. *Need-based scholarships/grants offered:* Federal Pell, SEOG, state scholarships/grants, private scholarships, school scholarship or grant aid from institutional funds. *Loan aid offered:* Direct Subsidized Stafford, Direct Unsubsidized Stafford, Direct PLUS, Federal Perkins, state loans. Federal Work-Study Program available. Off-campus job opportunities are good.

The Inside Word

Though not nearly as selective as some of its fellow Boston-area colleges, Stonehill students are no dummies. Half of them graduated in the top ten percent of their high school classes. Members of ethnic minorities may feel a bit isolated here.

THE SCHOOL SAYS "..."

From the Admissions Office

"Located twenty-two miles south of Boston, Stonehill is a selective Catholic college with an academically challenging, welcoming community on a beautiful, active campus. With an average class size of twenty, Stonehill's dedicated and supportive faculty make personal connections with each of our 2,400 students and mentor them throughout all four years and beyond. Stonehill offers more than seventy diverse majors and minors in the liberal arts, sciences, and business. Nearly ninety percent of our students participate in enriching opportunities such as competitive international and U.S. internships; nationally ranked study abroad programs; and top-notch undergraduate research, practicum, and field work experiences. Our proximity to America's premier college town allows you to join a network of 250,000 students and offers easy access to theatres, museums, professional sports games, restaurants, and more. But most importantly, Stonehill is a vibrant community where many minds come together for one purpose: to educate students for lives that make a difference."

SELECTIVITY

Admissions Rating	91
# of applicants	7,052
% of applicants accepted	64
% of acceptees attending	16
# accepting a place on wait list	67
% admitted from wait list	49
# of early decision applicants	49
% accepted early decision	90

FRESHMAN PROFILE

Range SAT Critical Reading	550–630
Range SAT Math	560–640
Range ACT Composite	24–28
Minimum paper TOEFL	550
Minimum computer TOEFL	213
Minimum web-based TOEFL	79
Average HS GPA	3.40
% graduated top 10% of class	35
% graduated top 25% of class	77
% graduated top 50% of class	98

DEADLINES

Early decision	
Deadline	11/1
Notification	12/25
Early action	
Deadline	11/1
Notification	1/15
Regular	
Deadline	1/15
Nonfall registration?	yes

APPLICANTS ALSO LOOK AT
AND OFTEN PREFER
Bentley College, Boston College, College of the Holy Cross, Fairfield University, Northeastern University, Providence College

AND SOMETIMES PREFER
University of Connecticut, University of Massachusetts Amherst, University of New Hampshire

AND RARELY PREFER
Assumption College

FINANCIAL FACTS

Financial Aid Rating	74
Annual tuition	$33,920
Room and board	$12,860
% frosh rec. need-based scholarship or grant aid	67
% UG rec. need-based scholarship or grant aid	63
% frosh rec. non-need-based scholarship or grant aid	11
% UG rec. non-need-based scholarship or grant aid	11
% frosh rec. need-based self-help aid	59
% UG rec. need-based self-help aid	57
% frosh rec. any financial aid	90
% UG rec. any financial aid	86
% UG borrow to pay for school	74
Average cumulative indebtedness	$30,435

SUFFOLK UNIVERSITY

EIGHT ASHBURTON PLACE, BOSTON, MA 02108 • ADMISSIONS: 617-573-8460 • FAX: 617-742-4291

CAMPUS LIFE

Quality of Life Rating	82
Fire Safety Rating	98
Green Rating	89
Type of school	private
Environment	metropolis

STUDENTS

Total undergrad enrollment	5,721
% male/female	45/55
% from out of state	30
% from public high school	68
% live on campus	23
# of fraternities	1
# of sororities	1
% African American	5
% Asian	7
% Caucasian	51
% Hispanic	8
% international	12
# of countries represented	103

SURVEY SAYS . . .
Great library
Diverse student types on campus
Students love Boston, MA
Great off-campus food
Dorms are like palaces
Student government is popular

ACADEMICS

Academic Rating	68
% students graduating within 4 years	40
% students graduating within 6 years	56
Calendar	semester
Student/faculty ratio	12:1
Profs interesting rating	78
Profs accessible rating	75
Most common reg class size	10–19 students
Most common lab size	10–19 students

MOST POPULAR MAJORS
business/corporate communication, interior design, sociology

STUDENTS SAY ". . ."

Academics

Located in "the heart of downtown Boston," Suffolk University offers a "happy environment" for "anyone who wants to be at a school and still be directly in the city." The university offers "a wide selection of interesting majors" and small class sizes throughout its College of Arts and Sciences and business school, giving this "united, diverse mass of students" a "global perspective in a real-world, urban setting." Students observe that depending on "[which] professor you have…you will like the class or not." Across the board, the teachers come across as being "very friendly" and genuine, and they "speak to you like an adult with respect." Some professors are "a bit dry;" however, "when you find [a great professor], they will be there for you through anything." Many here "wish the classes were more challenging," saying that coursework is "not as challenging as the school implies, but it is not easy." The school "offers students the resources they need should they want to put more effort into classes, job searching, and anything else, really;" students simply need to be self-motivated to take advantage of it. "Class participation comes naturally because class size is so small and the professor knows your name," says a freshman. "The administration is a little ridiculous sometimes with [its] rules," but overall it has "good relationships with the students."

Life

With the city as its "campus and playground," there is an "endless array of things to do" at Suffolk University, including shopping, museums, restaurants, and culture. "The students become part of the city," says a sophomore. "Suffolk doesn't really have a campus," though no one really seems to mind, as most students knew what they had signed on for when they enrolled. Due to space constraints, not all upperclassmen can live on campus, and many happily choose to live in Boston apartments. "My classes require me to walk through the Common everyday," says one student. For those who do live on campus, the university offers freshman orientation activities that "students can participate [in] to ease the tensions of moving into a dorm and being on your own." Most students take their social lives off campus, choosing to hang out at other colleges and in the city itself. Suffolk's campus is dry, so "students have to find other places in which to party" on the weekends (weeknights are typically dedicated to homework). As for the commuters, most "don't interact directly with [resident] students as much." Unsurprisingly, "there's a lot of Boston pride among Suffolk students." "Everyone loves the Red Sox, the Celtics, and the Bruins."

Student Body

Most of the kids here come out of "a medium to high income family" and are from "some town in Massachusetts," though Suffolk has a lot of international students. "It is very easy for a student to blend in due to Suffolk being a very diverse campus." Cultures and beliefs do indeed vary greatly—"that is definitely a part of what makes Suffolk so unique"—but "most students are friendly and interact with one another regardless of where they are from." However, there is a slight—though not tense—divide between two other classifications of Suffolk students: the large commuter populations and those who live in on-campus housing. "Suffolk is not very successful at integrating the two, but everyone seems to get along okay," says a student. Luckily, classes also require several group projects, "forcing students to work together." Preppy seems to be what the Suffolk student body preaches, and button downs, polo shirts, and Uggs abound—"most would *never* wear pajamas or sweatpants to class."

SUFFOLK UNIVERSITY

FINANCIAL AID: 617-573-8470 • E-MAIL: ADMISSION@SUFFOLK.EDU • WEBSITE: WWW.SUFFOLK.EDU

THE PRINCETON REVIEW SAYS

Admissions

Very important factors considered include: Rigor of secondary school record. *Important factors considered include:* Academic GPA, application essay, class rank, standardized test scores, character/personal qualities. *Other factors considered include:* Recommendation(s), alumni/ae relation, extracurricular activities, first generation, geographical residence, interview, level of applicant's interest, talent/ability, volunteer work, work experience. SAT or ACT required; ACT with writing component required. TOEFL required of all international applicants. High school diploma is required, and GED is accepted. *Academic units required:* 4 English, 3 mathematics, 2 science (1 science lab), 2 foreign language, 1 history, 4 academic elective. *Academic units recommended:* 4 English, 4 mathematics, 4 science (1 science lab), 3 foreign language, 4 history, 4 academic elective.

Financial Aid

Students should submit: FAFSA, institution's own financial aid form. Regular filing deadline is February 15. The Princeton Review suggests that all financial aid forms be submitted as soon as possible after January 1. *Need-based scholarships/grants offered:* Federal Pell, SEOG, state scholarships/grants, private scholarships, school scholarship or grant aid from institutional funds. *Loan aid offered:* Direct Subsidized Stafford, Direct Unsubsidized Stafford, Direct PLUS, Federal Perkins, state loans, university loans from institutional funds. Applicants will be notified of awards on a rolling basis beginning February 5. Federal Work-Study Program available. Off-campus job opportunities are excellent.

The Inside Word

Suffolk is unapologetic about its mission to provide access and opportunity to college-bound students. That said, test scores and high school GPA requirements are average. Applicants whose numbers are above-average have a good chance of gaining admission.

THE SCHOOL SAYS "..."

From the Admissions Office

"Ask any student, and they'll tell you: The best thing about Suffolk is the professors. They go the extra mile to help students to succeed. Suffolk faculty members are noted scholars and experienced professionals, but first and foremost, they are teachers and mentors. Suffolk's faculty is of the highest caliber. Ninety-four percent of the faculty hold PhDs. Suffolk maintains a thirteen to one student/faculty ratio with an average class size of nineteen.

"Career preparation is a high priority at Suffolk. Many students work during the school year in paid internships, co-op jobs, or work-study positions. Suffolk has an excellent job placement record. More than ninety-four percent of recent graduates are either employed or enrolled in graduate school at the time of graduation.

"The university's academic programs emphasize quality teaching, small class size, real-world career applications, and an international experience. There are more than fifty study abroad sites available to students. The undergraduate academic program offers more than seventy majors and 1,000 courses.

"We require applicants to submit the SAT with the essay score or the ACT taken with the writing component. Standardized tests are used for both placement and assessment. International students may submit any of the following tests for admission: the TOEFL or ELPT, IELTS, CPE, CAE, and FCE. The role of standardized testing is still a secondary role when considering admission to the university. The candidate's grades and the overall strength of curriculum are primary factors in the admission decision.

"Independent, eclectic, self-starters do best at Suffolk as do students who thrive in small classes and make the most of living in the city of Boston."

SELECTIVITY

Admissions Rating	73
# of applicants	9,145
% of applicants accepted	84
% of acceptees attending	17
# accepting a place on wait list	28
% admitted from wait list	4
# of early decision applicants	2,100
% accepted early decision	65

FRESHMAN PROFILE

Range SAT Critical Reading	450–560
Range SAT Math	460–570
Range SAT Writing	450–560
Range ACT Composite	20–24
Minimum paper TOEFL	525
Minimum computer TOEFL	197
Minimum web-based TOEFL	71
Average HS GPA	3.10
% graduated top 10% of class	12
% graduated top 25% of class	38
% graduated top 50% of class	72

DEADLINES

Early action	
Deadline	11/15
Notification	12/20
Regular	
Deadline	2/15
Notification	2/5
Nonfall registration?	yes

FINANCIAL FACTS

Financial Aid Rating	68
Annual tuition	$29,778
Room and board	$14,624
Required fees	$116
Books and supplies	$1,200
% frosh rec. need-based scholarship or grant aid	84
% UG rec. need-based scholarship or grant aid	81
% frosh rec. non-need-based scholarship or grant aid	24
% UG rec. non-need-based scholarship or grant aid	31
% frosh rec. need-based self-help aid	85
% UG rec. need-based self-help aid	13
% frosh rec. any financial aid	88
% UG rec. any financial aid	88

SUSQUEHANNA UNIVERSITY

514 UNIVERSITY AVENUE, SELINSGROVE, PA 17870 • ADMISSIONS: 570-372-4260 • FAX: 570-372-2722

STUDENTS SAY ". . ."

Academics

With its "beautiful" campus and "home-y" atmosphere, it's no surprise that Susquehanna University "is a school that really cares about its students." As one ecstatic freshman quips, "When I saw that even the squirrels were friendly, I knew this was the place!" Indeed, the college provides a "strong, inclusive community" where it seems as if everyone "knows your name." Academically, "SU offers so many different majors and minors and an amazing professor-to-student ratio." While there are a number of fantastic departments, undergrads give special praise to the "outstanding creative writing program," "great business school," and the "excellent" music education department. Though there might be the occasional "dud," the "majority of professors are excellent." As this biochemistry major shares, "They are passionate about what they teach, they want their students to succeed, and [they] are always willing to help." Additionally, "The class size is excellent, and you really get to know your teachers." Though one psych major does caution that there's "no sitting in the back where you think you won't be called on, because it will happen!" And one pleased senior sums up her professors and academic experience stating, "The passion they so clearly feel for their subject areas is inspiring and refreshing, the interest they take in their students is genuine and heartwarming, and the ease with which they can be contacted is impressive. For the most part, I have felt appropriately challenged by all of my classes and have taken valuable lessons away from each one."

Life

In a word, life at Susquehanna is "busy." Students here do an admirable job of juggling their academic demands with the myriad of activities available to them. Many undergrads appreciate that the "Student Activities Committee (SAC) tries really hard to keep us entertained, and usually does so quite successfully." A creative writing major chimes in, "Every weekend there is one event at the club on campus with free drinks and food, and there are often student recitals and performances. The coffee shop on campus has movie nights every week, as well as open mics and special events." Sadly, others sometimes grumble, "There's not much to do if you don't have a car." Fortunately, students are able to get creative and "learn to make [their] own fun by going sledding or playing board games [or with] impromptu dance parties or late-night word-association games." Additionally, "Most people are involved in sports or fraternities and sororities." One freshman assures us that while "partying is big on campus," you're "in no way pressured to drink or take part in it." Though some students find the surrounding area "quiet" and "small," others love to take advantage of the "cute little shops and cafes" that are "within walking distance."

Student Body

Undergrads at Susquehanna are "focused on their education" and very "involved with different clubs and organizations on campus." There's a friendliness that pervades the student body, and people are "not afraid to leave their doors open." Indeed, most "fit in quite easily," especially given the fact that there's "a spectrum of students with wide ranging interests." That being said, it often can feel as though the vast majority of undergrads either "join a sports team" or participate in Greek life. While students define their peers as "easygoing and fun to be with," nearly everyone also "has a very serious side when it comes to academics, their classes, and their commitments." On the surface, "Students tend to be well-off [and] very preppy." However, "Despite the general cookie-cutter facade, most students are really involved in diverse activities and are really curious and accepting of the world around them."

SUSQUEHANNA UNIVERSITY

FINANCIAL AID: 570-372-4450 • E-MAIL: SUADMISS@SUSQU.EDU • WEBSITE: WWW.SUSQU.EDU

THE PRINCETON REVIEW SAYS
Admissions
Very important factors considered include: Academic GPA, rigor of secondary school record. *Important factors considered include:* Application essay, class rank, recommendation(s), standardized test scores, alumni/ae relation, character/personal qualities, extracurricular activities, interview, level of applicant's interest, racial/ethnic status, talent/ability, volunteer work. *Other factors considered include:* First generation, geographical residence, religious affiliation/commitment, state residency. ACT with or without writing component accepted. TOEFL required of all international applicants. High school diploma is required, and GED is accepted. *Academic units required:* 4 English, 3 mathematics, 2 science (2 science labs), 2 foreign language, 2 social studies, 2 history, 2 academic elective. *Academic units recommended:* 4 English, 4 mathematics, 3 science (3 science labs), 4 foreign language, 4 social studies, 2 history, 3 academic elective.

Financial Aid
Students should submit: FAFSA. Regular filing deadline is May 1. The Princeton Review suggests that all financial aid forms be submitted as soon as possible after January 1. *Need-based scholarships/grants offered:* Federal Pell, SEOG, state scholarships/grants, private scholarships, school scholarship or grant aid from institutional funds. *Loan aid offered:* Federal Perkins, university loans from institutional funds. Federal Work-Study Program available. Off-campus job opportunities are good.

The Inside Word
Susquehanna is a selective university, and it's somewhat competitive to gain entry. Admissions officers are looking for bright, motivated candidates who greatly contribute to the Susquehanna community. They go to great lengths to consider the whole applicant and know that a candidate is more than their test results. To that end, they allow applicants to submit academic writing samples as opposed to SAT or ACT scores.

THE SCHOOL SAYS "..."
From the Admissions Office
"Susquehanna University prepares its graduates to achieve, lead and serve in a diverse and interconnected world. Graduates consistently say their Susquehanna experiences give them a competitive edge over other recent graduates entering the workplace. Susquehanna's new central curriculum includes GO (Global Opportunities). This distinctive program allows every student to have a cross-cultural experience away from campus, either in the United States or abroad. A cross-cultural experience is designed to take students out of their everyday environment. It might include a traditional semester study abroad program (GO Long), a short-term faculty/staff-led program (GO Short), a self-designed experience proposed and accepted in advance, or service in a cross-cultural setting."

"With more than fifty majors and minors, students find a fine balance of liberal arts and professional studies, and state-of-the-art facilities to support intellectual and personal growth. The Sigmund Weis School of Business is accredited by the Association to Advance Collegiate Schools of Business (AACSB). A new 'green' science facility opened in spring of 2010. As the largest academic building on campus, it includes nineteen teaching and research labs, thirty prep and support spaces, and a rooftop greenhouse."

"Susquehanna's success is demonstrated by its placement rate. Ninety-six percent of Susquehanna's graduates have a job or are attending graduate school within six months of graduation."

SELECTIVITY
Admissions Rating	83
# of applicants	3,186
% of applicants accepted	70
% of acceptees attending	29
# accepting a place on wait list	35
% admitted from wait list	17
# of early decision applicants	148
% accepted early decision	76

FRESHMAN PROFILE
Range SAT Critical Reading	500–610
Range SAT Math	520–610
Range SAT Writing	500–600
Range ACT Composite	22–26
Minimum paper TOEFL	550
Minimum computer TOEFL	213
Minimum web-based TOEFL	81
Average HS GPA	3.39
% graduated top 10% of class	29
% graduated top 25% of class	59
% graduated top 50% of class	86

DEADLINES
Early decision	
Deadline	11/15
Notification	12/1
Regular	
Priority	3/1
Deadline	3/1
Notification	12/15
Nonfall registration?	yes

APPLICANTS ALSO LOOK AT
AND OFTEN PREFER
Bucknell University, Dickinson College, Franklin & Marshall College, Gettysburg College, Lafayette College, Muhlenberg College, Villanova University

AND SOMETIMES PREFER
Ithaca College, Lehigh University, Quinnipiac University, Skidmore College, University of Delaware

AND RARELY PREFER
Elizabethtown College, Juniata College, Lebanon Valley College, Lycoming College, Ursinus College

FINANCIAL FACTS
Financial Aid Rating	81
Annual tuition	$35,860
Room and board	$9,600
Books and supplies	$850
% frosh rec. need-based scholarship or grant aid	70
% UG rec. need-based scholarship or grant aid	69
% frosh rec. non-need-based scholarship or grant aid	11
% UG rec. non-need-based scholarship or grant aid	8
% frosh rec. need-based self-help aid	58
% UG rec. need-based self-help aid	59
% frosh rec. any financial aid	97
% UG rec. any financial aid	93
% UG borrow to pay for school	73
Average cumulative indebtedness	$28,173

THE BEST 376 COLLEGES ■ 541

SWARTHMORE COLLEGE

500 COLLEGE AVENUE, SWARTHMORE, PA 19081 • ADMISSIONS: 610-328-8300 • FAX: 610-328-8580

CAMPUS LIFE

Quality of Life Rating	83
Fire Safety Rating	89
Green Rating	80
Type of school	private
Environment	village

STUDENTS

Total undergrad enrollment	1,509
% male/female	49/51
% from out of state	88
% from public high school	59
% live on campus	94
# of fraternities	2
% African American	6
% Asian	14
% Caucasian	45
% Hispanic	12
% international	7
# of countries represented	58

SURVEY SAYS . . .
No one cheats
Lab facilities are great
School is well-run
Low cost of living
Musical organizations are popular
Political activism is popular

ACADEMICS

Academic Rating	98
% students graduating within 4 years	89
% students graduating within 6 years	93
Calendar	semester
Student/faculty ratio	8:1
Profs interesting rating	97
Profs accessible rating	96
Most common reg class size	10–19 students
Most common lab size	fewer than 10 students

MOST POPULAR MAJORS
biology, economics, political science

STUDENTS SAY ". . ."

Academics

Swarthmore College "has a lovely campus, the people are almost unbelievably friendly, it's a safe environment, and it's really, really challenging academically," and "although it's not one of the most well-known schools, those who do know of it also know of its wonderful reputation. It's where to go for a real education—for learning for the sake of truly learning, rather than just for grades." Students warn that "academics here are definitely stressful, especially when you sign up for extracurricular activities that take up some more time—and almost everyone here's involved in something outside of just classes, because you don't want to just go to class, study, and sleep every day here." As a result, "Swarthmore is truly challenging. It teaches its students tough lessons not only about classes but about life, and though it may be extremely, almost unbearably difficult sometimes, it's totally worth it." Undergrads also note that "there are tons of resources to help you—professors, academic mentors, writing associates (who are really helpful to talk to when you have major papers), residential assistants, psychological counseling, multicultural support groups, queer/trans support groups—basically, whenever you need help with something, there's someone you can talk to." Swatties also love how "Swarthmore is amazingly flexible. The requirements are very limited, allowing you to explore whatever you are interested in and change your mind millions of times about your major and career path. If they don't offer a major you want, you can design your own with ease."

Life

The Swarthmore community is "a family of students who are engaged in academics, learning, politics, activism, and civic responsibility, with a work hard, play hard, intense mentality, who don't get enough sleep because they're too busy doing all they want to do in their time here, and who (this is kind of cheesy, but true) when you really think about it are really just smart students who care about the world and want to make it better." There "is a misconception that Swarthmore students do nothing but study, [but] while we certainly do a lot of it, we still find many ways to have fun." Not so much in hometown Swarthmore—"there isn't a lot to do right in the area"—but "with a train station on campus, Philly is very accessible." Additionally, "There are so many organizations and clubs on campus that you'd be pressed to find none of the activities interesting. Even then, you can start your own club, so that takes care of it." The small size of the school means that "opportunities to participate in many different programs" are usually available. On-campus activities "are varied, and there is almost always something to do on the weekend. There are student musical performances, drama performances, movies, speakers, and comedy shows," as well as "several parties every weekend, with and without alcohol, and a lot of pre-partying with friends." One student sums up, "While it is tough to generalize on the life of a Swarthmore student, one word definitely applies to us all: busy. All of us are either working on extracurriculars, studying, or fighting sleep to do more work."

Student Body

Students are "not sure if there is a typical Swattie" but suspect that "the defining feature among us is that each person is brilliant at something: maybe dance, maybe quantum physics, maybe philosophy. Each person here has at least one thing that [he or she does] extraordinarily well." A Swattie "is [typically] liberal, involved in some kind of activism group or multicultural group, talks about classes all the time, was labeled a nerd by people in high school, and is really smart—one of those people where you just have to wonder, how do they get all their homework done and manage their extracurriculars and still have time for parties?" The campus "is very diverse racially but not in terms of thought—in other words, pretty much everyone's liberal, you don't get many different points of view. Multicultural and queer issues are big here, but you don't have to be involved in that to enjoy Swarthmore. You just have to accept it."

SWARTHMORE COLLEGE

FINANCIAL AID: 610-328-8358 • E-MAIL: ADMISSIONS@SWARTHMORE.EDU • WEBSITE: WWW.SWARTHMORE.EDU

THE PRINCETON REVIEW SAYS

Admissions

Very important factors considered include: Academic GPA, application essay, class rank, recommendation(s), rigor of secondary school record, character/personal qualities. *Important factors considered include:* Standardized test scores, extracurricular activities. *Other factors considered include:* Alumni/ae relation, first generation, geographical residence, interview, level of applicant's interest, racial/ethnic status, talent/ability, volunteer work, work experience. Applicants are required to submit scores for any one of the three following testing scenarios: (1) SAT and any two SAT Subject tests; (2) the ACT with writing; or (3) SAT and ACT (with or without writing). Prospective engineers are encouraged to take the Mathematics Level 2 Subject Test, regardless of whether they opt for the SAT or ACT. High school diploma or equivalent isn't required. *Academic units recommended:* 4 English, 3 mathematics, 3 science.

Financial Aid

Students should submit: FAFSA, institution's own financial aid form, CSS/Financial Aid PROFILE. Regular filing deadline is February 15. The Princeton Review suggests that all financial aid forms be submitted as soon as possible after January 1. *Need-based scholarships/grants offered:* Federal Pell, SEOG, state scholarships/grants, private scholarships, school scholarship or grant aid from institutional funds. *Loan aid offered:* Direct Subsidized Stafford, Direct Unsubsidized Stafford, Direct PLUS, Federal Perkins, state loans, university loans from institutional funds. Federal Work-Study Program available. Off-campus job opportunities are good.

The Inside Word

Competition for admission to Swarthmore remains fierce, as the school consistently receives applications from top students across the country. Applicants should understand that Swarthmore receives more than enough applications from well-qualified students to fill its classrooms. At some point, perfectly good candidates get rejected simply because there's no more room. Admissions officers comb applications carefully for evidence of intellectually curious, highly motivated, and creative-minded candidates.

THE SCHOOL SAYS "..."

From the Admissions Office

"Swarthmore College, a highly selective college of liberal arts and engineering, celebrates the life of the mind. Since its founding in 1864, Swarthmore has given students the knowledge, insight, skills, and experience to become leaders for the common good. The college is private, yet open to all regardless of financial need, and decidedly global in outlook, drawing students from around the world and all fifty states. So much of what Swarthmore stands for, from its commitment to curricular breadth and rigor to its demonstrated interest in facilitating discovery and fostering social responsibility, lies in the quality and passion of its faculty. A student/faculty ratio of eight to one ensures that students have close, meaningful engagement with their professors, preparing them to translate the skills and understanding gained at Swarthmore into the mark they want to make on the world. The college's honors program features small groups of dedicated and accomplished students working closely with faculty; an emphasis on independent learning; students entering into a dialogue with peers, teachers, and examiners; and an examination at the end of two years study by outside scholars. Swarthmore's idyllic, 425-acre arboretum campus features rolling lawns, a creek, wooded hills, and hiking trails and is located just eleven miles from Philadelphia.

"Swarthmore maintains a need-blind admissions policy for U.S. citizens and permanent residents, wherein admission and financial aid decisions are made independently. Financial aid is also available for international students. All Swarthmore aid awards are loan-free and meet the full demonstrated need for admitted students."

SELECTIVITY	
Admissions Rating	98
# of applicants	6,041
% of applicants accepted	16
% of acceptees attending	40
# of early decision applicants	493
% accepted early decision	34

FRESHMAN PROFILE	
Range SAT Critical Reading	670–760
Range SAT Math	670–770
Range SAT Writing	680–770
Range ACT Composite	29–33
% graduated top 10% of class	84
% graduated top 25% of class	96
% graduated top 50% of class	100

DEADLINES	
Early decision	
Deadline	11/15
Notification	12/15
Regular	
Deadline	1/1
Nonfall registration?	no

FINANCIAL FACTS	
Financial Aid Rating	99
Annual tuition	$39,260
Required fees	$340
Books and supplies	$1,150
% frosh rec. need-based scholarship or grant aid	53
% UG rec. need-based scholarship or grant aid	50
% frosh rec. need-based self-help aid	52
% UG rec. need-based self-help aid	48
% frosh rec. any financial aid	53
% UG rec. any financial aid	52

SWEET BRIAR COLLEGE

PO Box B, Sweet Briar, VA 24595 • Admissions: 434-381-6142 • Fax: 434-381-6152

STUDENTS SAY ". . ."

Academics

A small, all-female, liberal arts college set in rural Virginia, Sweet Briar is "all about giving women the freedom to be leaders on campus and empowering them to do their best." With a "breathtakingly beautiful campus" and a "rich history and tradition that fosters growth and maturation for all those young women who are touched by it," "Sweet Briar is smarts, opportunity, and beauty all wrapped up in one." "Balancing very tough academics with involvement in multiple clubs," "everyone is so helpful, and there are so many opportunities for leadership and learning in and out of class." Here, "Academic integrity is valued, and hard work is rewarded." The faculty is always "incredibly involved and supportive." Says one student, "The nine to one student/faculty ratio was important to me. My professors even remembered me from my pre-acceptance visits." Another reflects, "Our president, Jo Ellen Parker, keeps an online blog…Our administration takes turns having cooking nights for students to learn how to cook different meals. I have personally had dinner with the Dean of Co-Curricular Life at her house along with other students." In essence, Sweet Briar "is about creating women for the future, whether it be a leading scientist in a cancer research facility or a homemaker in the suburbs of America." Every woman here has the opportunity "to be a big fish in a small, but nonetheless competitive, pond."

Life

Set in the beauty of the rural South, access to the outdoors is a big draw for many here. The "big campus" has "lots of trails for running and biking and lakes for swimming." In addition, "Horseback riding is extremely popular." Though some say Sweet Briar is a bit of a "suitcase school," set in a "middle-of-nowhere area," the women here don't let that get in the way of having fun. The motto seems to be, "work hard during the week" and "go off campus on the weekend to nearby Washington & Lee or Hampden-Sydney to party." During the week, "there are many things to do with the time you have outside of the classroom," "from parties at the Boathouse or on the Dell to enjoying a beautiful day on the trails to going to a movie in the Fitness and Athletics Center." Academics "are quite strong and allow students to take risks and challenge themselves," but with the help of enthusiastic professors and a little hard work, classes and assignments are "not too difficult to overcome." Students are always ready to strike a balance between setting their goals and enjoying their social lives: "Thursday nights are dedicated to the Boathouse parties, so we all appreciate it when teachers do not give Friday exams." The food on campus "could improve some; I feel like they try too hard sometimes to give us 'fancier' things and there is so much fried food."

Student Body

The typical Sweet Briar student is "pretty, smart, preppy, organized, [and a] multitasker." Harking back to their fondness for quirky traditions, one student jokingly reflects, "Sweet Briar has an archetype we fondly call 'Suzie Sweet Briar.' She is strong and intelligent and capable in a modern world but can still wear her pink and pearls." Though admittedly the school "attracts a lot of wealthy, Caucasian students," Sweet Briar women say they "would love to see a more diversified student population." "Very driven and involved," many here strive to be the best they can be in all worlds; "The typical Sweet Briar girl is a total overachiever. She has a boyfriend, gets good grades, is involved with several clubs, has an internship or job (on or off campus), plays at least one sport (riding counts), has a busy social life with friends all over the state, and loves caffeine." You can find people "who share almost any interest or hobby, whether it's needlepoint or partying." They "value tradition and interpersonal relationships."

FINANCIAL AID: 434-381-6156 • E-MAIL: ADMISSIONS@SBC.EDU • WEBSITE: WWW.SBC.EDU

THE PRINCETON REVIEW SAYS
Admissions

Very important factors considered include: Academic GPA, rigor of secondary school record. *Important factors considered include:* Application essay, recommendation(s), standardized test scores, interview. *Other factors considered include:* Class rank, alumni/ae relation, character/personal qualities, extracurricular activities, first generation, racial/ethnic status, talent/ability, volunteer work, work experience. SAT or ACT required; ACT with or without writing component accepted. TOEFL required of all international applicants. High school diploma is required, and GED is accepted. *Academic units required:* 4 English, 3 mathematics, 3 science (2 science labs), 2 foreign language, 3 social studies. *Academic units recommended:* 4 English, 4 mathematics, 4 science (3 science labs), 4 foreign language, 4 social studies.

Financial Aid

Students should submit: FAFSA. Regular filing deadline is February 15. The Princeton Review suggests that all financial aid forms be submitted as soon as possible after January 1. *Need-based scholarships/grants offered:* Federal Pell, SEOG, state scholarships/grants, private scholarships, school scholarship or grant aid from institutional funds. *Loan aid offered:* Direct Subsidized Stafford, Direct Unsubsidized Stafford, Direct PLUS, Federal Perkins, university loans from institutional funds. Federal Work-Study Program available. Off-campus job opportunities are fair.

The Inside Word

A fairly self-selecting applicant pool allows Sweet Briar to consider each application closely. The school looks not only for evidence of academic achievement and ability but also for "fit" with the school. How well will you meld with the Sweet Briar community? How well can the school deliver quality academics in your areas of interest? (A school this small can't provide in-depth instruction in every discipline, after all.) These are the questions that will determine your admission to Sweet Briar, especially if your test scores and/or high school grades are less than stellar.

THE SCHOOL SAYS "..."
From the Admissions Office

"The woman who applies to Sweet Briar is mature and far-sighted enough to know what she wants from her college experience. She is intellectually adventuresome, more willing to explore new fields, and more open to challenging her boundaries. Sweet Briar attracts the ambitious, confident woman who enjoys being immersed not only in a first-rate academic program, but in a variety of meaningful activities outside the classroom. Our students take charge and revel in their accomplishments. This attitude follows graduates, enabling them to compete confidently in the corporate world and in graduate school.

"The faculty and staff do not simply give students individual attention; rather they pay attention to individuals. As an institution, we commit to every student, and our mission is to provide a learning community that prepares her to be successful in whatever she chooses to do after college."

SELECTIVITY
Admissions Rating	81
# of applicants	629
% of applicants accepted	83
% of acceptees attending	38

FRESHMAN PROFILE
Range SAT Critical Reading	510–630
Range SAT Math	470–600
Range ACT Composite	22–27
Minimum paper TOEFL	550
Minimum computer TOEFL	213
Minimum web-based TOEFL	79
Average HS GPA	3.53
% graduated top 10% of class	28
% graduated top 25% of class	53
% graduated top 50% of class	88

DEADLINES
Regular	
Priority	2/1
Deadline	2/1
Nonfall registration?	yes

FINANCIAL FACTS
Financial Aid Rating	91
Annual tuition	$30,620
Room and board	$11,100
Required fees	$475
Books and supplies	$950
% frosh rec. need-based scholarship or grant aid	62
% UG rec. need-based scholarship or grant aid	53
% frosh rec. non-need-based scholarship or grant aid	33
% UG rec. non-need-based scholarship or grant aid	30
% frosh rec. need-based self-help aid	62
% UG rec. need-based self-help aid	53
% frosh rec. any financial aid	91
% UG rec. any financial aid	93
% UG borrow to pay for school	50
Average cumulative indebtedness	$20,118

SYRACUSE UNIVERSITY

100 CROSS-HINDS HALL, 900 SOUTH CROUSE AVE., SYRACUSE, NY 13244 • ADMISSIONS: 315-443-3611 • FAX: 315-443-4226

CAMPUS LIFE

Quality of Life Rating	66
Fire Safety Rating	86
Green Rating	95
Type of school	private
Environment	city

STUDENTS

Total undergrad enrollment	13,753
% male/female	44/56
% from out of state	53
% from public high school	71
% live on campus	75
# of fraternities	29
# of sororities	20
% African American	8
% Asian	9
% Caucasian	57
% Hispanic	8
% Native American	1
% international	7
# of countries represented	71

SURVEY SAYS . . .

Everyone loves the Orange
Frats and sororities dominate
social scene
Student publications are popular
Lots of beer drinking
Hard liquor is popular

ACADEMICS

Academic Rating	75
Calendar	semester
Student/faculty ratio	16:1
Profs interesting rating	76
Profs accessible rating	76
Most common reg class size	10–19 students
Most common lab size	20–29 students

MOST POPULAR MAJORS
commercial and advertising art,
psychology, radio and television

STUDENTS SAY ". . ."

Academics

Syracuse University "is cold weather, good academics, and amazing sports," one student sums up, and that about captures the prevailing sentiment among SU undergrads. Sure, Syracuse students recognize and appreciate the "top-quality education" they receive, but they typically frame it in the totality of Syracuse living, which includes not only "an excellent academic experience" but also athletics and extracurriculars that together create "the perfect balance of a great education and an amazing social atmosphere, [making] for an excellent college experience." The result is a student body fiercely proud of its school. "Syracuse bleeds Orange," students inform us. On the basis of academics alone, they would have just cause. Opportunities abound: "If you take advantage of all the great resources available to all students, it's impossible not to have a great college experience," one student observes. Most do. Syracuse students "are, for the most part, very serious about their work and know what they want to do in life after college." The school provides lots of choices. Its Newhouse School of Public Communications is "as good as it gets for journalism schools," students tell us. They're nearly as bullish on the school's separate colleges for citizenship and public affairs, architecture, engineering and computer science, and management. No wonder one student brags, "I'm a magazine journalism major with a specialization in fashion and a minor in theater. The best part about Syracuse is that it offers hundreds of specific programs that allow you to learn by doing."

Life

"People are very committed to their work Monday through Thursday" at SU, but "as soon as Thursday classes are over, people will start to party." Greek life attracts nearly one-fifth of the student body. The frats throw "a lot of parties, which are crowded, hot, noisy, and run out of alcohol frequently," but they are hardly the only game in town. "Social life is very well-rounded and consists of bars, fraternities/sororities, house parties, and apartment parties," students report. The perception that "there's not much to do off campus in Syracuse" amplifies the importance of the party scene. Students note, however, "There are many other options for students who don't drink." "During the winter, basketball season is huge, and we have one of the best student sections in the country. The school also provides free shuttles on the weekend to Carousel Mall, the country's fourth-largest mall." There are "easily accessible gyms" located "nearby both ends of the campus," and the school is home to "amazing musical groups" ranging from a cappella ensembles to jazz bands, an orchestra, and rock bands. In addition, "The university provides ways of having fun on the weekends as well, such as free movie screenings in lecture halls or activities such as water rafting (with a fee, of course)."

Student Body

Your standard issue Syracuse male "wears khakis, Polo, and Patagonias," while his female counterpart "wears American Apparel zip-ups, solid-colored v-neck tees, skinny jeans and leggings, Uggs, a North Face jacket, and a brand-name handbag" and "is glued to her Blackberry." Syracuse is a big university, though, with plenty of room for diversity, so pretty much everyone finds a comfortable niche here. There's "a huge population of hipsters…woodsy folk, city kids, and pretty average everyday people all over. It depends on what social scene you spend your time in." Dig deep enough and you'll find "students of every race, religion, and political background you can think of. There is a strong Asian and international student population as well as a noticeable percentage of gay, lesbian, and bisexual [students]." While groups "have their own cliques," there "is no animosity or unspoken status quo between different sorts of people."

SYRACUSE UNIVERSITY

FINANCIAL AID: 315-443-1513 • E-MAIL: ORANGE@SYR.EDU • WEBSITE: WWW.SYRACUSE.EDU

THE PRINCETON REVIEW SAYS

Admissions

Very important factors considered include: Academic GPA, application essay, class rank, recommendation(s), rigor of secondary school record, standardized test scores, character/personal qualities, extracurricular activities, interview, level of applicant's interest, talent/ability. *Important factors considered include:* Alumni/ae relation, first generation, volunteer work, work experience. *Other factors considered include:* Geographical residence, racial/ethnic status, state residency. SAT or ACT required; ACT with writing component required. TOEFL required of all international applicants. High school diploma is required, and GED is accepted. *Academic units required:* 4 English, 4 mathematics, 4 science (4 science labs), 3 foreign language, 4 social studies.

Financial Aid

Students should submit: FAFSA, CSS/Financial Aid PROFILE. Regular filing deadline is February 1. The Princeton Review suggests that all financial aid forms be submitted as soon as possible after January 1. *Need-based scholarships/grants offered:* Federal Pell, SEOG, state scholarships/grants, private scholarships, school scholarship or grant aid from institutional funds. Loan aid offered: Direct Subsidized Stafford, Direct Unsubsidized Stafford, Direct PLUS, Federal Perkins. Federal Work-Study Program available. Off-campus job opportunities are good.

The Inside Word

Syracuse University is divided into nine colleges, and applicants apply to the college in which they are interested. Some colleges make specific requirements of applicants (for example, a portfolio, or an audition in addition to SU's general admission requirements. Applicants are allowed to indicate a second or third choice program, so you may still gain admission even if you don't get into your first-choice program.

THE SCHOOL SAYS "..."

From the Admissions Office

"Syracuse University provides a dynamic learning environment with a focus on scholarship in action, in which excellence is connected to ideas, problems, and professions in the world. Students at SU focus on interactive, collaborative, and interdisciplinary learning while choosing their course of study from more than 200 options. About half of undergraduates study abroad. SU operates centers in Beijing, Florence, Hong Kong, London, Madrid, Santiago, and Strasbourg. New facilities continue to expand scholarship in action opportunities for students. The Newhouse three building houses various facilities for public communications students, including research centers, a high-tech convergence lab, and meeting rooms for student activities. The new Life Sciences Complex promotes interdisciplinary research and education, signaling a new era in scientific research.

"A distinction of the SU education is the breadth of opportunity combined with individualized attention. Average class size is less than twenty students. Only three percent of all classes have more than 100 students. Faculty members are experts in their field, who are dedicated to teaching while conducting research, writing, and experiments they can share with students to aid in the learning process.

"Outside of the classroom, students are encouraged to immerse themselves in organizations and take advantage of the opportunities available in the city of Syracuse. The university community collaborates with city residents, organizations, and businesses in such areas as the arts, entrepreneurship and economic development, and scientific research. The Connective Corridor, a three mile pedestrian pathway and shuttle bus circuit, links SU and downtown Syracuse's arts institutions, entertainment venues, and public spaces."

SELECTIVITY
Admissions Rating	89
# of applicants	22,935
% of applicants accepted	60
% of acceptees attending	25
# accepting a place on wait list	1,111
% admitted from wait list	1
# of early decision applicants	859
% accepted early decision	78

FRESHMAN PROFILE
Range SAT Critical Reading	520–620
Range SAT Math	540–650
Range SAT Writing	520–630
Range ACT Composite	23–28
Average HS GPA	3.60
% graduated top 10% of class	35
% graduated top 25% of class	72
% graduated top 50% of class	94

DEADLINES
Early decision	
Deadline	11/15
Notification	12/31
Regular	
Deadline	1/1
Notification	3/18
Nonfall registration?	yes

FINANCIAL FACTS
Financial Aid Rating	90
Annual tuition	$34,970
Room and board	$12,850
Required fees	$1,332
Books and supplies	$1,308
% frosh rec. need-based scholarship or grant aid	54
% UG rec. need-based scholarship or grant aid	54
% frosh rec. non-need-based scholarship or grant aid	3
% UG rec. non-need-based scholarship or grant aid	3
% frosh rec. need-based self-help aid	58
% UG rec. need-based self-help aid	59
% frosh rec. any financial aid	80
% UG rec. any financial aid	80
% UG borrow to pay for school	64
Average cumulative indebtedness	$30,813

THE BEST 376 COLLEGES ■ 547

TEMPLE UNIVERSITY

1801 NORTH BROAD STREET, PHILADELPHIA, PA 19122-6096 • ADMISSIONS: 215-204-7200 • FAX: 215-204-5694

STUDENTS SAY ". . ."

Academics

Temple University is "a large school" that "makes you feel at home in the city of Philadelphia" and offers "rigorous academic classes and many outside activities." This "wonderful" school is "located right in the city," and students praise the campus as being "one of the most diverse in the country." "Temple University is a place where everyone fits in and walks away with a little more knowledge than they had the day before," says one undergrad. This diversity also extends to classes. There's a "wide variety of classes" and "lots of awesome majors," all of which are supported by a "helpful and passionate set of professors who learn right along with students." There's also the "top-notch" honors program, which is a "favorite part of Temple by far," explains one student. "It's an outstanding program, and I feel very fortunate to be a part of it." Most here agree their academic experience has been "amazing." In the words of one undergrad, "Temple's standard of access and excellence is evident in its students' success." The "knowledgeable" professors "really want to see students succeed." While some feel that the administration "doesn't always run so smoothly," noting that "Temple is pretty much a small city, and it often runs like a bureaucracy," overall, students agree that administrators are "accessible at any time" and are "helpful when you need them."

Life

As you'd expect from a big school in a big city, "Temple has something for everyone." Whether you're looking for "city life," "friendly people," or "a million and one clubs or groups to join," you'll find it here at Temple. "There are tons of things to do," says one student. "If students get bored on campus, they were probably boring to begin with." Life on campus is "very interconnected," and "there's usually always something going on" thanks to "student organizations that appeal to every interest and social group." Most students keep busy during by "studying," "going to the gym," and "playing intramural sports," but even if nothing is happening on campus, "there's much to do in the city." Not surprisingly, Philadelphia plays a substantial part in students' social lives. "There are amazing bars in the city," says one undergrad. "The only nights that students do not go out for drinks are Sunday and Monday." That said, if imbibing isn't your cup of tea, not to worry—there's plenty more on offer than watering holes. "You can have tons of fun on campus without drinking," explains a student. "There are lots of fun things to do because of our close proximity to Center City Philadelphia." Some examples are "great clubs, shopping, hookah bars, and restaurants." Also, if you get tired of Temple's campus you can always check out another—"Drexel, LaSalle, and UPenn's campuses are close by."

Student Body

Diversity isn't just a word at Temple; it's a fact. "At Temple, the atypical students are the typical students," explains an undergrad. "The majority population is made up of ethnic minorities." The student body here is made up of "many different kinds of ethnicities, sexual orientations, and economic and political stances," all of whom "contribute to the overall sense of school spirit and pride." Students agree that everyone here is "unique," and that makes for a place where "everyone becomes comfortable with each other's differences." "Every student brings their own light to Temple, which is what makes the school shine so bright," says one student. Despite this "huge mixture of types," students here do share similarities, particularly in their "motivation" to do well. Students here fill their time with "studying" and "extracurricular activities," all while also "experiencing life in the city of Philadelphia." One thing that all students agree on is that "The typical student at Temple University is approachable and greatly accepts diversity." As one undergrad says, "Everyone just kind of fits in, which is why the students like Temple so much."

FINANCIAL AID: 215-204-2244 • E-MAIL: TUADM@TEMPLE.EDU • WEBSITE: WWW.TEMPLE.EDU

THE PRINCETON REVIEW SAYS

Admissions

Very important factors considered include: Academic GPA, rigor of secondary school record. *Important factors considered include:* Class rank, standardized test scores. *Other factors considered include:* Application essay, recommendation(s), alumni/ae relation, character/personal qualities, extracurricular activities, talent/ability, volunteer work, work experience. SAT or ACT required; ACT with writing component required. TOEFL required of all international applicants. High school diploma is required, and GED is accepted. *Academic units required:* 4 English, 3 mathematics, 2 science (1 science lab), 2 foreign language, 2 social studies, 1 history, 1 academic elective. *Academic units recommended:* 4 English, 4 mathematics, 3 science (2 science labs), 2 foreign language, 2 social studies, 2 history, 3 academic elective.

Financial Aid

Students should submit: FAFSA. The Princeton Review suggests that all financial aid forms be submitted as soon as possible after January 1. *Need-based scholarships/grants offered:* Federal Pell, SEOG, state scholarships/grants, private scholarships, school scholarship or grant aid from institutional funds, Federal Nursing Scholarships. *Loan aid offered:* Direct Subsidized Stafford, Direct Unsubsidized Stafford, Direct PLUS, Federal Perkins, Federal Nursing Loans, state loans, university loans from institutional funds. Applicants will be notified of awards on a rolling basis beginning February 15. Federal Work-Study Program available. Off-campus job opportunities are excellent.

The Inside Word

Temple is a well-recognized name in higher education, and its location is one of the nation's most popular cities. Competition can be steep when it comes to admissions, particularly if you aren't a resident of Pennsylvania. Admissions officers are fairly objective about their approach to application assessment in that they focus primarily on the solid numbers: class rank, GPA, and standardized test scores. That said, keep in mind that there are no minimum requirements, so if you have skills and talents that can't be mathematically calculated, it would behoove you to point them out in your application.

THE SCHOOL SAYS "..."

From the Admissions Office

"Temple combines the academic resources and intellectual stimulation of a large research university with the intimacy of a small college. The university experienced record growth in attracting new students from all fifty states and more than 125 countries. Students choose from 134 undergraduate majors. Special academic programs include honors, learning communities for first-year undergraduates, co-op education, and study abroad. Temple has seven regional campuses, including Main Campus and the Health Sciences Center in historic Philadelphia, suburban Temple University, Ambler, and overseas campuses in Tokyo and Rome. Main Campus is home to Alter Hall for the Fox School of Business, and the Tyler School of Art, both state-of-the-art facilities that opened in 2009. Our TECH Center has more than 600 computer workstations, 100 laptops, and a Starbucks. The Liacouras Center is a modern entertainment, recreation, and sports complex that hosts concerts, plays, trade shows, and college and professional athletics. It also includes the Independence Blue Cross Student Recreation Center, a major fitness facility for students now and in the future. Students can also take advantage of our Student Fieldhouse. The university is currently constructing a new residence hall, built to meet an unprecedented demand for main campus housing.

"Applicants are required to take the SAT (or the ACT with writing). The best critical reading, math and writing scores from either test will be considered."

SELECTIVITY

Admissions Rating	83
# of applicants	17,051
% of applicants accepted	65
% of acceptees attending	39
# accepting a place on wait list	602
% admitted from wait list	21

FRESHMAN PROFILE

Range SAT Critical Reading	500–600
Range SAT Math	510–610
Range SAT Writing	500–600
Range ACT Composite	20–26
Minimum paper TOEFL	550
Minimum computer TOEFL	213
Minimum web-based TOEFL	79
Average HS GPA	3.39
% graduated top 10% of class	18
% graduated top 25% of class	53
% graduated top 50% of class	90

DEADLINES

Regular	
Deadline	3/1
Notification	10/15
Nonfall registration?	yes

APPLICANTS ALSO LOOK AT

AND OFTEN PREFER

Drexel University, Penn State—University Park, Rutgers, The State University of New Jersey, University of Pittsburgh—Pittsburgh Campus, West Chester University of Pennsylvania

AND SOMETIMES PREFER

Syracuse University, University of Maryland—College Park, University of Massachusetts Amherst

AND RARELY PREFER

Holy Family University, Millersville University of Pennsylvania, Philadelphia University

FINANCIAL FACTS

Financial Aid Rating	79
Annual in-state tuition	$11,834
Annual out-of-state tuition	$21,662
Room and board	$9,550
Required fees	$590
Books and supplies	$1,000
% frosh rec. need-based scholarship or grant aid	69
% UG rec. need-based scholarship or grant aid	67
% frosh rec. non-need-based scholarship or grant aid	42
% UG rec. non-need-based scholarship or grant aid	30
% frosh rec. need-based self-help aid	60
% UG rec. need-based self-help aid	59
% frosh rec. any financial aid	86
% UG rec. any financial aid	85
% UG borrow to pay for school	76
Average cumulative indebtedness	$31,123

TEXAS A&M UNIVERSITY—COLLEGE STATION

ADMISSIONS COUNSELING, COLLEGE STATION, TX 77843-1265 • ADMISSIONS: 979-845-3741 • FAX: 979-847-8737

CAMPUS LIFE

Quality of Life Rating	87
Fire Safety Rating	86
Green Rating	83
Type of school	public
Environment	city

STUDENTS

Total undergrad enrollment	39,027
% male/female	52/48
% from out of state	3
% live on campus	24
# of fraternities	33
# of sororities	23
% African American	3
% Asian	5
% Caucasian	73
% Hispanic	16
% international	1
# of countries represented	127

SURVEY SAYS . . .

Great computer facilities
Athletic facilities are great
Students are friendly
Everyone loves the Aggies
Student publications are popular

ACADEMICS

Academic Rating	68
% students graduating within 4 years	46
% students graduating within 6 years	79
Calendar	semester
Student/faculty ratio	19:1
Profs interesting rating	71
Profs accessible rating	77
Most common reg class size	20–29 students
Most common lab size	20–29 students

MOST POPULAR MAJORS

biological and physical sciences, interdisciplinary studies, operations management and supervision

STUDENTS SAY ". . ."

Academics

"The excellence of a great research university filled with many traditions and the warm hospitality of a safe, small town" are the hallmarks of a Texas A&M education. United by the school's hallowed traditions, undergrads at this agriculture and engineering powerhouse "are the most fiercely loyal people to the school and other Aggies," and they can't stop bragging about how great their academic and extracurricular lives are. One student writes, "During the college search, I always heard about colleges looking for 'the well-rounded student.' Texas A&M's strength is being a 'well-rounded university,'" particularly for those interested in veterinary science, agricultural science, construction and engineering, business, and life sciences. Most departments hold students to "very high standards." As one student puts it, "At Texas A&M University, students generally get what they give. An A is well earned, [and] an F is deserved." Another adds, "Classes are extremely hard, but the Aggie ring is worth more this way." That ring provides access to "the Aggie network," alumni of A&M who "help make a lot of things possible," especially "finding a job. I've heard stories of some people getting hired at the sight of their Aggie ring." With A&M "taking many steps, especially in the past few years, to really make A&M an even stronger university and research institution"—including "hiring a lot of new faculty" and "construction of new facilities on campus"—there are now more reasons than ever to love being an Aggie. How great is it? Ultimately you have to find out for yourself, because, "from the outside looking in, you can't understand it, and from the inside looking out, you can't explain it!"

Life

A&M "is rich in tradition such as the Twelfth Man, Muster, Silvertaps, Reveille, 'Howdy,' the Corps of Cadets, Elephant Walk, and Maroon Out, just to name a few." If you're already familiar with these terms, you probably know how deeply they permeate campus life. Others should check out the school's website to learn more about them; how you feel about the traditions will strongly impact how much you enjoy life at A&M. Aggies tend to be enthusiastic about sports, both attending games and participating in club, intramural, and pickup games. Although social activities are bound to be extremely diverse at a campus this large, many students here tell us that Northgate, a "row of bars and restaurants off the north side of campus," is the place to go; live music ("Texas country music is really big at A&M"), drinks, and dancing are all on the menu. Hometown College Station "is a small city, so there aren't many activities available off campus, but the city is at the crossroads to the three major areas in Texas: Houston, Dallas—Fort Worth, and the Austin—San Antonio area. Weekend trips to these areas are fairly common."

Student Body

While "it is true that there is a very large Caucasian population at TAMU," there are also "large numbers of Middle Eastern, Asian, and Hispanic students" as well, providing a good deal of diversity on campus. It's Texas, and it's not Austin, so it should come as no surprise that A&M students tend to be politically conservative. Some point out that "conservative students are probably the most vocal, making it appear our school is more conservative [than it is]. From my experience, most students place themselves in the middle of left and right, making informed decisions when it comes to politics." Many here "are involved in student organizations and have a good social life as well." About five percent of the student body participates in the Corps of Cadets, "a senior military academy within the university." One cadet tells us that he and his peers "are the most visible people on campus and live with a structured military lifestyle."

TEXAS A&M UNIVERSITY—COLLEGE STATION

FINANCIAL AID: 979-845-3236 • E-MAIL: ADMISSIONS@TAMU.EDU • WEBSITE: WWW.TAMU.EDU

THE PRINCETON REVIEW SAYS

Admissions

Very important factors considered include: Academic GPA, class rank, rigor of secondary school record, standardized test scores, extracurricular activities, geographical residence, talent/ability. *Important factors considered include:* Application essay, first generation, geographical residence, state residency, volunteer work, work experience. *Other factors considered include:* Recommendation(s), character/personal qualities. SAT or ACT required; ACT with writing component required. TOEFL required of all international applicants. High school diploma is required, and GED is accepted. *Academic units required:* 4 English, 3 mathematics, 3 science (2 science labs), 2 foreign language, 2 social studies, 1 history. *Academic units recommended:* 4 English, 3 mathematics, 3 science (2 science labs), 2 foreign language, 2 social studies, 1 history, 1 computer science.

Financial Aid

Students should submit: FAFSA, institution's own financial aid form. The Princeton Review suggests that all financial aid forms be submitted as soon as possible after January 1. *Need-based scholarships/grants offered:* Federal Pell, SEOG, state scholarships/grants, private scholarships, school scholarship or grant aid from institutional funds. *Loan aid offered:* Direct Subsidized Stafford, Direct Unsubsidized Stafford, Direct PLUS, Federal Perkins, state loans, university loans from institutional funds. Applicants will be notified of awards on a rolling basis beginning April 1. Federal Work-Study Program available. Off-campus job opportunities are excellent.

The Inside Word

Texas A&M uses some cut-and-dried admissions criteria: Students graduating in the top ten percent of a recognized public or private high school in the state of Texas are automatically in; all they have to do is get their applications in on time. Applicants in the top quarter of their graduating class who have a combined SAT Math/Critical Reading score of 1300 (minimum score of 600 in each component) are also automatically in, as are such students who earn a composite ACT score of 30 (minimum 27 on the math and English sections). All other applications are deemed "Review Admits" to be sorted through by the admissions committee.

THE SCHOOL SAYS "..."

From the Admissions Office

"Established in 1876 as the first public college in the state, Texas A&M University has become a world leader in teaching, research, and public service. Located in College Station in the heart of Texas, it is centrally situated among three of the country's ten largest cities: Dallas, Houston, and San Antonio. Texas A&M is ranked nationally in these four areas: enrollment, enrollment of top students, value of research, and endowment.

"Freshman applicants are required to take the SAT or the ACT. We will use the applicant's best single testing date score in decision making."

SELECTIVITY
Admissions Rating	83
# of applicants	23,407
% of applicants accepted	69
% of acceptees attending	51
# accepting a place on wait list	1,470
% admitted from wait list	31

FRESHMAN PROFILE
Range SAT Critical Reading	530–650
Range SAT Math	570–680
Range SAT Writing	510–620
Range ACT Composite	24–30
Minimum paper TOEFL	550
% graduated top 10% of class	50
% graduated top 25% of class	87
% graduated top 50% of class	99

DEADLINES
Regular	
Priority	12/1
Deadline	1/15
Notification	4/1
Nonfall registration?	yes

APPLICANTS ALSO LOOK AT AND SOMETIMES PREFER
The University of Texas at Austin

FINANCIAL FACTS
Financial Aid Rating	86
Annual in-state tuition	$5,297
Annual out-of-state tuition	$19,727
Room and board	$8,008
Required fees	$3,090
Books and supplies	$1,350
% frosh rec. need-based scholarship or grant aid	37
% UG rec. need-based scholarship or grant aid	30
% frosh rec. non-need-based scholarship or grant aid	7
% UG rec. non-need-based scholarship or grant aid	3
% frosh rec. need-based self-help aid	21
% UG rec. need-based self-help aid	25
% frosh rec. any financial aid	77
% UG rec. any financial aid	65
% UG borrow to pay for school	51
Average cumulative indebtedness	$21,182

THE BEST 376 COLLEGES ■ 551

TEXAS CHRISTIAN UNIVERSITY

OFFICE OF ADMISSIONS, TCU BOX 297013, FORT WORTH, TX 76129 • ADMISSIONS: 817-257-7490 • FAX: 817-257-7268

CAMPUS LIFE

Quality of Life Rating	84
Fire Safety Rating	92
Green Rating	82
Type of school	private
Affiliation	Disciples of Christ
Environment	metropolis

STUDENTS

Total undergrad enrollment	7,804
% male/female	41/59
% from out of state	25
% from public high school	65
% live on campus	50
# of fraternities	15
# of sororities	18
% African American	5
% Asian	2
% Caucasian	74
% Hispanic	1
% Native American	1
% international	5
# of countries represented	88

SURVEY SAYS . . .
Great computer facilities
Athletic facilities are great
Students love Fort Worth, TX
Frats and sororities dominate
social scene

ACADEMICS

Academic Rating	76
% students graduating within 4 years	54
% students graduating within 6 years	74
Calendar	semester
Student/faculty ratio	13:1
Profs interesting rating	86
Profs accessible rating	84
Most common reg class size	20–29 students
Most common lab size	20–29 students

MOST POPULAR MAJORS
business administration and management, nursing, public relations, advertising, applied communication

STUDENTS SAY ". . ."

Academics
The popular conception of Texas is that everything there is big, big, big, but Texas Christian University is one Lone Star institution that bucks this trend, insisting on "smaller classroom sizes" that allows professors to be "very interested in [students] personally." One undergrad explains: "If I have a problem and need to talk with the profs, they go out of their way to meet with me, especially when it comes to career options and what my best options are in terms of what I want to do. They are very helpful." While "there are some programs with more students than others, overall the academic experience at TCU is very personal and rewarding. Many students are easily able to latch onto a professor's lab research...Getting involved in the academic programs at TCU will really pay off." Students enjoy a strong support network; the school "offers many resources such as the library, writing center, career center, student support services, and other educational and personal resources," and alumni "are really involved and give a lot back to the school." Business, education, and physical therapy are among the standout offerings here. Access to the Dallas–Fort Worth business community means plenty of good internship and networking opportunities.

Life
"Greek life is one of the most popular activities" at TCU; some say "the Greeks rule the social scene at the school," while others see slightly more diverse options. The school "puts a lot of its money to good use, such as new residence halls, a nice recreational facility, funding for numerous clubs and organizations, and great activities to bring the campus community together," creating "a focus on the student community" that extends beyond the Greek houses. TCU football is another pillar of campus life, and students "have a lot of pride" in both the program and the school itself. Beyond these choices, life at TCU "is what you make it. If you want to make grades your top priority, it's very easy to do so. If you want to go out and party a lot, it's very easy to do [that] as well. Lots of people drink on campus, but not everyone makes that their life. It's all about what your priorities are because it is easy to go either way." Off-campus opportunities are plentiful thanks to access to Dallas-Fort Worth, a major metropolis.

Student Body
"The student body is very Greek" at TCU. Students differ on how this impacts social dynamics; some insist that "if you aren't in a fraternity or sorority, it is very hard to fit in," while others point out that "there are other types of people on campus", and "if you are open-minded and have a good personality overall you won't find it hard to make friends inside and outside of Greek life and find yourself belonging at TCU." While "the student population is mostly made up of Caucasian students," there is "a growing minority student population," the largest segment of which is Latina. Undergrads tend to be "middle- to upper-class...in good physical shape, and like to have a good time." Many, "but not all, dress extremely well...First impressions mean a lot here, so do not mess up." Some complain about the pervasive materialism, but others think the issue is overblown; one tells us, "Some may find the money an issue, but that's only because they make it an issue. I've never been ashamed that I can't buy the latest Prada handbag, and no one has ever looked down on me because of that. If you don't bring it up, nobody cares. A lack of character may make these people feel left out."

FINANCIAL AID: 817-257-7858 • E-MAIL: FROGMAIL@TCU.EDU • WEBSITE: WWW.TCU.EDU

THE PRINCETON REVIEW SAYS

Admissions

Very important factors considered include: Academic GPA, application essay, class rank, recommendation(s), rigor of secondary school record, standardized test scores, character/personal qualities, geographical residence. *Important factors considered include:* Extracurricular activities, first generation, geographical residence, level of applicant's interest, racial/ethnic status, religious affiliation/commitment, talent/ability, volunteer work, work experience. *Other factors considered include:* Alumni/ae relation, interview. SAT or ACT required; ACT with writing component recommended. TOEFL required of all international applicants. *Academic units required:* 4 English, 3 mathematics, 3 science, 2 foreign language, 3 social studies, 2 academic elective. *Academic units recommended:* 4 English, 4 mathematics, 4 science, 4 foreign language, 4 social studies.

Financial Aid

Students should submit: FAFSA. Regular filing deadline is May 1. The Princeton Review suggests that all financial aid forms be submitted as soon as possible after January 1. *Need-based scholarships/grants offered:* Federal Pell, SEOG, state scholarships/grants, private scholarships, school scholarship or grant aid from institutional funds. *Loan aid offered:* Direct Subsidized Stafford, Direct Unsubsidized Stafford, Direct PLUS, Federal Perkins, Federal Nursing Loans, state loans. Applicants will be notified of awards on a rolling basis beginning March 15. Federal Work-Study Program available. Off-campus job opportunities are excellent.

The Inside Word

The sheer volume of applications sent to TCU—the school receives more than 14,000 each year—requires the school to apply some baseline criteria for winnowing out unlikely candidates. That said, the school works hard to consider applications holistically and to find mitigating evidence to offset sub-par performance in any one category (for example, standardized test scores).

THE SCHOOL SAYS "..."

From the Admissions Office

"TCU is a major teaching and research university with the feel of a small college. The TCU academic experience includes small classes with top faculty; cutting-edge technology; a liberal arts and sciences core curriculum; and real-life application though faculty-directed research, group projects, and internships. While TCU faculty members are recognized for research, their main focus is on teaching and mentoring students. The friendly campus community welcomes new students at Frog Camp before classes begin, where students find three days of fun meeting new friends, learning campus traditions, and serving the community. Campus life includes 200 clubs and organizations, a spirited NCAA Division I athletics program, and numerous productions from professional schools of the arts. More than half of the students participate in a wide array of intramural sports, and about forty percent are involved in Greek organizations, including ones emphasizing ethnic diversity as well as the Christian faith. The historic relationship to the Christian Church (Disciples of Christ) means that instead of teaching a particular viewpoint, TCU encourages students to consider and follow their own beliefs. The university's mission—to educate individuals to think and act as ethical leaders and responsible citizens in a global community—influences everything from course work to study abroad to the way Horned Frogs act and interact. From National Merit Scholars to those just now realizing their academic potential, TCU attracts and serves students who are learning to change the world.

"TCU will accept either the SAT or the ACT (with or without the writing component) in admission and scholarship processes. The writing sections will be considered alongside the TCU application essay."

SELECTIVITY

Admissions Rating	80
# of applicants	14,085
% of applicants accepted	53
% of acceptees attending	25
# accepting a place on wait list	478
% admitted from wait list	37

FRESHMAN PROFILE

Range SAT Critical Reading	520–630
Range SAT Math	530–650
Range SAT Writing	520–630
Range ACT Composite	23–29
Minimum paper TOEFL	550
Minimum computer TOEFL	213
Minimum web-based TOEFL	80
% graduated top 10% of class	33
% graduated top 25% of class	65
% graduated top 50% of class	92

DEADLINES

Early action	
Deadline	11/1
Notification	1/1
Regular	
Priority	2/15
Deadline	2/15
Nonfall registration?	yes

FINANCIAL FACTS

Financial Aid Rating	76
Annual tuition	$32,400
Room and board	$10,410
Required fees	$90
Books and supplies	$1,500
% frosh rec. need-based scholarship or grant aid	32
% UG rec. need-based scholarship or grant aid	54
% frosh rec. non-need-based scholarship or grant aid	59
% UG rec. non-need-based scholarship or grant aid	54
% frosh rec. any financial aid	79
% UG rec. any financial aid	78
% UG borrow to pay for school	45
Average cumulative indebtedness	$36,546

THOMAS AQUINAS COLLEGE

10000 NORTH OJAI ROAD, SANTA PAULA, CA 93060 • ADMISSION: 800-634-9797 • FAX: 805-525-9342

STUDENTS SAY ". . ."

Academics

Students at Thomas Aquinas College relish attending a school that "takes learning seriously for its own sake, not just as preparation for a job." With a "strong Catholic identity" and "rigorous curriculum," TAC offers a "holistic education" that's "demanding on every level." The college promotes a "Great Books education," which really forces its undergrads to "read and think critically." All classes are seminar-based, a method many students here feel "better facilitates learning." Importantly, the "Catholic/small-college setting creates an atmosphere of trust and faith that makes it easier to study, to live, and to grow at school." Unlike other colleges, "There aren't any majors at Thomas Aquinas." Students simply graduate with a bachelor's degree in liberal arts. Class time is solely "devoted to discussion of the [reading] material assigned" with professors (or tutors as they are known) facilitating said discussion. Undergrads happily report that professors are "more than happy to continue the discussion outside class and are always ready to help their students." Moreover, they're "welcoming" and "easy to talk to," and all seem to "have a passion for intellectual formation." As one content senior succinctly states, "The professors are great and lead you to truth without forcing it on you."

Life

TAC inspires and encourages a contemplative life, and students spend a large portion of their time in "an intellectual discussion." That being said, even TAC undergrads need to kick back every now and again. On this active campus, intramural sports are quite popular, and "running, hiking, basketball, soccer, and football are major pastimes on campus." Further, "Four times a year there is a formal dance hosted by one of the classes." As one enthusiastic sophomore explains, "I waltz, swing, lindy hop, tango, salsa, rumba, contra dance, polka, Virginia reel, and do other dances. People on this campus actually learn and know how to dance well." Students here also know how to make their own fun. As one freshman shares, there are "spontaneous student pranks, such as the day the freshmen men all wore blue while the freshmen women wore pink (officially titled 'Trip Out the Tudors Tuesday')." Additionally, "Once or twice a semester, the school arranges field trips to the Getty Center, Villa, operas, art galleries, science museums, and other points of interest in the wider LA area." It's also quite common for students to "leave campus for the weekend for fun activities either to Ventura Beach (thirty minutes), Santa Barbara (one hour), or Ojai (twenty minutes)."

Student Body

Undergrads at TAC might, in some respects, appear "homogenous." Indeed, the vast majority of students "are Catholic," "devoted to learning and their faith," and politically "conservative." That being said, a senior assures us, "Any student with any interest can usually find a group that shares his or her passion." Importantly, many agree that their peers are "very kind and inclusive" as well as "joyful and inviting." One junior elaborates saying, "You walk down the hallways and sidewalks and are personally greeted by freshmen and seniors alike." An overwhelming number of undergrads here declare their fellow students "intellectually curious" and "somewhat obsessed with philosophy." Indeed, the typical student "is a thinker [who] will never hesitate to get in[to] a philosophical argument." Naturally, people here are "committed to the academic life," and most students study "very hard." They're "focused [and] mature" and make a point of "coming prepared to class." As one honest and insightful senior admits, "Most [students] would probably be considered a bit geeky elsewhere." But perhaps this student sums up his TAC peers the best, "You get all different kinds of people here—but one thing they have in common is a desire to search for the truth."

FINANCIAL AID: 800-634-9797 • E-MAIL: ADMISSIONS@THOMASAQUINAS.EDU • WEBSITE: WWW.THOMASAQUINAS.EDU

THE PRINCETON REVIEW SAYS

Admissions

Very important factors considered include: Application essay, recommendation(s), rigor of secondary school record, standardized test scores, character/personal qualities, level of applicant's interest. *Important factors considered include:* Academic GPA. *Other factors considered include:* Class rank, extracurricular activities, interview, religious affiliation/commitment, talent/ability, volunteer work, work experience. SAT or ACT required; ACT with or without writing component accepted. TOEFL required of all international applicants High school diploma is required, and GED is accepted. *Academic units required:* 4 English, 3 mathematics, 2 science, 2 foreign language, 2 history *Academic units recommended:* 4 English, 4 mathematics, 3 science (2 science labs), 2 history, 3 academic elective.

Financial Aid

Students should submit: FAFSA, institution's own financial aid form. Regular filing deadline is March 2. The Princeton Review suggests that all financial aid forms be submitted as soon as possible after January 1. *Need-based scholarships/ grants offered:* Federal Pell, state scholarships/grants, private scholarships, school scholarship or grant aid from institutional funds. *Loan aid offered:* Direct Subsidized Stafford, Direct Unsubsidized Stafford, Direct PLUS, university loans from institutional funds. Applicants will be notified of awards on a rolling basis beginning February 1. Federal Work-Study Program not available. Off-campus job opportunities are fair.

The Inside Word

A unique academic institution, TAC thoroughly analyzes their applicants to ensure their accepted students will be a good fit. Academic prowess is a must, and candidates should also demonstrate intellectual curiosity. Because of their holistic approach, admissions officers pay close attention to the application essays. The college operates on a rolling admissions schedule and, if interested, you should apply as early as possible.

THE SCHOOL SAYS ". . ."

From the Admissions Office

"Thomas Aquinas College holds with confidence that the human mind is capable of knowing the truth about reality, that living according to the truth is necessary for human happiness, and that truth is best comprehended through the harmonious work of faith and reason. The intellectual virtues are understood to be essential, and the college considers the cultivation of those virtues the primary work of Catholic liberal education.

"The academic program designed to achieve this goal is comprehensive and unified—and it includes no textbooks or lecture classes. In every subject—from philosophy, theology, mathematics, and science to language, music, literature, and history—students read the greatest written works in those disciplines, both ancient and modern: Homer, Plato, Aristotle, Augustine, Aquinas, Newton, Maxwell, Einstein, the Founding Fathers of the American Republic, Shakespeare, and T. S. Eliot, to name just a few. Instead of attending lecture classes, students gather in small tutorials, seminars, and laboratories for Socratic-style discussions.

"One mark of the program's success is the variety of professions and careers that graduates enter. Many attend graduate and professional schools in a wide array of disciplines; among them, philosophy, theology, law, literature, and the sciences are most often chosen.

"SAT or ACT scores are required, and the writing component on each test is encouraged. However, scores in critical reading and math (SAT), or English and mathematics (ACT) are more central in the consideration of that aspect of a student's application."

SELECTIVITY

Admissions Rating	91
# of applicants	168
% of applicants accepted	76
% of acceptees attending	68
# accepting a place on wait list	5
% admitted from wait list	40

FRESHMAN PROFILE

Range SAT Critical Reading	630–730
Range SAT Math	570–670
Range SAT Writing	580–680
Range ACT Composite	27–31
Minimum paper TOEFL	570
Minimum computer TOEFL	230
Average HS GPA	3.79
% graduated top 10% of class	44
% graduated top 25% of class	78
% graduated top 50% of class	89

DEADLINES

Regular	
Notification	10/1
Nonfall registration?	no

APPLICANTS ALSO LOOK AT

AND OFTEN PREFER
University of Notre Dame

AND SOMETIMES PREFER
Benedictine College, Christendom College, Franciscan University of Steubenville, The Catholic University of America, University of Dallas

FINANCIAL FACTS

Financial Aid Rating	99
Annual tuition	$22,850
Room and board	$7,550
Books and supplies	$450
% frosh rec. need-based scholarship or grant aid	75
% UG rec. need-based scholarship or grant aid	69
% frosh rec. need-based self-help aid	82
% UG rec. need-based self-help aid	77
% frosh rec. any financial aid	86
% UG rec. any financial aid	81
% UG borrow to pay for school	82
Average cumulative indebtedness	$16,311

TRANSYLVANIA UNIVERSITY

300 NORTH BROADWAY, LEXINGTON, KY 40508-1797 • ADMISSIONS: 859-233-8242 • FAX: 859-233-8797

STUDENTS SAY ". . ."

Academics

Tucked away in the heart of Lexington, Kentucky, Transylvania University is able to marry a "small-school atmosphere" with "big-city" living. An "extremely close-knit campus," one truly feels a "strong sense of community" while strolling around the grounds. Undergrads here greatly appreciate that the school "values community, education for the sake of education, and producing students with the skills to tackle any career the job market has to offer." Moreover, Transy strives to provide "a holistic educational experience where one can grow intellectually and academically while participating in a vibrant social community." Students are quick to heap praise on their professors who "are both very knowledgeable and fun to be around." They're all "accomplished within their fields" and seem to "love teaching here at Transylvania." As one pleased Spanish and English double-major confidently declares, "It doesn't matter whether a class is lecture- or discussion-based, because either way you're guaranteed to learn something." One junior does warn that most professors "require students [to] participate in classroom discussion," which can be "intimidating" for some. Perhaps most important, their accessibility is "amazing," and they "are almost always willing to let you stop by during their office hours and discuss just about anything." And, as this anthropology major simply and smartly quips, "I am never bored."

Life

During the week, life at Transy can be fairly harried and "stressful," and most students have their noses "to the grindstone." In turn, because of working "ridiculously hard," students are pumped to "have some fun when [the week] is over." The vast majority of undergrads "are involved in Greek life," and "parties in the fraternity dorms are very popular." Fortunately, we have been assured that neither the fraternities nor sororities are "exclusive." Moreover, "every social event is practically open invitation." Of course, there's plenty to do aside from simply attending frat parties. For example, the "Student Activities Board [sponsors] a lot of activities that are pretty fun and have a relatively good turn out." There's always something to do as one freshman indicates, "This weekend I'll be going to a huge musical/talent show, then tomorrow I'll be volunteering to raise money for a local church, then after that I'll be going ice skating with some friends." Athletics are also fairly big, and "Transylvania has several perennially successful sports programs, some of which include men's and women's basketball, men's and women's soccer, and softball." Undergrads also love to take advantage of hometown Lexington, and you'll often find students "walking downtown to theaters, art exhibits, or other downtown events" as well as "the shopping district."

Student Body

Transylvania manages to attract students who "seem to be genuinely concerned with their education." Indeed, undergrads are quick to define their peers as "studious," "intellectually motivated," and full of "ambitious goals." As a result, "The average Transylvania student is extremely adept at balancing his or her academics with the many extracurricular activities available." Additionally, "Greek life is very prominent on campus." However, one student insists that overall, the "Transy campus has very diverse individuals." Of course, a handful of students begrudge the "lack of…geographic diversity," asserting that "most students come from the region around Lexington" and are "upper-middle-class." Others take issue with this sentiment, quickly stating, "We also have a huge population of individuals from different backgrounds including differences in sexual orientation, class, religion, region, and political orientation." Fortunately, undergrads do find their fellow students "approachable and friendly," and "most students will find themselves right at home on campus."

FINANCIAL AID: 859-233-8239 • E-MAIL: ADMISSIONS@TRANSY.EDU • WEBSITE: WWW.TRANSY.EDU

THE PRINCETON REVIEW SAYS

Admissions

Very important factors considered include: Academic GPA, rigor of secondary school record, standardized test scores. *Important factors considered include:* Application essay, recommendation(s), extracurricular activities. *Other factors considered include:* Alumni/ae relation, character/personal qualities, first generation, geographical residence, interview, talent/ability, volunteer work, work experience. SAT or ACT required; ACT with or without writing component accepted. TOEFL required of all international applicants. High school diploma is required, and GED is accepted. *Academic units required:* 4 English, 3 mathematics, 3 science (2 science labs), 2 social studies. *Academic units recommended:* 4 English, 4 mathematics, 4 science (2 science labs), 4 foreign language, 2 social studies, 1 history, 1 visual/performing arts, 1 academic elective.

Financial Aid

Students should submit: FAFSA. Regular filing deadline is February 1. The Princeton Review suggests that all financial aid forms be submitted as soon as possible after January 1. *Need-based scholarships/grants offered:* Federal Pell, SEOG, state scholarships/grants, private scholarships, school scholarship or grant aid from institutional funds. *Loan aid offered:* Direct Subsidized Stafford, Direct Unsubsidized Stafford, Direct PLUS, Federal Perkins, university loans from institutional funds. Applicants will be notified of awards on a rolling basis beginning March 15. Federal Work-Study Program available. Off-campus job opportunities are excellent.

Inside Word

The admissions committee at Transylvania University is tasked with finding a freshman class that will mesh well with the existing Transy community. That being the case, they do their utmost to consider the entire applicant. Of course, academic rigor is the most important factor. However, don't shirk on your essays, recommendations, or extracurricular involvement.

THE SCHOOL SAYS "..."

From the Admissions Office

"Bright, highly motivated students choose Transylvania for our personal approach to learning and our record of success in preparing them for rewarding careers and fulfilling lives. They attend small classes (many have fewer than ten students) with highly qualified professors (no teaching assistants) and tackle faculty-directed student research projects in intriguing subjects like neurotransmitters and receptors, computer animation, and local Hispanic culture. Transylvania graduates have won prestigious scholarships and distinguished themselves at highly selective graduate and professional schools.

"Transylvania students consider the world their classroom. They enjoy May term travel courses studying the ancient polis in Greece, language and culture in France, and tropical ecology in Hawaii. Study abroad takes them to Germany, England, Japan, Mexico, and other destinations for a summer, a semester, or a year.

"You'll find Transylvania, a small college, nestled in a big city. Transylvania students soak up the advantages of Lexington, Kentucky, with its population of 300,000, numerous internships and job opportunities, and lots of entertainment. On campus, we have more than fifty co-curricular activities, and eighteen varsity teams competing in NCAA Division III.

"While Transylvania is the nation's sixteenth oldest college and proud of its rich history, its commitments to the exploration of a variety of disciplines, to intellectual inquiry, and to critical thinking have never been more relevant than in today's rapidly changing twenty-first-century world.

"Applicants are not required to submit writing scores from the ACT or the SAT."

SELECTIVITY

Admissions Rating	87
# of applicants	1,319
% of applicants accepted	84
% of acceptees attending	27

FRESHMAN PROFILE

Range SAT Critical Reading	530–670
Range SAT Math	510–670
Range ACT Composite	24–29
Minimum paper TOEFL	550
Minimum computer TOEFL	213
Minimum web-based TOEFL	80
Average HS GPA	3.79
% graduated top 10% of class	45
% graduated top 25% of class	75
% graduated top 50% of class	94

DEADLINES

Early action	
Deadline	12/1
Notification	1/15
Regular	
Priority	12/1
Deadline	2/1
Notification	3/15
Nonfall registration?	yes

APPLICANTS ALSO LOOK AT AND SOMETIMES PREFER
Centre College, University of Kentucky

FINANCIAL FACTS

Financial Aid Rating	83
Annual tuition	$25,650
Room and board	$8,090
Required fees	$1,090
Books and supplies	$1,000
% frosh rec. need-based scholarship or grant aid	74
% UG rec. need-based scholarship or grant aid	68
% frosh rec. non-need-based scholarship or grant aid	25
% UG rec. non-need-based scholarship or grant aid	29
% frosh rec. need-based self-help aid	56
% UG rec. need-based self-help aid	55
% frosh rec. any financial aid	99
% UG rec. any financial aid	98
% UG borrow to pay for school	64
Average cumulative indebtedness	$22,433

TRINITY COLLEGE (CT)

300 SUMMIT STREET, HARTFORD, CT 06016 • ADMISSIONS: 860-297-2180 • FAX: 860-297-2287

STUDENTS SAY ". . ."

Academics

"[It's all] about getting a top-notch education in small classes with professors who know you and being able to also have a good time outside of class" at Trinity College, a small and prestigious liberal arts school located in Connecticut's state capital. A "great political science department" exploits TC's location "about two blocks away from the state capitol, which is great for internships." Other social sciences, including economics and history, earn students' praises, as do offerings in engineering and education. Strength across the liberal arts bolsters the school's Guided Studies Program, in which students undertake a fixed curriculum of interdisciplinary study to survey the entirety of Western civilization from the classical age to the present. In all disciplines, "small classes, very involved professors, and a very conscious student body" combine to provide "an excellent liberal arts education that will provide [students] with the skills to be thoughtful, independent adults." Professors "are always available to talk and offer help to students. They often invite students out to lunch." Likewise, administrators are easy to access. "Even the president of the school, James F. Jones, is accessible. He goes on the Quest Orientation hiking trip for first-year students and regularly attends various student events on campus." Students also appreciate that "the career services office is amazing" here.

Life

"The fraternity scene is the draw for the majority of campus" at Trinity College, where "On a typical weekend night, people go out to dinner, go back to their room and nap, get ready for the evening, and go meet up with a friend or two where they chill out and then go to someone's room for pregaming…Then when it's about 1:00 A.M. they go out and do some frat hopping. It's great for people who like their life to be predictable." The frats are hardly the only option, though; in fact, "There are a ton of underappreciated options on or near campus. Hartford has amazing restaurants, there are movie theaters and bowling alleys nearby, the Cinestudio is a ninety-second walk from the main dining hall, and there are two dorms on campus devoted specifically to alcohol-free activities. Plus, plenty of student groups hold events" in such places as "the arts and cultural houses." Trinity's theater and dance department offer regular performances. Hometown Hartford "may be [an economically] depressed city, but it is still a city, and it affords benefits that tiny college towns just can't match."

Student Body

The stereotype about Trinity undergrads is that "most…are from the tri-state area and appear to have just stepped off a yacht or out of a country club," and students confirm that while "there are a lot of students who are not" in this crowd, the preppy contingent is "the main group" and "socially dominant" here. "There are definitely some very preppy girls and boys—blond hair, sunglasses, Chanel flats, a polo," one student concedes before adding that "sometimes people identify these students as typical Trinity students; however there are many students who are not like that at all." All students tend to be "well-rounded" and "very passionate," "intelligent but also social," with "good verbal skills." They "care deeply about their work and really like to have fun when they can," and while many gravitate to the Greek community for their fun, "There are [also] communities here for those who do not enjoy the frat scene, for people who are passionate about music and acting, and [for] those who want to spend their weekends giving back to the community."

FINANCIAL AID: 860-297-2046 • E-MAIL: ADMISSIONS.OFFICE@TRINCOLL.EDU • WEBSITE: WWW.TRINCOLL.EDU

THE PRINCETON REVIEW SAYS

Admissions

Very important factors considered include: Rigor of secondary school record. *Important factors considered include:* Academic GPA, application essay, class rank, recommendation(s), standardized test scores, character/personal qualities, extracurricular activities, interview, racial/ethnic status, talent/ability. *Other factors considered include:* Alumni/ae relation, first generation, geographical residence, level of applicant's interest, volunteer work, work experience. SAT or ACT required; ACT with writing component recommended. High school diploma is required, and GED is accepted. *Academic units required:* 4 English, 3 mathematics, 2 science (2 science labs), 3 foreign language, 2 history.

Financial Aid

Students should submit: FAFSA, CSS/Financial Aid PROFILE. Regular filing deadline is March 1. The Princeton Review suggests that all financial aid forms be submitted as soon as possible after January 1. *Need-based scholarships/grants offered:* Federal Pell, SEOG, state scholarships/grants, private scholarships, school scholarship or grant aid from institutional funds. *Loan aid offered:* Direct Subsidized Stafford, Direct Unsubsidized Stafford, Direct PLUS, Federal Perkins, university loans from institutional funds. Federal Work-Study Program available. Off-campus job opportunities are good.

The Inside Word

Students describe Trinity as "the home of Yale rejects," an appraisal that accurately, if somewhat hyperbolically, characterizes the school's reputation as an Ivy safety. The hefty tuition and fees here ensure that a large percentage of the student body is made up of wealthy, preppy types, but the school does offer generous financial aid packages to top candidates who can't afford the considerable price of attending. The school would love to broaden its demographic, so competitive minority students should receive a very welcome reception here.

THE SCHOOL SAYS "..."

From the Admissions Office

"An array of distinctive curricular options—including an interdisciplinary neuroscience major and a professionally accredited engineering degree program, a unique Human Rights Program, a Health Fellows Program, and interdisciplinary programs such as the Cities Program, Interdisciplinary Science Program, and InterArts—is one reason record numbers of students are applying to Trinity. In fact, applications are up eighty percent over the past five years. In addition, the college has been recognized for its commitment to diversity; students of color have represented approximately twenty percent of the freshman class for the past four years, setting Trinity apart from many of its peers. Trinity's capital city location offers students unparalleled 'real-world' learning experiences to complement classroom learning. Students take advantage of extensive opportunities for internships for academic credit and community service, and these opportunities extend to Trinity's global learning sites in cities around the world. Trinity's faculty is a devoted and accomplished group of exceptional teacher-scholars; our 100-acre campus is beautiful; Hartford is an educational asset that differentiates Trinity from other liberal arts colleges; our global connections and foreign study opportunities prepare students to be good citizens of the world; and our graduates go on to excel in virtually every field. We invite you to learn more about why Trinity might be the best choice for you.

"Students applying for admission may submit the following testing options: SAT, ACT with writing."

SELECTIVITY

Admissions Rating	92
# of applicants	4,688
% of applicants accepted	43
% of acceptees attending	29
# accepting a place on wait list	517
% admitted from wait list	5
# of early decision applicants	417
% accepted early decision	69

FRESHMAN PROFILE

Range SAT Critical Reading	590–680
Range SAT Math	610–690
Range SAT Writing	610–700
Range ACT Composite	25–29
% graduated top 10% of class	56
% graduated top 25% of class	87
% graduated top 50% of class	99

DEADLINES

Early decision	
Deadline	11/15
Notification	12/15
Regular	
Deadline	1/1
Nonfall registration?	no

APPLICANTS ALSO LOOK AT AND OFTEN PREFER
Boston College, Boston University

AND SOMETIMES PREFER
Middlebury College, Wesleyan University

FINANCIAL FACTS

Financial Aid Rating	98
Annual tuition	$40,410
Room and board	$10,960
Required fees	$2,010
Books and supplies	$1,000
% frosh rec. need-based scholarship or grant aid	39
% UG rec. need-based scholarship or grant aid	41
% frosh rec. non-need-based scholarship or grant aid	8
% UG rec. non-need-based scholarship or grant aid	3
% frosh rec. need-based self-help aid	34
% UG rec. need-based self-help aid	35
% frosh rec. any financial aid	54
% UG rec. any financial aid	54
% UG borrow to pay for school	39
Average cumulative indebtedness	$21,671

TRINITY UNIVERSITY (TX)

ONE TRINITY PLACE, SAN ANTONIO, TX 78212 • ADMISSIONS: 210-999-7207 • FAX: 210-999-8164

CAMPUS LIFE

Quality of Life Rating	90
Fire Safety Rating	87
Green Rating	76
Type of school	private
Affiliation	Presbyterian
Environment	metropolis

STUDENTS

Total undergrad enrollment	2,416
% male/female	46/54
% from out of state	27
% from public high school	66
% live on campus	74
# of fraternities	7
# of sororities	6
% African American	3
% Asian	7
% Caucasian	61
% Hispanic	12
% Native American	1
% international	7
# of countries represented	69

SURVEY SAYS . . .

Great computer facilities
Great library
School is well-run
Great off-campus food
Dorms are like palaces
Campus feels safe

ACADEMICS

Academic Rating	88
% students graduating within 4 years	68
% students graduating within 6 years	78
Calendar	semester
Student/faculty ratio	9:1
Profs interesting rating	88
Profs accessible rating	93
Most common reg class size	10–19 students
Most common lab size	10–19 students

MOST POPULAR MAJORS

business, English language and literature, foreign languages and literatures

STUDENTS SAY ". . ."

Academics

"Trinity University is a place where one can be focused and diligent with studies—while also being in a great place to have fun on the side." In other words, this school is ideal for those seeking a well-rounded college experience and an "outstanding liberal arts education." Premed, accounting, and education are all popular majors, and the school offers "excellent science departments," and "the arts are amazing." Students praise the small class sizes and say they have access to "Ivy League smarts without the attitude." "The lectures are interesting, and class activities are unique and engaging." "The professors here, on the whole, are brilliant and helpful and are willing to work with you." "Professors are *always* accessible (some even give out home/cell phone numbers). They generally seem to enjoy students who stop by [during] office hours for help [or] just to chat." Slackers beware: While "the professors are usually very dedicated and excited to teach their subjects…that also means they expect each of their classes to be the most important class at Trinity." "Trinity professors assign a ridiculous amount of course work, but most will go to any length to help the students understand and complete the assignments." There are some complaints about the challenges of the current registration process, but overall, Trinity students are very happy with their classes, their extracurriculars, and their "gorgeous" campus.

Life

"Just about everybody at Trinity is involved in extracurricular activities," making the campus "fairly lively on its own, and it's easy to almost never leave it," though hometown San Antonio "is a great location: lots to do, lots to see, and it's right in the middle of everything exciting. Austin is only an hour away, and Padre Island is only a two-hour drive." Students have free admission to local art museums, too. But back to campus (students are required to live there for three years, after all): "There are plenty of clubs and organizations to get involved with, and Greek life at Trinity is great." Greek life and athletics are popular activities, but Trinity offers "something for everyone." Students tell us they're "always blown away by the stage productions on campus," and they enjoy working at the radio station, "which is an enormously respected jazz station by day and [broadcasts] quirky college indie radio by night." A typical week includes "a lecture one night, a cultural taste test the night after, and a concert over the weekend. There is always something to do." "There is always a party going on" at Trinity, "but they hardly dominate the social landscape." Plenty of students "watch movies or bake" for fun, and "it's not unusual to spend an afternoon with friends talking about a lecture from earlier in the day."

Student Body

"The typical student is pretty easygoing but hardworking. They want to embrace the college experience while still getting an education." Pretty much what you would expect at a university that offers such a well-balanced experience. Most students come from an "upper-middle-class upbringing…and likely came to Trinity to be a 'big fish in a small pond.'" Students do say "the school can be a bit clique-y at times," and "because [it] is so small, there is certainly a high school–like feel," but "there are many organizations and groups that anyone can join," and most students make friends easily in the dorms or via extracurricular activities. "The student body is very active in different organizations and athletics," and students note that "people who are happy at Trinity generally don't take advantage of all the different activities it has to offer." Lastly, "even though it's in Texas, it's a fairly liberal and tolerant school."

TRINITY UNIVERSITY (TX)

FINANCIAL AID: 210-999-8315 • E-MAIL: ADMISSIONS@TRINITY.EDU • WEBSITE: WWW.TRINITY.EDU

THE PRINCETON REVIEW SAYS

Admissions

Very important factors considered include: Academic GPA, class rank, rigor of secondary school record. *Important factors considered include:* Application essay, recommendation(s), standardized test scores, character/personal qualities, extracurricular activities, interview, talent/ability. *Other factors considered include:* Alumni/ae relation, first generation, geographical residence, level of applicant's interest, racial/ethnic status, volunteer work, work experience. SAT or ACT required; ACT with or without writing component accepted. TOEFL required of all international applicants. High school diploma is required, and GED is accepted. *Academic units required:* 4 English, 3 mathematics, 3 science (2 science labs), 2 foreign language, 3 social studies. *Academic units recommended:* 4 English, 3 mathematics, 3 science (3 science labs), 3 foreign language, 3 social studies, 3 academic elective.

Financial Aid

Students should submit: FAFSA. The Princeton Review suggests that all financial aid forms be submitted as soon as possible after January 1. *Need-based scholarships/grants offered:* Federal Pell, SEOG, state scholarships/grants, private scholarships, school scholarship or grant aid from institutional funds. *Loan aid offered:* Direct Subsidized Stafford, Direct Unsubsidized Stafford, Direct PLUS, Federal Perkins, state loans, university loans from institutional funds. Federal Work-Study Program available. Off-campus job opportunities are good.

The Inside Word

As Trinity embraces a small, close-knit community of students, admissions officers are looking for the complete package: bright, capable, motivated students who are ready to take advantage of all the school has to offer. While academic performance is the factor considered most heavily on each application, recommendations, extracurricular activities, and standardized test scores should all be very strong as well.

THE SCHOOL SAYS "..."

From the Admissions Office

"Three qualities separate Trinity University from other selective, academically challenging institutions around the country. First, Trinity is unusual in the quality and quantity of resources devoted almost exclusively to its undergraduate students. Those resources give rise to a second distinctive aspect of Trinity—its emphasis on undergraduate research. Our students prefer being involved over observing. With superior laboratory facilities and strong, dedicated faculty, our undergraduates fill many of the roles formerly reserved for graduate students, and our professors often go to their undergraduates for help with their research. Other hands-on learning experiences including internships, study abroad, and service projects are also available to students. Finally, Trinity stands apart for the attitude of its students. In an atmosphere of academic camaraderie and fellowship, our students work together to stretch their minds and broaden their horizons across academic disciplines. For quality of resources, for dedication to undergraduate research, and for the disposition of its student body, Trinity University holds a unique position in American higher education.

"Students applying for admission must submit either the SAT or the ACT. The highest composite test scores from one or multiple dates are evaluated. The SAT writing section and ACT writing component are not required."

SELECTIVITY

Admissions Rating	92
# of applicants	4,292
% of applicants accepted	63
% of acceptees attending	22
# accepting a place on wait list	105
% admitted from wait list	73
# of early decision applicants	50
% accepted early decision	88

FRESHMAN PROFILE

Range SAT Critical Reading	580–680
Range SAT Math	590–690
Range ACT Composite	26–33
Minimum paper TOEFL	600
Minimum computer TOEFL	250
Average HS GPA	3.52
% graduated top 10% of class	47
% graduated top 25% of class	79
% graduated top 50% of class	96

DEADLINES

Early decision	
Deadline	11/1
Notification	12/1
Early action	
Deadline	12/1
Notification	2/1
Regular	
Deadline	2/1
Nonfall registration?	no

APPLICANTS ALSO LOOK AT AND OFTEN PREFER
Rice University, The University of Texas at Austin

AND SOMETIMES PREFER
Texas A&M University—College Station, Tulane University

AND RARELY PREFER

FINANCIAL FACTS

Financial Aid Rating	88
Annual tuition	$29,832
Room and board	$10,312
Required fees	$180
Books and supplies	$950
% frosh rec. need-based scholarship or grant aid	52
% UG rec. need-based scholarship or grant aid	42
% frosh rec. non-need-based scholarship or grant aid	11
% UG rec. non-need-based scholarship or grant aid	7
% frosh rec. need-based self-help aid	42
% UG rec. need-based self-help aid	35
% frosh rec. any financial aid	91
% UG rec. any financial aid	83

TRUMAN STATE UNIVERSITY

RUTH W. TOWNE MUSEUM AND VISITOR'S CENTER, 100 EAST NORMAL, KIRKSVILLE, MO 63501 • ADMISSIONS: 660-785-4114 • FAX: 660-785-7456

CAMPUS LIFE

Quality of Life Rating	80
Fire Safety Rating	64
Green Rating	73
Type of school	public
Environment	village

STUDENTS

Total undergrad enrollment	5,675
% male/female	41/59
% from out of state	21
% from public high school	85
% live on campus	49
# of fraternities	18
# of sororities	11
% African American	4
% Asian	2
% Caucasian	81
% Hispanic	3
% Native American	1
% international	5
# of countries represented	49

SURVEY SAYS . . .

Students are friendly
Campus feels safe
Low cost of living
Students are happy
Very little drug use

ACADEMICS

Academic Rating	87
% students graduating within 4 years	43
% students graduating within 6 years	70
Calendar	semester
Student/faculty ratio	16:1
Profs interesting rating	83
Profs accessible rating	87
Most common reg class size	20–29 students
Most common lab size	10–19 students

MOST POPULAR MAJORS
biology, business, English language and literature

STUDENTS SAY ". . ."

Academics

Truman students aren't shy about discussing their school's "extremely well-deserved academic reputation," referring to it as "superior," "excellent," "the best public university in the state of Missouri," and even "the Harvard of the Midwest." Truman students are here to work, and many cite the school's financial aid and scholarships as allowing them to do so. "Truman State offers many scholarships that make getting a great education very affordable," says a freshman biology major, and a senior linguistics major says, "They gave me scholarships that ended up essentially paying me to come here." Students enjoy Truman's focus on its study abroad options, and they use the school's financial accessibility to participate. "I wanted to get a world-class education, but I didn't want the price of tuition to prevent me from exploring the world itself. I'm doing an internship in Tanzania this summer, which quite frankly would not have been financially possible" otherwise. Many Truman students choose to study English, business, and accounting, but as one junior told us, "I wanted a school that was well-rounded so that, regardless of what I ended up majoring [in], I knew it would be a solid program." Students also appreciate the ability to take classes outside their majors; as one junior tells us, "Even though I am an exercise science major, I have taken many classes in other majors such as art and literature."

Life

Students almost unanimously love life at Truman State. "The campus is beautiful, and the atmosphere is very welcoming." However, at a school of Truman's caliber one can expect students to spend most of their time studying. "Many people here really care about their education, so they do schoolwork and study," and "The thing that stands out the most is how everyone here is pretty grade conscious." Students have noticed that other students "would rather go to class hung-over than miss lectures." Students do have reservations about hometown Kirksville; "There is not a lot to do. It really is a rural town, but people make fun things to do on campus." Some students participate in Greek life and "go to planned social events with fraternities and sororities. There are also a few bars in town that of-age students go to on a regular basis." But Truman's social scene is far from one-sided; "Some people say there's nothing to do but drink, but from the amount of school organizations and activities, that's obviously not true. People make their own fun." "The trick to making life at Truman interesting is to find your niche, whether it's on a sports team… or in a musical ensemble…I got involved with the campus newspaper." Students also undertake social responsibility. "You can be a huge political advocate, involved in protests on the quad. You can become involved in community service locally and nationwide."

Student Body

All of the students at Truman are bonded by one thing; their respect for other students' academic abilities, and all students are here to study. Therefore, "It is easy to get to know other classmates and have study groups or friends to lean on in times of need." "Most people strive to excel here, so there is a healthy focus on academics within friends," and the "typical student is an overachiever with big dreams and goals." Also, many are "from Missouri, specifically St. Louis, and a high proportion are from Catholic, private schools." As one student tells us, "The typical student can be described as the typical American…there is no distinct description to identify the typical person."

TRUMAN STATE UNIVERSITY

FINANCIAL AID: 660-785-4130 • E-MAIL: ADMISSIONS@TRUMAN.EDU • WEBSITE: WWW.TRUMAN.EDU

THE PRINCETON REVIEW SAYS

Admissions

Very important factors considered include: Academic GPA, class rank, rigor of secondary school record, standardized test scores. *Important factors considered include:* Application essay. *Other factors considered include:* Recommendation(s), alumni/ae relation, character/personal qualities, extracurricular activities, first generation, geographical residence, racial/ethnic status, state residency, talent/ability, volunteer work, work experience. SAT or ACT required; ACT with or without writing component accepted. TOEFL required of all international applicants. High school diploma is required, and GED is accepted. *Academic units required:* 4 English, 3 mathematics, 3 science (2 science labs), 2 foreign language, 2 social studies, 1 history, 1 visual/performing arts, 5 academic elective. *Academic units recommended:* 4 English, 4 mathematics, 3 science (2 science labs), 2 foreign language, 2 social studies, 1 history, 1 visual/performing arts, 5 academic elective.

Financial Aid

Regular filing deadline is December 1. The Princeton Review suggests that all financial aid forms be submitted as soon as possible after January 1. Applicants will be notified of awards on a rolling basis beginning September 15. Federal Work-Study Program available. Off-campus job opportunities are good.

The Inside Word

Those interested in studying at Truman State had better get to work; the school places a large emphasis on GPA, class rank, and academic rigor. The selectivity and quality of education numbers are high, but annual tuition is low for all students. Although early application has no bearing on admission, greatest scholarship consideration is given to those who apply early.

THE SCHOOL SAYS " . . . "

From the Admissions Office

"Truman's talented student body enjoys small classes where undergraduate research and personal interaction with professors are the norm. Truman's commitment to providing an exemplary liberal arts and sciences education with over 270 student organizations and outstanding internship and study abroad opportunities allows students to compete in top graduate schools and the job market.

"Truman offers a variety of competitive scholarships, and there is no seperate scholarship application. Students wishing to be considered for all scholarship programs are strongly encouraged to apply for admission by December 5th.

"Students applying for admission to Truman State University can submit scores from both the ACT and the SAT. The best composite score from either test will be considered. The writing section is not currently required for admission to Truman."

SELECTIVITY

Admissions Rating	91
# of applicants	4,702
% of applicants accepted	74
% of acceptees attending	41

FRESHMAN PROFILE

Range SAT Critical Reading	570–710
Range SAT Math	560–680
Range ACT Composite	25–30
Minimum paper TOEFL	550
Minimum computer TOEFL	213
Minimum web-based TOEFL	79
Average HS GPA	3.76
% graduated top 10% of class	47
% graduated top 25% of class	77
% graduated top 50% of class	98

DEADLINES

Regular	
Priority	12/1
Notification	9/15
Nonfall registration?	yes

APPLICANTS ALSO LOOK AT AND OFTEN PREFER

Missouri State University, Saint Louis University, University of Missouri—Columbia

AND SOMETIMES PREFER

Washington University in St. Louis

FINANCIAL FACTS

Financial Aid Rating	84
Annual in-state tuition	$6,458
Annual out-of-state tuition	$11,856
Room and board	$7,350

TUFTS UNIVERSITY

BENDETSON HALL, MEDFORD, MA 02155 • ADMISSIONS: 617-627-3170 • FAX: 617-627-3860

CAMPUS LIFE

Quality of Life Rating	93
Fire Safety Rating	79
Green Rating	86
Type of school	private
Environment	town

STUDENTS

Total undergrad enrollment	5,187
% male/female	49/51
% from out of state	75
% from public high school	59
% live on campus	62
# of fraternities	11
# of sororities	3
% African American	5
% Asian	11
% Caucasian	57
% Hispanic	6
% international	6
# of countries represented	93

SURVEY SAYS . . .

Great computer facilities
Great food on campus
Great off-campus food
Campus feels safe
Student publications are popular
Political activism is popular

ACADEMICS

Academic Rating	91
% students graduating within 4 years	86
% students graduating within 6 years	91
Calendar	semester
Student/faculty ratio	9:1
Profs interesting rating	87
Profs accessible rating	86
Most common reg class size	10–19 students
Most common lab size	10–19 students

MOST POPULAR MAJORS

economics, English language and literature, international relations

STUDENTS SAY ". . ."

Academics

"Mid-sized" and "very internationally focused," Tufts University boasts "an incredible blend of academics, extracurriculars, and athletics, and really emphasizes the impact an individual can have on his or her community." Tufts is probably best known for its world-class science programs (especially pre-med) and its prestigious international relations programs. Full-year and semester-long study abroad options in places such as Chile, Ghana, and Oxford are so amazing that almost half the students here participate before heading off into the real-world. Back on campus, students have a lot of latitude in their studies: "They do internships; they devise their own research projects; they assist professors on their work." Most faculty members are "brilliant," "dedicated to students," and "extremely accessible and friendly." A few, however, are "out of touch with reality." Classes, especially at the lower levels, can be "bigger than you think they'll be." The academic atmosphere is tough overall but it really varies by department. "Some classes are disproportionately easy, while others are disproportionately hard." "If you're premed, life is going to be miserable," warns a biomedical engineering major. "If you're an English or psych major, there are great professors in those departments and the majors are cake." "[In] some classes, you're forced to learn a lot," adds a computer science major. "[In others] you need to do a lot of the learning yourself." The administration at Tufts is "always there when you want them," but is otherwise "neither awful nor particularly noteworthy." "Some things could be smoother, but that is true almost everywhere."

Life

This "beautiful" campus offers a "great view of Boston" but some of the facilities "are not outstanding." Dorms in particular "can be a little gross." "Rooms are on the small side and the common areas are really subpar." Social life at Tufts can be "as big or small" as you want it to be. "Everyone loves to meet up in the dining halls and socialize," and "There is always so much going on around campus." "Fantastic extracurricular opportunities" proliferate. "Everyone is involved in something." "I ride on the equestrian team and I'm a member of the classics and archaeology club," declares a sophomore. Tufts also "holds a few social events each semester that most of the student body attends, which is a lot of fun." Students tend to "work hard" and stay "very focused on studying" during the week. They also "love to be ridiculous" on weekends. While "non-drinkers and moderate drinkers will be comfortable here," "alcoholic partygoers" will be happy, too. "There's kind of an expectation during freshman year that you go to fraternities on the weekend and get drunk." Older students "tend to be a little choosier and will have more exclusive off-campus gatherings or go to the bars." "Going into Boston is always really fun" as well. Beantown is "a city full of opportunity and entertainment." Tufts runs a shuttle to public transportation in Somerville.

Student Body

Students say this campus is a paradise of "cosmopolitanism and ethnic tolerance." Students at Tufts range from "preppy North Face and Ugg wearers, to hipsters," to "self-aware dorky" types. "There are a lot of nerdy kids but it's great for them because they come here and find each other." "There are also a lot of international kids, which is great." Tufts students describe themselves as "generally very hardworking," "intellectually stimulating people." They're also "very real and unpretentious" and "very eclectic." "To be eccentrically passionate about something is absolutely necessary" here. "Some people are a little strange, but Tufts is known for that." "I have never met an unquirky person associated with Tufts," swears a senior.

FINANCIAL AID: 617-627-2000 • E-MAIL: ADMISSIONS.INQUIRY@ASE.TUFTS.EDU • WEBSITE: WWW.TUFTS.EDU

THE PRINCETON REVIEW SAYS

Admissions

Very important factors considered include: Academic GPA, application essay, rigor of secondary school record, character/personal qualities. *Important factors considered include:* Class rank, recommendation(s), standardized test scores, extracurricular activities, talent/ability, volunteer work, work experience. *Other factors considered include:* Alumni/ae relation, first generation, geographical residence, interview, racial/ethnic status. ACT with writing component required. TOEFL required of all international applicants. High school diploma is required, and GED is accepted. *Academic units recommended:* 4 English, 4 mathematics, 4 science, 4 foreign language, 4 social studies, 4 history.

Financial Aid

Students should submit: FAFSA, CSS/Financial Aid PROFILE. Regular filing deadline is February 15. The Princeton Review suggests that all financial aid forms be submitted as soon as possible after January 1. *Need-based scholarships/ grants offered:* Federal Pell, SEOG, state scholarships/grants, school scholarship or grant aid from institutional funds. *Loan aid offered:* Direct Subsidized Stafford, Direct Unsubsidized Stafford, Federal Perkins, university loans from institutional funds. Federal Work-Study Program available. Off-campus job opportunities are good.

The Inside Word

The admissions process is rigorous. Tufts rejects a little less than seventy-five percent of its applicants. You'll need to demonstrate fairly exceptional academic accomplishments and submit a thorough and well-prepared application to get admitted. On the bright side, Tufts is still a little bit of a safety school for aspiring Ivy Leaguers. Since many applicants will also get into an Ivy League school and will likely pass on Tufts, it has spots for "mere mortals" at the end of the day.

THE SCHOOL SAYS "..."

From the Admissions Office

"Tufts University, on the boundary between Medford and Somerville, sits on a hill overlooking Boston, five miles northwest of the city. The campus is a tranquil New England setting within easy access by subway and bus to the cultural, social, and entertainment resources of Boston and Somerville. Since its founding in 1852 by members of the Universalist church, Tufts has grown from a small liberal arts college into a nonsectarian university of more than 10,000 students with undergraduate programs in arts and sciences and engineering. By 1900 the college had added a medical school, a dental school, and graduate studies. The university now also includes the Fletcher School of Law and Diplomacy, the Graduate School of Arts & Sciences, the Cummings School of Veterinary Medicine, the Friedman School of Nutrition Science and Policy, the Sackler School of Graduate Biomedical Sciences, and the Gordon Institute of Engineering Management.

"Applicants are required to submit scores (including the writing assessment) from either the SAT or ACT. If an applicant submits the SAT, SAT Subject Tests are also required (candidates for the School of Engineering are encouraged to submit math and either chemistry or physics)."

SELECTIVITY

Admissions Rating	97
# of applicants	15,433
% of applicants accepted	24
% of acceptees attending	35
# accepting a place on wait list	0

FRESHMAN PROFILE

Range SAT Critical Reading	670–740
Range SAT Math	680–760
Range SAT Writing	680–760
Range ACT Composite	30–33
Minimum paper TOEFL	600
Minimum computer TOEFL	100
% graduated top 10% of class	85
% graduated top 25% of class	99
% graduated top 50% of class	100

DEADLINES

Early decision	
Deadline	11/1
Notification	12/15
Regular	
Deadline	1/1
Nonfall registration?	no

FINANCIAL FACTS

Financial Aid Rating	94
Annual tuition	$40,664
Room and board	$11,268
% frosh rec. need-based scholarship or grant aid	39
% UG rec. need-based scholarship or grant aid	38
% frosh rec. non-need-based scholarship or grant aid	2
% UG rec. non-need-based scholarship or grant aid	2
% frosh rec. need-based self-help aid	38
% UG rec. need-based self-help aid	38
% frosh rec. any financial aid	
% UG rec. any financial aid	50
% UG borrow to pay for school	41
Average cumulative indebtedness	$27,443

TULANE UNIVERSITY

6823 St. Charles Avenue, New Orleans, LA 70118 • Admissions: 504-865-5731 • Fax: 504-862-8715

STUDENTS SAY ". . ."

Academics

"Medium-sized" Tulane University is "small enough for individual attention but big enough that you don't know everybody." Students call Tulane "the perfect mix between top-fifty private college and party school." Its business school is nationally renowned, and a wealth of international programs provide opportunities to study abroad in more than forty countries. "Academics are rigorous but rewarding." "By no means is it a school for slackers," cautions a marketing major. "It's a challenging school," agrees an art major, "but not challenging to the point of mental insanity." Professors here are "really smart and even pretty funny." They "care a ton" and they're "extremely personable and easy to talk to." "Due to our small class sizes, individual attention is incredibly realistic," adds a neuroscience major. "Most professors know your name and who you are. Even intro classes have, at most, like eighty kids, and even then, there are smaller labs." The general sentiment is that Tulane's "visible" and "very accessible" administration "works hard to treat each student as an individual rather than a number."

Life

"Club and intramural sports are very popular" on this "absolutely beautiful campus." "Greek life is here, but it's not a huge deal." The administration works hard to provide alcohol-free events. Students say these events are "actually very fun," but that drinking, or at least being around drinking, is "inevitable" at Tulane. "Going out is part of the social culture," relates a senior. "Students embrace it." They "take full advantage of the party scene in New Orleans, a city where bars don't close and where Mardi Gras is a huge party in the spring semester." At the same time, you won't last long if you don't hit the books. "Tulane is about balance." Success "necessitates a large amount of self-control and willpower." "While the school has a reputation as a party school, it's more of a school in a party city," explains a sophomore. "Most people think we spend all our time on Bourbon Street, but [it's]…usually only reserved for twenty-first birthdays and a quick visit when friends from other colleges visit." "Laid-back, fun-loving," "thrilling," and "practically lawless," New Orleans is "the most incredible city in the world," though, and a fabulous asset. "There is always an amazing concert or festival going on." "New Orleans is abundant in culture and [offers] a surprise at every turn," and it's "very much an outdoors city because of the weather." You can explore "great historical restaurants and antique stores" or just "listen to a jazz band while eating a beignet, looking out onto the Mississippi River."

Student Body

Students describe themselves as "independent and confident," "happy kids" who "are academics-focused and want to get a good education while having a good time." "Everyone is very smart but a kind of cool smart," claims a junior. "The typical Tulane student is what I call a closet nerd," adds a sophomore. "Basically, you see them having fun and it looks like they never do work. But the truth is that they study way more than you think." While "Tulane could use a little more racial diversity," the population is very "geographically diverse." "There are large Jewish and Catholic populations. Many students are from the Northeast, Florida, Texas, and California." "There are a lot of wealthy kids here but there are also a lot of hardworking kids on scholarship." "People do dress well," notes a senior. "Sorority girls with their leggings" and guys with "gelled hair" certainly aren't uncommon. "You can wear whatever you want," but you'll fit in best if your attire is "kind of preppy." "We don't have so many artsy kids or crazy, pink-haired nonconformists," says a sophomore.

TULANE UNIVERSITY

FINANCIAL AID: 504-865-5723 • E-MAIL: UNDERGRAD.ADMISSION@TULANE.EDU • WEBSITE: WWW.TULANE.EDU

THE PRINCETON REVIEW SAYS
Admissions
Very important factors considered include: Academic GPA, class rank, rigor of secondary school record, standardized test scores. *Important factors considered include:* Application essay, recommendation(s), character/personal qualities. *Other factors considered include:* Alumni/ae relation, extracurricular activities, first generation, interview, talent/ability, volunteer work, work experience. SAT or ACT required; ACT with writing component recommended. TOEFL required of all international applicants. High school diploma is required, and GED is accepted. *Academic units recommended:* 4 English, 4 mathematics, 4 science (4 science labs), 3 foreign language, 3 social studies, 3 academic elective.

Financial Aid
Students should submit: FAFSA, CSS/Financial Aid PROFILE. The Princeton Review suggests that all financial aid forms be submitted as soon as possible after January 1. *Need-based scholarships/grants offered:* Federal Pell, SEOG, state scholarships/grants, school scholarship or grant aid from institutional funds. *Loan aid offered:* Direct Subsidized Stafford, Direct Unsubsidized Stafford, Direct PLUS, Federal Perkins, state loans. Applicants will be notified of awards on a rolling basis beginning March 18. Federal Work-Study Program available. Off-campus job opportunities are good.

The Inside Word
Students come to Tulane from all over the country, and admission is very competitive. Serious candidates need an excellent record of academic achievement. On the plus side, Tulane is perpetually on the cusp of truly elite college and universities, and it has to fight to get its share of ultra-accomplished students. If you're one of them, your financial aid package will likely be extremely generous.

THE SCHOOL SAYS "..."
From the Admissions Office
"More than 6,700 full-time undergraduate students in five schools, Tulane University offers the personal attention and teaching excellence traditionally associated with small colleges together with the facilities and interdisciplinary resources found only at major research universities. Following Hurricane Katrina, the university underwent a spectacular renewal: renovating facilities and restructuring academic programs. The opportunities for students to be involved in the rebirth of New Orleans offer an experience unavailable at any other place, at any other time.

"Tulane is committed to undergraduate education. Senior faculty members teach most introductory and lower-level courses, and most classes have twenty-five or fewer students. The close student-teacher relationship pays off. Tulane graduates are among the most likely to be selected for several prestigious fellowships that support graduate study abroad. Founded in 1834 and reorganized as Tulane University in 1884, Tulane is one of the major private research universities in the South.

"The Tulane campus offers a traditional collegiate setting in an attractive residential neighborhood, which is now thriving after Hurricane Katrina."

SELECTIVITY
Admissions Rating	97
# of applicants	43,815
% of applicants accepted	26
% of acceptees attending	14
# accepting a place on wait list	2,485
% admitted from wait list	4

FRESHMAN PROFILE
Range SAT Critical Reading	610–700
Range SAT Math	620–700
Range SAT Writing	620–710
Range ACT Composite	29–32
Minimum paper TOEFL	550
Minimum computer TOEFL	213
Average HS GPA	3.55
% graduated top 10% of class	60
% graduated top 25% of class	85
% graduated top 50% of class	98

DEADLINES
Early action	
Deadline	11/15
Notification	12/15
Regular	
Deadline	1/15
Nonfall registration?	yes

FINANCIAL FACTS
Financial Aid Rating	91
Annual tuition	$38,300
Room and board	$9,722
Books and supplies	$1,200
% frosh rec. need-based scholarship or grant aid	38
% UG rec. need-based scholarship or grant aid	36
% frosh rec. non-need-based scholarship or grant aid	16
% UG rec. non-need-based scholarship or grant aid	11
% frosh rec. need-based self-help aid	21
% UG rec. need-based self-help aid	24
% UG borrow to pay for school	47
Average cumulative indebtedness	$27,510

TUSKEGEE UNIVERSITY

OLD ADMINISTRATION BUILDING, SUITE 101, TUSKEGEE, AL 36088 • ADMISSIONS: 334-727-8500 OR 800-622-65311 • FAX: 334-727-4402

CAMPUS LIFE

Quality of Life Rating	61
Fire Safety Rating	80
Green Rating	79
Type of school	private
Environment	rural

STUDENTS

Total undergrad enrollment	2,479
% male/female	44/56
% from out of state	72
% live on campus	55
# of fraternities	5
# of sororities	6
% African American	84
% international	1
# of countries represented	19

SURVEY SAYS . . .

Registration is a pain
Students are friendly
Students don't like Tuskegee, AL
Low cost of living
Everyone loves the Golden Tigers
Frats and sororities dominate
social scene
Musical organizations are popular
Student government is popular
Hard liquor is popular

ACADEMICS

Academic Rating	68
% students graduating within 4 years	18
% students graduating within 6 years	46
Calendar	semester
Student/faculty ratio	12:1
Profs interesting rating	65
Profs accessible rating	61
Most common reg class size	10–19 students

MOST POPULAR MAJORS

electrical and electronics engineering,
veterinary medicine

STUDENTS SAY " . . . "

Academics

Tuskegee University is a smaller, Historically Black College steeped in "pride, history," "heritage, and tradition." A required core curriculum in the liberal arts and sciences ensures a well-rounded education, but this place is primarily known for its excellence in the hard sciences and its "top-notch" engineering programs. Tuskegee produces more African American aerospace science engineers than any other school in the country. The chemical, electrical, and mechanical engineering programs are also notable. (Incidentally, some three-quarters of the African American veterinarians on the planet went here as well.) Students tell us that the academic atmosphere is "wonderful." "Class sizes are small," explains a senior; "Only slightly larger than the average high school class at times." Opportunities for undergraduate research are definitely available. Professors are "always accessible" and "mostly good." Many are nothing less than "enlightening." Faculty members "are also very good mentors." They "break their necks to help students outside the class." In the past, the administration hasn't received the same reviews. Though some students have noted that Tuskegee is run "as smoothly as possible," other felt that the administrators were "hard to find." However, a vice president for student affairs was hired to recognize these issues. Additionally, a new online registration process has been implemented.

Life

Tuskegee is located in eastern Alabama, in an affordable but "boring" town "in the middle of nowhere." There are "very few distractions." "The students have a great sense of school spirit and unity," though, and they "make their own fun" on this "laid-back" campus. You can participate in more than 100 clubs and organizations. There are "all sorts of student activities, such as fashion shows, basketball tournaments, concerts," and game nights. "A lot of school clubs have movie nights and show really great movies," too. Tuskegee is home to "a great football team" that's "overwhelmingly supported." Don't leave your seat at halftime either, or you'll miss the Marching Crimson Pipers—"the best band in the land." Percentage-wise, Greek life isn't huge, but fraternities and sororities are extremely visible. Frat parties are common. House parties are also abundant. Drugs and alcohol are "available, but if it's not your style then you don't have to take part." When students grow tired of the campus scene, the relatively bright lights of Montgomery aren't far, and Auburn "is right up the road, so you can always go mingle with the Auburn University students."

Student Body

"As an HBCU, Tuskegee's student population is composed almost completely of African Americans." The only obvious exception is the smattering of white students who are enrolled in the veterinary school. "The typical student at Tuskegee is outgoing" "and easy to get along with." Most are very diligent when it comes to academics. "There may be a few slackers," one student says. Some Tuskegee students tell us, "Everyone has their own style" here. According to them, "you have the fraternity/sorority types, athletes," and all manner of other subgroups. Others beg to differ. They say that there isn't a lot of individuality. "Students at this university tend to dress the same." Either way, though, pretty much everyone agrees, "It's not hard to fit in unless you're just totally lame."

FINANCIAL AID: 334-727-8210 OR 800-416-2831 • E-MAIL: ADMI@TUSKEGEE.EDU • WEBSITE: WWW.TUSKEGEE.EDU

THE PRINCETON REVIEW SAYS

Admissions

Very important factors considered include: Academic GPA, class rank, recommendation(s), rigor of secondary school record, standardized test scores, talent/ability. *Important factors considered include:* Alumni/ae relation, character/personal qualities. *Other factors considered include:* Application essay, extracurricular activities, first generation, geographical residence, interview, state residency, volunteer work, work experience. SAT or ACT required. TOEFL required of all international applicants. High school diploma is required, and GED is accepted. *Academic units required:* 4 English, 3 mathematics, 2 science, 3 social studies, 4 academic elective.

Financial Aid

Students should submit: FAFSA, institution's own financial aid form, CSS/Financial Aid PROFILE. The Princeton Review suggests that all financial aid forms be submitted as soon as possible after January 1. *Need-based scholarships/grants offered:* Federal Pell, SEOG, state scholarships/grants, private scholarships, school scholarship or grant aid from institutional funds, United Negro College Fund, Federal Nursing Scholarships. *Loan aid offered:* Direct Subsidized Stafford, Direct Unsubsidized Stafford, Direct PLUS, Federal Perkins, Federal Nursing Loans, state loans, university loans from institutional funds. Federal Work-Study Program available. Off-campus job opportunities are good.

The Inside Word

Tuskegee presents its students with a myriad of opportunities for discovery and research. Therefore, Tuskegee seeks applicants who have proven themselves successful in the classroom. Admissions counselors consider each application holistically individually. What they really like to see, though, is a GPA of at least 3.0 and a composite ACT score of 21 or better. Note also that requirements for the nursing and engineering programs are more stringent. For example, you'll probably need four years of high school math if you want to major in engineering here. Prospective students interested in either field should investigate the specific criteria.

THE SCHOOL SAYS "..."

From the Admissions Office

"Tuskegee University, located in central Alabama, was founded in 1881 under the dynamic and creative leadership of Booker T. Washington. As a state-related, independent institution, Tuskegee offers undergraduate and graduate programs in five major areas: the College of Agriculture, Environmental, and Natural Sciences; the College of Engineering, Architecture, and Physical Sciences; the College of Business and Information Sciences; the College of Liberal Arts and Education; and the College of Veterinary Medicine, Nursing, and Allied Health. Substantial research and service programs make Tuskegee University an effective comprehensive institution, geared toward preparing tomorrow's leaders today.

"First-year applicants must take the SAT or ACT; the SAT is preferred. International applicants must complete the TOEFL. Nursing applicants must complete the National League of Nursing exam."

SELECTIVITY

Admissions Rating	81
# of applicants	2,471
% of applicants accepted	64
% of acceptees attending	44
# accepting a place on wait list	0

FRESHMAN PROFILE

Range SAT Critical Reading	400–500
Range SAT Math	398–490
Range ACT Composite	17–22
Minimum paper TOEFL	500
Minimum computer TOEFL	62
Average HS GPA	3.07
% graduated top 10% of class	20
% graduated top 25% of class	59
% graduated top 50% of class	100

DEADLINES

Regular	
Priority	3/31
Deadline	7/15
Notification	3/1
Nonfall registration?	yes

FINANCIAL FACTS

Financial Aid Rating	75
Annual tuition	$16,100
Room and board	$7,570
Required fees	$650
Books and supplies	$1,109
% frosh rec. need-based scholarship or grant aid	72
% UG rec. need-based scholarship or grant aid	54
% frosh rec. non-need-based scholarship or grant aid	86
% UG rec. non-need-based scholarship or grant aid	38
% frosh rec. need-based self-help aid	41
% UG rec. need-based self-help aid	43
% frosh rec. any financial aid	96
% UG rec. any financial aid	92
% UG borrow to pay for school	91
Average cumulative indebtedness	$23,000

UNION COLLEGE (NY)

GRANT HALL, SCHENECTADY, NY 12308 • ADMISSIONS: 518-388-6112 • FAX: 518-388-6986

STUDENTS SAY "..."

Academics

At Union College, challenging academic programs, friendly faculty, and diverse co-curricular experiences are all rolled up into one pretty little campus in upstate New York. Union "is small in size, yet prestigious in nearly every major it offers," making it a good choice for students interested in anything from the arts to engineering—or both! Here, "Students are encouraged to follow their passions and pursue all areas of interest." A current student chimes in, "As an engineering major, I am able to take courses that I would not normally take at a technical school, making the 'gen eds' [general education requirements] and electives enjoyable." In addition to diverse courses, "Union has fantastic research opportunities for undergraduate students (especially in the sciences)," and more than half the campus pursues studies or volunteer work overseas. Internships are also popular, and "Union has an awesome career center that is always reaching out to students to help them with life after college." Across disciplines, "Professors are wonderful, extremely qualified, compassionate, and interested in their students." Teaching is taken seriously, and "All of the professors do everything possible to engage their students and get discussions going." Relationships between students and faculty often extend beyond the classroom, and "Professors can often be seen sitting with students at lunch, literally bringing the classroom discussion into the lunchroom." You must be prepared to work at Union, as academic standards are high. Fortunately, most students feel "the workload is very manageable as long as you don't fall behind," not to mention "the rewards that come of those challenges make all the effort completely worthwhile." As a small private school, all of this doesn't come cheap, but "Union College is very generous with its financial aid and scholarship money" for qualified students.

Life

There are just 2,000 undergraduates at Union College, yet "There are always a million things to do" on the Union campus. During the week, "The homework load is pretty heavy," but come the weekend, Union students "like to go to a few off-campus bars on Wednesday nights and Thursday nights," while "Friday and Saturday are dominated by Greek life." For an alternative to parties, "Student activities and Minerva houses provide many nonalcohol[ic] events," including concerts and speakers. Union students can also be found going to "campus movie [screenings], going to [hear] a speaker, [attending] a hockey game, running around campus…going downtown for a bite to eat." School spirit is healthy, and "In the winter, our [Division I] hockey team's home games are the place to be." Hometown Schenectady draws few praises, and students would like to see the school promote "more involvement in the local community." For a break from campus life, "Some of the clubs on campus also organize ski trips or trips out of town such as to Montreal and New York City."

Student Body

On Union's small campus, "Students are always moving, always involved, always engaged," and most participate in "at least three organizations or clubs" on campus. Bright and motivated, students "are able to easily manage personal and professional time," and the typical student manages to "get great grades while volunteering and balancing a busy schedule." Located in upstate New York, this school draws a lot of students from the Northeast, and "the typical student is Caucasian, middle to upper-class, [and] from a private school or highly regarded public school." However, the student population is evolving, and "The college is clearly becoming more diverse, with more international and underrepresented student populations increasing by the year." Socially, "everyone seems to find their niche." In addition to the visible preppy contingent, "There is also a pretty strong indie scene that tends to be more involved in environmental awareness, community service, and the arts." In addition, "There are a lot of athletes."

FINANCIAL AID: 518-388-6123 • E-MAIL: ADMISSIONS@UNION.EDU • WEBSITE: WWW.UNION.EDU

THE PRINCETON REVIEW SAYS

Admissions

Very important factors considered include: Academic GPA, class rank, rigor of secondary school record. *Important factors considered include:* Recommendation(s), standardized test scores, character/personal qualities, extracurricular activities, talent/ability. *Other factors considered include:* Application essay, alumni/ae relation, first generation, geographical residence, interview, level of applicant's interest, racial/ethnic status, state residency, volunteer work, work experience. ACT with or without writing component accepted. TOEFL required of all international applicants. *Academic units required:* 4 English, 3 mathematics, 2 science (2 science labs), 2 foreign language, 1 social studies, 1 history. *Academic units recommended:* 4 English, 4 mathematics, 4 science (4 science labs), 4 foreign language, 2 social studies, 2 history.

Financial Aid

Students should submit: FAFSA, CSS/Financial Aid PROFILE. Regular filing deadline is February 1. The Princeton Review suggests that all financial aid forms be submitted as soon as possible after January 1. *Need-based scholarships/grants offered:* Federal Pell, SEOG, state scholarships/grants, private scholarships, school scholarship or grant aid from institutional funds. *Loan aid offered:* Direct Subsidized Stafford, Direct Unsubsidized Stafford, Direct PLUS, Federal Perkins, state loans, university loans from institutional funds. Federal Work-Study Program available. Off-campus job opportunities are good.

The Inside Word

Union College is an SAT-optional college. Students may simply indicate on their application if they would like the admissions committee to consider their test scores or not. However, applicants to the Leadership in Medicine Program (an eight-year MD/MBA program with Albany Medical College) and to the Law and Public Policy program (a combined BA and JD) must submit test scores for consideration. For students who know that Union is their first choice, the school offers two early decision deadlines.

THE SCHOOL SAYS ". . ."

From the Admissions Office

"The Union academic program is characterized by breadth and flexibility across a range of disciplines and interdisciplinary programs in the liberal arts and engineering. With nearly 1,000 courses to choose from, Union students may major in a single field, combine work in two or more departments or create their own organizing-theme major. Opportunities for undergraduate research are robust and give students a chance to work closely with professors year-round, take part in professional-level conferences and use sophisticated scientific equipment. More than half of Union's students take advantage of the college's extensive international study program, with new opportunities created regularly. A rich array of service learning programs and strong athletic, cultural, and social activities also enhance the overall Union experience. Union's seven student-run Minerva Houses are lively hubs for intellectual and social activities. They bring together students, faculty and staff for hundreds of events, from dinners with invited speakers, lectures, and live bands, to trips to local attractions.

"The Union community welcomes talented and diverse students, and we work closely with each one to help identify and cultivate their passions. Admission to the college is based on excellent academic credentials as reflected in the high school transcript, quality of courses selected, teacher and counselor recommendations, personal essays, and writing samples. Personal interviews are strongly recommended. All candidates who apply to Union receive a thorough and thoughtful review of their application. Submission of SAT and ACT scores is optional except for the law and medicine programs."

SELECTIVITY

Admissions Rating	95
# of applicants	4,946
% of applicants accepted	42
% of acceptees attending	26
# accepting a place on wait list	217
% admitted from wait list	43
# of early decision applicants	350
% accepted early decision	74

FRESHMAN PROFILE

Range SAT Critical Reading	580–670
Range SAT Math	610–700
Range SAT Writing	580–680
Range ACT Composite	27–30
Minimum paper TOEFL	600
Minimum computer TOEFL	250
Minimum web-based TOEFL	90
Average HS GPA	3.52
% graduated top 10% of class	62
% graduated top 25% of class	88
% graduated top 50% of class	98

DEADLINES

Early decision	
Deadline	11/15
Notification	12/15
Regular	
Deadline	1/15
Nonfall registration?	yes

APPLICANTS ALSO LOOK AT
AND OFTEN PREFER
Colgate University, Cornell University, Tufts University
AND SOMETIMES PREFER
Hamilton College, Lehigh University, Skidmore College
AND RARELY PREFER
Hobart and William Smith Colleges, Syracuse University, University of Rochester

FINANCIAL FACTS

Financial Aid Rating	90
Annual comprehensive tuition	$54,273
Books and supplies	$532
% frosh rec. need-based scholarship or grant aid	55
% UG rec. need-based scholarship or grant aid	49
% UG rec. non-need-based scholarship or grant aid	2
% frosh rec. need-based self-help aid	54
% UG rec. need-based self-help aid	50
% frosh rec. any financial aid	72
% UG rec. any financial aid	71
% UG borrow to pay for school	53
Average cumulative indebtedness	$25,621

UNITED STATES AIR FORCE ACADEMY

2304 CADET DRIVE, SUITE 2500, USAF ACADEMY, CO 80840-5025 • ADMISSIONS: 719-333-2520 • FAX: 719-333-3012

STUDENTS SAY ". . ."

Academics

The United States Air Force Academy is "a leadership laboratory" and "an incredibly prestigious institution" that provides "rigorous academic and military training" for future Air Force officers. Students here have "the opportunity to travel the world, making a difference in lives and in history." There's military free-fall parachute training, combat survival, skydiving, internships at national labs, and, of course, the best flying programs in the solar system. Everyone leaves here with a really cool skill set. There's "free tuition," too (and a nominal monthly stipend). "Very tough" professors bring "a lot of real-world experience" and "rival those of any of the top schools in the country." "Class sizes are very small," and extra help is copious. "The teachers are always there," promises a physics major. "The professors and officers who teach classes go the extra mile to make themselves available." "If you can get in, the tools are here to help you stay." You'll "owe at least five years of service" as an active-duty officer upon graduation, though, and nothing about this place is easy. The "very broad" core curriculum is "hard and tedious" and heavy on science and engineering. "Courses and course loads are very demanding." "You have to be on top of your game 24/7," cautions a first-year cadet. "Slacking is not tolerated, and constant professionalism is the minimum standard."

Life

"The Air Force Academy will break you down mentally and physically and then build you into something greater than you ever could have imagined." Like the other military academies, though, Air Force is "better to be from than to go to." "The campus has a pretty cold, sterile feel to it." "The dining facility and food quality are not the greatest." The "stressful, time-crunched environment" "challenges each cadet academically, militarily, and athletically." In addition to tons of homework, "There is military training almost every day." Rules are "strict." There are "room inspections." There are "random urine tests." "It's really easy to get in trouble." The "grueling" first year is especially difficult. You can leave the confines of the campus only rarely. "Your life is miserable, and the upperclassmen treat you with contempt." "Every action and word is under scrutiny." Life becomes a little easier, and free time becomes somewhat more abundant, as you rise through the ranks. "Weekends offer a good time to relax or get away, provided the weekend does not include military training." "Snowboarding and skiing are very popular in the winter." Drinking simply doesn't happen on campus, but "The cadets that are of age go out drinking a lot" when they can. Some students just catch up on sleep during their free time. "USAFA has made me appreciate and enjoy doing nothing," one cadet says.

Student Body

"We are all a bunch of college kids in a very different environment," explains one cadet. "This school forces you to grow up and obtain a more mature outlook on life, yet, at the same time, the kids are normal kids who know when and how to have fun." The population at Air Force is overwhelmingly male. It's a "tight-knit community," and people tend to be "similar in beliefs and backgrounds." The military aspect limits how "atypical" anyone can really be. "You probably will not do well here" if you don't fit the mold. Cadets describe themselves as "hardworking and motivated," "fairly conservative," and "very patriotic." "The sense of pride and duty that comes from serving your country is something that you cannot explain to a civilian," one student says. They're "inventive," "studious," "physically fit," and "smart as a whip." "The typical cadet is tired of being here and wants to go home on break" as well.

UNITED STATES AIR FORCE ACADEMY

E-MAIL: RR_WEBMAIL@USAFA.AF.MIL • WEBSITE: WWW.USAFA.AF.MIL

THE PRINCETON REVIEW SAYS

Admissions

Very important factors considered include: Academic GPA, application essay, class rank, recommendation(s), rigor of secondary school record, standardized test scores, character/personal qualities, interview. *Important factors considered include:* Extracurricular activities, talent/ability, volunteer work, work experience. *Other factors considered include:* Alumni/ae relation, first generation, geographical residence, level of applicant's interest, racial/ethnic status, state residency. SAT or ACT required; ACT with writing component recommended. High school diploma is required, and GED is accepted. *Academic units recommended:* 4 English, 4 mathematics, 4 science (4 science labs), 2 foreign language, 3 social studies, 3 history, 1 computer science.

Financial Aid

The Princeton Review suggests that all financial aid forms be submitted as soon as possible after January 1.

The Inside Word

The Air Force Academy promises a demanding four years, and the faint-hearted need not apply. Due to the arduous nature of the school, it's no wonder that applicants face stringent requirements right at the outset. Aside from an excellent academic record, successful candidates need to be physically fit. They also must win a nomination from their congressperson. Honor is a valued quality at the academy, and admissions officers will accept only those with the strength of character and determination necessary to succeed at one of the country's most elite institutions.

THE SCHOOL SAYS "..."

From the Admissions Office

"The Air Force Academy offers one of the most prestigious and respected undergraduate programs available. Each cadet completes a balanced sequence of core curriculum, which includes courses in basic sciences, engineering, humanities and social sciences. Air Force Academy graduates earn a Bachelor of Science degree from one of thirty-two majors and two minors. The academy education is tailored to develop future Air Force officers with innovative, analytical and resourceful minds. Upon graduation from the academy, one receives a commission as a second lieutenant in the United States Air Force.

"The academy's extensive athletic program includes intercollegiate or intramural sports, physical education courses, and physical fitness tests. These programs are tailored to help prepare you for Air Force leadership by building confidence, emotional control, physical courage, and the ability to perform under pressure. The twenty-seven men's and ten women's intercollegiate teams compete in the NCAA Division I and are members of the Mountain West Conference.

"The academy experience requires cadets to become active participants in leadership roles and opportunities that give a sense of honor and duty. The academy is a leadership laboratory, and our mission is to educate, train and inspire men and women to become officers of character motivated to lead the United States Air Force in service to our nation. If you choose to accept the challenges, you will be rewarded with unique experiences and opportunities incomparable to any other college experience."

SELECTIVITY

Admissions Rating	98
# of applicants	11,627
% of applicants accepted	13
% of acceptees attending	81

FRESHMAN PROFILE

Range SAT Critical Reading	590–680
Range SAT Math	620–700
Range SAT Writing	570–650
Range ACT Composite	29–32
Average HS GPA	3.86
% graduated top 10% of class	51
% graduated top 25% of class	80
% graduated top 50% of class	98

DEADLINES

Regular	
Deadline	1/31
Notification	10/15
Nonfall registration?	no

APPLICANTS ALSO LOOK AT AND SOMETIMES PREFER

United States Military Academy,
United States Naval Academy

FINANCIAL FACTS

Financial Aid Rating	60*
Annual in-state tuition	$0
Annual out-of-state tuition	$0
Room and board	$0
Required fees	$0
Books and supplies	$0

UNITED STATES COAST GUARD ACADEMY

31 MOHEGAN AVENUE, NEW LONDON, CT 06320-8103 • ADMISSIONS: 800-883-8724 • FAX: 860-701-6700

STUDENTS SAY ". . ."

Academics
Students at the United States Coast Guard Academy applaud their school for providing "an outstanding education" while affording undergrads the "opportunity to [become] America's leaders of tomorrow." Many appreciate the "regimented environment," which, according to one management major, "gives me a standard to live up to and hold myself to, even when I am away from here." Cadets are "pushed to [the] limits" "academically, emotionally, and physically," and they wouldn't have it any other way. Importantly, "The Academy fosters camaraderie amongst the Corps of Cadets that can't be found anywhere else. With a student body of less than 1,000, the Coast Guard Academy is truly unique in its ability to provide an environment where classmates become shipmates, friends, and eventually family." Though there are a number of excellent programs, cadets call the most attention to the strong engineering department. The academics are "challenging but rewarding." Professors are "extremely dedicated and expect the same from students." A third-year cadet elaborates about how professors are "willing to give up their time and stay after hours to help students succeed." As one impressed freshman proudly states, "You become a better person for going there."

Life
Day-to-day life at the Coast Guard Academy is "orderly and predictable." During the week, it's difficult for people to do anything "outside of their military, athletic, and academic obligations." As one honest marine and environmental science major reveals, "Every moment of every day is planned out." A government major chimes in that even "the times in which we are allowed to sleep are regulated (can't sleep between 6:20 A.M. and 4:00 P.M. without special permission)." Of course, life at the Academy isn't 100 percent work and stress. Many people "pass [the] time and unwind by playing computer/video games, surfing the Internet, working out, going to movies on weekends, etc." A senior shares, "Golf and outdoor activities are popular in the spring, and trips to Boston or NYC are often planned." While "students aren't allowed off campus during the week," "Most try and get away for the weekend." Another senior elaborates, "Underage students tend to go to the movies or the local mall. Of-age students usually spend their time off drinking at the BYO pizza place down the street or at the bars downtown." Additionally, "You can go out and have some fun at beaches or other local attractions in the summer, and snowboarding/skiing is a favorite in the winter." Though life can be "difficult" as one sage senior divulges, "The idea that gets most people through is the fact that they are serving their country and are part of something bigger than themselves."

Student Body
Coast Guard cadets admit, "Despite the academy's best efforts," the campus can appear fairly homogenous. Indeed, "The typical student is still an upper-middle-class, white, Christian from a coastal state, most likely the Northeast." Luckily, a civil engineering major assures us, "Those students of different backgrounds easily fit in with everyone else." Not surprisingly, the academy seems to attract "highly motivated [people] with a strong desire to serve in the Coast Guard." Certainly, another hallmark of Coast Guard cadets is that they're "smart, hardworking, and eager to work with each other." A naval architecture and marine engineering major adds, "Type-A personalities are most common among the Corps." A first-year cadet is quick to say that "everyone is very welcoming." He goes on to attribute this to the "lasting bonds and friendship" we all form "because of going through boot camp together." And this sophomore cheekily sums up his peers, "A typical student here is just like a typical student anywhere else but works harder, follows stricter rules, is in better shape, and is owned by the federal government."

UNITED STATES COAST GUARD ACADEMY

E-MAIL: ADMISSIONS@USCGA.EDU • WEBSITE: WWW.USCGA.EDU

THE PRINCETON REVIEW SAYS

Admissions

Very important factors considered include: Academic GPA, class rank, rigor of secondary school record, standardized test scores, character/personal qualities, extracurricular activities. *Important factors considered include:* Application essay, recommendation(s), talent/ability. *Other factors considered include:* Alumni/ae relation, first generation, geographical residence, interview, level of applicant's interest, racial/ethnic status, religious affiliation/commitment, volunteer work, work experience. SAT or ACT required; ACT with writing component required. TOEFL required of all international applicants. High school diploma is required, and GED is accepted. *Academic units required:* 4 English, 4 mathematics, 3 science (3 science labs).

Financial Aid

There's no financial aid necessary to attend. Tuition at the academy is free. As of November 2010, all entrance fees have been waved. In addition to free tuition, room, and board, all cadets receive an annual government stipend of totaling $11,150 per year, which covers the cost of books, uniforms, equipment, and other materials incidental to training. Upon graduation, the Coast Guard requires a five-year commitment to serve as a commissioned Coast Guard Officer.

The Inside Word

Gaining acceptance into the Coast Guard Academy is a highly competitive process. The admissions committee is looking not only for outstanding academic achievement but also for applicants who demonstrate leadership ability and strong moral character. In addition, unlike other colleges, you'll also need a physical fitness examination and evaluation.

THE SCHOOL SAYS ". . ."

From the Admissions Office

"Founded in 1876, the United States Coast Guard Academy enjoys a proud tradition of graduating leaders of character. The academy experience melds academic rigor, leadership development, and athletic participation to prepare you to graduate as a commissioned officer. Character development of cadets is founded on the core values of honor, respect, and devotion to duty. You build friendships that last a lifetime, study with inspiring professors in small classes, and train during the summer aboard America's tall ship Eagle, as well as the service's ships and aircraft. Top performers spend their senior summer traveling on exciting internships around the nation and overseas. Graduates serve for five years and have unmatched opportunities to attend flight school and graduate school, all funded by the Coast Guard.

"Appointments to the academy are based on a selective admissions process; Congressional nominations are not required. Your leadership potential and desire to serve your country are what counts. Our student body reflects the best America has to offer—with all its potential and diversity!

"Applicants are required to take the SAT (or the ACT with the writing section).

"The Coast Guard Academy boasts a prolific honor's program that has produces three consecutive Truman Scholars and several Fulbright Scholars over the last three years. The academy is ranked nationally among the top ten for women in STEM fields. The academy embraces a diversity of race and gender. Women comprise approximately thirty percent of the student body and approximately twenty percent of the student body are underrepresented minorities."

SELECTIVITY

Admissions Rating	96
# of applicants	2,223
% of applicants accepted	17
% of acceptees attending	72

FRESHMAN PROFILE

Range SAT Critical Reading	550–670
Range SAT Math	600–690
Range SAT Writing	530–650
Range ACT Composite	25–30
Minimum paper TOEFL	560
Minimum computer TOEFL	220
Average HS GPA	3.70
% graduated top 10% of class	51
% graduated top 25% of class	87
% graduated top 50% of class	99

DEADLINES

Early action	
Deadline	11/1
Notification	1/15
Regular	
Priority	11/1
Deadline	2/1
Notification	12/15
Nonfall registration?	no

FINANCIAL FACTS

Financial Aid Rating	60*
Annual in-state tuition	$0
Annual out-of-state tuition	$0
Room and board	$0
Required fees	$0
Books and supplies	$0

UNITED STATES MERCHANT MARINE ACADEMY

OFFICE OF ADMISSIONS, KINGS POINT, NY 11024-1699 • ADMISSIONS: 516-773-5391 • FAX: 516-773-5390

CAMPUS LIFE

Quality of Life Rating	61
Fire Safety Rating	60*
Green Rating	60*
Type of school	public
Environment	village

STUDENTS

Total undergrad enrollment	985
% male/female	88/12
% from out of state	86
% from public high school	71
% live on campus	100
% African American	3
% Asian	5
% Caucasian	84
% Hispanic	5
% Native American	1
% international	3
# of countries represented	5

SURVEY SAYS . . .

Class discussions are rare
Career services are great
Lousy food on campus
Low cost of living
Frats and sororities are unpopular
or nonexistent
Political activism is unpopular
or nonexistent
Very little drug use

ACADEMICS

Academic Rating	62
Calendar	trimester
Student/faculty ratio	11:1
Profs interesting rating	61
Profs accessible rating	69
Most common reg class size	10–19 students
Most common lab size	10–19 students

MOST POPULAR MAJORS
engineering, naval architecture and marine engineering, transportation and materials moving

STUDENTS SAY " . . ."

Academics
"The Merchant Marine Academy produces officers, leaders, and good citizens of honor and integrity to serve the economic and defense interests of the United States through the maritime industry and armed forces." This "prestigious academy, paid for by the federal government," has free tuition. With "strong alumni support," and "100 percent job placement," the USMMA offers "opportunities upon graduation [that] are endless." After gradation, students are automatically qualified to enter any branch of the armed forces as an officer, including Army, Navy, Air Force, Marines, Coast Guard, or NOAA. Students who choose to pursue civilian jobs after graduation are quick to note that the school provides the "best marine engineering education available," chock full of skills that are "highly sought after in the engineering industry." Known for having "the hardest academics out of all the military academies," "The school is regimented and very disciplined. The class load is very rigorous." Beyond the regular course load, "Spending a year studying at sea on merchant vessels gives the students a hands-on perspective that not many other engineering schools offer." Professors are "undoubtedly more than qualified in their fields of study (ranging from former NASA scientists to highly decorated and accomplished officers in the military). However, sometimes they experience difficulty in attempting to convey the subject matter." As one student notes, the United States Merchant Marine Academy "is academically challenging, which will push you far beyond what you thought you could do; it will also train you to assume a leadership role in any company."

Life
Life at the Merchant Marine Academy fosters "an environment that pushes you to the limit," and students say that it's "tough as hell, but worth every minute." Many midshipmen view "sea year" as the apex of their college experience because it is often considered "a gigantic study abroad term" during which students spend their time "traveling the world on merchant ships." Because of the school's focus on "teaching time-management, integrity, leadership, and discipline," students are "getting the best education in the field, while making the best friends of your life, all under stressful [and] sometimes painstaking conditions." For fun, students "will work out or play basketball or football." There are also "several clubs and activities to be involved in" and "several intramural tournaments held throughout the year." Because "New York City is sixteen miles east of school…students take frequent trips on the weekends and enjoy the city life." With their sights set on the future, many say, the Merchant Marine Academy is "a tough place to be at but the best place to be from."

Student Body
Students are quick to form a "mutual bond with one another" and "get along very well." "Outgoing and focused," "Everyone is strong-willed and generally respectful." The vast majority of students describe themselves as "white, male, intelligent, athletic, conservative, and competitive." Students are bonded by a fraternal patriotism and a strong work ethic. Regiments inspire an "esprit d'corps." "We are tight. We know everybody, and we are dedicated to everyone's success." Freshman year "is tough, both regimentally and academically." "As a plebe, a freshmen, you are an outcast from the rest of the regiment in order to build unity among their class. [Plebes] must complete a long series of steps before they become recognized." "Most time is spent doing academics, sports, and regiment. The few remaining hours a week are spent socializing with friends outside of school at bars."

FINANCIAL AID: 516-773-5295 • E-MAIL: ADMISSIONS@USMMA.EDU • WEBSITE: WWW.USMMA.EDU

THE PRINCETON REVIEW SAYS

Admissions

Very important factors considered include: Rigor of secondary school record, standardized test scores, character/personal qualities. *Important factors considered include:* Academic GPA, application essay, class rank, recommendation(s), extracurricular activities, level of applicant's interest, talent/ability. *Other factors considered include:* Geographical residence, interview, racial/ethnic status, state residency, volunteer work, work experience. SAT or ACT required; ACT with or without writing component accepted. TOEFL required of all international applicants. High school diploma is required, and GED is accepted. *Academic units required:* 4 English, 3 mathematics, 3 science (1 science lab), 8 academic elective. *Academic units recommended:* 4 English, 4 mathematics, 4 science (2 science labs), 2 foreign language, 4 social studies.

Financial Aid

Students should submit: FAFSA, institution's own financial aid form. Regular filing deadline is May 1. The Princeton Review suggests that all financial aid forms be submitted as soon as possible after January 1. *Need-based scholarships/grants offered:* Federal Pell, private scholarships. *Loan aid offered:* Direct Subsidized Stafford, Direct Unsubsidized Stafford, Direct PLUS. Applicants will be notified of awards on a rolling basis beginning January 31. Federal Work-Study Program not available. Off-campus job opportunities are poor.

The Inside Word

Prospective midshipmen face demanding admission requirements. The USMMA assesses scholastic achievement, strength of character, and stamina (applicants must meet specific physical standards). Candidates must also be nominated by a proper nominating authority, typically a state representative or senator.

THE SCHOOL SAYS "..."

From the Admissions Office

"What makes the U.S. Merchant Marine Academy different from the other federal service academies? The difference can be summarized in two phrases that appear in our publications. The first: 'The World Is Your Campus.' You will spend a year at sea—a third of your sophomore year and two-thirds of your junior year—teamed with a classmate aboard a U.S. merchant ship. You will visit an average of eighteen foreign nations while you work and learn in a mariner's true environment. You will graduate with seafaring experience and as a citizen of the world. The second phrase is 'Options and Opportunities.' Unlike students at the other federal academies, who are required to enter the service connected to their academy, you have the option of working in the seagoing merchant marine and transportation industry or applying for active duty in the Navy, Coast Guard, Marine Corps, Air Force, or Army. Nearly twenty-five percent of our most recent graduating class entered various branches of the armed forces with an officer rank. As a graduate of the U.S. Merchant Marine Academy, you will receive a Bachelor of Science degree, a government-issued merchant marine officer's license, and a Naval Reserve commission (unless you have been accepted for active military duty). No other service academy offers so attractive a package.

"Applicants must take the SAT or the ACT with the writing component. For homeschooled students, we recommend they also submit scores from SAT Subject Tests in chemistry and/or physics."

SELECTIVITY

Admissions Rating	90
# of applicants	1,734
% of applicants accepted	18
% of acceptees attending	100

FRESHMAN PROFILE

Range SAT Critical Reading	540–640
Range SAT Math	600–660
Range ACT Composite	25–29
Minimum paper TOEFL	533
Minimum computer TOEFL	200
Minimum web-based TOEFL	73
Average HS GPA	3.60
% graduated top 10% of class	18
% graduated top 25% of class	23
% graduated top 50% of class	85

DEADLINES

Regular	
Deadline	3/1
Notification	11/1
Nonfall registration?	no

APPLICANTS ALSO LOOK AT
AND OFTEN PREFER
United States Naval Academy

AND SOMETIMES PREFER
United States Air Force Academy, United States Coast Guard Academy, United States Military Academy

AND RARELY PREFER
State University of New York—Maritime College

FINANCIAL FACTS

Financial Aid Rating	90
Annual in-state tuition	$0
Annual out-of-state tuition	$0
Room and board	$0
Required fees	$7,020
Books and supplies	$0

UNITED STATES MILITARY ACADEMY

600 THAYER ROAD, WEST POINT, NY 10996-1797 • ADMISSIONS: 845-938-4041 • FAX: 845-938-3021

STUDENTS SAY " . . ."

Academics

West Point "is all about transforming a regular citizen into an intellectual soldier with unparalleled skills of leadership, fit to lead America's sons and daughters," a grueling process to be sure. The West Point experience entails "an intensive academic, physical, and military curriculum" in which students undergo "four years of breaking down to build up, unlearning to learn again, and narrowing purpose to open vast opportunities" in a highly regimented program in which "you need to be willing to put up with things you won't deal with anywhere else." Academics start with "a very large core curriculum" that some grouse about but most accept as "helping us become problem solvers…and critical thinkers" with "a broad base of knowledge to understand the world around us." The school employs the Thayer Method of instruction, "which means students prepare for class ahead of time and then discuss the material in class as opposed to the other way around." Cadets warn that it's "very difficult in some of the courses, particularly math and sciences," and also that there is often "not sufficient time to prepare for class" due to their busy academic and training schedules. Fortunately, professors are there to help cadets survive the challenging experience. They "are absolutely excellent" instructors who "put an incredible amount of effort and work into making sure the students succeed." "One-on-one tutoring from instructors is available on a daily basis," one grateful cadet reports.

Life

Asked to describe life at West Point, one cadet quoted Winston Churchill: "If you're going through hell, keep on going!" Campus life "is very structured. Everything is planned out and executed," with most time consumed by "a heavy course load, military duties and physical fitness," Cadets "are able to have fun, but not in the ways typical college students have fun. [Even] weekends can be busy with mandatory sporting events or other obligations." The demands of the West Point experience can doubtless seem overwhelming at times, but "there are bright moments…For fun, we have lots of athletic activities available and a surprisingly wide range of student clubs (ranging from a Korean American relations seminar to the fly-fishing club) compared to the size of the student body." Alcohol and drugs are strictly forbidden on campus, and "penalties for breaking [the rules] are harsh." Once students are of age, they can drink "at designated locations on campus, which many take advantage of on Thursdays, as they often leave on Fridays." New York City is the most frequently mentioned getaway for those procuring precious leaves. In sum, life can be monotonous at West Point, "but it's worth it" because "more is accomplished at this school in one day than anywhere else. No other school has such great commitment to [developing] a well-rounded student."

Student Body

"Physically fit," "type-A" "workaholics" fill the ranks at West Point, where "due to Army regulations, many people look the same in regards to facial hair and hair cuts. The uniform does not help either." There are a lot of "high school hero," "Captain America–type people" here. Not too many students stray from that prototype. One student warns, "Most people that do not eventually mold into the typical student do not make it through all four years. Cooperate and graduate." Although all students are "very competitive," there is a "great sense of duty to help out your classmates. Most students are very intelligent, polite, and professional." Other descriptors that pop up frequently include "patriotic," "religious," and "politically conservative." "While statistically the student body is probably mostly white and male," one student observes, "there is a good representation of all ethnic groups and both genders, and there are no discrimination issues that I have observed."

FINANCIAL AID: 845-938-4041 • E-MAIL: ADMISSIONS@USMA.EDU • WEBSITE: WWW.WESTPOINT.EDU

THE PRINCETON REVIEW SAYS

Admissions

Very important factors considered include: Academic GPA, application essay, class rank, recommendation(s), rigor of secondary school record, standardized test scores, character/personal qualities, extracurricular activities, nomination district, talent/ability. *Important factors considered include:* Geographical residence, interview, level of applicant's interest, volunteer work. *Other factors considered include:* Alumni/ae relation, state residency, work experience. SAT or ACT required. High school diploma is required, and GED is accepted. *Academic units recommended:* 4 English, 4 mathematics, 4 science (2 science labs), 2 foreign language, 3 social studies, 1 history, 3 academic elective.

Financial Aid

The Princeton Review suggests that all financial aid forms be submitted as soon as possible after January 1.

The Inside Word

The fact that you must be nominated by your Congressional representative in order to apply to West Point tells you all you need to know about the school's selectivity. Contact your district's Congressional representative to learn the deadline for nomination requests; typically these are made in the spring of your junior year. Successful candidates must demonstrate excellence in academics, physical conditioning, extracurricular involvement, and leadership. They must also be willing to commit to five years of active duty and three years of reserve duty upon graduation. The rigorous requirements and demanding commitments of a West Point education hardly dissuade applicants. Almost 15,000 applied for the 1,250 available slots.

THE SCHOOL SAYS "..."

From the Admissions Office

"West Point is searching for applicants who possess the leadership skills, cultural sensibilities, and the moral fiber to handle the volatile, uncertain, complex, and ambiguous contemporary operating environment of today's world as a future U.S. Army Officer. As a crucible for leadership, we are looking for critical thinkers that have who have the judgment and experience to become a leader of character upon graduation.

"To assess your ability and preparation, admissions looks at more than your GPA or standardized test scores. The applications of almost 15,000 students are evaluated based on academic, physical, and leadership potential to find approximately 1,250 candidates who are ready to be offered the challenge of admission into the Corps of Cadets. With an amazingly high offer-acceptance rate, only the most dedicated, enthusiastic applicants make it to the finish line for the report date each June.

"If you accept the challenge, you will be immersed in a military training program that ranges from marksmanship to orienteering, an academic program that offers forty-five majors ranging from electrical engineering to philosophy, and a physical program that finds every cadet participating in an intercollegiate, club, or intramural-level sport. The fully funded, four-year college education includes tuition, room, board, and full medical and dental care. In return, you will graduate with a Bachelor of Science degree and be commissioned as a U.S. Army Officer with an active duty service obligation of five years active and three years reserve. Complete admissions guidance found online."

SELECTIVITY

Admissions Rating	97
# of applicants	12,264
% of applicants accepted	13
% of acceptees attending	82

FRESHMAN PROFILE

Range SAT Critical Reading	560–670
Range SAT Math	580–680
Range SAT Writing	540–650
Range ACT Composite	25–30
Minimum computer TOEFL	580
Minimum web-based TOEFL	88
Average HS GPA	3.80
% graduated top 10% of class	47
% graduated top 25% of class	77
% graduated top 50% of class	99

DEADLINES

Regular	
Deadline	2/28
Notification	11/15
Nonfall registration?	no

APPLICANTS ALSO LOOK AT AND OFTEN PREFER

United States Air Force Academy,
United States Naval Academy

FINANCIAL FACTS

Financial Aid Rating	60*
Annual comprehensive tuition	$0
Books and supplies	$0

UNITED STATES NAVAL ACADEMY

117 DECATUR ROAD, ANNAPOLIS, MD 21402 • ADMISSIONS: 410-293-4361 • FAX: 410-295-1815

CAMPUS LIFE

Quality of Life Rating	80
Fire Safety Rating	70
Green Rating	60*
Type of school	public
Environment	town

STUDENTS

Total undergrad enrollment	4,603
% male/female	80/20
% from out of state	96
% from public high school	60
% live on campus	100
% African American	6
% Asian	4
% Caucasian	68
% Hispanic	12
% international	1
# of countries represented	28

SURVEY SAYS . . .
*Lab facilities are great
Great computer facilities
Athletic facilities are great
Career services are great
Campus feels safe
Everyone loves the Navy
Frats and sororities are unpopular
or nonexistent
Very little drug use*

ACADEMICS

Academic Rating	91
% students graduating within 4 years	88
% students graduating within 6 years	89
Calendar	semester
Student/faculty ratio	9:1
Profs interesting rating	81
Profs accessible rating	97
Most common reg class size	10–19 students

MOST POPULAR MAJORS
economics, history, political science

STUDENTS SAY ". . ."

Academics

Students at the United State Naval Academy are overjoyed about the amount of discipline involved, both academically and militaristically. Students feel "the structure is unparalleled, and the fact that PhDs routinely teach in class even for freshman core classes is amazing." Midshipmen here appreciate personalized attention saying, "You get more face time with your professors and actually get to know them better than you would at any other college." There's an intense focus not only on discipline, but also on the shaping of students moral character. Additionally, students note, "with such a wide selection of professors and an extra instruction system [that's] second-to-none, it is difficult to blame unsatisfactory academic performance on poor professors." There's a great deal of emphasis on personal and professional responsibility and on grooming the best possible naval officers while offering the best possible undergraduate education, free of charge. There's about a 50/50 split between civilian and military personnel, with students noting that "all civilian professors have PhDs, and all military professors have, at least, a master's." The course load is "very difficult," but the vast majority of the professors are "experts in their fields of study," and they "devote a lot of personal time to making sure we succeed."

Life

Students feel that the thing that makes USNA unique is "the combination of academic and military life. Our overall rank is determined not only by our grade. We are also being graded in our physical fitness, military knowledge, professionalism, and leadership abilities. World conflicts are always being discussed because in a few short years that is where we are possibly going to be. Monday to Friday midshipmen put every hour of their lives into their development. Sometimes training evolutions are on the weekends, and we have to sacrifice some fun time. Midshipmen life is very difficult, but the rewards are so great in four short years." Students note that their day-to-day "is very routine," with "classes from 0800 to 1545, then an athletic reserve period." There's "time to exercise every day," and "evenings are dedicated to studying and seeking out help in academics as well as extra curricular activities." "People tend to think about their jobs and tasks assigned, the people here are very locked on." Although classes at the academy follow a strict routine, life here is "enjoyable." But when given the chance and time to have fun, midshipmen have fun, "whether it's going out in town and socializing with friends and family or just staying back in the hall and having fun." Student privileges increase as midshipmen advance from freshmen to upperclassmen. As one student notes, "first year you get nothing; no media, no naps, must greet all upper-class by name, and you are only allowed to leave campus on Saturday from noon to midnight." As can be expected, USNA has a strict code when it comes to drugs and alcohol, which aren't permitted; the "punishment for drug abuse is very strict, and as it is a military school, random urinalysis and breathalyzer tests are taken." However, as the same student notes, "I love it here. Standards are enforced, people are safe, and we are learning."

Student Body

At USNA, the average student is a "type-A personality that works hard to uphold the standards of the academy and to ultimately receive the service selection of their choice." There's an intense camaraderie among the midshipmen here; "the initial summer training really brings students together into a good group that works well together for the remainder of their four years." The typical student is "a pretty well-rounded blend of academic, athletic, and cultural values."

UNITED STATES NAVAL ACADEMY

E-MAIL: WEBMAIL@GWMAIL.USNA.EDU • WEBSITE: WWW.USNA.EDU

THE PRINCETON REVIEW SAYS

Admissions

Very important factors considered include: Academic performance, GPA, class rank, teacher recommendations, rigor of secondary school, character/personal qualities, performance in leadership positions, interview. *Important factors considered include:* Standardized test scores, extracurricular activities, athletic ability. *Others factors considered include:* Geographic residence, alumni/ae relation, first generation to attend college, first generation American, unique life experiences, unique cultural or ethnic heritage, fluency in foreign language, science, technology, engineering, math (STEM) accomplishments, volunteer work, work experience. *Required:* SAT or ACT scores, medical exam. TOEFL required of all international applicants. *Academic units recommended:* 4 English, 4 mathematics, 2 science (1 science lab), 2 foreign language, 2 history.

Financial Aid

The Navy pays for the tuition, room and board, medical and dental care of Naval Academy Midshipmen. Midshipmen also earn a monthly salary while at the academy.

The Inside Word

USNA is an intensely rigorous and demanding program that requires and expects and receives the best possible candidates. The most important non-academic criteria are the personal interview, the applicant's character, and the desire of the applicant to attend the academy. It's the perfect program for anyone wanting to both serve in the U.S. Navy or Marines and receive a first-class education.

THE SCHOOL SAYS "..."

From the Admissions Office

"The Naval Academy offers you a unique opportunity to associate with a broad cross-section of the country's finest young men and women. You will have the opportunity to pursue a four-year program that develops you mentally, morally, and physically as no civilian college can. As you might expect, this program is demanding, but the opportunities are limitless and more than worth the effort. To receive an appointment to the academy, you need four years of high school preparation to develop the strong academic, athletic, and extracurricular background required to compete successfully for admission. You should begin preparing in your freshman year and apply for admission at the end of your junior year. Selection for appointment to the academy comes as a result of a complete evaluation of your admissions package and completion of the nomination process. Complete admissions guidance may be found online."

SELECTIVITY

Admissions Rating	95
# of applicants	17,419
% of applicants accepted	8
% of acceptees attending	85
# accepting a place on wait list	130
% admitted from wait list	12

FRESHMAN PROFILE

Range SAT Critical Reading	550–670
Range SAT Math	590–690
% graduated top 10% of class	56
% graduated top 25% of class	81
% graduated top 50% of class	96

DEADLINES

Regular	
Deadline	1/31
Notification	9/1
Nonfall registration?	no

**APPLICANTS ALSO LOOK AT
AND OFTEN PREFER**
United States Air Force Academy

AND SOMETIMES PREFER
United States Military Academy

FINANCIAL FACTS

Financial Aid Rating	60*
Annual in-state tuition	$0
Annual out-of-state tuition	$0
Room and board	$0
Required fees	$0
Books and supplies	$0

THE UNIVERSITY OF ALABAMA AT BIRMINGHAM

1530 3RD AVENUE SOUTH, BIRMINGHAM AL, 35294 • ADMISSIONS: 205-934-8221 • FAX: 205-975-7114

CAMPUS LIFE

Quality of Life Rating	90
Fire Safety Rating	88
Green Rating	60*
Type of school	public
Environment	metropolis

STUDENTS

Total undergrad enrollment	10,265
% male/female	42/58
% from out of state	6
% live on campus	20
# of fraternities	7
# of sororities	8
% African American	26
% Asian	4
% Caucasian	61
% Hispanic	2
% international	2
# of countries represented	86

SURVEY SAYS . . .

Registration is a breeze
Lab facilities are great
Athletic facilities are great
School is well-run
Diverse student types on campus
Different types of students interact
Students get along with local
community
Dorms are like palaces
Students are happy

ACADEMICS

Academic Rating	73
% students graduating within 4 years	17
% students graduating within 6 years	39
Calendar	semester
Student/faculty ratio	17:1
Profs interesting rating	81
Profs accessible rating	83
Most common reg class size	20–29 students
Most common lab size	10–19 students

MOST POPULAR MAJORS
accounting, biology, psychology

STUDENTS SAY ". . ."

Academics

At the University of Alabama at Birmingham, professors and administrators "care about you." "For many of the professors, it's not just about a grade in a class that you are taking. Rather it's an experience and preparation for any of our further endeavors." The professors here are "experts in their fields," they're "accessible and exciting," and "they're down-to-earth enough to give students a real view of what it's like to enter the world of academia." Despite the fact that this is a large university, there are "small class sizes in even the 100-level classes," and "many professors are available for help outside the classroom and care about teaching their subjects to the students." Of particular note, students say professors in the science departments "are great. They do a great job with interactive learning, and they really put forth every effort to make sure that those who want help get it." Academically, students feel that the workload is rigorous, but "certainly worth the challenge." As one student notes, a graduate tends to feel like "a better person for having experienced the challenge of UAB as well as the diversity." With an annual student forum, "The faculty and administration are very close with students and actively look to pursuing perfection and improving the collegiate experience."

Life

"Campus life is vibrant and exciting," boasts the student body. With UAB being "in the city of Birmingham, right outside of the school is something for everyone. There are malls, many restaurants, museums, and live music." UAB "strongly encourages their students to get involved on campus in some shape or form," presenting the student body with such opportunities as "the widely used Campus Recreation Center where students can take free U-Fit Classes (kickboxing, krunk/hip-hop class, yoga, spin, etc.), swim in the wave pool, climb the rock wall, or play intramurals (flag football, dodgeball, soccer, volleyball, slow pitch softball, etc.)." In addition, the surrounding city of Birmingham offers many venues for arts and entertainment; "students can dine or shop at the many malls located throughout the city. There are also many museums, art shows, concerts, dance clubs, [and] movie theaters to choose from." Students say that the list of attractions in Birmingham "goes on and on." "Students have the problem of having to narrow down their opportunities, rather than having to find something to do." Students "love the size of the school," finding it "like a small town in a big city." The impression is that "the campus is large enough that [you] meet and see new faces daily, but small enough to where [you] have personal relationships with teachers and the administration." Additionally, "there is a genuine interest among students in learning about the other cultures and religions represented on campus and in other cultures around the world."

Student Body

"Everyone is so diverse that there is literally something for everyone to get involved in." With more than 150 campus organizations, students say "you literally have to choose to not become involved." Many students love "how no one looks down on anyone," and how "everyone is so down-to-earth!" Most feel that they all come "from modest households." Regarding potential changes that could be made, "The meal plan situation could use some serious help." At UAB students feel, "It is easy to find a place where you fit in." Although the student body will insist that "there is no typical student!" In general, students are "hardworking and serious," while doing their best to always "enjoy weekend fun with friends."

The University of Alabama at Birmingham

FINANCIAL AID: 205-934-8223 • E-MAIL: UNDERGRADADMIT@UAB.EDU • WEBSITE: MAIN.UAB.EDU

THE PRINCETON REVIEW SAYS

Admissions

Very important factors considered include: Academic GPA, rigor of secondary school record, standardized test scores. SAT or ACT required; ACT with or without writing component accepted. TOEFL required of all international applicants. High school diploma is required, and GED is accepted. *Academic units required:* 4 English, 3 mathematics, 3 science (2 science labs), 1 foreign language, 3 social studies, 3 academic elective.

Financial Aid

Students should submit: FAFSA. The Princeton Review suggests that all financial aid forms be submitted as soon as possible after January 1. *Need-based scholarships/grants offered:* Federal Pell, SEOG, state scholarships/grants, private scholarships, school scholarship or grant aid from institutional funds, United Negro College Fund. *Loan aid offered:* Direct Subsidized Stafford, Direct Unsubsidized Stafford, Direct PLUS, Federal Perkins, state loans, university loans from institutional funds. Applicants will be notified of awards on a rolling basis beginning April 1. Federal Work-Study Program available. Off-campus job opportunities are excellent.

The Inside Word

UAB's incoming class tends to have an average GPA of 3.5. The most important factors for admission are GPA and test scores. At the minimum, students need a GPA of 2.25 and a 950 SAT score. Administrators here are looking to admit a student body that's friendly, diverse, and intelligent with students who strive to be active in the community.

THE SCHOOL SAYS "..."

From the Admissions Office

"Breakthrough...it's a great word to describe UAB. From undergraduate research and interest-specific honors programs to a cutting-edge medical center known internationally for discovery, UAB is a place where great minds come together to make a difference. We are an energetic, exciting place; one of the state's largest universities with eight undergraduate schools, a large graduate school, four medical professional schools, and a renowned medical center.

"UAB is the place for students who seek a world-class research university in the heart of a fun and diverse city and for students who want to take what they learn in the classroom directly to the best companies, career options, and graduate schools available. UAB is also for students who seek diversity in culture and thought, and who are creative, inquisitive, and motivated to get involved and to make a difference.

"On campus you'll discover more than 150 active student organizations and countless activities. And off campus, Alabama's largest city—recently named one of the most livable in America by a national organization—offers must-see attractions and can't-miss events just down the street or mere minutes away. So it's easy to explore your interests, try new experiences, create memories, enjoy old friends and make new ones.

"UAB...for students who expect more from college—students who take achievement seriously—students who want to make a *breakthrough*."

SELECTIVITY
Admissions Rating	78
# of applicants	4,418
% of applicants accepted	84
% of acceptees attending	41

FRESHMAN PROFILE
Range ACT Composite	21–27
Minimum paper TOEFL	500
Minimum computer TOEFL	173
Minimum web-based TOEFL	61
Average HS GPA	3.50
% graduated top 10% of class	27
% graduated top 25% of class	55
% graduated top 50% of class	77

DEADLINES
Regular Deadline	3/1
Nonfall registration?	yes

FINANCIAL FACTS
Financial Aid Rating	71
Annual in-state tuition	$5,806
Annual out-of-state tuition	$13,198
Books and supplies	$1,000
% frosh rec. need-based scholarship or grant aid	30
% UG rec. need-based scholarship or grant aid	33
% frosh rec. non-need-based scholarship or grant aid	32
% UG rec. non-need-based scholarship or grant aid	16
% frosh rec. need-based self-help aid	38
% UG rec. need-based self-help aid	42
% UG borrow to pay for school	53
Average cumulative indebtedness	$21,670

THE UNIVERSITY OF ALABAMA—TUSCALOOSA

Box 870132, Tuscaloosa, AL 35487-0132 • Admissions: 205-348-5666 • Fax: 205-348-9046

CAMPUS LIFE
Quality of Life Rating	79
Fire Safety Rating	67
Green Rating	87
Type of school	public
Environment	city

STUDENTS
Total undergrad enrollment	24,882
% male/female	48/52
% from out of state	31
% live on campus	30
# of fraternities	31
# of sororities	23
% African American	12
% Asian	1
% Caucasian	81
% Hispanic	2
% international	2
# of countries represented	75

SURVEY SAYS . . .
Athletic facilities are great
Everyone loves the Crimson Tide
Frats and sororities dominate
social scene
Student publications are popular

ACADEMICS
Academic Rating	74
% students graduating within 4 years	38
% students graduating within 6 years	67
Calendar	semester
Student/faculty ratio	19:1
Profs interesting rating	81
Profs accessible rating	81
Most common reg class size	10–19 students
Most common lab size	10–19 students

MOST POPULAR MAJORS
finance, marketing, accounting

STUDENTS SAY ". . ."

Academics
The University of Alabama is a ridiculously affordable, "technologically advanced," "student-centered" institution that enjoys an outrageous degree of alumni support. "Course offerings are pretty diverse," and there are "tons of majors." Highlights include a "great" engineering college and three honors programs. Other standout programs include business, communication studies, and nursing. Some students say that the "bold and visionary" top brass runs the school "fairly well." Others gripe that the administration is "very bogged down in red tape." "Working with the administration is really terrible sometimes," undergrads say. Professors here are "top researchers or writers in their fields," and some are "very enthusiastic about having undergraduate students helping them with research." The faculty as a whole is also "approachable" and "generally very easy to get in touch with for outside assistance." Teaching ability is "hit-or-miss," though. While many professors are "very animated and interesting to listen to," "Others do not have the same talent." "Being a great researcher does not necessarily make a person a good teacher," notes one student.

Life
"An atmosphere of almost antebellum charm" permeates this "pretty" campus. "On sunny days in the fall and spring, students enjoy studying and playing on the quad." Recreational facilities are "excellent." "Life during football season revolves around football." So does morale. Win or lose, though, UA boasts "one of the best college football atmospheres in the country. On Saturdays when the Crimson Tide plays at home, the campus is "a sea of tents for tailgating," "and Alabama fans are singing the fight song." Otherwise, "the Greek organizations rule this campus." They wield "an inordinate amount of power" in student government as well. Whether you pledge or not, though, students promise "an outstanding social atmosphere." "While not everyone participates in the party scene on campus, it is very popular." In addition to the house parties and the festivities at the frat houses, "people enjoying going to the bars on the strip." "Comfort" abounds in surrounding Tuscaloosa, and it is "definitely a college town." People are "very open and courteous" to the students, and virtually everything you need is within "walking distance." When students at UA hanker for more urban environs, "Birmingham is only an hour away, and there is plenty to do there."

Student Body
Students here are "extremely friendly" and "usually well-dressed and well-mannered." "People tend to be a bit conservative," and "a lot are religious." "The typical student is active in a few organizations, makes decent grades, and finds time to relax, too." African American students are the largest minority group. They represent more than ten percent of the student body. Some students maintain that UA is "not diverse socially, ideologically, and culturally." "The different ethnic groups stick together," they say. They look around campus and see "frat boys or sorority girls for the most part"—"same hair, same sunglasses with a string on the back, and stupid visors." Other students vigorously disagree. "We truly aren't a university filled with cookie-cutter people," asserts one student. "There are many diverse groups of students who all have their own roles on campus." "It is easy for someone to come from up north and say this campus is full of close-minded Southern Baptist Republicans, just like it is easy for someone to come from a small town…and think this campus is full of liberal heathens," points out another student. "Few people are really atypical, because no matter where you fall in any category, there are people around you who you can connect with."

THE UNIVERSITY OF ALABAMA—TUSCALOOSA

FINANCIAL AID: 205-348-6756 • E-MAIL: ADMISSIONS@UA.EDU • WEBSITE: WWW.UA.EDU

THE PRINCETON REVIEW SAYS

Admissions

Very important factors considered include: Academic GPA, rigor of secondary school record, standardized test scores. *Important factors considered include:* Class rank. *Other factors considered include:* Application essay, recommendation(s), alumni/ae relation, character/personal qualities, extracurricular activities, first generation, interview, talent/ability, volunteer work, work experience. SAT or ACT required; ACT with writing component required. TOEFL required of all international applicants. High school diploma is required, and GED is accepted. *Academic units required:* 4 English, 3 mathematics, 3 science (2 science labs), 1 foreign language, 4 social studies, 1 history, 5 academic elective. *Academic units recommended:* 4 English, 3 mathematics, 3 science (2 science labs), 1 foreign language, 4 social studies, 1 history, 5 academic elective.

Financial Aid

Students should submit: FAFSA. Priority filing deadline is March 1. The Princeton Review suggests that all financial aid forms be submitted as soon as possible after January 1. N*eed-based scholarships/grants offered:* Federal Pell, SEOG, state scholarships/grants, private scholarships, school scholarship or grant aid from institutional funds, Federal Nursing Scholarships. *Loan aid offered:* Direct Subsidized Stafford, Direct Unsubsidized Stafford, Direct PLUS, Federal Perkins, university loans from institutional funds. Applicants will be notified of awards on a rolling basis beginning April 1. Federal Work-Study Program available. Off-campus job opportunities are good.

The Inside Word

The University of Alabama relies heavily on objective data in the application process. Admission is not highly competitive, and applicants with satisfactory grades and modest test scores are likely to be accepted.

THE SCHOOL SAYS " . . ."

From the Admissions Office

"Since its founding in 1831 as the first public university in the state, the University of Alabama has been committed to providing the best, most complete education possible for its students. Our commitment to that goal means that as times change, we sharpen our focus and methods to keep our graduates competitive in their fields. By offering outstanding teaching in a solid core curriculum enhanced by multimedia classrooms and campus-wide computer labs, the University of Alabama keeps its focus on the future while maintaining a traditional college atmosphere. Extensive international study opportunities, internship programs, and cooperative education placements help our students prepare for successful futures. Consisting of eleven colleges and schools offering 220 degrees in more than 100 fields of study, the university gives its students a wide range of choices and offers courses of study at the bachelor's, master's, specialist, and doctoral levels. The university emphasizes quality and breadth of academic opportunities and challenging programs for well-prepared students through its Honors College, including the University Honors Program, International Honors Program, and Computer-Based Honors Programs and Blount Undergraduate Initiative (liberal arts program). Thirty-one percent of undergraduates are from out of state, providing an enriching social and cultural environment.

"Applicants may submit either the SAT or the ACT. The writing component is required for admission."

SELECTIVITY

Admissions Rating	88
# of applicants	20,112
% of applicants accepted	54
% of acceptees attending	51

FRESHMAN PROFILE

Range SAT Critical Reading	490–620
Range SAT Math	500–620
Range SAT Writing	480–600
Range ACT Composite	22–29
Minimum paper TOEFL	500
Minimum computer TOEFL	173
Minimum web-based TOEFL	61
Average HS GPA	3.50
% graduated top 10% of class	43
% graduated top 25% of class	60
% graduated top 50% of class	84

DEADLINES

Regular	
Priority	3/1
Notification	8/1
Nonfall registration?	yes

APPLICANTS ALSO LOOK AT AND OFTEN PREFER
Florida State University, University of Georgia, University of Tennessee—Knoxville

AND SOMETIMES PREFER
Auburn University

FINANCIAL FACTS

Financial Aid Rating	72
Annual in-state tuition	$7,900
Annual out-of-state tuition	$20,500
Room and board	$8,214
Books and supplies	$1,100
% frosh rec. need-based scholarship or grant aid	28
% UG rec. need-based scholarship or grant aid	28
% frosh rec. non-need-based scholarship or grant aid	46
% UG rec. non-need-based scholarship or grant aid	35
% frosh rec. need-based self-help aid	29
% UG rec. need-based self-help aid	34
% frosh rec. any financial aid	64
% UG rec. any financial aid	59
% UG borrow to pay for school	53
Average cumulative indebtedness	$26,701

UNIVERSITY OF ARIZONA

PO Box 210040, Tucson, AZ 85721-0040 • Admissions: 520-621-3237 • Fax: 520-621-9799

STUDENTS SAY ". . ."

Academics

In the simplest terms, University of Arizona is all about providing its students with "endless opportunities." Located on a "gorgeous" campus in vibrant Tucson, U of A offers a "great education" in a "relaxed community." Students here truly appreciate the university's "strong commitment to undergraduate research." Moreover, Arizona really "helps make the cost of education manageable," even "offering many scholarships to out-of-state students who qualify." While undergrads are impressed by a myriad of disciplines, they call special attention to the "excellent" agriculture department and the "great" engineering program. Students also highlight the physiology program and note that U of A is "the only university that offers an undergraduate major through its medical school." Undergrads do admit that professors can range from "very boring" to "extremely fun and interesting." One sophomore does assure us, by and large, "Professors are enthusiastic and genuinely care about students." And a knowledgeable junior adds, "As I get into the higher level classes or the classes that are more focused on my major, I find that the teachers are more enthusiastic and dedicated to their students to see that they succeed." Fortunately, "One thing that is consistent about all of them (and the TAs as well) is their availability through office hours for one-on-one instruction." As this public health major concludes, "The University of Arizona is an institution that provides a well-rounded education and numerous opportunities that prepare students for their future ambitions, whatever they may be."

Life

Students at the U of A are "motivated academically" and devote a decent percentage of their weekdays to hitting the books. Of course, undergrads here are also "very social," and as a sophomore enthusiastically shares, "There is always something to do on campus, and there are a variety of clubs to get involved in." Indeed, there are a number of activities available, ranging "from swing dance to intramural volleyball," which "help alleviate stress." Additionally, "people are really into the athletics. It builds school spirit for everyone involved, [and] tailgates are common on the weekends." Greek life is also extremely popular, and "on the weekends, frats have huge [theme] parties including ZBTahiti, AEPirates, Heaven and Hell, Swampwater, Pajama Jam, and many more." Undergrads also enjoy hometown Tucson, which has "great live music, art, and cinema." The city also "generally has a lot of community activities like Day of the Dead, which is extremely popular." Lastly, students also like to take advantage of the numerous outdoor recreation options available, and many often go "hiking or biking at the nearby mountain ranges."

Student Body

Undergrads at U of A report that the "relaxed" nature of their peers contributes to a "laid-back" atmosphere, which permeates the campus. While some students are most assuredly "in school to learn," others seem "to party their way through." However, an optical engineering major confidently states, "There is a place for you to fit in no matter what you want to get out of your college education." And a fellow engineering student adds, "Most students are very friendly and will greet each other around campus." U of A is quite "diverse," and you can easily find students of/from all different "socio-economic statuses, states, countries, races, ethnicities, ages, etc." A junior tells us that people often make friends by simply getting "involved with something they are interested in and meeting like-minded individuals." One thing that unites these undergrads? Nearly all these "Wildcats" are "full of pride for their school." Perhaps this content freshman says it best, "In a school of 30,000, there is really no typical student, but with such a great number of students, people find their niche."

FINANCIAL AID: 520-621-1858 • E-MAIL: APPINFO@ARIZONA.EDU • WEBSITE: WWW.ARIZONA.EDU

THE PRINCETON REVIEW SAYS

Admissions

Very important factors considered include: Academic GPA, rigor of secondary school record. *Other factors considered include:* Application essay, class rank, recommendation(s), standardized test scores, character/personal qualities, extracurricular activities, first generation, geographical residence, interview, racial/ethnic status, state residency, talent/ability, volunteer work. SAT or ACT reccommended; ACT with or without writing component accepted. TOEFL required of all international applicants. High school diploma is required, and GED is accepted. *Academic units required:* 4 English, 3 mathematics, 3 science (3 science labs), 2 foreign language, 1 social studies, 1 history. *Academic units recommended:* 4 English, 3 mathematics, 3 science (3 science labs), 2 foreign language, 2 social studies, 1 history.

Financial Aid

Students should submit: FAFSA. The Princeton Review suggests that all financial aid forms be submitted as soon as possible after January 1. *Need-based scholarships/grants offered:* Federal Pell, SEOG, state scholarships/grants, private scholarships, school scholarship or grant aid from institutional funds, Federal Nursing Scholarships. *Loan aid offered:* Direct Subsidized Stafford, Direct Unsubsidized Stafford, Direct PLUS, Federal Perkins, Federal Nursing Loans, university loans from institutional funds. Federal Work-Study Program available. Off-campus job opportunities are good.

The Inside Word

Admission to the U of A is competitive, and you'll need to demonstrate achievement in college prep courses. Arizona resident should take note: Candidates applying from within the state who graduate in the top twenty-five percent of their class and meet all course requirements gain automatic acceptance through the assured admission program. Applicants should also recognize that some programs, such as the College of Engineering and College of Fine Arts, mandate additional materials and requirements.

THE SCHOOL SAYS "..."

From the Admissions Office

"Surrounded by mountains and the dramatic beauty of the Sonoran Desert, the University of Arizona offers a top-drawer education in a resort-like setting. Some of the nation's highest-ranked departments make their homes at this oasis of learning in the desert. In addition to producing cloudless sunshine 350 days per year, the clear Arizona skies provide an ideal setting for one of the country's best astronomy programs. Other nationally rated programs include nursing, sociology, management information systems, anthropology, creative writing, and computer and aerospace engineering. The university balances a strong research component with an emphasis on teaching—faculty rolls include Nobel and Pulitzer Prize winners. Famous Chinese astrophysicist and political dissident Fang Lizhi continues his landmark studies here; he now teaches physics to undergraduates. A wealth of academic choices—the university offers 114 majors, with myriad academic concentration options within those majors—is supplemented by an active, progressive campus atmosphere; conference-winning and national title-winning basketball, baseball, swimming, softball, and football teams; and countless recreational opportunities."

SELECTIVITY

Admissions Rating	84
# of applicants	24,625
% of applicants accepted	78
% of acceptees attending	36

FRESHMAN PROFILE

Range SAT Critical Reading	460–600
Range SAT Math	490–620
Range ACT Composite	21–27
Average HS GPA	3.37
% graduated top 10% of class	34
% graduated top 25% of class	62
% graduated top 50% of class	88

DEADLINES

Regular	
Deadline	5/1
Notification	11/1
Nonfall registration?	yes

APPLICANTS ALSO LOOK AT

AND OFTEN PREFER
University of California—Irvine

AND RARELY PREFER
Arizona State University at the Tempe Campus, Northern Arizona University

FINANCIAL FACTS

Financial Aid Rating	78
Annual in-state tuition	$6,540
Annual out-of-state tuition	$21,949
Room and board	$8,614
Required fees	$315
Books and supplies	$1,000
% frosh rec. need-based scholarship or grant aid	36
% UG rec. need-based scholarship or grant aid	36
% frosh rec. non-need-based scholarship or grant aid	5
% UG rec. non-need-based scholarship or grant aid	3
% frosh rec. need-based self-help aid	20
% UG rec. need-based self-help aid	26
% frosh rec. any financial aid	65
% UG rec. any financial aid	64
% UG borrow to pay for school	43
Average cumulative indebtedness	$18,712

UNIVERSITY OF ARKANSAS—FAYETTEVILLE

232 Silas Hunt Hall, Fayetteville, AR 72701 • Admissions: 479-575-5346 • Fax: 479-575-7515

CAMPUS LIFE

Quality of Life Rating	89
Fire Safety Rating	84
Green Rating	94
Type of school	public
Environment	town

STUDENTS

Total undergrad enrollment	17,247
% male/female	52/48
% from out of state	30
% from public high school	84
% live on campus	30
# of fraternities	17
# of sororities	24
% African American	5
% Asian	3
% Caucasian	82
% Hispanic	4
% Native American	2
% international	3
# of countries represented	120

SURVEY SAYS . . .

Athletic facilities are great
Students love Fayetteville, AR
Everyone loves the Razorbacks
Frats and sororities dominate
social scene

ACADEMICS

Academic Rating	70
% students graduating within 4 years	34
% students graduating within 6 years	59
Calendar	semester
Student/faculty ratio	18:1
Profs interesting rating	71
Profs accessible rating	72
Most common reg class size	20–29 students
Most common lab size	20–29 students

MOST POPULAR MAJORS
finance, journalism, marketing

STUDENTS SAY ". . ."

Academics

The University of Arkansas is affordable, "student-centered," and large but not gargantuan. Though you'll see some sizeable lectures during your first year, most classes are "relatively small." "The facilities are exceptional" and otherwise "state-of-the-art." More than 100 undergraduate majors and programs are available. The Sam Walton College of Business is awash in cash and "one of the strongest assets." Engineering majors can participate in cutting-edge research. Agricultural programs are strong and diverse. The honors college is "wonderful." Also, some twenty-five percent of all Arkansas students study abroad. There are summer programs available in China and Egypt, just to a name two examples. Programs during the academic year take place in every nook and cranny of the globe. Student opinion is split with regard to the administration. Some students call the management "very friendly." "Things run pretty smoothly," they say. Others contend that UA is "overly bureaucratic." "The odds of being sent to three different buildings, none of which is right, are pretty much even," wagers one malcontent. Despite "a few really atrocious instructors," students generally praise Arkansas's "dynamic faculty." "The professors are almost always good teachers," and they "know their material." Outside of class, professors tend to be "accessible" and "willing to do anything it takes for the success of their students."

Life

"Parking is horrible," but UA boasts a "beautiful," "well-defined campus with lots of green space." The rolling hills provide plenty of "great exercise," too. Students here reportedly enjoy a "vibrant extracurricular and social scene." "There are lots of things to do that don't involve booze." With more than 300 clubs and groups to choose from "the vast majority of students participate in at least a few campus organizations." "Greek life is prevalent," according to some students. "Intramural sports are popular." Razorback football "is the big highlight of the fall," and the campus has "a lot of spirit" for the beloved Hogs. There are ample activities that do involve booze as well. "Parties are everywhere." "A lot of people will go to the fraternity houses" for revelry. There's also "great nightlife" and "a very enthusiastic bar scene" off campus. "Funky," "charming," and "not-too-expensive," Fayetteville is, by all accounts, a "pretty neat town." Eclectic restaurants and live music venues are ample. "The always-enticing Dickson Street," "located a couple blocks away," is the hub of it all. "On the weekends, it borders on insanity." For outdoorsy types, wilderness activities abound throughout northwestern Arkansas. "The nearby mountains" provide numerous opportunities for climbing, biking, and hiking.

Student Body

They typical student here is "overly friendly," "fun-loving," "at least somewhat religious, and has a southern accent." Most students come "from either Arkansas or Texas." There are "a lot of international students," but "there is little ethnic diversity." Like at virtually every other flagship state university, you'll find "all kinds of students" on this campus. Fayetteville is called "the melting pot of Arkansas." Politics range from "conservative" to "incredibly liberal." "Students come from all walks of life and have many different experiences to share with others." "Party-frat kids abound," as do "southern sorority girls who walk to class in pearls and heels." However, you'll also find "hicks," "artists, musicians, nerds," and "NPR listening, sandal-wearing, health-food-shopping people," as well as the occasional "middle-aged boomer returning to school to start a whole new career." "There is always someone just as weird as you to run with," and students generally "mesh well" even if "groups don't often commingle."

FINANCIAL AID: 479-575-3806 • E-MAIL: UOFA@UARK.EDU • WEBSITE: WWW.UARK.EDU/ADMISSIONS

THE PRINCETON REVIEW SAYS

Admissions

Very important factors considered include: Academic GPA, class rank, rigor of secondary school record, standardized test scores. *Other factors considered include:* Application essay, recommendation(s), alumni/ae relation, character/personal qualities, extracurricular activities, first generation, geographical residence, racial/ethnic status, state residency, talent/ability, volunteer work, work experience. SAT or ACT required; ACT with or without writing component accepted. TOEFL required of all international applicants. High school diploma is required, and GED is accepted. *Academic units required:* 4 English, 4 mathematics, 3 science (2 science labs), 3 social studies, 2 academic elective. *Academic units recommended:* 2 foreign language.

Financial Aid

Students should submit: FAFSA. The Princeton Review suggests that all financial aid forms be submitted as soon as possible after January 1. *Need-based scholarships/grants offered:* Federal Pell, SEOG, state scholarships/grants, private scholarships, school scholarship or grant aid from institutional funds. *Loan aid offered:* Direct Subsidized Stafford, Direct Unsubsidized Stafford, Direct PLUS, Federal Perkins, state loans, university loans from institutional funds. Applicants will be notified of awards on a rolling basis beginning April 1. Federal Work-Study Program available.

The Inside Word

The admissions policy at the University of Arkansas is very straightforward. You need a 3.0 grade-point average (on a 4.0 scale) in your serious academic coursework and at least a 20 on the ACT. The SAT is fine, too, as long as get a comparable minimum score. If you fail to meet these requirements, you still may gain admission based on a case-by-case review process. Also, UA has a rolling admissions policy. As such, candidates will find it in their best interest to apply early.

THE SCHOOL SAYS " . . . "

From the Admissions Office

"The University of Arkansas, the flagship campus of the University of Arkansas System, is located in Fayetteville and overlooks the beautiful Ozark Mountains. The university is both the major land-grant university for Arkansas and the state university, encompassing more than 130 buildings on 345 acres and providing more than 200 graduate and undergraduate academic programs—more than some universities twice its size.

"At the same time, the University of Arkansas maintains a low student-to-faculty ratio—currently eighteen to one—that makes personal attention possible. The university aggressively promotes undergraduate research in virtually every discipline and makes higher education affordable with competitively priced tuition and generous financial aid. In the last decade, university undergraduates have earned many honors: thirty-four received Goldwater Scholarships; twelve have been recognized by the USA Today All-USA College Academic Team. There have been thirty-eight National Science Foundation graduate fellows; thirty-two Fulbright scholars; three British Marshall scholars and six Truman scholars. Four undergraduates have received Udall scholarships; four earned Madison scholarships; three have received Tylenol scholarships; and one was named a Rhodes scholar. Quality programs, affordable tuition and the level of student achievement all contribute to the University of Arkansas consistently being ranked in the top tier of national universities.

"The city of Fayetteville is home to more than 73,000 people and is growing every day. Northwest Arkansas is the headquarters to several major international corporations that have close ties to the university: Tyson Foods, the world's largest protein producer; J.B. Hunt Transport Services Inc., a major transportation and logistics company; and Wal-Mart Stores Inc., the world's largest corporation. Fayetteville has been named "One of America's Most Livable Cities," "One of America's 'Hottest' Cities," one of the nation's "least stressful" metro areas, and among the "Best Places to Live in America" by publications such as Forbes,

SELECTIVITY

Admissions Rating	87
# of applicants	14,019
% of applicants accepted	60
% of acceptees attending	45

FRESHMAN PROFILE

Range SAT Critical Reading	500–610
Range SAT Math	520–640
Range ACT Composite	23–28
Minimum paper TOEFL	550
Minimum computer TOEFL	213
Minimum web-based TOEFL	79
Average HS GPA	3.56
% graduated top 10% of class	27
% graduated top 25% of class	56
% graduated top 50% of class	87

DEADLINES

Early action	
Deadline	11/15
Notification	12/15
Regular	
Priority	11/15
Deadline	8/1
Notification	9/1
Nonfall registration?	yes

FINANCIAL FACTS

Financial Aid Rating	70
Annual in-state tuition	$5,211
Annual out-of-state tuition	$14,443
Room and board	$8,042
Required fees	$1,557
Books and supplies	$1,162
% frosh rec. need-based scholarship or grant aid	29
% UG rec. need-based scholarship or grant aid	25
% frosh rec. non-need-based scholarship or grant aid	4
% UG rec. non-need-based scholarship or grant aid	2
% frosh rec. need-based self-help aid	23
% UG rec. need-based self-help aid	25
% frosh rec. any financial aid	72
% UG rec. any financial aid	65
% UG borrow to pay for school	43
Average cumulative indebtedness	$20,171

UNIVERSITY OF CALIFORNIA—BERKELEY

110 SPROUL HALL #5800, BERKELEY, CA 94720-5800 • ADMISSIONS: 510-642-3175 • FAX: 510-642-7333

CAMPUS LIFE

Quality of Life Rating	71
Fire Safety Rating	77
Green Rating	96
Type of school	public
Environment	city

STUDENTS

Total undergrad enrollment	35,838
% male/female	53/47
% from out of state	7
% live on campus	35
# of fraternities	38
# of sororities	19
% African American	3
% Asian	40
% Caucasian	30
% Hispanic	11
% Native American	1
% international	7
# of countries represented	74

SURVEY SAYS . . .
Great library
Great off-campus food
Everyone loves the Golden Bears
Student publications are popular
Political activism is popular

ACADEMICS

Academic Rating	86
% students graduating	
within 4 years	69
% students graduating	
within 6 years	96
Calendar	semester
Profs interesting rating	78
Profs accessible rating	67
Most common	
reg class size	fewer than
	10 students

MOST POPULAR MAJORS
computer engineering, English language
and literature, political science

STUDENTS SAY ". . ."

Academics
The University of California—Berkeley is a large public university where students feel that their "professors [are] all warm, open, and inviting." In fact, many students choose UC Berkeley because they feel "it's the best public university in the world." Students are quick to point out, "There are some amazing and inspiring minds at Berkeley." With an "all-star faculty and resources," professors here are "intelligent, accessible," with many departments boasting "the best [academics] in their field." Academics here are "on par with the best in the nation." For those students seeking a first-class education, UC Berkeley is "a place of incredible academic opportunity." Students here are a self-motivated lot. As some students note, "you don't get the coddling that the private universities show. You don't have a billion counselors catering to your every need." In addition, "there is no grade inflation." Though students note that survey classes here can sometimes be "enormous," professors "make themselves very accessible via e-mail and office hours." In addition, students find individual attention within "upper-division classes." These classes tend to have "smaller class sizes," while "lower-division classes" are pretty large and, in some cases, the quality "really depends on" the graduate student instructor. In general, UC Berkeley features the opportunity to work with "amazing professors from every department. Challenging, yet stimulating." However, students offer the occasional cautious caveat that, much like every public university in the country, "some professors obviously are more into research than teaching, but others make learning so enjoyable. I would say that the latter occurs way more than the former."

Life
Full of their signature optimism, students here say that "life at Berkeley has no limits;" we "study and hear obscure languages, meet famous scientists, engage with brilliant students, eat delicious food, and just relax with friends daily." Students also note, "The plus about Berkeley is that because of its location in the San Francisco Bay Area, there is a wealth of activities." For those who enjoy off-campus, outdoor recreation, there are "museums, parks, fairs, cultural events, plus gorgeous hiking trails and some of the best views in the bay." San Francisco is simply a short Bay Area Rapid Transit ride away. Though academics take up a large amount of students' free time, with a diversity of majors and interests, students note life here is "anything you want it to be." The general consensus is that "everyone here is not afraid to express themselves, and the opportunity to make a fresh start in college is amazingly liberating." Furthermore, "The friends you make here are closer than you have ever had and probably ever will have." Others note, "The amount of fun you'll have depends on your course load, though there are always events on campus, whether they are concerts, circus performances, club-sponsored activities or events in the dorms." Even "the busiest college student" finds time to attend campus events and his or her niche in the campus community. At UC Berkeley, "You simply won't have the chance to be bored."

Student Body
To simply label this school as "diverse" seems like a simplification. Here, people "think about everything." It's a place where "it's not uncommon to hear conversations vary from the wicked party last night...turn into debates about the roles of women in Hindu mythology to the specifics behind DNA replication." Students here "are ambitious, but fun to be around." For the most part, "Students fit in just fine, but the experience they have is what they make of it."

UNIVERSITY OF CALIFORNIA—BERKELEY

FINANCIAL AID: 510-642-6442 • WEBSITE: WWW.ADMISSIONS.BERKELEY.EDU

THE PRINCETON REVIEW SAYS

Admissions

Very important factors considered include: Academic GPA, application essay, rigor of secondary school record, state residency. *Important factors considered include:* Standardized test scores, character/personal qualities, extracurricular activities, talent/ability, volunteer work, work experience. *Other factors considered include:* First generation, geographical residence. ACT with writing component required. TOEFL required of all international applicants. High school diploma is required, and GED is accepted. *Academic units required:* 4 English, 3 mathematics, 2 science (2 science labs), 2 foreign language, 2 history, 1 visual/performing arts, 1 academic elective. *Academic units recommended:* 4 English, 4 mathematics, 3 science (3 science labs), 3 foreign language, 2 history, 1 visual/performing arts, 1 academic elective.

Financial Aid

Students should submit: FAFSA. Regular filing deadline is March 2. The Princeton Review suggests that all financial aid forms be submitted as soon as possible after January 1. *Need-based scholarships/grants offered:* Federal Pell, SEOG, state scholarships/grants, private scholarships, school scholarship or grant aid from institutional funds. *Loan aid offered:* Direct Subsidized Stafford, Direct Unsubsidized Stafford, Direct PLUS, Federal Perkins. Federal Work-Study Program available. Off-campus job opportunities are excellent.

The Inside Word

UC Berkeley is a top-notch public university with a well-regarded English and Literature department. Importance is placed on the totality of a student's application with a joint focus on the personal essay and academic excellence as noted by a student's GPA. Class rank isn't considered. The school is home to an incredible amount of students with as wide a range of interests. Successful applicants here are generally stellar both academically and personally. Applications, especially the essay, should create a picture of a unique candidate with a diversity of skills to offer this active community.

THE SCHOOL SAYS " . . ."

From the Admissions Office

"One of the top public universities in the nation and the world, the University of California—Berkeley offers a vast range of courses and a full menu of extracurricular activities. Berkeley's academic programs are internationally recognized for their excellence. Undergraduates can choose one of 100 majors. Thirty-five departments are top ranked, more than any other college or university in the country. Access to one of the foremost university libraries enriches studies. There are twenty-three specialized libraries on campus and distinguished museums of anthropology, paleontology, and science.

"All applicants must take the ACT plus writing or the SAT Reasoning Test. UC admissions requirements are found at http://www.universityofcalifornia.edu/admissions/freshman/requirements/index.html."

SELECTIVITY

Admissions Rating	97
# of applicants	52,945
# accepting a place on wait list	197
% admitted from wait list	0

FRESHMAN PROFILE

Range SAT Critical Reading	620–740
Range SAT Math	660–770
Range SAT Writing	650–750
Range ACT Composite	79–99
Average HS GPA	3.88

DEADLINES

Regular	
Deadline	11/30
Notification	late March
Nonfall registration?	yes

FINANCIAL FACTS

Financial Aid Rating	78
Annual in-state tuition	$12,461
Annual out-of-state tuition	$35,340
Room and board	$14,000
Books and supplies	$1,202

University of California—Davis

178 Mrak Hall, Davis, CA 95616 • Admissions: 530-752-2971 • Fax: 530-752-1280

CAMPUS LIFE

Quality of Life Rating	93
Fire Safety Rating	75
Green Rating	93
Type of school	public
Environment	town

STUDENTS

Total undergrad enrollment	24,497
% male/female	45/55
% from out of state	2
% from public high school	84
% live on campus	25
# of fraternities	28
# of sororities	21
% African American	3
% Asian	39
% Caucasian	34
% Hispanic	15
% Native American	1
% international	3
# of countries represented	121

SURVEY SAYS . . .

Athletic facilities are great
Student publications are popular

ACADEMICS

Academic Rating	74
% students graduating within 4 years	51
% students graduating within 6 years	82
Calendar	quarter
Student/faculty ratio	16:1
Profs interesting rating	73
Profs accessible rating	73
Most common reg class size	20–29 students
Most common lab size	20–29 students

MOST POPULAR MAJORS
biology, economics, psychology

STUDENTS SAY ". . ."

Academics

"UC Davis is a huge research university with the atmosphere of an intimate community." The agricultural and food sciences programs are excellent. There are more than 100 majors. Research opportunities for undergraduates are abundant. Study abroad and internship programs are "fantastic." "Registration is very nerve-racking," but on the whole, management is "invisible." "Things seem to work magically around here." "The administration is like Atlantis," offers a linguistics major; "it's rumored to exist, but you've never actually seen it." "As for your academic experience, 90 percent of it is dependent upon who your professor is, and 100 percent is dependent upon your personal interest," explains an international relations major. "I know that adds up to 190 percent. You can blame my statistics professor." UC Davis's quarter system affords "no time to fool around." "It is not really a school for a slacker." "Although the pace is fast, it's very doable," asserts a communications major. Classes can be quite large here, and the classrooms themselves "could do with some better desks." Some members of the "world-class faculty" are "very enthusiastic" and "really profound." "I have consistently found my professors to be wonderful teachers who care deeply about their students," boasts a biology major. "Professors vary a lot depending on subject." As a rule, "Upper-division professors are generally far better than lower-division ones."

Life

UC Davis is located in a "cozy," "rural," and "relaxed" college town in northern California not too far from Sacramento. Most students report a pretty high level of satisfaction with the atmosphere, though a few tell us that Davis "is boring, and ugly." "Downtown Davis is a great place that is located within walking distance of the dorms and most off-campus housing," says a sophomore. It's "filled with interesting non-chain stores" and "great places to eat all types of food." "There are bicycles everywhere." And "if Davis isn't your thing, you can always go to Sacramento or San Francisco." "Tahoe is about two hours away, so it's pretty easy to go snowboarding or skiing," too. On the "sprawling" campus "the food is repetitive," but Davis has "excellent" recreational facilities and "a wide variety of activities, clubs, and groups to get involved in." "The sense of community is pretty good." "Greek life is big;" and "keggers at frats" are definitely available. "There is a demographic that enjoys going to parties at the fraternities, but other people who do not enjoy that can easily stay out of it." "Davis is not mainly about parties," though. Mostly, "Davis is a place where you can really sit down and study," and "the best part is just finding a good group of people." "There is a niche for everyone."

Student Body

"Students here are the hardworking, studious, responsible kids," says a sophomore. "The student body is mostly made up of white and Asian students," but "Davis is a melting pot." "Many different cultures, ethnicities, and religions are present," and "everybody is really accepting." Students here describe themselves as "goal-oriented," "down-to-earth, well-rounded, balanced, amiable, and intelligent." "Some seem shy and timid." "There are some atypical students who care more about their looks and having fun than just studying, but I feel like they are a minority," says a sophomore. There are "the uber-serious premed students who spend all of their waking time in class or in the library having an aneurism." There's "the sorority girl; the band geek, the jock; the crazy, outspoken chick;" and "a lot of hippies," too. A pretty high percentage of these students is "really concerned about environmental issues," and many UC Davis students "take an active stand" on politics.

FINANCIAL AID: 530-752-2390 • E-MAIL: FRESHMANADMISSIONS@UCDAVIS.EDU • WEBSITE: WWW.UCDAVIS.EDU

THE PRINCETON REVIEW SAYS

Admissions

Very important factors considered include: Academic GPA, application essay, rigor of secondary school record, standardized test scores. *Important factors considered include:* Class rank, character/personal qualities, extracurricular activities, first generation, talent/ability, volunteer work. *Other factors considered include:* State residency, work experience. SAT or ACT required; ACT with writing component required. TOEFL required of all international applicants. High school diploma is required, and GED is accepted. *Academic units required:* 4 English, 3 mathematics, 2 science (2 science labs), 2 foreign language, 2 social studies, 1 visual/performing arts, 1 academic elective. *Academic units recommended:* 4 English, 4 mathematics, 3 science (3 science labs), 3 foreign language, 2 social studies, 1 visual/performing arts, 1 academic elective.

Financial Aid

Students should submit: FAFSA. Priority filing deadline is March 2. The Princeton Review suggests that all financial aid forms be submitted as soon as possible after January 1. *Need-based scholarships/grants offered:* Federal Pell, SEOG, state scholarships/grants, private scholarships, school scholarship or grant aid from institutional funds. *Loan aid offered:* Direct Subsidized Stafford, Direct Unsubsidized Stafford, Direct PLUS, Federal Perkins, university loans from institutional funds. Applicants will be notified of awards on a rolling basis beginning March 23.

The Inside Word

Admission to UC Davis is considerably easier than, say, admission to Berkeley. Nevertheless, every school in the UC system is world-class, and the UC system in general is geared toward the best and brightest of California's high school students.

THE SCHOOL SAYS ". . ."

From the Admissions Office

"UC Davis is characterized by a distinguished faculty of scholars, scientists, and artists; a treasured sense of community; and a dedication to innovative teaching, research, and public service. Student involvement in academics, leadership, and honors programs, as well as internships, education abroad, and research, typify the undergraduate experience. These experiences serve as vehicles for enhancing the quality of faculty-student interactions at a premier research university that addresses the critical issues facing our world today. Students can earn degrees in more than 100 majors, work alongside professional researchers, and receive pre-graduate advising in nearly any field imaginable.

"The friendly, supportive nature of the campus and Davis community also defines the undergraduate experience. More than 500 student-run clubs and organizations, themed residence hall programs, and cultural celebrations provide opportunities for students to learn about themselves and other cultures. UC Davis offers its active student body NCAA Division I athletics and stunning cultural, academic, and recreational facilities such as the Mondavi Center for the Performing Arts, the Robert Mondavi Institute for Wine and Food Science, and the Activities and Recreation Center. UC Davis also provides many resources to help undergraduates build social and career networks before they graduate, so that students are well-connected by the time they don their cap and gown.

"Freshman applicants are required to take the ACT assessment plus writing or the SAT Reasoning Test no later than December, the month following application to UC Davis. SAT Subject Tests are not required for fall 2012 admission or beyond."

SELECTIVITY

Admissions Rating	96
# of applicants	43,295
% of applicants accepted	45
% of acceptees attending	23
# accepting a place on wait list	1,510
% admitted from wait list	39

FRESHMAN PROFILE

Range SAT Critical Reading	530–650
Range SAT Math	570–690
Range SAT Writing	540–660
Range ACT Composite	24–30
Minimum paper TOEFL	550
Minimum computer TOEFL	213
Minimum web-based TOEFL	60
Average HS GPA	3.90
% graduated top 10% of class	100
% graduated top 25% of class	100
% graduated top 50% of class	100

DEADLINES

Regular	
Deadline	11/30
Nonfall registration?	no

APPLICANTS ALSO LOOK AT AND OFTEN PREFER

University of California—Berkeley,
University of California—Los Angeles,
University of California—San Diego

FINANCIAL FACTS

Financial Aid Rating	70
Annual in-state tuition	$10,152
Annual out-of-state tuition	$33,030
Room and board	$12,697
Required fees	$2,642
Books and supplies	$1,589
% frosh rec. need-based scholarship or grant aid	63
% UG rec. need-based scholarship or grant aid	60
% frosh rec. need-based self-help aid	45
% UG rec. need-based self-help aid	43
% frosh rec. any financial aid	65
% UG rec. any financial aid	62
% UG borrow to pay for school	60
Average cumulative indebtedness	$16,659

UNIVERSITY OF CALIFORNIA—LOS ANGELES

405 HILGARD AVENUE, BOX 951436, LOS ANGELES, CA 90095-1436 • ADMISSIONS: 310-825-3101 • FAX: 310-206-1206

STUDENTS SAY ". . ."

Academics

Undergrads at this esteemed university don't mince words when boasting about all that UCLA has to offer. As a geography and environmental science double-major proudly declares, "There's nothing that can't be accomplished at UCLA. The possibilities are endless, and the resources are unparalleled." Moreover, students appreciate the "ideal" location as well as the "pride of going to a Division I school with more NCAA championships than any other college/university." Perhaps more notable, "UCLA is the kind of school that pushes you to work hard academically but reminds you that interaction with people outside of the classroom is just as important." Students are continually impressed by their professors who are "leaders in their field." Indeed, most consider it "a privilege to study under them." While some undergrads caution that you might encounter some teachers simply "in it for the research," others insist, "Most professors care about their students." A political science major interjects, saying that professors "are willing to work extra hours with students and help us with anything we need." And an English major concurs, sharing, "I have never had a professor that I did not feel comfortable approaching, which has made my academic experience incredibly more beneficial." As this grateful junior succinctly explains, "UCLA is the campus. The people, the weather, the academics, the sports; it has absolutely everything I could ever want."

Life

There's so much "hustle and bustle" at UCLA that it would be virtually "impossible to [be] bored." While nearly everyone's "main focus is on school," most students also know how to "play hard." Indeed, "whether it be in Greek life, a club or organization, everybody has somewhere they can go to relax and have some fun. The apartments are close to campus, so nearly everybody lives in a small area with close proximity." Sports "are extremely popular here, and conversations about the Bruins are common." There are also "tons of movie showings on campus, recreation centers, pools, activities, [and] events." Additionally, students love being located in Los Angeles. A happy senior reveals, "You can take a five-minute drive and you'll be soaking in the Pacific Ocean, or take an hour drive where you can be hitting the slopes in Big Bear. You can walk down to the theater and run into Jennifer Lopez or head to the UCLA gym and watch…Kobe Bryant practicing. The possibilities are endless here, with or without money."

Student Body

UCLA "is the mold that fits you." Indeed, "26,000 students and more than 950 student groups," virtually assures that "there is no 'typical' student" to be found at UCLA. This wide range of individuals and activities guarantees that "everyone has their niche." Certainly, the Bruin community is a "vibrant" one, and "the unmatched diversity broadens students' horizons culturally and socially." Of course, undergrads here do tread some common ground. Many define their peers as "very hardworking and ambitious," and they typically "strive for success and to do their absolute best." They "know how to have a good time, but they also know when it is time to study." Further, it's an active student body, and it often "seems like everyone is in at least one club or organization." Friendliness is another trademark of UCLA undergrads as a physiology major assures us, "It is very easy to talk to and meet new people and make new friends." Fortunately, most people are "laid-back" and while "academically invested…[they're] not outright competitive with other students." This bio major sums up his peers easily by saying, "Everyone comes from different backgrounds with varied interests the only common denominator is truly an appetite for excellence."

FINANCIAL AID: 310-206-0400 • E-MAIL: UGADM@SAONET.UCLA.EDU • WEBSITE: WWW.UCLA.EDU

THE PRINCETON REVIEW SAYS

Admissions

Very important factors considered include: Academic GPA, application essay, rigor of secondary school record, standardized test scores. *Important factors considered include:* Character/personal qualities, extracurricular activities, talent/ability, volunteer work, work experience. *Other factors considered include:* First generation, geographical residence. SAT or ACT required; ACT with writing component required. TOEFL required of all international applicants. High school diploma is required, and GED is accepted. *Academic units required:* 4 English, 3 mathematics, 2 science (2 science labs), 2 foreign language, 2 history, 1 visual/performing arts, 1 academic elective. *Academic units recommended:* 4 English, 4 mathematics, 3 science (3 science labs), 3 foreign language, 2 history, 1 visual/performing arts, 1 academic elective.

Financial Aid

Students should submit: FAFSA. The Princeton Review suggests that all financial aid forms be submitted as soon as possible after January 1. *Need-based scholarships/grants offered:* Federal Pell, SEOG, state scholarships/grants, private scholarships, school scholarship or grant aid from institutional funds, United Negro College Fund, Federal Nursing Scholarships. *Loan aid offered:* Direct Subsidized Stafford, Direct Unsubsidized Stafford, Direct PLUS, Federal Perkins, Federal Nursing Loans, state loans, university loans from institutional funds. Applicants will be notified of awards on a rolling basis beginning March 15. Federal Work-Study Program available. Off-campus job opportunities are good.

The Inside Word

Competition is fierce to secure admittance to one of the nation's top public universities. Academic success is paramount, and your GPA and standardized test scores factor heavily into admissions decisions. You'll want to load up on challenging courses in high school. Indeed, taking advancement placement, IB, or honors classes is a must. Of course, UCLA also wants students who will actively contribute to their community, and it's also important to demonstrate commitment to extracurricular activities.

THE SCHOOL SAYS "..."

From the Admissions Office

"Undergraduates arrive at UCLA from throughout California and around the world with exceptional levels of academic preparation. They are attracted by our acclaimed degree programs, distinguished faculty, and the beauty of a park-like campus set amid the dynamism of the nation's second-largest city. UCLA's highly ranked undergraduate programs incorporate cutting-edge technology and teaching techniques that hone the critical-thinking skills and the global perspectives necessary for success in our rapidly changing world. The diversity of these programs draws strength from a student body that mirrors the cultural and ethnic vibrancy of Los Angeles. Generally ranked among the nation's top half-dozen universities, UCLA is at once distinguished and dynamic, academically rigorous and responsive.

"All applicants must take the ACT plus writing or the SAT Reasoning Test. In addition, all applicants must take two SAT Subject Tests in two different subject areas. (If a math SAT Subject Test is chosen by the applicant, he/she must take the math Level II exam.)"

SELECTIVITY

Admissions Rating	98
# of applicants	57,670
% of applicants accepted	23
% of acceptees attending	35

FRESHMAN PROFILE

Range SAT Critical Reading	570–680
Range SAT Math	600–740
Range SAT Writing	580–710
Range ACT Composite	25–31
Minimum paper TOEFL	560
Minimum computer TOEFL	220
Minimum web-based TOEFL	87
Average HS GPA	4.25
% graduated top 10% of class	97
% graduated top 25% of class	100
% graduated top 50% of class	100

DEADLINES

Regular	
Deadline	11/30
Notification	3/31
Nonfall registration?	no

FINANCIAL FACTS

Financial Aid Rating	82
Annual in-state tuition	$9,402
Annual out-of-state tuition	$32,281
Room and board	$13,734
Required fees	$2,466
Books and supplies	$1,608
% frosh rec. need-based scholarship or grant aid	54
% UG rec. need-based scholarship or grant aid	52
% frosh rec. non-need-based scholarship or grant aid	1
% UG rec. non-need-based scholarship or grant aid	1
% frosh rec. need-based self-help aid	37
% UG rec. need-based self-help aid	38
% frosh rec. any financial aid	56
% UG rec. any financial aid	55
% UG borrow to pay for school	44
Average cumulative indebtedness	$18,203

UNIVERSITY OF CALIFORNIA—RIVERSIDE

1138 HINDERAKER HALL, RIVERSIDE, CA 92521 • ADMISSIONS: 951-827-3411 • FAX: 951-827-6344

CAMPUS LIFE

Quality of Life Rating	61
Fire Safety Rating	88
Green Rating	95
Type of school	public
Environment	city

STUDENTS

Total undergrad enrollment	18,242
% male/female	48/52
% from out of state	1
% from public high school	91
% live on campus	32
# of fraternities	20
# of sororities	20
% African American	8
% Asian	40
% Caucasian	16
% Hispanic	31
% international	1
# of countries represented	102

SURVEY SAYS . . .
Great library
Athletic facilities are great
Diverse student types on campus
Different types of students interact
Frats and sororities dominate
social scene
Student publications are popular

ACADEMICS

Academic Rating	70
% students graduating within 4 years	39
% students graduating within 6 years	67
Calendar	quarter
Student/faculty ratio	19:1
Profs interesting rating	62
Profs accessible rating	64
Most common reg class size	20–29 students
Most common lab size	20–29 students

MOST POPULAR MAJORS
biology, business administration and
management, psychology

STUDENTS SAY "..."

Academics
The University of California—Riverside is an "underrated" and "research-oriented" school with an "extensive library" and heaps of "very up-to-date" technology. There are nearly eighty-eight majors available. Premed and the biological sciences are noteworthy strengths. Computer science, engineering, and business administration are also solid. "The honors program is fantastic." Cutting-edge research opportunities for undergraduates are ample "in virtually any area." If you have a passion for creepy crawly things, UCR boasts one of the best entomology departments in the nation. (The bug collection is astounding.) UCR is also a leader in agricultural research. "Lectures are huge" at the introductory level, and "overworked" teaching assistants are a fact of life. "Classes are smaller" as you get further along in your major, though, particularly in comparison to other UC schools. The academic atmosphere varies widely by department. "Fast-paced, challenging" course work is common in the hard sciences. "Most science students are always in the libraries." Other students report a radically different experience. "Some of my classes are a joke," gripes a history major. Similarly, "professors are either great or awful." There are "some very excellent teachers" here who "go out of their way to help students learn both inside and outside the classroom." Other professors "treat teaching as just a requirement. Student opinion regarding the administration also differs. Some undergrads declare them to be "helpful" and diligent about "keeping students on track." Others, however, assert that some administrators act as if helping the students is a burden."

Life
UCR students enjoy a "beautiful" campus with a lot of newer buildings and "a forest feel to it." With nearly 300 clubs and organizations, there are "plenty of extracurricular activities." The Greek system has a noticeable presence on campus. If you are athletic, the huge student recreation center is dreamy. Many intercollegiate athletic teams are formidable, too, though student support is generally low. The party scene isn't very happening. Many students are commuters, and on the weekends, "the campus is empty." The city of Riverside has a few advantages. For example, "the cost of living is cheap off campus." Just down the street from campus, there's also University Village, which has "a movie theater and food places." Riverside is also a mere "forty minutes from the snow at Big Bear." However, the general sentiment among students here is that the surrounding area is "lackluster" and "freaking boring." "UCR needs to be transplanted to another town," suggests one visionary student.

Student Body
UCR is "one of the most diverse of all the UC campuses." "It's hard to describe the typical student, because there are so many different types of people." There are "the fraternity freaks, the overachievers, the geeks, the recluses, the trendy people," and many other subgroups. At the same time, UCR is mostly full of "average college students." "Everybody is pretty relaxed and friendly." Sure, there "weirdoes here and there, "maybe a few people with green hair," but "no one is out of the ordinary." Just about everyone here is from California, and it's largely a middle-class crowd. Some seventy percent of all students receive financial aid. "Most of the students seem serious about being in college and are here for the right reasons," though not all of them. "There are the extremely bright students who spend all day studying," relates a sophomore. "There are also students who barely got in and do nothing at all."

UNIVERSITY OF CALIFORNIA—RIVERSIDE

FINANCIAL AID: 951-827-3878 • E-MAIL: UGADMISS@UCR.EDU • WEBSITE: WWW.UCR.EDU

THE PRINCETON REVIEW SAYS

Admissions

Very important factors considered include: Academic GPA, rigor of secondary school record, standardized test scores, state residency. *Important factors considered include:* Application essay. *Other factors considered include:* First generation. SAT or ACT required; ACT with writing component required. TOEFL required of all international applicants. High school diploma is required, and GED is accepted. *Academic units required:* 4 English, 3 mathematics, 2 science (2 science labs), 2 foreign language, 2 history, 1 visual/performing arts, 1 academic elective. *Academic units recommended:* 4 mathematics, 3 science (3 science labs), 3 foreign language.

Financial Aid

Students should submit: FAFSA. Regular filing deadline is March 2. The Princeton Review suggests that all financial aid forms be submitted as soon as possible after January 1. *Need-based scholarships/grants offered:* Federal Pell, SEOG, state scholarships/grants, private scholarships, school scholarship or grant aid from institutional funds. *Loan aid offered:* Direct Subsidized Stafford, Direct Unsubsidized Stafford, Direct PLUS, Federal Perkins, university loans from institutional funds. Applicants will be notified of awards on a rolling basis beginning March 1. Federal Work-Study Program available. Off-campus job opportunities are excellent.

The Inside Word

The UC—Riverside admissions process is based heavily on quantitative factors. Applicants who have strong GPAs and standardized test scores should have no problem gaining acceptance. There is a priority filing period, so students should apply as early as possible.

THE SCHOOL SAYS "..."

From the Admissions Office

"The University of California—Riverside offers the quality, rigor, and facilities of a major research institution, while assuring its undergraduates personal attention and a sense of community. Academic programs, teaching, advising, and student services all reflect the supportive attitudes that characterize the campus. Among the exceptional opportunities are the Thomas Haider Program in Biomedical Sciences, which provides an exclusive path to medical school: the University Honors Program, an extensive undergraduate research program, UC's largest undergraduate program is Business Administration, and UC's only bachelor's degree in creative writing. Additionally, the opening of UCR's School of Medicine is anticipated for August 2012. More than 300 student clubs and organizations and a variety of athletic and arts events give students a myriad of ways to get involved and have fun.

"Effective fall 2012, all applicants must take the ACT plus writing or the SAT Reasoning Test. The SAT Subject Tests will no longer be required for admission; however, students interested in admission to any major in the College of Natural and Agricultural Sciences or the Bourns College of Engineering are strongly recommended to take the SAT Subject Test math Level 2 and the SAT Subject Test in chemistry or physics."

SELECTIVITY

Admissions Rating	92
# of applicants	26,478
% of applicants accepted	78
% of acceptees attending	22

FRESHMAN PROFILE

Range SAT Critical Reading	450–560
Range SAT Math	480–610
Range SAT Writing	460–570
Range ACT Composite	19–24
Minimum paper TOEFL	550
Minimum web-based TOEFL	79
Average HS GPA	3.50
% graduated top 10% of class	94
% graduated top 25% of class	100
% graduated top 50% of class	100

DEADLINES

Regular	
Deadline	11/30
Notification	2/1
Nonfall registration?	no

APPLICANTS ALSO LOOK AT

AND OFTEN PREFER
University of California—Berkeley,
University of California—Los Angeles,
University of California—San Diego

AND SOMETIMES PREFER
University of California—Santa Barbara, University of California—Davis, University of California—Irvine

AND RARELY PREFER
University of California—Merced,
University of California—Santa Cruz

FINANCIAL FACTS

Financial Aid Rating	82
Annual in-state tuition	$11,683
Annual out-of-state tuition	$34,562
Room and board	$11,600
Required fees	$2,281
Books and supplies	$1,800
% frosh rec. need-based scholarship or grant aid	74
% UG rec. need-based scholarship or grant aid	69
% frosh rec. non-need-based scholarship or grant aid	2
% UG rec. non-need-based scholarship or grant aid	1
% frosh rec. need-based self-help aid	65
% UG rec. need-based self-help aid	57
% frosh rec. any financial aid	81
% UG rec. any financial aid	73
% UG borrow to pay for school	64
Average cumulative indebtedness	$18,094

UNIVERSITY OF CALIFORNIA—SAN DIEGO

9500 GILMAN DRIVE, 0021, LA JOLLA, CA 92093-0021 • ADMISSIONS: 858-534-4831 • FAX: 858-534-5723

CAMPUS LIFE

Quality of Life Rating	74
Fire Safety Rating	80
Green Rating	97
Type of school	public
Environment	metropolis

STUDENTS

Total undergrad enrollment	23,663
% male/female	49/51
% from out of state	3
% live on campus	34
# of fraternities	19
# of sororities	14
% African American	2
% Asian	44
% Caucasian	24
% Hispanic	13
% international	7
# of countries represented	70

SURVEY SAYS . . .
Great computer facilities
Great library
Athletic facilities are great
Low cost of living

ACADEMICS

Academic Rating	80
% students graduating within 4 years	57
% students graduating within 6 years	82
Calendar	quarter
Student/faculty ratio	19:1
Profs interesting rating	68
Profs accessible rating	68
Most common reg class size	10–19 students
Most common lab size	20–29 students

MOST POPULAR MAJORS
biology, economics

STUDENTS SAY ". . ."

Academics
UCSD is one of the world's premier research institutions, and the economic downturn hasn't diminished its importance or vitality. What began as an oceanography school that expanded into a university in the early 1960s has grown into a haven for neurosciences, chemistry, medicine, engineering, ocean studies, and even theater and dance. The faculty, filled with Nobel laureates, earns across-the-board praise from students for their knowledge and dedication. "My professors are amazing and truly want to teach every student," one says. "My professors have been phenomenal; always accessible, enthusiastic, and encouraging" adds another. Others say their classes got smaller and the instruction better as they progressed in their degree programs. "It's especially cool when you take a class on poli-sci immigration from the leader in the field, or take a physics class taught by (astronaut) Sally Ride." However, a common complaint is that some professors don't appear to be fully invested in the classroom experience: "A number of professors seemed to be focused more on their research rather than sharing knowledge with students." Libraries and research facilities get high marks. Best of all, students say, the school has a sterling reputation, so "I know my degree won't be meaningless." There's "always a good job market with so many biotech companies close by."

Life
Students are divided on whether this school in scenic but sleepy La Jolla has a boring social scene ("Some joke that UCSD stands for the University of California—Socially Dead/Sleep Deprived."), or that one simply has to look hard to find recreation ("There is always something to do on campus, and it is always changing! I never get bored!"). But one thing is certain: Some students work way too hard to afford the luxury of a social life, and this causes some friction between the science and non-science students. One student summed up the dichotomy perfectly: "My school is all about science and the beach." Trying to study the hard sciences despite the distraction of the Pacific only a few blocks away is a mammoth task. And a fine public transit system makes downtown San Diego very accessible. "If you enjoy constant fair weather and beautiful beaches, then this is the place for you," one student gushes. The school has tried to make campus a fun place to be. Price Center, the campus hub, is under expansion, and there are three free concerts per quarter, including the eagerly anticipated Sun God Festival in May. Then there's that cool outdoor art: seventeen commissioned installations (and counting), including a giant teddy bear made of boulders. Several students wish the NCAA Division II school would spring for a football team to create more campus unity. But to others, the six-college setup "makes everyone feel like they belong to a close-knit community within such a populous school."

Student Body
"The typical student at our school is Asian American and studious," one student reports. "Great professors and nice, dorky kids," is how one student sums up the demographic. "UCSD has very smart people doing really incredible things." They can "surf and dance and loads of other things, so it just goes to show that intelligence comes in all kinds of packages." As has been established, some view the nightlife as a dead zone, but many find kindred spirits through sports teams, whether it's university-sponsored or intramural. There are many campus groups, but some students wish there were a higher level of political involvement. "Many students are into their studies and hardly venture out of their comfort zone to take advantage of what college has to offer," one says.

UNIVERSITY OF CALIFORNIA—SAN DIEGO

FINANCIAL AID: 858-534-4480 • E-MAIL: ADMISSIONSINFO@UCSD.EDU • WEBSITE: WWW.UCSD.EDU

THE PRINCETON REVIEW SAYS

Admissions

Very important factors considered include: Academic GPA, application essay, rigor of secondary school record, standardized test scores, character/personal qualities, state residency, talent/ability. *Important factors considered include:* Extracurricular activities, volunteer work. *Other factors considered include:* First generation, work experience. SAT or ACT required; ACT with writing component required. TOEFL required of all international applicants. High school diploma is required, and GED is accepted. *Academic units required:* 4 English, 3 mathematics, 2 science (2 science labs), 2 foreign language, 2 history, 1 visual/performing arts, 1 academic elective. *Academic units recommended:* 4 English, 4 mathematics, 3 science (3 science labs), 3 foreign language, 2 history, 1 academic elective.

Financial Aid

Students should submit: FAFSA. The Princeton Review suggests that all financial aid forms be submitted as soon as possible after January 1. *Need-based scholarships/grants offered:* Federal Pell, SEOG, state scholarships/grants, private scholarships, school scholarship or grant aid from institutional funds. *Loan aid offered:* Direct Subsidized Stafford, Direct Unsubsidized Stafford, Direct PLUS, Federal Perkins, university loans from institutional funds. Applicants will be notified of awards on a rolling basis beginning March 15. Federal Work-Study Program available. Off-campus job opportunities are good.

The Inside Word

While not as lauded as Berkeley or UCLA, UCSD is quickly earning its place as one of the gems of the UC system. It continues to distinguish itself in a number of ways, including its individualized approach to admissions. Although admissions officers do implement a formula, they factor in extracurricular pursuits and personal experiences. Applicants will need to be strong in all areas if they hope to attend UCSD.

THE SCHOOL SAYS "..."

From the Admissions Office

"UCSD is recognized for the exceptional quality of its academic programs. UCSD ranks fifth in the nation and first in the University of California system for the amount of federal research dollars spent on research and development; and the university ranks tenth in the nation in the excellence of its graduate programs and the quality of its faculty, according to the most recent National Research Council college rankings."

"About forty percent of UCSD's undergraduates participate in research, developing critical thinking and effective communication skills as well as greater cultural understanding. Their faculty mentors are in the divisions and schools of arts and humanities, biology, engineering, medicine, pharmacy, physical sciences, social sciences, and UCSD's Scripps Institution of Oceanography, California Institute for Telecommunications and Information Technology and the San Diego Supercomputer Center. Undergraduates also participate in research at the Salk Institute for Biological Studies and other nearby research institutes and biotechnology companies."

"All applicants must take the ACT plus writing or the SAT Reasoning Test. In addition, all applicants must take two SAT Subject Tests in two different subject areas. (If a math SAT Subject Test is chosen by the applicant, he/she must take the math Level II exam.)"

SELECTIVITY

Admissions Rating	97
# of applicants	48,093
% of applicants accepted	38
% of acceptees attending	22

FRESHMAN PROFILE

Range SAT Critical Reading	540–670
Range SAT Math	610–720
Range SAT Writing	560–690
Range ACT Composite	25–31
Minimum paper TOEFL	550
Average HS GPA	3.98
% graduated top 10% of class	100
% graduated top 25% of class	100
% graduated top 50% of class	100

DEADLINES

Regular	
Deadline	11/30
Notification	3/15
Nonfall registration?	yes

APPLICANTS ALSO LOOK AT AND OFTEN PREFER

Stanford University,
University of California—Santa Barbara,
University of California—Berkeley,
University of California—Davis,
University of California—Los Angeles,
University of Southern California

FINANCIAL FACTS

Financial Aid Rating	76
Annual in-state tuition	$11,330
Annual out-of-state tuition	$32,281
Room and board	$11,719
Required fees	$1,904
Books and supplies	$1,573
% frosh rec. need-based scholarship or grant aid	62
% UG rec. need-based scholarship or grant aid	57
% frosh rec. non-need-based scholarship or grant aid	1
% frosh rec. need-based self-help aid	55
% UG rec. need-based self-help aid	49
% frosh rec. any financial aid	77
% UG rec. any financial aid	63
% UG borrow to pay for school	51
Average cumulative indebtedness	$17,679

UNIVERSITY OF CALIFORNIA—SANTA BARBARA

OFFICE OF ADMISSIONS, 1210 CHEADLE HALL, SANTA BARBARA, CA 93106-2014 • ADMISSIONS: 805-893-2881 • FAX: 805-893-2676

CAMPUS LIFE

Quality of Life Rating	94
Fire Safety Rating	91
Green Rating	97
Type of school	public
Environment	city

STUDENTS

Total undergrad enrollment	19,184
% male/female	47/53
% from out of state	3
% from public high school	87
% live on campus	33
# of fraternities	17
# of sororities	18
% African American	3
% Asian	14
% Caucasian	39
% Hispanic	18
% Native American	1
% international	1
# of countries represented	72

SURVEY SAYS . . .
Athletic facilities are great
Students are friendly
Student publications are popular
Lots of beer drinking
Hard liquor is popular

ACADEMICS

Academic Rating	74
% students graduating	
within 4 years	63
% students graduating	
within 6 years	80
Calendar	quarter
Student/faculty ratio	17:1
Profs interesting rating	79
Profs accessible rating	86
Most common	
reg class size	20–29 students
Most common	
lab size	20–29 students

MOST POPULAR MAJORS
biology, economics

STUDENTS SAY ". . ."

Academics

University of California—Santa Barbara is "a beautiful, laid-back learning institute on the beach," yet students say it's much more than a great place to get a tan. This prestigious public school is "one of the best research universities in the country," which "attracts many excellent professors" as well as a cadre of dedicated students. Maybe it's the sunny weather, but "professors here are more accessible than [at] other universities," and they are "genuinely interested in helping the students learn." To offset anonymity at this large school, high-achieving students can apply to the school's College of Creative Studies (CCS), "a selective and prestigious small college within the university," which allows students to pursue advanced coursework in their declared major from day one. Within the CCS, "The class sizes are very small, the teachers are experienced and knowledgeable, [and] the program is really great for learning without pressure." Throughout the university, undergraduates have the opportunity to participate in faculty projects or to "do original research," and "The library is enormous and is connected to the libraries of each UC campus, giving students access to the second largest library system in the world." Despite a myriad of resources, prospective students should be aware that, "The UC budget crisis is causing calamity when it comes to registering for the classes you want—especially if you are a lowly freshman."

Life

"Bordered by the mountains to the north, the ocean to the south, and the college town to the west," UCSB is a veritable paradise. Here, students have the luxury of deciding, "whether they want to go surf or spend the day playing volleyball in the park." "Greek life is not as large at UC Santa Barbara as it is at other universities;" however, the school is "widely known for its massive parties" in the Isla Vista neighborhood near campus. Expressive rather than exclusive, "The parties are as varied as the students, with an emphasis on having fun and not on drugs, violence, or risky behavior. Every person, no matter who they are, can find a party that they will enjoy." In addition to nightlife, students love "exploring downtown Santa Barbara—which is so much more than just State Street—hiking around campus, kayaking in the ocean, or simply spending quality time with friends." On campus, "a cappella groups, orchestras and bands, and theater groups provide outlets for artsy students," and many students "love playing sports with other students, both in intramural games and independently organized [games]." When describing the campus environment, the word "idyllic" comes to mind. A resident student details, "I step out of my door and am only a few steps away from Carrillo, one of the three on-campus dining halls. Directly next to Carrillo is a swimming pool, and right across the way there is a community center with a piano, televisions, a pool and ping-pong table, and comfortable chairs."

Student Body

At this beautiful, beachfront school, the typical undergraduate is a "white kid from California that likes to have fun, go out on the weekends, but knows when to take his or her studies seriously." UCSB has a reputation as a party school, and you'll certainly meet a student or two who "enjoys 'ragers' and [is] failing calculus because they were too busy surfing." But, on the opposite side of the spectrum, many students (especially those in the College of Creative Studies) "are highly driven toward the field that they choose for their major." UCSB does not have the diversity you might find at University of California's urban campuses. Nonetheless, "there are people from all sorts of backgrounds, levels of income, and religions," and "Almost everybody here at UCSB is extremely friendly. Nobody is judgmental or discriminatory." Given the school's spectacular surroundings, it's not surprising that "a general commonality among many people seems to be a love of the beach or at least an appreciation for the beautiful surroundings."

UNIVERSITY OF CALIFORNIA—SANTA BARBARA

FINANCIAL AID: 805-893-2432 • E-MAIL: ADMISSIONS@SA.UCSB.EDU • WEBSITE: WWW.UCSB.EDU

THE PRINCETON REVIEW SAYS

Admissions

Very important factors considered include: Academic GPA, application essay, rigor of secondary school record, standardized test scores. *Other factors considered include:* Class rank, character/personal qualities, extracurricular activities, first generation, state residency, talent/ability, volunteer work, work experience. SAT or ACT required; ACT with writing component required. TOEFL required of all international applicants. High school diploma is required, and GED is accepted. *Academic units required:* 4 English, 3 mathematics, (2 science labs), 2 foreign language, 2 history, 1 visual/performing arts, 1 academic elective. *Academic units recommended:* 4 mathematics, (3 science labs), 3 foreign language.

Financial Aid

Students should submit: FAFSA. Regular filing deadline is May 31. The Princeton Review suggests that all financial aid forms be submitted as soon as possible after January 1. *Need-based scholarships/grants offered:* Federal Pell, SEOG, state scholarships/grants, private scholarships, school scholarship or grant aid from institutional funds. *Loan aid offered:* Direct Subsidized Stafford, Direct Unsubsidized Stafford, Direct PLUS, Federal Perkins. Applicants will be notified of awards on a rolling basis beginning March 15. Federal Work-Study Program available. Off-campus job opportunities are good.

The Inside Word

To be considered for admission to UC—Santa Barbara, students must meet the minimum "eligibility index"—a formula based on your GPA and standardized test scores. In some cases, a lower GPA may be balanced out by higher test scores, or vice versa. Nonetheless, the minimum GPA for prospective students is 3.0 for California residents and 3.4 for non-residents. Applicants to the College of Creative Studies must submit a supplemental application.

The School Says "..."
From the Admissions Office

"The University of California—Santa Barbara is a major research institution offering undergraduate and graduate education in the arts, humanities, sciences and technology, and social sciences. Large enough to have excellent facilities for study, research, and other creative activities, the campus is also small enough to foster close relationships among faculty and students. The faculty numbers more than 900. A member of the most distinguished system of public higher education in the nation, UC—Santa Barbara is committed equally to excellence in scholarship and instruction. Through the general education program, students acquire good grounding in the skills, perceptions, and methods of a variety of disciplines. In addition, because they study with a research faculty, they not only acquire basic skills and broad knowledge but also are exposed to the imagination, inventiveness, and intense concentration that scholars bring to their work. UCSB is one of sixty-two members of the prestigous Association of American Universities.

"All applicants must take the ACT plus writing or the SAT Reasoning Test. In addition, all applicants must take two SAT Subject Tests in two different subject areas. (If a math SAT Subject Test is chosen by the applicant, he/she must take the math Level 2 exam.)"

SELECTIVITY

Admissions Rating	83
# of applicants	46,671
% of applicants accepted	46
% of acceptees attending	18
# accepting a place on wait list	1,276
% admitted from wait list	99

FRESHMAN PROFILE

Range SAT Critical Reading	540–650
Range SAT Math	560–680
Range SAT Writing	540–660
Range ACT Composite	25–30
Minimum paper TOEFL	550
Minimum computer TOEFL	213
Minimum web-based TOEFL	79
Average HS GPA	3.85

DEADLINES

Regular	
Deadline	11/30
Nonfall registration?	no

APPLICANTS ALSO LOOK AT
AND OFTEN PREFER
University of California—Berkeley,
University of California—Davis

AND SOMETIMES PREFER
University of California—Los Angeles

AND RARELY PREFER
California Polytechnic State University—San Luis Obispo, University of California—Santa Cruz

FINANCIAL FACTS

Financial Aid Rating	77
Annual in-state tuition	$11,686
Annual out-of-state tuition	$34,566
Books and supplies	$1,609
% frosh rec. need-based scholarship or grant aid	51
% UG rec. need-based scholarship or grant aid	45
% frosh rec. non-need-based scholarship or grant aid	1
% frosh rec. need-based self-help aid	43
% UG rec. need-based self-help aid	38
% frosh rec. any financial aid	55
% UG rec. any financial aid	66
% UG borrow to pay for school	47
Average cumulative indebtedness	$17,768

UNIVERSITY OF CALIFORNIA—SANTA CRUZ

ADMISSIONS, COOK HOUSE, 1156 HIGH STREET, SANTA CRUZ, CA 95064 • ADMISSIONS: 831-459-4008 • FAX: 831-459-4452

CAMPUS LIFE

Quality of Life Rating	84
Fire Safety Rating	76
Green Rating	99
Type of school	public
Environment	city

STUDENTS

Total undergrad enrollment	15,666
% male/female	47/53
% from out of state	3
% from public high school	87
% live on campus	48
# of fraternities	6
# of sororities	11
% African American	3
% Asian	23
% Caucasian	45
% Hispanic	20
% Native American	1
# of countries represented	87

SURVEY SAYS . . .
Great computer facilities
Students are friendly
Students are happy
Political activism is popular

ACADEMICS

Academic Rating	85
% students graduating within 4 years	50
% students graduating within 6 years	74
Calendar	quarter
Student/faculty ratio	19:1
Profs interesting rating	74
Profs accessible rating	77
Most common reg class size	10–19 students
Most common lab size	10–19 students

MOST POPULAR MAJORS
art studies, business/commerce

STUDENTS SAY ". . ."

Academics
The University of California—Santa Cruz offers one of the nation's best combinations of "focus on scholastic endeavors in a beautiful forest setting" and is, by all accounts "a great place to live and study!" Students attribute their enthusiasm to "intelligent, eloquent, and easily accessible professors," academics that are "impressive and challenging," and fellow students who are "happy, open-minded, and a little bit crazy." This school is best suited to those who can motivate themselves in a "chill" environment and the sort of student whose motto might be, "There's no point in learning if you're too stressed to enjoy it." The sciences are "world-class" at UCSC, and the school also boasts "one of the finest engineering programs in the UCs" as well as "a great marine biology program." While the "professors all do research," what sets them apart from those at the typical research-driven university is that "they are very passionate about their subject even when teaching undergrads," and they "also tend to be quite approachable despite having large class sizes and allow students to attend their office hours for extra help." The school also offers undergrads "a lot of opportunities in terms of internships, research opportunities, job opportunities, and networking." "There's a focus on undergraduate study" here, one student contentedly reports.

Life
Undergrads rave about the "take-your-breath-away beauty" of the heavily wooded UCSC campus; one says it's like "taking paths through the forest that resemble Endor only to find a lecture hall at the end." Another adds, "Almost every time my friends and I walk around outside, someone comments on how lucky we are to be surrounded by such beauty. Whether the silvery ocean, the fog in the trees, the wind in the fields of green, the wildlife such as deer, raccoons, squirrels, newts, etc., it all comes together like a painting." The school's setting means "there is much to do recreationally, such as hiking, biking, swimming, trail running, tree climbing, or rock-climbing. You can walk in any direction and find some hiking trail that leads to some other part of the forest." Students note that, "It is also nice to get off campus from time to time and enjoy the city of Santa Cruz. Downtown is lively and usually has something fun going on such as local farmer's markets and cultural festivals." Ambitious students "may head to San Jose or San Francisco on the weekend for a more rowdy bar or club scene." Both cities are "readily accessible via public transportation." The party scene on and off campus consists of "mostly decentralized, smaller parties, due to the near-absence of fraternities and sororities." It also includes "a lot of drug use" that is limited to "specific locations" and "easy to avoid" for abstaining students.

Student Body
"The 'stereotypical' Santa Cruz student is a hippie," and the school certainly has its fair share of those "The typical student is very hardworking until about 9:00 P.M., when hikes to the forest are common practice and returning to your room smelling like reefer is acceptable," one undergrad explains—but "there are many different types who attend UCSC." "It seems that almost every student here has a personal passion, whether it be an activism or cause of some sort, etc.," one student writes. "Everyone is so...alive." "Most are liberal," and there's a definite propensity for earnestness; it's the sort of place where students declare without irony that they "not only possess a great respect for one another but the world and life in general. The world to an average UCSC student is a sacred and beautiful place to be shared and enjoyed by all its inhabitants."

University of California—Santa Cruz

Financial Aid: 831-459-2963 • E-mail: ADMISSIONS@UCSC.EDU • Website: WWW.ADMISSIONS.UCSC.EDU

THE PRINCETON REVIEW SAYS

Admissions

Very important factors considered include: Academic GPA, application essay, rigor of secondary school record, standardized test scores, geographical residence, state residency. *Important factors considered include:* Class rank, character/personal qualities, extracurricular activities, first generation, geographical residence, talent/ability. *Other factors considered include:* Volunteer work, work experience. SAT or ACT required; ACT with writing component required. TOEFL required of all international applicants. High school diploma is required, and GED is accepted. *Academic units required:* 4 English, 3 mathematics, 2 science (2 science labs), 2 foreign language, 1 social studies, 1 history, 1 visual/performing arts, 1 academic elective. *Academic units recommended:* 4 English, 4 mathematics, 3 science (3 science labs), 3 foreign language.

Financial Aid

Students should submit: FAFSA. Regular filing deadline is March 2. The Princeton Review suggests that all financial aid forms be submitted as soon as possible after January 1. *Need-based scholarships/grants offered:* Federal Pell, SEOG, state scholarships/grants, private scholarships, school scholarship or grant aid from institutional funds. *Loan aid offered:* Direct Subsidized Stafford, Direct Unsubsidized Stafford, Direct PLUS, Federal Perkins. Applicants will be notified of awards on a rolling basis beginning April 1. Federal Work-Study Program available. Off-campus job opportunities are excellent.

The Inside Word

UC—Santa Cruz scores all applicants on a 9,200-point scale encompassing fourteen criteria. High school GPA accounts for 4,400 of those points; standardized test scores, 2,400 points; up to 700 points for academic accomplishment within life experiences; and lower point amounts in such areas as special talents, achievement, awards, geographic location, and outstanding performance in a particular academic discipline. UCSC's acceptance rate belies the high caliber of applicants it regularly receives.

THE SCHOOL SAYS "..."

From the Admissions Office

"UC—Santa Cruz students, faculty, and researchers are working together to make a world of difference. Within our extraordinary educational community, students participate in the creation of new knowledge, new technologies, and new forms of expressing and understanding cultures. From helping teachers improve their skills to building more efficient solar cells and working to save endangered sea turtles, our focus is on improving our planet and the lives of all its inhabitants. The academic programs at UCSC are challenging and rigorous, and many of them are in newer fields that focus on interdisciplinary thinking. At UCSC, undergraduates conduct and publish research, working closely with faculty on leading-edge projects. Taking advantage of the campus' proximity to centers of industry and innovation such as the Monterey Bay National Marine Sanctuary and Silicon Valley, many students at UC—Santa Cruz take part in fieldwork and internships that complement their studies and provide practical experience in their fields."

"All frosh applicants must take the ACT assessment plus the ACT writing test or the new SAT Reasoning Test."

SELECTIVITY

Admissions Rating	95
# of applicants	27,658
% of applicants accepted	65
% of acceptees attending	18
# accepting a place on wait list	592
% admitted from wait list	0

FRESHMAN PROFILE

Range SAT Critical Reading	500–630
Range SAT Math	520–640
Range SAT Writing	510–620
Range ACT Composite	22–27
Minimum paper TOEFL	550
Minimum computer TOEFL	220
Minimum web-based TOEFL	80
Average HS GPA	3.61
% graduated top 10% of class	96
% graduated top 25% of class	100
% graduated top 50% of class	100

DEADLINES

Regular	
Deadline	11/30
Notification	3/15
Nonfall registration?	yes

APPLICANTS ALSO LOOK AT

AND OFTEN PREFER
University of California—Berkeley,
University of California—Los Angeles

AND SOMETIMES PREFER
University of California—Santa Barbara, University of California—Davis, University of California—San Diego

AND RARELY PREFER
University of California—Merced,
University of California—Riverside

FINANCIAL FACTS

Financial Aid Rating	78
Annual out-of-state tuition	$22,878
Room and board	$14,610
Required fees	$12,447
Books and supplies	$1,407
% frosh rec. need-based scholarship or grant aid	53
% UG rec. need-based scholarship or grant aid	49
% frosh rec. need-based self-help aid	52
% UG rec. need-based self-help aid	48
% frosh rec. any financial aid	59
% UG rec. any financial aid	56
% UG borrow to pay for school	53
Average cumulative indebtedness	$16,024

UNIVERSITY OF CENTRAL FLORIDA

PO Box 160111, Orlando, FL 32816-0111 • Admissions: 407-823-3000 • Fax: 407-823-5625

CAMPUS LIFE

Quality of Life Rating	91
Fire Safety Rating	83
Green Rating	92
Type of school	public
Environment	city

STUDENTS

Total undergrad enrollment	47,652
% male/female	46/54
% from out of state	5
% from public high school	82
% live on campus	15
# of fraternities	11
# of sororities	9
% African American	10
% Asian	6
% Caucasian	64
% Hispanic	17
% Native American	1
% international	1
# of countries represented	167

SURVEY SAYS . . .

Great computer facilities
Athletic facilities are great
Great off-campus food
Student publications are popular
Student government is popular

ACADEMICS

Academic Rating	70
% students graduating within 4 years	34
% students graduating within 6 years	63
Calendar	semester
Student/faculty ratio	31:1
Profs interesting rating	69
Profs accessible rating	71
Most common reg class size	20–29 students
Most common lab size	20–29 students

MOST POPULAR MAJORS

engineering, business, hospitality
management

STUDENTS SAY ". . ."

Academics

The University of Central Florida is "a growing school with a solid academic image." "Its reputation needs to catch up with how it actually is," urges a junior. The engineering and science programs are renowned, and students laud the hospitality, management, and business programs. UCF undergrads also benefit from "awesome technology" all over campus. The Internet is everywhere. Much like the surrounding city of Orlando, UCF has experienced explosive growth in recent decades. Today, UCF is really quite gargantuan. "It's one of the largest schools in the nation." "The massive size of UCF can be intimidating for students who need a personal approach to higher education." "It is easy to feel a bit lost," admits a freshman. Classes are large, and most note that professors can be "hit-or-miss." "Some professors are amazing" and "willing to go out of their way to make sure you understand the lectures." Others "just stand in front of the class and read off PowerPoint slides." The foreign professors, while "highly specialized," can "be hard to understand." On the bright side, upper-level courses are "fun and taught by professors who are good and know what they're doing." "The administration seems to genuinely care but, because there are so many students, it is hard for them to really do anything about your concerns." Registration is pretty awful. "When you get to the end of your degree, you better plan out your schedule carefully because there are a lot of important classes that are only offered every three semesters," advises one student. In terms of initials, students used to say that "UCF" stood for "U Can't Finish." Now, it stands for "Under Construction Forever," but most don't mind "because the newer facilities are beautiful!"

Life

UCF boasts a "very scenic," "comfortable" campus. "Everything is relatively close together," which is great when it comes to getting to your next class, but not so much when parking your car. "No matter how many garages UCF builds, somehow parking still sucks." Socially, if you're bored here, you just aren't trying very hard. "The campus organizes a wide variety of social events." "We have a ridiculous number of clubs and organizations," boasts a sophomore. "There are about a million events going on at any given time." There is almost every imaginable intramural sport. There is "a huge three-story gym" that features "every kind of workout machine." "Football game days are amazing" as students root for the perennially "up-and-coming" team. Fraternities and sororities are here too, but they "constitute a minority of the culture." UCF's location is a big hit with students. Hot, sunny Orlando is "a large, thriving city," but the area around UCF has "the feel of a college town." "If you live in the dorms your first year, you will definitely get the typical college experience." The "many bars with dance floors around campus" are "a breeding ground for drunken debauchery." They "get packed every night." "Downtown Orlando is a different story, which "provides a nice refuge for upperclassmen trying to break away."

Student Body

"The only real thing that many students share in common is sandals," observes a business major. "At a given time, seventy-five percent of the campus is probably wearing sandals." UCF students hail overwhelmingly from in-state, too. And "the girls are insanely pretty." Otherwise, "it is difficult to generalize" about some 42,000 undergrads. "There is no possible way to describe a typical student." Students tend to have "their own set of friends, activities, and experiences at UCF." "This is a melting pot of culture," says one student. "Walking around campus you see a little bit of every culture, every race, and every ethnicity." "There are strong subcultures for the minorities" and ages, ranging from students "right out of high school" and those "older in years [who] are looking to further their careers."

FINANCIAL AID: 407-823-2827 • E-MAIL: ADMISSION@UCF.EDU • WEBSITE: WWW.UCF.EDU

THE PRINCETON REVIEW SAYS

Admissions

Very important factors considered include: Academic GPA, rigor of secondary school record, standardized test scores. *Important factors considered include:* Application essay, recommendation(s). *Other factors considered include:* Class rank, alumni/ae relation, character/personal qualities, extracurricular activities, first generation, geographical residence, interview, level of applicant's interest, state residency, talent/ability, volunteer work, work experience. SAT or ACT required; ACT with writing component required. TOEFL required of all international applicants. High school diploma is required, and GED is accepted. *Academic units required:* 4 English, 4 mathematics, 3 science (2 science labs), 2 foreign language, 3 social studies, 2 academic elective.

Financial Aid

Students should submit: FAFSA. Regular filing deadline is June 30. The Princeton Review suggests that all financial aid forms be submitted as soon as possible after January 1. *Need-based scholarships/grants offered:* Federal Pell, SEOG, state scholarships/grants, private scholarships, school scholarship or grant aid from institutional funds. *Loan aid offered:* Direct Subsidized Stafford, Direct Unsubsidized Stafford, Direct PLUS, Federal Perkins. Applicants will be notified of awards on a rolling basis beginning March 15. Federal Work-Study Program available.

Inside Word

As is the case at many state schools, it's all a numbers game here; students aren't required to interview or submit essays. It's also worth noting that when calculating your GPA, which is a very important criterion for admission, the Admissions Committee weights honors, AP, dual enrollment, and International Baccalaureate academic classes more heavily than regular classes.

THE SCHOOL SAYS "..."

From the Admissions Office

"The University of Central Florida offers competitive advantages to its student body. We're committed to teaching, providing advisement, and academic support services for all students. Our undergraduates have access to state-of-the-art wireless buildings, high-tech classrooms, research labs, web-based classes, and an undergraduate research and mentoring program.

"Our Career Services professionals help students gain practical experiences at NASA, schools, hospitals, high-tech companies, local municipalities, and the entertainment industry. With an international focus to our curricula and research programs, we enroll international students from 126 nations. Our study abroad programs and other study and research opportunities include agreements with ninety-eight institutions and thirty-six countries.

"UCF's 1,415-acre campus provides a safe and serene setting for learning, with natural lakes and woodlands. The bustle of Orlando lies a short distance away: the pro sport teams, the Kennedy Space Center, film studios, Walt Disney World, Universal Orlando, Sea World, and sandy beaches are all nearby.

"Applicants are required to take the SAT (or the ACT with the writing section). We will use a student's best scores from either test."

SELECTIVITY

Admissions Rating	90
# of applicants	32,876
% of applicants accepted	46
% of acceptees attending	40
# accepting a place on wait list	367
% admitted from wait list	28

FRESHMAN PROFILE

Range SAT Critical Reading	560–650
Range SAT Math	590–670
Range SAT Writing	530–620
Range ACT Composite	25–28
Minimum paper TOEFL	550
Minimum computer TOEFL	213
Minimum web-based TOEFL	80
Minimum IELTS	65
Average HS GPA	3.80
% graduated top 10% of class	33
% graduated top 25% of class	72
% graduated top 50% of class	96

DEADLINES

Regular	
Priority	1/1
Deadline	5/1
Notification	10/1
Nonfall registration?	yes

FINANCIAL FACTS

Financial Aid Rating	70
Annual in-state tuition	$5,020
Annual out-of-state tuition	$20,500
Room and board	$8,765
Books and supplies	$924
% frosh rec. need-based scholarship or grant aid	29
% UG rec. need-based scholarship or grant aid	31
% frosh rec. non-need-based scholarship or grant aid	59
% UG rec. non-need-based scholarship or grant aid	38
% frosh rec. need-based self-help aid	21
% UG rec. need-based self-help aid	29
% frosh rec. any financial aid	95
% UG rec. any financial aid	81
% UG borrow to pay for school	41
Average cumulative indebtedness	$17,044

UNIVERSITY OF CHARLESTON

2300 MacCorkle Ave SE, Charleston, WV 25304 • Admissions: 304-357-4750 • Fax: 304-357-4781

CAMPUS LIFE

Quality of Life Rating	79
Fire Safety Rating	80
Green Rating	66
Type of school	private
Environment	city

STUDENTS

Total undergrad enrollment	1,119
% male/female	41/59
% from out of state	37
% live on campus	61
# of fraternities	2
# of sororities	3
% African American	10
% Asian	1
% Caucasian	55
% Hispanic	1
% international	12
# of countries represented	35

SURVEY SAYS . . .

Diverse student types on campus
Students get along with local community
Low cost of living
Very little drug use

ACADEMICS

Academic Rating	72
% students graduating within 4 years	36
% students graduating within 6 years	43
Calendar	semester
Student/faculty ratio	16:1
Profs interesting rating	78
Profs accessible rating	81
Most common reg class size	10–19 students
Most common lab size	fewer than 10 students

MOST POPULAR MAJORS

biology, business administration and management, health services

STUDENTS SAY ". . ."

Academics

University of Charleston is a perfect place to prepare for life in the real world while benefiting from the friendliness and comfort of a small college environment. A private school in West Virginia's capital city, UC offers twenty-two undergraduate majors, including interior design, education, pre-pharmacy, science, and nursing. A sophomore enthuses, "I had high expectations, and those have been met. My dream [is] to attend medical school, and UC and the staff is there to make it happen." For those who don't have graduate programs in mind, the "school is located in an area where internships are plentiful and jobs are easy to find. Our job placement percentages are nearly at 100 percent every year." With about 1,000 undergraduates, class sizes are uniformly small, and "the professors are very open to interaction with students outside the classroom." You'll never feel like a face in the crowd at this small school, where "professors and administrators are always on hand and get to know you on a personal basis." Despite their accessibility, some feel that administrators "don't listen to students' concerns."

Life

Even though it is a small campus community, everybody at UC "finds ways to have their own fun, whether it comes in the form of playing video games, watching television sitcom reruns, or dabbling into an alcoholic beverage. It's all about individual tastes and preferences." Students lament the fact that "Charleston is a small town that usually stops functioning at about 8:00." Even so, "There is plenty to do on weekends," both on and off campus. In their free time, UC undergraduates "go shopping at the mall, watch movies, and go bowling, and sometimes we go dancing." For penny-pinching college students, "several local bars and dance clubs offer discount prices to UC students, and UC sponsored sports games and social events are always free to students." The Student Life department also offers activities "like dance lessons and Zumba classes." In addition, "many have on-campus and off-campus jobs" to help offset the high price of their educations.

Student Body

The typical UC student is "smart, social, and friendly;" invested in the campus community; and "truly cares about their academic success." Sports are a big part of campus life, and most students are "very involved throughout the university through various clubs, activities, or athletics." Students hail from more than thirty states, though predominantly from West Virginia and Ohio. There is also a smattering of international students from China, Nigeria, India, and the United Kingdom, among other countries. UC offers financial aid and scholarship packages (including athletic scholarships); however, tuition is pricey, and "students are typically from the middle- or upper-class." At the same time, there are also a "growing number of single parents and older students." No matter what your background, "ninety-eight percent of students fit in here at the University of Charleston and feel welcomed by the university residents and staff."

FINANCIAL AID: 304-357-4759 • E-MAIL: ADMISSIONS@UCWV.EDU • WEBSITE: WWW.UCWV.EDU

THE PRINCETON REVIEW SAYS

Admissions

Very important factors considered include: Academic GPA, standardized test scores. *Important factors considered include:* Class rank, rigor of secondary school record, alumni/ae relation, extracurricular activities. *Other factors considered include:* Application essay, recommendation(s), character/personal qualities, first generation, interview, level of applicant's interest, talent/ability, volunteer work, work experience. SAT or ACT required; ACT with or without writing component accepted. TOEFL required of all international applicants. High school diploma is required, and GED is accepted. *Academic units recommended:* 4 English, 3 mathematics, 3 science, 1 foreign language, 3 social studies, 2 history.

Financial Aid

Students should submit: FAFSA. Regular filing deadline is March 1. The Princeton Review suggests that all financial aid forms be submitted as soon as possible after January 1. *Need-based scholarships/grants offered:* Federal Pell, SEOG, state scholarships/grants, private scholarships, school scholarship or grant aid from institutional funds. *Loan aid offered: Federal Direct Loans,* Federal Perkins, Nursing Loans. Applicants will be notified of awards on a rolling basis beginning March 1. Federal Work-Study Program available. Off-campus job opportunities are good.

The Inside Word

With its nationally recognized "Learning Your Way" curriculum, intimate class sizes, and high graduate placement results, The University of Charleston is looking for students with the desire to excel in a small private university environment. Successful applicants reflect a commitment to personalizing their own education and a motivation to excel that exceeds just a competitive high school record. The University of Charleston reviews completed applications on a continuous or rolling basis.

THE SCHOOL SAYS ". . ."

From the Admissions Office

"Since our founding in 1888, the University of Charleston has been providing a dynamic educational experience in a welcoming environment that nurtures the strengths of each student to help them reach their highest potential. We are consistently ranked among the top regional colleges in the South, and almost one third of our graduates earn their degrees in less than four years.

"Our mission is to educate each student for a life of productive work, enlightened living, and community involvement. Our educational program focuses on 'Learning Your Way,' which means each student is allowed to demonstrate what they have learned in order to earn the credits necessary for graduation. This curriculum is a unique blend of learning outcomes, student needs, course delivery, experiential education, and continuous quality improvement.

"Our forty-acre campus is located directly across from the State Capitol complex along the banks of the Kanawha River in the beautiful city of Charleston, West Virginia. This location offers students the best of both worlds, with all the amenities of a major metropolitan community plus the renowned outdoor recreational attractions found in the Mountain State. Students love our new fitness center and modern residence halls. On-campus living options range from traditional double, single, and suite styles, to new two-, three-, and four-bedroom apartments.

"Because the university believes that students learn from their involvement in the community and campus activities, students are strongly encouraged to participate in one or more of the forty co-curricular organizations, and to get involved in community service both on campus and in the Charleston area. The UC athletic program is one of the university's most valuable assets with fourteen men's and women's teams competing in Division II of the NCAA."

SELECTIVITY

Admissions Rating	79
# of applicants	1,780
% of applicants accepted	56
% of acceptees attending	34

FRESHMAN PROFILE

Range SAT Critical Reading	430–520
Range SAT Math	450–550
Range ACT Composite	20–25
Minimum paper TOEFL	550
Minimum computer TOEFL	213
Minimum web-based TOEFL	79
Average HS GPA	3.35
% graduated top 10% of class	17
% graduated top 25% of class	44
% graduated top 50% of class	74

DEADLINES

Regular	
Notification	10/1
Nonfall registration?	yes

FINANCIAL FACTS

Financial Aid Rating	84
Annual tuition	$25,000
Room and board	$8,800
Books and supplies	$1,500
% frosh rec. need-based scholarship or grant aid	80
% UG rec. need-based scholarship or grant aid	59
% frosh rec. non-need-based scholarship or grant aid	80
% UG rec. non-need-based scholarship or grant aid	73
% frosh rec. need-based self-help aid	82
% UG rec. need-based self-help aid	81
% frosh rec. any financial aid	98
% UG rec. any financial aid	95
% UG borrow to pay for school	91
Average cumulative indebtedness	$23,250

THE UNIVERSITY OF CHICAGO

1101 EAST FIFTY-EIGHTH STREET, ROSENWALD HALL, SUITE 105, CHICAGO, IL 60637 • ADMISSIONS: 773-702-8650 • FAX: 773-702-4199

CAMPUS LIFE

Quality of Life Rating	77
Fire Safety Rating	82
Green Rating	86
Type of school	private
Environment	metropolis

STUDENTS

Total undergrad enrollment	5,225
% male/female	51/49
% from out of state	78
% from public high school	64
# of fraternities	10
# of sororities	3
% African American	5
% Asian	16
% Caucasian	43
% Hispanic	8
% international	9
# of countries represented	71

SURVEY SAYS . . .
No one cheats
Lab facilities are great
Great computer facilities
Great library
Athletic facilities are great
School is well-run
Students love Chicago, IL
Dorms are like palaces

ACADEMICS

Academic Rating	98
% students graduating within 4 years	87
% students graduating within 6 years	92
Calendar	quarter
Student/faculty ratio	7:1
Profs interesting rating	83
Profs accessible rating	81
Most common reg class size	fewer than 10 students
Most common lab size	10–19 students

MOST POPULAR MAJORS
biology, economics, political science

STUDENTS SAY ". . ."

Academics

"Dedication to enriching the 'life of the mind' is palpable" at the "incomparable" University of Chicago. It is home to "the best economics department in the country," and one of the best (and most monstrously ugly) main libraries on Earth. UChicago students believe that "no university offers a better academic experience," and there is "an unexpectedly vibrant school spirit that comes not from athletics, but [a] shared academic involvement." Undergraduates must complete an intense, "interdisciplinary" core curriculum that "teaches them how to think about literature and philosophy and science." The core is "rigorous" and "you will spend about a third of your time here on it. But it's [also] fantastic, and you come out an incredibly well-rounded thinker with opinions on a wide variety of subjects." Naturally, "courses are tough." "Once you're out of the fire," though, "you realize how much more enriched you've become intellectually, with respect [as] to how to learn and…knowledge itself." Professors at UChicago "are the best in the world" and are "real celebrities in their fields of study," but they "make every effort to help every student who asks." Still, "there are duds." "Not everyone with the intelligence to do amazing research is capable of teaching." The "incredibly supportive" administration "takes pains to engage the entire campus in a sort of collective, community-wide conversation…They bring in all sorts of speakers, allow student groups almost absolute freedom, and are very supportive of student initiatives."

Life

The quarter system "makes for a particularly fast-paced" schedule. "We wear t-shirts that say 'UChicago: Where fun comes to die,' and we're proud of it," explains a first-year student. "Don't come here if you don't plan to work very hard," an economics major warns. "We spend a large chunk of our time studying and should be studying much of the time that we are not." However, according to one student, "As much as a lot of people complain about the extremely rigorous academics at this school, we all secretly love it or we wouldn't be here." And "contrary to popular belief," students "certainly do know how to have fun." There are "concerts, plays, movies," and "tons of truly brilliant events on campus." Students also spend a lot of time "just talking" with "fascinating" classmates "who can hold their own on any topic under the sun." "The frat party scene is not much at all compared to other schools, but it's still there. Room parties with extended friends and random people from the building are usually more popular." While "scorn for the lovely neighborhood" surrounding the campus is "exceedingly common," downtown Chicago is "very accessible." The city "is a huge asset and resource," "whether it's for an internship," "a night out," or "just a day away from campus."

Student Body

Students at UChicago are "intense," "opinionated," "engaged with the world around them," and "somewhat zany." "Most everyone has a quirk," a senior reports. Without question, "the popular stereotype" of the UChicago student is "a nerdy, socially awkward person." Living up to the hype are an abundance of students "religiously dedicated to academic performance" and "a bunch of strange people," "usually clutching some fantastic book." However, "there aren't as many extremely strange and nerdy students as there have been in the past," and many say the stereotype is increasingly inaccurate. "There are loads of people who are fascinating," a sophomore writes, including many who are "cool and attractive." There are "artists, communists, fashionistas, activists." "Everyone who is at the University of Chicago considers themselves at the best possible university," concludes one student. "It's a self-selecting group," and most people are "happy to be here." UChicago students "look down on other schools, particularly the Ivies."

FINANCIAL AID: 773-702-8666 • WEBSITE: WWW.UCHICAGO.EDU

THE PRINCETON REVIEW SAYS

Admissions

Very important factors considered include: Application essay, recommendation(s), rigor of secondary school record, character/personal qualities, talent/ability. *Important factors considered include:* Academic GPA, class rank, extracurricular activities, volunteer work. *Other factors considered include:* Standardized test scores, alumni/ae relation, first generation, interview, level of applicant's interest, racial/ethnic status, work experience. SAT or ACT required; ACT with or without writing component accepted. TOEFL required of all international applicants. High school diploma or equivalent isn't required. *Academic units recommended:* 4 English, 4 mathematics, 4 science, 3 foreign language, 2 social studies, 2 history.

Financial Aid

Students should submit: FAFSA, institution's own financial aid form, CSS/Financial Aid PROFILE. Regular filing deadline is February 1. The Princeton Review suggests that all financial aid forms be submitted as soon as possible after January 1. *Need-based scholarships/grants offered:* Federal Pell, SEOG, state scholarships/grants, private scholarships, school scholarship or grant aid from institutional funds. *Loan aid offered:* Federal Perkins.

The Inside Word

The University of Chicago now uses the common application. Essay topics will continue to be of the thought provoking "uncommon" type, keeping the spirit of fun and inquiry in the application's supplement. People here dwell on deep thoughts and big ideas. In your application, you'll need to demonstrate outstanding grades in the tough courses and, most of all, that you will fit in with a bunch of thinkers. Interviews are recommended but are not required.

THE SCHOOL SAYS "..."

From the Admissions Office

"The University of Chicago is a place where talented young people—writers, politicians, activists, artists, mathematicians, and scientists—come to learn in a setting that rewards interesting thought and prizes initiative and creativity. UChicago is also a place where collegiate life is urban, yet friendly and open, and free of empty traditionalism and snobbishness. UChicago is the right choice for students who know that they would thrive in an intimate classroom setting. Classes at UChicago are small, emphasizing discussion with faculty members whose research is always testing the limits of their chosen fields. Students at UChicago take chances—delighting professors when they pursue a topic on their own for the fun of it—and display an articulate voice in papers and in discussion. Their good times include the normal collegiate good times— a highly successful Division III sports program, small but active Greek life, forty student theatrical productions a year, a rich musical life—and the extraordinary opportunities a major city offers our students, who enjoy the politics, music, theater, commerce, architecture, and neighborhood life of Chicago."

SELECTIVITY

Admissions Rating	99
# of applicants	19,340
% of applicants accepted	19
% of acceptees attending	38
# accepting a place on wait list	2,892
% admitted from wait list	3

FRESHMAN PROFILE

Range SAT Critical Reading	700–780
Range SAT Math	700–780
Range SAT Writing	690–770
Range ACT Composite	30–34
Minimum paper TOEFL	600
Minimum computer TOEFL	250
Minimum web-based TOEFL	104
Average HS GPA	3.79
% graduated top 10% of class	89
% graduated top 25% of class	98
% graduated top 50% of class	100

DEADLINES

Early action	
Deadline	11/1
Notification	mid-December
Regular	
Deadline	1/3
Nonfall registration?	no

APPLICANTS ALSO LOOK AT

AND OFTEN PREFER
Harvard College, Northwestern University, University of Pennsylvania, Yale University

AND SOMETIMES PREFER
University of California—Berkeley, Washington University in St. Louis

AND RARELY PREFER
Georgetown University, New York University

FINANCIAL FACTS

Financial Aid Rating	94
Annual tuition	$40,188
Room and board	$12,153
% frosh rec. need-based scholarship or grant aid	46
% UG rec. need-based scholarship or grant aid	47
% frosh rec. need-based self-help aid	35
% UG rec. need-based self-help aid	39
% frosh rec. any financial aid	48
% UG rec. any financial aid	46
% UG borrow to pay for school	50
Average cumulative indebtedness	$22,359

UNIVERSITY OF CINCINNATI

OFFICE OF ADMISSIONS, PO BOX 210091, CINCINNATI, OH 45221-0091 • ADMISSIONS: 513-556-1100 • FAX: 513-556-1105

CAMPUS LIFE

Quality of Life Rating	71
Fire Safety Rating	93
Green Rating	96
Type of school	public
Environment	metropolis

STUDENTS

Total undergrad enrollment	22,007
% male/female	49/51
% from out of state	10
% live on campus	20
# of fraternities	23
# of sororities	10
% African American	9
% Asian	3
% Caucasian	78
% Hispanic	2
% international	2
# of countries represented	111

SURVEY SAYS . . .
Great computer facilities
Athletic facilities are great
Diverse student types on campus

ACADEMICS

Academic Rating	65
% students graduating within 4 years	21
% students graduating within 6 years	56
Calendar	quarter
Student/faculty ratio	17:1
Profs interesting rating	71
Profs accessible rating	70
Most common reg class size	20–29 students

MOST POPULAR MAJORS
marketing, speech communication
and rhetoric

STUDENTS SAY ". . ."

Academics
The University of Cincinnati "offers students a balance of educational excellence and real-world experience" on an expansive campus comprised of twelve separate colleges. Students agree it's "a large school with many great programs and infinite opportunities that still retains the feeling of a small university." Many have praise for the "cooperative education program that gives students a real edge in the job market" by allowing them the opportunity to pursue competitive internships while enrolled. Students also feel confident that "UC provides excellent opportunities outside of the classroom to make me successful post-graduation." As one student puts it, "The University of Cincinnati is not only known for its great academics, but for all of the incredible opportunities students have including cooperative education, on-campus activities and clubs, along with athletics and one of the most beautiful campuses in the world." The university's size assures that there are "a wide variety of majors to choose from," and students name the Conservatory of Music, the School of Architecture and Design, and the engineering programs as stand outs. Nevertheless, many carp, "The school could be a little bit better at communicating" and say the "registration process is terrible." Overall, students feel that "the professors here have so much life experience in what they are teaching. It makes me trust and respect them more," and "Advisors have been helpful." However, they note, "The professors are as diverse as the classes offered here," which means that, "like anything else, there is variation. Some are horrible, and some are fantastic."

Life
It's common for students to remark on the "ample green spaces, [and] innovative architectural designs" that make up the "beautiful campus" at UC. One student explains, "The University of Cincinnati has rewarding educational programs and a beautiful urban campus with many opportunities to stay involved. What more can I ask for?" Although most feel that "campus is very safe," some note, "As soon as you step off of campus, it's a different story." However, many acknowledge, "The school does work hard on maintaining a safe environment for us to live and work in." The majority of students describe campus as having a "fun atmosphere" that makes "UC great" but are divided on the topic of university-sponsored activities. Some think the administration should provide "more afterschool activities," while others believe "UC offers a million and one activities for students to partake in during school and on the weekend. Friday Night Live is an extremely popular program offering awesome activities that don't involve alcohol or drugs." A significant portion of undergraduates are from Cincinnati and point out that UC "is a huge commuter school, so many of the students do things all over the city." However, all agree, "People are very passionate about sports here and have great school spirit." A common campus exclamation is "go Bearcats!!"

Student Body
The most common sentiment from UC students is that "there really isn't a typical student." Although "many students are from Cincinnati," most agree, "UC has students from all walks of life, which makes it extremely diverse and very interesting." While many say, "Students can find their niche, be it in LGBTQ groups, ethnic groups, or academic intercollegiate groups," some reveal that although "students fit in well…racial cliques are obvious around campus." However, all concur that the student body is "outgoing and expressive" and proclaim that "students come together to work on issues they care about such as sustainability." Most UC students can be found in a "sweatshirt, [and] jeans…[with a] coffee in hand," and students like to point out that "many students work as well so they seem to be more 'grounded' and well-rounded." Speaking about the student body, one UC student declares, "The majority are young sports fans that like to party, but being a research school there are some academic heavyweights as well." The consensus seems to be that "students at UC are open-minded, and everyone can find a place to fit in."

FINANCIAL AID: 513-556-1000 • E-MAIL: TRANSFER@UC.EDU • WEBSITE: WWW.ADMISSIONS.UC.EDU

THE PRINCETON REVIEW SAYS

Admissions

Very important factors considered include: Academic GPA, class rank, rigor of secondary school record, standardized test scores. *Other factors considered include:* Application essay, extracurricular activities. SAT or ACT required; ACT with writing component required. TOEFL required of all international applicants. High school diploma is required, and GED is accepted. *Academic units required:* 4 English, 3 mathematics, 2 science, 2 foreign language, 2 social studies, 2 academic elective. *Academic units recommended:* 4 mathematics, 3 science, 1 history.

Financial Aid

Students should submit: FAFSA. The Princeton Review suggests that all financial aid forms be submitted as soon as possible after January 1. *Need-based scholarships/grants offered:* Federal Pell, SEOG, state scholarships/grants, private scholarships, school scholarship or grant aid from institutional funds, United Negro College Fund, Federal Nursing Scholarships. *Loan aid offered:* Direct Subsidized Stafford, Direct Unsubsidized Stafford, Direct PLUS, Federal Perkins, Federal Nursing Loans, state loans, university loans from institutional funds. Applicants will be notified of awards on a rolling basis beginning March 26. Federal Work-Study Program available. Off-campus job opportunities are excellent.

The Inside Word

The UC offers hundreds of undergraduate majors and stresses the importance of exploring the specific admission criteria for your program of choice. Prospective students are reminded to work hard while still in high school, with admissions representative saying to hone your GPA from ninth grade on because "it counts!" UC seeks a student who shows evidence of self-reflection. Ideal candidates will exhibit this self-awareness through participation in extracurricular activities that speak to who they are, not to what they think an admissions board wants. Campus visits are strongly suggested.

THE SCHOOL SAYS ". . ."

From the Admissions Office

"Remarkable architecture, park-like open spaces, engaging student tour guides, and a welcoming admissions staff make the University of Cincinnati a must-visit destination. UC campus has been transformed over the past ten years and is drawing national and international attention for blending student life, learning, research, and recreation in a unique urban environment.

"Freshman application materials include high school transcripts, test scores, a personal statement, and a list of co-curricular activities. Some academic programs require additional materials.

"Sign up for a visit, become a Bearcat VIP, and apply online. Information about all UC majors is linked from the website. We also have Tuesday-night online chat sessions for students and parents. Nothing beats a visit, however, for assessing how well you'll fit in here.

"Either the SAT or ACT is required for students applying to bachelor's degree programs; the ACT writing component is required. SAT Subject Tests are not required."

SELECTIVITY

Admissions Rating	82
# of applicants	16,972
% of applicants accepted	62
% of acceptees attending	37

FRESHMAN PROFILE

Range SAT Critical Reading	500–620
Range SAT Math	510–640
Range SAT Writing	490–610
Range ACT Composite	22–27
Minimum paper TOEFL	515
Average HS GPA	3.44
% graduated top 10% of class	22
% graduated top 25% of class	51
% graduated top 50% of class	84

DEADLINES

Regular	
Priority	2/1
Deadline	7/1
Notification	10/1
Nonfall registration?	yes

FINANCIAL FACTS

Financial Aid Rating	69
Annual in-state tuition	$8,493
Annual out-of-state tuition	$23,016
Room and board	$9,702
Required fees	$1,572
Books and supplies	$1,308
% frosh rec. need-based scholarship or grant aid	28
% UG rec. need-based scholarship or grant aid	29
% frosh rec. non-need-based scholarship or grant aid	29
% UG rec. non-need-based scholarship or grant aid	20
% frosh rec. need-based self-help aid	11
% UG rec. need-based self-help aid	10
% frosh rec. any financial aid	81
% UG rec. any financial aid	75
% UG borrow to pay for school	66
Average cumulative indebtedness	$26,462

UNIVERSITY OF COLORADO—BOULDER

552 UCB, BOULDER, CO 80309-0552 • ADMISSIONS: 303-492-6301 • FAX: 303-492-7115

CAMPUS LIFE

Quality of Life Rating	79
Fire Safety Rating	87
Green Rating	91
Type of school	public
Environment	city

STUDENTS

Total undergrad enrollment	25,782
% male/female	53/47
% from out of state	33
% live on campus	24
# of fraternities	19
# of sororities	15
% African American	2
% Asian	6
% Caucasian	77
% Hispanic	7
% Native American	1
% international	2
# of countries represented	98

SURVEY SAYS . . .

Great computer facilities
Athletic facilities are great
Students love Boulder, CO
Great off-campus food
Everyone loves the
Colorado Buffaloes
Lots of beer drinking
Hard liquor is popular

ACADEMICS

Academic Rating	74
% students graduating within 4 years	41
% students graduating within 6 years	68
Calendar	semester
Student/faculty ratio	18:1
Profs interesting rating	67
Profs accessible rating	71
Most common reg class size	10–19 students
Most common lab size	20–29 students

MOST POPULAR MAJORS
international/global studies, physiology, psychology

STUDENTS SAY ". . ."

Academics

"It is all about the total college experience" at the University of Colorado; students enjoy both "excellent academics and a great social atmosphere." "The University of Colorado is all about getting an education for five days and spending the other two in the mountains," students repeatedly tell us, noting that "CU is an amazing place because you can find an array of challenges and opportunities whether your drive is research, the arts, sports, a job, or tough class work. However, at the same time, you can find a great social life outside of school being in an amazing place like Boulder." The sciences "are a huge strength" here, with students singling out chemistry, biology, and engineering for praise. "As an undergraduate student at CU—Boulder, I am able to research in one of my professor's labs while receiving a great education," one student explains; another points out that "being in a class taught by a Nobel laureate is not something everyone gets to experience." Business studies also excel. As at most large schools, CU has "a wide range when it comes to the quality of professors" but "for the most part [they are] very engaging in their lectures and encouraging of discussion. They are also very good about returning e-mails and [hanging] office hours." The administration can be cumbersome, but students generally appreciate how "In a tough economic climate and a gross lack of state funding, CU's administration does its best to make cuts without hurting the student body's quality of education."

Life

"The University of Colorado and the city of Boulder have so much to offer," students say. "The campus is gorgeous, as are most of the students, and there is always something to do," much of it outdoors. "People are very active in Boulder. Hiking, kayaking, mountain biking, and skiing or snowboarding is popular weekend (or weekday) activities." As one student puts it, "The mountains are a huge attraction, and during ski season the campus is considerably quieter on the weekends." CU football is also "huge, and so is the partying that is associated with it." Students concede that "the partying is pretty widespread" on and around campus but also note that "there are plenty of fun things to do that don't involve alcohol or drugs." The school "really encourages students to get involved with the ceaseless amounts of activities, groups, and clubs. Also, CU does a fantastic job of keeping students up-to-date on the goings-on and important news around school, town, and the world." Hometown Boulder is full of coffee shops and quaint shopping areas; students agree that they are blessed with "a beautiful campus and town."

Student Body

Most CU students "are very outdoors-prone"—it's what attracted them to the school in many cases—and tend to be "attractive, health-conscious," "liberal, [and] environmentally motivated" and they "live a bohemian-like lifestyle." The school is huge, so plenty students do not fit that description, of course; as one student observes, "Boulder is known for being a crazy, hippie town, but when I came here, I was surprised at the number of 'preppie kids' who are politically apathetic and more concerned with how they look than how the world around them looks." Most here "care about school but aren't superacademic." "Being social is extremely important to many people, and because of this, schoolwork sometimes takes a backseat." One student sums it up this way: "If you came to get a good education, then you will get one, but a lot of the students came here for the skiing and don't take school seriously." CU has "a large GLBTQ population, and the school is very supportive."

UNIVERSITY OF COLORADO—BOULDER

FINANCIAL AID: 303-492-5091 • E-MAIL: APPLY@COLORADO.EDU • WEBSITE: WWW.COLORADO.EDU

THE PRINCETON REVIEW SAYS

Admissions

Very important factors considered include: Academic GPA, application essay, class rank, rigor of secondary school record, standardized test scores. *Important factors considered include:* Recommendation(s), character/personal qualities, first generation, state residency. *Other factors considered include:* Alumni/ae relation, extracurricular activities, geographical residence, level of applicant's interest, talent/ability, volunteer work, work experience. SAT or ACT required; ACT with or without writing component accepted. TOEFL required of all international applicants. High school diploma is required, and GED is accepted. *Academic units required:* 4 English, 4 mathematics, 3 science (2 science labs), 3 foreign language, 3 social studies (including 1 history, 1 geography).

Financial Aid

Students should submit: FAFSA. Tax return required. The Princeton Review suggests that all financial aid forms be submitted as soon as possible after January 1. *Need-based scholarships/grants offered:* Federal Pell, SEOG, state scholarships/grants, private scholarships, school scholarship or grant aid from institutional funds. *Loan aid offered:* Direct Subsidized Stafford, Direct Unsubsidized Stafford, Direct PLUS, Federal Perkins, university loans from institutional funds. Applicants will be notified of awards on a rolling basis beginning March 1. Federal Work-Study Program available. Off-campus job opportunities are excellent.

The Inside Word

Applicants must indicate the school within CU to which they wish to be admitted. Engineering and Applied Science is most competitive, followed by the College of Music, the Leeds School of Business, and the College of Architecture and Planning. The College of Arts and Sciences is the least competitive; those applying to and not selected by the more competitive schools are automatically entered into consideration for admission to the College of Arts and Sciences. With nearly one-third of the student body from out of state, CU boasts far more geographic diversity than most state schools.

THE SCHOOL SAYS "..."

From the Admissions Office

"The University of Colorado—Boulder is a place of beauty and academic prominence at the foot of the Rocky Mountains. A sense of vitality and curiosity fills the campus, and yet it's comfortable and relaxed. It's a place you can be yourself and let your imagination soar. We have programs for you if you seek leadership training, research experience, academic honors, international experience (one in four graduates has studied abroad), community involvement, and more. There are a number of enrichment programs that give exceptionally talented and intellectually committed students the opportunity to expand their education outside the classroom, build a sense of community, and help prepare for post-graduate opportunities. Residential Academic Programs (RAPs) and Living and Learning Communities (LLCs) in several residence halls provide undergraduates with shared learning and living experiences.

"Getting involved is easy at CU—Boulder. If you are interested in student government, clubs, athletics, recreation, Greek life, volunteer work, theater, dance, film, exhibits, planetarium shows, or concerts, you will find them here.

"To find out if CU—Boulder is the place for you, we encourage you to visit. Contact the office of admissions, or take a virtual tour online. The University of Colorado at Boulder requires either SAT or ACT scores for admissions; the writing tests are currently not used in making decisions. SAT Subject Test scores are not required."

SELECTIVITY

Admissions Rating	83
# of applicants	21,145
% of applicants accepted	83
% of acceptees attending	30
# accepting a place on wait list	232
% admitted from wait list	33

FRESHMAN PROFILE

Range SAT Critical Reading	530–630
Range SAT Math	540–660
Range ACT Composite	23–28
Minimum paper TOEFL	500
Minimum computer TOEFL	173
Minimum web-based TOEFL	61
Average HS GPA	3.55
% graduated top 10% of class	26
% graduated top 25% of class	59
% graduated top 50% of class	93

DEADLINES

Early action	
Deadline	12/1
Notification	1/15
Regular	
Priority	12/1
Deadline	1/15
Nonfall registration?	yes

FINANCIAL FACTS

Financial Aid Rating	87
Annual out-of-state tuition	$28,000
Room and board	$10,792
Required fees	$1,493
Books and supplies	$1,748
% frosh rec. need-based scholarship or grant aid	36
% UG rec. need-based scholarship or grant aid	30
% frosh rec. non-need-based scholarship or grant aid	1
% UG rec. non-need-based scholarship or grant aid	1
% frosh rec. need-based self-help aid	36
% UG rec. need-based self-help aid	32
% frosh rec. any financial aid	86
% UG rec. any financial aid	64
% UG borrow to pay for school	43
Average cumulative indebtedness	$19,758

UNIVERSITY OF CONNECTICUT

2131 HILLSIDE ROAD, UNIT 3088, STORRS, CT 06268-3088 • ADMISSIONS: 860-486-3137 • FAX: 860-486-1476

STUDENTS SAY ". . ."

Academics

Brimming with sincere Husky pride, students at the University of Connecticut eagerly dole out praise for their school's fabulous athletic programs, world-class academics, friendly atmosphere, and remarkable affordability. At this large research university, professors are "extremely in-tune with recent developments in their fields," and "research opportunities are outstanding," even on the undergraduate level. A political science major shares, "My professors are the ones invited to the White House to discuss the Middle East crisis, flying across the world to solve issues of border disputes, and more. The professors bring their life experiences to the classroom, and it brings the material to life." While most professors maintain their professional pursuits outside the classroom, teaching is taken seriously at UConn, and instructors and administrators "genuinely care and want you to succeed." By all accounts, faculty is easily accessible during office hours, and, "if you can't make those, they'll work out a different time for you." Like professors, UConn's leadership is surprising friendly, down-to-earth, and accessible. Even so, students remind us that UConn is a big school, and students must take responsibility for their own educations. A senior explains, "UConn doesn't spoon-feed you education. Students do have to take the initiative to communicate with professors and the other resources on campus." "You have to put into it what you want to get out."

Life

UConn's "vibrant school spirit" is readily apparent because most UConn undergraduates are "in a million clubs, do community service, play sports, or simply have Husky pride and attend UConn events." "Some students are all about academics, and they live in Babbidge Library, others are all about partying and can be found at the off-campus apartments or the bar throughout the week." "From Sunday to Thursday, almost all students work diligently. Thursday nights bring some partying, followed by mass amounts of parties on Friday and Saturday nights." If you aren't interested in parties, there are plenty other options, "from athletics, to musical and theatrical performances, to events in the Student Union, UConn has so many different things to do!" In addition, there are more than "400 clubs and organizations," as well as an active intramural sports league, which is a great way to blow off steam. Division I athletics are the "heart of campus spirit." In their free time, UConn students (along with faculty and alumni) "love to go cheer on our nationally ranked UConn Huskies."

Student Body

More than seventy-five percent of UConn undergraduates come from Connecticut. While that fact may diminish the demographic diversity on campus, students reassure us that "there's a great mix at UConn. With more than 17,000 students enrolled, you're bound to run into just about every type of person." Students say you'll see a lot of students wearing North Face jackets and Ugg boots, but you'll also find an "animal science club, in which the students walk around with squirrel tails on." While UConn students exhibit varying degrees of academic seriousness, "the majority care about their grades, and the library is always packed during exams, midterms, and finals." More than anything else, "the real tie [among] students is the pride that we all have in our university." A senior insists, "I have not met one person who is unhappy and dislikes the university."

UNIVERSITY OF CONNECTICUT

FINANCIAL AID: 860-486-2819 • E-MAIL: BEAHUSKY@UCONN.EDU • WEBSITE: WWW.UCONN.EDU

THE PRINCETON REVIEW SAYS

Admissions

Very important factors considered include: Academic GPA, class rank, rigor of secondary school record, standardized test scores. *Important factors considered include:* Application essay, recommendation(s), character/personal qualities, extracurricular activities, first generation, racial/ethnic status, talent/ability, volunteer work. *Other factors considered include:* Alumni/ae relation, geographical residence, level of applicant's interest, state residency, work experience. SAT or ACT required; ACT with writing component required. TOEFL required of all international applicants. High school diploma is required, and GED is accepted. *Academic units required:* 4 English, 3 mathematics, 2 science (2 science labs), 2 foreign language, 2 social studies, 3 academic elective. *Academic units recommended:* 3 foreign language.

Financial Aid

Students should submit: FAFSA. The Princeton Review suggests that all financial aid forms be submitted as soon as possible after January 1. *Need-based scholarships/grants offered:* Federal Pell, SEOG, state scholarships/grants, private scholarships, school scholarship or grant aid from institutional funds, Federal Nursing Scholarships. *Loan aid offered:* Direct Subsidized Stafford, Direct Unsubsidized Stafford, Direct PLUS, Federal Perkins, Federal Nursing Loans. Applicants will be notified of awards on a rolling basis beginning March 1. Federal Work-Study Program available. Off-campus job opportunities are good.

The Inside Word

When reviewing applications, the UConn admissions committee evaluates students based on a wide range of factors, including standardized test scores, rigor of high school curriculum, classroom performance, extracurricular activities, and community involvement. Honors and AP classes aren't required, but they're viewed favorably by the admissions committee. Competitive applicants have a cumulative grade point average of 3.3 on a 4.0 scale and usually rank in the top quarter of their high school class.

THE SCHOOL SAYS " . . ."

From the Admissions Office

"Thanks to a $2.8 billion construction program that is impacting every area of university life, the University of Connecticut provides students a high-quality and personalized education on one of the most attractive and technologically advanced college campuses in the United States. Applications are soaring nationally as an increasing number of high-achieving students from diverse backgrounds are making UConn their school of choice. From award-winning actors to governmental leaders, students enjoy an assortment of fascinating speakers each year, while performances by premier dance, jazz, and rock musicians enliven student life. Our beautiful New England campus is convenient and safe, and most students walk to class or ride university shuttle buses. State-of-the-art residential facilities include interest-based learning communities and honors housing as well as on-campus suite-style and apartment living. Championship Division I athletics have created fervor known as Huskymania among UConn students.

"Freshman applicants seeking admittance are required to submit official score reports from the SAT or ACT with writing component."

SELECTIVITY

Admissions Rating	86
# of applicants	22,142
% of applicants accepted	54
% of acceptees attending	28
# accepting a place on wait list	1,397
% admitted from wait list	41

FRESHMAN PROFILE

Range SAT Critical Reading	550–640
Range SAT Math	580–670
Range SAT Writing	550–650
Range ACT Composite	25–29
Minimum paper TOEFL	550
Minimum computer TOEFL	213
Minimum web-based TOEFL	79
% graduated top 10% of class	44
% graduated top 25% of class	79
% graduated top 50% of class	98

DEADLINES

Early action	
Deadline	12/1
Notification	2/1
Regular	
Deadline	2/1
Notification	1/1
Nonfall registration?	yes

APPLICANTS ALSO LOOK AT

AND OFTEN PREFER
Boston College, University of Delaware, University of Maryland—College Park

AND SOMETIMES PREFER
Boston University, Northeastern University, Penn State—University Park

AND RARELY PREFER
Rutgers, The State University of New Jersey, University of Massachusetts Amherst, University of New Hampshire, University of Rhode Island, University of Vermont

FINANCIAL FACTS

Financial Aid Rating	71
Annual in-state tuition	$8,256
Annual out-of-state tuition	$25,152
Room and board	$11,050
Required fees	$2,414
Books and supplies	$850
% frosh rec. need-based scholarship or grant aid	46
% UG rec. need-based scholarship or grant aid	43
% frosh rec. non-need-based scholarship or grant aid	39
% UG rec. non-need-based scholarship or grant aid	27
% frosh rec. need-based self-help aid	40
% UG rec. need-based self-help aid	43
% frosh rec. any financial aid	49
% UG rec. any financial aid	48
% UG borrow to pay for school	63
Average cumulative indebtedness	$23,237

UNIVERSITY OF DALLAS

1845 EAST NORTHGATE DRIVE, IRVING, TX 75062 • ADMISSIONS: 972-721-5266 • FAX: 972-721-5017

CAMPUS LIFE

Quality of Life Rating	77
Fire Safety Rating	81
Green Rating	65
Type of school	private
Affiliation	Roman Catholic
Environment	city

STUDENTS

Total undergrad enrollment	1,337
% male/female	49/51
% from out of state	55
% from public high school	43
% live on campus	55
% African American	1
% Asian	4
% Caucasian	69
% Hispanic	16
% international	2
# of countries represented	33

SURVEY SAYS . . .
Students are friendly
Students are very religious
Low cost of living
Frats and sororities are unpopular
or nonexistent
Very little drug use

ACADEMICS

Academic Rating	83
% students graduating within 4 years	63
% students graduating within 6 years	74
Calendar	semester
Student/faculty ratio	10:1
Profs interesting rating	94
Profs accessible rating	90
Most common reg class size	20–29 students
Most common lab size	10–19 students

MOST POPULAR MAJORS
biology, business administration and
management, English language and
literature, social sciences

STUDENTS SAY "..."

Academics
This "Catholic University for Independent Thinkers" prides itself on its Core curriculum, in which students undertake "a deep and penetrating study of the Western tradition, from Ancient Greece to today" by reading "the greatest works of literature in all subjects." Students love the focus on primary sources throughout their four years. "The idea of learning politics from the writings of the democratic world's greatest minds is much more appealing to me than learning from a textbook," says one freshman. UD students are encouraged to approach everything—including their own faith—from a critical perspective. "The spirit of truth-seeking that pervades everything and everyone, both in and out of the classroom," can make for an "intense" environment. "I had one professor freshman year who said he was up until 3 A.M. doing the reading, so we better have done it, too," says a sophomore politics major. But it's easy to get motivated "when your professors care so much about what the students gain from the class discussions and the texts themselves." The small size of the school also adds to the academic intensity and makes students "feel like part of a big family." The administration gets poor marks: "They seem to be more concerned with keeping us from drinking and having sex than providing basic services all other college students take for granted." But any grumbling is overshadowed by enthusiasm for the school's unique character, including a study abroad program that sends most sophomores to Rome. The semester in Italy "brings our studies to life and helps us to connect what we learn in the classrooms with real, on-site visits to places like ancient Greece and Pompeii."

Life
At UD, "you're either studying, praying, or going to parties." The administration can be "very strict," and underage students are often written up for drinking. But that doesn't mean life here is boring. There are boisterous and popular celebrations for Groundhog Day and other holidays, weeknights bring "many, many on-campus activities organized by clubs, academic departments, or residence hall associations," and many students attend parties at off-campus apartments on weekends. Although Dallas is accessible by car, "undergraduate students (especially freshmen and sophomores) spend most of their time hanging out on campus." Students complain that the campus is in need of an overhaul: "A lot of the buildings are pretty ugly," and the school "needs to provide better facilities, [such as] library, computer lab, and study areas." But students find ways to have fun despite the barren surroundings. "We love to play intramurals, especially flag football and ultimate Frisbee. We like dancing, as evidenced by our very popular swing dancing club." And then there's that semester in Rome: "If you haven't gone yet, you're thinking about it, and if you have gone, you're talking about it and posting your photos."

Student Body
The typical UD student "studies one of the humanities (preferably English, history, or philosophy), is very, very studious and strongly committed to the Catholic faith but also knows how to have a good time." "It is not uncommon to encounter deep theological or philosophical discussions in diverse extracurricular settings—such as cross-country meets or weekend parties!" Students here take their studies seriously, and "few who are not enthusiastic about this intellectual pursuit come to the school." UD students are also serious about their faith: "Those who aren't very Catholic become more so." Campus nightlife is fun but not wild; most students "drink moderately or not at all," and there is no Greek scene. The student body is conservative politically, but everyone is "welcoming toward the liberal minority and dignifies alternative stances with respect and with very philosophical and very friendly discussions." Despite any differences, the core program unites the student body: "No matter what year you are, you have the same academic background as every student when it comes to discussing literary traditions, such as Dante or Homer, philosophy, politics, and more."

FINANCIAL AID: 972-721-5266 • E-MAIL: UGADMIS@UDALLAS.EDU • WEBSITE: WWW.UDALLAS.EDU

THE PRINCETON REVIEW SAYS

Admissions

Very important factors considered include: Academic GPA, application essay, recommendation(s), rigor of secondary school record, standardized test scores, character/personal qualities. *Important factors considered include:* Class rank, talent/ability. *Other factors considered include:* Alumni/ae relation, extracurricular activities, first generation, interview, level of applicant's interest, volunteer work, work experience. SAT or ACT required; ACT with writing component required. TOEFL required of all international applicants. High school diploma is required, and GED is accepted. *Academic units required:* 4 English, 3 mathematics, 3 science, 2 foreign language, 3 social studies, 3 history, 2 visual/performing arts, 4 academic elective. *Academic units recommended:* 4 English, 4 mathematics, 3 science (3 science labs), 3 foreign language, 4 social studies, 4 history, 2 visual/performing arts, 4 academic elective.

Financial Aid

Students should submit: FAFSA. Regular filing deadline is March 1. The Princeton Review suggests that all financial aid forms be submitted as soon as possible after January 1. *Need-based scholarships/grants offered:* Federal Pell, SEOG, state scholarships/grants, school scholarship or grant aid from institutional funds. *Loan aid offered:* Direct Subsidized Stafford, Direct Unsubsidized Stafford, Direct PLUS, state loans. Applicants will be notified of awards on a rolling basis beginning February 1. Federal Work-Study Program available. Off-campus job opportunities are fair.

The Inside Word

The university's conservative nature means that UD admissions officers place significant emphasis on the "fit" part of the admissions process. Having a solid academic background counts for a lot, but a dedication to the classics or just serious academic inquiry can be even more important.

THE SCHOOL SAYS "..."

From the Admissions Office

"Quite unabashedly, the curriculum at the University of Dallas is based on the supposition that truth and virtue exist and are the proper objects of search in an education. The curriculum further supposes that this search is best pursued through an acquisition of philosophical and theological principles on the part of a student and has for its analogical field a vast body of great literature—perhaps more extensive than is likely to be encountered elsewhere—supplemented by a survey of the sweep of history and an introduction to the political and economic principles of society. An understanding of these subjects, along with an introduction to the quantitative and scientific worldview and a mastery of a language, is expected to form a comprehensive and coherent experience, which, in effect, governs the intellect of a student in a manner that develops independence of thought in its most effective mode.

"Students applying for admission are required to take the SAT Reasoning Test or the ACT with writing assessment."

SELECTIVITY

Admissions Rating	86
# of applicants	1,041
% of applicants accepted	91
% of acceptees attending	40

FRESHMAN PROFILE

Range SAT Critical Reading	550–700
Range SAT Math	530–650
Range SAT Writing	540–680
Range ACT Composite	24–30
Minimum paper TOEFL	550
Minimum computer TOEFL	213
Minimum web-based TOEFL	79
Average HS GPA	3.75
% graduated top 10% of class	47
% graduated top 25% of class	64
% graduated top 50% of class	84

DEADLINES

Early action	
Deadline	11/1
Notification	1/15
Regular	
Deadline	3/1
Notification	4/1
Nonfall registration?	no

APPLICANTS ALSO LOOK AT

AND OFTEN PREFER
Texas A&M University—College Station, University of Notre Dame

AND SOMETIMES PREFER
Austin College, Texas Christian University, Trinity University

AND RARELY PREFER
Loyola University New Orleans, Pomona College, Saint Louis University, Trinity College, University of the Holy Cross

FINANCIAL FACTS

Financial Aid Rating	80
Annual tuition	$27,500
Room and board	$9,326
Required fees	$1,825
Books and supplies	$1,700
% frosh rec. need-based scholarship or grant aid	62
% UG rec. need-based scholarship or grant aid	61
% frosh rec. non-need-based scholarship or grant aid	7
% UG rec. non-need-based scholarship or grant aid	5
% frosh rec. need-based self-help aid	48
% UG rec. need-based self-help aid	51
% frosh rec. any financial aid	86
% UG rec. any financial aid	91
% UG borrow to pay for school	55
Average cumulative indebtedness	$28,020

UNIVERSITY OF DAYTON

300 COLLEGE PARK, DAYTON, OH 45469-1300 • ADMISSIONS: 937-229-4411 • FAX: 937-229-4729

CAMPUS LIFE

Quality of Life Rating	90
Fire Safety Rating	73
Green Rating	83
Type of school	private
Affiliation	Roman Catholic
Environment	city

STUDENTS

Total undergrad enrollment	7,750
% male/female	51/49
% from out of state	39
% from public high school	49
% live on campus	75
# of fraternities	11
# of sororities	7
% African American	4
% Asian	1
% Caucasian	87
% Hispanic	3
% international	3
# of countries represented	55

SURVEY SAYS . . .
School is well-run
Students are friendly
Students are happy
Intramural sports are popular
Lots of beer drinking

ACADEMICS

Academic Rating	76
% students graduating within 4 years	58
% students graduating within 6 years	76
Calendar	semester
Student/faculty ratio	15:1
Profs interesting rating	82
Profs accessible rating	91
Most common reg class size	20–29 students
Most common lab size	10–19 students

MOST POPULAR MAJORS
business, mechanical engineering

STUDENTS SAY ". . ."

Academics

The University of Dayton, a school "known for friendly students, strong academics, and Flyer basketball," is "academically challenging yet unpretentious [and] casual yet fun." Students at this mid-size Catholic school enjoy a "relaxed atmosphere. Academics are important at Dayton, but people aren't engaged in cut-throat rivalries with people to get ahead in the classroom. If you're struggling, it's easy to find someone to offer a helping hand." One student observes, "Dayton is about academics, but the school also stresses getting to know the people you study with. I thought the community aspect they repeated endlessly during my visit was just a way to get me to enroll at Dayton, but everyone is genuinely interested" in making sure that overall everyone around them has "a good college experience." Both academics and service "are taken very seriously" at UD. One undergrad notes, "You earn what you deserve. As long as you work hard, and your teachers can see that, you won't have a problem." Top programs include "a great premed program," "a wonderful engineering department," "an amazing teacher education program," and an "awesome business school" that includes the Davis Center for Portfolio Management, a "student-run fund that invests more than $11 million of the university's endowment." The number of options is unusual for an institution with such a small-school feel; students describe UD as "small enough that you get to know people very well, and you are always seeing someone you know, yet big enough that there are always new people to meet."

Life

"On top of great academic programs, the University of Dayton offers the full college experience—exciting athletic events, good dorm life, and the Ghetto," one student writes, alluding to UD's well-known student neighborhood, where "Porch sitting is a must on sunny days." One student explains, "Porches are symbolic of UD. Everyone sits out on the porch. It's one huge neighborhood where everyone is welcome to party or to chill. And when we party, everyone leaves their door wide open for anyone to come." As one student puts it, "Community is probably the first word that comes to the majority of the student body's minds." UD is situated near "a poverty-stricken area," but students point out that "It's never necessary to leave campus, even on the weekends," so the neighborhood isn't as large a factor as it might be. One student writes, "Going out to eat and seeing movies is the basic activity for when we get bored of hanging out at each other's houses on campus, but normally, we are content with going to the bars, going to house parties, or just staying in to watch a movie on the weekends…it just depends on the mood." And let's not forget Dayton basketball, "the gem of the community." True to its Marianist tradition, UD also has "the largest campus ministry in the country. We help both the local and global community with things ranging from one-time service days to immersion trips and even an entire year of service."

Student Body

"Many will say that the typical UD student comes from an upper-middle class suburb, went to a Catholic high school, and owns a North Face jacket," one student writes. "However, I know quite a few people who don't fit that description, and I think compared to similar schools, UD is much more diverse. Even though many people come from affluent backgrounds, many are also in need of a lot of financial aid, and it doesn't really matter. The idea of community and inclusiveness really helps everyone feel united." The typical undergrad here tends to be "semi-religious, overly friendly, welcoming, and accepting of the few diverse students who are here." Because of the school's Catholic focus, "The majority of students are Catholic, and some students who are not Catholic feel that the university incorporates too much religion in service-type activities."

FINANCIAL AID: 937-229-4311 • E-MAIL: ADMISSION@UDAYTON.EDU • WEBSITE: WWW.UDAYTON.EDU

THE PRINCETON REVIEW SAYS

Admissions

Very important factors considered include: Academic GPA, rigor of secondary school record, standardized test scores. *Important factors considered include:* Application essay, recommendation(s), alumni/ae relation. *Other factors considered include:* Class rank, character/personal qualities, extracurricular activities, first generation, racial/ethnic status, talent/ability, volunteer work, work experience. SAT or ACT required; ACT with or without writing component accepted. TOEFL required of all international applicants. High school diploma is required, and GED is accepted. *Academic units recommended:* 4 English, 4 mathematics, 4 science (1 science lab), 2 foreign language, 4 social studies, 4 history, 4 visual/performing arts, 4 computer science.

Financial Aid

Students should submit: FAFSA. Regular filing deadline is March 1. The Princeton Review suggests that all financial aid forms be submitted as soon as possible after January 1. *Need-based scholarships/grants offered:* Federal Pell, SEOG, state scholarships/grants, private scholarships, school scholarship or grant aid from institutional funds. *Loan aid offered:* Direct Subsidized Stafford, Direct Unsubsidized Stafford, Direct PLUS, Federal Perkins. Applicants will be notified of awards on a rolling basis beginning March 15. Federal Work-Study Program available. Off-campus job opportunities are good.

The Inside Word

University of Dayton is an excellent option for students who want to attend a Catholic university but don't meet the stringent criteria of Georgetown or Notre Dame. UD gives "balanced consideration" to all academic factors—for example, class rank, GPA—on the application. Candidates who demonstrate a modicum of success in the classroom and intellectual promise will most likely be accepted. Applicants must apply to one of the university's four divisions; admissions criteria vary slightly among the different divisions.

THE SCHOOL SAYS "..."

From the Admissions Office

"The University of Dayton founded in 1850 by the Society of Mary, is a top ten Catholic research university. The university seeks outstanding diverse faculty, staff, and students who value its mission and share its commitment to academic excellence in teaching, study, research and creativity, the development of the whole person, and leadership and service in the local and global community. More than seventy challenging academic programs are offered in the College of Arts and Sciences and the Schools of Business Administration, Education and Allied Professions, Engineering, and Law. Classes are small—twenty-six students on average. Our more than 1,000 full-time and part-time faculty are committed to teaching undergraduate students and involving them in their research projects. The University of Dayton Research Institute ranks second in the nation in the amount of materials research performed annually. Technology-enhanced learning ensures students gain expertise in the tools that will prepare them for the future. All areas of campus and surrounding neighborhoods have access to our high speed wireless network. Recent campus construction provides a modern home for the university's cutting-edge academic programs. New facilities include ArtStreet, Marianist Hall, and the Science Center. A new fitness and recreation complex, the RecPlex, provides 130,000 square feet of space for classrooms, courts, a natatorium, offices, and other recreational facilities. A strong sense of community is a hallmark feature of the university; a dual emphasis on leadership and service contributes to students' participation in more than 180 clubs and organizations. Division I intercollegiate athletics and club and intramural sports are also popular.

"Students applying for admission may provide scores from either the SAT or the ACT. The highest composite scores from either test will be used in admission and merit-based aid decisions."

SELECTIVITY
Admissions Rating	84
# of applicants	11,567
% of applicants accepted	77
% of acceptees attending	23

FRESHMAN PROFILE
Range SAT Critical Reading	510–610
Range SAT Math	520–630
Range SAT Writing	520–600
Range ACT Composite	22–28
Minimum paper TOEFL	523
Minimum computer TOEFL	193
Minimum web-based TOEFL	70
Average HS GPA	3.51
% graduated top 10% of class	27
% graduated top 25% of class	58
% graduated top 50% of class	87

DEADLINES
Early action	
Deadline	12/15
Notification	1/15
Regular	
Priority	12/15
Deadline	3/1
Notification	1/15
Nonfall registration?	yes

APPLICANTS ALSO LOOK AT
AND OFTEN PREFER
Miami University, The Ohio State University—Columbus

AND SOMETIMES PREFER
Indiana University at Bloomington, Purdue University—West Lafayette, Saint Louis University, University of Cincinnati, Xavier University (OH)

AND RARELY PREFER
Loyola University of Chicago, Marquette University, Ohio University—Athens

FINANCIAL FACTS
Financial Aid Rating	84
Annual tuition	$28,700
Required fees	$1,230
Books and supplies	$1,000
% frosh rec. need-based scholarship or grant aid	63
% UG rec. need-based scholarship or grant aid	55
% frosh rec. non-need-based scholarship or grant aid	98
% UG rec. non-need-based scholarship or grant aid	96
% frosh rec. need-based self-help aid	63
% UG rec. need-based self-help aid	54
% frosh rec. any financial aid	98
% UG rec. any financial aid	97
% UG borrow to pay for school	67
Average cumulative indebtedness	$35,421

UNIVERSITY OF DELAWARE

ADMISSIONS OFFICE, 116 HULLIHEN HALL, NEWARK, DE 19716-6210 • ADMISSIONS: 302-831-8123 • FAX: 302-831-6905

STUDENTS SAY ". . ."

Academics

If you're looking for a "well-rounded" college experience, University of Delaware delivers on every front. According to the school's satisfied undergraduates, "the University of Delaware is everything college should be," from its "gorgeous campus" and "amazing school spirit," to "top notch" academics and "vibrant campus life." At UD, as at many public schools, "College is what you make it: If you take easy classes, college is a breeze; if you challenge yourself, classes will be more difficult." First-year courses are often large and impersonal; fortunately, major classes are usually smaller and "electives are interesting and engaging." Highly qualified students may also apply to the school's "excellent" honors program, which provides access to "challenging, interesting classes taught by distinguished yet friendly professors." Through the touted undergraduate research program, students have access to "diverse research opportunities," and the school's extensive study abroad program is "one of the best in the nation." Overall, faculty get good reviews, though students warn it's a mixed bag: "Some professors shouldn't be allowed within ten miles of a classroom; others will change your life. It's up to you to weed out the bad ones." While you won't have your hand held, professors are responsive to student needs: "If you ever need any help, a quick e-mail or a phone call usually solves your problem." On a similar note, "The administration is extremely approachable and talks to students on the same level."

Life

Work and play come together at the University of Delaware, an institution that offers "the perfect balance of academic intensity and excellent social life." Come the weekend (or even during the week), "UD kids like to have their share of fun," and "There is always a party happening." For an alternative to the party scene, students go to "movies in the student center or to ice skating on Fridays," and "There are a lot of great guest speakers, bands, and cultural events on campus." In addition, "There are social groups for almost anything you can think of from the adventure club to organic cooking to ultimate Frisbee." While fraternities and sororities do exist, they do not dominate the social scene; still Greeks are "very spirited, have a ton of fun, and are widely supported by our campus community." Intramural and varsity sports are wildly popular, both for athletes and their raucous fans. In fact, "Homecoming is a university holiday where people wake up as early as 5:00 A.M. to start tailgating." What's more, the campus location can't be beat. Main Street, which runs right through campus, "is packed with great restaurants and shopping." For a fun day trip, "Philly is cheap and easy to get to by Septa train," and "the Chinatown bus costs thirty-five dollars round trip into NYC."

Student Body

It's a largely East Coast crowd at University of Delaware, drawing the vast majority of its undergraduates from "around NYC, Philly, or Baltimore." Within that demographic, "Preppy sorority kids are probably the most common, but no matter who you are or what your into, the school population is big enough [that] you're bound to find a group that shares your interest." At UD, "You'll have your jocks and frat boys, but you'll also find skaters, rockers, artsy types, and everything else in between." However, most UD students share an incredible enthusiasm for their school community, and "A typical student is engaged in coursework and a multitude of various extracurricular [activities]." Despite its long-standing repute as a party school, "students here have become more focused on academics. Most students here really do have a passion for learning and study really hard in order to get those grades and graduate." Even so, UD's reputation for revelry isn't lost on undergraduates: "The typical UD student cares about their school work but loves to have fun on the weekends."

FINANCIAL AID: 302-831-8761 • E-MAIL: ADMISSIONS@UDEL.EDU • WEBSITE: WWW.UDEL.EDU

THE PRINCETON REVIEW SAYS

Admissions

Very important factors considered include: Academic GPA, rigor of secondary school record, state residency. *Important factors considered include:* Application essay, recommendation(s), standardized test scores, character/personal qualities, extracurricular activities, talent/ability, volunteer work, work experience. *Other factors considered include:* Class rank, alumni/ae relation, first generation, geographical residence, interview, level of applicant's interest, racial/ethnic status. SAT or ACT required; ACT with writing component required. TOEFL required of all international applicants. High school diploma is required, and GED is accepted. *Academic units required:* 4 English, 3 mathematics, 3 science (2 science labs), 2 foreign language, 2 social studies, 2 history, 2 academic elective. *Academic units recommended:* 4 English, 4 mathematics, 4 science (3 science labs), 4 foreign language, 2 social studies, 2 history.

Financial Aid

Students should submit: FAFSA. Regular filing deadline is March 15. The Princeton Review suggests that all financial aid forms be submitted as soon as possible after January 1. *Need-based scholarships/grants offered:* Federal Pell, SEOG, state scholarships/grants, private scholarships, school scholarship or grant aid from institutional funds. *Loan aid offered:* Direct Subsidized Stafford, Direct Unsubsidized Stafford, Direct PLUS, Federal Perkins, Federal Nursing Loans, university loans from institutional funds. Applicants will be notified of awards on a rolling basis beginning March 15. Federal Work-Study Program available. Off-campus job opportunities are excellent.

Inside Word

Although UD is run by the state of Delaware, out-of-state students also benefit from the school's excellent academic and social offerings at a reasonable tuition. Even so, the school is expressly committed to supporting Delawarean students, who comprise about forty percent of the student body. More details and samples of qualifying high school curricula are available on the admissions department website. In all admissions decisions, UD considers the entirety of a student's application; there are no minimum test scores or grades.

THE SCHOOL SAYS "..."

From the Admissions Office

"An East Coast classic, the University of Delaware is a rich, historic campus in Newark, Delaware, midway between New York City and Washington, D.C. UD is known for its problem-based, hands-on learning in every college and a relatively small enrollment that engages students with interested, accessible faculty. Over ninety percent of our students land jobs within six months of graduation and continue their educations at the top graduate and professional schools in the world. Three signers of the Declaration of Independence were among our first class and recent alumni include the vice president of the United States, the governor of New Jersey, and the top campaign strategist for the president of the U.S. UD is also a talent magnet, attracting top scholars and innovators, including a recent Nobel Prize winner and a Rhodes Scholar. The University of Delaware is working on the most compelling social, civic, artistic, and scientific challenges of our age. As the flagship university in the first state of the union, we dare to be first in ways that matter—first in new energy technologies, first in global study, first in political leadership, first in interdisciplinary engineering, first in educating teachers, first in design innovation, first in championship athletics, first in translational medicine. We challenge our students to be first in what matters most to them."

SELECTIVITY

Admissions Rating	91
# of applicants	24,744
% of applicants accepted	57
% of acceptees attending	30
# accepting a place on wait list	669
% admitted from wait list	29

FRESHMAN PROFILE

Range SAT Critical Reading	520–630
Range SAT Math	540–650
Range SAT Writing	520–640
Range ACT Composite	24–28
Minimum paper TOEFL	550
Minimum computer TOEFL	213
Minimum web-based TOEFL	80
Average HS GPA	3.50
% graduated top 10% of class	37
% graduated top 25% of class	74
% graduated top 50% of class	96

DEADLINES

Regular	
Priority	12/1
Deadline	1/15
Nonfall registration?	yes

APPLICANTS ALSO LOOK AT

AND OFTEN PREFER
College of William and Mary, Princeton University, University of Pennsylvania

AND SOMETIMES PREFER
Brandeis University, Cornell University, Georgetown University, New York University, Syracuse University, The George Washington University, University of Florida, University of Michigan—Ann Arbor, University of North Carolina at Chapel Hill

AND RARELY PREFER
Indiana University at Bloomington, Northeastern University, Rutgers, The State University of New Jersey, State University of New York at Binghamton, University of Maryland—College Park, University of Massachusetts Amherst, University of Vermont, Villanova University

FINANCIAL FACTS

Financial Aid Rating	80
Annual in-state tuition	$8,540
Annual out-of-state tuition	$22,240
Room and board	$9,308
Required fees	$946
Books and supplies	$800
% frosh rec. need-based scholarship or grant aid	36
% UG rec. need-based scholarship or grant aid	39
% frosh rec. non-need-based scholarship or grant aid	22
% UG rec. non-need-based scholarship or grant aid	16
% frosh rec. need-based self-help aid	39
% UG rec. need-based self-help aid	48
% frosh rec. any financial aid	57
% UG rec. any financial aid	55
% UG borrow to pay for school	44
Average cumulative indebtedness	$17,200

UNIVERSITY OF DENVER

University Hall, Room 110, 2197 South University Boulevard, Denver, CO 80208 • Admissions: 303-871-2036 • Fax: 303-871-3301

STUDENTS SAY "..."

Academics

The University of Denver runs on a ten-week quarter system rather than the traditional semester schedule, which is "ideal to learn about many different subjects, since we take twelve to thirteen classes a year." "All of [the professors] seem to enjoy teaching," though they receive some mixed remarks from students, who aren't thrilled with their required classes but are very happy with the upper-level classes in their majors. The International Studies Department and Daniels School of Business receive special mention, and "opportunities to work with professors on their research have been abundant." "If you want to learn, professors will bend over backwards to accommodate you and your interests," and "almost all professors want to see their students succeed." Many students comment that "The academic experience at the University of Denver is whatever you want it to be. It can be as rigorous or as easy as the student wants." "If you just want to show up and count the minutes until you hit the mountains, you can. Or, if you really want to learn, you can do that, too." As is the case at many schools, student experiences with the administration vary wildly.

Life

At DU, "The people are very interested in playing outside, which is understandable with all the sunshine Denver gets." "Most people take advantage of the fact that we are only one hour away from some of the best skiing and snowboarding in the world." "There are free classes at the gym (which are *great*), a fantastic work-out facility, a beautiful park nearby to go running, great skiing within an hour of school, hiking trails, and camping sites." Students joke that life at DU generally consists of a shifting ratio of four activities: "skiing, hiking, drinking, and studying." "Substances may be used but, for the most part, with discretion." "Many kids go clubbing and go to parties. Others just enjoy hanging out and hitting the town. There is a good mix of the two here." "DU is a great size: big enough to never give off that small-town, high school feeling, but small enough to ensure that you will see friendly, recognizable faces everywhere." Life on campus is very active, with strong participation in intramural and club sports and a significant Greek presence. "Greek life can either be your whole social life, or you can not be involved in it at all and have a very active social life." Denver receives high marks as a college town: "Downtown Denver is…only eighteen minutes away by light rail, which has everything you would ever want to do or see that isn't right next to campus."

Student Body

Students at DU are pretty comfortable with themselves and each other. "Most people are just normal, friendly people who all have certain areas that they choose to be involved in, whether it is student government, alpine club, or Greek life." Also, most are probably "skiers or…snowboarders or involved in some sort of physical activity relating to Colorado, such as hiking, fishing, camping, etc." "There are not too many exclusive 'groups' on campus, and most people are very accepting of others." "Everyone is very laid-back." Though some students comment on the upper-middle-class majority—"the students are motivated but seem to be used to lives of accommodation." Many acknowledge that "DU puts a lot of emphasis on diversity," and "Denver has a combination of traditional students and nontraditional students, domestic and international students, liberals and conservatives." "There [is] a significant number of international students, which really adds to the university experience." "In general, everyone is friendly and gets along. Most people are a little quirky in their own way."

FINANCIAL AID: 303-871-4020 • E-MAIL: ADMISSION@DU.EDU • WEBSITE: WWW.DU.EDU/ADMISSION

THE PRINCETON REVIEW SAYS

Admissions

Very important factors considered include: Academic GPA, rigor of secondary school record, standardized test scores. *Important factors considered include:* Application essay, recommendation(s), character/personal qualities, extracurricular activities, interview, talent/ability. *Other factors considered include:* Alumni/ae relation, first generation, geographical residence, level of applicant's interest, racial/ethnic status, volunteer work, work experience. SAT or ACT required; ACT with or without writing component accepted. TOEFL required of all international applicants. High school diploma is required, and GED is accepted. *Academic units recommended:* 4 English, 3 mathematics, 3 science (2 science labs), 3 foreign language, 3 social studies.

Financial Aid

Students should submit: FAFSA, CSS/Financial Aid PROFILE. Regular filing deadline is April 1. The Princeton Review suggests that all financial aid forms be submitted as soon as possible after January 1. *Need-based scholarships/grants offered:* Federal Pell, SEOG, state scholarships/grants, private scholarships, school scholarship or grant aid from institutional funds. *Loan aid offered:* Direct Subsidized Stafford, Direct Unsubsidized Stafford, Direct PLUS, Federal Perkins. Applicants will be notified of awards on a rolling basis beginning early March. Federal Work-Study Program available. Off-campus job opportunities are excellent.

The Inside Word

DU admissions gives academic achievement top billing when reviewing applications. Last year's incoming freshman class had an average GPA of 3.7, but that's not all that counts: The admissions committee wants to see a roster of challenging classes as well. In particular, applicants to math or science programs and to the Daniels College of Business are expected to have strong quantitative skills. ACT and SAT scores are also important, though the writing components are not considered. Applicants are strongly encouraged to schedule an interview, which DU alumni, faculty, and staff conduct in thirty cities nationwide.

THE SCHOOL SAYS "..."

From the Admissions Office

"When you start from a higher place at the University of Denver—in our setting of great natural beauty, cultural richness, and intellectual energy—you'll experience meaningful interaction with professors who set you on paths toward personal discovery, paths that can change the course of your future. Our diverse student body, engaged faculty, and prime location provide a culture of opportunity that is unique and unrivaled. DU is continually developing educational initiatives that help students prepare for an ever-changing world. Our Living and Learning Communities provide extracurricular and co-curricular programming in specialized areas; the Partners in Scholarship (PinS) program funds undergraduate research for students wishing to pursue a topic of personal interest in greater depth; and sixty-five to seventy percent of our students are taking advantage of invaluable internship opportunities in laboratories, corporate offices, government agencies, and cultural settings. One of the university's signature offerings is the Cherrington Global Scholars program, which allows students to study abroad at the same cost of a quarter at DU. Nearly seventy-five percent of our students study abroad, which ranks DU fourth in the nation among doctoral and research institutions for percentage of students participating. Outside the classroom, DU students put ideas and ideals into action. They are active members of our community and they take advantage of the numerous recreational opportunities available to them, including club, intramural, and seventeen Division I sports. Whatever their majors and interests, DU students are groomed to excel in their life's work and to confront the great issues of the day."

SELECTIVITY
Admissions Rating	90
# of applicants	9,337
% of applicants accepted	72
% of acceptees attending	18
# accepting a place on wait list	523
% admitted from wait list	2

FRESHMAN PROFILE
Range SAT Critical Reading	540–650
Range SAT Math	560–660
Range SAT Writing	530–640
Range ACT Composite	25–30
Minimum paper TOEFL	525
Minimum web-based TOEFL	70
Average HS GPA	3.70
% graduated top 10% of class	45
% graduated top 25% of class	76
% graduated top 50% of class	96

DEADLINES
Early action	
Deadline	11/1
Notification	1/1
Regular	
Deadline	1/15
Nonfall registration?	yes

APPLICANTS ALSO LOOK AT
AND OFTEN PREFER
Colorado College, Colorado State University, University of Colorado—Boulder

AND SOMETIMES PREFER
Boston University, University of Puget Sound, University of Vermont

FINANCIAL FACTS
Financial Aid Rating	75
Annual tuition	$35,604
Room and board	$10,224
Required fees	$897
Books and supplies	$1,749
% frosh rec. need-based scholarship or grant aid	45
% UG rec. need-based scholarship or grant aid	43
% frosh rec. non-need-based scholarship or grant aid	39
% UG rec. non-need-based scholarship or grant aid	41
% frosh rec. need-based self-help aid	36
% UG rec. need-based self-help aid	35
% frosh rec. any financial aid	84
% UG rec. any financial aid	84
% UG borrow to pay for school	43
Average cumulative indebtedness	$25,578

UNIVERSITY OF FLORIDA

201 CRISER HALL, BOX 114000, GAINESVILLE, FL 32611-4000 • ADMISSIONS: 352-392-1365 • FAX: 352-392-3987

CAMPUS LIFE

Quality of Life Rating	85
Fire Safety Rating	60*
Green Rating	96
Type of school	public
Environment	city

STUDENTS

Total undergrad enrollment	32,660
% male/female	45/55
% from out of state	5
% from public high school	84
% live on campus	23
# of fraternities	38
# of sororities	26
% African American	9
% Asian	8
% Caucasian	58
% Hispanic	16
% international	1
# of countries represented	132

SURVEY SAYS . . .

Athletic facilities are great
Everyone loves the Gators
Intramural sports are popular
Frats and sororities dominate
social scene
Student publications are popular
Student government is popular
Lots of beer drinking
Hard liquor is popular

ACADEMICS

Academic Rating	68
% students graduating within 4 years	64
% students graduating within 6 years	84
Calendar	semester
Student/faculty ratio	20:1
Profs interesting rating	64
Profs accessible rating	73
Most common reg class size	10–19 students
Most common lab size	10–19 students

MOST POPULAR MAJORS
finance, political science, psychology

STUDENTS SAY ". . ."

Academics

"A top-tier research institute" that "is full of bright students who still know how to have fun," the University of Florida offers "an environment unparalleled by an other university in the world with its first-class amenities, athletics, academics, campus, and students," enthusiastic students insist. The school "has excellent academic programs all across the board: You're not limited to just a great engineering program or journalism program" here; the sciences (including premedical studies, which piggyback on "a strong teaching hospital on campus"), business, education, communications, and engineering are among the many standout offerings. In short, "UF is a great school" that's "not expensive, even for out-of-state students. Plus, there is a great sense of family here: You really are a part of the Gator Nation!" It is, of course, a very large university that at times "runs more [like] a machine than a place that fosters learning and growth." As one student reports, "The school never even knew I had a name. The first thing anyone ever asks you is 'What's your UF-ID?'" Also, students must be prepared for "the annoyance of the size of the more generalized prerequisite courses, e.g., lower-level courses required by two or three majors." Still, "the professors are almost always wonderful: They are helpful and definitely know their stuff."

Life

"The greatest strength [of this school] is UF's spirit," students agree, telling us that "there's just something about being a Gator. It doesn't matter where you are in the world, UF students and alumni are everywhere and ready to greet you with open arms and a hearty 'Go Gators!' You belong there." While here, you can party to your heart's content; the university "certainly lives up to its role of number one party school. Every day is a weekend in Gainesville, and you will always find something going on Sunday through Saturday. There's midtown, a strip right across from the stadium that has the infamous Swamp restaurant, clubs, bars, and plenty of food to satiate hunger in between classes. There's also 'downtown' Gainesville, which houses more bars, clubs, and restaurants and shopping to keep you busy throughout the entire semester." And "if you're not into the party scene, there's the Hippodrome Theatre, Lake Wauberg, and the local mall and movie theaters to keep you occupied. Gainesville is definitely a college town, and it is perfect for anyone looking for the true college experience." College sports are huge, "and there are hardly any people that aren't proud of Gator athletes and always ready to sport the orange and blue." UF's Greek community "is very prominent, and a large number of students belong [to] a fraternity/sorority or associate with students who do."

Student Body

The typical UF student "has a popular major like engineering or business," "is witty, loves Gator football, and likes to party. An atypical student may be someone who doesn't party or may deviate from mainstream beliefs, practices, or political parties, but for the most part, any student is accepted as a member of the Gator nation," and most "seem to maintain a well-balanced life of studying and socializing." While "the sorority/fraternity people are the most dominant group on campus," there's also "a really strong indie scene (the two never interact)." In fact, "There are people all over the spectrum," although the place is so big that "half of them you may never meet." "We are one of the most diverse campuses in the nation," one student explains, "and we are all Gators at heart, first and foremost."

UNIVERSITY OF FLORIDA

FINANCIAL AID: 352-392-1275 • WEBSITE: WWW.UFL.EDU

THE PRINCETON REVIEW SAYS

Admissions
SAT or ACT required; ACT with writing component required. High school diploma is required, and GED is accepted. *Academic units required:* 4 English, 3 mathematics, 3 science (2 science labs), 2 foreign language, 3 social studies, 3 academic elective.

Financial Aid
Students should submit: FAFSA. The Princeton Review suggests that all financial aid forms be submitted as soon as possible after January 1. *Need-based scholarships/grants offered:* Federal Pell, SEOG, state scholarships/grants, private scholarships, school scholarship or grant aid from institutional funds. *Loan aid offered:* Direct Subsidized Stafford, Direct Unsubsidized Stafford, Direct PLUS, Federal Perkins, university loans from institutional funds. Applicants will be notified of awards on a rolling basis beginning April 1. Federal Work-Study Program available. Off-campus job opportunities are fair.

The Inside Word
First-generation college students from disadvantaged backgrounds qualify for the Florida Opportunity Scholars program, which fully covers four years of educational costs. The program is not limited to minority students, the average family income of recipients is just less than $25,000 per year.

THE SCHOOL SAYS ". . ."

From the Admissions Office
"University of Florida students come from more than 100 countries, all fifty states, and every one of the sixty-seven counties in Florida. Twenty-three percent of the student body is comprised of graduate students. Approximately 4,300 African American students, 6,600 Hispanic students, and 4,100 Asian American students attend UF. Ninety percent of the entering freshmen rank above the national mean of scores on standard entrance exams. UF consistently ranks near the top among public universities in the number of new National Merit and Achievement scholars in attendance.

"Students must submit the SAT or ACT with the writing section. UF considers your highest section scores across all SAT test dates."

SELECTIVITY	
Admissions Rating	92
# of applicants	26,513
% of applicants accepted	44
% of acceptees attending	56

FRESHMAN PROFILE	
Range SAT Critical Reading	570–670
Range SAT Math	600–690
Range ACT Composite	26–30
Average HS GPA	3.90

DEADLINES	
Regular	
Deadline	11/1
Nonfall registration?	yes

FINANCIAL FACTS	
Financial Aid Rating	85
Annual in-state tuition	$5,020
Annual out-of-state tuition	$27,321
Room and board	$8,640
Books and supplies	$1,000
% frosh rec. need-based scholarship or grant aid	31
% UG rec. need-based scholarship or grant aid	31
% frosh rec. non-need-based scholarship or grant aid	47
% UG rec. non-need-based scholarship or grant aid	36
% frosh rec. need-based self-help aid	18
% UG rec. need-based self-help aid	22
% frosh rec. any financial aid	99
% UG rec. any financial aid	90
% UG borrow to pay for school	40
Average cumulative indebtedness	$16,013

UNIVERSITY OF GEORGIA

TERRELL HALL, ATHENS, GA 30602 • ADMISSIONS: 706-542-8776 • FAX: 706-542-1466

CAMPUS LIFE

Quality of Life Rating	92
Fire Safety Rating	77
Green Rating	92
Type of school	public
Environment	city

STUDENTS

Total undergrad enrollment	25,709
% male/female	42/58
% from out of state	9
% from public high school	78
% live on campus	28
# of fraternities	32
# of sororities	26
% African American	7
% Asian	7
% Caucasian	77
% Hispanic	4
% international	1
# of countries represented	126

SURVEY SAYS . . .
Athletic facilities are great
Great food on campus
Great off-campus food
Low cost of living
Everyone loves the Bulldogs

ACADEMICS

Academic Rating	72
% students graduating within 4 years	54
% students graduating within 6 years	82
Calendar	semester
Student/faculty ratio	19:1
Profs interesting rating	77
Profs accessible rating	71
Most common reg class size	20–29 students

MOST POPULAR MAJORS
biology, English language and literature, psychology

STUDENTS SAY " . . ."

Academics
As at many large universities, UGA has a "mixed bag of professors," but there are "more good teachers" than bad. Though students don't love the core curriculum classes due to their large size and the prevalence of TAs, "once [you're] in your particular program, the teachers are outstanding and easy to reach." "The professors really do want to see you at office hours if you have questions," and they "want to share their love of learning with you." "My major-related classes are very small, and each student receives individual attention." The honors program also receives raves: "Many of my best classes and favorite teachers have come from the honors program, but non-honors classes are generally good as well." "The study spaces are well-equipped and quiet," but "the school of social work is still housed in an old dorm." "Administration is a pain (not the people, only the requirements), but I think that describes academia in general." In general students "feel that the administration can be very accommodating at times, but at other times it can seem like it is full of red tape." Registration technology "needs to be brought out of the 1980s and into the twenty-first century." "The administration [can] seem like a bunch of penny-pinchers, but they must be to run a major research facility."

Life
Life at UGA seems to be a good mix of the two different worlds of sports and arts: football, frats, and tailgating on campus come together nicely with the coffee shops and music scene in downtown Athens. "On Saturday afternoons in the fall, nearly everyone on campus is at the football game. It's a way of life here." "Everybody really gets behind the team, and Saturdays in Athens feel like mini vacations." Fraternities and sororities dominate the party scene, but "there is definitely plenty to do, even if you don't go Greek." Students love to brag about the high number of bars per capita in Athens, but there's plenty more to boast about. "The Athens music and art scene is very inspiring, and there are tons of opportunities for creativity here." "Downtown Athens is fabulous! Whether you drink or don't drink, all are welcome and all congregate there." Campus life offers plenty of activity, too. "Fun is a part of daily life…with a dozen intramural sports each semester…and many community activities (multiple movie theaters, bowling allies, golf course)." "Ultimate Frisbee, walks around the multiple parks, days lounging on North Campus, and spending *lots* of time downtown are a couple ways I like to have fun at school." "There are so many organizations that everyone can find a place that will feel like home or find a place to meet new people." "It's no secret that UGA knows how to party. However, most of the students know how to manage social and academic time."

Student Body
"Students are generally white, upper-middle-class, smart, [and] involved, and [they] have a good time," "seem to be predominantly conservative," and "are usually involved in at least one organization whether it be Greek, a club, or sports." "The typical student at UGA is one who knows how and when to study but allows himself or herself to have a very active social life." The majority are Southerners, with many students from within Georgia. "The stereotype is Southern, Republican, football-loving, and beer-drinking. While many, many of UGA's students do not fit this description, there is no lack of the above," and "there is a social scene for everyone in Athens." "There are a great number of atypical students in the liberal arts," which "creates a unique and exciting student body with greatly contrasting opinions."

FINANCIAL AID: 706-542-6147 • E-MAIL: UNDERGRAD@ADMISSIONS.UGA.EDU • WEBSITE: WWW.UGA.EDU

THE PRINCETON REVIEW SAYS

Admissions

Very important factors considered include: Academic GPA, rigor of secondary school record. *Important factors considered include:* Standardized test scores. *Other factors considered include:* Application essay, recommendation(s), character/personal qualities, extracurricular activities, first generation, talent/ability, volunteer work, work experience. SAT or ACT required; ACT with writing component required. TOEFL required of all international applicants. High school diploma is required, and GED is accepted. *Academic units required:* 4 English, 4 mathematics, 3 science (2 science labs), 2 foreign language, 3 social studies. *Academic units recommended:* 4 English, 4 mathematics, 3 science (2 science labs), 3 foreign language, 1 social studies, 2 history, 1 academic elective.

Financial Aid

Students should submit: FAFSA. Regular filing deadline is rolling. The Princeton Review suggests that all financial aid forms be submitted as soon as possible after January 1. *Need-based scholarships/grants offered:* Federal Pell, SEOG, state scholarships/grants, private scholarships, school scholarship or grant aid from institutional funds. *Loan aid offered:* Direct Subsidized Stafford, Direct Unsubsidized Stafford, Direct PLUS, Federal Perkins, state loans, university loans from institutional funds. Applicants will be notified of awards on a rolling basis beginning May 15.

The Inside Word

A school as large as UGA must start winnowing applicants by the numbers. If you fail to meet certain baseline curricular, GPA, and standardized-test-score floors, only exceptional talent elsewhere (a gift for the arts or, better still, throwing a football) will get you past the first cut. Some students here are Georgia residents reaping the benefits of the state's HOPE scholarship program, which pays tuition and most school-related fees for state residents who earn at least a 3.7 GPA in high school, a 1200 SAT or 26 ACT score, and maintain a 3.3 in college. George state residents who earn at least a 3.0 in high school will also have a large portion of their tuition paid.

THE SCHOOL SAYS "..."

From the Admissions Office

"The University of Georgia offers students the advantages and resources of a top public research university, including a wide range of majors and exceptional academic facilities such as the 200,000-square-foot Miller Learning Center. At the same time, UGA provides opportunities more common to smaller, private schools, such as first-year seminars led by distinguished faculty and learning communities that connect students with similar academic interests. The university is committed to challenging its academically superior students in the classroom and beyond, with increased emphasis on undergraduate research, service-learning, and study abroad. UGA students taking advantage of such offerings find themselves well positioned to compete with the best undergraduates in the country, as evidenced by their recent string of successes in winning Rhodes, Marshall, Truman, and other major scholarships.

"The UGA campus, considered one of the most beautiful in the nation, adjoins vibrant downtown Athens. While Athens is renowned for its local music scene, UGA also houses the Performing Arts Center, the Hugh Hodgson School of Music, the Lamar Dodd School of Art, and the Georgia Museum of Art. Sports—from football to gymnastics—are also a major attraction, with UGA teams perennially ranked among the best in the country. "To experience the excitement of UGA, most prospective students visit campus, a ninety-minute drive northeast of the Atlanta airport. See the admissions website to sign up for a tour with the Visitors Center, view the weekday schedule of admissions information sessions, and find application details.

"Applicants for first-year admission will be required to submit either the SAT or ACT. Students submitting only the ACT must also submit the optional ACT writing test."

SELECTIVITY	
Admissions Rating	93
# of applicants	17,408
% of applicants accepted	59
% of acceptees attending	45
# accepting a place on wait list	709
% admitted from wait list	7

FRESHMAN PROFILE	
Range SAT Critical Reading	560–660
Range SAT Math	560–670
Range SAT Writing	560–660
Range ACT Composite	25–29
Minimum paper TOEFL	550
Minimum computer TOEFL	213
Average HS GPA	3.82
% graduated top 10% of class	53
% graduated top 25% of class	90
% graduated top 50% of class	98

DEADLINES	
Early action	
Deadline	10/15
Notification	12/15
Regular	
Priority	10/15
Deadline	1/15
Notification	4/1
Nonfall registration?	yes

APPLICANTS ALSO LOOK AT
AND OFTEN PREFER
Georgia Institute of Technology

AND SOMETIMES PREFER
Auburn University, Clemson University, Emory University, Oxford College of Emory University, University of North Carolina at Chapel Hill, Vanderbilt University

AND RARELY PREFER
University of South Carolina—Columbia

FINANCIAL FACTS	
Financial Aid Rating	78
Annual in-state tuition	$8,736
Annual out-of-state tuition	$26,946
Room and board	$8,460
Books and supplies	$1,030
% frosh rec. need-based scholarship or grant aid	40
% UG rec. need-based scholarship or grant aid	34
% frosh rec. non-need-based scholarship or grant aid	11
% UG rec. non-need-based scholarship or grant aid	6
% frosh rec. need-based self-help aid	19
% UG rec. need-based self-help aid	23
% frosh rec. any financial aid	48
% UG rec. any financial aid	43
% UG borrow to pay for school	45
Average cumulative indebtedness	$15,938

UNIVERSITY OF HOUSTON

OFFICE OF ADMISSIONS, 4400 UNIVERSITY, HOUSTON, TX 77204-2023 • ADMISSIONS: 713-743-1010 • FAX: 713-743-9633

CAMPUS LIFE

Quality of Life Rating	75
Fire Safety Rating	88
Green Rating	87
Type of school	public
Environment	metropolis

STUDENTS

Total undergrad enrollment	29,378
% male/female	50/50
% from out of state	1
% from public high school	92
% live on campus	15
# of fraternities	24
# of sororities	19
% African American	14
% Asian	21
% Caucasian	31
% Hispanic	26
% international	4
# of countries represented	127

SURVEY SAYS . . .
Great library
Career services are great
Students are friendly
Diverse student types on campus
Great off-campus food
Athletic facilities are great

ACADEMICS

Academic Rating	67
% students graduating within 4 years	15
% students graduating within 6 years	46
Calendar	semester
Student/faculty ratio	23:1
Profs interesting rating	73
Profs accessible rating	70
Most common reg class size	20–29 students
Most common lab size	20–29 students

MOST POPULAR MAJORS
biology, business administration and
management, psychology

STUDENTS SAY ". . ."

Academics
High student-class involvement and a multitude of activities "amplify school pride and success" at the University of Houston, located in—you guessed it—Houston, Texas. This "potential powerhouse" school's engineering and business programs make it a favorite among local residents, who constitute a large portion of the school's student body, and are just a couple of the reasons that the school offers an "outstanding education at an affordable price." Professors are "very active and inviting of comments and suggestions," and "discussion is certainly promoted and encouraged." There's great accessibility to faculty, who "encourage feedback" and are "friendly and will talk to you even if you are not currently enrolled in their class." The diverse array of courses is "really enjoyable," and the Honors College allows students to take special classes, "creating an environment of a small private college with the diversity and resources of a large public university." Of course, there are "a couple of professors who have been so-so," but for the most part, everyone is more than pleased. UH also has a "good relationship with industry," placing an "emphasis on internships, research, and job placement." Students laud the school's ability to "help prepare you for the real-world," and the opportunities for jobs after graduation. "I have had the opportunity to become involved in undergraduate research and author many publications in peer-reviewed journals," says one physics major. Communication is key to the satisfaction level at the school, where students are always "kept up-to-date and sent reminders of lectures, internships, competitions, scholarships, and upcoming events." Some administrative offices do lack for responsiveness (such as financial aid), but the staff is "overall productive." "University of Houston is on the road to becoming a premier tier one university and competitive on all scales and programs."

Life
The campus is centrally located close to "exciting" downtown Houston, and it has been compared to a "robust beehive." "Think of it as a small city where people from all over the world converge, whether to learn, talk, eat, or hang out together," says a student. You can walk outdoors on a warm day and see students studying in the grass, visit the "amazing" recreation center, and "harness up for one of the largest rock-climbing walls in North America." Those who want to imbibe a bit can have one at "The Den," which is an "alumni-owned, on-campus pub and a delicious sandwich shop," where "politics, music, and opinions on current events are widely discussed." There's plenty of school spirit, making sports (both intramural and Division I) popular, and the cafeteria "is a popular spot since it just got remodeled." With so many commuters, many say that parking is "horrible" at the school, but UH is building new parking garages and making new student housing and apartment options available to those who want to live on campus, which will hopefully help alleviate the problem.

Student Body
This is one heckuva "multicultural campus," with "all ages, races, religions, and...varying languages." This diversity is a beloved aspect of the school, and "Everyone, no matter who they are or where they're from, seems to fit in." "You meet so many different people with different cultures, which helps you grow and expand your world views," adds a student. Texas being Texas, this "loud and friendly" group goes about it their own way: "It's easy to fit in. You just start talking to someone." Still, common threads do run throughout, and the "majority of the students are commuters," with many holding down full-time jobs and families. People most often fit in immediately with their similar races and social groups, but "Over time, almost everyone breaks through that initial shell," and "Most networking and meeting people is done through clubs and study groups."

FINANCIAL AID: 713-743-9051 • E-MAIL: ADMISSIONS@UH.EDU • WEBSITE: WWW.UH.EDU

THE PRINCETON REVIEW SAYS

Admissions

Very important factors considered include: Class rank, rigor of secondary school record. *Important factors considered include:* Academic GPA, standardized test scores. *Other factors considered include:* Recommendation(s), character/personal qualities, extracurricular activities, first generation, level of applicant's interest, talent/ability, volunteer work, work experience. SAT or ACT required; ACT with or without writing component accepted. TOEFL required of all international applicants. High school diploma is required, and GED is accepted. *Academic units recommended:* 4 English, 3 mathematics, 2 science, 2 foreign language, 3 social studies.

Financial Aid

Students should submit: FAFSA. The Princeton Review suggests that all financial aid forms be submitted as soon as possible after January 1. *Need-based scholarships/grants offered:* Federal Pell, SEOG, state scholarships/grants, private scholarships, school scholarship or grant aid from institutional funds. *Loan aid offered:* Direct Subsidized Stafford, Direct Unsubsidized Stafford, Direct PLUS, Federal Perkins, state loans. Federal Work-Study Program available. Off-campus job opportunities are excellent.

Inside Word

The school's 37,000 strong student body means that acceptance is easier to achieve than at some smaller schools. Students who meet the State of Texas Uniform Admission Policy and satisfy a certain scale of requirements for class ranking and SAT or ACT scores are assured admission. But even if your grades aren't seemingly up to par, the admissions committee will consider students individually based on a holistic review of certain aspects, such as first-generation, socioeconomic background, rigor of high school curriculum, family responsibilities, special talents, public service, and strong letters of recommendation or a persuasive statement explaining your special circumstances.

THE SCHOOL SAYS "..."

From the Admissions Office

"The University of Houston is a Carnegie-designated Tier-One public research university that is recognized throughout the world as a leader in energy research, which is centered in a visionary Energy Research Park, law, business, and environmental education. Located in America's fourth-largest city, the University of Houston is the most ethnically diverse metropolitan research university in the United States. Its 38,500 students hail from 127 countries.

"In addition to preparing its students to succeed in today's global economy, the University of Houston also is a catalyst within its own community—changing lives through health, education, and outreach projects that help build a future for children in Houston, in Texas, and in the world.

"Other distinctive merits of the University of Houston include a strong student experience, a historic Division I athletic programs, top-level arts programs, and an internationally recognized faculty including a Nobel Laureate; winners of the National Medal of Science, Pulitzer, and Tony awards; and members of prestigious National Academies. The Princeton Review has chosen the University of Houston for inclusion in its guidebook of the nation's best colleges.

"Discover the greatness of the University of Houston's dynamic tree-lined campus of more than 650 acres—nestled just minutes from Houston's bustling theater and museum districts—where world-class teaching, revolutionary research, and nationally recognized students work together to create a globally competitive educational environment."

SELECTIVITY	
Admissions Rating	72
# of applicants	12,571
% of applicants accepted	70
% of acceptees attending	41

FRESHMAN PROFILE	
Range SAT Critical Reading	470–580
Range SAT Math	510–620
Range ACT Composite	20–25
Minimum paper TOEFL	550
Minimum computer TOEFL	213
Minimum web-based TOEFL	79
% graduated top 10% of class	27
% graduated top 25% of class	59
% graduated top 50% of class	86

DEADLINES	
Regular	
Priority	12/1
Deadline	4/1
Nonfall registration?	yes

FINANCIAL FACTS	
Financial Aid Rating	79
Annual in-state tuition	$6,270
Annual out-of-state tuition	$15,570
Room and board	$7,300
Required fees	$2,730
Books and supplies	$1,100
% frosh rec. need-based scholarship or grant aid	57
% UG rec. need-based scholarship or grant aid	51
% frosh rec. non-need-based scholarship or grant aid	3
% UG rec. non-need-based scholarship or grant aid	1
% frosh rec. need-based self-help aid	44
% UG rec. need-based self-help aid	49
% frosh rec. any financial aid	85
% UG rec. any financial aid	68
% UG borrow to pay for school	44
Average cumulative indebtedness	$14,922

UNIVERSITY OF IDAHO

IDAHO ADMISSIONS OFFICE, PO BOX 444264, MOSCOW, ID 83844-4264 • ADMISSIONS: 208-885-6326 • FAX: 208-885-9119

STUDENTS SAY ". . ."

Academics

While huge lectures and inaccessible administrators beleaguer many other state schools, the University of Idaho comes with a friendly and intimate academic environment. Even better, this school comes with a tremendously affordable price tag. Idaho residents attend UI for a pittance, and students from more than a dozen other states pay only a little more. "We don't cost a lot," dryly notes a senior. All students must complete a straightforward core curriculum. Beyond that, you can choose from more than 150 majors. The engineering programs here are nationally recognized. The College of Natural Resources boasts excellent forestry and ecology programs as well as one of the biggest genetics laboratories in the country. Students describe the academic atmosphere here as "relaxed," and they report a high level of satisfaction with their academic experiences. "The administration is active and visible." Many facilities are world-class. Classes are usually small, particularly once you get past the introductory courses. "With a few exceptions," the faculty is "very knowledgeable" and generally "incredible." Professors are "pretty easy to get a hold of after class and are always willing to help you." Also, many are "constantly involved in doing research," in a good way. As a result, undergraduate research opportunities are ample.

Life

The University of Idaho's "beautiful" campus is chock full of trees, expansive lawns, and traditionally collegiate buildings. Students laud the fact that UI "isn't too big or too small." Students portray a lively campus atmosphere and a thriving party scene. Cultural events include the Lionel Hampton Jazz Festival, which attracts big name musicians each year. Intramural sports are popular. The student recreation center boasts saunas, professional massage therapy, and a massive fifty-five-foot climbing wall. There are "many student organizations"—more than 200, in fact. When it comes to social life, though, "Greek life rules the school." While that may be a bit of an exaggeration (only twenty percent of the student body is actually part of the Greek system), students here take full advantage and "party a lot." Some are thrilled about this situation. Still others find the focus on frats and sororities to be a bit much. Off campus, "podunk" Moscow "is not and will never be a big city," but students assure us that it is "the perfect college town." Restaurants and bars are plentiful. Coffee shops are "numerous." "Good music" abounds. You can't really beat Moscow for organic food. Also, the social amenities at Washington State University are "right next door" (about 10 miles west). Another big draw here is the great outdoors. The plethora of nearby rivers, lakes, and mountains provides opportunities galore for adrenaline sports and wilderness recreation.

Student Body

The student population at UI has a "laid-back" vibe. "It is really easy to meet people." If you are having any trouble, just head over to the famed Hello Walk, a sidewalk on campus where it's customary for students and everyone else to greet "one another with a friendly hello." "A lot of UI students are Greek," but there are also plenty of rugged, "earthy-hippie, outdoorsy types." You'll find every personality type, though, "from cowboys to cosmopolitan city residents." That said, pretty much everyone is "white, middle-class," and "from the Northwest." There are few minorities. Some students lament the lack of ethnic diversity. Others call our attention to the school's geographic limitations in this regard. "It's Idaho," says a senior. "Idaho just isn't diverse."

FINANCIAL AID: 208-885-6312 • E-MAIL: ADMAPPL@UIDAHO.EDU • WEBSITE: WWW.UIDAHO.EDU

THE PRINCETON REVIEW SAYS

Admissions

Very important factors considered include: Academic GPA, standardized test scores. *Other factors considered include:* Recommendation(s). SAT or ACT required; ACT with or without writing component accepted. TOEFL required of all international applicants. High school diploma is required, and GED is accepted. *Academic units required:* 4 English, 3 mathematics, 3 science (1 science lab).

Financial Aid

Students should submit: FAFSA. The Princeton Review suggests that all financial aid forms be submitted as soon as possible after January 1. *Need-based scholarships/grants offered:* Federal Pell, SEOG, state scholarships/grants, private scholarships, school scholarship or grant aid from institutional funds. *Loan aid offered:* Direct Subsidized Stafford, Direct Unsubsidized Stafford, Direct PLUS, Federal Perkins, university loans from institutional funds. Applicants will be notified of awards on a rolling basis beginning March 30. Federal Work-Study Program available. Off-campus job opportunities are good.

The Inside Word

The University of Idaho's straightforward approach to admissions is a welcome change for students completing more involved applications. In a way that's typical of large, public universities; admissions officers arrive at decisions based on high school GPA and test scores. Most applicants are admitted and welcome the opportunity to attend a strong school at an affordable price.

THE SCHOOL SAYS "..."

From the Admissions Office

"A leading public research university in the West, the University of Idaho offers a traditional residential campus experience in a spectacular natural setting. It provides more than 130 undergraduate degree options and graduate degrees in forty-seven discipline areas, which helps provide unprecedented undergraduate research opportunities. Idaho has become known for its academic excellence, student-centered, experiential learning, and an exceptional student living environment that coupled with dedicated faculty, world-class facilities, and renowned research has produced a proven track record of high-achieving graduates. The student population of 12,000 includes first-generation college students and ethnically diverse scholars, who select from hands-on learning experiences in the colleges of Agricultural and Life Sciences; Art and Architecture; Business and Economics; Education; Engineering; Law; Letters, Arts, and Social Sciences; Natural Resources; and Science. The university also provides medical education for the state through the WWAMI program. Increasingly its interdisciplinary teams involved in environmental, sustainability, engagement, and resource management have gained national recognition. Idaho combines the strength of a large, land grant university with the intimacy of a small learning community to help students succeed and become leaders. It is home to the Vandals and competes in the Western Athletic Conference.

"Students applying for admission are required to take either the SAT or the ACT. The writing component is not required from the ACT. SAT Subject Test scores are not used for admission purposes."

SELECTIVITY

Admissions Rating	78
# of applicants	5,101
% of applicants accepted	79
% of acceptees attending	43

FRESHMAN PROFILE

Range SAT Critical Reading	480–600
Range SAT Math	490–610
Range SAT Writing	460–570
Range ACT Composite	20–26
Minimum paper TOEFL	525
Minimum computer TOEFL	193
Minimum web-based TOEFL	70
Average HS GPA	3.37
% graduated top 10% of class	19
% graduated top 25% of class	44
% graduated top 50% of class	77

DEADLINES

Regular	
Priority	2/15
Deadline	8/1
Nonfall registration?	yes

APPLICANTS ALSO LOOK AT
AND SOMETIMES PREFER
Utah State University

AND RARELY PREFER
Idaho State University

FINANCIAL FACTS

Financial Aid Rating	70
Annual in-state tuition	$5,402
Annual out-of-state tuition	$11,592
Room and board	$7,194
Required fees	$5,402
Books and supplies	$1,474
% frosh rec. need-based scholarship or grant aid	38
% UG rec. need-based scholarship or grant aid	41
% frosh rec. non-need-based scholarship or grant aid	56
% UG rec. non-need-based scholarship or grant aid	53
% frosh rec. need-based self-help aid	46
% UG rec. need-based self-help aid	51
% frosh rec. any financial aid	56
% UG rec. any financial aid	58
% UG borrow to pay for school	66
Average cumulative indebtedness	$24,396

University of Illinois at Urbana-Champaign

901 West Illinois Street, Urbana, IL 61801 • Admissions: 217-333-0302 • Fax: 217-333-9758

STUDENTS SAY ". . ."

Academics

The epically large flagship campus of the University of Illinois "is very challenging and gives you freedom to do anything." Students here enjoy "all the benefits of a great public university." There are more than 150 undergraduate programs. The colleges of engineering and business are of the "most prestigious and hardest to get into," but there are dozens of other "very strong and reputable" departments as well. "The research resources are amazing," raves a Russian literature major. "The library has almost any resource an undergraduate or even an advanced researcher would ever need." However, the drawbacks that come with such an expansive campus are present as well. Lower-level class sizes "are horrendously large." "My largest class had 800 students," says a biochemistry major. "The massive bureaucracy" is a constant source of irritation. "Simple things like adding or dropping a class a few weeks into a semester can require five or six trips to different buildings to talk to different people, each time requiring you to explain your situation." "Professors are more impersonal to freshmen but seem to warm up to upperclassmen," explains one student. "There are some professors that should not be teaching anywhere," though. "A lot of times, it's a toss-up with bad/good professors," counsels a geology major. "You can learn a lot and have a great teacher, but you need to ask around and find out who that good teacher is." "There are professors and classes that you come across that certainly leave something to be desired," agrees a women's studies major. "But overall, I am very pleased with my academic experience at UIUC, and I have met some astoundingly intelligent, influential professors."

Life

At the University of Illinois, there is "never a dull moment, despite the surrounding cornfields." More than a thousand clubs and organizations provide students with a wide array of options. "Anything that you are interested in, you can do," gloats an engineering major. "It's a huge campus, but it's not too spread out," says a Spanish major. "You can get around anywhere by bike or bus, and you don't need a car." "The campus is very Greek-oriented," and the students who pledge the myriad of frats and sororities "love the Greek life." Some students notice serious animosity between the independent students and students involved in the frat scene. "It seems at times to take over our campus," says one independent. Other students just don't see the problem. "I think plenty of non-Greeks associate with Greeks," asserts a finance major. "Drinking is a big thing at U of I," and there is an "outstanding bar culture." "If you don't want to party all the time, there are plenty of other options." "Intramural sports and playing sports on the quad and in frat park are popular." The campus is "alive with the Big Ten spirit," and students are very supportive of their beloved Illini. "Awesome concerts" proliferate, and "there is a really good artsy theater, which runs foreign and indie films."

Student Body

The U of I has a decidedly Midwestern feel, and "Midwestern hospitality" is abundant. "Kids from out-of-state and small-town farm students" definitely have a presence, but, sometimes, it seems like "practically everyone is from the northwest suburbs of Chicago." There's a lot of ethnic diversity "visible on campus." On the whole, the majority of students are "very smart kids who like to party." "The typical student is involved and really good at balancing schoolwork, clubs and organizations, and a social life." "They really study fairly hard, and when you ask, it turns out that they're majoring in something like rocket science." "There is a niche for everyone."

FINANCIAL AID: 217-333-0100 • E-MAIL: ADMISSIONS@OAR.UIUC.EDU • WEBSITE: WWW.UIUC.EDU

THE PRINCETON REVIEW SAYS

Admissions

Very important factors considered include: Academic GPA, application essay, class rank, rigor of secondary school record, standardized test scores. *Important factors considered include:* Character/personal qualities, extracurricular activities, first generation, talent/ability, volunteer work, work experience. *Other factors considered include:* Geographical residence, racial/ethnic status, state residency. SAT or ACT required; ACT with writing component required. TOEFL required of all international applicants. High school diploma is required, and GED is accepted. *Academic units required:* 4 English, 3 mathematics, 2 science (2 science labs), 2 foreign language, 2 social studies, 2 academic elective.

Financial Aid

Students should submit: FAFSA. The Princeton Review suggests that all financial aid forms be submitted as soon as possible after January 1. *Need-based scholarships/grants offered:* Federal Pell, SEOG, state scholarships/grants, private scholarships, school scholarship or grant aid from institutional funds, United Negro College Fund. *Loan aid offered:* Direct Subsidized Stafford, Direct Unsubsidized Stafford, Direct PLUS, Federal Perkins, university loans from institutional funds. Federal Work-Study Program available. Off-campus job opportunities are excellent.

The Inside Word

Few candidates are deceived by Illinois's relatively high acceptance rate; the university has a well-deserved reputation for expecting applicants to be strong students, and those who aren't usually don't bother to apply. Despite a jumbo applicant pool, the admissions office reports that every candidate is individually reviewed, which deserves mention as rare in universities of this size.

THE SCHOOL SAYS "..."

From the Admissions Office

"The campus has been aptly described as a collection of neighborhoods constituting a diverse and vibrant city. The neighborhoods are of many types: students and faculty within a department; people sharing a room or house; the members of a professional organization, a service club, or an intramural team; or simply people who, starting out as strangers sharing a class or a study lounge or a fondness for a weekly film series, have become friends. And the city of this description is the university itself—a rich cosmopolitan environment constructed by students and faculty to meet their educational and personal goals. The quality of intellectual life parallels that of other great universities, and many faculty and students who have their choice of top institutions select Illinois over its peers. While such choices are based often on the quality of individual programs of study, another crucial factor is the 'tone' of the campus life that is linked with the virtues of Midwestern culture. There is an informality and a near-absence of pretension, which, coupled with a tradition of commitment to excellence, creates an atmosphere that is unique among the finest institutions.

"Applicants are required to take the SAT or the ACT with the writing section."

SELECTIVITY

Admissions Rating	85
# of applicants	27,273
% of applicants accepted	67
% of acceptees attending	38
# accepting a place on wait list	142
% admitted from wait list	89

FRESHMAN PROFILE

Range SAT Critical Reading	530–660
Range SAT Math	680–770
Minimum paper TOEFL	550
Minimum computer TOEFL	213
Minimum web-based TOEFL	79
% graduated top 10% of class	56
% graduated top 25% of class	93
% graduated top 50% of class	99

DEADLINES

Early action	
Deadline	11/10
Notification	12/14
Regular	
Priority	11/10
Deadline	1/2
Nonfall registration?	no

APPLICANTS ALSO LOOK AT

AND OFTEN PREFER
Northwestern University,
University of Michigan—Ann Arbor

AND SOMETIMES PREFER
Indiana University at Bloomington, University of Iowa,
University of Wisconsin—Madison, Washington
University in St. Louis

AND RARELY PREFER
Purdue University—West Lafayette

FINANCIAL FACTS

Financial Aid Rating	81
Annual in-state tuition	$9,484
Annual out-of-state tuition	$23,626
Room and board	$9,714
Required fees	$2,510
Books and supplies	$1,200
% frosh rec. need-based scholarship or grant aid	38
% UG rec. need-based scholarship or grant aid	34
% frosh rec. non-need-based scholarship or grant aid	13
% UG rec. non-need-based scholarship or grant aid	12
% frosh rec. need-based self-help aid	39
% UG rec. need-based self-help aid	39
% frosh rec. any financial aid	54
% UG rec. any financial aid	56
% UG borrow to pay for school	51
Average cumulative indebtedness	$16,866

UNIVERSITY OF IOWA

107 CALVIN HALL, IOWA CITY, IA 52242 • ADMISSIONS: 319-335-3847 • FAX: 319-333-1535

CAMPUS LIFE
Quality of Life Rating	84
Fire Safety Rating	80
Green Rating	94
Type of school	public
Environment	city

STUDENTS
Total undergrad enrollment	20,493
% male/female	48/52
% from out of state	38
% from public high school	90
% live on campus	30
# of fraternities	20
# of sororities	19
% African American	2
% Asian	3
% Caucasian	79
% Hispanic	4
% international	6
# of countries represented	101

SURVEY SAYS . . .
Low cost of living
Everyone loves the Hawkeyes
Lots of beer drinking
Hard liquor is popular

ACADEMICS
Academic Rating	67
% students graduating within 4 years	44
% students graduating within 6 years	70
Calendar	semester
Student/faculty ratio	16:1
Profs interesting rating	71
Profs accessible rating	75
Most common reg class size	10–19 students
Most common lab size	20–29 students

MOST POPULAR MAJORS
biology, business/commerce, engineering

STUDENTS SAY ". . ."

Academics

The University of Iowa "is a large school that…becomes small" once you find your place in it, students tell us. Or rather, places: Your academic specializations, extracurricular activities, and social circles all contribute to "each person finding their own niche here." This comfort doesn't come at the expense of opportunity, as it might at a smaller school; here undergrads enjoy "the opportunity to take advantage of the resources…and seek out everything from research to internships in the areas [they] are studying." Those opportunities are available across disciplines, as "University of Iowa is all about serious professions such as medicine and engineering but is also good with the arts as well." Students report that Iowa has "strong science programs," a "good business school," a "prestigious journalism school," a "strong art program," and "one of the best creative writing programs in the country." Most professors here "are approachable and seem interested in helping students learn," although not all are stellar lecturers. Students majoring in the sciences and engineering in particular complain that for some professors, "English is a very distant second language." Teaching assistants are ubiquitous. As one student explains, "Unless it's an honors class or a grad class that you asked permission to join as [an] undergrad, you mostly deal with the TAs. The TAs are hit-and-miss, but a lot of them are really great and helpful."

Life

"Football season is the best time of year" at University of Iowa, where "tailgating is great" and "most of the student body is out tailgating before 8:00 A.M. on Saturdays in the fall." "Even those who aren't football fans take part in the atmosphere," and at game time more than "70,000 fans fill the stadium to cheer the Hawks on to victory." The bar scene is also quite popular. "Loads of popular and underground music acts come through" each week and where students often congregate to watch out-of-town football games. But while "going to bars is pretty common," "there are plenty of other things to do" in and around campus, including "Campus Activities Board events, student organizations…intramurals, and Night Games," in which the school opens the field house one night a month for recreational sports and activities. Greek life "makes up around twelve percent of the population on campus, which is big enough to mean something but also not super overwhelming." Iowa City is no major metropolis but students enjoy its "many restaurants and bars;" "great places to shop, eat, and hang out;" and the "great relationship between the residents and the students."

Student Body

Iowa's undergraduate population is about 20,000 strong, large enough to encompass numerous subpopulations. The student body consists of a mix of kids "who grew up in rural Iowa, kids from the Chicago suburbs, and several students from every state in the country and various countries from around the world." You'll find everything "ranging from city to country kids, liberal to conservative, regional to international" here, with "so many things you can get involved in to channel those traits" that you'll inevitably "find your fit." Your job will be easiest if you blend well with the majority, who are "white, middle-class, decent at school," and "involved in at least one student organization," have "a great interest in [Iowa] athletics," and "take their social [lives] rather seriously." Iowa hosts "many students from other countries, especially China, so there is plenty of opportunity to broaden your cultural base if you choose. If you want to be a typical partying college student, you can definitely fit right in, but if you don't, you can find your own social group as well."

FINANCIAL AID: 319-335-1450 • E-MAIL: ADMISSIONS@UIOWA.EDU • WEBSITE: WWW.UIOWA.EDU

THE PRINCETON REVIEW SAYS

Admissions

Very important factors considered include: Academic GPA, class rank, rigor of secondary school record, standardized test scores. *Other factors considered include:* Recommendation(s), character/personal qualities, state residency, talent/ability. SAT or ACT required; ACT with writing component recommended. TOEFL required of all international applicants. High school diploma is required, and GED is accepted. *Academic units required:* 4 English, 3 mathematics, 3 science, 2 foreign language, 3 social studies. *Academic units recommended:* 4 mathematics, 4 foreign language.

Financial Aid

Students should submit: FAFSA, institution's own financial aid form. The Princeton Review suggests that all financial aid forms be submitted as soon as possible after January 1. *Need-based scholarships/grants offered:* Federal Pell, SEOG, state scholarships/grants, private scholarships, school scholarship or grant aid from institutional funds. *Loan aid offered:* Direct Subsidized Stafford, Direct Unsubsidized Stafford, Direct PLUS, Federal Perkins, Federal Nursing Loans, university loans from institutional funds. Applicants will be notified of awards on a rolling basis beginning March 15. Federal Work-Study Program available. Off-campus job opportunities are good.

The Inside Word

University of Iowa uses a formula to calculate your Regent Admission Index (RAI), a number that is "strongly predictive" of your likelihood of gaining admission. You can find the formula (and an online calculator) at Iowa's admissions website, where you will also find the cutoff number for likely successful candidates (it's currently 245). Price and academic opportunities make Iowa a popular choice, so the cutoff is fairly high. Students interested in business or nursing should apply to the College of Liberal Arts and Sciences; space in these programs is especially limited, making admission even more competitive. Engineers must apply to the School of Engineering, where admissions requirements are also relatively stringent.

THE SCHOOL SAYS "..."

From the Admissions Office

"The University of Iowa has outstanding programs in the creative arts, notably the Iowa Writers' Workshop and the world-renowned International Writing Program. It also has strong programs in business, communication studies, journalism, English, engineering, political science, and psychology, and was the birthplace of the discipline of speech pathology and audiology. It offers excellent programs in the basic health sciences and health care programs, led by the top ranked College of Medicine and the closely associated University Hospitals and Clinics.

"The University of Iowa will accept either the SAT or the ACT. The ACT writing test is not required but we recommend you take it."

SELECTIVITY

Admissions Rating	82
# of applicants	17,220
% of applicants accepted	84
% of acceptees attending	32

FRESHMAN PROFILE

Range SAT Critical Reading	460–640
Range SAT Math	560–700
Range SAT Writing	490–640
Range ACT Composite	23–28
Minimum paper TOEFL	540
Minimum computer TOEFL	197
Minimum web-based TOEFL	80
Average HS GPA	3.59
% graduated top 10% of class	24
% graduated top 25% of class	56
% graduated top 50% of class	91

DEADLINES

Regular	
Deadline	4/1
Notification	9/15
Nonfall registration?	yes

APPLICANTS ALSO LOOK AT
AND OFTEN PREFER
University of Illinois at Urbana-Champaign

AND SOMETIMES PREFER
Indiana University at Bloomington, Iowa State University, University of Northern Iowa

FINANCIAL FACTS

Financial Aid Rating	82
Annual in-state tuition	$6,436
Annual out-of-state tuition	$23,770
Room and board	$8,750
Required fees	$1,329
Books and supplies	$1,090
% frosh rec. need-based scholarship or grant aid	32
% UG rec. need-based scholarship or grant aid	29
% frosh rec. non-need-based scholarship or grant aid	28
% UG rec. non-need-based scholarship or grant aid	17
% frosh rec. need-based self-help aid	36
% UG rec. need-based self-help aid	39
% frosh rec. any financial aid	80
% UG rec. any financial aid	79
% UG borrow to pay for school	54
Average cumulative indebtedness	$27,391

UNIVERSITY OF KANSAS

OFFICE OF ADMISSIONS & SCHOLARSHIPS, 1502 IOWA STREET, LAWRENCE, KS 66045 • ADMISSIONS: 785-864-3911 • FAX: 785-864-5017

CAMPUS LIFE

Quality of Life Rating	96
Fire Safety Rating	82
Green Rating	83
Type of school	public
Environment	city

STUDENTS

Total undergrad enrollment	19,983
% male/female	51/49
% from out of state	21
% live on campus	22
# of fraternities	22
# of sororities	13
% African American	3
% Asian	4
% Caucasian	79
% Hispanic	5
% Native American	1
% international	5
# of countries represented	112

SURVEY SAYS . . .

Athletic facilities are great
Great off-campus food
Everyone loves the Jayhawks
Student publications are popular

ACADEMICS

Academic Rating	70
% students graduating within 4 years	32
% students graduating within 6 years	61
Calendar	semester
Student/faculty ratio	20:1
Profs interesting rating	81
Profs accessible rating	83
Most common reg class size	20–29 students
Most common lab size	10–19 students

MOST POPULAR MAJORS

biology, business/commerce, psychology

STUDENTS SAY ". . ."

Academics

The University of Kansas—KU for short—"can offer an unbelievable education but can also provide the quintessential college sports and party scene if the student so chooses. It is a school where the student chooses [his or] her own experience." For those seeking them, the school "provides numerous, wonderful opportunities to every student" through "the integration of tradition and new media...to form a new level of excellence." University resources allow KU to excel in a broad range of disciplines, from business to biology to social welfare to art to engineering to architecture, and, thanks to state sponsorship, can do so "at an affordable price." Universities mean research, of course, and "KU has great undergrad research opportunities. Since it is such a big school, there are some great facilities and a lot of funding. Also, the professors are very interested in helping undergrads, and not just graduate students, start working on research." For those up to the challenge, the Honors Program "is an unbelievable resource" that "offers fabulous classes...[and] plenty of opportunities for students to connect with each other and faculty."

Life

"Life at KU is extraordinary," undergraduates gloat. "From going downtown to Mass Street to attending basketball and football games, there is always something to do in Lawrence." Division I athletics "are fantastic" here; "a certain awe seems to radiate throughout Allen Fieldhouse as an energetic student section cheers for their team," according to one die-hard Jayhawks fan. Greek life attracts a substantial number of KU undergraduates, and the Greek houses serve as a center of weekend fun. Students "work hard to get through classes and activities and work during the week so that they can party hard on the weekends. It's pretty easy to find several frat parties or keggers and go party-hopping." KU's first-rate recreation center is also "a popular place, offering a huge climbing wall, basketball courts, equipment, and other programs," and the campus is home to "every club imaginable...If you like something, someone else does too. If the club does not already exist, you can start it." Hometown Lawrence "has a pretty nice bar scene, and there are enough bands that come through and local concerts to keep things entertaining. One thing that is great about Lawrence is the city really supports local business[es], so there are several local restaurants, coffee shops, etc. It has a unique feel to it." Lawrence is "halfway between Kansas City and Topeka as well as Omaha and Wichita, [so] even if you can't find something to do in Lawrence, you can head to another city and catch a concert or show or just go on a road trip."

Student Body

The typical KU student "would be from one of the big suburbs in Kansas such as Overland Park, Topeka, or Wichita," but "because the university is so big with many different colleges, there is a place for everyone." On this campus you'll find everything "from international students from across the globe to white Republicans to gays and lesbians." The student body divides into "two distinct categories: the Greeks and everyone else. There is no animosity between the two groups but they don't intermingle very much." They are also divided by their devotion to academics. As one student explains, "There are those who come to KU, take large lecture classes (which they sleep through), party on the weekend, and catch every basketball game. Then there are those who have three separate majors, two internships, four jobs, and no sleep. The rest of us fall somewhere between those two extremes." "Lawrence is very liberal," at least by Kansas standards, and many students follow suit, although "there are some very conservative students here" who "are generally accepted and their views respected." Wondering what the uniting factor is among this diverse student body? Most everyone "is a loyal Jayhawk," passionate about KU sports.

FINANCIAL AID: 785-864-4700 • E-MAIL: ADM@KU.EDU • WEBSITE: WWW.KU.EDU

THE PRINCETON REVIEW SAYS

Admissions

Very important factors considered include: Academic GPA, class rank, standardized test scores. SAT or ACT required; ACT with or without writing component accepted. TOEFL required of all international applicants. High school diploma is required, and GED is accepted. *Academic units required:* 4 English, 3 mathematics, 3 science, 3 social studies. *Academic units recommended:* 4 English, 4 mathematics, 3 science, 2 foreign language, 3 social studies.

Financial Aid

Students should submit: FAFSA. The Princeton Review suggests that all financial aid forms be submitted as soon as possible after January 1. *Need-based scholarships/grants offered:* Federal Pell, SEOG, state scholarships/grants, private scholarships, school scholarship or grant aid from institutional funds. *Loan aid offered:* Direct Subsidized Stafford, Direct Unsubsidized Stafford, Direct PLUS, Federal Perkins, university loans from institutional funds. Applicants will be notified of awards on a rolling basis beginning April 1. Federal Work-Study Program available. Off-campus job opportunities are excellent.

The Inside Word

You want instant gratification? KU will process your application in forty-eight hours if you apply to the College of Liberal Arts and Sciences (CLAS) or the School of Engineering (with the exception of the architectural engineering program). Formulas drive admissions at this large state school, and the right combination of test scores and high school grades can get you in without too much sweat. In-state applicants with average test scores and at least a 2.0 GPA in the Kansas Board of Regents high school curriculum are shoo-ins; out-of-state applicants need slightly better test scores and at least a 2.5 GPA. Any applicant who ranks in the top third of his high school class is admitted regardless of test scores or GPA. Requirements at the School of Engineering are considerably more rigorous (at least 3.0 GPA just to be considered).

THE SCHOOL SAYS "..."

From the Admissions Office

"The University of Kansas has a long and distinguished tradition for academic excellence. Outstanding students from Kansas and across the nation are attracted to KU because of its strong academic reputation, beautiful campus, affordable cost of education, and contagious school spirit. KU provides students extraordinary opportunities in honors programs, service learning, research, internships, and study abroad. The university is located in Lawrence (forty minutes from Kansas City), a community of 88,000 regarded as one of the nation's best small cities for its arts scene, live music, and historic downtown.

"Students applying for admissions may submit an ACT or SAT score, and KU will only look at math and critical reading (verbal) section of SAT for admissions purposes."

SELECTIVITY

Admissions Rating	79
# of applicants	10,157
% of applicants accepted	93
% of acceptees attending	39

FRESHMAN PROFILE

Range ACT Composite	22–28
Minimum paper TOEFL	540
Minimum web-based TOEFL	70
Average HS GPA	3.50
% graduated top 10% of class	2
% graduated top 25% of class	55
% graduated top 50% of class	89

DEADLINES

Regular	
Priority	9/1
Deadline	4/1
Nonfall registration?	yes

FINANCIAL FACTS

Financial Aid Rating	75
Annual in-state tuition	$7,875
Annual out-of-state tuition	$20,680
Room and board	$6,982
Required fees	$858
Books and supplies	$800
% frosh rec. need-based scholarship or grant aid	31
% UG rec. need-based scholarship or grant aid	30
% frosh rec. non-need-based scholarship or grant aid	19
% UG rec. non-need-based scholarship or grant aid	12
% frosh rec. need-based self-help aid	38
% UG rec. need-based self-help aid	35
% frosh rec. any financial aid	65
% UG rec. any financial aid	66
% UG borrow to pay for school	48
Average cumulative indebtedness	$23,319

UNIVERSITY OF KENTUCKY

100 FUNKHOUSER BUILDING, LEXINGTON, KY 40506 • ADMISSIONS: 859-257-2000 • FAX: 859-257-3823

CAMPUS LIFE
Quality of Life Rating	74
Fire Safety Rating	81
Green Rating	60*
Type of school	public
Environment	city

STUDENTS
Total undergrad enrollment	19,927
% male/female	51/49
% from out of state	20
% live on campus	27
# of fraternities	23
# of sororities	19
% African American	7
% Asian	2
% Caucasian	82
% Hispanic	2
% international	2
# of countries represented	110

SURVEY SAYS . . .
Great computer facilities
Great library
Athletic facilities are great
Everyone loves the Wildcats
Student publications are popular

ACADEMICS
Academic Rating	63
% students graduating within 4 years	32
% students graduating within 6 years	58
Calendar	semester
Student/faculty ratio	18:1
Profs interesting rating	68
Profs accessible rating	62
Most common reg class size	20–29 students
Most common lab size	20–29 students

MOST POPULAR MAJORS
biology, nursing, psychology, business, mechanical engineering

STUDENTS SAY ". . ."

Academics
The University of Kentucky in Lexington is "all about making a name for yourself by preparing for and getting involved in future career goals while having fun and enjoying what college is all about." "Making a name for yourself" here requires distinguishing yourself in a crowd of almost 19,000 undergraduates; daunting as that sounds, students tell us it can be done. "Getting involved in future career goals" is easy enough, given the "great selection of courses and majors" available. Kentucky offers undergraduate degrees in twelve of its nineteen divisions. Choices include the College of Agriculture (with popular majors in animal science, agricultural economics, and hospitality management), the College of Business and Management, the College of Education, the College of Engineering, the College of Communications and Information Studies (advertising, journalism, and library science), and the College of Arts and Sciences (biology, history, and political science). Students here laud the "impressive teaching staff, dedicated to enhancing student knowledge and teaching students about the future." UK's brand-new library "is also quite amazing. It is the perfect place to go study because usually the dorms can be a bit too distracting." All told, go-getters willing to take initiative will find UK offers "a safe and fun atmosphere where you have unlimited opportunities to get involved at a reasonable price."

Life
"Everyone is a Wildcat" at UK, because "UK has tremendous sports programs and big fans all around the United States." Men's basketball fans "are among the craziest in the nation," and students "would be football fanatics if our team would win a game every now and then." "Because UK is dry, most parties are held off campus." Social life for many revolves around the off-campus Greek houses where "There is always a party going on, but you have to be a part of a fraternity or sorority to really know about it and attend." Some students report, "There are a lot of nonalcoholic parties in the dorms that might be crazier than the alcoholic parties," although others advise, "It's better to live off campus because the residence halls are pretty bad (except for the new ones), the meal plan is awful, and everything off campus is a lot cheaper." Hometown Lexington "is a great city with much to do and lots of opportunities. It offers many different clubs, bars, and restaurants that college students can go to as well as horse racing. All of these venues have a 'College Day' where students get discounts." One sophomore warns, however, "Small-town students can become distracted by the lights of the city."

Student Body
"The typical UK student has a Southern accent, likes to party, and often shops at J. Crew," but, "as the undergraduate population is about 19,000, there are a lot of people who do not fit that description." True, one of the most common "types"—or at least the most conspicuous one—are the "beautiful people, the hot girls and guys who roam the campus and dress up to go to class." But for every "collar-popping, stuck-up frat boy" there's also "your typical country Kentucky boy, boots and all." What you won't find many of at UK are "liberals—they are few and far between—and the type of atypical student with wild hair colors or other style extremes." Most "lean right politically, but generally the student body is apathetic." School spirit is rampant, so much so that "on an average day, one in three students will have some sort of UK clothing on."

UNIVERSITY OF KENTUCKY

FINANCIAL AID: 859-257-3172 • E-MAIL: ADMISSION@UKY.EDU • WEBSITE: WWW.UKY.EDU

THE PRINCETON REVIEW SAYS

Admissions

Very important factors considered include: Academic GPA, rigor of secondary school record, standardized test scores. *Other factors considered include:* Application essay, class rank, recommendation(s), alumni/ae relation, character/personal qualities, extracurricular activities, geographical residence, interview, racial/ethnic status, talent/ability, volunteer work. SAT or ACT required; ACT with or without writing component accepted. TOEFL required of all international applicants. High school diploma is required, and GED is accepted. *Academic units required:* 4 English, 3 mathematics, 3 science, 2 foreign language, 3 social studies, 5 academic elective. *Academic units recommended:* 4 English, 4 mathematics, 4 science, 2 foreign language, 3 social studies, 3 academic elective.

Financial Aid

Students should submit: FAFSA. Regular filing deadline is February 15. The Princeton Review suggests that all financial aid forms be submitted as soon as possible after January 1. *Need-based scholarships/grants offered:* Federal Pell, SEOG, state scholarships/grants, private scholarships, school scholarship or grant aid from institutional funds. *Loan aid offered:* Direct Subsidized Stafford, Direct Unsubsidized Stafford, Direct PLUS, Federal Perkins, state loans, university loans from institutional funds. Applicants will be notified of awards on a rolling basis beginning April 1.

The Inside Word

The University of Kentucky's admissions team is about as objective as they come. If you have the GPA, class rank, and test scores, you'll in all likelihood be welcomed into the Wildcat community. The university is continually looking to improve its selectivity, so hitting the books is a must if you want to be a serious contender.

THE SCHOOL SAYS "..."

From the Admissions Office

"The University of Kentucky offers you an outstanding learning environment and quality instruction through its excellent faculty. Of the 1,892 full-time faculty, ninety-eight percent hold the doctorate degree or the highest degree in their field of study. Many are nationally and internationally known for their research, distinguished teaching, and scholarly service to Kentucky, the nation, and the world. UK's scholars (students, faculty, and alumni) have been honored by Nobel, Pulitzer, Rhodes, Fulbright, Guggenheim, and Grammy awards, and most recently the Metropolitan Opera and the Marshall Foundation. Yet, with a student to teacher ratio of only seventeen to one, UK faculty are accessible and willing to answer your questions and discuss your interests.

"UK will accept the SAT. The writing sections of the ACT and SAT will not be used in the admission process."

SELECTIVITY

Admissions Rating	82
# of applicants	13,537
% of applicants accepted	69
% of acceptees attending	46

FRESHMAN PROFILE

Range SAT Critical Reading	490–620
Range SAT Math	500–630
Range SAT Writing	480–590
Range ACT Composite	22–28
Minimum paper TOEFL	527
Minimum computer TOEFL	197
Average HS GPA	3.40
% graduated top 10% of class	32
% graduated top 25% of class	60
% graduated top 50% of class	87

DEADLINES

Regular	
Priority	2/15
Deadline	2/15
Notification	10/1
Nonfall registration?	yes

FINANCIAL FACTS

Financial Aid Rating	81
Annual in-state tuition	$7,656
Annual out-of-state tuition	$16,724
Room and board	$9,439
Required fees	$954
Books and supplies	$800
% frosh rec. need-based scholarship or grant aid	18
% UG rec. need-based scholarship or grant aid	17
% frosh rec. non-need-based scholarship or grant aid	41
% UG rec. non-need-based scholarship or grant aid	29
% frosh rec. need-based self-help aid	28
% UG rec. need-based self-help aid	28
% frosh rec. any financial aid	45
% UG rec. any financial aid	39
% UG borrow to pay for school	33
Average cumulative indebtedness	$22,943

UNIVERSITY OF LOUISIANA AT LAFAYETTE

PO DRAWER 41210, LAFAYETTE, LA 70504 • ADMISSIONS: 337-482-6457 • FAX: 337-482-6195

CAMPUS LIFE

Quality of Life Rating	86
Fire Safety Rating	86
Green Rating	60*
Type of school	public
Environment	city

STUDENTS

Total undergrad enrollment	14,715
% male/female	43/57
% from out of state	4
% live on campus	12
# of fraternities	11
# of sororities	9
% African American	20
% Asian	2
% Caucasian	72
% Hispanic	2
% international	2
# of countries represented	97

SURVEY SAYS . . .
Students are friendly
Students get along with local community
Students love Lafayette, LA
Great off-campus food
Student publications are popular
Student government is popular

ACADEMICS

Academic Rating	61
% students graduating within 4 years	13
% students graduating within 6 years	40
Calendar	semester
Student/faculty ratio	23:1
Profs interesting rating	70
Profs accessible rating	69
Most common reg class size	20–29 students
Most common lab size	20–29 students

MOST POPULAR MAJORS
biology, business administration and management

STUDENTS SAY ". . ."

Academics
At the "medium-sized" University of Louisiana at Lafayette—in "the heart of Cajun country"—many students feel "under the shadow" of their mammoth cousin, LSU. We really don't know why. UL Lafayette offers "serious bang for your buck;" tremendously generous grant and scholarship programs and out-of-state fee waivers make UL Lafayette one of the best bargains in the country. Programs in "education, computer science, and engineering" are "ranked as some of the best in the nation." The nursing program is the "third largest" in the country and "one of the best" anywhere. "Seasoned" and "overwhelmingly helpful" professors are "friendly, fun," and "honestly interested in having you learn." "The experience has been absolutely wonderful academically," gushes a senior. "In more than 120 hours of course study, I cannot remember having one bad professor." Other students disagree; they remember a "couple of bad apples." A perennial complaint among students at UL Lafayette is that many professors from other countries "cannot be understood by the students." The administration is generally unpopular. "The bureaucracy is ridiculous," reports a general studies major. "The university is run like an out-of-date chicken farm," adds a finance major. "No one knows the answer to anything" and "Getting financial aid in a timely manner is a real problem." Students are generally very satisfied, though. "My overall college experience at University of Louisiana at Lafayette has been terrific," asserts a junior. "I would recommend this college to anyone."

Life
UL Lafayette's "beautiful campus" is "full of big trees and handsome Southern architecture." Unfortunately, "It always floods when it rains," some "lousy buildings" "need updating," and the parking situation is just "painful." Nevertheless, "school spirit is really high." "Football games are huge events," and Lafayette is, by all accounts, a "great" college town. "Believe me," swears a wide-eyed first-year student, "it is an experience." The Strip "is right by campus" and "lined with numerous bars and clubs." "Most people," however, "congregate downtown," where it's "almost like Bourbon Street in New Orleans." The local music scene is hopping, and festivals are frequent, including a very large International Music Festival and a gigantic Mardi Gras celebration. If partying isn't your bag, or if you get sick of it, Lafayette also offers an "abundance of coffee shops" and "numerous art venues." "There is so much history and culture in Louisiana" that, frankly, it's hard to "ever be bored or without something fun to do on any day of the week," and you can find "great food anywhere." "If you're looking for a good, inexpensive college education that is packed with good food, cold beer, and excitement, look no further than UL Lafayette."

Student Body
Students at UL Lafayette are "friendly and fun" and "always seem to be in a good mood." They have "Southern flair with a little bit of our Cajun cayenne," a marketing major quips. They're also "very strongly rooted in their religions;" in that regard, "Catholic conservatives" seem to dominate. Many "are from the surrounding area of Acadiana," are "lower- to upper-middle-class," and "receive some financial support from [their] parents." Many also "have part-time job[s]." Beyond that, "there are many different types of people," and "everyone seems to get along together." One undergrad reports, "Our campus includes a very diverse group of students from various religious and racial backgrounds." There are also "a few oddballs" who "try to get themselves noticed by the way they dress and their eccentric hair." For the most part, however, "everyone blends in." "No one really points out or harasses other students here at UL Lafayette, unless that student happens to be wearing LSU paraphernalia."

FINANCIAL AID: 337-482-6506 • E-MAIL: ADMISSIONS@LOUISIANA.EDU • WEBSITE: WWW.LOUISIANA.EDU

THE PRINCETON REVIEW SAYS

Admissions

Very important factors considered include: Academic GPA, class rank, rigor of secondary school record, standardized test scores. *Other factors considered include:* State residency. SAT or ACT required; ACT with or without writing component accepted. TOEFL required of all international applicants. High school diploma is required, and GED is accepted. *Academic units required:* 4 English, 4 mathematics, 3 science, 2 foreign language, 1 social studies, 2 history, 1 visual/performing arts.

Financial Aid

Students should submit: FAFSA. The Princeton Review suggests that all financial aid forms be submitted as soon as possible after January 1. *Need-based scholarships/grants offered:* Federal Pell, SEOG, state scholarships/grants, private scholarships, school scholarship or grant aid from institutional funds, Federal Nursing Scholarships. *Loan aid offered:* Federal Perkins, Federal Nursing Loans. Applicants will be notified of awards on a rolling basis beginning April 1. Federal Work-Study Program available. Off-campus job opportunities are good.

The Inside Word

UL Lafayette is still a fallback school for many applicants. You are pretty much guaranteed admission if you carry an ACT score of at least 18 and complete a basic college-prep high school curriculum with a GPA of 2.5 or better. If your numbers are a little lower, you can submit an essay and some other credentials for possible admission through UL Lafayette's admission by committee. It should be noted, however, that admission by committee is limited to seven percent of each incoming class.

THE SCHOOL SAYS "..."

From the Admissions Office

"The University of Louisiana at Lafayette offers students from throughout the United States and more than ninety countries strong academic training and personal enrichment opportunities in a friendly, comfortable, student-centered environment. UL Lafayette students are taught, mentored, and advised by some of the brightest and most accomplished faculty members in the United States. Although UL Lafayette offers more than 100 programs of study and the research opportunities, internship possibilities, and facilities of a major research-intensive university, average class size is approximately the same as that at many high schools and smaller higher education institutions. "UL students receive a good deal of individual attention and support—both personal and academic—from faculty and staff.

"A wide range of cultural, recreational, and social activities are available on and off campus, including more than 150 campus organizations and clubs, NCAA Division I and intramural athletics, a state-of-the-art aquatic center, a thriving arts scene, a wide range of live music venues, shopping, a great variety of excellent restaurants, theaters, the second largest Mardi Gras in the nation, and an international music festival. In fact, Utne Reader magazine selected the city of Lafayette as Louisiana's 'Most Enlightened Town.'

"Our relatively low tuition and generous financial aid and scholarship programs, including an out-of-state tuition waiver for qualified students, make UL Lafayette one of the most affordable universities in the nation. "Students who have completed the required college preparatory core curriculum in high school may qualify for admission on the basis of a combination of their high school cumulative grade point average and ACT or SAT scores. Writing scores are not required."

SELECTIVITY
Admissions Rating	71
# of applicants	8,426
% of applicants accepted	67
% of acceptees attending	52

FRESHMAN PROFILE
Range ACT Composite	20–24
Minimum paper TOEFL	525
Minimum computer TOEFL	195
Average HS GPA	3.25
% graduated top 10% of class	15
% graduated top 25% of class	41
% graduated top 50% of class	75

DEADLINES
Regular	
Priority	7/20
Nonfall registration?	yes

FINANCIAL FACTS
Financial Aid Rating	67
Annual in-state tuition	$3,002
Annual out-of-state tuition	$11,574
Room and board	$8,236
Required fees	$1,454
Books and supplies	$1,200
% frosh rec. need-based scholarship or grant aid	49
% UG rec. need-based scholarship or grant aid	41
% frosh rec. non-need-based scholarship or grant aid	8
% UG rec. non-need-based scholarship or grant aid	4
% frosh rec. need-based self-help aid	25
% UG rec. need-based self-help aid	29
% frosh rec. any financial aid	87
% UG rec. any financial aid	72

UNIVERSITY OF MAINE

5713 CHADBOURNE HALL, ORONO, ME 04469-5713 • ADMISSIONS: 207-581-1561 • FAX: 207-581-1213

STUDENTS SAY ". . ."

Academics
The University of Maine is proud to have "one of the top engineering schools in the Northeast!" Students describe the atmosphere as "engineering with a dash of liberal art," and also praise the forestry and business programs. However, some point out, "As with many schools focused on funding their science departments, the arts programs tend to suffer and feel like the neglected, malnourished stepchildren." Yet, the overall consensus is that "UMaine has challenging courses that push students to reach their potential." Many students say they chose UMaine for its balance of "the friendly, small feeling while still at a state university," and Maine residents cite the "financially feasible" in-state tuition combined with the fact that "it's close to home but far enough away and large enough to feel different and exciting" as big selling points. Most agree, "The faculty and administrators take an active interest in the students" and say, "Education is top priority." Professor reviews offer a mixed bag, with some students saying, "The professors here are open-minded and teach with enthusiasm," and others finding, "There is the occasional dud professor." One zoology major sums up the disparity this way: "Professors in the lower-level courses tend to be more focused on lecturing than anything else. As you move up in the course levels, and classes get smaller, the professors tend to pay more attention to class discussion and the opinions of individual students."

Life
Despite the fact that "it can get rather gloomy with the long winters" and "winters are pretty harsh," UMaine students agree, "The administration, in conjunction with the student government, does whatever they can to make it better." One business administration major says, "We have a saying: If you're bored, you're doing something wrong. There is stuff going on six nights a week, and there is lots to do in the Bangor area. Hiking, dining, arts, sports, anything you need, really." Most students point to the overall "outdoorsyness" of campus life, saying, "The only thing more plentiful than the friendly people are the deer and the squirrels." UMaine students "love to use the recreation facilities and explore the great outdoors," and they're proud to add, "Our school has a really strong campus culture." A common sentiment is that "UMaine is a great place to work and play." One sophomore says, "Hockey is life; the rest is just classes." The Division I hockey team at UMaine has many shouting, "Go Black Bears!" and all agree that "UMaine Hockey is a huge event for any Maine student." While some rave about the recently upgraded gym complex, others grumble that some "facilities are old and falling apart," and some students believe the university should focus on "upgrading outdated classroom buildings in some majors." The most common complaint about the administration: "They could start by backing off with the parking tickets…It's crazy."

Student Body
The majority of students here hail from Maine and the Northeast. However, despite a lack of external diversity, students say, "There is a wide range of diversity in thought and belief," and students say that although "diversity is rare because of the school's location…it is encouraged and accepted." One thing's for sure, in the "winter, we all look like Eskimos." In fact, most students agree, "One of the best aspects of UMaine is the camaraderie that everyone has for each other," and agree, "Students have many opportunities to meet people in and out of class." In fact, one theater major proclaims, "The majority of the students who attend the University of Maine are either athletes or soon-to-be scientists…however, both groups tend to mix fairly well with each other." Another student concurs, "I've seen former high school jocks socializing with brilliant engineers." UMaine has a reputation for its lively social life; "There is no denying that most everybody drinks for fun," but students are careful to point out, "The campus is huge, so if partying isn't your scene it's easy to find another one."

FINANCIAL AID: 207-581-1324 • E-MAIL: UM-ADMIT@MAINE.EDU • WEBSITE: WWW.UMAINE.EDU

THE PRINCETON REVIEW SAYS

Admissions

Very important factors considered include: Academic GPA, class rank, rigor of secondary school record, standardized test scores. *Important factors considered include:* Application essay, recommendation(s). *Other factors considered include:* Character/personal qualities, extracurricular activities, geographical residence, interview, state residency, talent/ability, volunteer work, work experience. SAT or ACT required; ACT with or without writing component accepted. TOEFL required of all international applicants. High school diploma is required, and GED is accepted. *Academic units required:* 4 English, 3 mathematics, 2 science (2 science labs), 2 foreign language, 2 social studies, 4 academic elective. *Academic units recommended:* 4 English, 4 mathematics, 4 science (3 science labs), 2 foreign language, 2 social studies, 1 history, 4 academic elective.

Financial Aid

Students should submit: FAFSA. Regular filing deadline is March 1. The Princeton Review suggests that all financial aid forms be submitted as soon as possible after January 1. *Need-based scholarships/grants offered:* Federal Pell, SEOG, state scholarships/grants, private scholarships, school scholarship or grant aid from institutional funds. *Loan aid offered:* Direct Subsidized Stafford, Direct Unsubsidized Stafford, Direct PLUS, Federal Perkins, state loans. Applicants will be notified of awards on a rolling basis beginning March 15. Federal Work-Study Program available. Off-campus job opportunities are good.

The Inside Word

UMaine has rolling admissions but cautions that deadlines are still important, particularly for early action students who want to be considered for merit scholarships. The university recommends campus visits; tours are available at the Buchanan Alumni House. While interviews aren't required, they're considered mutually beneficial and informative for prospective students and admissions representatives.

THE SCHOOL SAYS "..."

From the Admissions Office

"The University of Maine offers you the best of both worlds—the excitement, breadth and depth that are available at a land grant, sea grant, research university with the personal attention and community feel of a smaller college. Five academic colleges and an Honors College offer you the chance to belong to a supportive academic community, while providing the specialization, resources and opportunities for research, internships and scholarly activity you would expect at a major university. Academics are a priority at UMaine; most programs hold the highest level of accreditation possible, setting UMaine apart nationally.

"And at UMaine there is always something to do—there are more than 200 clubs and student organizations, lots of volunteer opportunities, an active student government, a new multimillion dollar student recreation center with an busy intramural schedule and Division I varsity athletics to keep you busy. A special First Year Residence Experience (FYRE) will help support your transitions to college—this unique program includes special activities and theme living communities. It is located between the new Student Recreation Center and the newly renovated Hilltop dining complex. Check out our website to learn more—or better yet, come visit us in person and see the campus for yourself!"

SELECTIVITY

Admissions Rating	77
# of applicants	7,247
% of applicants accepted	78
% of acceptees attending	31

FRESHMAN PROFILE

Range SAT Critical Reading	480–590
Range SAT Math	480–600
Range SAT Writing	470–580
Range ACT Composite	21–27
Minimum paper TOEFL	530
Minimum computer TOEFL	197
Minimum web-based TOEFL	71
Average HS GPA	3.25
% graduated top 10% of class	22
% graduated top 25% of class	50
% graduated top 50% of class	87

DEADLINES

Early action	
Deadline	12/15
Notification	1/31
Regular	
Priority	2/1
Notification	2/1
Nonfall registration?	yes

APPLICANTS ALSO LOOK AT
AND OFTEN PREFER
University of New Hampshire, University of Southern Maine, University of Vermont

AND SOMETIMES PREFER
University of Connecticut, University of Massachusetts Amherst, University of Rhode Island

FINANCIAL FACTS

Financial Aid Rating	82
Annual in-state tuition	$8,010
Annual out-of-state tuition	$23,040
Room and board	$8,766
Required fees	$2,158
Books and supplies	$1,000
% frosh rec. need-based scholarship or grant aid	62
% UG rec. need-based scholarship or grant aid	56
% frosh rec. non-need-based scholarship or grant aid	4
% UG rec. non-need-based scholarship or grant aid	3
% frosh rec. need-based self-help aid	65
% UG rec. need-based self-help aid	66
% frosh rec. any financial aid	76
% UG rec. any financial aid	83
% UG borrow to pay for school	76
Average cumulative indebtedness	$21,487

UNIVERSITY OF MARY WASHINGTON

1301 COLLEGE AVENUE, FREDERICKSBURG, VA 22401 • ADMISSIONS: 540-654-2000 • FAX: 540-654-1857

CAMPUS LIFE

Quality of Life Rating	77
Fire Safety Rating	86
Green Rating	78
Type of school	public
Environment	city

STUDENTS

Total undergrad enrollment	4,271
% male/female	36/64
% from out of state	20
% from public high school	78
% live on campus	57
% African American	5
% Asian	5
% Caucasian	58
% Hispanic	4
# of countries represented	23

SURVEY SAYS . . .
No one cheats
Athletic facilities are great
Students are friendly
Great off-campus food
Students are happy
Frats and sororities are unpopular
or nonexistent

ACADEMICS

Academic Rating	74
% students graduating within 4 years	65
% students graduating within 6 years	72
Calendar	semester
Student/faculty ratio	15:1
Profs interesting rating	90
Profs accessible rating	75
Most common reg class size	20–29 students
Most common lab size	20–29 students

MOST POPULAR MAJORS
business administration and management, English language and literature

STUDENTS SAY ". . ."

Academics

The University of Mary Washington is known as a "lovely state university that gives you a private school education." A political science major raves, "Even though it's a public university it feels like a small liberal arts school." In fact, students laud the "small student body and class sizes" for facilitating "individual interactions with professors." Most students agree, "The professors really make UMW shine." Although they admit that "the professors vary, just like at any other university," they say, "The professors are always available outside of class." The overall sentiment is that "Mary Washington is a solid academic school that could use a little growth," but students believe UMW is "a hidden jewel that delivers on a historical campus" and say courses are "engaging and intellectually stimulating." Students are particularly enthusiastic about the historic preservation and education programs, and many take pride in the university's honor code, which they believe "provides a good environment for students to build a community" and "encourages people to try hard in an honest way." Overall, students agree, "Mary Washington is all about getting a well-rounded education while becoming a part of a great community" and point out that "professors are included in that as well."

Life

Students say, "The population size and the layout of the campus make it impossible to not bump into someone you know," and admit that the "beautiful campus" and "Jeffersonian architecture" are a large part of UMW's draw. A large proportion feels that "the atmosphere is incredibly friendly," and say, "Community and campus participation is paramount." However, some students complain that UMW "could use improvement in school spirit," and point out that "the student activities and clubs aren't as abundant here as they are at other schools." Still, there's a consensus that the clubs in existence are "welcoming" and that it's "easy to get involved." Most students agree, "The administration needs to do a better job of communicating with students," especially in relation to "the upcoming campus remodel." An English major clarifies, saying, "Our school needs to understand how important the integrity of our current campus is to us." Students grumble, "The registration process is a mess," and say, "Although having smaller classes is nice, sometimes it is hard…to get into a desired class because of this." Despite these grievances, students agree that UMW is "a small school with a big heart," and "It is a tight-knit community with an atmosphere that pushes you to your potential."

Student Body

UMW students describe their fellow classmates as "typically bright, fairly hardworking but easygoing for the most part," and say, "Most students fit in very well." An anthropology major says, "There are prepsters with pearls and Ralph Lauren, athletes sporting sweats, punks with gauges and flannel, and everyone in between." However, one student notes, "We have lots of diversity in terms of religious background, sexual orientation, and the gender ratio, but the school needs to work on becoming more racially balanced." "As with anywhere, groups tend to form," but students say, "There isn't a feeling of exclusivity," and they assert that "students have a lot of opportunity to connect… through the mandatory two years they need to live on campus." A common freshman complaint is that "there is nothing to do on the weekends," but upperclassmen insist that "below the surface, Mary Wash is a hotspot of activity" and rave about programs like "Cheap Seats," which sponsors dollar movies on campus. Either way, it's commonly held that "there are not many raging parties, usually just low key house parties." However, many students praise UMW's location, exclaiming that "Fredericksburg is a fantastic town" and pointing out that the school is "within an hour's distance to Richmond or D.C., so there are frequent trips for class or for fun."

UNIVERSITY OF MARY WASHINGTON

FINANCIAL AID: 800-468-5614 • E-MAIL: ADMIT@UMW.EDU • WEBSITE: WWW.UMW.EDU

THE PRINCETON REVIEW SAYS

Admissions

Very important factors considered include: Academic GPA, rigor of secondary school record. *Important factors considered include:* Application essay, class rank, recommendation(s), standardized test scores, extracurricular activities. *Other factors considered include:* Alumni/ae relation, character/personal qualities, first generation, geographical residence, racial/ethnic status, state residency, talent/ability, volunteer work, work experience. SAT or ACT required; ACT with or without writing component accepted. TOEFL required of all international applicants. High school diploma is required, and GED is accepted. *Academic units required:* 4 English, 3 mathematics, 3 science (3 science labs), 2 foreign language, 2 social studies, 1 history. *Academic units recommended:* 4 English, 4 mathematics, 4 science (4 science labs), 4 foreign language, 2 social studies, 2 history.

Financial Aid

Students should submit: FAFSA. Regular filing deadline is May 31. The Princeton Review suggests that all financial aid forms be submitted as soon as possible after January 1. *Need-based scholarships/grants offered:* Federal Pell, SEOG, state scholarships/grants, private scholarships, school scholarship or grant aid from institutional funds. *Loan aid offered:* Direct Subsidized Stafford, Direct Unsubsidized Stafford, Direct PLUS, Federal Perkins. Federal Work-Study Program available. Off-campus job opportunities are good.

The Inside Word

UMW seeks to enroll a well-rounded student body and doesn't follow a particular blueprint when evaluating applicants. The admissions team gives each application a focused review, looking for students with a strong secondary school curriculum that has prepared them for successful study at the university level. Honors level and AP work is highly encouraged as evidence of this.

THE SCHOOL SAYS "..."

From the Admissions Office

"The University of Mary Washington has long been known for its commitment to providing a stellar undergraduate, liberal arts education. Our faculty are devoted to teaching—without teaching assistants—and are able to provide individualized attention to their students. An education at UMW, with multi ple opportunities for student research and service learning, prepares graduates for outstanding careers or for entry into graduate school. Internship opportunities abound not only in Fredericksburg, but also an hour's drive away in either Washington, D.C., or Richmond, Virginia. A wide range of programs includes strong majors in political science/international affairs, English, biology, psychology, earth/environmental science, history, visual and performing arts, economics, and business. Also distinctive are historic preservation and a concentration in creative writing. UMW's campus is one of the nation's most beautiful, with classic Jeffersonian architecture, spacious grounds, and a park-like character. Historic Fredericksburg's forty-square-block historic district is walking distance from campus. Several large, modern shopping and entertain ment complexes are nearby. UMW provides a variety of residential options, from traditional residence halls to modern apartments. A new retail and luxury student apartment complex opened in fall 2010. More than 100 clubs and organizations are offered along with a top NCAA Division III athletic program. The university's recently renovated Lee Hall offers an expanded facility providing enhanced student services, a spacious bookstore, and 'Underground' snack bar/coffee house. UMW students are bright, multi-talented, and involved."

SELECTIVITY

Admissions Rating	76
# of applicants	4,766
% of applicants accepted	77
% of acceptees attending	26
# accepting a place on wait list	165
% admitted from wait list	50

FRESHMAN PROFILE

Range SAT Critical Reading	530–640
Range SAT Math	520–610
Range SAT Writing	520–620
Range ACT Composite	23–27
Minimum paper TOEFL	570
Minimum computer TOEFL	230
Minimum web-based TOEFL	88
Average HS GPA	3.58

DEADLINES

Early action	
Deadline	11/15
Regular	
Priority	1/15
Deadline	2/1
Nonfall registration?	yes

APPLICANTS ALSO LOOK AT
AND OFTEN PREFER
College of William and Mary, University of Virginia

AND SOMETIMES PREFER
James Madison University, University of Richmond, Virginia Tech

AND RARELY PREFER
Christopher Newport University, George Mason University

FINANCIAL FACTS

Financial Aid Rating	67
Annual in-state tuition	$4,460
Annual out-of-state tuition	$16,190
Room and board	$8,900
Required fees	$4,340
Books and supplies	$1,000
% frosh rec. need-based scholarship or grant aid	18
% UG rec. need-based scholarship or grant aid	15
% frosh rec. non-need-based scholarship or grant aid	17
% UG rec. non-need-based scholarship or grant aid	9
% frosh rec. need-based self-help aid	23
% UG rec. need-based self-help aid	18
% frosh rec. any financial aid	56
% UG rec. any financial aid	58
% UG borrow to pay for school	44
Average cumulative indebtedness	$15,630

UNIVERSITY OF MARYLAND—BALTIMORE COUNTY

1000 HILLTOP CIRCLE, BALTIMORE, MD 21250 • ADMISSIONS: 410-455-2291 • FAX: 410-455-1094

STUDENTS SAY ". . ."

Academics

The University of Maryland, Baltimore County has a "great regional reputation" as a "quiet academic school" where "students take education seriously." Undergraduates are enthusiastic about the "academic opportunities and scholarship programs available," and say, "UMBC wants to see every student succeed—they provide you with the tools, people, and resources to make sure you get where you want to go in life." The university is particularly known for its "strong" science and mathematics programs and a commitment to the performing arts. Some students grumble, "The school needs to serve those with different majors apart from the sciences," but others are quick to point out that "UMBC is changing a bit to offer more to the fine arts students," including construction of a new technologically advanced fine arts building. Most agree the university has "extremely intelligent professors that have a knack for inspiring the students," and say, "UMBC is a place where professors aren't just talking heads." Although some complain about dull lectures, a common consensus is that "this is a university where teaching comes first, followed by research, and it shows," and say, "Most of the professors are so helpful, you can find most of them sitting in their office and they don't mind if you come and ask them questions."

Life

UMBC has a large contingent of commuters and one ancient studies major says, "There are a lot of activities held by student organizations on campus during the week and on the weekends, but many students live close to campus and choose to go home for the weekend." While some may see this as a downside others say, "The location of UMBC is true brilliance—so close to Baltimore. We hop over there on the weekdays even to go shopping or go out to eat." Most lament the absence of a football team and say, "The only real issue with UMBC is the lack of visible school spirit…People have made efforts to try and pump up the school, but nothing's come to fruition yet." In fact, students give the administration poor marks, saying, "Students are not given adequate attention on the matters of housing, financial aid, and advising," and there are complaints about the parking facilities, as well as a desire for "better buildings and food options." Despite these criticisms, a sociology major says, "Everyone on campus is nice and helpful to other students. People will always hold a door for you, help you pick up a dropped folder, or offer to share their notes with a student who missed class."

Student Body

More than one student says, "UMBC is a place where it is cool to be smart, and everything about the campus, including the students, exudes 'nerd-chic.'" In fact, an English major says that even "our president likes to say that it's cool to be smart at UMBC." This mentality is captured by a student who remarks, "Life at UMBC, aside from special events, revolves around classes and learning," and most undergrads agree, "The typical student at UMBC is interested in doing well academically and not just here to party until graduation." However, despite their dedication to hard work, UMBC students call themselves "enthusiastic and bright" and say "that almost every student at UMBC is involved with at least a couple of extracurricular activities, which connect them to the campus." The school has a strong reputation for diversity and students feel "it enriches our school and everyone gets to know everyone despite culture or ethnicity." A mechanical engineering student says, "This is even reflected in the high number of interracial couples I see on campus." Overall, it seems, "People fit in by being intellectually creative and finding a community with which to discuss important issues."

UNIVERSITY OF MARYLAND—BALTIMORE COUNTY

FINANCIAL AID: 410-455-2387 • E-MAIL: ADMISSIONS@UMBC.EDU • WEBSITE: WWW.UMBC.EDU

THE PRINCETON REVIEW SAYS

Admissions

Very important factors considered include: Academic GPA, rigor of secondary school record, standardized test scores. *Important factors considered include:* Application essay, recommendation(s). *Other factors considered include:* Class rank, character/personal qualities, extracurricular activities, talent/ability, volunteer work, work experience. SAT or ACT required; ACT with or without writing component accepted. TOEFL required of all international applicants. High school diploma is required, and GED is accepted. *Academic units required:* 4 English, 3 mathematics, 3 science, 2 foreign language. *Academic units recommended:* 4 English, 4 mathematics, 3 science, 2 foreign language.

Financial Aid

Students should submit: FAFSA. The Princeton Review suggests that all financial aid forms be submitted as soon as possible after January 1. *Need-based scholarships/grants offered:* Federal Pell, SEOG, state scholarships/grants, private scholarships, school scholarship or grant aid from institutional funds. *Loan aid offered:* Direct Subsidized Stafford, Direct Unsubsidized Stafford, Direct PLUS. Applicants will be notified of awards on a rolling basis beginning March 15. Federal Work-Study Program available. Off-campus job opportunities are excellent.

The Inside Word

UMBC maintains an Admissions Counselor Blog where prospective students can connect with current members of the admissions team to questions during the application process. The admissions committee considers the strength of your secondary school curriculum and class rank in combination with traditional factors, such as GPA, test scores, and essay when making an acceptance decision. Additionally, it's suggested that at least one letter of recommendation be written by a teacher.

THE SCHOOL SAYS "..."

From the Admissions Office

"When it comes to universities, a mid-sized school can be just right. Some students want the resources of a large community. Others are looking for the attention found at a smaller one. With an undergraduate population of over 9,000, UMBC can offer the best of both. There are always new people to meet and things to do—from Division I sports to more than 170 student clubs. As a research university, we offer an abundance of programs, technology, and opportunities for hands-on experiences. Yet we are small enough that students don't get lost in the shuffle. More than eighty percent of our classes have fewer than forty students. Among public research universities, UMBC is recognized for its success in placing students in the most competitive graduate programs and careers. Of course, much of the success of UMBC has to do with the students themselves—highly motivated students who get involved in their education."

"Freshman applicants are required to take the SAT or ACT."

SELECTIVITY

Admissions Rating	85
# of applicants	6,987
% of applicants accepted	63
% of acceptees attending	34
# accepting a place on wait list	497
% admitted from wait list	67

FRESHMAN PROFILE

Range SAT Critical Reading	540–640
Range SAT Math	560–670
Range SAT Writing	530–660
Range ACT Composite	24–29
Minimum paper TOEFL	460
Minimum computer TOEFL	140
Minimum web-based TOEFL	48
Average HS GPA	3.57
% graduated top 10% of class	30
% graduated top 25% of class	53
% graduated top 50% of class	83

DEADLINES

Early action	
Deadline	11/1
Notification	12/15
Regular	
Priority	11/1
Deadline	2/1
Notification	12/15
Nonfall registration?	yes

APPLICANTS ALSO LOOK AT

AND OFTEN PREFER
Johns Hopkins University, Virginia Tech

AND SOMETIMES PREFER
Johns Hopkins University, Penn State—University Park, University of Maryland—College Park, Virginia Tech

AND RARELY PREFER
Towson University

FINANCIAL FACTS

Financial Aid Rating	78
Annual in-state tuition	$6,678
Annual out-of-state tuition	$16,616
Room and board	$9,620
Books and supplies	$1,200
% frosh rec. need-based scholarship or grant aid	36
% UG rec. need-based scholarship or grant aid	37
% frosh rec. non-need-based scholarship or grant aid	5
% UG rec. non-need-based scholarship or grant aid	3
% frosh rec. need-based self-help aid	27
% UG rec. need-based self-help aid	32
% frosh rec. any financial aid	73
% UG rec. any financial aid	65
% UG borrow to pay for school	46
Average cumulative indebtedness	$19,122

UNIVERSITY OF MARYLAND—COLLEGE PARK

MITCHELL BUILDING, COLLEGE PARK, MD 20742-5235 • ADMISSIONS: 800-422-5867 • FAX: 301-314-9693

CAMPUS LIFE

Quality of Life Rating	65
Fire Safety Rating	79
Green Rating	97
Type of school	public
Environment	metropolis

STUDENTS

Total undergrad enrollment	26,194
% male/female	53/47
% from out of state	23
% live on campus	42
# of fraternities	36
# of sororities	27
% African American	12
% Asian	15
% Caucasian	58
% Hispanic	7
% international	2
# of countries represented	125

SURVEY SAYS . . .

Athletic facilities are great
Diverse student types on campus
Everyone loves the Terrapins
Student publications are popular
Lots of beer drinking

ACADEMICS

Academic Rating	77
% students graduating within 4 years	62
% students graduating within 6 years	81
Calendar	semester
Student/faculty ratio	18:1
Profs interesting rating	71
Profs accessible rating	67
Most common reg class size	20–29 students
Most common lab size	20–29 students

MOST POPULAR MAJORS
criminology, economics, psychology

STUDENTS SAY ". . ."

Academics

The University of Maryland—College Park is a grand mix of "twenty-minute walks to class across one of the country's most beautiful campuses, [an introduction] to high-level courses taught by the nation's top researchers, [and] a motivated 'green' campus" as well as "crowded, smelly frat parties, [and] living-learning communities that can make the gigantic campus much smaller." Students are quick to boast about sports, too, especially the school's titles as "the 2008 national champions in men's soccer and women's field hockey." In short: It's a quintessential large university, offering "a great experience with a variety of opportunities that are what you make of them." Students crow about Maryland's "nationally recognized business program," a "top-ranked criminology program," a solid engineering school, a great political science department that capitalizes on the school's proximity to Washington, D.C., and the "top-notch honors program." Most of all, they love the "great price. This school gives you a great education for a really cheap price." Low cost doesn't translate to budget accommodations. On the contrary, "the administration shows a desire to always upgrade facilities, as can be witnessed by the tremendous business school and the brand new engineering building." In conclusion, students applaud "the widely diverse opportunities available at UMD. You can never get bored because there is always something to do."

Life

"Life at UMD is awesome," with "a good mix of fun activities" including "school-sponsored parties, games," a "campus recreation center that has virtually everything you could wish for, including pools, an extensive gym, a rock wall, squash courts, an indoor track," and a student union "loaded with fun places like the arcade area, bowling alley," and "tons of places to eat as well." In addition, "there are always open games of soccer, football, or ultimate Frisbee being played on the mall and elsewhere." There are bars close to campus, and "students are always having parties," especially along College Park's raucous Frat Row. Terrapin sports are a passion for many. And if all that isn't enough, "the proximity to D.C., makes clubbing, nights out on the town, and general visits to D.C. frequent." With all this going on, no wonder students say that "the social life at UMD is unsurpassed." Some warn the surrounding area is dicey; "It's pretty annoying and scary to get crime alerts from the police informing us of incidents close to campus," one student explains. Undergrads also warn that parking regulations are brutal. "Bus transportation around campus provided by the university is great, but for students and visitors with cars, it's a huge hassle. Permits are expensive, and free parking for visitors is impossible to find. School officials are strict with violations, and tickets are seventy-five dollars. They are hard to refute and very costly."

Student Body

"The University of Maryland is a very large school," so "there is no 'typical' student here. Everyone will find that they can fit in somewhere." Better still, "different groups are very accepting of other groups. Students in Greek life are just as accepting of students in non-Greek life. Athletes blend in with non-athletes. UMD provides a great environment for students to meet people they would normally not know and helps to provide great connections with these people." UMD is "an especially diverse school," and this makes people "more tolerant and accepting of people from different backgrounds and cultures." A student from New Jersey explains it this way: "Coming from a very diverse area, I thought it was going to be hard to find a school that had that same representation of minority and atypical students until I found Maryland. I don't think I have ever learned so much about different religions, cultures, orientations, or lifestyles. All of them are accepted and even celebrated" at UMD.

FINANCIAL AID: 301-314-9000 • E-MAIL: UM-ADMIT@UMD.EDU • WEBSITE: WWW.MARYLAND.EDU

THE PRINCETON REVIEW SAYS

Admissions

Very important factors considered include: Academic GPA, rigor of secondary school record, standardized test scores. *Important factors considered include:* Application essay, class rank, recommendation(s), first generation, state residency, talent/ability. *Other factors considered include:* Alumni/ae relation, character/personal qualities, extracurricular activities, geographical residence, racial/ethnic status, volunteer work, work experience. SAT or ACT required; ACT with writing component required. TOEFL required of all international applicants. High school diploma is required, and GED is accepted. *Academic units required:* 4 English, 4 mathematics, 3 science (2 science labs), 2 foreign language, 3 history or social science.

Financial Aid

Students should submit: FAFSA. Regular filing deadline is February 15. The Princeton Review suggests that all financial aid forms be submitted as soon as possible after January 1. *Need-based scholarships/grants offered:* Federal Pell, SEOG, state scholarships/grants, private scholarships, school scholarship or grant aid from institutional funds. *Loan aid offered:* Direct Subsidized Stafford, Direct Unsubsidized Stafford, Direct PLUS, Federal Perkins. Applicants will be notified of awards on a rolling basis beginning April 1. Federal Work-Study Program available. Off-campus job opportunities are good.

The Inside Word

Maryland admissions officers don't simply crunch numbers and apply a formula. The school considers no fewer than twenty-five factors when determining who's in and who's out. Essays, recommendations, extracurricular activities, talents and skills, and demographic factors all figure into the mix along with high school transcript and standardized test scores. Give all aspects of your application your utmost attention; admissions are very competitive.

THE SCHOOL SAYS "..."

From the Admissions Office

"Commitment to excellence, to diversity, to learning—these are the hallmarks of a Maryland education. As the state's flagship campus and one of the nation's leading public universities, Maryland offers students and faculty the opportunity to come together to explore and create knowledge, to debate and discover our similarities and our differences, and to serve as a model of intellectual and cultural excellence for the state and the nation's capital. With leading programs in engineering, business, journalism, architecture, and the sciences, the university offers an outstanding educational value."

SELECTIVITY

Admissions Rating	95
# of applicants	26,358
% of applicants accepted	44
% of acceptees attending	34

FRESHMAN PROFILE

Range SAT Critical Reading	580–680
Range SAT Math	610–710
Minimum paper TOEFL	575
Average HS GPA	3.98
% graduated top 10% of class	71
% graduated top 25% of class	91
% graduated top 50% of class	100

DEADLINES

Early action	
Deadline	11/1
Notification	1/31
Regular	
Priority	11/1
Deadline	1/20
Notification	4/1
Nonfall registration?	yes

FINANCIAL FACTS

Financial Aid Rating	65
Annual in-state tuition	$6,763
Annual out-of-state tuition	$23,178
Room and board	$9,599
Required fees	$1,653
Books and supplies	$1,076
% frosh rec. need-based scholarship or grant aid	21
% UG rec. need-based scholarship or grant aid	26
% frosh rec. non-need-based scholarship or grant aid	23
% UG rec. non-need-based scholarship or grant aid	16
% frosh rec. need-based self-help aid	24
% UG rec. need-based self-help aid	27
% frosh rec. any financial aid	72
% UG rec. any financial aid	63
% UG borrow to pay for school	43
Average cumulative indebtedness	$22,696

UNIVERSITY OF MASSACHUSETTS AMHERST

UNIVERSITY ADMISSIONS CENTER, AMHERST, MA 01003-9291 • ADMISSIONS: 413-545-0222 • FAX: 413-545-4312

CAMPUS LIFE

Quality of Life Rating	90
Fire Safety Rating	82
Green Rating	88
Type of school	public
Environment	town

STUDENTS

Total undergrad enrollment	21,373
% male/female	50/50
% from out of state	19
% live on campus	60
# of fraternities	21
# of sororities	15
% African American	4
% Asian	7
% Caucasian	70
% Hispanic	5
% international	1
# of countries represented	51

SURVEY SAYS . . .

Lots of liberal students
Class discussions are rare
Great computer facilities
Great library
Students aren't religious
Great off-campus food
Low cost of living
Student publications are popular

ACADEMICS

Academic Rating	69
% students graduating within 4 years	53
% students graduating within 6 years	61
Calendar	semester
Student/faculty ratio	19:1
Profs interesting rating	72
Profs accessible rating	75
Most common reg class size	10–19 students
Most common lab size	20–29 students

MOST POPULAR MAJORS
biology, psychology, speech communication and rhetoric

STUDENTS SAY ". . ."

Academics

It's all about "finding out where you fit in" at the University of Massachusetts Amherst, where students say the experience is "all what you make of it. If you want to party, there is one available to you almost every night," but a pre-law student warns that "academics are challenging," and other students agree, especially in the engineering program, the hard sciences, the sports management program ("one of the oldest and best in the country"), and at the Isenberg School of Management. As at many big schools, "It is easy to not go to class because they are so large, although many teachers now use the PRS [a hand-held wireless interactive remote unit], which quizzes you and is a method of [taking] attendance during each class." You will also have the opportunity to get a degree with an "individual concentration" that allows you to design your own interdisciplinary majors. Students can also enroll—at no extra charge—in courses at Amherst, Hampshire, Mount Holyoke, and Smith colleges through the Five College Consortium. The consortium includes open library borrowing, a meal exchange, and a free bus system connecting the campuses. Unlike many major research institutions, UMass Amherst has a surprising number of professors who "show a passion for teaching. I have yet to see a professor who just teaches for money," a sports management major reports. By all accounts, "More than half of the professors are awesome." Students agree that "UMass Amherst has countless opportunities for one to get involved and improve his or her leadership and responsibilities."

Life

"There is so much to do on campus here that you rarely have to leave the school to find something," students report, pointing out that, in addition to attending one of the school's ubiquitous sporting events, "You can go ice skating on campus, go to a play, see bands play, see a movie, etc." Are you sitting down? "Most of these things are also free of charge, or available for a reduced fee." When the weather permits, "Numerous people are outside doing some sort of activity, whether it's playing catch, playing a sport with a bunch of people, or just laying out in the sun. In the Southwest Residential area, there is a horseshoe that people call Southwest Beach because on nice days it is packed with hundreds of people." If you're into socializing, "There is something going on every night of the week somewhere." One student says, "Drinking is big here but not totally out of control like some say." And another student assures us that, "It is more than possible to stay in on a Friday night, do your laundry, and watch a movie with friends. Parties are available, but not required." More students seem to want to live on campus now, lured perhaps by the new apartment style residence halls and dining services. Hometown Amherst provides "great restaurants and shows." Northampton and Holyoke, both close by, are "good places to go shopping."

Student Body

"There is no such thing as a typical student at UMass Amherst." An undergraduate population of more than 20,000 makes that impossible; however, students do seem to fall into a few readily identified groups. There are "plenty of students who are here strictly for academics," people who are here for the party scene," and a "lot of people who came here for academics but fell into the party scene." Most learn to balance fun and work; those who don't exit long before graduation. Students also "tend to fit the mold of their residence," undergrads tell us. one student writes, "Southwest houses students of mainstream culture. Students there can be seen wearing everything from UMass Amherst sweats to couture. Students in Central (especially Upper Central) tend to be the 'hippie' or scene type kids. Northeast houses…the more reserved types. Orchard Hill typically houses the more quiet types as well."

UNIVERSITY OF MASSACHUSETTS AMHERST

FINANCIAL AID: 413-545-0801 • E-MAIL: MAIL@ADMISSIONS.UMASS.EDU • WEBSITE: WWW.UMASS.EDU

THE PRINCETON REVIEW SAYS

Admissions

Very important factors considered include: Academic GPA, rigor of secondary school record. *Important factors considered include:* Class rank, standardized test scores. *Other factors considered include:* Application essay, recommendation(s), character/personal qualities, extracurricular activities, first generation, geographical residence, level of applicant's interest, racial/ethnic status, state residency, talent/ability, volunteer work, SAT or ACT required; ACT with writing component recommended. TOEFL required of all international applicants. High school diploma is required, and GED is accepted. *Academic units required:* 4 English, 3 mathematics, 3 science (2 science labs), 2 foreign language, 2 social studies, 2 academic elective.

Financial Aid

Students should submit: FAFSA. The Princeton Review suggests that all financial aid forms be submitted as soon as possible after January 1. *Need-based scholarships/grants offered:* Federal Pell, SEOG, state scholarships/grants, private scholarships, school scholarship or grant aid from institutional funds. *Loan aid offered:* Direct Subsidized Stafford, Direct Unsubsidized Stafford, Direct PLUS, Federal Perkins, state loans. Applicants will be notified of awards on a rolling basis beginning March 1. Federal Work-Study Program available. Off-campus job opportunities are good.

The Inside Word

University of Massachusetts Amherst requires applicants to identify a first-choice and a second-choice major; admissions standards are tougher in the school's most prestigious programs (such as engineering, business, communications and journalism, economics, computer science, and sports management). It is possible to be admitted for your second-choice major but not your first; it is also possible to be admitted as an "undeclared" student if you fail to gain admission via your chosen majors. You can transfer into either major later, although doing so will require you to excel in your freshman and sophomore classes.

THE SCHOOL SAYS ". . ."

From the Admissions Office

"The University of Massachusetts Amherst is the largest public university in New England, offering its students an almost limitless variety of academic programs and activities. Over eighty-five majors are offered, including a unique program called Bachelor's Degree with Individual Concentration (BDIC) in which students create their own program of study. The outstanding full-time faculty of over 1,100 is the best in their fields and they take teaching seriously. Students can take courses through the honors program and sample classes at nearby Amherst, Hampshire, Mount Holyoke, and Smith Colleges at no extra charge. First-year students participate in the Residential First-Year Year Experience with opportunities to explore every possible interest through residential life. The extensive library system is the largest at any public institution in the Northeast. The Center for Student Development brings together more than 200 clubs and organizations, fraternities and sororities, multicultural and religious centers. The campus completes in NCAA Division I sports for men and women, with teams winning national recognition. Award-winning student-operated businesses, the largest college daily newspaper in the region, and an active student government provide hands-on experience. About 5,000 students a year participate in the intramural sports program. The picturesque New England Town of Amherst offers shopping and dining, and the ski slopes of western Massachusetts and southern Vermont are close by. SAT or ACT scores are required for admission to the university. The school takes a holistic view of the student's application package and considers these scores as only part of the evaluation criteria. Additionally, any Advanced Placement, Honors, and SAT Subject Test scores are considered when reviewing each applicant. Increased applications in recent years have made admission more selective."

SELECTIVITY
Admissions Rating	86
# of applicants	30,853
% of applicants accepted	68
% of acceptees attending	21
# accepting a place on wait list	1,308
% admitted from wait list	102

FRESHMAN PROFILE
Range SAT Critical Reading	520–620
Range SAT Math	540–640
Range ACT Composite	23–28
Minimum paper TOEFL	550
Minimum computer TOEFL	213
Average HS GPA	3.61
% graduated top 10% of class	25
% graduated top 25% of class	65
% graduated top 50% of class	97

DEADLINES
Early action	
Deadline	11/1
Notification	12/15
Regular	
Deadline	1/15
Nonfall registration?	yes

APPLICANTS ALSO LOOK AT
AND OFTEN PREFER
Boston College, Boston University, Syracuse University, Tufts University, University of Delaware

AND SOMETIMES PREFER
Northeastern University, University of Connecticut

AND RARELY PREFER
University of New Hampshire, University of Rhode Island, University of Vermont

FINANCIAL FACTS
Financial Aid Rating	82
Annual in-state tuition	$11,917
Annual out-of-state tuition	$23,414
Room and board	$8,480
Books and supplies	$1,000
% frosh rec. need-based scholarship or grant aid	52
% UG rec. need-based scholarship or grant aid	53
% frosh rec. non-need-based scholarship or grant aid	5
% UG rec. non-need-based scholarship or grant aid	5
% frosh rec. need-based self-help aid	47
% UG rec. need-based self-help aid	49
% frosh rec. any financial aid	85
% UG rec. any financial aid	90
% UG borrow to pay for school	68
Average cumulative indebtedness	$24,420

UNIVERSITY OF MIAMI

OFFICE OF ADMISSION, PO BOX 248025, CORAL GABLES, FL 33124-4616 • ADMISSIONS: 305-284-4323 • FAX: 305-284-2507

CAMPUS LIFE

Quality of Life Rating	96
Fire Safety Rating	86
Green Rating	88
Type of school	private
Environment	town

STUDENTS

Total undergrad enrollment	10,368
% male/female	49/51
% from out of state	50
% from public high school	63
% live on campus	40
# of fraternities	20
# of sororities	13
% African American	7
% Asian	5
% Caucasian	43
% Hispanic	23
% international	9

SURVEY SAYS . . .

Athletic facilities are great
Diverse student types on campus
Low cost of living

ACADEMICS

Academic Rating	86
% students graduating within 4 years	68
% students graduating within 6 years	80
Calendar	semester
Student/faculty ratio	11:1
Profs interesting rating	80
Profs accessible rating	83
Most common reg class size	10–19 students
Most common lab size	10–19 students

STUDENTS SAY ". . ."

Academics

"A force, much like a real hurricane, to be reckoned with academically and in athletics," the "heavily sports-oriented" University of Miami offers "academic excellence along with cultural diversity." The reputation is a result of the efforts of the university's president, Donna Shalala, whose "forward thinking" has "transformed this university into an academic leader." In addition to its "top-notch" nursing program, the school's other notable programs include business and communications. "Coursework is often challenging, even for those students who got straight A's in high school." Class size ranges from "200-plus person classes" to "small interactive classes," and students are generally pleased with their professors who "are always available and very willing to talk to students." One student says, "The majority of the teachers were good, and those that weren't made up for it with sheer enthusiasm." The school's administration is both "very visible and approachable" and "is working hard to improve the quality of the university through facility improvements and additions, as well as program restructuring and evaluation." "It is not uncommon to see multiple administrators showing their support at school events and club meetings." During final exams, "faculty, trustees, and student government executives served free breakfast to students from 9:00 P.M. [to] past midnight" and also "strung up thirty-some hammocks between the palm trees behind the library for [students] to study or sleep."

Life

Depending on which student you talk to, the University of Miami "can be the hottest party spot" or "the ideal place to gain experience in almost any field of work or research while living in a beautiful place with a culture mix that is truly unique." One international student raves that "the school's rich culture and proud spirit acted like a sponge and soaked me into the Canes culture." Students compare their "very mellow" campus to "a country club" that is "secluded from the poverty and sham politics of Miami, where students live in a party-life bubble, protected from the real world." The "vibrant student life" includes "going out clubbing" as well as "following the football team" and "tailgating." Students also agree that "sorority/fraternity life is also a major part of life." "Every day, there are dozens of programs (cultural, social, physical, or academic) to participate in," and students can get involved in "theater productions, musical performances, cultural events, student shows and showcases, on-campus movie showings, service events, leadership opportunities, and seminars." For off-campus fun, "the beach is a popular weekend destination," and "people either go to Coconut Grove or South Beach."

Student Body

At first glance, "it can appear that the University of Miami admits only super-thin or super-buff students looking for the perfect spot for a tan while cruising in their Mercedes down the ritzy streets of Coral Gables." University of Miami students "all love warm weather and not wearing an excess amount of clothing" and "develop an urge to wear shades at one point or another." However, "the students at Miami are not all about tanning and partying; [they] are a competitive bunch." "The typical Miami student is probably from either Miami-Dade/Broward Counties or the Northeast" and is "into athletics." Students seem to fall into three categories: "those who go to South Beach, those who just have fun and party, and those who choose to remain for the most part academic." "While "students are not politically active," "most students perform community service." The student body "is very diverse," and "international students have formed various cultural organizations that reach out to their respective cultures." Although "it can seem that people are a little 'clique-y' when it comes to their culture," University of Miami students seem "widely accepting of many cultural groups" and manage to "all live together symbiotically."

FINANCIAL AID: 305-284-5212 • WEBSITE: WWW.MIAMI.EDU/ADMISSIONS

THE PRINCETON REVIEW SAYS

Admissions

Very important factors considered include: Academic GPA, application essay, class rank, recommendation(s), rigor of secondary school record, standardized test scores, character/personal qualities, extracurricular activities, volunteer work, work experience. *Other factors considered include:* Alumni/ae relation, first generation, geographical residence, level of applicant's interest, racial/ethnic status, talent/ability. SAT or ACT required; ACT with or without writing component accepted. TOEFL required of all international applicants. High school diploma is required, and GED is accepted. *Academic units recommended:* 4 English, 4 mathematics, 3 science (2 science labs), 2 foreign language, 3 social studies, 2 history, 1 visual/performing arts, 1 computer science.

Financial Aid

Students should submit: FAFSA. The Princeton Review suggests that all financial aid forms be submitted as soon as possible after January 1. *Need-based scholarships/grants offered:* Federal Pell, SEOG, state scholarships/grants, private scholarships, school scholarship or grant aid from institutional funds, Federal Nursing Scholarships. *Loan aid offered:* Direct Subsidized Stafford, Direct Unsubsidized Stafford, Direct PLUS, Federal Perkins, Federal Nursing Loans, university loans from institutional funds. Applicants will be notified of awards on a rolling basis beginning March 1. Federal Work-Study Program available. Off-campus job opportunities are excellent.

The Inside Word

The University of Miami's campaign to overcome its reputation as a "football school" is an unqualified success. Each recent academic year has seen an increase in applications, and UM's selectivity is on the rise. The school partially attributes this accomplishment to its alumni and gladly repays them by giving legacies a boost during the admissions process. Of course, having a Cane for a parent isn't enough; students must demonstrate achievement in arduous classes, intellectual promise, and strong moral character.

THE SCHOOL SAYS "..."

From the Admissions Office

"The University of Miami in Coral Gables, is an innovative private research university in a location unlike any other in the country. Located ten miles from the vibrant international city of Miami, UM's more than 9,000 undergraduates come from every state and 114 nations, allowing people of many cultures to challenge and champion each other. Faculty work closely with students, and internships and research experiences are integral to academic life. Students work hard as community volunteers and exert leadership in a range of lively clubs and organizations, including the student-managed TV station, radio station, and newspaper.

"The University of Miami will accept the critical reading and math scores from the SAT, as well as the ACT with or without the writing component."

SELECTIVITY

Admissions Rating	96
# of applicants	25,895
% of applicants accepted	39
% of acceptees attending	21
# of early decision applicants	1,310
% accepted early decision	18

FRESHMAN PROFILE

Range SAT Critical Reading	590–680
Range SAT Math	620–700
Range SAT Writing	580–680
Range ACT Composite	28–32
Minimum paper TOEFL	550
Minimum web-based TOEFL	80
Average HS GPA	4.20
% graduated top 10% of class	68
% graduated top 25% of class	90
% graduated top 50% of class	97

DEADLINES

Early decision	
Deadline	11/1
Notification	12/15
Early action	
Deadline	11/1
Notification	2/1
Regular	
Deadline	1/15
Nonfall registration?	yes

FINANCIAL FACTS

Financial Aid Rating	83
Annual tuition	$18,481
Room and board	$11,270
% frosh rec. need-based scholarship or grant aid	50
% UG rec. need-based scholarship or grant aid	47
% frosh rec. non-need-based scholarship or grant aid	19
% UG rec. non-need-based scholarship or grant aid	15
% frosh rec. need-based self-help aid	43
% UG rec. need-based self-help aid	43
% UG borrow to pay for school	54
Average cumulative indebtedness	$26,438

UNIVERSITY OF MICHIGAN—ANN ARBOR

1220 STUDENT ACTIVITIES BUILDING, ANN ARBOR, MI 48109-1316 • ADMISSIONS: 734-764-7433 • FAX: 734-936-0740

STUDENTS SAY ". . ."

Academics

Among the many allures of the University of Michigan—Ann Arbor is that the school offers "a great environment both academically and socially." One student explains, "It has the social, fun atmosphere of any Big Ten university, but most people are still incredibly focused on their studies. It's great to be at a place where there is always something to do, but your friends completely understand when you have to stay in and get work done." With "an amazing honors program," a "wide range of travel-abroad opportunities," and "research strength" all available "at a low cost," it's no wonder students tell us that UM "provides every kind of opportunity at all times to all people." Academically, Michigan "is very competitive, and the professors have high academic standards for all the students." In fact, some here insist that "Michigan is as good as Ivy League schools in many disciplines." Standout offerings include business ("We have access to some of the brightest leaders" in the business world, students report), a "great engineering program," and "a good undergraduate program for medical school preparation." Those seeking add-on academic experiences here will find "a vast amount of resources. Internships, career opportunities, tutoring, community service projects, a plethora of student organizations, and a wealth of other resources" are all available, but "you need to make the first move" because no one "will seek you out."

Life

Michigan is a huge university, meaning that students have endless extracurricular options here. One explains: "If you seek it out, you can find organizations for *any* interest. There are always people out there who share your interests. That's part of the benefit of 40,000-plus students!" There is a robust party scene. Students tell us that "most students go to house parties [or] hit the bars." There's also a vigorous social scene for the non-drinking crowd, with "great programs like UMix…phenomenal cultural opportunities in Ann Arbor especially music and movies," and "the hugely popular football Saturdays. The sense of school spirit here is impressive." Michigan students tend to be both academically serious and socially outgoing, which "is great because you can have a stimulating conversation with someone one day, and, the next day, be watching a silly movie or playing video games with this person."

Student Body

The Michigan student body "is hugely diverse," which "is one of the things Michigan prides itself on." "If you participate in extracurricular activities and make an effort to get to know other students in class and elsewhere, you'll definitely end up with a pretty diverse group of friends," undergrads assure us. Although varied, students tend to be similar in that they "are social but very academically driven." A number of students "are on the cutting edge of both research and progressive thinking," and there is a decided liberal tilt to campus politics. Even so, there's a place for everyone here, because "there are hundreds of mini-communities within the campus, made of everything from service fraternities to political organizations to dance groups. If you have an interest, you can find a group of people who enjoy the same thing."

FINANCIAL AID: 734-763-6600 • WEBSITE: WWW.ADMISSIONS.UMICH.EDU, WWW.FINAID.UMICH.EDU

THE PRINCETON REVIEW SAYS

Admissions

Very important factors considered include: Rigor of secondary school record. *Important factors considered include:* Academic GPA, application essay, recommendation(s), standardized test scores, character/personal qualities, first generation, level of applicant's interest. *Other factors considered include:* Class rank, alumni/ae relation, extracurricular activities, geographical residence, state residency, talent/ability, volunteer work, work experience. SAT or ACT required; ACT with writing component required. TOEFL required of all international applicants. High school diploma is required, and GED is accepted. *Academic units required:* 4 English, (1 science lab), 3 social studies, 3 history, 1 academic elective. *Academic units recommended:* 4 English, 4 mathematics, 4 science (1 science lab), 4 foreign language, 3 social studies, 4 history, 2 visual/performing arts, 1 computer science.

Financial Aid

Students should submit: FAFSA, CSS/Financial Aid PROFILE. Regular filing deadline is May 31. The Princeton Review suggests that all financial aid forms be submitted as soon as possible after January 1. *Need-based scholarships/grants offered:* Federal Pell, SEOG, state scholarships/grants, private scholarships, school scholarship or grant aid from institutional funds. *Loan aid offered:* Direct Subsidized Stafford, Direct Unsubsidized Stafford, Direct PLUS, Federal Perkins, Federal Nursing Loans, university loans from institutional funds. Applicants will be notified of awards on a rolling basis beginning March 15. Federal Work-Study Program available. Off-campus job opportunities are excellent.

The Inside Word

Michigan admissions are extremely competitive. Generally, about a quarter of the incoming freshman class graduates in the top one percent of their high school class. The volume of applications—Michigan receives nearly 30,000 applications—means the admissions office must rely heavily on numbers to make its decision, so do what you can to get those test scores and GPA as high as you can. Michigan admits on a rolling basis, a process that favors those who apply early.

THE SCHOOL SAYS "..."

From the Admissions Office

"Michigan is a place of incredible possibility. Students shape that possibility according to their diverse interests, goals, energy, and initiative. Undergraduate education is in the academic spotlight at Michigan, offering more than 220 fields of study in twelve schools and colleges; more than 150 first-year seminars with twenty or fewer students taught by senior faculty; composition classes of twenty or fewer students; more than 1,200 first- and second-year students in undergraduate research partnerships with faculty; and numerous service learning programs linking academics with volunteerism. Some introductory courses have large lectures, but these are combined with labs or small group discussions where students get plenty of individualized attention. A Michigan degree is one of distinction and promise; graduates are successful in medical, law, and graduate schools all over the nation and world. A year after graduation, more than ninety-five percent of UM alumni report that they are in the "next step" of their career—whether that is graduate or professional school, working, or volunteering."

SELECTIVITY

Admissions Rating	97
# of applicants	31,613
% of applicants accepted	51
% of acceptees attending	41
# accepting a place on wait list	3,724
% admitted from wait list	2

FRESHMAN PROFILE

Range SAT Critical Reading	590–690
Range SAT Math	640–750
Range SAT Writing	610–710
Range ACT Composite	27–31
Minimum paper TOEFL	570
Minimum computer TOEFL	230
Minimum web-based TOEFL	88
Average HS GPA	3.76
% graduated top 10% of class	84
% graduated top 25% of class	97
% graduated top 50% of class	100

DEADLINES

Early action	
Deadline	10/31
Notification	12/22
Regular	
Priority	11/1
Deadline	1/31
Notification	12/23
Nonfall registration?	yes

APPLICANTS ALSO LOOK AT

AND OFTEN PREFER
Michigan State University, Northwestern University, University of Illinois at Urbana-Champaign, University of Pennsylvania

AND SOMETIMES PREFER
Cornell University, New York University, Washington University in St. Louis

AND RARELY PREFER
University of California-Berkeley, University of Wisconsin—Madison

FINANCIAL FACTS

Financial Aid Rating	91
Annual in-state tuition	$11,648
Annual out-of-state tuition	$35,812
Room and board	$9,192
Required fees	$189
Books and supplies	$1,048
% frosh rec. need-based scholarship or grant aid	48
% UG rec. need-based scholarship or grant aid	48
% frosh rec. non-need-based scholarship or grant aid	39
% UG rec. non-need-based scholarship or grant aid	33
% frosh rec. need-based self-help aid	51
% UG rec. need-based self-help aid	53
% frosh rec. any financial aid	89
% UG rec. any financial aid	87
% UG borrow to pay for school	46
Average cumulative indebtedness	$27,828

UNIVERSITY OF MINNESOTA—TWIN CITIES

240 WILLIAMSON HALL, 231 PILLSBURY DRIVE SOUTHEAST, MINNEAPOLIS, MN 55455-0213 • ADMISSIONS: 612-625-2008

CAMPUS LIFE

Quality of Life Rating	88
Fire Safety Rating	82
Green Rating	95
Type of school	public
Environment	metropolis

STUDENTS

Total undergrad enrollment	33,607
% male/female	48/52
% from out of state	25
% live on campus	21
# of fraternities	24
# of sororities	12
% African American	5
% Asian	9
% Caucasian	72
% Hispanic	3
% Native American	1
% international	6
# of countries represented	130

SURVEY SAYS . . .

Students love Minneapolis, MN
Great off-campus food
Student publications are popular

ACADEMICS

Academic Rating	69
% students graduating within 4 years	50
% students graduating within 6 years	70
Calendar	semester
Student/faculty ratio	21:1
Profs interesting rating	70
Profs accessible rating	69
Most common reg class size	20–29 students
Most common lab size	10–19 students

MOST POPULAR MAJORS

journalism, psychology, business, education, biology, engineering, kinesiology, nutrition

STUDENTS SAY ". . ."

Academics

The University of Minnesota is an "insanely huge" "research institution" and Big Ten school "in the heart of" the Twin Cities. You'll find a wealth of majors here. Business is "superb." Engineering is strong across the board. The U is also "a great place to study an obscure language" or virtually anything else you can imagine. There are more than 300 opportunities to work and study abroad. Local internships "and hands-on opportunities" are also ample. "The professors run the whole gamut." "There are some amazing ones and some really terrible ones," says a civil engineering major. Some faculty members are "brilliant" and "inspired people" who "enjoy teaching the material and getting to know the students personally." Other professors "are knowledgeable but not always great at conveying the concepts." "There are a few who can really be GPA wreckers," too. Lower-level classes can be full of "massive crowds of students," though freshman seminars have fifteen to twenty students. The teaching assistants who "do the dirty work" are frequently "from foreign countries" and "have really thick accents," especially in the hard sciences. "As your progress into upper-division course, the lectures rarely eclipse 100," though, and you have more interaction with real professors. "The administration really seems to care about the students" and "the U is run very well for a university of its size." Also, advising can be "beyond terrible."

Life

The "beautiful," "very environmentally friendly" campus here is "spread over two cities and a river." "Frigid," "crazy winters" are perennial. "By January, all you can see of students is their eyes," observes a sophomore. "The rest of them are wrapped in coats, hats, and scarves." "The snow is great for outdoor fun like sledding and ice skating" but "don't come here if you can't handle the cold." Socially, "the U has everything, plain and simple." You can have a "totally different experience than someone else." "There's a group for just about every interest," and "there is always something to do, even on a random Tuesday night." The campus provides a variety of events and "always has something going on during the weekends." "Hockey games are always great" and sports are a "big thing." "Partying is very popular but there are also a lot of people who don't" participate. If you want to imbibe, though, "keggers," house parties, and frat blowouts are frequent. There's also quite a bit happening off campus. According to students here, "Minneapolis is one of the greatest places in the country." "The music scene is unreal." "Great art" and "gorgeous parks" abound. "Shopping at the Mall of America" is another favorite pastime. The neighborhoods near campus are generally "very young and energetic" and public transportation is "readily available and cheap."

Student Body

"Students are generally from the Midwest somewhere." More often than not, they are "right out of suburbia" or from "small to medium-sized towns" in "Minnesota or Wisconsin." There are a lot of "tall," "blond," "pasty, white people" who "are 'Minnesota Nice.'" "The U of M is a human zoo," though. "It's a school that embraces diversity." "There are a lot of different ethnicities." Some people are "snooty." Others "grew up poor." Some are "bubbly." Some are "antisocial." Also, "there is a microcosm for just about every subculture imaginable." There are "the math nerds," the "frat boys," and "lots of hippies and artsy people." There's "a huge gay population." "Preppy, athletic, emo," and nontraditional students are also visible. Politically, "the conservatives add a good balance to the grand scheme of things," but the campus leans left. Some students are "very politically aware." "There always seems to be some group protesting or trying to convince me of something," notes one student. Not surprisingly, "there is a limited sense of community" at the U, but sooner or later, most everyone "is able to find their niche." After that, "most people stick to their cliques."

UNIVERSITY OF MINNESOTA—TWIN CITIES

Fax: 612-626-1693 • Financial Aid: 612-624-1665 • Website: ADMISSIONS.TC.UMN.EDU

THE PRINCETON REVIEW SAYS

Admissions

Very important factors considered include: Academic GPA, class rank, rigor of secondary school record, standardized test scores. *Other factors considered include:* Alumni/ae relation, character/personal qualities, extracurricular activities, first generation, geographical residence, racial/ethnic status, talent/ability, volunteer work, work experience. SAT or ACT required; ACT with writing component required. TOEFL required of all international applicants. High school diploma is required, and GED is accepted. *Academic units required:* 4 English, 3 mathematics, 3 science, 2 foreign language, 3 social studies, 1 history, 1 visual/performing arts. *Academic units recommended:* 4 English, 4 mathematics, 4 science (1 science lab), 2 foreign language, 3 social studies, 1 history, 1 visual/performing arts.

Financial Aid

Students should submit: FAFSA. The Princeton Review suggests that all financial aid forms be submitted as soon as possible after January 1. *Need-based scholarships/grants offered:* Federal Pell, SEOG, state scholarships/grants, private scholarships, school scholarship or grant aid from institutional funds, Federal Nursing Scholarships. *Loan aid offered:* Direct Subsidized Stafford, Direct Unsubsidized Stafford, Direct PLUS, Federal Perkins, Federal Nursing Loans, state loans, university loans from institutional funds. Applicants will be notified of awards on a rolling basis beginning February 15. Federal Work-Study Program available.

The Inside Word

Despite what looks to be a fairly choosy admissions rate, it's the sheer volume of applicants that creates a selective situation at Minnesota.

THE SCHOOL SAYS "..."

From the Admissions Office

"The University of Minnesota is one of the nation's top public research universities. That means your college experience will be enhanced by world-renowned faculty, state-of-the-art learning facilities, and an unprecedented variety of options (such as 135 majors). Eighty-three percent of our classes have fewer than fifty students, and our caring advisers will help you find opportunities that are right for you.

"Hands-on courses, volunteer opportunities, internships, study abroad, and undergraduate research are part of the U of M experience. Students benefit from programs and traditions designed to support their success, like Welcome Week, where freshmen explore campus, meet their classmates, and connect with faculty and staff before the school year begins. Our classic Big Ten campus is located in the heart of the vibrant Twin Cities. Just minutes away, intern at a Fortune 500 company, volunteer at a major hospital, or relax at the beautiful Chain of Lakes. With a wealth of cultural, career, and recreational opportunities, there's no better place to earn your degree.

"The University of Minnesota offers a fantastic education and prestigious degree at a great value. Residents of Minnesota benefit from in-state tuition. Minnesota residents may also qualify for the University of Minnesota Promise Scholarship, which guarantees tuition aid to eligible students with a family income up to $100,000."

"Residents of North Dakota, South Dakota, Wisconsin, or Manitoba qualify for special reciprocity tuition rates. Out-of-state students benefit from the most affordable non-resident tuition in the Big Ten. Last year, we awarded over $12 million in four-year scholarship packages."

SELECTIVITY

Admissions Rating	87
# of applicants	36,853
% of applicants accepted	48
% of acceptees attending	30
# accepting a place on wait list	0

FRESHMAN PROFILE

Range SAT Critical Reading	530–690
Range SAT Math	600–720
Range SAT Writing	550–670
Range ACT Composite	25–30
Minimum paper TOEFL	550
Minimum computer TOEFL	213
% graduated top 10% of class	43
% graduated top 25% of class	83
% graduated top 50% of class	99

DEADLINES

Regular	
Priority	12/15
Nonfall registration?	yes

FINANCIAL FACTS

Financial Aid Rating	82
Annual in-state tuition	$12,369
Annual out-of-state tuition	$16,369
Room and board	$7,576
Books and supplies	$1,000
% frosh rec. need-based scholarship or grant aid	55
% UG rec. need-based scholarship or grant aid	53
% frosh rec. non-need-based scholarship or grant aid	8
% UG rec. non-need-based scholarship or grant aid	6
% frosh rec. need-based self-help aid	50
% UG rec. need-based self-help aid	47
% frosh rec. any financial aid	56
% UG rec. any financial aid	55
% UG borrow to pay for school	63
Average cumulative indebtedness	$27,578

UNIVERSITY OF MISSISSIPPI

145 MARTINDALE, UNIVERSITY, MS 38677 • ADMISSIONS: 662-915-7226 • FAX: 662-915-5869

CAMPUS LIFE

Quality of Life Rating	98
Fire Safety Rating	60*
Green Rating	89
Type of school	public
Environment	village

STUDENTS

Total undergrad enrollment	13,983
% male/female	47/53
% from out of state	32
% live on campus	33
# of fraternities	18
# of sororities	13
% African American	16
% Asian	1
% Caucasian	77
% Hispanic	2
% international	1

SURVEY SAYS . . .

Great off-campus food
Everyone loves the Ole Miss Rebels
Frats and sororities dominate
social scene
Student publications are popular
Lots of beer drinking
Hard liquor is popular

ACADEMICS

Academic Rating	66
Calendar	semester
Student/faculty ratio	18:1
Profs interesting rating	70
Profs accessible rating	74
Most common	
reg class size	10–19 students
Most common	
lab size	20–29 students

MOST POPULAR MAJORS

accounting, elementary education and
teaching, marketing

STUDENTS SAY ". . ."

Academics

The University of Mississippi (or "Ole Miss," as it is familiarly known) is an institution "steeped in rich traditions" that its students praise for having "great people, a beautiful campus, and a hospitable community." Familial connections and affection for the school's past (which includes graduating "numerous senators and representatives, among them Trent Lott, Thad Cochran, and Roger Wicker") draw many to Ole Miss, but that doesn't mean the school is content to rest on its laurels. On the contrary, in recent years the school has taken major strides toward "making itself one of America's great public universities." The 1997 establishment of the Croft Institute for International Studies, "recently ranked second best in the nation by the State Department in the areas of job placement," represents one such step. Another was the 1999 creation of the Lott Leadership Institute; together the two resources "provide unique and challenging fields of study that help distinguish Ole Miss academically." Solid programs in journalism, music, accounting, forensic chemistry, engineering, pharmacy, premedicine, and Southern studies help round out the academic picture. Those who can gain access to the Sally McDonnell Barkesdale Honors College should take advantage of the opportunity. The program "is so strongly supported by the administration and alumni that you can literally eat dinner with fourteen other honor students and a visiting senator, and then the next day go talk with a visiting ambassador about opportunities for working with the State Department. Honors college students receive many perks, including the chance to go on a 'ventures' trip to a major city, paid for by the Honors College."

Life

Undergrads at Mississippi are generally a content lot. As one student happily exclaimed, "The school spirit and pride people have at Ole Miss is contagious!." Indeed, many undergrads view the university as, "a great Southern school with amazing traditions and great standards that knows how to have a good time." Popular traditions include pregaming in The Grove, "a social setting jam-packed with friends and families all bound by the same values of hospitality and friendship." An "extremely popular" Greek system is another tradition that hasn't lost any steam. For many undergrads, "most activities outside of class or studying are centered on Greek life," which includes not only "an enormous amount of drinking and partying," but also "being among the most involved and active people on campus." Hometown Oxford "may be small, but there is always something to do. Oxford has some of the best restaurants in the South. Also, Oxford gets great live music, poetry readings, and famous authors frequently. Lake Sardis is also nearby. Many people go boating on free days."

Student Body

Ole Miss is home to almost 14,000 undergraduates, a size that makes generalizations about the entire population difficult and necessarily imprecise. That said, students detect an undeniable presence of "students who are pretty wealthy and take pride in that." This group is personified by the "preppy girl or boy wearing expensive labels and going to school to follow in his or her mom or dad's footsteps. "Sums up one undergrad, "Ole Miss students are charming and very social; it is as if everyone has been raised attending cocktail parties and debutante balls forever. We are primarily conservative, white southerners who are unashamed of our Southern culture and heritage. Those who fit this mold love Ole Miss; [others] seem to view the Southern elitism as 'snobbery.'" This perceived snobbery may be at least a partial result of the fact that the school is "not very diverse."

FINANCIAL AID: 662-915-7175 • E-MAIL: ADMISSIONS@OLEMISS.EDU • WEBSITE: WWW.OLEMISS.EDU

THE PRINCETON REVIEW SAYS

Admissions

Very important factors considered include: Academic GPA, rigor of secondary school record. *Important factors considered include:* Class rank, standardized test scores. *Other factors considered include:* Alumni/ae relation, state residency, talent/ability. TOEFL required of all international applicants. High school diploma is required, and GED is accepted. *Academic units required:* 4 English, 3 mathematics, 3 science (2 science labs), 1 foreign language, 1 social studies, 2 history, 1 academic elective. *Academic units recommended:* 4 mathematics, 4 science, 2 foreign language, 2 social studies.

Financial Aid

Students should submit: FAFSA. The Princeton Review suggests that all financial aid forms be submitted as soon as possible after January 1. *Need-based scholarships/grants offered:* Federal Pell, SEOG, state scholarships/grants, private scholarships, school scholarship or grant aid from institutional funds. *Loan aid offered:* Federal Perkins, university loans from institutional funds. Applicants will be notified of awards on a rolling basis beginning April 1. Federal Work-Study Program available. Off-campus job opportunities are fair.

The Inside Word

While Ole Miss offers students tremendous educational opportunities, the university's admissions policies are less than strenuous. Applicants who demonstrate moderate success in college prep curricula will most likely secure admittance.

THE SCHOOL SAYS "..."

From the Admissions Office

"The flagship university of the state, The University of Mississippi, widely known as Ole Miss, offers extraordinary opportunities through more than 100 areas of study, including programs such as the Sally McDonnell Barksdale Honors College and the Croft Institute for International Studies. UM students are the only public university students in the state who have the opportunity to be tapped by the nation's oldest and most prestigious honor society, Phi Beta Kappa. Strong academic programs and a rich and varied campus life have helped Ole Miss graduate twenty-four Rhodes Scholars, and eleven Truman Scholars. Since 1998 alone, UM has produced five Goldwater Scholars, a Marshall Scholar, and four Fulbright Scholars.

"The campus is diverse; thirty-two percent come from other states and countries and thirteen percent are black American. Recent significant campus improvements include the $25 million Gertrude Ford Performing Arts Center and the privately funded Paris-Yates Chapel and Peddle Bell Tower. UM ranks thirty-third in the nation among public universities for endowment per student. Ole Miss is home to twenty research centers, including the National Center for Justice and the Rule of Law, which provides training on investigating and prosecuting cybercrime; the William Winter Institute for Racial Reconciliation; and the National Center for Natural Products Research.

"The university is located in Oxford, consistently recognized as a great college town and as a center for writers and other artists. Like Ole Miss, Oxford is modest in size and large in the opportunities it provides residents, offering many of the advantages of a larger place in a friendly and open environment.

"Students applying will be allowed to take the SAT or the ACT but are not required to take the ACT writing section. The university will not consider the writing section of either exam when evaluating students for admission, but certain specialty programs may request these scores."

SELECTIVITY

Admissions Rating	78
# of applicants	10,909
% of applicants accepted	78
% of acceptees attending	36

FRESHMAN PROFILE

Range SAT Critical Reading	470–590
Range SAT Math	470–600
Range ACT Composite	20–29
Minimum paper TOEFL	550
Minimum computer TOEFL	213
Average HS GPA	3.30
% graduated top 10% of class	32
% graduated top 25% of class	57
% graduated top 50% of class	79

DEADLINES

Regular	
Priority	6/15
Deadline	7/20
Notification	9/15
Nonfall registration?	yes

FINANCIAL FACTS

Financial Aid Rating	76
Annual in-state tuition	$5,436
Annual out-of-state tuition	$13,890
% frosh rec. need-based scholarship or grant aid	40
% UG rec. need-based scholarship or grant aid	42
% frosh rec. non-need-based scholarship or grant aid	7
% UG rec. non-need-based scholarship or grant aid	4
% frosh rec. need-based self-help aid	30
% UG rec. need-based self-help aid	37
% UG borrow to pay for school	41
Average cumulative indebtedness	$23,637

UNIVERSITY OF MISSOURI

230 JESSE HALL, COLUMBIA, MO 65211 • ADMISSIONS: 573-882-7786 • FAX: 573-882-7887

STUDENTS SAY "..."

Academics

The University of Missouri—"Mizzou" to students, alumni, staff, and Tigers fans—"is the total package for a college experience," offering "great professors, [a] beautiful campus, and many social activities." The sum of all these parts helps make Mizzou "an outstanding school with incredible students that bleed black and gold. We are excited to learn, meet new people, and find ourselves." The school is best known for its journalism program, "the first and best journalism school in the country" according to its students, but that's hardly the only standout offering. Mizzou also boasts "a great engineering program," a College of Agriculture Food and Natural Resources with "a family environment," and strong programs in business, nursing, and education. Academics "are integrated into our professional fields accordingly so we get to show our knowledge in the classroom and [in the] field simultaneously." Undergraduates warn, however, "Mizzou represents the typical big state school in Missouri, with all the benefits and drawbacks that go along with that," meaning that everything is "big. Big money, big campus, big sports, big research, big construction. While this is great for those looking for big-world opportunities, it can also mean anonymity for most."

Life

Students here tell us that "Greek life is huge on campus" and that downtown Columbia—which is "right next to the campus"—offers an enticing "array of bars and restaurants." In addition, during the fall "Mizzou football is a huge deal. The world stops on football Saturday, between the game and tailgating. Even without a ticket, you'll have a good time." But while many undergraduates certainly do like to get their party on when the weekend rolls around, "there are definitely other ways to keep yourself occupied in Columbia," an "excellent college town" with "theaters, stores, coffee shops, cafes, an independent theatre, art galleries, bookstores, concert venues and more." There are also "several free events on campus for students like movies, a comedy troupe, and concerts," and an easy way to keep track of them: a page on the school's main website entitled "Stuff to Do," which provides "a listing of events or activities that students can get involved in. Some revolve around certain holidays, such as Valentine's Day, where students can participate in speed dating." When they need a change of scenery, undergrads "head to Kansas City or St. Louis for fun." No wonder students describe Mizzou as "the perfect mix of work and play. The education is wonderful...[and] social life here is equally awesome."

Student Body

"There really is no typical student at Mizzou," where a huge student population creates room for "tons of unique and diverse students on campus." Many students define their peers as, "friendly, smart and enjoying life." Indeed, most undergrads are "fairly dedicated to classes, like to attend football and basketball games, involved in at least one or two activities on campus, and like to have fun with their friends on the weekends." As one student puts it, "It is a wonderful mix between a Big 12 school, an urban and rural population, and social challenges brought to light from students and Columbia citizens. People are encouraged to speak their opinion[s] and express themselves no matter what." Mizzou undergrads are "driven" and career-oriented but not always the most rigorous students; they "go to class for the most part, will usually cram for tests rather than [study] the entire semester, and will balance social life with academics fairly well." There is "a pretty sizable and visible LGBTQ population" here.

UNIVERSITY OF MISSOURI

E-MAIL: MIU4U@MISSOURI.EDU • WEBSITE: WWW.MISSOURI.EDU

THE PRINCETON REVIEW SAYS

Admissions

Very important factors considered include: Academic GPA, class rank, standardized test scores. *Important factors considered include:* Rigor of secondary school record. *Other factors considered include:* Application essay, recommendation(s), first generation, level of applicant's interest, racial/ethnic status, talent/ability, volunteer work, work experience. SAT or ACT required; ACT with or without writing component accepted. TOEFL required of all international applicants. High school diploma is required, and GED is accepted. *Academic units required:* 4 English, 4 mathematics, 3 science (1 science lab), 2 foreign language, 3 social studies.

Financial Aid

Students should submit: FAFSA. Regular filing deadline is March 1. The Princeton Review suggests that all financial aid forms be submitted as soon as possible after January 1. *Need-based scholarships/grants offered:* Federal Pell, SEOG, state scholarships/grants, private scholarships, school scholarship or grant aid from institutional funds. *Loan aid offered:* Direct Subsidized Stafford, Direct Unsubsidized Stafford, Direct PLUS, Federal Perkins, Federal Nursing Loans, state loans, university loans from institutional funds. Applicants will be notified of awards on a rolling basis beginning April 1. Federal Work-Study Program available. Off-campus job opportunities are excellent.

The Inside Word

Mizzou admitted eighty-four percent of all applicants for admission to the class 2014. The message is clear: If your application suggests that you can handle the workload here, the school will find a place for you. Average test scores in conjunction with a college-prep high school curriculum should be all it takes. Even those who don't meet these criteria have a chance; admissions officers consider essays, recommendations, and special talents in the cases of borderline candidates.

THE SCHOOL SAYS "..."

From the Admissions Office

"Founded in 1839 as the first public university west of the Mississippi River, MU is a member of the nation's most prestigious group of sixty-one public and private teaching/research institutions: the Association of American Universities. The National Science Foundation has recognized MU as one of the top ten universities in the country for integrating research into undergraduate education; Mizzou offers undergraduate research to some students as early as their freshman year.

"Service learning is important at Mizzou. The Service Learning Center at MU integrates service to others into students' academic experiences through collaborative partnerships on campus and throughout the community.

"Nearly thirty percent of the fall 2010 freshman class came from another state or another country, and a strong international community thrives in Columbia. At the same time, Mizzou also has a growing Study Abroad program, with nearly 400 programs in more than sixty countries.

"Mizzou offers many strong, unique programs. Some in the sciences are taught in collaboration with MU's medical school, and humanities classes include such areas as music composition and creative writing where students frequently win national awards.

"Students can find admissions requirements at missouri.edu. As students apply online, it is clear whether they are admissible or not. That may partially explain Missouri's high acceptance rate."

SELECTIVITY	
Admissions Rating	73
# of applicants	17,465
% of applicants accepted	84
% of acceptees attending	42

FRESHMAN PROFILE	
Range SAT Critical Reading	540–650
Range SAT Math	530–650
Range ACT Composite	23–28
Minimum paper TOEFL	500
Minimum web-based TOEFL	61
% graduated top 10% of class	25
% graduated top 25% of class	55
% graduated top 50% of class	86

DEADLINES	
Regular	
Priority	5/1
Notification	rolling
Nonfall registration?	yes

FINANCIAL FACTS	
Financial Aid Rating	77
Annual in-state tuition	$7,368
Annual out-of-state tuition	$19,383
Room and board	$8,607
Required fees	$1,133
Books and supplies	$1,070
% frosh rec. need-based scholarship or grant aid	43
% UG rec. need-based scholarship or grant aid	39
% frosh rec. non-need-based scholarship or grant aid	3
% UG rec. non-need-based scholarship or grant aid	2
% frosh rec. need-based self-help aid	37
% UG rec. need-based self-help aid	37
% UG borrow to pay for school	57
Average cumulative indebtedness	$20,689

THE UNIVERSITY OF MONTANA—MISSOULA

101 LOMMASSON CENTER, MISSOULA, MT 59812 • ADMISSIONS: 406-243-6266 • FAX: 406-243-5711

CAMPUS LIFE

Quality of Life Rating	84
Fire Safety Rating	80
Green Rating	95
Type of school	public
Environment	city

STUDENTS

Total undergrad enrollment	12,673
% male/female	47/53
% from out of state	17
% from public high school	44
% live on campus	27
# of fraternities	5
# of sororities	4
% African American	1
% Asian	1
% Caucasian	83
% Hispanic	2
% Native American	4
% international	2
# of countries represented	69

SURVEY SAYS . . .

Athletic facilities are great
Students love Missoula, MT
Low cost of living
Student publications are popular

ACADEMICS

Academic Rating	70
% students graduating within 4 years	22
% students graduating within 6 years	44
Calendar	semester
Student/faculty ratio	20:1
Profs interesting rating	82
Profs accessible rating	71
Most common reg class size	20–29 students
Most common lab size	20–29 students

MOST POPULAR MAJORS

business administration and management, education, psychology

STUDENTS SAY ". . ."

Academics

Perhaps it stands to reason a school boasting "the best wildlife program in the country" would be found in Missoula, a "beautiful city" that is "five minutes from a designated wilderness area." While the wildlife biology program has garnered the most acclaim from students, the university is no one-trick pony. The school also boasts "great anthropology, biology, forestry, and nursing programs" taught by professors who are "nationally known." Raves one student, "I feel like I have [an] Ivy-League professor for Montana prices." Indeed, there is nearly unanimous agreement that "academics at UM are facilitated by great instructors" who would do "anything and everything for their students." Despite the university's size, "professors provide individual attention and provide numerous methods for contact (some including home phone numbers)." While TAs are spoken of in lesser terms, ranging from "[not] quite as good" to "horrible," the enthusiasm for the university's professors seems to carry the day. In addition to "great professors that care about your education," the university also has "tutors for many subjects that students may need help with" and "really encourages internships, studying abroad, and community service."

Life

"Life at UM combines a love for the Grizzlies with the outdoors." "And while "football is very popular, [it] does not overshadow academic progress." Indeed, Missoula seems to offer the best of many worlds, as "you can be in a good-sized city with 65,000 people and be completely isolated on a hiking trail looking across a beautiful landscape." For every activity, there is a season. "In the summer, hundreds of college kids grab tubes and float the river. In the winter, snowboarding is popular. Longboarding, cycling, and golf are also popular." And while the university clearly appeals to the outdoorsy types, one needn't fear a lack of choice. "There are a great number of social and academic clubs available for students to partake in" as well as "great art shows downtown on Friday nights, and the bar life is fun on weekends, too." While some feel that the administration could be "more strict with underage drinking," students who are "twenty-one or older have a wide choice of small bars downtown to attend." And though "The University of Montana prides itself for having a beautiful campus," the most common complaint relates to the recent and disruptive "construction at every corner of campus."

Student Body

A certain level of diversity can be expected from students living in "a barnacle of liberalism and intellectual pursuits in the red state of Montana." While the school is sometimes described as being split into the two factions of "Montanans who love football and big trucks and out-of-state hippies who love the mountains," the truth is that "Missoula is a very accepting town. People don't have to fit in here; they simply are who they choose to be. The diversity makes for a more interesting experience." The student body is demographically dominated by students who are "Caucasian, middle-class, outdoor-orientated, environmentally conscious," some of whom "are very active in the volunteer community, school organizations, political campaigns and much more. They are very open to different views and pursue healthy interactions about opinions." On campus, "There seems to be very little pressure to act or dress a certain way," and students tend to appreciate "the libertarian 'Live and Let Live' mentality of many of the people in this area."

THE UNIVERSITY OF MONTANA—MISSOULA

FINANCIAL AID: 406-243-5373 • E-MAIL: ADMISS@UMONTANA.EDU • WEBSITE: WWW.UMT.EDU

THE PRINCETON REVIEW SAYS

Admissions

Very important factors considered include: Academic GPA, class rank, rigor of secondary school record, standardized test scores. *Important factors considered include:* Extracurricular activities, talent/ability. *Other factors considered include:* Application essay, recommendation(s). SAT or ACT required; ACT with writing component recommended. TOEFL required of all international applicants. High school diploma is required, and GED is accepted. *Academic units required:* 4 English, 3 mathematics, 2 science (2 science labs), 3 social studies, 2 history. *Academic units recommended:* 2 foreign language, 2 visual/performing arts, 2 computer science.

Financial Aid

Students should submit: FAFSA. The Princeton Review suggests that all financial aid forms be submitted as soon as possible after January 1. *Need-based scholarships/grants offered:* Federal Pell, SEOG, state scholarships/grants, private scholarships, school scholarship or grant aid from institutional funds. *Loan aid offered:* Direct Subsidized Stafford, Direct Unsubsidized Stafford, Direct PLUS, Federal Perkins. Applicants will be notified of awards on a rolling basis beginning April 1. Federal Work-Study Program available. Off-campus job opportunities are good.

The Inside Word

The University of Montana operates on a rolling admissions basis, and the admissions game here is relatively straightforward. Decisions are based largely upon numbers. Applicants who enrolled in a college prep curriculum and earned average or better grades should be able to secure entry—especially if they apply earlier in the admissions cycle.

THE SCHOOL SAYS "..."

From the Admissions Office

"There's something special about this place. It's something different for each person. For some, it's the blend of academic quality and outdoor recreation. The University of Montana ranks fifth in the nation among public institutions for producing Rhodes scholars, and Outside Magazine lists Missoula in its 'Top Ten Amazing Places for Outdoor Recreation.'" For others, it's size—not too big, not too small. The University of Montana is a midsized university in the heart of the Rocky Mountains—accessible in both admission and tuition bills—that produces graduates considered among the best and brightest in the world. It is located in a community that could pass for a cozy college town or a bustling big city, depending on your point of view. There's a lot happening, but you won't get lost. People are friendly and diverse. They come from all over the world to study and learn and to live a good life. They come to a place to be inspired, a place where they feel comfortable yet challenged. Some never leave. Most never want to."

SELECTIVITY

Admissions Rating	74
# of applicants	4,630
% of applicants accepted	83
% of acceptees attending	49

FRESHMAN PROFILE

Range SAT Critical Reading	490–610
Range SAT Math	480–590
Range SAT Writing	470–580
Range ACT Composite	20–26
Minimum paper TOEFL	500
Minimum computer TOEFL	173
Minimum web-based TOEFL	61
Average HS GPA	3.23
% graduated top 10% of class	16
% graduated top 25% of class	39
% graduated top 50% of class	71

DEADLINES

Regular	
Priority	3/1
Notification	9/15
Nonfall registration?	yes

FINANCIAL FACTS

Financial Aid Rating	69
Annual out-of-state tuition	$17,662
Room and board	$6,900
Required fees	$1,510
Books and supplies	$900
% frosh rec. need-based scholarship or grant aid	39
% UG rec. need-based scholarship or grant aid	41
% frosh rec. non-need-based scholarship or grant aid	2
% UG rec. non-need-based scholarship or grant aid	1
% frosh rec. need-based self-help aid	46
% UG rec. need-based self-help aid	50
% frosh rec. any financial aid	82
% UG rec. any financial aid	77
% UG borrow to pay for school	61
Average cumulative indebtedness	$20,223

UNIVERSITY OF NEBRASKA—LINCOLN

313 NORTH THIRTEENTH STREET, VAN BRUNT VISITORS CENTER, LINCOLN, NE 68588-0256 • ADMISSIONS: 402-472-2023

CAMPUS LIFE

Quality of Life Rating	92
Fire Safety Rating	73
Green Rating	68
Type of school	public
Environment	city

STUDENTS

Total undergrad enrollment	18,995
% male/female	54/46
% from out of state	17
% from public high school	0
% live on campus	41
# of fraternities	29
# of sororities	18
% African American	3
% Asian	3
% Caucasian	83
% Hispanic	4
% Native American	1
% international	3
# of countries represented	117

SURVEY SAYS . . .

Athletic facilities are great
Everyone loves the Cornhuskers
Intramural sports are popular
Student publications are popular

ACADEMICS

Academic Rating	69
% students graduating within 4 years	29
% students graduating within 6 years	64
Calendar	semester
Student/faculty ratio	20:1
Profs interesting rating	72
Profs accessible rating	79
Most common reg class size	20–29 students
Most common lab size	20–29 students

MOST POPULAR MAJORS

business administration, psychology, pre-health

STUDENTS SAY ". . ."

Academics

"A big research university with a small school feel," the University of Nebraska—Lincoln provides "the best of both worlds…the benefits and amenities of a large school, but the community atmosphere of a smaller school." At UNL, "If you have questions about anything, it is so easy to find the answer." With "lots of amenities" and "ample opportunities for research and growth, both academically and socially in a college-town environment," UNL students enjoy "the strong sense of community" of this large state school, and say "it's amazingly personal for such a large amount of students." The community-like feel extends to how students regard those who run the school. Students say the administration is "very accessible and always friendly," and the members of the faculty "care enough to know more than your name." Students are also very positive when it comes to their professors. "Most of my professors are genuinely interested in the well-being of their students and want to aid in learning." In addition, when classes prove quite challenging, there are "plenty of available resources" at students' disposal. Students come to UNL for "the range of academic strengths" and to pursue a variety of majors including strong business and engineering programs. "Academically, the honors program is a real challenge—and it has the added benefit of small class sizes." It also "provides above-average classroom experience and education." At UNL, according to the students, "if you want to make an excellent educational experience for yourself, the opportunities here make it possible."

Life

Life in Lincoln is "all about the Husker spirit," because "nearly the entire student body…rallies around Husker football," and "being a Husker really is a big deal for most people at UNL." In addition to strong student of support of athletics, UNL boasts several fun intramural sports opportunities year-round, and students are eagerly awaiting the updates to the health and fitness centers, "luckily, plans are being made." "The amount and variety of organizations and activities that UNL has is outrageous." And "the fact that each student is given the opportunity to create their own [organization] if they wish leaves no room for complaint." When asked for an area of improvement, students mention that UNL "can work on being conscious about the environment a bit more," but students have already noted that they are "seeing more and more recycling bins around campus." UNL is a dry campus, and "off-campus house parties are popular" and "for those of age, there's a large bar-scene a few blocks from campus." The school's location in Nebraska's capital city is "convenient for almost anything you want to do." "Just a short walk away from city campus," students also venture into Lincoln since "the downtown scene has a lot to offer: theaters, bars, boutiques, coffee shops, restaurants, etc."

Student Body

At UNL, "students here like to socialize and better their communities," and most "students are friendly, willing to meet new friends and…help out even a perfect stranger." Though according to students, UNL's student body is comprised of "typical Midwestern people" and "a lot of white students that are relatively religious," "there are a lot of international students," and "differences are pretty well tolerated, even though we aren't the most ethnically diverse student body." Students also mention a division between those "that are Greek and those that aren't." Also, "groups of students seem to be localized in dorms—the honors students in Neihardt, the international and music students at Selleck, the athletes at Harper-Schramm-Smith, the partiers at Abel, etc."

UNIVERSITY OF NEBRASKA—LINCOLN

Fax: 402-472-0670 • Financial Aid: 402-472-2030 • E-mail: ADMISSIONS@UNL.EDU • Website: WWW.UNL.EDU

THE PRINCETON REVIEW SAYS

Admissions

Very important factors considered include: Class rank, standardized test scores. *Important factors considered include:* Rigor of secondary school record. *Other factors considered include:* Academic GPA, recommendation(s), first generation, talent/ability. SAT or ACT required; ACT with or without writing component accepted. TOEFL required of all international applicants. High school diploma is required, and GED is accepted. *Academic units required:* 4 English, 4 mathematics, 3 science (1 science lab), 2 foreign language, 3 social studies. *Academic units recommended:* 1 history.

Financial Aid

Students should submit: FAFSA. The Princeton Review suggests that all financial aid forms be submitted as soon as possible after January 1. *Need-based scholarships/grants offered:* Federal Pell, SEOG, state scholarships/grants, private scholarships, school scholarship or grant aid from institutional funds. *Loan aid offered:* Direct Subsidized Stafford, Direct Unsubsidized Stafford, Direct PLUS, Federal Perkins, university loans from institutional funds. Applicants will be notified of awards on a rolling basis beginning April 1. Federal Work-Study Program available. Off-campus job opportunities are excellent.

The Inside Word

UNL offers 150 majors and 285 programs of study. All applications will be weighed on the combined strength of coursework, GPAs, and test scores. In order to gain direct acceptance to a specific school of study at UNL, interested applicants should take into account those school's specialized requirements as they may include additional high school coursework than what is required by UNL's general studies program.

THE SCHOOL SAYS "..."

From the Admissions Office

"The University of Nebraska—Lincoln offers one of today's most dynamic college experiences. The university has developed a national reputation for its substantial out-of-state scholarship program, and now for its participation in the Big Ten Conference. As a result, more students nationwide are finding that the university, with all its strength in undergraduate research and education, its tradition of student engagement, its lively campus atmosphere, and its connection to downtown Lincoln, is uniquely suited to provide an enriching student experience. It is an exciting time on the University of Nebraska—Lincoln campus. One of the most notable changes is our acceptance into the Big Ten Conference. Students attending UNL in the fall of 2011 will be the first class of new, undergraduate students able to take advantage of all the Big Ten Conference has to offer including more academic opportunities, collaboration, student discovery and value.

"Established in 1869, the University of Nebraska—Lincoln has a rich tradition of excellence. Students join more than 200,000 alumni who have made their mark as industry leaders in business, engineering, the arts, journalism, education, and the sciences. Employers and grad schools have always held UNL degrees in high regard, and the added value of Big Ten affiliation gives UNL alumni an even bigger advantage in the U.S. and around the world.

"Freshman students seeking admission should either be ranked in the upper one-half of their high school class, or have received an ACT composite score of 20 or higher or an SAT total score of 950 or higher (critical reading and math only; writing portion not considered)."

SELECTIVITY

Admissions Rating	76
# of applicants	9,610
% of applicants accepted	81
% of acceptees attending	51

FRESHMAN PROFILE

Range SAT Critical Reading	510–650
Range SAT Math	530–660
Range ACT Composite	22–28
Minimum paper TOEFL	525
Minimum computer TOEFL	193
Minimum web-based TOEFL	70
% graduated top 10% of class	24
% graduated top 25% of class	52
% graduated top 50% of class	84

DEADLINES

Regular	
Priority	1/15
Deadline	5/1
Nonfall registration?	yes

FINANCIAL FACTS

Financial Aid Rating	81
Annual in-state tuition	$7,312
Annual out-of-state tuition	$19,012
Room and board	$8,196
Books and supplies	$950
% frosh rec. need-based scholarship or grant aid	36
% UG rec. need-based scholarship or grant aid	33
% frosh rec. non-need-based scholarship or grant aid	5
% UG rec. non-need-based scholarship or grant aid	3
% frosh rec. need-based self-help aid	30
% UG rec. need-based self-help aid	34
% frosh rec. any financial aid	41
% UG rec. any financial aid	36
% UG borrow to pay for school	61
Average cumulative indebtedness	$19,075

UNIVERSITY OF NEW HAMPSHIRE

FOUR GARRISON AVENUE, DURHAM, NH 03824 • ADMISSIONS: 603-862-1360 • FAX: 603-862-0077

CAMPUS LIFE

Quality of Life Rating	70
Fire Safety Rating	92
Green Rating	98
Type of school	public
Environment	village

STUDENTS

Total undergrad enrollment	12,183
% male/female	45/55
% from out of state	40
% from public high school	80
% live on campus	59
# of fraternities	11
# of sororities	7
% African American	1
% Asian	2
% Caucasian	87
% Hispanic	2
% international	1
# of countries represented	61

SURVEY SAYS . . .
Great library
Athletic facilities are great
Diversity lacking on campus
Frats and sororities dominate
social scene
Lots of beer drinking
Hard liquor is popular

ACADEMICS

Academic Rating	65
% students graduating within 4 years	61
% students graduating within 6 years	75
Calendar	semester
Student/faculty ratio	18:1
Profs interesting rating	62
Profs accessible rating	62
Most common reg class size	20–29 students
Most common lab size	20–29 students

MOST POPULAR MAJORS
business administration and
management, English language and
literature, psychology

STUDENTS SAY ". . ."

Academics
The benefits of going to a large, well-established state school, such as the University of New Hampshire, are exactly what one expects—its low in-state tuition, firmly established reputation, and place in the system allow it to offer "many resources to help students out in life." Located in tiny, beautiful Durham, the school "emphasizes research in every field, including non-science fields," and a lot of importance is placed "on the outdoors and the environment." The small town really fosters "lots of school spirit," and the laid-back denizens of UNH make it known that "having a good time" is a priority in their lives: "Weekends are for the Warriors." Most professors "truly care" about the students' learning so that "you never feel like a number at the school but rather a respected student," and professors "will get down and dirty when it comes to experiencing what they're teaching firsthand." Though there are definitely complaints that some can be "sub-par," a student "just needs to posses the initiative to go to their office hours" and they will get all the help they need. Some of the general education classes "are *huge*," and TAs can be difficult to understand, but for the most part, students report that they've had a "good experience" and that their academic careers has been "very successful." The Honors program is particularly challenging (in a very positive way) and offers "great seminar/inquiry classes that have about fifteen students." Students universally pan the administration, claiming it "is a massive bureaucracy that gets little done," partially due to poor communication, or one student puts it that "the left hand has no idea what the right hand is doing." "The school is way more challenging than I thought it would be because the administration makes things harder than they need to be," says a sophomore.

Life
The school is just "fifteen minutes to the beach, one hour to the mountains, and one hour to Boston," making the world a Wildcat's oyster. Partying is big here, and the weekends are crazy; "Everyone goes out pretty much every Thursday, Friday, and Saturday night." The small number of bars in town "makes the age limit pretty well enforced." After a hard night out, "there are many late night convenience stores and food places to go to." In fact, it can be "difficult to find activities to do on the weekend that don't involve drinking," though UNH does a good job of bringing in "popular comedians, musicians, bands, political figures, etc.," and the school has tons of "amazing" a capella groups, so there is "almost always something to go see." Sports are also big here: "We love our hockey and football," says a student. Though there's a pretty big housing crunch, the oft-used athletic and recreational facilities here are both convenient and excellent, and since everything on this "beautiful" campus is only about ten minutes away, "you walk pretty much everywhere," though public transportation and school-provided buses run often. Students do a lot of socializing over meals at the "eight cafés or in any of the three dining halls."

Student Body
This being New Hampshire, people are "very politically and socially aware." Students here are mostly middle-class and hail from New England (especially from New Hampshire, naturally), and a main point of contention among students is that there "is not a lot of ethnic/racial diversity," though the school is working on it. The size of UNH means that "even the most unique individual will find a group of friends," and even the most atypical students "fit in perfectly well." Most of these "laid-back" and "easy-to-get-along-with" Wildcats party, and it can be "hard to find one that doesn't." "*Everyone* skis or snowboards," and in the cold weather "Uggs and North Face fleece jackets abound."

UNIVERSITY OF NEW HAMPSHIRE

FINANCIAL AID: 603-862-3600 • E-MAIL: ADMISSIONS@UNH.EDU • WEBSITE: WWW.UNH.EDU

THE PRINCETON REVIEW SAYS

Admissions

Very important factors considered include: Class rank, rigor of secondary school record. *Important factors considered include:* Academic GPA, recommendation(s). *Other factors considered include:* Application essay, standardized test scores, alumni/ae relation, character/personal qualities, extracurricular activities, first generation, geographical residence, racial/ethnic status, state residency, talent/ability, volunteer work, work experience. SAT or ACT required; ACT with writing component required. TOEFL required of all international applicants. High school diploma is required, and GED is accepted. *Academic units required:* 4 English, 3 mathematics, 3 science (2 science labs), 2 foreign language, 3 social studies. *Academic units recommended:* 4 English, 4 mathematics, 4 science (3 science labs), 3 foreign language, 3 social studies, 1 academic elective.

Financial Aid

Students should submit: FAFSA. Regular filing deadline is March 1. The Princeton Review suggests that all financial aid forms be submitted as soon as possible after January 1. *Need-based scholarships/grants offered:* Federal Pell, SEOG, state scholarships/grants, private scholarships, school scholarship or grant aid from institutional funds. *Loan aid offered:* Direct Subsidized Stafford, Direct Unsubsidized Stafford, Direct PLUS, Federal Perkins. Applicants will be notified of awards on a rolling basis beginning March 1. Federal Work-Study Program available. Off-campus job opportunities are excellent.

The Inside Word

New Hampshire's emphasis on academic accomplishment in the admissions process makes it clear that the admissions committee is looking for students who have taken high school seriously. Standardized tests take as much of a backseat here as is possible at a large, public university.

THE SCHOOL SAYS "..."

From the Admissions Office

"The University of New Hampshire is an institution best defined by the students who take advantage of its opportunities. Enrolled students who are willing to engage in a high-quality academic community in some meaningful way, who have a genuine interest in discovering or developing new ideas, and who believe in each person's obligation to improve the community they live in typify the most successful students at UNH. Undergraduate students practice these three basic values in a variety of ways: by undertaking their own, independent research projects; by collaborating in faculty research; and by participating in study abroad, residential communities, community service, and other cultural programs.

"University of New Hampshire will require all high school graduates to submit results from the new SAT or the ACT (with the writing component). The Writing portions will not be used for admissions decisions during the first two to three admissions cycles. Students graduating from high school prior to 2006 can submit results from the old SAT or ACT. The UNH admissions process does not require SAT Subject tests."

SELECTIVITY
Admissions Rating	77
# of applicants	16,545
% of applicants accepted	73
% of acceptees attending	23

FRESHMAN PROFILE
Range SAT Critical Reading	500–600
Range SAT Math	520–620
Range SAT Writing	525–625
Range ACT Composite	23–27
Minimum paper TOEFL	550
Minimum computer TOEFL	213
Minimum web-based TOEFL	80
% graduated top 10% of class	25
% graduated top 25% of class	59
% graduated top 50% of class	96

DEADLINES
Early action	
Deadline	11/15
Notification	1/15
Regular	
Deadline	2/1
Notification	2/1
Nonfall registration?	yes

APPLICANTS ALSO LOOK AT
AND OFTEN PREFER
University of Connecticut, University of Massachusetts Amherst, University of Vermont

AND SOMETIMES PREFER
Boston University, Northeastern University, Providence College, University of Rhode Island

AND RARELY PREFER
Boston College, Syracuse University, University of Maine

FINANCIAL FACTS
Financial Aid Rating	75
Annual in-state tuition	$10,730
Annual out-of-state tuition	$24,700
Room and board	$9,052
Required fees	$2,942
Books and supplies	$1,200
% frosh rec. need-based scholarship or grant aid	45
% UG rec. need-based scholarship or grant aid	41
% frosh rec. non-need-based scholarship or grant aid	7
% UG rec. non-need-based scholarship or grant aid	4
% frosh rec. need-based self-help aid	60
% UG rec. need-based self-help aid	60
% frosh rec. any financial aid	84
% UG rec. any financial aid	79
% UG borrow to pay for school	76
Average cumulative indebtedness	$32,323

THE BEST 376 COLLEGES ■ 667

UNIVERSITY OF NEW MEXICO

OFFICE OF ADMISSIONS, PO BOX 4895, ALBUQUERQUE, NM 87196-4895 • ADMISSIONS: 505-277-2446 • FAX: 505-277-6686

CAMPUS LIFE

Quality of Life Rating	76
Fire Safety Rating	73
Green Rating	93
Type of school	public
Environment	metropolis

STUDENTS

Total undergrad enrollment	20,655
% male/female	45/55
% from out of state	10
% live on campus	10
# of fraternities	9
# of sororities	10
% African American	3
% Asian	3
% Caucasian	41
% Hispanic	40
% Native American	6
% international	1
# of countries represented	92

SURVEY SAYS . . .

Great computer facilities
Diverse student types on campus
Different types of students interact
Students get along with local
community
Great off-campus food
Low cost of living
Students are happy
Student publications are popular

ACADEMICS

Academic Rating	61
Calendar	semester
Profs interesting rating	72
Profs accessible rating	67
Most common	
reg class size	20–29 students
Most common	
lab size	20–29 students

MOST POPULAR MAJORS

biology, business administration and
management, psychology

STUDENTS SAY ". . ."

Academics

Offering a "solid education" in a beautiful setting, the University of New Mexico offers "academic excellence...through some of the best teachers and tough classes." Students also cited affordability and excellent scholarships awarded to both in-state and out-of-state applicants as a decisive factor in attending UNM. The affordability also extends to "amazing opportunities to travel abroad." At UNM, "there is something here for everyone." The education program and variety of science programs—including Earth and planetary sciences, biology, and the premed and nursing programs—also attract students. Some students express frustration with it at times being "difficult to work your way around the student services system," but the "very knowledgeable" teaching faculty are roundly praised as "teachers who care." UNM students also agree that "professors are helpful [and] genuinely interested in your personal success." Professors are approachable both in class and out and "talk to and with you and not just at you." "It's very easy to come to instructors outside of class with questions," and "most professors are willing to meet with you at your convenience." As for UNM's greatest strengths, students cite both the "research-oriented staff" and "the research opportunities available. Oftentimes the research can be done with top-of-the-line equipment" nearby at Sandia National Labs, Los Alamos National Labs, and other well-known research institutes. In UNM's collaborative environment, students also often work together and "are eager to form study groups." Also, students who need additional help can rely on academic support with "tutoring, study groups and, supplemental instruction for most courses."

Life

With "ways for everyone to get involved," UNM offers "hundreds of great student organizations" providing "opportunities for fun events." There is a student group "that will fit everyone," and at UNM, "everyone seems to find their niche." Offering another opportunity to become more involved on campus, the Greek community "makes up a lot of the senate and other extracurricular activities" and "with them, any activity has fun attached." UNM students are divided in their support of the school's athletics program. With some thinking "this school should concentrate less on sports and more on academics," other students feel "attending games is a must." Students enjoy spending time at the Student Union Building (SUB), because "there is always something going on." Even with a dry campus, "a lot of people drink, just like at any college." Students often leave campus for Albuquerque and its "excellent night life." UNM students also mentioned attending concerts and art shows for fun. Students also go to the weekly free movies at The Cellar, and to stay active, students frequent the Johnson Gym. Students say that "hanging out at the duck pond is a great way to pass time between classes in warmer months" and, "during the winter season, there are numerous ski resorts and places to go snowboarding that are not far away."

Student Body

Time and time again, students select UNM's "diversity" as its greatest strength, and one student even stated "no one will ever feel ethnically alone since there are so many different kinds of people." This also means at UNM, "people never get boring," and "you meet someone different every day." In addition to the diversity, the prevailing atmosphere is a friendly one where "people get along regardless of origin," but "like any school there are cliques...but that does not mean they do not interact with each other." One student reserved special praise for the university, "UNM is sensitive and very engaged with its diverse population of students...concerned with facilitating in-depth inquiry and learning," and more than one student observed that at UNM, "everyone brings something to the table."

FINANCIAL AID: 505-277-2041 • E-MAIL: APPLY@UNM.EDU • WEBSITE: WWW.UNM.EDU

THE PRINCETON REVIEW SAYS

Admissions

Very important factors considered include: Academic GPA, rigor of secondary school record. *Important factors considered include:* Class rank, standardized test scores. *Other factors considered include:* Application essay, character/personal qualities, extracurricular activities, first generation, talent/ability, volunteer work, work experience. SAT or ACT required; ACT with writing component recommended. TOEFL required of all international applicants. High school diploma is required, and GED is accepted. *Academic units required:* 4 English, 3 mathematics, 3 science (1 science lab), 2 foreign language, 2 social studies, 1 history.

Financial Aid

Students should submit: FAFSA. The Princeton Review suggests that all financial aid forms be submitted as soon as possible after January 1. *Need-based scholarships/grants offered:* Federal Pell, SEOG, state scholarships/grants, private scholarships, school scholarship or grant aid from institutional funds, United Negro College Fund, Federal Nursing Scholarships. *Loan aid offered:* Direct Subsidized Stafford, Direct Unsubsidized Stafford, Direct PLUS, Federal Perkins, Federal Nursing Loans, state loans, university loans from institutional funds. Applicants will be notified of awards on a rolling basis beginning April 15.

The Inside Word

UNM offers online applications through its website, and you will also find specific scholastic standards for traditional and nontraditional students interested in applying to UNM. Traditional applicants should have completed core coursework, taken the ACT or SAT exam and have an average or above-average GPA if they would like to be considered for admission at UNM.

THE SCHOOL SAYS "..."

From the Admissions Office

"The University of New Mexico is a major research institution nestled in the heart of multicultural Albuquerque on one of the nation's most beautiful and unique campuses. Students learn in an environment graced by distinctive Southwestern architecture, beautiful plazas and fountains, spectacular art and a national arboretum...all within view of the 10,000-foot Sandia Mountains. At UNM, diversity is a way of learning with education enriched by a lively mix of students being taught by a world-class research faculty that includes a Nobel laureate, a MacArthur Fellow, and members of several national academies. UNM offers more than 200 degree programs and majors and has earned national recognition in dozens of disciplines, ranging from primary care medicine and clinical law to engineering, photography, Latin American history, and intercultural communications. Research and the quest for new knowledge fuels the university's commitment to an undergraduate education where students work side-by-side with many of the finest scholars in their fields.

"The university will continue to accept SAT or ACT scores, but the University of New Mexico does not require the writing component at this time. The SAT critical reading portion will be used with the SAT Math to be considered in any admission decision based on formula. The use of ACT composite remains unchanged. These requirements are subject to change."

SELECTIVITY

Admissions Rating	79
# of applicants	11,220
% of applicants accepted	66
% of acceptees attending	48

FRESHMAN PROFILE

Range SAT Critical Reading	480–620
Range SAT Math	480–620
Range ACT Composite	19–25
Minimum paper TOEFL	520
Minimum computer TOEFL	190
Minimum web-based TOEFL	68
Average HS GPA	3.29
% graduated top 10% of class	27
% graduated top 25% of class	44
% graduated top 50% of class	75

DEADLINES

Regular	
Priority	6/15
Nonfall registration?	yes

FINANCIAL FACTS

Financial Aid Rating	60*
Annual in-state tuition	$5,506
Annual out-of-state tuition	$18,691
Room and board	$7,638
Required fees	$1,158
Books and supplies	$944

UNIVERSITY OF NEW ORLEANS

AD 103, LAKEFRONT, NEW ORLEANS, LA 70148 • ADMISSIONS: 504-280-6595 • FAX: 504-280-5522

CAMPUS LIFE

Quality of Life Rating	67
Fire Safety Rating	66
Green Rating	65
Type of school	public
Environment	metropolis

STUDENTS

Total undergrad enrollment	8,345
% male/female	50/50
% from out of state	3
% from public high school	63
% live on campus	9
# of fraternities	7
# of sororities	7
% African American	16
% Asian	7
% Caucasian	55
% Hispanic	7
% Native American	1
% international	5
# of countries represented	83

SURVEY SAYS . . .
Great computer facilities
Athletic facilities are great
Diverse student types on campus
Students get along with local community

ACADEMICS

Academic Rating	67
Calendar	semester
Student/faculty ratio	18:1
Profs interesting rating	72
Profs accessible rating	71
Most common reg class size	20–29 students

MOST POPULAR MAJORS
accounting, business administration and management, general studies

STUDENTS SAY "..."

Academics

The University of New Orleans provides "an equal opportunity for all people to get a superior education at an affordable price." You'll find a "diverse community of students" and "some of the best academics in the country." Classes are "challenging," "rewarding," and "offered at a variety of times, so it is easier for working students to attend class," but there are few bells and whistles. UNO "is geared to get students an education and doesn't fool around with extras." While "it is easy to get in" to UNO, it can be "hard to get out." "Classes are not easy." "UNO is for hard workers," a computer science major asserts. "It isn't an escalator for rich people to send their spoiled kids like the other schools in New Orleans." Faculty members are "accessible," "dedicated," and "extremely knowledgeable." They "have had extensive careers" and retain "good connections to the real world." Students note, however, that the bad professors are "really bad." On the upside, "UNO is a great school academically and has one of the best business programs in the city." Other academic standouts include engineering, naval architecture, and hotel, restaurant, and tourism administration. There is also a "great jazz program."

Life

UNO is now bigger and better than ever. "UNO has brand new apartments for incoming freshman, who always receive first pick and also just recently received a six million dollar grant to update the Earl K. Long Library." While "more people are living on campus" now, UNO remains "primarily a commuter campus." Students here are "almost completely focused on academics." Generally, when classes end, students "leave ASAP." "Job opportunities for college students are pretty good," and "most students work either full- or part-time." "The overall experience at UNO is a very independent one," an English major reports. "There are clubs and organizations in which to be involved," but "it is hard to get people involved in extracurricular activities." "If you want a college life, you must join a fraternity or sorority or some type of group on campus," a business major ventures. On the plus side, UNO boasts a "world-class" gym, and, of course, the "amazing" city of New Orleans is still brimming "with a lot of opportunity." "It's New Orleans. My god!" exclaims a junior. The campus is "less than ten minutes to the French Quarter." "There's so much to do," and the food "is unmatched anywhere." "We live in a city that is immersed in culture and entertainment so fun is not too hard to find," says a senior. "You can find an open bar at any time of any day, but it isn't impossible to find a quiet spot and work out some math."

Student Body

UNO boasts "an eclectic assortment of students" who are "very serious" about academics, yet "very friendly." "Many different ethnic and social backgrounds" are represented here and it's definitely not "a regular 'all-American' college." "Because the school is a commuter school, the student population is made up mostly of local folks," observes an anthropology major. "But that doesn't stop the school from being extremely diverse." "Classmates range from high school grads to grandparents." "It's just a big gumbo of people," a sophomore writes. "The typical student" at UNO is probably "mid-twenties, working full or part time while attending classes, [and] living off-campus in New Orleans." "I think the typical student at UNO is one who is excited to be in college, often entering or returning to college after spending some time in the workforce," a political science major reports. Many students are "married, have kids, and live in the suburbs," and many are "making a second or third try at college." In recent years, though, "the contingency of on-campus, fresh-out-of-high-schoolers" has grown by "leaps and bounds."

FINANCIAL AID: 504-280-6603 • E-MAIL: ADMISSIONS@UNO.EDU • WEBSITE: WWW.UNO.EDU

THE PRINCETON REVIEW SAYS

Admissions

Very important factors considered include: Academic GPA, class rank, rigor of secondary school record, standardized test scores. *Other factors considered include:* Recommendation(s), geographical residence, state residency. SAT or ACT required; ACT with or without writing component accepted. TOEFL required of all international applicants. High school diploma is required, and GED is accepted. *Academic units required:* 4 English, 3 mathematics, 3 science, 2 foreign language, 1 social studies, 2 history, 1 visual/performing arts, 1 additional math or science, 0.5 computer science.

Financial Aid

Students should submit: FAFSA. The Princeton Review recommends students submit their FAFSA as soon as possible after January 1. *Need-based scholarships/grants offered:* Federal Pell, Federal SEOG, state scholarships/grants, private scholarships, institutional scholarships (Priority date is January 15.), or grant aid from institutional funds. *Loan aid offered:* Federal Direct Subsidized and Direct Unsubsidized, Direct PLUS, Federal Perkins, alternative loans. Federal Work-Study program available, affording job opportunities on and off campus.

The Inside Word

Admission is straightforward here. Complete a basic college-bound high school curriculum with a GPA of at least 2.5, get at least an 23 on your ACT, or graduate in the top twenty-five percent of your high school class. Nontraditional students who don't want to pay the exorbitant prices of the more well-known private universities in New Orleans can find their niche at UNO; if you are twenty-five or older, the only requirement for admission is a legitimate high school diploma or a GED.

THE SCHOOL SAYS ". . ."

From the Admissions Office

"The University of New Orleans has a wide array of academic programs. Quality student life programs include a campus bar, first-run movies, and a host of exciting student activities."

"UNO embraces its mission by providing the best educational opportunities for undergraduate and graduate students, conducting world-class research, and serving a diverse and cultured community in critical areas. UNO's most outstanding offerings include a doctoral program in conservation biology, providing training in the most advanced molecular biological techniques; the largest U.S. undergraduate program in Naval Architecture and Marine Engineering; a leading jazz studies program; one of the top five film programs in the country; and the only graduate arts administration program in the Gulf South.

"UNO will use the total score from the critical reading/verbal and math sub sections of the SAT or the composite score for the ACT. The writing components of the ACT and SAT will be used for placement purposes, but not for admission purposes, at the time."

SELECTIVITY

Admissions Rating	77
# of applicants	3,467
% of applicants accepted	56
% of acceptees attending	55

FRESHMAN PROFILE

Range SAT Critical Reading	470–583
Range SAT Math	450–580
Range SAT Writing	450–580
Range ACT Composite	20–24
Minimum paper TOEFL	525
Minimum computer TOEFL	195
Minimum web-based TOEFL	71
Average HS GPA	3.07
% graduated top 10% of class	15
% graduated top 25% of class	35
% graduated top 50% of class	64

DEADLINES

Regular	
Priority	7/1
Deadline	11/30
Notification	10/1
Nonfall registration?	yes

FINANCIAL FACTS

Financial Aid Rating	67
Annual in-state tuition	$4,152
Annual out-of-state tuition	$13,740
Room and board	$8,127
Required fees	$659
Books and supplies	$1,300
% frosh rec. need-based scholarship or grant aid	53
% UG rec. need-based scholarship or grant aid	37
% frosh rec. non-need-based scholarship or grant aid	45
% UG rec. non-need-based scholarship or grant aid	19
% frosh rec. need-based self-help aid	30
% UG rec. need-based self-help aid	30
% frosh rec. any financial aid	72
% UG rec. any financial aid	56
% UG borrow to pay for school	20
Average cumulative indebtedness	$16,427

THE UNIVERSITY OF NORTH CAROLINA AT ASHEVILLE

CPO #1320, 117 UNIVERSITY HALL, ASHEVILLE, NC 28804-8510 • ADMISSIONS: 828-251-6481 • FAX: 828-251-6482

CAMPUS LIFE

Quality of Life Rating	92
Fire Safety Rating	83
Green Rating	83
Type of school	public
Environment	town

STUDENTS

Total undergrad enrollment	3,418
% male/female	44/56
% from out of state	12
% from public high school	87
% live on campus	33
# of fraternities	1
# of sororities	2
% African American	2
% Asian	1
% Caucasian	87
% Hispanic	4
% international	1
# of countries represented	20

SURVEY SAYS . . .
No one cheats
Students are friendly
Students get along with local
community
Students love Asheville, NC
Great off-campus food
Dorms are like palaces
Students are happy
Political activism is popular

ACADEMICS

Academic Rating	85
% students graduating within 4 years	30
% students graduating within 6 years	56
Calendar	semester
Student/faculty ratio	14:1
Profs interesting rating	92
Profs accessible rating	86
Most common reg class size	10–19 students
Most common lab size	20–29 students

MOST POPULAR MAJORS
business management, English
language and literature, psychology

STUDENTS SAY ". . ."

Academics

Undergrads at UNC—Asheville rave about their top-notch academic experience. Professors are "devoted and passionate [about] their fields of study, and it shows in the classroom." Importantly, "even though you may not be totally fascinated by the subject initially, the professors' enthusiasm for each course is contagious." Students also appreciate Asheville's "liberal arts ideology." As one senior English lit major says, "It's wonderful when every semester, at least two seemingly unrelated classes end up teaching the same lessons through different means and subjects." Though "course material is challenging," students take solace in knowing that "an A is totally achievable." This is due in part to the fact that "professors are available and more than willing to assist students outside of class." One environmental studies major adds, "The classes are small enough that the professors know you by name and seem to care if you do well." Furthermore, "tutoring sessions…are free and plentiful" for those undergrads who feel that they require more assistance. There are some undergrads who feel that the administration is "relatively detached from school life" and "out of touch with the students," others taut the deans as being "unusually accessible."

Life

With roughly "two-thirds of [the] student [body] living off-campus," some undergrads warn that life "can be slow on the weekends." Fortunately, one senior confidently declares that campus life "has started to pick up in the last few years." Freshman are required to live on campus their first year. Indeed, "students enjoy a wide range of activities" from playing "Frisbee golf on the quad" to attending one of many "lectures" or "basketball games" held on campus. While there is a Greek system, "partying does not define the school." Many students are "environmentally conscious" and spend a lot of energy helping shape "campus policies, including [instituting] new, reusable take-out boxes from the school cafeteria." Undergrads love the fact that they are nestled "in the Blue Ridge Mountains." The university offers a fantastic "outdoors program that [hosts] popular rock-climbing, caving, hiking, and kayaking [trips]." Students also give hometown Asheville high marks. One student says, "You can't take three steps downtown without tripping over some kind of festival or street performance." A favorite Asheville activity for many students is "the drum circle" where "people gather every Friday evening (in warm weather), circulating, dancing, thrumming, and drumming. Drummers, amateur to experienced, bring their own instruments to bang upon. People without personal beat abilities twist through the crowds to dance or simply watch from the sidelines."

Student Body

UNC—Asheville seems to hold appeal for self-described "hippies." One sophomore says, "This school attracts the sort of people who get excited about local, organic, dairy-free muffins and sandals made from recycled flax." Indeed many undergrads "care about the environment, [are] liberal-leaning, enjoy the outdoors, [and are] pretty sociable." Happily, the university "fosters the idea that individuality is essential," and students assure us that everyone "is easily accepted here" regardless of political affiliation. Perhaps this acceptance stems from the fact that the campus welcomes students from a variety of "economic backgrounds, religious backgrounds and sexual orientations." Asheville does manage to attract both a large number of "commuter students" as well as "a lot of nontraditional students."

THE UNIVERSITY OF NORTH CAROLINA AT ASHEVILLE

FINANCIAL AID: 828-251-6535 • E-MAIL: ADMISSIONS@UNCA.EDU • WEBSITE: WWW.UNCA.EDU

THE PRINCETON REVIEW SAYS

Admissions

Very important factors considered include: Academic GPA, rigor of secondary school record. *Important factors considered include:* Application essay, class rank, recommendation(s), standardized test scores. *Other factors considered include:* Alumni/ae relation, extracurricular activities, first generation, geographical residence, interview, level of applicant's interest, racial/ethnic status, state residency, talent/ability, volunteer work, work experience. SAT or ACT required; ACT with writing component required. TOEFL required of all international applicants. *Academic units required:* 4 English, 4 mathematics, 3 science (1 science lab), 2 foreign language, 1 social studies, 1 history. *Academic units recommended:* 4 academic elective.

Financial Aid

Students should submit: FAFSA. The Princeton Review suggests that all financial aid forms be submitted as soon as possible after January 1. *Need-based scholarships/grants offered:* Federal Pell, SEOG, state scholarships/grants, private scholarships, school scholarship or grant aid from institutional funds. *Loan aid offered:* Direct Subsidized Stafford, Direct Unsubsidized Stafford, Direct PLUS, Federal Perkins, state loans, university loans from institutional funds. Applicants will be notified of awards on a rolling basis beginning March 15. Federal Work-Study Program available. Off-campus job opportunities are good.

The Inside Word

UNC—Asheville provides a sound public education in a small campus atmosphere, and an increasing number of students are setting their sights on it each year. In kind, the school works diligently to create a diverse student body and thoroughly analyzes each application it receives. Although selectivity is rising, candidates who demonstrate reasonable academic success and involvement in a variety of extracurricular activities should be able to secure admittance.

THE SCHOOL SAYS "..."

From the Admissions Office

"If you want to learn how to think, how to analyze and solve problems on your own, and how to become your own best teacher then, a broad-based liberal arts education is the key. UNC Asheville focuses on undergraduates, with a core curriculum covering natural science, math, social sciences, humanities, language and culture, arts and ideas, and health and fitness. Students thrive in small classes, with a faculty dedicated first of all to teaching. The liberal arts emphasis develops discriminating thinkers, expert and creative communicators with a passion for learning. These are qualities you need for today's challenges and the changes of tomorrow.

"The University of North Carolina at Asheville requires the SAT or for students submitting an ACT score, the ACT with the writing component."

SELECTIVITY
Admissions Rating	84
# of applicants	2,362
% of applicants accepted	77
% of acceptees attending	33

FRESHMAN PROFILE
Range SAT Critical Reading	540–650
Range SAT Math	520–620
Range SAT Writing	510–620
Range ACT Composite	22–27
Minimum paper TOEFL	550
Minimum computer TOEFL	213
Minimum web-based TOEFL	79
Average HS GPA	3.91
% graduated top 10% of class	22
% graduated top 25% of class	58
% graduated top 50% of class	95

DEADLINES
Early action	
Deadline	11/15
Notification	12/15
Regular	
Priority	11/15
Deadline	2/15
Nonfall registration?	yes

FINANCIAL FACTS
Financial Aid Rating	86
Annual in-state tuition and fees	$5,393
Annual out-of-state tuition and fees	$19,025
Room and board	$7,302
Books and supplies	$950
% frosh rec. need-based scholarship or grant aid	44
% UG rec. need-based scholarship or grant aid	46
% frosh rec. non-need-based scholarship or grant aid	8
% UG rec. non-need-based scholarship or grant aid	6
% frosh rec. need-based self-help aid	27
% UG rec. need-based self-help aid	32
% frosh rec. any financial aid	71
% UG rec. any financial aid	66
% UG borrow to pay for school	48
Average cumulative indebtedness	$15,443

THE UNIVERSITY OF NORTH CAROLINA AT CHAPEL HILL

JACKSON HALL 153A, CAMPUS BOX #2200, CHAPEL HILL, NC 27599 • ADMISSIONS: 919-966-3621 • FAX: 919-962-3045

CAMPUS LIFE

Quality of Life Rating	94
Fire Safety Rating	84
Green Rating	95
Type of school	public
Environment	town

STUDENTS

Total undergrad enrollment	17,943
% male/female	41/59
% from out of state	18
% from public high school	80
% live on campus	46
# of fraternities	33
# of sororities	21
% African American	9
% Asian	6
% Caucasian	66
% Hispanic	11
% Native American	1
% international	2
# of countries represented	63

SURVEY SAYS . . .

Low cost of living
Everyone loves the Tar Heels
Student publications are popular

ACADEMICS

Academic Rating	80
% students graduating within 4 years	76
% students graduating within 6 years	90
Calendar	semester
Student/faculty ratio	14:1
Profs interesting rating	81
Profs accessible rating	77
Most common reg class size	10–19 students
Most common lab size	10–19 students

MOST POPULAR MAJORS
biology, mass communication/media
studies, psychology

STUDENTS SAY ". . ."

Academics

It's quite an understatement to say students at UNC—Chapel Hill are proud of their school. One calls it his "dream school," while another calls it the "perfect mixture of academics, sports, and social life." Although its relative low cost makes UNC a great bargain in higher education, academic rigor doesn't take a back seat, and the vast majority of students say it's one of the main reasons they chose the school. The journalism, business, and nursing programs are ranked among the best in the country, but the students hail the overall liberal arts curriculum because it creates well-rounded adults who "can handle any intellectual obstacle." In describing the instructors, students use words like "world-class," "brilliant," and "incredible," while also noting that they're "warm," "welcoming," and "passionate" about their work and their students. "Most of my professors have been great, and some have been phenomenal." Faculty members are generous with their time outside of class, patiently explaining "even the most difficult material" and using e-mail to announce changes. Some complain about large classes and warn incoming students that they will have to take the initiative and "speak up," because they won't be "coddled." The school's academic-advising system still comes in for sharp criticism. "Students are on their own there," one student says.

Life

With more than 17,000 undergrads, UNC is large enough that students rarely are lacking for something to do. Tar Heel men's basketball probably is at the top of the list; indeed, for many rabid fans, the Dean Smith Center is the center of the universe, especially when Duke is the opponent. One student sums up the school's essence this way: "It's the feeling of running through the beautiful old quad by Davie Poplar on the way to Franklin Street after a big win." The consensus is maintaining grades requires such an effort, letting off steam on weekends is a reward. "Life at UNC is full throttle. People work hard and play hard." Many flock to the bars, restaurants and coffee shops of Franklin Street, but others prefer the music scene in nearby Carrboro or staying on campus to participate in a function sponsored by one of the hundreds of student groups. The campus itself is gorgeous and filled with history. Although only seventeen percent of students belong to a fraternity or sorority, the Greek organizations are a big part of the social scene. "When you're writing thirty-page papers on twentieth-century German philosophy and working two jobs, a night where you get to dress up as a biker chick and listen to AC/DC all night at the bar is a welcome reprieve," one sorority member says.

Student Body

One student after another comments about the feeling of generosity that pervades UNC—"the epitome of Southern hospitality"—and how it extends beyond mere school spirit and the wearing of Carolina blue and white on game days. "Carolina is family," one student says. "Most of us here are crazy about sports, but most will do anything at all to help a fellow UNC student." "Although the student body is very diverse, a commonality among students is the desire to serve others and work for humanitarian efforts." One reason for the closeness is that the vast majority of students hail from the Tar Heel state. So there are "lots of down-home, North Carolina types who excelled in their rural high schools." Students and faculty are viewed as leaning liberal politically, which makes for some interesting exchanges. "Political activism is huge here," a student says. But even though it's a vast school, "it has a place for everyone." "There are really only two common denominators: commitment to some kind of excellence (academic, extracurricular, etc.) and rooting against Duke."

THE UNIVERSITY OF NORTH CAROLINA AT CHAPEL HILL

FINANCIAL AID: 919-962-8396 • E-MAIL: UNCHELP@ADMISSIONS.UNC.EDU • WEBSITE: WWW.UNC.EDU

THE PRINCETON REVIEW SAYS

Admissions

Very important factors considered include: Academic GPA, application essay, class rank, recommendation(s), rigor of secondary school record, standardized test scores, character/personal qualities, extracurricular activities, state residency, talent/ability. *Important factors considered include:* Alumni/ae relation, first generation, racial/ethnic status, volunteer work, work experience. SAT or ACT required; ACT with writing component required. TOEFL required of all international applicants. *Academic units required:* 4 English, 4 mathematics, 3 science (1 science lab), 2 foreign language, 1 social studies, 1 history. It's recommended that students enroll in course levels beyond these minimum requirements. For more information, visit the school's website.

Financial Aid

Students should submit: FAFSA, CSS/Financial Aid PROFILE. The Princeton Review suggests that all financial aid forms be submitted as soon as possible after January 1. *Need-based scholarships/grants offered:* Federal Pell, SEOG, state scholarships/grants, private scholarships, school scholarship or grant aid from institutional funds. *Loan aid offered:* Direct Subsidized Stafford, Direct Unsubsidized Stafford, Direct PLUS, Federal Perkins, state loans, university loans from institutional funds. Applicants will be notified of awards on a rolling basis beginning March 15. Federal Work-Study Program available. Off-campus job opportunities are good.

The Inside Word

UNC's admissions process is highly selective. North Carolina students compete against other students from across the state for eighty-two percent of all spaces available in the freshman class; out-of-state students compete for the remaining eighteen percent of the spaces. State residents will find the admissions standards high, and out-of-state applicants will find that it's one of the hardest offers of admission to come by in the country.

THE SCHOOL SAYS "..."

From the Admissions Office

"One of the leading research and teaching institutions in the world, UNC Chapel Hill offers first-rate faculty, innovative academic programs, and students who are smart, friendly, and committed to public service. Students take full advantage of extensive undergraduate research opportunities, a study abroad program with programs on every continent except Antarctica, and 600-plus clubs and organizations. We offer all this in Chapel Hill, one of the greatest and most welcoming college towns anywhere.

"Carolina's commitment to excellence, access, and affordability is reflected in premier scholarships, such as the prestigious Morehead and Robertson Scholarships, as well the Carolina Covenant, a national model that enables students from low-income families to graduate from Carolina debt-free. We invite you to visit—talk with our professors, attend a class, spend time with our students, and stroll across our beautiful residential campus, where friendly people and exciting events are within easy walking distance.

"All first-year applicants are required to submit an SAT or an ACT writing component score. While test scores are important, our holistic review process includes other important factors such course work, grades, and extracurricular activities."

SELECTIVITY

Admissions Rating	98
# of applicants	23,272
% of applicants accepted	32
% of acceptees attending	52
# accepting a place on wait list	1,114
% admitted from wait list	44

FRESHMAN PROFILE

Range SAT Critical Reading	590–700
Range SAT Math	610–710
Range SAT Writing	590–690
Range ACT Composite	27–31
Minimum paper TOEFL	600
Minimum web-based TOEFL	100
Average HS GPA	4.47
% graduated top 10% of class	78
% graduated top 25% of class	95
% graduated top 50% of class	99

DEADLINES

Early action	
Deadline	10/15
Notification	1/31
Regular	
Deadline	1/15
Notification	3/31
Nonfall registration?	no

APPLICANTS ALSO LOOK AT
AND SOMETIMES PREFER
Duke University, University of Virginia

AND RARELY PREFER
North Carolina State University, Wake Forest University

FINANCIAL FACTS

Financial Aid Rating	94
Annual in-state tuition	$4,815
Annual out-of-state tuition	$23,430
Room and board	$9,470
Required fees	$1,850
Books and supplies	$1,150
% frosh rec. need-based scholarship or grant aid	39
% UG rec. need-based scholarship or grant aid	36
% frosh rec. non-need-based scholarship or grant aid	18
% UG rec. non-need-based scholarship or grant aid	11
% frosh rec. need-based self-help aid	17
% UG rec. need-based self-help aid	19
% frosh rec. any financial aid	69
% UG rec. any financial aid	63

THE UNIVERSITY OF NORTH CAROLINA AT GREENSBORO

1400 SPRING GARDEN STREET, GREENSBORO, NC 27402-6170 • ADMISSIONS: 336-334-5243 • FAX: 336-334-4180

CAMPUS LIFE

Quality of Life Rating	78
Fire Safety Rating	73
Green Rating	76
Type of school	public
Environment	city

STUDENTS

Total undergrad enrollment	14,310
% male/female	34/66
% from out of state	7
% from public high school	95
% live on campus	29
# of fraternities	11
# of sororities	11
% African American	24
% Asian	4
% Caucasian	65
% Hispanic	5
% international	1
# of countries represented	12

SURVEY SAYS . . .

Great computer facilities
Diverse student types on campus
Different types of students interact
Students get along with local community
Students are happy

ACADEMICS

Academic Rating	64
% students graduating within 4 years	29
% students graduating within 6 years	53
Calendar	semester
Student/faculty ratio	17:1
Profs interesting rating	77
Profs accessible rating	74
Most common reg class size	20–29 students
Most common lab size	20–29 students

MOST POPULAR MAJORS

biology, business administration and management

STUDENTS SAY "..."

Academics

Students describe the University of North Carolina at Greensboro as "about a half-and-half commuter school with great specialized programs and schools such as nursing, education, dance, and music." Undergrads here praise the "high quality of education at a significantly reduced rate, while having the smaller classes allowing closer bonds between faculty and students" than one could reasonably expect for the tuition charged. The key here is the faculty, because according to one student, "UNCG places a big emphasis on having great teachers. There are some duds, but overall, more of them are fantastic than anything else." The school excels in some off-the-beaten-path areas like programs in kinesiology, deaf education, human development, and family studies, which all receive enthusiastic praise from students. Undergrads also love the "opportunities that are given to network with businesses and people outside of campus" and the "great internships" the school helps them find. Nontraditional students appreciate the "great support system for adult students." As the school's reputation continues to improve, some worry this "historically moderate-sized university where student well-being was the first priority...will change into a large research university where the focus is raising more and more money." One undeniable upside of the school's increased stature is that "you feel like you are respected in the community when you tell someone that you are a student at UNCG."

Life

UNCG is conveniently located "a mile from downtown and close to surrounding schools: Guilford College, NC A&T, Greensboro College, Elon, UNC, NC State." One student observes, "With six colleges around UNCG, a metropolis of 250,000-plus (1.1 million in the metro area), and access within a three-hour drive to both beaches and mountains, there is always something to do." On campus "UNCG makes it easy for anyone and everyone to fit in and feel included. Through clubs, students have the ability to offer ideas and have them implemented. There's also intramural sports and free events." The high-profile arts programs on campus yield some wonderful cultural opportunities. "The Weatherspoon Museum of Art is amazing at showcasing the most modern American art and keeps this provincial little town on its toes," writes one artist. A performing arts student adds, "There are wonderful concerts and plays and lectures here. It's a great cultural center and you can always have something to do as long as you look for it." Intercollegiate athletics, students tell us, "are not as popular as they could be, even though they are often ranked nationally, or at least ranked in the conference." Many here feel the addition of a football team (the school has none) would change that. "It would really bring the school spirit up," opines one undergrad. The school's many commuters warn that "parking is horrendous."

Student Body

UNCG is a big school with "many people from all walks of life, social/cultural backgrounds, etc. The university promotes cultural diversity and acceptance and tolerance of people of different backgrounds." One student reports, "One minute you see a bunch of music majors talking about how much Bach has affected their life, and the next minute, you see a bunch of sorority girls discussing the Gap. Mainly, I have observed that sorority girls stick together, jocks stick together, etc." As at many state schools, "about half of the students at UNCG came here to party. The other half consists of hard-working students who are generally frustrated with the slacker mentality in a lot of our classes. This is less of a problem once you get past the intro-level lectures."

THE UNIVERSITY OF NORTH CAROLINA AT GREENSBORO

FINANCIAL AID: 336-334-5702 • E-MAIL: ADMISSIONS@UNCG.EDU • WEBSITE: WWW.UNCG.EDU

THE PRINCETON REVIEW SAYS

Admissions

Very important factors considered include: Academic GPA, rigor of secondary school record. *Important factors considered include:* Standardized test scores. *Other factors considered include:* Application essay. SAT or ACT required; ACT with writing component required. TOEFL required of all international applicants. *Academic units required:* 4 English, 4 mathematics, 3 science (1 science lab), 2 foreign language, 2 social studies.

Financial Aid

Students should submit: FAFSA. The Princeton Review suggests that all financial aid forms be submitted as soon as possible after January 1. *Need-based scholarships/grants offered:* Federal Pell, SEOG, state scholarships/grants, private scholarships, school scholarship or grant aid from institutional funds. *Loan aid offered:* Direct Subsidized Stafford, Direct Unsubsidized Stafford, Direct PLUS, Federal Perkins, university loans from institutional funds. Applicants will be notified of awards on a rolling basis beginning March 15. Federal Work-Study Program available. Off-campus job opportunities are good.

The Inside Word

UNCG has yet to gain much attention outside of regional circles so, at least for the moment, gaining admission is not particularly difficult. The usual public university considerations apply; expect the admissions office to focus on grades and test scores, and not much else. Out-of-staters will find a much smoother path to admission here than at Chapel Hill and will still be within reasonable reach of internship and career possibilities in the Research Triangle.

THE SCHOOL SAYS " . . ."

From the Admissions Office

"UNCG is committed to student success. Exceptional teaching and first-rate academic programs provide a solid learning foundation. Hands-on experiences in internships, undergraduate research, and service-learning programs prepare students to take on the challenges of the twenty-first century. An ambitious expansion of on-campus housing and learning communities helps to promote a sense of community that is engaging and supportive.

"In addition to excellence in our academic programs, we are looking for students with outstanding records who will benefit from these challenging programs. As admission to UNCG becomes more competitive, our goal is to assess students' entire academic record, beginning with a combination of their overall cumulative grade point average and SAT or ACT scores. Freshmen applicants must submit at least one SAT or ACT score (including the writing component). We also will review other factors such as students' entire high school record, course selection, senior class schedule, and a short essay.

"UNCG students can broaden their college experience by taking advantage of one of the most extensive and affordable study abroad programs in the country. The Lloyd International Honors College offers a unique opportunity for talented students in any major to benefit from a rich intellectual life with a global perspective. UNCG's ideal size and close-knit campus atmosphere enable students to excel as individuals and get connected through more than 180 student organizations, intramural, club and intercollegiate sports, Greeks, outdoor adventures, a vibrant arts community, and a friendly Southern city that quickly starts to feel like home."

SELECTIVITY

Admissions Rating	79
# of applicants	11,574
% of applicants accepted	58
% of acceptees attending	38

FRESHMAN PROFILE

Range SAT Critical Reading	460–560
Range SAT Math	460–560
Range SAT Writing	440–550
Minimum paper TOEFL	550
Minimum computer TOEFL	213
Minimum web-based TOEFL	79
Average HS GPA	3.59
% graduated top 10% of class	18
% graduated top 25% of class	48
% graduated top 50% of class	86

DEADLINES

Early action	
Deadline	1/15
Notification	4/1
Regular	
Priority	11/1
Deadline	3/1
Notification	12/15
Nonfall registration?	yes

FINANCIAL FACTS

Financial Aid Rating	75
Annual in-state tuition	$3,243
Annual out-of-state tuition	$15,004
Room and board	$6,655
Required fees	$1,730
Books and supplies	$1,282
% frosh rec. need-based scholarship or grant aid	45
% UG rec. need-based scholarship or grant aid	45
% frosh rec. non-need-based scholarship or grant aid	59
% UG rec. non-need-based scholarship or grant aid	55
% frosh rec. need-based self-help aid	47
% UG rec. need-based self-help aid	49
% frosh rec. any financial aid	77
% UG rec. any financial aid	71
% UG borrow to pay for school	67
Average cumulative indebtedness	$23,772

UNIVERSITY OF NORTH DAKOTA

PO BOX 8135, GRAND FORKS, ND 58202 • ADMISSIONS: 800-225-5863 • FAX: 701-777-4857

CAMPUS LIFE
Quality of Life Rating	71
Fire Safety Rating	75
Green Rating	87
Type of school	public
Environment	town

STUDENTS
Total undergrad enrollment	11,139
% male/female	55/45
% from out of state	56
% from public high school	92
% live on campus	32
# of fraternities	13
# of sororities	7
% African American	1
% Asian	1
% Caucasian	82
% Hispanic	2
% Native American	2
% international	6
# of countries represented	78

SURVEY SAYS . . .
Great computer facilities
Athletic facilities are great
Students are friendly
Everyone loves the Fighting Sioux
Student publications are popular
Lots of beer drinking
Hard liquor is popular

ACADEMICS
Academic Rating	61
Calendar	semester
Student/faculty ratio	19:1
Profs interesting rating	67
Profs accessible rating	65
Most common reg class size	20–29 students
Most common lab size	20–29 students

MOST POPULAR MAJORS
commercial aviation, nursing, biology

STUDENTS SAY ". . ."

Academics

"Size and affordability are very nice draws" at the University of North Dakota. The number of undergrads here is ideal, and UND offers "the best bang for the buck anywhere." North Dakota residents can attend for a song, and reciprocity agreements provide enticing tuition breaks for students from a number of Western states. There are nearly ninety undergraduate majors. Nursing and engineering are reportedly solid. The aviation and aerospace programs are some of the very best anywhere in the world. UND owns the biggest non-military fleet of training aircraft on the planet, and students boast that a UND degree has quite a bit of prestige among airlines and in the aviation industry generally. "If you're considering air-traffic control, this is the school to be at," advises one student. Another unique program is the Center for Innovation, which provides internships for undergrads who want to launch a business. Additionally, there are more than thirty specialized academic programs for American Indians. Students describe the overall academic experience at UND as "pretty good" "and not too stressful." Despite some frustrating bureaucracy, most students appreciate the "helpful" administration. The faculty is "highly qualified" but sometimes hit-or-miss in the classroom. Some professors are "excellent teachers who genuinely care for their students." Others "seem to be distant at times." As a result, courses can range "from absolutely awesome to really annoying."

Life

UND's "very safe" campus is "pretty no matter what time of year," and the "rural" locale of Grand Forks serves up plenty of "small-town atmosphere." It's important to understand this school is "located in the tundra of the world," though. Winters are long and brutal. "It's way too cold up here" (like "grimacing-in-pain" cold). Student activities at UND run the gamut. There are more than 200 clubs and organizations. The student recreation center is enormous and state of the art. Intramural sports are quite popular, and many students are "huge supporters of the Fighting Sioux," the intercollegiate athletic teams. Specifically, "hockey is king here." The team is formidable year in and year out, and it has won several national championships. Home games in the "breathtaking" arena are well attended and "extremely fun." About ten percent of the student population is involved in the Greek scene. Students report the fraternities and sororities loom large in the social scheme of things, though, so that percentage often seems higher. Beginning on Friday (or maybe Thursday), "everybody is on a quest to entertain themselves, usually through alcohol consumption." Many students "drink every weekend," either at the frats or at "bars or house parties."

Student Body

Students here describe themselves as "really friendly." They "have their head on straight," and they know how to handle seriously frigid weather. According to UND, there's somebody on this campus from every state. However, the overwhelming majority of students come "from rural areas in the Midwest." A little under half of the undergrads are North Dakota residents. Nearly one-third hails from neighboring Minnesota. (The school is essentially located on the state line.) South Dakota residents have a presence, too. Students from anywhere else usually end up at UND because of the aviation program, and those students tend to form their own little worlds. "This is Scandinavian country," so you'll see "a lot of Nordic-descended people." Tall, blue-eyed blonds are pretty common. Native Americans make up the largest non-white ethnic group. "There are not too many minority students," but that information shouldn't be surprising given UND's rural location and the regional demographics.

FINANCIAL AID: 701-777-3121 • E-MAIL: ENROLLMENTSERVICES@MAIL.UND.EDU • WEBSITE: WWW.UND.EDU

THE PRINCETON REVIEW SAYS

Admissions

Very important factors considered include: Academic GPA, standardized test scores. *Other factors considered include:* Class rank, rigor of secondary school record. SAT or ACT required; ACT with or without writing component accepted. TOEFL required of all international applicants. High school diploma is required, and GED is accepted. *Academic units required:* 4 English, 3 mathematics, 3 science (3 science labs), 3 social studies. *Academic units recommended:* 1 foreign language.

Financial Aid

Students should submit: FAFSA. The Princeton Review suggests that all financial aid forms be submitted as soon as possible after January 1. *Need-based scholarships/grants offered:* Federal Pell, SEOG, state scholarships/grants, private scholarships, school scholarship or grant aid from institutional funds, Federal Nursing Scholarships. *Loan aid offered:* Federal Perkins, Federal Nursing Loans. Applicants will be notified of awards on a rolling basis beginning May 15. Federal Work-Study Program available. Off-campus job opportunities are excellent.

The Inside Word

UND's loose admissions standards belie the national reputation it has earned. Akin to most state schools, it's all about meeting GPA and standardized test minimums. The lack of subjective criteria makes for a relatively painless application process, and a majority of students are admitted.

THE SCHOOL SAYS "..."

From the Admissions Office

"More than 10,000 undergraduate students come to the University of North Dakota each year, from every state in the nation and more than thirty countries. They're impressed by our academic excellence, more than 200 programs, our dedication to the liberal arts mission, and alumni success record. Nearly all of the university's new students rank in the top half of their high school classes, with about half in the top quarter. As the oldest and most diversified institution of higher education in the Dakotas, Montana, Wyoming, and western Minnesota, UND is a comprehensive teaching and research university. Yet the university provides individual attention that may be missing at very large universities. UND graduates are highly regarded among prospective employers. Representatives from more than 200 regional and national companies recruit UND students every year. Our campus is approximately ninety-eight percent accessible.

"Students applying for admission to UND are required to take either the ACT or SAT unless they are older than twenty-five. The ACT writing component is not a requirement for admission, and SAT results considered include only the math and critical reading sections."

SELECTIVITY
Admissions Rating	74
# of applicants	4,796
% of applicants accepted	70
% of acceptees attending	62

FRESHMAN PROFILE
Range ACT Composite	20–25
Minimum paper TOEFL	525
Minimum computer TOEFL	195
Average HS GPA	3.38
% graduated top 10% of class	16
% graduated top 25% of class	43
% graduated top 50% of class	77

DEADLINES
Regular	
Notification	9/1
Nonfall registration?	yes

APPLICANTS ALSO LOOK AT AND OFTEN PREFER
Saint Cloud State University, University of Minnesota Duluth

AND SOMETIMES PREFER
Concordia College (Moorhead, MN), Minot State University, University of Minnesota—Crookston

FINANCIAL FACTS
Financial Aid Rating	72
Annual in-state tuition	$6,726
Annual out-of-state tuition	$15,091
Room and board	$5,950
Required fees	$1,282
Books and supplies	$800
% frosh rec. need-based scholarship or grant aid	41
% UG rec. need-based scholarship or grant aid	37
% frosh rec. non-need-based scholarship or grant aid	1
% frosh rec. need-based self-help aid	50
% UG rec. need-based self-help aid	48
% frosh rec. any financial aid	71
% UG rec. any financial aid	79
% UG borrow to pay for school	83
Average cumulative indebtedness	$45,369

UNIVERSITY OF NOTRE DAME

220 MAIN BUILDING, NOTRE DAME, IN 46556 • ADMISSIONS: 574-631-7505 • FAX: 574-631-8865

STUDENTS SAY ". . ."

Academics

Notre Dame has many traditions, including a "devotion to undergraduate education" you might not expect from a school with such an athletic reputation. Professors here are, by all accounts, "wonderful": "Not only are they invested in their students," they're "genuinely passionate about their fields of study," "enthusiastic and animated in lectures," and "always willing to meet outside of class to give extra help." Wary that distance might breed academic disengagement, professors ensure "large lectures are broken down into smaller discussion groups once a week to help with class material and…give the class a personal touch." For its part, "the administration tries its best to stay on top of the students' wants and needs." They make it "extremely easy to get in touch with anyone." Like the professors, administrators try to make personal connections with students. For example, "our president (a priest), as well as both of our presidents emeritus, make it a point to interact with the students in a variety of ways—teaching a class, saying mass in the dorms, etc." Overall, "while classes are difficult," "students are competitive against one another," and "it's necessary to study hard and often, [but] there's also time to do other things."

Life

Life at Notre Dame is centered around two things—"residential life" and "sports." The "dorms on campus provide the social structure" and supply undergrads with tons of opportunities to get involved and have fun." "During the school week" students "study a lot, but on the weekends everyone seems to make up for the lack of partying during the week." The school "does not have any fraternities or sororities, but campus is not dry, and drinking/partying is permitted within the residence halls." The administration reportedly tries "to keep the parties on campus due to the fact that campus is such a safe place and they truly do care about our safety." In addition to parties the dorms are really competitive in the Interhall Sport System, and "virtually every student plays some kind of sport [in] his/her residence hall." Intercollegiate sports, to put it mildly, "are huge." "If someone is not interested in sports upon arrival, he or she will be by the time he or she leaves." "Everybody goes to the football games, and it's common to see 1,000 students at a home soccer game." Beyond residential life and sports, "religious activities," volunteering, "campus publications, student government, and academic clubs round out the rest of ND life."

Student Body

Undergrads at Notre Dame report "the vast majority" of their peers are "very smart" "white kids from upper- to middle-class backgrounds from all over the country, especially the Midwest and Northeast." The typical student "is a type-A personality that studies a lot, yet is athletic and involved in the community. They are usually the outstanding seniors in their high schools," the "sort of people who can talk about the BCS rankings and Derrida in the same breath." Additionally, something like "eighty-five percent of Notre Dame students earned a varsity letter in high school." "Not all are Catholic" here, though most are, and it seems that most undergrads "have some sort of spirituality present in their daily lives." "ND is slowly improving in diversity concerning economic backgrounds, with the university's policy to meet all demonstrated financial need." As things stand now, those who "don't tend to fit in with everyone else hang out in their own groups made up by others like them (based on ethnicity, sexual orientation, etc.)."

UNIVERSITY OF NOTRE DAME

FINANCIAL AID: 574-631-6436 • E-MAIL: ADMISSIONS@ND.EDU • WEBSITE: WWW.ND.EDU

THE PRINCETON REVIEW SAYS

Admissions

Very important factors considered include: Rigor of secondary school record. *Important factors considered include:* Academic GPA, application essay, class rank, recommendation(s), standardized test scores, alumni/ae relation, character/personal qualities, extracurricular activities, talent/ability, volunteer work. *Other factors considered include:* First generation, level of applicant's interest, racial/ethnic status, religious affiliation/commitment, work experience. SAT or ACT required; ACT with or without writing component accepted. TOEFL required of all international applicants. *Academic units required:* 4 English, 3 mathematics, 2 science (2 science labs), 2 foreign language, 2 history, 3 academic elective. *Academic units recommended:* 4 English, 4 mathematics, 4 science (2 science labs), 4 foreign language, 4 history.

Financial Aid

Students should submit: FAFSA, CSS/Financial Aid PROFILE. Regular filing deadline is February 15. The Princeton Review suggests that all financial aid forms be submitted as soon as possible after January 1. *Need-based scholarships/grants offered:* Federal Pell, SEOG, state scholarships/grants, private scholarships, school scholarship or grant aid from institutional funds. *Loan aid offered:* Direct Subsidized Stafford, Direct Unsubsidized Stafford, Direct PLUS, Federal Perkins. Off-campus job opportunities are fair.

The Inside Word

Notre Dame is one of the most selective colleges in the country. Almost everyone who enrolls is in the top ten percent of their graduating class and possesses test scores in the highest percentiles. But, as the student respondents suggest, strong academic ability isn't enough to get you in here. The school looks for students with other talents, and seems to have a predilection for athletic achievement. Legacy students get a leg up but are by no means assured of admission.

THE SCHOOL SAYS ". . ."

From the Admissions Office

"Notre Dame is a Catholic university, which means it offers unique opportunities for academic, ethical, spiritual, and social service development. The First Year of Studies program provides special assistance to our students as they make the adjustment from high school to college. The first-year curriculum includes many core requirements, while allowing students to explore several areas of possible future study. Each residence hall is home to students from all classes; most will live in the same hall for all their years on campus. An average of ninety-three percent of entering students will graduate within five years.

"The highest critical reading score and the highest math score from either test will be accepted; the writing component score is not required. The ACT is also accepted (with or without writing component) in lieu of the SAT."

SELECTIVITY

Admissions Rating	95
# of applicants	14,357
% of applicants accepted	29
% of acceptees attending	50
# accepting a place on wait list	1,060
% admitted from wait list	24

FRESHMAN PROFILE

Range SAT Critical Reading	650–750
Range SAT Math	680–760
Range SAT Writing	640–730
Range ACT Composite	31–34
Minimum paper TOEFL	560
Minimum computer TOEFL	250
Minimum web-based TOEFL	100

DEADLINES

Early action	
Deadline	11/1
Notification	12/20
Regular	
Deadline	12/21
Nonfall registration?	yes

APPLICANTS ALSO LOOK AT AND SOMETIMES PREFER
Duke University, Georgetown University, Northwestern University

AND RARELY PREFER
Boston College

FINANCIAL FACTS

Financial Aid Rating	92
Annual tuition	$39,412
Room and board	$10,866
Required fees	$507
Books and supplies	$950
% frosh rec. need-based scholarship or grant aid	51
% UG rec. need-based scholarship or grant aid	47
% frosh rec. non-need-based scholarship or grant aid	34
% UG rec. non-need-based scholarship or grant aid	29
% frosh rec. need-based self-help aid	41
% UG rec. need-based self-help aid	42
% UG borrow to pay for school	57
Average cumulative indebtedness	$28,371

UNIVERSITY OF OKLAHOMA

1000 ASP AVENUE, NORMAN, OK 73019-4076 • ADMISSIONS: 405-325-2252 • FAX: 405-325-7124

CAMPUS LIFE

Quality of Life Rating	87
Fire Safety Rating	91
Green Rating	90
Type of school	public
Environment	city

STUDENTS

Total undergrad enrollment	20,498
% male/female	48/52
% from out of state	29
% live on campus	33
# of fraternities	31
# of sororities	20
% African American	5
% Asian	6
% Caucasian	65
% Hispanic	4
% Native American	6
% international	2
# of countries represented	85

SURVEY SAYS . . .

Athletic facilities are great
Low cost of living
Everyone loves the Sooners

ACADEMICS

Academic Rating	71
% students graduating	
within 4 years	33
Calendar	semester
Student/faculty ratio	17:1
Profs interesting rating	76
Profs accessible rating	77
Most common	
reg class size	20–29 students
Most common	
lab size	20–29 students

MOST POPULAR MAJORS

interdisciplinary studies, journalism,
organizational behavior studies

STUDENTS SAY ". . ."

Academics

Students "just swell with school pride" when they talk about the University of Oklahoma. They note, for example, that this "dynamic," "affordable," and "very research-oriented" institution reels in a slew of national merit scholars. They extol the "extensive" study abroad program. The meteorology program is "outstanding." "The engineering facilities are fantastic," and the campus as a whole is "gorgeous" and "well-kept." "The library is beautiful," reports a journalism major. "I could live in there." Like at any similar "big-time university," "The education here is what you make of it." "Anyone who truly wants to learn and achieve can find all sorts of opportunities." Then again, "If you just want to get by," you can "take easy blow-off classes." The faculty runs the gamut as well. "Most professors are great," relates an industrial engineering major. They "know what they are talking about," and they're "approachable." Professors "usually lecture more than they promote discussions." "The best can keep you riveted until the very end of the class period," promises an economics major. Others are "dry" and "overeager" teaching assistants "could use some work." Also, lower-level courses are often "huge," and they tend occur in "ancient coliseum-type" spaces.

Life

"There are tons of organizations" on OU's campus, and "There's no way you could possibly be bored." "From the Indonesian Student Association to the Bocce Ball League of Excellence, there's a group for" you. "The programming board here brings in a lot of great acts and keeps us very entertained in the middle of Oklahoma," adds one student. "School spirit is rampant," and intercollegiate athletics are insanely popular—particularly football. "Not everyone likes Sooner football," but it sure seems that way. Students at OU "live and breathe football" "to the point of near-frightening cultism." Game days in the fall are "an unforgettable experience," because "the campus goes into a frenzy." Fraternities and sororities are also "a large part of social life." Some students insist that the Greek system isn't a dominant feature of the OU landscape. "You hardly notice their presence" if you're not involved, they say, and "The majority of students aren't involved." Other students disagree. "Greek life is really big, unfortunately," they tell us. "It feels as though everyone here is Greek," and "There is a division" between the students who pledge and the students who don't. The "friendly and cute little town" of Norman is reportedly an ideal place to spend a day when not in class. Right next to campus is an area "full of" boutique shops and "a fine selection of bars and restaurants." "Norman is such a great town," gushes one student. "It's not too little to be boring but not too big to be impersonal."

Student Body

The typical student here is "pretty laid-back," "very good at prioritizing," "in some sort of organization or club," and "from Oklahoma or Texas." That student also "loves football," has "a penchant for fun," and has "no outrageous features." OU is home to "a wide variety of students with different political, religious, and economic backgrounds" though, and "There are plenty of options for every major and lifestyle." A lot of students come from a "suburban background" while "many come from small towns." There's also a "quite impressive" contingent of international students. Many students are "vaguely to devoutly Christian." Politically, "The atmosphere on campus tends to be conservative," but the left is well-represented. "We have a ton of liberals," relates one student, "and they are very much liberal." "There are the fraternity dudes and sorority girls" dressed in "North Face apparel and Nike shorts." "You have your partiers, hardcore studiers, and those in between who may lean one way or the other."

FINANCIAL AID: 405-325-4521 • E-MAIL: ADMREC@OU.EDU • WEBSITE: WWW.OU.EDU

THE PRINCETON REVIEW SAYS

Admissions

Very important factors considered include: Academic GPA, class rank, rigor of secondary school record, standardized test scores. *Other factors considered include:* Application essay, recommendation(s), state residency. SAT or ACT required; ACT with or without writing component accepted. TOEFL required of all international applicants. High school diploma is required, and GED is accepted. *Academic units required:* 4 English, 3 mathematics, 3 science (3 science labs), 2 social studies, 1 history, 2 academic elective. *Academic units recommended:* 4 mathematics, 2 foreign language, 1 computer science.

Financial Aid

Students should submit: FAFSA. The Princeton Review suggests that all financial aid forms be submitted as soon as possible after January 1. *Need-based scholarships/grants offered:* Federal Pell, SEOG, state scholarships/grants, private scholarships, school scholarship or grant aid from institutional funds, United Negro College Fund. *Loan aid offered:* Direct Subsidized Stafford, Direct Unsubsidized Stafford, Direct PLUS, Federal Perkins, university loans from institutional funds. Applicants will be notified of awards on a rolling basis beginning March 15. Federal Work-Study Program available. Off-campus job opportunities are excellent.

The Inside Word

Like at a lot of large public schools, the admissions process at the University of Oklahoma is a fairly standardized affair that favors state residents. Students who graduate in the top half of their high school class and have decent grades in college prep courses and solid standardized test scores, stand a good chance at admission. Also worth noting: national merit scholars get a lot of perks here including a sweet scholarship package.

THE SCHOOL SAYS "..."

From the Admissions Office

"Ask yourself some significant questions. What are your ambitions, goals, and dreams? Do you desire opportunity, and are you ready to accept challenge? What do you hope to gain from your educational experience? Are you looking for a university that will provide you with the tools, resources, and motivation to convert ambitions, opportunities, and challenges into meaningful achievement? To effectively answer these questions you must carefully seek out your options, look for direction, and make the right choice. The University of Oklahoma combines a unique mixture of academic excellence, varied social cultures, and a variety of campus activities to make your educational experience complete. At OU, comprehensive learning is our goal for your life. Not only do you receive a valuable classroom learning experience, but OU is also one of the finest research institutions in the United States. This allows OU students the opportunity to be a part of technology in progress. It's not just learning, it's discovery, invention, and dynamic creativity, a hands-on experience that allows you to be on the cutting edge of knowledge. Make the right choice and consider the University of Oklahoma!

"The SAT (or ACT) will be used when considering freshman applicants for admission. The writing component of either test is not required of students and is not used in determining admission to the university. The student's best composite score from any one test will be used."

SELECTIVITY

Admissions Rating	84
# of applicants	9,996
% of applicants accepted	85
% of acceptees attending	44
# accepting a place on wait list	1,545
% admitted from wait list	73

FRESHMAN PROFILE

Range SAT Critical Reading	510–650
Range SAT Math	530–660
Range ACT Composite	23–29
Minimum paper TOEFL	550
Minimum computer TOEFL	213
Minimum web-based TOEFL	79
Average HS GPA	3.60
% graduated top 10% of class	35
% graduated top 25% of class	67
% graduated top 50% of class	93

DEADLINES

Regular	
Deadline	4/1
Nonfall registration?	yes

FINANCIAL FACTS

Financial Aid Rating	86
Annual in-state tuition	$7,853
Annual out-of-state tuition	$18,284
% frosh rec. need-based	
scholarship or grant aid	27
% UG rec. need-based	
scholarship or grant aid	28
% frosh rec. non-need-based	
scholarship or grant aid	34
% UG rec. non-need-based	
scholarship or grant aid	24
% frosh rec. need-based	
self-help aid	31
% UG rec. need-based	
self-help aid	35
% frosh rec. any financial aid	83
% UG rec. any financial aid	90
% UG borrow to pay for school	57
Average cumulative indebtedness	$23,671

UNIVERSITY OF OREGON

1217 UNIVERSITY OF OREGON, EUGENE, OR 97403-1217 • ADMISSIONS: 541-346-3201 • FAX: 541-346-5815

STUDENTS SAY "..."

Academics

Ask University of Oregon students what they like best about their school and a surprising number will mention intercollegiate athletics. Press them a bit harder, however, and they'll start to identify the school's many outstanding academic programs: a business school with "a great faculty" and "amazing facilities;" solid and popular foreign language programs, including robust offerings in Japanese and Chinese; an "esteemed" and "extremely challenging" journalism school; a "very strong program in psychology and neuroscience;" an architecture program that "is increasing in popularity;" and a music program that students tout as "one of the best in the country." The school also offers "a strong study abroad program" that provides a "good outlet for all of the creative types at the university to pursue wild adventures or projects around the world," "tons of opportunities for internships," and "a whole world of unrecognized undergraduate lab research opportunities. Any, let alone all of these opportunities would give any student a foot in the door for a future in research." In other words, an ocean of opportunities awaits anyone here willing to seek it out. UO "is a place where you can get involved as deeply as you care to in social causes/politics, where you can become closely connected to your professors and their research, and where a sense of community (on campus and off) permeates your entire educational career." University of Oregon: come for the football and basketball, stay for the "incredible academics."

Life

"Life at UO is amazing all year round," undergrads report. In the fall "there is football, warm but crisp weather, and our campus is gorgeous." During the winter "there are basketball games and a lot of indoor parties." Spring and summer "are gorgeous" and the best time to enjoy the area's many outdoor opportunities, because "the rain keeps people inside during the fall and winter." Hometown Eugene "is great for the outdoors...There are mountains to hike, rivers to float, and lakes to swim in all within fifteen minutes. The coast is an hour away; the mountains are only an hour away (if you ski during the winter)." The school's outdoor program "has several trips each week. Depending on the season, they have rock-climbing, snow excursions, white water rafting, and camping trips." Eugene is also great for cultural life. "The Hult Center and other venues host extensive arts and entertainment opportunities including the annual Bach Festival, numerous other music festivals, art walks, the Saturday Market crafts fair—the list is extensive." Enthusiasm for sports permeates the campus, and "there's always a party going on" if that's what you're looking for. In short, "Whatever interests students hold, Eugene and the university usually have something going on that captures their attention."

Student Body

"There is a significant blend of students with different ethnicities, religious views, sexual orientations, and genders" at the University of Oregon, where students tend to be "laid-back, environmentally conscious, and politically inclined...usually to the left." The population includes "more than its fair share of nerds, preps, theater kids, hippies, and maybe more pot smokers, but everyone seems to be super friendly, and most people just want to get along." The student body is "pretty white-bread," though, partly in reflection of the state of Oregon's demographics (the state is ninety-three percent white). "If they lowered out-of-state costs, more people would attend who are from ethnically diverse cities," one student suggests. A "large Asian and Middle Eastern population" accounts for much of the racial diversity here.

FINANCIAL AID: 541-346-3211 • E-MAIL: UOADMIT@OREGON.UOREGON.EDU • WEBSITE: WWW.UOREGON.EDU

THE PRINCETON REVIEW SAYS

Admissions

Very important factors considered include: Academic GPA, rigor of secondary school record. *Important factors considered include:* Standardized test scores. *Other factors considered include:* Application essay, class rank, recommendation(s), extracurricular activities, first generation, geographical residence, racial/ethnic status, state residency, talent/ability, volunteer work, work experience. SAT or ACT required; ACT with writing component required. TOEFL required of all international applicants. High school diploma is required, and GED is accepted. *Academic units required:* 4 English, 3 mathematics, 2 science, 2 foreign language, 3 social studies. *Academic units recommended:* (1 science lab).

Financial Aid

Students should submit: FAFSA. Regular filing deadline is March 1. The Princeton Review suggests that all financial aid forms be submitted as soon as possible after January 1. *Need-based scholarships/grants offered:* Federal Pell, SEOG, state scholarships/grants, private scholarships, school scholarship or grant aid from institutional funds. *Loan aid offered:* Direct Subsidized Stafford, Direct Unsubsidized Stafford, Direct PLUS, Federal Perkins, university loans from institutional funds. Applicants will be notified of awards on a rolling basis beginning April 15. Federal Work-Study Program available. Off-campus job opportunities are good.

The Inside Word

Give your grades, rank, and serial number—sorry, make that test scores—and wait for the admissions office to crunch the numbers. A GPA of 3.0 in a college prep curriculum pretty much guarantees entry here; the school is willing to overlook substandard test scores for anyone meeting this threshold. Applicants whose personal circumstances may have hindered their academic achievement should inform the school, as the admissions office may show leniency in their cases.

THE SCHOOL SAYS " . . ."

From the Admissions Office

"At the UO, you'll be part of a community dedicated to making a difference in the world. Whether you want to change a community, a law, or one person's mind, the UO will provide you with the inspiration and resources you'll need to succeed. You'll attend classes alongside students from all fifty states, three U.S. territories, and eighty-six other countries, learn from people with diverse cultural, ethnic, and spiritual heritages, and have opportunities to participate in cutting-edge research and engage in intellectual dialog with renowned faculty. You'll graduate from the UO with the knowledge, experience, and research, writing, and critical thinking skills necessary to succeed in an increasingly global and diverse community. Set in a 295-acre arboretum, the UO is literally green. Both academic and outdoor programs will bring you into contact with forests, mountains, rivers, and lakes. The first facilities of their kind in the nation, the Green Chemistry Laboratory uses only nontoxic materials and the Tyler Instrumentation Center provides the full range of instruments needed in green chemistry. The Lillis Business Complex is the country's most environmentally friendly business school facility, and nationally recognized programs in sustainable business, architecture, and technology demonstrate the UO's ongoing commitment to the environment. With a student/teacher ratio of twenty to one, average class size of twenty-two students, 273 academic programs, and more than 250 student organizations, you'll find that the UO is uniquely able to provide the advantages of a smaller liberal arts university in addition to all the resources of a major research institution. To be eligible for freshman admission, you must have a high school GPA of at least 3.0, be a graduate of a standard or accredited high school, and submit SAT or ACT scores."

SELECTIVITY

Admissions Rating	84
# of applicants	18,515
% of applicants accepted	79
% of acceptees attending	27
# accepting a place on wait list	306
% admitted from wait list	46

FRESHMAN PROFILE

Range SAT Critical Reading	492–607
Range SAT Math	499–611
Minimum paper TOEFL	500
Minimum web-based TOEFL	61
Average HS GPA	3.52
% graduated top 10% of class	28
% graduated top 25% of class	65
% graduated top 50% of class	94

DEADLINES

Early action	
Deadline	11/1
Notification	12/15
Regular	
Priority	11/1
Deadline	1/15
Notification	4/1
Nonfall registration?	yes

FINANCIAL FACTS

Financial Aid Rating	65
Annual in-state tuition	$6,930
Annual out-of-state tuition	$24,570
Room and board	$9,429
Required fees	$1,260
Books and supplies	$1,050
% frosh rec. need-based scholarship or grant aid	22
% UG rec. need-based scholarship or grant aid	26
% frosh rec. non-need-based scholarship or grant aid	23
% UG rec. non-need-based scholarship or grant aid	15
% frosh rec. need-based self-help aid	37
% UG rec. need-based self-help aid	37
% frosh rec. any financial aid	71
% UG rec. any financial aid	66
% UG borrow to pay for school	56
Average cumulative indebtedness	$20,928

UNIVERSITY OF THE PACIFIC

3601 PACIFIC AVENUE, STOCKTON, CA 95211 • ADMISSIONS: 209-946-2211 • FAX: 209-946-2413

CAMPUS LIFE

Quality of Life Rating	75
Fire Safety Rating	90
Green Rating	79
Type of school	private
Environment	city

STUDENTS

Total undergrad enrollment	3,740
% male/female	45/55
% from out of state	11
% from public high school	82
% live on campus	57
# of fraternities	21
# of sororities	22
% African American	3
% Asian	31
% Caucasian	36
% Hispanic	14
% Native American	1
% international	3
# of countries represented	66

SURVEY SAYS . . .

Low cost of living
Diverse student types interact
Very little drug use

ACADEMICS

Academic Rating	82
% students graduating within 4 years	44
% students graduating within 6 years	69
Calendar	semester
Student/faculty ratio	14:1
Profs interesting rating	85
Profs accessible rating	85
Most common reg class size	fewer than 10 students
Most common lab size	10–19 students

MOST POPULAR MAJORS
biology, business/commerce,
engineering

STUDENTS SAY "..."

Academics

University of the Pacific is "a student-centered school with opportunities for growth" in "many areas" of students' "academic, social, and professional" lives. The school places a premium on "very strong" academics and "personalized learning" that is bolstered by "the relationships between students and faculty" being "really good." "If you ever have any questions, there's always someone there to answer them and help you out academically and socially," says one undergrad. "You won't get lost at Pacific." Indeed, the "small school" atmosphere "creates a sense of community on campus" which allows plenty of "opportunities for students to be somebody...instead of just another person at a large university." Overall, students here praise the "great academics," "small classes," "beautiful campus," "amazing faculty," "strong alumni support," and "great student involvement." However, on every college education a little rain must fall. In line with that, reviews of the administration are decidedly mixed. Some students feel that it's "pretty awesome" and that it is "always working to make sure the school is running properly." The administration makes "informed and useful choices based on student need," explains one student. Others aren't as convinced, noting that the administration can be a "mess of petitions." One thing that all students do agree on is that Pacific is "a school that you can be proud of going to." As one undergrad explains, "I grew up in Stockton, and this school made me realize all the great opportunities that Pacific offers in the way of career development and networking."

Life

Most students at Pacific agree that "life at this school revolves around studying and attending classes." Due to the "rigorous curriculum" offered in any major, "most of the time people are talking about when the next exam is and when they are going to study." That said, this "work hard" atmosphere fades on the weekend, when students "tend to relieve stress and party." "There are always parties on the weekends," explains one student, "usually at Greek houses, but if not there then in the dorms." Outside of parties, many "balance" their academic workloads "by joining social clubs and participating in many volunteer services." Some find the "small campus" "awesome" because "you always run into someone you know when walking from class to class." Off campus, the social options decidedly lessen because many students view Stockton as being "unsafe." Many at Pacific wish the school would "reach out to more students when it comes to activities" and that they would "work with the [city] community to develop activities off campus." On the weekends, a fair amount of the student body heads "home, or to San Francisco if home isn't close enough."

Student Body

At first glance, the typical Pacific student can be described most broadly as "very friendly, active, and sociable." However, beyond that, the descriptions run the gamut from those who "like to party all the time" to those who are "solely focused on academics." "It's a very diverse student body," says one undergrad. "Various ethnic, academic, religious, and personal backgrounds are represented." Others agree, noting that "the greatest strength of the school would have to be the diversity," which is supported by "many out-of-state and international students." Despite all the "different types" of students, everyone "fits into their respective niche on campus." One thing that they share is a tendency to "be quite studious" and "very active in the community and extracurricular activities." The small campus means that students "can recognize a lot of faces around campus even if they aren't friends with them."

UNIVERSITY OF THE PACIFIC

FINANCIAL AID: 209-946-2421 • E-MAIL: ADMISSIONS@PACIFIC.EDU • WEBSITE: WWW.PACIFIC.EDU

THE PRINCETON REVIEW SAYS

Admissions

Very important factors considered include: Rigor of secondary school record. *Important factors considered include:* Academic GPA, application essay, recommendation(s), standardized test scores, extracurricular activities, first generation. *Other factors considered include:* Class rank, alumni/ae relation, character/personal qualities, geographical residence, level of applicant's interest, talent/ability, volunteer work, work experience. SAT or ACT required; ACT with or without Writing component accepted. TOEFL required of all international applicants. High school diploma is required, and GED is accepted. *Academic units recommended:* 4 English, 2 foreign language, 2 social studies, 1 history, 1 visual/performing arts, 1 academic elective.

Financial Aid

Students should submit: FAFSA. Priority filing deadline is February 15. The Princeton Review suggests that all financial aid forms be submitted as soon as possible after January 1. *Need-based scholarships/grants offered:* Federal Pell, SEOG, state scholarships/grants, private scholarships, school scholarship or grant aid from institutional funds. *Loan aid offered:* Direct Subsidized Stafford, Direct Unsubsidized Stafford, Direct PLUS, Federal Perkins. Applicants will be notified of awards on a rolling basis beginning March 15.

The Inside Word

As you'd expect in a state as educationally rich as California, the competition between colleges for students is fierce, meaning that high acceptance rates don't necessarily correlate with low entrance requirements. In fact, it's often the reverse, as is the case with University of the Pacific. While the admissions officers consider a variety of factors when considering applicants, a challenging course load is of utmost importance. In other words, enroll in all the honors and advanced placement courses you can if you're keen on making Pacific the place where you'll hang your graduation cap.

THE SCHOOL SAYS "..."

From the Admissions Office

"One of the most concise ways of describing the University of the Pacific is that it is 'a major university in a small college package.' Our 3,740 undergraduates get the personal attention that you would expect at a small, residential college. But they also have the kinds of opportunities offered at much larger institutions, including more than ninety majors and programs; hundreds of student organizations; drama, dance, and musical productions; sixteen NCAA Division I athletic teams; and two dozen club and intramural sports. We offer undergraduate major programs in the arts, sciences and humanities, business, education, engineering, international studies, music, pharmacy, and health sciences. Some of the unique aspects of our academic programs include the following: We have the only independent, coed, nonsectarian liberal arts and sciences college located between Los Angeles and central Oregon; we have the only undergraduate professional school of international studies in California—and it's the only one in the nation that actually requires you to study abroad; we have the only engineering program in the West that requires students to complete a year's worth of paid work experience as part of their degree; our Conservatory of Music focuses on performance but also offers majors in music management, music therapy, and music education; and we offer several accelerated programs in business, dentistry, dental hygiene, education, law, engineering, and pharmacy. Our beautiful New England–style main campus is located in Stockton (population: 287,245) and is within two hours or less of San Francisco, Santa Cruz, Yosemite National Park, and Lake Tahoe. SAT Subject Tests recommended: mathematics, chemistry (natural science majors only)."

SELECTIVITY

Admissions Rating	92
# of applicants	19,811
% of applicants accepted	38
% of acceptees attending	13
# accepting a place on wait list	30
% admitted from wait list	100

FRESHMAN PROFILE

Range SAT Critical Reading	510–630
Range SAT Math	530–660
Range SAT Writing	510–630
Range ACT Composite	22–28
Minimum paper TOEFL	475
Minimum computer TOEFL	150
Minimum web-based TOEFL	52
Average HS GPA	3.49
% graduated top 10% of class	42
% graduated top 25% of class	76
% graduated top 50% of class	95

DEADLINES

Early action	
Deadline	11/15
Notification	1/15
Regular	
Priority	11/15
Deadline	1/15
Notification	3/15
Nonfall registration?	yes

APPLICANTS ALSO LOOK AT
AND OFTEN PREFER
University of California—Berkeley,
University of California—Davis

AND SOMETIMES PREFER
California Polytechnic State University—San Luis
Obispo, University of California—Los Angeles,
University of Southern California

FINANCIAL FACTS

Financial Aid Rating	70
Annual tuition	$33,600
Room and board	$11,142
Required fees	$500
Books and supplies	$1,620
% frosh rec. need-based scholarship or grant aid	76
% UG rec. need-based scholarship or grant aid	71
% frosh rec. need-based self-help aid	72
% UG rec. need-based self-help aid	70
% frosh rec. any financial aid	91
% UG rec. any financial aid	83

UNIVERSITY OF PENNSYLVANIA

ONE COLLEGE HALL, PHILADELPHIA, PA 19104 • ADMISSIONS: 215-898-7507 • FAX: 215-898-9670

CAMPUS LIFE

Quality of Life Rating	87
Fire Safety Rating	73
Green Rating	89
Type of school	private
Environment	metropolis

STUDENTS

Total undergrad enrollment	9,865
% male/female	49/51
% from out of state	81
% from public high school	59
% live on campus	62
# of fraternities	36
# of sororities	13
% African American	7
% Asian	19
% Caucasian	46
% Hispanic	7
% international	11
# of countries represented	126

SURVEY SAYS . . .

Athletic facilities are great
Diverse student types on campus
Great off-campus food
Students are happy
Student publications are popular
Student government is popular
Hard liquor is popular

ACADEMICS

Academic Rating	95
% students graduating within 4 years	88
% students graduating within 6 years	96
Calendar	semester
Student/faculty ratio	6:1
Profs interesting rating	73
Profs accessible rating	79
Most common reg class size	fewer than 10 students

MOST POPULAR MAJORS

economics, finance, nursing

STUDENTS SAY "..."

Academics

At the University of Pennsylvania, everyone shares an intellectual curiosity and top-notch resources but doesn't "buy into the stigma of being an Ivy League school." Students here are "very passionate about what they do outside the classroom" and the "flexible core requirements." The university is composed of four undergraduate schools (and "a library for pretty much any topic"). "You can take courses in any of the schools, including graduate-level courses." Luckily, there's a vast variety of disciplines available to students: "I can take a course in old Icelandic and even another one about the politics of food," says a student. Wharton, Penn's highly regarded, "highly competitive undergraduate business school" attracts "career-oriented" students who don't mind a "strenuous course load." There are "more than enough" resources, funding, and opportunity here for any student to take advantage of, and "Penn encourages students to truly take advantage of it all!" Professors can "sometimes seem to be caught up more in their research than their classes," but all "are incredibly well-versed in their subject (as well as their audience)." If you're willing to put in the time and effort, your professors "will be happy to reciprocate." In general, the instructors here are "very challenging academically" and are "always willing to offer their more than relevant life experience in class discussion."

Life

Penn students don't mind getting into intellectual conversations during dinner—"Politics and religion come up often, but so does baseball, types of wine, and restaurants"—but some "partying is a much higher priority here than it is at other Ivy League schools." "Campus is split between the downtown club scene and the frat/bar scene, depending on your preference." However, when it comes down to midterms and finals, "People get really serious and...buckle down and study." There's easy access to downtown Philadelphia, yet "still the comfortable feeling of having our own campus," giving students plenty of access to restaurants (BYO restaurants in Philly are "a huge hit"), shopping, concerts, and sports games, as well as plain old "hanging out with hallmates playing Mario Kart." "It's the perfect mix between an urban setting a traditional college campus." The school provides plenty of guest speakers, cultural events, clubs, and organizations for students to channel their energies (all of which "makes the campus feel smaller"), and seniors can even attend "Feb Club" in the month of February, which is essentially an event every night. The weekend buses to/from New York and D.C. "are always packed." It's a busy life at Penn, and "People are constantly trying to think about how they can balance getting good grades academically and their weekend plans."

Student Body

This "determined" bunch "is either focused on one specific interest, or very well-rounded." Pretty much everyone "was an overachiever ('that kid') in high school," and some students "are off-the-charts brilliant," making everyone here "sort of fascinated by everyone else." Everyone has "a strong sense of personal style and his or her own credo," but no group deviates too far from the more mainstream stereotypes. There's a definite lack of "emos" and hippies. There's "the career-driven Wharton kid who will stab you in the back to get your interview slot" and "the nursing kid who's practically nonexistent," but on the whole, there's tremendous school diversity, with "people from all over the world of all kinds of experiences of all perspectives."

UNIVERSITY OF PENNSYLVANIA

FINANCIAL AID: 215-898-1988 • E-MAIL: INFO@ADMISSIONS.UGAO.UPENN.EDU • WEBSITE: WWW.UPENN.EDU

THE PRINCETON REVIEW SAYS

Admissions

Very important factors considered include: Application essay, recommendation(s), rigor of secondary school record, character/personal qualities. *Important factors considered include:* Academic GPA, standardized test scores, extracurricular activities. *Other factors considered include:* Class rank, alumni/ae relation, first generation, geographical residence, interview, racial/ethnic status, talent/ability, volunteer work, work experience. ACT with writing component required. TOEFL required of all international applicants. High school diploma or equivalent is required. *Academic units recommended:* 4 English, 4 mathematics, 3 science (3 science labs), 4 foreign language, 2 social studies, 3 history. Calculus strongly recommended for Wharton and engineering applicants. Physics strongly recommended for engineering applicants.

Financial Aid

Students should submit: FAFSA, institution's own financial aid form, CSS/Financial Aid PROFILE. The Princeton Review suggests that all financial aid forms be submitted as soon as possible after January 1. *Need-based scholarships/grants offered:* Federal Pell, SEOG, state scholarships/grants, private scholarships, school scholarship or grant aid from institutional funds. *Loan aid offered:* Federal Perkins, Federal Nursing Loans, university loans from institutional funds. Applicants will be notified of awards upon admittance. Federal Work-Study Program available. Off-campus job opportunities are good.

The Inside Word

After a small decline four cycles ago, applications are once again climbing at Penn—the fifth increase in six years. The competition in the applicant pool is formidable. Applicants can safely assume that they need to be one of the strongest students in their graduating class in order to be successful.

THE SCHOOL SAYS " . . ."

From the Admissions Office

"Founded by Benjamin Franklin in 1740 to push the frontiers of knowledge, teaching, and problem solving to benefit society, Penn combines opportunities for practical training with foundations in the liberal arts and sciences all in one institution. A community that reflects the diversity of our world, with one of the largest international undergraduate student population in the Ivy League, our students and faculty work toward the shared goal of enacting change by questioning, thinking, and doing—often across traditional academic disciplines. The integration of knowledge and learning is created through access to four undergraduate schools: the College of Arts & Sciences, the School of Engineering & Applied Science, the Wharton School of Business, and the School of Nursing. Penn offers more than ninety majors, eighty minors, and the ability to earn more than one degree in four years.

"Penn believes that learning is only realized when put to use. The Penn community thrives on the open exchange of ideas and shared learning experiences, engaging students to access courses in twelve graduate schools, collaborate with faculty on research, and actively participate in over 450 clubs and organizations. Education through engagement is made possible by Penn's extensive partnerships for transformative civic outreach—around the world and close to our Philadelphia campus. More than 150 Academically Based Community-Service courses link Penn students to work in the community.

"Penn understands that the best minds should have access to the finest education, regardless of their families' ability to pay. To achieve this, Penn practices need-blind admissions, meets 100 percent of demonstrated financial need, and provides a no-loan aid package for all undergraduates receiving financial aid. Our goal is to allow students to pursue their aspirations without assuming a burden of debt, which is why we provide students the opportunity to graduate debt-free."

SELECTIVITY

Admissions Rating	99
# of applicants	26,941
% of applicants accepted	14
% of acceptees attending	63
# accepting a place on wait list	1,760
% admitted from wait list	3
# of early decision applicants	3,851
% accepted early decision	34

FRESHMAN PROFILE

Range SAT Critical Reading	660–750
Range SAT Math	690–780
Range SAT Writing	680–770
Range ACT Composite	30–34
Average HS GPA	3.89
% graduated top 10% of class	96
% graduated top 25% of class	99
% graduated top 50% of class	100

DEADLINES

Early decision	
Deadline	11/1
Notification	12/15
Regular	
Deadline	1/1
Nonfall registration?	no

APPLICANTS ALSO LOOK AT
AND OFTEN PREFER
Harvard College, Massachusetts Institute of Technology, Princeton University, Stanford University, Yale University

AND SOMETIMES PREFER
Brown University, Columbia University, Duke University

AND RARELY PREFER
Cornell University, Georgetown University

FINANCIAL FACTS

Financial Aid Rating	97
Annual tuition	$42,098
Room and board	$11,878
Books and supplies	$1,160
% frosh rec. need-based scholarship or grant aid	45
% UG rec. need-based scholarship or grant aid	44
% frosh rec. need-based self-help aid	46
% UG rec. need-based self-help aid	46
% frosh rec. any financial aid	47
% UG rec. any financial aid	45
% UG borrow to pay for school	43
Average cumulative indebtedness	$17,013

UNIVERSITY OF PITTSBURGH—PITTSBURGH CAMPUS

4227 FIFTH AVENUE, FIRST FLOOR, ALUMNI HALL, PITTSBURGH, PA 15260 • ADMISSIONS: 412-624-7488 • FAX: 412-648-8815

STUDENTS SAY ". . ."

Academics

Students at the University of Pittsburgh—Pittsburgh Campus call their school an "under-recognized treasure of opportunity and scholasticism," with "brilliant professors doing fantastic things in their fields." As a large research university, some students say that "Administrators are generally unavailable for 'normal' students." However, others laud the effectiveness of the school's "Deans' Hours" where "students can ask questions and administrat[ors] can better learn of the needs of the student community" which "can help you get around the red tape." "The advising system isn't super strong, but is sufficient for someone [who is] relatively independent." Nevertheless, "Administrators and professors are both surprisingly eager to involve students and are sincerely interested in our happiness and success." In large lecture courses and in classes that meet general education requirements, "you have to go to office hours to get to know the professors"; however, if you reach out they will "push you to bring out the best of your abilities." In essence, "Pitt provides all the resources of a large research university (which it is), but [it] also retains a small college atmosphere with its Honors College to provide the best opportunities for its students." One of the benefits of being a major research university is that research opportunities abound and "there is definitely a professor willing to take on pretty much anyone." The in-class experience gets mixed reviews, with accolades for "brilliant" professors that are "passionate" about their fields coupled with concerns about those "who leave [students] behind" and aren't as focused about teaching. The key to avoiding the duds, "like at any other institution," "is to do your research."

Life

Pitt offers a great balance between a college environment "that offers a lot of opportunities for fun," and a medium-sized, affordable city "with a ton of places to eat and shop." As one student observes, "Something that unifies Pitt students is passion—be it [for] Pitt's renowned medical program, Division I athletics, copious quantities of clubs, or [for] the many internships available." On the weekends, "most students [go] to frat parties or house and apartment parties in Oakland." Oakland is also home to a "lively" college bar scene for Pitt students of age, and "There are a lot of informal get-togethers within the dorms." Even though "typical students study hard, party harder," "there are so many alternatives for things to do because of being in the city." Pitt (both the campus and the city) is home to "major sports teams [that] are also a big source of involvement and pride." So it's no surprise that participating in intramurals or watching sporting events—"college and professional"—are major pastimes. A "variety" of clubs and activities offer opportunities for any interest. Taking advantage of hometown Pittsburgh's many offerings is also easy, convenient, and free with a Pitt ID. "There are opportunities to do everything…for a reduced price," including attending professional sporting events. Moreover, "PittArts provides…free arts activities on weekends." As one sophomore sums up, "Pitt is the smallest big school, and the campus is truly the city."

Student Body

Roughly three-quarters of Pitt students are from Pennsylvania, and overall, students are "middle-class" and "personable and accepting." "You're going to find slackers at every school, but the majority of people [here] work very hard and have heavy workloads." Going to Pitt is about "being in the middle of everything with the greatest people you can find." Beyond that, "We're big enough that there's a group for everyone" and that students "can develop a group of friends" while still being "accepted with open arms" by the larger student community. Says one Pitt student, "There are many atypical students when considering backgrounds, ethnicity, and beliefs, but a common interest in positive academic pursuits and community development brings us all together."

UNIVERSITY OF PITTSBURGH—PITTSBURGH CAMPUS

FINANCIAL AID: 412-624-7488 • E-MAIL: OAFA@PITT.EDU • WEBSITE: WWW.PITT.EDU

THE PRINCETON REVIEW SAYS

Admissions

Very important factors considered include: Academic GPA, rigor of secondary school record, standardized test scores. *Other factors considered include:* Application essay, class rank, recommendation(s), character/personal qualities, extracurricular activities, first generation, geographical residence, level of applicant's interest, racial/ethnic status, state residency, talent/ability, volunteer work. SAT or ACT required; ACT with writing component recommended. TOEFL required of all international applicants. *Academic units required:* 4 English, 3 mathematics, 3 science (3 science labs), 2 foreign language, 2 social studies, 3 academic elective. *Academic units recommended:* 4 English, 4 mathematics, 4 science (4 science labs), 3 foreign language, 3 social studies, 5 academic elective.

Financial Aid

Students should submit: FAFSA. Priority filing deadline is March 1. The Princeton Review suggests that all financial aid forms be submitted as soon as possible after January 1. *Need-based scholarships/grants offered:* Federal Pell, SEOG, state scholarships/grants, private scholarships, school scholarship or grant aid from institutional funds, Federal Nursing Scholarships. *Loan aid offered:* Direct Subsidized Stafford, Direct Unsubsidized Stafford, Direct PLUS, Federal Perkins, Federal Nursing Loans, state loans, university loans from institutional funds. Applicants will be notified of awards on a rolling basis beginning March 15. Federal Work-Study Program available. Off-campus job opportunities are excellent.

The Inside Word

Despite the large number of applications Pitt receives, admissions counselors review each application individually with a holistic perspective. Essays and recommendation are taken into consideration. That said, strong secondary school records and test scores rank high on the admit list. Applicants with honors classes, advanced placement classes, and solid grades have the best chance of admission.

THE SCHOOL SAYS ". . ."

From the Admissions Office

"The University of Pittsburgh is one of sixty-three members of the Association of American Universities, a prestigious group whose members include the major research uni versities of North America. There are nearly 440 degree programs available at the sixteen Pittsburgh campus schools (one offering only undergraduate degree programs, six offering graduate degree programs, and eight offering both) and four regional campuses, allowing students a wide latitude of choices, both academically and in setting and style, size, and pace of campus. Programs ranked nationally include philosophy, history and philosophy of science, chemistry, economics, English, his tory, physics, political science, and psychology. Some of the company the University of Pittsburgh keeps: For the fourth consecutive year Pitt ranks in the very top cluster of U.S. public research universities according to the 2009 edition of the Top American Research Universities annual report, issued by the Center for Measuring University Performance, along with Berkeley, Illinois, Michigan, UCLA, UNC, and Wisconsin; it has a notable record of high achieving graduates—since 1995 Pitt undergraduates have won three Rhodes, seven Marshall, five Truman, five Udall, one Churchill, one Gates Cambridge, thirty-five Goldwater scholarships, and three Mellon Humanities Fellowships. In research, Pitt ranks fifth among all U.S. universities in terms of competitive grants awarded to faculty by the National Institutes of Health. In inter national education, Pitt's University Center for International Studies offers seven area studies centers, three of which are designated National Resource Centers by the U.S. Department of Education."

SELECTIVITY

Admissions Rating	93
# of applicants	22,616
% of applicants accepted	58
% of acceptees attending	29
# accepting a place on wait list	234
% admitted from wait list	6

FRESHMAN PROFILE

Range SAT Critical Reading	570–680
Range SAT Math	600–690
Range SAT Writing	560–660
Range ACT Composite	25–30
Minimum paper TOEFL	550
Minimum computer TOEFL	213
Minimum web-based TOEFL	80
Average HS GPA	3.91
% graduated top 10% of class	51
% graduated top 25% of class	85
% graduated top 50% of class	99

DEADLINES

Regular	
Notification	10/1
Nonfall registration?	yes

APPLICANTS ALSO LOOK AT
AND OFTEN PREFER
Boston University, Carnegie Mellon University, New York University, University of Pennsylvania

AND SOMETIMES PREFER
Penn State—University Park, University of Delaware, University of Maryland—College Park, University of Michigan—Ann Arbor

AND RARELY PREFER
Duquesne University, Temple University

FINANCIAL FACTS

Financial Aid Rating	81
Annual in-state tuition	$14,076
Annual out-of-state tuition	$23,732
Required fees	$860
% frosh rec. need-based scholarship or grant aid	41
% UG rec. need-based scholarship or grant aid	39
% frosh rec. non-need-based scholarship or grant aid	23
% UG rec. non-need-based scholarship or grant aid	16
% frosh rec. need-based self-help aid	44
% UG rec. need-based self-help aid	45
% frosh rec. any financial aid	63
% UG rec. any financial aid	62
% UG borrow to pay for school	63
Average cumulative indebtedness	$26,612

UNIVERSITY OF PUGET SOUND

1500 NORTH WARNER STREET, TACOMA, WA 98416-1062 • ADMISSIONS: 253-879-3211 • FAX: 253-879-3993

CAMPUS LIFE
Quality of Life Rating	88
Fire Safety Rating	78
Green Rating	60*
Type of school	private
Environment	city

STUDENTS
Total undergrad enrollment	2,582
% male/female	41/59
% from out of state	76
% from public high school	76
% live on campus	58
# of fraternities	4
# of sororities	4
% African American	2
% Asian	9
% Caucasian	73
% Hispanic	5
% Native American	1
% international	1
# of countries represented	11

SURVEY SAYS . . .
Lab facilities are great
School is well-run
Musical organizations are popular

ACADEMICS
Academic Rating	92
% students graduating within 4 years	70
% students graduating within 6 years	80
Calendar	semester
Student/faculty ratio	12:1
Profs interesting rating	94
Profs accessible rating	99
Most common reg class size	10–19 students
Most common lab size	10–19 students

MOST POPULAR MAJORS
business/commerce, English language and literature, psychology

STUDENTS SAY ". . ."
Academics
University of Puget Sound "is all about creating an intimate learning environment in order to encourage a well-rounded educational experience." Indeed, one of the most common reasons students give for choosing to attend Puget Sound is the "close-knit community," with strong financial aid and the beautiful campus running close behind. Puget Sound is a small liberal arts school that offers a business major—a rare combination with big appeal. Other popular majors include the sciences, psychology, and music programs, and "Most classes in all majors emphasize writing and communicating ideas effectively." Professors are almost universally praised, and students are very happy with the "personal attention to undergraduates" here. "It's small, so students have greater access to professors, and many professors are willing to work outside of class with students." "All are genuinely passionate about their subjects, and accessible for extra help or attention." "Professors care a lot about your understanding of the material and if you can't make the [three or four] hours that they have scheduled as office hours, every professor will find a time that works for your schedule." In the classroom, "They bring enthusiasm and a lively approach," "they make class very interesting and are good at articulating the material in a way that makes learning easy," and "they also expect a high quality of work from all the students." Overall, Puget Sound "provides the 360 [degree] education; not only do students get a rich and rigorous academic experience, but they are also strongly encouraged to explore the urban and natural world around them" (though "the administration could do better to find new innovative ways to implement more green strategies such as composting [food waste]").

Life
While Puget Sound offers an active campus life, the surrounding area holds many attractions: The Puget Sound, the Cascades, and the Olympic National Park are all nearby and "people love being outdoors, walking down to the waterfront… taking bike rides, going to Mount Rainier." Camping, hiking, and whitewater rafting are all popular outdoor activities, and "There are usually people playing Frisbee-golf or Ultimate Frisbee out on the quad." Seattle is forty-five minutes away by car, and it "has an awesome live music scene (that definitely spills over into Tacoma), and being able to go to live shows all the time is a big draw." On campus, "There [is] a considerable amount of leadership opportunities" and "so much to do! There are clubs for everything, and if there isn't one for what you want, you can create it. There's dancing, movie nights, boat cruises." "There's a lot to do and a lot to think about. [Students have] conversations ranging from the latest video game to the presidential election, from the best joke a professor has told to how to get away with swimming naked in the fountain. People do all sorts of things for fun. There is drinking, of course, but it's definitely not a 'requirement'—there is plenty else to do." Greek life is popular but not dominant, as there are a lot of extracurricular offerings here, and "The theme houses are something completely unique and absolutely wonderful for meeting people and being introduced to new interests." All around, students say, "We know how to have an amazing time on the weekend, but during the week and during finals, the library is full to the gills with students working hard."

Student Body
On one hand, students in this "easygoing and friendly" community are loathe to generalize about themselves—"Everybody here is a very unique and exciting person and we are all passionate about our diverse areas of study!"—and on the other, some will admit, "Generally, the students are left wing, outdoorsy, committed to sustainability efforts," and suggest, "If you don't own flannel, get the hell out!" Overall, though, "There are people from all walks of life" on this campus, and "You're bound to find somewhere you fit in whether it is through BGLAD [the gay/straight alliance group], sports, classes, events, or the Greek system," and one student sums up the environment, saying, "I haven't ever been in a place that is more accepting of all backgrounds."

FINANCIAL AID: 800-396-7192 • E-MAIL: ADMISSION@PUGETSOUND.EDU • WEBSITE: WWW.PUGETSOUND.EDU

THE PRINCETON REVIEW SAYS

Admissions

Very important factors considered include: Academic GPA, rigor of secondary school record, essay, character/personal qualities. *Important factors considered include:* Test scores, recommendation(s), alumni/ae relation, extracurricular activities, talent/ability. *Other factors considered include:* Class rank, first generation, interview, racial/ethnic status, level of applicant's interest, volunteer work, work experience. SAT or ACT required. TOEFL required of all international applicants. High school diploma is required, and GED is accepted. *Academic units recommended:* 4 English, 4 mathematics, 4 science (4 science labs), 3 foreign language, 3 social studies, 3 history, 1 visual/performing/fine arts.

Financial Aid

Students should submit: FAFSA. Priority filing deadline is February 1. The Princeton Review suggests that all financial aid forms be submitted as soon as possible after January 1. *Need-based scholarships/grants offered:* Federal Pell, SEOG, state scholarships/grants, private scholarships, school scholarship or grant aid from institutional funds. *Loan aid offered:* Direct Subsidized Stafford, Direct Unsubsidized Stafford, Direct PLUS, Federal Perkins. Applicants will be notified of awards no later than April 1. Federal Work-Study Program available. Off-campus job opportunities are excellent.

The Inside Word

Puget Sound supplies students with detailed information about the selection process, which can help alleviate some of that college application angst. While academic background is the primary consideration of every admissions committee (and that includes both grades and the rigor of the classes in which those grades were obtained), Puget Sound considers the whole candidate, and demonstrated interest in a particular issue or extracurricular activity will strengthen any application. Applicants can count on a considerate and caring attitude before, during, and after the review process.

THE SCHOOL SAYS "..."

From the Admissions Office

"For over more than 100 years, students from many locations and backgrounds have chosen to join our community. It is a community committed to excellence in the classroom and in student organizations and activities. Puget Sound students are serious about rowing and writing, management and music, skiing and sciences, leadership and languages. At Puget Sound you'll be challenged—and helped—to perform at the peak of your ability."

SELECTIVITY

Admissions Rating	90
# of applicants	6,586
% of applicants accepted	52
% of acceptees attending	18
# accepting a place on wait list	246
% admitted from wait list	26
# of early decision applicants	151
% accepted early decision	82

FRESHMAN PROFILE

Range SAT Critical Reading	570–680
Range SAT Math	560–660
Range SAT Writing	560–670
Range ACT Composite	26–30
Minimum paper TOEFL	550
Minimum computer TOEFL	213
Average HS GPA	3.52
% graduated top 10% of class	36
% graduated top 25% of class	68
% graduated top 50% of class	93

DEADLINES

Early decision	
Deadline	11/15
Notification	12/15
Regular	
Deadline	1/15
Notification	4/1
Nonfall registration?	yes

APPLICANTS ALSO LOOK AT
AND OFTEN PREFER
Stanford University

AND SOMETIMES PREFER
Colorado College, Lewis & Clark College, University of Washington, Whitman College, Willamette University

FINANCIAL FACTS

Financial Aid Rating	84
Annual tuition	$38,510
Room and board	$10,020
Required fees	$375
Books and supplies	$1,000
% frosh rec. need-based scholarship or grant aid	66
% UG rec. need-based scholarship or grant aid	64
% frosh rec. non-need-based scholarship or grant aid	25
% UG rec. non-need-based scholarship or grant aid	26
% frosh rec. need-based self-help aid	50
% UG rec. need-based self-help aid	48
% frosh rec. any financial aid	88
% UG rec. any financial aid	90
% UG borrow to pay for school	88
Average cumulative indebtedness	$27,648

UNIVERSITY OF REDLANDS

1200 EAST COLTON AVENUE, REDLANDS, CA 92373 • ADMISSIONS: 909-335-4074 • FAX: 909-335-4089

CAMPUS LIFE
Quality of Life Rating	87
Fire Safety Rating	81
Green Rating	79
Type of school	private
Environment	town

STUDENTS
Total undergrad enrollment	2,335
% male/female	44/56
% from out of state	29
% live on campus	66
# of fraternities	5
# of sororities	5
% African American	2
% Asian	4
% Caucasian	55
% Hispanic	17
% Native American	1
% international	1
# of countries represented	6

SURVEY SAYS . . .
Lab facilities are great
Great computer facilities
Athletic facilities are great
Students are friendly
Students are happy
Musical organizations are popular

ACADEMICS
Academic Rating	89
% students graduating within 4 years	58
% students graduating within 6 years	64
Calendar	semester
Student/faculty ratio	15:1
Profs interesting rating	88
Profs accessible rating	91
Most common reg class size	10–19 students

MOST POPULAR MAJORS
business/commerce, liberal arts and sciences, psychology

STUDENTS SAY "..."

Academics
The University of Redlands is a smallish liberal arts college in Southern California that offers "great financial aid" and "emphasizes a balanced, broad education." "Small class sizes provide a more hands-on learning experience" and "personal attention." Class discussions are "often spicy and provoking." Professors are "friendly," "always prepared," and "willing to help you with anything." Some students call the coursework here "demanding." Whatever the case, there are "endless academic opportunities," and Redlands has the "resources for just about anything" you can conjure up to study. Through the College of Arts and Sciences (CAS), the majority of students follow a conventional undergraduate curriculum, declaring majors and minors. About 200 students choose the innovative approach of the Johnston Center for Integrative Studies. They design their own majors, work with professors to create contracts for their courses, and receive narrative evaluations of their work (instead of letter grades). Other academic highlights at Redlands include an impressive school of music, an uncommon major in communicative disorders, and excellence across the hard sciences. The study abroad program is also awesome. Some forty percent of these undergrads take coursework in places far-flung, either for a traditional semester or during the fairly unique May Term, an intensive four-week period when students focus on one class. As far as complaints, red tape is pretty annoying—especially for a school this size. "Any bureaucratic task takes a million years to accomplish." Also, "A lot of courses aren't offered every year," and the ones that are available tend to "fill up fast."

Life
No one could deny that the Redlands campus "has incredible aesthetic appeal" and eye-popping scenery. It's also "bustling with fun people and tons of activities." "The whole campus is full of creativity." "There are programs and things to do every night, usually so much that you end up overbooking yourself and having to run from one thing to another in order to be everywhere you want to be." Though some note, "Some of the facilities are really old and outdated." This doesn't flag students' enthusiasm. "There is a lot of school spirit," and intercollegiate sports are popular. The Greek system, which consists of a handful of sororities and fraternities that are "not nationally affiliated," is pretty popular. However, "The party scene is only one part of life on campus and does not take over social life by any means." "There's a real spectrum of hard partiers and stone-cold sober people." The town of Redlands is "quirky" but "a bit isolated." Critics gripe that "there is not a lot to do" off campus. Devotees of the surrounding area tell us that there's "an excellent downtown" "with coffee shops, restaurants, and bars." "If you give the town half a chance," they maintain, "it actually has some cool features." In addition, the school sponsors a wealth of outdoor adventures and "rents out equipment such as snowboards, backpacks, sleeping bags, and anything else you would need in the wilderness." Students also take "trips up to Joshua Tree and Big Bear" or, for more urban fare, trek to Los Angeles.

Student Body
Students at Redlands are "passionate." They have a "sense of wonder and enthusiasm" and "a huge variety of interests." As a whole, students are "quite liberal" politically. Most students are "fairly involved in many aspects of school," and they promise that "everyone can find a niche somewhere on campus." The undergraduate population melds pretty well. There's "no separation of athletes, geeks, Greeks, etc." To the extent that there's any division, it's between Johnston students and students in the CAS. Johnston students—the ones who make their own majors and get evaluations instead of grades—definitely "pride themselves on their uniqueness," and they can be "eccentric." "There are colorful characters on both sides of the spectrum," though, and students assure us that any segregation is self-imposed. "I really don't see a line between the CAS and Johnston," observes one student. "It is only there for those who want it to be."

FINANCIAL AID: 909-335-4047 • E-MAIL: ADMISSIONS@REDLANDS.EDU • WEBSITE: WWW.REDLANDS.EDU

THE PRINCETON REVIEW SAYS

Admissions

Very important factors considered include: Academic GPA, recommendation(s), rigor of secondary school record, character/personal qualities,talent/ability. *Important factors considered include:* Application essay, standardized test scores. *Other factors considered include:* Alumni/ae relation, extracurricular activities, first generation, geographical residence, interview, volunteer work, work experience. SAT or ACT required; ACT with writing component recommended. TOEFL required of all international applicants. High school diploma is required, and GED is accepted. *Academic units required:* 4 English, 3 mathematics, 2 science (1 science lab), 2 foreign language, 2 social studies. *Academic units recommended:* 4 English, 4 mathematics (including Algebra II), 3 science (1 science lab), 3 foreign language, 2 social studies, 1 history.

Financial Aid

Students should submit: FAFSA. The Princeton Review suggests that all financial aid forms be submitted as soon as possible after January 1. *Need-based scholarships/grants offered:* Federal Pell, SEOG, state scholarships/grants, private scholarships, school scholarship or grant aid from institutional funds. *Loan aid offered:* Federal Perkins, university loans from institutional funds. Applicants will be notified of awards on a rolling basis beginning February 28. Federal Work-Study Program available. Off-campus job opportunities are fair.

The Inside Word

The admit rate here is reasonably high and students with above-average high school records and respectable standardized test scores should could the school as a target. Candidates who are interested in pursuing the self-designed programs available through the Johnston Center will find the admissions process to be distinctly more personal. Note, though, that you have to be admitted as a regular student in the CAS first.

THE SCHOOL SAYS "..."

From the Admissions Office

"We've created an unusually blended curriculum of the liberal arts and pre-professional study because we think education is about learning how to think and learning how to do. For example, our environmental studies students have synthesized their study of sociology, biology, and economics to develop an actual resource management plan for the local mountain communities. Our creative writing program encourages internships with publishing or television production companies. We educate managers, poets, environmental scientists, teachers, musicians, and speech therapists to be reflective about culture and society so that they can better understand and improve the world they'll enter upon graduation.

"First-year students applying for admission are required to submit the results of either the SAT or the ACT. We do not require the writing section of either test."

SELECTIVITY
Admissions Rating	90
# of applicants	3,587
% of applicants accepted	66
% of acceptees attending	27

FRESHMAN PROFILE
Range SAT Critical Reading	520–620
Range SAT Math	520–620
Range ACT Composite	22–27
Minimum paper TOEFL	550
Minimum computer TOEFL	213
Minimum web-based TOEFL	81
Average HS GPA	3.58
% graduated top 10% of class	30
% graduated top 25% of class	67
% graduated top 50% of class	93

DEADLINES
Regular	
Priority	12/15
Deadline	5/1
Notification	11/1
Nonfall registration?	yes

APPLICANTS ALSO LOOK AT
AND OFTEN PREFER
Occidental College

AND SOMETIMES PREFER
Chapman University, Loyola Marymount University

FINANCIAL FACTS
Financial Aid Rating	85
Annual tuition	$35,240
Room and board	$10,832
Required fees	$300
Books and supplies	$1,650
% frosh rec. need-based scholarship or grant aid	79
% UG rec. need-based scholarship or grant aid	74
% frosh rec. non-need-based scholarship or grant aid	15
% UG rec. non-need-based scholarship or grant aid	8
% frosh rec. need-based self-help aid	61
% UG rec. need-based self-help aid	61
% frosh rec. any financial aid	82
% UG rec. any financial aid	81
% UG borrow to pay for school	67
Average cumulative indebtedness	$20,364

UNIVERSITY OF RHODE ISLAND

14 Upper College Road, Kingston, RI 02881-1391 • Admissions: 401-874-7100 • Fax: 401-874-5523

STUDENTS SAY ". . ."

Academics

The University of Rhode Island "is a school that challenges me to think big and outside the box," says one student. URI is known for having "excellent science programs," including a "marine biology program [that] is one of the best in the Northeast." Other stand-out majors include "nursing, pharmacy, and engineering." Praise for teachers and staff garners varied reactions, as this student notes, "You have bad mixed in with good, but I will say that the good professors are top-notch." As far as transitioning to the workplace, a sophomore says, "URI has impressive programs that help get your career started as soon as possible and also act as a bridge to graduate school." Another student observes that the staff is also "great at helping freshmen transferring from home to college, and there are lots of different programs offered to help students excel academically." Overall, URI is known to have a solid liberal ideology with "openness to creative and critical exploration." This engineering major finds the environment to be rather "forward-thinking [with an] emphasis on today's global workforce." URI is described as providing a "great sense of community" with a philosophical message that students should be connected to the world around them.

Life

The school's proximity to the beach and to other major cities like Providence and Boston make it appealing to students from all over the Northeast. "I think its beauty is definitely a strength, and the location near the beach is great," says a communication major. If fine dining is meaningful to your quality of life, it's worth noting that URI's dining hall has "won a national award the past two years in a row." There are complaints about the dry campus. One senior says, "Because we have a dry campus, people usually live in the surrounding neighborhoods, so you can travel to your friends' houses and party." Others say that students who live nearby still choose to stay on campus during weekends, since this is where their social life is centered. Life isn't all about "getting wasted," chides one sophomore. "Sometimes we get together [to] make dinner and just have a movie night inside our apartment." Students are said to have a "two brain track" in terms of serious attention to study followed by equal attention to "relaxing and having a good time." One student says, "Basketball games are really fun to watch," and "Newport cliff walks are popular during the nice weather." Greek life is a big part of URI's campus yet many students don't feel obliged to pledge; still they enjoy the Greek life's social offerings, "which accounts for the majority of on-campus activities."

Student Body

URI, as an affordable state school, naturally attracts a large percentage of Rhode Islanders. Rumor has it that this group "sticks to their friends from high school," yet one undergrad observes, "Rhody-borns are so afraid of college turning into another four years of high school that we go searching for new people to meet." As far as categorizing a "typical student," undergrads are reluctant to stereotype. "URI is diverse, and the students cannot be generalized into a certain type." Campus diversity is strong, and most groups intermingle without issue. One junior sums it up: "Just like any other college, some come to party and some come to learn, but in the end they are all good people."

UNIVERSITY OF RHODE ISLAND

FINANCIAL AID: 401-874-9500 • E-MAIL: URIADMIT@ETAL.URI.EDU • WEBSITE: WWW.URI.EDU/ADMISSIONS

THE PRINCETON REVIEW SAYS

Admissions

Very important factors considered include: Rigor of secondary school record. *Important factors considered include:* Academic GPA, application essay, class rank, standardized test scores. *Other factors considered include:* Recommendation(s), alumni/ae relation, character/personal qualities, extracurricular activities, first generation, geographical residence, level of applicant's interest, racial/ethnic status, state residency, talent/ability, volunteer work. SAT or ACT required; ACT with writing component recommended. TOEFL required of all international applicants. High school diploma is required, and GED is accepted. *Academic units required:* 4 English, 3 mathematics, 2 science (1 science lab), 2 foreign language, 2 social studies, 5 academic elective.

Financial Aid

Students should submit: FAFSA. The Princeton Review suggests that all financial aid forms be submitted as soon as possible after January 1. *Need-based scholarships/grants offered:* Federal Pell, SEOG, state scholarships/grants, private scholarships, school scholarship or grant aid from institutional funds. *Loan aid offered:* Direct Subsidized Stafford, Direct Unsubsidized Stafford, Direct PLUS, Federal Perkins, Federal Nursing Loans, university loans from institutional funds. Applicants will be notified of awards on a rolling basis beginning March 31. Federal Work-Study Program available. Off-campus job opportunities are good.

The Inside Word

Early decision deadline is December 1. Don't forget to apply to URI's merit-based scholarships, which are open to international students as well. Remember if you're a resident of another New England state (besides Rhode Island) you may be eligible, depending on your major, for discounted tuition.

THE SCHOOL SAYS " . . . "

From the Admissions Office

"Outstanding freshman candidates admission with a minimum SAT score of 1200 (combined Critical Reading and Math) or ACT composite score of 25 who rank in the top quarter of their high school class are eligible to be considered for a Centennial Scholarship. These merit-based scholarships range up to full tuition and are renewable each semester if the student maintains full-time continuous enrollment and a 3.0 average or better. In order to be eligible for consideration, all application materials must be received in the Admission Office by the December 1, early action deadline. Applications are not considered complete until the application fee, completed application, official high school transcript, list of senior courses, personal essay, and SAT or ACT scores (sent directly from the testing agency) are received.

"If a student is awarded a Centennial Scholarship, and his or her residency status changes from out-of-state to regional or in-state, the amount of the award will be reduced to reflect the reduced tuition rate.

"The SAT math and critical reading scores are used for admission evaluation and Centennial Scholarship consideration. The writing score is not currently used for admission evaluation or Centennial Scholarship consideration."

SELECTIVITY

Admissions Rating	77
# of applicants	19,564
% of applicants accepted	78
% of acceptees attending	19

FRESHMAN PROFILE

Range SAT Critical Reading	470–560
Range SAT Math	470–580
Range SAT Writing	470–570
Range ACT Composite	21–25
Minimum paper TOEFL	550
Minimum computer TOEFL	213
Minimum web-based TOEFL	79
Average HS GPA	3.12
% graduated top 10% of class	14
% graduated top 25% of class	42
% graduated top 50% of class	81

DEADLINES

Early action	
Deadline	12/1
Notification	1/31
Regular	
Deadline	2/1
Notification	12/1
Nonfall registration?	yes

FINANCIAL FACTS

Financial Aid Rating	78
Annual in-state tuition	$9,014
Annual out-of-state tuition	$25,720
Room and board	$10,854
Required fees	$1,462
Books and supplies	$1,200
% frosh rec. need-based scholarship or grant aid	53
% UG rec. need-based scholarship or grant aid	62
% frosh rec. non-need-based scholarship or grant aid	5
% UG rec. non-need-based scholarship or grant aid	5
% frosh rec. need-based self-help aid	53
% UG rec. need-based self-help aid	60
% frosh rec. any financial aid	60
% UG rec. any financial aid	55
% UG borrow to pay for school	63
Average cumulative indebtedness	$22,750

UNIVERSITY OF RICHMOND

28 WESTHAMPTON WAY, RICHMOND, VA 23173 • ADMISSIONS: 804-289-8640 • FAX: 804-287-6003

CAMPUS LIFE

Quality of Life Rating	87
Fire Safety Rating	82
Green Rating	95
Type of school	private
Environment	city

STUDENTS

Total undergrad enrollment	2,945
% male/female	46/54
% from out of state	79
% from public high school	60
% live on campus	91
# of fraternities	8
# of sororities	8
% African American	7
% Asian	5
% Caucasian	63
% Hispanic	5
% international	6
# of countries represented	67

SURVEY SAYS . . .
Great computer facilities
Athletic facilities are great
Great food on campus
Campus feels safe
Low cost of living

ACADEMICS

Academic Rating	92
% students graduating within 4 years	81
% students graduating within 6 years	87
Calendar	semester
Student/faculty ratio	9:1
Profs interesting rating	91
Profs accessible rating	91
Most common reg class size	10–19 students
Most common lab size	10–19 students

MOST POPULAR MAJORS
business administration and
management, English language
and literature, social sciences

STUDENTS SAY ". . ."

Academics

The University of Richmond provides "the resources of a large university with the personal attention of a small college" and just "a hint of Southern charm." Financial aid is "generous." Facilities are "outstanding." "Students have access to state-of-the-art technologies and research labs that normally only graduate students would be able to work with." Among the sixty or so undergraduate majors, students call our attention to the "great business program" and the "excellent premed program." "Another of Richmond's strengths is its study abroad programs." Every year, a few hundred Richmond students take classes in more than thirty countries or complete a summer internship in one of six countries. The "core liberal arts program" here is reasonably broad and pretty much all coursework is "rigorous." "There are no easy classes," "and there is a significant amount of homework." The degree of difficulty notwithstanding, though, faculty members are overwhelmingly "brilliant," "insightful, accommodating," and "extremely accessible." "They genuinely care about their students and they make themselves totally available," gushes a political science major. "We're a school where professors know all of their students' names," expounds an English major, "and where the president of the university stops and talks to you on the way to your next class."

Life

This "gorgeous," "peaceful," "isolated" suburban campus comes complete with "glistening lake in the center of it." During the week, "Students get down to business" academically. "Everybody is in the library." However, "Every single student is involved with an extracurricular activity or two" as well, "and since there aren't 20,000 students here, everyone has a chance to make a difference." A solid contingent of students plays intercollegiate or intramural sports or is "extremely invested" in a club sport. Fraternities and sororities also play a "very big" social role. However, some students "really dislike Greek life," and they insist that the Greek system "does not dominate the social scene." Other students flatly assert, "Greek life rules the Richmond campus." Parties are popular at the "frat lodges" (essentially an edifice containing a large dance floor with an area to serve beer, a deck, and a backyard). For those looking for a more intimate scene, apartment parties are also popular. "There are concerts, sporting events, movies, and just groups of friends doing a wide variety of things" as well. Off campus, "Richmond is a great city that most students will never explore" because not many of these undergrads leave campus with any regularity.

Student Body

Nearly eighty percent of the students at Richmond come from out of state. "A large percentage of the students here are attending on scholarship or with a very generous financial aid package," and "more and more, the school is starting to diversify from its stereotype as just rich white kids" "who seem to have unlimited spending budgets." There's also a "growing number of" international students. Nevertheless, "Richmond is pretty homogenous." The typical student is "from 'outside Philly' or 'outside Boston'" or is a "Mid-Atlantic prep school kid" "who probably owns several pairs of Sperrys." Many students "dress well" and "obviously care about their physical appearance." There are "lots of Polos, button-downs, and sundresses." Otherwise, these "clean cut," and (if they don't mind saying so themselves) "good looking" students are "ambitious," "friendly," "outgoing," "overcommitted, and usually a little stressed." There's also "a great mixture of nerds and athletes," and "Everyone brings their own sense of individuality."

UNIVERSITY OF RICHMOND

FINANCIAL AID: 804-289-8438 • E-MAIL: ADMISSIONS@RICHMOND.EDU • WEBSITE: WWW.RICHMOND.EDU

THE PRINCETON REVIEW SAYS

Admissions

Very important factors considered include: Academic GPA, rigor of secondary school record. *Important factors considered include:* Application essay, class rank, standardized test scores, character/personal qualities, talent/ability. *Other factors considered include:* First generation, recommendation(s), alumni/ae relation, extracurricular activities, geographical residence, interview, racial/ethnic status, state residency, volunteer work, work experience. SAT or ACT required; ACT with or without writing component accepted. TOEFL required of all international applicants. High school diploma is required, and GED is accepted. *Academic units required:* 4 English, 3 mathematics, 2 science (2 science labs), 2 foreign language, 2 social science. *Academic units recommended:* 4 English, 4 mathematics, 4 science (4 science labs), 4 foreign language, 4 social science.

Financial Aid

Students should submit: FAFSA, CSS PROFILE, copies of federal tax returns. Regular filing deadline is February 15. The Princeton Review suggests that all financial aid forms be submitted as soon as possible after January 1. *Need-based scholarships/grants offered:* Federal Pell, SEOG, state scholarships/grants, private scholarships, school scholarships or grant aid from institutional funds. *Loan aid offered:* Direct Subsidized Stafford, Direct Unsubsidized Stafford, Direct PLUS, Federal Perkins. Applicants will be notified of awards beginning in April. Federal Work-Study Program and institutional work program available. Off-campus job opportunities are excellent.

The Inside Word

While the University of Richmond remains a little bit of a safety school for students with loftier goals, the standardized test scores and grades of incoming students at Richmond are tremendous and most undergraduates here finished in the top quarter of their high school classes. Note also the pile of financial aid that's available here to students with exceptional credentials.

THE SCHOOL SAYS "..."

From the Admissions Office

"The University of Richmond combines the characteristics of a small college with the dynamics of a large university. The unique size, beautiful suburban campus, and world-class facilities offer students an extraordinary mix of opportunities for personal growth and intellectual achievement. At Richmond, students are encouraged to engage themselves in their environment. Discussion and dialogue are at the forefront of the academic experience, while research, internships, and international experiences are important components of students' co-curricular lives. The university is committed to providing under-graduate students with a rigorous academic experience, while integrating these studies with opportunities for experiential learning and promoting total individual development. The university also places a high value on diversity and believes in taking full advantage of the rich benefits of learning in a com-munity of individuals from varied backgrounds.

"The University of Richmond requires either the SAT or the ACT. We do not prefer either test. We evaluate all three sections of the SAT (critical reading, math, and writing); the writing section of the ACT is optional. If multiple tests are submitted, the admission committee considers those results that are most favorable to the applicant. We do not require or recommend SAT Subject Tests."

SELECTIVITY
Admissions Rating	92
# of applicants	8,661
% of applicants accepted	33
% of acceptees attending	29
# accepting a place on wait list	984
% admitted from wait list	8
# of early decision applicants	585
% accepted early decision	55

FRESHMAN PROFILE
Range SAT Critical Reading	580–680
Range SAT Math	600–700
Range SAT Writing	600–690
Range ACT Composite	27–31
Minimum paper TOEFL	550
Minimum computer TOEFL	213
Minimum web-based TOEFL	80
% graduated top 10% of class	54
% graduated top 25% of class	86
% graduated top 50% of class	99

DEADLINES
Early decision	
Deadline	11/15
Notification	12/15
Regular	
Priority	4/1
Deadline	1/15
Nonfall registration?	no

APPLICANTS ALSO LOOK AT
AND OFTEN PREFER
Boston College, College of William and Mary, Georgetown University, Princeton University, University of Virginia, Wake Forest University

AND SOMETIMES PREFER
University of North Carolina at Chapel Hill, Vanderbilt University, Villanova University, Washington and Lee University

FINANCIAL FACTS
Financial Aid Rating	97
Annual tuition	$43,170
Room and board	$9,250
Books and supplies	$1,050
% frosh rec. need-based scholarship or grant aid	47
% UG rec. need-based scholarship or grant aid	47
% frosh rec. non-need-based scholarship or grant aid	11
% UG rec. non-need-based scholarship or grant aid	18
% frosh rec. need-based self-help aid	39
% UG rec. need-based self-help aid	40
% frosh rec. any financial aid	63
% UG rec. any financial aid	70
% UG borrow to pay for school	42
Average cumulative indebtedness	$23,070

UNIVERSITY OF ROCHESTER

300 WILSON BOULEVARD, PO BOX 270251, ROCHESTER, NY 14627 • ADMISSIONS: 585-275-3221 • FAX: 585-461-4595

CAMPUS LIFE

Quality of Life Rating	73
Fire Safety Rating	81
Green Rating	83
Type of school	private
Environment	metropolis

STUDENTS

Total undergrad enrollment	5,416
% male/female	49/51
% from out of state	50
% from public high school	73
% live on campus	83
# of fraternities	17
# of sororities	13
% African American	4
% Asian	11
% Caucasian	63
% Hispanic	6
% international	9
# of countries represented	92

SURVEY SAYS . . .
Great library
Low cost of living
Musical organizations are popular
Very little drug use

ACADEMICS

Academic Rating	84
% students graduating within 4 years	74
% students graduating within 6 years	84
Calendar	semester
Student/faculty ratio	9:1
Profs interesting rating	76
Profs accessible rating	82
Most common reg class size	10–19 students

MOST POPULAR MAJORS
biology, economics, psychology

STUDENTS SAY ". . ."

Academics

Students at the University of Rochester praise its "great atmosphere, superior academics," and "beautiful campus" by simply saying: "What more could you want?" Indeed, this college "couples strong academics without the cutthroat competitive atmosphere" meaning that students feel "relaxed" while being "pushed to do their best and forge their own paths." As one undergrad explains, "Rochester balances the academic prestige of an Ivy League school with a small, close-knit community and the drive to ensure that every student reaches their full potential." The "intimate" classes allow students to get to know their "knowledgeable and enthusiastic" professors, who "on the whole" are "stellar in terms of their qualifications, their accessibility, and their ability to teach." The faculty is widely known for "making time for students"; however, some students note, "Most science professors are here to do research as a first priority, not to teach." Also worth mentioning are the "great" career center and study abroad offices. The administration is "usually helpful," and most note that they have "open doors and ears to students." Students agree the "academic experience" at Rochester leaves "very little to be desired." After all, notes one student, "You cannot escape this place without learning a hell of a lot."

Life

At this "academic school," expect life to be "very busy" thanks to "a lot of studying," but don't worry: "There's always time for fun." Whether your interests involve "movies, music, parties," or "bars," you'll find something to occupy your time away from the books. "There's always something to do at school," says one undergrad, "which is in large part due to the student-run clubs. There are clubs in almost all areas of interest, and each club makes a true effort to organize interesting programs for the student population." When the weekend arrives, "Most people hang out at the frat quad," which is "generally bustling with parties." "There's drinking just like [at] any college," says one student, "but generally people are much more in control than at a big state school." For those less inclined to imbibe, there are "bajillions of clubs and organizations" on campus, and then there's always the city of Rochester itself. The school has a "bus system" that provides free access for students to "various places around town." The city boasts a "pretty awesome" music scene, and "There's always a show or concert on the weekends." And while Rochester's notoriously brutal winters might make some stay indoors, outdoor enthusiasts will find plenty on offer in any season, including lots of "hiking" and "skiing."

Student Body

Most students at Rochester are hard-pressed to describe the "typical" student here. Expect a "very high level" of "ethnic, religious, and social" diversity here thanks to the "wide variety of opportunities" the school offers. "Rochester is all about smart, fun, and interesting people who take their classes and their work seriously but still know how to have a good time," says one undergrad. These "driven" and "hardworking" students often have "a unique set of interests and are dedicated to pursing them" within "the university and the outside community." Because of this wide range of interests "everyone finds their niche" here. Though this can yield a "sometimes cliquish" atmosphere, students note "there's plenty of opportunity for interaction between different groups."

FINANCIAL AID: 585-275-3226 • E-MAIL: ADMIT@ADMISSIONS.ROCHESTER.EDU • WEBSITE: WWW.ROCHESTER.EDU

THE PRINCETON REVIEW SAYS

Admissions

Very important factors considered include: Recommendation(s), rigor of secondary school record, character/personal qualities. *Important factors considered include:* Application essay, standardized test scores, extracurricular activities, interview, talent/ability. *Other factors considered include:* Class rank, alumni/ae relation, first generation, geographical residence, level of applicant's interest, racial/ethnic status, volunteer work, work experience. SAT or ACT required; ACT with or without writing component accepted. TOEFL required of all international applicants. High school diploma is required, and GED is accepted.

Financial Aid

Students should submit: FAFSA, CSS/Financial Aid PROFILE. Regular filing deadline is February 1. The Princeton Review suggests that all financial aid forms be submitted as soon as possible after January 1. *Need-based scholarships/grants offered:* Federal Pell, SEOG, state scholarships/grants, school scholarship or grant aid from institutional funds. *Loan aid offered:* Direct Subsidized Stafford, Direct Unsubsidized Stafford, Direct PLUS, Federal Perkins, Federal Nursing Loans. Federal Work-Study Program available. Off-campus job opportunities are excellent.

The Inside Word

With nearly 5,300 undergrads, applicants to Rochester can expect a highly individualized academic experience—something that makes this school not only a great place to learn, but also an increasingly competitive institution when it comes to admissions. The most important consideration for admission is grades and standardized test scores, followed closely by the rigor of class work and recommendations. Keep in mind that Rochester is looking for students who will fit well within the school's academic environment and demonstrate a true interest in attending—that is, scheduling an interview could go a long way in increasing your odds.

THE SCHOOL SAYS "..."

From the Admissions Office

"Rochester believes that excellence requires freedom. In the Rochester Curriculum, students are free to select the courses that appeal to them most. There are no required subjects; students' interests drive their education. Students major in either sciences and engineering, humanities, or social sciences and complete a "cluster" of at least three related courses in each of the other two areas. Because Rochester is among America's smallest research universities, its students can pursue advanced studies and research in graduate courses, in arts and science or in any one of Rochester's nationally ranked schools of engineering, medicine, nursing, music, education, and business.

"Learning here takes place on a personal scale. Rochester remains one of the most collegiate among top research universities, with smaller classes and a nine to one student-faculty ratio—all within a university setting that attracts more than $400 million in research funding each year. Rochester faculty publish articles across the globe, win awards for their work, and collaborate with undergraduate students on a level that is rare in higher education.

"The expectation is that each student will live up to Rochester's motto, "Meliora" (ever better), recognizing that they are future leaders in industry, education, and culture. Navigating through world-renowned facilities and resources, a day in the life of two Rochester students—or any two days in the life of a single student—is never the same."

SELECTIVITY

Admissions Rating	96
# of applicants	12,805
% of applicants accepted	38
% of acceptees attending	24
# accepting a place on wait list	582
% admitted from wait list	1
# of early decision applicants	579
% accepted early decision	48

FRESHMAN PROFILE

Range SAT Critical Reading	600–690
Range SAT Math	630–730
Range SAT Writing	600–700
Range ACT Composite	29–32
Minimum paper TOEFL	600
Minimum computer TOEFL	250
Minimum web-based TOEFL	100
Average HS GPA	3.77
% graduated top 10% of class	79
% graduated top 25% of class	93
% graduated top 50% of class	100

DEADLINES

Early decision	
Deadline	11/1
Notification	12/15
Regular	
Deadline	1/1
Nonfall registration?	yes

FINANCIAL FACTS

Financial Aid Rating	92
Annual tuition	$39,480
Room and board	$11,640
Required fees	$802
Books and supplies	$1,250
% frosh rec. need-based scholarship or grant aid	57
% UG rec. need-based scholarship or grant aid	55
% frosh rec. non-need-based scholarship or grant aid	6
% UG rec. non-need-based scholarship or grant aid	4
% frosh rec. need-based self-help aid	50
% UG rec. need-based self-help aid	51
% frosh rec. any financial aid	88
% UG rec. any financial aid	88
% UG borrow to pay for school	64
Average cumulative indebtedness	$28,100

UNIVERSITY OF SAN DIEGO

5998 ALCALA PARK, SAN DIEGO, CA 92110-2492 • ADMISSIONS: 619-260-4506 • FAX: 619-260-6836

CAMPUS LIFE

Quality of Life Rating	89
Fire Safety Rating	77
Green Rating	89
Type of school	private
Affiliation	Roman Catholic
Environment	metropolis

STUDENTS

Total undergrad enrollment	5,299
% male/female	45/55
% from out of state	38
% from public high school	59
% live on campus	46
# of fraternities	5
# of sororities	6
% African American	2
% Asian	6
% Caucasian	59
% Hispanic	16
% international	4
# of countries represented	64

SURVEY SAYS . . .
Lab facilities are great
Great computer facilities
Students get along with local community
Students love San Diego, CA
Great off-campus food
Dorms are like palaces
Campus feels safe
Students are happy

ACADEMICS

Academic Rating	84
% students graduating within 4 years	60
% students graduating within 6 years	73
Calendar	4-1-4
Student/faculty ratio	15:1
Profs interesting rating	82
Profs accessible rating	86
Most common reg class size	30–39 students
Most common lab size	10–19 students

MOST POPULAR MAJORS
accounting, business administration and management, communications studies

STUDENTS SAY ". . ."

Academics
This "academically challenging, Roman Catholic" institution couples "amazing academics" and "wonderful teachers and programs" with "great weather and a beautiful campus." As one liberal studies major notes, "I just felt an overwhelming sense of belonging the very first time I stepped on campus. I fell in love right away." USD "strives and puts into action ways to create a well-rounded student who is able to succeed out in the real world." Major draws to the curriculum here include "small class sizes, potential relationships with professors, and the caring nature of the faculty." The professors "are there for you and want you to do your best…I love that the classes are taught by instructors with PhDs rather than TAs. It is great having your professor know you personally." Beyond the picturesque coastal campus—"It is in San Diego"—"undergraduate research opportunities are great!" In addition, USD has a strong undergraduate business program. USD is all about "discovering one's passions in the classroom in order to fulfill them in the real world." Besides the high caliber academics, "It is vacation weather year round. I went to the beach and tanned in January; very few other college students can say that."

Life
Life at USD boasts "beauty and brains!" USD is a "laid-back school overlooking the ocean, so people are happy to be at school and in class every day." Many tout a picture of the campus as a "country club escape from the city with outstanding professors, a friendly student body, and a five-minute drive to the beach." It's a "beach town, so surfing, laying out, bathing suits, sunglasses, and flip-flops are very prevalent." Going to the beach "is easy, you can see the ocean from campus." A car "is not totally necessary, the campus is equipped with everything you need and we have Zipcar on campus!" "It's a very active and fit" community. Some note that they "would love to see more diversity on campus." "There is a big difference between students with scholarships and those who don't need scholarships to attend." Yet others note that there are "tremendous opportunities to get involved at USD, local community and abroad!" "San Diego is about working hard for what you want, but it has everything you need to enjoy your undergraduate years." At USD, "There is always something to do for fun." There "is a party scene, but it is not overbearing to the point where it is necessary to drink." A typical day in the life of a USD student "is to go to class, get a delicious breakfast burrito at La Paloma (served all day) and hit the beach for parties on the weekend." Those adventurers looking to relax "can go to the pool, beach, parties at the beach, downtown's Gaslamp District, and Sea World on the weekends." Plus, "You are only 1.5 hours away from Disneyland and Los Angeles and four hours from Las Vegas!" Surrounding San Diego is "an amazing city."

Student Body
USD "produces students who have a desire to pursue their dreams with philanthropy." In general, all students at USD are "motivated" and "looking to better themselves and achieve personal success." As one student says, "The students here are like the protagonists in a TV series." However, "Don't let the students' good looks, high fashion, or athletic prowess and wealth fool you, these students had 4.0s in high school, have intense internships, compete for graduate and professional school spots, and are constantly serving the community." Others concede, the typical student "comes from substantial wealth, [is] white, has a strong work ethic, [and is] laid-back, athletic, outgoing, and friendly." Though, others note, "There are exceptions to the USD stereotype." Many students "receive financial aid" and thus join the leagues of those who "are very motivated to get good grades." Since USD is a Catholic school, "There are quite a few of us who are religious." Others note, "It feels a lot like high school…all the groups keep to themselves." Yet others say with the wealth of campus clubs, sporting events, internship, and community service opportunities, "There seems to be a niche for everyone."

UNIVERSITY OF SAN DIEGO

FINANCIAL AID: 619-260-4514 • E-MAIL: ADMISSIONS@SANDIEGO.EDU • WEBSITE: WWW.SANDIEGO.EDU/ADMISSIONS/UNDERGRADUATE

THE PRINCETON REVIEW SAYS

Admissions
Very important factors considered include: Academic GPA, rigor of secondary school record, standardized test scores. *Important factors considered include:* Application essay, class rank, recommendation(s), character/personal qualities, extracurricular activities, religious affiliation/commitment, talent/ability, volunteer work. *Other factors considered include:* Alumni/ae relation, first generation, geographical residence, interview, level of applicant's interest, racial/ethnic status, work experience. SAT or ACT required; ACT with writing component required. TOEFL required of all international applicants. High school diploma is required, and GED is accepted. *Academic units required:* 4 English, 3 mathematics, 3 science (2 science labs), 2 foreign language, 3 social studies. *Academic units recommended:* 4 English, 4 mathematics, 4 science (3 science labs), 3 foreign language, 4 social studies.

Financial Aid
Students should submit: FAFSA. Regular filing deadline is March 2. The Princeton Review suggests that all financial aid forms be submitted as soon as possible after January 1. *Need-based scholarships/grants offered:* Federal Pell, SEOG, state scholarships/grants, private scholarships, school scholarship or grant aid from institutional funds, Federal Nursing Scholarships. *Loan aid offered:* Direct Subsidized Stafford, Direct Unsubsidized Stafford, Direct PLUS, Federal Perkins, university loans from institutional funds. Applicants will be notified of awards on a rolling basis beginning March 1. Federal Work-Study Program available. Off-campus job opportunities are good.

The Inside Word
USD offers a broad liberal arts core, small classes, and close interaction between students and professors. The dazzling campus and an unbeatable location are just gravy. As such, admission here is competitive. Solid test scores and outstanding grades should be a given for applicants.

THE SCHOOL SAYS "..."

From the Admissions Office
"Looking at the University of San Diego is easy on the eyes. But really seeing our true character demands a little work. It is easy to focus on the obvious: the incredible beauty of the campus, the region's unparalleled climate and livability, long lists of recreational and co-curricular opportunities, the vitality of students walking through the central plaza, or even the obvious expressions of USD's Catholic character. But to focus on the superficial would be misleading.

"Long known for having one of the most beautiful campuses in the country, the University of San Diego is also quickly becoming known for offering one of the best educational experiences in the country. USD offers a values-based education in which ethics and intellectual inquiry form the foundation of the learning experience. As our profile indicates, our students are very bright and passionate about learning. Our faculty are equally passionate about providing them with the resources they need to succeed. They focus on teaching our undergraduates, but also provide them with research opportunities, help them get meaningful internships, support them as they take part in our study abroad programs, and serve as their advisors and mentors.

"A USD education is characterized by the strong liberal arts foundation, research, internships, and a wide array of international experiences. We have the second highest participation rate in study abroad programs of any school in the country. Through all these experiences our students are prepared to engage the world around them and make a difference. Giving back to the community is an integral part of our Catholic heritage and service is something many of our students are committed to.

"All these opportunities in the backdrop of America's Finest City make the USD experience a very special one."

SELECTIVITY
Admissions Rating	93
# of applicants	12,141
% of applicants accepted	51
% of acceptees attending	18
# accepting a place on wait list	463
% admitted from wait list	23

FRESHMAN PROFILE
Range SAT Critical Reading	550–640
Range SAT Math	570–660
Range SAT Writing	550–650
Range ACT Composite	25–29
Minimum paper TOEFL	550
Minimum computer TOEFL	213
Minimum web-based TOEFL	80
Average HS GPA	3.81
% graduated top 10% of class	42
% graduated top 25% of class	77
% graduated top 50% of class	97

DEADLINES
Early action	
Deadline	11/15
Notification	1/31
Regular	
Priority	1/15
Deadline	3/1
Nonfall registration?	yes

APPLICANTS ALSO LOOK AT
AND OFTEN PREFER
University of Southern California

AND SOMETIMES PREFER
Loyola Marymount University

AND RARELY PREFER
University of California—San Diego

FINANCIAL FACTS
Financial Aid Rating	76
Annual tuition	$19,075
Room and board	$5,876
Required fees	$216
% frosh rec. need-based scholarship or grant aid	55
% UG rec. need-based scholarship or grant aid	45
% frosh rec. non-need-based scholarship or grant aid	34
% UG rec. non-need-based scholarship or grant aid	21
% frosh rec. need-based self-help aid	44
% UG rec. need-based self-help aid	39
% frosh rec. any financial aid	80
% UG rec. any financial aid	68
% UG borrow to pay for school	53
Average cumulative indebtedness	$29,928

UNIVERSITY OF SAN FRANCISCO

2130 FULTON STREET, SAN FRANCISCO, CA 94117 • ADMISSIONS: 415-422-6563 • FAX: 415-422-2217

CAMPUS LIFE

Quality of Life Rating	82
Fire Safety Rating	60*
Green Rating	80
Type of school	private
Affiliation	Roman Catholic
Environment	metropolis

STUDENTS

Total undergrad enrollment	5,329
% male/female	36/64
% from out of state	39
% from public high school	49
% live on campus	38
# of fraternities	4
# of sororities	4
% African American	3
% Asian	19
% Caucasian	38
% Hispanic	18
% Native American	1
% international	11
# of countries represented	75

SURVEY SAYS . . .
Great library
Athletic facilities are great
Diverse student types on campus
Students get along with local
community
Students love San Francisco, CA
Great off-campus food

ACADEMICS

Academic Rating	80
% students graduating within 4 years	53
% students graduating within 6 years	70
Calendar	4-1-4
Student/faculty ratio	13:1
Profs interesting rating	82
Profs accessible rating	80
Most common reg class size	10–19 students
Most common lab size	10–19 students

MOST POPULAR MAJORS
business/commerce, psychology

STUDENTS SAY ". . ."

Academics
With its "Jesuit morals" and "close-knit" community, this "academically rigorous school" focuses on "promoting social justice, tolerance, and community spirit." USF "teaches its students about the importance of helping others and making a difference in today's society." The curriculum here not only focuses "a lot on education but on making students aware of issues in the world and, on a smaller scale, the local community." Classes here are about "educating minds and hearts to change the world." As one student notes, "I wanted to go to a small school in a big city that promotes important issues like social justice and community service." Many tout the school's "diversity" and "remarkable education." "Because the school is small, classes are too." "One-on-one attention from professors is common." "Professors are sincerely passionate about their subject and try to engage students and share their passion while ensuring learning and comprehension." "Most of the professors are really enthusiastic about their classes because most of them have already worked in the areas they're teaching and can enlighten us on their past failures and successes." "During my junior and senior semesters at USF, I began to really appreciate my professors of upper-division courses that are really devoted to their teachings."

Life
"People here love to go out and have a good time." Living in San Francisco, "There is always something to do." People "go out into the city to enjoy the beach, parks, downtown, city landmarks, club events, social justice groups, protests, and rallies for causes." When looking for a place to spend an idle-while afternoon, students "go to Golden Gate Park [or] take MUNI downtown." "There are too many places to eat!" Chinatown "is always fun; Fisherman's wharf and Pier 39 are always fun too." On campus, students are "very involved." This typical motto reverberates, "I have two on campus jobs, and I'm active in three clubs!" When it comes to socializing, "People think and discuss a lot of things; topics like religion, politics, international issues, [and] the environment." Using the gym "is also something to do since you get free membership to Koret Gym if you are a student at USF." On the weekend, for fun, students go to "the free festivals that are going on in the city…go shopping in downtown, hang out at the park, or check out a neighborhood or area I've never been to before with my friends." Those with an outdoors bent "enjoy going on bike rides through Golden Gate Park or to China Beach and watching the sunset." In general, life here is all about "managing my time in a way that I can get all my work done and still have time to hang out with friends." Dorms are generally well accommodated, but "like any other campus," students note, "The facilities in some of the building could be updated and the computer labs could be updated."

Student Body
A typical student at USF "cannot clearly be defined" as "the students at the University of San Francisco are from all walks of life"; "Students easily fit in to the school," which is "extremely diverse." Students "are very accepting of all cultures." True to their Jesuit values and passion for community service, students here call out the following attributes like roll call. Students are "outgoing, cheerful, fashionable, and active socially, politically, [and] environmentally." "Everyone is very friendly and tolerant," and "There are always new people to meet." While "there is no 'typical student'" at USF, "Many students here are definitely involved in a green movement, sustainability, community service or international affairs." Those who are quick to affix a label cast the following stereotype, "Guys [at USF] are more of the grungy or hipster types. For girls, the school is a show…you find out quickly that many intend to see and be seen. Athletes [tend to] stick together." Whatever cues their fashion code may call for, the average student here "studies a lot [and is] always on the move helping out someone in need." "Ambitious goals" pervade student thinking, and everyone is "kind toward others." In essence, "San Francisco is home to a wide variety of people and, as such, so is USF."

UNIVERSITY OF SAN FRANCISCO

FINANCIAL AID: 415-422-6303 • E-MAIL: ADMISSION@USFCA.EDU • WEBSITE: WWW.USFCA.EDU

THE PRINCETON REVIEW SAYS

Admissions

Very important factors considered include: Academic GPA, recommendation(s), rigor of secondary school record, standardized test scores. *Important factors considered include:* Application essay, class rank. *Other factors considered include:* Alumni/ae relation, character/personal qualities, extracurricular activities, interview, talent/ability, volunteer work. SAT or ACT required; ACT with writing component required. TOEFL required of all international applicants. High school diploma is required, and GED is accepted. *Academic units recommended:* 4 English, 3 mathematics, 2 science (2 science labs), 2 foreign language, 3 social studies, 6 academic elective.

Financial Aid

Students should submit: FAFSA. The Princeton Review suggests that all financial aid forms be submitted as soon as possible after January 1. *Need-based scholarships/grants offered:* Federal Pell, SEOG, state scholarships/grants, private scholarships, school scholarship or grant aid from institutional funds, Federal Nursing Scholarships. *Loan aid offered:* Direct Subsidized Stafford, Direct Unsubsidized Stafford, Direct PLUS, Federal Perkins, Federal Nursing Loans, university loans from institutional funds. Applicants will be notified of awards on a rolling basis beginning April 1. Federal Work-Study Program available. Off-campus job opportunities are excellent.

The Inside Word

The admissions committee at USF isn't purely numbers-focused. They'll evaluate your full picture here, using your academic strengths and weaknesses along with your personal character strengths, essays, and recommendations to assess your suitability for admission. It's matchmaking. If you fit well in the USF community, you'll be welcome.

THE SCHOOL SAYS " . . ."

From the Admissions Office

"The University of San Francisco has experienced a significant increase in applications for admission over the past five years. We select applicants with strong academic credentials who will make the most of the university's academic opportunities, location in San Francisco, and its mission to educate minds and hearts to challenge the world. Community outreach and service to others, along with academic excellence, are characteristics that help distinguish those offered admission.

"The University has just completed a major upgrade to all administrative computer systems, including software that will help with student compatibility matching in residence halls.

"Applicants are required to take the SAT reasoning test (or the ACT with the writing section). The writing sections will be used for advising and placement purposes. SAT subject test scores will also be accepted."

SELECTIVITY

Admissions Rating	86
# of applicants	9,179
% of applicants accepted	68
% of acceptees attending	19
# of early action applicants	3,469
# accepted early action	2,569

FRESHMAN PROFILE

Range SAT Critical Reading	500–610
Range SAT Math	510–610
Range SAT Writing	510–610
Range ACT Composite	22–27
Minimum paper TOEFL	550
Minimum computer TOEFL	213
Minimum web-based TOEFL	79
Average HS GPA	3.52
% graduated top 10% of class	21
% graduated top 25% of class	56
% graduated top 50% of class	90

DEADLINES

Early action	
Deadline	11/15
Notification	1/16
Regular	
Priority	1/15
Nonfall registration?	yes

APPLICANTS ALSO LOOK AT

AND OFTEN PREFER
Santa Clara University, Stanford University, University of California—Berkeley, University of California—Davis, University of Southern California

AND SOMETIMES PREFER
Loyola Marymount University, Seattle University, University of California—Santa Barbara, University of California—Santa Cruz, University of San Diego

AND RARELY PREFER
Boston College, Fordham University

FINANCIAL FACTS

Financial Aid Rating	71
Annual tuition	$37,040
Room and board	$12,050
Required fees	$384
Books and supplies	$1,500
% frosh rec. need-based scholarship or grant aid	65
% UG rec. need-based scholarship or grant aid	52
% frosh rec. non-need-based scholarship or grant aid	39
% UG rec. non-need-based scholarship or grant aid	11
% frosh rec. need-based self-help aid	59
% UG rec. need-based self-help aid	53
% UG borrow to pay for school	64
Average cumulative indebtedness	$26,886

UNIVERSITY OF SCRANTON

800 LINDEN STREET, SCRANTON, PA 18510-4699 • ADMISSIONS: 570-941-7540 FAX: 570-941-5928

STUDENTS SAY ". . ."

Academics
With "an outstanding record for admission to graduate programs, not only in law and medicine but also in several other fields," The University of Scranton is a good fit for ambitious students seeking "a Jesuit school in every sense of the word. If you come here, expect to be challenged to become a better person, to develop a strong concern for the poor and marginalized, and to grow spiritually and intellectually." The school manages to accomplish this without "forcing religion upon you, which is nice." Undergraduates also approve of the mandatory liberal-arts-based curriculum that "forces you to learn about broader things than your own major." Strong majors here include "an amazing occupational therapy program. "This is a great place for premeds and other sciences," students agree. While the workload can be difficult, "a tutoring center provides free tutoring for any students who may need it, and also provides work-study positions for students who qualify to tutor." Need more help? Professors "are extremely accessible. They will go to any lengths to help you understand material and do well," while administrators "are here for the students, and show that every day inside and outside of the classroom." Community ties here are strong; as one student points out, "the Jesuits live in our dorms, creating an even greater sense of community, because we don't view them as just priests, we view them as real people who can relate on our level."

Life
"There is a whole range of activities to do on the weekends" at The University of Scranton, including "frequent trips, dances, and movies that are screened for free." Students tell us "the school and student organizations provide plenty of options, such as retreats, talent shows, and other various activities." There are also "many intramurals to become involved in, and the varsity sports (specifically the women's) are very successful." Furthermore, "being a Jesuit school, social justice issues are huge. They are taught in the classroom, and students spend a lot of time volunteering." Hometown Scranton is big enough to provide "movie theaters, two malls, parks, a bowling alley, and a skiing/snowboarding mountain." In short, there are plenty of choices for the non-partier at Scranton. Many we heard from in our survey reported busy extracurricular schedules. But those seeking a party won't be disappointed here, either. Scranton undergrads "party a lot, but they balance it with studying. Parties are chances to go out, see people, dance, and drink if you want." You "can find a party any time of day, seven days a week" here, usually with a keg tapped and pouring. Few here feel the party scene is out of hand, however a typical student writes, "It's very different than at schools with Greek systems. It is a lot more laid-back, and all about everyone having a good time."

Student Body
While "the typical Scranton student is white, Catholic, and from the suburbs," students hasten to point out "within this sameness, there is much diversity. There are people who couldn't care at all about religion, and there are people who are deeply religious. Even in the Catholic atmosphere of the school, the school only requires that you learn about Catholicism as it stands. Theology classes…are prefaced with the idea that 'You do not have to believe this!'" Undergrads here are generally "friendly and welcoming. Cliques are pretty much nonexistent, and anyone who would be classified as 'popular' is only considered so because they are extremely friendly, outgoing, and seek out friendships with as many people as possible." Students tend to be on the Abercrombie-preppy side, with lots of undergrads of Italian, Irish, and Polish descent.

FINANCIAL AID: 570-941-7700 • E-MAIL: ADMISSIONS@SCRANTON.EDU • WEBSITE: WWW.SCRANTON.EDU

THE PRINCETON REVIEW SAYS

Admissions

Very important factors considered include: Academic GPA, class rank, rigor of secondary school record, standardized test scores. *Important factors considered include:* Extracurricular activities. *Other factors considered include:* Application essay, recommendation(s), alumni/ae relation, character/personal qualities, interview, level of applicant's interest, talent/ability, volunteer work, work experience. SAT or ACT required; ACT with or without writing component accepted. TOEFL required of all international applicants. High school diploma is required, and GED is accepted. *Academic units required:* 4 English, 3 mathematics, 3 science (1 science lab), 2 foreign language, 2 social studies, 2 history, 4 academic elective. *Academic units recommended:* 4 English, 4 mathematics, 3 science (1 science lab), 2 foreign language, 3 social studies, 3 history, 4 academic elective.

Financial Aid

Students should submit: FAFSA. The Princeton Review suggests that all financial aid forms be submitted as soon as possible after January 1. *Need-based scholarships/grants offered:* Federal Pell, SEOG, state scholarships/grants, private scholarships, school scholarship or grant aid from institutional funds. *Loan aid offered:* Direct Subsidized Stafford, Direct Unsubsidized Stafford, Direct PLUS, Federal Perkins, Federal Nursing Loans. Applicants will be notified of awards on a rolling basis beginning March 15. Federal Work-Study Program available. Off-campus job opportunities are good.

The Inside Word

Admission to Scranton gets harder each year. A steady stream of smart kids from the tristate area keeps classes full and the admit rate low. Successful applicants will need solid grades and test scores. As with many religiously affiliated schools, students should be a good match philosophically as well.

THE SCHOOL SAYS "..."

From the Admissions Office

"A Jesuit institution in Pennsylvania's Pocono Northeast, The University of Scranton is known for its outstanding academics, state-of-the art campus, and exceptional sense of community. Founded in 1888, the University offers more than eighty undergraduate and graduate academic programs of study through four colleges and schools.

"The Princeton Review included Scranton among The Best Colleges in the nation in past years. For years, Scranton was the only college in Pennsylvania and the only Jesuit university to have a student named to the first academic team.

"Freshman applicants are required to take the SAT or ACT exam. The writing scores will not be considered in the admissions decision process. Students are encouraged to apply early for admission and can do so online with no application fee."

SELECTIVITY

Admissions Rating	85
# of applicants	7,810
% of applicants accepted	74
% of acceptees attending	16
# accepting a place on wait list	276
% admitted from wait list	16

FRESHMAN PROFILE

Range SAT Critical Reading	500–600
Range SAT Math	520–610
Minimum paper TOEFL	500
Minimum computer TOEFL	173
Average HS GPA	3.35
% graduated top 10% of class	26
% graduated top 25% of class	59
% graduated top 50% of class	87

DEADLINES

Early action	
Deadline	11/15
Notification	12/15
Regular	
Priority	3/1
Deadline	3/1
Notification	12/15
Nonfall registration?	yes

APPLICANTS ALSO LOOK AT AND OFTEN PREFER

Fairfield University, Saint Joseph's University (PA), University of Delaware, Villanova University

AND SOMETIMES PREFER

Loyola College in Maryland, Penn State—University Park

FINANCIAL FACTS

Financial Aid Rating	73
Annual tuition	$34,236
Room and board	$11,862
Required fees	$300
Books and supplies	$1,150
% frosh rec. need-based scholarship or grant aid	70
% UG rec. need-based scholarship or grant aid	66
% frosh rec. non-need-based scholarship or grant aid	7
% UG rec. non-need-based scholarship or grant aid	5
% frosh rec. need-based self-help aid	59
% UG rec. need-based self-help aid	58
% frosh rec. any financial aid	85
% UG rec. any financial aid	82
% UG borrow to pay for school	75
Average cumulative indebtedness	$30,920

UNIVERSITY OF SOUTH CAROLINA—COLUMBIA

UNIVERSITY OF SOUTH CAROLINA, COLUMBIA, SC 29208 • ADMISSIONS: 803-777-7700 • FAX: 803-777-0101

STUDENTS SAY ". . ."

Academics

At the University of South Carolina's flagship campus, you'll find "a mixture of deep South tradition and an increasingly progressive education." You can get "a good degree in just about any field" here. The nationally recognized business school is "definitely a strength." There's a "great nursing program" as well. USC also excels in journalism, chemistry, and hospitality management. In most majors, the academic atmosphere is "not impossible, but a good amount of time goes into studying outside of class." "It is just the right amount of work to still have a good social life," opines a broadcast journalism major. Students in the "fantastic" honors college enjoy "small, discussion-based classes and a lot of personal attention." Meanwhile, for the run of USC-ers, classes are much bigger, teaching assistants are common, and the professors "vary vastly." A lot of professors are "very well-prepared," "very approachable," and "passionate about their subjects." "Most of the teachers I have had here have been outstanding," reports a business major. Other faculty members "just read through slides." Still others are "generally unhelpful, unapproachable, and more concerned with their research." USC's administration is "very friendly" and "student-oriented." Getting things done "can be slow" and advising can be "completely unorganized," but "the bureaucracy is easy to navigate," which definitely isn't the norm at your average state school.

Life

Students here enjoy "awesome" weather and a "pretty," "historical campus." "A lot of the buildings are very old" and could use a serious makeover, though. "Parking is a problem," too. For many students, "Attending college sporting events is the most fun thing to do at USC." "The school spirit is crazy," reports a senior. "In the fall, student life revolves strongly around football." Home games "are an all-day event." "The tailgating is epic." However, you can have "good fun year-round." "It's a big school, so there's a little of everything." "There are tons of resources for the students to use," including "a world-class gym." "Intramural sports are very popular." Guest speakers and big-name performers are numerous. Greek life is "huge" and Columbia is a "fun college town." "People party hard here at USC." It's easy to "get trashed on the weekends" because "the campus is surrounded by nightlife." Five Points is a bar district within "walking distance" "that is super fun." The Vista, which is similar to Five Points but a bit more upscale, is another bar-filled area of town that "students love to visit." When the hankering for road trips arises, students appreciate that the campus is "close to Charleston and Charlotte, and not too far from Atlanta."

Student Body

Archetypal students at USC are "politically conservative, openly religious (mostly Christian), and traditionally Southern." The atmosphere "can be intimidating to non-Southerners at times." "If you are from a different part of the country," counsels a first-year student, "it's a culture shock." Students here are also "very involved on campus" and exceedingly proud of their school. "We all have Gamecock pride," explains a sophomore. Otherwise, this place is "a huge melting pot," with "a wide range" of students and organizations. Students who pledge fraternities and sororities constitute the most visible bloc. "A lot of the girls are the classic blond Southern girl and many of the guys are preppy" types sporting "boat shoes," "sunglasses around their necks," and a "frat-boy swoop" hairdo. "There is a different group for everyone down here," though. "Good old boys and some more progressive types," "artsy" kids, "gothic" kids, "theater kids, ROTC kids," and "self-proclaimed honors college nerds" all have their respective niches. "Every type of person goes to this school," says a sophomore.

UNIVERSITY OF SOUTH CAROLINA—COLUMBIA

FINANCIAL AID: 803-777-8134 • E-MAIL: ADMISSIONS-UGRAD@SC.EDU • WEBSITE: WWW.SC.EDU

THE PRINCETON REVIEW SAYS

Admissions

Very important factors considered include: Academic GPA, rigor of secondary school record, standardized test scores. *Important factors considered include:* Class rank. *Other factors considered include:* Application essay, recommendation(s), alumni/ae relation, character/personal qualities, extracurricular activities, first generation, racial/ethnic status, state residency, talent/ability, volunteer work, work experience. SAT or ACT required; ACT with writing component required. TOEFL required of all international applicants. High school diploma is required, and GED is accepted. *Academic units required:* 4 English, 4 mathematics, 3 science (3 science labs), 2 foreign language, 2 social studies, 1 history, 1 academic elective.

Financial Aid

Students should submit: FAFSA. The Princeton Review suggests that all financial aid forms be submitted as soon as possible after January 1. *Need-based scholarships/grants offered:* Federal Pell, SEOG, state scholarships/grants, private scholarships, school scholarship or grant aid from institutional funds, United Negro College Fund, Federal Nursing Scholarships. *Loan aid offered:* Direct Subsidized Stafford, Direct Unsubsidized Stafford, Direct PLUS, Federal Perkins, Federal Nursing Loans. Applicants will be notified of awards on a rolling basis beginning January 4. Federal Work-Study Program available. Off-campus job opportunities are good.

The Inside Word

Provided that you've completed a strong and serious college preparatory curriculum, it's not tremendously difficult to get admitted here. Like at most large schools, the process is largely based on grades and test scores. Applicants with a B-plus average and SAT section scores in the mid 500s (or an ACT composite in the low 20s) usually get in. With higher standardized scores, you can sneak in with spottier grades. Likewise, if your grades are really good, your test scores can be lower.

THE SCHOOL SAYS "..."

From the Admissions Office

"In just six years, the number of annual undergraduate applicants to USC has doubled, making it more critical than ever for students to meet the university's priority application deadline. The University of South Carolina's national prominence in academics and research activities also has increased. USC is one of only sixty-two public research institutions to earn a designated status of 'very high research activity' by the Carnegie Foundation. As early as their freshman year, undergraduates are encouraged to compete for research grants. As South Carolina's flagship institution, USC offers more than 350 degree programs. More than 27,000 students seek baccalaureate, masters, or doctoral degrees. USC is known for its top-ranked academic programs, including its international business and exercise science programs—both rated number one nationally. Other notable programs include chemical and nuclear engineering; health education; hotel, restaurant, and tourism; marine science; law; medicine; nursing; and psychology, among others. USC is recognized for its pioneering efforts in freshman outreach. Its honors college is one of the nation's best, offering an Ivy League–caliber education at state college costs. USC offers student support in such areas as career development, disability services, pre-professional planning, and study abroad. On campus, students enjoy a state-of-the-art fitness center, an 18,000-seat arena, an 80,000-seat stadium, and nearly 300 student organizations. Off campus, South Carolina's world-famous beaches and the Blue Ridge Mountains are each less than a three-hour drive away. The University of South Carolina is located in the state's capital city, making it a great place for internships and job opportunities."

SELECTIVITY

Admissions Rating	87
# of applicants	18,485
% of applicants accepted	65
% of acceptees attending	35
# accepting a place on wait list	0

FRESHMAN PROFILE

Range SAT Critical Reading	530–630
Range SAT Math	560–650
Range ACT Composite	24–29
Minimum paper TOEFL	550
Minimum computer TOEFL	210
Minimum web-based TOEFL	77
Average HS GPA	3.89
% graduated top 10% of class	28
% graduated top 25% of class	60
% graduated top 50% of class	90

DEADLINES

Early action	
Deadline	10/15
Notification	12/20
Regular	
Priority	12/1
Deadline	12/1
Notification	3/15
Nonfall registration?	yes

APPLICANTS ALSO LOOK AT AND OFTEN PREFER
University of North Carolina at Chapel Hill

AND SOMETIMES PREFER
Clemson University

FINANCIAL FACTS

Financial Aid Rating	79
Annual in-state tuition	$9,386
Annual out-of-state tuition	$24,962
Room and board	$7,764
Required fees	$400
Books and supplies	$936
% frosh rec. need-based scholarship or grant aid	21
% UG rec. need-based scholarship or grant aid	25
% frosh rec. non-need-based scholarship or grant aid	40
% UG rec. non-need-based scholarship or grant aid	29
% frosh rec. need-based self-help aid	32
% UG rec. need-based self-help aid	38
% frosh rec. any financial aid	82
% UG rec. any financial aid	72
% UG borrow to pay for school	49
Average cumulative indebtedness	$21,811

THE UNIVERSITY OF SOUTH DAKOTA

414 EAST CLARK, VERMILLION, SD 57069 • ADMISSIONS: 605-677-5434 • FAX: 605-677-6323

STUDENTS SAY "..."

Academics

With an honors program that is "the best-kept secret in the country" and professors who are "nearly always willing to go the extra mile for students," the University of South Dakota offers a "great student to faculty communicative experience at a reasonable price." Numerous departments garner praise from students, and the University boasts winners "almost every year for big scholarships like the Goldwater and Truman, competing with big, Ivy League, private colleges that charge quadruple the amount for the same education." While the nursing school is the most frequently praised, the "business, biology, premed, law, and psychology classes are very solid," and the "dental hygiene, music, and journalism schools" also stand out, with the most copious laurels heaped on the music department's professors who are "some of the best." All told, the wide selection of quality academics "gives students many options as far as majors go," and for students willing to throw themselves into their studies "the odds of getting into a professional or graduate program are good."

Life

"We work hard, so we can play hard," sums up the undergraduate philosophy at USD. "Although there is a lot of partying that happens, the students keep themselves occupied with school work, intramural sports, and hanging out with their friends." Vermillion's small size seems to be a double-edged sword; some insist that "the size of the town means no one is more than a 10-minute walk/bike ride away!" and that "since it is a smaller campus students have more opportunities to be involved in internships and various other activities." But the fact remains that "Many of the upperclassmen live in the larger cities to the north and south." In general, "students have to make their own fun, which often involves partying or taking small road trips to other cities in the area." For those planning to roam further afield, "Vermillion is located very close to Yankton, Sioux City (IA), and Sioux Falls (all within an hour). They are bigger cities and offer everything a person would want to do (shopping, movies, entertainment)."

Student Body

A typical USD student "would be a conservative Midwesterner. He or she would be Caucasian" and would most likely have originated in "small towns in South Dakota, Iowa, and Nebraska." "Many people join a Greek system or are athletes or musicians. Those who do not fit into these three main groups seem to focus on their academics" and "[fit] in fine with the majority because of the open mindedness of most students." For example, "Gay students are able to get along with the rest of student population." There's no denying that "partying is a definite part of the culture, though many of the 'smart' kids both party and work hard." Student organizations call out to many, and "it seems like every person on campus is part of at least one of them. It is a great way to meet new people and [to participate in] activities."

FINANCIAL AID: 605-677-5446 • E-MAIL: ADMISS@USD.EDU • WEBSITE: WWW.USD.EDU

THE PRINCETON REVIEW SAYS

Admissions

Very important factors considered include: Academic GPA, class rank, rigor of secondary school record, standardized test scores. *Important factors considered include:* Alumni/ae relation. *Other factors considered include:* Application essay, recommendation(s), character/personal qualities, extracurricular activities, geographical residence, racial/ethnic status, state residency, talent/ability, volunteer work, work experience. SAT or ACT required; ACT with or without writing component accepted. TOEFL required of all international applicants. High school diploma is required, and GED is accepted. *Academic units required:* 4 English, 3 mathematics, 3 science (3 science labs), 3 social studies. *Academic units recommended:* 4 mathematics, 4 science, 2 foreign language.

Financial Aid

Students should submit: FAFSA. The Princeton Review suggests that all financial aid forms be submitted as soon as possible after January 1. *Need-based scholarships/grants offered:* Federal Pell, SEOG, private scholarships, school scholarship or grant aid from institutional funds, Federal Nursing Scholarships. *Loan aid offered:* Federal Perkins, Federal Nursing Loans, university loans from institutional funds. Applicants will be notified of awards on a rolling basis beginning March 1. Federal Work-Study Program available. Off-campus job opportunities are good.

The Inside Word

To be a candidate for general admission to USD, you must meet one of three general requirements: rank in the top fifty percent of your graduating class or obtain an ACT/SAT composite score of 21/990 or higher or have a minimum grade point average of at least 2.6 on a 4.0 scale in all high school courses. An applicant's high school curricula must also meet certain minimum requirements.

THE SCHOOL SAYS " . . ."

From the Admissions Office

"The University of South Dakota is the perfect fit for students looking for a smart educational investment. USD is South Dakota's only designated liberal arts university and is consistently rated among the top doctoral institutions in the country. Annually, USD awards scholarships to more than 800 first-year students, and more than eighty percent of USD students receive some form of financial aid through grants, loans, and work-study jobs.

"USD students earn the nation's most prestigious scholarships. Our quality of teaching and research prepares students to pursue their passions all over the world, at institutions such as Columbia, Johns Hopkins, The University of Chicago, and beyond. Fifty-nine students have been awarded prestigious Fulbright, Rhodes, National Science Foundation, Boren, Truman, Udall, Gilman, and Goldwater scholarships and grants for graduate study. Personal attention from our award-winning faculty and our welcoming environment makes students feel right at home.

"As the flagship liberal arts institution in South Dakota, USD—founded in 1862—has long been regarded as a leader in the state and the region. Notable undergraduate and postgraduate alumni include journalist Ken Bode, author and former news anchor Tom Brokaw, writer and Emmy Award–winner Dorothy Cooper Foote, U.S. Senator Tim Johnson, USA Today founder Al Neuharth, and U.S. Senator John Thune.

"Applicants are not required to take the writing test for either SAT or ACT. USD recommends taking the ACT over the SAT. Students who wish to send their SAT scores will have their scores converted to ACT scores for placement and scholarship consideration."

SELECTIVITY

Admissions Rating	74
# of applicants	3,452
% of applicants accepted	85
% of acceptees attending	30

FRESHMAN PROFILE

Range SAT Critical Reading	440–630
Range SAT Math	450–610
Range ACT Composite	20–25
Minimum paper TOEFL	550
Minimum computer TOEFL	213
Minimum web-based TOEFL	79
Average HS GPA	3.25
% graduated top 10% of class	13
% graduated top 25% of class	34
% graduated top 50% of class	69

DEADLINES

Regular	
Notification	9/20
Nonfall registration?	yes

APPLICANTS ALSO LOOK AT
AND OFTEN PREFER
University of Nebraska—Lincoln

AND SOMETIMES PREFER
Augustana College (SD), South Dakota State University

AND RARELY PREFER
Dakota State University

FINANCIAL FACTS

Financial Aid Rating	88
Annual in-state tuition	$3,429
Annual out-of-state tuition	$5,144
Room and board	$6,543
Required fees	$3,780
Books and supplies	$1,100
% frosh rec. need-based scholarship or grant aid	32
% UG rec. need-based scholarship or grant aid	32
% frosh rec. non-need-based scholarship or grant aid	45
% UG rec. non-need-based scholarship or grant aid	30
% frosh rec. need-based self-help aid	54
% UG rec. need-based self-help aid	58
% frosh rec. any financial aid	94
% UG rec. any financial aid	91

UNIVERSITY OF SOUTH FLORIDA

4202 EAST FOWLER AVENUE, SVC-1036, TAMPA, FL 33620-9951 • ADMISSIONS: 813-974-3350 • FAX: 813-974-9689

STUDENTS SAY ". . ."

Academics

Conveniently located in Tampa, Florida, this top-tier state university attracts students for whom "price, diversity, and opportunities" are as important as a location that's "close to home." The University of South Florida "is all about community." One student says, "It was close to home, offered the degree that I wanted, offered me the most financial aid, and had many ties to the community and surrounding areas culturally and academically." USF may be huge, but this "does not affect the level of personal attention that students receive." Many here laud the honors program: "Classes are almost always discussion-based." In general, professors here "really want you to succeed." Students universally cheer, "The campus is beautiful!" "This is the only poly university in Florida and offers a unique and more real-world learning environment." Most of the professors "have worked twenty plus years in the field and are not strictly academia experienced, which results in more content-related discussions." Another adds, "Most professors, especially the business and philosophy related people, know their material and provide an open forum for learning." The College of Education has a sterling reputation for building "a caring community that expects excellence." With a large commuter population, there's a great diversity in the student body, "not just ethnically or culturally, but older students that bring experience and students from all socioeconomic levels." In addition, USF "is a top school for medical-related studies." USF offers the total package; "Fair tuition prices, a great city/location, excellent professors and [an excellent] learning atmosphere." USF is "doing everything within its capacity to provide the best education it can to every student, regardless of major, background, or ethnicity." This is an institution "dedicated to enriching their students and communities lives through eclectic methods."

Life

Life at USF "strongly promotes building a cohesive, comfortable community." The university enjoys "a diverse student population on a beautiful urban campus surrounded by a bustling city." Tampa "has a lot to offer for students. USF has so many clubs that each have various events, there is always something going on." Popular recreations include the "flea markets, poster sales, Patio Tuesdays (social event in the student center), clubs and organizations, free speech areas, residence hall parties, coffee houses, performances put on by the orchestras, bands, and theater, sports (Go Bulls!), guest speakers, etc." Many students enjoy the bustling club scene in Ybor City, a historic-district-turned-night-clubbing-district in Tampa's Latin Quarter where "there are a plethora of local bars and clubs to hang out at for fun."

Student Body

The USF student body is "a diverse mix socioeconomically, culturally, religiously, and racially." As one returning student testifies, "I am a non-traditional student in my fifties, and [I] feel completely comfortable in classes with students half my age. It's a very friendly school. All walks of life. I could not describe a typical student." USF "is a huge university." Every student "is completely different, so it's impossible to describe a 'typical' one." This makes for a welcome mix of professional and extracurricular interests; "So far, in every class it's been incredibly easy to get along with other classmates and everyone is really accepting of each other, no matter your background." As is often noted at many large universities with an active nightlife, "Most people here have two personalities. One is extremely studious persona and the other is a party animal. Basically when it's time to let loose we let loose." On-campus students "are involved in campus and community activities, friendly, busy, and often have active social lives." There's "a strong sense of community fostered by club and organization involvement." USF "offers plenty of places to gather on campus." Despite the size of the school, social life is filled by "all sorts of activities and organizations that make it very easy to interact with people who share your views and interests."

FINANCIAL AID: 813-974-4700 • WEBSITE: WWW.USF.EDU

THE PRINCETON REVIEW SAYS

Admissions

Very important factors considered include: Academic GPA, rigor of secondary school record. *Important factors considered include:* Standardized test scores, first generation. *Other factors considered include:* Application essay, class rank, recommendation(s), character/personal qualities, extracurricular activities, geographical residence, state residency, talent/ability, volunteer work, work experience. SAT or ACT required; ACT with writing component required. TOEFL required of all international applicants. High school diploma is required, and GED is accepted. *Academic units required:* 4 English, 4 mathematics, 3 science (2 science labs), 2 foreign language, 3 social studies, 3 academic elective. *Academic units recommended:* 4 English, 4 mathematics, 3 science (3 science labs), 4 foreign language, 3 social studies, 3 academic elective.

Financial Aid

Students should submit: FAFSA. The Princeton Review suggests that all financial aid forms be submitted as soon as possible after January 1. *Need-based scholarships/grants offered:* Federal Pell, SEOG, state scholarships/grants, private scholarships, school scholarship or grant aid from institutional funds. *Loan aid offered:* Direct Subsidized Stafford, Direct Unsubsidized Stafford, Direct PLUS, Federal Perkins, university loans from institutional funds. Applicants will be notified of awards on a rolling basis beginning March 15. Federal Work-Study Program available. Off-campus job opportunities are good.

The Inside Word

A traditional college-prep high school course load is required for admission to USF. Beyond making sure that you complete all prerequisite classes, however, keep two other things in mind when applying to USF. First, admissions decisions are made on a rolling basis, so the earlier one applies, the better his or her chance of acceptance since there are more unfilled seats early in the admissions cycle. Second, AP and international baccalaureate classes are looked on favorably in the admissions office, so if your school offers them, load up on them and do well.

THE SCHOOL SAYS "..."

From the Admissions Office

"Located in the Tampa Bay metropolitan area, USF is recognized as one of the nation's top research universities. USF takes great pride in its faculty. Professors in all academic areas are responsible for discovering new solutions to existing and emerging problems. As an undergraduate at USF, you can participate actively in the creation of the knowledge that will be taught on other college campuses for decades to come. And, the faculty at USF is diverse as well. Among top tier research universities, USF ranks third in the number of black faculty, seventh in the number of Hispanic faculty, and first in the number of female faculty.

"As students begin the application process, they should become familiar with USF's admission requirements. USF used extensive institutional research to validate that the high school GPA coupled with grade trends and the rigor of student's curriculum in high school are the most critical factors in student academic success at USF. Preference in admission, therefore, is given to students who complete at least three AP or IB courses, at least two college-level courses through dual enrollment, and additional coursework in math, science or foreign language beyond minimum requirements. "SAT and ACT scores, while important, are less critical in USF's admission decisions when the high school GPA and rigor of curriculum are both strong. USF does use the SAT writing and the ACT English/writing components to make decisions, as scores of 550 and 24 respectively are additional indicators of potential for academic success. USF also takes into account special talents in and outside of the classroom as well as whether a student would be in the first generation of the family to attend college.

"With some of the best weather in the country, it's always a great time to visit USF. Campus tours, information sessions and tours of the residence halls are offered on weekdays throughout the year and on most Saturday mornings from September through April. Reservations are strongly encouraged."

SELECTIVITY
Admissions Rating	85
# of applicants	26,366
% of applicants accepted	41
% of acceptees attending	39

FRESHMAN PROFILE
Range SAT Writing	530–620
Range ACT Composite	23–28
Minimum paper TOEFL	550
Minimum web-based TOEFL	79
Average HS GPA	3.78
% graduated top 10% of class	24
% graduated top 25% of class	57
% graduated top 50% of class	81

DEADLINES
Regular	
Priority	3/1
Deadline	3/1
Notification	10/1
Nonfall registration?	yes

APPLICANTS ALSO LOOK AT AND OFTEN PREFER
University of Florida

AND SOMETIMES PREFER
Florida State University, University of Central Florida

FINANCIAL FACTS
Financial Aid Rating	67
Annual in-state tuition	$5,200
Annual out-of-state tuition	$16,010
Room and board	$9,000
Books and supplies	$1,500
% frosh rec. need-based scholarship or grant aid	45
% UG rec. any financial aid	79

UNIVERSITY OF SOUTHERN CALIFORNIA

700 CHILDS WAY, LOS ANGELES, CA 90089-0911 • ADMISSIONS: 213-740-1111 • FAX: 213-740-6364

STUDENTS SAY ". . ."

Academics

The University of Southern California boasts "a dynamic and culturally diverse campus located in a world-class city which is equally dynamic and culturally diverse." Everything related to cinema is "top notch." Among the other 150 or so majors here, programs in journalism, business, engineering, and architecture are particularly notable. The honors programs are "very good," too. One of the best perks about USC is its "large and enthusiastic alumni network." Becoming "part of the Trojan Family" is a great way to jumpstart your career because USC graduates love to hire other USC graduates. "Almost everyone talks about getting job offers based solely on going to USC." "The school seems to run very smoothly, with few administrative issues ever being problematic enough to reach the awareness of the USC student community," says an international relations major. The top brass "is a bit mysterious and heavy handed," though. Also, "they milk every dime they can get from you." Academically, some students call the general education courses "a complete waste of time." There are a few "real narcissists" on the faculty as well as some professors "who seem to just be there because they want to do research." Overall, though, students report professors "make the subject matter come alive" and make themselves "very available" outside the classroom. "My academic experience at USC is fabulous," gushes an aerospace engineering major. "I would not choose any other school."

Life

On campus, life is "vibrant." There are more than 600 student organizations. Theatrical and musical productions are "excellent." School spirit is "extreme" and "infectious." "Football games are huge." "There is absolutely nothing that can top watching our unbelievable football team throttle the competition," says a merciless sophomore. "Drinking is a big part of the social scene" as well. "We definitely have some of the sickest parties ever," claims an impressed freshman. "Greek life is very big" and, on the weekends, a strong contingent of students "religiously" visits "The Row, the street lined with all the fraternity and sorority houses." Students also have "the sprawling city of Los Angeles as their playground." It's an "eclectic place with both high and low culture and some of the best shopping in the world." "Hollywood clubs and downtown bars" are popular destinations. Art exhibits, concerts, and "hip restaurants" are everywhere. However, "you need a car." Los Angeles traffic may be "a buzz kill" but students report that it's considerably preferable to the "absolutely terrible" public transportation system.

Student Body

The one thing that unites everyone here is "tons of Trojan pride." USC students are also "intensely ambitious" and, while there are some "complete slackers," many students hit the books "harder than they let on." Otherwise, students insist that, "contrary to popular belief, USC has immense diversity." "The stereotypical USC student is a surfer fraternity bro or a tan, trendy sorority girl from the O.C." You'll find plenty of those. Many students are also "extremely good looking." "No one cares what your orientation is," says a first-year student. There are "prissy Los Angeles types" and "spoiled" kids. In some circles, "family income and the brands of clothes you wear definitely matter." However, "though there are quite a few who come from mega wealth, there are also many who are here on a great deal of financial aid." There are "lots of nerds," too, and a smattering of "band geeks and film freaks."

UNIVERSITY OF SOUTHERN CALIFORNIA

FINANCIAL AID: 213-740-1111 • E-MAIL: ADMITUSC@USC.EDU • WEBSITE: WWW.USC.EDU

THE PRINCETON REVIEW SAYS
Admissions
Very important factors considered include: Academic GPA, application essay, recommendation(s), rigor of secondary school record, standardized test scores. *Important factors considered include:* Extracurricular activities, talent/ability. *Other factors considered include:* Class rank, alumni/ae relation, character/personal qualities, first generation, interview, racial/ethnic status, volunteer work, work experience. SAT or ACT required; ACT with writing component required. *Academic units required:* 4 English, 3 mathematics, 2 science (2 science labs), 2 foreign language, 2 social studies, 3 academic elective. *Academic units recommended:* 4 English, 4 mathematics, 3 science (3 science labs), 3 foreign language, 3 social studies, 3 history, 3 academic elective.

Financial Aid
Students should submit: FAFSA, CSS/Financial Aid PROFILE. The Princeton Review suggests that all financial aid forms be submitted as soon as possible after January 1. *Need-based scholarships/grants offered:* Federal Pell, SEOG, state scholarships/grants, private scholarships, school scholarship or grant aid from institutional funds. *Loan aid offered:* Direct Subsidized Stafford, Direct Unsubsidized Stafford, Direct PLUS, Federal Perkins. Applicants will be notified of awards on a rolling basis beginning March 15. Federal Work-Study Program available. Off-campus job opportunities are excellent.

The Inside Word
USC doesn't have the toughest admissions standards in California but it's up there. Your grades and test scores need to be outstanding to compete. Even if you are a borderline candidate, though, USC is certainly worth a shot. Few schools on the planet have a better alumni network and the "Trojan Family" really does create all kinds of opportunities for its members upon graduation.

THE SCHOOL SAYS "..."
From the Admissions Office
"One of the best ways to discover if USC is right for you is to walk around campus, talk to students, and get a feel for the area both as a place to study and a place to live. If you can't visit, we hold admission information programs around the country. Watch your mailbox for an invitation, or send us an e-mail if you're interested.

"Freshman applicants are required to submit a standardized writing exam. We will accept either the SAT or the ACT with its optional writing section."

SELECTIVITY
Admissions Rating	98
# of applicants	35,794
% of applicants accepted	24
% of acceptees attending	34

FRESHMAN PROFILE
Range SAT Critical Reading	620–720
Range SAT Math	640–740
Range SAT Writing	640–740
Range ACT Composite	29–32
Average HS GPA	3.69
% graduated top 10% of class	86
% graduated top 25% of class	97
% graduated top 50% of class	100

DEADLINES
Regular	
Priority	12/1
Deadline	1/10
Nonfall registration?	yes

APPLICANTS ALSO LOOK AT
AND OFTEN PREFER
Brown University, California Institute of Technology, Columbia University, Duke University, Harvard College, Massachusetts Institute of Technology, Stanford University, University of Pennsylvania, Yale University

AND SOMETIMES PREFER
Cornell University, Georgetown University, Johns Hopkins University, Northwestern University, Princeton University, Rice University, University of California—Berkeley, University of Virginia, Washington University in St. Louis

AND RARELY PREFER
Emory University, New York University, Univeristy of California—Los Angeles, University of California—San Diego, University of Michigan—Ann Arbor, Vanderbilt University

FINANCIAL FACTS
Financial Aid Rating	93
Annual tuition	$40,384
% frosh rec. need-based scholarship or grant aid	34
% UG rec. need-based scholarship or grant aid	36
% frosh rec. non-need-based scholarship or grant aid	21
% UG rec. non-need-based scholarship or grant aid	17
% frosh rec. need-based self-help aid	35
% UG rec. need-based self-help aid	38
% frosh rec. any financial aid	72
% UG rec. any financial aid	66
% UG borrow to pay for school	44
Average cumulative indebtedness	$30,090

THE BEST 376 COLLEGES ■ 715

THE UNIVERSITY OF TENNESSEE AT KNOXVILLE

320 STUDENT SERVICE BUILDING, CIRCLE PARK DRIVE, KNOXVILLE, TN 37996-0230 • ADMISSIONS: 865-974-2184

CAMPUS LIFE

Quality of Life Rating	74
Fire Safety Rating	83
Green Rating	88
Type of school	public
Environment	city

STUDENTS

Total undergrad enrollment	20,849
% male/female	51/49
% from out of state	13
% live on campus	26
# of fraternities	23
# of sororities	18
% African American	8
% Asian	3
% Caucasian	84
% Hispanic	2
% Native American	1
% international	1
# of countries represented	115

SURVEY SAYS . . .
Great library
Athletic facilities are great
Students are happy
Everyone loves the Volunteers
Student publications are popular

ACADEMICS

Academic Rating	71
% students graduating within 4 years	31
% students graduating within 6 years	61
Calendar	semester
Student/faculty ratio	16:1
Profs interesting rating	70
Profs accessible rating	75
Most common reg class size	20–29 students
Most common lab size	20–29 students

MOST POPULAR MAJORS
business administration and management, journalism, psychology

STUDENTS SAY ". . ."

Academics

The University of Tennessee "provides a family-like atmosphere full of opportunity and support!" Life at UT is all about "atmosphere, affordability, and school spirit." Many here tout "the school spirit and sense of community." In addition, the "in-state tuition and scholarship money" make "Tennessee a good deal for the amount you pay. I have fabulous teachers, great friends, fun activities to participate in, nice housing, a decent meal plan, and I pay $2,000 for all of it." "Although [UT is] a large school, you're not just a number; you're a face, a person, and a name." In general, "Professors greatly appreciate an appetite to learn, and they welcome challenges that help us learn and grow as students." Most are "very intelligent, open to debate, well-versed on their topics, and willing to meet with students outside of class for any reason." One student says, "The majority of my experience with academia and professors has been diverse and excellent." UT embraces a classic liberal arts core dedicated to "helping students find their passions by providing a friendly and intellectually enriching environment to learn, lead, and grow." UT offers "many opportunities for involvement" and "sets a high standard for success." Attending the UT "is about pursuing excellence in all areas of your life and using the knowledge you gain to prepare you for your future." It also "has a well-known medical program" and—for many—is "close to home."

Life

The typical UTK student "loves all aspects of the university's life from its sports to its long-standing traditions." Students flock here for "family history, athletics, and to sing 'Rocky Top.'" "We love football just about as much as academics." However, academics here are just as intense as athletics, "Being a larger university, I have had many more opportunities than people I know at smaller schools in education as well as extracurriculars." "The University of Tennessee combines the best of all worlds: great education for a great price, sports, social life, and a ton of extracurriculars to choose from." In fact, many say, "There are so many clubs and groups that on a social level UT doesn't feel large at all." "There's also a great selection of food and a wonderful gym." Life at UT is all "about education, community, and becoming a true Tennessee volunteer." "There's a great sense of unity." The faculty "tries extremely hard to encourage acceptance of several kinds of diversity." A "LGBTQ Resource Center [recently] opened on campus." "There is also a large 'Stop Bias' program that is promoted." In general, there are "tons of clubs and organizations to get involved with if you are passionate about something." If pressed to note a campus flaw, students say UT is "stuck between a river and downtown Knoxville, so it now has no room to expand and way too many hills. So they've crammed all these buildings into too small of a space."

Student Body

"There is not one 'popular' group of students. We have athletes, artists, musicians, dancers, religious students, scientists, Greeks, volunteers, etc." In general a live-and-let-live atmosphere pervades this "friendly" "energetic," "personable" campus; "All students fit in extremely well." The Greek community here "is especially prevalent." Some wonder "how non-Greeks fit in." "The conservative, upper-class attitude is definitely the one with the strongest voice." However, others counter this stalwart image. "The best thing about being an average student here? If you don't want to conform, you don't have to." "Once you go beyond the surface and away from the jocks and sorority girls, there are all types of students at UT." Others enthusiastically concede, "The literary snob crowd is small, but it's here, they do cool stuff, and they welcome new folks all the time with open arms." A typical student "studies hard, but parties even harder at the appropriate times." Classical entrees to social life include "to become part of the Greek system here or be an athlete." Most students exhibit the hallmark "Southern hospitality" and are "industrious, honest, charitable, and compassionate."

THE UNIVERSITY OF TENNESSEE AT KNOXVILLE

FINANCIAL AID: 865-974-3131 • E-MAIL: ADMISSIONS@UTK.EDU • WEBSITE: WWW.UTK.EDU

THE PRINCETON REVIEW SAYS

Admissions

Very important factors considered include: Academic GPA, rigor of secondary school record, standardized test scores. *Other factors considered include:* Application essay, class rank, recommendation(s), alumni/ae relation, character/personal qualities, extracurricular activities, first generation, geographical residence, level of applicant's interest, racial/ethnic status, state residency, talent/abili SAT or ACT required; ACT with or without writing component accepted. TOEFL required of all international applicants. High school diploma is required, and GED is accepted. *Academic units required:* 4 English, 3 mathematics, 2 science (1 science lab), 2 foreign language, 1 social studies, 1 history, 1 visual/performing arts.

Financial Aid

Students should submit: FAFSA. The Princeton Review suggests that all financial aid forms be submitted as soon as possible after January 1. *Need-based scholarships/grants offered:* Federal Pell, SEOG, state scholarships/grants, private scholarships, school scholarship or grant aid from institutional funds, Federal Nursing Scholarships. *Loan aid offered:* Direct Subsidized Stafford, Direct Unsubsidized Stafford, Direct PLUS, Federal Perkins, Federal Nursing Loans, university loans from institutional funds. Applicants will be notified of awards on a rolling basis beginning March 15. Off-campus job opportunities are fair.

The Inside Word

UT must winnow through more than 12,000 freshman applications each year. That sort of volume doesn't allow for nuance. Students with above-average high school GPAs (achieved in a reasonable college prep curriculum) and above-average standardized test scores pretty much all make the cut. The school will consider additional evidence of an applicant's potential (school and community involvement, awards, essays, special talents, and recommendations) in making admissions decisions, particularly for marginal candidates.

THE SCHOOL SAYS "..."

From the Admissions Office

"The University of Tennessee, Knoxville, offers students the great program diversity of a major university, opportunities for research or original creative work in every degree program, and a welcoming campus environment. Nine colleges offer more than 170 undergraduate majors and concentrations to students from all fifty states and 100 foreign countries, and UTK students can make the world their campus through study abroad programs. More than 400 clubs and organizations on campus allow students to further individualize their college experience in service, recreation, academics, and professional development. UTK blends more than 200 years of history, tradition, and 'Volunteer Spirit' with the latest technology and innovation."

SELECTIVITY

Admissions Rating	88
# of applicants	12,234
% of applicants accepted	73
% of acceptees attending	42

FRESHMAN PROFILE

Range SAT Critical Reading	510–640
Range SAT Math	530–650
Range ACT Composite	24–29
Minimum paper TOEFL	523
Minimum computer TOEFL	193
Minimum web-based TOEFL	70
Average HS GPA	3.78
% graduated top 10% of class	39
% graduated top 25% of class	70
% graduated top 50% of class	92

DEADLINES

Regular	
Deadline	12/1
Nonfall registration?	yes

FINANCIAL FACTS

Financial Aid Rating	80
Annual in-state tuition	$5,918
Annual out-of-state tuition	$19,714
Room and board	$6,652
Required fees	$932
Books and supplies	$1,366
% frosh rec. need-based scholarship or grant aid	51
% UG rec. need-based scholarship or grant aid	44
% frosh rec. need-based self-help aid	26
% UG rec. need-based self-help aid	31
% frosh rec. any financial aid	53
% UG rec. any financial aid	50
% UG borrow to pay for school	47
Average cumulative indebtedness	$24,593

THE UNIVERSITY OF TEXAS AT AUSTIN

PO Box 8058, Austin, TX 78713-8058 • Admissions: 512-475-7440 • Fax: 512-475-7475

CAMPUS LIFE
Quality of Life Rating	92
Fire Safety Rating	75
Green Rating	60*
Type of school	public
Environment	metropolis

STUDENTS
Total undergrad enrollment	36,711
% male/female	48/52
% from out of state	4
# of fraternities	26
# of sororities	22
% African American	5
% Asian	18
% Caucasian	54
% Hispanic	18
% international	4
# of countries represented	125

SURVEY SAYS . . .
Athletic facilities are great
Students love Austin, TX
Everyone loves the Longhorns
Student publications are popular
Political activism is popular

ACADEMICS
Academic Rating	71
% students graduating within 4 years	48
% students graduating within 6 years	78
Calendar	semester
Student/faculty ratio	17:1
Profs interesting rating	70
Profs accessible rating	62
Most common reg class size	10–19 students
Most common lab size	10–19 students

MOST POPULAR MAJORS
biology, business/commerce, liberal arts and sciences

STUDENTS SAY ". . ."

Academics
Students insist that the University of Texas at Austin has "everything you want in a college: academics, athletics, social life, location," and it's hard to argue with them. UT is "a huge school and has a lot to offer," meaning students have "an infinite number of possibilities open to them and can use them in their own way to figure out what they want for their lives." As one student tells us about arriving on campus, "I did not realize how much was available to me just as an enrolled student. There is free tutoring, gym membership, professional counseling, doctors visits, legal help, career advising, and many distinguished outside speakers. The campus is crawling with experts in every field you can imagine." Standout academic departments are numerous: from the sciences to the humanities to creative arts, UT makes a strong bid for the much-sought-after mantle of "Harvard of the south." Also, the school does a surprisingly good job of avoiding the factory-like feel of many large schools. One student observes: "Coming to a large university, there was a prejudgment that the huge classes will make it impossible to know your professor and vice versa. The university has dispelled that myth with professors who want to know you and [who] provide opportunities to get to know them." And while professors "can vary greatly across a spectrum from 'I'm smarter than him' to 'I want to follow in his footsteps,'" "the class offerings at UT are generally vast and diverse, and students can often avoid taking the less-qualified professors with a little research."

Life
Life at UT—Austin is "very relaxed…Students usually wear shorts and a t-shirt to class. When the weather gets cold, you might find students wearing the same shorts and T-shirt with a sweatshirt. Students and faculty frequently picnic all over campus. There are plenty of outdoor tables and grassy areas to sit." Undergrads "are often found throwing a Frisbee outside the tower or taking a nap under a tree. It's truly what you see in one of those cheesy brochures with everyone studying and smiling. Of course, the smiles aren't so bright during finals. We switch to an over-caffeinated, glazed-eye look instead." Hometown Austin "provides a social education that a college student newly out on his own would not find anywhere else," with "festivals or fairs of some kind going on downtown all the time" and "the infamous 6th Street with nightlife that dies down only after the bars close." Campus and the surrounding area offer "many hike-and-bike trails and fitness organizations. It's possible for students to train for marathons, half marathons, and triathlons while in school. Barton Springs pool is a natural spring that is very popular year-round. On any giving Saturday you will find students throwing a football, going for a run, biking through the hills, kayaking in the river, having a late lunch at one of Austin's great restaurants, or just sleeping in."

Student Body
"Because of the huge Greek life at UT, a 'typical student' would be a sorority girl or fraternity boy," but—and it's a big but—such students "are hardly the majority, since UT is actually made of more 'atypical' people than most other schools. Everyone here has his own niche, and I could not think of any type of individual who would not be able to find one of his own." Indeed, "Everyone at Texas is different! When you walk across campus, you see every type of ethnicity. There are a lot of minorities at Texas. Also, I see many disabled people, whom the school accommodates well. Everyone seems to get along. The different types of students just blend in together." Especially by Texas standards, "Austin is known for being 'weird.' If you see someone dressed in a way you've never seen before, you just shrug it off and say 'That's Austin!'"

THE UNIVERSITY OF TEXAS AT AUSTIN

FINANCIAL AID: 512-475-6282 • WEBSITE: WWW.UTEXAS.EDU

THE PRINCETON REVIEW SAYS

Admissions

Very important factors considered include: Class rank, rigor of secondary school record. *Important factors considered include:* Application essay, standardized test scores, extracurricular activities, talent/ability, volunteer work, work experience. *Other factors considered include:* Recommendation(s), character/personal qualities, first generation, level of applicant's interest, racial/ethnic status, state residency. SAT or ACT required; ACT with writing component required. TOEFL required of all international applicants. High school diploma is required, and GED is accepted. *Academic units required:* Applicants must meet the state's requirements of 4 English, 4 mathematics, 4 sciences, 3.5 social studies, 0.5 economics, 1 physical education, 1 fine arts, 2 foreign language, 0.5 speech, 6 electives. (Exemptions are available.)

Financial Aid

Students should submit: FAFSA. The Princeton Review suggests that all financial aid forms be submitted as soon as possible after January 1. *Need-based scholarships/grants offered:* Federal Pell, SEOG, state scholarships/grants, private scholarships, school scholarship or grant aid from institutional funds. *Loan aid offered:* Direct Subsidized Stafford, Direct Unsubsidized Stafford, Direct PLUS, Federal Perkins, state loans. Applicants will be notified of awards on a rolling basis beginning March 15. Federal Work-Study Program not available. Off-campus job opportunities are fair.

The Inside Word

The university is required to automatically admit enough Texas applicants to fill seventy-five percent of available spaces set aside for students from Texas. The university will admit applicants from Texas who are in the top nine percent of their high school class for the summer/fall 2012 and the spring 2013 entering freshman class. The rank needed for automatic admission for future classes will be announced each September. All students, including those eligible for automatic admission, should submit the strongest possible application to increase the likelihood of admission to the university and to their requested major. Admissions are quite competitive. Space for out-of-state students is limited, meaning they'll have even higher hurdles to clear.

THE SCHOOL SAYS "..."

From the Admissions Office

"For more than 120 years, students from all over the world have come to The University of Texas at Austin to obtain a first-class education. Recognized for research, teaching, and public service, the university boasts more than 130 undergraduate academic programs, more than 350 study abroad programs, outstanding student services, cultural centers, and volunteer and leadership opportunities designed to prepare students to make a difference in the world. Along with its nationally ranked athletic programs, the university's spirit is enhanced by cultural, artistic, and scientific opportunities that help to make Austin one of the most inviting destinations in the country. The Performing Arts Center hosts plays, Austin's opera and symphony, and visiting musical and dance groups. Students access more than eight million volumes in the university's seventeen libraries and study prehistoric fossils at the Texas Memorial Museum, Renaissance and Baroque paintings in the Blanton Museum, original manuscripts at the Ransom Center, and life in the 1960s at the Lyndon B. Johnson Library and Museum. Each year the university enrolls about 50,000 students from richly varied ethnic and geographic backgrounds. Every day graduates contribute to the world community as volunteers, teachers, journalists, artists, engineers, business leaders, scientists, and lawyers. With world-renowned faculty, top-rated academic programs, successful alumni, and such an enticing location, it's no surprise that The University of Texas at Austin ranks among the best universities in the world."

SELECTIVITY

Admissions Rating	91
# of applicants	29,501
% of applicants accepted	44
% of acceptees attending	52

FRESHMAN PROFILE

Range SAT Critical Reading	540–660
Range SAT Math	570–690
Range SAT Writing	540–670
Range ACT Composite	24–30
Minimum paper TOEFL	550
Minimum computer TOEFL	213
Minimum web-based TOEFL	79
% graduated top 10% of class	75
% graduated top 25% of class	95
% graduated top 50% of class	99

DEADLINES

Regular Deadline	12/15
Nonfall registration?	yes

FINANCIAL FACTS

Financial Aid Rating	90
Annual in-state tuition	$8,986
Annual out-of-state tuition	$31,218
Room and board	$10,112
Books and supplies	$874
% frosh rec. need-based scholarship or grant aid	57
% UG rec. need-based scholarship or grant aid	44
% frosh rec. need-based self-help aid	60
% UG rec. need-based self-help aid	51
% frosh rec. any financial aid	60
% UG rec. any financial aid	54
% UG borrow to pay for school	42
Average cumulative indebtedness	$17,000

UNIVERSITY OF TORONTO

172 GEORGE STREET, TORONTO, ON M5R0A3 • ADMISSIONS: 416-978-2190 • FAX: 416-978-7022

STUDENTS SAY ". . ."

Academics

With "an excellent reputation and a huge selection of courses" as well as "a world-class city" to call home, the University of Toronto "provides expert knowledge in every field" to its 50,000-plus undergraduates and nearly 11,000 graduate students. True, it can be "hard to relate to the instructors given that the class sizes are so huge," and those looking for an intimate and supportive academic environment might not find a good fit at U of T. "The general attitude is one of professionalism and very little mercy [here]." Still, self-starters will find the limitless opportunities outweigh the drawbacks. As one puts it, "Most of the professors are premier representatives of their respective industries." Another adds, "The fact that you are learning from Nobel Prize winners in a city full of adventures is unbeatable." "Excellent research facilities" are among the other assets here. The school also capitalizes on its location in the center of Toronto: "The city and the university draw on each other in a variety of ways—clinical opportunities and research flow in both directions." On top of that, industrious undergrads tell us, "The libraries and other research facilities here are excellent and contribute much to the overall academic experience."

Life

When they aren't hitting the books, University of Toronto students enjoy life in "one of the coolest cities in North America" where "there's always something new happening: the Toronto International Film Festival, skating in Nathan Phillips Square, etc." Students benefit from the fact that "the Royal Ontario Museum is on campus, a ton of pubs and art galleries are within walking distance, and a nightlife to suit just about any type of person" can be found in Toronto. When it comes to campus life, many students feel the school's spirit and unity is negatively affected by the large number of commuter students. "Off-campus students, of whom there are many, rarely participate in extracurricular activities," one student complains adds that "Interest in varsity sports is just pathetic" among all undergraduates. Others focus on the positives, pointing out the social and recreational opportunities available to those willing to look. A junior says, "Getting involved here takes some research in terms of navigating the 300 clubs and endless academic/research opportunities, but once I did some searching, I found several places where I fit in well and have fun." For those who live on campus, sororities and fraternities help nurture social bonds, and "most of the residential colleges have tons of events, from campus-wide capture the flag [games] to movie nights" or "intramural sports."

Student Body

At this large public school, the demographics on campus reflect those of surrounding Toronto, "one of the most diverse cities around." As one junior puts it, "It can be said that all students here have in common an excellent academic record prior to university. Beyond that, anything goes: There are huge variances in race, religion, sexual orientation, academic focus, postgraduate aspirations, socioeconomic background, disability, nationality, athleticism, and community involvement." A freshman chimes in, "On my floor alone there are kids from at least ten different countries and, even with the different cultures, we have blended together to make a big family." Most students say it's relatively easy to find a social group among like-minded individuals, despite the school's impressive size and diversity. According to one senior, "Most students will find a niche where they feel comfortable; there's a place for everyone."

UNIVERSITY OF TORONTO

FINANCIAL AID: 416-978-2190 • E-MAIL: ADMISSIONS.HELP@UTORONTO.CA • WEBSITE: WWW.UTORONTO.CA

THE PRINCETON REVIEW SAYS
Admissions
Very important factors considered include: Academic GPA, standardized test scores. SAT or ACT required; ACT with writing component required. TOEFL required of all international applicants. High school diploma is required, and GED is accepted.

Financial Aid
The Princeton Review suggests that all financial aid forms be submitted as soon as possible after January 1. U.S. citizens can apply for financial assistance from the U.S. Federal Family Education Program (FFELP). University of Toronto is a recognized post-secondary institution for Federal Stafford Loans (PLUS, Subsidized, and Unsubsidized). Education Savings Plans and U.S. Federal Education Tax credits are also applicable. Complete details can be found at www.adm.utoronto.ca. To obtain a study permit, international students must demonstrate to Citizenship and Immigration Canada (www.cic.gc.ca) that they have sufficient resources to cover tuition and expenses for at least one year of university.

The Inside Word
University of Toronto takes a numbers-based approach to admissions. American students must submit not only high school transcripts and SAT/ACT scores but also results for three SAT subject tests/APs/IBs. Only those who perform well by all these metrics are likely to gain admission. Candidates should be aware that qualifications vary from program to program, and as an international student you'll have more paperwork to file. The University of Toronto is a recognized postsecondary institution for Federal Stafford Loans. All applicants are automatically considered for admission scholarships.

THE SCHOOL SAYS "..."
From the Admissions Office
"The University of Toronto is committed to being an internationally significant research university with undergraduate, graduate, and professional programs of study.

"For arts, science, commerce/management, concurrent teacher education, music, physical education & health/kinesiology, U.S. Grade 12 in an accredited high school with a high grade point average and high scores on SAT Reasoning/ACT exams and a minimum of two appropriate SAT Subject Tests/APs/IBs (or a combination of SAT Subject Tests/APs/IBs covering different subjects). English Grade 12/AP is required for all programs. Those seeking admission to science or commerce programs are strongly advised to complete AP Calculus.

"The minimum admission requirements are an excellent CGPA and Grade 12 GPA; scores of at least 1800 on SAT Reasoning and 26 on the ACT; no score below 500 on SAT Subject Tests. SAT scores below 500 in any part of the SAT Reasoning or Subject Tests are not acceptable.

"For engineering, applicants must present AP/IB Calculus, as well as AP/IB or SAT Subject Tests in both chemistry and physics. English Grade 12/AP is required for all programs. Applicants seeking admission to engineering after one year of university in the U.S. are required to present a GPA of at least 3.5 with two semesters of math, physics and chemistry. Refer to www.engineering.utoronto.ca for complete information."

SELECTIVITY

Admissions Rating	60*
# of applicants	63,955
% of applicants accepted	71
% of acceptees attending	30

FRESHMAN PROFILE

Minimum paper TOEFL	600
Minimum computer TOEFL	250

DEADLINES

Regular	
Deadline	3/1
Notification	3/15
Nonfall registration?	no

FINANCIAL FACTS

Financial Aid Rating	60*
Annual in-state tuition	$5,331
Annual out-of-state tuition	$23,994
Room and board	$8,165–$14,148
Books and supplies	$1,500

THE UNIVERSITY OF TULSA

800 SOUTH TUCKER DRIVE, TULSA, OK 74104 • ADMISSIONS: 918-631-2307 • FAX: 918-631-5003

CAMPUS LIFE
Quality of Life Rating	89
Fire Safety Rating	88
Green Rating	76
Type of school	private
Affiliation	Presbyterian
Environment	metropolis

STUDENTS
Total undergrad enrollment	3,059
% male/female	55/45
% from out of state	42
% from public high school	75
% live on campus	72
# of fraternities	7
# of sororities	9
% African American	5
% Asian	3
% Caucasian	62
% Hispanic	4
% Native American	4
% international	16
# of countries represented	62

SURVEY SAYS . . .
Great computer facilities
Athletic facilities are great
Students are friendly
Students get along with local community
Students are happy

ACADEMICS
Academic Rating	85
% students graduating within 4 years	47
% students graduating within 6 years	65
Calendar	semester
Student/faculty ratio	11:1
Profs interesting rating	86
Profs accessible rating	85
Most common reg class size	10–19 students
Most common lab size	10–19 students

MOST POPULAR MAJORS
business administration and management, petroleum engineering, psychology

STUDENTS SAY ". . ."

Academics
The University of Tulsa is a mid-size, private school that provides a superior learning environment and a myriad of academic opportunities to its 3,000 undergraduate students. Across disciplines, the academic experience is high quality and stimulating, incorporating "rigorous and invigorating lectures and well instructed lab periods." In addition to coursework, undergraduates benefit from unmatched "academic and professional opportunities reserved only for graduate students at other schools." A current student attests, "I had no trouble getting undergraduate research experience in biochemistry as early as sophomore year." Students rave about TU's outgoing professors, saying that "the faculty and staff at TU seem to take a personal interest in the students here. They are accessible and love to help students in any way possible, not only academically, but professionally and personally as well." How's this for involved? "I have even received a text message from a professor when I forgot to turn in a homework assignment," reports a sophomore. While course selection is occasionally limited by the school's size, "professors will frequently tailor independent study projects with students." When it comes to the administration, some students worry that they are too preoccupied with improving the college's rankings. Others insist that the administrative offices are just as student-friendly as the teaching staff. A sophomore shares, "I became involved in student government my third semester here, and I am so impressed by how accessible the administration is. The deans and president of the university really care about students."

Life
Student life at TU reflects the school's unequivocal emphasis on academics. Studious undergraduates agree that the University of Tulsa "is definitely not a big party school. Most of the students here are focused on studies." Nonetheless, there are plenty of opportunities for extracurricular involvement, and campus clubs range "from honor societies to multicultural groups to religious gatherings." The campus isn't too big, so students looking for leadership experience will be pleased to learn that "anyone can be involved and 'be someone' on campus." In addition to student clubs, "collegiate, intramural, and pick-up sports are really popular." About twenty percent of the campus is involved in a Greek organization, and "a lot of student life revolves strongly around sororities and fraternities." However, students reassure us that "even non-Greek students can visit the houses and hang out on a Friday night." If you don't feel like partying at fraternities, there's plenty more to do, on and off campus. A sophomore shares, "For fun my friends and I go bowling, explore the parks of Tulsa, watch movies, do arts and crafts, and go to the occasional party." While students readily admit that Tulsa isn't New York City, they appreciate the myriad of pleasures of their manageable mid-size city, which boasts "some really great restaurants and coffee shops around TU and in historic Tulsa."

Student Body
Defined in broad strokes, most TU undergraduates hail from affluent, Christian families in the Midwest. However, TU students insist that, while there are some similarities within the campus community, they cannot be summed up so easily. In addition to the array of "jocks, computer geeks, fashionistas, 'good' students, loners, and partygoers," The University of Tulsa has a "strong international community. Programs such as the petroleum engineering department attract a diverse international populace. One can hear five different languages simply walking to class!" Thanks, in part, to the international students, there is "a diverse religious life on campus, several activist groups that meet on campus, and countless student organizations." No matter what your background, "The majority of students I know at TU are very open and accepting of everyone else, regardless of religion, race, sexual orientation, athletic ability, major, and Greek affiliation." In fact, it's easy to feel at home on the TU campus. A junior explains, "Because the campus is small, even if you don't know somebody's name, you normally recognize their face from somewhere; this leads to a great sense of community."

FINANCIAL AID: 918-631-2526 • E-MAIL: ADMISSION@UTULSA.EDU • WEBSITE: WWW.UTULSA.EDU

THE PRINCETON REVIEW SAYS

Admissions

Very important factors considered include: Academic GPA, class rank, rigor of secondary school record, standardized test scores, level of applicant's interest. *Important factors considered include:* Application essay, recommendation(s), character/personal qualities, interview. *Other factors considered include:* Alumni/ae relation, extracurricular activities, first generation, racial/ethnic status, talent/ability, volunteer work, work experience. SAT or ACT required; ACT with or without writing component accepted. TOEFL required of all international applicants. High school diploma is required, and GED is accepted. *Academic units recommended:* 4 English, 3 mathematics, 3 science (2 science labs), 2 foreign language, 3 social studies, 1 computer science.

Financial Aid

Students should submit: FAFSA. The Princeton Review suggests that all financial aid forms be submitted as soon as possible after January 1. *Need-based scholarships/grants offered:* Federal Pell, SEOG, state scholarships/grants, private scholarships, school scholarship or grant aid from institutional funds. *Loan aid offered:* Direct Subsidized Stafford, Direct Unsubsidized Stafford, Direct PLUS, Federal Perkins. Applicants will be notified of awards on a rolling basis beginning March 1. Federal Work-Study Program available. Off-campus job opportunities are good.

The Inside Word

TU is a university with solid academic offerings, a strong sense of community, lots of student-faculty interaction, and attainable admission standards. The school's commitment to undergrads is clear. One of TU's most impressive programs, The Tulsa Undergraduate Research Challenge (TURC), allows undergrads to complete research along with faculty.

THE SCHOOL SAYS " . . . "

From the Admissions Office

"The University of Tulsa is a private university with a comprehensive scope. Students choose from more than eighty majors offered through three undergraduate colleges—Arts and Sciences, Business Administration, and Engineering and Natural Sciences. Curricula can be customized with collaborative research, joint undergraduate and graduate programs, and an honors program, among others. Professors are equally committed to teaching undergraduates and to scholarly research. This results in extraordinary individual achievement, resulting in the nationally competitive scholarships students have won since 1995: forty-six Goldwaters, thirty-one National Science Foundation scholars, nine Trumans, seven Department of Defense scholars, seven Fulbrights, eight Phi Kappa Phi, six Udalls, and four British Marshalls. Over the past decade over 700,000 square feet of facilities have been added costing over $200 million. These include athletic venues, 400 additional apartments, fitness center, Legal Information Center, literacy expansion and renovation, and a new performing arts center. Over 160 registered clubs, and interest groups, including intramural and recreational sports teams exist along with six fraternities and nine sororities. The 8,300 seat Reynolds Center is home to the standout Golden Hurricane NCAA Division I men's basketball team, campus events, and concerts. A forty-acre sports complex includes the fitness center and indoor tennis center that hosted the 2008 NCAA Division I Men's and Women's tennis finals. An outdoor freshman orientation program launches an entire first-year experience dedicated to developing students' full potential.

"Applicants are required to submit the SAT or ACT. The writing component is not required. For admission and scholarship review, the best composite score of submitted tests will be used."

SELECTIVITY

Admissions Rating	95
# of applicants	5,737
% of applicants accepted	39
% of acceptees attending	30
# accepting a place on wait list	285
% admitted from wait list	62

FRESHMAN PROFILE

Range SAT Critical Reading	560–700
Range SAT Math	570–700
Range ACT Composite	26–32
Minimum paper TOEFL	500
Minimum computer TOEFL	173
Minimum web-based TOEFL	61
Average HS GPA	3.80
% graduated top 10% of class	74
% graduated top 25% of class	94
% graduated top 50% of class	99

DEADLINES

Early action	
Deadline	11/1
Notification	11/22
Regular	
Priority	2/1
Notification	12/1
Nonfall registration?	yes

APPLICANTS ALSO LOOK AT
AND OFTEN PREFER
Oklahoma State University, Southern Methodist University, Texas Christian University, University of Oklahoma

AND SOMETIMES PREFER
Baylor University, Tulane University, Washington University in St. Louis

AND RARELY PREFER
Texas A&M University—College Station, University of Kansas, University of Missouri—Columbia

FINANCIAL FACTS

Financial Aid Rating	89
Annual tuition	$30,866
Room and board	$9,464
Required fees	$685
Books and supplies	$1,200
% frosh rec. need-based scholarship or grant aid	19
% UG rec. need-based scholarship or grant aid	19
% frosh rec. non-need-based scholarship or grant aid	87
% UG rec. non-need-based scholarship or grant aid	77
% frosh rec. need-based self-help aid	37
% UG rec. need-based self-help aid	34
% frosh rec. any financial aid	94
% UG rec. any financial aid	88
% UG borrow to pay for school	52
Average cumulative indebtedness	$29,684

UNIVERSITY OF UTAH

201 SOUTH 1460 EAST, ROOM 250 S, SALT LAKE CITY, UT 84112 • ADMISSIONS: 801-581-7281 • FAX: 801-585-7864

CAMPUS LIFE

Quality of Life Rating	76
Fire Safety Rating	91
Green Rating	89
Type of school	public
Environment	metropolis

STUDENTS

Total undergrad enrollment	23,370
% male/female	55/45
% from out of state	20
% from public high school	94
% live on campus	13
# of fraternities	7
# of sororities	6
% African American	1
% Asian	4
% Caucasian	77
% Hispanic	6
% Native American	1
% international	6
# of countries represented	129

SURVEY SAYS . . .

Registration is a breeze
Great computer facilities
Great library
Students get along with local
community
Students love Salt Lake City, UT
Great off-campus food
Campus feels safe
Students are happy
Everyone loves the Utes
Student publications are popular

ACADEMICS

Academic Rating	69
% students graduating	
within 4 years	23
% students graduating	
within 6 years	57
Calendar	semester
Student/faculty ratio	15:1
Profs interesting rating	73
Profs accessible rating	66
Most common	
reg class size	20–29 students
Most common	
lab size	20–29 students

MOST POPULAR MAJORS
economics, mass communication/media
studies, psychology

STUDENTS SAY " . . . "

Academics

Nestled amid Salt Lake City's snowcapped mountains, the University of Utah is a large public school that offers extensive academic programs, ample research opportunities, and a surprisingly student-friendly atmosphere. No matter what your interests, you'll find like minds at U of U. "I have studied everything from Tai Chi/Yoga movement and stage combat to differential equations and linear algebra," says a junior. "The one thing that has remained consistent throughout is the appreciation and dedication the people have for the topic they are involved in." U of U is a research university that actually takes teaching seriously, and "every teacher that I've had shows incredible knowledge in their area, as well as personality and wit." "Classes are informative, challenging, and genuinely enjoyable." As is the case in many larger universities, "most general education courses are taught by grad students," whose teaching abilities can range from great to below average. "Ninety percent of my professors are fantastic; the ones that aren't are usually grad students," explains a junior. On this large campus, students have little contact with the school's administration and "there's definitely no hand-holding at the U of U. If you're unsure of your major or career plans, it's easy to slip through the cracks." However, students assure us. "The administration puts student interests first whenever possible with a focus on keeping tuition low, creating a diverse environment, and providing opportunities and experience in order to prepare students to be productive citizens."

Life

While a large percentage of the undergraduate community at the University of Utah commutes to campus, there are still plenty of activities for the school's 4,000 resident students. There are many people "active in politics, environmental issues, and international issues," and, after hours, "the school holds different events throughout the year, such as Crimson Nights that feature activities such as bowling, crafts, games, food, and music." Socially, "Greek life is not as large as at other schools but is definitely a lot of fun and the best way to get to know more people your age." In addition, "during football season there are great tailgate parties with friends, drinks, and food." Right off campus, there are a range of great restaurants, and "the nightlife is hard to keep up with." There's always something good going on—whether it's at the bars and clubs downtown, or at small music venues." For outdoorsy types, U of U is a paradise. "We have all four seasons and some of the best outdoors in the nation," explains one student. "Killer snow, amazing hills, mountains, lakes, and streams." In this natural wonderland, "hiking, biking, boating, snow-skiing, and snowboarding are just a few of the hundreds of activities available to students."

Student Body

Located in Salt Lake City, hometown to the Church of Latter Day Saints, "a majority of students at the U of U are Mormon, but not a vast majority. There are plenty of social niches to fall into, and none of them are rigidly exclusive." A current student adds, "About half the student body is the typical Utah Mormon, and the other half is a mix of everything. The two halves usually stay separate but they get along." U of U students agree that "there is more diversity here than in any other part of the state." However, out-of-state students are uncommon, and "those of us not from Utah are definitely in the minority." While there are a number of residential students, a very large percentage of students also chose to commute to school while living with their parents or family. In addition, "there are a lot of older students and a lot of married students." Academically, however, U of U undergraduates are "independent, smart, and come to class ready to discuss ideas."

FINANCIAL AID: 801-581-6211 • E-MAIL: FAWIN1@SA.UTAH.EDU • WEBSITE: WWW.UTAH.EDU

THE PRINCETON REVIEW SAYS

Admissions

Very important factors considered include: Academic GPA, rigor of secondary school record, standardized test scores. *Important factors considered include:* Talent/ability. *Other factors considered include:* Class rank, recommendation(s), extracurricular activities, interview, racial/ethnic status. SAT or ACT required; ACT with or without writing component accepted. TOEFL required of all international applicants. High school diploma is required, and GED is accepted. *Academic units required:* 4 English, 2 mathematics, 3 science (1 science lab), 2 foreign language, 1 history, 4 academic elective.

Financial Aid

Students should submit: FAFSA, institution's own financial aid form. The Princeton Review suggests that all financial aid forms be submitted as soon as possible after January 1. *Need-based scholarships/grants offered:* Federal Pell, SEOG, state scholarships/grants, private scholarships, school scholarship or grant aid from institutional funds, Federal Nursing Scholarships. *Loan aid offered:* Direct Subsidized Stafford, Direct Unsubsidized Stafford, Direct PLUS, Federal Perkins, Federal Nursing Loans, university loans from institutional funds. Applicants will be notified of awards on a rolling basis beginning April 15. Federal Work-Study Program available. Off-campus job opportunities are excellent.

The Inside Word

Utah is another state in which low numbers of high school grads keep selectivity down at its public flagship university. Admission is based primarily on the big three: Course selection, grades, and test scores. If you have a 3.0 GPA or better and average test scores, you're close to a sure bet for admission.

THE SCHOOL SAYS "..."

From the Admissions Office

"The University of Utah is a distinctive community of learning in the American West. Today's 30,819 students are from every state and 129 foreign countries. The university has research ties worldwide, with national standing among the top comprehensive research institutions. The university offers 100 undergraduate and more than ninety graduate degree programs. Nationally recognized honors and undergraduate research programs stimulate intellectual inquiry. Undergraduates collaborate with faculty on important investigations. In 2011–2012, the university's intercollegiate athletes will begin competing in the NCAA PAC-12 Conference. The football team has been nationally ranked for several years, as have our women's gymnastics and skiing teams. The university's location in Salt Lake City provides easy access to the arts, theater, Utah Jazz basketball, and hockey. Utah's great outdoors—skiing, hiking, and five national parks—are nearby. The university was the site for the opening and closing ceremonies and the Athletes Village for the 2002 Winter Olympic Games.

"Housing and residential education has greatly expanded the opportunity for students to live on campus with a new and wide variety of housing. Heritage Commons, constructed during the 2002 Olympics, is located in historic Fort Douglas on campus, and consists of twenty-one buildings, which accommodate more than 2,500 students. The university also has apartment housing available for students located minutes from campus in downtown Salt Lake City. In addition, construction is underway for a 'living/learning community' that will house approximately 300 honors students.

"Applicants are required to submit ACT scores. SAT scores are also accepted, although ACT scores are preferred. Students are urged to take the ACT near the end of their junior year or early in the senior year of high school."

SELECTIVITY

Admissions Rating	80
# of applicants	8,364
% of applicants accepted	83
% of acceptees attending	45

FRESHMAN PROFILE

Range SAT Critical Reading	490–630
Range SAT Math	510–630
Range SAT Writing	490–610
Range ACT Composite	21–27
Minimum paper TOEFL	500
Minimum web-based TOEFL	61
Average HS GPA	3.52
% graduated top 10% of class	26
% graduated top 25% of class	50
% graduated top 50% of class	82

DEADLINES

Regular	
Priority	12/15
Deadline	4/1
Nonfall registration?	yes

FINANCIAL FACTS

Financial Aid Rating	72
Annual in-state tuition	$5,850
Annual out-of-state tuition	$20,476
Room and board	$6,699
Required fees	$913
Books and supplies	$1,090
% frosh rec. need-based scholarship or grant aid	32
% UG rec. need-based scholarship or grant aid	34
% frosh rec. non-need-based scholarship or grant aid	2
% UG rec. non-need-based scholarship or grant aid	1
% frosh rec. need-based self-help aid	25
% UG rec. need-based self-help aid	31
% frosh rec. any financial aid	39
% UG rec. any financial aid	42
% UG borrow to pay for school	42
Average cumulative indebtedness	$17,343

UNIVERSITY OF VERMONT

194 SOUTH PROSPECT STREET, BURLINGTON, VT 05401-3596 • ADMISSIONS: 802-656-3370 • FAX: 802-656-8611

CAMPUS LIFE

Quality of Life Rating	79
Fire Safety Rating	87
Green Rating	91
Type of school	public
Environment	town

STUDENTS

Total undergrad enrollment	10,461
% male/female	44/56
% from out of state	66
% from public high school	70
% live on campus	51
# of fraternities	9
# of sororities	6
% African American	1
% Asian	2
% Caucasian	87
% Hispanic	4
% international	1
# of countries represented	51

SURVEY SAYS . . .

Students are friendly
Students love Burlington, VT
Great off-campus food
Political activism is popular
Lots of beer drinking
Hard liquor is popular

ACADEMICS

Academic Rating	71
% students graduating within 4 years	61
% students graduating within 6 years	77
Calendar	semester
Student/faculty ratio	17:1
Profs interesting rating	75
Profs accessible rating	76
Most common reg class size	10–19 students
Most common lab size	10–19 students

MOST POPULAR MAJORS

biology, business administration and management, psychology

STUDENTS SAY ". . ."

Academics

Quality of life issues are important to most University of Vermont undergrads; when discussing their reasons for choosing UVM, they're as likely to cite the "laid-back environment," the "proximity to skiing facilities," the "great parties," and their "amazing" hometown of Burlington as they are to mention the academics. But, students remind us, "That doesn't mean that there are not strong academics [at UVM]." On the contrary, UVM is made up of several well-established colleges and offers "a wide variety of majors." "You can jump around between majors, and then leave with a recognized diploma in hand for something you love to do." Students single out the business school, the "top-notch" education program, the psychology department, premedical sciences, and "the amazing animal science program" for praise, and are especially proud of The Rubenstein School of Natural Resources. It's home to UVM's environmental science majors; students tell us it "is a great college that feels like it's much smaller, [more] separate, and just cozier than the rest of the school." No matter which discipline, "You get out what you put in." "Teachers are readily available and are willing to help you do well in your classes. They encourage you to get help if you need it and are enthusiastic about what they teach. It's all there; you just have to take advantage of it." The size of the university, we're told, is just right. UVM is "a moderately large school," and it allows undergrads "to feel at home while still offering just about any activity possible."

Life

"UVM is known to be a party school," "even though the university has cracked down on drinking." Indeed, students tell us that one can find "a good balance of having fun and academics" at UVM, "but it's tough, because there's always a party going on somewhere." Students who want to dodge the party scene will find "there is always something" happening in Burlington. The town has "lots of wonderful restaurants, a few movie theaters, a rockin' music scene, several bars, some dancing, and various environmental and social activities downtown." "On campus, there is typically at least one university-sponsored event each night, including interesting lectures, movies, games, or social events." Students love outdoor activities. "When it snows, it's very popular to go to the ski resorts around here and ski or snowboard for the day. When it's still warm out, going to the waterfront and swimming in Lake Champlain is popular too." UVM is an intercollegiate hockey powerhouse, and "in the fall and winter, hockey games are huge social events." They're so popular "that you have to get tickets to them the Monday before the game, or they will be sold out!"

Student Body

There's a "great variety of students" at UVM "because it's a big university," undergrads report, but they also note that "students at UVM are mostly white" and there's "a lot of money at this school." While the most prevalent UVM archetype is "the guitar-loving, earth-saving, relaxed hippie" who "care[s] strongly about the environment" and "social justice," the student body also includes "your athletic types, your artsy people, and a number of other groups" including "vocal LGBTQ and ALANA populations" who, "usually hang out in their own groups," but "are also active in all sorts of clubs across campus." Not surprisingly, there are many "New England types," "potheads," and "snow bums." Students report they "pretty much get along well with everyone." They either come here loving the outdoors or learn to love the outdoors by the time they leave.

FINANCIAL AID: 802-656-3156 • E-MAIL: ADMISSIONS@UVM.EDU • WEBSITE: WWW.UVM.EDU

THE PRINCETON REVIEW SAYS
Admissions
Very important factors considered include: Rigor of secondary school record. *Important factors considered include:* Academic GPA, application essay, class rank, standardized test scores, character/personal qualities, state residency. *Other factors considered include:* Class rank, recommendation(s), alumni/ae relation, extracurricular activities, first generation, geographical residence, interview, level of applicant's interest, racial/ethnic status, talent/ability, volunteer work, work experience. SAT or ACT required; ACT with writing component required. TOEFL required of all international applicants. High school diploma is required, and GED is accepted. *Academic units required:* 4 English, 3 mathematics, 2 science (1 science lab), 2 foreign language, 3 social studies.

Financial Aid
Students should submit: FAFSA. The Princeton Review suggests that all financial aid forms be submitted as soon as possible after January 1. *Need-based scholarships/grants offered:* Federal Pell, SEOG, state scholarships/grants, private scholarships, school scholarship or grant aid from institutional funds, Federal Nursing Scholarships. *Loan aid offered:* Federal Perkins, Federal Nursing Loans, university loans from institutional funds. Applicants will be notified of awards on a rolling basis beginning March 15. Federal Work-Study Program available. Off-campus job opportunities are good.

The Inside Word
UVM is a very popular choice among out-of-state students, whom the school welcomes; more than half the student body originates from outside of Vermont. While admissions standards are significantly more rigorous for out-of-staters, solid candidates (B-plus/A-minus average, about a 600 on each section of the SAT) should do fine here. The school assesses applications holistically, meaning students who are weak in one area may be able to make up for it with strengths or distinguishing skills and characteristics in other areas.

THE SCHOOL SAYS "..."
From the Admissions Office
"The University of Vermont blends the close faculty-student relationships most commonly found in a small liberal arts college with the dynamic exchange of knowledge associated with a research university. This is not surprising, because UVM is both. A comprehensive research university offering nearly 100 undergraduate majors and extensive offerings through its Graduate College and College of Medicine, UVM is one of the nation's premier public research universities. UVM prides itself on the richness of its undergraduate experience. Distinguished senior faculty teach introductory courses in their fields. They also advise not only juniors and seniors, but also first- and second-year students, and work collaboratively with undergraduates on research initiatives. Students find extensive opportunities to test classroom knowledge in field through practicums, academic internships, and community service. More than 100 student organizations (involving eighty percent of the student body), eighteen Division I varsity teams, fifteen intercollegiate club and fourteen intramural sports programs, and a packed schedule of cultural events fill in where the classroom leaves off.

"Applicants for the entering class and beyond are required to take the SAT, or the ACT with the writing section, and they must submit official test scores. SAT Subject Tests are neither required nor recommended for the admission application."

SELECTIVITY
Admissions Rating	80
# of applicants	22,317
% of applicants accepted	71
% of acceptees attending	16
# accepting a place on wait list	982
% admitted from wait list	1

FRESHMAN PROFILE
Range SAT Critical Reading	540–640
Range SAT Math	545–640
Range SAT Writing	540–640
Range ACT Composite	24–29
Minimum paper TOEFL	550
Minimum computer TOEFL	213
% graduated top 10% of class	27
% graduated top 25% of class	69
% graduated top 50% of class	98

DEADLINES
Early action	
Deadline	11/1
Notification	12/15
Regular	
Deadline	1/15
Nonfall registration?	yes

FINANCIAL FACTS
Financial Aid Rating	75
Annual in-state tuition	$12,180
Annual out-of-state tuition	$30,744
Room and board	$9,352
Required fees	$1,886
Books and supplies	$1,200
% frosh rec. need-based scholarship or grant aid	52
% UG rec. need-based scholarship or grant aid	50
% frosh rec. non-need-based scholarship or grant aid	25
% UG rec. non-need-based scholarship or grant aid	22
% frosh rec. need-based self-help aid	52
% UG rec. need-based self-help aid	49
% frosh rec. any financial aid	81
% UG rec. any financial aid	81
% UG borrow to pay for school	63
Average cumulative indebtedness	$27,696

UNIVERSITY OF VIRGINIA

OFFICE OF ADMISSION, PO BOX 400160, CHARLOTTESVILLE, VA 22906 • ADMISSIONS: 434-982-3200 • FAX: 434-924-3587

CAMPUS LIFE

Quality of Life Rating	88
Fire Safety Rating	73
Green Rating	92
Type of school	public
Environment	city

STUDENTS

Total undergrad enrollment	14,232
% male/female	44/56
% from out of state	26
% from public high school	74
% live on campus	42
# of fraternities	29
# of sororities	16
% African American	8
% Asian	12
% Caucasian	59
% Hispanic	5
% international	5
# of countries represented	136

SURVEY SAYS . . .

Athletic facilities are great
Low cost of living
Lots of beer drinking
Hard liquor is popular

ACADEMICS

Academic Rating	85
% students graduating within 4 years	85
% students graduating within 6 years	93
Calendar	semester
Student/faculty ratio	16:1
Profs interesting rating	82
Profs accessible rating	78
Most common reg class size	10–19 students
Most common lab size	20–29 students

MOST POPULAR MAJORS

business/commerce, economics,
international relations

STUDENTS SAY ". . ."

Academics

Founded by Thomas Jefferson, the University of Virginia takes its history and traditions seriously, but that doesn't mean it's trapped in the past. The school "ranks among the world's best and offers every imaginable subject," combining "the academic advantages of the Ivy League" with the social life—and price—of a large state school. Academics here are "definitely tough" but "straightforward:" "Go to class, do the reading, [and] you'll get the grade you deserve." Although class sizes can be large and it can take "some maneuvering to get into the more popular courses," students rave about their professors. "My professors have been my heroes; they are personable, wise, funny, prepared, engaging, and inspiring." However, that doesn't mean they'll hand your education to you on a platter: Professors "are really willing to help out students after class" if you have "the guts to go up to them." The expectation of student involvement extends across university life; student bodies administer the honor code, "which says that you will not lie, cheat, or steal while at the university." While sanctions for violations like plagiarism can be harsh, one student points out that "it is nice to be able to leave my stuff in the library or dining hall while I get up for a little while and not worry about it getting stolen."

Life

UVA students embody the "work-hard, play-hard" ethos. Life here "is all about balance between studying and partying. The same students who talk nonstop about how much they drank last weekend are the ones who ace their chem exams and dream of med school." The Greek scene is popular, and alcohol "is definitely a big and visible part of campus life." But there is also "lots going on in Charlottesville" and plenty to do off campus, like "hiking at Old Rag or Humpback Rock, apple picking at Carter Mountain, and other fun, outdoorsy things. There is always the downtown mall for shopping and cool places to eat." And then, of course, there is UVA athletics. Students here "go crazy for football games," which take up "most of a Saturday" during football season. But it's not all party, all the time: "Volunteering is big. Most students are involved in a variety of activities, [like] adopt-a-grandparent, student council, or honor committee." Students complain about the lack of parking and the "bland and repetitive" dining hall food, but they rave about the "beautiful grounds" and "historical architecture." The central location of dorms is "really convenient and good for social interaction."

Student Body

Students here "often get typecast as homogeneous and preppy." While this type certainly exists on campus, "there is a place for everyone at UVA. There are a lot of preppy kids, but there are also tomboys, Goths, skaters, and I even know of one kid who wears a kilt on a regular basis." Some students say that UVA has "room for improvement" when it comes to diversity: "There is some truth behind the rumor that the majority of students here are white, but by no means does this mean that the other ethnic groups here are segregated," since people here are "incredibly friendly" and the school is "a bastion of southern gentility." The student body is a happy group: "Everyone here loves it—you can't find a school with more enthusiastic and dedicated students." UVA students "are really serious about succeeding, but they want to get all they can out of every part of college, too." They're apt to "party Thursday through Saturday" and spend the rest of the week hitting the books and participating in the many clubs and organizations on campus.

UNIVERSITY OF VIRGINIA

FINANCIAL AID: 434-982-6000 • E-MAIL: UNDERGRADADMISSION@VIRGINIA.EDU • WEBSITE: WWW.VIRGINIA.EDU

THE PRINCETON REVIEW SAYS
Admissions
Very important factors considered include: Academic GPA, class rank, recommendation(s), rigor of secondary school record. *Important factors considered include:* Application essay, standardized test scores, character/personal qualities, extracurricular activities, talent/ability, alumni/ae relation, first generation, racial/ethnic status, state residency. *Other factors considered include:* Geographical residence, volunteer work, work experience. SAT or ACT required; ACT with writing component required. TOEFL required of all international applicants who haven't been in an English-speaking high school system. High school diploma is required, and GED is accepted. *Academic units required:* 4 English, 4 mathematics, 2 science, 2 foreign language, 1 social studies. *Academic units recommended:* 5 mathematics, 4 science, 5 foreign language, 4 social studies.

Financial Aid
Students should submit: FAFSA, CSS PROFILE. Regular filing deadline is March 1. The Princeton Review suggests that all financial aid forms be submitted as soon as possible after January 1. *Need-based scholarships/grants offered:* Federal Pell, SEOG, state scholarships/grants, private scholarships, school scholarship or grant aid from institutional funds, Federal Nursing Scholarships. *Loan aid offered:* Federal Nursing Loans. Applicants will be notified of awards on a rolling basis beginning. Federal Work-Study Program available.

The Inside Word
As one of the premier public universities in the country, UVA holds its applicants to high standards. While admissions officers don't set minimum requirements, all viable candidates have stellar academic records. Intellectual ability is imperative, and prospective students are expected to have taken a rigorous course load in high school. Applicants should be aware that geographical location holds significant weight, as Virginia residents are given preference.

THE SCHOOL SAYS "..."
From the Admissions Office
"Admission to competitive schools requires strong academic credentials. Students who stretch themselves and take rigorous courses (honors-level and Advanced Placement courses, when offered) are significantly more competitive than those who do not. Experienced admissions officers know that most students are capable of presenting superb academic credentials, and the reality is that a very high percentage of those applying do so. Other considerations, then, come into play in important ways for academically strong candidates, as they must be seen as 'selective' as well as academically competitive.

"SAT or ACT is required. Neither is preferred. It is strongly recommended that applicants take two SAT Subject Tests of the applicant's choice."

SELECTIVITY
Admissions Rating	99
# of applicants	22,124
% of applicants accepted	33
% of acceptees attending	45
# accepting a place on wait list	2,112
% admitted from wait list	14

FRESHMAN PROFILE
Range SAT Critical Reading	600–710
Range SAT Math	620–740
Range SAT Writing	610–720
Range ACT Composite	28–32
Average HS GPA	4.17
% graduated top 10% of class	90
% graduated top 25% of class	97
% graduated top 50% of class	99

DEADLINES
Regular	
Deadline	1/1
Nonfall registration?	no

APPLICANTS ALSO LOOK AT
AND OFTEN PREFER
College of William and Mary, Virginia Tech
AND SOMETIMES PREFER
Duke University, University of North Carolina at Chapel Hill
AND RARELY PREFER
James Madison University

FINANCIAL FACTS
Financial Aid Rating	94
Annual in-state tuition	$8,356
Annual out-of-state tuition	$31,302
Room and board	$8,652
Required fees	$2,472
Books and supplies	$1,167
% frosh rec. need-based scholarship or grant aid	31
% UG rec. need-based scholarship or grant aid	28
% frosh rec. non-need-based scholarship or grant aid	4
% UG rec. non-need-based scholarship or grant aid	3
% frosh rec. need-based self-help aid	20
% UG rec. need-based self-help aid	19
% frosh rec. any financial aid	59
% UG rec. any financial aid	50
% UG borrow to pay for school	32
Average cumulative indebtedness	$19,384

UNIVERSITY OF WASHINGTON

1410 NORTHEAST CAMPUS PARKWAY, 320 SCHMITZ BOX 355840, SEATTLE, WA 98195-5840 • ADMISSIONS: 206-543-9686

STUDENTS SAY "..."

Academics

Students find "a great combination of high-powered academics, an excellent social life, and a wide variety of courses, all in the midst of the exciting Seattle life" at the University of Washington, the state's flagship institution of higher learning. UW offers "a lot of really stellar programs and the best bang for the buck, especially for in-state students or those in the sciences." Indeed, science programs "are incredible. The research going on here is cutting-edge and the leaders of biomedical sciences, stem cell research, etc. are accessible to students." Undergrads warn, however, that science programs are extremely competitive, "high pressure," and "challenging," with "core classes taught in lectures that seat more than 500 people," creating the sense that "professors don't seem to care too much whether you succeed." Pre-professional programs in business, law, nursing, medicine and engineering all earn high marks, although again with the caveat that the workload is tough and the hand-holding nominal. As one student puts it, "The University of Washington provides every resource and opportunity for its students to succeed. You just have to take advantage of them. No one will do it for you." For those fortunate enough to get in, the Honors Program "creates a smaller community of highly motivated students...It puts this school on top."

Life

UW students typically "have a good balance in their lives of education and fun." They "generally study hard and work in the libraries, but once the nighttime hits, they look forward to enjoying the night with their friends." Between the large university community and the surrounding city of Seattle, undergrads have a near-limitless selection of extracurricular choices. As one student explains, "There are tons of options for fun in Seattle. Going down to Pike's Market on a Saturday and eating your way through is always popular. There are tons of places to eat on 'The Ave,'" the shopping district that abuts campus, "and the UVillage shopping mall is a five minute walk from campus with chain-store comfort available. Intramural sports are big for activities, and going to undergraduate theater productions is never a disappointing experience. And during autumn or spring renting a canoe and paddling around lake Washington down by the stadium is fun." Husky football games "are amazing," and the Greek community "is very big" without dominating campus social life. In short, "the UW has anything you could want to do in your free time."

Student Body

"At such a large university, there is no 'typical' student," undergrads tell us, observing "one can find just about any demographic here and there is a huge variety in personalities." There "are quite a lot of yuppies, but then again, it's Seattle," and by and large "the campus is ultraliberal. Most students care about the environment, are not religious, and are generally accepting of other diverse individuals." Otherwise, "You've got your stereotypes: the Greeks, the street fashion pioneers, the various ethnic communities, the Oxford-looking grad students, etc." In terms of demographics, "The typical student at UW is white, middle-class, and is from the Seattle area," but "There are a lot of African American students and a very large number of Asian students." All groups "seem to socialize with each other."

University of Washington

FAX: 206-685-3655 • FINANCIAL AID: 206-543-6101 • E-MAIL: ASKUWADM@U.WASHINGTON.EDU • WEBSITE: WWW.WASHINGTON.EDU

THE PRINCETON REVIEW SAYS

Admissions

Very important factors considered include: Academic GPA, application essay, rigor of secondary school record. *Important factors considered include:* Standardized test scores, character/personal qualities, extracurricular activities, first generation, talent/ability, volunteer work, work experience. *Other factors considered include:* State residency. SAT or ACT required; ACT with writing component required. TOEFL required of all international applicants. High school diploma or equivalent isn't required. *Academic units required:* 4 English, 3 mathematics, 2 science (2 science labs), 2 foreign language, 3 social studies. *Academic units recommended:* 4 English, 4 mathematics, 4 science (3 science labs), 4 foreign language, 4 social studies, 1 visual/performing arts, 1 academic elective.

Financial Aid

Students should submit: FAFSA. The Princeton Review suggests that all financial aid forms be submitted as soon as possible after January 1. *Need-based scholarships/grants offered:* Federal Pell, SEOG, state scholarships/grants, private scholarships, school scholarship or grant aid from institutional funds. *Loan aid offered:* Direct Subsidized Stafford, Direct Unsubsidized Stafford, Direct PLUS, Federal Perkins, Federal Nursing Loans, university loans from institutional funds. Federal Work-Study Program available. Off-campus job opportunities are excellent.

The Inside Word

In recent years, UW committed to a thorough review of all freshman applications, abandoning the previous process by which a formula was used to rank applicants according to high school GPA and standardized test scores. The new, holistic approach allows admissions officers to take into account a student's background, the degree to which he or she has overcome personal adversity, and such intangibles as leadership quality and special skills. The move has so far resulted in increased racial and socioeconomic diversity, a result praised by some and criticized by others, who regard the new system as a poorly disguised affirmative action program.

THE SCHOOL SAYS "..."

From the Admissions Office

"Are you curious about everything, from comet dust to computer game design, salmon to Salman Rushdie, ancient Rome to the atmospherics of Mars? Do you seek the freedom to chart your own course—and work on breakthrough research? Are you ready to cheer on the Division I Huskies and spend your weekends sea kayaking? Would you like to walk to class on a 700-acre stunning, ivy-covered campus, yet be only fifteen minutes from downtown Seattle? If the answers are yes, then the University of Washington may be the place for you. Offering more than 140 majors and 450 student organizations, the UW is looking for students who are both excited about the vast academic and social possibilities available to them and eager to contribute to the campus' cultural and intellectual life.

"We encourage you to take advantage of every opportunity in the application, especially the personal statement and activities summary, to tell us why Washington would be good fit for you and how you will contribute to the freshman class.

"Freshman applicants to the University of Washington are required to submit scores from either the SAT or ACT (with the writing component)."

SELECTIVITY

Admissions Rating	91
# of applicants	22,843
% of applicants accepted	57
% of acceptees attending	42
# accepting a place on wait list	1,308
% admitted from wait list	30

FRESHMAN PROFILE

Range SAT Critical Reading	530–650
Range SAT Math	570–690
Range SAT Writing	520–640
Range ACT Composite	24–30
Minimum paper TOEFL	537
Minimum computer TOEFL	207
Minimum web-based TOEFL	76
% graduated top 10% of class	85
% graduated top 25% of class	95
% graduated top 50% of class	100

DEADLINES

Regular	
Deadline	12/1
Notification	3/15
Nonfall registration?	yes

APPLICANTS ALSO LOOK AT
AND OFTEN PREFER
University of Southern California

AND SOMETIMES PREFER
Gonzaga University, Western Washington University

AND RARELY PREFER
Washington State University

FINANCIAL FACTS

Financial Aid Rating	74
Annual in-state tuition	$8,122
Annual out-of-state tuition	$25,329
Room and board	$8,169
Required fees	$272
Books and supplies	$1,008
% frosh rec. need-based scholarship or grant aid	29
% UG rec. need-based scholarship or grant aid	29
% frosh rec. non-need-based scholarship or grant aid	7
% UG rec. non-need-based scholarship or grant aid	4
% frosh rec. need-based self-help aid	21
% UG rec. need-based self-help aid	24
% frosh rec. any financial aid	50
% UG rec. any financial aid	50
% UG borrow to pay for school	50
Average cumulative indebtedness	$16,800

UNIVERSITY OF WISCONSIN—MADISON

702 WEST JOHNSON STREET 1101, MADISON, WI 53715-1007 • ADMISSIONS: 608-262-3961 • FAX: 608-262-7706

CAMPUS LIFE

Quality of Life Rating	88
Fire Safety Rating	66
Green Rating	87
Type of school	public
Environment	city

STUDENTS

Total undergrad enrollment	28,897
% male/female	48/52
% from out of state	32
% live on campus	25
# of fraternities	26
# of sororities	11
% African American	2
% Asian	5
% Caucasian	78
% Hispanic	4
% international	6
# of countries represented	132

SURVEY SAYS . . .

Students love Madison, WI
Great off-campus food
Everyone loves the Badgers
Student publications are popular
Political activism is popular
Lots of beer drinking
Hard liquor is popular

ACADEMICS

Academic Rating	76
% students graduating within 4 years	51
% students graduating within 6 years	84
Calendar	semester
Student/faculty ratio	17:1
Profs interesting rating	71
Profs accessible rating	70
Most common reg class size	10–19 students
Most common lab size	20–29 students

MOST POPULAR MAJORS

biology, economics, political science

STUDENTS SAY ". . ."

Academics

"The resources are phenomenal" at University of Wisconsin—Madison. "If you are proactive, you basically have the means and resources to pursue any academic or creative feat," promises a journalism major. "The liberal arts majors are fantastic." However, Madison is mostly known as "an amazing research institution," and the hard sciences and engineering programs get most of the pub. They iodized salt here, after all, and cultivated the first lab-based embryonic stem cells. The school of business is "excellent" as well and boasts "some of the best facilities on campus." Overall the school runs surprisingly smoothly" despite some "red tape." Many lecture courses are large and "impersonal." But class sizes often "plummet" after the intro courses, and the academic atmosphere is "challenging." Madison "definitely makes you earn your grades." "Some professors are amazing, and some suck." Also, "a lot of the classes for the undergrads are taught by teaching assistants who are not so good." "It becomes clear within the first few weeks which of your professors actually have lectures that are worthwhile for you to attend, which is probably about half," suggests a first-year student.

Life

UW—Madison's "reputation as a party school" is legendary. Halloween and the Mifflin Street Block Party are epic. "The weekend pretty much starts on Thursday night" as the streets of Madison "fill to the brim with drunk co-eds." There are house parties and frat parties galore. "Getting up at 9:00 a.m." to "bong a few beers for breakfast" before football games in the fall is common, and "nothing—absolutely nothing—can beat being in the student section at a Badger home football game." "The stadium is usually full" for hockey games, too. However, "no one looks at you differently if you choose not to drink" or attend sporting events. And, for everyone, "if you don't have a strong dedication to your education, you will slip up." Beyond the party and sports scene, UW is "energetic" and mammoth. "No one's going to hold your hand and point you to what it is you want." At the same time, whoever you are, "there is a group for you and a ton of activities for you." Two daily student newspapers "serve as the penultimate example of free speech in action." UW's lakefront campus provides "gorgeous" scenery. Many of the buildings "aren't that appealing," though, and some dorms are "absolutely horrible." Off-campus, "having the streets crawling with the homeless isn't so great," but Madison is teeming with culture, "live music," "late-night coffee shops," and "exceptional" chow from around the globe.

Student Body

Ethnic diversity at Madison is in the eye of the beholder. "If you're from a big city, it's pretty white," proposes a sophomore. "But, then again, I've met people here who had one black person in their high school and had never met a Jewish person." Without question, socioeconomic diversity flourishes. "There is a prevalent rivalry between [Wisconsin] students (sconnies) and the coasties who are generally wealthier and from the East or West Coast." Beyond that, it's impossible to generalize. "All types of people make up the student body here, ranging from the peace-preaching grass-root activist, to the protein-shake-a-day jock, to the overly privileged coastie, to the studious bookworm, to the computer geek," explains a first-year student. "There is a niche for everyone." "There are a lot of atypical students, but that is what makes UW—Madison so special," adds a senior. "Normal doesn't exist on this campus." Politically, "Madison is a hotbed for political and social debate." "Many people are passionate about many things, and it provides a great opportunity to see things from others' points of view."

FINANCIAL AID: 608-262-3060 • E-MAIL: ONWISCONSIN@ADMISSIONS.WISC.EDU • WEBSITE: WWW.WISC.EDU

THE PRINCETON REVIEW SAYS

Admissions

Very important factors considered include: Academic GPA, class rank, rigor of secondary school record. *Important factors considered include:* Application essay, standardized test scores, state residency. *Other factors considered include:* Recommendation(s), alumni/ae relation, character/personal qualities, extracurricular activities, first generation, level of applicant's interest, racial/ethnic status, talent/ability, volunteer work, work experience. SAT or ACT required; ACT with writing component required. TOEFL required of all international applicants. High school diploma is required, and GED is accepted. *Academic units required:* 4 English, 3 mathematics, 3 science, 2 foreign language, 3 social studies, 2 academic elective. *Academic units recommended:* 4 English, 4 mathematics, 4 science, 4 foreign language, 4 social studies, 4 academic elective.

Financial Aid

Students should submit: FAFSA, institution's own financial aid form. The Princeton Review suggests that all financial aid forms be submitted as soon as possible after January 1. *Need-based scholarships/grants offered:* Federal Pell, SEOG, state scholarships/grants, private scholarships, school scholarship or grant aid from institutional funds, Federal Nursing Scholarships. *Loan aid offered:* Direct Subsidized Stafford, Direct Unsubsidized Stafford, Direct PLUS, Federal Perkins, Federal Nursing Loans, state loans. Applicants will be notified of awards on a rolling basis beginning April 1. Federal Work-Study Program available. Off-campus job opportunities are excellent.

The Inside Word

Though it's not at the top tier of selectivity, Wisconsin has high expectations of its candidates. Admissions officers are most concerned with the high school transcript (course selection and grades), although test scores are also important. And they won't ignore compelling essays, recommendations, or extracurricular achievements.

THE SCHOOL SAYS " . . ."

From the Admissions Office

"UW—Madison is the university of choice for some of the best and brightest students. Our freshman class has an average ACT score of 28 and an average SAT of 1276. Almost sixty percent are from the top ten percent of their high school class, and nearly all are from the top quarter.

"These factors combine to make admission to UW—Madison both competitive and selective. We consider academic record, course selection, strength of curriculum (honors, AP, IB, etc.), grade trend, class rank, results of the ACT/SAT, and non-academic factors. There is no prescribed minimum test score, GPA, or class rank criteria. Rather, we admit the best and most well-prepared students—students who have challenged themselves and who will contribute to Wisconsin's strength and diversity—for the limited space available.

"Each application is personally reviewed by our admission counselors. All domestic freshman applications completed by February 1 receive full and equal consideration. We offer two notification periods for domestic freshman applicants. To receive a decision during the First Notification Period, you must complete the application and submit all required materials (application fee, official high school transcript, official test scores, personal statements, and recommendations) postmarked by November 1. Admission decisions for these students will be made on or by January 15. All students who complete their applications during the Second Notification Period (after November 1 but before the February 1 deadline) will have decision made on or by March 15. All students receive equal consideration for admission whether they apply during the First or Second Notification Periods."

SELECTIVITY
Admissions Rating	93
# of applicants	25,522
% of applicants accepted	57
% of acceptees attending	41

FRESHMAN PROFILE
Range SAT Critical Reading	530–670
Range SAT Math	620–750
Range SAT Writing	580–680
Range ACT Composite	26–30
Minimum paper TOEFL	550
Minimum computer TOEFL	213
Minimum web-based TOEFL	80
Average HS GPA	3.69
% graduated top 10% of class	56
% graduated top 25% of class	93
% graduated top 50% of class	99

DEADLINES
Regular	
Priority	2/1
Deadline	2/1
Notification	10/1
Nonfall registration?	yes

FINANCIAL FACTS
Financial Aid Rating	74
Annual in-state tuition	$4,157
Annual out-of-state tuition	$11,532
Room and board	$8,040
Books and supplies	$1,040
% frosh rec. need-based scholarship or grant aid	21
% UG rec. need-based scholarship or grant aid	23
% frosh rec. non-need-based scholarship or grant aid	28
% UG rec. non-need-based scholarship or grant aid	27
% frosh rec. need-based self-help aid	29
% UG rec. need-based self-help aid	31
% frosh rec. any financial aid	47
% UG rec. any financial aid	46
% UG borrow to pay for school	48
Average cumulative indebtedness	$22,837

UNIVERSITY OF WYOMING

DEPARTMENT 3435, 1000 EAST UNIVERSITY AVENUE, LARAMIE, WY 82071 • ADMISSIONS: 307-766-5160 • FAX: 307-766-4042

CAMPUS LIFE

Quality of Life Rating	72
Fire Safety Rating	83
Green Rating	85
Type of school	public
Environment	town

STUDENTS

Total undergrad enrollment	9,893
% male/female	48/52
% from out of state	29
% live on campus	20
# of fraternities	9
# of sororities	6
% African American	1
% Asian	1
% Caucasian	81
% Hispanic	5
% Native American	1
% international	3
# of countries represented	95

SURVEY SAYS . . .

Great computer facilities
Athletic facilities are great
Students are friendly
Students get along with local
community
Everyone loves the Cowboys
Lots of beer drinking
Hard liquor is popular

ACADEMICS

Academic Rating	71
Calendar	semester
Student/faculty ratio	14:1
Profs interesting rating	78
Profs accessible rating	80
Most common reg class size	20–29 students
Most common lab size	20–29 students

MOST POPULAR MAJORS

elementary education and teaching,
nursing, secondary education and
teaching

STUDENTS SAY " . . ."

Academics

Why choose University of Wyoming? "Wyoming scholarships rock!" Hathaway Scholarships allow state residents to graduate virtually debt free, and financial aid for out-of-state students isn't too shabby, either. This allows students to get "an outstanding education for pennies on the dollar." This is a large university, though, which means "you have to make the commitment to do well." In other words, those grades aren't going to earn themselves! The business school, engineering school, and English departments all receive high marks from students, and the school's agricultural programs also have an excellent reputation. "They are on top of developing degree programs and courses focused on sustainability, green design, and climate change." There's "a 50/50 [split between] professors who love what they do and those who are just going with the flow," but "Nine times out of ten they will go well out of their way to help you." Many faculty members "have real-world job experience that helps bring their lectures to life." Many students complain about the registration process, which favors athletes and members of the honors program, but others suggest that kicking up a fuss will get you into the classes you want, or they suggest applying for the honors program: "They pull in the best professors across campus, and the requirements are a piece of cake. Plus, you get free printing," semester-long book checkout at the library, and priority registration. (Conservatives take note: Some students describe the honors classes as "very biased and liberal.") "The new library is great and full of awesome resources," and study abroad resources are "absolutely amazing" as well.

Life

"Cowboy football is a blast! We may not have the best team or biggest crowd, but we make up for it in dedicated fans!" Supporting UW's Division I football team is a bit pastime in the fall. Winter in Laramie, Wyoming, may be freezing (student wish lists include reopening underground tunnels for travel between buildings, and/or "fire pits for staying warm on your way to your next class!"), but it's "a great town if you enjoy the outdoors," and "Skiing, mountain biking, hiking, camping, fishing, mountain climbing, hunting are all popular activities." "People often say that there is nothing to do in Laramie but drink," and UW has its fair share of partying, though members of the large religious and nontraditional student populations are quick to point out that not everyone is searching for a house party every weekend. "The school offers a wide breadth of other activities from free ice skating to free movies, fly-fishing classes to a capella concerts, and many of these are run by students and are widely attended." Fort Collins and Denver, Colorado, are both about two and a half hours away by car, though if you're bringing a vehicle to campus, four-wheel drive is strongly recommended.

Student Body

"The majority of the students are Wyoming residents with a large portion of the rest coming from Colorado." Students tend to be "good-natured kids [who have] grown up on ranches or farms where a strong work ethic has been established," "usually nice with strong family values and a conservative upbringing." Politically, there seems to be a bit of a divide among students, which reflects the geography of the university: Laramie is considered a more liberal enclave in a traditionally conservative state. "The school creates an open-minded atmosphere within one of the most conservative states in the union," but on the other hand, "Many of the Christian campus ministries are very outspoken." Students say, "We are not incredibly diverse ethnically, but we are diverse in so many other ways," and "Every semester brings more and more minority and foreign students." There's "a huge amount of nontrad students as well."

UNIVERSITY OF WYOMING

FINANCIAL AID: 307-766-2116 • E-MAIL: WHY-WYO@UWYO.EDU • WEBSITE: WWW.UWYO.EDU

THE PRINCETON REVIEW SAYS

Admissions

Very important factors considered include: Academic GPA, rigor of secondary school record, standardized test scores. *Important factors considered include:* Level of applicant's interest. *Other factors considered include:* Application essay, recommendation(s), character/personal qualities, extracurricular activities, interview, state residency, talent/ability. SAT or ACT required; ACT with or without writing component accepted. TOEFL required of all international applicants. High school diploma is required, and GED is accepted. *Academic units required:* 4 English, 3 mathematics, 3 science (3 science labs). *Academic units recommended:* 4 English, 4 mathematics, 4 science (3 science labs), 2 foreign language.

Financial Aid

Students should submit: FAFSA. The Princeton Review suggests that all financial aid forms be submitted as soon as possible after January 1. *Need-based scholarships/grants offered:* Federal Pell, SEOG, state scholarships/grants, private scholarships, school scholarship or grant aid from institutional funds. *Loan aid offered:* Direct Subsidized Stafford, Direct Unsubsidized Stafford, Direct PLUS, Federal Perkins, state loans. Applicants will be notified of awards on a rolling basis beginning March 15. Federal Work-Study Program available. Off-campus job opportunities are good.

The Inside Word

The admissions process at UW is formula-driven. State residents need a minimum high school GPA of 2.75 to gain admission, and nonresidents need a 3.0 GPA. That combined with some solid test scores will open the door to this university.

THE SCHOOL SAYS "..."

From the Admissions Office

"The University of Wyoming and the town of Laramie are relatively small, affording students the opportunity to get the personal attention and develop a close rapport with their professors. They can easily make friends and find peers with similar interests and values. More than 200 student organizations offer students a great way to get involved and encourage growth and learning. Couple the small size with a great location, and you have a winning combination. Laramie sits between the Laramie and Snowy Range Mountains. There are numerous outdoor activities in which one can participate. Furthermore, the university works hard to attract other great cultural events. Major-label recording artists come to UW as well as some of today's great minds. In all, the University of Wyoming is a great place to be because of its wonderful blend of small-town atmosphere with 'big city' activities.

"The University of Wyoming requires first-time, incoming freshmen to submit scores from either the ACT or SAT. The writing component of the ACT and SAT is not required."

SELECTIVITY

Admissions Rating	76
# of applicants	3,713
% of applicants accepted	95
% of acceptees attending	42

FRESHMAN PROFILE

Range SAT Critical Reading	490–600
Range SAT Math	490–610
Range ACT Composite	21–27
Minimum paper TOEFL	525
Minimum computer TOEFL	197
Minimum web-based TOEFL	71
Average HS GPA	3.43
% graduated top 10% of class	23
% graduated top 25% of class	51
% graduated top 50% of class	79

DEADLINES

Regular	
Priority	3/1
Deadline	8/10
Nonfall registration?	yes

FINANCIAL FACTS

Financial Aid Rating	71
Annual in-state tuition	$2,970
Annual out-of-state tuition	$11,280
Room and board	$8,360
Required fees	$957
Books and supplies	$1,200
% frosh rec. need-based scholarship or grant aid	24
% UG rec. need-based scholarship or grant aid	27
% frosh rec. non-need-based scholarship or grant aid	40
% UG rec. non-need-based scholarship or grant aid	29
% frosh rec. need-based self-help aid	25
% UG rec. need-based self-help aid	28
% frosh rec. any financial aid	95
% UG rec. any financial aid	84
% UG borrow to pay for school	56
Average cumulative indebtedness	$20,759

URSINUS COLLEGE

URSINUS COLLEGE, ADMISSIONS OFFICE, COLLEGEVILLE, PA 19426 • ADMISSIONS: 610-409-3200 • FAX: 610-409-3662

CAMPUS LIFE

Quality of Life Rating	81
Fire Safety Rating	86
Green Rating	84
Type of school	private
Environment	city

STUDENTS

Total undergrad enrollment	1,655
% male/female	45/55
% from out of state	42
% from public high school	61
% live on campus	95
# of fraternities	7
# of sororities	7
% African American	6
% Asian	4
% Caucasian	73
% Hispanic	3
% international	1
# of countries represented	13

SURVEY SAYS . . .

Athletic facilities are great
Different types of student interact
Lots of beer drinking

ACADEMICS

Academic Rating	91
% students graduating within 4 years	72
% students graduating within 6 years	76
Calendar	semester
Student/faculty ratio	12:1
Profs interesting rating	85
Profs accessible rating	90
Most common reg class size	fewer than 10 students
Most common lab size	10–19 students

MOST POPULAR MAJORS

biology, economics, psychology

STUDENTS SAY ". . ."

Academics

Set in Collegeville, Pennsylvania, this "small, close-knit college community" offers "an exceptional academic record" and "small-school atmosphere," which "provides accessibility to professors and successful students, enabling a better learning experience." This is "a campus filled with motivated students and professors who worked toward every student's success." "Academic integrity" is "high," "yet fostering leadership, community and personal growth [is] also extremely prided." The "greatest strengths" of Ursinus's program "are probably the focus on community service, the strength of the academic programs, and programs such as CIE (common intellectual experience, an entire class [where the focus is on] the whole campus reading and discussing the same books or movies." Ursinus is also known for its "strong biology and science program," which "allow students to maintain strong connections in other fields, from art to education." Classes "are small," and professors "are accessible and have extensive knowledge in their fields." The academic bar here is high. Professors expect "students to be engaged." They "tend to be very attentive to your performance in class and are available to help if you need it." While "[professors] expect a lot from you, and it is challenging," the workload is "very doable because of the relationships with professors and students." Overall, this small, rigorous program is "about creating free-thinking, intelligent, [and] contributing members of society" and "letting people be who they are without fear and while accomplishing learning beyond the classroom."

Life

During the week, "Mostly everyone goes to class and then to the library or another study room to finish homework and study." "There is always something happening on campus, which is contrary to the big misconception about smaller schools." "Because the student population is low, everyone receives e-mails about everything going on." In addition, there "is a large athletic population, and games are highly attended." "Almost every night there is some party going on, and on weekends it can get crazy, but the drinking scene is easily avoidable." Others agree, "The school offers a lot of weekend activities for those of us who do not partake in drinking. They have movie nights, casino nights, game show nights, special dinners, [and] a lot of off campus events." While "the town [of Collegeville] is small, they are expanding and building upon it. Philadelphia is close as is King of Prussia, Phoenixville, Skippack, and Limerick so students have places to go off campus and have fun." "Most students stay on weekends and either attend a campus event or hang out with friends." "Partying does happen; it happens only Thursday through Saturday because most students are extremely serious about their academics."

Student Body

Ursinus students are "well-rounded, mature, and friendly." Everyone at Ursinus "has an interest in their academics as well as their social life." "Because of various requirements, students interact with all sorts of students with different majors, especially our CIE class, which requires a lot of introspection." Most students "can find a group of students they fit in with easily." The typical student "has a core group of friends, friends that they have classes with, many are involved with some kind of sport (intramural or collegiate), and many are involved with community service." While some tout the stereotypical badge of being "upper-middle- or middle-class, involved in a sport in some way"; however, by in large the student body here is "very open to other beliefs and opinions" and "willing to branch out into different areas other than their specified major." Overall, a "supportive and friendly" atmosphere pervades. Ursinus students "are all hard-working and must go above and beyond to compete academically." Students at Ursinus tend to balance their "very studious" academic aspirations "with an active and healthy extracurricular lifestyle." They're "outgoing to others [and] involved in campus and in the society." "Many students are athletes," and "About twenty percent of the campus is affiliated with a Greek organization." In a sentence, "Ursinus students are overachievers."

FINANCIAL AID: 610-409-3600 • E-MAIL: ADMISSIONS@URSINUS.EDU • WEBSITE: WWW.URSINUS.EDU

THE PRINCETON REVIEW SAYS

Admissions

Very important factors considered include: Class rank, rigor of secondary school record, extracurricular activities. *Important factors considered include:* Academic GPA, application essay, recommendation(s), standardized test scores, alumni/ae relation, racial/ethnic status, talent/ability, volunteer work, work experience. *Other factors considered include:* Character/personal qualities, first generation, geographical residence, interview, level of applicant's interest. ACT with writing component recommended. TOEFL required of all international applicants. High school diploma is required, and GED is accepted. *Academic units required:* 4 English, 3 mathematics, 1 science (1 science lab), 2 foreign language, 1 social studies. *Academic units recommended:* 4 English, 4 mathematics, 4 science (2 science labs), 4 foreign language, 4 social studies.

Financial Aid

Students should submit: FAFSA, institution's own financial aid form, CSS/Financial Aid PROFILE. Regular filing deadline is February 15. The Princeton Review suggests that all financial aid forms be submitted as soon as possible after January 1. *Need-based scholarships/grants offered:* Federal Pell, SEOG, state scholarships/grants, private scholarships, school scholarship or grant aid from institutional funds. *Loan aid offered:* Direct Subsidized Stafford, Direct Unsubsidized Stafford, Direct PLUS, Federal Perkins. Federal Work-Study Program available. Off-campus job opportunities are excellent.

The Inside Word

Grades, test scores, and class rank count for more than anything else, and unless you're academically inconsistent, you'll likely get good news. If you're hoping to snag a scholarship, it's essential that you visit campus for an interview, and interviews are strongly encouraged anyway. Students in the top ten percent of their graduating classes rank out of having to submit SAT scores.

THE SCHOOL SAYS "..."

From the Admissions Office

"Located a half-hour from center-city Philadelphia, the college boasts a beautiful 168-acre campus that includes the Residential Village (renovated Victorian-style homes that decorate the Main Street and house our students) and the nationally recognized Berman Museum of Art. Ursinus is a member of the Centennial Conference, competing both in academics and in intercollegiate athletics with institutions such as Dickinson, Franklin & Marshall, Gettysburg, and Muhlenberg. The academic environment is enhanced with such fine programs as a chapter of Phi Beta Kappa, an early assurance program to medical school with the Medical College of Pennsylvania, and myriad student exchanges both at home and abroad. A heavy emphasis is placed on student research—an emphasis that can only be carried out with the one-on-one attention Ursinus students receive from their professors.

"Ursinus will continue to ask applicants for writing samples—both a series of application essays and a graded high school paper."

SELECTIVITY

Admissions Rating	93
# of applicants	6,192
% of applicants accepted	55
% of acceptees attending	32
# accepting a place on wait list	260
% admitted from wait list	3
# of early decision applicants	197
% accepted early decision	62

FRESHMAN PROFILE

Range SAT Critical Reading	570–680
Range SAT Math	570–670
Range SAT Writing	560–660
Range ACT Composite	25–29
Minimum paper TOEFL	500
Minimum computer TOEFL	173
Average HS GPA	3.67
% graduated top 10% of class	48
% graduated top 25% of class	78
% graduated top 50% of class	96

DEADLINES

Early decision	
Deadline	1/15
Notification	2/15
Early action	
Deadline	12/1
Regular	
Priority	2/15
Deadline	2/15
Nonfall registration?	yes

FINANCIAL FACTS

Financial Aid Rating	84
Annual tuition	$38,500
Room and board	$9,250
Books and supplies	$1,000
% frosh rec. need-based scholarship or grant aid	64
% UG rec. need-based scholarship or grant aid	66
% frosh rec. non-need-based scholarship or grant aid	17
% UG rec. non-need-based scholarship or grant aid	16
% frosh rec. need-based self-help aid	50
% UG rec. need-based self-help aid	55
% frosh rec. any financial aid	92
% UG rec. any financial aid	91
% UG borrow to pay for school	75
Average cumulative indebtedness	$21,171

VALPARAISO UNIVERSITY

KRETZMANN HALL, 1700 CHAPEL DRIVE, VALPARAISO, IN 46383 • ADMISSIONS: 219-464-5011 • FAX: 219-464-6898

STUDENTS SAY ". . ."

Academics

Valparaiso University, a small Lutheran university, "is a serious academic community with strong, but not forceful, religious background" that "prepares, motivates, and challenges tomorrow's leaders, engineers, nurses, and teachers while giving the opportunity for religious growth." Business, education, and engineering are the most popular general areas of study, and are among Valpo's most celebrated departments. Other standout disciplines include nursing, music, theater ("the department involves touring professional directors a couple times a year, which speaks for itself" and "puts on great plays"), and one of the nation's largest meteorology programs (which "just erected a state-of-the-art Doppler radar, putting Valpo at the forefront for undergrad meteorology"). Undergrads here appreciate the breadth of excellent offerings as well as "the school's ability to integrate the liberal arts with a variety of majors...As a student, I have been able to study engineering as well as hermeneutics, child development, and read classic texts ranging from Aristotle and Plato to Chuang Tzu and Derrida." Valpo operates under an honor code students say, "creates an environment of trust and high moral responsibility." "People follow the honor code, especially because the punishments are strict, such as failing the class for a first offense," one student tells us. A few dissenters feel "the honor code may reduce some cheating, but I don't think it comes near to eliminating it." Outstanding students may enroll in Christ College, an honors college, which they describe as "very intense but very rewarding."

Life

"There are several activities to choose from on Valparaiso's campus on a typical weekend, ranging from philanthropic dance parties at fraternity houses to music recitals to special guests speakers (to name just a few)," students tell us. Religious groups are active, and not just the Lutherans. The Catholic Church "is very active" here, offering "a student mass Sunday nights with a meal afterward, which is very nice" and "at least three events each week." Athletics are also popular. "We have Division I athletics, so it's fun to watch if you don't play, but Valpo also offers club sports (like Ultimate Frisbee) and intramurals for all student to participate in." The VU campus is officially dry, but that doesn't mean students don't drink. An aggressive campus police force means "there is lots of fear of getting arrested when drinking, but people do it anyway." Fraternities "have parties every Friday night," which helps to offset the perception that "the city of Valpo is horrible" because "there's not much to do" there. "If you can't entertain yourself, this is not the place for you," students warn. When they need big-city diversion, students will "hop on the train to go over to Chicago, an hour ride, for about six dollars, and get a CTA day pass for four dollars (to ride Chicago's transit all day)."

Student Body

One student estimates that "conservative, churchgoing studiers" make up about two-thirds of the Valpo student body. Most "come from somewhere in the Midwest," with many "from the Chicagoland area." The typical student is "here to learn. There are some who are just here for the party, but there are not many." Because "meteorology and engineering are large areas of study, there are some students who are 'nerdy,' but no one is left out of university activities." Valpo has "few minority students," and "it would be nice to have a little bit more diversity."

VALPARAISO UNIVERSITY

FINANCIAL AID: 219-464-5015 • E-MAIL: UNDERGRAD.ADMISSIONS@VALPO.EDU • WEBSITE: WWW.VALPO.EDU

THE PRINCETON REVIEW SAYS

Admissions

Very important factors considered include: Academic GPA, rigor of secondary school record, standardized test scores. *Important factors considered include:* Class rank, alumni/ae relation, character/personal qualities, extracurricular activities, talent/ability. *Other factors considered include:* Application essay, recommendation(s), first generation, interview, level of applicant's interest, racial/ethnic status, religious affiliation/commitment, volunteer work. SAT or ACT required; ACT with writing component recommended. Proof of English proficiency required of all international applicants. High school diploma is required, and GED is accepted. *Academic units required:* 4 English, 3 mathematics, 2 science (2 science labs), 2 foreign language, 2 history, 3 academic elective. *Academic units recommended:* 4 English, 4 mathematics, 3 science (3 science labs), 2 foreign language, 1 social studies, 2 history, 3 academic elective.

Financial Aid

Students should submit: FAFSA. Priority filing deadline is March 1. The Princeton Review suggests that all financial aid forms be submitted as soon as possible after January 1. *Need-based scholarships/grants offered:* Federal Pell, SEOG, state scholarships/grants, private scholarships, school scholarship or grant aid from institutional funds. *Loan aid offered:* Direct Subsidized Stafford, Direct Unsubsidized Stafford, Direct PLUS, Federal Perkins, university loans from institutional funds. Applicants will be notified of awards on a rolling basis beginning March 1. Federal Work-Study Program available. Off-campus job opportunities are good.

The Inside Word

Valparaiso's ninety percent admit rate suggests a pretty generous admissions office. The figure is somewhat misleading; Valpo's applicant pool consists largely of students familiar enough with the school to know whether it's worth their while to apply here. In other words, the school doesn't receive a lot of 'reach' applications. Applicants indicating an interest in meteorology should expect a more rigorous review, as space in the program is limited.

THE SCHOOL SAYS " . . . "

From the Admissions Office

"Valpo provides students a blend of academic excellence, social experience, and spiritual exploration. The concern demonstrated by faculty and administration for the total well-being of students reflects a long history as a Lutheran-affiliated university."

SELECTIVITY	
Admissions Rating	83
# of applicants	3,506
% of applicants accepted	85
% of acceptees attending	23

FRESHMAN PROFILE	
Range SAT Critical Reading	490–600
Range SAT Math	510–620
Range SAT Writing	480–590
Range ACT Composite	23–29
Minimum paper TOEFL	550
Minimum computer TOEFL	213
Minimum web-based TOEFL	80
Average HS GPA	3.52
% graduated top 10% of class	32
% graduated top 25% of class	65
% graduated top 50% of class	91

DEADLINES	
Regular	
Priority	12/1
Notification	10/1
Nonfall registration?	yes

APPLICANTS ALSO LOOK AT
AND OFTEN PREFER
Butler University, Indiana University at Bloomington, Purdue University—West Lafayette

AND SOMETIMES PREFER
Ball State University, Bradley University, Marquette University

AND RARELY PREFER
Indiana University—Purdue University Indiana, University of Illinois at Chicago

FINANCIAL FACTS	
Financial Aid Rating	77
Annual tuition	$28,590
Room and board	$8,330
Required fees	$992
Books and supplies	$1,200
% frosh rec. need-based scholarship or grant aid	78
% UG rec. need-based scholarship or grant aid	72
% frosh rec. non-need-based scholarship or grant aid	10
% UG rec. non-need-based scholarship or grant aid	7
% frosh rec. need-based self-help aid	59
% UG rec. need-based self-help aid	57
% frosh rec. any financial aid	98
% UG rec. any financial aid	98
% UG borrow to pay for school	72
Average cumulative indebtedness	$33,024

VANDERBILT UNIVERSITY

2305 WEST END AVENUE, NASHVILLE, TN 37203 • ADMISSIONS: 615-322-2561 • FAX: 615-343-7765

STUDENTS SAY ". . ."

Academics

Vanderbilt University "is a school where everyone has countless opportunities at their fingertips and students are encouraged to excel academically, extracurricularly and socially." Slackers, be warned: the academic environment here is challenging and intense. As one neuroscience major reveals, "The courses are meant to push students to their absolute limit and this can be overwhelming. Doing well in classes is very hard." Thankfully, undergrads feel that the experience is "rewarding" nonetheless. This is no doubt due in large part to the "fantastic" professors who "take a genuine interest in [students'] education and development." As a satisfied junior concurs, "My professors are always readily available to help with academic and life issues that I may be facing. They truly care about me, and they are extremely prompt in their response to my needs and questions." A content senior goes further, sharing, "I've been to dinner with professors, [attended] brunches at professors' houses with foreign dignitaries, and [attended] barbeques in professors' backyards." Certainly, this speaks to the "feeling of community between the faculty, staff, and students." It's therefore not surprising that undergrads are also quick to applaud Vanderbilt's administrators. They are very "visible and accessible" and it's quite common "to see deans at the lunch halls eating with students."

Life

Vanderbilt students "like to stay busy" and life here is all about "balancing friends and extracurriculars with schoolwork." Indeed, undergrads "take studying and partying equally seriously. Everyone has some excellent party stories from a Wednesday [night] and everyone has pulled at least one all-nighter." When students want to unwind they typically head to frat parties, as "Greek life is big" at Vanderbilt. Fortunately, "fraternity parties are mostly open events, so anyone, Greek or non-Greek, can enjoy the social scene." Sporting events are "also a great time. Everyone tailgates for the football games and the men's basketball team is very popular as well." Undergrads "are admitted [to games] for free by displaying their VU student ID." Those wary of frats or indifferent to athletics need not worry about being bored on campus, as one sophomore assures us: "We do a huge range of things for fun, [from] attending a movie showing in student center cinema [to] having an Apples to Apples or Pictionary tournament." Additionally, "student groups also organize campus-wide events regularly." Hometown Nashville also serves "as a playground for infinite fun for Vandy students." The city has "a great nightlife" and students frequently take advantage of both the restaurant and the arts scenes.

Student Body

A sophomore admits, "The stereotype of a typical Vandy student used to be wealthy, conservative, white, Southern, etc." However, he continues, "While some still fit the stereotype there is much more diversity on campus. At Vanderbilt, you'll find an undergraduate population that's "hardworking, sociable, and enjoys having fun." Indeed, many Vanderbilt students "definitely fit the 'work hard, play hard' personality type." An "overachieving" and "accomplished" lot, undergrads at Vanderbilt are "very involved in something, be it a sorority or fraternity, dance group, [or] religious group." "This is not a school where students lock themselves in the room to study 24/7. It's rare to find a student who is involved in only one club or not involved in anything." "The commitment to community service at Vanderbilt is incredible. The amount of time, effort, and innovation my fellow students put into serving others truly astounds me."

VANDERBILT UNIVERSITY

FINANCIAL AID: 615-322-3591 • E-MAIL: ADMISSIONS@VANDERBILT.EDU • WEBSITE: WWW.VANDERBILT.EDU

THE PRINCETON REVIEW SAYS

Admissions

Very important factors considered include: Academic GPA, application essay, class rank, rigor of secondary school record, standardized test scores, character/personal qualities, extracurricular activities, recommendation(s), talent/ability. *Other factors considered include:* Alumni/ae relation, first generation, geographical residence, interview, racial/ethnic status, state residency, volunteer work, work experience. SAT or ACT required; ACT with writing component required. TOEFL or IELTS required of all international applicants. High school diploma is required, and GED is accepted. *Academic units required:* 4 English, 3 mathematics, 3 science (2 science labs), 2 foreign language, 2 social studies, 1 history, 3 academic elective. *Academic units recommended:* 4 English, 4 mathematics, 4 science (3 science labs), 2 foreign language, 3 social studies, 1 history, 3 academic elective.

Financial Aid

Students should submit: FAFSA, CSS/Financial Aid PROFILE. Regular filing deadline is February 5. The Princeton Review suggests that all financial aid forms be submitted as soon as possible after January 1. *Need-based scholarships/grants offered:* Federal Pell, SEOG, state scholarships/grants, private scholarships, school scholarship or grant aid from institutional funds. Need-based financial aid awards don't include loans to meet demonstrated need. *Loan aid available:* Direct Subsidized Stafford, Direct Unsubsidized Stafford, Direct PLUS, Federal Perkins, Federal Nursing Loans, university loans from institutional funds. Federal Work-Study Program available. Off-campus job opportunities are excellent.

The Inside Word

Vanderbilt receives twenty-five percent more early decision applications each academic year than it did for the previous academic year, and as a result, competition has increased for those spaces. Still, if you consider early decision here (or anywhere for that matter), remember that you will not learn about financial aid until long after you've received your binding decisions.

THE SCHOOL SAYS " . . ."

From the Admissions Office

"The Vanderbilt undergraduate experience is often described as uniquely balanced. Within the context of an outstanding academic landscape, students are encouraged to participate in a broad spectrum of campus organizations (more than 350) among a highly diverse population. Many students take classes in all four undergraduate schools, stretching their intellectual experience far beyond that of their declared major. Students live on campus all four years beginning with a year at The Commons, Vanderbilt's living and learning residential community. Students take full advantage of Nashville, Tennessee, by participating in government-related internships, getting involved in area secondary schools, working in any one of many Nashville-based industries, and enjoying the cultural offerings of a major metropolitan area.

"Vanderbilt makes a three-pronged commitment regarding financial aid:

1. Applications are considered without regard for financial need (need-blind).

2. Vanderbilt meets 100 percent of a family's demonstrated financial need for all admitted U.S. citizens and eligible non-citizens.

3. Financial aid awards do not include loans. Instead of offering need-based loans, Vanderbilt offers additional grant assistance.

"Early decision applicants who submit the CSS Profile at the time of application will be provided with a provisional award of need-based financial aid. The admissions process is holistic—the student's complete academic and non-academic record is reviewed in conjunction with recommendations and personal essays. The audition is of primary importance for students applying to the Blair School of Music. Students admitted to Vanderbilt typically show exceptional academic accomplishment within the context of their high school, and are highly engaged in their communities, often serving in leadership roles."

SELECTIVITY

Admissions Rating	99
# of applicants	21,811
% of applicants accepted	18
% of acceptees attending	41
# accepting a place on wait list	1,733
% admitted from wait list	19
# of early decision applicants	2,150
% accepted early decision	32

FRESHMAN PROFILE

Range SAT Critical Reading	670–760
Range SAT Math	690–770
Range SAT Writing	660–750
Range ACT Composite	30–34
Minimum paper TOEFL	570
Average HS GPA	3.70
% graduated top 10% of class	85
% graduated top 25% of class	96
% graduated top 50% of class	100

DEADLINES

Early decision	
Deadline	11/1
Notification	12/15
Regular	
Priority	1/3
Deadline	1/3
Nonfall registration?	no

APPLICANTS ALSO LOOK AT
AND OFTEN PREFER
Columbia University, Dartmouth College, Harvard College, Massachusetts Institute of Technology, Princeton University, Stanford University, Yale University

AND SOMETIMES PREFER
Brown University, Cornell University, Duke University, Georgetown University, Johns Hopkins University, Northwestern University, Rice University, University of Chicago, University of North Carolina at Chapel Hill, University of Notre Dame, University of Pennsylvania, University of Virginia, Washington University in St. Louis

AND RARELY PREFER
Boston College, Emory University, Georgia Institute of Technology, Tulane University, University of Florida, University of Georgia, University of Illinois at Chicago, University of Michigan—Ann Arbor, Wake Forest University

FINANCIAL FACTS

Financial Aid Rating	96
Annual tuition	$38,952
Room and board	$13,058
Required fees	$978
Books and supplies	$1,344
% frosh rec. need-based scholarship or grant aid	44
% UG rec. need-based scholarship or grant aid	43
% frosh rec. non-need-based scholarship or grant aid	29
% UG rec. non-need-based scholarship or grant aid	22
% frosh rec. need-based self-help aid	25
% UG rec. need-based self-help aid	28
% frosh rec. any financial aid	64
% UG rec. any financial aid	63
% UG borrow to pay for school	37
Average cumulative indebtedness	$18,605

VASSAR COLLEGE

124 RAYMOND AVENUE, POUGHKEEPSIE, NY 12604 • ADMISSIONS: 845-437-7300 • FAX: 845-437-7063

STUDENTS SAY ". . ."

Academics

Vassar College gives students "the chance to experiment with [their] life in an encouraging and stimulating environment," providing an unusual amount of academic freedom because "there's no real core curriculum. All you need in the way of requirements are one quantitative class and one foreign language credit. Plus, one-quarter of your credits must be outside of your major." This approach, students agree, "really encourages students to think creatively and pursue whatever they're passionate about, whether medieval tapestries, neuroscience, or unicycles. Not having a core curriculum is great because it gives students the opportunity to delve into many different interests." Of course, a system like this only works if students are motivated and teachers are dedicated. Fortunately, that's exactly how it shakes out at Vassar. The school boasts "world-class professors, small classes, and a faculty that really is interested in us as students. Every teacher and member of the faculty goes the extra mile to [be] available outside of class and [to] meet students for lunch or dinner." Vassar places "a real focus on the undergraduate students. There is big-time research just like at major universities, but there are no graduate students to fill all the spots. All assisting positions go to undergraduates." The school excels in the visual and performing arts—the "drama department is huge"—as well as in English, psychology, history, life sciences, and natural sciences.

Life

"Life is very campus-centered" at Vassar; the farthest off campus people regularly go is the twenty-four-hour diner two blocks north of campus. This is partly because hometown Poughkeepsie "does not offer much in the way of entertainment." For whatever reason, insularity is a defining characteristic of life at Vassar, so much so that students speak of "The Vassar Bubble. This is a term any student will immediately become familiar with. Essentially, Vassar is an island closed off from the rest of the town and community. It would be entirely possible (and not even rare) for a student to not leave campus once in an entire semester. While this is good for some, others will likely go a little crazy stuck on campus." Some escape to New York City whenever possible, but unfortunately the trip to the city is a relatively "expensive endeavor for weekly entertainment; it's about thirty-five dollars round-trip, and that doesn't include doing stuff once you get there." Fortunately, "there is a huge array of things to do every night on campus. Comedy shows, improv, an incredibly wide array of theater productions"—including "several shows a year and three student groups devoted to drama"—"four comedy groups, five a cappella groups," and "interesting lectures create numerous opportunities to get out of the dorms at night." Weekends are for parties; there's "no Greek life, so lots of parties are awesome, school-sponsored, theme events." There's also "lots of socializing at senior housing," and "Halloween is huge. People really go all out."

Student Body

There are "lots of hipsters" at Vassar including kids who are "very left-wing politically" and "very into the music scene." The school is "not entirely dominated by hipsters," however; there are "lots of different groups" on campus. "Walking around you'll see students who walked out of a thrift store next to students who walked out of a *J. Crew* catalog," one student tells us. Another adds that Vassar is a comfortable respite for "indie-chic students who revel in obscurity, some socially awkward archetypes, and some prep school pin-ups with their collars popped. But the majority of kids on campus are a mix of these people, which is why we mesh pretty well despite the cliques that inevitably form." What students share is having "an amazing talent or something they passionately believe in" that makes them distinctive. "Vassar admissions works tremendously hard to ensure every student at Vassar is unique and mold-breaking," students brag.

VASSAR COLLEGE

FINANCIAL AID: 845-437-5230 • E-MAIL: ADMISSIONS@VASSAR.EDU • WEBSITE: WWW.VASSAR.EDU

THE PRINCETON REVIEW SAYS

Admissions

Very important factors considered include: Rigor of secondary school record. *Important factors considered include:* Academic GPA, application essay, class rank, recommendation(s), standardized test scores, character/personal qualities, extracurricular activities, talent/ability. *Other factors considered include:* Alumni/ae relation, first generation, geographical residence, interview, racial/ethnic status, volunteer work, work experience. ACT with writing component required. TOEFL required of all international applicants. High school diploma is required, and GED is accepted. *Academic units required:* 4 English, 4 mathematics, 4 science (3 science labs), 3 foreign language, 2 social studies, 2 history, 4 academic elective. *Academic units recommended:* 4 English, 4 mathematics, 4 science (3 science labs), 4 foreign language, 2 social studies, 2 history.

Financial Aid

Students should submit: FAFSA, CSS/Financial Aid PROFILE. Regular filing deadline is February 1. The Princeton Review suggests that all financial aid forms be submitted as soon as possible after January 1. *Need-based scholarships/grants offered:* Federal Pell, SEOG, state scholarships/grants, private scholarships, school scholarship or grant aid from institutional funds. *Loan aid offered:* Direct Subsidized Stafford, Direct Unsubsidized Stafford, Direct PLUS, Federal Perkins. Federal Work-Study Program available. Off-campus job opportunities are fair.

The Inside Word

With acceptance rates hitting record lows, stellar academic credentials are a must for any serious Vassar candidate. Importantly, the college prides itself on selecting students who will add to the vitality of the campus. Once admissions officers see you meet their rigorous scholastic standards, they'll closely assess your personal essay, recommendations, and extracurricular activities. Demonstrating an intellectual curiosity that extends outside the classroom is as important as success within it.

THE SCHOOL SAYS "..."

From the Admissions Office

"Vassar presents a rich variety of social and cultural activities, clubs, sports, living arrangements, and regional attractions. Vassar is a vital, residential college community recognized for its respect for the rights and individuality of others.

"Candidates must submit either the SAT Reasoning Test and two SAT Subject Tests taken in different subject fields, or the ACT exam (the optional ACT writing component is required)."

SELECTIVITY

Admissions Rating	98
# of applicants	7,822
% of applicants accepted	24
% of acceptees attending	36
# accepting a place on wait list	568
% admitted from wait list	0
# of early decision applicants	639
% accepted early decision	41

FRESHMAN PROFILE

Range SAT Critical Reading	670–740
Range SAT Math	640–720
Range SAT Writing	660–750
Range ACT Composite	29–32
Minimum paper TOEFL	600
Minimum computer TOEFL	250
Minimum web-based TOEFL	100
Average HS GPA	3.77
% graduated top 10% of class	65
% graduated top 25% of class	96
% graduated top 50% of class	100

DEADLINES

Early decision	
Deadline	11/15
Notification	12/15
Regular	
Deadline	1/1
Nonfall registration?	no

APPLICANTS ALSO LOOK AT

AND OFTEN PREFER
Amherst College, Brown University, Harvard College, Williams College, Yale University

AND SOMETIMES PREFER
Columbia University, Tufts University, Wesleyan University

AND RARELY PREFER
New York University, Skidmore College

FINANCIAL FACTS

Financial Aid Rating	99
Annual tuition	$42,560
Room and board	$10,080
Required fees	$630
Books and supplies	$860
% frosh rec. need-based scholarship or grant aid	64
% UG rec. need-based scholarship or grant aid	62
% frosh rec. need-based self-help aid	64
% UG rec. need-based self-help aid	63
% frosh rec. any financial aid	64
% UG rec. any financial aid	63
% UG borrow to pay for school	49
Average cumulative indebtedness	$18,153

VILLANOVA UNIVERSITY

800 LANCASTER AVENUE, VILLANOVA, PA 19085-1672 • ADMISSIONS: 610-519-4000 • FAX: 610-519-6450

CAMPUS LIFE

Quality of Life Rating	94
Fire Safety Rating	86
Green Rating	85
Type of school	private
Affiliation	Roman Catholic
Environment	village

STUDENTS

Total undergrad enrollment	7,146
% male/female	49/51
% from out of state	76
% from public high school	56
% live on campus	70
# of fraternities	10
# of sororities	10
% African American	5
% Asian	6
% Caucasian	77
% Hispanic	7
% international	3
# of countries represented	54

SURVEY SAYS . . .
School is well-run
Low cost of living
Everyone loves the Wildcats

ACADEMICS

Academic Rating	91
% students graduating within 4 years	85
% students graduating within 6 years	90
Calendar	semester
Student/faculty ratio	11:1
Profs interesting rating	88
Profs accessible rating	88
Most common reg class size	10–19 students
Most common lab size	20–29 students

MOST POPULAR MAJORS
finance, nursing, speech communication and rhetoric

STUDENTS SAY ". . ."

Academics

"Villanova emphasizes not only the importance of academics but also service and connection with the community." A Catholic university just outside Philadelphia, the school's emphasis on community and "dedication to service" is an important factor in its reputation. Villanova's "well-rounded academic focus," "excellent nursing and business school programs," and "outstanding" faculty are definitely strong draws. Villanova "requires students to take classes based on a core curriculum, which [leads] to a well-rounded education." "You will work hard," warns one student, "but if you put in the work, you will do well." "The professors at Villanova are fantastic!" says another. "I've had professors give out e-mail addresses, cell, home, and office numbers, even an AIM screenname in order to make contacting them as easy as possible." The professors for the most part are "PhDs and love to teach. You are never taught by a grad student." Even the harshest critique has an element of praise in it: "You either get someone you completely click with and is very interactive with students, or you get a PhD who just has to teach a class and isn't very good at teaching, but is really, really smart." The administration gets high marks as well. "If I wanted to meet with Father Peter, the president of Villanova, I could go see him tomorrow. Everyone is accessible." Keep in mind, though. "You need to be your own advocate—you can get anything you want if you ask nicely (or not so nicely, if need be), but nothing will happen if you don't ask."

Life

The "idea of community is extremely important" at Villanova. "The average student works hard four days a week, parties harder two days a week, and spends the seventh day working for some cause," explains one student. "Life at Villanova seems to be a work hard during the day, play hard during the night atmosphere," says another. "People are serious about their schoolwork and do many activities. However, once it becomes nighttime, especially Thursday through Saturday, many people drink and throw parties. People generally like to have a good time." "Basketball and frat parties" seem to make up a majority of the social life. But, "There is always stuff to do for fun that does not involve partying." "Sporting events are huge here at the school as our basketball program is fantastic." It's worth pointing out, "If you don't like basketball, you will learn to like it even if you never actually understand it." Villanova is only twelve miles and a short train ride away from Center City Philadelphia, where "many people go out to dinner or shopping," or to watch basketball at the Wachovia Center. The school also provides free shuttle buses to the huge King of Prussia mall nearby. Because "there are no frat, sorority, or sports houses on campus," much of the Greek life takes place at off-campus houses and apartments, and "parties are usually hard to get to." Ultimately, "The community of students is very tight-knit," and "there are always activities on campus that involve volunteer work or group projects in the surrounding areas."

Student Body

"Good-looking, white, overachievers who like to have a good time" seems to be the prevailing consensus. "However, that seems to be changing more and more every year," one student says. "We are starting to see many more minorities, which obviously is a great and refreshing thing to see." "Villanova is not as preppy, conservative, or homogeneous as it was…The newer students seem a bit more liberal and academic than the students of years before." Regardless of race or politics, the typical Villanova student "is very service oriented and excels academically," not to mention a "basketball fanatic." "In general, everyone gets along nicely, and the multitude of student organizations and trips foster school unity." Many people note, "students outside the Villanova norm can easily find their own niche in the community."

VILLANOVA UNIVERSITY

FINANCIAL AID: 610-519-4010 • E-MAIL: GOTOVU@VILLANOVA.EDU • WEBSITE: WWW.VILLANOVA.EDU

THE PRINCETON REVIEW SAYS

Admissions

Very important factors considered include: Academic GPA, class rank, rigor of secondary school record, standardized test scores. *Important factors considered include:* Application essay, recommendation(s), character/personal qualities, extracurricular activities, talent/ability, volunteer work, work experience. *Other factors considered include:* Alumni/ae relation, first generation, geographical residence, level of applicant's interest, racial/ethnic status, state residency. SAT or ACT required; ACT with writing component required. TOEFL required of all international applicants. High school diploma is required, and GED is accepted. *Academic units required:* 4 English, 4 mathematics, 4 science (2 science labs), 2 foreign language, 2 academic elective. *Academic units recommended:* 4 English, 4 mathematics, 4 science (3 science labs), 4 foreign language, 2 academic elective.

Financial Aid

Students should submit: FAFSA, CSS/Financial Aid PROFILE, noncustodial profile. Regular filing deadline is February 7. The Princeton Review suggests that all financial aid forms be submitted as soon as possible after January 1. *Need-based scholarships/grants offered:* Federal Pell, SEOG, state scholarships/grants, private scholarships, school scholarship or grant aid from institutional funds. *Loan aid offered:* Direct Subsidized Stafford, Direct Unsubsidized Stafford, Direct PLUS, Federal Perkins, Federal Nursing Loans. Applicants will be notified of awards on or around April 1. Federal Work-Study Program available. Off-campus job opportunities are excellent.

The Inside Word

Villanova's growing academic reputation means its application process is growing more competitive as well: ninety percent of the most recent freshman class ranked in the top twenty-five percent of their high school graduating class. But while academic achievement is important, the university looks at the whole package when considering applicants and expects candidates to do the same. As a private university, Villanova is not exactly cheap, but the school offers a wide variety of scholarships and aid to qualifying students.

THE SCHOOL SAYS ". . ."

From the Admissions Office

"Villanova is the oldest and largest Catholic university in Pennsylvania, founded in 1842 by the Order of Saint Augustine. Students of all faiths are welcome. The university tends to attract students who are interested in volunteerism. Villanovans provide more than 200,000 hours of service annually and host the largest student-run Special Olympics in the nation. Villanova's scenic campus is located twelve miles west of Philadelphia. The university offers programs through four undergraduate colleges: Liberal Arts and Sciences, Engineering, Nursing, and the Villanova School of Business. There are 250 student organizations and thirty-six National Honor Societies at Villanova. Incoming freshmen can opt to be part of a Learning Community, through which student groups live together in specially-designated residence halls and learn together in courses and co-curricular programs. The university offers Naval and Marine Reserve Officers Training Corps (ROTC) programs and hundreds of options for studying abroad. 'Nova's alumni body is comprised of 108,000 people. Some prominent grads include: Maria Bello, Golden Globe-Nominated Actress; Rear Admiral Christine Bruzek-Kohler, Executive Director of Healthcare Operations, Joint Task Force—National Capital Region; Sean McDermott, CEO of Winward IT Solutions; Robert Moran, President and COO of PetSmart; James O'Donnell, CEO of American Eagle Outfitters; and Dianna Sugg, Pulitzer Prize Recipient for Journalism.

"If you're looking to join 'Nova Nation, be prepared: The competition for admission is getting tougher every year."

SELECTIVITY

Admissions Rating	95
# of applicants	14,361
% of applicants accepted	45
% of acceptees attending	25
# accepting a place on wait list	2,420
% admitted from wait list	16

FRESHMAN PROFILE

Range SAT Critical Reading	590–680
Range SAT Math	620–710
Range ACT Composite	28–31
Minimum paper TOEFL	550
Minimum computer TOEFL	213
Average HS GPA	3.82
% graduated top 10% of class	59
% graduated top 25% of class	90
% graduated top 50% of class	98

DEADLINES

Early action	
Deadline	11/1
Notification	12/20
Regular	
Priority	12/15
Deadline	1/7
Nonfall registration?	no

APPLICANTS ALSO LOOK AT

AND OFTEN PREFER
Georgetown University, University of Notre Dame, University of Pennsylvania

AND SOMETIMES PREFER
Boston College, Bucknell University, Holy Cross College, Lehigh University, Penn State—University Park

AND RARELY PREFER
Drexel University, Loyola College in Maryland, Saint Joseph's University (PA), University of Delaware

FINANCIAL FACTS

Financial Aid Rating	73
Annual tuition	$39,350
Room and board	$10,620
Required fees	$730
Books and supplies	$950
% frosh rec. need-based scholarship or grant aid	42
% UG rec. need-based scholarship or grant aid	42
% frosh rec. non-need-based scholarship or grant aid	12
% UG rec. non-need-based scholarship or grant aid	13
% frosh rec. need-based self-help aid	44
% UG rec. need-based self-help aid	43
% frosh rec. any financial aid	47
% UG rec. any financial aid	47
% UG borrow to pay for school	55
Average cumulative indebtedness	$37,267

VIRGINIA POLYTECHNIC INSTITUTE AND STATE UNIVERSITY (VIRGINIA TECH)

UNDERGRADUATE ADMISSIONS, 201 BURRUSS HALL, BLACKSBURG, VA 24061 • ADMISSIONS: 540-231-6267 • FAX: 540-231-3242

CAMPUS LIFE

Quality of Life Rating	98
Fire Safety Rating	76
Green Rating	99
Type of school	public
Environment	town

STUDENTS

Total undergrad enrollment	23,600
% male/female	58/42
% from out of state	25
% live on campus	37
# of fraternities	31
# of sororities	12
% African American	4
% Asian	8
% Caucasian	76
% Hispanic	4
% international	2
# of countries represented	113

SURVEY SAYS . . .

Athletic facilities are great
Great food on campus
Everyone loves the Hokies
Student publications are popular

ACADEMICS

Academic Rating	71
Calendar	semester
Student/faculty ratio	16:1
Profs interesting rating	75
Profs accessible rating	79
Most common reg class size	20–29 students
Most common lab size	20–29 students

MOST POPULAR MAJORS
biology, engineering

STUDENTS SAY ". . ."

Academics

Students at tech schools don't typically brag about their quality of life, but then again, Virginia Polytechnic Institute and State University, otherwise known as Virginia Tech, is not your typical tech school. Here, students happily discover that they can enjoy "a diverse community," "an accepting atmosphere," "a football program that takes priority for all but the most dedicated students," and the opportunity "to have a blast in college while still staying focused on their education." Without losing access to "a great science program" (in which "undergraduate research is huge"), strong engineering programs, and outstanding offerings in architecture, agricultural science, forestry, and business. Throughout this large school, undergrads are pleasantly surprised to find this school offers a well-rounded experience. Profesors "who are always willing to help answer questions," although they warn that "there are a few classes where you can't understand anything the professor says, and he can't figure out how to explain it." Sometimes the result of a language barrier, other times the result of the difficulty of the concept being taught. Fortunately, "even if your teacher can't help you understand something, is not very hard to find someone who can." About one in five students here pursues engineering, a degree that "provides a mixture of practical and theoretical teaching in the classes, experimental labs, a design capstone" and "a cooperative education program that places great value on applying knowledge in the real world."

Life

Virginia Tech may be located "in the middle of nowhere," but students don't seem to mind, because "the people you meet and the cozy town of Blacksburg can be so much fun. Being part of the Hokie nation is really special." That's especially true during football season, because the football team "is king in Blacksburg. It's hard not to be excited about football when you are tailgating with friends and seeing 60,000 people pack the stadium." While "most people are very serious about school work," they "still have time to go party" or "to have fun in a place called the Break Zone, where you can go bowling, play pool, or just hang out." Greek life is also "pretty big and a really great thing." Whenever weather permits, "you can always find people outside playing volleyball or basketball, or using the Drillfield for games of pickup soccer and football" at Tech; lots of students exploit the "perfect location for outdoor activities." According to one undergrad, "Within thirty minutes from campus, you can be hiking on the Appalachian Trail, floating down the New River, picnicking in the Jefferson National Forest, or listening to live old-time music at the Floyd Country Store on Friday nights." Shopping has been a problem in the past, but students report that "they are beginning to bring more sites into Blacksburg" and that there's "some shopping in Christianburg," which is about ten miles away.

Student Body

School spirit is strong at Virginia Tech, where students "are typically clad head to toe in maroon and orange with a Virginia Tech/HokieBird logo at least somewhere on their outfit." Students regard themselves as "well-rounded and friendly," the sort of people who "enjoy going out and partying but also know when to study and get their work done." There are lots of folks who fit the description: "Caucasian; middle class; and from the Northern Virginia, Richmond, or Virginia Beach areas," but the school is "very open to student diversity. That's actually an aspect that is being pushed in the student population," where you'll also find "a lot of students from other countries like India and China." With more than 23,000 undergraduates, Virginia Tech's "large student body makes it easy to find many people that have the same interests and are able to become good friends."

VIRGINIA POLYTECHNIC INSTITUTE AND STATE UNIVERSITY (VIRGINIA TECH)

FINANCIAL AID: 540-231-5179 • E-MAIL: VTADMISS@VT.EDU • WEBSITE: WWW.VT.EDU

THE PRINCETON REVIEW SAYS

Admissions

Very important factors considered include: Academic GPA, rigor of secondary school record, standardized test scores. *Other factors considered include:* Personal statement, alumni/ae relation, character/personal qualities, extracurricular activities, first generation, geographical residence, major requested, racial/ethnic status, state residency, talent/ability, volunteer work. SAT or ACT required; ACT with writing component required. TOEFL required of all international applicants. High school diploma is required, and GED is accepted. *Academic units required:* 4 English, 3 mathematics, 2 science (2 science labs), 1 social studies, 1 history, 4 academic elective. *Academic units recommended:* 4 mathematics, 3 science, 3 foreign language.

Financial Aid

Students should submit: FAFSA. Priority filing deadline is March 1. The Princeton Review suggests that all financial aid forms be submitted as soon as possible after January 1. *Need-based scholarships/grants offered:* Federal Pell, SEOG, state scholarships/grants, private scholarships, school scholarship or grant aid from institutional funds. *Loan aid offered:* Direct Subsidized Stafford, Direct Unsubsidized Stafford, Direct PLUS, Federal Perkins, university loans from institutional funds. Applicants will be notified of awards on a rolling basis beginning March 30. Off-campus job opportunities are excellent.

The Inside Word

It's a numbers game at Virginia Tech, a byproduct of the almost 20,000 applications that flood into the admissions office each year. High school grades and curriculum figure most prominently into the admissions decision, followed by standardized test scores. There are no published cutoffs, but solid performers should expect little resistance here, except perhaps in more competitive disciplines (for example, engineering, architecture).

THE SCHOOL SAYS "..."

From the Admissions Office

"Virginia Tech offers the opportunities of a large research university in a small-town setting. Undergraduates choose from more than seventy majors in seven colleges, including nationally ranked architecture, business, forestry, and engineering schools, as well as excellent computer science, biology, and communication studies, and architecture programs. Technology is a key focus, both in classes and in general. All first-year students are required to own a personal computer, each residence hall room has Ethernet connections, and every student is provided e-mail and Internet access. Faculty incorporate a wide variety of technology into class, utilizing chat rooms, online lecture notes, and multimedia presentations. The university offers cutting-edge facilities for classes and research, abundant opportunities for advanced study in the honors program, undergraduate research opportunities, study abroad, internships, and cooperative education. Students enjoy nearly 700 organizations which offer something for everyone. Tech offers the best of both worlds—everything a large university can provide and a small-town atmosphere.

"Freshman applicants must take the SAT or ACT with writing section. We will use the highest scores from any SAT or ACT test scores submitted."

SELECTIVITY

Admissions Rating	91
# of applicants	19,981
% of applicants accepted	67
% of acceptees attending	39
# accepting a place on wait list	1,349
% admitted from wait list	0
# of early decision applicants	2,079
% accepted early decision	55

FRESHMAN PROFILE

Range SAT Critical Reading	540–640
Range SAT Math	580–680
Range SAT Writing	540–630
Minimum paper TOEFL	550
Average HS GPA	3.96
% graduated top 10% of class	45
% graduated top 25% of class	85
% graduated top 50% of class	99

DEADLINES

Early decision	
Deadline	11/1
Notification	12/15
Regular	
Deadline	1/15
Nonfall registration?	yes

APPLICANTS ALSO LOOK AT AND OFTEN PREFER
College of William and Mary, University of Virginia

AND RARELY PREFER
College of William and Mary, University of North Carolina at Chapel Hill

FINANCIAL FACTS

Financial Aid Rating	73
Annual in-state tuition	$7,308
Annual out-of-state tuition	$23,216
Books and supplies	$1,100
% frosh rec. need-based scholarship or grant aid	28
% UG rec. need-based scholarship or grant aid	30
% frosh rec. non-need-based scholarship or grant aid	36
% UG rec. non-need-based scholarship or grant aid	34
% frosh rec. need-based self-help aid	30
% UG rec. need-based self-help aid	32
% frosh rec. any financial aid	62
% UG rec. any financial aid	69
% UG borrow to pay for school	52
Average cumulative indebtedness	$23,100

WABASH COLLEGE

PO Box 352, 301 West Wabash Avenue, Crawfordsville, IN 47933 • Admissions: 765-361-6225 • Fax: 765-361-6437

STUDENTS SAY ". . ."

Academics

A "small, personalized, rigorous, elite institution" with an all-male student body, "Wabash College is a powerful small school that changes lives." In a word, Wabash is all about "tradition." The men here "live by a Wabash motto: 'Think Critically, Act Responsibly, Live Humanely, and Lead Effectively.'" With a "ninety-five percent acceptance rate into law school and a ninety percent acceptance rate into medical school," academics here are nothing to shake a stick at. Wabash is "a very challenging academic environment," "but you are provided with every opportunity needed to succeed and excel." Students flock here for the "devoted alumni network, strong, academically focused Greek system, small classes, personal professors, [and] emphasis on reading and writing." "One of the best things about Wabash is the opportunities it provides." The campus boasts "a state-of-the-art athletic center, an incredibly supportive faculty and staff, and an extensive alumni network." "Whether you strive for academic, athletic, community, or professional success, Wabash provides the means to achieve your goals." Professors here "are, generally speaking, the biggest selling point for Wabash." "They are world-class teachers [and] researchers." When not teaching, "Professors are nearly always available, and most departments have a tutoring center led by upperclassmen open every night of the week if you need assistance." "Many of the professors are also active in the social life of the school and can be seen tailgating with students before games or participating in different student-run clubs." All members of this unique community tout the understanding that Wabash College "is a school where boys come to become men, and men come to become gentlemen."

Life

The campus as a whole "is incredibly intimate." "The depth of the relationships between students and faculty is incredible." Furthermore, "The type of scholastic discourse that takes place both within and outside of the classroom is unparalleled." The school has a strict "honesty policy, which most, if not everybody, take seriously." Must hold fast to the credo that "what makes this place special [is] the life blood of our school: exceptional men who wish to learn and lead." "We work hard at classes five days a week, but the upperclassmen often make time to go to the Neon Cactus at Purdue on Thursday." "Friday and Saturday are devoted to releasing the stress from the week with a lot of cold beer." "In the warm months, we grill outside and have drinks with professors. In the cold months, we hang out in the fraternity house talking about movies, or world events, or what the pledges did last week." The academic buildings are built around a grassy field, called the "mall," and "There are frequently pickup games of soccer or ultimate Frisbee." Some say that "the absence of women is hard to bear." "After a while, you begin to embrace the lifestyle." "When you are done with class you might go to ESH (Employment Self-Help), an on-campus job, or you might go relax with your friends at your fraternity."

Student Body

A typical Wabash student "is an athlete who is willing to work long hours to get good grades." "Studious, eager to learn and to get work done, [and] serious about school," students here are "almost treated like peers by professors." "Everyone at Wabash works very hard and benefits from the rigorous academic requirements." "Lower-class to upper-class backgrounds allow for a variety of perspectives and previous educations." Regardless of where they hail from, "Students embrace the backgrounds of their classmates and work together to learn." Others say, "It's an all-male college, but that's where the universal attributes end." "There could stand to be some more ethnic diversity"; however, others say, "I think that's got more to with self-selection than anything else." "The library is packed Sunday through Thursday evening"; on the weekends, everyone "cuts loose and hangs out with friends." The most dominant social factor "is fraternity, followed by sports." The typical student is "from the Midwest, plays a sport, and will be going into business or grad school after graduation."

WABASH COLLEGE

FINANCIAL AID: 765-361-6370 • E-MAIL: ADMISSIONS@WABASH.EDU • WEBSITE: WWW.WABASH.EDU

THE PRINCETON REVIEW SAYS

Admissions

Very important factors considered include: Academic GPA, class rank, rigor of secondary school record. *Important factors considered include:* Recommendation(s), standardized test scores, extracurricular activities, interview, level of applicant's interest, talent/ability. *Other factors considered include:* Application essay, alumni/ae relation, character/personal qualities, first generation, geographical residence, racial/ethnic status, volunteer work, work experience. SAT or ACT required; ACT with writing component required. TOEFL required of all international applicants. High school diploma is required, and GED is accepted. *Academic units recommended:* 4 English, 4 mathematics, 2 science (2 science labs), 2 foreign language, 2 social studies, 2 history.

Financial Aid

Students should submit: FAFSA, CSS/Financial Aid PROFILE. Regular filing deadline is March 1. The Princeton Review suggests that all financial aid forms be submitted as soon as possible after January 1. *Need-based scholarships/grants offered:* Federal Pell, state scholarships/grants, private scholarships, school scholarship or grant aid from institutional funds. *Loan aid offered:* Direct Subsidized Stafford, Direct Unsubsidized Stafford, Direct PLUS, university loans from institutional funds. Federal Work-Study Program available. Off-campus job opportunities are good.

The Inside Word

Wabash is one of the few remaining all-male colleges in the country, and like the rest of the brotherhood, it has a small applicant pool. The pool is highly self-selected, and the academic standards for admission, while selective, aren't especially demanding. Graduating is a whole other matter. Don't consider applying if you're not ready to do the grueling work required for success here.

THE SCHOOL SAYS " . . . "

From the Admissions Office

"Wabash College is different—and distinctive—from other liberal arts colleges. Different in that Wabash is an outstanding college for men only. Distinctive in the quality and character of the faculty, in the demanding nature of the academic program, in the farsightedness and maturity of the men who enroll, and in the richness of the traditions that have evolved throughout its 178-year history. Wabash is preeminently a teaching institution, and fundamental to the learning experience is the way faculty and students talk to each other—with mutual respect for the expression of informed opinion. For example, students who collaborate with faculty on research projects are considered their peers in the research—an esteem not usually extended to undergraduates. The college takes pride in the sense of community that such a learning environment fosters. But perhaps the single most striking aspect of student life at Wabash is personal freedom. The college has only one rule: 'The student is expected to conduct himself at all times, both on and off the campus, as a gentleman and a responsible citizen.' Wabash College treats students as adults, and such treatment attracts responsible freshmen and fosters their independence and maturity.

"For students seeking admission, Wabash will accept the SAT or the ACT. Wabash will use the student's best scores from either examination and will accept the SAT or ACT writing portions in place of an essay. Wabash does not require SAT Subject Tests."

SELECTIVITY

Admissions Rating	89
# of applicants	1,535
% of applicants accepted	56
% of acceptees attending	29
# accepting a place on wait list	98
% admitted from wait list	17
# of early decision applicants	43
% accepted early decision	88

FRESHMAN PROFILE

Range SAT Critical Reading	510–615
Range SAT Math	540–660
Range SAT Writing	490–610
Range ACT Composite	22–28
Minimum paper TOEFL	550
Minimum computer TOEFL	213
Average HS GPA	3.58
% graduated top 10% of class	43
% graduated top 25% of class	67
% graduated top 50% of class	93

DEADLINES

Early decision	
Deadline	11/15
Notification	12/1
Early action	
Deadline	12/1
Notification	12/22
Regular	
Priority	12/1
Notification	12/1
Nonfall registration?	yes

APPLICANTS ALSO LOOK AT

AND OFTEN PREFER
Indiana University at Bloomington, Purdue University—West Lafayette

AND SOMETIMES PREFER
DePauw University, Hanover College

FINANCIAL FACTS

Financial Aid Rating	95
Annual tuition	$30,400
Room and board	$8,300
Required fees	$650
Books and supplies	$800
% frosh rec. need-based scholarship or grant aid	82
% UG rec. need-based scholarship or grant aid	77
% frosh rec. non-need-based scholarship or grant aid	12
% UG rec. non-need-based scholarship or grant aid	10
% frosh rec. need-based self-help aid	73
% UG rec. need-based self-help aid	68
% frosh rec. any financial aid	86
% UG rec. any financial aid	79
% UG borrow to pay for school	81
Average cumulative indebtedness	$29,897

WAGNER COLLEGE

ONE CAMPUS ROAD, STATEN ISLAND, NY 10301-4495 • ADMISSIONS: 718-390-3411 • FAX: 718-390-3105

STUDENTS SAY ". . ."

Academics
At Wagner College, "You get a small, lively, personal community tucked away on Grymes Hill of Staten Island," with "stunning views of the Atlantic and of Manhattan" and "the heart of New York City" just a "ferry ride away." This "small, private campus" located in one of the nearby boroughs of Manhattan" couples "great academics," with strong "internship opportunities" and a "convenient location." The "small classes" and "well-rounded liberal arts education" "focus on discussion and experiential learning rather than large lectures." Many students laud "the student/ teacher ratio." "It's a small school, so I don't feel like just a number. I can actually get to know my professors." In addition, Wagner offers "a very unique curriculum" known as "The Wagner Plan," which uses "experiential learning in tying together course material and field work to give students a practical, real-world liberal arts experience." "The opportunities Wagner College offers are great." Students continually align the "convenient location by Manhattan, its majors, its internship opportunities, and its strong pre-medical program!" In addition, the "theater program is one of the best in the nation." The "nursing/physician's assistant programs are [also] very strong." Professors are "brilliant"; "They really know their material and enthusiastically convey the information to their students." Wagner is "all about learning through doing and putting what you learn into practice." "Also, what's not to love about New York City?!"

Life
Students consistently laud Wagner's "breathtaking scenery and spectacular views of Manhattan." The Big Apple is definitely a large draw. "Because my school is so close to Manhattan, most people spend their time there as opposed to on campus or on Staten Island." Others concur, "My experiences and memories related to Manhattan and New York City in general are inseparable from my overall college experience." Wagner students "take advantage of the opportunities, resources, and certainly entertainment available to them" in nearby Manhattan. Many "go out with friends on a weekend and go out to eat, see a Broadway show, [or] simply walk around." On campus, however, "There are several clubs and organizations to participate in." "Our student body is small—about 1,900 undergraduates—so there is small town gossip, but people recognize or know each other a lot of the time, and people are very social and engaging—always willing to make new friends." Another happy Wagner student concurs, "There is always something to do here, whether it's a free show at the theater or a fundraiser in the coffee house. Wagner is always having guest speakers come for lectures and even book readings." For fun, others "participate in community service activities" as well as become "a part of clubs and organizations."

Student Body
The typical Wagner student is "driven, smart, funny, friendly, and loves New York City." "They might have a sense of adventure and like to explore the city." In this sense, the campus is a reflection of the nearby metropolis itself. Wagner is "a melting pot." The student body here celebrates its "diverse" makeup. Students "fit in through common interests (major/minor, hobbies) through joining organizations." "Areas of study tend to play a large role in where students fit in, such as the theater majors and the business majors." Greek life is "also popular." Students here practice "a balance of discipline and freedom, studying through the week and relaxing on the weekend." "There are different social groups, but students are free to interact with other social groups and all groups are fairly accepting." Others note a "divide between the 'theater kids' and 'athletes,'" "which is very disappointing because it creates tension at times." "Three distinct types of students" tend to emerge at Wagner: "the theater students, the athletes, and everyone else." However, others say, "Students usually find friends within their major" but still "are open-minded."

WAGNER COLLEGE

FINANCIAL AID: 718-390-3183 • E-MAIL: ADMISSIONS@WAGNER.EDU • WEBSITE: WWW.WAGNER.EDU

THE PRINCETON REVIEW SAYS

Admissions

Very important factors considered include: Academic GPA, class rank, rigor of secondary school record. *Important factors considered include:* Application essay, recommendation(s), character/personal qualities, extracurricular activities, interview, talent/ability. *Other factors considered include:* Standardized test scores, level of applicant's interest, volunteer work, work experience. ACT with or without writing component accepted. TOEFL required of all international applicants. High school diploma is required, and GED is accepted. *Academic units required:* 4 English, 3 mathematics, 2 science (1 science lab), 2 foreign language, 1 social studies, 3 history, academic elective.

Financial Aid

Students should submit: FAFSA, institution's own financial aid form. Regular filing deadline is February 15. The Princeton Review suggests that all financial aid forms be submitted as soon as possible after January 1. *Need-based scholarships/grants offered:* Federal Pell, SEOG, state scholarships/grants, private scholarships, school scholarship or grant aid from institutional funds. *Loan aid offered:* Direct Subsidized Stafford, Direct Unsubsidized Stafford, Direct PLUS, Federal Perkins, Federal Nursing Loans. Applicants will be notified of awards on a rolling basis beginning March 1. Federal Work-Study Program available. Off-campus job opportunities are good.

The Inside Word

As far as grades and test scores, the profile of the average freshman class at Wagner is solid. Standardized tests are optional, and there is more value placed on the strength of your course work and your grades in those classes. The admissions staff here is dedicated to finding the right students for their school. Wagner is looking for students who like to be involved in community events, so make sure your application reflects your extracurriculars. An interview bodes well for serious applicants.

THE SCHOOL SAYS " . . ."

From the Admissions Office

"At Wagner College, we attract and develop active learners and future leaders. Wagner College has received national acclaim (Time magazine, American Association of Colleges and Universities) for its innovative curriculum, The Wagner Plan for the Practical Liberal Arts. At Wagner, we capitalize on our unique geography; we are a traditional, scenic, residential campus, which happens to sit atop a hill on an island overlooking lower Manhattan. Our location allows us to offer a program that couples required off-campus experiences (experiential learning), with 'learning community' clusters of courses. This program begins in the first semester and continues through the senior capstone experience in the major. Fieldwork and internships, writing-intensive reflective tutorials, connected learning, 'reading, writing, and doing': At Wagner College our students truly discover 'the practical liberal arts in New York City.'"

SELECTIVITY

Admissions Rating	85
# of applicants	2,581
% of applicants accepted	65
% of acceptees attending	29
# accepting a place on wait list	145
% admitted from wait list	8
# of early decision applicants	72
% accepted early decision	81

FRESHMAN PROFILE

Range SAT Critical Reading	530–640
Range SAT Math	520–650
Range SAT Writing	520–650
Range ACT Composite	24–28
Minimum paper TOEFL	550
Minimum computer TOEFL	217
Minimum web-based TOEFL	17
Average HS GPA	3.60
% graduated top 10% of class	14
% graduated top 25% of class	71
% graduated top 50% of class	92

DEADLINES

Early decision	
Deadline	12/1
Notification	12/15
Regular	
Priority	2/15
Deadline	3/15
Nonfall registration?	yes

APPLICANTS ALSO LOOK AT
AND OFTEN PREFER
Fairfield University, New York University

AND SOMETIMES PREFER
Drew University, Hobart and William Smith Colleges, Muhlenberg College

AND RARELY PREFER
Manhattan College, Marist College, Quinnipiac University

FINANCIAL FACTS

Financial Aid Rating	78
Annual tuition	$35,620
Room and board	$10,680
Required fees	$200
Books and supplies	$745
% frosh rec. need-based scholarship or grant aid	71
% UG rec. need-based scholarship or grant aid	62
% frosh rec. need-based self-help aid	56
% UG rec. need-based self-help aid	51
% frosh rec. any financial aid	92
% UG rec. any financial aid	90
% UG borrow to pay for school	55
Average cumulative indebtedness	$36,988

WAKE FOREST UNIVERSITY

Box 7373, REYNOLDA STATION, WINSTON-SALEM, NC 27109 • ADMISSIONS: 336-758-5201 • FAX: 336-758-4324

STUDENTS SAY ". . ."

Academics

Wake Forest University is a smaller, private school that offers "the best of both worlds—a big university's resources with small liberal arts college's sense of community." Business and accounting are probably the most notable programs, but you really can't go wrong with any of the various majors available. The alumni network is "incredible," and technology is fabulous. Upon enrollment, "every student receives a laptop." "Studying abroad is a huge deal at Wake Forest," too. More than half of the students participate at some point, taking courses in exotic locales all over the world. Wake Forest owns residential study centers in Venice, Vienna and London. Students at Wake proudly assert theirs are "perhaps the hardest working" students attending a school with the "most beautiful campus in the country." There's definitely quite a bit of "academic rigor" here. "The workload is excessive at times," and professors are "committed to both grade and ego deflation." "Small classes with a lot of discussion are common," though, and students rave about the "wonderful" faculty. "They make class interesting and people rarely skip." "Contacting them out of class is a piece of cake" as well. The administration is also "very easily accessible," and "the school seems to be run well." "There are no needs that are not met by the administration," says a finance major, "and there are no wants by the majority of the students."

Life

Academic pressures are "intense," and students tend to really let loose when they are finally done hitting the books. "Drinking is pretty big at Wake, especially hard liquor." "Frat parties are wildly popular" "on the weekends (and Wake Wednesdays)." Students say the "Greek scene is massive," but the number of students pledging each year has been steadily decreasing. "A large portion of the student body is a member of a fraternity or sorority." "All of the frats and sororities have really different personalities," explains a senior, "so you can find a group that fits you no matter what." Intercollegiate sports are another big pastime, "basketball, field hockey, and football in particular." Wake students love their Demon Deacons, and the teams fight well above their weight, pulling down ACC championships against far larger and less academically renowned schools. Intramurals are also very popular. Students are split regarding the appeal of hometown Winston-Salem. On one hand, it's "a very spread-out city" located in a residential area with no easy access to commerce. On the other hand, it's also "a perfectly gorgeous southern location" filled with "plenty of art galleries, theaters, coffeehouses, bookstores, shops, etc."

Student Body

"There is a lot of Southern prep at Wake Forest" and "a slight air of materialism." "Most people fit into the preppy white kid stereotype," observes a first-year student, "even the non-white students." The typical undergrad is basically "your all-American" kid. Nearly two-thirds of the students here receive some form of financial aid. Many students come from "well-to-do" families. "Pearl-wearing, North Face jacket-owning, Kate Spade-toting, Greek letter-wearing" types are quite common. Students tell us they range from "really friendly" to "exceedingly perky." They also tend to be athletic. "Everyone works out a bunch, and the few overweight students do stick out." "Politically, most kids are moderates—perhaps a bit right of center, but not drastically so," and "rightwing and leftwing groups tend to be vocal about their views." Some students suggest that Wake "could do with more diversity," and the school has been listening: last year, Wake Forest enrolled its most diverse freshman class ever.

FINANCIAL AID: 336-758-5154 • E-MAIL: ADMISSIONS@WFU.EDU • WEBSITE: WWW.WFU.EDU

THE PRINCETON REVIEW SAYS

Admissions

Very important factors considered include: Academic GPA, application essay, class rank, rigor of secondary school record, character/personal qualities. *Important factors considered include:* Recommendation(s), extracurricular activities, interview, talent/ability. *Other factors considered include:* Standardized test scores, alumni/ae relation, first generation, geographical residence, level of applicant's interest, racial/ethnic status, religious affiliation/commitment, state residency, volunteer work. TOEFL required of all international applicants. High school diploma is required, and GED is accepted. *Academic units required:* 4 English, 3 mathematics, 1 science, 2 foreign language, 2 social studies. *Academic units recommended:* 4 English, 4 mathematics, 4 science, 4 foreign language, 4 social studies.

Financial Aid

Students should submit: FAFSA, CSS/Financial Aid PROFILE. Regular filing deadline is March 1. The Princeton Review suggests that all financial aid forms be submitted as soon as possible after January 1. *Need-based scholarships/grants offered:* Federal Pell, SEOG, state scholarships/grants, private scholarships, school scholarship or grant aid from institutional funds. *Loan aid offered:* Direct Subsidized Stafford, Direct Unsubsidized Stafford, Direct PLUS, Federal Perkins, state loans, university loans from institutional funds. Applicants will be notified of awards on a rolling basis beginning April 1. Federal Work-Study Program available. Off-campus job opportunities are excellent. Students wishing to be considered for merit-based scholarships must apply by December 1. Regular decision deadline January 1.

The Inside Word

Wake Forest's considerable application numbers afford admissions officers the opportunity to be rather selective. In particular, admissions officers remain diligent in their matchmaking efforts—finding students who are good fits for the school—and their hard work is rewarded by a high graduation rate. Candidates will need to be impressive in all areas to gain admission, since all areas of their applications are considered carefully. A relatively large number of qualified students find themselves on Wake Forest's wait list.

THE SCHOOL SAYS "..."

From the Admissions Office

"Wake Forest University has been dedicated to the liberal arts for over a century and a half; this means education in the fundamental fields of human knowledge and achievement. It seeks to encourage habits of mind that ask why, that evaluate evidence, that are open to new ideas, that attempt to understand and appreciate the perspective of others, that accept complexity and grapple with it, that admit error, and that pursue truth.

"Wake Forest is among a small, elite group of American colleges and universities recognized for their outstanding academic quality. It offers small classes taught by full-time faculty—not graduate assistants—and a commitment to student interaction with those professors. Students are provided ThinkPad computers. Classroom and residence halls are fully networked. Students are admitted based on the unique qualities they bring to our community. Wake Forest's generous financial aid program allows deserving students to enroll regardless of their financial circumstances.

"Wake Forest is the first top thirty national university in the United States to make standardized tests such as the SAT and ACT with writing optional in the admissions process. If applicants feel that their SAT or ACT with writing scores are a good indicator of their abilities, they may submit them and they will be considered in the admissions decision. If, however, a prospective student does not feel that their scores accurately represent their academic abilities, they do not need to submit them until after they have been accepted and choose to enroll. Wake Forest takes a holistic look at each applicant."

SELECTIVITY
Admissions Rating	94
# of applicants	10,553
% of applicants accepted	38
% of acceptees attending	30
# of early decision applicants	805
% accepted early decision	42

FRESHMAN PROFILE
Range SAT Critical Reading	580–690
Range SAT Math	600–700
Range ACT Composite	27–31
Minimum paper TOEFL	600
Minimum computer TOEFL	250
% graduated top 10% of class	75
% graduated top 25% of class	89
% graduated top 50% of class	99

DEADLINES
Early decision	
Deadline	11/15
Regular	
Deadline	1/1
Nonfall registration?	no

APPLICANTS ALSO LOOK AT AND SOMETIMES PREFER
Duke University, University of North Carolina at Chapel Hill, University of Virginia

FINANCIAL FACTS
Financial Aid Rating	90
Annual tuition	$39,544
Room and board	$11,010
Required fees	$426
Books and supplies	$930
% frosh rec. need-based scholarship or grant aid	28
% UG rec. need-based scholarship or grant aid	35
% frosh rec. non-need-based scholarship or grant aid	17
% UG rec. non-need-based scholarship or grant aid	25
% frosh rec. need-based self-help aid	24
% UG rec. need-based self-help aid	32
% frosh rec. any financial aid	39
% UG rec. any financial aid	34
% UG borrow to pay for school	38
Average cumulative indebtedness	$24,561

WARREN WILSON COLLEGE

PO Box 9000, Asheville, NC 28815-9000 • Admissions: 828-771-2073 • Fax: 828-298-1440

CAMPUS LIFE

Quality of Life Rating	86
Fire Safety Rating	63
Green Rating	99
Type of school	private
Affiliation	Presbyterian
Environment	town

STUDENTS

Total undergrad enrollment	923
% male/female	40/60
% from out of state	84
% from public high school	71
% live on campus	90
% African American	1
% Asian	1
% Caucasian	91
% Hispanic	2
% international	3
# of countries represented	13

SURVEY SAYS . . .

Lots of liberal students
Students are friendly
Low cost of living
Frats and sororities are unpopular
or nonexistent
Political activism is popular

ACADEMICS

Academic Rating	79
% students graduating within 4 years	33
% students graduating within 6 years	45
Calendar	semester
Student/faculty ratio	13:1
Profs interesting rating	85
Profs accessible rating	85
Most common reg class size	10–19 students
Most common lab size	10–19 students

MOST POPULAR MAJORS

biological and physical sciences,
environmental studies, outdoor
leadership

STUDENTS SAY ". . ."

Academics

Warren Wilson's unique approach to education is encapsulated in its "Triad program." This distinctive curriculum combines academics with "work and service." And though this program might demand more of your time, under-grads here speak quite highly of it. As one psych major shares, Triad "allows students to deepen their understanding of the world's needs and prepares them for a lifestyle of service beyond college." Additionally, it's an "active style of learning" that "really pushes students…to become well-rounded individuals." Undergrads are especially enthusiastic about the college's "environmental focus and strong science programs." There's "a working farm on campus that students run, and it [lends] excellent opportunity for hands-on experience." Undergrads also laud the "good creative writing department." Importantly, "the majority of the faculty are genuinely interested in the well-being of each and every student." Professors are "easy to talk to and highly available." This accessibility extends to the administration as well. As one impressed junior tells us, "We know our administration by first name, and if we want to talk to them, it's no problem to schedule an appointment or have the admin attend a student government meeting."

Life

Undergrads at Warren Wilson tend to lead hectic lives. Many concur that "students are really busy during the week" and therefore view the weekend as "a time for release." However, the intellectual debates don't just stop because it's leisure time. As one freshman shares, life often "revolves around political arguments and philosophical discussions held over cans of Pabst Blue Ribbon." Of course, activities extend beyond delightful and thought-provoking conversation. Students "greatly enjoy" the outdoors, and many can often be found "exploring trails, visiting the animals on the farm, swimming, kayaking, and canoeing on the Swannanoa River." Additionally, "fall soccer games, Friday night themed dance parties…and Thursday night contra dances" are all well attended. And one senior adds that "poetry slams, talent shows, theatrical productions, and parties that are held in the common areas of the dorms" are all great fun. Students are also "very politically and environmentally active, and community service" is extremely popular. Venturing into downtown Asheville is common as well. The town center is only "a fifteen-minute ride from campus, and there is a bus that goes back and forth during specific hours." The "funky" area has "a great arts and music scene," and "there are lots of concerts, performances, restaurants and local stores to visit."

Student Body

Warren Wilson is a college that "is very open to the idea of individuality" and thus manages to attract "a wide range of students." Many undergrads proclaim their peers to be "dynamic people" who are all "atypical." As a sophomore proudly boasts, "The great thing about this school is that a person, in all their weirdness, is loved and embraced by the community." Of course, for all this diversity, some commonalities do seep through. The "vast majority of people who go here are liberal" and are concerned "with social justice issues." Indeed, the mantle "hippie" is frequently bandied about. While some might object to this stereotype, many undergrads are "committed to environmental awareness." And a freshman notes that his fellow students "care about the outdoors, recycle, unplug appliances not in use, and would rather eat an organic salad than a steak." Additionally, most undergrads are hardworking and very industrious, constantly thinking of new projects to do and coming up with interesting ideas." But perhaps this math major sums up his peers best, "If you like people with weird haircuts, people with a different gender identity, vegans, feminists, and future organic farmers—or are one of these people— you will probably fit right in."

WARREN WILSON COLLEGE

THE PRINCETON REVIEW SAYS

Admissions

Very important factors considered include: Application essay, rigor of secondary school record, standardized test scores, character/personal qualities, interview, volunteer work, work experience. *Important factors considered include:* Academic GPA, class rank, recommendation(s). *Other factors considered include:* Class rank, alumni/ae relation, extracurricular activities, state residency, talent/ability. SAT or ACT required. TOEFL required of all international applicants. High school diploma is required, and GED is accepted. *Academic units required:* 4 English, 3 mathematics, 2 science (2 science labs), 3 history. *Academic units recommended:* 2 foreign language.

Financial Aid

Students should submit: FAFSA, institution's own financial aid form. The Princeton Review suggests that all financial aid forms be submitted as soon as possible after January 1. *Need-based scholarships/grants offered:* Federal Pell, SEOG, state scholarships/grants, school scholarship or grant aid from institutional funds. *Loan aid offered:* Federal Perkins, university loans from institutional funds. Applicants will be notified of awards on a rolling basis beginning March 2. Federal Work-Study Program available. Off-campus job opportunities are good.

The Inside Word

At Warren Wilson College, one's sense of social commitment is as vital to the admissions process as one's high school transcript—the college desires students who are actively engaged in their communities. Admissions officers are interested in applicants who seek to make connections and who understand how to apply what they learn in the classroom to outside projects and activities.

THE SCHOOL SAYS "..."

From the Admissions Office

"This book is *The Best 376 Colleges,* but Warren Wilson College may not be the best college for many students. There are 3,500 colleges in the U.S., and there is a best place for everyone. The 'best college' is one that has the right size, location, programs, and above all, the right feel for you, even if it is not listed here. Warren Wilson College may be the best choice if you think and act independently, actively participate in your education, and want a college that provides a sense of community. Your hands will get dirty here, your mind will be stretched, and you'll not be anonymous. If you are looking for the traditional college experience with football and frats and a campus on a quad, this probably is not the right place. However, if you want to be a part of an academic community that works and serves together, this might be exactly what you are looking for.

"Students applying for fall admission should provide results of the SAT or ACT."

SELECTIVITY

Admissions Rating	81
# of applicants	1,060
% of applicants accepted	74
% of acceptees attending	29
# accepting a place on wait list	0
# of early decision applicants	96
% accepted early decision	90

FRESHMAN PROFILE

Range SAT Critical Reading	540–660
Range SAT Math	500–610
Range SAT Writing	520–630
Range ACT Composite	23–28
Minimum paper TOEFL	550
Minimum computer TOEFL	0
Average HS GPA	3.24
% graduated top 10% of class	23
% graduated top 25% of class	51
% graduated top 50% of class	83

DEADLINES

Early decision	
Deadline	11/15
Notification	12/1
Regular	
Deadline	2/15
Nonfall registration?	yes

APPLICANTS ALSO LOOK AT
AND OFTEN PREFER
Earlham College

AND RARELY PREFER
Guildford College

FINANCIAL FACTS

Financial Aid Rating	77
Annual tuition	$26,675
Room and board	$8,213
Required fees	$300
Books and supplies	$870
% frosh rec. need-based scholarship or grant aid	52
% UG rec. need-based scholarship or grant aid	54
% frosh rec. non-need-based scholarship or grant aid	14
% UG rec. non-need-based scholarship or grant aid	10
% frosh rec. need-based self-help aid	57
% UG rec. need-based self-help aid	60
% frosh rec. any financial aid	90
% UG rec. any financial aid	90
% UG borrow to pay for school	44
Average cumulative indebtedness	$17,533

WASHINGTON COLLEGE

300 WASHINGTON AVENUE, CHESTERTOWN, MD 21620 • ADMISSIONS: 410-778-7700 • FAX: 410-778-7287

STUDENTS SAY ". . ."

Academics

Washington College is all about "gaining a distinctive and strong education in the liberal arts through personalized programs and hands-on experience." Located in small-town Chestertown, Maryland, this "small, tight-knit" community fosters a "high level of education" and an "intimate and personalized education experience." Washington College is a place where "students learn to think outside of the box while becoming better people and having the time of their lives." Centrally located between "three major employment markets: Washington, D.C., Philadelphia, and Baltimore," this "beautiful campus" "provides the perfect setting for a learning environment." "There are not as many distractions, but there is enough to keep you busy." Professors here are "highly educated, very personal, and willing to bend over backwards to ensure your education." Unlike at large research universities, faculty at Washington College are "here to teach, and they love to teach." The "attention given to the students by faculty is undeniable." The English and creative writing programs are among "the best in the country," earning Washington College a reputation "as a writing school," with the famous "Rose O'Neill Literary House, and the Sophie Kerr Prize." Students say all in one breath, "The professors are world-class, and the campus is beautiful. Also the Eastern Shore of Maryland is an incredible place to be."

Life

Living at Washington College "is as good as a college experience can get." "No matter what your interests are there is plenty to do." Some note that because of "the small-town environment, we have to make our own fun on weekends, but there's usually something on-campus to make it less of a challenge." "I personally love the environment and being outdoors. I spend a lot of time kayaking at our boat house on the Chester River, fishing on the Eastern Shore of Maryland, and supporting our athletic teams." "The school's rather small, so we know almost all of the athletes, so we're not only supporting a program, we're supporting our best friends." On campus, "There are plenty of student-run activities." When it comes to facilities, "The athletic department is great, and the dining hall is new and wonderful." For fun, students "often go to plays hosted by the drama department, attend interesting guest lectures, play Wii in the dorm rooms, play Frisbee on the campus green, play pool in the student center, go to movies, or stroll around Chestertown and the waterfront." We drink in the dorms and suites because almost everyone lives on campus." Washington College "is located within a rural town; however, we are not completely isolated. We are about forty minutes away from Annapolis." Students do warn, "Being in a rural town was hard at first."

Student Body

A typical Washington College student "is preppy—from the way they dress to the way that they interact with each other and their professors." It's "an athletic campus, as even non-athletes are generally fit and participate in intramural sports." Most students "come from a somewhat affluent background, and the majority study and work very hard, but they also party very hard on the weekends." Though some note "there is very little diversity on campus," others say while the campus "might lack in racial diversity, people have diverse morals, values, and political views." There seem to be "two major, distinct campus cultures: the athletic/Greek life people and the English/drama people. People generally gravitate to one or the other." "It isn't hard to find your 'place,' though." Most students are "involved in several different types of activities." Students "usually fit in by playing a sport or joining Greek life, but there is always a club for everyone." Others concur, Washington College is a "melting pot of individuals from different backgrounds, but the typical student is open-minded, ambitious, and extremely innovative." Athletes and burgeoning writers alike "have strong pride and love for our school."

FINANCIAL AID: 410-778-7214 • WEBSITE: HTTP://ADMISSIONS.WASHCOLL.EDU

THE PRINCETON REVIEW SAYS

Admissions

Very important factors considered include: Academic GPA, rigor of secondary school record, interview. *Important factors considered include:* Application essay, class rank, standardized test scores, level of applicant's interest, work experience. *Other factors considered include:* Recommendation(s), alumni/ae relation, character/personal qualities, extracurricular activities, first generation, geographical residence, racial/ethnic status, state residency, talent/ability, volunteer work. SAT or ACT required; ACT with or without writing component accepted. High school diploma is required, and GED is accepted. *Academic units required:* 4 English, 3 mathematics, 3 science (2 science labs), 2 foreign language, 2 social studies, 2 history. *Academic units recommended:* 4 English, 4 mathematics, 4 science (3 science labs), 4 foreign language, 4 social studies, 2 history.

Financial Aid

Students should submit: FAFSA, institution's own financial aid form. Regular filing deadline is February 15. The Princeton Review suggests that all financial aid forms be submitted as soon as possible after January 1. *Need-based scholarships/grants offered:* Federal Pell, SEOG, state scholarships/grants, private scholarships, school scholarship or grant aid from institutional funds. *Loan aid offered:* Direct Subsidized Stafford, Direct Unsubsidized Stafford, Direct PLUS, Federal Perkins. Applicants will be notified of awards on a rolling basis beginning February 1. Federal Work-Study Program available. Off-campus job opportunities are good.

The Inside Word

The profile of a typical successful applicant at Washington College is that of the solid but not exceptional high school student. Above-average standardized test scores and respectable grades in a college-prep high school curriculum should be enough to get you past the gatekeepers here. Students who rank in the top ten percent of their high school class or have a GPA above 3.5 can request a "score optional" admissions review. Washington College is up front about its preference for students who visit campus and/or complete an interview; the school says that such applicants "are processed and admitted before qualified non-visitors." Proceed accordingly.

THE SCHOOL SAYS "..."

From the Admissions Office

"We tell our students, 'Your revolution starts here,' because the person who graduates from Washington College is not the same one who matriculated four years earlier; and because through your experiences here, you can be empowered and emboldened to change the world. Your education reflects the maxims of our founder, George Washington: The strength of America's democracy depends on critical and independent thinkers who persevere in the face of challenge and assume the responsibilities and privileges of informed citizenship. We provide a truly personalized education that tests—and stretches—each student's talents and potentials. We create challenges and opportunities that expand your brainpower and creativity through collaborative research with faculty and through independent study."

"All this happens on a campus that has been through its own physical revolution in the past several years: some $70 million in improvements that include a brand new Commons with a food court, coffee shop, student center and game room; a totally renovated and expanded Arts Center; two new residence halls with geothermal heating, and dramatic landscape improvements. Beyond campus, a wonderfully distinct setting—historic Chestertown, on the Chester River, amid the ecological bounty of Maryland's Chesapeake Bay—helps define us and enriches our programs in history, literature and ecology."

"Admission to Washington College is selective; decisions are based primarily on a student's record of academic achievement. SAT/ACT scores are optional for students who rank in the top ten percent of their class. Interviews are strongly recommended."

SELECTIVITY

Admissions Rating	87
# of applicants	3,980
% of applicants accepted	74
% of acceptees attending	14
# accepting a place on wait list	68
% admitted from wait list	19
# of early decision applicants	55
% accepted early decision	93

FRESHMAN PROFILE

Range SAT Critical Reading	540–630
Range SAT Math	530–620
Range SAT Writing	520–620
Range ACT Composite	23–27
Average HS GPA	3.45
% graduated top 10% of class	38
% graduated top 25% of class	64
% graduated top 50% of class	92

DEADLINES

Early decision	
Deadline	11/1
Notification	12/1
Early action	
Deadline	12/1
Notification	1/15
Regular	
Priority	2/15
Notification	10/1
Nonfall registration?	yes

FINANCIAL FACTS

Financial Aid Rating	85
Annual tuition	$36,078
Room and board	$7,834
Required fees	$660
Books and supplies	$1,250
% frosh rec. need-based scholarship or grant aid	68
% UG rec. need-based scholarship or grant aid	58
% frosh rec. non-need-based scholarship or grant aid	27
% UG rec. non-need-based scholarship or grant aid	26
% frosh rec. need-based self-help aid	57
% UG rec. need-based self-help aid	52
% frosh rec. any financial aid	95
% UG rec. any financial aid	85
% UG borrow to pay for school	52
Average cumulative indebtedness	$35,831

WASHINGTON & JEFFERSON COLLEGE

OFFICE OF ADMISSIONS, 60 SOUTH LINCOLN STREET, WASHINGTON, PA 15301 • ADMISSIONS: 888-W-AND-JAY OR 724-223-6025

CAMPUS LIFE

Quality of Life Rating	67
Fire Safety Rating	85
Green Rating	84
Type of school	private
Environment	village

STUDENTS

Total undergrad enrollment	1,425
% male/female	51/49
% from out of state	26
% from public high school	82
% live on campus	90
# of fraternities	6
# of sororities	4
% African American	3
% Asian	1
% Caucasian	83
% Hispanic	2
# of countries represented	14

SURVEY SAYS . . .
Low cost of living
Frats and sororities dominate
social scene
Very little drug use

ACADEMICS

Academic Rating	85
% students graduating within 4 years	68
% students graduating within 6 years	71
Calendar	4-1-4
Student/faculty ratio	11:1
Profs interesting rating	91
Profs accessible rating	91
Most common reg class size	10–19 students
Most common lab size	10–19 students

MOST POPULAR MAJORS
business/commerce, English language and literature, psychology

STUDENTS SAY ". . ."

Academics
Washington & Jefferson College is an "intimate" and "prestigious" bastion of the liberal arts in western Pennsylvania. The 4-1-4 academic calendar here is fairly unique. In addition to two conventional semesters, a January term allows students to focus on a single course or to pursue an internship or study abroad in places like Japan, Germany, and Tanzania. A broad set of graduation requirements and "the liberal arts aspect creates well-rounded individuals." More than 40 majors and programs are available. W&J boasts "a great track record with law school admissions." Premed is also "excellent." The academic atmosphere is "wonderfully rigorous." "Small classes make for some good discussions." Coursework ranges from "intense" to "outrageously challenging." Students rarely miss class. "Absences are regarded as strange." The faculty receives high marks. "There are a few who really ought to retire," but most professors are "very knowledgeable and seem to fully enjoy the classes they are teaching." They are "dedicated" and "really personable." They "go out of their way to make themselves accessible" and "do whatever they can to help you." "They all care about me," says a satisfied econ major. "They want me to do well. They want me to learn a lot." The administration is "down-to-earth" and "always looking for student input." Career Services is "extremely helpful" as well. Employment placement is "impressive." "Great alumni connections" definitely help in this regard. "Alumni are always offering to take students under their wings," notes a biology major.

Life
During the week, students are "very busy." Academics are "pivotal." Scores of students play varsity, club, or intramural sports as well. "Almost everyone is involved in a couple different activities." "Sunday through Friday afternoon is all work, for sure," counsels a junior. "When the weekend rolls around," justifies a junior, "we deserve to have some fun." "Going to the frats is the most common weekend fun." "It gets repetitive, but it's all we have," relates a sophomore. However, "If the party scene is not for a student, there are usually other forms of entertainment offered by the school." The hilly campus here is "beautiful" and traditional-looking. The dorms in particular "could be updated and made a lot nicer." "They force you to live on campus," complains a junior. "Getting off campus is like fighting your own personal war." Other complaints include "limited" wireless internet access and the meal plans, which are "a rip off." Off-campus, the surrounding town is "dull" at best and "scary" at worst. Pittsburgh is "only thirty minutes away," though, and expeditions there are "a frequent thing."

Student Body
W&J is "extremely homogenous." "We're pretty much all the same," admits a junior. "Mostly, the school consists of white students from relatively average or high socioeconomic backgrounds." You'll fit in especially well if you come from "suburban" "western Pennsylvania or Ohio." "If you are 'different' or eclectic in personal expression in some way and really want to develop that, then I would pick a different school," advises a senior. "If you like to wear sweats to class all the time but don't mind looking cute every now and then, then this is a good school for you." Students here are "fit" and "preppy." Many are "athletes who really break the dumb-jock mold." They are "laid-back but ambitious." They are "goal-oriented." They "take their academics fairly seriously" and have a "great work ethic." Some students tell us the campus is "close-knit." Others say "there are a lot of cliques." Whatever the case, "everyone seems to get along."

WASHINGTON & JEFFERSON COLLEGE

Fax : 724-223-6534 • Financial Aid: 724-223-6019 • E-mail: ADMISSION@WASHJEFF.EDU • Website: WWW.WASHJEFF.EDU

THE PRINCETON REVIEW SAYS

Admissions

Very important factors considered include: Academic GPA, application essay, class rank, recommendation(s), rigor of secondary school record, character/personal qualities, interview. *Important factors considered include:* Standardized test scores, extracurricular activities. *Other factors considered include:* Alumni/ae relation, geographical residence, level of applicant's interest, racial/ethnic status, state residency, talent/ability, volunteer work, work experience. ACT with or without writing component accepted. TOEFL required of all international applicants. High school diploma is required, and GED is accepted. *Academic units required:* 3 English, 3 mathematics, 1 science (1 science lab), 2 foreign language, academic elective. *Academic units recommended:* 4 English, 4 mathematics, 2 science (2 science labs), 3 foreign language, 6 academic elective.

Financial Aid

Students should submit: FAFSA. The Princeton Review suggests that all financial aid forms be submitted as soon as possible after January 1. *Need-based scholarships/grants offered:* Federal Pell, SEOG, state scholarships/grants, private scholarships, school scholarship or grant aid from institutional funds. *Loan aid offered:* Direct Subsidized Stafford, Direct Unsubsidized Stafford, Direct PLUS, Federal Perkins, university loans from institutional funds. Applicants will be notified of awards on a rolling basis beginning March 1. Federal Work-Study Program available. Off-campus job opportunities are good.

The Inside Word

In a reflection of the students the school aims aim to admit, Washington & Jefferson College takes a well-rounded approach to admissions. Academic record, class rank, personal statement, and extracurricular activities are all thoroughly evaluated. Most prospective students work diligently to secure admittance. The lucky applicants who receive a fat letter in the mail are welcomed into a distinctive community that promises to broaden their horizons and to prepare them for a successful future.

THE SCHOOL SAYS " . . ."

From the Admissions Office

"There is an exciting sense of momentum and energy at Washington & Jefferson College, where the entire community is devoted to ensuring student success. In the last three years, 100 percent of W&J graduates taking the Pennsylvania bar exam passed, and we regularly see admission rates of ninety percent for graduates headed to medical and law school. The college has added $100 million dollars in new facilities since 2002, including residence halls, athletic facilities, a state-of-the-art technology center, the Burnett Center (housing accounting, business, economics, education, entrepreneurial studies, and modern languages), and the new Swanson Science Center (dedicated to the physical sciences, including physics, chemistry, biochemistry, and bioinformatics). Unique to W&J is the Magellan Project, providing stipends for innovative internships, research fellowships, and independent study travel programs, domestic or international. You dream it; we help make it happen. Our students are balanced, goal-oriented, active, engaged, and involved, and we look for applicants who demonstrate these qualities in every stage of the admissions process. If you are a student who thrives on academic rigor, wants a close personal relationship with top-notch faculty, and values being a member of a true college community, we encourage you to consider W&J. Finally, W&J recommends but does not require scores from the SAT (or ACT). We will use the best scores from either test. The new version of the SAT (or the ACT with the writing section) is not required. And be sure to check out our new four-year On-Time Graduation Guarantee at washjeff.edu."

SELECTIVITY

Admissions Rating	88
# of applicants	6,820
% of applicants accepted	39
% of acceptees attending	15
# accepting a place on wait list	28
% admitted from wait list	18
# of early decision applicants	12
% accepted early decision	33

FRESHMAN PROFILE

Range SAT Critical Reading	530–610
Range SAT Math	530–630
Range ACT Composite	23–28
Minimum paper TOEFL	563
Minimum computer TOEFL	223
Minimum web-based TOEFL	84
Average HS GPA	3.35
% graduated top 10% of class	41
% graduated top 25% of class	71
% graduated top 50% of class	94

DEADLINES

Early decision	
Deadline	12/1
Notification	12/15
Early action	
Deadline	1/15
Notification	2/15
Regular	
Priority	1/15
Deadline	3/1
Notification	10/1
Nonfall registration?	yes

FINANCIAL FACTS

Financial Aid Rating	75
Annual tuition	$35,960
Room and board	$9,560
Required fees	$460
Books and supplies	$800
% frosh rec. need-based scholarship or grant aid	66
% UG rec. need-based scholarship or grant aid	64
% frosh rec. non-need-based scholarship or grant aid	75
% UG rec. non-need-based scholarship or grant aid	66
% frosh rec. need-based self-help aid	70
% UG rec. need-based self-help aid	68
% frosh rec. any financial aid	99
% UG rec. any financial aid	98
% UG borrow to pay for school	75
Average cumulative indebtedness	$30,000

WASHINGTON STATE UNIVERSITY

370 LIGHTY STUDENT SERVICES, PULLMAN, WA 99164-1067 • ADMISSIONS: 888-468-6978 • FAX: 509-335-4902

CAMPUS LIFE

Quality of Life Rating	74
Fire Safety Rating	81
Green Rating	86
Type of school	public
Environment	town

STUDENTS

Total undergrad enrollment	21,816
% male/female	48/52
% from out of state	8
% from public high school	99
% live on campus	33
# of fraternities	25
# of sororities	14
% African American	2
% Asian	6
% Caucasian	71
% Hispanic	7
% Native American	1
% international	4
# of countries represented	98

SURVEY SAYS . . .

Athletic facilities are great
Everyone loves the Cougars
Frats and sororities dominate
social scene
Student publications are popular
Lots of beer drinking
Hard liquor is popular

ACADEMICS

Academic Rating	65
% students graduating within 4 years	40
% students graduating within 6 years	69
Calendar	semester
Student/faculty ratio	15:1
Profs interesting rating	64
Profs accessible rating	67
Most common reg class size	20–29 students

MOST POPULAR MAJORS

business administration and
management, nursing, social sciences

STUDENTS SAY ". . ."

Academics

It's "all about big-school pride in a small-town atmosphere" at Washington State University, a large state school in eastern Washington where students are "challenged and learn in an open and diverse community." For a big school, WSU offers a surprising degree of conviviality. It's the sort of school "where you will run into your professor at the grocery store and you'll stop to chat." "It has all the opportunities of a large research university but it still has that small-town feel," one student explains. A "reputable communications program," a "good business school," and a strong education program are among the top draws here; hospitality, veterinary medicine, and pharmacy studies are also reportedly strong. WSU professors "challenge us daily" but "are available when we're struggling and need extra help." They also point students toward "terrific resources outside of class," including "good books, conferences, and even articles that are related to our degrees that we might find interesting." The administration "works with students, especially on hot[-button] issues, but obviously not everyone can always be accommodated."

Life

Washington State "is very much like other universities. Some people party... and some focus on school." While hometown "Pullman has a reputation for partying, especially since some people look around the town and assume there is nothing else to do," most here insist that the school is not a big party school. There are "plenty of other opportunities for fun" on and around campus, including "free movies in the union every weekend, a movie theater, bowling alley, multiple restaurants, and many stores in Pullman." Performing arts, religious groups, school clubs and associations, Greek life, and intercollegiate and intramural sports all occupy prominent places in campus life. One student explains, "Because our school is in a fairly remote part of the state, the school and the various student groups are usually putting on some kind of event every weekend. There's the improv theater group 'Nuthouse,' which costs between nothing and three dollars." Pullman offers lots of outdoor entertainment options, so students "hang out at the river in areas called The Cliffs and The Dunes" and also "ski and snowboard in the winter." Moscow, Idaho, home to the University of Idaho, "is only eight miles away and offers even more opportunities for shopping and dining."

Student Body

WSU "is a very large school, so as long as the student puts in some effort they can find a group of people that they fit in with." Undergrads enjoy "great student support systems for multicultural students, women, and the queer population" as well as "resource centers for anyone who wants to seek support in their college experience." The student body includes a mix of kids "from a big city or rural area, and these two backgrounds blend well." All that said, some warn that "There is not a ton of diversity on our campus, but [that's] understandable given the rural location of the university." School officials note, however, that diversity is increasing across the board. Cougars "like to have a good time." So much so that WSU has something of a reputation for "partying it up," but most here insist that "there is plenty of time dedicated to studying" and that only a small minority are "irresponsible." As one student points out, the popular perception is "that the typical student is a partier, but if you look at statistics taken, more than fifty percent of students living on campus chose not to party or drink."

WASHINGTON STATE UNIVERSITY

FINANCIAL AID: 509-335-9711 • E-MAIL: ADMISS2@WSU.EDU • WEBSITE: WWW.WSU.EDU

THE PRINCETON REVIEW SAYS

Admissions

Very important factors considered include: Academic GPA, standardized test scores. *Important factors considered include:* Application essay, rigor of secondary school record. *Other factors considered include:* Class rank, recommendation(s), character/personal qualities, grading trends, extracurricular activities, talent/ability, volunteer work, work experience. SAT or ACT required; ACT with or without writing component accepted. English language proficiency required of all international applicants. High school diploma is required, and GED is accepted. *Academic units required:* 4 English, 3 mathematics, 2 lab science, 2 foreign language, 3 social studies, 1 visual/performing arts. *Academic units recommended:* 4 English, 4 mathematics, 2 lab science, 2 foreign language, 3 social studies, 1 visual/performing arts.

Financial Aid

Students should submit: FAFSA. Priority filing deadline is February 15. The Princeton Review suggests that all financial aid forms be submitted as soon as possible after January 1. *Need-based scholarships/grants offered:* Federal Pell, SEOG, state scholarships/grants, private scholarships, school scholarship or grant aid from institutional funds, United Negro College Fund, Federal Nursing Scholarships. *Loan aid offered:* Direct Subsidized Stafford, Direct Unsubsidized Stafford, Direct PLUS, Federal Perkins, Federal Nursing Loans. Applicants will be notified of awards on a rolling basis beginning April 15. Federal Work-Study Program available. Off-campus job opportunities are good.

The Inside Word

The huge number of applications WSU must process each year should leave admissions officers little time to consider anything other than grades, quality of curriculum, and standardized test scores. Yet WSU encourages applicants to submit a personal statement, which strongly suggests officers take time to read them, at least in the case of borderline candidates. Those on the cusp would be well served to take advantage of this opportunity. Use your essay to sell yourself as someone who can contribute substantially to the campus community.

THE SCHOOL SAYS "..."

From the Admissions Office

"At Washington State University, you work side-by-side with nationally renowned faculty who help you succeed. Many academic programs rank among the nation's best. Programs are designed to give you real-world experience through internships, community service, in-depth labs, and study abroad experiences. Plus, many disciplines encourage you to participate in faculty research or conduct your own. If you have top grades and a passion for learning, the highly acclaimed Honors College challenges you with interdisciplinary studies, rich classroom discussions, and research opportunities.

"The campus forms the heart of a friendly college town where faculty and fellow students help you achieve your greatest potential. More than 300 campus organizations connect you with others who share your interests. Each year employers return to campus seeking WSU graduates. The university stands among the top twenty-five in the nation that best prepare students for workforce success (2010 Wall Street Journal survey). The main Pullman campus was named the safest among peers nationwide. WSU also has three non-residential urban campuses in Spokane, the Tri-Cities (Richland), and Vancouver.

"The priority date to apply for admission and the deadline to apply for scholarships is January 31. For your candidacy to be considered, you must complete the high school core curriculum and provide official scores from the SAT or ACT. We urge you to deliver a strong personal statement (essay). If you apply by January 31 and are among the top ten percent of your high school class or have at least a 3.5 GPA, you're assured admission."

SELECTIVITY

Admissions Rating	82
# of applicants	12,427
% of applicants accepted	69
% of acceptees attending	38
# accepting a place on wait list	125
% admitted from wait list	61

FRESHMAN PROFILE

Range SAT Critical Reading	480–580
Range SAT Math	500–610
Range SAT Writing	470–570
Range ACT Composite	21–26
Minimum paper TOEFL	520
Minimum web-based TOEFL	68
Average HS GPA	3.44
% graduated top 10% of class	32
% graduated top 25% of class	53
% graduated top 50% of class	86

DEADLINES

Regular	
Priority	1/31
Notification	11/1
Nonfall registration?	yes

APPLICANTS ALSO LOOK AT

AND OFTEN PREFER
Central Washington University, Eastern Washington University, University of Washington, Western Washington University

AND SOMETIMES PREFER
Gonzaga University, Oregon State University, Seattle University, University of Idaho, University of Oregon, University of Portland

AND RARELY PREFER
Pacific Lutheran University, Seattle Pacific University, Whitworth College

FINANCIAL FACTS

Financial Aid Rating	74
Annual in-state tuition	$8,080
Annual out-of-state tuition	$19,122
Room and board	$9,644
Required fees	$1,409
Books and supplies	$936
% frosh rec. need-based scholarship or grant aid	34
% UG rec. need-based scholarship or grant aid	37
% frosh rec. non-need-based scholarship or grant aid	31
% UG rec. non-need-based scholarship or grant aid	20
% frosh rec. need-based self-help aid	42
% UG rec. need-based self-help aid	48
% frosh rec. any financial aid	52
% UG rec. any financial aid	53

WASHINGTON UNIVERSITY IN ST. LOUIS

CAMPUS BOX 1089, ONE BROOKINGS DRIVE, ST. LOUIS, MO 63130-4899 • ADMISSIONS: 314-935-6000 • FAX: 314-935-4290

CAMPUS LIFE

Quality of Life Rating	98
Fire Safety Rating	86
Green Rating	60*
Type of school	private
Environment	city

STUDENTS

Total undergrad enrollment	6,542
% male/female	51/49
% from out of state	91
% from public high school	60
% live on campus	79
# of fraternities	12
# of sororities	6
% African American	6
% Asian	15
% Caucasian	57
% Hispanic	5
% international	6
# of countries represented	87

SURVEY SAYS . . .

Lab facilities are great
School is well-run
Students are friendly
Great food on campus
Great off-campus food
Dorms are like palaces

ACADEMICS

Academic Rating	96
% students graduating within 4 years	86
% students graduating within 6 years	94
Calendar	semester
Student/faculty ratio	7:1
Profs interesting rating	85
Profs accessible rating	88
Most common reg class size	10–19 students
Most common lab size	10–19 students

MOST POPULAR MAJORS
psychology, biology/biological sciences, finance

STUDENTS SAY ". . ."

Academics

Washington University "is a top-tier university" that "offers students an opportunity to explore interests in a number of areas both academically and extra-curricularly" and, "manages to maintain core Midwestern values." As one student notes, "While it may not be as well known on the East Coast, it is a hidden gem in the Midwest, rich with great people, amazing extracurricular opportunities, an underrated city just down the street, and an education that will challenge you." "I was impressed by students' abilities to pursue academically rigorous classes, balance numerous activities, and still find time to spend at various campus events with friends." "Collaboration" over competition here "is key." Washington University "provides the education of an Ivy League university with the atmosphere and warmth of home." The co-curricular programs "are flexible enough to allow students to pursue academic interests in business, arts and sciences, art and architecture, and engineering all at once." Undergraduates "truly have the flexibility to study what you want: You can take any class offered in any college, double major or minor across colleges, or even get dual degrees." Professors "are engaged and lively." Their "passion for the subject is contagious for the student body." "Community is probably [Wash U's] greatest asset." "It's a very positive, vibrant environment."

Life

Wash U boasts "a beautiful campus" and "an active and friendly student body." Students are also "genuinely concerned about the city of St. Louis and actively participate in social justice measures." The food "is delicious," the dorms "are beautiful," and students "are happy." Be it "an intramural sport, organizing a charity event, Greek life, the radio station, or the new live sketch comedy show, every student takes part in non-academic activities that build friendships and make college life far more colorful." During their downtime, students "go to concerts, movies, the local mall, etc., for fun." The popular Delmar Loop is "just a ten-minute walk from main campus." Loaded with restaurants and small storefronts, "It's an extremely popular place for students to walk around, shop at small boutiques, and grab a bite to eat." Whether it's "seeing a show," "eating out on the Loop," "chilling with friends," or "watching a movie," "There is always something to do." "Thursdays, Fridays, and Saturdays are party night." Though some confess, "A lot of people drink on the weekends…the fraternities' parties are primarily open to all grades and are not exclusive," others say, "There is very little pressure for people to drink, even for students involved in Greek Life." Beyond campus parties and Greek life, there are "a ton of options for social events." Headline-grabbing events include "W.I.L.D.," "a huge all-day concert held in the quad with great musical performers." Other "big draws" include the "performances held on campus, such as Diwali, Carnival, Mr. WU, and Black Anthology, which are always sold out." Recently, "There has been a lot of programming in our student center, where we recently broke the world record for the largest nerf gun fight with more than 470 students participating."

Student Body

Students here quickly fall captive to the "positive atmosphere." "Everyone here is happy! Seriously, you'll always see smiles everywhere you go on campus." Students say there's not "a 'typical' student at Wash U…I guess the best way to describe students here is that they defy the typical stereotypes. You'll have a fraternity brother who's a dancer [or] a premed student who's minoring in architecture, etc." Students "embrace that their fellow classmates have their own interests, even picking up new hobbies from their friends." Wash U provides the backdrop for "a diverse set of social circles." "There are the suburban East-coasters, the liberal Texans, the local kids from St. Louis, the California jocks, etc." "The typical Wash U student graduated in the top two percent of her high school class, participated in at least four different clubs with an office in at least one (but probably two), was homecoming queen, and volunteered at an animal shelter on the weekends." Students here are "very involved and take both academics and extracurriculars (particularly community service) very seriously."

WASHINGTON UNIVERSITY IN ST. LOUIS

FINANCIAL AID: 888-547-6670 • E-MAIL: ADMISSIONS@WUSTL.EDU • WEBSITE: WUSTL.EDU

THE PRINCETON REVIEW SAYS

Admissions

Very important factors considered include: Academic GPA, application essay, class rank, recommendation(s), rigor of secondary school record, standardized test scores, character/personal qualities, extracurricular activities, talent/ability, volunteer work, work experience. *Other factors considered include:* Alumni/ae relation, first generation, interview, level of applicant's interest, racial/ethnic status. SAT or ACT required; ACT with or without writing component accepted. TOEFL required of all international applicants. High school diploma is required, and GED is accepted. *Academic units required: Academic units recommended:* 4 English, 4 mathematics, 4 science (4 science labs), 2 foreign language, 4 social studies, 4 history.

Financial Aid

Students should submit: FAFSA, CSS/Financial Aid PROFILE, non-custodial profile, student and parent 1040 tax return or signed waiver, if there's no tax return. Regular filing deadline is February 1. The Princeton Review suggests that all financial aid forms be submitted as soon as possible after January 1. *Need-based scholarships/grants offered:* Federal Pell, SEOG, state scholarships/grants, private scholarships, school scholarship or grant aid from institutional funds, Federal Academic Competitive Grant, Federal SMART Grant. *Loan aid offered:* Direct Subsidized Stafford, Direct Unsubsidized Stafford, Direct PLUS, Federal Perkins, state loans, university loans from institutional funds. Applicants will be notified of awards on or about April 1. Federal Work-Study Program available. Institutional employment available. Off-campus job opportunities are excellent.

The Inside Word

The fact that Wash U doesn't have much play as a nationally respected car-window decal is about all that prevents it from being among the most selective universities. In every other respect—that is, in any way that really matters—this place is hard to beat and easily ranks as one of the best. No other university with as impressive a record of excellence across the board has a more accommodating admissions process. Not that it's easy to get in here, but lack of instant name recognition does affect Wash U's admission rate. Students with above-average academic records who aren't quite Ivy material are the big winners. Marginal candidates with high financial need may find difficulty; the admissions process at Wash U isn't need-blind and may take into account candidates' ability to pay if they're not strong applicants.

THE SCHOOL SAYS "..."

From the Admissions Office

"Washington University in St. Louis is a research university that offers a unique environment for undergraduate students to learn and grow. Unparalleled curriculum flexibility and learning opportunities in a friendly and supportive community inspire undergraduates to explore their interests and to develop new ones. Working with their advisors, undergraduates may choose a traditional single major, as many do. Others combine majors with minors, second majors, and pre-professional programs—all within their four-year undergraduate experience. We encourage our students to participate in internships, study abroad programs, research and scholarship, and more than 200 clubs and organizations, rounding out Washington University's commitment to help each student identify and pursue his or her passion. Our students pursue their passions every day. Visit campus and ask them about their experiences. As part of this commitment to help our students, Washington University is working to eliminate need-based loans as part of its undergraduate financial aid awards to students from low-income families. This new initiative and its goal of helping families with the most need will not lessen our desire, responsibility, or ability to work with all families to ensure they have the financial resources they need. We remain committed to a flexible and independent approach to delivering financial aid to those who need it most. Applicants are required to submit scores from either the SAT or ACT test. Applicants who submit scores from the ACT test may submit with or without the writing component."

SELECTIVITY

Admissions Rating	98
# of applicants	24,939
% of applicants accepted	21
% of acceptees attending	31

FRESHMAN PROFILE

Range SAT Critical Reading	680–750
Range SAT Math	710–790
Range ACT Composite	32–34
% graduated top 10% of class	96
% graduated top 25% of class	100
% graduated top 50% of class	100

DEADLINES

Early decision	
Deadline	11/15
Notification	12/15
Regular	
Deadline	1/15
Notification	4/1
Nonfall registration?	no

APPLICANTS ALSO LOOK AT
AND OFTEN PREFER
Harvard College, Princeton University, Stanford University, University of Pennsylvania, Yale University

AND SOMETIMES PREFER
Cornell University, Duke University, Northwestern University, Rice University, University of Chicago

AND RARELY PREFER
Emory University, Tufts University, Tulane University, University of Michigan—Ann Arbor

FINANCIAL FACTS

Financial Aid Rating	97
Annual tuition	$40,950
Room and board	$13,119
Required fees	$1,042
Books and supplies	$1,390
% frosh rec. need-based scholarship or grant aid	35
% UG rec. need-based scholarship or grant aid	40
% frosh rec. non-need-based scholarship or grant aid	5
% UG rec. non-need-based scholarship or grant aid	3
% frosh rec. need-based self-help aid	28
% UG rec. need-based self-help aid	29
% frosh rec. any financial aid	37
% UG rec. any financial aid	41
% UG borrow to pay for school	38

WEBB INSTITUTE

298 CRESCENT BEACH ROAD, GLEN COVE, NY 11542 • ADMISSIONS: 516-671-2213 • FAX: 516-674-9838

CAMPUS LIFE

Quality of Life Rating	93
Fire Safety Rating	72
Green Rating	60*
Type of school	private
Environment	village

STUDENTS

Total undergrad enrollment	80
% male/female	85/15
% from out of state	70
% from public high school	83
% live on campus	100
% Asian	8
% Caucasian	85
% Hispanic	2

SURVEY SAYS . . .

Registration is a breeze
Career services are great
Different types of students interact
Dorms are like palaces
Frats and sororities are unpopular
or nonexistent
Student government is popular
Political activism is unpopular
or nonexistent
Very little drug use

ACADEMICS

Academic Rating	95
% students graduating	
within 4 years	88
% students graduating	
within 6 years	85
Calendar	semester
Student/faculty ratio	7:1
Profs interesting rating	89
Profs accessible rating	99
Most common	
reg class size	20–29 students

STUDENTS SAY ". . ."

Academics

Webb Institute on Long Island is a very small school that focuses on the complex field of ship design engineering. If you feel destined to become one of "America's future ship designers and engineers," enroll here. Every student receives a four-year, full-tuition scholarship. The only costs are books and supplies, Room and board, and personal expenses. Everyone majors in naval architecture and marine engineering, although non-engineering electives are available to juniors and seniors. Webbies are exposed to a smattering of the liberal arts and a ton of advanced math and physics. Virtually every other course involves ship design. There's also a senior thesis and a "required internship program." In January and February, all students get real, paying jobs in the marine industry. Job prospects are phenomenal. Newly minted Webb graduates enjoy "a 100 percent placement rate in grad schools and careers." Coursework is "rigorous," but the academic atmosphere is very intimate. "A huge plus of Webb's small size is that everyone knows everyone," relates a junior. "You're not just another number." "The administration, professors, and students all work in the same building every day, every week." "The [President] can get carried away when he perceives a problem," but the faculty is "approachable," "always accessible," and "very dedicated to the school and students." "Professors have a great deal of respect for the students and work closely with us to accomplish our goals," says a sophomore. "If you're passionate about architecture and engineering, you cannot hope for a better learning environment."

Life

Webb has a "family-like atmosphere." It's "a tiny student body living, eating, sleeping, and learning ship design in a mansion" "in a residential area overlooking the beautiful Long Island Sound." There's an honor code "that is strictly adhered to by all students." Cheating and stealing just don't happen here. "You can leave your wallet lying in the reception room, and if someone doesn't return it to you just because they know what your wallet looks like compared to the other 90 wallets in the school, it will still be there the next day and even the next week." Life at Webb "revolves around course load and the attempts to find distractions from it." "We average about five to seven hours of homework per night," advises a freshman. At the end of the semesters, life [can get crazy] due to a ton of projects." "People generally think about homework and spend most of their time discussing class assignments." When students find some down time, movies and unorganized sports are common. Not surprisingly, "many people turn to the water" for amusement as well. "Sailing is popular." "The school has a skiff and sailboats, which are frequently used during the warm months," says a sophomore. Annual whitewater rafting and ski trips are well attended. New York City is a little less than an hour away, and "a bunch of people venture into" Manhattan on the weekends. "A lot of spontaneous and off-the-wall things occur" too, and "a fair amount of partying goes on at least once a week."

Student Body

The average Webbie is a "middle-class, white male who enjoys engineering and sciences." "Everyone is motivated and works hard." Basically, you have your bookworms who "don't socialize as much" and your more social students who get their work done but also play sports and "have a good time." Camaraderie is reportedly easy due to the academic stress and Webb's small size. Everyone interacts with everyone else, regardless of background. With fewer than 100 students, it's "impossible to completely isolate yourself." "There are no social cliques, and everyone is included in anything they'd like to be included in." As at most engineering schools, the ratio between males and females is pretty severely lopsided here. "We want more women!" plead many students.

FINANCIAL AID: 516-671-2213 • E-MAIL: ADMISSIONS@WEBB-INSTITUTE.EDU • WEBSITE: WWW.WEBB-INSTITUTE.EDU

THE PRINCETON REVIEW SAYS

Admissions

Very important factors considered include: Academic GPA, class rank, rigor of secondary school record, standardized test scores, character/personal qualities, interview, level of applicant's interest. *Important factors considered include:* Recommendation(s), extracurricular activities. *Other factors considered include:* Talent/ability, volunteer work, work experience. *Academic units required:* 4 English, 4 mathematics, 2 science (2 science labs), 2 social studies, 4 academic elective.

Financial Aid

Students should submit: FAFSA. Regular filing deadline is July 1. The Princeton Review suggests that all financial aid forms be submitted as soon as possible after January 1. *Need-based scholarships/grants offered:* Federal Pell, state scholarships/grants, private scholarships, school scholarship or grant aid from institutional funds. *Loan aid offered:* Direct Subsidized Stafford, Direct Unsubsidized Stafford, Direct PLUS. Federal Work-Study Program not available. Off-campus job opportunities are fair.

The Inside Word

Let's not mince words; admission to Webb is mega-tough. Webb's Admissions Counselors are out to find the right kid for their curriculum—one that can survive the school's rigorous academics. The applicant pool is highly self-selected because of the focused program of study: naval architecture and marine engineering.

THE SCHOOL SAYS "..."

From the Admissions Office

"Webb, the only college in the country that specializes in the engineering field of naval architecture and marine engineering, seeks young men and women of all races from all over the country who are interested in receiving an excellent engineering education with a full-tuition scholarship. Students don't have to know anything about ships, they just have to be motivated to study how mechanical, civil, structural, and electrical engineering come together with the design elements that make up a ship and all its systems. Being small and private has its major advantages. Every applicant is special and the President will interview all entering students personally. The student/faculty ratio is eight to one, and since there are no teaching assistants, interaction with the faculty occurs daily in class and labs at a level not found at most other colleges. The entire campus operates under the Student Organization's honor system that allows unsupervised exams and twenty-four-hour access to the library, every classroom and laboratory, and the shop and gymnasium. Despite a total enrollment of between eighty-five and ninety students and a demanding workload, Webb manages to field six intercollegiate teams. Currently more than sixty percent of the members of the student body play on one or more intercollegiate teams. Work hard, play hard and the payoff is a job for every student upon graduation. The placement record of the college is 100 percent every year.

"Freshman applicants must take the SAT. We also require scores from two SAT Subject Tests: Math Level I or II and either physics or chemistry."

SELECTIVITY

Admissions Rating	97
# of applicants	72
% of applicants accepted	44
% of acceptees attending	56
# of early decision applicants	15
% accepted early decision	33

FRESHMAN PROFILE

Range SAT Critical Reading	640–700
Range SAT Math	700–740
Range SAT Writing	620–720
Average HS GPA	3.90
% graduated top 10% of class	63
% graduated top 25% of class	88
% graduated top 50% of class	100

DEADLINES

Early decision	
Deadline	10/15
Notification	12/15
Regular	
Priority	10/15
Deadline	2/15
Notification	4/15
Nonfall registration?	no

APPLICANTS ALSO LOOK AT
AND OFTEN PREFER
United States Coast Guard Academy, United States Naval Academy

AND SOMETIMES PREFER
The Cooper Union for the Advancement of Science and Art, Virginia Tech

AND RARELY PREFER
State University of New York—Maritime College, University of Michigan—Ann Arbor

FINANCIAL FACTS

Financial Aid Rating	83
Annual tuition	$0
Annual in-state tuition	$0
Annual out-of-state tuition	$0
Annual comprehensive tuition	$0
Room and board	$12,600
Required fees	$0
Books and supplies	$950
% UG rec. need-based scholarship or grant aid	11
% UG rec. non-need-based scholarship or grant aid	8
% frosh rec. need-based self-help aid	16
% UG rec. need-based self-help aid	21
% frosh rec. any financial aid	25
% UG rec. any financial aid	20
% UG borrow to pay for school	33
Average cumulative indebtedness	$8,545

WELLESLEY COLLEGE

BOARD OF ADMISSION, 106 CENTRAL STREET, WELLESLEY, MA 02481-8203 • ADMISSIONS: 781-283-2270 • FAX: 781-283-3678

CAMPUS LIFE
Quality of Life Rating	95
Fire Safety Rating	85
Green Rating	89
Type of school	private
Environment	town

STUDENTS
Total undergrad enrollment	2,296
% male/female	0/100
% from out of state	84
% from public high school	62
% live on campus	97
% African American	6
% Asian	22
% Caucasian	46
% Hispanic	9
% international	10
# of countries represented	70

SURVEY SAYS . . .
No one cheats
Lab facilities are great
Great computer facilities
School is well-run
Diverse student types on campus
Dorms are like palaces
Campus feels safe
Frats and sororities are unpopular
or nonexistent
Student government is popular
Political activism is popular

ACADEMICS
Academic Rating	98
% students graduating within 4 years	84
% students graduating within 6 years	87
Calendar	semester
Student/faculty ratio	8:1
Profs interesting rating	99
Profs accessible rating	98
Most common reg class size	10–19 students
Most common lab size	10–19 students

MOST POPULAR MAJORS
economics, political science,
psychology

STUDENTS SAY ". . ."

Academics
Widely considered to be the top women's college in the nation, "Wellesley grooms its students to be strong leaders" through rigorous academic programs, "an intense intellectual environment," and "fierce commitment to social change." As a small college, Wellesley offers ample "personal attention" and a "comfortable environment;" however, choice and opportunity separate Wellesley from other similar institutions. While enrolling just 2,300 undergraduates, Wellesley offers a remarkable array of more than 1,000 courses and fifty-four major programs; plus, "You can cross-register at MIT (and to a limited extent at Brandeis, Babson, and Olin.)" From research to internships to overseas studies, Wellesley "provides great resources and opportunities to all its students." A senior shares, "I have had opportunities for research and independent study in both of my majors (and in at least one other field of interest.)" Attracting "fiercely driven and deeply passionate women," a Wellesley education "can be stressful and intense." At the same time, "It is a very friendly, respectful, intellectual environment where professors believe in your ability to do great things and the whole world seems to open up to you." When it comes to the teaching staff, "Not only are many of the professors notable in their fields, they are all excellent teachers. Classes in all departments are exciting, challenging, and engaging." And the benefits don't stop on your graduation day. Thanks to a "very strong alumni network" and a strong career placement program, Wellesley women are ready to enter the workplace. No matter what your field, "Wellesley women are everywhere. It's very helpful when you're looking for internships or jobs."

Life
"Students tend to be very driven academically." Fortunately, no matter how busy they are, "People always try to make time for friends…whether it's a group study session or just dinner together." "Outspoken and well-informed," students are eager to engage in "insightful discussions about politics, religion, sexuality, etc., at the lunch table." In addition, "there are always seminars and panel discussions and cultural events to attend" on campus. "Private parties are often broken up due [to] the Draconian alcohol and party policies imposed by the administration." Therefore, many Wellesley students "go into Boston or Cambridge for parties, concerts, shopping, protests, or people-watching." For others, "The ideal night would [include having] a handful of friends clustered around the kitchen table in the Shakespeare house, debating, drinking, and laughing about politics, literature, and the latest celebrity events." For those concerned about meeting members of the opposite sex, "You can interact with Harvard and MIT men, as well as men from the many institutions in Boston and the surrounding area."

Student Body
While many students describe Wellesley as an "ethnically and financially diverse campus," a typical Wellesley undergraduate is "white, very liberal, very intelligent, [and] politically active, does a lot of community service, and has fashion sense like you wouldn't believe." Others describe their classmates as "intelligent, engaged, curious, quick-witted, articulate, politically aware, outspoken, thoughtful, passionate, ambitious, and poised." Wellesley women come in a "variety of packages, from women who brag about showering in the Science Library to those who party [in] Cambridge every weekend to rugby players and Shakespearean actors to sorority-girl-esque 'society' members." Students also point out that "alternative gender expressions and sexual orientations are also quite common" on the Wellesley campus. Friendly and welcoming, "everyone is accepted" within the college community, though students note that "deeply religious students are less common, and Republicans are quite the minority."

WELLESLEY COLLEGE

FINANCIAL AID: 781-283-2360 • E-MAIL: ADMISSION@WELLESLEY.EDU • WEBSITE: WWW.WELLESLEY.EDU

THE PRINCETON REVIEW SAYS

Admissions

Very important factors considered include: Academic GPA, application essay, recommendation(s), rigor of secondary school record, standardized test scores, character/personal qualities. *Important factors considered include:* Class rank, extracurricular activities, talent/ability. *Other factors considered include:* Alumni/ae relation, first generation, geographical residence, interview, level of applicant's interest, racial/ethnic status, state residency, volunteer work, work experience. ACT with writing component required. High school diploma or equivalent isn't required. *Academic units required:* 4 English, 4 mathematics, 3 science (2 science labs), 4 foreign language, 4 social studies, 4 history.

Financial Aid

Students should submit: FAFSA, CSS/Financial Aid PROFILE. Regular filing deadline is January 15. The Princeton Review suggests that all financial aid forms be submitted as soon as possible after January 1. *Need-based scholarships/grants offered:* Federal Pell, SEOG, state scholarships/grants, private scholarships, school scholarship or grant aid from institutional funds. *Loan aid offered:* Direct Subsidized Stafford, Direct Unsubsidized Stafford, Direct PLUS, Federal Perkins, state loans, university loans from institutional funds. Federal Work-Study Program available. Off-campus job opportunities are excellent.

The Inside Word

When making an admissions decision, Wellesley considers a broad range of factors, including a student's academic record, the difficulty of her high school curriculum, participation in extracurricular activities, class rank, recommendations, personal essay, standardized test scores, leadership, and special talents (students may submit art, music, or theater supplements along with their application). Personal interviews are highly recommended, but not required, though they can be a useful way to help you stand out in Wellesley's extraordinary applicant pool.

THE SCHOOL SAYS "..."

From the Admissions Office

"Widely acknowledged as the nation's best women's college, Wellesley College provides students with numerous opportunities on campus and beyond. With a long-standing commitment to and established reputation for academic excellence, Wellesley offers more than 1,000 courses in fifty-four established majors and supports 180 clubs, organizations, and activities for its students. The college is easily accessible to Boston, a great city in which to meet other college students and to experience theater, art, sports, and entertainment. Considered one of the most diverse colleges in the nation, Wellesley students hail from seventy countries and all fifty states.

"As a community, we are looking for students who possess intellectual curiosity: the ability to think independently, ask challenging questions, and grapple with answers. Strong candidates demonstrate both academic achievement and an excitement for learning. They also display leadership, an appreciation for diverse perspectives, and an understanding of the college's mission to educate women who will make a difference in the world.

"The SAT and SAT Subject Tests or ACT with writing component are required. Two SAT Subject Tests are required, one of which should be quantitative (math or Science). We strongly recommend that students planning to apply early decision complete the tests before the end of their junior year and no later than October of their senior year."

SELECTIVITY	
Admissions Rating	96
# of applicants	4,267
% of applicants accepted	34
% of acceptees attending	44
# accepting a place on wait list	495
% admitted from wait list	0
# of early decision applicants	235
% accepted early decision	59

FRESHMAN PROFILE	
Range SAT Critical Reading	640–740
Range SAT Math	630–740
Range SAT Writing	650–750
Range ACT Composite	28–31
% graduated top 10% of class	78
% graduated top 25% of class	95
% graduated top 50% of class	99

DEADLINES	
Early decision	
Deadline	11/1
Notification	12/15
Regular	
Deadline	1/15
Nonfall registration?	no

FINANCIAL FACTS	
Financial Aid Rating	98
Annual tuition	$39,420
Room and board	$12,284
Required fees	$246
Books and supplies	$800
% frosh rec. need-based scholarship or grant aid	60
% UG rec. need-based scholarship or grant aid	61
% frosh rec. need-based self-help aid	53
% UG rec. need-based self-help aid	58
% frosh rec. any financial aid	61
% UG rec. any financial aid	63
% UG borrow to pay for school	58
Average cumulative indebtedness	$12,495

WELLS COLLEGE

ROUTE 90, AURORA, NY 13026 • ADMISSIONS: 315-364-3264 • FAX: 315-364-3227

CAMPUS LIFE

Quality of Life Rating	71
Fire Safety Rating	84
Green Rating	71
Type of school	private
Environment	rural

STUDENTS

Total undergrad enrollment	552
% male/female	29/71
% from out of state	32
% from public high school	88
% live on campus	84
% African American	6
% Asian	2
% Caucasian	67
% Hispanic	4
% Native American	1
% international	2
# of countries represented	13

SURVEY SAYS . . .
No one cheats
Lousy food on campus
Low cost of living
Frats and sororities are unpopular
or nonexistent
Musical organizations are popular
Very little drug use

ACADEMICS

Academic Rating	87
% students graduating within 4 years	53
% students graduating within 6 years	61
Calendar	semester
Student/faculty ratio	10:1
Profs interesting rating	91
Profs accessible rating	87
Most common reg class size	10–19 students

MOST POPULAR MAJORS
English language and literature,
molecular biology, psychology

STUDENTS SAY ". . ."

Academics
Undergrads at Wells are full of praise for their academic experience. The "intimate" size of the college ensures a "personal" education that stresses "individual attention." The professors "genuinely care about their students" and often "form lasting friendships" with them. However, this doesn't mean the classroom is a cakewalk. One junior stressed the professors "set very high academic standards for their students." And a freshman revealed the workload, at times, can be "overwhelming." Indeed, it's "not a school where you will be able to get an easy A." Luckily, it's a supportive environment, and professors are "almost always willing to go the extra step to make sure you understand the material." Moreover, "they encourage you to explore beyond their own subject and connect your subjects with each other." It's clearly evident to these undergrads their profs "teach for the love it." While acclaim for the academics is virtually unanimous, opinions regarding the administrators definitely run the gamut. Some undergrads feel "the administration tend to do as they please with little regard for the students." And one senior adds that they "make it very obvious they are running a business." However, another undergrad counters by saying "students are allowed to have a voice, and can meet with the administration to discuss changes to controversial policies."

Life
Wells students agree "there isn't a lot to do" in "rural" hometown Aurora. Fortunately, that just means entertainment is centered around the college. One junior reveals, "The traditions on campus are superior and amazing!" In turn, they foster "a great sense of community." The school sponsors a number of activities such as "concerts, parties, dances, and guest speakers." Additionally the college theater is pretty popular because the "performing arts are very high quality" at Wells. Of course many students love to simply "chill out with close friends, have an intellectual conversation, or host their own dance party." And a number of students "get creative" and "make their own fun." Indeed, an intrepid freshman regales with tales of "riding mattresses down stairs," and another shares that when it snows "students ride sleds or make snowmen or other types of sculptures." Though Aurora is "small," one sophomore gushes "the surrounding area is beautiful and there are lots of places to go hiking." When undergrads are itching to get a little farther away, they typically head to either "Ithaca or Auburn." Both towns offer ample opportunity for fun such as "movies, bowling, ice skating, a mall, [and] dining out."

Student Body
When Wells made the decision to go co-ed back in 2005, the college was forced to "restructure its student identity." Naturally, the transition was fraught with some growing pains. And while there's still some lingering tension, many undergrads assure us "one of the beautiful things about Wells is that, in general, everyone is welcome." A content English major expands upon this sentiment stating, "Everyone is important and has a place here." This can partly be attributed to the fact the college "has a strong emphasis on community." Additionally, Wells seems to attract "friendly, eccentric people" who are "socially and politically conscious, academic minded, and tolerant." And these "fun" students "aren't afraid to be different." Undergrads find common ground in that most everyone is "concerned about their education." Indeed, the "typical student at Wells is very studious [and] spends many hours studying or in the library." Perhaps this happy freshman sums up by sharing, "It is a diverse environment, but everyone can find someone that is like them. There is no such thing as not fitting in!"

FINANCIAL AID: 315-364-3289 • E-MAIL: ADMISSIONS@WELLS.EDU • WEBSITE: WWW.WELLS.EDU

THE PRINCETON REVIEW SAYS

Admissions

Very important factors considered include: Academic GPA, recommendation(s), rigor of secondary school record, standardized test scores, extracurricular activities. *Important factors considered include:* Application essay, interview. *Other factors considered include*: Class rank, alumni/ae relation, character/personal qualities, level of applicant's interest, talent/ability, volunteer work, work experience. SAT or ACT required; ACT with or without writing component accepted. TOEFL required of all international applicants. High school diploma is required, and GED is accepted. *Academic units required:* 4 English, 3 mathematics, 2 science (2 science labs), 1 social studies, 3 history, 2 academic elective. *Academic units recommended:* 4 mathematics, 3 science (3 science labs), 2 foreign language, 2 social studies, 2 history, 3 academic elective.

Financial Aid

Students should submit: FAFSA. The Princeton Review suggests that all financial aid forms be submitted as soon as possible after January 1. *Need-based scholarships/grants offered:* Federal Pell, SEOG, state scholarships/grants, private scholarships, school scholarship or grant aid from institutional funds. *Loan aid offered:* Direct Subsidized Stafford, Direct Unsubsidized Stafford, Direct PLUS, Federal Perkins. Applicants will be notified of awards on a rolling basis beginning March 1. Federal Work-Study Program available. Off-campus job opportunities are poor.

The Inside Word

Wells is engaged in that age-old admissions game called matchmaking. There are no minimums or cutoffs in the admissions process here. But don't be fooled by the high admit rate. The admissions committee will look closely at your academic accomplishments. However, they will also give attention to your essay, recommendations, and extracurricular pursuits. The committee also recommends an interview; we suggest taking them up on it.

THE SCHOOL SAYS "..."

From the Admissions Office

"Wells College believes the twenty-first century needs well-educated individuals with the ability, self-confidence, and vision to contribute to an ever-changing world. Wells offers an outstanding classroom experience and innovative liberal arts curriculum that prepares students for leadership in a variety of fields, including business, government, the arts, sciences, medicine, and education. By directly connecting the liberal arts curriculum to experience and career development through internships, off-campus study, study abroad, research with professors, and community service, each student has an ideal preparation for graduate and professional school as well as for the twenty-first century."

SELECTIVITY

Admissions Rating	85
# of applicants	1,673
% of applicants accepted	71
% of acceptees attending	12
# accepting a place on wait list	56
% admitted from wait list	100
# of early decision applicants	15
% accepted early decision	27

FRESHMAN PROFILE

Range SAT Critical Reading	500–630
Range SAT Math	480–600
Range SAT Writing	480–590
Range ACT Composite	22–27
Minimum paper TOEFL	550
Minimum computer TOEFL	213
Average HS GPA	3.50
% graduated top 10% of class	31
% graduated top 25% of class	65
% graduated top 50% of class	91

DEADLINES

Early decision	
Deadline	12/15
Notification	1/15
Early action	
Deadline	12/15
Notification	2/1
Regular	
Priority	12/15
Deadline	3/1
Nonfall registration?	yes

APPLICANTS ALSO LOOK AT

AND OFTEN PREFER
Hobart and William Smith Colleges, Mount Holyoke College, Smith College

AND SOMETIMES PREFER
Alfred University, State University of New York at Binghamton, State University of New York at Geneseo

AND RARELY PREFER
Elmira College, LeMoyne College

FINANCIAL FACTS

Financial Aid Rating	78
Annual tuition	$28,180
Room and board	$9,000
Required fees	$1,500
Books and supplies	$800
% frosh rec. need-based scholarship or grant aid	86
% UG rec. need-based scholarship or grant aid	83
% frosh rec. non-need-based scholarship or grant aid	57
% UG rec. non-need-based scholarship or grant aid	49
% frosh rec. need-based self-help aid	78
% UG rec. need-based self-help aid	80
% frosh rec. any financial aid	96
% UG rec. any financial aid	95
% UG borrow to pay for school	82
Average cumulative indebtedness	$24,182

WESLEYAN COLLEGE

4760 FORSYTH ROAD, MACON, GA 31210-4462 • ADMISSIONS: 478-757-5206 • FAX: 912-757-4030 • 800-447-6610

CAMPUS LIFE

Quality of Life Rating	85
Fire Safety Rating	60*
Green Rating	78
Type of school	private
Affiliation	Methodist
Environment	city

STUDENTS

Total undergrad enrollment	630
% male/female	0/100
% from out of state	7
% from public high school	81
% live on campus	82
% African American	28
% Asian	1
% Caucasian	45
% Hispanic	2
% international	20
# of countries represented	21

SURVEY SAYS . . .
Lab facilities are great
Diverse student types on campus
Low cost of living
Very little drug use

ACADEMICS

Academic Rating	90
% students graduating within 4 years	51
% students graduating within 6 years	52
Calendar	semester
Student/faculty ratio	8:1
Profs interesting rating	95
Profs accessible rating	85
Most common reg class size	fewer than 10 students

MOST POPULAR MAJORS
business, international business, psychology

STUDENTS SAY "..."

Academics
The Wesleyan College motto, "First for Women," encompasses the school's commitment to women's education since it was founded in 1836. The first accredited college to offer degrees to women, this small school is not your typical college environment, maintaining a strong focus on sisterhood between students, rigorous academic programs, and an intimate and interactive academic atmosphere. With an excellent faculty-to-student ratio, "you get one-on-one time with your professors," and "most classes are done discussion-style, with many diverse viewpoints presented." At the same time, the close-knit atmosphere does not translate into slack academic expectations. A junior explains, "The overall academic experience is tough due to the small classes and extra attention; teachers expect you to turn [in] quality work on time." Fortunately, students appreciate the benefits of their unique education, saying, "Everyone brings something different to the table, which enriches the academic experience." Tuition is a bit more reasonable at Wesleyan College than at other private schools, and more than half of current students receive some form of financial assistance. Despite affordability, "the campus facilities are impressive, especially for such a small school" and the 200-acre campus includes athletic and equestrian facilities, as well as a new, world-class science center. When it comes to the nuts and bolts, many students feel the school's administration, though friendly, could improve its organizations skills. A student points out, "Getting to the administration is the easy, but the paperwork can be difficult."

Life
"The academic load can be quite stressful, a lot of time is spent studying." Even in their downtime, students like to "talk about the interesting things we discussed in classes or about plays or art shows we've recently been to." Those who do have wheels often "leave campus to party and drink because alcohol is not allowed on campus." In the surrounding city, the "Cherry Blossom festival is also a great program to enjoy during the spring semester," and students "frequent many of the clubs on Cherry Street in downtown Macon." Wesleyan is affiliated with the United Methodist Church, and many students take part in community service activities, religious groups, and campus clubs. In addition, "the sense of sisterhood and camaraderie on campus" is one of the school's distinguishing characteristics. Wesleyan promotes class spirit and frequently organizes "pep rallies and different events that get students involved." In fact, "during lunch in the cafeteria you can usually hear class cheers." A sophomore enthuses, "Sisterhood enables you to make friends and interact with people you would have never met otherwise." On the other hand, if you want to fraternize with the opposite sex, "boys (and students from neighboring colleges) rarely come to our campus events!"

Student Body
There are just 600 undergraduates at Wesleyan College, yet "Wesleyan students come from all kinds of backgrounds, countries, ethnic groups, and religions." Within the Wesleyan community, you'll meet "artsy kids, hippies, science geeks, religious girls, political activists." "Wesleyan truly embraces how you are, no matter who you are." A junior attests, "Everybody is different here, but since diversity is so celebrated, there are very few people who just don't fit in." "The top students are strong-willed [and] outspoken and passionately love the work they do." At the same time, the average student "maintains a balance between their academics, extracurricular activities, and community service." On that note, most students are involved in their school and community, as the student body's small size "allows for you to be involved in student activities as much as you want."

FINANCIAL AID: 800-447-6610 • E-MAIL: ADMISSION@WESLEYANCOLLEGE.EDU • WEBSITE: WWW.WESLEYANCOLLEGE.EDU

THE PRINCETON REVIEW SAYS

Admissions

Very important factors considered include: Rigor of secondary school record. *Important factors considered include:* Academic GPA, class rank, recommendation(s), standardized test scores, extracurricular activities, interview, talent/ability. *Other factors considered include:* Application essay, alumni/ae relation, level of applicant's interest, volunteer work, work experience. SAT or ACT required; ACT with or without writing component accepted. TOEFL required of all international applicants. High school diploma is required, and GED is accepted. *Academic units required:* 4 English, 3 mathematics, 3 science (2 science labs), 2 foreign language, 3 social studies. *Academic units recommended:* 4 English, 4 mathematics, 4 science (3 science labs), 4 foreign language, 4 social studies, 2 academic elective.

Financial Aid

Students should submit: FAFSA, institution's own financial aid form. Regular filing deadline is June 3. The Princeton Review suggests that all financial aid forms be submitted as soon as possible after January 1. *Need-based scholarships/ grants offered:* Federal Pell, SEOG, state scholarships/grants, private scholarships, school scholarship or grant aid from institutional funds. *Loan aid offered:* Direct Subsidized Stafford, Direct Unsubsidized Stafford, Direct PLUS, Federal Perkins, state loans, university loans from institutional funds. Applicants will be notified of awards on a rolling basis beginning March 1. Off-campus job opportunities are good.

The Inside Word

Wesleyan College values diversity. At this small college, you'll find students from more than twenty countries and twenty-one states, with a wide range of interests. To evaluate a student's qualitative characteristics, Wesleyan recommends that applicants submit a teacher recommendation and have a personal interview with the admissions staff (though neither is required.) Students are also encouraged to submit samples of their creative work, such as poetry, music, or research projects.

THE SCHOOL SAYS ". . ."

From the Admissions Office

"Mention the term 'women's college' and most people envision ivy-covered towers in the Northeastern U.S. However, Wesleyan College in Macon, Georgia was founded in 1836 as the first college in the world chartered to grant degrees to women. Today it is recognized as one of the nation's most diverse and affordable selective four-year liberal arts colleges. Students value the college's tradition of service and rigorous academic program renowned for its quality. An exceptional faculty teaches classes in seminar style. A student/faculty ratio of ten to one ensures that students are known by more than just a grade or a number. The acceptance rate of Wesleyan students into medical, law, business, and other graduate programs is exemplary. Undergraduate degrees are offered in thirty-two majors and twenty-nine minors including self-designed majors and interdisciplinary programs, plus eight pre-professional programs that include seminary, engineering, medicine, pharmacy, veterinary medicine, health sciences, dental, and law. A $12.5 million science center added to the college's offerings for 2007. Master of Arts degrees in education and an accelerated Executive Master of Business Administration program enroll both men and women.

"Beyond the academic, Wesleyan offers a thriving residence life program, NCAA Division III athletics, championship IHSA equestrian program, and meaningful opportunities for community involvement and leadership. The college's beautiful 200-acre wooded campus, along with thirty historically significant buildings, is listed in the National Register of Historic Places as the Wesleyan College Historic District. Wesleyan is nestled in a northern suburb of Macon, the third largest city in the state. First-year applicants must take either the SAT or ACT."

SELECTIVITY

Admissions Rating	85
# of applicants	516
% of applicants accepted	40
% of acceptees attending	50
# accepting a place on wait list	0

FRESHMAN PROFILE

Range SAT Critical Reading	420–660
Range SAT Math	400–610
Range ACT Composite	18–25
Minimum paper TOEFL	550
Minimum computer TOEFL	213

DEADLINES

Early decision	
Deadline	11/15
Notification	12/15
Early action	
Deadline	2/15
Notification	3/15
Regular	
Priority	3/1
Deadline	6/1
Notification	10/1
Nonfall registration?	yes

APPLICANTS ALSO LOOK AT AND SOMETIMES PREFER

Agnes Scott College, Emory University, Oxford College, University of Georgia

FINANCIAL FACTS

Financial Aid Rating	86
Annual tuition	$18,000
Room and board	$8,500
Books and supplies	$1,000
% frosh rec. need-based scholarship or grant aid	70
% UG rec. need-based scholarship or grant aid	61
% frosh rec. non-need-based scholarship or grant aid	22
% UG rec. non-need-based scholarship or grant aid	15
% frosh rec. need-based self-help aid	48
% UG rec. need-based self-help aid	46
% frosh rec. any financial aid	96
% UG rec. any financial aid	91
% UG borrow to pay for school	62
Average cumulative indebtedness	$20,896

WESLEYAN UNIVERSITY

STEWART M. REID HOUSE, 70 WYLLYS AVENUE, MIDDLETOWN, CT 06459-0265 • ADMISSIONS: 860-685-3000 • FAX: 860-685-3001

CAMPUS LIFE

Quality of Life Rating	87
Fire Safety Rating	84
Green Rating	85
Type of school	private
Environment	town

STUDENTS

Total undergrad enrollment	2,837
% male/female	49/51
% from out of state	92
% from public high school	53
% live on campus	98
# of fraternities	9
# of sororities	4
% African American	6
% Asian	7
% Caucasian	56
% Hispanic	9
% international	7
# of countries represented	42

SURVEY SAYS . . .

Lots of liberal students
No one cheats
Great computer facilities
Great library
Athletic facilities are great
Students are friendly
Students aren't religious
Students are happy
Political activism is popular

ACADEMICS

Academic Rating	98
% students graduating within 4 years	88
% students graduating within 6 years	93
Calendar	semester
Student/faculty ratio	9:1
Profs interesting rating	88
Profs accessible rating	94
Most common reg class size	10–19 students
Most common lab size	10–19 students

MOST POPULAR MAJORS
economics, psychology

STUDENTS SAY ". . ."

Academics

Tucked away in Middletown, Connecticut, Wesleyan University is a dynamic institution "committed [to] catering to its undergraduates." The school certainly attracts those with a high level of "intellectual interest and curiosity" and students "really engage their education in a meaningful way." Fortunately, there's a "lack of...competitive cutthroat [behavior which] really promotes a community of learning." Undergrads at Wesleyan also appreciate "the lack of core curriculum," which gives students the flexibility to really "explore new areas" and "obtain a broad education." Academics here are "very challenging" but students find their classes immensely "rewarding." This is wholly due to professors that are "always available and eager to speak with students, and have a terrific passion for their work." Many of them maintain "intimate relationships with students" and a junior tells us that "having a meal with a professor at their home is not a rare occurrence." While a few students find that "the administration is full of red tape," others insist that they are "generally very responsive to student needs" and "very invested in the happiness of the students." As one senior concludes, "I feel that the administration as well as faculty work hard to make Wesleyan a strong community where everyone's voice matters."

Life

Wesleyan students have eclectic interests and passions and the social scene really reflects that. An intellectual group, undergrads can frequently be found deep in conversation with their peers, discussing anything from "the ethics of grading [or] the rendering of astrophysics into tangible graphics [to] the analysis of the feminist meanings of a Spanish worksheet." Of course, you shouldn't let this deceive you. These students also know how to kick back and have fun. "From the traditional frat party, to a gathering at a program house, [to] a performance or movie with friends in somebody's living room, Wesleyan offers a variety of social scenes for students to get involved in." Activities certainly run the gamut. An African American studies major shares, "For fun, people go to performances, sporting events, lectures, protests, restaurants, open mics, parties, campus events, etc." On any given day these lucky students might enjoy "anything from an Indian dance festival to an open forum on the economic recession to a frat party that's also a charity event for a school in Kenya." Of course, Wesleyan students are also quite adept at making their own fun and they can be found "sledding on the snow, rolling down the hill, playing Duck Duck Goose, [and] having awesome corny dance parties."

Student Body

Undergrads at Wesleyan are fairly adamant about the fact that they cannot "be pigeon-holed." While many insist "there are no typical students," others concede that there "are a few traits that often connect [everyone]." Most people "are interested in engaging with the world around them, often in hopes of improving it." Indeed this is a "passionate" group who are very "socially-conscious, politically aware, and [into] activism." Moreover, Wesleyan students are "driven," "intellectually curious" and "eager to learn and experience new things." These are kids who are "serious about academics" but also know how to "relax and have fun." They are also "very proud to be part of a diverse community" and are always excited to "meet new people." Another commonality is that undergrads here tend to "have a variety of interests." As a Spanish and film studies double-major illustrates, "Your best friend might be captain of the football team and double-majoring in chemistry and art studio." Perhaps most importantly, students at Wesleyan "aren't afraid to associate with many different kinds of people." A content senior sums up, "Students here are committed to creating a strong and close-knit community made up of open-minded people."

FINANCIAL AID: 860-685-2800 • E-MAIL: ADMISS@WESLEYAN.EDU • WEBSITE: WWW.WESLEYAN.EDU

THE PRINCETON REVIEW SAYS

Admissions

Very important factors considered include: Rigor of secondary school record. *Important factors considered include:* Academic GPA, application essay, class rank, recommendation(s), standardized test scores, character/personal qualities, first generation, racial/ethnic status, talent/ability. *Other factors considered include:* Alumni/ae relation, extracurricular activities, geographical residence, interview, volunteer work, work experience. ACT with writing component recommended. TOEFL required of all international applicants. High school diploma is required, and GED is accepted. *Academic units recommended:* 4 English, 4 mathematics, 4 science (3 science labs), 4 foreign language, 4 social studies, 4 history.

Financial Aid

Students should submit: FAFSA, CSS/Financial Aid PROFILE. Regular filing deadline is February 15. The Princeton Review suggests that all financial aid forms be submitted as soon as possible after January 1. *Need-based scholarships/grants offered:* Federal Pell, SEOG, state scholarships/grants, private scholarships, school scholarship or grant aid from institutional funds. *Loan aid offered:* Direct Subsidized Stafford, Direct Unsubsidized Stafford, Direct PLUS, Federal Perkins, university loans from institutional funds. Federal Work-Study Program available. Off-campus job opportunities are good.

The Inside Word

You want the inside word on Wesleyan admissions? Read The Gatekeepers: Inside the Admissions Process at a Premier College, by Jacques Steinberg. The author spent an entire admissions season at the Wesleyan admissions office. His book is a wonderfully detailed description of the Wesleyan admissions process (which is quite similar to processes at other private, highly selective colleges and universities).

THE SCHOOL SAYS "..."

From the Admissions Office

"Wesleyan faculty believe in an education that is flexible and affords individual freedom and that a strong liberal arts education is the best foundation for success in any endeavor. The broad curriculum focuses on essential communication skills and analytical abilities through course content and teaching methodology, allowing students to pursue their intellectual interests with passion while honing those capabilities. As a result, Wesleyan students achieve a very personalized but broad education. Wesleyan's Dean of Admission and Financial Aid, Nancy Hargrave Meislahn, describes the qualities Wesleyan seeks in its students: 'Our very holistic process seeks to identify academically accomplished and intellectually curious students who can thrive in Wesleyan's rigorous and vibrant academic environment; we look for personal strengths, accomplishments, and potential for real contribution to our diverse community.'

"Applicants will meet standardized testing requirements one of two ways: by taking the SAT plus two SAT Subject Tests of the student's choice or by taking the ACT (writing component recommended)."

SELECTIVITY

Admissions Rating	98
# of applicants	10,657
% of applicants accepted	21
% of acceptees attending	34
# accepting a place on wait list	645
% admitted from wait list	14
# of early decision applicants	854
% accepted early decision	41

FRESHMAN PROFILE

Range SAT Critical Reading	635–740
Range SAT Math	660–740
Range SAT Writing	650–750
Range ACT Composite	30–33
Minimum paper TOEFL	600
Minimum computer TOEFL	250
Minimum web-based TOEFL	100
Average HS GPA	3.77
% graduated top 10% of class	68
% graduated top 25% of class	91
% graduated top 50% of class	99

DEADLINES

Early decision	
Deadline	11/15
Notification	12/15
Regular	
Deadline	1/1
Nonfall registration?	no

APPLICANTS ALSO LOOK AT

AND OFTEN PREFER
Brown University, Harvard College, Stanford University, Yale University

AND SOMETIMES PREFER
Amherst College, Swarthmore College

AND RARELY PREFER
Oberlin College, Tufts University, Vassar College

FINANCIAL FACTS

Financial Aid Rating	98
Annual tuition	$41,814
Room and board	$11,592
% frosh rec. need-based scholarship or grant aid	44
% UG rec. need-based scholarship or grant aid	43
% frosh rec. need-based self-help aid	47
% UG rec. need-based self-help aid	48
% frosh rec. any financial aid	47
% UG rec. any financial aid	48
% UG borrow to pay for school	39
Average cumulative indebtedness	$29,227

WEST VIRGINIA UNIVERSITY

ADMISSIONS OFFICE, PO BOX 6009, MORGANTOWN, WV 26506-6009 • ADMISSIONS: 304-293-2121 • FAX: 304-293-3080

CAMPUS LIFE

Quality of Life Rating	81
Fire Safety Rating	91
Green Rating	92
Type of school	public
Environment	town

STUDENTS

Total undergrad enrollment	22,303
% male/female	55/45
% from out of state	46
% live on campus	26
# of fraternities	14
# of sororities	9
% African American	4
% Asian	1
% Caucasian	87
% Hispanic	3
% international	2
# of countries represented	67

SURVEY SAYS . . .

Great computer facilities
Athletic facilities are great
Students are friendly
Everyone loves the WV Mountaineers
Student publications are popular
Lots of beer drinking
Hard liquor is popular

ACADEMICS

Academic Rating	62
Calendar	semester
Student/faculty ratio	23:1
Profs interesting rating	66
Profs accessible rating	74
Most common reg class size	20–29 students
Most common lab size	20–29 students

MOST POPULAR MAJORS
engineering, health professions and related clinical sciences

STUDENTS SAY "..."

Academics

Set in the "heart of the mountains of West Virginia," West Virginia University combines pastoral charm with an emphasis on providing a strong academic tradition to a large student body. With a strident regional appeal, West Virginia University couples "affordable" tuition with the resources of "a large university." "Close to home" for many, in-state students are quick to note the school's alluring trio of "proximity, money, and opportunity." "The journalism school is well-accepted," as are the advertising and communication programs. "If you apply yourself, the opportunities at WVU are endless." Though "every professor is different," "Most professors are available and willing to provide extra help outside of the classrooms." Like most large universities, "with a variety of majors," "Life at WVU is what you make of it...If you're able to handle making a commitment to your work, you can have a great time doing both!" West Virginia's academic curriculum excels in numerous areas, including engineering, premedicine, journalism, psychology, forensics, advertising, music, and athletic training. It also offers a rigorous intellectual program through its elite Honors College. "Professors are usually great. I love it here overall; it's a large university in a small state."

Life

West Virginia University is "very school spirited," legendary for its "good football team" and "a fun, relaxing atmosphere to learn." Full of "genuine people" who enjoy "working hard in the classroom," life on campus involves "meeting lots of people, getting involved," and occasionally "letting the good times roll." In a word, it's all about "unity." Students tell us, "When you go to a football game you'll feel it." An average week involves "going bowling or to dinner with friends for fun." Many take advantage of the surrounding mountains and rugged setting of a university "hidden away in the hills of West Virginia" and enjoy participating in outdoor activities and sporting events. Others are quick to comment on Morgantown's status as one of the best small cities in the country, noting that it "is one of the fastest growing cities in the nation." On the weekend, "People either go to WVU sporting events, party, go to bars/clubs, or spend time at the rec center," which is state-of-the-art and draws rave reviews. Though many note the abundance of "athletics and partying," "a typical student goes to class, makes time to study and get work done, and definitely finds time to go out and enjoy [himself]."

Student Body

Though many affectionately tout the "cheers, beers, and mountaineers" slogan, "most students are at WVU to learn." "Easygoing, kind, good people," "the typical student is an outgoing person that likes to have fun and can multitask and balance an abundant social life." Always "ready to succeed and have fun," "There are a few typical students that include 'the party animals,' 'the religious kids,' and the 'very academically focused kids.'" Students assure us, "Everyone fits in if they try." Reflective of the school's regional appeal coupled with its nationally recognized journalism and honors program, array of majors and quality academics, "There are a lot of down-home, WV country boys. But then again, there are a lot of people from New Jersey as well." Overall, life at West Virginia University is "about growing socially, academically, and personally," and students are "kind and polite."

WEST VIRGINIA UNIVERSITY

FINANCIAL AID: 304-293-5242 • E-MAIL: WVUADMISSIONS@ARC.WVU.EDU • WEBSITE: WWW.WVU.EDU

THE PRINCETON REVIEW SAYS

Admissions

Very important factors considered include: Academic GPA, standardized test scores. *Important factors considered include:* Rigor of secondary school record, level of applicant's interest, state residency. *Other factors considered include:* Recommendation(s), extracurricular activities, talent/ability, work experience. SAT or ACT required; ACT with writing component required. TOEFL required of all international applicants. High school diploma is required, and GED is accepted. *Academic units required:* 4 English, 4 mathematics, 3 science (3 science labs), 2 foreign language, 3 social studies, 1 visual/performing arts.

Financial Aid

Students should submit: FAFSA. Regular filing deadline is March 1. The Princeton Review suggests that all financial aid forms be submitted as soon as possible after January 1. *Need-based scholarships/grants offered:* Federal Pell, SEOG, state scholarships/grants, private scholarships, school scholarship or grant aid from institutional funds. *Loan aid offered:* Direct Subsidized Stafford, Direct Unsubsidized Stafford, Direct PLUS, Federal Perkins. Applicants will be notified of awards on a rolling basis beginning April 15. Federal Work-Study Program available. Off-campus job opportunities are good.

The Inside Word

While standards for general admission to WVU aren't especially rigorous, you'll find admission to its premier programs to be quite competitive. Admission to the College of Business and Economics, for example, requires a high school GPA of at least 3.75 and an SAT math score of at least 610. Programs in computer science, education, engineering, fine arts, forensics, journalism, medicine, and nursing all require fairly impressive credentials. If you're not admitted to the program of your choice, you may be able to transfer to it later if your grades are good enough, but it won't be easy.

THE SCHOOL SAYS ". . ."

From the Admissions Office

"From quality academic programs and outstanding, caring faculty, to incredible new facilities and a campus environment that focuses on students' needs, WVU is a place where dreams can come true. The university's tradition of academic excellence attracts some of the region's best high school seniors. WVU has produced twenty-five Rhodes Scholars, thirty-two Goldwater Scholars, twenty-one Truman Scholars, six members of the USA Today's All-USA College Academic First Team, and two Udall Scholarship winners. Whether your goal is to be an aerospace engineer, reporter, physicist, athletic trainer, opera singer, forensic investigator, pharmacist, or CEO, WVU's 190 degree choices can make it happen. Unique student-centered initiatives help students experience true education beyond the classroom. Resident Faculty Leaders live next to the residence halls to mentor students, and WVUp All Night provides a way to relax and have fun with free food and activities every weekend. The Mountaineer parents club connects more than 20,000 families and a parents' helpline (800-WVU-0096) leads to a full-time parent advocate. A Student Recreation Center includes athletic courts, pools, weight/fitness equipment, and a fifty-foot indoor climbing wall. Also, a life science building and completely renovated library complex are cutting edge academic facilities. With programs for studying abroad, a Center from Black Culture and Research, and Office of Disability Services, and a student body that comes from every WV county, fifty states, and 100 different countries, WVU encourages and nurtures diversity. More than $152 million in annual grant funding makes WVU a major research institution where undergraduates can participate. All applicants are required to take the ACT writing assessment as part of the ACT exam, or take the SAT to be considered for admission."

SELECTIVITY

Admissions Rating	77
# of applicants	14,905
% of applicants accepted	86
% of acceptees attending	39

FRESHMAN PROFILE

Range SAT Critical Reading	460–560
Range SAT Math	480–580
Range ACT Composite	21–26
Minimum paper TOEFL	550
Minimum computer TOEFL	173
Minimum web-based TOEFL	61
Average HS GPA	3.32
% graduated top 10% of class	19
% graduated top 25% of class	45
% graduated top 50% of class	76

DEADLINES

Regular	
Priority	3/1
Deadline	8/1
Notification	9/15
Nonfall registration?	yes

APPLICANTS ALSO LOOK AT
AND OFTEN PREFER
Penn State—University Park,
University of Maryland—College Park, Virginia Tech

AND SOMETIMES PREFER
James Madison University, Marshall University,
University of Pittsburgh—Pittsburgh Campus

AND RARELY PREFER
Fairmont State College, Shepherd University, The Ohio
State University—Columbus

FINANCIAL FACTS

Financial Aid Rating	72
Annual in-state tuition	$5,406
Annual out-of-state tuition	$17,002
Room and board	$8,120
Books and supplies	$1,160
% frosh rec. need-based scholarship or grant aid	36
% UG rec. need-based scholarship or grant aid	36
% frosh rec. non-need-based scholarship or grant aid	33
% UG rec. non-need-based scholarship or grant aid	36
% frosh rec. need-based self-help aid	40
% UG rec. need-based self-help aid	42
% frosh rec. any financial aid	72
% UG rec. any financial aid	75

WESTMINSTER COLLEGE (PA)

319 SOUTH MARKET STREET, NEW WILMINGTON, PA 16172 • ADMISSIONS: 800-942-8033 • FAX: 724-946-7171

CAMPUS LIFE

Quality of Life Rating	86
Fire Safety Rating	96
Green Rating	60*
Type of school	private
Affiliation	Presbyterian
Environment	village

STUDENTS

Total undergrad enrollment	1,467
% male/female	41/59
% from out of state	25
% from public high school	91
% live on campus	73
# of fraternities	5
# of sororities	5
% African American	2
% Asian	1
% Caucasian	95
% Hispanic	2
# of countries represented	4

SURVEY SAYS . . .
Career services are great
Students are friendly
Students get along with local
community
Campus feels safe
Students are happy
Frats and sororities dominate
social scene
Student government is popular

ACADEMICS

Academic Rating	81
% students graduating within 4 years	67
% students graduating within 6 years	77
Calendar	semester
Student/faculty ratio	12:1
Profs interesting rating	86
Profs accessible rating	87
Most common reg class size	10–19 students
Most common lab size	10–19 students

MOST POPULAR MAJORS
biology, business/commerce, education

STUDENTS SAY ". . ."

Academics
Since 1852, Westminster College has remained intent crafting a personalized learning process for students, with the aim of turning out well-rounded individuals who "can live and affect the world around us in a positive way." The "challenging" liberal arts curriculum provides a broad foundation for academic study, and the school heavily stresses the application of what's learned by pushing students "to prepare themselves for the future using real life simulations." At this "very happy place," the administration always "keeps the interests of the students in mind," the classes are small, and "Students get the attention they need." Westminster runs on personal relationships between faculty and students, and "Even the janitor knows your name." The low student/teacher ratio means the "extremely accessible and helpful" professors are devoted to ensuring that every last student understands the material, and "Office doors are always open." This care extends far beyond the classroom, as professors love to see students involved in interesting activities outside of classes, and they "pretty much beg you to study abroad because they know it will be so beneficial for you as a person." "If you see some slacking there is always someone there, whether a classmate or professor, to bring you up," says one student. A few students do remark on the school's rather slow adoption of modern technology ("We just got wireless Internet this year"), but this is more than made up for by the "variety of courses," "student-teacher bonds," and "opportunities to get involved." "Contrary to popular belief, Westminster College, not Disneyland, is the happiest place on earth," says a student.

Life
"This school has so much going on that it is almost impossible to not be involved," says one student of the busy hive that is Westminster. There are more than 100 clubs and a wide range of activities offered, including "concerts, competitions, Humans versus Zombies, a Frisbee team, philosophy club, jazz band, flute choir, an equestrian team, an ice skating class, [and] karate class." The administration plan events all throughout the week ("Most people stay on campus on the weekends"), such as "movies on weekends, concerts on Friday or Saturday nights, sports events at least once a week, [and] special cuisine nights at the [cafeteria]." Located in the heart of Amish country, the dry town and campus "creates a great place to focus and learn" with "small-town appeal and charm that's irresistible." Greek life "is especially important for socialization," and many join it in some form or another (whether a social sorority or fraternity, or an honors society). Some students do choose to party off campus, but "It's far enough off of campus that you don't feel pressured to join in if you don't want to." Off-campus malls, restaurants, and cities "are not too far away," but "So much is happening on campus during the week and weekends that I do not see much need to go off-campus often."

Student Body
The typical Titan is "extremely friendly" and academically driven; students "know how to have fun but also know when to study and hit the books." Though the majority of Westminster students are white and Christian, "No one at Westminster is discriminatory towards other races, genders, religions, or sexual orientations." The student body is small enough that it can be called "tight-knit," and there's a lot of frequent interaction among students, because almost all who go to school here "get involved with a number of extracurricular activities" or "community service and philanthropic events." This easygoing crowd "gets along very well," and "Just about everyone fits in to the mix somewhere." Many students say, "Westminster is your family," and "It is a quick and easy process to make friends and find a niche."

WESTMINSTER COLLEGE (PA)

FINANCIAL AID: 724-946-7102 • E-MAIL: ADMIS@WESTMINSTER.EDU • WEBSITE: WWW.WESTMINSTER.EDU

THE PRINCETON REVIEW SAYS

Admissions

Very important factors considered include: Rigor of secondary school record, standardized test scores, interview. *Important factors considered include:* Application essay, class rank, recommendation(s), character/personal qualities. *Other factors considered include:* Alumni/ae relation, extracurricular activities, racial/ethnic status, talent/ability, volunteer work, work experience. SAT or ACT required; ACT with or without writing component accepted. TOEFL required of all international applicants. High school diploma is required, and GED is accepted. *Academic units required:* 4 English, 3 mathematics, 2 science (2 science labs), 2 foreign language, 2 social studies, 1 history, 3 academic elective.

Financial Aid

Students should submit: FAFSA, institution's own financial aid form. The Princeton Review suggests that all financial aid forms be submitted as soon as possible after January 1. *Need-based scholarships/grants offered:* Federal Pell, SEOG, state scholarships/grants, private scholarships, school scholarship or grant aid from institutional funds. *Loan aid offered:* Direct Subsidized Stafford, Direct Unsubsidized Stafford, Direct PLUS, Federal Perkins. Applicants will be notified of awards on a rolling basis beginning November 1.

The Inside Word

Westminster offers both early action and rolling admissions (following the December 15 deadline). The school will accept either the SAT or ACT test scores and also has an organization of student volunteers dedicated to assisting the Office of Admissions in the recruitment of qualified students. Most of your competition will be from Pennsylvania, with the rest mostly coming from Ohio.

THE SCHOOL SAYS "..."

From the Admissions Office

"Since its founding, Westminster has been dedicated to a solid foundation in today's most crucial social, cultural, and ethical issues. Related to the Presbyterian Church (USA), Westminster is home to people of many faiths. Our students and faculty, tradition of campus, and small-town setting all contribute to an enlightening educational experience.

"For purposes of admission and merit scholarships Westminster College will evaluate applicants using the composite score of the math and critical reading sections of the SAT or the composite score of the ACT. Westminster will collect new writing section scores and compare with national percentiles for possible inclusion in admission and scholarship criteria for the future."

SELECTIVITY	
Admissions Rating	80
# of applicants	4,296
% of applicants accepted	59
% of acceptees attending	16

FRESHMAN PROFILE	
Range SAT Critical Reading	470–580
Range SAT Math	480–590
Range ACT Composite	20–25
Minimum paper TOEFL	550
Minimum computer TOEFL	213
Average HS GPA	3.45
% graduated top 10% of class	26
% graduated top 25% of class	59
% graduated top 50% of class	91

DEADLINES	
Early action	
Deadline	11/15
Notification	11/15
Regular	
Deadline	4/15
Notification	9/1
Nonfall registration?	no

FINANCIAL FACTS	
Financial Aid Rating	64
Annual tuition	$29,150
Room and board	$9,200
Required fees	$1,160
Books and supplies	$1,000
% frosh rec. need-based scholarship or grant aid	84
% UG rec. need-based scholarship or grant aid	83
% frosh rec. non-need-based scholarship or grant aid	97
% UG rec. non-need-based scholarship or grant aid	97
% frosh rec. need-based self-help aid	65
% UG rec. need-based self-help aid	67
% UG borrow to pay for school	80
Average cumulative indebtedness	$23,262

WESTMINSTER COLLEGE (UT)

1840 SOUTH 1300 EAST, SALT LAKE CITY, UT 84105 • ADMISSIONS: 801-832-2200 • FAX: 801-832-3101

STUDENTS SAY ". . ."

Academics

Westminster College "has the perfect balance of everything: it focuses on being academically challenging but [that] is also equally weighted by all the fun events." The opportunity "to ski, climb, work, attend classes, hang out with friends, and be active on campus every day" makes the Westminster experience "the absolute best package of any college available," according to the many boosters among its student body. Academics are by no means neglected here; they are "challenging but manageable," students report. About one in three undergrads pursue a business major in a program that "prepares you for a global career [and] being able to work in many different cultures." The nursing program is also "highly respected," and the education program is "very good." In all fields, small class sizes "give all students the opportunity to be seen and heard by their professors and also give classes a chance to turn from strict lecturing to a more discussion-based learning that allows everyone to say something if they desire." "The small class sizes are amazing," one student writes. "You don't feel as though you are just a number and no one cares about you like at some big universities." Many also appreciate Westminster's reputation as "a liberal oasis" in the "sea of conservatism" known as Utah.

Life

"There are a lot of physically active students" at Westminster, "so it's not hard to find someone to work out with. In fact, it's not hard to find someone to do anything with: walk to a local restaurant, study with, party with, etc." That's both because "everyone is friendly and helpful" and because the school "has somehow made it very easy to meet people as well as do many different things in the local area." The student-run Associated Students of Westminster College organization "provides many opportunities for students to have fun and meet other students, from Casino Night to Pizza Tasting to bringing in popular comedians from around the state." Students also enjoy "lots of…skiing and other outdoor activities" such as hiking, camping, kayaking, and snowboarding. The school is especially hospitable to rock climbers, with "an indoor gym and outdoor bouldering wall, outdoor locations nearby, and several gyms in the city" for their use. On weekends, some here "like to unwind and enjoy the weekend with some partying" that includes "drinking games" and "beer runs," but (this being Utah) there is also a considerable population that will have none of that. Sugar House, the college-friendly neighborhood surrounding the school, accommodates both types of students well.

Student Body

"There is a large concentration of skiers and snowboarders" at Westminster, as one might expect from its location, but "there are also other types of students… that don't do snow sports." Likewise, the student body "is primarily Caucasian, much like Utah as a whole," but "the ethnic variety on campus is improving." An influx of Asian students "due to an exchange program within China and increased international recruiting efforts by the administration" contributes substantially to the diversity. There's a distinct Western vibe here, as students tend to be "liberal, environmentally friendly, laid-back, achieving, and accepting." Their ranks include the requisite kids who "don't really care," and many more who are "very studious" and "engaged in many opportunities on campus."

FINANCIAL AID: 801-832-2500 • E-MAIL: ADMISSION@WESTMINSTERCOLLEGE.EDU • WEBSITE: WWW.WESTMINSTERCOLLEGE.EDU

THE PRINCETON REVIEW SAYS

Admissions

Very important factors considered include: Academic GPA, rigor of secondary school record. *Important factors considered include:* Application essay, class rank, standardized test scores, interview. *Other factors considered include:* Recommendation(s), alumni/ae relation, character/personal qualities, extracurricular activities, geographical residence, talent/ability. SAT or ACT required; ACT with writing component recommended. TOEFL required of all international applicants. High school diploma is required, and GED is accepted. *Academic units required:* 4 English, 2 mathematics, 3 science, 2 foreign language, 2 social studies, 1 history, 2 academic elective. *Academic units recommended:* 4 English, 3 mathematics, 3 science, 3 foreign language, 2 social studies, 1 history, 3 academic elective.

Financial Aid

Students should submit: FAFSA. Regular filing deadline is April 15. The Princeton Review suggests that all financial aid forms be submitted as soon as possible after January 1. *Need-based scholarships/grants offered:* Federal Pell, SEOG, state scholarships/grants, private scholarships, school scholarship or grant aid from institutional funds. *Loan aid offered:* Direct Subsidized Stafford, Direct Unsubsidized Stafford, Direct PLUS, Federal Perkins. Applicants will be notified of awards on a rolling basis beginning March 1. Federal Work-Study Program available. Off-campus job opportunities are excellent.

The Inside Word

You don't need to clear lofty hurdles to gain admission to Westminster. Solid grades in a college-prep curriculum—we're not talking straight A's here, just mostly A's and B's—should make the grade. Test scores need to be decent (at or above the national average) but needn't be astronomical. If your record shows you can handle the workload at Westminster, you're likely to gain admission. The school reviews applications closely, allowing applicants who fall somewhat short in the GPA or test score department to impress through essays, extracurricular achievement, and demonstration of special skills or talent.

THE SCHOOL SAYS "..."

From the Admissions Office

"Founded in 1875, Westminster College is a private, comprehensive, liberal arts college dedicated to students and their learning, and offers one of the most unique learning environments in the country. Located where the Rocky Mountains meet the vibrant city of Salt Lake, Westminster blends classroom learning with experiences derived from its unique location to help students develop skills and attributes critical for success in a rapidly changing world. Impassioned teaching and active learning are the hallmarks of the Westminster experience.

"Each application is read and reviewed individually by an admissions committee who takes into account both level of challenge in course work and grades received. Either the SAT or ACT exam is accepted. Writing ability will be assessed through the writing sections of the SAT, ACT, application essays, and in some cases, other writing samples such as graded papers.

"Westminster College has a rolling application deadline and will accept applications until the class is filled. To be eligible for the widest array of financial aid—and more than ninety-seven percent of freshmen receive some financial aid—April 15 is the priority consideration deadline for fall semester, and May 15 is the deadline for on-campus housing applications."

SELECTIVITY

Admissions Rating	82
# of applicants	1,963
% of applicants accepted	78
% of acceptees attending	35

FRESHMAN PROFILE

Range SAT Critical Reading	500–620
Range SAT Math	510–630
Range ACT Composite	22–27
Minimum paper TOEFL	550
Minimum computer TOEFL	213
Minimum web-based TOEFL	100
Average HS GPA	3.51
% graduated top 10% of class	24
% graduated top 25% of class	55
% graduated top 50% of class	85

DEADLINES

Regular	
Priority	3/1
Deadline	8/27
Notification	rolling
Nonfall registration?	yes

APPLICANTS ALSO LOOK AT
AND OFTEN PREFER
University of Denver, University of Puget Sound

AND SOMETIMES PREFER
Brigham Young University (UT), Colorado College, University of Colorado—Boulder, University of Vermont

AND RARELY PREFER
Lewis & Clark College

FINANCIAL FACTS

Financial Aid Rating	84
Annual tuition	$26,712
Room and board	$7,584
Required fees	$470
Books and supplies	$1,000
% frosh rec. need-based scholarship or grant aid	63
% UG rec. need-based scholarship or grant aid	61
% frosh rec. non-need-based scholarship or grant aid	8
% UG rec. non-need-based scholarship or grant aid	6
% frosh rec. need-based self-help aid	44
% UG rec. need-based self-help aid	54
% frosh rec. any financial aid	98
% UG rec. any financial aid	94
% UG borrow to pay for school	65
Average cumulative indebtedness	$20,002

WHEATON COLLEGE (IL)

501 COLLEGE AVENUE, WHEATON, IL 60187 • ADMISSIONS: 630-752-5005 • FAX: 630-752-5285

CAMPUS LIFE

Quality of Life Rating	97
Fire Safety Rating	88
Green Rating	76
Type of school	private
Affiliation	Christian-nondenominational
Environment	town

STUDENTS

Total undergrad enrollment	2,406
% male/female	49/51
% from out of state	76
% from public high school	57
% live on campus	90
% African American	3
% Asian	8
% Caucasian	83
% Hispanic	4
% international	1
# of countries represented	26

SURVEY SAYS . . .

Students are very religious
Students get along with local community
Great food on campus
Frats and sororities are unpopular or nonexistent
Very little beer drinking
Very little drug use

ACADEMICS

Academic Rating	89
% students graduating within 4 years	79
% students graduating within 6 years	88
Calendar	semester
Student/faculty ratio	12:1
Profs interesting rating	90
Profs accessible rating	91
Most common reg class size	10–19 students
Most common lab size	10–19 students

MOST POPULAR MAJORS

business/managerial economics,
English language and literature,
health services

STUDENTS SAY "..."

Academics

Wheaton College strives to cultivate students' knowledge and to "prepare them to enter the world as strong and capable individuals who serve Christ and His Kingdom." This "academically rigorous" and deeply religious liberal arts school is equally as interested in the character of each student, with a focus on "developing yourself in ways [that] will affect you long after you've left the school campus." Professors here are "the heart and soul of this campus," and they're "exceptional teachers who genuinely care for the academic and spiritual well-being of their students." They "attempt to connect with students in ways other than the material they are told to teach," and it's "not unusual to meet professors outside of class, whether that be for a meal, coffee, or fun activities." That's not to say that there aren't a few bad apples or that the grading isn't tough; professors "rarely curve," but they do provide "many mentoring and tutoring sessions" to those in need. There's a "serious integration of faith and learning" that "places a high emphasis on opening up our eyes to serious issues going on around the world." "When you see other people using their gifts for God and hear them encouraging you to do the same, it's inspiring," says one student. Class sizes at Wheaton are pleasantly small, and one-on-one interaction is very common through "internships, teaching assistants, research opportunities, and the 'Dine with a Mind' program." This student body that's truly "sincere about learning" goes on to form a "very close-knit network of graduates" that's easily accessible after graduation. Other than that, students laud the "successful career placement, top-notch music conservatory, [and] excellent science facilities."

Life

All Wheaton students adhere to a community covenant, which is a set of rules and regulations governing students that forbids things, such as drinking, smoking, and "spontaneous" dancing. While several students wish that the school was "more lenient in their punishment system," most are happy to comply and even claim that it "forces us to come up with super-creative ways to have fun." "Everyone has at least one costume—bring one if you come here because you will need it," says a mysterious student. Drink-wise, "Wheaton students don't need alcohol to have an awesome time," and food-wise, the school has what some students call the "greatest college food in the country." The train station is a few minutes' walk from campus, which can bring you to nearby Chicago, but most students "just find fun activities to do on campus... like bond with [students who live on their housing] floor or play campus-wide Sardines." The college offers lots of activities during the weekend and has tons of "random traditions," such as a "student 'Iron Chef' competition in the dining hall." Students here are very passionate about social justice issues and "just as likely to be found discussing theology or philosophy as the latest sports game." ESL tutoring, mentoring, and serving on spring break service trips are also popular extracurricular activities for Wheaties.

Student Body

Pretty much the entirety of Wheaton is composed of "academically strong, driven, and Christian students," and the phrase "type-A personality" is oft-used. The school draws students from all over the country (including "quite a lot of homeschooled and international students"), and the diversity isn't as strong as some students would like, though "they are making a lot of efforts to change that in the admissions office." Students at Wheaton "take their studies extremely seriously and work very hard to keep high grades," but most still get involved with student activities, ministries, and sports, and enjoy the groups of friends that form when people share a "common identity." In their downtime, people "have a respectful and creative sense of fun and do not waste their time." All in all, "Most students find some way to fit in."

WHEATON COLLEGE (IL)

FINANCIAL AID: 630-752-5021 • E-MAIL: ADMISSIONS@WHEATON.EDU • WEBSITE: WWW.WHEATON.EDU

THE PRINCETON REVIEW SAYS

Admissions

Very important factors considered include: Academic GPA, application essay, recommendation(s), rigor of secondary school record, standardized test scores, character/personal qualities, interview, religious affiliation/commitment. *Important factors considered include:* Extracurricular activities, talent/ability, volunteer work, work experience. *Other factors considered include:* Class rank, alumni/ae relation, first generation, geographical residence, level of applicant's interest, racial/ethnic status, state residency. SAT or ACT required; ACT with writing component required. TOEFL required of all international applicants. High school diploma is required, and GED is accepted. *Academic units recommended:* 4 English.

Financial Aid

Students should submit: FAFSA, institution's own financial aid form. The Princeton Review suggests that all financial aid forms be submitted as soon as possible after January 1. *Need-based scholarships/grants offered:* Federal Pell, SEOG, state scholarships/grants, school scholarship or grant aid from institutional funds. *Loan aid offered:* Direct Subsidized Stafford, Direct Unsubsidized Stafford, Direct PLUS, Federal Perkins. Applicants will be notified of awards on a rolling basis beginning March 10. Federal Work-Study Program available. Off-campus job opportunities are excellent.

The Inside Word

Although Wheaton College looks for students who are strong academically, the college doesn't have any minimum requirements for GPA, class rank, or standardized test scores. The school does look for evidence of Christian faith when making its decision, and proof of Christian commitment is necessary for admission, but you'll also have to prove the quality of your high school courses.

THE SCHOOL SAYS " . . ."

From the Admissions Office

"At Wheaton, we're commited to being a community that fearlessly pursues truth, upholds an academically rigorous curriculum, and promotes virtue. The college takes seriously its impact on society. The influence of Wheaton is seen in fields ranging from government (the former speaker of the house) to sports (two NBA coaches) to business (the CEO of John Deere) to music (Metropolitan Opera National Competition winners) to education (over forty college presidents) to global ministry (Billy Graham). Wheaton seeks students who want to make a difference and are passionate about their Christian faith and rigorous academic pursuit.

"Applicants are required to submit results from the SAT or the ACT with writing section. Wheaton will use the highest of these scores from either test in evaluating a student's application."

SELECTIVITY

Admissions Rating	94
# of applicants	2,010
% of applicants accepted	66
% of acceptees attending	45
# accepting a place on wait list	126
% admitted from wait list	46

FRESHMAN PROFILE

Range SAT Critical Reading	600–730
Range SAT Math	610–700
Range SAT Writing	590–710
Range ACT Composite	26–32
Minimum paper TOEFL	587
Minimum computer TOEFL	213
Minimum web-based TOEFL	80
Average HS GPA	3.73
% graduated top 10% of class	58
% graduated top 25% of class	82
% graduated top 50% of class	98

DEADLINES

Early action	
Deadline	11/1
Notification	12/31
Regular	
Deadline	1/10
Nonfall registration?	no

APPLICANTS ALSO LOOK AT AND SOMETIMES PREFER
Grove City College, Taylor University

AND RARELY PREFER
Baylor University, Bethel University (MN), Calvin College, College of William and Mary, Davidson College, Gordon College, Houghton College, Indiana Wesleyan University, Westmont College

FINANCIAL FACTS

Financial Aid Rating	81
Annual tuition	$27,316
Room and board	$7,900
Books and supplies	$800
% frosh rec. need-based scholarship or grant aid	52
% UG rec. need-based scholarship or grant aid	51
% frosh rec. non-need-based scholarship or grant aid	18
% UG rec. non-need-based scholarship or grant aid	16
% frosh rec. need-based self-help aid	51
% UG rec. need-based self-help aid	50
% frosh rec. any financial aid	76
% UG rec. any financial aid	71
% UG borrow to pay for school	50
Average cumulative indebtedness	$21,241

WHEATON COLLEGE (MA)

OFFICE OF ADMISSION, NORTON, MA 02766 • ADMISSIONS: 508-286-8251 • FAX: 508-286-8271

CAMPUS LIFE

Quality of Life Rating	65
Fire Safety Rating	82
Green Rating	82
Type of school	private
Environment	village

STUDENTS

Total undergrad enrollment	1,635
% male/female	36/64
% from out of state	66
% from public high school	62
% live on campus	93
% African American	5
% Asian	2
% Caucasian	74
% Hispanic	5
% international	6
# of countries represented	40

SURVEY SAYS . . .

Frats and sororities are unpopular
or nonexistent
Student government is popular
Lots of beer drinking
Hard liquor is popular

ACADEMICS

Academic Rating	90
% students graduating within 4 years	71
% students graduating within 6 years	75
Calendar	semester
Student/faculty ratio	10:1
Profs interesting rating	89
Profs accessible rating	87
Most common reg class size	35 students
Most common lab size	20 students

MOST POPULAR MAJORS

psychology, economics, English
language and literature

STUDENTS SAY ". . ."

Academics

Wheaton College is a historic private liberal arts college located in Southeastern Massachusetts, where an intimate campus and small student body create a tight-knit community and much-appreciated "small class sizes." There's certainly a "rigor of the academics" here, but "Work in class is very reasonable," and there are "resources available to help students...everywhere." Administration "is very good with letting us know what is going on," and "The school's honor code is taken very seriously," creating "a strong bond between students and staff all over campus." Faculty are "easily the strong point of Wheaton," as "tenured, associate, and visiting professors are all extremely well-educated and aren't pretentious in their teaching style." No TAs teach classes, and the "well-informed" professors encourage dialogue in all classrooms, are "super accessible" to students that need extra help or counsel, and "make an honest effort to know and understand you as a person, not just a student." The professors don't talk at us, they discuss with us," says a student of Wheaton's classes, many of which have a participation grade. Each student also has the unique option to take classes at surrounding schools (Brown, Wellesley, the Boston Aquarium, etc.). Many people at Wheaton go on to postgraduate studies, and the close relationships between professors and students open doors for numerous research opportunities and useful connections; there are also "many funds available for individual projects and studies." Study abroad programs are a popular, robust option here. Really, "Wheaton provides every individual with the opportunities to try anything and everything that you are interested in."

Life

Classes demand that a student works hard during the week, but that means "they can relax and have a little fun on the weekend." Sundays are "sort of a transition day for students to get ready for the week ahead." The vast majority of students live on campus and stick around for Friday and Saturday, but the school's restrictive drug and alcohol policies (which many students believe "could be changed") relegate most partying to off-campus locales, creating some tension with the local community. Wheaton doesn't have fraternities or sororities, but "There is still a pretty big party scene at Wheaton." The small town location "is not the most ideal" ("Norton is not a college town," says one student emphatically), but there's a bus that runs from the school to the nearest train station, which is "very, very, very convenient to go to Boston or Providence." "Having a car makes you a god for getting off campus." Students are active in all sorts of clubs and community service activities, and individuals "usually manage to fit it once they find a club, organization, or group of some kind that they enjoy being a part of." Luckily, there are many at Wheaton, and "There are always events going on around the school." Dance and music shows are "well-attended," and popular movies are shown every weekend. "If students cannot find something to do, it's because they aren't trying," says one. The historic upper campus, designed by Ralph Adams Cram, is "a beautiful addition to life," but the food is "a big issue" here, even though "it's improving."

Student Body

There's a wide range of students at Wheaton, but the standard issue is "studious but not obsessive" and "involved in a variety of activities." "Any student could fit in this community pretty easily," and most "acclimate to the 'New England' style by the end of freshman year." On this "fairly liberal" campus, "artists, activists, and average Joes are as common as athletes"; or, as one student puts it, "There are bros and activists and party animals and computer science people...You have to seek out 'your people.'" Everyone is "very open to multicultural students," and the school is "surprisingly diverse." There's "a moderate level of political discussion" that abounds.

WHEATON COLLEGE (MA)

FINANCIAL AID: 508-286-8232 • E-MAIL: ADMISSION@WHEATONCOLLEGE.EDU • WEBSITE: WWW.WHEATONCOLLEGE.EDU

THE PRINCETON REVIEW SAYS

Admissions

Very important factors considered include: Academic GPA, application essay, rigor of secondary school record, character/personal qualities, extracurricular activities, first generation, talent/ability. *Important factors considered include:* Class rank, recommendation(s), alumni/ae relation, interview, volunteer work, work experience. *Other factors considered include:* Geographical residence, level of applicant's interest, racial/ethnic status, state residency. ACT with or without writing component accepted. TOEFL required of all international applicants. High school diploma is required, and GED is accepted. *Academic units recommended:* 4 English, 4 mathematics, 3 science (2 science labs), 4 foreign language, 3 social studies, 2 history.

Financial Aid

Students should submit: FAFSA, CSS/Financial Aid PROFILE. Regular filing deadline is February 1. The Princeton Review suggests that all financial aid forms be submitted as soon as possible after January 1. *Need-based scholarships/grants offered:* Federal Pell, SEOG, state scholarships/grants, private scholarships, school scholarship or grant aid from institutional funds. *Loan aid offered:* Federal Perkins. Federal Work-Study Program available. Off-campus job opportunities are good.

The Inside Word

Wheaton gives applicants the option of not submitting standardized test scores. The school also invites applicants to submit optional personal academic portfolios, collections of completed schoolwork that demonstrates talents the applicant wants to highlight. All applicants should seriously consider this option; for those who do not submit test scores, an academic portfolio is practically imperative, both as an indicator of the applicant's seriousness about Wheaton and as evidence of academic excellence (evidence that standardized test scores might otherwise provide).

THE SCHOOL SAYS " . . ."

From the Admissions Office

"What makes for a 'best college'? Is it merely the hard-to-define notions of prestige or image? We don't think so. We think what makes college 'best' and best for you is a school that will make you a first-rate thinker and writer, a pragmatic professional in your work, and an ethical practitioner in your life. To get you to all these places, Wheaton takes advantage of its great combinations: a beautiful, secluded New England campus combined with access to Boston and Providence; a high quality, classic liberal arts and sciences curriculum combined with award-winning internship, job, and community-service programs; and a campus that respects your individuality in the context of the larger community. What's the 'best' outcome of a Wheaton education? A start on life that combines meaningful work, significant relationships, and a commitment to your local and global community. Far more than for what they've studied or for what they've gone on to do for a living, we're most proud of Wheaton graduates for who they become.

"Wheaton does not require students to submit the results of any standardized testing. The only exception is the TOEFL for students for whom English is a second language. Students who choose to submit standardized testing may use results from the SAT or the ACT."

SELECTIVITY

Admissions Rating	89
# of applicants	3,272
% of applicants accepted	62
% of acceptees attending	22
# accepting a place on wait list	133
% admitted from wait list	31
# of early decision applicants	164
% accepted early decision	87

FRESHMAN PROFILE

Range SAT Critical Reading	580–690
Range SAT Math	570–660
Range ACT Composite	26–30
Minimum paper TOEFL	580
Minimum computer TOEFL	243
Minimum web-based TOEFL	90
Average HS GPA	3.42
% graduated top 10% of class	40
% graduated top 25% of class	32
% graduated top 50% of class	93

DEADLINES

Early decision I	
Deadline	11/15
Notification	12/15
Early decision II	
Deadline	11/15
Notification	2/15
Regular	
Deadline	1/15
Notification	4/1
Nonfall registration?	yes

APPLICANTS ALSO LOOK AT
AND OFTEN PREFER
Bates College, Connecticut College

AND SOMETIMES PREFER
Hamilton College, Skidmore College, University of Vermont

AND RARELY PREFER
Boston University, Brandeis University, Clark University

FINANCIAL FACTS

Financial Aid Rating	90
Annual tuition	$41,600
Room and board	$10,670
Required fees	$294
Books and supplies	$940
% frosh rec. need-based scholarship or grant aid	58
% UG rec. need-based scholarship or grant aid	55
% frosh rec. non-need-based scholarship or grant aid	16
% UG rec. non-need-based scholarship or grant aid	15
% frosh rec. need-based self-help aid	6
% UG rec. need-based self-help aid	57
% frosh rec. any financial aid	77
% UG rec. any financial aid	72
% UG borrow to pay for school	58
Average cumulative indebtedness	$27,546

WHITMAN COLLEGE

345 BOYER AVENUE, WALLA WALLA, WA 99362-2083 • ADMISSIONS: 509-527-5176 • FAX: 509-527-4967

CAMPUS LIFE
Quality of Life Rating	97
Fire Safety Rating	74
Green Rating	82
Type of school	private
Environment	town

STUDENTS
Total undergrad enrollment	1,535
% male/female	42/58
% from out of state	62
% from public high school	75
% live on campus	67
# of fraternities	4
# of sororities	3
% African American	1
% Asian	7
% Caucasian	68
% Hispanic	6
% Native American	1
% international	3
# of countries represented	29

SURVEY SAYS . . .
Great computer facilities
Athletic facilities are great
School is well-run
Students are friendly
Dorms are like palaces
Intramural sports are popular
Musical organizations are popular

ACADEMICS
Academic Rating	98
% students graduating within 4 years	80
% students graduating within 6 years	85
Calendar	semester
Student/faculty ratio	10:1
Profs interesting rating	99
Profs accessible rating	99
Most common reg class size	10–19 students
Most common lab size	20–29 students

MOST POPULAR MAJORS
biology, English language and literature, political science

STUDENTS SAY ". . ."

Academics
If learning can be both rigorous and laid-back at the same time, it happens at Whitman College in Walla Walla, WA. The "challenging" academics here are coupled with a "relaxed attitude" in order to give students "the best education possible without sacrificing all the fun one expects of college." Populated mainly by "intelligent, ambitious liberals with far-reaching goals," this somewhat idealistic school seeks to build critical thinking skills through "an earnest discourse about 'life, the universe, and everything.'" So no one starts off with a blank slate, all first-year students are required to take a course referred to as "Encounters" which offers a survey of Western thought, starting with The Odyssey, working through Socrates, Plato, Augustine, up through Marx, Voltaire, and other thinkers who shaped modern thought. Distribution requirements ensure that all students get a breadth of courses, and a lack of TAs ensures that they get all the attention they need. Although there's always a dud or two in the mix, professors are "genuinely brilliant and interesting people" and "love to spend time with students outside of class," whether it be for academic help or just conversation. "It is not uncommon to have potlucks, classes, or movie night over at your professor's house with your class," says one student.

On the administrative side of things, bureaucracy and red tape are kept to a minimum in this chill environment through "effortless use of the 'system'" and the administration gets raves all around for its devotion to "maintaining quality student life," which is something of a rarity. "I have never heard of *any* college being as supportive as this place has been to me in just the past two years," says a student. "Whitman's president gave me a ride to campus one semester after I met him at the airport," says another. As one can imagine, all these things come together to form a student body that's "happy, well-balanced, and well-cared-for."

Life
Most people stay on campus for their fun, "especially first-years," and throughout this "bubble" the "sense of closeness and comradeship is very evident through attendance at student-run concerts, art shows, etc." Everything is within ten minutes' walking distance. Academics take precedence for almost everyone, but "most students find time to party on the weekends" at the frats, due to a "lenient and fair" alcohol policy. Thanks to the campus activities board, "there's almost always something fun going on, whether or not a person chooses to drink," such as Drive-In Movie Night and Casino Night. With "four beautiful seasons," outdoor activities are also very popular, thanks to "a great gear rental program that gets people outside hiking, biking, kayaking, and rock-climbing," and "Frisbees are everywhere when it's warm." In fact, there's so much going on "if someone says they are bored, students laugh and wish they could relate."

Student Body
It's a sociable bunch at Whitman, where most students "are interested in trying new things and meeting new people" and "everyone seems to have a weird interest or talent or passion." The quirky Whitties "usually have a strong opinion about *something*," and one freshman refers to her classmates as ""cool nerds." Diversity has risen steadily over the past several years, as the school has made an effort to recruit beyond the typical "mid- to upper-class and white" contingent. Everyone here is pretty outdoorsy and environmentally aware ("to the point where you almost feel guilty for printing an assignment"), and a significant number of students have won fellowships and scholarships such as the Fulbright, Watson, Truman, and Udall."

WHITMAN COLLEGE

FINANCIAL AID: 509-527-5178 • E-MAIL: ADMISSION@WHITMAN.EDU • WEBSITE: WWW.WHITMAN.EDU

THE PRINCETON REVIEW SAYS

Admissions

Very important factors considered include: Academic GPA, application essay, rigor of secondary school record, character/personal qualities. *Important factors considered include:* Recommendation(s), standardized test scores, extracurricular activities, racial/ethnic status, talent/ability. *Other factors considered include:* Class rank, alumni/ae relation, first generation, geographical residence, interview, level of applicant's interest, state residency, volunteer work, work experience. SAT or ACT required; ACT with writing component required. TOEFL required of all international applicants. High school diploma is required, and GED is accepted. *Academic units recommended:* 4 English, 4 mathematics, 3 science (2 science labs), 2 foreign language, 2 social studies, 2 history.

Financial Aid

Students should submit: FAFSA, CSS/Financial Aid PROFILE. Regular filing deadline is February 1. The Princeton Review suggests that all financial aid forms be submitted as soon as possible after January 1. *Need-based scholarships/grants offered:* Federal Pell, SEOG, state scholarships/grants, private scholarships, school scholarship or grant aid from institutional funds. *Loan aid offered:* Direct Subsidized Stafford, Direct Unsubsidized Stafford, Direct PLUS, Federal Perkins. Applicants will be notified of awards upon admission. Federal Work-Study Program available. Off-campus job opportunities are good.

The Inside Word

Whitman's admissions committee emphasizes essays and extracurriculars more than SAT scores. The college cares much more about who you are and what you have to offer if you enroll than it does about what your numbers will do for the freshman academic profile. Whitman is a mega-sleeper. Educators all over the country know it as an excellent institution, and the college's alums support it at one of the highest rates of giving at any college in the nation. Students seeking a top-quality liberal arts college owe it to themselves to take a look.

THE SCHOOL SAYS "..."

From the Admissions Office

"Whitman College is a national, highly selective, residential liberal arts college located in Walla Walla, a historic town of 30,000 in sunny southeastern Washington State known for its ideal weather, charming Main Street, and vibrant arts and wine culture. Whitman has a history of graduating ethical, engaged, and unpretentious leaders who have made a difference in their local and international communities.

"Whitman is known for the balance of academic rigor and collaboration. The Penrose Library is open 24/7 for good reason. Students complete comprehensive capstone projects in their majors, oral exams as well as a thesis or written examination. This experience is excellent preparation for sixty-five percent of students who will attend graduate school.

"Signature programs include Encounters, a first-year seminar course; Semester in the West, an experiential, on-the-road study of economic, cultural, and environmental issues throughout the Western United states; Undergraduate Conference, at which about 150 students share their original research with the campus community; and the Outdoor Program, the most varied, comprehensive outdoor program in the nation.

"Whitman enrolls a diverse of active learners, dedicated volunteers, and campus leaders. There are over 100 student organizations. Athletic competition includes Division III, club sports, and intramurals. Whitman has fielded nationally ranked teams in tennis, cross-country, cycling, and Ultimate Frisbee. In recent years, Whitman has been a leader in the number of students who have won fellowships and scholarships such as the Fulbright, Watson, Truman, and Udall."

SELECTIVITY
Admissions Rating	96
# of applicants	3,164
% of applicants accepted	47
% of acceptees attending	28
# accepting a place on wait list	188
% admitted from wait list	1
# of early decision applicants	176
% accepted early decision	80

FRESHMAN PROFILE
Range SAT Critical Reading	610–720
Range SAT Math	610–720
Range SAT Writing	610–710
Minimum paper TOEFL	550
Minimum computer TOEFL	220
Minimum web-based TOEFL	85
Average HS GPA	3.80
% graduated top 10% of class	62
% graduated top 25% of class	94
% graduated top 50% of class	100

DEADLINES
Early decision	
Deadline	11/15
Notification	12/21
Regular	
Priority	11/15
Deadline	1/15
Nonfall registration?	yes

APPLICANTS ALSO LOOK AT
AND OFTEN PREFER
Carleton College, Middlebury College, Pomona College, Stanford University

AND SOMETIMES PREFER
Colorado College, Macalester College

AND RARELY PREFER
Lewis & Clark College, University of Puget Sound, University of Washington, Willamette University

FINANCIAL FACTS
Financial Aid Rating	92
Annual tuition	$38,450
Room and board	$9,720
Required fees	$320
Books and supplies	$1,400
% frosh rec. need-based scholarship or grant aid	43
% UG rec. need-based scholarship or grant aid	40
% frosh rec. non-need-based scholarship or grant aid	54
% UG rec. non-need-based scholarship or grant aid	47
% frosh rec. need-based self-help aid	25
% UG rec. need-based self-help aid	17
% frosh rec. any financial aid	76
% UG rec. any financial aid	78
% UG borrow to pay for school	50
Average cumulative indebtedness	$14,285

WHITTIER COLLEGE

13406 PHILADELPHIA STREET, PO BOX 634, WHITTIER, CA 90608 • ADMISSIONS: 562-907-4238 • FAX: 562-907-4870

CAMPUS LIFE

Quality of Life Rating	65
Fire Safety Rating	85
Green Rating	75
Type of school	private
Environment	city

STUDENTS

Total undergrad enrollment	1,444
% male/female	47/53
% from out of state	25
% live on campus	60
# of fraternities	4
# of sororities	5
% African American	5
% Asian	10
% Caucasian	39
% Hispanic	30
% Native American	1
% international	2
# of countries represented	24

SURVEY SAYS . . .

Great computer facilities
Great library
Diverse student types on campus
Different types of students interact
Great off-campus food
Student publications are popular
Lots of beer drinking
Hard liquor is popular

ACADEMICS

Academic Rating	78
% students graduating within 4 years	55
% students graduating within 6 years	61
Calendar	4-1-4
Student/faculty ratio	13:1
Profs interesting rating	84
Profs accessible rating	87
Most common reg class size	10–19 students
Most common lab size	20–29 students

MOST POPULAR MAJORS

criminal justice/safety studies,
elementary education and teaching,
psychology

STUDENTS SAY ". . ."

Academics

At tiny Whittier College in California, there's a proud emphasis placed on the interconnectedness of all of the liberal arts disciplines. Students are challenged to learn things relevant to their field and "encouraged to take courses in seemingly unrelated fields and then make connections to see how they actually all relate." In being allowed "to pursue their educations in a comfortable and friendly environment," students enjoy how the school allows for a "strengthening of student integrity" by providing a tight-knit community. Professors are "all passionate about their subject material," and their understanding and flexibility are spoken of highly; although "a course [may be] geared to a particular subject, the professors make it a point to relate the discipline to others we may be interested in, too." "All of your professors will know you by name, and not by number, because you matter to them." Aside from being knowledgeable and sincere, faculty also help students to "pursue larger goals in life," and encourage students "to take their own initiative in developing their goals and future." Small class sizes (and an "amazing" range of classes) at Whittier provide students with the opportunity to ask questions and to receive personalized attention, and teachers "make you feel welcome and always informed." Academics are "challenging, but not…difficult to where it is impossible." Whittier also offers a January term to help students graduate on time [or] early, and there's free tutoring to help with homework and studies. Internships, work study, and leadership are all available starting as a freshman, and it's "easy to travel abroad." Basically, "If you utilize the resources available on campus, you can truly make your own experience."

Life

When schoolwork is done, busy Whittier students "do their best to promote their own strengths in extracurricular activities." This is a true California school at heart, and "You can always find students laying out on the quad soaking up the beautiful Southern California sun." "On sunny days (which is basically everyday), I have seen slip-n-slides on the quad." The whole town "is supportive of Whittier College," and "There are several unique mom-and-pop shops and eateries throughout Uptown, along with a movie theater," all within walking distance. Still, a lot of students get out of Whittier by driving to Los Angeles or the nearby beach, and "getting a Disneyland annual pass is very popular." In recent years, housing has been overcrowded, resulting in some busy cafeterias and creative living arrangements. On weekends, some "like to party at the houses off campus that certain students rent out," but for those who don't, there are a "lot of on-campus activities are offered in the evening." "The school does not revolve around the 'party scene' like other campuses, although one does exist if it's desired," says a student. Societies, intramurals, and clubs on campus "are constantly organizing events" though some commuter students who aren't able to participate in these events speak of feeling disconnected from the Whittier community.

Student Body

Predictably, there are a number of California natives at Whittier, but those from out-of-state find themselves happily adopted. Students here are extremely friendly and "mostly fit in with their types," but there's a fair amount of cross-pollination among the groups because "everyone sort of meets each other in all the different classes." Everyone at Whittier "has a niche," and for the most part, "Everyone respects, as well as embraces, each others' uniqueness." The Division III school is athletically inclined, and a fair number of people play sports, though "it's not 'that' athletic of a student body."

FINANCIAL AID: 562-907-4285 • E-MAIL: ADMISSION@WHITTIER.EDU • WEBSITE: WWW.WHITTIER.EDU

THE PRINCETON REVIEW SAYS

Admissions

Very important factors considered include: Application essay, rigor of secondary school record. *Important factors considered include:* Academic GPA, recommendation(s), standardized test scores, character/personal qualities, extracurricular activities, interview, talent/ability, volunteer work. *Other factors considered include:* Class rank, alumni/ae relation, first generation, geographical residence, racial/ethnic status, state residency, work experience. SAT or ACT required; ACT with writing component required. TOEFL required of all international applicants. High school diploma is required, and GED is accepted. *Academic units required:* 3 English, 2 mathematics, 1 science (1 science lab), 2 foreign language, 1 social studies. *Academic units recommended:* 4 English, 3 mathematics, 2 science, 3 foreign language, 2 social studies.

Financial Aid

Students should submit: FAFSA, institution's own financial aid form. Regular filing deadline is June 30. The Princeton Review suggests that all financial aid forms be submitted as soon as possible after January 1. *Need-based scholarships/grants offered:* Federal Pell, SEOG, state scholarships/grants, private scholarships, school scholarship or grant aid from institutional funds. *Loan aid offered:* Direct Subsidized Stafford, Direct Unsubsidized Stafford, Direct PLUS, Federal Perkins. Applicants will be notified of awards on a rolling basis beginning February 15. Federal Work-Study Program not available. Off-campus job opportunities are good.

The Inside Word

Whittier is looking for well-rounded students, and so activities and recommendations are just as important as scores and grades—the admissions office hates to focus just on numbers. Though sixty-five percent of students hail from California, no preference is given to state of origin. Through the Whittier Scholars program, students may construct a personalized major that fits academic and career goals.

THE SCHOOL SAYS " . . . "

From the Admissions Office

"Faculty and students at Whittier share a love of learning and delight in the life of the mind. They join in understanding the value of the intellectual quest, the use of reason, and a respect for values. They seek knowledge of their own culture and the informed appreciation of other traditions, and they explore the interrelatedness of knowledge and the connections among disciplines. An extraordinary community emerges from teachers and students representing a variety of academic pursuits, individuals who have come together at Whittier in the belief that study within the liberal arts forms the best foundation for rewarding endeavor throughout a lifetime.

"Whittier College is a vibrant, residential, four-year liberal arts institution where intellectual inquiry and experiential learning are fostered in a community that promotes respect for diversity of thought and culture. A Whittier College education produces enthusiastic, independent thinkers who flourish in graduate studies, the evolving global workplace, and life."

SELECTIVITY

Admissions Rating	79
# of applicants	2,263
% of applicants accepted	72
% of acceptees attending	22

FRESHMAN PROFILE

Range SAT Critical Reading	470–580
Range SAT Math	470–590
Range SAT Writing	470–570
Range ACT Composite	19–25
Minimum paper TOEFL	550
Minimum computer TOEFL	230
Average HS GPA	3.05
% graduated top 10% of class	30
% graduated top 25% of class	42
% graduated top 50% of class	82

DEADLINES

Early action	
Deadline	12/1
Notification	12/30
Regular	
Priority	2/1
Notification	12/30
Nonfall registration?	yes

APPLICANTS ALSO LOOK AT

AND OFTEN PREFER
Occidental College, University of Redlands

AND SOMETIMES PREFER
Loyola Marymount University

AND RARELY PREFER
Chapman University

FINANCIAL FACTS

Financial Aid Rating	85
Annual tuition	$31,950
Room and board	$9,050
Required fees	$520
Books and supplies	$1,566
% frosh rec. need-based scholarship or grant aid	62
% UG rec. need-based scholarship or grant aid	58
% frosh rec. non-need-based scholarship or grant aid	60
% UG rec. non-need-based scholarship or grant aid	61
% frosh rec. need-based self-help aid	69
% UG rec. need-based self-help aid	70
% frosh rec. any financial aid	92
% UG rec. any financial aid	89
% UG borrow to pay for school	78
Average cumulative indebtedness	$40,220

WILLAMETTE UNIVERSITY

900 STATE STREET, SALEM, OR 97301 • ADMISSIONS: 503-370-6303 • FAX: 503-375-5363

STUDENTS SAY ". . ."

Academics

Willamette University offers "serious academics without the snobbery." In both its educational and extracurricular offerings, "Willamette is very focused on learning in a team environment," and the school "cultivates a strong feeling of community" throughout its academic programs. Students are encouraged to work together, and there is a "designated 'hearth' (common area) for every department where students can go for tutoring, group project collaboration, or just to do homework with classmates." Willamette's "knowledgeable" professors are "dedicated to what they teach and genuinely interested in helping students learn." Students warn, however, that, "Classes are demanding and instructors expect you to come to class prepared to discuss, not just listen." A sophomore agrees, "Professors expect the most out of us as true adults instead of as 'students,' thus I do my best to live up to that high expectation." Beyond academics, Willamette promotes a well-rounded lifestyle, and professors are "always checking to make sure that everything is going well both in the class and outside." In fact, "many professors socialize with students outside of class," and "It's not unusual to be asked to dinner at a professor's house." Located in the capital city of Salem, Oregon, co-curricular opportunities are abundant. Through the school, there are many "community service options, internship options, [and] on-campus job options," and students praise the "ease of getting state government internships" at the Oregon State capitol—just across the street!

Life

"The library on Sunday nights is a great merging of social and academic worlds— [you're] practically guaranteed to find a table of people working on assignments for your class or in your department." In addition to schoolwork, "There is a huge population that is involved in clubs on campus, anything from soccer club to juggling club or knitting club." In particular, "Lots of people are involved in sports," whether varsity or intramural, and many socially minded students "do a lot of community volunteering." Laid-back and casual, at Willamette "parties do happen but they're low-key compared to larger schools." There are also "two substance-free dorms" for those who don't like to indulge. For fun, students hit "the local bars on the weekends, or stick around campus and go to an a cappella night, a movie being shown on campus, or a Greek event, such as a dance." Surrounding Salem is a sleepy town, and "most everything off campus closes early"; however, there are "tons of coffee shops" in the local area, as well as "a mall easily within walking distance." "Students take trips to Portland and the ocean, and also head out to the mountains for skiing as well as hiking along paths decorated with waterfalls (weather permitting)."

Student Body

Willamette students are "smart, politically focused, interested, social, outgoing, [and] athletic or outdoorsy in some way," as well as "environmentally conscious." The community is varied, "open-minded," and mature: "Though there are many communities on campus (i.e., community service groups, Greek houses, clubs, sports teams, etc.), nearly every student is involved in more than one community and thus floats freely between groups, eliminating cliquishness." A student adds, "Regardless of if you're a football player, or environmentalist, or bio-chem double major, everyone fits in because we are all very open and inclusive people." Willamette students are "involved in many campus activities, including classes, clubs, and on-campus jobs." Outside the classroom, they are "active in leadership, eager to volunteer, [and] interested in a well-rounded education instead of primarily a 'book' education." Almost seventy percent of Willamette's undergraduates are from the West Coast, and some students say, "Our campus is not very culturally diverse." However, through a partner program with Tokyo International University, about 100 Japanese students come to Willamette each year to study English and liberal arts.

FINANCIAL AID: 503-370-6273 • E-MAIL: LIBARTS@WILLAMETTE.EDU • WEBSITE: WWW.WILLAMETTE.EDU

THE PRINCETON REVIEW SAYS

Admissions

Very important factors considered include: Academic GPA, application essay, class rank, rigor of secondary school record, standardized test scores. *Important factors considered include:* Recommendation(s), interview. *Other factors considered include:* Alumni/ae relation, character/personal qualities, extracurricular activities, first generation, geographical residence, racial/ethnic status, talent/ability. SAT or ACT required; ACT with writing component required. TOEFL required of all international applicants. High school diploma is required, and GED is accepted. *Academic units recommended:* 4 English, 4 mathematics, 3 science (3 science labs), 4 foreign language, 1 social studies, 2 history, 2 academic elective.

Financial Aid

Students should submit: FAFSA. Regular filing deadline is February 1. The Princeton Review suggests that all financial aid forms be submitted as soon as possible after January 1. *Need-based scholarships/grants offered:* Federal Pell, SEOG, state scholarships/grants, private scholarships, school scholarship or grant aid from institutional funds. *Loan aid offered:* Direct Subsidized Stafford, Direct Unsubsidized Stafford, Direct PLUS, Federal Perkins. Applicants will be notified of awards on a rolling basis beginning April 1. Federal Work-Study Program available. Off-campus job opportunities are good.

The Inside Word

When evaluating prospective students, Willamette places the most emphasis on academic record, including rigor of high school coursework, grades, and grade trends. Drastic variations in academic performance during high school will not be viewed favorably by Willamette's admissions officers. As a residential campus, Willamette is also interested in accepting students who will contribute something to the campus community. Evidence of community service and extracurricular involvement reflect a habit of participation that will only enhance your application in the eyes of Willamette's discerning admissions officers.

THE SCHOOL SAYS ". . ."

From the Admissions Office

"As one of the nation's premier liberal arts universities, Willamette has superb academic programs and noted professors who work with students one-on-one. Ten of the past twenty-two Oregon Professors of the Year come from Willamette, illustrating our faculty's teaching excellence.

"Our faculty help you develop the skills necessary to succeed in our global workforce: critical reading, writing, thinking, and verbal communication. Willamette also helps you hone your creativity, critical thinking, and global perspective outside of class. Half of our students study abroad, twenty-five percent perform joint research with faculty members, and seventy percent complete one or more internships. You'll learn how to analyze issues from a variety of perspectives preparing you to creatively address the challenges of the world.

"College is more than preparation for the future; it's about friends and fun. Willamette has 100-plus student organizations, twenty varsity sports, many club and intramural teams, and countless social activities on campus to bring students together. You can also get involved in Willamette's nationally recognized sustainability efforts. You'll build lifelong friendships in addition to building your intellect.

"Our graduates credit their Willamette education with developing the expertise they needed for successful careers at businesses, government agencies and nonprofits. They frequently find careers at companies such as Nike, Intel, and Microsoft, and many enter top-notch graduate programs across the country. Our students and graduates often earn competitive, national awards that provide money for research or graduate school."

SELECTIVITY

Admissions Rating	94
# of applicants	7,785
% of applicants accepted	42
% of acceptees attending	13
# accepting a place on wait list	88
% admitted from wait list	25

FRESHMAN PROFILE

Range SAT Critical Reading	570–680
Range SAT Math	570–660
Range SAT Writing	570–670
Range ACT Composite	27–30
Minimum paper TOEFL	560
Minimum computer TOEFL	220
Minimum web-based TOEFL	83
Average HS GPA	3.79
% graduated top 10% of class	51
% graduated top 25% of class	80
% graduated top 50% of class	100

DEADLINES

Early action	
Deadline	11/1, 12/1
Notification	12/15, 1/15
Regular	
Priority	2/1
Deadline	2/1
Notification	3/15
Nonfall registration?	yes

APPLICANTS ALSO LOOK AT

AND OFTEN PREFER
Whitman College

AND SOMETIMES PREFER
Claremont McKenna College, Lewis & Clark College, Occidental College, Santa Clara University, University of Puget Sound, University of Washington

AND RARELY PREFER
University of Oregon

FINANCIAL FACTS

Financial Aid Rating	84
Annual tuition	$38,800
Room and board	$9,350
Required fees	$212
Books and supplies	$920
% frosh rec. need-based scholarship or grant aid	71
% UG rec. need-based scholarship or grant aid	63
% frosh rec. non-need-based scholarship or grant aid	22
% UG rec. non-need-based scholarship or grant aid	12
% frosh rec. need-based self-help aid	66
% UG rec. need-based self-help aid	60
% frosh rec. any financial aid	94
% UG rec. any financial aid	93
% UG borrow to pay for school	65
Average cumulative indebtedness	$23,248

WILLIAM JEWELL COLLEGE

500 COLLEGE HILL, LIBERTY, MO 64068 • ADMISSIONS: 816-415-7511 • FAX: 816-415-5040

CAMPUS LIFE

Quality of Life Rating	86
Fire Safety Rating	83
Green Rating	61
Type of school	private
Environment	town

STUDENTS

Total undergrad enrollment	1,060
% male/female	40/60
% from out of state	34
% from public high school	90
% live on campus	77
# of fraternities	3
# of sororities	4
% African American	3
% Asian	1
% Caucasian	84
% Hispanic	4
% Native American	1
% international	3
# of countries represented	14

SURVEY SAYS . . .

No one cheats
Career services are great
Students are friendly
Students get along with local
community
Great off-campus food
Students are happy
Frats and sororities dominate
social scene
Musical organizations are popular
Student publications are popular
Very little drug use

ACADEMICS

Academic Rating	88
% students graduating within 4 years	56
% students graduating within 6 years	65
Calendar	semester
Student/faculty ratio	12:1
Profs interesting rating	92
Profs accessible rating	89
Most common reg class size	fewer than 10 students
Most common lab size	fewer than 10 students

MOST POPULAR MAJORS

biology, elementary education
and teaching, secondary education
and teaching

STUDENTS SAY ". . ."

Academics

Often called "the Harvard of the Midwest," William Jewell College is a prestigious small school with a strong sense of community. In both philosophy and practice, "Jewell is the quintessential liberal arts college, thoroughly engaging students in critical study of both the self and the world as a whole." Undergraduate programs are "extremely academically challenging" and the workload is heavy. However, students assure us that Jewell offers "an incredible learning opportunity, available to all who are willing to put in the work." Jewell students have the opportunity to shape their education in a way they couldn't do at larger schools; "If you want something to be changed in the cafe they'll do it; if you want to design your own major they'll do it." More importantly, the school's "incredibly brilliant" professors are accessible and supportive; "Most teachers will work with you personally should you have a problem with the class, or even on a personal level." Through internships and service projects, "Jewell is big on getting [its] students into real-world situations as soon as possible," and the career counseling office excels at "getting students a job in their field of study directly after graduating." While most are highly satisfied with the Jewell experience, students admit that, "there have been rough patches for the administration," who aren't always responsive to student concerns. Fortunately, the winds of change are in the air, as "President Sallee is a very competent and popular administrator."

Life

At Jewell, life never slows down. In addition to keeping up with academic demands, "The typical student is involved in a bazillion activities, from sports to Greek life and clubs." "Participation in school functions is pretty high" and there is always something going on, "whether it's bowling, or Sundae night on Sunday, or free movie night, worship jams, pool, study groups, or just hanging out with your friends." Friendships blossom in this unique environment, and students say "It's amazing how well we all get to know each other in such a short amount of time." Chats in the cafeteria "range from very deep, philosophical inquiries to lighthearted bantering." Socially, "Lots of students are involved in Greek life and enjoy Greek-related activities." On the weekends, "it is easy to find a party"; however, "If you like to stay in and have fun, there are always people to hang out with." Under any circumstance, academics come first: "When Monday hits, we know how to stop partying and start studying." All students (except seniors) are required to live on campus, yet "the weekends are pretty dead" because most students go home or travel to a nearby city. A student explains, "After spending five days stuck in what we call the 'bubble,' we want to get away and do something different."

Student Body

At this competitive, small college, students are "incredibly bright," and most "were in the top twenty-five percent of the class" in high school. Ambitious by nature, academics are first priority for most of Jewell's "hardworking" students, who are "here to succeed." You'll meet a largely "Midwestern, middle-class" crowd at this college, yet one that encompasses "various personalities, interests, [and] communication skills." Recently, the school community has become even more open: "Since our split with the Baptist church, Jewell has been making efforts to attract students of other ethnicities and sexual orientations, and such students seem to feel welcome." In fact, "We have a strong group that supports the GLBT community and a group called Unity that promotes understanding of people from other cultures and colors." Most students are "extremely busy and involved" with campus activities, and the school community is often described as "close-knit." At Jewell, "everyone says hi, even if you don't know them," and "even the freshmen feel that they can just go sit down at an all-senior table and fit in just fine."

FINANCIAL AID: 888-2-JEWELL • E-MAIL: ADMISSION@WILLIAM.JEWELL.EDU • WEBSITE: WWW.JEWELL.EDU

THE PRINCETON REVIEW SAYS

Admissions

Very important factors considered include: Rigor of secondary school record. *Important factors considered include:* Academic GPA, class rank, recommendation(s), standardized test scores. *Other factors considered include:* Application essay, alumni/ae relation, character/personal qualities, extracurricular activities, first generation, interview, talent/ability, volunteer work, work experience. SAT or ACT required; ACT with writing component recommended. TOEFL required of all international applicants. High school diploma is required, and GED is accepted. *Academic units required:* 4 English, 3 mathematics, 3 science (1 science lab), 2 foreign language, 3 social studies. *Academic units recommended:* 4 English, 4 mathematics, 3 science (1 science lab), 3 foreign language, 3 social studies, 2 academic elective.

Financial Aid

Students should submit: FAFSA. The Princeton Review suggests that all financial aid forms be submitted as soon as possible after January 1. *Need-based scholarships/grants offered:* Federal Pell, SEOG, state scholarships/grants, school scholarship or grant aid from institutional funds. *Loan aid offered:* Federal Perkins, Federal Nursing Loans. Applicants will be notified of awards on a rolling basis beginning February 15. Federal Work-Study Program available. Off-campus job opportunities are excellent.

The Inside Word

Jewell brings a personal touch to the admissions process. Prospective students can make arrangements for a personal visit—or "individual experience"—at Jewell, through which they can meet with their admissions counselor, as well as current students. If you've already submitted an application, you can even stay overnight in the dorms. All students who apply by the priority deadline will be considered for admission and merit-based scholarships, and will be notified of the decision before winter break.

THE SCHOOL SAYS "..."

From the Admissions Office

"William Jewell College is committed to bringing together talented students and gifted faculty mentors within a vibrant community sparked by a rigorous and intentional liberal arts curriculum. A full range of personal and professional development experiences are presented by the selective national liberal arts college's location within the Kansas City metroplex of more than 1.5 million. The William Jewell College experience focuses on enhancing the student's ability to apply learning to complex ethical, scientific and cultural problems. The College places a high value on experiential learning and gives students the opportunity to "live what they learn." By completing the College's thirty-eight-hour liberal arts core plus three applied learning experiences, Jewell students can receive a second major in Applied Critical Thought and Inquiry. This means that all students can graduate with double majors and some with triple majors. The internationally recognized Oxbridge Honors Program combines British tutorial methods of instruction with opportunities for a year of study in Oxford or Cambridge. It is the only program of its kind in the nation. Jewell's undergraduate Nonprofit Leadership major is one of only thirteen nationwide and ranks among the top three in academic rigor. The Pryor Leadership Studies Program includes course work, community service projects and internships that help students enhance their leadership skills in a variety of settings. William Jewell students graduate equipped with deep content knowledge in their major(s), a host of social and real-world experiences, personal maturity and the intellectual habits of mind for success in a world of change and challenge."

SELECTIVITY

Admissions Rating	89
# of applicants	3,032
% of applicants accepted	50
% of acceptees attending	18

FRESHMAN PROFILE

Range SAT Critical Reading	510–700
Range SAT Math	500–620
Range ACT Composite	23–29
Minimum paper TOEFL	550
Minimum computer TOEFL	213
Minimum web-based TOEFL	80
Average HS GPA	3.69
% graduated top 10% of class	32
% graduated top 25% of class	66
% graduated top 50% of class	91

DEADLINES

Regular	
Priority	12/1
Deadline	8/15
Notification	9/15
Nonfall registration?	yes

APPLICANTS ALSO LOOK AT

AND OFTEN PREFER
Truman State University,
University of Missouri—Columbia

AND SOMETIMES PREFER
Rockhurst University

AND RARELY PREFER
Northwest Missouri State University

FINANCIAL FACTS

Financial Aid Rating	75
Annual tuition	$29,600
Room and board	$7,560
Required fees	$300
Books and supplies	$1,100
% frosh rec. need-based scholarship or grant aid	80
% UG rec. need-based scholarship or grant aid	73
% frosh rec. non-need-based scholarship or grant aid	77
% UG rec. non-need-based scholarship or grant aid	68
% frosh rec. need-based self-help aid	66
% UG rec. need-based self-help aid	61
% frosh rec. any financial aid	99
% UG rec. any financial aid	96
% UG borrow to pay for school	77
Average cumulative indebtedness	$23,210

WILLIAMS COLLEGE

33 STETSON COURT, WILLIAMSTOWN, MA 01267 • ADMISSIONS: 413-597-2211 • FAX: 413-597-4052

STUDENTS SAY ". . ."

Academics

Williams College is a small bastion of the liberal arts "with a fantastic academic reputation." "Williams students tend to spend a lot of time complaining about how much work they have" but they say the academic experience is "absolutely incomparable." Classes are "small" and "intense." "The facilities are absolutely top-notch in almost everything." Research opportunities are plentiful. A one-month January term offers study abroad programs and a host of short pass/fail courses that are "a college student's dream come true." "The hard science departments are incredible." Economics, art history, and English are equally outstanding. Despite the occasional professor "who should not even be teaching at the high school level," the faculty at Williams is one of the best. Most professors "jump at every opportunity to help you love their subject." "They're here because they want to interact with undergrads." "If you complain about a Williams education then you would complain about education anywhere," wagers an economics major.

Life

Students at Williams enjoy a "stunning campus." "The Berkshire mountains are in the background every day as you walk to class" and opportunities for outdoor activity are numerous. The location is in "the boonies," though, and the surrounding "one-horse college town" is "quaint" at best. "There is no nearby place to buy necessities that is not ridiculously overpriced." Student life happens almost exclusively on campus. Dorm rooms are "large" and "well above par" but the housing system is "very weird." While some students like it, there is a general consensus that its creators "should be slapped and sent back to Amherst." Entertainment options include "lots of" performances, plays, and lectures. Some students are "obsessed with a capella groups." Intramurals are popular, especially broomball ("a sacred tradition involving a hockey rink, sneakers, a rubber ball, and paddles"). Intercollegiate sports are "a huge part of the social scene." For many students, the various varsity teams "are the basic social blocks at Williams." "Everyone for the most part gets along, but the sports teams seem to band together," explains a sophomore. "Booze-laden parties" "and general disorder on weekends" are common. "A lot of people spend their lives between homework and practice and then just get completely smashed on weekends." Nothing gets out of hand, though. "We know how to unwind without being stupid," says a sophomore.

Student Body

The student population at Williams is not the most humble. They describe their peers as "interesting and beautiful" "geniuses of varying interests." They're "quirky, passionate, zany, and fun." They're "athletically awesome." They're "freakishly unique" and at the same time "cookie-cutter amazing." Ethnic diversity is stellar and you'll find all kinds of students including "the goth students," "nerdier students," "a ladle of environmentally conscious pseudo-vegetarians," and a few "west coast hippies." However, "a typical student looks like a rich white kid" who grew up "playing field hockey just outside Boston" and spends summers "vacationing on the Cape." Sporty students abound. "There definitely is segregation between the artsy kids and the athlete types but there is also a significant amount of crossover." "Williams is a place where normal social labels tend not to apply," reports a junior. "Everyone here got in for a reason. So that football player in your theater class has amazing insight on Chekhov and that outspoken environmental activist also specializes in improv comedy."

FINANCIAL AID: 413-597-4181 • E-MAIL: ADMISSION@WILLIAMS.EDU • WEBSITE: WWW.WILLIAMS.EDU

THE PRINCETON REVIEW SAYS

Admissions

Very important factors considered include: Academic GPA, application essay, recommendation(s), rigor of secondary school record, standardized test scores. *Important factors considered include:* Class rank, extracurricular activities, talent/ability. *Other factors considered include:* Alumni/ae relation, character/personal qualities, first generation, geographical residence, racial/ethnic status, volunteer work, work experience. SAT or ACT required; ACT with writing component required. High school diploma or equivalent isn't required. *Academic units recommended:* 4 English, 4 mathematics, 3 science (3 science labs), 4 foreign language, 3 social studies.

Financial Aid

Students should submit: FAFSA, CSS/Financial Aid PROFILE. Regular filing deadline is February 1. The Princeton Review suggests that all financial aid forms be submitted as soon as possible after January 1. *Need-based scholarships/grants offered:* Federal Pell, SEOG, state scholarships/grants, private scholarships, school scholarship or grant aid from institutional funds. *Loan aid offered:* Direct Subsidized Stafford, Direct Unsubsidized Stafford, Direct PLUS, Federal Perkins, university loans from institutional funds. Federal Work-Study Program available.

The Inside Word

As is typical of highly selective colleges, at Williams high grades and test scores work more as qualifiers than to determine admissibility. Beyond a strong record of achievement, evidence of intellectual curiosity, noteworthy non-academic talents, and a non-college family background are some aspects of a candidate's application that might make for an offer of admission. But there are no guarantees—the evaluation process here is rigorous. The admissions committee (the entire admissions staff) discusses each candidate in comparison to the entire applicant pool. The pool is divided alphabetically for individual reading; after weak candidates are eliminated, those who remain undergo additional evaluations by different members of the staff. Admission decisions must be confirmed by the agreement of a plurality of the committee. Such close scrutiny demands a well-prepared candidate and application.

THE SCHOOL SAYS "..."

From the Admissions Office

"Special course offerings at Williams include Oxford-style tutorials, where students (in teams of two) research and defend ideas, engaging in weekly debate with a faculty tutor. Half of Williams' students pursue study abroad at some point, with about thirty students annually spending at year at Oxford. Four weeks of winter study each January provide time for individualized projects, research, and novel fields of study. Students compete in thirty-two Division III athletic teams, perform in twenty-five musical groups, stage ten theatrical productions, and volunteer in thirty service organizations. The college receives several million dollars annually for undergraduate science research and equipment. The town offers two distinguished art museums, the Williams College Museum of Art and the Clark Art Institute, and 2.200 forest acres—complete with a treetop canopy walkway—for environmental research and recreation.

"Students are required to submit either the SAT or the ACT including the optional writing section. Applicants should also submit scores from any two SAT Subject Tests. To limit the debt obligations of its graduates, Williams maintains one of the lowest loan expectations of any college or university in the country. Often the aid packages of students whose families demonstrate high financial need are made up entirely of grants and a campus job—and do not include any loans."

SELECTIVITY

Admissions Rating	99
# of applicants	6,631
% of applicants accepted	19
% of acceptees attending	44
# accepting a place on wait list	494
% admitted from wait list	7
# of early decision applicants	538
% accepted early decision	40

FRESHMAN PROFILE

Range SAT Critical Reading	660–770
Range SAT Math	650–760
Range ACT Composite	29–34
% graduated top 10% of class	90
% graduated top 25% of class	98
% graduated top 50% of class	100

DEADLINES

Early decision	
Deadline	11/10
Notification	12/15
Regular	
Deadline	1/1
Nonfall registration?	no

APPLICANTS ALSO LOOK AT AND OFTEN PREFER
Harvard College, Yale University

AND RARELY PREFER
Amherst College

FINANCIAL FACTS

Financial Aid Rating	96
Annual tuition	$41,190
Room and board	$10,906
Required fees	$244
Books and supplies	$800
% frosh rec. need-based scholarship or grant aid	53
% UG rec. need-based scholarship or grant aid	54
% frosh rec. need-based self-help aid	53
% UG rec. need-based self-help aid	54
% frosh rec. any financial aid	53
% UG rec. any financial aid	53
% UG borrow to pay for school	41
Average cumulative indebtedness	$8,369

WITTENBERG UNIVERSITY

PO Box 720, Springfield, OH 45501 • Admissions: 877-206-0332 • Fax: 937-327-6379

CAMPUS LIFE

Quality of Life Rating	74
Fire Safety Rating	97
Green Rating	76
Type of school	private
Affiliation	Lutheran
Environment	town

STUDENTS

Total undergrad enrollment	1,894
% male/female	44/56
% from out of state	26
% from public high school	80
% live on campus	83
# of fraternities	6
# of sororities	5
% African American	6
% Asian	1
% Caucasian	82
% Hispanic	2
% international	2
# of countries represented	23

SURVEY SAYS . . .
Students are friendly
Students are happy
Everyone loves the Tigers
Intramural sports are popular
Frats and sororities dominate
social scene
Student government is popular

ACADEMICS

Academic Rating	88
% students graduating within 4 years	59
% students graduating within 6 years	66
Calendar	semester
Student/faculty ratio	11:1
Profs interesting rating	96
Profs accessible rating	95
Most common reg class size	10–19 students
Most common lab size	10–19 students

MOST POPULAR MAJORS
biology, business/commerce, education

STUDENTS SAY ". . ."

Academics

At Wittenberg University, a Lutheran-affiliated liberal arts college, the motto, "Having light, we pass it on to others," rings throughout the minds of every student. This small community of students and faculty in Springfield, Ohio, emphasizes personal attention and development of the person as a whole, and the administration "encourages students to try new things" both inside and outside of the classroom to "broaden student horizons." In doing so, students become "committed to their own success and the success of the greater school community." Almost every Wittenberg student speaks glowingly of their professors, for both their teaching abilities and their caring nature. ("They treat us more like peers instead of people younger than they are," says one.) Most classes are in lecture format, and all are taught by professors who "do a great job of creating a dialogue in the classroom with students and between students that extends beyond the classroom." And professors "are always willing to meet up and discuss anything that is on our minds." "We work extra hard, because we know we can't get away with slacking (for better or for worse)." "Even in my largest class of seventy-five people (which is one of the largest at the university), my professor still knew who I was," says one student. The faculty also makes teaching their current students and advisees as "a top priority over their own research interests." While Wittenberg is "intellectually challenging," there are many great resources that students can avail themselves of, such as the Math Workshop, Writing Center, Oral Communication Center, and Foreign Language Learning Center. The administration "[wants] you to do well, but also love what you are doing."

Life

It's a friendly and "home-y" environment at Wittenberg, where "you know most people, but there's always new faces as well." The school has a strong freshman acclimation program called "The First-Year Experience," which allows for incoming students to meet each other and make friends at school-sponsored events, but "new friendships develop through clubs, sports, and other activities." Many friends come from the multitude of living options offered (dorms, off-campus housing, etc.). Everyone agrees, "The food is not the best," and the meal plans can be restrictive. Springfield is big enough that there are movie theaters and bowling alleys that students can go to off campus, but "Most students end up staying on campus for the weekends." Though the campus itself is "gorgeous," there are "some safety concerns with Springfield residents" when you leave it at night. Greek life here is "pretty epic," with more than a third of all students participating; students typically work "very hard at times that call for hard work, but weekends are time for play." Though a fair amount of drinking takes place, there are plenty of alternatives offered, such as "Witt Wednesday" events, and there are also games "for just about every sport on almost every day of the week."

Student Body

Tigers are a "relaxed, friendly" group who are "more than happy to make new friends all the time." While there's a "tolerant community" at Wittenberg where "everyone is accepted," students admit, "We are rather...homogeneous." However, similarities end at appearance, because "interests are as variant as Lady Gaga's dress collection." Everyone agrees that as long as you make an effort, there's "always a group or club and friends with the same interests." Wittenberg has a fair number of athletes and Ohioans, in no particular order, and no one has any trouble learning "how to balance play with studies."

FINANCIAL AID: 800-677-7558 • E-MAIL: ADMISSION@WITTENBERG.EDU • WEBSITE: WWW.WITTENBERG.EDU

THE PRINCETON REVIEW SAYS

Admissions

Very important factors considered include: Academic GPA, class rank, rigor of secondary school record. *Important factors considered include:* Application essay, recommendation(s), character/personal qualities, extracurricular activities, talent/ability, volunteer work. *Other factors considered include:* Standardized test scores, alumni/ae relation, first generation, interview, work experience. ACT with or without writing component accepted. TOEFL required of all international applicants. High school diploma is required, and GED is accepted. *Academic units required:* 4 English, 3 mathematics, 3 science (2 science labs), 2 foreign language, 2 history. *Academic units recommended:* 4 English, 4 mathematics, 5 science (2 science labs), 3 foreign language, 3 history.

Financial Aid

Students should submit: FAFSA. The Princeton Review suggests that all financial aid forms be submitted as soon as possible after January 1. *Need-based scholarships/grants offered:* Federal Pell, SEOG, state scholarships/grants, private scholarships, school scholarship or grant aid from institutional funds. *Loan aid offered:* Federal Perkins, university loans from institutional funds. Applicants will be notified of awards on a rolling basis beginning March 1. Federal Work-Study Program available. Off-campus job opportunities are excellent.

The Inside Word

Wittenberg's applicant pool is small but quite solid coming off of a couple of strong years. Students who haven't successfully reached an above-average academic level in high school will meet with little success in the admissions process. Candidate evaluation is thorough and personal; applicants should devote serious attention to all aspects of their candidacy.

THE SCHOOL SAYS ". . ."

From the Admissions Office

"At Wittenberg, you will experience an active and engaged learning environment, a setting where you can refine your definition of self yet gain exposure to the varied kinds of knowledge, people, views, activities, options, and ideas that add richness to our lives. Wittenberg is a university where students are able to thrive in a small campus environment with many opportunities for intellectual and personal growth in and out of the classroom. Campus life is as diverse as the interests of our students. Wittenberg attracts students from all over the United States and from many other countries. Historically, the university has been committed to geographical, educational, cultural, and religious diversity. With their varied backgrounds and interests, Wittenberg students have helped initiate many of the more than 125 student organizations that are active on campus. The students will be the first to tell you there's never a lack of things to do on or near the campus any day of the week, if you're willing to get involved.

"Wittenberg University is test score optional. Freshman applicants can choose to submit either ACT (with or without writing component) or SAT scores."

SELECTIVITY

Admissions Rating	83
# of applicants	3,120
% of applicants accepted	73
% of acceptees attending	22
# of early decision applicants	68
% accepted early decision	57

FRESHMAN PROFILE

Range SAT Critical Reading	510–630
Range SAT Math	510–610
Range ACT Composite	22–28
Minimum paper TOEFL	550
Minimum computer TOEFL	213
Average HS GPA	3.44
% graduated top 10% of class	26
% graduated top 25% of class	52
% graduated top 50% of class	82

DEADLINES

Early decision	
Deadline	11/15
Notification	12/15
Early action	
Deadline	12/1
Notification	1/1
Regular	
Priority	3/15
Deadline	11/30
Notification	1/1
Nonfall registration?	yes

APPLICANTS ALSO LOOK AT AND OFTEN PREFER

Denison University, Miami University,
Ohio University—Athens, Ohio Wesleyan University,
The College of Wooster, The Ohio State University—
Columbus

AND SOMETIMES PREFER

Capital University, Ohio Northern University

FINANCIAL FACTS

Financial Aid Rating	86
Annual tuition	$34,324
Room and board	$9,032
Required fees	$550
Books and supplies	$1,000
% frosh rec. need-based scholarship or grant aid	82
% UG rec. need-based scholarship or grant aid	75
% frosh rec. non-need-based scholarship or grant aid	18
% UG rec. non-need-based scholarship or grant aid	24
% frosh rec. need-based self-help aid	82
% UG rec. need-based self-help aid	74
% frosh rec. any financial aid	100
% UG rec. any financial aid	99
% UG borrow to pay for school	83
Average cumulative indebtedness	$29,506

WOFFORD COLLEGE

429 North Church Street, Spartanburg, SC 29303-3663 • Admissions: 864-597-4130 • Fax: 864-597-4147

STUDENTS SAY ". . ."

Academics

Students agree Wofford is "an extremely challenging institution with a strong local and increasing national reputation." Undergrads are quick to heap praise on their professors, stating they "genuinely care about their students and…are willing to do everything it takes for each student to succeed." Perhaps even more importantly, Wofford profs "clearly love to teach," which "creates a fun and interesting academic environment." In turn, as one junior shares, this frequently fosters a "desire to continue learning about the course material." Additionally, professors encourage students to explore their own passions. However, slackers be warned, "You cannot come to Wofford, play around, and still make an A. You need to work." Undergrads are also quite pleased with the folks who keep the college running smoothly. Indeed, administrators "are very nice and [always] willing to hear student opinion." And one sophomore boasts, "Deans go out of their way to assist the students." The highly visible administration can often be seen "eating lunch on the Quad, at football games and other athletic events, and [at] various academic and extracurricular functions on campus." Perhaps Wofford can be summed up best by this junior who simply states it's "an educational dream."

Life

Students at Wofford are academically oriented and tend to put "their education first." That means weekdays are generally reserved for classes and studying. However, when Friday rolls around, these Terriers are ready to let loose. "A very high Greek population" typically means many students will flock to "fraternity row" on the weekends. Luckily, "All students are welcome" regardless of affiliation. Fortunately, "The student activities council ensures that plenty of non-Greek events are planned each semester also." Activities can range from "movies" and "paintball and ice skating" to "the occasional hot air balloon ride or bull riding." Additionally, with rampant school spirit, it's not surprising "football games…are very popular." Indeed, these "games are a big event where girls wear dresses and guys wear a coats, ties, and croakies." With all these options, it's no surprise an excited freshman shares, "There are so many activities on campus that you don't want to leave!" However, when undergrads do want to venture off campus, hometown "Spartanburg always has festivals and community gatherings, and there are plenty of restaurants to choose from." Students looking for additional adventure can easily escape to Greenville, a city about thirty minutes away, or the always entertaining Asheville, which is roughly an hour trip by car.

Student Body

Easily characterized with their "polo and pearls," Wofford undergrads admit the typical student is "Southern, Protestant, rich," and heavily "involved in Greek life." However, fret not if you don't find any of those adjectives applicable. A junior assures us "everyone interacts together, and there are no exclusive groups on campus." Indeed, most people are "friendly…and outgoing," and even atypical students will find it "easy to fit in…and get involved." Regardless of background, Wofford undergrads are an intellectual and curious lot. By and large, they tend to be academically "driven…and hardworking" and "motivated to do well" both in and out of the classroom. A few students bemoan the fact that Wofford seems to lack diversity, citing that most of their peers are "Caucasian" and "conservative." While others concede to this fact, they are quick to highlight this is slowly changing. As one experienced senior shares, "Despite the largely homogenous campus, diversity is growing rapidly." And this sentiment is echoed by a hopeful sophomore who confidently states, "Each year the number of students who defy this 'Wofford stereotype' is rising."

FINANCIAL AID: 864-597-4160 • E-MAIL: ADMISSIONS@WOFFORD.EDU • WEBSITE: WWW.WOFFORD.EDU

THE PRINCETON REVIEW SAYS

Admissions

Very important factors considered include: Academic GPA, rigor of secondary school record. *Important factors considered include:* Application essay, class rank, standardized test scores, character/personal qualities, extracurricular activities, talent/ability, volunteer work. *Other factors considered include:* Recommendation(s), alumni/ae relation, first generation, geographical residence, interview, racial/ethnic status, work experience. SAT or ACT required; ACT with writing component required. TOEFL required of all international applicants. High school diploma is required, and GED is accepted. *Academic units recommended:* 4 English, 4 mathematics, 3 science (3 science labs), 3 foreign language, 3 social studies, 1 history, 1 visual/performing arts, 1 computer science.

Financial Aid

Students should submit: FAFSA. The Princeton Review suggests that all financial aid forms be submitted as soon as possible after January 1. *Need-based scholarships/grants offered:* Federal Pell, SEOG, state scholarships/grants, private scholarships, school scholarship or grant aid from institutional funds. *Loan aid offered:* Direct Subsidized Stafford, Direct Unsubsidized Stafford, Direct PLUS, Federal Perkins. Federal Work-Study Program available. Off-campus job opportunities are good.

The Inside Word

Wofford College distinguishes itself by providing its students with an extremely supportive environment. This concern extends to the applications it receives, each of which is given careful consideration. Students who have earned decent grades in challenging courses should find themselves with an opportunity to attend a school that is gaining a reputation as one of the South's premier liberal arts colleges.

THE SCHOOL SAYS "..."

From the Admissions Office

"A century ago, Wofford athletics teams chose the Boston Terrier as their mascot. These dogs proved to be a perfect fit. Terriers are small, but full of intelligence and energy. As evident in recent Graduation Success Rate numbers and NCAA Division I Southern Conference championships in football, baseball, soccer and basketball, our teams are 'world-class.' The same is true for our Phi Beta Kappa liberal arts college of 1,450 students, located in Spartanburg, South Carolina. Our 'new urban' Village Housing for seniors and our new environmental studies center have won an impressive series of architectural awards. Recently, Wofford's student-led project was the national winner of the ONE Campus Challenge, competing against 1,400 colleges and universities in a global advocacy campaign dedicated to fighting extreme poverty and preventable disease, particularly in Africa. For the past two years, Wofford also has been listed 'with distinction' on the President's Community Service Honor Roll. The faculty/student ratio is one to eleven, and graduation rates exceed eighty percent of entering first-year students. According to the 'Open Doors' survey of participation in international programs, the college ranks in the national top ten. Our scores on the National Survey of Student Engagement (NSSE) are among the nation's best. Wofford thus remains committed to its historic mission—turning out graduates who can make international connections and become difference makers in a variety of vocations and professions."

SELECTIVITY

Admissions Rating	93
# of applicants	2,595
% of applicants accepted	62
% of acceptees attending	27
# accepting a place on wait list	49
% admitted from wait list	16
# of early decision applicants	711
% accepted early decision	70

FRESHMAN PROFILE

Range SAT Critical Reading	560–675
Range SAT Math	590–680
Range SAT Writing	545–650
Range ACT Composite	22.25–28
Minimum paper TOEFL	550
Minimum computer TOEFL	213
Average HS GPA	3.56
% graduated top 10% of class	56
% graduated top 25% of class	80
% graduated top 50% of class	98

DEADLINES

Early decision	
Deadline	11/15
Notification	12/5
Regular	
Deadline	2/1
Nonfall registration?	yes

APPLICANTS ALSO LOOK AT

AND SOMETIMES PREFER
Furman University

AND RARELY PREFER
Clemson University,
University of South Carolina—Columbia

FINANCIAL FACTS

Financial Aid Rating	89
Annual tuition	$31,710
Room and board	$8,870
Books and supplies	$1,076
% frosh rec. need-based scholarship or grant aid	57
% UG rec. need-based scholarship or grant aid	55
% frosh rec. non-need-based scholarship or grant aid	20
% UG rec. non-need-based scholarship or grant aid	19
% frosh rec. need-based self-help aid	30
% UG rec. need-based self-help aid	29
% frosh rec. any financial aid	91
% UG rec. any financial aid	88
% UG borrow to pay for school	47
Average cumulative indebtedness	$23,103

WORCESTER POLYTECHNIC INSTITUTE

100 INSTITUTE ROAD, WORCESTER, MA 01609 • ADMISSIONS: 508-831-5286 • FAX: 508-831-5875

CAMPUS LIFE

Quality of Life Rating	83
Fire Safety Rating	84
Green Rating	83
Type of school	private
Environment	city

STUDENTS

Total undergrad enrollment	3,537
% male/female	70/30
% from out of state	51
% from public high school	66
% live on campus	50
# of fraternities	13
# of sororities	5
% African American	3
% Asian	6
% Caucasian	71
% Hispanic	7
% Native American	1
% international	10
# of countries represented	75

SURVEY SAYS . . .

Lab facilities are great
Great computer facilities
Career services are great
School is well-run
Dorms are like palaces
Students are happy
Frats and sororities dominate
social scene
Student government is popular

ACADEMICS

Academic Rating	87
% students graduating within 4 years	72
% students graduating within 6 years	80
Calendar	quarter
Student/faculty ratio	14:1
Profs interesting rating	77
Profs accessible rating	84
Most common reg class size	20–29 students
Most common lab size	20–29 students

MOST POPULAR MAJORS

computer science, electrical and
electronics engineering, mechanical
engineering

STUDENTS SAY ". . ."

Academics

Learning "is project-based and very hands on" at Worcester Polytechnic Institute, a prestigious engineering, mathematics, and science university located in central Massachusetts. Here, "students are encouraged to do some hands-on work in almost every class" through a "project-based curriculum," in which "students are given the opportunity to work on projects with minimal guidance from their advisors." Students describe this approach as "a good and realistic experience that is helpful for future career plans." The project-based system "emphasizes the understanding of technical concepts, the practical implementation of these concepts, and also an appreciation for how technological advances can benefit mankind." WPI's unique grading system of A/B/C/NR—"fail a class and it won't show up on your transcript," one student explains—means "there is a lot of freedom to take riskier classes" and the school "promotes a culture of cooperation over competition." "Even though the curriculum is hard, [and] even though we have homework due every day, we are all happy because we know that failing is just another chance to try again. It's a good philosophy." A quarterly academic calendar "allows students to take a more diverse array of classes, and forces them to learn quickly or fall behind," but also means "if you're sick for two weeks, you have lots of make-up work to do." "Incredible technological resources" are the cherry on the sundae here.

Life

"Students are very involved with schoolwork, studying, and homework" during the week at WPI, where a heavy workload and rapid-paced academic calendar keep kids busy ("With classes that last only seven weeks, midterms hit fast, and then by the time they're over, it's already time to start up on finals," one student warns). Thank goodness "the social life is unbeatable." The campus hosts "a very large amount of active clubs and organizations," including a student-run social committee that "is always holding really outrageous and fun events," including "concerts with really good and popular bands." WPI also has a well supported "sports scene—football and basketball are pretty popular," and intramurals draw plenty of participants as well. WPI's "awesome," "strong and very popular" Parties "are really fun," drawing "people from all the neighboring schools," and students insist that the parties "are always fun-themed and not sketchy. You can have a fun time and not have to be concerned about your safety" due to "a driving service with a no-questions-asked policy" and "a detail cop so nothing goes wrong."

Student Body

"We have a very nice mix of students here who do not fit the typical engineering student [profile]," which "stands us apart from other engineering schools," one student writes. Even so, most here concede that "the typical student is nerdy." "We're all nerdy in our own way, whether it be a love of calculus or getting excited over video games," one undergrad relates. Another student breaks down the population this way: "There are four groups of students at WPI. One group consists of the kids who are involved on campus, one consists of kids who never leave their rooms because they are playing video games, one consists of kids who spend all their time studying, and the final group consists of kids who go to class but just want to go to parties the rest of the time." Nearly everyone here is "very driven and self-motivated," because you can't survive WPI long without those qualities. The population includes "a lot of stereotypical Massachusetts or general New England people" and "lots of international students," with China and India especially well represented.

FINANCIAL AID: 508-831-5469 • E-MAIL: ADMISSIONS@WPI.EDU • WEBSITE: WWW.WPI.EDU

THE PRINCETON REVIEW SAYS

Admissions

Very important factors considered include: Academic GPA, rigor of secondary school record. *Important factors considered include:* Class rank, recommendation(s), standardized test scores, character/personal qualities, extracurricular activities. *Other factors considered include:* Application essay, alumni/ae relation, first generation, geographical residence, interview, level of applicant's interest, racial/ethnic status, talent/ability, volunteer work, work experience. ACT with or without writing component accepted. TOEFL required of all international applicants. High school diploma is required, and GED is accepted. *Academic units required:* 4 English, 4 mathematics, 2 science (2 science labs). *Academic units recommended:* 4 science, 2 foreign language, 2 social studies, 1 history, 1 computer science.

Financial Aid

Students should submit: FAFSA, CSS/Financial Aid PROFILE. Regular filing deadline is February 1. The Princeton Review suggests that all financial aid forms be submitted as soon as possible after January 1. *Need-based scholarships/ grants offered:* Federal Pell, SEOG, state scholarships/grants, private scholarships, school scholarship or grant aid from institutional funds. *Loan aid offered:* Direct Subsidized Stafford, Direct Unsubsidized Stafford, Direct PLUS, Federal Perkins, state loans, university loans from institutional funds. Federal Work-Study Program available. Off-campus job opportunities are good.

The Inside Word

WPI's high admission rate is the result of a self-selecting applicant pool; those who don't have a decent chance of getting in here rarely bother to apply. The relatively low rate of conversion of accepted students to enrollees is due to the fact that WPI is a 'safety' school for many applicants. Those who get in here and at MIT, CalTech, Cornell, or Carnegie Mellon usually wind up elsewhere.

THE SCHOOL SAYS "..."

From the Admissions Office

"Projects and research enrich WPI's academic program. WPI believes that in these times simply passing courses and accumulating theoretical knowledge is not enough to truly educate tomorrow's leaders. Tomorrow's professionals ought to be involved in project work that prepares them today for future challenges. Projects at WPI come as close to professional experience as a college program can possibly achieve. In fact, WPI works with more than 200 companies, government agencies, and private organizations each year. These groups provide opportunities where students get a chance to work in real, professional settings. Students gain invaluable experience in planning, coordinating team efforts, meeting deadlines, writing proposals and reports, making oral presentations, doing cost analyses, and making decisions.

Applicants are required to submit SAT or ACT scores, or in lieu of test scores may submit supplemental materials through WPI's Flex Path program. Students who choose the Flex Path are encouraged to submit examples of academic work or extracurricular projects that reflect a high level of organization, motivation, creativity and problem-solving ability."

SELECTIVITY

Admissions Rating	94
# of applicants	6,660
% of applicants accepted	59
% of acceptees attending	23
# accepting a place on wait list	436
% admitted from wait list	4

FRESHMAN PROFILE

Range SAT Critical Reading	560–660
Range SAT Math	630–730
Range SAT Writing	560–660
Range ACT Composite	26–31
Minimum paper TOEFL	550
Minimum computer TOEFL	213
Minimum web-based TOEFL	79
Average HS GPA	3.80
% graduated top 10% of class	63
% graduated top 25% of class	91
% graduated top 50% of class	99

DEADLINES

Early action	
Deadline	11/10
Notification	12/20
Regular	
Deadline	2/1
Nonfall registration?	yes

APPLICANTS ALSO LOOK AT

AND OFTEN PREFER
Brown University, Carnegie Mellon University, Cornell University, Massachusetts Institute of Technology

AND SOMETIMES PREFER
Boston University, Rensselaer Polytechnic Institute, Tufts University, University of Rochester

AND RARELY PREFER
Northeastern University, Rochtester Institute of Technology, University of Connecticut, University of Massachusetts Amherst

FINANCIAL FACTS

Financial Aid Rating	80
Annual tuition	$39,450
Room and board	$11,934
Books and supplies	$1,000
% frosh rec. need-based scholarship or grant aid	77
% UG rec. need-based scholarship or grant aid	64
% frosh rec. non-need-based scholarship or grant aid	27
% UG rec. non-need-based scholarship or grant aid	18
% frosh rec. need-based self-help aid	53
% UG rec. need-based self-help aid	54
% frosh rec. any financial aid	99
% UG rec. any financial aid	95

XAVIER UNIVERSITY OF LOUISIANA

One Drexel Drive, Box 132, New Orleans, LA 70125-1098 • Admissions: 504-520-7388 • Fax: 504-520-7941

STUDENTS SAY "..."

Academics

One of the top Historically Black Colleges/Universities (HBCU), Xavier University of Louisiana prides itself on educating students in a range of subjects, to provide a "thriving underlying foundation, upon which students can achieve the very best for themselves." Though perhaps best known for its science departments, the New Orleans-based school has both a College of Arts and Sciences and a College of Pharmacy and requires "high academic standards" for all of majors across the board. Between its academic reputation and the emphasis placed on community leadership, no matter the reason that you go to XU, you leave "fully educated." "I was challenged academically, but not broken. The workload was not overwhelming," says a student. Small class sizes means great interaction with professors, and the ensuing "close-knit relationships" are cited by many as a major part of their satisfaction with the school. Also on that list? "The education you receive at XU, considering the extremely low tuition cost and financial aid opportunities for a private university, is unparalleled." Professors at XU are dedicated to ensuring that all students "are proficient, if not masters, in the materials taught," and they provide "an excellent foundation for further academic and career success." XU produces a tremendous number of graduates who go on to medical school and other professional schools in "the pursuit of success." Most faculty members are "almost always available in some form or fashion to help you with any questions you may have," and the school itself provides "multiple resources for any problems that need reinforcement." One exception, however, is the financial aid and fiscal services departments, which "have very little time to discuss things with students."

Life

Despite its location, XU "is by no means a party school." Because the student body is mostly composed of science majors, people "are always studying," and "Study groups are a common thing." Students "will take occasional breaks," but for the most part, grades are the important thing at XU. "We are not a school that places as much emphasis on 'fun' as we do making sure we are productive and contributing citizens by the time we graduate," says a student. Though the school offers "lots of opportunities to volunteer," many students complain that there aren't enough social activities to keep students occupied, and school spirit suffers as a result. "We have a strong academic standing, but our campus life is pretty limited," says one student. The dry campus also enforces a curfew ("Sometimes it feels like a boarding school"), so the typical college experience and hair-letting-loose happens off-campus: "Campus is a place to work." Not everyone is familiar with the city (there's no off-campus housing associated with XU), so going out to movies, clubs, and shopping on weekends usually happens in groups. There's also a fair amount of interaction with neighboring schools like Tulane, Loyola, and Dillard. "There are so many things to do right around the corner from Xavier; I can see musicals, watch the Saints, see the Hornets play, salsa dance, get amazing Southern cuisine, listen to 'bounce' music, and learn how to dance, see parades and second lines," sums up a Big Easy lover.

Student Body

Studious, studious, studious. Most students are "very focused, driven, and destined for success," and unsurprisingly, you run into a lot of "aspiring" doctors and pharmacists. The majority of students are African American or Asian, and the female-to-male ratio is quite high. The student body as a whole has a "conservative mentality." It's "very easy" to make friends here, particularly through study groups, and the small campus means that "everyone recognizes everyone" and "gets along with each other."

FINANCIAL AID: 504-520-7517 • E-MAIL: APPLY@XULA.EDU • WEBSITE: WWW.XULA.EDU

THE PRINCETON REVIEW SAYS

Admissions

Very important factors considered include: Academic GPA, recommendation(s), rigor of secondary school record, standardized test scores. *Important factors considered include:* Application essay, class rank. *Other factors considered include:* Alumni/ae relation, character/personal qualities, extracurricular activities, interview, talent/ability, volunteer work, work experience. SAT or ACT required; ACT with or without writing component accepted. TOEFL required of all international applicants. High school diploma is required, and GED is accepted. *Academic units required:* 4 English, 2 mathematics, 1 science, 1 social studies, 8 academic elective. *Academic units recommended:* 4 mathematics, 3 science, 1 foreign language, 1 history.

Financial Aid

Students should submit: FAFSA. The Princeton Review suggests that all financial aid forms be submitted as soon as possible after January 1. *Need-based scholarships/grants offered:* Federal Pell, SEOG, state scholarships/grants, private scholarships, school scholarship or grant aid from institutional funds, United Negro College Fund. *Loan aid offered:* Direct Subsidized Stafford, Direct Unsubsidized Stafford, Direct PLUS, Federal Perkins. Applicants will be notified of awards on a rolling basis beginning April 1. Federal Work-Study Program available. Off-campus job opportunities are good.

Inside Word

This HBCU has a rolling admissions process, and applicants typically receive notification of the school's decision within one month of completed application submission. Campus visits are encouraged. If you want to be considered for scholarships, you'll need to include a strong personal statement that reflects evidence of leadership. Admission to the school's College of Pharmacy is separate from that of the College of Arts and Sciences and is subject to a different set of requirements.

THE SCHOOL SAYS "..."

From the Admissions Office

A Message from the SGA president:

"It is my pleasure to invite you to a college experience that will change and enhance your life. Xavier alumni are known for being exceptional doctors, lawyers, educators, business leaders, journalists, and the like.

"As a graduating biology major, I know Xavier has prepared me for my career in medicine while nurturing me academically and socially.

"With hardship often comes an opportunity to rise to greater heights. In its own way, Hurricane Katrina in 2005 may have added to the character of our people and enhanced the very principles upon which this university was founded.

"St. Katharine Drexel clearly understood when she founded Xavier, the necessity to provide minority students with a quality education and the skills needed to become leaders in their communities. Her vision was to help build a more just and humane society. What better time than now to become a part of the rebuilding of one of America's most unique cities, New Orleans.

"Higher education is not only about gaining intellectual knowledge, but acquiring social and community skills as well. At Xavier we offer a wide array of clubs, organizations and teams to suit the needs and interests of the student body."

SELECTIVITY

Admissions Rating	79
# of applicants	3,397
% of applicants accepted	69
% of acceptees attending	33
# accepting a place on wait list	0

FRESHMAN PROFILE

Range SAT Critical Reading	430–530
Range SAT Math	420–530
Range SAT Writing	410–530
Range ACT Composite	18–23
Minimum paper TOEFL	550
Minimum computer TOEFL	220
Average HS GPA	3.16
% graduated top 10% of class	26
% graduated top 25% of class	52
% graduated top 50% of class	76

DEADLINES

Early action	
Deadline	1/15
Notification	2/15
Regular	
Priority	3/1
Deadline	7/1
Nonfall registration?	yes

FINANCIAL FACTS

Financial Aid Rating	63
Annual tuition	$16,100
Room and board	$7,200
Required fees	$1,000
Books and supplies	$1,200
% frosh rec. need-based scholarship or grant aid	64
% UG rec. need-based scholarship or grant aid	61
% frosh rec. non-need-based scholarship or grant aid	78
% UG rec. non-need-based scholarship or grant aid	64
% frosh rec. need-based self-help aid	84
% UG rec. need-based self-help aid	84
% frosh rec. any financial aid	92
% UG rec. any financial aid	24
% UG borrow to pay for school	84
Average cumulative indebtedness	$23,291

XAVIER UNIVERSITY (OH)

3800 VICTORY PARKWAY, CINCINNATI, OH 45207-5311 • ADMISSIONS: 513-745-3301 • FAX: 513-745-4319

CAMPUS LIFE

Quality of Life Rating	81
Fire Safety Rating	79
Green Rating	78
Type of school	private
Affiliation	Roman Catholic-Jesuit
Environment	metropolis

STUDENTS

Total undergrad enrollment	4,186
% male/female	46/54
% from out of state	40
% from public high school	52
% live on campus	45
% African American	11
% Asian	2
% Caucasian	80
% Hispanic	4
% international	1
# of countries represented	43

SURVEY SAYS . . .
School is well-run
Students are friendly
Dorms are like palaces
Everyone loves the Musketeers
Frats and sororities are unpopular
or nonexistent
Student government is popular

ACADEMICS

Academic Rating	84
% students graduating within 4 years	70
% students graduating within 6 years	79
Calendar	semester
Student/faculty ratio	12:1
Profs interesting rating	83
Profs accessible rating	86
Most common reg class size	20–29 students
Most common lab size	10–19 students

MOST POPULAR MAJORS
business/commerce, liberal arts and sciences, nursing

STUDENTS SAY ". . ."

Academics

Xavier University, a medium-sized Jesuit institution "in the heart of Cincinnati," instills "a real sense of community and social conscience" while still "giving students the needed skills to succeed in all of their life endeavors." Xavier even tosses in a broad liberal arts education for good measure, courtesy of a core curriculum and distribution requirements that include lots of theology, philosophy, English, history, and foreign language. But it's business that many students—one in four, to be more precise—major in here. Undergrads tout the "great entrepreneurship program" and XU's "great record" for placing accounting students in graduate schools. XU's nursing program is also "very strong," with "an excellent" "pass rate on the NCLEX," and the education program earns similar plaudits. In all areas, XU offers "relatively small" classes, "which can make it hard when it's time for registration, but when you're in class it's great." Academics are "challenging, but the teachers and administration help make the transition [from high school] smooth and are there whenever you need their help." "Academically, it is nearly impossible to fail," a freshman adds. "There are always tutoring centers and help [is] available for any subject, whenever you need it." The school also "excels at real-world placement. If you want an internship, just ask. There's even a team of people here whose only job is to find internships and co-ops for students." Undergrads also appreciate their classmates' low-key approach; they "care but are very laid-back in classes."

Life

"Xavier University has a little bit of everything—service projects, strong academics, social events, religious events, weekend trips, and lots of other activities to get involved in." A good number of the aforementioned activities "are put on by [the] Student Activities Council and by student government." Many Xavier students "go to the sporting events," with a heavy focus on the men's basketball team, which "is obviously a huge deal here" (the team was the Atlantic 10 champion for five years straight). Students say XU parties "usually don't get too out of control. I've never really heard or experienced any…of the typical bad college party experiences," a sophomore reports. They also tell us "there are few bars around (mainly only one, for upper classmen) so people generally party at houses." Big-city living lures some students off campus. Cincinnati "is a great city to go out in—there are areas such as Mt. Adams and Newport that provide entertainment and dining for both college-aged students and young professionals."

Student Body

"I'd say ninety-five percent of the students at this school are friendly and always willing to meet new people or help you if you have a problem," writes one student, expressing a commonly held perception of Xavier undergrads. Students "spend a lot of time with varieties of people—not just a 'clique' or single group of people—[so] it is fairly easy to get to know a large percentage of your classmates, especially the peers in your graduating class." In terms of demographics, "Lots of kids come from suburban areas and went to Catholic schools, so there is a large population of wealthy, religious students." Adding some ethnic diversity are "significant populations of minority students (black, Asian, international, etc.) who each have [a] strong voice on campus." Alternative culture is hardly found here, one student notes; "It's rare to find a kid with a mohawk unless the rugby team shaved his head. Most kids are clean-cut." An accounting and finance major adds, "There are no real emo/goth kids at this school (thank God)." However, a weekend degree program and night classes draw a substantial, nontraditional population to the school.

XAVIER UNIVERSITY (OH)

FINANCIAL AID: 513-745-3142 • E-MAIL: XUADMIT@XAVIER.EDU • WEBSITE: WWW.XAVIER.EDU

THE PRINCETON REVIEW SAYS

Admissions

Very important factors considered include: Rigor of secondary school record. *Important factors considered include:* Academic GPA, application essay, class rank, recommendation(s), standardized test scores, character/personal qualities. *Other factors considered include:* Alumni/ae relation, extracurricular activities, first generation, level of applicant's interest, talent/ability, volunteer work, work experience. SAT or ACT required; ACT with or without writing component accepted. TOEFL required of all international applicants. High school diploma is required, and GED is accepted. *Academic units recommended:* 4 English, 3 mathematics, 3 science, 2 foreign language, 3 social studies, 5 academic elective.

Financial Aid

Students should submit: FAFSA. The Princeton Review suggests that all financial aid forms be submitted as soon as possible after January 1. *Need-based scholarships/grants offered:* Federal Pell, SEOG, state scholarships/grants, private scholarships, school scholarship or grant aid from institutional funds. *Loan aid offered:* Direct Subsidized Stafford, Direct Unsubsidized Stafford, Direct PLUS, Federal Perkins. Applicants will be notified of awards on a rolling basis beginning February 15. Federal Work-Study Program available. Off-campus job opportunities are excellent.

The Inside Word

Above-average students should encounter little difficulty in gaining admission to Xavier. Others may be able to finagle their way in with some elbow grease, credible demonstrations of commitment to academics and Jesuit ideals of service, and a Catholic approach to academics.

THE SCHOOL SAYS " . . ."

From the Admissions Office

"Founded in 1831, Xavier University is the fourth oldest of the twenty-eight Jesuit colleges and universities in the United States. The Jesuit tradition is evident in the university's core curriculum, degree programs, and involvement opportunities. Xavier is home to approximately 7,000 total students; 4,000 degree-seeking undergraduates. The student population represents more than forty-five states and forty-three foreign countries. Xavier offers more than eighty undergraduate academic majors and more than fifty minors in the College of Arts and Sciences; the Williams College of Business; and the College of Social Sciences, Health, and Education. Most popular majors include business, natural sciences, communication arts, education, psychology, biology, sport management/marketing, and pre-professional study. Other programs of note include University Scholars; Honors AB; Philosophy, Politics, and the Public; Army ROTC, study abroad, academic service-learning, and community engagement fellowship. There are more than 100 academic clubs, social and service organizations, and recreational sports activities on campus. Students participate in groups such as student government, campus ministry, performing arts, and intramural sports as well as one of the largest service-oriented Alternative Break clubs in the country. Xavier is a member of the Division I Atlantic 10 Conference and fields teams in men's and women's basketball, cross-country, track, golf, soccer, swimming, and tennis, as well as men's baseball and women's volleyball.

"Xavier is situated on more than 148 acres in a residential area of Cincinnati, Ohio. The face of Xavier continues to change with the addition of the technology-based Conaton Learning Commons and Smith Hall, a new building for the Williams College of Business, both which opened in fall 2010, and a new student residence/dining hall complex scheduled for occupancy in fall 2011.

"Applicants must submit results from the SAT or ACT. The student's best score(s) from either test will be used. The writing portion of the SAT/ACT is not required and will not be used in admission and scholarship decisions."

SELECTIVITY

Admissions Rating	84
# of applicants	9,353
% of applicants accepted	69
% of acceptees attending	16
# accepting a place on wait list	19
% admitted from wait list	47

FRESHMAN PROFILE

Range SAT Critical Reading	500–610
Range SAT Math	500–620
Range SAT Writing	490–610
Range ACT Composite	22–28
Minimum paper TOEFL	530
Minimum computer TOEFL	197
Minimum web-based TOEFL	71
Average HS GPA	3.54
% graduated top 10% of class	24
% graduated top 25% of class	55
% graduated top 50% of class	81

DEADLINES

Regular	
Deadline	2/1
Notification	10/15
Nonfall registration?	yes

APPLICANTS ALSO LOOK AT

AND OFTEN PREFER
University of Notre Dame

AND SOMETIMES PREFER
Indiana University at Bloomington, John Carroll University, Loyola University of Chicago, Marquette University, Miami University, Purdue University—West Lafayette, Saint Louis University, The Ohio State University—Columbus, University of Dayton

AND RARELY PREFER
Ohio University—Athens, University of Cincinnati

FINANCIAL FACTS

Financial Aid Rating	72
Annual tuition	$14,650
Room and board	$4,950
% frosh rec. need-based scholarship or grant aid	61
% UG rec. need-based scholarship or grant aid	56
% frosh rec. non-need-based scholarship or grant aid	9
% UG rec. non-need-based scholarship or grant aid	6
% frosh rec. need-based self-help aid	48
% UG rec. need-based self-help aid	47
% frosh rec. any financial aid	100
% UG rec. any financial aid	95
% UG borrow to pay for school	63
Average cumulative indebtedness	$29,296

YALE UNIVERSITY

PO BOX 208234, NEW HAVEN, CT 06520-8234 • ADMISSIONS: 203-432-9316 • FAX: 203-432-9392

CAMPUS LIFE

Quality of Life Rating	95
Fire Safety Rating	60*
Green Rating	94
Type of school	private
Environment	city

STUDENTS

Total undergrad enrollment	5,279
% male/female	49/51
% from out of state	93
% from public high school	56
% live on campus	88
% African American	6
% Asian	14
% Caucasian	17
% Hispanic	9
% Native American	1
% international	10
# of countries represented	108

SURVEY SAYS . . .
School is well-run
Musical organizations are popular
Theater is popular
Student publications are popular
Political activism is popular

ACADEMICS

Academic Rating	96
% students graduating within 4 years	90
% students graduating within 6 years	98
Calendar	semester
Student/faculty ratio	6:1
Profs interesting rating	87
Profs accessible rating	87
Most common reg class size	10–19 students

MOST POPULAR MAJORS
economics, biology, political science

STUDENTS SAY ". . ."

Academics

Listening to Yale students wax rhapsodic about their school, one can be forgiven for wondering whether they aren't actually describing the platonic form of the university. By their own account, students here benefit not only from "amazing academics and extensive resources" that provide "phenomenal in-and out-of-class education," but also from participation in "a student body that is committed to learning and to each other." Unlike some other prestigious, prominent research universities, Yale "places unparalleled focus on undergraduate education," requiring all professors to teach at least one undergraduate course each year. "[You know] the professors actually love teaching, because if they just wanted to do their research, they could have easily gone elsewhere." A residential college system further personalizes the experience. Each residential college "has a Dean and a Master, each of which is only responsible for 300 to 500 students, so administrative attention is highly specialized and widely available." Students further enjoy access to "a seemingly never-ending supply of resources (they really just love throwing money at us)" that includes "the twelve million volumes in our libraries." In short, "The opportunities are truly endless." "The experiences you have here and the people that you meet will change your life and strengthen your dreams," says ones student. Looking for the flip side to all this? "If the weather were a bit nicer, that would be excellent," one student offers. Guess that will have to do.

Life

Yale is, of course, extremely challenging academically, but students assure us that "Aside from the stress of midterms and finals, life at Yale is relatively carefree." Work doesn't keep undergrads from participating in "a huge variety of activities for fun. There are more than 300 student groups, including singing, dancing, juggling fire, theater...the list goes on. Because of all of these groups, there are shows on-campus all the time, which are a lot of fun and usually free or less than five dollars. On top of that, there are parties and events on campus and off campus, as well as many subsidized trips to New York City and Boston." Many here "are politically active (or at least politically aware)" and "a very large number of students either volunteer or try to get involved in some sort of organization to make a difference in the world." When the weekend comes around, "there are always parties to go to, whether at the frats or in rooms, but there's definitely no pressure to drink if you don't want to. A good friend of mine pledged a frat without drinking and that's definitely not unheard of (but still not common)." The relationship between Yale and the city of New Haven "sometimes leaves a little to be desired, but overall it's a great place to be for four years."

Student Body

A typical Yalie is "tough to define because so much of what makes Yale special is the unique convergence of different students to form one cohesive entity. Nonetheless, the one common characteristic of Yale students is passion—each Yalie is driven and dedicated to what he or she loves most, and it creates a palpable atmosphere of enthusiasm on campus." True enough, the student body represents a wide variety of ethnic, religious, economic, and academic backgrounds, but they all "thrive on learning, whether in a class, from a book, or from a conversation with a new friend." Students here also "tend to do a lot." "Everyone has many activities that they are a part of, which in turn fosters the closely connected feel of the campus." Undergrads tend to lean to the left politically, but for "those whose political views aren't as liberal as the rest of the campus...there are several campus organizations that cater to them."

FINANCIAL AID: 203-432-2700 • E-MAIL: UNDERGRADUATE.ADMISSIONS@YALE.EDU • WEBSITE: WWW.YALE.EDU/ADMIT

THE PRINCETON REVIEW SAYS

Admissions

Very important factors considered include: Academic GPA, application essay, class rank, recommendation(s), rigor of secondary school record, standardized test scores, character/personal qualities, extracurricular activities, talent/ability. *Other factors considered include:* Alumni/ae relation, first generation, geographical residence, interview, level of applicant's interest, racial/ethnic status, state residency, volunteer work, work experience. ACT with writing component required. TOEFL required of all international applicants. High school diploma or equivalent isn't required.

Financial Aid

Students should submit: FAFSA, CSS/Financial Aid PROFILE. Regular filing deadline is March 1. The Princeton Review suggests that all financial aid forms be submitted as soon as possible after January 1. *Need-based scholarships/grants offered:* Federal Pell, SEOG, state scholarships/grants, private scholarships, school scholarship or grant aid from institutional funds, United Negro College Fund. *Loan aid offered:* Direct Subsidized Stafford, Direct Unsubsidized Stafford, Direct PLUS, Federal Perkins, state loans, university loans from institutional funds. Federal Work-Study Program available.

The Inside Word

Yale estimates that over three-quarters of all its applicants are qualified to attend the university, but less than ten percent get in. That adds up to a lot of broken hearts among kids who, if admitted, could probably handle the academic program. With so many qualified applicants to choose from, Yale can winnow to build an incoming class that is balanced in terms of income level, racial/ethnic background, geographic origin, and academic interest. For all but the most qualified, getting in typically hinges on offering just what an admissions officer is looking for to fill a specific slot. Legacies (descendents of Yale grads) gain some advantage—although they still need exceptionally strong credentials.

THE SCHOOL SAYS "..."

From the Admissions Office

"The most important questions the admissions committee must resolve are 'Who is likely to make the most of Yale's resources?' and 'Who will contribute significantly to the Yale community?' These questions suggest an approach to evaluating applicants that is more complex than whether Yale would rather admit well-rounded people or those with specialized talents. In selecting a class of 1,300 from more than 22,000 applicants, the admissions committee looks for academic ability and achievement combined with such personal characteristics as motivation, curiosity, energy, and leadership ability. The nature of these qualities is such that there is no simple profile of grades, scores, interests, and activities that will assure admission. Diversity within the student population is important, and the admissions committee selects a class of able and contributing individuals from a variety of backgrounds and with a broad range of interests and skills.

"Applicants for the entering class will be required to take the two SAT Subject Tests of their choice. Applicants may take the ACT, with the writing component, as an alternative to the SAT and SAT Subject Tests."

SELECTIVITY

Admissions Rating	99
# of applicants	25,869
% of applicants accepted	8
% of acceptees attending	67
# accepting a place on wait list	727
% admitted from wait list	11

FRESHMAN PROFILE

Range SAT Critical Reading	700–800
Range SAT Math	700–780
Range SAT Writing	700–790
Range ACT Composite	30–34
Minimum paper TOEFL	600
Minimum computer TOEFL	250
Minimum web-based TOEFL	100
% graduated top 10% of class	96
% graduated top 25% of class	100
% graduated top 50% of class	100

DEADLINES

Early action	
Deadline	11/1
Notification	12/15
Regular	
Deadline	12/31
Nonfall registration?	no

FINANCIAL FACTS

Financial Aid Rating	99
Annual tuition	$40,500
Room and board	$12,200
Books and supplies	$1,000
% frosh rec. need-based scholarship or grant aid	60
% UG rec. need-based scholarship or grant aid	54
% frosh rec. need-based self-help aid	42
% UG rec. need-based self-help aid	45
% frosh rec. any financial aid	60
% UG rec. any financial aid	54
% UG borrow to pay for school	28
Average cumulative indebtedness	$10,717

PART 4

INDEXES

INDEPENDENT COUNSELING

There are currently two professional organizations for independent counselors that require professional credential review: Independent Educational Consultants Association (IECA) and National Association for College Admission Counseling (NACAC). Counselors affiliated with both groups provide varied and detailed services to students and families exploring future educational opportunities. Should you consider seeking the services of an independent counselor, I encourage you to visit both the IECA and NACAC websites for up-to-date information and listings.

Sincerely,

Robert Franek

Lead Author, *The Best 376 Colleges*

SVP—Publisher

The Princeton Review

IECA—The Independent Educational Consultants Association is a national nonprofit professional association of independent consultants.

www.iecaonline.com

NACAC—The National Association for College Admission Counseling is an organization of 9,000 global professionals dedicated to serving students as they make choices in pursuing postsecondary education.

www.nacacnet.org

INDEX OF SCHOOLS

INDEX OF SCHOOLS BY LOCATION

Price categories are based on figures the schools reported to us in early spring 2011 for tuition (out-of-state tuition for public schools) and do not include fees, room, board, transportation, or other expenses.

LESS THAN $15,000

Angelo State University	64
Brigham Young University (UT)	106
California State University Stanislaus	118
City University of New York—Baruch College	142
City University of New York—Brooklyn College	144
City University of New York—Hunter College	146
City University of New York—Queens College	148
College of the Ozarks	174
Flagler College	234
Grove City College	266
Hampton University	278
Indiana University of Pennsylvania	308
Louisiana State University	338
McGill University	364
Salisbury University	476
Sonoma State University	498
Spelman College	504
State University of New York at Binghamton	522
State University of New York at Geneseo	524
State University of New York—Purchase College	526
State University of New York—Stony Brook University	528
State University of New York—University at Albany	530
State University of New York—University at Buffalo	532
Truman State University	562
United States Air Force Academy	572
United States Coast Guard Academy	574
United States Merchant Marine Academy	576
United States Military Academy	578
United States Naval Academy	580
University of Alabama at Birmingham	582
University of Arkansas—Fayetteville	588
University of Idaho	630
University of Louisiana at Lafayette	640
University of Mississippi	658
University of New Orleans	670
University of South Dakota, The	710
University of Wisconsin—Madison	732
University of Wyoming	734
Webb Institute	764
Xavier University (OH)	802

$15,000–$30,000

Albion College	56
Alfred University	58
Arizona State University	66
Auburn University	68
Austin College	70
Baylor University	82
Bellarmine University	84
Berea College	92
Birmingham-Southern College	94
Bradley University	102
Calvin College	120
Catawba College	128
Centenary College of Louisiana	132
Champlain College	136
Christopher Newport University	140
College of Idaho, The	170
Creighton University	194

DePaul University	204
Duquesne University	216
Elon University	220
Emerson College	222
Eugene Lang College The New School for Liberal Arts	226
Evergreen State College, The	228
Fisk University	232
Florida Southern College	236
Florida State University	238
George Mason University	248
Georgia Institute of Technology	254
Gonzaga University	258
Green Mountain College	262
Guilford College	268
Gustavus Adolphus College	270
Hanover College	280
Hillsdale College	290
Hiram College	292
Howard University	300
Indiana University—Bloomington	306
Iowa State University	310
James Madison University	314
Kansas State University	322
Lynchburg College	348
Marist College	354
Marywood University	360
Miami University	368
Michigan State University	370
Michigan Technological University	372
Millsaps College	378
Missouri University of Science and Technology	380
Monmouth University (NJ)	382
Montana Tech of the University of Montana	384
National University of Ireland Maynooth	392
Nazareth College	394
New College of Florida	396
New Jersey Institute of Technology	398
North Carolina State University	402
Oglethorpe University	412
Ohio State University—Columbus, The	416
Ohio University—Athens	418
Pennsylvania State University—University Park	422
Portland State University	430
Prescott College	432
Purdue University—West Lafayette	438
Randolph College	442
Rider University	452
Ripon College	454
Rutgers, The State University of New Jersey—New Brunswick	464
Saint Anselm College	468
Samford University	478
Seton Hall University	488
St. Bonaventure University	506
St. Mary's College of Maryland	516
Suffolk University	538
Temple University	548
Texas A&M University—College Station	550
Thomas Aquinas College	554
Transylvania University	556

Robert Franek is a graduate of Drew University and vice president and publisher for The Princeton Review. He has proudly been a part of the company since 1999. Robert comes to The Princeton Review with an extensive admissions background. In addition, he owns a walking tour business, leading historically driven, yet not boring, walking tours of his favorite town, New York City!

Christopher Maier is a graduate of Dickinson College. During the past five years, he's lived variously in New York City, coastal Maine, western Oregon, central Pennsylvania, and eastern England. Now he's at an oasis somewhere in the Midwestern cornfields—the University of Illinois—where he's earning his MFA in fiction. Aside from writing for magazines, newspapers, and The Princeton Review, he's worked as a radio disc jockey, a helping hand in a bakery, and a laborer on a highway construction crew. He's trying to avoid highway construction these days.

Carson Brown graduated from Stanford University in 1998, and after getting paid too much for working for various Internet companies for several years, sold her BMW and moved to Mexico. She has now overstayed her welcome south of the border and is returning to San Francisco to be responsible and further her career working as a writer and editor.

Julie Doherty is a freelance writer, web designer, and preschool teacher. She lives in Mexico City.

Andrew Friedman graduated in 2003 from Stanford University, where he was a President's Scholar. He lives in New York City.

"COW TIPPING IS DEFINITELY PASSÉ HERE."

Our survey has seven questions that allow students to answer in narrative form. We tell students that we don't care what they write: If it is "witty, informative, or accurate," we try to get it into this book. We use all the informative and accurate essays to write the "Students Speak Out" sections; below are excerpts from the wittiest, pithiest, and most outrageous narrative responses to our open-ended questions.

FOOD...

"When students first arrive, they call the Observatory Hill Dining Facility 'O-Hill.' They soon learn to call it 'O-Hell,' because the food here is beyond revolting."

—Greg F.,
University of Virginia

"If I had known that I'd be rooming with roaches and poisoned by the cafeteria staff I would have gone to Wayne State. I really can't complain, though, because I have met my husband here, like my mom did 20 years before."

—M.L.P., Fisk University

HOMETOWN...

"In my experience New York is a place that allows people to be anyone they want to be. You can wear a zebra-striped bikini in the middle of winter on a snow-covered street here, and people would hardly look twice."

—Sophomore, Barnard College

"Connecticut is a cute state. It's a great place to go to school, but I wouldn't want to live here."

—Claire S., NJ native,
Fairfield University

"Socially, the surrounding area is so dead that the Denny's closes at night."

—Thomas R., UC—Riverside

"The local liquor stores and towing companies make a lot of money."

—Katherine R.,
University of Rhode Island

"It is definitely important to have a car, as the population of Canton frequently matches our winter temperature. 'Canton gray,' our perennial sky color, is one Crayola missed."

—Daniel R., St. Lawrence University

"Montreal is the sh*@!"

—Elizabeth R., McGill University

SECURITY...

"Campus security is made up of a bunch of midget high school dropouts with Napoleonic complexes who can spot a beer can from a mile away."

—Anonymous, UC—San Diego

"Public safety here is a joke. The public safety officers are like the Keystone Kops on Thorazine."

—Anonymous, Bryn Mawr College

"If you're thinking of applying to MIT, go ahead. Because, believe it or not, most people here are at least as stupid as you are."

—Patrick L., MIT

"The typical student is mostly an easygoing, skirt-wearing, intelligent, procrastinating kid. Although, there [are] of course, many many many variations on this. Not all kids wear skirts. Not all the boys in skirts are straight. Not all the girls in skirts are straight. 'Everybody here looks like Jesus!' was a pretty accurate description from an outsider."

—Amy P., New College of Florida

"Students here mostly get along, and since it is a business school we all have a common goal of being rich."

—Female Sophomore, Babson College

"People who go to school here are all pretty good looking, especially the women. It should be renamed UKB, the University of Ken and Barbie."

—Tony H., Arizona State University

"Mt. Holyoke students are friendly and respectful with the exception of the occasions when the entire campus gets PMS."

—Abigail K., Mount Holyoke College

"A school can be defined by its graffiti and its level of cleverness. Three-quarters of our school graffiti is pro- or anti- a specific fraternity, with the other one-quarter devoted to homophobic or misogynist theories."

—Matthew E., College of William & Mary

"This is a great university if you're not studying sciences involving animal research, politics, teacher education (certification), or anything that offends any long-haired leftist who's a vegetarian."

—Brock M., University of Oregon

"Everyone here is too smart for their own good. As one upper-level executive in the Houston area put it, 'The students at Rice know how to make it rain, but they don't know to come in out of it.'"

—John B., Rice University

"Bates is so diverse! Yesterday I met somebody from Connecticut!"

—Ellen H., Bates College

"We have this typical student stereotype we call 'Wendy Wellesley.' Wendy takes copious notes, is a devoted member of 10 organizations, always has an internship, goes over the page limit on every assignment, takes six classes, goes to all the office hours, triple majors, and is basically diligent, overcommitted, extroverted, overachieving, and energetic (but without a sense of humor or ability to relax)."

—R.D., Wellesley College

"I am constantly impressed with the creativity of hell-raisers on campus. One day I walked past the Manor House to find a dozen plastic babies climbing all over the roof! Right before Parents' Weekend, some people hung up signs saying 'Princeton Review reports: "LC students ignore herpes on a regular basis." Please visit the health clinic!'"

—Anonymous, Lewis & Clark College

"Diversity in the female population means different shades of hair color . . . we often joke that Burberry is SMU Sorority Camouflage."

—Male Senior,
Southern Methodist University

ADMINISTRATION...

"Despite the best efforts of the administration to provide TCNJ students with an inefficient, cold-hearted, red-tape-infested, snafu-riddled Soviet-style administrative bureaucracy, The College of New Jersey is a pretty decent place to go for a fairly reasonable amount of money."

—Anonymous,
The College of New Jersey

"Administration is like the stock market, you invest time and money, sometimes you get a return, other times you don't."

—J.W.R., Albertson College of Idaho

"Columbia is like a fruit truck. It picks up varied and exotic fruits and deposits them rotten at their destination."

—Paul L., Columbia University

"The University of Minnesota is a huge black hole of knowledge. It sucks things into it from far and wide, compressing to the essence. Unfortunately, it is very hard to get anything out of a black hole. What I have managed to eke out has been both rewarding and depressing."

—James McDonald,
University of Minnesota

"The strangest incident I've ever had in class was when one of my journalism profs burnt our tests in the microwave. But he decided to give everyone in the class an A, instead of retesting."

—Ashlea K., Ohio University

"Going to Northwestern is like having a beautiful girlfriend who treats you like crap."

—Jonathan J. G., Northwestern University

"Getting an education from MIT is like getting a drink from a firehose."

—Juan G., MIT

"Intro classes have the consistency of Cheez Whiz: They go down easy, they taste horrible, and they are not good for you."

—Pat T., University of Vermont

SEX, DRUGS, ROCK & ROLL...

"Beam, Bud, beer, babes—the four essential B's."

—"Jim Beam," Wittenberg University

"Yeah, there aren't any guys, but who doesn't like doing homework on a Saturday night?"

—Nicole C., Wellesley College

"The dances here are a riot because I love watching nerds and intellectuals dance."

—Male Senior, Columbia University

"Any campus attempt to provide drug-free entertainment shuts down at 10:20 P.M. to allow plenty of time to be drunk. The general campus motto is 'If you weren't wasted, the night was.'"

—Junior, Lehigh University

"Drug use here is extremely prevalent. People smoke pot everywhere, even outdoors."

—Freshman, New College of Florida

SCHOOL SAYS . . .

In this section you'll find advertisements directly from colleges with information they'd like you to consider about their schools. The editorial in these pages is entirely the responsibility of the colleges. It does not reflect any opinion of The Princeton Review about the schools, and The Princeton Review did not create the advertisements. The Princeton Review charges the schools a fee to offset the cost of printing their advertisements in this section which has been added to the book.

The Princeton Review does not charge schools a fee to be profiled in this book, or in any of our books. The company has never required colleges, universities, or any institutions to pay a fee for their profiles or inclusions in our books.

For information about how we selected the 376 outstanding schools in this book, see page 18, "How and Why We Produce This Book."

Experience Champlain College

A Smarter Way to Learn

Champlain College stays ahead of the curve to offer an unmatched professional education in some of the nation's most promising career fields. Our career-driven majors and our approach to developing well-educated, highly skilled professionals make Champlain College unlike any other institution of higher education in the country.

VISIT: **WWW.CHAMPLAIN.EDU**

CHAMPLAIN
COLLEGE
BURLINGTON, VERMONT

What the world needs now is you.

The world can sometimes appear to be pretty empty.

Perhaps it's because the world desperately needs what only you have to offer.
Perhaps the world simply needs an irreplaceable, indispensable you.

The you who looks at the world and asks: why is it like this?
What's in me that can make it better – rather than just "what's in it for me?"

We're Grove City College. We have a reputation as one of the finest
liberal arts colleges in the country – and yet we're one of the most affordable.
Our graduates succeed not just in their careers, but at life.

God gave you a mind for higher things. We'll help you learn to use it well.

And that is the first step to changing the world.

Grove City College • 100 Campus Drive • Grove City, PA 16127

724.458.2100 • www.gcc.edu/review

Michigan Tech
Create the Future

Smart.
We do that.

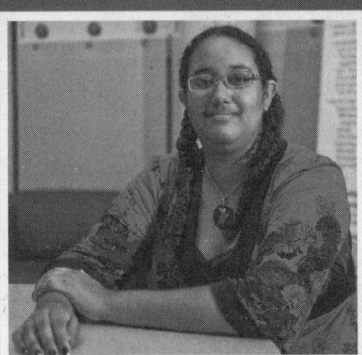

Raven Rebb, a second-year computer science major at Michigan Technological University, enjoys her college experience so much that she can't help but share it with others.

"I'm the president of Michigan Tech's Women in Computing Science organization," she says. "One of the things we do is hold a community outreach program each year for girls in kindergarten through twelfth grade that encourages interest in computing. We want to show girls that there are plenty of opportunities for women in computer science."

Raven knows firsthand that the Michigan Tech name is known far and wide for its academics, community, and extracurricular activities.

"I actually heard about Michigan Tech from one of my high school teachers," she says. "He told me that there's always a lot going on and lots of ways to get involved on campus—and he was definitely right."

Since coming to Tech, Raven has found student organizations tailored exactly to her interests.

"I've never heard of another university having a group specifically for Linux users or for women in computer science."

Although Raven says she initially came for the cold weather, low student-to-professor ratio, and great science and engineering programs, she says she's staying because of the many doors she knows her degree will open after graduation.

"Even though college is definitely an investment, I know it will pay off in the long run," she says. "It's a highly regarded degree, and it's worth it financially. I might even stay here for graduate school. I love Tech—especially the research going on here."

Study engineering; forest resources; computing; technology; business; economics; natural, physical, and environmental sciences; arts; humanities; and social sciences—we have more than 130 degree programs and a reputation for extraordinary hands-on education. In addition, our Enterprise program allows students to manage their own corporate-sponsored, real-world research projects and business ventures.

In your free time, join a student organization—we've got more than 200, from sailing and swing dancing to environmental sustainability and Engineers Without Borders. And with the Experience Tech initiative, you'll enjoy unlimited skiing, golf, tennis, intramural sports, and athletic and performing arts events (they're included in your tuition fees).

FLORIDA SOUTHERN COLLEGE

A Great Education
at a Great Destination

- 12:1 student-faculty ratio
- Guaranteed internships
- Guaranteed study-travel experience
- More than 50 academic programs
- 94% of recent graduates report landing great jobs or entering graduate schools

Learn more at: www.flsouthern.edu/ownit

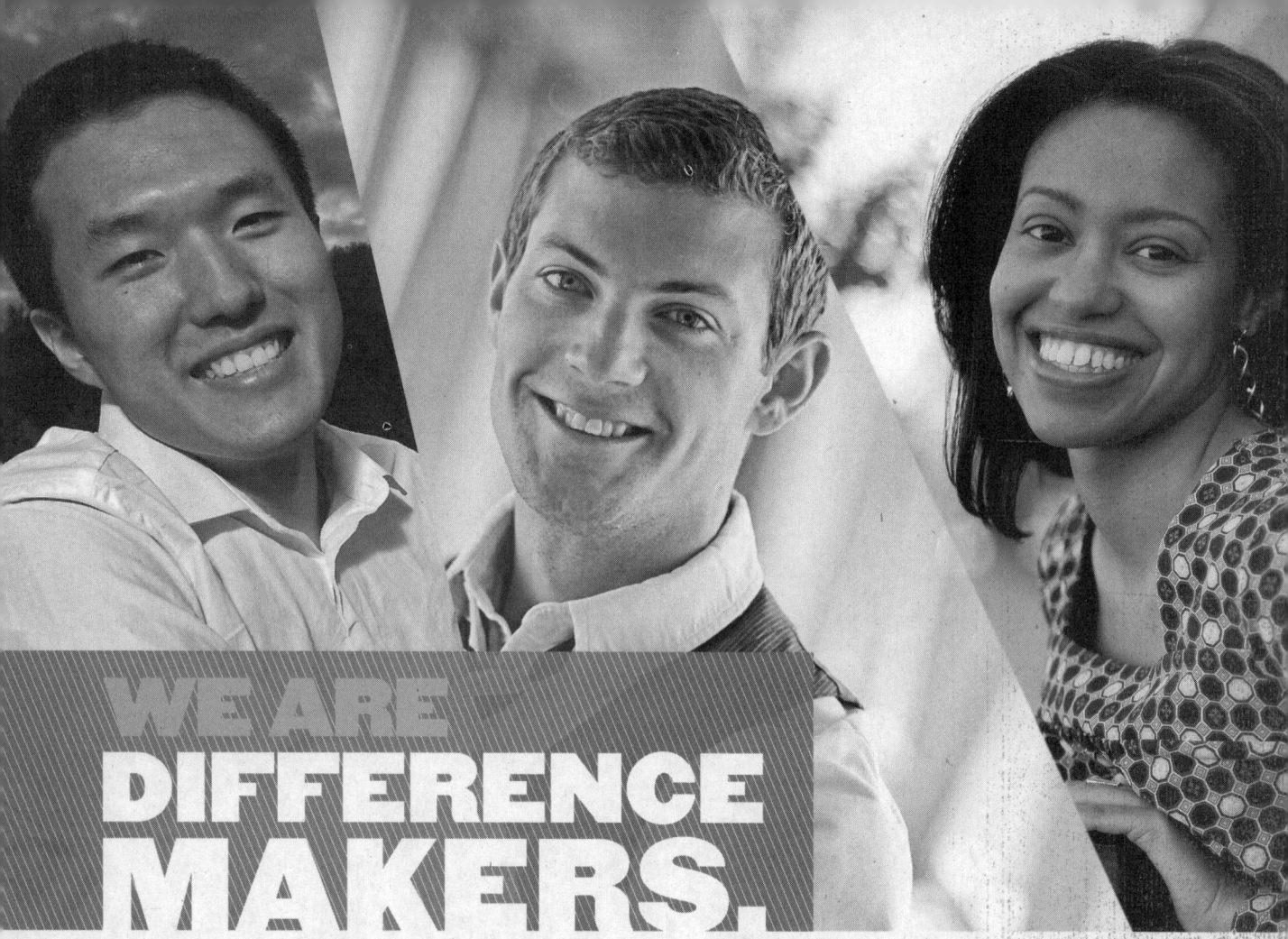

WE ARE
DIFFERENCE
MAKERS.

PURDUE STUDENTS BELIEVE THAT WORK SHOULD BE ABOUT MAKING THINGS WORK. SMARTER. FASTER. BETTER. THEY ARE EASILY INSPIRED — BUILDING BRIDGES BETWEEN WHAT'S KNOWN AND WHAT'S NOT. BOILERMAKERS HAVE AN INSATIABLE DESIRE TO UNCOMPLICATE THE COMPLICATED. TO SEEK OUT POTENTIAL AT EVERY TURN. AND TO PUT IMAGINATION INTO ACTION.

TOP 20 PUBLIC UNIVERSITY
U.S. NEWS AND WORLD REPORT

#4 IN PREPARING STUDENTS FOR THE WORK FORCE
WALL STREET JOURNAL

TOP 70 BEST VALUES IN EDUCATION
KIPLINGER PERSONAL FINANCE

WE ARE PURDUE.
WHAT WE MAKE
MOVES THE WORLD FORWARD

APPLY ONLINE AT **www.purdue.edu**

PURDUE
UNIVERSITY

EA/EOU

Challenge Convention

CHANGE OUR WORLD

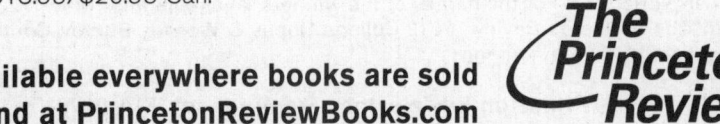

WE KNOW APPLYING TO COLLEGES IS STRESSFUL.

Why Not Win $1,000 for It?

Participate in our 2012 "College Hopes & Worries Survey."

You might win our college scholarship prize.

The Princeton Review has conducted this survey of high school students applying to colleges and parents of applicants since 2002. Why? We're curious to know what concerns you the most about your application experiences and what your dream college would be.

Our survey has just fifteen questions—way shorter than any college app. You can zip through it in less than three minutes. Plus, in addition to the $1,000 scholarship prize we'll give to one lucky participant chosen at random, we'll give another twenty-five participants (also chosen at random) a free copy of one of our college-related guidebooks. They can chose either our book, *Paying for College without Going Broke,* or our book, *ACT or SAT?: Choosing the Right Exam For You,* or our book, *The Portable Guidance Counselor.* In March 2012, about the time you'll (hopefully) be receiving college acceptance and financial aid award letters, we'll post the survey findings on our site and inform the scholarship winner and book winners. For more information, see "OFFICIAL RULES" below.

We know how exciting and how stressful college applications can be. We hope the information on our site and in our books helps you find, get in to, and get aid from the college best for you. We wish you great success in your applications and your college years ahead.

Official Rules:

Princeton Review 2012 "College Hopes & Worries Survey" Prize Sweepstakes

NO PURCHASE NECESSARY. OPEN TO RESIDENTS OF THE FIFTY UNITED STATES (AND WASHINTON, DC) THIRTEEN YEARS OF AGE AND OLDER ONLY.

1. HOW TO ENTER: To enter via the Internet, visit www.princetonreview.com/go/survey. LIMIT ONE ENTRY PER PERSON. All online entries must be received by 11:59 P.M. EDT on February 28, 2012. To enter without Internet access or answering the questionnaire, handwrite your name, complete address, and phone number on a postcard and mail to: The Princeton Review, 2012 College Hopes & Worries Survey c/o Robert Franek, 317 Madison Ave. 4th Fl, New York, NY 10017. Mail-in entries must be received by February 21, 2012. Not responsible for lost, late, or misdirected mail.

2. ELIGIBILITY: Open to residents of the fifty United States and Washington, DC, thirteen years of age and older, except for employees of The Princeton Review, Inc. ("Sponsor"); its affiliates, subsidiaries, and agencies (collectively "Promotion Parties"); and members of their immediate family or persons living in the same household. Void where prohibited.

3. RANDOM DRAWINGS: A random drawing will be held on or about March 31, 2012. Odds of winning will depend upon the number of eligible entries received. Winner will be notified by e-mail/mail and/or telephone, at Sponsor's option and will be required to sign and return any required Affidavit of Eligibility, Release of Liability and Publicity Release within seven (7) days of attempted delivery or prize will be forfeited and an alternate winner may be selected. The return of any prize or prize notification as undeliverable may result in disqualification and an alternate winner may be selected.

4. PRIZES: One (1) Grand Prize: $1,000.00 Scholarship, awarded as a check. Twenty-Five (25) First Prizes: winner's choice of one of the following Princeton Review books: *Paying for College without Going Broke, ACT or SAT?: Choosing the Right Exam for You,* or *The Portable Guidance Counselor.* Approximate Retail Value: $16.00. Total prize value: $1,425.00. Limit one prize per family/household. All prizes will be awarded.

5. GENERAL RULES: All income taxes resulting from acceptance of prize are the responsibility of winner. By entering sweepstakes, entrant accepts and agrees to these Official Rules and the decisions of Sponsor, which shall be final in all matters. By accepting prize, winner agrees to hold Promotion Parties, their affiliates, directors, officers, employees and assigns harmless against any and all claims and liability arising out of use of prize. Acceptance also constitutes permission to the Promotion Parties to use winner's name and likeness for marketing purposes without further compensation or right of approval, unless prohibited by law. Promotion Parties are not responsible for lost or late mail, or for technical, hardware or software malfunctions, lost or unavailable network connections, or failed, incorrect, inaccurate, incomplete, garbled or delayed electronic communications whether caused by the sender or by any of the equipment or programming associated with or utilized in this sweepstakes, or by any human error which may occur in the processing of the entries in this sweepstakes. If, in the Sponsor's opinion, there is any suspected evidence of tampering with any portion of the promotion, or if technical difficulties compromise the integrity of the promotion, the Sponsor reserves the right to modify or terminate the sweepstakes in a manner deemed reasonable by the Sponsor, at the Sponsor's sole discretion. In the event a dispute arises as to the identity of a potentially winning online entrant, entries made by internet will be declared made by the name on the online entry form. All federal and state laws apply.

6. WINNERS LIST: For the names of the winners, available after May 1, 2012 send a self-addressed, stamped (#10) envelope to: The Princeton Review, 2012 College Hopes & Worries Survey Contest Winners, c/o Robert Franek, 317 Madison Ave. 4th Fl., New York, NY, 10017.

SPONSOR: The Princeton Review, Inc., Framingham, MA 01701.

College Hopes & Worries Survey 2012

Mail to Robert Franek, The Princeton Review, 317 Madison Ave., 4th Fl., New York, NY 10017 (mailed entries must be received by February 21, 2012) or fill out online (online entries can be submitted between February 1 and February 28, 2012) at www.PrincetonReview.com/go/survey.

Name _____

Address (optional) _____

City / State / ZIP _____

Daytime phone _____

E-mail address _____

I am _____ a parent of a student _____ a student applying to attend college beginning in

_____ Spring or Fall 2012 _____ Spring or Fall 2013 _____ Later (indicate year: _____).

1   What would be your "dream" college? What college would you most like to attend (or see your child attend) if chance of being accepted or cost were not an issue?   (Please write full name of school, not initials such as "OU".)

_____

2   How many colleges will you (your child) apply to?

_____ 1 to 4

_____ 5 to 8

_____ 9 to 12

_____ 13 or more

3   What is (or will be) the toughest part of your (your child's) college application experience? (Choose one.)

_____ Researching colleges and deciding which schools to apply to

_____ Taking the SAT, ACT, or AP exams

_____ Completing all the applications for admission and financial aid

_____ Waiting for the decision letters and choosing which college to attend

4   What do you estimate your (or your child's) college degree will cost, including four years of tuition, room and board, fees, books and other expenses? (Choose one.)

_____ More than $100,000

_____ $75,000 to $100,000

_____ $50,000 to 75,000

_____ $25,000 to $50,000

_____ Up to $25,000

5   How necessary will financial aid (education loans, scholarships, or grants) be to pay for your (your child's) college education? (Choose one.)

_____ Extremely

_____ Very

_____ Somewhat

_____ Not at all

6   As you research and compare colleges to find the best ones for you (your child) to apply to, which of the following topics would be useful to have more information about (than what you've been able to find out so far about the schools)? Would you say, "I wish I knew more about the schools' ___ ." (Choose one.)

_____ Academic and Course Offerings

_____ Financial Aid Award and Scholarship Opportunities

_____ Student Activities, Campus Life, and Extracurriculars

7   What's your biggest concern about applying to or attending college? (Choose one.)

_____ Won't get into first-choice college

_____ Will get into first-choice college, but won't be able to attend it due to insufficient financial aid and high cost

_____ Amount of loans I (my child) will take out to pay for the degree

_____ Choosing a college I (my child) may not be happy attending

8   How would you gauge your stress level about the college application process? (Choose one.)

_____ Very High

_____ High

_____ Average

_____ Low

_____ Very Low

9   Ideally, how far from home would you like the college you (your child) attend(s) to be? (Choose one.)

_____ 0 to 250 miles

_____ 250 to 500 miles

_____ 500 to 1,000

_____ 1,000 miles or more

10 When it comes to choosing the college you (your child) will attend, which of the following do you think it is most likely to be? (Choose one.)

_____ College with best academic reputation

_____ College with best program for my (my child's) career interests

_____ College that will be the most affordable

_____ College that will be the best overall fit

11 If you (your child) had a way to compare colleges based on their commitment to environmental issues (from academic offerings to practices concerning energy use, recycling, etc.), how much would this contribute to your (your child's) decision to apply to or attend a school?

_____ Strongly

_____ Very much

_____ Somewhat

_____ Not much

_____ Not at all

12 Has the state of the economy affected your (your child's) decisions about applying to or attending college? (Choose one.)

_____ Yes: Extremely

_____ Yes: Very much

_____ Yes: Somewhat

_____ No: Not at all

13 If your answer to the previous question was one of the three "Yes" choices, how would you describe the major way the economy has affected your (your child's) college application decisions. (Choose one.)

_____ Am applying to colleges with lower "sticker" prices.

_____ Am applying to more 'financial aid safety' schools.

_____ Am applying to colleges closer to home to save on travel costs.

14 If you (your child) had a way to compare colleges based on their commitment to making their degree affordable (from their generosity with scholarships to how satisfied their students are with their financial aid), how much would this contribute to your (your child's) decision to apply to or attend a school? (Choose one.)

_____ Strongly

_____ Very much

_____ Somewhat

_____ Not much

_____ Not all

15 What will be the biggest benefit of your (your child) getting a college degree?

_____ The education overall

_____ The experience: exposure to new ideas, places, and people

_____ The potentially better job/higher income and career preparation

Optional: What advice would you give to college applicants or parents of applicants going through this experience next year?

_____

_____

_____

_____

_____

_____

_____

NOTES

NOTES

NOTES